REAL AND PER CAPITA DATA

LESS	EQUALS	LESS: PERSONAL OUTLAYS			EQUALS	PERCENT OF DISPOSABLE PERSONAL INCOME				Gross national product		Disposable personal income		
						Personal outlays								
(15)	(16)	(17)	(18)	(19)	(20)	(21)	(22)	(23)		(24)	(25)	(26)	(27)	
						Total	Personal consumption expenditures	Personal saving		Current prices	1972 prices	Current prices	1972 prices	
Personal tax and nontax payments	Disposable personal income	Total	Personal consumption expenditures	Interest paid by consumers	Personal saving	Total	Personal consumption expenditures	Personal saving		Per capita dollars	Billions of dollars	Per capita dollars	Billions of dollars	
Billions of dollars						Percent								
2.6	83.3	79.1	77.2	1.5	4.2	95.0	92.7	5.0		846	298	683	221	1929
2.5	74.5	71.1	69.9	0.9	3.4	95.4	93.8	4.6		734	268	605	203	1930
1.9	64.0	61.4	60.5	0.7	2.6	95.9	94.4	4.1		610	247	516	197	1931
1.5	48.7	49.3	48.6	0.5	−0.6	101.3	99.8	− 1.3		464	211	390	166	1932
1.5	45.5	46.5	45.8	0.5	−0.9	102.0	100.6	− 2.0		442	207	362	165	1933
1.6	52.4	52.0	51.3	0.5	0.4	99.3	98.0	0.7		514	225	414	176	1934
1.9	58.5	56.4	55.7	0.5	2.1	96.3	95.2	3.7		566	247	459	194	1935
2.3	66.3	62.7	61.9	0.6	3.6	94.6	93.3	5.4		644	283	518	218	1936
2.9	71.2	67.4	66.5	0.7	3.8	94.7	93.4	5.3		700	296	552	225	1937
2.9	65.5	64.8	63.9	0.7	0.7	98.9	97.6	1.1		652	282	504	212	1938
2.4	70.3	67.7	66.8	0.7	2.6	96.3	95.0	3.7		690	306	537	229	1939
2.6	75.7	71.8	71.0	0.8	3.8	94.9	93.6	5.1		754	332	573	242	1940
3.3	92.7	81.7	80.8	0.9	11.0	88.2	86.9	11.8		933	385	695	277	1941
6.0	116.9	89.3	88.6	0.7	27.6	76.4	75.7	23.6		1,170	436	867	311	1942
17.8	133.5	100.1	99.4	0.5	33.4	75.0	74.4	25.0		1,402	493	976	326	1943
18.9	146.3	109.1	108.2	0.5	37.3	74.5	74.0	25.5		1,518	528	1,057	339	1944
20.9	150.2	120.7	119.5	0.5	29.6	80.3	79.7	19.7		1,514	518	1,074	336	1945
18.7	158.6	145.2	143.8	0.7	13.4	91.5	90.6	8.5		1,482	476	1,122	332	1946
21.4	168.4	163.5	161.7	1.0	4.9	97.1	96.1	2.9		1,616	468	1,169	319	1947
21.0	187.4	176.9	174.7	1.4	10.6	94.3	93.2	5.7		1,767	488	1,278	336	1948
18.5	187.1	180.4	178.1	1.7	6.7	96.4	95.2	3.6		1,729	491	1,254	336	1949
20.6	205.5	194.7	192.0	2.3	10.8	94.7	93.4	5.3		1,887	534	1,355	362	1950
28.9	224.8	210.0	207.1	2.5	14.8	93.4	92.1	6.6		2,140	577	1,457	372	1951
34.0	236.4	220.4	217.1	2.9	16.0	93.2	91.8	6.8		2,211	599	1,506	382	1952
35.5	250.7	233.7	229.7	3.6	17.0	93.2	91.6	6.8		2,294	622	1,571	398	1953
32.5	255.7	240.1	235.8	3.8	15.6	93.9	92.2	6.1		2,256	614	1,575	402	1954
35.4	273.4	258.5	253.7	4.4	14.9	94.6	92.8	5.4		2,416	655	1,654	426	1955
39.7	291.3	271.6	266.0	5.1	19.7	93.2	91.3	6.8		2,501	669	1,732	445	1956
42.4	306.9	286.4	280.4	5.5	20.6	93.3	91.4	6.7		2,585	681	1,792	454	1957
42.1	317.1	295.4	289.5	5.6	21.7	93.2	91.3	6.8		2,578	680	1,821	459	1958
46.0	336.1	317.3	310.8	6.1	18.8	94.4	92.5	5.6		2,747	720	1,898	477	1959
50.4	349.4	332.3	324.9	7.0	17.1	95.1	93.0	4.9		2,800	737	1,934	487	1960
52.1	362.9	342.7	335.0	7.3	20.2	94.4	92.3	5.6		2,847	755	1,976	501	1961
56.8	383.9	363.5	355.2	7.8	20.4	94.7	92.5	5.3		3,020	799	2,058	522	1962
60.3	402.8	384.0	374.6	8.8	18.8	95.3	93.0	4.7		3,140	831	2,128	539	1963
58.6	437.0	410.9	400.4	9.9	26.1	94.0	91.6	6.0		3,309	874	2,278	577	1964
64.9	472.2	441.9	430.2	11.1	30.3	93.6	91.1	6.4		3,536	926	2,430	612	1965
74.5	510.4	477.4	464.8	12.0	33.0	93.5	91.1	6.5		3,822	981	2,597	644	1966
82.1	544.5	503.7	490.4	12.5	40.9	92.5	90.0	7.5		3,999	1,008	2,740	670	1967
97.1	588.1	550.1	535.9	13.3	38.1	93.5	91.1	6.5		4,317	1,052	2,930	695	1968
115.4	630.4	595.3	579.7	14.7	35.1	94.4	92.0	5.6		4,615	1,079	3,111	712	1969
115.3	685.9	635.4	618.8	15.5	50.6	92.6	90.2	7.4		4,795	1,075	3,348	742	1970
116.3	742.8	685.5	668.2	16.2	57.3	92.3	90.0	7.7		5,136	1,108	3,588	769	1971
141.2	801.3	751.9	733.0	17.9	49.4	93.8	91.5	6.2		5,607	1,171	3,837	801	1972
150.8	901.7	831.3	809.9	20.2	70.3	92.2	89.8	7.8		6,210	1,235	4,285	855	1973
170.3	984.6	913.0	889.6	22.4	71.7	92.7	90.3	7.3		6,666	1,219	4,646	842	1974
168.8	1,086.7	1,003.0	979.1	23.0	83.6	92.3	90.1	7.7		7,158	1,202	5,088	860	1975
197.1	1,184.5	1,115.9	1,089.9	25.1	68.6	94.2	92.0	5.8		7,910	1,273	5,504	892	1976
226.4	1,305.1	1,240.2	1,210.0	29.3	65.0	95.0	92.7	5.0		8,758	1,341	6,017	930	1977
259.0	1,458.4	1,386.4	1,350.8	34.8	72.0	95.1	92.6	4.9		9,733	1,399	6,672	973	1978
299.9	1,623.2	1,550.4	1,509.8	39.6	72.8	95.5	93.0	4.5		10,743	1,431	7,363	994	1979

CONTEMPORARY ECONOMICS

Fourth Edition

Contemporary Economics

Fourth Edition

Milton H. Spencer

Professor of Economics and
Director of the Center for
Business and Economic Education
School of Business Administration
Wayne State University

Worth Publishers, Inc.

Contemporary Economics, Fourth Edition

Printed in the United States of America

Library of Congress Catalog Card No. 79-56789

ISBN: 0-87901-113-0

First printing, February 1980

Editor: Betty Jane Shapiro

Production: George Touloumes

Design: Malcolm Grear Designers

Picture Editor: Rita Longabucco

Composition: New England Typographic Service, Inc.

Printing and binding: Rand McNally & Company

Worth Publishers, Inc.

444 Park Avenue South

New York, New York 10016

Preface

Economics is exciting and important. Anyone who thinks otherwise has failed to realize that economic ideas and practices have moved people to rebellion, and nations to war. Many of the great social problems that confront us today—among them unemployment, inflation, poverty, discrimination, urban blight, and ecological decay—have economic roots. In order to diagnose and cure these ailments, we must first understand their complex nature.

Distinguishing Features

In this book I have tried to convey a vivid sense of the pertinence and importance of economics by presenting a balanced treatment of theory, problems, and policies. A list of special features will best convey the ways in which this balance has been achieved.

ORGANIZATION

The sequence of topics conforms to the preferences of most instructors. Although the coverage is comprehensive, I have tried throughout to be concise. I believe that most instructors will find the book comfortable to teach from and easily adaptable to both long and short courses.

EXHIBITS, BOXED ESSAYS, AND PHOTOGRAPHS

A great many charts, tables, and illustrations are employed—considerably more than are found in most texts. Short boxed essays, often containing photographs, are used to highlight important ideas and to provide pleasant but pertinent diversions.

LEADERS IN ECONOMICS—HISTORICAL AND CONTEMPORARY

Essays on many of the great economists of the past and present are introduced at appropriate places throughout the book. These essays are primarily substantive, not biographical. That is, they stress the individual's main ideas and contributions as they relate to the topic being presented in the text, thus providing brief but interesting side trips into the history of economic thought.

ISSUES, CASES, AND PORTFOLIOS

Optional issues and case problems involving topics of current interest are presented at the ends of most chapters. Each issue and case concludes with several questions. Some of the questions involve discussion;

others require pencil-and-paper computation, graphing, and problem solving. All provide excellent vehicles for oral or written analysis. In addition, portfolios (photographic essays), both historical and current, have been included where they are particularly useful in providing an appreciation of institutions, events, and situations.

DICTIONARY

All technical terms and concepts are defined when they are first introduced. These expressions, and many others not mentioned in the text, are catalogued in a substantial dictionary at the back of the book. The text can thus serve as a convenient reference—not only for this course, but for other courses in economics, business administration, and the social sciences.

Study Guide and Teaching Aids

The following supplementary items are available with the text (the various teaching aids can be obtained by instructors only, upon written request to the publisher):

STUDENT STUDY GUIDE

Each chapter corresponds to a chapter in the text and includes the following:

○ A concise list of the concepts to be learned.

○ Fill-in questions that focus on definitions, key terms, and concepts.

○ Problems, many of which are analytical, requiring graphing or simple computation.

○ Self-tests, both true–false and multiple-choice.

○ Learning objectives—what the students should be able to do after reading each chapter.

○ Questions for discussion.

○ Answers to the fill-in questions, problems, and self-test questions.

TEACHING AIDS

A complete set of pedagogical aids is available to the instructor, including an *Instructor's Manual, Test Bank, Model Examinations,* and *Transparency Masters.*

The Fourth Edition

The basic organization of the book remains the same as in previous editions. However, a substantial proportion (more than one-third) of this edition is either entirely new or has been revised from the previous edition. Some topics were dropped, and much new material has been added. All in all, many chapters have undergone significant change—thanks to the suggestions of numerous instructors and students.

Here, for example, is a summary of what is new or has been substantially revised from the previous edition.

PART 1. THE PROBLEM AND ITS SETTING

Mixed economy—a more concise discussion of resources, goals, and the institutions of capitalism, combined with new visual material amplifying resource classification and specialization.

Supply and demand—largely rewritten and reorganized, introducing equilibrium before undertaking a discussion of shifts of the curves.

Private sector (households and businesses)—condensed to one chapter, with new material on income distribution, recent gains in income equality, and issues involving business size and responsibility.

Public sector (government)—new topics on public choice, government budgeting, benefit-cost analysis, and collective decision making.

PART 2. NATIONAL INCOME, EMPLOYMENT, AND FISCAL POLICY

National income and wealth—a new section on the measurement of national wealth (i.e., the construction of the nation's balance sheet as well as the conventional income statement).

Economic instability—new material on forecasting methods, the measurement of unemployment, and the growing significance of underemployment.

Income, employment, and fiscal policy—explanations of the absolute, relative, and permanent income hypotheses; a clarification of the marginal efficiency of investment as a rate of return; and a new, clearer explanation of the distinction between planned and realized investment. There are also two historical portfolios: (1) "The Classical Economists: Adam Smith's 'Sons' and 'Daughters'" and (2) "The Great Depression and the Keynesian Revolution." Both provide opportunities to examine today's problems in the light of previous attitudes, beliefs, and experiences.

PART 3. MONEY, BANKING, AND MONETARY POLICY: THE FISCAL-MONETARY MIX

Monetary and banking system—new definitions and measures of the money supply, a fuller explanation of monetary standards, and an account of how monetary panics led to the creation of the Federal Reserve System. A new portfolio, "The Story of Money and Banking," provides a lively photographic history of government's attempts to control the money supply.

Commercial and central banking—a practical case study of bank portfolio management by (graphic) linear programming. Also, relationships between bond prices and bond yields, portfolio effects of business investment decisions, and practical difficulties faced by the Fed in carrying out its functions.

Macro equilibrium, fiscalism, and monetarism—a fuller explanation of the distinction between the Keynesian and classical models; a substantial revision of the neo-Keynesian and monetarist views with emphasis on the "transmission mechanism"; and new findings relating money, interest, and prices.

Stagflation—alternative policy proposals and theories, including "new" Phillips curves, acceleration curves, rational expectations, market and nonmarket policies, the Laffer curve, tax-based incomes policy (TIP), indexation, employment programs, productivity improvement, and economic planning.

PART 4. ECONOMIC GROWTH AND RESOURCE POLICIES

Growth theory and problems—a more concise discussion, with revised data and charts providing international comparisons and sources of growth.

Less developed countries—a special case of "the growth problem," with explanations of growth policies and the reasons for successes and failures.

PART 5. USING SUPPLY AND DEMAND. THE LAWS OF PRODUCTION AND COST

Supply, demand, and elasticity—new material on the income elasticity of demand and the cross elasticity of demand, based on recent consumer-goods studies, plus a discussion of the DuPont cellophane case as an example of cross elasticity used in the courtroom.

Utility, consumer demand, and costs of production—a generally tighter and more structured treatment, facilitating the recognition of important relationships.

PART 6. THE ECONOMICS OF THE FIRM: HOW ARE PRICES AND OUTPUTS DETERMINED?

Perfect competition—a more concise discussion, and a simplified explanation of the derivation of supply curves from marginal cost curves.

Monopoly—a fuller explanation of the natural-monopoly concept as a basis for full-cost pricing by public utilities.

Imperfect competition—an expanded discussion of the role of research and development, an essay on Nobel laureate Herbert Simon, and a new issue on some economic aspects of advertising.

General equilibrium and welfare economics—a new issue on gasoline rationing, permitting a discussion of intersector implications.

PART 7. DOMESTIC PROBLEMS: STRIVING FOR EFFICIENCY AND EQUITY

Antitrust, labor, poverty, and urban problems—new illustrative material on government and business; a substantial essay on Galbraith's views of big business in today's economy; problems and data on financing social security; and a generally more concise discussion of domestic issues.

PART 8. INTERNATIONAL ECONOMICS AND THE WORLD'S ECONOMIES

International economics—new illustrative material and a fuller discussion of world trade, the Eurocurrency market, and current international problems.

Economic planning—recent developments in China concerning industrialization and planning, and a new portfolio on China's Four Modernizations and "The New Long March."

Student Involvement

> I hear and I forget
> I see and I remember
> I do and I understand
> Confucius

The most effective and interesting way of learning any subject is by "doing" it. To an extent not found in most other texts, this book abounds with applications—many of them integrated within the text, others developed independently in the form of practical end-of-chapter questions, issues, and case studies. Some of the applications require students to perform simple computations or to sketch graphs in order to solve real-world problems. Other applications ask students to use previously learned principles for dealing with economic controversies. As a general rule, *all* the applications—developed in the form of questions, problems, issues, and cases—lend themselves both to individual and to small-group participative efforts, thereby enabling instructors to heighten classroom interest by providing a variety of educational experiences in addition to lectures and discussions. The result of these approaches is that students become more deeply *involved* in the learning process by "practicing" economics, largely through debating and evaluating ideas instead of merely hearing or reading about them.

In short, the book permits a blending of both *case* and *clinical methods*. These have long been used with eminent success by business, law, and medical schools—in large classes as well as small ones. There is ample evidence that the methods are highly effective and that they provide stimulating alternatives to more conventional pedagogical approaches.

Acknowledgments

It is a pleasure to acknowledge the help and cooperation I have received in the preparation of this book.

A general expression of thanks goes to Muriel Converse. She is not only the author of the accompanying *Study Guide*, but my severest critic. Her demanding standards have made the book much better than it might otherwise have been.

Professor Mona Hersh, a prominent economic educator, and her students at Texas Woman's University helped immeasurably in improving the consistency of the Dictionary.

Patrice Zemenick typed a substantial portion of the material and was helpful in many other ways.

Over the life of this book, I have benefited greatly from the advice and criticisms of hundreds of dedicated academicians. Unfortunately, I cannot list them all. However, it is a privilege to mention the names of those who reviewed substantial portions of this edition, thank them for their constructive suggestions, and absolve them of any shortcomings in the final product.

Sue Adams, TARRANT COUNTY JUNIOR COLLEGE
Donald T. Buck, SOUTHERN CONNECTICUT STATE COLLEGE
Deborah Chollet, TEMPLE UNIVERSITY
William H. Collins, EAST CAROLINA UNIVERSITY
Robert Coston, GEORGIA SOUTHERN COLLEGE
Martha A. Eppley, ELIZABETHTOWN COLLEGE
Frank Fato, WESTCHESTER COMMUNITY COLLEGE
Theodore Frickel, UTAH STATE UNIVERSITY
Curtis Harvey, UNIVERSITY OF KENTUCKY
Leon P. Jorgensen, UNIVERSITY OF NORTH CAROLINA, CHARLOTTE
Sidney Kronish, MONTCLAIR STATE COLLEGE
Allen Larsen, ST. CLOUD STATE UNIVERSITY
Ronald A. Madsen, UNIVERSITY OF NORTH CAROLINA, CHARLOTTE
Robert Payne, PORTLAND COMMUNITY COLLEGE
Richard Romano, BROOME COMMUNITY COLLEGE
Arthur Schreiber, GEORGIA STATE UNIVERSITY
Francis Shieh, PRINCE GEORGE'S COMMUNITY COLLEGE
Mark Soskin, SUNY AT POTSDAM
George Tzannetakis, SETON HALL UNIVERSITY
Darwin Wassink, UNIVERSITY OF WISCONSIN, EAU CLAIRE
Ann Witte, UNIVERSITY OF NORTH CAROLINA, CHAPEL HILL
Paul D. Zook, THE UNIVERSITY OF TEXAS AT EL PASO

MILTON H. SPENCER
January 1980

for Cathy

Contents in Brief

Contents

Suggested Outlines for One-Semester Courses

These recommendations are flexible. Many other chapter combinations are possible.

Chapter topic	Macro-economic emphasis	Micro-economic emphasis	Balanced macro/micro emphasis	Problems and policy emphasis
Introduction	○	○	○	○
1. Our Mixed Economy: Resources, Goals, and Institutions	○	○	○	○
2. The Laws of Supply and Demand	○	○	○	○
3. The Private Sector: Households and Businesses	○	○	○	○
4. The Public Sector: Government	○	○	○	○
5. National Income and Wealth	□		□	□
6. Economic Instability	□		□	□
7. Consumption, Saving, and Investment	□		□	□
8. Income and Employment Determination	□		□	□
9. Fiscal Policy for Efficiency and Stability	□		□	□
10. Our Monetary and Banking System	□		□	□
11. Commercial Banking: How Banks Create Money	□		□	□
12. Central Banking: How the Fed Manages Our Money	□		□	□
13. Macroeconomic Equilibrium	□		□	□
14. Fiscalism, Monetarism, and the Fiscal–Monetary Mix	□		□	□
15. Can We Overcome Stagflation?	□		□	□
16. Understanding Economic Growth	⊡		⊡	
17. Problems of Economic Growth				⊡
18. The Less Developed Countries				⊡
19. Managing Our Resources: Energy and the Environment				⊡
20. Working with Supply, Demand, and Elasticity *(can follow Chapter 2 if desired)*	○	○	○	○
21. Utility and Consumer Demand		□	□	
22. Costs of Production		□	□	
23. Perfect Competition		□	□	
24. Monopoly Behavior		□	□	
25. Imperfect Competition		□	□	
26. Marginal Productivity and Income Distribution		⊡		
27. Determination of Factor Prices		⊡		
28. Stability, General Equilibrium, and Welfare Economics		□		
29. Business Behavior and the Antitrust Laws		□		⊡
30. Labor Practices and Collective Bargaining		⊡		⊡
31. Insecurity and America's Poor		⊡		⊡
32. Urban Problems: Can the Cities Be Saved?		⊡		⊡
33. International Trade	⊡	⊡		
34. International Finance	□	⊡		
35. International Economic Problems and Policies	□	⊡		⊡
36. Radical Viewpoints, Old and New	⊡	□		⊡
37. Economic Planning	⊡	□		⊡

○ = Common core of chapters.   □ = Chapters for kinds of emphasis desired.

⊡ = Optional topic, time permitting.

Part 1

The Problem and Its Setting

Introduction

What is economics?

Why should you study it?

What errors should you watch for in reasoning about economic problems?

How are graphs, which are fundamental tools of economics, constructed and interpreted?

You cannot bring about prosperity by discouraging thrift. You cannot strengthen the weak by weakening the strong. You cannot help the wage-earner by pulling down the wage payer. You cannot further the brotherhood of man by encouraging class hatred.

You cannot help the poor by destroying the rich. You cannot keep out of trouble by spending more than you earn. You cannot build character and courage by taking away a person's initiative and independence. You cannot help people permanently by doing for them what they could and should do for themselves.

Abraham Lincoln (1861)

Lincoln had a profound understanding of social problems. Many of his economic beliefs are as meaningful today as when he first expressed them. Through self-education and experience, he came to realize that economics is an activity in which nearly everyone is engaged but about which relatively few have any knowledge.

Today, such knowledge is more vitally needed than ever before. For economics is concerned with most of society's complex issues. These include inflation, unemployment, and poverty; pollution, urban decay, and shortages of raw materials; taxes, monopoly, and the role of government. Every day we are asked to express an opinion on economic matters. Sometimes we do this by voting. More often we take part in a discussion or we evaluate a current government proposal or news item. In any case we are continually being flooded with information and advice, some of it right and much of it wrong.

Economics helps us to form valid opinions about many crucial problems. Although economics does not provide a fixed set of rules that guarantees solutions, it does offer a systematic way of thinking and some useful tools for understanding and coping with many of society's ills.

What Is Economics About?

Anyone beginning the study of a subject likes to have a concise description of its nature and content. Here is a modern definition of economics—one you will use frequently:

> *Economics* is a social science concerned chiefly with the way society chooses to employ its limited resources, which have alternative uses, to produce goods and services for present and future consumption.

Thus, economics explains how human and material resources are used to provide people with the commodities they want. Therefore, *economics is concerned with the production and delivery of a standard of living.*

Our definition of economics needs some amplification.

First, why is economics a *social* science? Because it deals with an aspect of human behavior, and is therefore related intimately to other social or behavioral sciences: psychology, sociology, anthropology, history, and political science.

Second, what does it mean to say that a society's resources are limited? Simply that people everywhere want more goods and services than there are means to produce them. An economy's human and material resources are thus scarce when compared with society's wants. Society must therefore decide how to utilize those limited resources most effectively. Economics is concerned both with those choices and with the forces that determine the choices.

Finally, what does it mean to say that resources have alternative uses? Only this: That just as you cannot simultaneously read at home *and* visit the movies, so must society choose between allocating resources to, say, constructing highways or constructing buildings. The same resources cannot be used for both purposes simultaneously.

This book will show how nations cope with the problems of *what, how,* and *for whom* society's limited resources are used to produce the desired goods and services. The solution to these problems affects the whole structure and nature of a society. These include its political system, the character of its insti-

tutions, the degree of choice open to its members, and the distribution of its wealth and income.

Of course, every society operates according to its own rules and regulations. These determine the ways in which resources are used. Therefore, a society's laws, customs, and practices, and their relationships to an economy's business firms, households, and government, constitute an *economic system*. Today, the two major types of economic systems are capitalism and socialism. The nature of these "isms," and modern variations of them, will concern us frequently in this book.

MICROECONOMICS AND MACROECONOMICS

Economists traditionally divide their studies into two broad categories: microeconomics and macroeconomics.

Microeconomics is concerned with the specific economic units or parts that make up an economic system and the relationships between those parts. In microeconomics, emphasis is placed on understanding the behavior of individual firms, industries, and households and the ways in which such entities interact.

Macroeconomics is concerned with the economy as a whole, or large segments of it. Macroeconomics focuses on such problems as the rate of unemployment, the changing level of prices, the nation's total output of goods and services, and the ways in which government raises and spends money.

Stated differently:

> Microeconomics looks at the trees, while macroeconomics looks at the forest. Both categories involve the construction of theories and formulations of policies—activities that are the heart of economics.

Working with Theories and Models

Economists, like all scientists, study relationships between variables and formulate theories about them. At one time it was popular to call a relationship a *hypothesis* if there was no evidence to support it; a *theory* if there was some evidence; and a *law* or *principle* if it was certain. Scientists no longer emphasize these distinctions. They know that no hypothesis can be made about a subject of which one is completely ignorant, and that no scientific law is ever certain. Consequently, they use "theory," "law," and "principle" interchangeably.

A theory may be stated in the form of a *model*. This is a representation of the essential features of a theory or of a real-world situation. A model may be expressed in the form of words, diagrams, tables of data, graphs, mathematical equations, or combinations of these. A model is easier to manipulate than the reality it represents because only the *relevant* properties of reality are presented. A road map, for example, is a model. It does not show vegetation or climatic variations because these are not relevant to its purposes, but it will still guide you across the country.

A theory or model usually fits the observed facts only approximately. Therefore, it might have to be changed or even discarded as time passes and the facts themselves alter. In recent years, some new economic theories have revised and replaced older ones to provide better explanations of today's problems.

COMMON FALLACIES IN REASONING

Like physicists and chemists, economists try to use observed, verifiable facts as stepping-stones to an understanding of how their portion of the world works. But physicists and chemists can usually discover rather quickly when they are in error, because at best an experiment goes wrong, or at worst it causes an explosion. Economists, on the other hand, may labor for years under misapprehensions and formulate policies that affect thousands or even millions of people. Consequently, it is important to discern at the outset whether economic ideas are rational or misleading. One way of doing this is to examine them very carefully with the help of formal logic—a kind of microscope of the mind.

In common usage the word "fallacy" designates any mistaken idea or false belief. In a stricter sense, fallacy means an error in reasoning or argument. This is what we are looking for when we analyze economic ideas. Of course, an argument may be so incorrect that it deceives nobody. But for our purposes we shall reserve the word "fallacy" for certain types of reasoning which, although incorrect, are nevertheless persuasive—a dangerous combination. Here are some typical fallacies in economic thinking that will enable you to pinpoint the errors in other people's reasoning as well as your own.

Fallacy of False Cause

Every science tries to establish cause-and-effect relationships. The fallacy of false cause, or *post hoc fallacy,* is often encountered in such efforts. (The fallacy comes from the Latin expression *post hoc ergo propter hoc,* which means "after this, therefore, because of this.") This fallacy is committed when a person mistakenly assumes that because one event follows an-

other, or both events occur simultaneously, one is the cause and the other the effect.

The fallacy of false cause may be illustrated by the following "if–then" form of argument:

> If A occurs, then B occurs.
> Therefore, A causes B.

Is this good grounds for concluding that A causes B? Not necessarily. There are other possible explanations:

1. B may occur by chance.

2. B may be caused by factors other than A (or by a third factor C, which is a common cause of both A and B).

3. B may cause A.

Some possibilities are illustrated in the following examples:

EXAMPLE 1   Company X hired a new sales manager, and the firm's sales soared during the ensuing year.
    Therefore, the growth in sales was due to the new sales manager.

This argument is obviously a false cause or *post hoc* fallacy. It fails to point out that although some of the growth in sales may be due to the manager's efforts, much or even most of it may be the result of other factors. Among them: lower prices, higher incomes of buyers, and/or a larger number of buyers in the market.

EXAMPLE 2   The severity of hay fever varies inversely with the price of corn. That is, the lower the price of corn, the greater the severity of hay fever, and vice versa.
    Therefore, the price of corn is the cause of hay fever.

It is true that the price of corn and the severity of hay fever are inversely related. However, the fact is that ragweed is a cause of hay fever. The summer conditions that will produce a bumper crop of ragweed—high temperatures and adequate rainfall—will also produce a bumper crop of corn. This usually results in a lower corn price. Thus, it may *seem* as if corn prices affect hay fever. In reality these factors are independent of each other and a third factor is operating which is a common cause of both.

Fallacious relationships frequently occur in economics. Because they are not often apparent, a careful study of the subject is necessary before we can learn to recognize such errors and to avoid the fallacy of false cause.

Fallacies of Composition and Division

Now let us look at two additional fallacies. The *fallacy of composition* is committed when one reasons that what is true of the parts of a whole is also true of the whole. The *fallacy of division* is committed when one contends that something which is true only of the whole is also true of its parts taken separately.

The following *true* statements from macro- and microeconomics illustrate these fallacies:

1. In a recession it may be desirable for a family to increase its savings by cutting down on its consumption expenditures. However, if all families do this, spending in the economy will decline. As a result, firms will lay off workers, the level of total income will fall, and families will find themselves saving *less* rather than more.

2. If prices in a specific industry were to increase tomorrow by X percent, the firms in that industry would probably experience an increase in profits. But if prices of everything throughout the economy were to increase tomorrow by X percent, no firms would experience an increase in profits.

3. Economic policies that may be wise for a *nation* are not necessarily wise for an *individual,* and vice versa.

The fallacies of composition and division are thus particularly relevant to micro- and macroeconomics. To summarize:

> The fallacy of composition warns us that what is true of the parts is not necessarily true of the whole. Thus, generalizations of a microeconomic nature may not always be applicable to a macroeconomic situation. The fallacy of division warns us that what is true of the whole is not necessarily true of the parts. Thus, generalizations of a macroeconomic nature may not always be applicable to a microeconomic situation.

These ideas may seem obvious when they appear in a textbook, but they can be remarkably subtle in discussions of actual economic problems.

What You Have Learned

1. Economics is a *social* science because it deals with an aspect of human behavior—how people earn a living and distribute the proceeds.

2. Like all sciences, social or physical, economics uses theories and models to represent reality. However, a model is a simplified version of reality. As such it may need to be adjusted or even abandoned as facts change or new ones come to light.

3. Many types of fallacies can be committed in economic reasoning. Perhaps the most common are the fallacy of false cause and the fallacies of composition and division.

For Discussion

1. *Terms and concepts to review:*

economics	macroeconomics	law
economic system	hypothesis	principle
microeconomics	theory	model

2. "Everyone knows that the United States is one of the richest countries in the world. Therefore, economics as it is defined may be correct for poor countries, but certainly not for America, where the problem is one of abundance, not scarcity." True or false? Explain.

3. Senator Jason is campaigning for a tax reduction. He argues that tax cuts in other major industrial nations have stimulated their rapid economic growth. Senator Blaine replies that what happens in nations thousands of miles away is no guide to what will happen here. Do you agree with Senator Blaine? Why or why not?

Identify at least one fallacy in each of the following:

4. All rich nations have steel industries, so the surest way for a poor nation to become rich is to develop its own steel industry.

5. The students who do best in economics have some working experience, so the surest way to receive a good grade in this course is to go out and get a job.

6. "To press forward with a properly ordered wage structure in each industry is the first condition for curbing competitive bargaining; but there is no reason why the process should stop there. What is good for each industry can hardly be bad for the economy as a whole."

Twentieth Century Socialism, New York, Penguin Books, 1956, p. 74

7. "Each person's happiness is a good to that person, and the general happiness, therefore, a good to the aggregate of all persons."

John Stuart Mill, *Utilitarianism*

8. In a capitalist system, each manufacturing plant is free to set its own price on the product it produces. Therefore, there can't be anything wrong with all manufacturers getting together to agree on the prices of the products they produce.

9. All economics textbooks are long and dull, so we can't expect this one to be short and interesting.

10. "Roger Babson, who was best known for his predictions of the stock market, once became ill with tuberculosis. Against his doctor's advice, he chose to convalesce at his home in Massachusetts rather than remain in the West. During the freezing winter, he kept his windows open and wore a coat with an electric heating pad in the back. He had his secretary do her typing by wearing mittens and hitting the keys with rubber hammers. Babson recovered and remained a fresh-air fiend ever since. He believed that air from pine woods had chemical and/or electrical qualities of great medicinal value.

"On another occasion, Babson wrote an article in which he contended that gravity affects weather and crops, crops influence business, and business affects elections. He supported his thesis with an analysis of 27 presidential elections, from 1844 to 1948. In 75 percent of the cases, he said, the party in power remained in power when weather and business were good, and was voted out when weather and business were bad."

Martin Gardner, *Fads and Fallacies in the Name of Science,* New York, Dover Publications, 1957, p. 97

Working with Graphs

Economic ideas are often expressed with models. One of the most common ways of presenting a model is in the form of a line graph. Such a graph shows relationships between variables—that is, how one quantity varies with another. The procedure for making line graphs is illustrated in the following paragraphs and in Charts (a) through (f).

In Chart (a) a common sheet of graph paper is shown. Two intersecting straight lines at right angles to each other are drawn on the graph paper. The horizontal line is called the X axis, the vertical line the Y axis, and the point of intersection the origin. The two lines divide the chart into four parts called quadrants. These quadrants are identified by starting with the upper right-hand corner and numbering them counterclockwise. Observe that positive numbers on the X axis are to the right of the origin, and negative numbers are to the left. Positive numbers on the Y axis are above the origin, and negative numbers are below. For brevity, we write the coordinates of a point in the form (x,y), where x represents the value on the X axis, and y the value on the Y axis. These procedures for labeling and numbering are used in all branches of science.

You can now locate any point on the chart with two numbers—one for x and one for y—in much the same way as you would locate a ship at sea by its latitude and longitude. The two numbers are called the coordinates of the point. Thus, the coordinates of point A

are (3,5), those of point B are (5,2), and those of point C are (4,0). The horizontal coordinate is always stated first and the vertical coordinate second. Can you give the coordinates of the remaining points?

Charts such as these are used to show how one quantity varies with another. In Chart (b), for example, the values of x and y are plotted from the data in the accompanying table. First, the points representing each pair of x,y values are located and marked. The points are then connected with a smooth curve, in this case a straight line. Since the line slopes upward from left to right, the two variables are said to be directly related. Thus, as x increases, y increases; as x decreases, y decreases. In contrast, the line in Chart (c) slopes downward from left to right. Therefore, the two variables are said to be inversely related. Thus, as x increases, y decreases; as x decreases, y increases.

In economics, the lines plotted usually fall entirely in the first quadrant because the data on which they are based are positive, although there are important exceptions. Sometimes two or more lines are plotted on the same chart in order to examine the relationships between them, as in Chart (d). Can you read the coordinates of the points determining these lines? Try filling in the table.

Different scales and labels may be used on the horizontal and vertical axes, to suit the particular purpose of the graph. This is shown in Chart (e). The curve in this chart shows what happened to the price, $P, of a particular bond t years after it was purchased. For example, at $t = 0$, $P = \$1,204$; and at $t = 2$ years, $P = \$1,190$. Can you fill in the table? Try to estimate the numbers from the graph where necessary.

Finally, Chart (f) shows the unit costs, $\$C$, which a certain firm experiences as a result of producing different quantities, Q, of a commodity. You should be able to fill in the table from the chart.

x	-3	-2	-1	0	1	2	3	4
y	-2	-1	0	1	2	3	4	5

x	-3	-2	-1	0	1	2	3	4
y	5	4	3	2	1	0	-1	-2

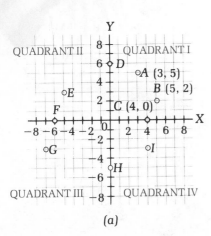

(a)

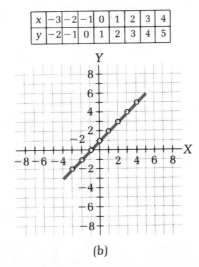

(b)

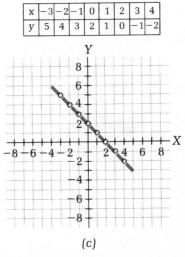

(c)

Chart (a). The two intersecting straight lines divide the chart into four quadrants numbered counterclockwise. Positive values are measured to the right along the X axis and upward along the Y axis. Negative values are measured to the left along the X axis and downward along the Y axis. Any point on the chart can be located by its coordinates.

Chart (b). A line that slopes upward from left to right exhibits a direct relation between the two variables. As one variable increases, so does the other; as one decreases, so does the other.

Chart (c). A line that slopes downward from left to right exhibits an inverse relation between the two variables. As one variable increases, the other decreases; as one decreases, the other increases.

x	2	3	4	5	6
y	3			4	
y	7	6			

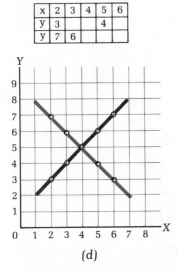

(d)

t	0	4	8	12	16
p					

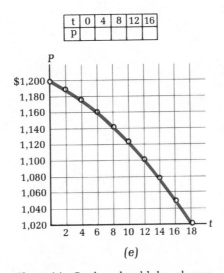

(e)

Q		2		4		6	
C	90		30		30		90

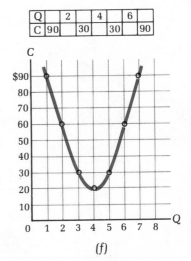

(f)

Chart (d). Two or more lines may be graphed on the same chart in order to study their interrelationships. Can you complete the table from the graph?

Chart (e). Scales should be chosen and axes labeled in the manner that best suits a particular problem. Can you use the graph to estimate the missing numbers in the table?

Chart (f). The points should be connected with care because the resulting curve may be quite pronounced. Can you fill in the table from the graph?

Exercises in Graphing

Sketch the graphs of the following relationships:

1.

x	1	2	3	4	5	6	7	8
y	1	2	3	4	5	6	7	8

2.

x	1	2	3	4	5	6	7
y	7	6	5	4	3	2	1

3.

x	−2	0	2	4
y	−8	−4	0	4

4. Sketch the graphs of the following data on the same chart. Estimate the coordinates of the point of intersection of the two lines.

x	1	2	3	4
y	2	3	4	5

x	1	2	3	4
y	5	4	3	2

5. Sketch the graph of hog prices as a function of time:

time (t)	0	1	2	3	4	5	6	7	8
hog prices (P)	8	33	40	35	24	13	8	15	40

Our Mixed Economy: Resources, Goals, and Institutions

Chapter Preview

What are the human and nonhuman resources of our economy?

What are the goals of our economic system? What do we want to accomplish?

How can we make economic use of our scarce resources? What, how, and for whom should goods be produced? How can we depict a society's production possibilities?

What is capitalism? How did it evolve? What are its main features?

This evening it would be nice if you could (1) read this chapter, (2) do all your homework, (3) earn some money, (4) engage in pleasant recreational activity, and (5) relax and enjoy a leisurely dinner at the best restaurant in town. But you cannot do all these things. You will have to give up one or more because you are faced with limitations of time, and possibly of money.

Every economic system also faces limitations. But they are of the human and nonhuman resources needed to produce the goods and services that society wants. This chapter describes the nature of those limitations and how an economy adjusts to them in the light of the objectives it tries to attain.

Resources of Our Economic System: What Do We Have?

Every economic system has various resources at its disposal to produce the goods and services that are wanted. These resources are of two broad types:

1. *Property Resources*   Includes such things as natural resources, raw materials, machinery and equipment, buildings, and transportation and communication facilities.

2. *Human Resources*   Consists of the productive physical and mental abilities of the people who comprise an economy.

This classification of resources is occasionally too general for some practical problems. Economists therefore divide property resources into two subcategories, "land" and "capital," and human resources into two subcategories, "labor" and "entrepreneurship." These four types of resources are known as the *factors of production*.

FACTORS OF PRODUCTION

The four factors of production—land, capital, labor, and entrepreneurship—are the basic ingredients or "inputs" which any society must use to obtain the "outputs" that it desires.

Land

Land includes all nonhuman or "natural" resources, such as land itself, mineral deposits, timber, and water. Land thus consists of all the basic and natural physical stuff on which any civilization must be built.

You may be surprised to learn that many countries, even some of the poorest, have vast quantities of untapped natural resources. This is true because world demand for the resources is not sufficient to make their extraction profitable with existing technology. When these conditions change, as they often do, a country's physical resources may take on new economic significance.

Because of this, a nation's "stock" of natural resources should not be thought of as a fixed physical quantity. Instead, it should be viewed as a variable one whose size is determined by changing economic and technological conditions. The United States, for example, has large untapped quantities of oil and natural gas. However, these resources will not be extracted until higher prices resulting from increased demand, or lower costs resulting from technological advancements, make production profitable. Thus, the physical volume of these resources may be constant. However, their economic quantity may be variable, depending on their prices and costs of production.

Capital

Capital may be defined as a produced means of further production. In this sense, capital means *capital goods* or *investment goods,* the things that are used by business. Examples are raw materials, tools, machinery and equipment, factory buildings, freight cars, and office furniture. Capital is thus an economic resource that is used to help produce consumer goods and services. *Consumer goods* are those bought and used by households—food, cars, appliances, clothing, health services, and so on.

An important distinction between *physical* capital (goods used in production) and *finance* capital (money) must be kept in mind. Business managers, *but not economists,* generally use the term "capital" to mean money—the funds owned or borrowed to purchase capital goods and to finance the operation of a business. But for the economy as a whole, money is not a productive resource. If it were, nations could become rich simply by printing money. Instead, money's chief function is to facilitate exchange of goods and services. Money therefore serves as a "lubricant" rather than as a factor of production within the economic system.

Labor

Land and capital are of no use unless they can be made productive. That requires *labor*, the hired workers whose efforts or activities are directed toward production.

In a broader sense, "labor" includes everyone who works for a living. We often refer to the labor force of a nation, that is, all the employable population above a certain age. The meaning of "labor force" and the notion of labor as a factor of production are different concepts in economics. Although they are sometimes related in economic discussions, the distinction between the two is always clear from the context in which the terms are used.

Entrepreneurship

The three factors of production described above must be organized and combined in order to produce. In other words, labor must be given a purpose if it is to work with land and capital to turn out goods and services. This is where *entrepreneurship* enters the picture. The entrepreneur recognizes a need and the opportunities to be gained from production. Accordingly, he or she generates new ideas and puts them into effect. The entrepreneur assembles the factors of production, raises the necessary money, organizes the management, makes the basic business policy decisions, and reaps the gains of success or the losses of failure. Some entrepreneurs act as their own managers; others do not. But regardless of who acts as manager, the *entrepreneurial function* is necessary.

Something to Think About

Is there such a thing as "human" capital? Are scientists, engineers, teachers, doctors, lawyers, and skilled workers, for example, part of a nation's capital? What criteria would you use when deciding whether something is qualified to be called capital?

RETURNS TO RESOURCE OWNERS

In a capitalistic system the factors of production are privately owned. In other types of economic systems, one or more of the productive resources might be owned by society. Because there are not enough factors of production to satisfy everyone, their owners can command a price for them in the market.

For example, those who supply land receive a payment called *rent*. The suppliers of finance capital, the money that business firms borrow for the purchase of capital goods, receive a return called *interest*. Workers who sell their labor receive a payment called *wages*, which includes salaries, commissions, and the like. Finally, those who perform the entrepreneurial function receive *profits* (or losses). These ideas are summarized in Exhibit 1.

Although the factors of production are grouped into four broad classes, you can appreciate the fact that there is generally a considerable degree of specialization within each class. Machines, for example, are designed to do specific jobs, and people are often trained

Exhibit 1
Classifying the Factors of Production

The classification of factors of production and their corresponding income payments is an outgrowth of the social structure that prevailed in England during most of the nineteenth century. At that time it was customary to distinguish between landowners, capitalists, and wage earners, representing the upper, middle, and lower classes. By the turn of the century, economists recognized a fourth factor of production, enterprise. Profits then became the share of income attributed to entrepreneurship, and interest became the income received by suppliers of finance capital.

Resource or factor of production	Description or activity	Payment or reward
Land	Natural resources (e.g., minerals, water, timber)	Rent
Capital	Produced resources (e.g., tools, factories, machines)	Interest
Labor	Physical and mental efforts (e.g., hired workers and professionals)	Wages
Entrepreneurship	Organizing and risk taking	Profit

to perform specific tasks. The result is a much larger volume of production, but often at the cost of substantial personal dissatisfaction. This is explained in Box 1.

Goals of Our Economic System: What Do We Want to Accomplish?

When we refer to the economy as a "system," we imply there is purpose or order in its structure. What do we want our economy to do? What do we want it to be?

Every society seeks to attain certain objectives. Four goals that are fundamental to all economic systems, capitalistic as well as socialistic, are (1) efficiency, (2) equity, (3) stability, and (4) growth. The meanings of these terms are worth examining because they are universal standards used for judging the success of economic practices and policies.

EFFICIENCY: FULL EMPLOYMENT OF RESOURCES

Because every society possesses only limited resources or factors of production, they must be used with maximum efficiency. What does this mean? In general, *efficiency* is the ability to make the best use of what is available to attain a desired result. This definition is adequate for most purposes, but for use in economic reasoning a clear distinction must be made between technical and economic efficiency.

Technical Efficiency

Engineers measure physical efficiency by the ratio of physical output to total physical input. The greater the ratio, the greater the physical efficiency. If a motor, for example, uses 100 units of energy input to produce 80 units of energy output, the motor is said to be 80 percent efficient. If the motor produced 75 units of energy output for 100 units of energy input, the motor would be 75 percent efficient.

When a system has attained its greatest physical efficiency, it is at a point of *technical efficiency*. A firm, an industry, or an economy is said to be technically efficient when it is achieving maximum output by making the fullest utilization of available inputs. Further, when a production system has attained technical efficiency, its resources are fully utilized in the most effective way. Therefore, no change in the combination of inputs can be made that will increase the output of one product without decreasing the output of another.

Box 1

Specialization: Learning More and More About Less and Less

Most members of society specialize. _Specialization_ is the division of productive activities among individuals and regions so that no one person or area is self-sufficient. _Division of labor_ is specialization by workers. The result of specialization is an enormous gain in productivity. This fact was pointed out as long ago as 1776 by Adam Smith, the founder of modern economics, in what has become a classic quotation.

The Bettmann Archive, Inc.

Division of Labor in a Pin Factory

A workman not educated to this business . . . could scarce, perhaps, with his utmost industry, make one pin in a day, and certainly could not make twenty. But in the way in which this business is now carried on, not only the whole work is a peculiar trade, but it is divided into a number of branches. . . . One man draws out the wire, another straights it, a third cuts it, a fourth points it, a fifth grinds it at the top for receiving the head: to make the head requires two or three distinct operations; to put it on, is a peculiar business, to whiten the pins is another; it is even a trade by itself to put them into the paper; and the important business of making a pin is, in this manner, divided into about eighteen distinct operations, which, in some manufactories, are all performed by distinct hands, though in others the same man will sometimes perform two or three of them. I have seen a small manufactory of this kind where ten men only were employed, and where some of them consequently performed two or three distinct operations. But . . . those ten persons . . . could make among them upwards of forty-eight thousand pins in a day.

Adam Smith, _An Inquiry into the Nature and Causes of the Wealth of Nations_ (1776)

Eleutheran Mills.

The assembly line was not invented by Henry Ford but by an anonymous Frenchman. This factory, observed by Adam Smith on a visit to France, increased output tenfold by instituting the division of labor in the production of pins.

Paul Conklin, Monkmeyer Press Photo Service.

Workers on an automobile assembly line, 1914 and today.

To generalize from Smith, specialization and division of labor increase production because they:

○ Allow the development and refinement of skills.

○ Avoid the time that is wasted in going from one job to another.

○ Simplify human tasks, thus permitting the introduction of laborsaving machines.

Specialization has its shortcomings. It may alienate many workers because they have contributed only one small part to the completed product. Their jobs can dull the mind and become naked means of subsistence. There is little personal satisfaction to those who must learn more and more about less and less in order to survive in an advancing age of technology.

This idea can be illustrated with an example. A farmer growing as much corn as possible with existing quantities of labor, capital, and land has achieved technical efficiency. Under these circumstances, it would be impossible to transfer some resources out of corn production and into wheat production without decreasing the output of corn.

The concept of technical efficiency can be broadened from simple production systems to more complex ones, such as firms, industries, or the entire economy. An economic system, for example, is technically efficient if every firm in the system has attained technical efficiency—the greatest ratio of physical output to available physical inputs. No change in the combination of society's resources can then be made which will increase the output of one commodity without decreasing the output of another.

Economic (Allocative) Efficiency

As you have already learned, economics is concerned with the way a society allocates its scarce resources to meet social goals. Therefore, a standard is needed for determining success. This standard is called *economic,* or *allocative, efficiency.* An economy is said to have achieved economic (allocative) efficiency when it is producing that combination of goods that people prefer, given their incomes. No change can then be made in the combination of resources or output that will make someone better off without making someone else worse off—each in his or her own estimation.

These concepts, involving both technical and economic efficiency, contain some interesting implications. Here are a few that are especially important for our present purposes:

1. A society that has achieved technical efficiency is making full utilization of available resources. But the society is not economically efficient unless it is producing the goods that people prefer to purchase with their given incomes.

2. A society that has achieved economic efficiency has also achieved technical efficiency. That is, the society is not only producing the largest possible output with available resources but it is also satisfying consumer preferences. Economic efficiency is thus a general concept that includes technical efficiency.

These ideas suggest a useful guide for judging various economic practices and policies.

One of the fundamental goals of our society is to achieve *full employment*—maximum, efficient utilization of the economy's available resources. In practical terms involving human resources, this means that everyone who wants to work is working, except for those who may be temporarily out of work or those who are changing jobs.

Efficiency thus means *full employment of resources.* You will find more complete definitions of "full employment" and "efficiency" in the Dictionary at the back of the book.

EQUITY: FAIRNESS OR ECONOMIC JUSTICE

Economic efficiency is concerned with the way a society can make the best use of scarce resources to fulfill consumers' preferences. Economic efficiency does not deal with the question of how society's goods are shared among you, me, and everyone else. This is a problem of _income distribution_—the division of society's output (i.e., the income society earns) among people. Because income distribution concerns the matter of who gets how much, it raises basic issues of equity or justice which every society must resolve.

Equity is both a philosophical concept and an economic goal. However, there is no scientific way of concluding that one distribution of income is fair and therefore "good" while another is unfair and therefore "bad." For example, in the United States a neurosurgeon may earn twenty times as much as a schoolteacher; in Britain, four times as much; in Israel, twice as much; and in Cuba and China, an even smaller proportion. Which proportion is equitable depends on the rules or standards of income distribution society establishes. You will learn about such standards in later chapters. Meanwhile, the following considerations should be kept in mind:

Wide differences in income exist in our economy. Among the causes are native ability and intelligence, racial and sexual discrimination, education and training, and the extent of property ownership. One of the major goals of our society is to achieve an equitable distribution of income. Because equitable means "fair" or "just" (*not* "equal"), the attainment of equity requires that we seek reasonable methods of altering the controllable factors that cause undesirable differences in income.

STABILITY AND GROWTH

Stability of prices and growth of total output are two remaining fundamental goals of every economic system. These terms have close economic interrelationships. By maintaining stability, an economy avoids substantial price fluctuations and is better able to encourage continuous full employment of all resources. This, in turn, leads to a robust volume of economic activity and to steady economic growth—a rising level of real output per capita. As a result, all income groups in society can benefit even if each receives a constant proportion of an expanding economic pie.

This idea can be stated somewhat differently:

Every economy seeks stable prices and a growing volume of output. By maintaining stability, both efficiency and continuous economic growth are encouraged. This makes it possible for everyone to share in the benefits of expansion regardless of a society's pattern of income distribution.

CONCLUSION: A PROPER MIX OF GOALS

The goals listed above seem reasonable enough. However, their realization may involve certain sacrifices—for the following two reasons.

Private Choice Versus Governmental Direction

In a democracy there is a close connection between political freedom and economic freedom. Citizens vote for legislators who influence government policy; consumers choose the goods they want; workers select their occupations; and holders of wealth employ their assets as they see fit. Government, of course, may impose certain restrictions for what it believes are in the public's interest. And social or racial discrimination may deprive some people of equal opportunities. Nevertheless, the preservation and enhancement of freedom of choice are ideals of our democratic political and economic system.

Unfortunately, failure to attain efficiency, equity, stability, and growth may sometimes tempt us to rely heavily on government direction and control. This could cause us to sacrifice some of our political and economic freedoms. Therefore, unless we know the extent to which we are prepared to make such sacrifices, implementation of the goals outlined above will remain difficult for government policy makers.

Conflicting Goals

A second reason for sacrifice arises from the fact that certain goals tend to conflict with each other. For example, the goal of full employment can conflict with that of stability if a rising proportion of resource utilization exerts upward pressure on prices. Similarly, the goal of economic growth can conflict with that of equity if a rising volume of output per person benefits some groups at the expense of others.

Where such conflicts occur, government may try through legislation or regulation to promote the desirable goals while minimizing the undesirable consequences. However, such efforts are likely to entail some costs. For instance, legislation in the form of wage and price controls may succeed in curbing inflation but will also limit freedom of choice for consumers, workers, and businesspersons. In view of this, would you recommend such legislation?

Decisions Involve Trade-Offs

It is evident from these considerations that every decision involves a choice between alternatives. If the choices are to be made rationally, a system of trade-offs must be established. This would enable us to understand the alternative cost or sacrifice of choosing one objective over another, or of formulating compromises between them. Thus, an overall problem faced by society is to establish a proper mix of goals. As a rule:

The goals of nations vary according to their political as well as their economic philosophies. To achieve certain objectives, such as full employment and rapid economic growth, autocratic socialistic countries such as the Soviet Union, China, and Cuba have sacrificed much political and economic freedom. In contrast, democratic countries such as the United States, Canada, Japan, and many Western European nations have tried to achieve those objectives without sacrificing these freedoms.

Scarcity: A Fundamental Economic Challenge

In economics, *scarcity* is the name of the game and *economizing* is the way it is played. Every society has to cope with a fundamental economic challenge: How can that society best use its limited resources to satisfy its unlimited wants? This is the problem of scarcity.

For the majority of people, scarcity is a fact of life. Most of the things they want and need are economic goods in that they have a price. In this sense, they differ from free goods for which the market price is zero. But even "free goods" may be scarce in some circumstances. Sunshine and surf are free for residents of Hawaii, but not for tourists who must expend time, effort, and money to get there. Fish in a mountain lake are free goods, but in a city they are scarce. These facts suggest an important law:

Law of scarcity. Economic resources are scarce. There are never enough at any given time to produce all the things that people want. Scarce resources can be increased, if at all, only through effort or sacrifice.

Scarcity of resources forces every economic system to make choices. A decision to produce one thing frequently implies a decision to produce less of some other things. All societies thus face the basic problem of deciding what they are willing to sacrifice to get the things they want. This is the central problem of economics. In general:

Economics is fundamentally concerned with choice or decision in the use of resources. Problems of choice arise when there are alternative ways of achieving a given objective. Economics develops specific criteria that define the conditions for making the best use of society's resources. These criteria are then used as guidelines for formulating and evaluating public policy.

THE GREAT QUESTIONS: WHAT? HOW? FOR WHOM?

It is the task of an economic system to combine efficiently its *resources, wants,* and *technologies.* To do so, it must answer three fundamental and interdependent questions.

WHAT Goods and Services Should Society Produce—and in What Quantities?

How should a society's scarce resources be allocated? Should some of them be taken out of the production of consumer goods (food, clothing, automobiles, and appliances) and put into the production of capital goods (tools, machines, tractors, and factories)? Would the reverse be better? For instance, by enlarging its proportion of capital goods now the economy will be able to produce more consumer goods in the future. It is necessary, then, to decide how much consumption should be sacrificed today to provide for increased output of consumer goods later.

A related question is: *How much* of each good should society produce? How many automobiles? How much food and clothing? How many tractors, factories, and so on? The values and priorities involved in such decisions are extremely complex. Nevertheless, in answering this question society is again choosing between present and future satisfactions. It is making a trade-off between the amount of consumption to be sacrificed today in return for increased consumption at a later time.

HOW Should Resources Be Organized for Production?

Most goods can be produced in more than one way by using resources in different quantities and combinations. In the early days of America, for example, agricultural commodities were produced by farming large quantities of land extensively, while using only small quantities of labor. This was because labor was relatively more scarce than land. In parts of the Far East, on the other hand, land is farmed intensively because it is relatively more scarce than labor. Similarly, in manufacturing it is often possible to vary the combinations of resources. Automobiles, for example, can be produced with different combinations of materials such as steel, aluminum, or fiber glass, as well as different combinations of labor and capital. Any society, therefore, must decide how it will *organize* its scarce resources in order to use them efficiently.

FOR WHOM Shall the Goods Be Produced?

Who is to receive what share of the economic pie? This question is of enormous significance, because an economic system is often judged by the way in which it distributes its goods and services. It is also a question of direct concern to each of us, because the answer determines not only the nation's well-being but our individual standard of living as well.

The three great questions—WHAT, HOW, and FOR WHOM—are fundamental in all societies. Each society meets these challenges in different ways. At one extreme is a *command economy.* This is one in which an authoritarian government exercises primary control over decisions concerning what and how much to produce. Government may also, but does not necessarily, decide for whom to produce. Countries such as the Soviet Union, China, and Cuba are among the best examples. At the other extreme is the *market economy.* Here all three questions are decided in open markets through competitive forces of supply and demand. This is the ideal of "pure" capitalism, also called "theoretical capitalism." It is an extremely useful model which cannot be represented by real-world economies but which is examined in later chapters. However:

Between the two extremes of a command economy and a market economy is the *mixed economy.* Here the three great questions, or specific applications of them, are decided partially by the free market and partially by a central governmental authority. Most of the advanced nations fall into this category. However, they vary in the degree of reliance they place on the market mechanism as distinct from governmental direction.

Society's Production Possibilities

For every society, the answers to the questions of WHAT, HOW, and FOR WHOM are intimately related to the need for economizing. In reality, the problem of economizing is a complex one. Therefore, we must simplify it in order to focus on the basic concepts involved.

We may begin by constructing a model of the economizing process for a hypothetical society. The model is based on four assumptions:

1. *The economy produces only two types of goods: agricultural, such as crops and livestock, and capital, such as machines and factories.* This assumption permits us to derive principles for a simple two-good economy. These principles are also applicable to a complex economy producing many goods.

2. *The same resources can be used to produce either or both of the two classes of goods and can be shifted freely between them.* This means, for example, that labor and other factors of production can be used to produce either food or machines, or different combinations of both.

3. *The supply of resources and the state of technological knowledge are fixed.* This is equivalent to assuming a short-run state of affairs. In the long run, the supply of resources and the level of technological knowledge are expandable.rather than fixed.

4. *Society's resources are fully employed in the most (technically) efficient way.* This assumption emphasizes the fact that in the short run the economy may be able to increase the production of one class of goods by taking resources away from the production of an-other class of goods. However, the economy cannot increase the production of *both* classes of goods.

The model is illustrated by Exhibit 2. The table is called a *production-possibilities schedule.* Note that if society chooses production alternative *A,* it will be devoting all its resources to the production of agricultural goods. None of its resources will be used in the production of capital goods. Society will thus be producing 14 units of agricultural goods and zero units of capital goods.

At the other extreme, if society chooses alternative *G,* it will be putting all its resources into the production of capital goods. Society will thus be producing 6 units of capital goods and zero units of agricultural goods.

These two alternatives are extremes. Realistically, the society must seek a balance. As society tries to increase its capital goods production by choosing any of alternatives *B, C, D,* and so on, it must *sacrifice* some agricultural goods. The amount of sacrifice for each production alternative is shown by the negative numbers in the fourth column of the table.

All the information in the production-possibilities schedule can be transferred directly to the accompa-

---

Exhibit 2
Society's Production-Possibilities Curve: Achieving Technical Efficiency

A society that is on its production-possibilities curve has achieved technical efficiency. This means that the society has attained the largest possible output with available inputs. Therefore, no change in the combination of inputs can be made that will increase the output of one product without decreasing the output of another.

However, the society will not have achieved economic efficiency unless it is producing the combination of goods that people prefer to purchase with their existing incomes.

PRODUCTION-POSSIBILITIES SCHEDULE

Production alternatives	Capital goods production	Agricultural goods production	Sacrifice of agricultural goods for capital goods
A	0	14	−1
B	1	13	−2
C	2	11	−2
D	3	9	−2
E	4	7	−3
F	5	4	−4
G	6	0	

[NOTE   When you sketch a production-possibilities curve freehand, you should draw it smooth like the one in Chart *(a).* The smooth curve is an idealization or model of a real situation. Therefore, a smooth curve is easier to interpret than a jagged line.]

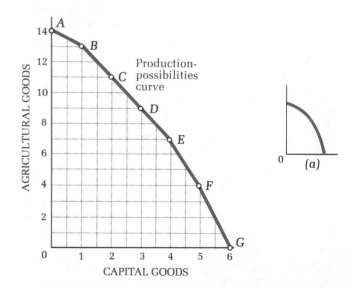

nying chart. Note that the units of capital goods are scaled on the horizontal axis and those for agricultural goods on the vertical axis. The line that connects the various production alternatives *A* through *G* is called a *production-possibilities curve*. It reveals all possible combinations of total output for the society it represents.

LAW OF INCREASING COSTS

The production-possibilities curve raises two challenging questions:

1. *Is there an optimum or best combination of agricultural and capital goods?* The production-possibilities curve alone cannot tell us what combination of the two goods to produce. For example, some countries, such as the Soviet Union and China, have sought rapid economic growth by emphasizing production of capital goods at the expense of consumer goods. Other nations, such as New Zealand and Uruguay, have traditionally allocated larger proportions of their resources to agricultural than to capital goods production. Choices such as these are based on each society's value judgments and goals, and hence involve questions which economics per se cannot answer.

2. *Why does the sacrifice of agricultural products increase as society gets more capital goods?* Greater and greater sacrifices of agricultural output must be made to get more capital goods. This is because the economy's factors of production differ and are not all equally suitable for producing the two types of goods. Fertile land, for example, is more suitable for crops than for factories, and unskilled farm workers are more adaptable to agriculture than to manufacturing. Even though an economy's resources may be substitutable within wide limits for given production purposes, the resources are relatively more efficient in some uses than in others. Thus, as society tries to increase its production of capital goods, it must take increasing amounts of resources out of agriculture. This is necessary even though the resources are relatively more productive in agriculture.

These points suggest the operation of an important law:

> *Law of increasing costs*. An economy's production-possibilities curve relates two kinds of goods. The real cost of acquiring either good is not the money that must be spent for it. The real cost is the increasing amount of the *alternative* good that the society must sacrifice because it cannot have all it wants of both goods.

Thus, referring back to the fourth column of the table in Exhibit 2, note again that the sacrifices are shown with negative numbers. This is because they represent the amount of agricultural goods that society must *give up* to acquire 1 more unit of capital goods. For example, if society is at point *D* and wants to go to point *E*, it must give up 2 units of agricultural goods to get 1 more unit of capital goods. Similarly, if it is at point *E* and wants to get to point *F*, it must give up 3 units of agricultural goods to get 1 more unit of capital goods. As explained in Exhibit 2, this means that the society has achieved technical efficiency but not necessarily economic efficiency.

Some Interesting Problems

Production-possibilities curves can be used to depict several interesting situations. For example, can you demonstrate each of the following propositions by sketching the appropriate freehand graphs? (SUGGESTION   Use arrows to show possible directions of movement.) Label points and curves as needed to illustrate clearly the concepts involved.

1. An economy that underutilizes its resources is producing at some point *inside* its production-possibilities curve. Three of the moves that it can make to get back on the curve are to produce more capital goods, more agricultural goods, or more of both.

2. Increases in resources or improvements in technology will shift an economy's production-possibilities curve to the right (i.e., outward from the origin). The resulting expansion represents *economic growth*—a higher level of real output per capita.

3. A nation that allocates more resources in the present to the production of capital goods relative to consumer goods will have more of both kinds of goods in the future. The nation will thus experience more economic growth.

To repeat: *Each of the foregoing statements is true.* However, your understanding of them will be greatly improved if you can illustrate them with graphs.

Capitalism and Our Mixed Economy

The economic system of our nation and of many other countries of the Western world is commonly known as "capitalism," "free enterprise," or "private enterprise." These terms are synonymous. What do they mean?

> *Capitalism* is a system of economic organization characterized by private ownership of the means of production and distribution (land, factories, railroads, etc.) and their operation for profit under predominantly competitive conditions.

On what foundations does the theory of capitalism rest? Is our economic system typical of theoretical, or pure, capitalism?

INSTITUTIONS OF CAPITALISM

If you take a course in sociology, you will learn that social systems are often characterized by their _institutions_. These may be defined as those traditions, beliefs, and practices that are well established and widely held as a fundamental part of a culture. Because capitalism is a type of social system—or more precisely _socioeconomic_ system—it has its own particular institutions. Together they comprise the following pillars on which a pure capitalistic system rests.

Private Property

The institution of _private property_ is the most basic element of capitalism. It assures each person the right to acquire economic goods and resources by legitimate means, enter into contracts involving their use, and dispose of them as he or she wishes. This concept originated in the writings of the late-seventeenth-century English philosopher John Locke. He justified private ownership and control of property as a "natural right" independent of the power of the state. This right, he maintained, provides maximum benefits for society as a whole. (In contrast, socialist views prevailing since the nineteenth century have held that private property is a means of exploiting the working class—the so-called "proletariat.")

The granting of property rights fulfills three important economic functions:

1. It provides individuals with personal incentives to make the most productive use of their assets.

2. It strongly influences the distribution of wealth and income by allowing individuals to accumulate assets and pass them on to others at the time of death.

3. It permits a high degree of exchange, because individuals must have property rights before they can transfer those rights.

The social and economic consequences of these functions, as we shall see, have been instrumental in the development of capitalism.

Self-Interest—The "Invisible Hand"

In 1776, a Scottish professor, Adam Smith, published _The Wealth of Nations_. In this book he described his principle of the _"invisible hand."_ This means that individuals pursuing their self-interests without interference by government would be led as if by an invisible hand to achieve the best good for society. In Smith's words:

> An individual neither intends to promote the public interest, nor knows he is promoting it. . . . He intends only his own gain, and he is led by an invisible hand to promote an end which was no part of his intention. . . . It is not from the benevolence of the butcher, the brewer, or the baker that we expect our dinner, but from their regard to their self-interest. We address ourselves not to their humanity, but to their self-love, and never talk to them of our necessities, but of their advantages.

Self-interest drives people to action, but alone it is not enough. People must think rationally if they are to make the right decisions. This requirement ultimately led economists to introduce the concept of _economic man_—the notion that each individual in a capitalistic society is motivated by economic forces. Therefore, each individual will always act in such a way as to obtain the greatest amount of satisfaction for the least amount of sacrifice or cost. These satisfactions may take the form of profits for a businessperson, higher wages or more leisure time for a worker, and greater pleasure from goods purchased for a consumer.

Of course, these assumptions are not always realistic. People may be motivated by forces other than self-interest. Nevertheless, the assumption of economic man does serve as a reasonable approximation of the way people tend to pattern their economic behavior in a capitalistic society. And in economics, as in other social sciences, reasonable approximations are often the most that can be made.

Economic Individualism—Laissez-Faire

In the late seventeenth century, Louis XIV reigned as King of France. His famous finance minister, Jean Baptiste Colbert, asked a manufacturer by the name of Legendre how the government might help business. Legendre's reply was _"laissez nous faire"_ (leave us alone). The expression became a watchword and motto of capitalism.

Today we interpret _laissez-faire_ to mean that absence of government intervention leads to economic individualism and economic freedom. People's economic activities are their own private affairs. As consumers, they are free to spend their incomes as they choose. As producers, they are free to purchase the economic resources they desire and to utilize these resources as they wish. In reality, this concept of laissez-faire is significantly limited, because economic freedom is subject to restraints imposed by society for its protection and general welfare. Can you give some examples?

Competition and Free Markets

Capitalism operates under conditions of _competition_. This means that there is rivalry among sellers of similar goods to attract customers and among buyers to secure the goods that are wanted. There is rivalry among workers to obtain jobs and among employers to obtain workers. And there is rivalry among buyers and sellers of resources to transact business on the best terms that each can get from the other.

Theoretical capitalism is often described as a free-market system. Competition and free markets are closely related. In their most complete or pure form, free markets have two characteristics:

1. There are a large number of buyers and sellers, each with a small enough share of the total business so that no individual can affect the market price of the commodity.

2. Buyers and sellers are unencumbered by economic or institutional restrictions, and possess full knowledge of market prices and alternatives. As a result, they enter or leave markets as they see fit.

Under such circumstances, the market price of a particular commodity is established by the interacting forces of demand and supply. Each buyer and each seller, acting in his or her own best interest as an economic being, decides whether or not to transact business at the going price. No individual has control over the price because no one exerts any perceptible influence in the market.

In the real world, competition does not exist in this pure form. The closest we get to a pure free market is in organized exchanges such as the Chicago Board of Trade and the New York Cotton Exchange. These markets, which are open to all buyers and sellers, deal in standardized commodities such as soybeans, grains, basic metals, and cotton. Markets of this type are studied in considerable detail in microeconomics.

A free market performs a number of important functions. Among them:

1. It establishes competitive prices for both consumer goods and the factors of production.

2. It encourages the efficient use of economic resources.

Free markets may fail to perform these functions if there is a growth of monopolistic or restrictive practices. When this occurs, society (through government) will frequently intervene in the market to regulate such practices.

The Price System

Who tells workers where to work or what occupations to choose? Who decides that automobiles should be made in Detroit and steel in Pittsburgh? Who declares how many cars should be produced and how many homes should be built? Who specifies the predominant style of women's dresses or men's suits?

The greater the degree of competition, the more these matters will be decided impersonally and automatically by the *price system* or the *market system*. This essentially is a system of rewards and penalties.

Rewards consist of profits for firms and individuals who are able to survive. Penalties take the form of losses or possibly bankruptcy for those who fail. The price system is fundamental to the traditional concept of capitalism.

The price system basically operates on the principle that everything that is exchanged—every good, every service, and every resource—has its price. In a free market with many buyers and sellers, the prices of these things reflect the quantities that sellers make available and the quantities that buyers wish to purchase.

Thus, if buyers want to purchase more of a certain good, its price will rise. This will encourage suppliers to produce and sell more of it. On the other hand, if buyers want to purchase less of a certain good, this will cause a fall in its price. Suppliers will then find it to their advantage to produce and sell less of the good.

This interaction between sellers and buyers in a competitive market, and the resulting changes in prices, are what most people refer to by the familiar phrase "supply and demand."

Government: Rule-Maker; Protector; Umpire

The doctrine of laissez-faire came into prominence in the eighteenth century as a result of its popularization by Adam Smith in *The Wealth of Nations*. The concept has strong political as well as economic implications. According to this doctrine, the functions of government in a capitalistic system should be confined to certain traditional activities. These include maintaining order, defining property rights, enforcing contracts, promoting competition, and defending the realm. They also include issuing money, prescribing standards of weights and measures, raising funds to meet operating expenses, and adjudicating disputes over the interpretation of the rules.

Government is thus essential to the existence of capitalism. When society's economic, social, or political values are violated, they must be corrected. When personal freedoms conflict, one individual's freedom must be limited so that another's may be preserved. In theoretical capitalism government fulfills the roles of rule-maker, protector, and umpire. Government does this by imposing minimum restrictions on personal freedoms to protect the well-being of society and by reconciling conflicts of values resulting from the free exercise of property rights.

CONCLUSION: OUR MIXED ECONOMY

Is the doctrine of laissez-faire observed in our economy? Does the "invisible hand" perform as smoothly as Adam Smith said it would, thereby resulting in the best of all possible economic worlds?

The answers to these questions are neither completely positive nor completely negative. Over the years our economy has become increasingly complicated, and the role of government has expanded.

Through the use of legislation of various types, government has come to play a significant role as a protector and regulator of certain groups within the economy. Government has promoted the interests of agriculture, labor, and the consumer. It has controlled competition among such regulated industries as domestic transportation, communication, and power. It has sought to maintain effective competition in the unregulated industries that comprise the bulk of the business sector. Government has assumed the responsibility of keeping the economy's total production and spending in balance to achieve the long-run objectives of economic growth and full employment. And government has become a large provider of many goods and services, among them education, highways, and national defense.

These historical trends suggest the following conclusion:

> The American economy is neither a pure market economy nor a pure command economy. It is a mixed but capitalistically oriented economy in which both private individuals and government exercise their economic influence in the marketplace. *The same is true in all capitalistic countries today.*

The Circular Flow of Economic Activity

It is appropriate for us to consider some important features of a capitalistic system. These are illustrated in a simplified way in Exhibit 3, which summarizes the *circular flow of economic activity*. This model assumes that the total economy is divided into two sectors: households and businesses. The model shows how the two sectors meet one another in two sets of markets: the product markets and the resource markets.

In the *product markets*, households buy the goods and services that businesses sell. Payments for these goods and services are represented by consumption expenditures that become the receipts of businesses. In the *resource markets*, businesses buy the factors of production that households sell. Payments for these factors of production are costs that become the money incomes of households.

All these transactions are accomplished in free markets by a price system that registers the wishes of buyers and sellers. Through the price system, therefore, the product markets are the places where busi-

nesses decide WHAT to produce, whereas the resource markets are the places where businesses decide HOW to produce.

One other feature of the diagram should be noted. The outer loop portrays the physical flow of goods and resources in one direction. The inner loop shows the corresponding flow of money in the opposite direction. If this model depicted a barter economy instead of a monetary one, only goods and resources would be exchanged and there would be no money flows.

LIMITATIONS OF THE CIRCULAR-FLOW MODEL

The circular-flow model is a simplified representation of an economic system. The chief function of the model is to illustrate important aggregate economic relationships. But, like any model, it is an abstraction from reality and therefore omits certain features. Among them:

1. The model says nothing about the behavior of individual buyers and sellers. Nor does it show the ways in which they react to determine prices and quantities in the product and resource markets. Hence, it is a *macroeconomic* rather than a microeconomic model.

2. The model assumes a stable, rather than a fluctuating, circular flow. It does not disclose the effects of variations in the flow on the economy's production and employment. It therefore overlooks the problems of recession and inflation, which are among the most critical economic issues of our time.

Despite these shortcomings, the circular-flow concept provides many useful insights. They will become increasingly apparent as we seek to amplify the underlying implications and ideas of the model in order to gain a better understanding of our modern mixed economy. (See *Leaders in Economics*, pages 22 and 23.)

What You Have Learned

1. A society's resources are the ingredients of its production. The four classes of resources—labor, land, capital, and entrepreneurship—are commonly referred to as the factors of production. The returns received by the owners of these resources are wages, rent, interest, and profits.

2. Every economic system seeks to attain certain objectives. The chief ones are (a) *efficiency* in the use of scarce resources, (b) *equity* in the distribution of income, (c) *stability* of prices and incomes, and (d) *growth* of real output per capita. In democratic, capitalistic countries these goals are sought within a framework of political and economic freedoms. Each society, however, must decide the priorities it wishes to place on these goals and the sacrifices to be made in attaining them.

Exhibit 3
The Circular Flow of Economic Activity

Households and businesses are linked through the product markets, where goods and services are exchanged, and through the resource markets, where the factors of production are exchanged. The questions of WHAT and HOW to produce are answered in these markets. Households act as buyers in the product markets and as sellers in the resource markets, whereas the reverse is true of businesses.

The outer loop shows physical flows in one direction, and the inner loop shows money flows in the opposite direction. (NOTE The question, FOR WHOM? is not directly apparent in this chart. The answer depends on factor prices which are determined in the resource markets, and on other considerations.)

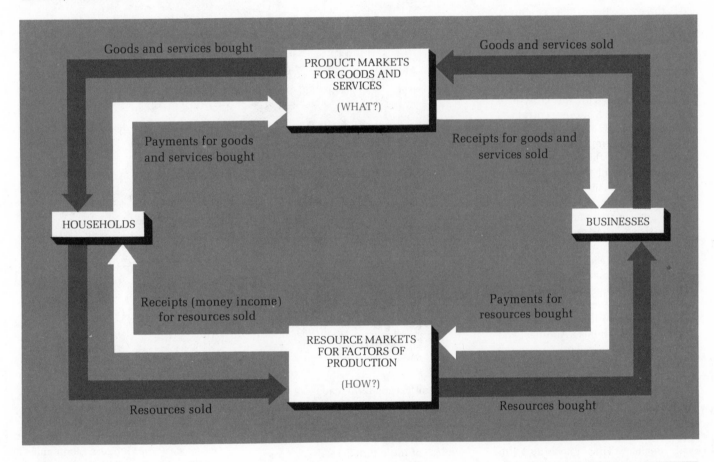

3. All societies are faced with the problem of scarcity because they have limited resources and apparently unlimited wants. Therefore, most economic problems are aspects of the three big questions that every society must answer: WHAT to produce—and in what quantities? HOW to produce? FOR WHOM to produce? These questions are answered differently in mixed and in command economies.

4. In an economy characterized by technical efficiency (i.e., full employment of resources), any increase in the output of some goods and services causes a reduction in the output of some others. With given resources and technology, the production choices open to an economy can be summarized by its production-possibilities curve. The shape of this curve reflects the operation of the law of increasing costs.

5. A society's production-possibilities curve can be used to illustrate several basic economic concepts.

(a) Any point inside the curve indicates some underutilization of resources.

(b) An outward shift of the curve represents an increase in the supply of resources or in technological capability.

(c) A choice between the present proportions of production of consumption goods and capital goods will affect the degree of outward shift of the economy's future curve.

6. The economic system of the United States and many other countries of the Western world is capitalistic. Capitalism is a type of economic organization in which the

Leaders in Economics
St. Thomas Aquinas   1225–1274

The Great Scholastic of Early Capitalism

The period known as the Middle Ages covers approximately one thousand years—from the fall of the Roman Empire in A.D. 476 to about 1500.

Modern capitalism took root in the last three of these ten centuries. Money and credit instruments gained wider acceptance in trade among European towns and cities. The ownership of tools of production became separated from their use. And a wage system emerged with the growth of urbanization and more centralized production.

The outstanding intellectual accomplishment of the late Middle Ages was the system of thought known as Scholasticism. The participants in this system are referred to as Scholastics or Schoolmen. Essentially, Scholasticism was an attempt to harmonize reason with faith. The method consisted of integrating philosophy and theology primarily on the basis of rationalism or logic rather than science and experience.

The greatest of the Scholastic philosophers was Thomas Aquinas, and his most famous work was the *Summa Theologica*. The English translation runs to some twenty volumes. In his writings on economic problems Aquinas applied the principles of Aristotelian philosophy and logic to biblical teachings and canonical dogma. Thus, according to Aquinas:

○ The individual's right to private property accords with natural law.

○ Production under private ownership is preferred to production under communal ownership.

○ Trade is to be condoned to the extent that it maintains the household and benefits the country.

○ Sellers are bound to be truthful with their buyers.

○ Fairness exists when goods are exchanged at equal values and at a "just" price which reflects the customary price.

Brown Brothers.

○ Wealth is good if it leads to a virtuous life.

○ "Usury," the charging of excess interest on loans, is among the most vulgar of trade practices.

Aquinas and the Schoolmen were not in sympathy with many of the economic practices of their time. However, they could do little to change the practices and hence proceeded to make them as respectable as possible. This was done by establishing moral and ethical rules of economic behavior. Many of these rules are now an integral part of modern capitalistic philosophy.

For example, Aquinas decried usury, which he defined as any return for the use of a loan. But he permitted usury if a lender had to forgo an alternative investment that would have yielded an income. This was the principle of *lucrum cessans*—a concept similar to what is known as "opportunity cost" in modern economics. Aquinas also justified the idea that buyers on credit could pay more than the cash price and that discounts were allowed on promissory notes. He also believed that many business transactions could involve specialized charges and payments.

Aquinas was canonized in 1323. For centuries his teachings have been held in the highest esteem by most Catholic as well as by many non-Catholic educators. He is perhaps the foremost authority among Catholics on social subjects, especially since his views were endorsed by Pope Leo XIII in an 1879 encyclical.

Leaders in Economics
Adam Smith 1723–1790

Founder of Economics; Apostle of Economic Liberalism

The year 1776 was marked by two great events in man's struggle for emancipation. In North America, representatives of the British colonies adopted the *Declaration of Independence*—an eloquent statement setting forth a doctrine of political freedom. In Europe, a former Scottish professor of philsophy at the University of Glasgow published a monumental book entitled *An Inquiry into the Nature and Causes of the Wealth of Nations.* Usually known simply as *The Wealth of Nations,* it is an eloquent statement expounding a doctrine of economic freedom. Both the *Declaration of Independence* and *The Wealth of Nations* stand as milestones in the Age of Enlightenment and Liberalism that blossomed during the eighteenth century.

Born in Scotland and educated at Glasgow and Oxford, Adam Smith became a lecturer on literature and philosophy in his mid-twenties. At twenty-eight he was appointed professor of logic and moral philosophy at the University of Glasgow. His great book, *The Wealth of Nations,* took him ten years to write. It earned for him the title of "founder of economics" because it was the first complete and systematic study of the subject.

"The Economic Problem"
The book is a masterful synthesis of centuries of accumulated but separate economic ideas. In it, Smith argues that labor, rather than land or money, is the basic source of a nation's wealth. He points out that individuals know best what is good for them. Therefore, if unrestricted by government controls or private monopolies, workers will be motivated by the quest for profit to turn out the goods and services that society wants most. Consequently, through free trade and free markets, self-interest will be harnessed to the common good.

Brown Brothers.

Smith discussed many topics in *The Wealth of Nations.* Among them: labor; value and price determination; the theory of income distribution involving wages, rent, and profit; the accumulation of capital; and the principles of public finance. These and other topics are fundamental in modern economics textbooks. However, Smith's view of "the economic problem" was somewhat narrower than the modern one.

Smith conceived the central task of economics as man's struggle to conquer nature in the production of material wealth. Hence, Smith's concern was with increasing the productivity of labor and expanding the size of the market. Today, on the other hand, the basic problem of economics is seen to be a broader one. It is concerned with allocating scarce resources among different uses so as to maximize consumers' satisfaction and achieve full employment and steady economic growth without inflation.

Permanent Legacy
Through his approach to economic

questions and his organization of the science, Smith cast a mold for the body of nineteenth-century economic thought. His substantive theory provided scores of economists with points of departure for elaboration and refinement. His views on public policy, which became a semiofficial doctrine of the British government, left their imprint on parliamentary debates and governmental reports. For these reasons, and because of his enormous influence upon succeeding generations of scholars, Smith's unique position in the history of economic thought is forever assured.

Reading *The Wealth of Nations* today, one can see why the influence of this book reached out beyond the borders of economics. Like the Bible, Smith's treatise contains familiar concepts and well-worn truths on almost every page. As a result, "the shy and absentminded scholar," as Smith was affectionately called, became the apostle of economic liberalism— meaning laissez-faire in his time. Today we refer to such ideas as "conservatism."

means of production and distribution are privately owned and used for private gain.

7. Pure capitalism rests on certain pillars. These include private property, self-interest, economic individualism or laissez-faire, competition, and the price system. The economic role of government in a pure capitalistic system is relatively minor. Since the nineteenth century, however, capitalistic or market economies have become increasingly complex. As a result, the economic functions of government have gained in importance. Capitalistic economies today are neither pure market economies nor pure command economies. Instead, they are mixed economies in which both private individuals and government exercise their economic influence in the marketplace.

8. The circular-flow model is a simplified representation of our economy. It focuses on aggregate relationships by depicting the streams of money, goods, and resources that link major sectors and markets.

For Discussion

1. *Terms and concepts to review:*

factors of production	production-possibilities
land	curve
capital	capitalism
labor	private property
entrepreneurship	"invisible hand"
efficiency	economic man
income distribution	laissez-faire
equity	competition
economic good	price system
law of scarcity	circular flow of economic
mixed economy	activity
law of increasing costs	

2. Would entrepreneurship exist in a pure communistic society in which all citizens live and work by the motto: "From each according to his ability, to each according to his needs"?

3. "No one in a rich society has to starve or go naked. Therefore, it is incorrect to say that scarcity pervades our economy. Food and clothing are available to all and hence are not scarce." True or false? Explain.

4. It is sometimes contended that the act of exchange does not *create* wealth because it merely results in a redistribution of goods already in existence. Evaluate this argument.

5. Denmark produces some of the world's best butter. Yet most Danish butter producers use margarine in their homes instead of butter. Does this make sense? Explain.

6. Money is a resource because a person who has it can put it to productive use. The same is true of a nation. Do you agree?

7. The question, FOR WHOM shall goods be produced? is concerned with distributing total output among the members of society. Can you suggest at least three different criteria or rules to decide who gets how much? Which criterion is best?

8. A conventional production-possibilities curve illustrates the law of increasing costs. Can you draw curves that illustrate (a) constant costs and (b) decreasing costs? Define the meaning of each case.

9. Suppose that an economy produces only agricultural goods and capital goods. Using production-possibilities curves, illustrate the effect of a new invention, assuming that the invention has *no direct impact* on agriculture (although it may have some indirect effects). Describe the possible adjustment paths that society may take as a result of the invention.

10. Distinguish between the concepts of *capital* and *capitalism.*

11. The "profit motive" is sometimes said to be the most fundamental feature of capitalism. (a) What do you suppose is meant by the "profit motive"? (b) Why wasn't it explicitly listed in this chapter as one of the pillars of capitalism?

12. (a) "In a free competitive economy, the consumer is king." What does this mean? (b) "The producer, not the consumer, is king. After all, the producer is the one who advertises. Therefore, he or she is the one who creates wants and thereby influences what consumers will purchase." True or false? Explain

13. A shortcoming of a capitalistic society, as compared to a collectivist or socialistic one, is that people are not compensated in proportion to the usefulness and difficulty of their work. True or false? Explain.

Issue
Libertarianism: Capitalism, Raw and Pure

What sort of people want to abolish all laws protecting women, children, and minorities; remove all controls over the use of natural resources; do away with all government subsidies to agriculture, business, the arts, and education; eliminate all taxes, tariffs, and import quotas; repeal legislation that outlaws "victimless" crimes such as gambling, homosexuality, and attempted suicide; and "deregulate" the economy by abolishing not only all government regulatory agencies but— in the long run—even government? Answer: *Libertarians*.

Libertarians are not the sort of fringe crackpot people often associated with revolutionary movements. Indeed, many Libertarians are distinguished community and national leaders. But they are also superconservatives dedicated to a belief in complete political and economic freedom—so much so that they sometimes make most traditional conservatives look like left-wing radicals.

Potpourri of Beliefs, and No Coercion

Libertarians are, first and foremost, capitalists. Their philosophy, however, is a blend of several beliefs. Among them: *hedonism*—devotion to pleasure; *social Darwinism*—survival of the fittest; *objectivism*—enlightened selfishness; and *laissez-faire* economics—free markets unhampered by legislation or central authority. It follows that Libertarians are staunch defenders of civil and personal rights and of the belief that everyone should be free to sell whatever goods and services he or she wishes in an open market.

For example, among the things that Libertarians want legalized—or rather "decriminalized" as they call it—are hard drugs, child labor, voluntary "slavery," sodomy, pornography, and prostitution. The attitudes of Libertarians are thus extraordinarily consistent. They oppose censorship and oppression of any kind and practically all forms of centralized control. Stated briefly, then, the essence of

Virginia Hamilton/FPG.

libertarianism is *opposition to coercion*.

Voluntarism—and Pay As You Go

Perhaps the single biggest thorn in the side of most Libertarians—and the issue which irks them most—is taxation. Libertarians do not merely want a reduction of taxes, but an elimination of them. Taxation is "legalized theft"—and must be outlawed just as any other form of theft.

But if taxes are abolished, how will public services such as police and fire protection and education be provided, and who will care for the poor? The answer, say the Libertarians, is "voluntarism—and pay as you go." In a utopian free society, property owners who want police and fire protection will pay private firms to provide it. Parents who want their children educated will pay teachers to do the job. As for the poor, voluntary charity will take care of their needs. If private donations are insufficient for this purpose, communities could run lotteries and bazaars to raise the necessary funds. And if this fails, the indigent could always sell themselves into voluntary "slavery" in return for food, clothing, and shelter. Stripped

to its bare essentials the goal of Libertarians is a *voluntary, noncoercive society* in which people who want a service pay for what they get.

Conclusion: What Future?

Does Libertarianism have a future? According to its adherents, it does. The movement has grown from a group composed of less than two dozen intellectuals a few decades ago to a political party whose membership today numbers in the thousands. Among its supporters are state governors, Supreme Court justices, members of Congress, business executives, scientists, educators, and journalists. Although many Libertarians are not party members, they profess sympathy for any movement in our society that seeks to reduce the scope of government.

If Libertarianism has a future, it may be due to a general disillusionment with government. In the words of one prominent observer, "Libertarianism appeals to the overtaxed, overregulated, overburdened, and underpowered millions of the American middle class. It offers the only real alternative—the only one worth voting for." To some Libertarians, however, even that is not a desirable alternative. One anarchist faction opposes all forms of government and wants the right to reject any or all candidates at the voting booth.

QUESTIONS

1. How does Adam Smith's view of the role of government contrast with the views held by Libertarians?

2. Libertarians believe that only the people who want a service should pay for what they get—and that those who do not want a particular service should not be required to pay for it. How could this belief be implemented with respect to such services as fire protection, the administration of justice, and national defense? In other words, how could people who do not pay for these services be prevented from receiving them?

Chapter 2

The Laws of Supply and Demand: The Price System in a Pure Market Economy

Chapter Preview

What are the laws of supply and demand? How do they determine prices?

How does a market economy operate? What is a price system?

What can be said about the pros and cons of a market economy? How well does it answer the questions: WHAT? HOW? FOR WHOM?

One unusual thing about economics is that even a parrot can answer many important questions with just three simple words, *supply and demand*. Here are a few examples.

QUESTION   Why are Rembrandts expensive while water is cheap—especially since everyone needs water more than Rembrandts?
ANSWER   Supply and demand.

QUESTION   Why is the cost of medical care rising faster than prices generally?
ANSWER   Supply and demand.

QUESTION   Why are some luxurious apartments vacant, while there is a shortage of low-cost housing?
ANSWER   Supply and demand.

QUESTION   Why do the prices of some commodities fluctuate, while the prices of others remain stable?
ANSWER   Supply and demand.

Such simplistic answers to complex problems are not very illuminating. Nevertheless, much of economics is concerned with supply and demand. In this chapter you discover more about this apparently simple, but actually complicated, subject.

What Do We Mean by Demand?

If pizzas were $5 each, how many would you buy per month? What if the price were $3? $2? Would you buy twice as many at $2 as at $4?

These are typical of the questions that arise in the study of demand. What is demand? In economics it has a special meaning:

> Demand is a relation showing the various amounts of a commodity that buyers would be willing and able to purchase at possible alternative prices during a given period of time, all other things remaining the same.

The commodity can be anything—pizzas, shoes, television sets, haircuts, labor time, computers, or any other good or service bought by consumers, businesses, or government agencies. The definition assumes that demand means both desire and ability to pay. Either of these taken separately is of no economic significance in the marketplace.

Thus, if you want a steak but cannot pay for it—or if you can pay but prefer hamburger—you exercise no economic influence in the market for steaks. But if you have both the desire and the ability to pay, these together will affect your demand for the product.

THE DEMAND SCHEDULE

Suppose that you were a merchant dealing in grain—for example, wheat, corn, barley, or oats. What is your demand for a specific commodity such as wheat?

According to the definition of demand above, you must first ask, "At what prices and for how long?" It seems likely that within a given period you would buy more wheat at a lower price than at a higher one. Also, at a given price you would probably buy more in a longer period than in a shorter one. In view of this, you might prepare a hypothetical list of the number of bushels of wheat you would buy at different prices during a particular time interval. The interval could be of any length—a day, a week, a month, and so on.

Exhibit 1
An Individual's Demand Schedule for Wheat

A demand schedule is a list showing the number of units of a product that would be purchased at various possible prices during a given period of time.

	Price per bushel	Quantity demanded per day
A	$5	5
B	4	10
C	3	20
D	2	35
E	1	60

During the interval, *your income and the prices of other commodities are assumed to remain the same.*

Economists call such a list a <u>demand schedule,</u> as shown in Exhibit 1. This schedule represents your individual demand for wheat over the price range shown. The schedule tells you that at $5 per bushel you would buy 5 bushels per day. At a price of $4 per bushel you would buy 10 bushels per day, and so on. The schedule can be made more detailed by extending the price scale upward and by quoting the prices in dollars and cents instead of just dollars. But such detail is not necessary. As you will see, the schedule already gives you the highlights of your demand for wheat. This is all you need in order to draw a graph.

SKETCHING A DEMAND CURVE

Most people prefer to look at a chart instead of a table of figures. This is easily done by converting the information in Exhibit 1 to the diagram in Exhibit 2. The graphing process is done in three steps.

Step 1   Draw the vertical and horizontal axes of the chart and put the labels on them as shown. Once you become accustomed to sketching these charts, you may simply label the vertical axis *P* for price and the horizontal axis *Q* for quantity. The starting point or origin of the chart is always at the lower left-hand corner, labeled 0.

Exhibit 2
An Individual's Demand Curve for Wheat

A demand curve is the graph of a demand schedule. Each point along the curve represents a different price–quantity combination. A demand curve slopes downward from left to right, reflecting the fact that the quantity demanded of a product varies inversely with the price. This is called the *law of demand.*

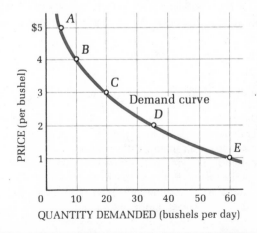

Step 2 Plot the corresponding prices and quantities with large dots, and label them with the appropriate letters *A*, *B*, *C*, *D*, *E* from the demand schedule in Exhibit 1. The letters help you identify the points. After you gain some experience in graphing, the emphasized points and letters will no longer be necessary.

Step 3 Connect the points with a smooth curve.

What you now have is called a <u>demand curve</u>. It represents the graphic equivalent of the demand schedule in Exhibit 1. The advantage of the curve is that it enables you to "see" the relationship between price and quantity demanded. Thus, you can read off the values at a glance, much as you would use a map to locate a ship at sea by its latitude and longitude.

For instance, point *C* represents 20 bushels of wheat demanded per day at a price of $3 per bushel. Would you agree that at $1.50 per bushel the quantity demanded is 45 bushels per day? Can you verify that at a quantity demanded of 35 bushels per day, the *highest price* you would be willing to pay (called the <u>demand price</u>) is $2 per bushel? Can you explain why we use an agricultural product rather than a manufactured one? (See Box 1.)

THE LAW OF DEMAND

A look at the demand curve in Exhibit 2 reveals its most fundamental property. *The curve slopes downward from left to right—from northwest to southeast.* This characteristic illustrates the law of demand. The law applies to virtually all commodities: wheat, houses, cars, books, stereo records, or practically anything you care to name. Here is a definition:

> *Law of demand.* The quantity demanded of a good varies inversely with its price, assuming that other things which may affect demand remain the same. These include the buyer's income, tastes, and the prices of other commodities. (NOTE In the definition, "inversely" means that as the price of a good decreases, the corresponding quantity demanded increases. Also, as the price of a good increases, the corresponding quantity demanded decreases.)

Why does the law of demand operate as it does? This question can be answered in several ways.

1. If the price of a good decreases, you can *afford* to buy more of it if your income, tastes, and the prices of

---

Box 1
Why Wheat?

Why are we using wheat as an example? Why not use a more familiar product—cars or television sets?

The answer is that we want to show how the price is established for a uniform or standardized product in a highly competitive market. That is, the market should be characterized by a great many buyers and sellers, each acting independently according to his or her best interests. This type of situation or model will result in a *single market price* for the product at any given time. Clearly, autos and television sets do not meet these requirements, for at least three reasons.

1. Each is produced by a relatively small number of sellers.

2. Each is nonstandardized or differentiated by brand name, model, year, style, color, and so on.

3. Each is characterized by different prices rather than by single prices.

These conditions are true in varying degrees for nearly all the other products we buy every day.

On the other hand, products such as wheat, as well as the other commodities shown on the accompanying list, approximate the requirements rather closely. Any one of them may be used in a model to illustrate the "pure" operation of supply and demand. Prices of these commodities, which are bought and sold in national and international markets, are quoted daily in several major newspapers.

COMMODITIES: CASH PRICES AT NATIONAL MARKETS
(quotations as of 4 P.M. Eastern time)

	Monday	Friday	Year Ago
Foods			
Flour, hard winter, per cwt.	$11.65	$11.60	$ 8.10
Coffee, Santos 4s, per lb.	.70	.70	.57
Cocoa, Accra, per lb.	.77	.79	.37
Sugar, raw, per lb.	.11	.10	.09
Butter, fresh, per lb.	.74	.75	.69
Eggs, per doz.	.64	.66	.39
Broilers, dressed "A," per lb.	.36	.39	.28
Grains and feeds			
Pepper, black, per lb.	.59	.58	.45
Wheat, No. 2, per bu.	4.64	4.65	2.21
Oats, No. 1, per bu.	1.40	1.36	.85
Rye, No. 2, per bu.	2.45	2.48	1.15
Barley, per bu.	2.66	2.65	1.35
Miscellaneous			
Cottonseed oil, per lb.	.19	.18	.10
Soybean oil, per lb.	.19	.19	.09
Peanut oil, per lb.	.24	.21	.17
Cotton, 1 in., per lb.	.72	.71	.29
Print cloth, 64 x 60, 45 in., per yd.	.50	.51	.23
Steel scrap, per ton	86.00	86.00	38.00
Lead, per lb.	.16	.16	.14
Zinc, per lb.	.20	.20	.18

SOURCE: Adapted from *The Wall Street Journal.*

other goods remain the same. For instance, if you like pizza, but find it too expensive to buy frequently, a lower price might induce you to purchase it more often.

2. When the price of a product is reduced, you may buy more of it because it becomes a better bargain than other goods are. This assumes, as before, that your income, tastes, and the prices of other goods remain constant. Thus, if the price of steak falls, you might buy more steak and fewer substitutes, such as hamburger or hot dogs. On the other hand, if the price of steak rises, you would tend to buy less steak and more substitutes.

3. Finally, the downward-sloping demand curve tells you that you would be willing to pay a relatively high price for a small amount of something. However, the more you have of it—other things remaining the same—the less you would care to pay for one more unit. Why? *Because each extra unit gives you less additional satisfaction or "utility" than the previous unit gave you.* For example, however crazy you are about ice-cream sundaes, there is a limit to the number you can eat in any given period. After the first few sundaes, you would probably get sick.

No matter how much you like a product, your demand curve will slope downward for the three sets of reasons given above. And people in business, of course, often operate as if they believe a law of (downward-sloping) demand exists. Why else would they advertise bargains that encourage people to buy more goods at lower prices?

MARKET DEMAND IS THE SUM OF INDIVIDUAL DEMANDS

If you were the only buyer of wheat in the market, your individual demand schedule would also be the total market demand schedule. In reality there are many other buyers, so the total market demand schedule is obtained by simply adding up the quantities demanded by all buyers at each possible price.

Exhibit 3 shows how this is done. This assumes there are only three buyers in the market—Mr. X, Ms. Y, and Mr. Z. However, the example can easily be expanded to include as many buyers as you wish. Note that the individual demand curves have all been labeled so that they can be referred to as they are needed.

Exhibit 3
Market Demand for Wheat, Three Buyers

The total market demand is obtained by summing all the individual quantities demanded at each price.

Price per bushel	Quantity demanded by Mr. X		Quantity demanded by Ms. Y		Quantity demanded by Mr. Z		Total market demand per day
$5	0	+	15	+	20	=	35
4	9	+	20	+	26	=	55
3	22	+	27	+	33	=	82
2	42	+	38	+	43	=	123
1	80	+	65	+	60	=	205

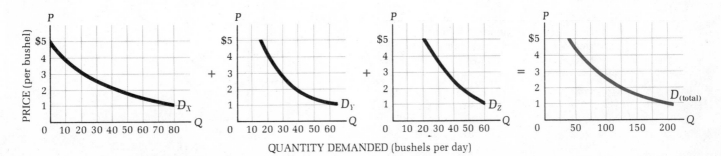

QUANTITY DEMANDED (bushels per day)

What Is Supply?

You now have a basic knowledge of demand. The other half of the picture involves supply. What do we mean by supply? Is there a law of supply?

Supply is a relation showing the various amounts of a commodity that sellers would be willing and able to make available for sale at possible alternative prices during a given period of time, all other things remaining the same.

How does this definition of supply compare with the definition of demand given near the beginning of this chapter? Are there any similarities? Any differences?

SUPPLY SCHEDULES AND SUPPLY CURVES

Each seller in the market has his own *supply schedule* for a product, just as each buyer has his own demand schedule. Thus, if you were a wheat farmer, Exhibit 4 might represent your individual supply schedule for wheat. This schedule indicates that at a price of $1 per bushel you would not be willing to supply any wheat at all. At a price of $2 per bushel you would be willing to supply 21 bushels of wheat per day, and so on. Plotting these data on a chart gives the *supply curve* shown in Exhibit 5. What is your estimate of the quantity supplied at a price of $2.50 per unit? What is the *least price,* approximately, that will persuade you to supply 40 bushels per day?

REMARK   The "least price" is more often called the *supply price.* This is the price necessary to call forth a given quan-

tity. What do you estimate the supply price to be for 25 bushels per day?

An example of the supply schedules for three individual producers, Ms. A, Mr. B., and Ms. C, is presented in Exhibit 6. When you plot the data, you get the corresponding supply curves shown on the charts. Note that the total market supply schedule is obtained by adding up the quantities supplied by all sellers at each market price. How does this compare with the way in which the total market demand schedule was derived earlier?

THE LAW OF SUPPLY

The supply curve as drawn has a distinguishing feature. *The curve slopes upward from left to right—from southwest to northeast.* This feature reflects the law of supply:

Law of supply. The quantity supplied of a commodity usually varies *directly* with its price, assuming that all other factors that may determine supply remain the same. (NOTE   In the definition, "directly" means that the quantity of a product produced and offered for sale will increase as the price of the product rises, and decrease as the price falls.)

Observe that according to the definition, the direct relation between quantity and price is "usually" true,

Exhibit 4
An Individual's Supply Schedule for Wheat

A supply schedule is a list showing the number of units of a product that sellers would be willing and able to make available for sale at various prices during a given period of time.

	Price per bushel	Quantity supplied per day (bushels)
A'	$5	50
B'	4	42
C'	3	33
D'	2	21
E'	1	0

Exhibit 5
An Individual's Supply Curve for Wheat

A supply curve is the graph of a supply schedule. Each point along the curve represents a different price–quantity combination. A supply curve slopes upward from left to right, reflecting the fact that the quantity supplied of a product varies directly with the price. This is called the *law of supply.*

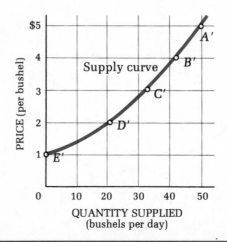

Exhibit 6
Market Supply of Wheat, Three Sellers

The total market supply of wheat is obtained by summing all the individual quantities supplied at each price.

Price per bushel	Quantity supplied by Ms. A		Quantity supplied by Mr. B		Quantity supplied by Ms. C		Total market supply per day
$5	52	+	56	+	60	=	168
4	46	+	49	+	50	=	145
3	36	+	42	+	40	=	118
2	26	+	28	+	26	=	80
1	0	+	15	+	10	=	25

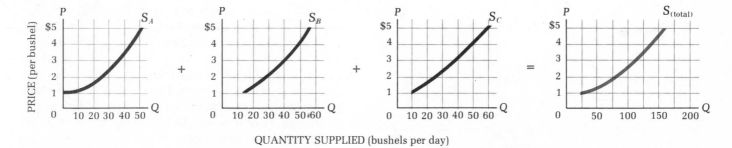

QUANTITY SUPPLIED (bushels per day)

but not always. This is because there can be some supply curves where larger quantities are offered for sale at the *same* price or even at *lower* prices. These ideas are examined more fully in the study of micro-economics.

If you were a producer—say, a farmer cultivating both wheat and corn—the law of supply would prompt you to act in the following way. When the price of wheat rose relative to the price of corn, you would make greater profits by reorganizing your methods of production. That is, you would shift your limited resources—fertilizer, land, labor, machinery, and so on—out of corn production into wheat production. If the price of wheat rose high enough, you would even find it worthwhile to grow wheat on land where you previously grew nothing. It seems, therefore, that the law of supply does, indeed, make sense.

Supply and Demand Together Make a Market

The concepts of supply and demand must be united to provide an explanation of how prices are determined in competitive markets.

A market exists whenever and wherever one or more buyers and sellers can negotiate for goods or services and thereby participate in determining their prices. A market, therefore, can be anywhere—on a street corner, on the other side of the world, or as close as the nearest telephone. *Competitive markets* are composed of buyers and sellers so numerous that no single one can influence the market price by deciding to buy or not to buy, to sell or not to sell.

BUYERS AND SELLERS IN THE MARKETPLACE

By using the *total* demand and supply information derived in Exhibits 3 and 6, we can discover how the market price of a product and the quantity bought and sold are determined. The total market demand and supply schedules and their corresponding curves are reproduced in Exhibit 7. Note that the curves, abbreviated D and S, are identical with the total market curves that were graphed in Exhibits 3 and 6. The only difference is that both curves are now graphed on the same chart so that their interactions can be studied.

The most important thing to observe is that the supply and demand curves intersect at an *equilibrium* point. A dictionary will tell you that "equilibrium" is a state of balance between opposing forces. Let us see what this means in terms of Exhibit 7.

Exhibit 7
The Equilibrium Price and Quantity for Wheat

The intersection of the supply and demand curves determines the equilibrium price and the equilibrium quantity. At any price above the equilibrium price, the quantity supplied exceeds the quantity demanded and the price tends to fall. At any price below the equilibrium price, the quantity demanded exceeds the quantity supplied and the price tends to rise. At the equilibrium price, the quantity supplied precisely equals the quantity demanded, and hence there is no tendency for the price to change.

Price per bushel	Total market supply per day (bushels)	Total market demand per day (bushels)
$5	168	35
4	145	55
3	118	82
2	80	123
1	25	205

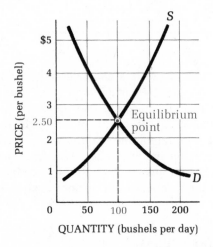

At any price above $2.50 per bushel, the quantity supplied exceeds the quantity demanded. For example, at a price of $5 per bushel, the quantity supplied is 168 bushels per day, and the quantity demanded is 35 bushels per day. This means that at the price of $5 per bushel there is a surplus of 168 − 35 = 133 bushels per day. Because sellers thus have more wheat available than buyers want, sellers will compete with one another to dispose of their product and thereby drive the price down.

At any price below $2.50 per bushel, the quantity demanded exceeds the quantity supplied. At $1 a bushel, for example, the quantity demanded is 205 bushels per day and the quantity supplied is 25 bush-els per day. At this price there is thus a shortage of 205 − 25 = 180 bushels per day. Because buyers want more wheat than sellers have available at this price, buyers will compete with one another to acquire the product and thereby drive the price up.

ARRIVING AT MARKET EQUILIBRIUM

At a price of $2.50 per bushel, the quantity demanded just equals the quantity supplied, 100 bushels per day. At this price there will be no surpluses or shortages. We refer to this price as the equilibrium price and to the corresponding quantity as the equilibrium quantity.

Thus, when the quantity demanded equals the quantity supplied, there is a state of market equilibrium because the price of the product and the corresponding quantities bought and sold are "in balance." That is, they have no tendency to change as a result of the opposing forces of demand and supply. On the other hand, when the quantities demanded and supplied at a given price are unequal or "out of balance," prices and quantities will be changing, so the market is then in a state of disequilibrium.

Two Kinds of Changes in Demand

Demand and supply curves are extremely practical. You can employ them to answer many fundamental questions in economics. However, in order to give them even wider use, it is necessary to realize that two kinds of changes in the curves may occur. With respect to demand, there may be (1) changes in the quantity demanded and (2) changes in demand. With respect to supply, similar changes can take place. The various types of changes can be best understood by first examining those for demand.

CHANGES IN THE QUANTITY DEMANDED

Take a look back again at Exhibit 2. According to the law of demand, a downhill movement along the same curve in the general direction A, B, C, ... signifies an increase in the quantity demanded as the price is reduced. On the other hand, an upward movement along the curve in the general direction E, D, C, ... signifies a decrease in the quantity demanded as the price is raised. Any such movement along the same curve, whether downward or upward, is called a change in the quantity demanded. Note that this expression refers to changes in the quantities purchased by buyers due to changes in price.

CHANGES IN DEMAND

The law of demand says that the quantity demanded of a good varies inversely with its price, assuming that all other things remain the same. What are these "all other" things? What happens if they do not remain the same?

Among the "all other" factors that will influence the demand for a commodity are (1) buyers' money incomes, (2) prices of related commodities, and (3) non-monetary factors. These three demand-determining conditions are not measured on the axes, and are assumed to be constant when you draw a demand curve. Therefore, a change in any one of them will cause a shift of the demand curve to a new position. When this happens, we say that there has been a *change in demand*. The change may take either of two forms—an increase or a decrease.

1. An increase in demand can be visualized on a chart as a shift of the demand curve to the right. This is shown in Exhibit 8. The shift takes place from the old demand curve *D* to the new demand curve *D'*.

What does this increase in demand tell you? It shows that, *at any given price, buyers are now willing to purchase more than they were willing to purchase before.* For example, the dashed lines on the chart indicate that at a price of $30 per unit, buyers were

previously willing to purchase 300 units per week. After the increase in demand, they are willing to buy 400 units per week at the same price of $30 per unit.

2. A decrease in demand, shown in Exhibit 9, can be visualized as a shift of the demand curve to the left. This time the chart illustrates that, *at any given price, buyers are now willing to purchase less than they were willing to purchase before.* Thus, at $30 per unit, people were willing to buy 300 units per week. Now, after the decrease in demand, they are willing to buy only 200 units per week at the same price of $30 per unit.

Test Yourself 1

An increase in demand also means that for any given quantity demanded, buyers are now willing to pay a *higher price* per unit than they were willing to pay before.

1. Can you define a decrease in demand in a parallel way?

2. Look at Exhibit 8. What is your estimate of the highest price per unit that buyers were willing to pay for 300 units per week, before and after the increase in demand?

3. Look at Exhibit 9. What is your estimate of the highest price per unit that buyers were willing to pay for 200 units per week, before and after the decrease in demand?

Exhibit 8
Increase in Demand

An increase in demand can be represented by a shift of the demand curve to the right. At any given price, people are now willing to buy more than they were willing to buy before.

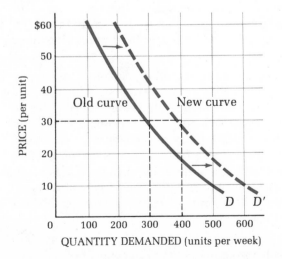

Exhibit 9
Decrease in Demand

A decrease in demand can be represented by a shift of the demand curve to the left. At any given price, people are now willing to buy less than they were willing to buy before.

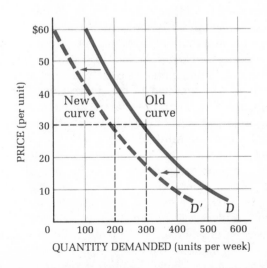

How do changes in any of the three demand determinants mentioned above bring about a change in demand? That is, how do the changes cause a shift of the demand curve either to the right or to the left?

Buyers' Incomes   The demands for most goods vary directly with buyers' incomes. This means the demand curves shift to the right when incomes rise and to the left when incomes fall. Goods whose demand curves behave in this way are known as *superior goods,* or more popularly as *normal goods*. They are called this because they represent the "normal" situation. Examples include most food, clothing, cars, appliances, and other items that people typically buy.

For some goods, however, changes in consumption (prices remaining constant) vary inversely with changes in income over a certain range of income. Such goods are called *inferior goods*. Typical examples are bread, potatoes, beans, and used clothing, bought by poor families. As the incomes of these families rise, they can afford to buy better qualities of goods. Thus, they spend less on bread and potatoes and more on fruits and vegetables, less on beans and more on steaks, less on used clothing and more on new clothing.

Prices of Related Goods   A second factor determining the demand for any good is the price of related goods. The degree of relationship depends on the extent to which consumers regard the products as competitive or complementary with each other. Thus, if buyers' incomes remain constant, the commodities that consumers purchase may be placed in one of two categories.

Some products are *substitute goods*. The more that people consume of one product, the less they consume of the other. Thus, an increase in the price of one leads to an increase in the demand for the other. Similarly, a decrease in the price of one leads to a decrease in the demand for the other. For example, if the price of Coca-Cola increases, people will probably buy less Coca-Cola and more Pepsi-Cola. The market demand curve for Pepsi-Cola will therefore shift to the right. On the other hand, if the price of Coca-Cola decreases, people will be inclined to buy more Coca-Cola and less Pepsi-Cola. Then the market demand curve for Pepsi-Cola will shift to the left. What other substitute products can you think of?

Some products are *complementary goods*. The more that people consume of one, the more they consume of the other. An increase in the price of one leads to a decrease in the demand for the other. Conversely, a decrease in the price of one leads to an increase in the demand for the other. For example, if the price of cameras increases, people will buy fewer cameras—and less film. The market demand curve for film will shift to the left.

Products that are neither substitutes nor complements are unrelated. The consumption of one does not affect the consumption of the other. Therefore, a change in the price of one does not cause a change in the demand for the other. Some examples are salt and pencils, chewing gum and paper clips, thumbtacks and mustard.

Keep in mind, however, that expenditures on unrelated pairs of commodities must represent a relatively small percentage of the consumer's budget. Otherwise, if a buyer's expenditure on a good absorbs a relatively large proportion of his or her budget, a change in its price may affect the buyer's demand for another product. This is true even if the latter is neither competitive nor complementary with the former. One example of this is housing and entertainment. Can you give some other examples?

To generalize thus far:

> Suppose that buyers' incomes remain constant. Then the market demand curve of any commodity will move in the same direction as a change in the price of its substitute. Conversely, the market demand curve will move in the opposite direction from a change in the price of its complement. This means that for substitute products the relationship between a change in the price of one commodity and the resulting change in demand for the other is *direct*. For complementary products the relationship is *inverse*.

Expectations   Of course, buyers' *expectations* of incomes and prices can also influence demands for commodities. If buyers expect higher incomes or higher prices in the near future, larger quantities of goods may be bought in anticipation of the increases. This causes the demands for those goods to shift to the right. On the other hand, if buyers expect lower incomes or lower prices, fewer quantities of goods may be bought. This causes demands to shift to the left. For these reasons, economists who are engaged in economic forecasting often try to incorporate the effects of buyers' expectations in their predictive models.

Nonmonetary Factors   Many factors other than prices and incomes influence the demands for commodities. These factors include all nonmonetary determinants of demand, such as the age, occupation, sex, race, religion, education, tastes, and number of consumers. Changes in these factors can affect the preferences, composition, and quantity of buyers. It is customary to assume, however, that for large numbers of consumers these nonmonetary factors are stable—for two reasons:

1. They vary widely among individuals so that their effects in the market tend to cancel out.

2. They change slowly over the long run because they

are primarily the result of demographic characteristics and cultural traditions.

For both reasons, therefore, short-run changes in demand caused by economic factors can be analyzed exclusively in terms of prices and incomes.

CONCLUSION: IMPORTANT DISTINCTIONS

You have learned that demand can be represented by a schedule or curve that reflects buyers' attitudes at the time. If the demand curve does not shift, a change in price leads to a *change in the quantity demanded*, not to a change in demand. This means that there has been either an increase in the quantity demanded, as represented by a movement downward along the curve, or a decrease in the quantity demanded, as represented by a movement upward along the curve. The change is due either to a decrease or an increase in the price of the product (while all other demand determinants remain the same).

A *change in demand* means that the schedule itself has changed. Therefore, the demand curve has either shifted to the right, if there has been an increase in demand, or to the left, if there has been a decrease in demand. The shift is due to a change in any of the demand determinants that were assumed to remain constant when the curve was initially drawn.

It is easy to commit errors in economic reasoning by failing to understand the important distinctions between a change in the quantity demanded and a change in demand.

Test Yourself 2

Which of the following involve a change in the quantity demanded and which involve a change in demand?

1. People buy more bathing suits in the summer than in the winter.

2. Consumer incomes fall and the number of automobiles purchased declines.

3. Honda reduces the prices of its motorcycles by 10 percent and its sales increase.

4. State College raises its tuition and student enrollments fall off.

Two Kinds of Changes in Supply

As with demand, so too with supply, two types of changes may occur. One is called a "change in the quantity supplied"; the other is known as a "change in supply." On the basis of what you now know about the theory of demand, can you guess the meanings of these two concepts before we explain them?

CHANGES IN THE QUANTITY SUPPLIED

Look back at Exhibit 5. According to the law of supply, an upward movement along the same curve signifies an increase in the quantity supplied as the *price is raised*. On the other hand, a downward movement along the curve signifies a decrease in the quantity supplied as the *price is reduced*. Any such movement along the same curve, whether upward or downward, is called a *change in the quantity supplied*. Note that such movements are due exclusively to a *change in price*.

CHANGES IN SUPPLY

The law of supply says that the quantity supplied of a product usually varies directly with its price, assuming that all other things remain the same. The "other things" that may have an influence in determining supply are (1) resource prices or the costs of the factors of production, (2) prices of other goods, and (3) nonmonetary factors. If any of these conditions change, a new relationship is established between price and quantity offered. In terms of a graph, this means a shift of the supply curve to a new position. When that happens, we get what is called a *change in supply*.

1. An increase in supply is a shift of the supply curve to the right, as shown in Exhibit 10. *At any given price sellers are now willing to supply more than they were willing to supply before.* For example, the dashed black lines indicate that at a price of $30 per unit sellers were previously willing to supply a total of 300 units per week. Now, after the increase in supply, they are willing to sell a total of 400 units per week at the same price of $30 per unit.

2. A decrease in supply is represented by a shift of the supply curve to the left. *At any given price, sellers are now willing to supply less than they were willing to supply before.* In Exhibit 11 they were previously willing to supply a total of 300 units per week at a price of $30 per unit. Now, after the decrease in supply, they are willing to sell a total of 200 units per week at the same price of $30 per unit.

How will a change in any of the supply determinants listed above bring about a change in supply—that is, a shift of the supply curve?

Resource Prices Ordinarily, a decrease in resource prices (such as wages) in a particular industry will reduce production costs and thus broaden the profit potentials. However, if there is vigorous competition among businesses within the industry, those firms will increase their output at each possible price in order to

Exhibit 10
Increase in Supply

An increase in supply can be represented by a shift of the supply curve to the right. At any given price, sellers are now willing to supply more than they were willing to supply before.

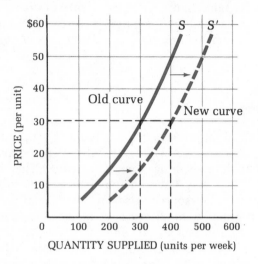

Exhibit 11
Decrease in Supply

A decrease in supply can be represented by a shift of the supply curve to the left. At any given price, sellers are now willing to supply less than they were willing to supply before.

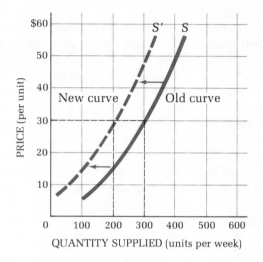

capture some of these profits. This action will shift the total market supply curve to the right. Conversely, an increase in resource prices (such as wages) in a given industry would tend to have the opposite effect, because it raises production costs and decreases profits. This encourages businesses in that industry to reduce their output at each possible price. The market supply curve thus shifts to the left.

Prices of Related Goods   Business firms produce goods to make profits. Changes in the relative prices of goods which compete in production may change the relative profitabilities of those goods. This brings about changes in their respective supply curves. For instance, if the price of wheat increases relative to the price of corn, farmers may find it more profitable to transfer some land and other resources out of corn and into wheat. This would shift the market supply curve of corn to the left and the market supply curve of wheat to the right.

Of course, sellers' *expectations* of prices will also influence their supply decisions. Some producers may decide to hold back on their current output because they anticipate higher prices for their goods—and therefore higher profits. Other producers may decide to increase their current output because they anticipate lower prices for their goods—and, therefore, lower profits or possibly losses.

Nonmonetary Factors   Various factors other than prices can affect the supply of a commodity. The most important are the state of technology and the number of sellers in the market. For example, the adoption of a new production method, such as a new machine in place of labor, may improve technical efficiency and increase supply by shifting the market supply curve to the right. A decline in technical efficiency due to a failure to modernize can have the opposite effect. Similarly, an increase in the number of sellers in the market will result in a rightward shift of the market supply curve. A decrease in the number of sellers will cause a leftward shift of the curve.

CONCLUSION: IMPORTANT DISTINCTIONS

You have seen that supply can be represented by a schedule or curve that reflects sellers' attitudes at the time. If the supply curve does not shift, a change in price leads to a *change in the quantity supplied*, not to a change in supply. This can mean there has been a movement upward along the curve in the case of an increase in the quantity supplied. Alternatively, it can mean a movement downward along the curve in the case of a decrease in the quantity supplied.

A *change in supply* means that the schedule itself has changed. That is, the curve has shifted to the right if there has been an increase in supply or to the left if there has been a decrease in supply. The shift is the result of a change in any of the supply determinants that were assumed to remain constant when the curve was initially drawn.

As with demand, so with supply, these important distinctions must be understood to avoid errors in economic reasoning.

Test Yourself 3

An increase in supply also means that for any given quantity supplied sellers are now willing to accept a *lower price* per unit than before.

1. Can you define a decrease in supply in a parallel way?

2. Look back at Exhibit 10. What is your estimate of the lowest price per unit that sellers were willing to accept for a supply of 300 units per week, before the increase in supply? After the increase in supply?

3. Look at Exhibit 11. What is your estimate of the lowest price per unit that sellers were willing to accept for a supply of 200 units per week, before the decrease in supply? After the decrease in supply?

Combined Changes in Demand and Supply

Demand and supply curves rarely remain fixed for very long. This is because the factors determining them, such as buyers' incomes, resource costs, or prices of related products, are continually changing, causing the curves to shift. Because we are interested in learning about the behavior of prices and quantities in competitive markets, we must be able to analyze such shifts to evaluate their effects.

What happens when a demand or supply curve moves to a new position? The answer is that there may also be a change in the equilibrium price, the equilibrium quantity, or both. Some examples are presented in Exhibit 12, with the arrows indicating the directions of change.

REMARK Supply and demand curves may be drawn as straight lines rather than as curved lines. This is because straight lines are often simpler to work with and are usually just as informative for most practical purposes. However, even when they are drawn as straight lines, we still refer to them as supply and demand *curves*.

What can you say about Exhibit 12?

In each of Charts (a) through (d), one of the curves shifted while the other remained unchanged. The effects on the equilibrium price and quantity in each case are depicted by the arrows. In Chart (a), an increase in demand resulted in an increase in both the equilibrium price and the equilibrium quantity. The

Exhibit 12
Changes in Demand and Supply

Shifts in the demand or supply curves will cause changes in equilibrium price, equilibrium quantity, or both.

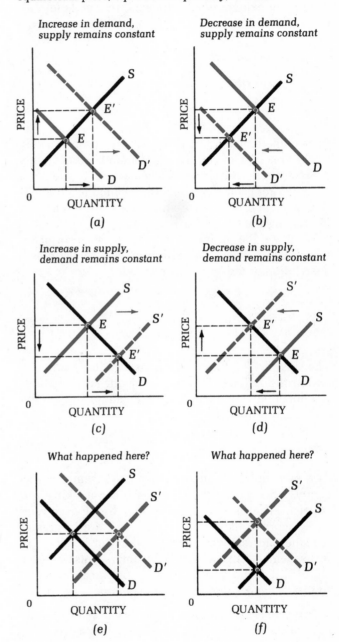

(a) Increase in demand, supply remains constant

(b) Decrease in demand, supply remains constant

(c) Increase in supply, demand remains constant

(d) Decrease in supply, demand remains constant

(e) What happened here?

(f) What happened here?

TEST YOURSELF

In Charts (e) and (f), what would have happened to price and/or quantity if the change in one of the curves was not exactly "offset" by the change in the other? Try sketching a few diagrams and see for yourself. Can you suggest some general conclusions?

opposite situation occurred in Chart (b) as a result of a decrease in demand. In Chart (c), on the other hand, an increase in supply resulted in a decrease in the equilibrium price and an increase in the equilibrium quantity. The opposite situation occurred in Chart (d), as a result of a decrease in supply.

Can you explain what happened in Charts (e) and (f)?

The Market Economy: Is It "Good" or "Bad"?

In a competitive market, prices are determined solely by the free play of supply and demand. An economy characterized entirely by such markets would be a _pure market economy_, sometimes called a "competitive economy." The two expressions are often used interchangeably.

What are the desirable features of such an economy? Does it have shortcomings? Is it realistic as a description of the capitalistic system?

THE PRINCIPAL FEATURES OF A PURE MARKET ECONOMY

The answers to these questions can be expressed within the familiar framework of our society's four fundamental economic goals: efficiency, equity, stability, and growth.

Efficiency

In a competitive economy there is _consumer sovereignty_. This means that the consumer is "king"—or "queen." That is, consumers "vote" by offering relatively more dollars for products that are in greater demand and relatively fewer dollars for products in lesser demand. In this way, consumers cause relative shifts in demand curves. How do producers respond to these changes in demand? In general:

> In a pure market economy resources will be used as efficiently as possible, to the extent that supply and demand reflect all costs and benefits of production and consumption. The efficient use of resources occurs because firms in each industry compete for the dollar "votes" of consumers. As a result, each firm, and therefore the economy as a whole, achieves technical efficiency by making the fullest utilization of available inputs. The economy also achieves economic efficiency by fulfilling consumer preferences, producing the combination of goods that people are willing and able to purchase with their incomes.

In other words, a pure market economy achieves maximum output at the lowest prices consistent with existing costs, technology, and incomes. What is most important, perhaps, is that these results are realized without direct intervention by government. Indeed, they come about through the free interactions of market supply and demand forces. These forces, like an "invisible hand," guide the allocation of society's resources to their most efficient uses.

Equity

A second feature of a pure market economy is that it distributes society's income in proportion to an individual's contribution to production. If Smith adds twice as much to the value of total output as Johnson does, then competition among employers and among suppliers of resources will see to it that Smith earns twice as much as Johnson.

The reason for this is not hard to see. No employer will pay either Smith or Johnson more than the value that each contributes. And neither Smith nor Johnson need accept less. Why? Because there is always some other employer who would find it profitable to pay them slightly more. Competition among employers would thus bid up Smith's and Johnson's earnings until each is paid precisely what he or she is worth. The result is that the "invisible hand" of competition—the forces of supply and demand—guide both Smith and Johnson into the occupations that each performs best. Stated in more general terms:

> In a pure market economy, the factors of production tend to move into their most remunerative employments. This ensures that the entire income of society is distributed to the owners of resources in proportion to their contribution to the economy's total output.

Can we conclude in any _scientific_ way that this method of apportioning society's income is fair or equitable? Not really. Equity considerations are based on value judgments of what is "right" and what is "wrong," what is "good" and what is "bad." In such matters, your own opinion is not necessarily better or worse than someone else's. However, we will examine this problem in considerable detail at later points.

Stability and Growth

There are two other important features of a pure market economy. The first concerns price, output, and employment fluctuations. This is the problem of economic stability. The second concerns the expansion of real output. This is the problem of economic growth.

A pure market economy may be represented by a simple circular-flow chart, like the one in Chapter 1. With respect to stability, this economy maintains a level of total spending sufficient to sustain full employment (or full utilization) of society's available resources. Of course, innovations and changes in production methods may cause lapses in full employment. However, such lapses tend to be temporary. Because of the competitive nature of both the product and resource markets, the supplies and demands for goods and for factors of production adjust quickly to changing economic conditions. As a result, the economy's output and employment tend to remain relatively stable while prices fluctuate around a long-run level corresponding to full employment.

Concerning economic growth, part of the income received by the household sector is spent for consumption. The rest is borrowed by the business sector to finance innovations—new production techniques, new plant and equipment, and the like. As a consequence, society's stock of capital increases, and the economy's production-possibilities curve shifts outward to the right. This means, as you have already learned, that society realizes a larger quantity of both consumer goods and capital goods, that is, economic growth.

To summarize:

With respect to stability and growth, a pure market economy has several characteristics.

1. Prices fluctuate relatively more than output and employment to accommodate short-run changes in the supplies of and demands for goods and resources.

2. Economic growth takes place in response to innovations by entrepreneurs who seek new and better ways of improving production methods.

These are among the more important features of a pure market economy. Their implications will become increasingly apparent in later chapters as you learn more about the achievements and failures of modern capitalism. (See Box 2.)

SOME REAL-WORLD SHORTCOMINGS

The properties of efficiency, equity, stability, and growth that characterize a pure market economy have been the subject of much debate. In particular, critics argue that our capitalistic system is not a prototype of the "pure" model. Therefore, they say, the system does not achieve the results claimed by some advocates. The more important criticisms are described below.

Market Imperfections and Frictions

The market, it is said, does not always work as neatly in the real world as the theoretical model suggests. Imperfections and frictions, such as imperfect knowl-

---

Box 2
Freedom Versus Power

A pure market economy is the prototype of capitalism. As such, it has the advantage of combining maximum economic freedom with minimum economic power—for two reasons:

1. *Private Property and Economic Freedom*   Freedom of enterprise is an extension of the institution of private property. This is the most fundamental pillar of a capitalistic system and, hence, of a pure market economy. Freedom of enterprise means that owners of resources are free to employ them where they see fit. The owners are subject only to the minimal governmental restraints needed to protect the welfare of society. Unlike a command economy, therefore, a pure market economy has no central authority that decides WHAT, HOW, and FOR WHOM economic resources should be used. Instead, these decisions are made individually by producers seeking to earn profits by allocating resources according to the ways in which consumers freely register their preferences through the price system.

2. *Dispersion of Economic Power*   Economic power exists when a buyer or seller can exert an influence on the market price of a good or resource. The fragmentation of economic power is an integral feature of a pure market economy and is closely related to economic freedom. Economic power does not exist in a highly competitive system. This is because the market price of a commodity is established by the bids and offers of numerous buyers and sellers. An individual buyer or seller can either accept or reject the going market price, but cannot influence it. Each is a passive participant whose presence or absence has no influence on the economic process because each is an insignificant part of it.

---

edge, resource immobility, and barriers to entry, impede the smooth functioning of the system.

For example, buyers and sellers of goods and resources do not usually have complete market information about alternative prices, working conditions, and the like. Unemployed people frequently must be retrained before they can qualify for new jobs. And even when they are retrained, they may not be willing to bear the economic or psychic costs of moving long distances to accept employment. Entrepreneurs and workers are often prevented from entering new industries because they lack the large amount of capital or the specialized know-how required. Or perhaps they cannot overcome monopolistic barriers, such as patent rights and apprenticeship requirements, that protect various business firms and unions from increased competition.

These and other obstacles retard the rate at which the factors of production shift out of declining industries and into expanding ones. As a result, shortages and surpluses arise in various product and resource markets. These imbalances would not ordinarily occur, or at best would be short-lived, if a real market-oriented economy functioned as smoothly as the theory assumes.

Economic Inequality and Inequity

In a market economy, incomes are distributed in proportion to one's contribution to production. As we have seen, if Smith adds twice as much to the value of total output as Johnson does, then Smith's income will tend to be twice that of Johnson's.

However, this difference can be further magnified by the right of inheritance. This fundamental institution of capitalism permits the accumulation and concentration of wealth within families. Such disparities in income and wealth can lead to economic and social inequities. As critics point out, in a market economy a rich person has more dollar votes than does a poor person. As a result, the former can satisfy his or her whims, whereas the latter may find it hard to satisfy even basic needs.

Technology and Large-Scale Production

The model of a pure market economy makes the unrealistic assumption that industries are composed of numerous small firms, as envisioned by Adam Smith. Yet modern technology dictates that in many industries, such as automobiles and steel, firms must be very large if they are to make use of the most efficient means of production. In such industries a few large firms are dominant, and small firms cannot survive. In fact, the massive scale of operations dictated by modern technology helps explain why many major industries are dominated by one or a few large firms.

Social Effects and "Externalities"

A fourth criticism is that the market system fails to reflect *all* the costs and benefits associated with production and consumption. As a result, there are side effects, or "externalities."

For example, production of some commodities, such as steel, rubber, and chemicals, pollutes the environment and so contributes to social costs. At the same time, production of other commodities, such as education, sanitation services, and park facilities, adds to community satisfactions and so contributes to social benefits.

These externalities are not fully reflected in the market prices of commodities. Therefore, supply and demand curves fail to incorporate *all* the costs and benefits of production. As a result, either too large or too small a quantity of goods is produced, and resources are misallocated.

CONCLUSION: RELEVANT IF NOT ALWAYS REALISTIC

For these reasons, the model of a pure market economy does not convey a true picture of the way in which the price system operates in a modern capitalistic society.

For example, in many markets we do not have large numbers of buyers and sellers in rivalry with one another, as envisioned by Adam Smith. Instead, we have big business, big unions, and big government. Consequently, concentrations of market power influence commodity and factor prices, and distort the allocation of resources. This is hardly the type of economy that Adam Smith had in mind. Nevertheless, as we will see later, our pure market model provides a useful framework for evaluating the performance of a capitalistic system. Hence, the model is extremely relevant, if not always realistic.

What You Have Learned

1. The purpose of studying supply and demand is to learn how a competitive or pure market economy works. This helps answer the three great questions: WHAT to produce, HOW to produce, and FOR WHOM to produce.

2. Demand is a relationship between the price of a commodity and the quantity of it that buyers are willing and able to purchase at a given time. Other things affecting demand, such as buyers' income, prices of related goods, and number of buyers or other nonmonetary determinants, are assumed to remain the same. The law of demand states that the relationship between price and quantity demanded is inverse. Therefore, demand curves slope downward from left to right.

3. Supply is a relationship between the price of a commodity and the quantity of it that sellers are willing and able to sell at a given time. Other things affecting supply, such as resource costs, prices of related goods in production, and technology, number of sellers, or other nonmonetary determinants, are assumed to remain the same. The law of supply states that the relationship between price and quantity supplied is usually direct. Hence, supply curves typically slope upward from left to right.

4. The intersection of a market demand curve with a market supply curve determines the equilibrium price and quantity of a commodity. Demand or supply curves may shift either left or right as a result of changes in any of the determinants assumed to remain constant when the curves were drawn. When such shifts occur, we refer to them either as a change in demand or a change in supply, depending on which curve has shifted.

5. Movements along supply and demand curves may occur. These movements result from changes in the price of the commodity while the other underlying determinants of demand and supply remain constant. Such movements are called either a change in the quantity demanded or a change in the quantity supplied, depending on the particular curve.

6. In the real world, demand and supply curves are always shifting. A change in demand or a change in supply may result in either a new equilibrium price, a new equilibrium quantity, or both. The change depends on the relative shifts of the curves.

7. A market economy is highly competitive. Prices and quantities are determined by numerous buyers and sellers through the free operation of supply and demand. Organized commodity markets, such as the New York or London Cotton Exchange, or the Chicago Board of Trade, typify this situation. However, most of the markets in our economy differ from the competitive market in varying degrees.

For Discussion

1. *Terms and concepts to review:*

demand	equilibrium quantity
demand schedule	disequilibrium
demand curve	change in quantity
demand price	demanded
law of demand	change in demand
supply	normal goods
supply schedule	inferior goods
supply curve	substitute goods
supply price	complementary goods
law of supply	change in quantity
equilibrium	supplied
surplus	change in supply
shortage	social cost
equilibrium price	social benefit

In the following problems, use graphs whenever possible to verify your answer.

2. Do the numerical quantities of a demand schedule characterize buyers' behavior? If not, what is the fundamental property of a demand schedule?

3. Evaluate the following editorial comments on the basis of what you know about the meaning of demand and scarcity in economics. (HINT   How meaningful are the italicized words?)

Our community *needs* more schools and better teachers; after all, what could be more *critical* than the education of our children as future citizens?

Lynwood *Times*

The health of our citizens is uppermost in our minds. Ever since the rate of garbage pick-up in our northwest suburbs deteriorated to its present deplorable levels, it has been evident that our *shortage* of collection facilities has reached *emergency* proportions.

Lexington *Daily Explicit*

4. Some people would buy more of a good (such as jewelry or furs) at a high price than at a low price. This results in an upward-sloping "demand" curve. Would such a curve be an exception to the law of demand? Explain.

5. What would happen to the market demand curve for steak as a result of each of the following: (a) an increase in the average level of income; (b) an increase in the number of families; (c) an increased advertising campaign for veal and pork; (d) an increase in the prices of veal and pork; (e) a decrease in the prices of veal and pork?

6. What would happen to the demand for Pepsi-Cola if the price of Coca-Cola were doubled? Why would it happen?

7. Determine the effect on the supply of office buildings if each of the following things happened: (a) the price of land rose; (b) the price of steel fell; (c) the price of cement fell; (d) a new and faster method of construction were adopted; (e) the number of firms building offices declined; (f) rents for office buildings were expected to decline.

8. Analyze the following:

(a) What would happen to the equilibrium price and quantity of butter if the price of margarine rose substantially?

(b) What would happen if there were an increase in the cost of producing butter?

9. "Wheat is wheat. Therefore, the price of wheat at any given time should be the same in Chicago as it is in Kansas City." Do you agree? Explain.

10. In organized commodity markets, buyers often become sellers and sellers often become buyers, depending on the price of the good. Examine the following schedule of five individuals, A, B, C, D, and E.

Price per unit	Quantities that individuals will buy (+) or sell (−) at each market price				
	A	B	C	D	E
$1	+6	+5	+3	+8	−2
2	+3	+4	+2	+7	−5
3	0	+3	+1	+6	−8
4	−2	+2	0	+5	−10
5	−2	−3	−1	+4	−10
6	−4	−5	−2	+3	−11
7	−5	−6	−3	+2	−12

(a) Draw the market supply and demand curves, and estimate the equilibrium price and quantity.

(b) Show the effects on the supply and demand curves if C drops out of the market.

Case
Directory Assistance—At a Price

For telephone subscribers in parts of New York, Ohio, Wisconsin, and certain other areas, free information service is a thing of the past. Led by Cincinnati Bell in 1974, more and more phone companies (there are about 1,600 in the United States) have applied for and received permission from state regulatory commissions to charge a fee for directory assistance. In most cases the telephone subscriber is allowed up to three free information calls a month. Beyond that a service charge—generally equal to the price of a local call from a coin telephone—is imposed.

Phone companies that have adopted the policy consider the results spectacular. Directory-assistance calls have dropped an average of 75 percent in some affected areas. "By invoking the price system, people pay for what they get—and don't pay for what they don't want," a telephone company executive remarked. "Otherwise, 5 percent of telephone subscribers—those who are not too lazy to use a phone book—pay for 95 percent of directory-assistance billings. That, by any standard, is grossly unjust and inefficient."

The phone companies have not as yet worked out a consistent policy. For example, some companies charge for new listings that are not yet published; other companies do not. Some exempt handicapped customers and public phones from charges; other companies do not. And some have been permitted to charge for directory-assistance calls in lieu of being granted a general rate increase, while others have not.

Despite these inconsistencies, the idea of the information charge is a natural for telephone companies.

They are seeking to cut labor costs to keep rates from rising faster than they already are. Further, charging for information is a way for phone companies to make more money by getting fewer calls. That, of course, is good for stockholders.

QUESTIONS
1. Studies by telephone companies show that when no specific charge is made for information calls, a small percentage of subscribers is responsible for a large percentage of such calls. What does this indicate with respect to the two fundamental economic goals—efficiency and equity?

2. Do you think that charging for directory assistance is a good idea? Why? How would you answer if you were a stockholder in the phone company?

Charging for information reduces the number of calls for directory assistance, which in turn can reduce labor costs.

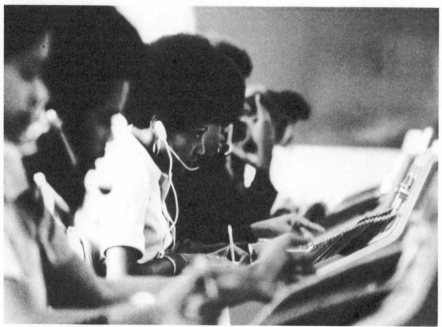

AT&T Photo Center.

Chapter 3

The Private Sector: Households and Businesses

Chapter Preview

Why are some people rich? Some poor? How much inequality of income and wealth exists today?

What standards exist for distributing income? Are the standards equitable?

How are businesses organized? Does business have a responsibility to society? How does responsibility relate to efficiency and equity?

Our mixed economy is like a three-legged stool—one leg representing "households," the second "businesses," and the third "government." The first two comprise the private sector of the economy and are explored in this chapter. The last is the public sector, and is the subject of the next and several subsequent chapters.

You and I are part of the household segment of the private sector. So too are some 80 million families. Households are the ultimate suppliers of the economy's inputs of human resources and the major purchasers of its outputs of goods and services. Businesses, of which there are over 15 million, including farmers and professional people, are the second major group within the system. This group is chiefly responsible for producing the things society wants.

These are just a few of the basic facts concerning the private sector. Some of the fundamental issues that confront it are explained in this chapter.

Households: Income, Wealth, and Equity

In the United States, concern with the distribution of income and wealth is as old as the nation itself. Alexander Hamilton believed that liberty without inequality of property is impossible because the latter "would unavoidably result from that very liberty itself." Thomas Jefferson remarked that the perpetuation of wealth through inheritance "sometimes does injury to the morals of youth by rendering them independent of, and disobedient to, their parents." And James Madison supported legislation that "would reduce extreme income and wealth toward a state of mediocrity and raise extreme indigence toward a state of comfort."

What constitutes an equitable or fair distribution of income and wealth among individuals? This question has been debated for centuries by economists, politicians, and social critics. In this chapter we shall be primarily concerned with the problem of economic equity among households. Households, together with businesses, comprise the *private sector* of our mixed economy. The *public sector,* which embraces all levels of government, is discussed in later chapters.

A LOOK AT THE FACTS

Many people believe that income and wealth in our economy have been distributed inequitably, and that this maldistribution is one of the fundamental social problems of our time. This belief is not new; it has had cyclical upswings and downswings since the early nineteenth century. Whether it is correct is a question we try to answer in this and in later chapters.

To begin with, we have to examine the facts. This is not easy, because there are different concepts of income and wealth. To most of us, income is simply money that people receive from various sources; wealth is the value of the goods and property they own. But a significant part of many people's income consists of more than wages and salaries. Income also consists of money and nonmoney benefits which are never reported to the tax authorities or to census takers. A similar situation exists in the reporting of wealth holdings. As a result, no government or private source provides complete and accurate information about the distribution of income and wealth. With these deficiencies in mind, let us turn our attention to the available facts. First, however, we need two definitions:

Income is the gain derived from the use of human or material resources; it is a flow of dollars per unit of time. *Wealth* is anything that has value because it is capable of producing income. Wealth is a "stock" of value as distinct from a "flow" of income.

Personal Income Distribution

How are incomes distributed in the United States? Who is rich and who is poor, and what is the gap between them? This is the problem of *personal income distribution*—the relative allocation of income among people.

The percentage of all families in the lower-income groups—below the $10,000 level—has been declining in recent decades. The percentage of families in the upper-income groups has been rising. The median income has also been rising. (A *median* is a type of average that divides a distribution of numbers into two equal parts. One-half of the cases are equal to or less than this value and one-half are equal to or greater than it.) However, there are still significant gaps in median income levels among various groups—especially racial groups—within the economy. This situation causes serious equity problems for our society.

Exhibit 1 shows the relative share of total money income before taxes received by each fifth and the top 5 percent of all families. This table reveals three long-run characteristics:

1. The lowest one-fifth of families has consistently received less than 6 percent of total *money* income. (Money income is distinguished from in-kind income such as food stamps, subsidized housing, subsidized medical care, etc.) The highest one-fifth has received over 40 percent. This represents a long-run average of almost eight times as much.

2. The ratio of the share received by the top 5 percent to the share received by the lowest 20 percent has declined substantially. However, the former is still more than twice the latter.

3. The entire distribution has remained remarkably stable.

As a result of these factors, many observers believe that the pattern of income distribution will continue

---

Exhibit 1

Percent of Aggregate Income (Total Money Income Before Taxes) Received by Each One-Fifth and Top 5 Percent of Families*

Income rank	1950	1960	1970	1975	1980
Lowest fifth	4.5	4.8	5.4	5.4	5.1
Second fifth	11.9	12.2	12.2	11.8	11.8
Middle fifth	17.4	17.8	17.8	17.6	17.5
Fourth fifth	23.6	24.0	23.8	24.1	24.2
Highest fifth	42.7	41.3	40.9	41.0	41.5
Top 5%	17.3	15.9	15.6	15.5	15.7
Ratio of top 5% to lowest 20%	3.8	3.3	2.9	2.9	3.1

* Because figures are rounded, columns may not add to 100.
SOURCE: U.S. Department of Commerce.

to remain about the same as it is now. As you will see, the issue of whether incomes should be more equal or less involves serious ethical considerations that will be taken up later in the chapter.

Distribution of Wealth

The distribution of income is concerned with who *gets* how much. The distribution of wealth is concerned with who *has* how much. The same inequality that exists in the distribution of income also exists in the distribution of wealth. However, the inequality in the distribution of wealth is more pronounced. There is a much heavier concentration at the top and a considerably thinner scattering at the bottom.

Wealth consists of both income- and non-income-producing assets. Stocks, bonds, savings accounts, land, houses, and automobiles are examples. Holdings of both types are important. Unfortunately, facts and figures about the distribution of wealth are limited and are not published periodically. As a result, we must rely on infrequent studies and reports.

Exhibit 2 shows that the wealthiest 1 percent of families own one-fourth of the total wealth. In fact, this small proportion of people owns about as much wealth as the lowest 80 percent of families. The wealthiest 20 percent, on the other hand, owns somewhat less than three times as much wealth as the bottom 80 percent.

Concentration of wealth is thus considerably greater than concentration of income. And the concentration of the most influential form of wealth—income-producing wealth—is even more pronounced. The top one-fifth owns the great bulk of both corporate stock and corporate and municipal bonds (not shown in the table).

Thus, although stocks and bonds are owned by millions of people, the vast majority of these securities is owned directly by a relatively small percentage of the population. Indirectly, however, a large and growing proportion of the population owns stocks and bonds—through retirement and pension funds, which invest heavily in such securities.

MEASURING INEQUALITY AND EXPLAINING THE FACTS

The commonest method of depicting and measuring income and wealth inequality is by a *Lorenz diagram.* An illustration for income is shown in Exhibit 3. Both the table and chart show what percentage of people, ranked from the poorest to the richest, received what percentage of the nation's total income in a given year.

The diagram is constructed by laying off on the horizontal axis the number of income recipients—not in absolute terms but in percentages. Families, rather than individuals, are usually represented. The point marked 20 denotes the lowest 20 percent of the number of families; the point 40, the lowest 40 percent; and so on. The vertical axis measures percentages of total income. Both axes have the same length and equal scales. Therefore, by enclosing the diagram in a square, a diagonal line can be drawn representing a curve of complete equality.

You can now verify certain facts from the chart. For example, along the diagonal line of equal distribution, the lowest 20 percent of the families would receive 20 percent of total income, the lowest 40 percent of the families would receive 40 percent of total income, and so on. This line is compared with the curve of actual distribution—called a *Lorenz curve*—derived from the data in the table. The area between the diagonal line of equal income distribution and the curved line of actual income distribution reflects the degree of income inequality. Thus, the more that the curved line is bowed downward in a southeasterly direction, the greater is the inequality of income distribution.

How does the distribution of income compare with the distribution of wealth? The answer, given in terms of two Lorenz curves, is shown in Exhibit 4. As explained there, it is difficult to determine which curve is most responsible for the other.

Why Are Some People Rich? Some Poor?

What factors account for differences in income among households? That is, why do some people earn more money than others? There are many reasons. Among them:

1. *Differences in Wealth* Because wealth is a significant source of income, it appears obvious that a widely distorted distribution of wealth is perhaps the most important cause of income inequality.

Exhibit 2
Percent of Total Wealth Held by Each One-Fifth, Top 5 Percent, and Top 1 Percent of Families

Wealth rank	Percent
Lowest fifth	Less than 1
Second fifth	2
Third fifth	5
Fourth fifth	18
Highest fifth	74
Top 5 percent	39
Top 1 percent	25

SOURCE: U.S. Treasury, Internal Revenue Service.

Exhibit 3
Illustrating Inequality with a Lorenz Diagram

PERCENT OF AGGREGATE INCOME RECEIVED BY EACH
ONE-FIFTH OF FAMILIES

Income rank of families	1980
Lowest fifth	5
Second fifth	12
Middle fifth	18
Fourth fifth	24
Highest fifth	42

SOURCE: U.S. Department of Commerce.

You can use the data from the table to construct a *Lorenz curve*. This curve shows the extent of departure between an equal distribution of income and the actual distribution of income.

From the curved line showing actual distribution, can you estimate the percent of income received by the lowest 20 percent of families? The lowest 40 percent? 60 percent? 80 percent? 100 percent? Check your estimates against the results in the table to see if you are correct.

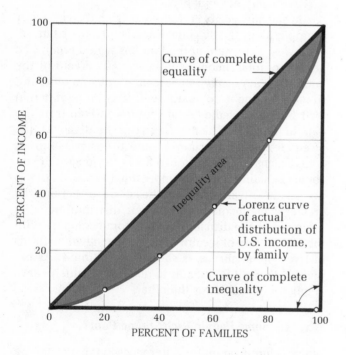

The colored axes in the lower half of the diagram represent the curve of *complete inequality*. Thus, on the horizontal axis, a point near the right end of the scale is designated, showing where 99 percent of the families receive no income, and the remaining 1 percent receive it all.

Exhibit 4
Lorenz Curves of Income and Wealth Distribution

The distribution of wealth is considerably more unequal than the distribution of income. However, it is not clear which is the cause and which the effect. High income leads to higher savings, which enables further accumulation of wealth. This in turn begets still higher income.

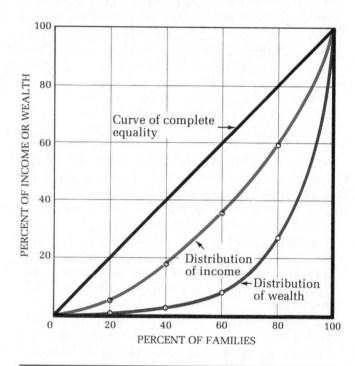

2. *Differences in Earning Ability and Opportunity* People differ widely in education, intelligence, skill, motivation, energy, and talent. Also, they face job barriers because of age, sex, race, religion, and nationality. Legislation has made some of these barriers less formidable, but they are still responsible for many of the inequalities in income distribution.

3. *Differences in Resource Mobility* The factors responsible for differences in earning ability and opportunity also make for differences in resource mobility. Many people, for example, are prevented by lack of information or financial means from moving into higher-paying occupations or locations. Consequently, low incomes and even poverty may exist unchanged for years in the same regions. This is true in certain parts of the South where sharecroppers, migratory farm workers, and some factory laborers eke out a substandard living.

4. *Differences in Luck* An individual born into the right environment and provided with opportunities to

develop inherited talents stands a greater chance of earning a higher income than one not so fortunate. This has been borne out by sociological studies of "vertical mobility"—the climb up the socioeconomic ladder. Unfortunately, what is not known is how changes in vertical mobility are affected by changes in income l istribution and in the degree of equality.

5. *Differences in Age*   Young people who have recently entered the job market, and old people who have left it, will have significantly lower incomes than those in midcareer.

6. *Differences in Human-Capital Investment*   Some people make heavier investments in their future earning capacity than do others. Sales clerks, for instance, may begin earning income after graduating from high school. Most professionals, on the other hand, must spend many additional years in training, often without income and living on borrowed funds, before realizing higher financial rewards for their time and effort.

7. *Differences in Risk, Uncertainty, and Security*   Some occupations are more risky, and some have more uncertain futures, than others. These differences are reflected in earnings. Many people prefer security, in return for lower incomes, in the less risky and more certain fields of employment. Witness the fact that employees in relatively stable industries, such as civil service, banking, and public utilities, generally earn less than their counterparts in more unstable industries, such as manufacturing. Admittedly, lower incomes in some stable industries may be partly offset by nonmonetary factors, such as longer vacations, shorter working hours, and better fringe benefits. But the fact remains that coal miners earn more than ditch diggers, window washers in skyscrapers command a higher wage than dish washers in restaurants, and college professors earn less but live longer than corporate executives. The clash between risk, uncertainty, and security reveals itself in many ways.

These and other factors affecting individuals' incomes help explain why the Lorenz curve of income distribution will always show some degree of inequality. A method of measuring inequality is explained in Box 1.

Evaluating the Data: The Trouble with Lorenz Curves

Both the table on income distribution and its accompanying Lorenz curve have long been used as standard devices for measuring income inequality. Do they accomplish their objective? The answer is not a simple yes or no, because the measurement of inequality requires consideration of several factors.

Equivalent Spendable Income   The data on income distribution are based on what the U.S. Census Bureau (which compiles the figures) calls "money income." This is not the same as income available for spending—for three reasons:

1. Personal income taxes and social security taxes are included in money income. When these taxes are paid by families, their income available for spending is reduced.

2. Noncash income is not counted as part of money income. Noncash income consists of benefits that poor families receive in the form of government subsidies or "in-kind" transfers of goods and services. Examples are food stamps, low-income housing, rent supplements, and free medical services.

3. Money income does not reflect differences in average family size within each quintile (i.e., each fifth) of the population. As a result, small families may sometimes be better off than large ones, and vice versa, depending on their relative money incomes.

In view of these factors, what happens when the appropriate allowances are made for them? That is, how do the figures change when (1) personal and social security taxes are subtracted from money income, (2) noncash income is added in, and (3) the data are converted to a per capita basis to adjust for differences in average family size within each quintile? The results are startling: *The overall distribution of income shows a remarkable trend toward greater equality since 1950.* In that year, according to various studies, the lowest fifth of families received approximately 8 percent of total income and the highest fifth about 37 percent. Since the early 1970s, the lowest fifth of families has averaged between 12 and 15 percent of total income and the highest fifth between 30 and 33 percent.

Lifetime Earnings   A second difficulty concerning the measurement of inequality with a Lorenz curve is that it reflects the distribution of income at a given time. The curve therefore fails to consider the incomes that people earn over their lifetimes. For example, a schoolteacher and a professional athlete may each earn about the same total incomes during their lifetimes. But the schoolteacher's income will be spread over a period of forty years, whereas most of the athlete's income will be realized in less than ten years. Yet in any given year the two incomes will be highly unequal.

Age Distribution of Earnings   Another problem in measuring inequality involves relationships between age and income. To a large extent, income inequalities at any given time result from differences in the age and therefore the earning power of individuals. We do not ordinarily expect young people who have recently

Box 1
Application: Measuring Inequality

Social scientists customarily measure the precise degree of income inequality with the *Gini coefficient of inequality* (named after an early twentieth-century Italian statistician). In terms of a Lorenz diagram, the Gini coefficient may be defined as the numerical value of the area between the Lorenz curve and the diagonal line, divided by the entire area beneath the diagonal line. As can be visualized from the diagram, the Gini coefficient is the ratio of the inequality area to the entire triangular area under the diagonal:

$$\text{Gini coefficient of inequality} = \frac{\text{inequality area}}{\text{triangular area}}$$

The value of the ratio may therefore vary from 0 to 1. For example, as incomes become more equal, the inequality

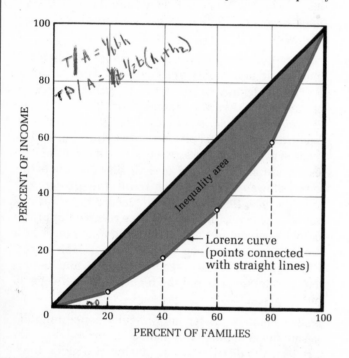

area narrows relative to the triangular area under the diagonal and the Gini coefficient approaches zero (no inequality). On the other hand, as incomes become more unequal, the inequality area widens relative to the triangular area and the Gini coefficient approaches 1 (absolute inequality).

HOW TO DO IT

You can calculate the Gini coefficient of inequality quite easily by connecting the successive points of the Lorenz curve with straight lines. The area under the Lorenz curve will then consist of one triangle and four trapezoids. In a problem at the end of the chapter, a simple procedure for making the calculation is explained. Meanwhile, you may want to see if you can figure the calculation out for yourself.

TRENDS TOWARD GREATER EQUALITY

From the mid-1930s to the present, the distribution of incomes in the United States has become somewhat more even. That is, the inequality area on the Lorenz chart has narrowed. Most of the shift toward greater income equality occurred between 1935 and 1945 as the economy's laborers and farmers became considerably more prosperous. During that period the Gini coefficient of inequality declined from 0.44 to 0.38. Since 1945 the shift has been less pronounced. The Gini coefficient has shown a slight downward trend, decreasing to about 0.35 at present. This means that on a scale such as the following, ranging from 0 to 1.00, the degree of income equality in the United States is currently about 0.65.

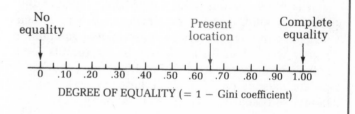

entered the job market, or old people who have left it, to be earning the same incomes as those in midcareer. The Lorenz curve, however, does not distinguish incomes by ages, and therefore reflects income inequalities across all ages.

The last factor involving age and incomes is especially significant—as you will see. It leads to an important criticism:

The conventional Lorenz curve and the data on which the curve is based are the most common methods of measuring income inequality. These methods, however, are invalid for measuring income inequality over time. One reason is that the young and old are concentrated at

the low ends of the income scale. To correct this situation, family incomes should be calculated by age groups and compared for the *same age groups at different times*. For example, incomes should be compared between 25-year-olds several decades ago and 25-year-olds today.

Conclusion: Substantial Gains in Equality

What happens when these revisions in the data are made? Economists who have conducted such studies covering both income and wealth distribution have come up with new and interesting findings. Among them:

○ Conventional data on *age-unadjusted* income and wealth inequality, like the tables of figures shown earlier, tend to overstate the degree of inequality by about 50 percent. But when the data are adjusted for age differences, the evidence shows a dramatic change. Since 1950, the overall degree of income inequality among families has actually declined by more than 25 percent, and wealth inequality by more than 35 percent.

○ There is no evidence to support those critics who argue that because the data on *money* income distribution (shown earlier in Exhibit 1) have remained stable for several decades, the lowest fifth of families is assigned to a "permanent state of poverty." On the contrary, the 20 percent of families on the lowest end of the income scale have raised their share of *age-adjusted* total income from 5 percent to over 8 percent. This is an increase of more than 60 percent since 1950.

○ The proportion of employed people among families in the upper half of the income scale has increased sharply as many more women have entered the job market. On the other hand, a strong reverse trend toward more unemployment among families in the lower end of the income scale has also occurred. Because of this, low-income families have received, over the years, increasing amounts of government assistance. This has taken the form of cash payments, food allotments, subsidized housing, and free health care.

As a result of these and related findings, you can better understand why our government has devoted increasing proportions of its budget to *transfer payments*. These are expenditures within and between sectors of the economy for which there are no corresponding contributions to current production. Examples include unemployment compensation, relief payments, and other "free" benefits. They are usually intended to reduce what society regards as inequities in the distribution of income and wealth.

To summarize:

1. The distributions of income and wealth, adjusted for age differences, have become substantially *more equal* in recent decades.

2. The distribution of income as a reward for labor or paid employment has become considerably *less equal* in recent decades. This is because there is a larger percentage of employment among families in the upper half, and a smaller percentage of employment among families in the lower half, of the income scale.

3. The conventional Lorenz standard of *age-unadjusted* inequality greatly overstates the degree of inequality. This may lead to the implication that the distributions of income and wealth are in more urgent need of revision than is actually the case.

DISTRIBUTIVE CRITERIA AND EQUITY— THE ETHICS OF DISTRIBUTION

The seventeenth-century English philosopher and essayist Francis Bacon remarked that "Money is like manure; not good except it be spread." But what criteria can be used for spreading money? In other words, who should get *how much*? This is the age-old problem of economic justice. Unfortunately, the problem has no completely satisfactory solution because justice in any form is at best a tolerable accommodation of the conflicting interests of society. Nevertheless, a number of distributive standards have been proposed over the long history of discussions on the subject. Most of these standards derive from three basic criteria:

1. Distribution based on productive contribution.

2. Distribution based on needs.

3. Distribution based on equality.

Contributive Standard

Most people would agree that an individual should be paid what he or she deserves. This criterion, which fundamentally hinges on *merit*, represents one of the oldest concepts of justice known to man.

Unfortunately, merit is a criterion that is difficult to define and impossible to measure. How can we decide, in a manner acceptable to everyone, what each person merits or deserves? Surely, responsibility in a job is not the criterion, because commercial-aircraft mechanics earn less but have greater responsibility than heart surgeons. Nor are years of formal education a criterion, because most plumbers are more highly paid than schoolteachers. Certainly, the difficulty of a job is not a criterion, because difficulty depends on individual aptitudes and interests. Some people can master advanced mathematics more easily than they can learn to play tennis. These, as well as almost all other standards of merit, lead to similar contradictions. However, there is one measure of merit that is unique to capitalism:

> The criterion of distribution in a capitalist society can be expressed by the phrase, "To each according to what he or she produces." This may be called a *contributive standard* because it is based on the principle of payment according to contribution.

How is one's productive contribution measured? The most objective measure is the value placed upon it in a free market. Here the price of the factors of production are established by the interactions of supply and demand. The contribution to the total product made by a particular factor of production and the payment received for the contribution can then be measured. This is done by multiplying the price per unit of the factor by the number of units supplied. Thus, under these conditions, if the market price of your labor is $6 per hour, and if you work 2,000 hours each year, your contribution to the total product and the payment you receive are both equal to $12,000. However, much more is involved in determining factor contributions and payments than is implied by this simple example. Nevertheless, the illustration emphasizes an important principle:

In a capitalistic or market economy the payment received for a factor of production is the measure of its worth. This payment, which reflects the value of the factor's contribution to total product, is determined by the impersonal pressure of market forces—not by the judgment of a central authority.

Of course, society also recognizes obligations to its nonproducers—the aged, the disabled, the very young, the involuntarily unemployed, and so on. As a result, society employs some noncontributive criteria for apportioning income. Nevertheless, the contributive standard is the dominant one in our economy.

Needs Standard

The distributive principle of capitalism, as we have seen, is expressed by the phrase, "To each according to what he or she produces." In contrast, the distributive principle of pure communism may be described by the expression, "To each according to his or her needs."

It is interesting to note that the latter standard is not just a distributive principle of communist philosophy. This standard serves roughly as a criterion of distribution within most families, and in time of war or other emergency is adopted by all kinds of governments as a means of rationing a limited supply of goods.

Distribution according to need has wide appeal. But upon close examination its implementation poses two major difficulties.

1. No impersonal mechanism exists for measuring need. Thus, decisions to allocate goods according to need—whether such decisions are made within a family or a nation—must be based on the subjective judgment of a central authority.

2. Even if individual needs could be measured, it is likely that the implementation of a needs standard would not precisely utilize the economy's entire output. There would be either shortages or surpluses, depending on whether the sum of needs was greater or less than the total product. This is less likely to occur when output is distributed according to the contributive criterion of capitalism. Under such a system,

there is a tendency for the market to equate the incomes people receive with the values of what they contribute.

To summarize:

Individual needs are impossible to measure. As a result, if distribution of income according to needs were to be adopted, it would have to be based on some central authority's personal judgment of what constitutes "needs." In addition, peoples' different needs would somehow have to be matched up with available products if surpluses and shortages were to be avoided.

Equality Standard

A third criterion of distribution, which was debated as far back as biblical times, is the *equality standard*. It is expressed most simply by the phrase, "To each equally."

The equality standard is a just standard only if we assume that all individuals are alike in the *added* satisfaction or utility they receive from an extra dollar of income. In reality, an additional dollar of income may provide a greater gain in utility to some people than to others. In that case, justice is more properly served by distributing most of any increase in society's income to those who will enjoy it more. However, there is no conclusive evidence that people are either alike or unlike in the satisfactions they derive from additional income. Therefore, the equalitarians (also called "egalitarians") argue that, because we cannot prove that people are unlike, we should assume they are alike and distribute all incomes equally.

This conclusion, regardless of how plausible it may seem, illustrates a logical fallacy in reasoning. This fallacy is called "argument from ignorance." It is committed whenever someone argues that a proposition is true simply because it has not been proved false, or that it is false because it has not been proved true. In terms of the equality standard, this implies that we must go beyond the stage of theorizing about individual utilities and consider instead some of the realistic effects of an equality standard. Among the most important are the "motivational" ones:

An equal distribution of income would eliminate incentives of rewards. Therefore, it would provide no economic motivation for people to develop or apply their skills, or to use economic resources efficiently, because there is no commensurate return. The result would be declining economic progress and probable stagnation.

This argument assumes, of course, that economic progress attributable to inequality and material incentives is desirable in itself. Some critics think it is not. We shall have more to say about this issue in later chapters.

Conclusion: An "Optimal" Distribution?

The foregoing arguments suggest that there is some "ideal" degree of income inequality—a distribution that is not too extreme either way. What can be said about this hypothesis?

In a society characterized by a very unequal distribution of income, the economic surplus or savings of the rich minority can finance investment in capital. The result is material and cultural advancement. This was true of such ancient civilizations as Egypt, Greece, and Rome, whose economies were based on slavery—the most unequal distributive system of all. Because of this, they were able to produce magnificent art, architecture, and other cultural achievements.

On the other hand, in a society whose limited income is distributed equally among the masses, virtually all of its income is spent on needed consumption goods. This leaves little if any savings with which to acquire capital goods. (This is the familiar production-possibilities concept of earlier chapters. It involves the notion that every society must make choices between the proportions of consumption goods and capital goods that it wishes to have.) Such a society, although it has an egalitarian (i.e., equal) income distribution, would tend to remain poor because of its distributive policy.

To conclude:

Every society seeks the best compromise—the "optimum"—between two extremes of income distribution: substantial inequality and complete equality. But each society's concept of optimum differs, depending on the society's goals and institutions. Therefore, it is impossible to state objectively whether a particular distribution of income is "good" or "bad."

Businesses—Organization, Size, and Social Responsibility

The private sector includes businesses as well as households. Business is a major institution. It is powerful, and its decisions and policies influence the nature, structure, and goals of our society. This makes business highly controversial, and its motives the subject of ceaseless debate.

How are business firms organized? Why are some of them large and some small? Does business have responsibilities to society? These are the questions that concern us. Before answering them, a definition of a business firm will be helpful:

A *firm* is a business organization that brings together and coordinates the factors of production—capital, land, labor, and entrepreneurship—for the purpose of producing a good or service.

ORGANIZATIONAL STRUCTURE

Business firms may be classified in various ways. One way is to group them in terms of products produced. Firms that turn out either similar or identical products are said to be in the same *industry*. Thus, General Motors and Ford are in the automobile industry. But General Motors also produces trucks, buses, and diesel locomotives, among other things. Therefore, it would be correct to say that General Motors is also in the truck industry, the bus industry, and the diesel locomotive industry. Indeed, most of the largest companies make more than one product. Can you name at least five industries in which General Electric is an important producer?

Another method of classifying firms is by their legal form of organization. Three types are particularly common: the individual proprietorship, the partnership, and the corporation. More than 75 percent of all firms in the United States are proprietorships, about 10 percent are partnerships, and the remainder are corporations. Although the proportion of corporations is relatively small, this form of business organization is responsible for most of our economy's total output.

The Proprietorship

The simplest, oldest, and commonest form of business is the *proprietorship*. This is a firm in which the owner (proprietor) is solely responsible for the activities and liabilities of the business. Most of the firms you see every day, such as bakeries, barber shops, beauty salons, restaurants, gas stations, and radio and TV repair shops, are examples of proprietorships. Why are proprietorships so common? Because they are relatively easy to establish. They usually do not require special business skills, experience, or large amounts of money capital (although there are some exceptions). These advantages, however, should be weighed against certain disadvantages of proprietorships. They tend to lack stability and permanence, it is difficult for them to raise funds for expansion, and their owners are personally liable for all unpaid debts of the business.

The Partnership

A partnership is simply a modified version of a proprietorship. That is, a *partnership* is an association of two or more individuals to carry on, as co-owners, a business for profit. A partnership has the same kinds of advantages and disadvantages of a proprietorship—but on a somewhat different scale. For example, partners can pool their funds to establish a business, and they can combine their talents to manage it. However, they are jointly and personally liable for all unpaid debts of the business.

The Corporation

The third, and from an economic standpoint the most important, form of business organization is the corporation. Here is a definition that will be amplified in the following paragraphs:

A *corporation* is an association of stockholders (owners) created under law, but regarded by the courts as an artificial person existing only in the contemplation of law. The chief economic characteristics of a corporation are (1) limited liability of its stockholders, (2) stability and permanence, and (3) the ability to accumulate large sums of capital for expansion through the sale of stocks and bonds.

Some of the ideas behind this definition may already be familiar to you. For example:

The ownership of a corporation is divided into units represented by shares of *stock*. A stockholder who owns 100 shares of stock in a corporation has twice as much "ownership" as a stockholder with only 50 shares. Each stockholder participates in the profits of the corporation by receiving *dividends* in the form of a certain amount of dollars or cents per share. If there are no profits, there may be no dividends.

One of the distinguishing features of a corporation is the *limited liability* of its stockholders. The owners of a proprietorship or partnership can be held personally liable for the debts of the business. However, stockholders in corporations cannot be held liable for any of the firm's debts. For almost all practical purposes, the most that stockholders can lose if the business goes bankrupt is the money they paid for stock.

The corporation has durability. Stockholders may come and go, but the corporation itself lives on. Indeed, some corporations in existence today were originally chartered hundreds of years ago. This permanence makes the corporation highly flexible. It can raise large amounts of capital by selling stocks and *bonds* (promises to pay money plus interest in future years) to the public, and can adapt itself to changing market needs and conditions.

Stockholders elect a board of directors, which is responsible for the management of the corporation. Each stockholder gets one vote for each share of stock owned. Some stockholders may thus elect themselves to the board if they own enough shares or if they can get the support of enough of the other stockholders. In large corporations, the board employs officers—a president and vice-presidents—to manage day-to-day operations and report back to it the results of these operations. In smaller corporations it is common to find one or more members of the board serving as officers as well.

BUSINESS SIZE: HOW BIG IS BIG?

Most corporations in the United States are "small," with assets (cash, buildings, equipment, inventories, etc.) totaling less than a few hundred thousand dollars each. At the other extreme are dozens of corporations belonging to the "billion dollar-plus club." These are companies whose total assets, annual sales, and annual net profits after taxes are far in excess of $1 billion. Each corporation employs hundreds of thousands of workers and distributes profits to hundreds of thousands or even millions of stockholders. Together these companies control a large share of the nation's income-producing wealth. The names of most of these corporations are already familiar to you. In fact, you are probably a customer for many of their products. Several of the firms are shown in Exhibit 5.

How big is big? By way of comparison, General Motors' annual sales often rank with the value of output produced by Argentina and Belgium. And General Motors, like a number of other U.S. corporations, has annual sales exceeding, by many billions of dollars, the total outputs of several dozen nations.

Is Bigness a Curse or a Blessing?

Is it "good" or "bad" to have an economy whose major industries are dominated by a few giant corporations? Are such companies as U.S. Steel in the steel industry, General Motors in the automobile industry, and AT&T in the electronic communications industry beneficial or harmful? Would we be better or worse off if we had

Culver Pictures.

A bond issued by the city of Philadelphia in 1884.

Exhibit 5

Who's Who Among the Giants? Average Sales of America's Ten Largest Corporations, 1978–1980

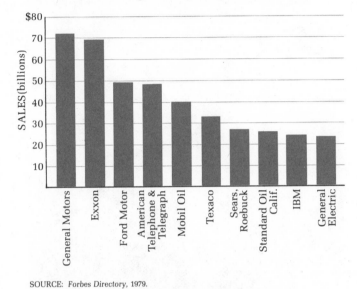

SOURCE: *Forbes Directory, 1979.*

an economy whose industries were composed of many small firms in active competition?

There are no simple answers. The best that we can do is sketch the main aspects of the problem and leave you to think out some tentative conclusions. As you study later chapters, you may very well come to see some of these conclusions in a different light.

Separation of Ownership and Control   A striking feature of the modern large corporation is the *separation of ownership and control*—the distinction between those who own the business (the stockholders) and those who control it (the hired managers). In most large corporations stock ownership is widely dispersed among hundreds of thousands or even millions of people. These stockholders are usually not interested in who manages the corporation. Consequently, a corporation's board of directors and officers may be able to keep themselves in power for their own benefit rather than for the primary benefit of the company and its stockholders. To some extent this problem has been reduced over the years as a result of government regulations and laws to protect the interests of stockholders. But the difficulty still exists in varying degrees and will probably never be eliminated completely.

Market Domination   Many important industries are dominated by a few large companies. Examples include aluminum, automobiles, telephone equipment, steel, cigarettes, breakfast foods, and many others. The giants in these industries exercise varying degrees of monopoly power over the markets in which they deal. This means, among other things, that:

○ They may charge prices higher than would occur if the industries were very competitive.

○ They may not improve their efficiency and productivity as much as they would do if they were subject to greater competition.

○ They may have the power to influence the very legislators and federal agencies responsible for regulating them.

However, many of today's corporate giants are the same companies whose productive resources and scientific know-how are vital to the country for peace as well as war. As many of the severest critics of big business have acknowledged, these firms have been instrumental in providing us with the standard of living we now possess.

Conclusion: Free Markets for Greater Efficiency

In light of these considerations, we cannot state unqualifiedly that big business is either "good" or "bad" for society. There are important advantages as well as disadvantages of large corporations, as you will see in some later chapters. Meanwhile, the following conclusions should be kept in mind.

> With respect to business size, the task of modern capitalism is not one of choosing between large firms and small ones. Both types are here to stay. The really practical problem is to find ways of making the free market work to improve the efficiency of businesses in general, both large and small. In this way, firms will utilize their resources more fully for the betterment of society.

Some further aspects of business size are described in Box 2.

DOES BUSINESS HAVE A SOCIAL RESPONSIBILITY? EFFICIENCY VERSUS EQUITY

According to traditional philosophy, social progress under capitalism is a by-product of economic efficiency. As Adam Smith asserted in 1776, the individual pursuing his or her own self-interest would be led by an invisible hand to do the most good for society. Such a person would do this not out of a sense of duty or responsibility to other human beings, but out of a drive for personal gain.

Box 2
How and Why Do Firms Become Big?

A business may expand through internal growth by plowing most of its profits back into the business. Or it can sell securities such as stocks and bonds to the public. In this way it acquires the funds it needs to pay for new equipment, research, and product development.

A classic example of both types of growth is the Ford Motor Company. For several decades after its formation, it remained a privately (mostly family) held corporation. After its stock became available to the public, it often paid out as little as 33 to 40 percent of its profits as dividends to stockholders. It kept the rest of the profits for reinvestment in plant, equipment, research, and so on. At the same time other major industrial firms were distributing between 50 and 65 percent of their profits.

A firm may also expand by combining or merging with others. This has been the most prevalent method of growth in American industry. Indeed, many of our largest firms achieved their present huge size through "marriages" with others.

EXPANSION MOTIVES

Why do some firms become large? Their ultimate objective is usually to strengthen their financial position.

For instance, a firm may combine with other firms in the same or in related types of activity for various reasons. Among them are the desire to gain economies in production or distribution, regularize supplies, or round out a product line. Thus, some container manufacturers also make tin cans, glass jars, and plastics. Some automobile producers own rubber companies, iron mines, and steel mills.

Many companies have also chosen to grow by combining with firms in totally unrelated activities. This may reflect various goals on the part of the acquiring company. Among these are the desire to spread risks, find investments for idle

Ford Motor Company.

capital funds, add products that can be sold with the firm's merchandising knowledge and skills, or simply to gain greater economic power on a broader front.

Businesses have accepted this capitalistic credo for two centuries. By seeking to maximize profits and technical efficiency—subject to such constraints as honest dealing with customers, fair dealing with workers, and no "dealing" with competitors—corporate executives have believed they would simultaneously be creating wealth for themselves as well as jobs, goods, and wealth for others.

Although this fundamental doctrine of capitalism has not been nullified, it has undergone substantial modification in recent decades. According to conventional belief, a corporation can only fulfill its obligations to society if it continues to be a profitable investment for its stockholders. More recently, many observers both in and out of the executive suite have argued in favor of a reversal of priorities. These critics believe that a corporation can only continue to be a profitable investment for its stockholders if it fulfills its obligations to society.

Responsibilities Beyond Profit

What are these obligations? Corporations, partly because of the failure of government and other institutions, have become increasingly involved in social improvement efforts. For example, many companies have participated in training and assisting poorly educated minorities, building and providing financing for ghetto housing, operating child-care centers, strengthening and improving urban school systems, and cleaning up the environment. In short, firms have taken on social problems which, not so long ago, would have been inconceivable. In fact, so pervasive has been this trend that it is a rare large corporation today that does not have an active social program.

Despite the widespread existence of such programs, however, their stability is not always assured. An economic recession, for example, cuts deeply into business profits, causing sharp reductions in social spending by corporations. And corporate executives, who must weigh the benefits and costs of social spending programs, are not always convinced of their worth. For these and similar reasons, the social role of business in modern society continues to be controversial.

A Critical View: Friedman

Interestingly enough, not everyone views the "social responsibility doctrine" in the same way. Many critics claim that it is a euphemism for socialism, breeding conditions that will eventually undermine the basis of a free society. The best known modern exponent of this view is the noted economist and Nobel laureate Milton Friedman. According to him, discussions that proclaim a "social consciousness" for business are ill-conceived and ill-defined, rooted more in emotion than in logic. The essence of his argument can be reduced to several fundamental propositions:

1. In a capitalistic system, a corporate executive is an employee of the stockholders (owners) of the business. The executive's responsibility is to conduct the business in accordance with the stockholders' wishes. Generally, this means to make as much money as possible without violating the law or the ethical customs of society.

2. Corporate executives, are, of course, also individuals in their own right. As such, they may assume whatever social responsibilities they choose—to community, church, favorite charities, country. However, any time or money that they devote to social causes, regardless of worthiness, must be their own, not their employers'.

3. Corporate executives may fail to adhere to these rules. For example, they may choose to make their companies better "citizens" by involving them, beyond the levels required by law, in socially responsible activities. However, in doing so they are spending money that rightfully belongs to others. To the extent that their actions result in a reduction in corporate profits, they are spending stockholders' money. To the extent that their actions result in higher prices, they are spending consumers' money. And to the extent that their actions result in lower wages, they are spending employees' money.

4. The stockholders, customers, and employees could each spend their own money for social causes if they wished to do so. By exercising corporate social responsibility, executives are acting in an unauthorized capacity for these groups. They are, in effect, taxing the groups and deciding how the tax proceeds are to be spent.

5. Such executives are, therefore, usurping governmental functions pertaining to the imposition of taxes and the expenditure of tax proceeds. These are functions for which society has established elaborate legislative and judicial provisions to assure that taxes are imposed where possible in accordance with public preferences and desires. Indeed, "taxation without representation" was one of the contributing factors to the American Revolution.

To summarize:

Friedman believes that the acceptance by corporate executives of responsibility other than to make as much money for the stockholders as possible is fundamentally subversive of free enterprise. The "social responsibility" doctrine, he contends, parallels the socialist view that exhortations and policies of political leaders, rather than market forces of supply and demand, are better able to determine the allocation of society's scarce resources.

What do you think? Should self-appointed private individuals decide not only what the social interest is, but also how great a burden others should share in serving that interest?

Private–Public "Partnership": Galbraith

Another viewpoint concerning the role of business in modern capitalism has gained considerable popularity. It emphasizes the need for a "partnership" between large corporations and the public sector. Among the advocates of this point of view is the widely known economist John Kenneth Galbraith. According to him, there comes a point in the development of a business firm when its size and market power no longer permit it to be considered "private." At that point the organization becomes both a political system and social enterprise—a "public institution." In the United States, firms that fall into this category include Exxon, General Motors, Ford Motor Company, General Electric, International Business Machines, and several hundred other giant corporations.

It is held that large organizations such as these possess substantial market power. As a result, they can fix their prices, persuade—and sometimes bamboozle—their customers, control supplies and prices of many raw materials, and even influence government legislation. For such firms the traditional concept of a competitive market is a myth. Instead, there is a clash between corporate goals and the public interest. Examples occur in the areas of product safety, industrial effects on the environment, the impact of price and wage settlements on the economy, and elsewhere. Galbraith thus concludes that under such circumstances, the large corporation has no natural right to be left alone.

To summarize:

> According to Galbraith and some others, today's markets do not resemble the traditional competitive model. Instead, they are dominated by large firms which, because of their monopolistic power, misallocate economic resources and engage in practices that conflict with the public interest. Therefore, closer ties between big corporations and government are necessary if business is to meet society's needs.

This means that today's large corporations should be treated not only as business firms, but as "political institutions" designed to help meet social goals.

Conclusion: Balancing Efficiency and Equity

Placed in proper perspective, the corporate-responsibility issue is actually a conflict between two goals—efficiency and equity.

A growing proportion of the public has come to believe that certain aspects of corporate behavior conflict with the welfare of society. To remedy the situation, these people say, the corporation should be left alone to compete in the market place. This would assure that economic resources will be allocated efficiently in accordance with society's preferences. Other people contend that giant corporations are too large to be left alone. A closer relationship with government is needed to assure that equity is not sacrificed on the altar of efficiency.

As with most social and economic problems, there are merits to both arguments. In view of this, can a compromise be reached between the goals of efficiency and equity?

In most cases, corporate officials can best fulfill their obligations to stockholders and to the public by striving for efficiency. But when socioeconomic conditions warrant it, the drive for efficiency may have to be tempered. Large corporations, for example, may find it prudent to restrain inflationary price increases or to restrict profits because society demands these things. This does not mean that corporations should stop thinking in businesslike terms and start shouldering more responsibility for correcting society's ills. Corporations have neither the desire nor the ability to do either. What they must do if they are to survive as business institutions in free markets is to *become*

more attentive to the public interest. This suggests the following conclusion:

> Corporations should strive not only for efficiency but for equity, and executives should learn to think not only economically but "politically." For if efficiency is the primary goal of economics, equity is the indispensable condition of practical politics. And in a democratic society, equity is defined by the public, not by corporate officials.

What You Have Learned

1. Income and wealth are among the chief measures of society's well-being. Therefore, their distributions within society and the forces determining the distributions are of central concern.

2. The Lorenz diagram and the corresponding Gini coefficient are the most common methods of measuring inequality. However, they are only as reliable as the data on which they are based. Therefore, the data should always be analyzed with a critical eye.

3. There are many reasons for income inequality. Among the more important are differences in wealth, earning ability and opportunity, resource mobility, luck, age, human-capital investment, and occupational risk.

4. Critics who contend that the personal distribution of income has remained stable since 1950 are basing their argument on unadjusted data. When the figures are adjusted for age differences among income receivers, the results show substantial gains in income equality during recent decades.

5. Ethical criteria exist for allocating income. Three major ones are (a) productive contribution, (b) needs, and (c) equality. The first is the primary standard of distribution in capitalistic economies. The second and third criteria are philosophical goals of pure communistic and of egalitarian societies—neither of which exist anywhere on a national scale.

6. Economic history shows that the higher a nation's per capita real income, the more that nation tends to progress toward greater income equality. This is because a high-income economy enables people to save enough to provide the capital accumulation necessary for a society's material advancement.

7. The business sector of the economy consists primarily of proprietorships, partnerships, and corporations. The number of proprietorships greatly exceeds the number of partnerships and corporations. However, corporations produce by far the largest proportion of the nation's goods and services. This is mainly because of two of their principal advantages: (a) the possibility of accumulating large sums of money to finance expansion and (b) the limited liability of stockholders.

8. The consequences of bigness are mixed. On the one hand, it has created separation of ownership and control in the large corporation, and resulted in increased monopoly

power for the largest firms in many industries. On the other hand, the largest firms have also been significantly responsible for some of the major advances in our standard of living and in our military preparedness.

9. The controversy over business responsibility concerns the question of which corporate goal is more important—efficiency or equity. Experience indicates that in most circumstances, the public permits efficiency to take precedence over equity as long as equity is not impaired. But corporate executives should recognize that equity is defined by society, and changes with the times. Therefore, if business firms are to minimize the chances of inviting government involvement, corporate officials must become more attentive to the public interest.

For Discussion

1. Terms and concepts to review:

private sector	firm
public sector	industry
income	proprietorship
wealth	partnership
personal income	corporation
distribution	stock
median	dividend
Lorenz diagram	limited liability
Gini coefficient of	bond
inequality	separation of ownership
transfer payments	and control

2. What are the chief causes of income inequality among households? Would it be better if all incomes were equal? Explain.

3. Is it a necessary condition of capitalism that some people be rich and some poor? Is it morally right for the government to tax the incomes of the rich and redistribute them to the poor? Defend your answer.

4. Suppose that a society consists of only five families with a combined money income of $100,000. The distribution of income among the families is shown in the accompanying table. Construct a Lorenz curve and calculate the Gini coefficient of inequality. Here are some helpful hints and suggestions:

(a) Fill in the table. Then derive the Lorenz curve from the last three columns. Note that the lowest 20 percent of the families receive 5 percent of the income; label this point B on the curve. The lowest 40 percent receive 15 percent of the income; label this point C on the curve. And so on.

(b) Connect the points with straight lines. If there had been many more income classes than five, the Lorenz curve would be a smooth, rounded line instead of a series of straight-line segments.

(c) The entire area under the Lorenz curve is equal to the sum of the separate triangular and trapezoidal areas beneath it. (A trapezoid is a four-sided plane figure having two parallel and two nonparallel sides.)

To perform the necessary calculations, make use of the fact that the area A in terms of the base b and height h is found as follows:

$$\text{for a triangle} \quad A = \tfrac{1}{2}bh$$
$$\text{for a trapezoid} \quad A = \tfrac{1}{2}b(h_1 + h_2)$$

where h_1 and h_2 represent, respectively, the heights of the left-hand and right-hand vertical sides.

5. We cannot distribute goods according to needs because we do not know how to determine peoples' needs. Therefore, why not solve the problem by (a) distributing incomes according to needs, and (b) permitting goods to be allocated through the price system, thereby preserving freedom of consumer choice?

6. The principle of payment according to product (i.e., the contribution standard) assures that people get what they deserve. Therefore, it is more democratic than payment based on needs or on equality. Do you agree? Explain.

7. "If payments to individuals are based on needs or on equality, some people are bound to be exploited for the benefit of others." What does "exploitation" mean? Explain.

8. In a democracy, we do not allocate political votes in proportion to one's intelligence and ability to use them. Instead, everyone gets an equal vote. Therefore, the same should be true of dollar votes (income); everyone's should be equal. Do you agree? Explain.

9. "The value of a culture is measured by its peak accomplishments, not by its average level of achievement. Thus, a society of mud huts and a great cathedral is better than a society of stone huts and no cathedral. To put it differently, it is by the quality of its saints and heroes, not its common people, and by its masterpieces and not by its domestic utensils, that a culture should be judged." What implications does this have for income distribution?

10. What are the two most important economic features of the corporate form of organization, as distinguished from the proprietorship or partnership form?

Percent of families	Income received (thousands)	Percent income received	Cumulative percent of families	Cumulative percent of income received	Point on Lorenz curve
0	$ 0	0			A
Lowest fifth	5	5			B
Second fifth	10	10			C
Third fifth	15	15			D
Fourth fifth	20	20			E
Highest fifth	50	50			

11. How and why do firms become big? Explain.

12. Is big business "good" or "bad"? Give some pros and cons of big business.

13. Some critics contend that the corporate search for "social responsibility" is the result of the market's failure to do its job. More fundamentally, it is a search for a stable standard of behavior. Can you explain what this means?

14. An eminent political scientist, Robert A. Dahl of Yale University, has challenged the assumption that stockholders should control the direction of a company. "I can discover absolutely no moral or political basis," he says, "for such a special right. Why investors and not consumers, workers, or, for that matter, the general public?" What implications does this statement have for the future of capitalism?

15. One way to give shareholders more voice in the affairs of a corporation is to revise the voting procedure from one share, one vote to one person, one vote. Those who support this view point out that in political elections, people with unequal economic stakes in society nevertheless get one vote each. Therefore, the same should be true in corporate elections. What do you think of this proposal? Explain.

Issue
Economic Justice: Is Equity Possible?

The human search for a just society has been long, arduous, and unsuccessful. In no society recorded by historians have all its members agreed that they are being treated justly. All too often, burning grievances have caused a group within society to overturn its institutions, peacefully or violently. The new society the group creates may seem to be just; to the vanquished opponents the new society seems the opposite. Yet the dream of a just society remains. Is it an impossible dream? Can a society ever be constructed that treats all its citizens justly?

The problems start with the term itself. Is a "just society" one that seeks the greatest degree of equality among its members, or one that regards the rights of individuals as inviolate? The question has been discussed in two classic books. Each was written by a gifted and distinguished young philosopher at Harvard University: John Rawls, *A Theory of Justice* (Harvard University Press, 1971), and Robert Nozick, *Anarchy, State, and Utopia* (Basic Books, 1974). Both books were highly acclaimed by critics, received national awards for originality, and even reached the best-seller lists. These are rare achievements for treatises dealing with such complex topics as justice, equality, and human rights.

Rawls's "Just Society": Optimum Differences
Rawls begins his discussion with the assertion that every society has a collection of human talents. These are the society's assets. The problem is to distribute these assets in a way that will be beneficial to all—without restricting anyone's liberty. To accomplish this, we must assume that "justice is the first virtue of social institutions." Two principles of justice—both of which serve as criteria for judging the efficiency of social change—may then be established:

1. **Equality Principle**   Each person has an equal right to the same liber-ties and opportunities available to others. This means that no individual may be deprived of choices that other individuals possess.

2. **Difference Principle**   Justice is realized when social and economic inequalities have been arranged so that their differences yield the greatest satisfaction to the least advantaged without reducing the satisfactions of anyone. In other words, inequalities of income, wealth, and natural abilities are justifiable only to the extent that they contribute to the improvement of the least fortunate.

Rawls thus recognizes that social and economic inequalities exist in every society. The problem, he says, is to rearrange these inequalities so that they work for the benefit of society rather than against it. When this happens, the society will be a "just" one. It will have achieved an optimum distribution of inequalities.

Of course, it helps to have some sort of criterion for rearranging inequalities. The following rule, derived from the two principles stated above, serves as a guideline:

Rawls: *Inequalities are justifiable if they contribute to the improvement of the least fortunate.*

Any social action should be undertaken if it will make the least advantaged person better off without making anyone else worse off.

According to Rawls, adherence to this guideline improves equity. How? By assuring that those who have been favored by nature with talent, wealth, or other social advantages may gain from their good fortune only when it improves those who have lost out. With respect to income inequality, for example, any policy action that increases the income of the lowest-income person without reducing the well-being of anyone else will clearly enhance social justice. Therefore, according to Rawls, the policy should be adopted.

Nozick's "Just Society": You're Entitled
Rawls's colleague, Robert Nozick, starts off with a different assumption. "Individuals have rights," Nozick argues, "and there are things no persons or group may do to them (without violating their rights). . . . The fact of our separate existences [means that] there is no moral outweighing of one of our lives by others so as to lead to a greater overall *social* good. *There is no justified sacrifice of some of us for others.*"

On the basis of this, Nozick proposes what he calls an "entitlement theory of justice":

A just society is one which acknowledges that people are entitled to their possessions—no matter how unequal the distribution of goods in society as a whole. This is true provided that the goods have been acquired legitimately without making anyone else "worse off."

The entitlement theory leads Nozick to deduce a number of interesting conclusions. Among them:

○ Any "patterned" distribution of goods—any allocation based on contribution, need, effort, or whatever—is necessarily coercive. It therefore violates peoples' fundamental rights to use their property and talents as they wish.

○ Egalitarianism (the doctrine of equality) is unjust because it "forbids capitalist acts between consenting adults." That is, it deprives people of their natural right to pay for what they want in order to be "different."

○ Free competition enables us to benefit from market information by reflecting buyers' and sellers' knowledge and anticipations. Market information is transmitted most effectively in a price system that is unhampered by government restraints and regulations.

○ Government has no right to tax the rich to help the poor, nor to forbid people to abuse or endanger themselves. Neither does government have the right to levy a progressive income tax, engage in welfare activities, provide public health care, impose compulsory social security, legislate equal opportunity, or sponsor public education. "I do believe," Nozick says, "that you should aid people in need. I would personally do it, and I would encourage it. But I don't believe the state has a right to force me to do it, or that my fellow citizens, if they're in the majority, have a right to force me to do it."

Nozick: *Equality is unjust because it forbids capitalist acts between consenting adults.*

In short, Nozick believes that the task of a theory of justice is *not* to describe the pattern that a society ought to fit. Any imposed pattern is necessarily coercive. Further, "on the entitlement theory of justice there is no overall pattern that will fit. People are entitled to what they have if they got it in a legitimate way"—in free exchange among consenting parties to a transaction. By this standard, Nozick says, "the most serious intervention in the free labor market in the United States was slavery. We're still learning the consequences of that in serious fashion. I think reparations may be in order. And Indians are another problem."

QUESTIONS

1. Rawls emphasizes the primacy of liberty—including the assurance of equal opportunity. However, he also argues that our legal, political, and social institutions should be modified to bestow maximum benefits on the disadvantaged. From Nozick's viewpoint, is it possible to achieve both these goals? Discuss.

2. Rawls advocates legislation designed to improve the well-being of the least fortunate. Nozick opposes such legislation—or for that matter, any legislation that interferes with individual rights. In view of these conflicting opinions, can you propose a "rule" or guide for legislation that would satisfy both Rawls and Nozick? Is your rule "workable"? Discuss.

Chapter 4

The Public Sector: Government

Chapter Preview

What are the scope and functions of government?

How should goods and services provided by government be allocated? Are there basic guidelines for making such decisions?

What have been the trends of government spending at the federal, state, and local levels? How are expenditures allocated among alternative uses? What principles exist for achieving efficiency in government budgeting?

What is the nature of our tax system? Are our taxes fair? How can we judge the relative merits of a tax?

One of the most remarkable trends in contemporary history has been the growing importance of government in economic life. As measured by government purchases of goods and services, the public sector bought 10 percent of the nation's total output in 1930. By 1960, this figure had risen to 20 percent. Today it is close to 25 percent. These facts raise many problems concerning the economic functions of government in our mixed economy. This chapter examines a few of the more important ones and provides some basic concepts for understanding them.

Of course, any serious discussion of government is bound to raise questions of taxes. Taxes, if you recall your study of history, have been the cause of wars and revolutions. Obviously, anything that can have such widespread influences ought to be worth knowing something about.

When we speak of government, we ordinarily mean the federal government. But in this chapter we shall say some things about government at the state level and also at the local level. The local level includes counties, cities, villages, townships, school districts, and so on.

Economic Scope and Functions of Government

For centuries, political scholars have theorized about the purposes and functions of the state. In *The Wealth of Nations* Adam Smith said that government's role should be limited to national defense, the administration of justice, the facilitation of commerce, and the provision of certain public works. Many social scientists today would agree with Smith, although some might add a few provisos of their own. For present purposes, the economic role of government can be described within a framework of two broad areas. These are (1) promotion and regulation of the private sector and (2) provision of social goods.

PROMOTION AND REGULATION OF THE PRIVATE SECTOR

Government promotes and regulates the private sector in many ways. Sometimes it does this to the net advantage and sometimes to the net disadvantage of society as a whole. A complete listing of the public sector's economic activities is impossible, but six major areas can be identified.

1. Government *provides a stable environment* in which firms and households can engage in orderly exchange. Government performs this basic function by defining property rights, upholding contracts, adjudicating disputes, setting standards for weights and measures, enforcing law and order, and maintaining a monetary system. These conditions are so fundamental to organized society that they have existed even in the most ancient civilizations. The Code of Hammurabi (circa 2100 B.C.), and the later laws of ancient Egypt and Rome, went into considerable detail in defining property rights and related matters pertaining to commerce.

2. Government *performs public welfare activities*. It establishes health and safety standards in industry, regulates minimum wages for certain classes of workers, and provides old-age, disability, sickness, and unemployment benefits for those who qualify. Social welfare measures are enacted primarily for humanitarian reasons. Nevertheless, some of the measures may be a tacit admission that the private sector has failed to fulfill society's needs in an equitable manner.

3. Government *grants economic privileges* to specific groups. Through selective subsidies, tariffs, quotas, credit programs, price supports, legal provisions, and taxes, government favors particular consumers, industries, unions, and other segments of the economy. This elaborate network of privileges and controls results as much from political pressures as from economic logic. Hence, to a large extent government privileges cause higher prices, reduced efficiencies, and misallocations of society's resources.

4. Government is empowered to *maintain competition* within the economy. Specific laws forbid unre-

gulated monopolies and unfair trade and labor practices. If government enforces these laws vigorously, it ensures the perpetuation of a strong private sector.

5. Government seeks to *maintain high employment* through appropriate tax, expenditure, and monetary policies. At the same time, government seeks to encourage a steady rate of economic growth while curbing inflation and minimizing environmental decay. These activities are undertaken primarily by the federal government, but state and local governments also influence them through their own taxing, spending, and legislative policies.

6. Government *redistributes income and wealth* among firms and households through income taxes, inheritance taxes, property taxes, zoning ordinances, and other types of controls. Thus, through taxation and regulation, all major levels of government reallocate within the private sector some of the income and wealth that is generated therein.

This brief sketch of government practices and policies leads to an important observation:

> The promotional and regulatory activities of government are complex and widespread. Ostensibly, some of these actions are undertaken to correct for market failures. That is, they address the inability of the private sector, if left to itself, to achieve the goals of efficiency, equity, stability, and growth that all societies seek. However, the extent to which government activities contribute to the realization of these goals is often debatable. This will be seen here and in many subsequent chapters.

PROVISION OF SOCIAL GOODS

All economic systems are concerned with the three fundamental questions of WHAT will be produced, HOW it will be produced, and WHO will receive the final output. In mixed capitalistic economies such as ours, these questions are answered primarily by the market system. But certain types of commodities are not adequately provided by a free market. Their supply then usually becomes a function of government. We refer to such commodities as *social goods*, of which there are several different types.

Public (Collective) Goods

Certain social products may be classified as *public*, or *collective*, *goods*. Examples are national defense, law and order, the administration of justice, air traffic control, and public safety. These products have three common characteristics:

1. *Inclusiveness*   The benefits of a public good are indivisible. This means that they cannot be denied to

anyone, regardless of whether he or she pays for them. This is not the case with *nonpublic goods*. These are private goods, such as food or clothing, or certain social goods, such as toll highways or national parks. Someone who does not pay for nonpublic goods can conceivably be excluded from their use. Hence, a nonpublic good is subject to what is technically known as the exclusion principle, whereas a public good is not. This method of distinguishing between a public and nonpublic good is crucial. Can you formulate a definition of the principle in your own words? How does your definition compare with the one given in the Dictionary at the back of the book?

2. *Zero Incremental or Marginal Costs*   There is no increase in the cost of a public good if it is provided to one more consumer. Therefore, we say that the additional or incremental cost—commonly called *marginal cost*—of the commodity is zero. Thus, the cost of national defense, law and order, or any other commodity mentioned above does not increase with unitary gains in the population. However, this characteristic is also true of many private as well as other social goods. For example, within wide limits, up to the point of overcrowding, there are no significant marginal costs to a theater or to a library resulting from the admittance of one more patron.

3. *Spillover Effects*   A public good creates spillovers. These are external benefits or costs resulting from activities for which no compensation is made. Spillovers are also referred to as externalities. For example, air traffic control at busy airports reduces noise for some nearby residents while increasing it for others. This is an unpaid-for benefit to the former and an uncompensated "cost" to the latter. Similarly, in the private sector a factory may provide income and employment benefits to a community while polluting its environment. Thus, spillover effects, like zero incremental costs, are not a unique property of public goods.

These characteristics provide the basis for a definition:

Public goods are those not subject to the exclusion principle. This is because the benefits of public goods are indivisible. Therefore, no one can be excluded from receiving them, whether he or she pays or not. For this reason, public goods are commodities that the private sector is usually unable or unwilling to produce. Two additional but not unique characteristics of public goods are zero incremental or marginal costs and spillover effects.

REMARK   Radio and most television transmissions are public goods because they are not subject to the exclusion principle. Yet they are provided (in the United States and some other countries) by the private sector. Can you suggest why? Can you think of some other exceptions?

Other Social Goods

Public goods are not the only commodities supplied by government. Other social goods are also provided, each sharing in different degrees some of the properties of both public and private goods. Examples are highways, national parks, libraries, museums, elementary and secondary education, public housing, and public hospitals. These goods are subject to the exclusion principle, even though the principle may not always be invoked. Therefore, they are not public goods. People could be charged for the use of these goods instead of receiving them "free" or at less than market value. As you will see, this raises interesting problems about the effects of social goods on society's welfare.

CONCLUSION: IDENTIFYING THE PUBLIC'S CHOICES

Throughout the nation's history, government has served as a savior, subsidizer, owner, and regulator of special interests. It has financed roads and canals, subsidized firms and industries, sheltered workers, protected consumers and businesses, stabilized credit, refereed competition, and regulated markets.

In addition, government has become the chief producer of social goods, including public and nonpublic goods. The benefits of the former are received by everyone. The benefits of the latter are widely available and, in most cases, are provided at below-market prices. Therefore, since many social goods are not sold in the market, how does government decide WHAT and HOW MUCH to produce?

Unlike private goods that businesses produce in response to the dollar "votes" of consumers, social goods are produced by government in response to the public's choices. Through their elected representatives at the voting booths, people make known, in a broad sense, the social goods that are wanted. Therefore, methods are needed to identify the public's choices so they can be fulfilled with reasonable efficiency.

As you will now see, the task of identifying what the public wants can pose some interesting and challenging problems.

Public Choice and Public Goods

In our mixed economy, as you have already learned, society's resources are allocated to the production of private goods in accordance with market forces. But what about public goods such as national defense, public safety, air-traffic control, and other examples given earlier? These, unlike private goods, are not subject to the exclusion principle. Therefore, no one can be prevented from consuming public goods, whether he or she pays or not. Further, the benefits of such goods are not sold in the market. Therefore, the allocation of society's resources for the production of public goods raises special problems. These come under the heading of *public choice*. This is a branch of economics dealing with nonmarket collective decision making, or the application of economics to political science.

EFFICIENCY: ALLOCATING PUBLIC GOODS

When you studied demand and supply curves earlier, you saw how the total market demand curve for a commodity is derived by summing horizontally the individual demand curves. A similar procedure is used in the case of supply. To refresh your memory, the idea is illustrated in Exhibit 1 for a demand curve. For simplicity, this model assumes there are only three people in the market—individuals *A, B,* and *C.* The conclusions can then be extended to include a market composed of any number of people.

In Chart *(a)*, the total demand for a private good is simply the *horizontal* sum of the individual demand curves, D_A, D_B, and D_C. For example, at a price of $2 per unit, individual *A* will demand 4 units, individual *B* will demand 8 units, and individual *C* will demand 10 units. Therefore, the total market demand at a price of $2 will be $4 + 8 + 10 = 22$ units. Similarly, at a price of $6 per unit, the specific quantities demanded will be $2 + 4 + 8 = 14$ units. If we connect each pair of points for each individual with a straight line, we get the three individual demand curves. The total market demand curve is then seen to be the horizontal sum of the individual curves at each price.

In contrast, Chart *(b)* shows the individual demand curves for a public good. Unlike a private good, whose benefits must be purchased by those who want them, the benefits of a public good—such as guided missiles, street lighting, and disease control—are shared by everyone. As a result, the total demand curve for a public good must be derived in a different way.

Thus, in Chart *(b)*, the total demand for the good is the *vertical* sum of the individual demand curves D_A, D_B, and D_C. For example, to share in the benefits of 1 unit of the good, such as 1 missile, individual *A* would be willing to pay (in the form of increased taxes) $2. Similarly, individual *B* would be willing to pay $4,

---

Exhibit 1
Deriving Demand Curves and Allocating a Public Good

Chart (a). *For a private good, each point on the total demand curve is obtained by starting with a given price and finding the horizontal sum—the total quantity that individuals are willing to purchase.*

Chart (b). *For a public good, each point on the total demand curve is obtained by starting with a given quantity and finding the vertical sum—the total price (in the form of taxes) that individuals are willing to pay.*

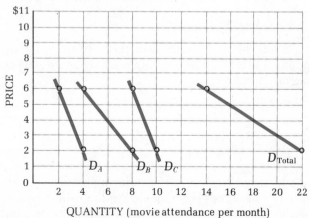

(a) DERIVING A DEMAND CURVE FOR A PRIVATE GOOD (example: movie attendance)

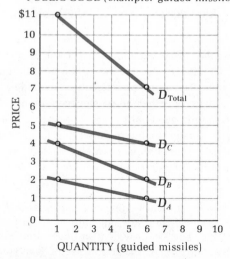

(b) DERIVING A DEMAND CURVE FOR A PUBLIC GOOD (example: guided missiles)

and individual C would be willing to pay $5. Therefore, the total *demand price*—the highest price per unit that buyers are willing to pay for a given quantity of the commodity—is $2 + $4 + $5 = $11 for 1 unit. For a quantity of 6 units, the total demand price is $1 + $2 + $4 = $7. As before, if we connect each pair of points for each individual with straight lines, we get three individual demand curves. The total curve, of course, is simply the vertical sum of the individual curves at each quantity.

We can now use supply and demand curves to determine the equilibrium quantity of a public good. The equilibrium quantity is the amount that society will produce with its limited resources. This is shown in Chart (c). Note that the supply curve in this case is horizontal. This is true of most public goods. The horizontal supply curve tells you that the additional or marginal cost of supplying one more unit of the good remains the same. Therefore, government is willing to supply additional units at a constant price per unit.

How much will actually be supplied, and at what price? The answer is determined by the intersection of the demand and supply curves. Thus, the equilibrium quantity of the good will be at M units and the equilibrium price at P dollars per unit.

These ideas can be summarized briefly:

Chart (c). *For many public goods, the supply curve is horizontal. This indicates that government will provide any number of units of the commodity at the given price. The actual amount provided is determined, as with a private good, by the intersection of the total demand and supply curves. Thus, the equilibrium quantity is at M, and the equilibrium price at P.*

(c) ALLOCATING A PUBLIC GOOD

For a *private good*, each point on the total demand curve is obtained by starting with a given price and finding the *horizontal sum*—the total quantity that people are willing to purchase. For a *public good*, each point on the total demand curve is obtained by starting with a given quantity and finding the *vertical sum*—the total price that people are willing to pay. If the supply and demand curves of the public are known, the equilibrium price and quantity are determined in the same way as for a private good—by the intersection of the two curves.

Test Yourself

1. For a private good, the supply curve is likely to be upward-sloping. What does such a curve tell you? (Think in terms of the law of supply.)

2. For most public goods, the supply curve is horizontal. For some public goods, however, the supply curve may be vertical. What would a vertical curve tell you? Does it conform to the law of supply?

PRACTICAL DIFFICULTIES: PSEUDO DEMAND CURVES AND THE FREE-RIDER PROBLEM

This analysis of how a public good is allocated may seem strange if not confusing. The reason is that it involves at least two practical problems.

1. The demand curves shown in Chart (b) are actually "false" or "counterfeit" demand curves. This is because they are based on the unrealistic assumption that consumers voluntarily state their demand prices. If this were in fact the case, government could achieve greater efficiency and equity in the financing of public goods by charging consumers the amounts they were willing to pay. Instead, public goods are usually financed through taxes and subsidies, which, for reasons shown later in the chapter, may often fall far short of achieving maximum efficiency and equity.

2. A second problem arises from the fact that a public good is one that is not subject to the exclusion principle. Therefore, no individual can be prevented from receiving the benefits of a public good, whether he or she pays or not. In view of this, why would anyone be willing to state his or her demand price for a public good, as was assumed in Chart (b)?

This second difficulty results in what is known as the *free-rider problem*. It may be defined as the tendency of people to avoid paying for a good's benefits when the benefits can be obtained free. The free-rider problem exists because public goods, more than any others, create extensive spillover benefits. Those who receive the benefits without paying are thus "free riders." It follows that if many people become free riders, the demand curves shown in Chart (b) become ineffective. That is, they serve as a useful guide for thinking about the problem of allocating a public good, but they do not provide a practical means for doing so. Thus, an alternative approach is needed.

CONCLUSION: ALLOCATION BY COLLECTIVE ACTION

The inability of the market system to allocate resources for the production of public goods is an example of *market failure*. When markets fail, democratic societies resort to various nonmarket methods to provide the desired goods. Because voters as well as their elected representatives have different attitudes about what constitutes the optimal amount of public goods, differences of opinion must be reconciled through the political process. How is this accomplished? In general:

> The nonmarket method used by democratic societies to allocate resources for the production of public goods is *collective action*—the rule of majority vote. This method does not always lead to equitable results because it may not be capable of reconciling conflicting preferences. However, through vote trading and compromise by legislators, collective action has proven to be a workable and relatively "fair" system—as evidenced by its long history of acceptability.

Public Budgeting and Collective Decision Making

In the past few decades the public sector has been characterized by a remarkable growth of expenditures at all levels of government—federal, state, and local. This means that a rising volume of the nation's output is being allocated by collective rather than by private decision making. Several major reasons for the growth of government spending are given in Exhibit 2.

Any discussion of public-sector expenditures is bound to raise questions about public-sector revenues. The methods used by governments to manage their revenues and expenditures comprise what is known as "public budgeting." This is a branch of economics and political science concerned with governmental financial planning and control. Exhibit 3 provides some illustrations of government budgets.

Budgeting for a government, like budgeting for a family, is an activity dealing with hopes, daydreams, and hard facts. What is a budget? It is an itemized estimate of expected revenues and expenditures for a given period in the future. The federal budget covers a

Exhibit 2
Growth of Government Expenditures

The size of the public sector, measured by government expenditures, has expanded rapidly—for several reasons.

1. *Increased Demand for Social Goods and Services*   The public sector has increased its expenditures on social goods such as education, transportation, public assistance, health care, housing, and consumer protection.

2. *War and National Defense*   A large part of the increase in federal spending can be attributed to expenditures on wars, defense-related activities, and interest on the federal debt, much of which resulted from the financing of our recent major wars.

3. *Inflation and Lagging Productivity*   The costs of social benefits provided by government have climbed with inflation (i.e., rising prices). At the same time, productivity in the delivery of those services has lagged far behind rising costs. Government has thus found that the salaries it pays out—for education, public safety, health, and so on—are growing faster than the efficiency of the services it performs.

[NOTE   The vertical axis of this chart is a "ratio" or logarithmic scale on which equal distances are represented by equal percentage changes. For example, the changes from 100 to 200, 200 to 400, 300 to 600, and so on, all equal 100 percent, and hence are presented by equal distances on the chart. This permits better comparisons to be made of both small and large (i.e., *relative*) changes in the data.]

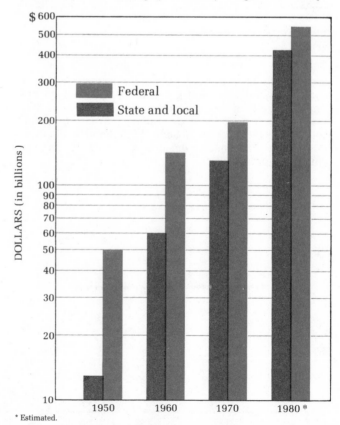

* Estimated.

SOURCE: U.S. Department of Commerce.

Exhibit 3
Federal, State, and Local Budgets: What Happens to Your Tax Dollars?

(a) FEDERAL BUDGET RECEIPTS AND OUTLAYS: 1960–1980

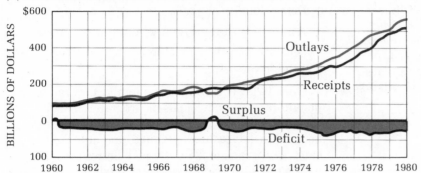

Chart (a). *The government's total revenues and expenditures for any given year are rarely equal. When they are, the budget is said to be* balanced. *On the other hand, when total revenues exceed total expenditures in any given year, the budget is said to have a* surplus; *when total revenues are less than total expenditures, the budget has a* deficit.

(b) ANNUAL FEDERAL BUDGET: AVERAGE, 1975–1980

WHERE IT COMES FROM: RECEIPTS

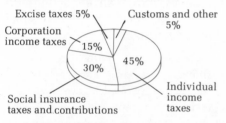

Excise taxes 5%
Customs and other 5%
Corporation income taxes 15%
30%
45%
Social insurance taxes and contributions
Individual income taxes

WHERE IT GOES: OUTLAYS

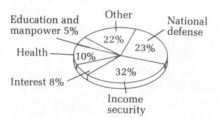

Education and manpower 5%
Other
National defense
Health 22%
23%
10%
32%
Interest 8%
Income security

Chart (b). *For the federal government, income taxes, both individual and corporate, comprise the largest source of receipts. Income security payments, including social security benefits, unemployment compensation, public assistance (welfare), and federal employment retirement and disability benefits, constitute the largest category of outlays.*

(c) STATE AND LOCAL GOVERNMENT BUDGETS: AVERAGE, 1975–1980

WHERE IT COMES FROM: RECEIPTS

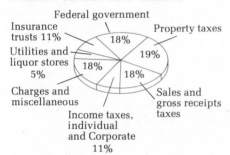

Federal government
Insurance trusts 11%
Property taxes
18%
Utilities and liquor stores 5%
19%
18%
18%
Charges and miscellaneous
Sales and gross receipts taxes
Income taxes, individual and Corporate 11%

WHERE IT GOES: OUTLAYS

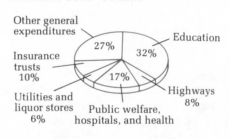

Other general expenditures
Education
Insurance trusts 10%
27%
32%
17%
Utilities and liquor stores 6%
Highways 8%
Public welfare, hospitals, and health

Chart (c). *For state and local governments combined, property taxes (on land, buildings, etc.) and sales taxes make up the chief sources of tax income. Education is the largest category of expenditure.*

(d) PER CAPITA TAX REVENUE, BY LEVEL OF GOVERNMENT

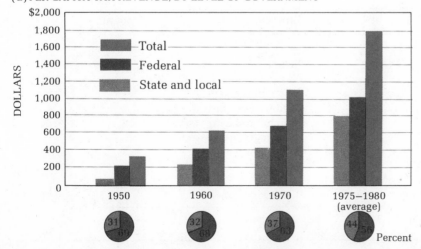

Total
Federal
State and local

1950   1960   1970   1975–1980 (average)
31   32   37   44
Percent

Chart (d). *Over the long run, state and local governments have received a rising, and the federal government a declining, percentage share of total tax revenues. These trends reflect the growing economic influence of the state and local sector relative to the federal sector—particularly the need of the former to finance its accelerating public functions.*

SOURCE: U.S. Department of Commerce.

fiscal year. The budgets of some state and local governments cover a fiscal period which may involve one year or even two years.

You will often hear people complain of waste in government spending. Can financial controls be developed to reduce public-sector inefficiencies? Although improvements in budgeting have been made from time to time, two scientific approaches have gained considerable popularity at certain levels of government. The two approaches are (1) program-planning-budgeting systems and (2) benefit-cost analyses.

PROGRAM-PLANNING-BUDGETING SYSTEMS (PPBS)

A budget is a financial road map. It tells you where revenues are expected to come from and where expenditures are expected to go. Most traditional budgets are called "administrative" budgets. They classify expected money inflows and outflows by administrative units such as departments or agencies, or by activities describing the work to be performed. Administrative budgets do not ordinarily explain why or how the funds are to be coordinated to fulfill objectives.

A budget that is designed to avoid this shortcoming is a "program budget." It is part of a larger complex called a *program-planning-budgeting system (PPBS)*. This may be defined as a method of revenue and expenditure management based on:

1. Determination of goals.

2. Assessment of their relative importance to society.

3. Allocation of those resources needed to attain the goals at least cost.

Thus, PPBS is a budgetary method that relates expenditures to specific goals or programs. This is done so that the costs of achieving a particular program can be identified, measured, planned, and controlled. You can best appreciate the difference between an administrative budget and a program budget by the examples shown in Exhibit 4.

In government departments where PPBS has been adopted, it has frequently improved budgeting efficiency. However, it has also been found to have some important limitations. In particular:

Outputs are usually in the form of indivisible services, and are therefore difficult to measure. For example, neither the quantity nor the quality of most governmentally provided social goods—such as education, health care, police protection, space exploration, and so on—can be broken down and measured in precise units. As a result,

---

Exhibit 4
Application: U.S. Coast Guard—Alternative Budget Structures

In an administrative budget, funds are allocated by administrative agencies and by activities. In a program budget, funds are allocated for the purpose of attaining certain objectives, that is, undertaking specific programs. The totals in both budgets may be the same, but the ways in which the expenditures are broken down are quite different. As explained in the text, a program budget is part of a larger planning and control system.

Administrative budget	Amount	Program budget	Amount
General funds: finance division			
Operating expenses	×	Search and rescue	×
Retired pay	×	Navigational aids	×
Reserve training	×	Law enforcement	×
Activities funds: departments		Military readiness	×
Vessel operations	×	Merchant Marine safety	×
Aviation operations	×	Oceanography projects	×
Training and recruiting	×	Supporting services	×
Administration	×		
Other expenses	×		
Total	×	Total	×

SOURCE: U.S. Department of Transportation. Adapted.

the establishment of budgetary goals and priorities is generally based on value judgments rather than on scientific determinations.

Despite this shortcoming, PPBS is a useful tool for facilitating overall budgetary decision making. However, when specific alternatives must be evaluated to decide whether certain large-scale projects and expenditures should be undertaken, a more scientific approach is needed.

BENEFIT-COST ANALYSIS

A scientific approach to budgeting and financial planning that has gained increasing use both in government and in corporations is *benefit-cost analysis*. Stated in simplest terms, it is a method of comparing the advantages and disadvantages of alternative investment projects to decide which should be undertaken. Thus, if you were thinking of purchasing a house, a car, or even a vacation, benefit-cost analysis would help you make the choice that best meets your goals. A formal definition of benefit-cost analysis appears in the Dictionary at the back of the book.

As a concrete example based on an actual situation, look at Exhibit 5, which analyzes a water-resource construction project. Four tributaries in a national forest flow together to form the Harrison River. Flooding occurs annually, causing significant damage within a large area. By building an earthwork dam on each tributary, water levels would be controlled and

future damage avoided. In the exhibit, the first column of the table shows the number of dams to be considered. The second and third columns show the total costs and the total benefits resulting from dollars saved due to damage reduction.

Columns (4) and (5) of the table convey some special information. Column (4) tells you the incremental or *marginal cost*—the additional cost of one more dam—and column (5) shows the incremental or *marginal benefit*—the additional benefit of that dam. Each marginal cost figure is the change in total cost, and each marginal benefit figure is the change in total benefit, resulting from a change in quantity—the number of dams. Therefore, to calculate the marginal figures, you divide the changes in their corresponding totals by the changes in quantity. The results are then entered between the horizontal rows of figures in the table to emphasize the fact that the marginal numbers are simply the *changes* in the totals. Finally, column (6) discloses the dams' net benefit—the difference between total benefit and total cost.

To yield the greatest net benefit, how many dams should be constructed? As you can see from Exhibit 6, which shows the graphs of the data, the correct answer is three. This quantity of output represents the number of dams that yields the largest difference between total benefit and total cost—the greatest net benefit. This is shown in both the top and bottom charts. You can verify this fact by following the vertical dashed line downward. Note also from the middle chart that this production quantity occurs at the out-

Exhibit 5
Application: Benefit-Cost Analysis for Harrison River Flood-Control Project
(annual data, thousands of dollars)

(1) Quantity of output (number of dams)	(2) Total cost, TC, estimated*	(3) Total benefit, TB, estimated†	(4) Marginal cost, MC $\dfrac{\text{Change in (2)}}{\text{Change in (1)}}$	(5) Marginal benefit, MB $\dfrac{\text{Change in (3)}}{\text{Change in (1)}}$	(6) Net benefit, NB (3) − (2)
0	$ 0	$ 0			$ 0
			$150	$400	
1	150	400			250
			150	300	
2	300	700			400
			150	200	
3	450	900			450
			150	100	
4	600	1,000			400

* Equal to equivalent annual cost (i.e., construction cost plus a forecast of annual maintenance costs) expressed in today's dollars.
† Equal to equivalent annual benefit (i.e., a forecast of the annual value of damage reduction to crops, homes, and recreational facilities) expressed in today's dollars.

Exhibit 6
Benefit and Cost Curves for Harrison River Flood-Control Project
(thousands of dollars per year)

Chart (a) Total Curves. *Maximum net benefit is determined where the distance between total benefit TB and total cost TC is greatest—as shown by the vertical dashed line. This occurs at an output quantity of 3 units.*

Chart (b) Marginal Curves. *Maximum net benefit is determined where MC = MB, as explained in the text. This is also evident by following the vertical dashed line downward at 3 units of output.*

Chart (c) Net Benefit Curve. *Maximum net benefit is determined where the net benefit curve NB (= TB − TC) is a maximum. The vertical dashed line at 3 units of output emphasizes these net benefit-maximizing principles in all three charts.*

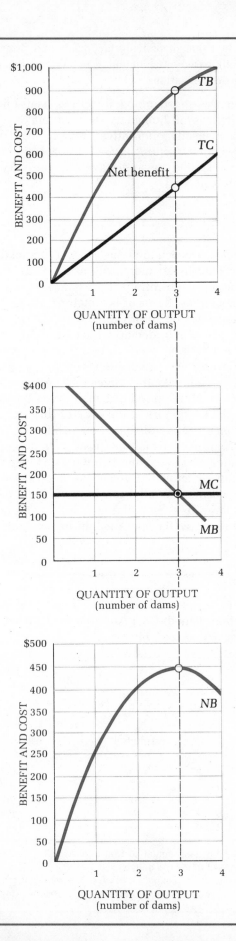

put level where marginal cost, *MC*, equals marginal benefit, *MB*. This suggests the following useful rule:

> Production of a social good should continue as long as the addition to total benefit (called "marginal benefit") exceeds the addition to total cost (called "marginal cost"). This is because net benefit will be rising over that range of output. When the difference between total benefit and total cost is greatest, net benefit will be at a maximum. At that level of output, marginal benefit will equal marginal cost.

NOTE   For graphing purposes, the marginal values in the middle chart are plotted to the *midpoints* of the integers on the horizontal axis. This is because marginal cost and marginal benefit reflect, respectively, the *change* in total cost and in total benefit resulting from a unit *change* in quantity.

CONCLUSION: EFFICIENCY THROUGH "MARGINAL" THINKING

The growth of the public sector has fostered many proposals for achieving efficiency in government. PPBS and benefit-cost analysis are two related approaches to budgeting that have been in use at various levels of government for several decades.

In practice, benefit-cost analysis suffers from several handicaps. Chief among them is the fact that many types of government expenditures produce benefits which are widespread, intangible, and therefore difficult to measure. As a result, the public sector's adoption of benefit-cost analysis has been limited to specific types of projects. These include flood control, electric power production, transportation systems, and certain service activities. The benefits from these kinds of projects are more clearly identifiable and measurable. Despite limited applications, however, benefit-cost analysis has certain fundamental advantages.

> In a conventional budgeting system, funds tend to be allocated according to expected "needs" or "requirements." Little or no effort is made to establish in any precise way how those needs are determined—and whether they are worth the costs. In a benefit-cost budgeting system, each marginal (additional) expenditure is compared to its marginal benefit. The expenditure is not undertaken unless it is at least equaled by its benefit. Therefore, net benefit is increased and scarce resources are thus allocated more efficiently—through "marginal" as opposed to "needs" or "requirements" thinking.

The American Tax System

Government budgets deal not only with expenditures, but with revenues. Governments raise revenues through taxation. In view of this, we must ask: What is the nature of our tax system?

A <u>tax</u> is a compulsory payment to government. The purpose of a tax is to achieve one or more of four objectives:

Efficiency—full use of society's available resources to produce the goods and services that consumers want to purchase, given their incomes.

Equity—a distribution of income and wealth that society regards as fair.

Stability—a steady, high level of employment without sharp inflations or deflations.

Growth—a rising level of output for all members of society.

Taxes can be levied and classified in many ways. In the United States and many other Western countries there are three principal types of taxes:

1. Taxes on income

   (a) Personal income taxes.

   (b) Corporation income taxes.

2. Taxes on wealth (including its ownership and transfer)

   (a) Property taxes.

   (b) Death (estate and inheritance) and gift taxes.

3. Taxes on activities (consumption, production, employment, etc.)

   (a) Sales and excise taxes.

   (b) Social security taxes.

Dozens of other less important kinds of taxes exist, but nearly all can be placed in one of these three main categories.

TAXES ON INCOME

Income taxes are based on net income—what remains after certain items are deducted from gross income. The items that can be deducted and the tax rates that are applied are specified by law and differ between the personal income tax and the corporation income tax.

Personal Income Tax

In the spring a young man's fancy turns to thoughts of love. But for millions of American taxpayers, spring is the season when their thoughts turn to more mundane and certainly less romantic activities as they begin to sort their previous year's income and expense records. As shown in Exhibit 7, this is the first step that must be completed to determine the personal income tax.

Exhibit 7
Logical Structure of the Federal Personal Income Tax

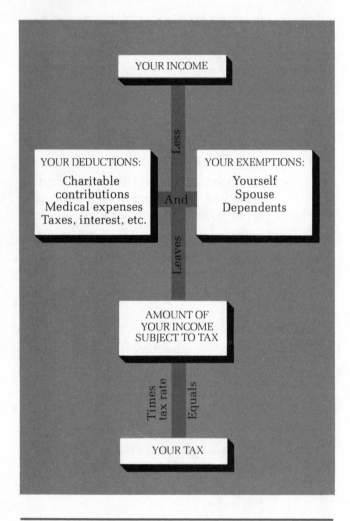

In calculating this tax you would be allowed to take specific types of deductions and exemptions. For instance, some deductions that may be made (within limits) from your income are donations to the Red Cross, to your alma mater, and to various other nonprofit organizations. You may also deduct some payments for doctors' bills, X rays, and medicine; taxes paid to state and local governments; interest paid on loans; and various other outlays. In addition, tax allowances or exemptions are permitted for support of yourself, your family, and your dependents. In this way the government acknowledges the fact that larger families require more funds than smaller ones to meet their living costs.

The amount of income tax you would have to pay at a given income level depends on several things. These include whether you are single or married and what the particular tax rates happen to be at the time. The rates are usually revised by Washington every few years. Nevertheless, certain features of a tax-rate schedule never change—as explained in Exhibit 8.

Some controversial aspects of the personal income tax should be noted.

Incentives The steepness of the marginal tax-rate schedule (explained in the exhibit) may have serious economic consequences. It must be high enough at all income levels to yield the desired amounts of revenues. However, rates that are too high at the upper-income levels may discourage investment and risk taking. Rates that are too high at the lower levels may reduce the incentive for taking on overtime work or second jobs. Is there a "best" or optimum schedule for the economy as a whole? There probably is, but it changes with different needs and conditions, reflecting political as well as economic circumstances of the times.

Loopholes Through legal methods of *tax avoidance*, many taxpayers are able to reduce their average rates. This is because our tax system contains dozens of legal "loopholes" which permit relative tax advantages for people in almost every income class. Although changes in the tax laws have, over the years, closed many of these loopholes, it is not likely that they will ever be entirely eliminated. (In contrast, illegal methods of escaping taxes, such as lying or cheating about income or expenses, come under the general heading of *tax evasion*.) On the whole, just about every taxpayer, rich and poor alike, benefits from tax loopholes of one form or another. However, the greatest share of benefits from tax loopholes goes to the taxpayer group with above-average incomes. This group is also the one that pays more than half the total individual tax bill. (See Box 1.)

Corporation Income Tax

The federal government's second largest source of revenue is the corporate income tax. (Many states also tax corporate incomes, but at lower rates.) The corporate income tax is simple to calculate because it is based on the difference between a company's total income and its total expenses—its net profit. The tax rate has varied over the years. During recent decades it has averaged close to 50 percent.

The corporate income tax raises many important issues. Among them:

1. Some experts argue that lower rates would leave corporations with more profits to use for expanding their operations, thereby creating more jobs. Other authorities, however, contend that the rates should be

Exhibit 8
Personal Income Tax Schedule
(hypothetical data)

The income taxes people pay are determined from government tax schedules such as the one shown here. Although the numbers in the table change frequently with revisions in the tax laws, certain characteristics of the schedule remain the same. For example:

Columns (1), (2), and (3) As the level of taxable income increases, the amount paid out in income taxes also increases. The average tax rate tells you what percentage of income is paid in taxes. This percentage increases as income rises.

Columns (4) and (5) Each increase in income results in a corresponding increase in taxes. These columns enable you to compare the *amounts* of increase in both.

Column (6) This tells you the *percent* of each increase in income that is paid out in taxes. The distinction between the *average tax rate* in column (3) and the *marginal tax rate* in column (6) is shown by the formulas beneath the table.

In comparing columns (3) and (6), note that the marginal tax rate is always higher than the average tax rate in going from one income level to the next. Observe also that, according to the marginal tax-rate schedule, you can never find yourself worse off by making an extra dollar. No matter how high your total taxable income may be, you would still be able to keep some percentage of every additional dollar you earned.

Although this is not an actual tax schedule, the basic ideas and relationships conveyed are reasonably representative.

(1) Total taxable annual income	(2) Total personal income tax	(3) Average tax rate* (percent) (2) ÷ (1)	(4) Change in column (1)	(5) Change in column (2)	(6) Marginal tax rate† (percent) (5) ÷ (4)
$ 5,000	$ 500	10			
			$ 5,000	$ 1,000	20
10,000	1,500	15			
			10,000	3,500	35
20,000	5,000	25			
			30,000	15,000	50
50,000	20,000	40			
			50,000	30,000	60
100,000	50,000	50			
			100,000	70,000	70
200,000	120,000	60			
			200,000	140,000	70
400,000	260,000	65			
			600,000	420,000	70
1,000,000	680,000	68			

* Average tax rate $= \dfrac{\text{total personal income tax}}{\text{total taxable income}}$.

† Marginal tax rate $= \dfrac{\text{change in total personal income tax}}{\text{change in total taxable income}}$.

higher, enabling government to reduce other taxes, especially personal income taxes.

2. There is much controversy over who ultimately bears the burden of the corporate income tax. Some economists believe that the tax is shifted "forward" to consumers in the form of higher prices. Other observers contend that most of the tax is shifted "backward" to resource owners in the form of lower wages, rents, and so on. Still other authorities believe that the tax is borne by the owners (stockholders) of the corporation because the tax is imposed on corporate net profit.

3. The tax is actually a form of *double taxation*. This is because the corporation pays a tax on its profits, and the stockholder pays a personal income tax on the dividends received from those profits. Therefore, it is often argued that the tax is not only inequitable, but

may impede the attainment of other economic goals as well.

There are no simple answers to these controversial issues. Each has valid aspects which you will often read or hear about in the news media.

The remaining two categories that make up the structure of the American tax system—taxes on wealth and taxes on activities—can be sketched briefly.

TAXES ON WEALTH

Property taxes are levied primarily on land and buildings. The taxes vary from low rates in some rural areas where services are minor to high rates in localities with good streets, schools, and public safety facilities.

Box 1
Tax Loopholes—Something for Everyone

Our federal tax system is riddled with loopholes containing something for everyone— rich and poor, large taxpayers and small ones. A complete list of loopholes would contain over 100 items. These tax preferences cost the federal government hundreds of billions annually in lost revenues.

Individuals	Corporations
Income not taxed	Exemptions, deductions, and credits
Pension plans	Investment tax credit
Company-paid benefits	Progressive tax rate on profits
Social security benefits	Interest on municipal bonds
Interest on life insurance savings	Special employment allowances
Interest on municipal bonds	Extra depreciation deductions
Military and veterans benefits	Foreign-trade exemptions and credits
Scholarships and fellowships	Research and development expenses
Sick pay	Excess depletion allowances
Deductions and credits	Capital gains
State, local, income, and sales taxes	Charitable contributions
Charitable contributions	Special bad-debt reserves
Mortgage interest on owner-occupied homes	Exploration and developmental costs
State and local property taxes	Construction-period interest, taxes
Medical expenses	Investment credit, employee stock plans
Interest on debt	Credit-union income exemption
Casualty losses	
Exemptions for aged and blind	

SOURCE: U.S. Department of the Treasury.

Death taxes are levied on estates by the federal government and on inheritances by some state governments. The rates depend on values and amounts. Like income taxes, death taxes exempt small estates and inheritances but tax the unexempt portions at progressive rates. Many wealthy people would try to avoid these taxes by distributing most of their property before death. Therefore, _gift taxes_ are imposed on the transfer of assets beyond certain values. However, various legal devices, such as trust funds and family foundations, have enabled many wealthier individuals to lighten the weight of these taxes.

TAXES ON ACTIVITIES

Sales taxes are imposed by many state and local governments. These taxes are flat percentage levies on the retail prices of items. In some states or cities such commodities as food, medicine, and services are exempt. In other places they are not. The federal government imposes no "general" sales tax on the final sale of goods. However, it does impose special sales taxes, called _excise taxes_, on the manufacture, sale, or consumption of liquor, gasoline, and other products. From time to time, in order to raise more money, political and economic efforts are exerted to introduce a value-added tax (VAT). This is a type of national sales tax paid by manufacturers and merchants on the value contributed to a product at each stage of its production and distribution. However, this form of tax, although common in Europe, has not yet gained sufficiently wide acceptance for adoption in the United States.

Social security taxes are payroll taxes levied by the federal government. The taxes finance our compulsory social insurance program covering old-age and unemployment benefits. The contributions come from both employees and employers and are based on the incomes of the former. These taxes are actually a "reverse" form of income tax. After a person has earned a certain amount each year, his or her income above that level is exempt from the tax. This assures that every income earner is covered.

Theories of Taxation

"The power to tax is one great power upon which the whole national fabric is based. It is not only the power to destroy but also the power to keep alive."

So stated the U.S. Supreme Court in a famous case in 1899. Today hardly anyone would disagree. For this reason, economists have developed several broad standards for judging the relative merits of a tax:

1. *Equity*   Tax burdens should be distributed justly among the people.

2. *Efficiency, Stability, Growth*   A tax should contribute toward improving resource allocation, economic stabilization, and the total output of goods and services.

3. *Enforceability*   A tax should be adequate for its purpose and acceptable to the public, or else it will be impossible to enforce.

These criteria are simple and persuasive. But implementation, especially of equity, has caused a good deal of controversy. Let us see why.

PRINCIPLES OF TAX EQUITY

A good tax system should be fair. If people believe it is unfair—that too many loopholes benefit some individuals and not others—taxpayers' morale and the effectiveness of the tax system will deteriorate. Therefore, two standards of tax equity have evolved over the years.

Horizontal Equity   "Equals should be treated equally." This means that people who are economically equal should bear equal tax burdens. That is, if people have the same income, wealth, or other taxpaying ability, they should pay the same amount of tax.

Vertical Equity   "Unequals should be treated unequally." This means that people who are economically unequal should nevertheless bear equal tax burdens. To accomplish this, people with different incomes, wealth, or other taxpaying abilities should pay different amounts of tax.

Horizontal and vertical equity are standards for judging the fairness of a tax. Efforts to apply the standards have resulted in two fundamental principles of taxation—the benefit principle and the ability-to-pay principle.

Benefit Principle

The *benefit principle* holds that people should be taxed according to the benefits they receive. For example, the tax you pay on gasoline reflects the benefit you receive from driving on public roads. The more you drive, the more gasoline you use and the more taxes you pay. These tax revenues are typically set aside for financing highway construction and maintenance. Similarly, local governments pay for at least part of the construction of streets and sewers by taxing those residents who benefit directly from the services of these goods.

What is wrong with the benefit principle as a general guide for taxation? There are two major difficulties:

1. Relatively few publicly provided goods and services exist for which all benefits can be readily determined. For many goods and services the benefits would be impossible to determine. The entire nation benefits from public education, health and sanitation facilities, police and fire protection, and national defense. How can we decide which groups should pay the taxes for these things and which should not?

2. Those who receive certain benefits may not be able to pay for them. For instance, it would be impossible to finance public welfare assistance or unemployment compensation by taxing the recipients.

Ability-to-Pay Principle

About 2,400 years ago, in his classic work, *The Republic,* the philosopher Plato remarked: "When there is an income tax, the just man will pay more and the unjust less on the same amount of income."

Plato was speaking of an ideal world—a utopia in which all individuals strive to do what will be best for society. Unfortunately, with human nature as it is, most people are not inclined to pay any more taxes than the law requires of them.

However, the *ability-to-pay principle* is actually a modern and realistic restatement of Plato's ancient dictum. It states that the fairest tax a government can impose is one that is based on the financial ability of the taxpayer, regardless of any benefit derived from the tax. This means that the more wealth an individual has or the higher his or her income, the greater the taxes should be. This is based on the assumption that each dollar of taxes paid by a rich person "hurts" less than each dollar paid by a poor one. The personal income tax in the United States is structured on this principle.

There are two major difficulties in the use of this principle as a general guide for taxation:

1. Ability to pay is a debatable concept—difficult to determine and impossible to measure. How can we really know that an additional thousand dollars a year in income means less to a rich person than to a poor person? A rich person may not want for any material things. Nevertheless, he or she may derive a greater

increase in satisfaction from earning an extra thousand dollars than a poor person gains from spending it. Therefore, although we ordinarily *assume* that certain taxes should be based on ability to pay, the entire concept involves deep psychological and philosophical issues that economics cannot explore.

2. Even if we could really be clear about what we mean by ability to pay, how could we distinguish between *degrees* of ability among different individuals? You may feel that a person who earns $50,000 a year is able to pay more in taxes than someone who earns $15,000. But *how much* more? As with the benefit principle, the hardest problem is to develop a way of measuring the right concepts.

SOME PRACTICAL COMPROMISES

As a result of these philosophical difficulties, it has become necessary to adopt convenient methods of implementing the benefit and ability principles. Unfortunately, the methods may not always be ideal. Nevertheless, three major classes of tax rates have evolved over the years: proportional, progressive, and regressive. They differ from each other according to the way in which the amount is related to the <u>tax base</u>. This is the item being taxed. Examples are the value of a taxpayer's property (in the case of a property tax), income (in the case of an income tax), or the value of goods sold (in the case of a sales tax). When the amount of the tax is divided by the tax base, the resulting figure, expressed as a percentage, is called the <u>tax rate</u>. Thus, a $10 tax on a tax base of $100 represents a tax rate of 10 percent. It follows that the tax base times the tax rate equals the tax yield to the government.

Proportional Tax

A <u>*proportional tax*</u> is one whose percentage rate remains *constant* as the tax base increases. Consequently, the amount of the tax paid is proportional to the tax base. The property tax is an example. If the tax rate is constant at 5 percent, a person who owns property valued at $10,000 pays $500 in taxes. Someone who owns property valued at $100,000 pays $5,000 in taxes.

Progressive Tax

A <u>*progressive tax*</u> is one whose percentage rate *increases* as the tax base increases. In the United States, the federal personal income tax is the best example. The tax is graduated so that theoretically a person with a higher income pays a greater percentage in tax

than a person with a lower income. We say "theoretically" because in reality, certain loopholes in the tax structure distort and sometimes even prevent the progressive principle from operating over the full range of income.

Regressive Tax

A <u>*regressive tax*</u> is one whose percentage rate *decreases* as the tax base increases. In this narrow technical sense there is no regressive tax in the United States. However, in practice the term "regressive" is applied to any tax that takes a larger share of income from the low-income taxpayer than from the high-income taxpayer. Most proportional taxes, such as sales taxes, are thus seen to have regressive effects. For instance, a 4 percent sales tax is the same rate for everyone, rich and poor alike. But people with smaller incomes spend a larger percentage of their incomes. Therefore, the sales taxes they pay are a greater proportion of their incomes.

To summarize:

> In the narrow *technical* sense, definitions of proportional, progressive, and regressive taxes are expressed in terms of their actual tax bases. These are the things that are taxed, such as income, property, or value of goods sold. But for *equity* purposes, the base chosen for reference is always income—regardless of the actual tax base. (See Exhibit 9.)

How do the foregoing principles and compromises apply to the American tax system? Generally speaking, some of our taxes tend to lean more toward the benefit principle and others toward ability to pay. Social security, license, and gasoline taxes are some examples of the former; income and death (estate and inheritance) taxes are illustrative of the latter.

We can also find examples of progressive, regressive, and proportional taxes. Income and death taxes are progressive in both the technical and equity sense because their percentage rates increase with the tax base. Property taxes, general sales taxes, and excise taxes are proportional in their technical structure, because their rates are a constant percentage of the tax base. However, they tend to have regressive effects from an equity standpoint when related to the *incomes* of the taxpayers.

TAX SHIFTING AND INCIDENCE: DIRECT OR INDIRECT TAXES?

Surprisingly enough, the person or business firm upon whom a tax is initially imposed does not always bear

Exhibit 9
Proportional, Progressive, and Regressive Tax-Rate Structures in Equity Terms
(hypothetical data)

The structure of a tax is usually evaluated in equity terms by comparing the tax rate to the taxpayer's income—regardless of the actual tax base to which the tax is applied.

Chart (a) Proportional Tax. *The tax takes the same percentage of income from high-income taxpayers as from low-income taxpayers. In this example the tax is 40 percent of a $10,000 income, 40 percent of a $20,000 income, and so on.*

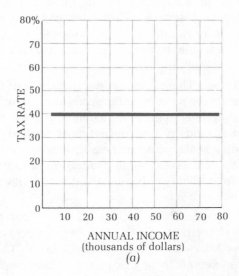

ANNUAL INCOME
(thousands of dollars)
(a)

Chart (b) Progressive Tax. *The tax takes a larger percentage of income from high-income taxpayers than from low-income taxpayers. In this example the tax is 10 percent of a $10,000 income, 20 percent of a $20,000 income, and so on.*

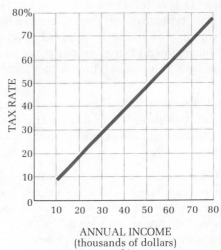

ANNUAL INCOME
(thousands of dollars)
(b)

Chart (c) Regressive Tax. *The tax takes a smaller percentage of income from high-income taxpayers than from low-income taxpayers. In this example the tax is 60 percent of a $10,000 income, 50 percent of a $20,000 income, and so on.*

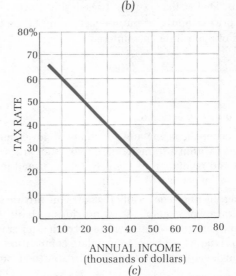

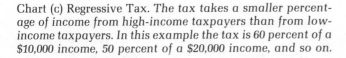

ANNUAL INCOME
(thousands of dollars)
(c)

its burden. For instance, a company may be able to *shift* all or part of a tax "forward" to its customers by charging them higher prices for its goods. Or it may be able to shift a tax "backward" to the owners of its factors of production by paying them less for their materials and services. When a tax has been shifted, its burden or *incidence* is on someone else. It thus proves convenient to classify taxes into two categories: direct and indirect.

Direct Taxes   These taxes are not shifted; their burden is borne by the persons or firms originally taxed. Typical examples are personal income taxes, social security taxes paid by employees, most property taxes (excluding rental and business property), and death taxes. Certain taxes, notably those on corporate income, are probably only partially direct. Can you suggest why?

Indirect Taxes   These include all taxes that can be shifted either partially or entirely to someone other than the individual or firm originally taxed. The most familiar example is the sales tax. Contrary to popular belief, this tax is imposed on sellers, not buyers. Sellers, however, typically shift the tax burden to buyers. Other examples of indirect taxes are excise taxes, taxes on business and rental property, social security taxes paid by employers, and most corporate income taxes.

In what direction will a tax be shifted, assuming that it is shifted at all? This is a thorny problem in economic theory, and the experts do not always agree. In general:

Most taxes are like an increased cost to the taxpayer. Therefore, each taxpayer will try to pass them on to someone else. As a result, once a tax is imposed, it tends—like lightning or water—to follow the path of least resistance through the markets in which the taxpayer deals. That is, the taxpayer tries to shift the tax by altering prices, inputs, or outputs according to the least degree of opposition encountered.

What You Have Learned

1. The economic scope and functions of government may be viewed within a framework of two major areas: (a) promotion and regulation of the private sector and (b) provision of social goods.

2. Government promotes and regulates the private sector in many ways. For example, it (a) provides a stable environment, (b) performs social welfare activities, (c) grants economic privileges, (d) seeks to maintain competition, (e) promotes high employment, and (f) redistributes income.

3. Government provides social goods consisting of (a) public goods such as national defense, law and order, and fire protection; and (b) nonpublic goods such as libraries, museums, highways, and many other commodities. A unique feature of public goods is that they are not subject to the exclusion principle. Other social goods are subject to this principle, even though it is not always invoked. All public goods as well as many other social goods have two additional characteristics: zero incremental or marginal costs, and spillover effects.

4. The market demand curve for a private good is determined graphically by summing horizontally the quantity demanded at each price. In contrast, the market demand curve for a public good is determined graphically by summing vertically the demand price at each quantity. In reality, most public goods are not allocated by free markets because of the exclusion principle and the free-rider problem. As a result, democratic societies generally allocate public goods by nonmarket methods, namely by collective action through majority vote.

5. The last several decades have witnessed a remarkable growth of expenditures at all levels of government. This has been due primarily to (a) increased demand for collective goods and services, (b) war and national defense, and (c) inflation and lagging productivity.

6. In the federal budget, income taxes, both individual and corporate, are the chief source of revenue. The main expenditure items are income security payments and national defense. In state and local budgets, the chief sources of revenue are property taxes and sales taxes. The main expenditure items are education (especially schools) and public welfare and health.

7. Two closely related approaches to scientific budgeting are program-planning-budgeting systems (PPBS) and benefit-cost analysis. The former method emphasizes revenue and expenditure planning based on identifiable objectives. The latter focuses on the relative worth of a program, project, or other economic activity by comparing its marginal (incremental) benefits and marginal costs. Net benefit is maximized at the output where the difference between total benefit and total cost is greatest. This is also the output where marginal benefit and marginal cost are equal. Benefit-cost analysis thus allocates expenditures by marginal as opposed to "needs" considerations.

8. The American tax structure consists of taxes on income, taxes on wealth, and taxes on activities. Taxes on income, both personal and corporate, are graduated or progressive.

9. A chief requirement of a good tax system is that it be fair. Accepted standards of fairness are horizontal equity and vertical equity. Two principles of taxation that seek to apply these standards are the benefit principle and the ability-to-pay principle. However, these principles are often difficult to apply. Therefore, they are usually implemented in practice by the use of proportional, progressive, and regressive taxes.

10. Those upon whom a tax is levied may sometimes be able to shift it forward or backward through changes in prices, inputs, or outputs. Thus, the burden or incidence of the tax falls on someone else. Such taxes are therefore indirect, as contrasted with direct taxes, which cannot be shifted.

For Discussion

1. *Terms and concepts to review:*

exclusion principle	death tax
externalities	sales tax
public goods	excise tax
public choice	horizontal equity
free-rider problem	vertical equity
program-planning-budgeting system (PPBS)	benefit principle
	ability-to-pay principle
	proportional tax
benefit-cost analysis	progressive tax
marginal cost	regressive tax
marginal benefit	direct tax
double taxation	indirect tax
property tax	

2. Since public goods are not subject to the exclusion principle, how do you explain the fact that some public goods are, nevertheless, provided by the private sector? Give some examples.

3. What are PPBS's major problems in our system of government? How does benefit-cost analysis relate to PPBS?

4. Can you explain the formal definition of benefit-cost analysis given in the Dictionary at the back of the book? In particular, what does the word "discounted" in the definition mean?

5. (a) Suppose that the *additional* or *incremental* social cost of a unit of output is $50,000 and the *additional* or *incremental* social benefit is $80,000. Assuming that you want *net* social benefit—the difference between social benefit and social cost—to be as large as possible, would you recommend that the unit be produced? Explain. (b) What if the figures for additional social cost and social benefit were reversed? (SUGGESTION Look up the meanings of *social benefit* and *social cost* in the Dictionary at the back of the book.)

6. Net social benefit represents the difference between social benefit and social cost. Can you use the concept of net social benefit to determine the optimum size of a government program in terms of *incremental* social benefit and *incremental* social cost?

7. How can the costs of benefits provided by government be reduced?

8. Some economists and legislators contend that the present federal income tax reaches too far down into low-income brackets. Assuming that you disagree with this contention, what arguments can you offer to defend your position?

9. If you were considering taking on an extra part-time job, would you base the decision on your average tax rate or on your marginal tax rate? Why?

10. The ability-to-pay principle of taxation may also be called the "equal-sacrifice principle." Can you explain why?

11. How can a market-oriented economy such as ours justify the large expenditures made by government on free public education?

12. Is the desire to maximize net social benefit a goal useful only to capitalistic economies, or does it apply to socialistic economies, too?

13. If you were advising a legislator on whether the government should spend an additional $2 billion on space exploration as opposed to public transportation, what approach would you use? What difficulties would you expect to encounter?

14. When the private costs of a decision are equal to its social costs, *all* the costs are borne by the decision maker. Do you agree? Explain.

15. What is wrong with using figures showing expenditures by government as a measure of the importance of government in our society?

Issue
Tax Consumption, Not Income

The Irish wit and playwright George Bernard Shaw had his own explanation of what was wrong with the world. According to him, society's seven deadly sins were food, clothing, firing, rent, respectability, children, and taxes. Although many people might disagree over the first six, few would argue about the seventh.

Taxation is a major instrument of social and economic policy. Yet the U.S. tax code, as taxpayers know, is incredibly complicated. It consists of dozens of volumes whose maze of rules and requirements are riddled with exemptions, deductions, and special provisions. Despite occasional legislative efforts toward simplification, the wheels of tax reform grind agonizingly slowly. This is because the issues involved are as much political as economic. The various loopholes that people and businesses enjoy were written into the tax code piecemeal by Congress over many years. It is not likely, therefore, that these special provisions will ever be entirely eliminated.

Consumption Tax
Nevertheless, a significant step toward improving the present tax system can be made. It consists of replacing personal and corporate income taxes with a tax on consumption. A consumption tax may be thought of as simply an income tax that allows deductions from income for the amounts that are saved or invested. Unlike an income tax, however, a consumption tax is extremely simple to understand. Almost any high-school graduate could fill out a consumption-tax form and know exactly what is owed and why.

The chief features of a consumption tax can be judged in terms of the economy's four major goals—efficiency, equity, stability, and growth.

Efficiency   The arguments in favor of a consumption tax are largely the arguments against an income tax. A consumption tax, for example, would not penalize savings by taxing interest income. Nor would it punish success (i.e., higher incomes or profits from improved efficiency). It would also be an easy tax to administer because it treats all transactions on a cash-flow basis. Thus, when any income-producing assets, such as stocks, bonds, or buildings, are purchased, their prices would be deducted from income. When the assets are later sold, the tax would be paid on the total amount realized—not just the profit. Complexities involving capital gains, depreciation, mergers, and related matters, which pose some of the thorniest problems of income taxation, would thus cease to be relevant under consumption taxation.

Equity   A consumption tax is one of the fairest taxes conceivable—for several reasons:

○ It would exempt interest income on savings as well as income from capital that is later reinvested. In contrast, an income tax allows unrealized capital gains (i.e., profits from the sale of assets) to accrue untaxed while wages and savings-account interest are taxed immediately.

○ A consumption tax would be based on how much a person takes out of the economy (in contrast to an income tax, which is based on how much is put in). Therefore, with a consumption tax, lower-income families would pay a lower tax because they spend a smaller amount on consumption.

Richard Davis/DPI.

○ A consumption tax could easily be made progressive by exempting such necessities as food, clothing, shelter, and medicine; by graduating the rates; and by other methods. The tax could thus be designed to fit specific objectives.

Stability The consumption tax would provide a good source of revenue because it encompasses a broad base—total expenditures on consumption. It would also help stabilize the economy by raising larger revenues in boom periods when consumption is high and lower revenues during recessions when consumption declines.

Growth A consumption tax would encourage personal saving and business expenditures on plant and equipment. It would thereby stimulate economic activity and promote a rising volume of production—the key to economic growth.

Conclusion: Political Obstacles
Most legislators and economists who have studied the problem agree that a consumption tax is far superior to an income tax. A consumption tax would not discriminate between saving and spending, nor would it punish investment and growth. On the other hand, an income tax discriminates against capital by favoring consumption while penalizing saving and investment—the income from which is taxed repeatedly.

Despite these considerations, a consumption tax is not likely to be passed by Congress—for political rather than economic reasons. "A consumption tax would be perceived by the public as extremely inequitable—a disguised tax on wages," said the chairman of a congressional tax committee. "What President would dare to go on record advocating a tax only on wages?"

QUESTIONS
1. Critics of a consumption tax claim it would impose a heavier burden on the poor than on the rich. How can this be? After all, the rich have higher incomes; therefore, they spend more for consumption and consequently would pay higher taxes.

2. How can *vertical* equity be improved under a consumption tax? Do efforts at improving vertical equity affect horizontal equity? Explain.

Part 2

National Income, Employment, and Fiscal Policy

Chapter 5

National Income and Wealth: Measuring the Nation's Economic Health

Chapter Preview

What measures do we use to evaluate the nation's economic health? What do these measures tell us? What do they fail to tell us?

How are the various measures of the nation's economic health related? What have been their historical trends?

Americans like to take their own pulse, tirelessly searching for signs of normality, abnormality, and other statistical measurements of health—or illness.

Economic diagnoses and prognoses are as much a part of the daily news as football and baseball scores, and arouse similarly partisan feelings. That is unfortunate. The economic system is highly complicated, and more a subject for cool, rational analysis than hot, emotional debate.

The tools for analyzing the economy's performance, strengths, and weaknesses are the tables, charts, and data published by the federal government and some other public and private agencies. Since the early 1930s the U.S. Department of Commerce has been the nation's bookkeeper. Its methods, terms, and concepts are the foundation on which economists have built what they call "national-income accounting."

Gross National Product—The Basic Measure of a Nation's Output

The most comprehensive measure of a nation's economic activity, and the one quoted most frequently in newspapers and magazines, is *gross national product* (GNP). It is always stated in money terms, representing the total value of a nation's annual final output.

More precisely:

> GNP is the total market value of all final goods and services produced by an economy during a year.

The items that comprise GNP range from apples and automobiles to zinc and zippers. However, because you cannot add these different things, you must first express these diverse items in terms of their monetary values. Then, when you add X dollars' worth of automobiles to Y dollars' worth of oranges to Z dollars' worth of doctors' services, and so on, you arrive at a total dollar figure. If you do this for all final goods and services produced in the economy during any given year, the result is GNP. And if you repeat this process for several years, the different GNPs can be compared. In that way you can tell whether there has been a long-run growth or decline.

However, there are several pitfalls to avoid.

Watch Out for Price Changes

If the prices of goods and services change from one year to the next, the GNP may also change—even if there has been no change in physical output. For instance, if apples cost 10 cents each this year, five apples will have a market value of 50 cents. But next year if the price rises to 15 cents each, five apples will have a market value of 75 cents.

How can we tell whether the variations in GNP are due to differences in prices or to differences in _real output_—that is, output unaffected by price changes? The answer is shown in Exhibit 1. Observe that GNP is expressed in two ways. One is in _current dollars_, reflecting actual prices as they existed each year. The other is in _constant dollars_, reflecting the actual prices of a previous year, or the average of actual prices in some previous period.

The use of constant dollars is thus a way of compensating for the distorting effects of inflation—the long-run upward trend of prices—by a reversing process of _deflation_. You can get an idea of how this is done by studying Exhibit 2.

Avoid Double Counting of Intermediate Goods

Note that the definition of GNP covers only _final_ goods and services purchased for last use, as distinguished from _intermediate_ goods and services which enter into production of final commodities. For example, if you purchase a new automobile this year, it is a final good. However, the materials of which the automobile is made, such as steel, engine, tires, and paint, are intermediate goods. Because the values of final goods include the values of all intermediate goods, only final goods are included in calculating GNP. If you allow intermediate goods to enter the picture, you will commit the cardinal sin of _double counting_—or even triple and quadruple counting.

Exhibit 3 shows this in terms of producing a loaf of bread. As you can see in column (2), the "total sales values" of $1.44 include all the intermediate stages. This is an incorrect statement of the actual value of the product. However, the sales value of the final product, or the total _value added_ for all the stages of

Exhibit 1
Gross National Product
(current and constant dollars)

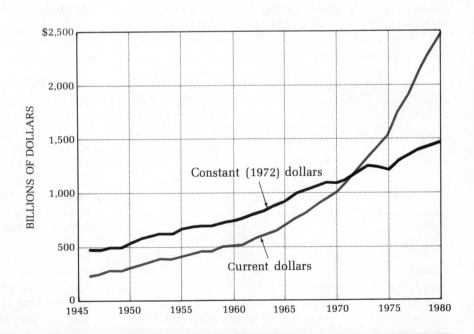

Exhibit 2
Deflating with a Price Index

HOW A VALUE SERIES IN *CURRENT DOLLARS* IS CONVERTED INTO A VALUE SERIES IN *CONSTANT DOLLARS* OF ANOTHER YEAR

Index numbers are percentages of some previous base period. They are widely used by government and private sources in reporting business and economic data. Column (4) expresses the prices of column (3) in the form of index numbers. Ordinarily, the base period chosen is assumed to be fairly "normal." In this illustration, because the data are hypothetical, Year 2 has been arbitrarily selected as the base.

When the value series in *current dollars* [column (5)] is divided by these index numbers, the result is a new value series in *constant dollars* of the base year. This is shown in column (6). The two value series are plotted for comparison in the accompanying chart.

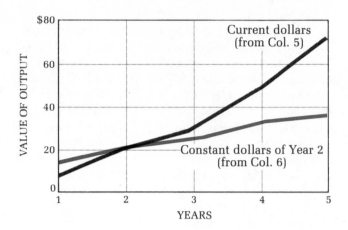

(1)	(2)	(3)	(4)	(5)	(6)
Year	Units of output	Price per unit of output	Price index; data in col. (3) as percent of price in Year 2	Value of output in *current dollars* of each year (2) × (3)	Value of output in *constant dollars* of Year 2 (5) ÷ (4)
1	3	$2	2/4 = 0.50 or 50%	$ 6	6/0.50 = $12
2 = base period	5	4	4/4 = 1.00 or 100%	20	20/1.00 = 20
3	6	5	5/4 = 1.25 or 125%	30	30/1.25 = 24
4	8	6	6/4 = 1.50 or 150%	48	48/1.50 = 32
5	9	8	8/4 = 2.00 or 200%	72	72/2.00 = 36

production, given in column (3), shows the true value of the total output. It also shows the total income—the sum of wages, rent, interest, and profit—derived from the production process.

We can summarize with an important principle:

GNP may be calculated by totaling either the market values of all final goods and services or the values added at all stages of production. The latter are equal to the sum of all incomes—wages, rent, interest, and profit—generated from production.

Include Productive Activities; Exclude Nonproductive Ones

The purpose of deriving GNP is to develop a measure of the economy's total output, based on the market values of final goods and services, produced. However, even if all these market values are estimated, some *productive* activities still do not show up in the market but should nevertheless be included in GNP. There are also some *nonproductive* activities which

do appear in the market but should be excluded from GNP.

Here are some examples of productive nonmarket activities:

Rent of Owner-Occupied Homes   The rent that people pay to landlords enters into GNP. However, more than half the dwellings in the United States are owner-occupied. Therefore, the rental value of this housing—the rent which people "save" by living in their own homes—may be thought of as the value of shelter produced. This value is assumed to be the same amount that individual homeowners would receive if they became landlords and rented out their homes to others. Hence, this amount is included in GNP.

Farm Consumption of Home-Grown Food   The value of food that people buy is included in GNP. But the value of food that farmers grow and consume themselves also is a part of the nation's productive output and is therefore included in GNP.

Exhibit 3
Sales Values and Value Added at Each Stage of Producing a Loaf of Bread

(1)	(2)	(3)
		Value added (income payments: wages, rent, interest, profit) (cents per loaf)
Stages of production	Sales values (cents per loaf)	
Stage 1: Fertilizer, seed, etc.	$ .02	$.02
Stage 2: Wheat growing	.14	.12
Stage 3: Flour milling	.24	.10
Stage 4: Bread baking, final	.44	.20
Stage 5: Bread retailer, value	.60	.16
Total sales values	$1.44	—
Total value added (= total income)		$.60

Stage 1   A farmer purchases 2 cents worth of seed and fertilizer which he applies to his land.

Stage 2   The farmer grows wheat, harvests it, and sells it to a miller for 14 cents. The farmer has thereby added 12 cents worth of value. His factors of production then receive this 12 cents in the form of income: wages, rent, interest, and profit.

Stage 3   The miller, after purchasing the wheat for 14 cents, adds 10 cents worth of value by milling the wheat into flour. The miller's factors of production receive this 10 cents as income: wages, rent, interest, and profit.

Stage 4   The baking company buys the flour from the miller for 24 cents, then adds 20 cents worth of value to it by baking it into bread. This 20 cents becomes factor incomes in the form of wages, rent, interest, and profit.

Stage 5   The retailer buys the bread from the baker for 44 cents and sells it to you, the final user, for 60 cents. The retailer has thus added 16 cents in value, which shows up as factor incomes in the form of wages, rent, interest, and profit.

Note that the value of the final product, 60 cents, equals the sum of the values added.

Some productive nonmarket activities never enter into GNP because their values are either too difficult to estimate or involve complex definitional issues. These include such things as the labor time of a do-it-yourselfer who performs his or her own repairs and maintenance around the house. Similar activities include the productive services of homemakers in their capacities as cooks, housekeepers, tutors, dieticians, chauffeurs, and so on, for which no salaries are received. No wonder a famous British economist once remarked that if you marry your housekeeper, you reduce the nation's output and income. Can you see why?

Here are some examples of nonproductive market activities:

Transfer Payments   As you recall, these are shifts in funds within or between sectors of the economy with no corresponding contribution to current production. Hence, they are excluded from GNP. Some examples of transfer payments are social security benefits, unemployment insurance, and welfare payments.

Securities Transactions   When you buy or sell stocks or bonds, you exchange one form of asset for another—either money for securities or securities for money. These financial transfers add nothing to current production and therefore are excluded from GNP. (However, broker commissions on security transactions are included in GNP, since brokers perform a productive service by bringing buyers and sellers together.)

Used-Goods Sales   Billions of dollars are paid each year for used automobiles, houses, machines, factory buildings, and so on. But these goods are omitted from the calculation of current GNP because they were already counted as part of GNPs in the years in which they were sold new. (As with brokers, however, the value added by dealers in used-merchandise transactions is included in current GNP.)

IS GNP A MEASURE OF SOCIETY'S WELL-BEING?

GNP is a comprehensive indicator of the economy's output. However, it is an imperfect measure of society's "well-being" because it fails to tell anything about:

1. The growth of leisure time, that is, the substantial reduction in the workweek that has taken place during the past several decades.

2. The composition of the nation's total output in terms of the quality and variety of goods and services.

3. The growth and distribution of total output among the members of society.

On the basis of the first two factors, the long-run trend of our economy is better than the GNP figures indicate. As for the third, you will often see GNP quoted on a per capita basis over the years. This reflects the share that each person would have in the nation's total output if it were distributed equally to every man, woman, and child. What does it mean in terms of the economy's growth if the trend of GNP per capita increases over the years? Decreases? Remains the same?

WHAT ABOUT GROSS NATIONAL "DISPRODUCT"?

The gross national product, which is our standard index of economic output, measures everything from the cost of hospital care to the wages of belly dancers. But it is only an index of dollar values—not social benefits.

In other words, GNP makes no distinction between the useful and the frivolous—regardless of the price that has been paid. For example, GNP includes cloth coats for people as well as mink coats for dogs, life-saving antibiotics as well as useless patent medicines. Further, there is no measure of the amount of "disproduct," or *social cost*, that results from producing the GNP. Thus, to society:

1. The cost of air and water pollution is the disproduct of the nation's factories.

2. The cost of treating lung cancer victims is the disproduct of cigarette production.

3. The cost of geriatric medicine is the disproduct of good medical care in the earlier years, which results in increased longevity.

4. The cost of commuter transportation is the disproduct of suburbia.

5. The cost of aspirin for headaches resulting from TV commercials is the disproduct of advertising.

Can you suggest some more examples?

If this process were carried through our whole product list, the sum would be *gross national disproduct*. And if the total were then set against the aggregate of production as measured by GNP, it would indicate our degree of progress toward (or departure from) social welfare. In fact, if we could discover a true "net" between disproduct and product, we would have our first great "social" indicator of what the country has accomplished.

The results would be disillusioning. We would find that while satisfying human wants from today's productivity, we were simultaneously generating present and future wants to repair the damage created by current production.

CONCLUSION: GNP AND SOCIAL WELFARE

Because GNP measures the market value of final goods and services, it can only reflect the amount of money that society exchanges for commodities. As a result, many important activities that affect our level of living are excluded from the calculation of GNP. For example, some activities that are excluded—and corresponding ones that are included—are:

1. The nonpaid value of homemakers' services—but not the salaries paid to housekeepers.

2. The benefits received from the public sector—but not the costs of providing them.

3. The environmental pollution that results from production—but not the money spent to clean it up.

4. The social value of education—but not the expenditures incurred to acquire it.

5. The rising level of crime—but not the funds allocated to fight it.

Some economists are trying to devise a better measure of the economy's true output by incorporating the negative as well as positive contributions of production. If this can be done, GNP will come closer to measuring *social welfare* rather than just the market value of final commodities.

However, many informed observers disagree with the idea that GNP should serve as an indicator of society's well-being. They point out that "social welfare" is a multidimensional concept with too many deep psychological and economic implications to permit precise definition, let alone measurement. As a result, they conclude:

The conversion of GNP from a measure of output to a one-dimensional summary measure of society's satisfaction may be dangerous. It can mislead the nation into believing that GNP is at last measuring social welfare when in fact it is not. This misunderstanding might impede progress toward urgently needed social legislation.

Something to Think About

1. Would it be better to produce wool suits and vaccines instead of mink coats and patent medicines, so that the nation moves closer to "worthwhile" national goals?

2. Does the GNP of an advanced, interdependent economy necessarily contain a considerable amount of disproduct in comparison to a relatively simple type of economic system?

3. Are the costs of the disproducts of our economy borne in the present or in the future?

Two Ways of Looking at GNP

Because GNP is the market value of the nation's output of final goods and services, it can be expressed conceptually by the simple diagram in Exhibit 4. Equivalently, it can be expressed by the following

fundamental identity, which says that the *total amount spent equals the total amount received:*

$$\left.\begin{array}{l}\text{total flow of}\\\text{expenditures}\\\text{on final output}\end{array}\right\} \text{GNP} = \text{GNI} \left\{\begin{array}{l}\text{total flow of}\\\text{income from}\\\text{final output}\end{array}\right.$$

The left side of the identity or upper pipeline of Exhibit 4 views GNP as a sum of expenditures or flow of product. The right side or lower pipeline views it as a sum of incomes or values added at each stage of production. This lower pipeline thus represents gross national income (GNI). It is the sum of wages, rent, interest, and profit earned in the production of GNP, and is always equal to GNP. This diagram illustrates a *simple* circular-flow system. It provides a "first look" at the relation between an economy's output and income, whereas a more elaborate model is necessary for understanding the underlying forces at work. Such a model is presented in Exhibit 5.

Exhibit 4
Gross National Product = Gross National Income

A TWO-SECTOR MODEL
(without a government or foreign sector)

A simplified circular-flow model can be used to illustrate the fundamental principle that gross national product and gross national income are actually two sides of the same coin. The nation's flow of output in the upper pipeline

equals the nation's flow of income in the lower pipeline. Profit is the residual or "balancing item" that brings this equality about. Can you explain why? How is the model affected if profits are positive? Zero? Negative (i.e., losses)?

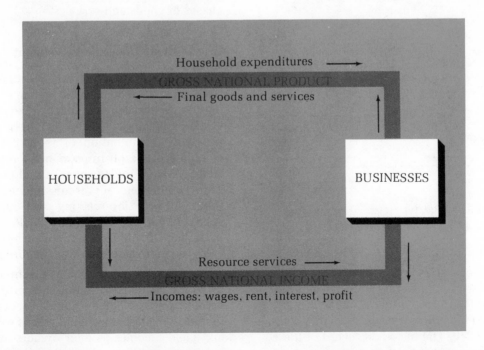

Exhibit 5
Gross National Product = Gross National Income

A FOUR-SECTOR MODEL

The data for measuring the nation's total output can be estimated from two points of view:

○ The product side—showing the value of goods and services produced.

○ The income side—showing the costs incurred and payments received in producing those goods and services.

The product side is divided into four sectors representing the major markets for the output of the economy: households, government, business, and foreign. The sum of their expenditures on final products comprises GNP. The income side summarizes the payments or costs incurred by business firms to produce final products. These costs are wages, rent, interest, profit, indirect business taxes, and capital consumption allowances or depreciation. Their sum comprises GNI.

Can you explain why it must be true that for any given period, GNP = GNI? What is the meaning of the expression "national income at factor cost"? Why is profit listed as a "cost"?

EXPENDITURE VIEWPOINT: FLOW OF PRODUCT		INCOME VIEWPOINT: FLOW OF COSTS	
HOUSEHOLD SECTOR		NATIONAL INCOME (AT FACTOR COST)	
Personal consumption expenditures	$×	Wages	$×
+		Rent	×
BUSINESS SECTOR		Interest	×
Gross private domestic investment	×	Profit	×
+		+	
GOVERNMENT SECTOR		NONINCOME (EXPENSE) ITEMS	
Government purchases of goods and services	×	Indirect business taxes	×
+		Capital consumption allowance (depreciation)	×
FOREIGN SECTOR			
Net exports of goods and services	×		
GNP	$× =	GNI	$×

GNP FROM THE EXPENDITURE VIEWPOINT: A FLOW-OF-PRODUCT APPROACH

On the left side of the diagram in Exhibit 5, the economy is divided into four major sectors: households, government, business, and foreign. These are the major markets for the output of the economy. In any one year, the total expenditures of these sectors comprise the nation's GNP. The historical record of these expenditures is presented in the first four columns of the front endpapers (the inside front cover) of this book. GNP is presented in the fifth column. What major trends can you discern from the table over the past 10 years? In particular:

1. What have been the trends of personal consumption expenditures, government purchases of goods and services, and gross private domestic investment?

2. What has been the trend of net exports?

You can answer these questions by referring directly to the front endpapers. However, you will also find it useful to prepare a chart showing the graphs of the four classes of expenditures over the past decade. Meanwhile, what can be said about the meaning of these four categories?

Personal Consumption Expenditures

Frequently referred to as "consumption expenditures" or simply "consumption," this category includes household expenditures on consumer goods. Some examples are food, clothing, appliances, automobiles, services, and recreation.

Government Purchases of Goods and Services

The items in this category are purchased by all levels of government. They include guided missiles, school buildings, fire engines, pencils, and the services of clerks, administrators, and all other government employees. However, recall that a significant part of government expenditures—transfer payments—is omitted because it does not represent current output or purchases of goods and services.

Gross Private Domestic Investment

This category includes total investment spending by business firms. The term "investment" has two meanings: (1) In everyday language, a person makes an investment when buying stocks, bonds, or other properties with the intention of receiving an income or making a profit. (2) In economics, _investment_ means additions to or replacement of real productive assets. Thus, investment represents spending by business firms on new job-creating and income-producing goods which thereby add to GNP. This concept of investment is the one that concerns us in this book.

Investment goods fall into two broad classes:

1. New capital goods, such as machines, factories, offices, and residences, including apartment houses and owner-occupied homes. (Owner-occupied homes are included because they could just as well be rented out and yield incomes to their owners, as do apartment houses.) Recall that when a firm buys a used machine

or existing factory, it merely exchanges money assets for physical assets. The purchase itself creates no additional GNP. But when a firm buys *new* machines or *new* buildings it creates jobs and incomes for steelworkers, carpenters, bricklayers, and other workers, thereby contributing to the nation's GNP.

2. Increases in *inventories* (including raw materials, supplies, and finished goods on hand) are as much a part of business firms' physical capital as are plant and equipment. Therefore, the market values of any additions to inventories are part of the current flow of product that makes up GNP. On the other hand, any declines in inventories are reductions from the flow of product that makes up GNP.

In the process of producing goods during any given year some existing plant and equipment is used up, or *depreciated*. Therefore, a part of the year's gross private domestic investment goes to replace it. Any amount left over is called *net private domestic investment* because it represents a net addition to the total stock of capital. For example, if

gross private domestic investment	= $50 billion
and replacement for depreciation	= 30 billion
then net private domestic investment	= $20 billion

An economy will tend to grow, remain static, or decline according to whether:

1. Gross investment exceeds depreciation, in which case net investment is positive. The economy is thus adding to its capital stock and expanding its productive base.

2. Gross investment equals depreciation, in which case net investment is zero. The economy is merely replacing its capital stock and is neither expanding nor contracting its productive base.

3. Gross investment is less than depreciation, in which case net investment is negative. The economy is diminishing, or *disinvesting*, its capital stock and is thereby contracting its productive base.

To summarize:

Investment is spending by business firms on job-creating and income-producing goods. It consists of replacements or additions to the nation's stock of capital, including its plant, equipment, and inventories, that is, its nonhuman productive assets.

Net Exports

Some domestic expenditures are made to purchase foreign goods. These are our imports. Some foreign expenditures are made to purchase domestic goods. These are our exports. To measure GNP in terms of total expenditures we have to add the value of ex-

ported goods and services to our total expenditures. This is because the value of our exports represents the amount that foreigners spent on purchasing some of our total output. Then we subtract the value of *imported goods and services* from our total expenditures, because we are interested only in measuring the value of domestic output. In performing these adjustments it is simpler to combine the separate figures for exports and imports into a single figure called *net exports,* according to the formula

$$\text{net exports} = \text{total exports} - \text{total imports}$$

Thus, if a nation's total exports in any given year amount to $20 billion, and its total imports are $15 billion, its net exports of $5 billion are part of that year's GNP. (Look back at Exhibit 5.) Of course, its imports may exceed its exports in any particular year, in which case its net exports will be negative and will reduce its GNP. If you have any doubts about this, look again at Exhibit 5 and note what the effect would be on GNP if net exports were negative.

GNP FROM THE INCOME VIEWPOINT: A FLOW-OF-COSTS APPROACH

Now turn your attention to the right side of the diagram in Exhibit 5. This shows a second method of calculating GNP. It is expressed in terms of the flow of costs or payments that businesses incur as a result of production. The sum of these payments comprises *gross national income* (GNI). However, only the first four items—wages, rent, interest, and profit—represent incomes paid to the owners of the factors of production for their contribution to the nation's output. The remaining two types of payments—indirect business taxes and capital consumption allowance (depreciation)—do not. Let us see why.

Wages

The broad category of *wages* embraces all forms of remuneration for work. It thus includes not only wages but also executive salaries and bonuses, commissions, payments in kind, incentive payments, tips, and fringe benefits.

Rent

Income earned by persons for the use of their real property, such as a house, store, or farm, is *rent*. This category also includes the estimated rental value of owner-occupied nonfarm dwellings, and royalties received by persons from patents, copyrights, and rights to natural resources.

Interest

Interest is expressed in net rather than gross terms. It represents the excess of interest paid by the domestic business sector over its interest receipts from all other sectors, plus net interest received from abroad. Interest payments within a sector, such as interest paid by one individual to another, or by one business firm to another, or by one government agency to another, have no net effect on the sector and are excluded from this category. Interest payments by government and by consumers, even when they flow between sectors as in the case of interest paid on government debt or on consumer loans, are considered unproductive and are also excluded here. Instead, they are counted as transfer payments.

Profit

Profit, in our model, combines proprietors' income and corporate profits before taxes. (These items are treated separately, however, by Commerce Department statisticians.) The former represents the earnings of unincorporated businesses—proprietorships, partnerships, and producers' cooperatives. The latter measures the profits of corporations before payments of corporate income taxes or disbursements of dividends to stockholders.

To generalize:

> *National income (at factor cost)* is part of gross national income. It represents the sum of wages, rent, interest, and profit. These are the payments that business firms must make to the owners of the factors of production in return for the services provided by those factors.

The two remaining components of gross national income are indirect business taxes and capital consumption allowances (depreciation). Because these two items are not payments to the owners of productive resources, their inclusion in GNI requires some explanation.

Indirect Business Taxes

Indirect business taxes consist primarily of sales, excise, and real property taxes incurred by businesses. (Direct taxes on factor payments, such as employer contributions for social security or corporate income taxes, are not counted here. This is because they were already included in wages, profits, and other specific items comprising national income at factor cost.) For accounting purposes, an indirect business tax is actually "paid"—that is, turned over to the government—by a business firm. Therefore, the tax is regarded as a business expense, although the real burden of the tax may be borne by the firm's customers in the form of a higher price. As a result, the tax is included in GNI as a cost item.

To put it somewhat differently, indirect business taxes tend to be passed on or shifted "forward" by business firms to buyers. Sales taxes are typical. If you live in a state or city that has a 5 percent general sales tax and you buy a product whose price is $1, your total *expenditure* is actually $1.05. Of this, $1 goes to pay incomes—the wages, rent, interest, and profit—earned for making the product, and 5 cents goes to the local government, which has not contributed directly to production. It follows, therefore, that indirect business taxes cause the expenditure side of GNP to be greater than the income side. In view of this, indirect business taxes must be added to total incomes (or subtracted from GNP) if the two sides are to be brought closer together.

Capital Consumption Allowance (Depreciation)

In the process of producing GNP, some decline in the value of existing physical capital occurs due to wear and tear, obsolescence, and accidental loss. To reflect this decline, firms deduct as part of their costs a *capital consumption allowance*—or simply "depreciation." The allowance consists primarily of depreciation on business plant and equipment and on owner-occupied dwellings. For purposes of national-income accounting, depreciation may be thought of as the portion of the current year's GNP that goes to replace the physical capital "consumed" or used up in the process of production.

Depreciation is thus the difference between gross and net private domestic investment, as already explained. If there were no such thing as depreciation, and if the government returned all indirect business taxes to households, the nation's income from production would be identical to its output. However, because depreciation does exist, it causes the income side of GNP to be less than the expenditure side. Therefore, depreciation must be added to incomes (or subtracted from GNP) to bring the two sides closer together.

To conclude:

> Business firms view indirect business taxes and depreciation as part of their *costs,* and hence charge higher prices for their goods in order to cover these costs. Therefore, these nonincome expense items must be added to the other income payments or expense items (wages, rent, interest, and profit) in order for the total expenditures on GNP to equal the total payments or expenses incurred in producing it.

Four Other Concepts—All Related

What relationship exists between the value of the nation's output and the money that households actually have available for spending? We may proceed by examining the items listed in the nation's income statement of Exhibit 6.

From Gross National Product to Net National Product

GNP is the total market value of the nation's annual output of final goods and services. But, as you know, this figure does not equal the actual dollar incomes available to households. To arrive at a closer measure of the dollars received by society, we must subtract the proportion that was spent to replace used up capital goods. This is the *capital consumption allowance,* or depreciation, figure. The number that results is net national product or simply NNP.

Exhibit 6
The Nation's Income Statement
Gross National Product and Related Accounts
(billions of dollars)

Can you fill in the figures for the most recent year? See the endpapers in the front of the book.

	19__
Gross national product (GNP)	$____
Minus:	
Capital consumption allowance (depreciation)	____
Equals: **Net national product (NNP)**	
Minus:	
Indirect business taxes	____
Equals: **National income (NI)**	____
Minus: Income earned but not received	
Corporate income taxes	____
Undistributed corporate profits	____
Social insurance contributions	____
Plus: Income received but not earned	
Transfer payments	____
Equals: **Personal income (PI)**	____
Minus:	
Personal taxes	____
Equals: **Disposable personal income (DPI)**	____
Out of which:	
Personal consumption expenditures	____
Personal saving	____

From Net National Product to National Income

Net national product (NNP) measures the total sales value of goods and services available for society's consumption and for adding to its stock of capital equipment. As such, NNP may be thought of as "national income at market prices." But it still does not represent the dollars people actually had available to spend. This is because NNP is overstated by the amount of indirect business taxes—such as sales taxes—which are shifted forward by sellers to consumers in the form of higher prices. These indirect business taxes must be deducted from NNP in order to arrive at a closer estimate of the dollars available to people for actual spending. This deduction results in national income at factor cost.

From National Income to Personal Income

National income (at factor cost), NI, is the total of all incomes earned by the factors of production. Thus, NI is the sum of wages, rent, interest, and profit earned by the suppliers of labor, land, capital, and entrepreneurship. Does NI represent the dollars that people actually had available for spending? Once again the answer is *no.* Some people earned income they did not receive; others received income they did not earn.

The stockholders in a corporation are its owners and hence earn the corporation's profits. However, stockholders do not receive all the profits, for two reasons. Some profits are paid to the government in the form of corporation income taxes. Some profits are also plowed back into the business for future expansion instead of being distributed to stockholders as dividends. Likewise, social security contributions are taken out of workers' current earnings, and thus are also part of income earned but not received.

As for income received but not earned, the major items are transfer payments. These are merely shifts of funds within the economy, primarily from the government sector to households—for reasons other than current production.

To measure the dollars people actually had available for spending, we therefore adjust the NI in two ways. (1) We *subtract* income earned but not received, and (2) we *add* income received but not earned. These two steps result in a figure called personal income.

From Personal Income to Disposable Personal Income

Personal income (PI) is the total received by persons from all sources. It is the dollars that you and I receive for performing our jobs and thereby contributing to GNP. Does *PI* measure the dollars actually available to people for spending? The answer is still *no,* because out of personal income people must first pay their personal taxes. This amount must therefore be deducted from *PI,* leaving a figure called *disposable personal income (DPI).* It is this amount that people actually have available for spending. As you can see from the front endpapers of this book, the great bulk of *DPI* goes for personal consumption, while the rest is saved.

There are thus five measures of income and output for the economy:

1. Gross national product.

2. Net national product.

3. National income.

4. Personal income.

5. Disposable personal income—or simply, disposable income.

All five measures are closely interrelated, can be derived from one another, and tend approximately to parallel one another over the years. In many economic discussions (except those involving specific accounting practices as described in this chapter) *economists use the term "national income" or simply "income" to represent all five terms.* A complete circular-flow model is shown in Exhibit 7.

Wealth of a Nation: How Much Is America "Worth"?

If you wanted to buy the United States—its land, buildings, machines, people's personal belongings, government property, everything—what would you have to pay? In 1776 the answer was $3.7 billion; in

Exhibit 7
The Flow of National Income and Related Concepts

Can you fill in the data for the most recent year? See the front endpapers.

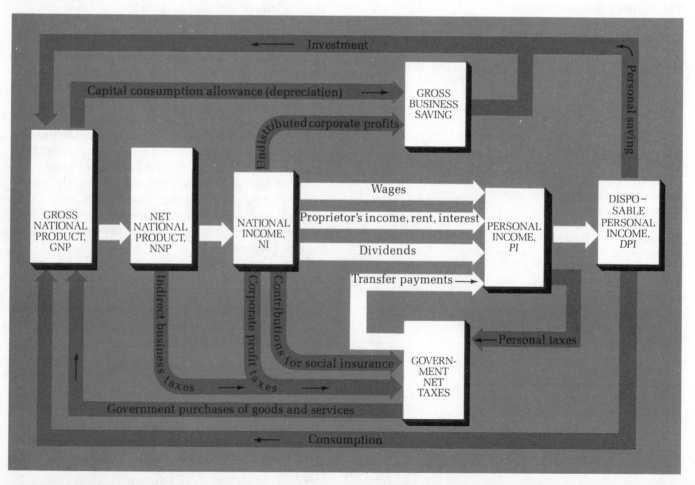

1976 it was $6 trillion. In the year 2000, according to trends in recent decades, the figure is likely to be about $13 trillion.

This sum includes only physical wealth, that is, wealth consisting of tangible assets. Items such as cash, corporate stocks and bonds, and savings and checking accounts are excluded because they represent intangible assets—claims against physical wealth.

What kinds of items enter into the calculation of a nation's wealth? You can get an idea by examining the table in Exhibit 8. This illustrates a balance sheet for the country as a whole. When used in conjunction with the nation's income statement shown in Exhibit 6, two important types of information are revealed:

The nation's balance sheet shows the country's financial position on a *given date*. The nation's income statement shows the country's output and income for a *given period*. Therefore, the balance sheet is like a "snapshot" of the nation's financial status, whereas the income statement is like a "motion picture."

As you probably know, business firms regularly

prepare balance sheets and income statements. The meanings of these terms are defined *for businesses* in the Dictionary at the back of the book. How do these definitions compare with the concepts of a national balance sheet and a national income statement? (See also *Leaders in Economics,* page 96.)

What You Have Learned

1. GNP, the basic and most comprehensive measure of a nation's output, represents the total market value of all final goods and services produced during a year.

Three pitfalls to avoid in calculating GNP are (a) the effects of price changes, (b) the possibility of double (actually multiple) counting, and (c) the inclusion of nonproductive transactions.

2. From the expenditure standpoint, GNP is the sum of personal consumption expenditures, government purchases of goods and services, investment, and net exports. GNP can be viewed from the income standpoint as gross national income (GNI) or the sum of wages, rent, interest, and profit, plus two nonincome business expense items: indirect business taxes and depreciation.

3. The items that make up the nation's income accounts are GNP, NNP, *NI, PI,* and *DPI.* All five measures are closely related and can be derived from one another. They are among the most important measures of our economy's performance. In economic discussions (except those involving actual accounting practices) we often refer to all five measures as "national income" or simply "income."

4. The financial status of a nation is reflected by its income statement, showing gross national product and related accounts. Financial status is also reflected by a nation's balance sheet, showing assets, liabilities, and net worth. Taken together, these financial statements provide an overall picture of the economy's income and wealth.

Exhibit 8
The Nation's Balance Sheet
Household, Business, and Government Sectors
(billions of dollars)

Assets are what we own; *liabilities* are what we owe; *net worth* is the difference between the two. Can you explain why liabilities to domestic residents is the same as intangible assets?

		19__
Assets		
Tangible		
Buildings and other structures	$	×
Land		×
Durable goods, equipment, and inventories		×
Intangible		
Currency and checking accounts		×
Other bank deposits and shares		×
Insurance and pension reserves		×
Credit, securities, and other claims		×
Total assets		×
Liabilities		
To domestic residents (same as intangible assets)		×
To foreigners		×
Total liabilities		×
Net worth (or net national wealth)		
Total assets less total liabilities	$	×

For Discussion

1. *Terms and concepts to review:*

gross national product	depreciation
real output	disinvestment
current dollars	national income
constant dollars	(at factor cost)
deflation	capital consumption
index numbers	allowance
value added	net national product
transfer payments	personal income
gross national income	disposable personal
investment	income
inventory	

2. Suppose that a nation's GNP increased from $100 billion to $200 billion. What has happened to its *real* GNP during that period if

(a) Prices remained the same?

(b) Prices doubled?

(c) Prices tripled from their constant level in (a)?

(d) Prices fell by 50 percent of their constant level in (a)?

Leaders in Economics
Simon Smith Kuznets   1901–

Father of National-Income Accounting

Few scholars in any field are capable of deciding, by their mid-twenties, the precise type of work they want to do for the remainder of their professional careers. One person who made that decision, and has earned lasting fame for his accomplishments, is Simon Kuznets.

Born in Russia, Kuznets migrated to the United States as a young man. After receiving his doctorate from Columbia University, he joined the staff of one of the nation's major research organizations, the National Bureau of Economic Research. While there, he also did occasional work for the Commerce Department. In addition, he taught for many years at the University of Pennsylvania, Johns Hopkins, and Harvard.

More than anyone else, Kuznets pioneered the development of national-income data. When the nation plunged into the Great Depression of the early 1930s, the amount of factual information available was, said Kuznets, "a scandal. No one knew what was happening. The data available then were neither fish nor flesh nor even red herring."

It remained for Kuznets to point out the kind of information that was needed. When the Senate ordered official income estimates, the Commerce Department turned to the National Bureau of Economic Research for assistance. Kuznets went to Washington as a consultant, lecturing government economists and statisticians on his concepts. On January 4, 1934, a Senate document was pub-

Wide World Photos.

lished containing the country's first national-income figures, for 1929 to 1932. This was the beginning of one of the most significant advances in the history of economics. The measurement of GNP and related concepts was not fully developed by the Commerce Department until the 1940s. And although the technical structure is quite different from Kuznets' original conceptual scheme, he is still recognized as the person most responsible for its statistical formulation.

Kuznets was well aware that national income served as an imperfect measure of society's well-being. He gave two reasons. First, nonmarket activities, such as the services of homemakers, amateur gardeners, and others engaged in productive pursuits, do not enter the national-income accounts. As a result of these omissions, our national-income data are less than they otherwise would be.

Second, certain "occupational expenses" are included in national-income accounts, even though they may not all yield positive returns to us from the economic system. Such expenses include the costs of commut-

ing to work, buying banking services because we live in a money economy, and other necessary "costs" of carrying out our daily activities. Because these expenses are included, the accounts tend to be higher than they otherwise would be.

These and other shortcomings, Kuznets pointed out, introduce biases in national-income accounts which make it difficult to compare one economy with another. For example, in 1953 he wrote: "That such [errors] are hardly in the nature of minutiae may be illustrated by a tentative calculation made in attempting a comparison of per capita income in the United States and China and purifying the former for what may be called inflated costs of urban civilization: the inflation in question amounted to from 20 to 30 percent of all consumers' outlay . . . as estimated by the Department of Commerce."

Kuznets' whole career has been devoted to closely related tasks. Sifting through mountains of historical data, he has estimated the changing effects of capital, labor, income distribution, productivity, and other variables on the economic growth of this and other countries. To a degree rarely equaled by any other economist, he has the ability to generate and analyze masses of data from which he draws many provocative socioeconomic hypotheses about long-term economic development.

Kuznets' lifework has been crowned with honors. In 1971, when he was 70, the Swedish Royal Academy of Science awarded him the Alfred Nobel Memorial Prize in Economic Science.

3. What happens when you "deflate" a *rising* current-dollar series, as in Exhibit 1? Obviously, the constant-dollar series lies below the current-dollar series for all years after the base year, and above it for all years prior to the base year. What would happen if you deflated a current-dollar series that was *declining* rather than one that was rising? Explain why.

4. Why is "value added" a logically correct method of measuring the nation's output?

5. The level of inventories serves as a "balancing" item between sales to final users and current production. True or false? Can sales to final users exceed current production? Can sales be less than current production? Explain, in terms of changes in inventories and their effects on GNP.

6. How is the growth or decline of an economy related to its net investment? Do you think an economy's percentage growth or decline is related to its percentage change in net investment? Explain.

7. What is the effect on national income if you (a) marry your housekeeper; (b) take an unpaid vacation? Is there any effect on social welfare from either act?

8. Which of the following is included, and which is not included, in calculating GNP?

(a) One hundred shares of General Motors stock purchased this week on the New York Stock Exchange.

(b) Wages paid to teachers.

(c) A student's income from a part-time job.

(d) A student's income from a full-time summer job.

(e) Value of a bookcase built by a do-it-yourselfer.

(f) Purchase of a used car.

(g) A monthly rent of $250 which a homeowner "saves" by living in his or her own home instead of renting it out to a tenant.

9. Each year the total amount of dollar payments by checks and cash far exceeds—by many billions of dollars—the GNP. If GNP is the market value of the economy's final output, how can this huge difference exist?

10. Gross business saving represents that part of business income available for various forms of investment. Examine the following hypothetical data (in billions of dollars):

Corporate profits	$90
Corporate income taxes	43
Dividends to stockholders	25
Retained profits	22
Depreciation	75

(a) How much is gross business saving? Show your method of calculation.

(b) Of what significance is depreciation in your calculation?

(c) Can gross business saving be larger than corporate profits *before* taxes and dividends? Can it be smaller? Explain.

11. Examine the following hypothetical data (all in billions of dollars) for a particular year:

(1)	Gross private domestic investment	$ 59
(2)	Contributions for social insurance	8
(3)	Interest paid by consumers	3
(4)	Personal consumption expenditures	206
(5)	Transfer payments	20
(6)	Undistributed corporate profits	13
(7)	Indirect business taxes	25
(8)	Net exports of goods and services	4
(9)	Capital consumption allowance	21
(10)	Government purchases of goods and services	59
(11)	Corporate income taxes	22
(12)	Personal tax and nontax payments	29

On the basis of these data, calculate (a) gross national product; (b) net national product; (c) national income; (d) personal income; (e) disposable income.

12. Examine the following hypothetical data (all in billions of dollars) for a particular year:

(1)	Indirect business taxes	$ 32
(2)	Corporate profits before taxes	47
(3)	Capital consumption allowance	32
(4)	Compensation of employees	225
(5)	Undistributed corporate profits	17
(6)	Proprietors' income	42
(7)	Contributions for social insurance	11
(8)	Corporate income taxes	22
(9)	Net interest	4
(10)	Transfer payments	27
(11)	Personal tax and nontax payments	36
(12)	Rental incomes	14
(13)	Personal consumption expenditures	254

On the basis of these data, calculate the five types of national income discussed in this chapter. (HINT Do not try to calculate GNP first.)

13. A country's gross national product rose from $285 billion in 1960 to $504 billion in 1970. During the same period the country's Consumer Price Index (1977 = 100) rose from 72.1 to 88.7.

(a) What was the percentage increase of GNP over the decade?

(b) By how much have average prices, measured by the Consumer Price Index, risen over the decade?

(c) How would you calculate GNP for 1960 and for 1970, expressed in 1977 dollars?

(d) Is the percentage change of GNP in constant dollars greater or less than the percentage change in current dollars? Show your calculations.

14. Convert personal consumption expenditures into 1977 dollars for the years shown in the following table. What is the economic significance of your calculations? Have you "deflated" or "inflated"? Explain.

Year	Personal consumption expenditures (regional data, billions)	Consumer Price Index (1977 = 100)
1960	$191.0	72.1
1965	254.4	80.2
1970	325.2	88.7
1975	432.8	94.5

15. Which measure of national income best tells you

(a) The amount by which the economy's production exceeds the capital equipment used up in producing it?

(b) The amount of income available to consumers for spending?

(c) The market value of commodities produced for final use?

(d) The amount of income available to people for government taxation?

(e) The incomes earned by resource owners engaged in production?

Which measure of national income is best?

Case
Tax-Free GNP: The Underground Economy

Fred Henderson owns his own Jeep and snowplow, earns enough during the winter months to cover an entire year's college expenses, and files no income tax return. Janet Brennan works full time as a waitress, files an annual income tax return, but generally declares only about 50 percent of her tips as income. Dr. S. J. Jackson, a physician, exchanges medical care for car maintenance services with a patient who is an automobile mechanic; as a result, no money passes between them.

Although the names in these scenarios are fictitious, the cases are not. They illustrate some of the activities that take place in the underground economy—a segment of the private sector in which transactions go unreported to government agencies, especially to the Internal Revenue Service.

The results are by no means trivial. Indeed, some experts estimate that the amount of unreported income each year equals about 10 percent of actual GNP, and that the percentage is probably growing. Further, most of this income comes from legal activities, not from illegal ones like prostitution, gambling, or drugs.

Some Implications

If the estimate is correct, or even if it is only half accurate, the income "lost" amounts to hundreds of billions of dollars annually. The implications for economic policy are staggering. They indicate that if the subterranean economy is large and growing, the nation's economic health is quite different from what the official figures disclose. For example:

○ The unemployment rate is much lower than is generally believed. According to some estimates, many more people, perhaps a third of those listed as unemployed, are actually working full time and earning incomes which are either unreported or understated.

○ Actual GNP figures are significantly higher than the official data.

Christa Armstrong, Rapho/Photo Researchers.

Businesses such as these are part of the growing underground economy.

Therefore, the nation's rate of economic growth—the output of its goods and services—is rising faster than is generally believed.

○ Taxes on unreported income are lost to the government. In any given year, this loss in tax revenues could be enough to erase a large portion of the deficit in the federal budget.

Because of these and other considerations, government officials are seeking ways to reduce the scope of the underground economy.

Experiences Overseas

Unfortunately, the task is not easy, as the experiences of advanced foreign countries bear out. Subterranean economies have thrived much longer and are considerably more extensive in western Europe and Japan than in the United States.

In Italy, where dodging the tax collector is a national sport, more than 15 percent of the labor force earns unreported income from second jobs. The Italian government, which places highest priority on full employment, prefers to ignore the matter. This is because the government prefers not to risk the loss in jobs that might occur if employers had to pay legal wages and benefits.

In France, high income and sales taxes have driven increasing numbers of workers into second jobs. Most are service occupations in which cheating on taxes is relatively easy. French officials estimate that as many as half the scientists and engineers in Paris engage in such part-time activities as television repair and automobile maintenance. "And if you go out for dinner or have your house painted," says a French tax authority, "the odds are better than even that the person who services you will be a police officer, firefighter, or schoolteacher."

Similar conditions exist in Belgium, Britain, West Germany, Scandinavia (Denmark, Norway, and Sweden), and Japan. A major reason is the steepness of tax rates in these countries. When taxes rise sharply with increases in income, the pressure on people to seek ways of escaping taxes, through illegal means if necessary, becomes pronounced. As a result, unless governments face up to the need for major tax reforms, a growing proportion of their economies will continue to go underground.

QUESTIONS

1. One of the chief problems of the underground economy involves the vital issue of equity. Can you explain why?

2. Can you suggest measures to reduce the importance of the underground economy?

Chapter 6

Economic Instability: Business Cycles, Unemployment, and Inflation

Chapter Preview

What are business cycles? What causes them? Can they be predicted and controlled?

How significant is unemployment in our economy? What are the "costs" of unemployment? Who pays these costs?

What is inflation? Who benefits from it? Who suffers from it? Can inflation be avoided?

Fluctuations in economic activity—or "business cycles" as they are often called—have been an unending plague for capitalistic nations. Inflation and unemployment are the costs of that plague—costs we have paid throughout much of our history.

This chapter examines the nature of business cycles, unemployment, and inflation, and their interrelationship. Once we understand their characteristics, we can attempt to do something about the problems themselves, which are among the most potent challenges confronting affluent Western nations.

Essentially, as you will learn, our government tries to keep all three ailments at bay simultaneously. However, our nation's policy makers are not consistently successful, because both the ailments themselves and their cure are still subjects of controversy.

Business Cycles—A Long History of Fluctuations

Business history repeats itself, but always with a difference.

Wesley C. Mitchell,
Business Cycles (1913)

What are business cycles? You can get a preliminary idea by looking ahead at the historical picture in Ex-

Exhibit 1
How Do Business Cycles Look?

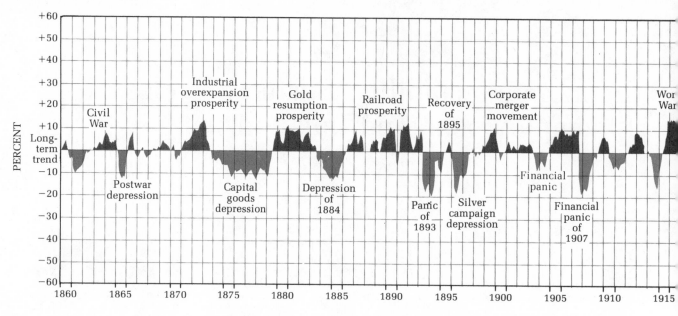

When data such as GNP, sales, prices, employment, or any other figures are arranged chronologically, they are referred to as *time series*. The measurement of "time" may be in years, months, weeks, days, or other units, and is usually scaled on the horizontal axis when depicted graphically.

According to the definition of business cycles, fluctuations may occur in production, prices, income, employment, or in any other time series of economic data. In order to measure business cycles for the economy as a whole, therefore, it is necessary to combine many different time series into a single index of business activity. Then, if the value of the index for each year is expressed as a percentage of the long-term average or trend, the resulting data when graphed might look like the fluctuations in the chart.

Note how the actual cycle differs from the idealized one. Actual business cycles are recurrent but not periodic—their scope and intensity differ. Idealized cycles are both recur-

rent *and* periodic—their peaks and valleys occur at regular intervals.

Can you see why the various cyclical phases are called *prosperity, recession, depression,* and *recovery*? If not, look up the meanings of these terms in the Dictionary at the back of the book.

The four phases of the cycle are by no means equal in scope or intensity and do not always come in the order shown. For example, an economy may fluctuate between contractions and expansions for many years without experiencing either high prosperity or deep depression. Further, the transition from one phase of a cycle into the next is occasionally imperceptible; it may be almost impossible to distinguish between the end of one phase and the beginning of another. For these reasons, the names of the four phases should be viewed only as convenient descriptions and the diagram as a highly simplified picture.

hibit 1. The meaning of this chart will be examined shortly. Meanwhile, you can see that although we no longer have the frequent booms and busts that characterized the economy prior to World War II, we do have fluctuations in business activity. The following modern definition of business cycles is therefore appropriate:

Business cycles are fluctuations in general economic activity. The fluctuations are recurrent but nonperiodic (i.e., irregular). They occur in such aggregate variables as income, output, employment, and prices, most of which move at about the same time in the same direction but at different rates.

Business cycles, therefore, are not just cumulative fluctuations in the absolute level of important economic variables, but are a speeding up and a slowing down in their rates of growth. Note that the definition is important for what it excludes:

1. Business cycles are not *seasonal fluctuations*, such as the upswing in retail sales that occurs each year during the Christmas and Easter periods.

2. Business cycles are not *secular trends*, such as the long-run growth or decline that characterizes practically all economic data over a long period of years.

A more complete explanation of the nature of business cycles is given in Exhibit 1.

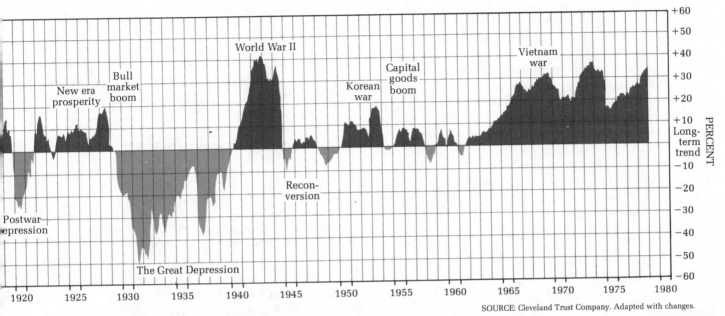

SOURCE: Cleveland Trust Company. Adapted with changes.

An Historical Picture of American Business Cycles. *Fluctuations are recurrent but not periodic (i.e., the peaks and troughs do not occur at regular intervals).*

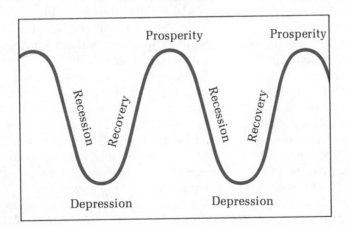

An idealized business cycle is one in which fluctuations are recurrent and periodic. The peaks and troughs occur at regular intervals, like a sine or cosine curve in trigonometry, or an alternating electric current.

SOME FACTS ABOUT BUSINESS CYCLES

Economists who have analyzed business cycles have learned a great deal about them, from studies going back to the nineteenth century.

For instance:

Over the course of a business cycle, the durable or "hard goods" industries tend to experience relatively wide fluctuations in output and employment and relatively small fluctuations in prices. The nondurable or "soft goods" industries tend to experience relatively wide fluctuations in prices and relatively small fluctuations in output and employment.

The reasons for this are based primarily on two sets of factors: durability and competition.

Durability

Durable goods—precisely because they are durable—do not have to be replaced at a particular time. They can be repaired and made to last longer if necessary. What effect does this have on business executives, who buy capital goods such as iron and steel, cement, and machine tools? What effect does it have on consumers, who purchase durable goods such as automobiles, furniture, and appliances?

In a recession or depression, total demand for the

economy's output is likely to be low. Business managers thus find themselves with excess production capacity. Therefore, they see little prospect of profiting from investment in capital goods. Likewise, consumers find they can get along with their existing cars and other durable goods rather than purchase new ones. As a result, the "hard goods" industries experience sharp decreases in demand.

During recovery and prosperity, on the other hand, the reverse situation occurs. Aggregate demand is high, and business executives and consumers are ready to replace as well as add to their existing stocks of capital and durable goods. The hard goods industries therefore experience sharp increases in demand.

Purchase of capital goods and consumer durables can be postponed to a later date. The contrary, however, is true of nondurables and semidurables—the "soft goods"—such as fresh food, some clothing, and certain services. Their purchase is not readily postponable. Therefore, the change in demand for them over the course of a business cycle is much less pronounced.

Competition

The degree of competition in an industry, as determined by the number of sellers, usually has a bearing on the way in which the industry adjusts its prices and outputs to changes in demand. In view of this, how does a fall in aggregate demand affect hard goods producers as compared to soft goods producers?

Many durable goods industries tend to be characterized by relatively small numbers of dominant sellers. The aluminum, locomotive, automobile, aircraft engine, and telephone equipment industries, among others, are typical. The "big three" or "big four" producers in these industries control a large proportion of the total output of their commodity. Consequently, they can influence the prices they charge and can formulate stable pricing policies despite fluctuations in sales. As a result, when they are confronted with a decline in aggregate demand, they try to reduce costs and maintain profit margins by cutting back production and employment. Eventually, if market sluggishness continues, some hard-pressed firms may seek to reduce their inventories by cutting prices. But even then, price decreases are likely to be small relative to the declines in output and employment.

The opposite situation tends to occur in industries producing nondurable and semidurable goods—such as ladies' dresses, men's suits, millinery, and toilet preparations. In these industries, unlike most durable goods industries, a considerable number of sellers are usually competing in the same market. Each firm, therefore, is likely to have too small a share of the market to ignore the importance of price reduction as a means of countering a decrease in demand. Consequently, when aggregate demand falls, firms in such industries tend to reduce their prices while holding output and employment relatively steady.

To summarize:

Two factors—durability and competition—help account for different degrees of price and output changes when aggregate demand declines. During a recession, for example, we first hear about production cutbacks and layoffs in such industries as automobiles and steel—not in food processing or textiles. The latter industries may also reduce their output and employment, but for them the percentage decreases are usually much smaller.

CAN WE FORECAST BUSINESS CYCLES?

If we could first know where we are and whither we are tending, we could better judge what to do and how to do it.

Abraham Lincoln

These words are more than a century old, but they explain as well as any the necessity of forecasting. As long as we live in a world in which no one can predict the future with certainty, virtually all business and economic decisions rest upon forecasts.

For example, if you were a business executive, would you invest without knowing something about future economic conditions in your industry or in the economy? As a consumer, would you delay buying a house or a car if you thought the price was going to drop in the near future? If you were a speculator in commodities or in common stocks, would you buy and sell if you did not expect to make a profit? If you were a member of Congress, would you vote for measures to help curb inflation if you thought that prices were going to leap upward next year?

Each of these questions involves a prediction of the future. Forecasting is a means of reducing the uncertainty that surrounds the making of business and economic decisions.

How are the forecasts made? Several methods are employed by economic forecasters working in industry, government, and universities.

Statistical Projections—Extrapolations

Suppose that GNP has increased at an average rate of 5 percent a year for a number of years. If on that basis you predict a 5 percent increase in GNP for next year, you are forecasting by statistical projection.

This simple example illustrates the idea that a statistical projection is basically an extrapolation or extension into the future of past trends, averages, or other quantitative relationships. Some statistical projection methods are quite sophisticated, employing elaborate mathematical procedures requiring computer solutions. Regardless of their sophistication, however, all extrapolation procedures are mechanical forecasting devices because they involve straightforward projections of one form or another. That is, they pay little or no attention to the underlying economic relationships that determine the data because very little is known about them.

Opinion Polling—Intentions Surveys

A second approach to forecasting is to survey a representative group of people from the business and household sectors. For example, executives and consumers might be asked: "What major economic decisions do you plan to make and when do you plan to make them?" The information obtained can then be blown up to a national scale for making predictions about the economy as a whole.

Several privately and publicly sponsored organizations conduct periodic surveys along these lines. Some of the surveys seek to determine business managers' intentions to spend on plant, equipment, and inventories. Other surveys focus on households, their finances, and on consumers' intentions to purchase automobiles, homes, and major appliances.

In general, surveys have frequently been successful in foretelling by a few months some of the major upward or downward turning points of economic activity. However, the surveys have not been as useful for predicting economic activity over longer periods. This is because people's spending decisions are affected by a wide array of economic and emotional complexities. As a result, factors determining spending cannot be unraveled and used as a basis for future buying plans beyond several months.

Econometric Models

Economics, like every science, seeks to discover relationships between variables. You are already familiar with some of them. For example, the quantities demanded and supplied of a commodity are each dependent upon (related to) its price. You will learn about many other economic relationships in subsequent chapters.

Relationships may be formulated in terms of mathematical equations. If the equations are then verified by statistical methods, the resulting system of relationships is called an _econometric model_.

Econometric models are frequently used for forecasting. They can be constructed for firms, industries, regions, or the entire economy. In addition to being predictive devices, econometric models may also serve as guides for policy making. Consequently, in order to be useful in today's complex economy, modern econometric models contain hundreds of equations reflecting numerous relationships. Because of this, econometric models require a large computer as well as staffs of economists and statisticians to keep them up to date.

Economic Indicators

In 1878, British economist W. S. Jevons astounded the scientific world by announcing that he had discovered a close relationship between business cycles and sunspots. These are the dark patches that appear from time to time on the surface of the sun. The explanation that Jevons gave became known as the _sunspot theory_. It held that sunspot cycles occur regularly, thereby affecting the weather. This causes cycles in agricultural production, which in turn influence total economic activity.

Jevons' theory received worldwide popularity when it was first introduced. But it soon fell into disrepute when the near-perfect 20-year correlation between sunspots and agricultural cycles which Jevons discovered did not last. The high correlation turned out to be the result of accidental rather than causal factors.

Economic science has advanced considerably since Jevons' time. Today forecasters look at hundreds of economic time series. Among them: retail sales, new construction activity, labor productivity, and stock market prices. The purpose is to judge not only what is happening but what is likely to happen. The time series that are continuously scrutinized are too numerous to list, but most of them can be classified into one of three categories:

Coincident Indicators These time series tend to move approximately in phase with the aggregate economy and therefore are measures of current economic activity. _Examples:_ GNP; industrial production; retail sales.

Leading Indicators These time series tend to move ahead of aggregate economic activity, thus reaching peaks and troughs before the economy as a whole. _Examples:_ New orders for plant and equipment; new building permits; stock market prices.

Lagging Indicators These time series tend to follow or trail behind aggregate economic activity. _Examples:_ Business loans outstanding; manufacturing and trade inventories; unit labor costs.

The trouble with all three types of indicators (especially the leading ones) is that they often give false signals by temporarily reversing their upward or downward direction. This, of course, impairs their usefulness for interpreting and forecasting economic trends. (See Exhibit 2.)

Exhibit 2
Forecasting with Economic Indicators

Ideally, the three types of indicators might look like the ones shown here, illustrating distinct leads and lags in terms of the peaks and troughs. In reality, the leads and lags are not always so definite or consistent. If they were, forecasting would be a simple task. (Note that the shaded area is a reference range. It covers a temporary downturn for the economy as a whole, represented by the coincident indicator. Note also that the vertical axis is not labeled. This is because actual indicators are measured in different units, such as dollars, tons, hours, etc.)

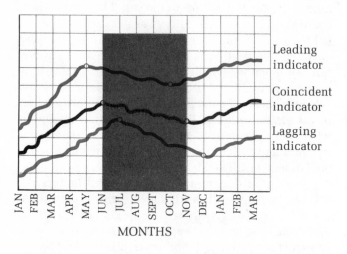

CONCLUSION: STABILITY AND FREEDOM

Some people contend that the business cycle can readily be cured if only certain fundamental adjustments are made. This belief is especially popular during economic recessions. "Find a proper balance between wages and prices." "Improve labor–management relations." "Reform our tax system." If these and other measures are adopted, it is said, economic instability would be eliminated.

Unfortunately, such beliefs are false. Even if these desirable objectives could be achieved, we would still experience economic fluctuations. The reasons are not difficult to see:

Business cycles are an inherent characteristic of mixed economies. This is because households, which express their demands for goods and services in the marketplace, are not the same as businesses that seek to fulfill those demands. Each group is composed of different people with different motivations. Consequently, the economic actions of both groups—their decisions to spend or not to spend—generally differ. The result is that waves of economic activity are always being created.

In view of this, you will find that one of the major goals of macroeconomics is not to eliminate instability, because that would be impossible in our type of economy. Instead, a chief goal is to reduce instability without sacrificing our capitalistic institutions and freedoms.

Unemployment

You will often hear it said that one of our primary national objectives is to maintain the economy's resources at a "full" or "high" level of employment. What do these terms mean?

Before this question can be answered, it is necessary to understand some basic terms and concepts that are part of the modern language of economics. The first is the _labor force_. It is defined as all people 16 years of age or older who are employed, plus all those unemployed who are actively seeking work. The total labor force includes those in the armed services plus the civilian labor force. However, only the _civilian labor force_ is of interest to us here, because this is the segment that experiences unemployment.

TYPES OF UNEMPLOYMENT

The U.S. Department of Labor encounters certain difficulties when it tries to measure unemployment. It finds that the circumstances and conditions of unemployment vary widely among individuals. Accordingly, a distinction is made between several different kinds of unemployment.

Frictional (Transitional) Unemployment

A certain amount of unemployment, which is of a short-run nature and is characteristic of a dynamic economy, may be called _frictional unemployment_. It exists because of "frictions" in the economic system resulting from imperfect labor mobility, imperfect knowledge of job opportunities, and the economy's inability to match people with jobs instantly and smoothly. Typically, frictional unemployment consists of people temporarily out of work because they are between jobs or in the process of changing jobs. Frictional unemployment can be reduced by improving labor mobility and knowledge, but cannot—and in a democratic society should not—be completely eliminated. To do so would greatly reduce people's freedom to change jobs. In view of the nature of frictional unemployment, an equally suitable and more descriptive name for it might be _transitional unemployment_.

Cyclical Unemployment

In mixed economies such as ours, a major type of unemployment has been _cyclical_. This type of unemployment is the result of business recessions and depressions. Obviously, society would like to reduce cyclical unemployment as much as possible, but this can be done only by conquering the business cycle. Although substantial progress in this direction has been made in recent decades, cyclical unemployment continues to be one of our economy's most serious ills. Therefore, its treatment is a topic of major importance in subsequent chapters.

Structural Unemployment

Unlike cyclical unemployment, which results from economic instability, _structural unemployment_ arises from deep-rooted conditions and changes in the economy. Two major groups of people make up structural unemployment:

The first group consists of the _hard-core unemployed,_ who lack the education and skills needed in today's complex economy, and who are often the victims of discrimination. This class is composed mainly of minorities: blacks, Puerto Ricans, Mexicans, the "too young," the "too old," the high-school dropouts, and the permanently displaced victims of technological change.

The second group is a completely different type. It consists of skilled workers, many college graduates, and professionals whose talents have been made obsolete by changes in technology, markets, or national priorities.

Because the existence of both groups constitutes one of our society's major economic challenges, much of macroeconomics is concerned with efforts to solve the problems posed by structural unemployment. (See Exhibit 3.)

FULL EMPLOYMENT AND "NORMAL" UNEMPLOYMENT

Ideally, the economy should maintain _full employment_—maximum efficient utilization of all resources available for employment. In terms of society's human resources, this means that the entire civilian labor force should be working, except for the proportion which is frictionally unemployed—typically about 3 percent. This is equivalent to saying there should be no _involuntary unemployment_. This is a condition in which people who want to work are unable to find jobs at going wage rates for the skills and experiences they have to offer.

For convenience, the goal of full employment is generally expressed in terms of a percentage of the labor force. What minimum unemployment percentage constitutes full employment? There is always some disagreement on this question, and the figure chosen is likely to be revised upward from time to time.

For instance, it used to be widely accepted that full employment existed when the "normal" unemployment rate was no more than 3 percent of the labor force. Presently, we hear figures of 4, 5, or even 6 percent. This reflects the growing significance of structural unemployment as well as other factors explained in the following paragraphs. You may think such relatively small differences in percentages are unimportant. However, remember that even a difference of only 1 percentage point can involve the employment or unemployment of hundreds of thousands of people—depending on the size of the labor force. Take a look at the recent labor-force figures in the back endpapers of this book and estimate the consequences for yourself.

Causes of "Normal" Unemployment

How much higher is the "normal" unemployment level likely to go? Some experts predict that before the end of this century perhaps 15 percent unemployed will constitute "full employment." They base their beliefs on three major trends:

Changing Composition of the Labor Force The proportion of secondary income earners in the labor force, such as teenagers and part-time jobholders, has been increasing relative to the proportion of primary breadwinners. The percentage of unemployed within these groups is usually relatively high—in some instances as much as 20 or 30 percent. As a result, the growing importance of secondary income earners within the labor force helps to boost the overall unemployment rate.

Rising Minimum-Wage Rate According to many studies, continued increases in the minimum-wage rate will intensify unemployment. Such increases eliminate jobs that cannot be done productively at the required wage rate. Many unskilled, low-paying occupations could be held by teenagers, but will not be, because employers will find it unprofitable to pay the minimum wage. These jobs, therefore, will not be done unless cheaper methods can be found to do them. Various studies conducted by economists in universities and the Labor Department support this view. The studies show that teenage unemployment rates are remarkably low or virtually nonexistent in many industrial countries that have no minimum-wage laws.

Exhibit 3
Who Is Unemployed?

Unemployment figures are always subject to attack, especially when they are high. Critics point out that the overall unemployment rate may at times either be overstated or understated—because of the inclusion or exclusion of three categories of workers:

1. *Marginally Employed*   The jobless total is swollen by the inclusion of many people, among them some homemakers and students, who may be only marginally dependent on regular paychecks.

2. *Discouraged Workers*   The unemployment total is understated by its failure to include the "hidden unemployed"—those discouraged people who have given up trying to find work.

3. *Partially Employed*   The published unemployment statistics do not reflect the fact that many jobholders are only partially employed because they cannot find full-time jobs.

For these and other reasons, unemployment data are always somewhat ambiguous. Perhaps their chief value,

therefore, is not so much their amounts, but what they reveal about the direction in which unemployment is going.

MEASURING UNEMPLOYMENT

In view of this, how should unemployment be measured? The answer depends on how the concept is defined. The U.S. Department of Labor, which compiles the unemployment data, publishes seven different measures, ranging from the narrowest to the broadest. In the accompanying chart, the narrowest, U_1, consists of those people unemployed for 15 weeks or more. The broadest, U_7, includes *all* types of unemployed—full-time, part-time, and so on. The most widely used measure, U_5, may be thought of as a base. Those measures above it are additions to the base; those below are subtractions.

There is thus no single "true" measure of unemployment. Instead, there are different measures, reflecting different points of view about the economic and psychological hardship caused by unemployment.

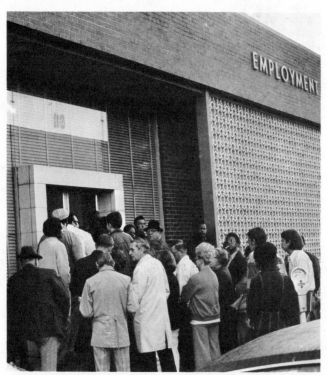

Bruce Roberts, Rapho/Photo Researchers.

The entrances to Employment Security Commission offices are sometimes jammed with people trying to get inside.

SEVEN MEASURES OF UNEMPLOYMENT

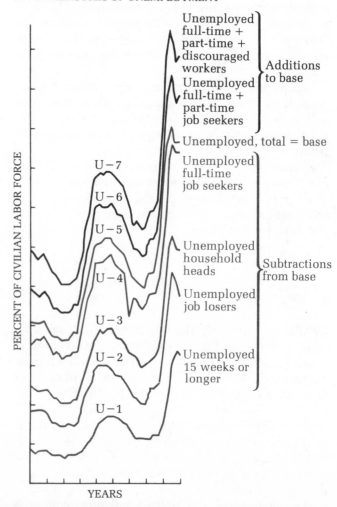

Advances in Technology Accelerations in science and technology have been occurring at particularly rapid rates in recent decades. As a result, increasing proportions of unskilled and untrained workers have been permanently displaced, thereby aggravating the problem of structural unemployment. The trend will continue unless methods are developed—through training programs, subsidies, tax incentives, and other devices—to absorb the displaced workers in new jobs. We shall have more to say about this problem in later chapters.

These are among the major factors contributing to a rising level of "normal" unemployment. But what are the costs to society of unemployment beyond the frictional level—that is, of involuntary unemployment? There are two:

Society suffers both an economic cost and a social cost of unemployment.

1. The economic cost is what the nation forgoes and never gets back. This includes not only lost consumer goods and capital goods that society fails to produce, but deterioration of human capital resulting from loss of skills.

2. The social cost includes not only the economic cost, but also the human misery, deprivation, and social and political unrest brought on by large-scale unemployment.

Of course, social cost is usually more difficult to measure than is economic cost. Nevertheless, both are important and are matters of deep and general concern. Some implications are shown in Exhibit 4.

Inflation

What is it that hits the consumer's pocketbook by eroding the purchasing power of the dollar, sometimes acts as a hidden tax, reduces a nation's competitiveness in world markets, and can have a general debilitating effect on almost all types of economic activity? Answer: Inflation.

Inflation is a rise in the general price level (or average level of prices) of all goods and services. The general price level thus varies inversely with the purchasing power of a unit of money (such as the dollar). For example, if prices double, purchasing power decreases by one-half; if prices halve, purchasing power doubles. Therefore, inflation is also a reduction in the purchasing power of a unit of money.

The opposite of inflation is *deflation*. Can you formulate your own definition?

Does inflation mean that all prices rise? Clearly not.

Exhibit 4
What About Underemployment?

If you get a college degree and end up working as an office clerk, are you unemployed? The answer, of course, is no. However, you may be "underemployed."

Underemployment (also called disguised employment) is a condition that exists when employed resources are not being used in their most efficient ways. This happens when individuals are employed below their training or capabilities.

Underemployment is an interesting problem that raises some thought-provoking questions. For example:

1. If a scientist who is unable to find work in the field of science takes a job as a taxi driver, should his or her unused scientific skills be counted as unemployed? If so, then the taxi-driving skills should not be counted as employed. Otherwise, the same individual would be counted as two people—an unemployed scientist and an employed taxi driver.

2. Is a taxi-driving scientist an economic loss to society? Apparently not—from a *social* viewpoint. The fact that the scientist was able to get a job as a taxi driver rather than as a scientist indicates that society valued the services of an additional taxi driver more highly than the services of an additional scientist.

In view of this, perhaps the taxi-driving scientist should not be classified as underemployed.

What do you think?

In almost any inflation some prices rise, some are fairly constant, and some even fall. However, the "average" level of prices—the *general price level*—rises.

TYPES OF INFLATION: IS THE UNITED STATES INFLATION-PRONE?

Different explanations for inflation have been given from time to time. Here are the more common types you are likely to encounter in the news media and should know something about. Note that some of them may be overlapping in their causes and effects.

Demand-Pull Inflation

The traditional type of inflation, known as *demand-pull inflation,* takes place when aggregate demand is rising while the available supply of goods is becoming increasingly limited. Goods may be in short supply because resources are fully utilized or because production cannot be increased rapidly enough to meet the growing demand. As a result, the general level of prices begins to rise in response to a situation sometimes described as "too much money chasing too few goods."

This is the meaning behind the conventional "demand-pull" model in Exhibit 5. It assumes a time period in which the stock of resources and their productivity are constant. The model can be analyzed in terms of its three stages.

No-Inflation Phase   In this stage the economy has excess resources. Therefore, as total demand rises from a depressed level, producers can increase the output of goods while competitive pressures remain strong enough to keep prices from rising.

Inflation Phase   In this stage the economy comes closer to utilizing all its available labor and other productive factors. Less efficient resources are brought into use, some inputs become substantially scarcer than others, and labor markets become tighter. This strengthens the bargaining position of unions and exerts upward pressure on wages. Consequently, businesses find it easier to raise prices and also to pass on wage increases to buyers. Output and employment thus reach a point where further increases in aggregate demand cause more than proportional increases in the general price level.

Hyperinflation Phase   Once the full-employment level of labor and other resources is attained, additional increases in output are no longer possible during the given period. Any further rise in aggregate demand, therefore, drives the economy into a hyperinflationary phase, characterized by spiraling prices as producers bid against each other for the same fixed supply of resources.

Cost-Push (Market-Power) Inflation

A second type of inflation is *cost-push inflation*. It occurs when prices increase because factor payments to one or more groups of resource owners rise faster than productivity or technical efficiency. Typical forms of cost-push inflation are "wage-push," "profit-push," and "commodity."

Wage-push inflation occurs when strong labor unions manage to force wage increases in excess of productivity gains. This raises unit costs of production and exerts pressure on sellers to increase prices to maintain profit margins.

Profit-push inflation occurs when sellers try to increase their profit margins by raising prices rather than by reducing costs through improved efficiency. Rising prices prompt workers and other factor owners to "catch up" by seeking higher resource payments. This increases unit costs of production and stimulates inflation.

Exhibit 5
Inflation and Employment: Conventional Demand-Pull Type

Increases in aggregate demand or total spending may result in moderate increases in the general price level as full employment is approached. Thereafter, further increases in total spending result in pure or hyperinflation as the general price level rises without any increases in output.

(NOTE   This does not mean that hyperinflation is synonymous with full employment. The underlying conditions of each are vastly different—as explained in the text.)

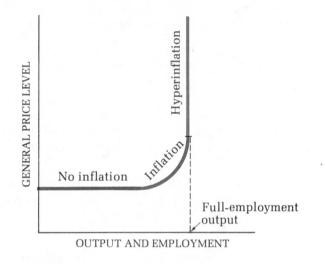

Commodity inflation occurs when prices of material inputs rise sufficiently to cause significant increases in costs of production, prompting firms to respond by raising finished-goods prices. Worldwide commodity inflations that have resulted from rising costs of energy and other raw materials provide common examples.

These facts suggest the following conclusion:

Cost-push inflation is usually attributable to monopolistic "market power." This is the effective degree of discretion which those who control resources, such as unions or firms, have to set wages and prices. Market power is generally stronger in prosperity periods because labor is in relatively short supply and consumers are less sensitive to price increases. Conversely, market power tends to be weaker in recession periods—for opposite reasons. Therefore, our society may have to tolerate some degree of cost-push (market-power) inflation as a necessary condition for maintaining high levels of income and employment.

Structural Inflation, Creeping Inflation, and Hyperinflation

Demand-pull and cost-push inflation are the fundamental types of inflation. Any other kinds of inflation that you may read or hear about in the news media are simply different aspects of these basic forms. The ones that are most often mentioned are structural inflation, creeping inflation, and hyperinflation. On the basis of what you have already learned, can you formulate definitions of these terms? Explanations are given in the Dictionary at the back of the book.

Inflations in our economy have resulted at various times from demand-pull as well as from cost-push factors. These forces have been at work in different degrees, suggesting that our nation is inflation-prone or that it has a built-in inflationary bias. Some of the implications of this will be examined shortly.

WHO SUFFERS FROM INFLATION? WHO BENEFITS?

Everyone is aware that many things bought today cost more than they did a few years ago. This fact suggests that the long-run trend of prices has been upward. By how much? You can gain some idea from the graphs in Exhibit 6 showing important price indexes.

The *Consumer Price Index* (CPI) is an average of prices of goods and services commonly purchased by

---

Exhibit 6
Price Indexes   (1967 = 100)

The Consumer Price Index and the Producer Price Index, prepared by the U.S. Department of Labor, are the most widely used measures of inflationary price trends in our economy. Can you project the indexes to the year 2000? What are you assuming when you make such projections?

[TECHNICAL NOTE   The vertical axis of this chart is scaled logarithmically. This facilitates comparison of relative (percentage) changes in the graphs. To understand why, look up the meaning of *logarithmic scale* in the Dictionary at the back of the book.]

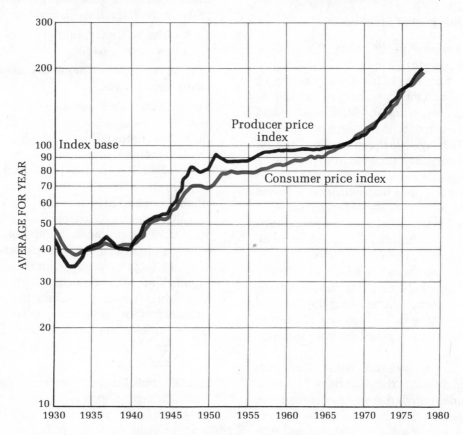

SOURCE: U.S. Department of Labor.

families in urban areas. Generally referred to as a "cost-of-living index," the CPI is published by the Bureau of Labor Statistics of the U.S. Department of Labor.

The *Producer Price Index* (PPI) is a weighted average of selected items priced in wholesale markets, including raw materials, semifinished products, and finished goods. The PPI, like the CPI, is also published by the Department of Labor.

Should we conclude from the graphs that the rising trend of the price indexes imposes an inflationary burden on all of us? Not necessarily. The effects of inflation are not distributed equally; most people suffer from it, but others sometimes benefit.

To see why this is so, we must understand the difference between two kinds of income:

1. *Money Income*   This is the amount of money received for work done.

2. *Real Income*   This is the purchasing power of money income as measured by the quantity of goods and services that it can buy. Clearly, your money income may be quite different from your real income. This is because the latter is determined not only by your money income but also by the prices of the commodities you buy.

Expected Versus Unexpected Inflation

If the rate of inflation were fairly steady, it would be easier for people to plan for it. They could do this by *anticipating* future increases in the average prices of goods and services. Then they could adjust their *present* earning, buying, borrowing, and lending activities in such ways as to overcome the expected depreciation of the dollar. However, if they failed to forecast the rate of inflation correctly, they might experience a transfer of wealth to other groups in society.

As an illustration, suppose that you lend a friend $100 for one year. If you expect the general price level to remain stable, and if you want to earn a real return (in terms of constant purchasing power) of 5 percent, you will charge 5 percent interest on the loan. Assume, however, that you expect the average level of prices to rise by 10 percent. In that case, you should charge your friend about 15 percent interest on the loan. Of this, 5 percent represents a real return and 10 percent represents compensation for your loss in purchasing power.

Suppose that a year elapses and your friend pays you what is owed, but the rise in prices has been greater than you anticipated. Are you better or worse off? Obviously, the repaid loan plus interest has not provided full compensation for your decreased purchasing power. Hence, your change in real wealth is less than you anticipated. You have suffered a loss from inflation. Your friend, on the other hand, has

repaid the loan in terms of less purchasing power than was originally borrowed. Your friend has thus experienced an increase in wealth—a gain from inflation. On the whole, therefore, there has been a redistribution of wealth—in this case from you to your friend—because of your failure to make a full adjustment to inflation.

Conversely, if the rise in prices has been less than you anticipated, you are better off. You will experience an increase in wealth—a redistribution from your friend to you. Can you explain why?

To generalize:

> People who do not predict inflation correctly are unable to adjust their economic behavior to compensate for it. As a result, some people experience gains while others experience losses. The net outcome is a redistribution of wealth between debtors and creditors.

Redistributive Effects: Problems of Equity

What, then, is wrong with unanticipated inflation? One of the chief criticisms is that it redistributes wealth arbitrarily—that is, in a manner that may not always accord with society's goals. This can be explained in terms of the net monetary financial position of the economy's three major sectors. The explanation rests on the following distinction:

1. A sector is a *net monetary debtor* if it owes more than it is owed.

2. A sector is a *net monetary creditor* if it is owed more than it owes.

Public Sector   This sector—particularly because of the federal government—has long had a rising national debt. (The national debt, which is the debt owed by the federal government, is more commonly called the public debt. It is incurred by selling bonds to the public. The size of the debt is listed in the back endpapers of this book.) Government is by far the largest net monetary debtor in our economy and therefore benefits from unanticipated inflation. Because government belongs to all of us, the gains that accrue to it are passed along to everyone. *But the distributions are not equal.* Your income, wealth, age, occupation, or certain other factors can affect the various forms and amounts of benefits you receive from government. These benefits include subsidies, financial aids, and even the "benefit" of reducing your taxes through legal loopholes.

Nonfinancial Business Sector   This sector (i.e., the business sector, excluding banks, insurance companies, etc.) is also a net monetary debtor, but on a much smaller scale than the public sector. Therefore, the owners (stockholders) of those firms that are net monetary debtors are the ultimate beneficiaries of unanticipated inflation. (Keep in mind, however, that even though the nonfinancial business sector *as a whole* is a net monetary debtor, many business firms within the sector are net monetary creditors.)

Household Sector This sector is the economy's largest net monetary creditor. This is because it is the ultimate source of most of the funds borrowed by the public and private sectors. Consequently, those households that are net monetary creditors suffer from unanticipated inflation. (Keep in mind, of course, that many households are net monetary debtors, even though the sector *as a whole* is a net monetary creditor.)

To summarize:

Both the business and household sectors contain net monetary debtor and creditor units. As a result, unexpected price-level changes cause a redistribution of wealth among these units by taking from some and giving to others. The redistribution is not on the basis of income levels, number of dependents, or other socially acceptable economic criteria. Instead, the redistribution is haphazard and inequitable in a manner unrelated to society's objectives.

International Impacts: Efficiency and Growth

In today's interdependent world, inflation may have adverse international consequences, as well. If prices and costs rise faster in this country than abroad, our ability to compete in world markets is impaired. This may cause a decrease in exports, an increase in imports, and therefore a general decline in efficiency and growth. Situations of this type occur frequently and create international economic problems of major significance.

CONCLUSION: THE NEED FOR PRICE STABILITY

The term "inflation" means rising prices. However, it is important to distinguish between anticipated and unanticipated inflation.

If *all* prices rose at a fairly steady rate, people would learn to anticipate inflation and to adjust their asset and liability holdings accordingly. The impact of inflation on unsuspecting individuals and groups would thus be greatly reduced.

In reality, *all* prices never rise at the same rate, nor does the average price level expand at a steady pace. As a result, inflation tends to be erratic and unanticipated, leaving far more losers than winners within the household sector. In fact, even if households could anticipate inflation perfectly, they would still lose wealth to the extent that they held money during periods of rising prices.

This leads to the following conclusion:

Unanticipated inflation has three major adverse consequences:

1. It creates general economic instability.

2. It results in individual inequities and costs. Inequities occur in terms of haphazard redistributions of wealth. Costs arise in terms of the efforts that people must put forth to anticipate and adjust their asset and liability holdings to unanticipated increases in prices.

3. It retards efficiency and growth by impairing productive capacity and the ability to compete in world markets.

For these reasons, a major goal of society is to achieve sufficient price stability in order to encourage a steady high level of economic activity. A number of subsequent chapters are devoted to understanding the difficulties of achieving this goal. (See *Leaders in Economics,* page 112.)

What You Have Learned

1. Capitalistic economies suffer from recurrent but nonperiodic fluctuations in economic activity known as business cycles. The four phases of cycles are prosperity, recession, depression, and recovery.

2. Industries in the economy react to business cycles in different ways. Most durable goods industries tend to be less competitive than nondurable goods industries, and therefore experience relatively wide fluctuations in output. The opposite situation tends to occur in many nondurable goods industries. In these, prices fluctuate relatively more than output and employment.

3. If economists can learn how to forecast business cycles, they will be in a better position to recommend government policies for avoiding downturns in economic activity. Today the most scientific methods of business-cycle forecasting involve the use of surveys and opinion polling, econometric models, and economic indicators.

4. The rate of unemployment is expressed as a percentage of the labor force. A jobless rate of 4 to 5 percent is generally regarded as constituting "full" to "high" employment. Unemployment rates may continue to rise in future years because of (a) the changing composition of the labor force, (b) a rising level of minimum-wage rates, and (c) advances in technology.

5. Inflation is a rise in the general price level or a reduction in the purchasing power of a unit of money. Inflations are commonly attributed to demand-pull or cost-push forces. Although there is widespread agreement on the former as a cause of inflation, there is much disagreement over the latter. In general, inflation tends to redistribute wealth haphazardly without regard to social goals. It may also impair a nation's efficiency, growth, and competitiveness in world markets.

Leaders in Economics
Wesley Clair Mitchell 1874–1948
Arthur Frank Burns 1904–

Pioneers in Business-Cycle Research

Few economists have devoted as much attention to the analysis of business cycles as have Wesley C. Mitchell and Arthur F. Burns.

Mitchell served as a professor of economics at Columbia University in New York. He was a founder and, for many years, research director of the National Bureau of Economic Research, one of the world's major centers devoted to the study of aggregate economic activity.

Mitchell inspired original investigations into many aspects of capitalism. In the 1930s and 1940s, he worked closely with his friend and collaborator, Arthur Burns, who succeeded Mitchell in 1945 as director of the NBER. In 1952, Burns went to Washington to serve as head of the Council of Economic Advisers under President Eisenhower. Later he became Chairman of the Board of Governors of the Federal Reserve System, the nation's central bank.

Broadly, Mitchell and Burns viewed business cycles as self-generating processes based on mutual interdependencies of causes and effects. Perhaps their greatest contribution was the impetus they gave to the use of empirical data and quantitative model building, which have characterized much of macroeconomic research for decades.

Wide World Photos.

Wesley Clair Mitchell.

Wide World Photos.

Arthur Burns.

Modern macroeconomic models are not designed to give detailed accounts of economic phenomena. However, if we make meaningful assumptions about the data and about the relationships among such variables as income, consumption, saving, and investment, we can construct models that convey many of the essential workings of an economy. Such models help explain past economic changes, predict future changes, and serve as guides for policy makers. But models can never give results with certainty because they represent the "highlights" of reality rather than the complete picture.

---

6. There is considerable evidence that virtually all mixed economies, including our own, have an "inflationary bias." This means they are inflation-prone. Therefore, a desirable social objective is not only to reduce inflation, but to make it less erratic. People would then be better able to adjust to inflation by altering their asset and liability holdings, thereby minimizing adverse redistributive effects.

For Discussion

1. *Terms and concepts to review:*

business cycles	time series
seasonal fluctuations	econometrics
trend	economic indicators
labor force	general price level
frictional unemployment	demand-pull inflation
cyclical unemployment	cost-push inflation
structural unemployment	Consumer Price Index
involuntary	Producer Price Index
unemployment	money income
inflation	real income

2. If business cycles were recurrent and periodic, would they be easily predictable? Why? What, precisely, would you be able to predict about them?

3. If you were to compare two industries, automobiles and agricultural products, over the course of a business cycle, which would be more stable with respect to (a) output and employment; (b) prices? Explain why.

4. Economists prefer to remove both the seasonal and long-term trend influences from their data before undertaking an analysis of cyclical forces. Although there are no unusual controversies concerning removal of the seasonal factor, there is considerable disagreement over removal of the trend. Can you suggest why?

5. Can you suggest how the interaction of changes in consumption and investment may cause business cycles?

6. What do you suppose are some of the chief difficulties in using leading indicators for forecasting purposes?

7. Is an increasing level of aggregate demand likely to cure the problems of cyclical unemployment and structural unemployment—without encouraging inflation? Explain.

8. Is it better to have full employment with mild inflation or moderate unemployment with no inflation? Explain.

9. "Because of the changing composition of the labor force, a single measure of full employment proves to be an inadequate goal." In view of this statement, what alternatives can you suggest? Discuss.

10. It is often said that our economy has a built-in inflationary bias and is inflation-prone. Can you give reasons to account for this statement?

11. Minimum-wage legislation, despite its good intention, has been called "the most racially discriminating law on the books"? Can you explain why? Can you show, with supply and demand curves, how minimum-wage legislation results in unemployment? What market solution can you suggest to increase employment among low-skilled members of the labor force?

12. "Reduce working hours. Spread the work. That's the way to solve the unemployment problem." So say many critics, union leaders, and social reformers. They argue for a reduction in working time—with no loss of pay—as a cure for unemployment. Do you agree with them?

Issue
Inflation: The 6% Solution

When can you take a friend to dinner at a modest restaurant, hand the waiter a $50 bill, and not get back enough change to leave an appropriate tip? Answer: Pretty soon, if inflationary trends of 6 to 12 percent, or even more, are as common in the future as they have been in the past.

Table 1 shows average prices of some familiar commodities in 1980. If inflation proceeds at an annual rate of "only" 6 percent—the rate often heralded as reasonable—prices by 1990 will have nearly doubled. By the year 2000 they will have more than tripled.

But, you say, your income will be going up accordingly, so you won't be any worse off. *Not true.* Our progressive income tax is such that you pay a larger proportion of any increase in income you receive. Therefore, even if your income keeps up with inflation, your real take-home pay is likely to drop because the government will take away an increasing amount in taxes. This assumes, as has been the case in recent decades, that future tax cuts by Washington will not be enough to compensate for inflation.

Table 2 provides some examples. The projected tax rates are averages based on a wide range of considerations, but the rates are nevertheless reasonable.

Note that even though the attorney's gross earnings figure grows at 6 percent a year, the tax rate grows faster. As a result, the attorney suffers a decline in real income of over $7,000 annually by 1990 and more than $25,000 annually by the year 2000. Even the salesclerk will be worse off; taxes will rise from 15 percent in 1980 to 20 percent by 1990, and to 30 percent by the year 2000.

Conclusion: 6% Is No Solution

How does inflation affect you personally? You can get an idea from Table 3. At a 6 percent rate of inflation, for example, your dollar today will lose half of its value in only 12 years. At higher inflationary rates, the loss will be much faster. Inflation, therefore, hurts all of us to the extent that we are unable to anticipate it and adjust accordingly. Unfortunately, hardly anyone can.

QUESTIONS

1. Suppose that you were able to predict inflation accurately. What would you do to avoid its adverse effects?

2. What are *real assets* as distinguished from *monetary assets*? Is this distinction important in light of your answer to Question 1?

Table 1. WHAT THINGS WILL COST
(rounded to nearest dollar)

Goods and services	1980	Future cost, assuming 6% inflation	
		1990	2000
House	$60,000	$107,460	$192,420
Boat	10,000	17,910	32,070
Automobile	6,000	10,746	19,242
Tuition cost—state college	1,300	2,328	4,002
Two-week vacation	1,000	1,791	3,207
Steak dinner	15	26	56
Haircut	10	18	32
Pizza	4	7	13
Paperback novel	3	5	10
Hamburger, french fries	2	4	6

Table 2. WHAT YOU MAY EARN
(assuming growth of gross earnings at 6% annually)

Occupation	1980	1990	2000
Attorney			
Gross earnings	$40,000	$71,640	$128,300
Taxes	12,000	28,656	64,150
After-tax earnings	28,000	42,984	64,150
Tax rate	30%	40%	50%
Decline in real income		7,164	25,646
Salesclerk			
Gross earnings	$12,000	$21,492	$38,490
Taxes	1,800	4,298	11,547
After-tax earnings	10,200	17,194	26,943
Tax rate	15%	20%	30%
Decline in real income		1,074	5,768

Table 3. PURCHASING POWER OF THE DOLLAR AT VARIOUS RATES OF INFLATION

Years hence	Inflationary rate at:					
	2%	4%	6%	8%	10%	12%
0	$1.00	$1.00	$1.00	$1.00	$1.00	$1.00
2	.96	.92	.89	.86	.83	.80
4	.92	.85	.79	.74	.68	.64
6	.89	.79	.70	.63	.56	.51
8	.85	.73	.63	.54	.47	.40
10	.82	.68	.56	.46	.39	.32
12	.79	.62	.50	.40	.32	.26
14	.76	.58	.44	.34	.26	.20
16	.73	.53	.39	.29	.22	.16

Consumption, Saving, and Investment: Elements of the Theory of Income and Employment

Chapter Preview

Can a predominantly market or capitalistic economy such as ours achieve and maintain economic efficiency—*full employment* of resources?

How did earlier, so-called "classical economists" view the problem of attaining full employment? Are their ideas useful today?

The modern theory of income and employment is built on such fundamental concepts as consumption, saving, and investment. What do these terms mean? What relationships do they involve?

Our mixed economy faces an awesome task. It must find ways to put millions of unemployed people to work. At the same time it must learn how to reduce upward pressures on prices. These are the problems of unemployment and inflation. In a broader sense, as you already know, they are the fundamental problems of efficiency and stability.

To solve these problems, we first need a logical explanation of why they occur. We can do this by developing a body of principles known as "the theory of income and employment." The theory is built on three types of economic activity: consumption, saving, and investment. Each plays a distinctive role in our economy. As you will see, acting in combination they help to determine our society's material well-being. Therefore, they are the foundations upon which much of modern economic policy is built.

The Classical Explanation of Income and Employment

Scientists in 'most disciplines are often inclined to separate traditional from modern viewpoints. Economists are not exceptions—as evidenced by a distinction that is often made between "old" and "new" economics.

The "old" economics, known as *classical economics*, started mainly with Adam Smith. It developed until by the 1930s it was the predominant body of economic theory in the non-Communist world. The *New Economics*, which we think of as "modern economics," started with a British scholar, John Maynard Keynes (pronounced "canes"), in the late 1930s. Since then it has been refined and modified, and its basic analytical tools and methods are now widely used by practically all economists.

But in the social sciences, great theories, like the phenomena they try to describe, rarely remain constant. Today's modern economic ideas represent a broad synthesis of the best thinking from the "old" and the "new" economics, as the following pages and chapters point out.

SAY'S LAW: "SUPPLY CREATES ITS OWN DEMAND"

In the early nineteenth century, a French economist, Jean Baptiste Say, wrote:

> ... a product is no sooner created than it, from that instant, offers a market for other products to the full extent of its own value.... Thus, the mere circumstance of the creation of one product immediately opens a market for other products.

This conclusion has come to be known as *Say's Law*. But the idea has been expressed more pointedly by David Ricardo, a British contemporary of Say and a great pioneer in economic thought:

> No man produces but with a view to consume or sell, and he never sells but with an intention to purchase some other commodity which may be immediately useful to him or which may contribute to future production. By producing, then, he necessarily becomes either the consumer of his own goods, or the purchaser and consumer of the goods of some other person.

Say's Law—whether expressed in its original form by Say or as restated by Ricardo—amounts to saying that *supply creates its own demand*. This occurs because in a specialized, or exchange, economy, as distinct from a self-sufficient, "Robinson Crusoe" economy, people are interdependent. That is, people work at the occupation in which they are relatively most efficient. They then exchange the surplus of what they produce above their own needs for the products of others. Thus, the shoemaker, the butcher, and the baker acquire one another's wares by exchanging the portions of their outputs which they do not consume themselves.

These ideas can be expressed in monetary rather than in barter terms. Thus, the income a person receives from production is spent to purchase goods produced by others. For the economy as a whole, therefore, total income equals total production, and aggregate demand equals aggregate supply. Consequently, any addition to output generates an equal addition to income, which in turn is spent on the added output. Thus:

> It follows from Say's Law that firms will always find it profitable to hire unemployed resources up to the point of full employment. This is true provided that the owners of unemployed resources are willing to be paid no more than their physical productivities justify. If this condition is granted, there can be no prolonged period of unemployment—for two reasons:

> 1. Workers and other resource suppliers will be receiving what they are worth, as measured by the value of their contribution to production.

> 2. The additional income earned from increased production will be spent on purchasing the additional output.

This belief was central to classical economic thought of the nineteenth and early twentieth centuries. It is a belief that is widely held with varying degrees of conviction today. In view of this, what does the classical model really tell us? What are its implications for our economic system? The answers to these questions are fundamental to modern economics.

Essentials of the Classical Theory

The classical model assumes the operation of a free-enterprise, highly competitive economic system. This is a system in which there are many buyers and sellers in both the product and resource markets. It is also a system in which all prices are flexible so that they can quickly adjust upward or downward to changing supplies and demands in the marketplace. In this type of economic system the output and resource markets will automatically adjust to full-employment levels as if guided by an "invisible hand" because *aggregate demand equals aggregate income or output*. Let us examine this idea more closely.

Aggregate Demand = Aggregate Income or Output

We have learned that an economy's aggregate output (GNP) equals its aggregate income (GNI). But the classicists argued that the purpose of earning income is to spend it on output. Hence, the level of *aggregate demand*—the total value of output that all sectors of the economy are willing to purchase—always equals the level of aggregate income or output.

This does not mean that oversupply of some particular items cannot occur. Overproduction of specific commodities can and does occur when business managers misjudge the markets for their goods. But these errors are temporary and are corrected as entrepreneurs shift resources out of production of less profitable commodities into production of more profitable ones. Only *general* overproduction, or a deficiency in aggregate demand, is impossible according to the classical view.

But what if households choose to *save*—that is, not spend a certain proportion of their income on goods and services? Will these savings represent a withdrawal or "leakage" of funds from the income stream? Will aggregate demand then fall below aggregate output or supply, resulting in excess production, increasing unemployment, and decreasing incomes? The classical economists' answer is no, because *all savings are invested*. Let us see why.

All Savings Are Invested

Say's Law tells us that total spending will always be high enough to maintain full employment. Thus, if some people save part of their income, there will always be businesspersons who will borrow those savings and pay a price for them called *interest*. This borrowed money will be invested in capital goods in order to carry on profitable production. In classical theory, therefore, saving by households leads directly to spending by businesses on capital or investment goods. And because aggregate income is always spent, part of it is spent for consumption and part for investment.

What mechanism ensures equality between saving and investment at full employment? The classicist's answer was the interest rate, which they view as a reward for saving. That is, the interest rate is a price that businesses pay households to persuade the latter to consume less in the present so that they can consume more at a later date. The equilibrium rate of interest is determined in a competitive money market where households' supply of savings interacts with businesses' demand for them.

This is illustrated in Chart (a) of Exhibit 1. The model is based on the classical assumption that no household will save (and thereby forgo the pleasure of spending) unless it is offered interest in return. Also, no businessperson will borrow (and thereby pay interest) unless he or she plans to invest. Therefore, a flexible interest rate assures that every dollar saved by households will be borrowed and invested by businesses, thus *automatically* maintaining a full-employment level of aggregate spending.

Exhibit 1
Markets in the Classical Theory of Income and Employment

In the classical model, all markets are assumed to be competitive and all resources mobile. Therefore, prices and quantities are flexible and adjust *automatically* to their full-employment equilibrium levels through the free play of market forces.

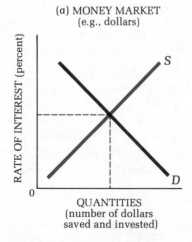
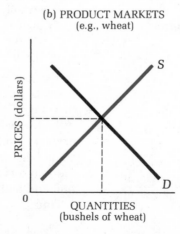
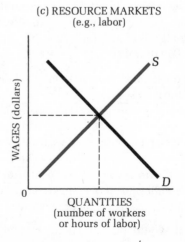

Prices and Wages Are Flexible

But suppose some unemployment *did* develop, causing a decline in aggregate income or purchasing power. Would such a situation be more than temporary? The classicists answered no, because *prices and wages are flexible*. In classical theory, prices in *all* markets—the money market, the product markets, and the resource markets—are assumed to move freely. Therefore, they *automatically* adjust to their individual full-employment equilibrium levels, as shown in Exhibit 1. Thus, if the price in any market is below its particular equilibrium level, the quantity demanded will exceed the quantity supplied. Competition among buyers (demanders) in that market will therefore drive the price up. If the price in any market is above its equilibrium level, the quantity supplied will exceed the quantity demanded. Competition between sellers (suppliers) in that market will therefore drive the price down. At the equilibrium price in each market, the quantity that sellers want to sell is equal to the quantity that buyers want to buy. At these prices *there are no shortages and no surpluses* in any of the product, resource, or money markets. Therefore, there must be full employment and full production throughout the economy.

Classical Conclusion: Capitalism Is a Self-Regulating Economic System

In the classical economists' view it follows that a capitalistic economic system will tend *automatically* toward full employment through the free operation of the price system. Therefore, the functions of government, as Adam Smith emphasized, should be limited to national defense, the administration of justice, the facilitation of commerce, and the provision of certain public works. Adherence to such a policy would establish *laissez-faire* (freedom from government intervention) as the watchword of capitalism. It would place government in an economically neutral position, leaving the economy to allocate its resources optimally as if guided by an "invisible hand."

To summarize:

Classical economics dominated the Western world from the late eighteenth century until the late 1930s. Among its chief proponents were Adam Smith (1723–1790), Jean Baptiste Say (1767–1832), and David Ricardo (1772–1823). It emphasized people's self-interest and the operation of universal economic laws. These would tend automatically to guide the economy toward full-employment equilibrium if the government adheres to a policy of laissez-faire or noninterventionism.

It would be a mistake to infer from the foregoing discussion that all economists of the pre-1930s pre-sented a united classical front. In fact, many economists differed substantially in their beliefs. Thus, some adhered to the classical tradition but advocated government spending programs as short-term measures to stimulate production and employment. Others departed from the classical tradition by adopting socialistic ideologies (i.e., government ownership of the means of production). And still others turned to descriptive studies of the economy based on sociological and legal institutions. However, despite these dissentions from strict orthodox theory, the basic ideas of classicism represented the mainstream of economic thinking prior to the birth of the New Economics in the 1930s.

The Modern (Keynesian) Explanation of Income and Employment

The Great Depression of the 1930s was long and painful. At the bottom of the business cycle in 1933, unemployment in the United States reached almost 13 million, approximately 25 percent of the labor force. For the remainder of the decade it never recovered beyond 8 million, or 14 percent of the labor force. Comparable rates of unemployment existed in the United Kingdom during this period. Such a prolonged and deep depression was contrary to classical thinking. As a result, many economists were inclined to explain the situation away by saying it was the "world" and not the theory that was at fault. For example, one of the most distinguished classicists of that era, Professor Arthur C. Pigou of England's Cambridge University, in a famous book entitled *The Theory of Unemployment* (1933), wrote:

> With perfectly free competition . . . there will always be a strong tendency toward full employment. The implication is that such unemployment as exists at any time is due wholly to the fact that frictional resistances [caused by monopolistic unions and firms maintaining rigid wages and prices] prevent the appropriate wage and price adjustments from being made instantaneously.

A flexible wage and price policy, Pigou and other classical economists contended, would "abolish fluctuations of employment" entirely. In America, many orthodox economists added the proviso that the government under President Roosevelt's administration should also stop interfering with the free operation of the markets through its extensive regulatory legislation and activities.

Thus:

The classicists strongly believed that the economic system *automatically* tends toward full-employment equilibrium. They contended that frictional maladjustments alone are responsible for temporary short-run fluctuations.

In response to this general view—and to Pigou's book in particular—an eminent British scholar named John Maynard Keynes published in 1936 a monumental treatise, *The General Theory of Employment, Interest and Money.* In this book Keynes undermined the classical theory and founded what came to be called the New Economics. (See *Leaders in Economics,* page 122.)

KEYNES AND MODERN MACROECONOMIC THEORY

Much of modern macroeconomic theory is rooted in the work done by Keynes. However, the theory has been greatly refined and extended since then—in many instances by some of Keynes' strongest critics. As a result, most of the major controversial economic issues you read and hear about—taxes, inflation, national debt, unemployment, balance of payments, interest rates, and so on—are analyzed within the framework of modern theory. The remainder of this chapter deals with the elements of this theory as Keynes and his followers developed it. Subsequent chapters will then build on these elements.

How does modern macroeconomic theory—the theory of income and employment determination—contrast with the classical theory?

Aggregate Demand May Not Equal Full-Employment Aggregate Income

Keynesian theory rejects the classical notion that aggregate demand always equals full-employment aggregate income, and that the economic system automatically tends toward its full-employment equilibrium level. Keynesian theory demonstrates that the economic system may be in equilibrium at less than full employment, and may remain so indefinitely.

Changes in aggregate demand play a critical role in the modern (Keynesian) theory. An economy may be operating at a level equal to or below full employment, and may experience a drop in aggregate demand and a consequent decline in real output and resource use. On the other hand, an economy may be operating at a level below full employment and may experience an increase in aggregate demand and a consequent rise in real output and resource use. Further, if aggregate demand continues to increase above full-employment levels, the result will be rising prices and demand-pull inflation—a situation sometimes described as "too many dollars chasing too few goods."

Savers and Investors Are Different People with Different Motivations

An important feature of the modern (Keynesian) theory concerns the roles of saving and investment.

Keynes pointed out that in a primitive economy, saving and investing are undertaken largely by the same groups for the same reasons. But in an advanced economy, saving and investing are undertaken by different groups for different reasons. In our own economy, for example, households such as yours and mine may save for several reasons. Among them: to purchase a new car, finance an education, make a down payment on a house, or pay for a vacation. They may also save to provide for future security, to amass an estate that can be passed on to future generations, or to buy stocks and bonds for income or future profit. And, of course, many households may save simply to accumulate funds without a specific purpose in mind.

Business firms save when they retain some of their profits instead of distributing them to stockholders. Their reasons for saving, however, are different from those of households. Businesses usually save in order to invest in plant, equipment, and inventories; they may also borrow for the same purposes. In any case, they invest primarily on the basis of the rate of profit they anticipate. Thus:

Savers and investors are different people with different motivations. Much of the economy's saving is done by households, whereas its investment is done primarily by businesses on the basis of profit expectations. The amount businesses want to invest fluctuates widely from year to year and is not likely to equal the amount households want to save. The interest rate, therefore, is *not* a mechanism that brings about the equality of saving and investment at full employment, as the classicists assumed.

Prices and Wages Are Not Flexible

Do prices and wages exhibit the flexibility the classicists assumed? The answer is no. Our economy is characterized by big unions and big businesses, and there is great resistance to reductions in prices and wages. We almost always hear of prices and wages going up, but we rarely hear of them going down.

Nevertheless, let us assume for the moment that wages and prices are flexible, and that the fall in wages during a period of unemployment is greater than the fall in prices. This is what the classical economists postulated. If wage decreases are experienced by one firm only, its profits will increase and it will be encouraged to expand its production and employment. But if wage decreases are experienced by all firms in the economy, *real wages* (i.e., money wages relative to the general price level) or general purchasing power will decline. The result is likely to be a further reduction in output and employment instead of the reverse. And if the interest rate happens to be "sticky" rather than flexible, as is often the case, its failure to adjust downward helps to perpetuate or worsen an already depressed situation.

To summarize: A reduction in real wages within a single firm is not likely to affect the overall demand for that firm's product. However, it cannot be assumed that a general reduction in real wages of *all* workers throughout the economy will have no effect on aggregate demand. The classical economists failed to recognize this distinction between the "particular" and the "general," and thereby committed a logical fallacy in their thinking. Can you name the fallacy?

Keynesian Conclusion: Laissez-Faire Capitalism Cannot Ensure Full Employment

In contrast to the classicists, Keynes concluded with the following ideas:

A capitalistic economy provides *no automatic tendency* toward full employment. The levels of aggregate output and employment are determined by the level of aggregate demand, and there is no assurance that aggregate demand will always equal full-employment aggregate income. As aggregate demand increases, so do aggregate output and employment—up to the level of full employment.

Most economists since Keynes have subscribed to these beliefs. In view of this, let us now see what the Keynesian theory says about the concept of *aggregate demand*. This, you recall from the study of national-income accounting, is the sum of consumption demand, private investment demand, government demand for goods and services, and net export demand.

Consumption Demand

Consumption demand is by far the largest component of aggregate demand. What factors determine consumption demand, that is, personal consumption expenditures on goods and services in our economy?

Take your own case. What determines the amount spent by *your* family on goods and services? You can probably think of several factors, but first and foremost is your family's disposable income—the amount it has left after paying personal taxes.

The situation is much the same with other families. *Disposable income is usually the single most important factor affecting a family's consumption expendi-* tures. Other conditions, such as the size of the family, the ages of its members, its past income, and its expectations of future income, will also have some influence.

Although no two families spend their incomes in the same way, some generalizations about family expenditure patterns can be made. These generalizations are known as *Engel's Laws*. They are derived from the work of a German statistician, Ernst Engel, who first conducted such research in 1857. Here is a modernized version of Engel's Laws, based on budgetary studies of family expenditures.

As a family's income increases:

1. The percentage spent on food decreases.

2. The percentage spent on housing and household operations remains approximately constant (except for fuel, light, and refrigeration, which decrease).

3. The percentage spent on all other categories and the amount saved increases (except for medical care and personal care items, which remain fairly constant).

Note that the *total amount spent increases as a family's income increases.* The decreases occur only as a percentage of the total.

THE PROPENSITY TO CONSUME

The relationship between a family's disposable income and its consumption expenditures is illustrated by the schedule in the first two columns of Exhibit 2. The difference between disposable income and consumption is saving, shown in column (3). The first thing to notice is that as disposable income increases, consumption increases and so does saving.

The consumption and saving data are graphed in Exhibit 3. Let us consider the upper chart first. Note that consumption expenditures are measured on the vertical axis and disposable income on the horizontal. Observe also that both axes are drawn to the same scale. Therefore, the 45-degree diagonal is a line along which consumption C is 100 percent of disposable income DI. That is, the ratio $C/DI = 1$.

The consumption curve C is the graph of the data in columns (1) and (2) of the table. The intersection of this curve with the diagonal line is the family's "break-even point." This is the point at which consumption is exactly equal to disposable income. At this level the family is just getting by, neither borrowing nor saving.

To the right of the break-even point the vertical distance representing consumption is less than the horizontal distance denoting disposable income. The difference, saving, is represented by the vertical distance between the consumption line and the diagonal.

Exhibit 2
A Family's Consumption and Saving Schedule
(annual data)

These hypothetical figures show that as a family's disposable income increases, the amount it spends on consumption and the amount it saves also increase. The meanings of the various columns are explained in the text.

HOW DO CONSUMPTION AND SAVING RELATE TO INCOME?

(1)	(2)	(3)	(4)	(5)	(6)	(7)
			Average propensity to consume, APC	Average propensity to save, APS	Marginal propensity to consume, MPC	Marginal propensity to save, MPS
Disposable income (after taxes), DI	Consumption, C	Saving, S (1) − (2)	(2) ÷ (1)	(3) ÷ (1)	Change in (2) / Change in (1)	Change in (3) / Change in (1)
$ 8,000	$ 9,200	−$1,200	1.15	−0.15		
					0.70	0.30
10,000	10,600	− 600	1.06	−0.06		
					0.70	0.30
12,000	12,000	0	1.00	0.00		
					0.70	0.30
14,000	13,400	600	0.96	0.04		
					0.70	0.30
16,000	14,800	1,200	0.93	0.07		
					0.70	0.30
18,000	16,200	1,800	0.90	0.10		
					0.70	0.30
20,000	17,600	2,400	0.88	0.12		
					0.70	0.30
22,000	19,000	3,000	0.86	0.14		
					0.70	0.30
24,000	20,400	3,600	0.85	0.15		

To the left of the break-even point the family is consuming more than its disposable income. The difference is called *dissaving*. How does a family dissave or live beyond its means? Either by spending its previous savings, by borrowing, or by receiving gifts from others (i.e., by being subsidized). Here are some important ideas to remember:

> The level of consumption depends on the level of income (i.e., disposable income). The dependency is such that as income increases, consumption increases, but not as fast as income. This relation between consumption and income is called the *propensity to consume*, or the *consumption function*. The word "function" is thus used here in its mathematical sense. It means a quantity whose value depends on the value of another quantity (e.g., the amount of consumption *depends* on the level of income).

Note that the consumption curve C is the family's propensity-to-consume curve. It assumes that, apart from income, all other factors that may affect consumption remain constant. Do you recall these factors? If not, refresh your memory by referring back to the beginning of this section.

THE PROPENSITY TO SAVE

You know that saving is the difference between income and consumption, and that consumption depends on income. Therefore saving also depends on income. (Keep in mind that the term "income" as used here means disposable income.)

The data on saving in column (3) of Exhibit 2, taken together with column (1), are shown in the graph in the lower panel of Exhibit 3. Here, disposable income is again measured on the horizontal axis, but saving is now scaled vertically. The saving curve S depicts the vertical differences between the diagonal line and the consumption curve in the upper chart.

Leaders in Economics
John Maynard Keynes   1883–1946

Founder of the New Economics

"You have to know that I believe myself to be writing a book on economic theory which will largely revolutionize . . . the way the world thinks about economic problems." So wrote John Maynard Keynes to the Irish wit and author George Bernard Shaw in 1935.

Keynes was right. He did indeed write a book that revolutionized economic thinking. As a result, he became recognized as one of the most brilliant and influential economists of all time. In fact, as one who helped shape the thinking of future generations of scholars, Keynes ranks with Adam Smith and Karl Marx.

Keynes was born in Cambridge, England, the son of a noted economist, John Neville Keynes. The younger Keynes was educated at Eton and Cambridge, where he first majored in mathematics but later turned his attention to philosophy and economics. After college he took a civil service post in the India Office. Later, he returned to England and served as a teaching fellow at Cambridge, where his talents were quickly recognized. He became editor of the *Economic Journal*, Britain's most distinguished economic publication—a position which he held for 33 years.

Many-Sided Genius

To say that Keynes was brilliant is an understatement. He was a genius with diverse talents who combined teaching at Cambridge with an active and highly successful business life in the fields of insurance, investments, and publishing. In addition to his many publications in economics, he wrote a remarkable book on the philosophical foundations of probability which is required reading by graduate students in mathematical logic and philosophy. And he amassed a fortune of

Wide World Photos.

over $2 million by speculating in the international currency and commodity markets. Perhaps most impressive, however, is the fact that he accomplished these feats in his "spare time"; he wrote his mathematics book while employed in government service, and accumulated his fortune by analyzing financial reports and phoning orders to his broker for a half-hour each morning before breakfast.

Keynes' most celebrated work, *The General Theory of Employment, Interest and Money* (1936), is one of the most influential books ever written in economics. Here he made it clear that he was departing significantly from traditional economic theory, which held that there is a natural tendency

for the economy to reach equilibrium at full employment. Indeed, Keynes showed that equilibrium can be reached and maintained at a level of output less than full employment. He thus advocated reduction in the bank interest rate to stimulate investment. He also believed in progressive income taxation to make incomes more equal and thereby increase the percentage of aggregate income that people spend on consumption. And he argued for government investment through public works as a "pump priming" process when private investment expenditures fall off. Today, these and several related ideas are part of a larger family of concepts that make up macroeconomic theory and policy.

Depression vs. Inflation Theory

Nowadays, practically all economists use many of the fundamental theoretical tools and concepts that Keynes developed. However, economists may not always agree on the ways in which those ideas should be implemented in matters of public policy.

For example, most informed observers agree that Keynesian economics works well when applied to deflation and depression. In these situations expenditures and, therefore, purchasing power can be increased to stimulate demand and promote higher employment and production. But the Keynesian model seems less than adequate for coping with inflation. This is especially true if a high level of employment is to be maintained. Consequently, much effort continues to be devoted to developing tools for dealing with these and related problems of today's economy.

Exhibit 3
A Family's Consumption and Saving in Relation to Its Income
(annual data)

The vertical distances show you how much will be consumed and saved at each income level. For example, at an income of $22,000 the amount spent on consumption is $19,000 and the amount saved is $3,000.

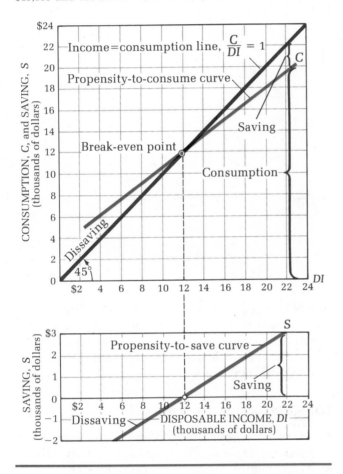

The level of saving depends on the level of income. This relation between saving and income is called the *propensity to save*, or the *saving function*.

Thus, the saving curve S is the family's propensity-to-save curve.

AVERAGE PROPENSITIES TO CONSUME AND TO SAVE

What will the family's *average* consumption be in relation to its income? What will be its *average* amount of saving? The answers are given in columns (4) and (5) of Exhibit 2.

The *average propensity to consume (APC)* is simply the ratio of consumption to income:

$$APC = \frac{\text{consumption}}{\text{income}}$$

The *APC* tells you the proportion of each income level that the family will spend on consumption. Similarly, the *average propensity to save (APS)* is the ratio of saving to income. The *APS* tells you the proportion of each income level that the family will save—that is, will not spend on consumption:

$$APS = \frac{\text{saving}}{\text{income}}$$

For example, at an income level of $20,000, the family will spend 88 cents of each dollar or a total of $17,600. It will save 12 cents of each dollar or a total of $2,400. In other words, the family will spend 88 percent of its income and save 12 percent.

Note that as income increases, *APC* decreases; therefore, *APS* increases because both must total 1 (or 100 percent) at each income level. What can you learn from the fact that *APC* declines with rising incomes? Basically, this tendency confirms the everyday observation that the rich save a larger proportion of their incomes than the poor. You probably would have guessed this without looking at the figures in the table; but they help to fix this important idea more firmly in your mind.

MARGINAL PROPENSITIES TO CONSUME AND TO SAVE

It is important to know the amount of each *extra* dollar of income that the family will spend on consumption, and the amount it will save. These amounts are shown in columns (6) and (7) of Exhibit 2.

The *marginal propensity to consume (MPC)* is the change in consumption resulting from a unit change in income. As you can see from the table, the formula for calculating *MPC* is

$$MPC = \frac{\text{change in consumption}}{\text{change in income}}$$

The *MPC* tells you the *fraction of each extra dollar of income that goes into consumption*. An *MPC* of 0.70, for instance, means that 70 percent of any increase in income will be spent on consumption.

The *marginal propensity to save* (MPS) is the change in saving resulting from a unit change in income:

$$MPS = \frac{\text{change in saving}}{\text{change in income}}$$

The MPS tells you the *fraction of each extra dollar of income that goes into saving.* An MPS of 0.30, for example, means that 30 percent of any increase in income will be saved.

What is the difference between APC and MPC? Between APS and MPS? At any given level of income, the APC relates total consumption to income. On the other hand, the MPC relates a *change* in the amount of consumption to a *change* in income. The "average" may thus be quite different from the "marginal," as you can see from the table. The same kind of reasoning applies to APS and MPS. The "average" and the "marginal" tell you two distinctly different things. Note from the table, however, that just as APC and APS must always total 1 (or 100 percent) at any income *level,* MPC and MPS must always total 1 (or 100 percent) for each *change* in income.

The MPC and MPS are of great practical value, especially when applied at the macroeconomic level. Suppose that the nation is in recession and the MPC for the economy as a whole is 0.70. This means that to increase the volume of consumption by $700 million in order to move the economy closer to full employment, the level of aggregate disposable income must be raised by $1 billion. As shown in later chapters, government can adopt various economic measures to achieve such a goal.

By now you have probably recognized an important idea about MPC. Because it is the change in total consumption resulting from a unit change in income, it measures the _slope_ (steepness) of the consumption function or line. The slope of any straight line is defined as the number of units it changes vertically for each unit of change horizontally. Thus, in Exhibit 4, the line rises 4 units on the vertical axis for a run of 6 units on the horizontal. Therefore, the slope, which is measured by the rise over the run, is 2/3.

Similarly, the MPS measures the slope of the saving line. You should be able to verify that the slope of a straight line is the same at every point. This is why the table shows all values of MPC as equal and all values of MPS as equal. That is, the consumption and saving curves in this example are each straight lines.

TWO KINDS OF CHANGES INVOLVING CONSUMPTION

The consumption function (propensity-to-consume curve) expresses a relation between consumption ex-

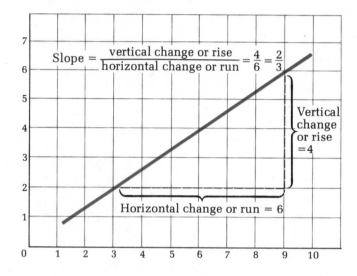

Exhibit 4
Slope of a Line

penditures and income. Your understanding of this concept can serve as a basis for distinguishing between two kinds of variations in consumption. One is called a change in the amount consumed. The other is a change in consumption.

Change in the Amount Consumed

Examine the diagrams in Exhibit 5. In the upper chart any movement along the consumption curve represents a *change in the amount consumed*. The change will consist of an increase in the amount consumed if income rises and a decrease in the amount consumed if income falls. This is indicated by the vertical dashed lines. Thus:

1. A movement to the right always signifies an increase in income and hence a movement upward along the existing C curve.

2. A movement to the left indicates a decrease in income and therefore a movement downward along the existing C curve.

Note also in the lower chart that saving, like consumption, varies directly with income. Therefore, a change in the amount saved—either an increase or decrease—occurs for the same reason as a change in the amount consumed, namely, a change in income.

Exhibit 5
Changes in the Amounts Consumed and Saved

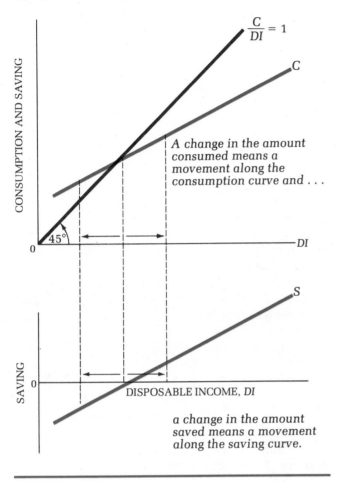

A change in the amount consumed means a movement along the consumption curve and . . .

a change in the amount saved means a movement along the saving curve.

Exhibit 6
Changes in Consumption and Saving

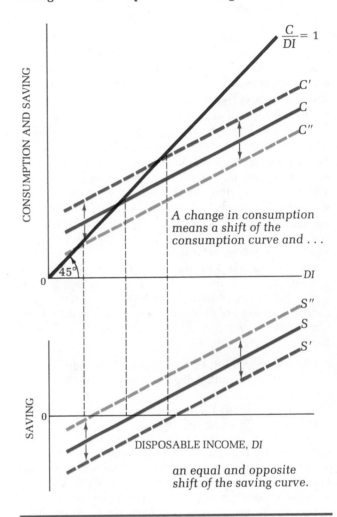

A change in consumption means a shift of the consumption curve and . . .

an equal and opposite shift of the saving curve.

Change in Consumption

A second type of movement, shown in Exhibit 6, is a *change in consumption*. This may take the form of an increase in consumption, whereby the curve shifts to a higher level. Or it may take the form of a decrease in consumption, shown by a shift of the curve to a lower level. An increase in consumption from curve C to curve C' means that at any given level of income, people are now willing to consume more and save less than before. What does a decrease from curve C to curve C'' mean?

As with supply and demand curves, the consumption curve may shift as a result of a change in any one of the "all other" things that were assumed to remain constant when the curve was initially drawn. What are these factors? Some of the more important ones are:

1. The volume of liquid assets (e.g., currency, stocks, bonds, etc.) owned by households.

2. Expectations of future prices and incomes.

3. Anticipations of product shortages (resulting, for example, from wars, strikes, etc.).

4. Credit conditions.

An increase in any one of these factors (and several others you may be able to think of) can cause an increase in consumption and shift the curve upward. Also, a decrease in any one can cause a decrease in consumption and shift the curve downward. Because these factors do not remain constant over the long run, the *true* consumption function for the economy is likely to vary. (See also Exhibit 7.)

Exhibit 7
The Consumption Function: Three Ideas in One Principle

There is general agreement that consumption depends on income. But the nature of the dependency has long intrigued economists. Over the years, three major explanations—called "hypotheses"—have been explored:

Absolute Income Hypothesis A family's consumption depends on its *level* of income—the absolute amount available for spending. This concept of the propensity to consume was the one used by Keynes.

Relative Income Hypothesis A family's consumption depends on its previous peak level of income and/or the relative position that the family occupies along the income scale. In other words, spending behavior is influenced by the highest past income levels to which people become accustomed and by the incomes of other individuals in the same socioeconomic environment.

Permanent Income Hypothesis A family's consumption depends on its anticipated long-run or permanent income, that is, the average income expected to be received over a number of years. In addition, a family's consumption expenditures are approximately proportional to its permanent income.

All three theories fit the definition of the *propensity to consume*—the law stating that consumption increases with income, but not as fast. However, the two latter explanations have been found, for certain purposes, to be significant improvements over the first.

For example, the relative income hypothesis recognizes that people try to maintain their previous higher standard of living when their incomes decline. The theory also acknowledges that a family's consumption patterns are influenced by social pressures as well as by income.

The permanent income hypothesis helps explain why people's expectations of their long-run income determines their purchases of large-expenditure items, such as houses, expensive jewelry, and furs.

As you can see from these theories, consumer behavior is strongly affected by psychological as well as economic factors.

Private Investment Demand

"The economy turns on capital investment, and capital investment turns on confidence, and confidence turns on certainty, and certainty turns on predictability." These words, spoken by a major corporation president, suggest that investment is of critical importance to our economy.

Investment, of course, means spending by business firms on physical capital, such as additions to plant, equipment, and inventories. As you know, the private sector's consumption demand and investment demand are the two major components of aggregate demand. Therefore, having studied consumption demand, we must now turn our attention to investment demand.

INVESTMENT AND RATE OF RETURN

If you were a business executive, what would determine your decision to invest? The fundamental answer, of course, is your profit expectation. If you think a new machine would add to your profit, you will try to purchase it. If you believe that an additional wing on your factory would yield greater profits, you will try to build it.

In the business world, the money you get back each year from an investment, in relation to the investment, is called the rate of return. It is always measured in percentage terms. Thus, if you buy land for $1,000 and rent it out for $100 annually, the rate of return on your investment is 10 percent:

$$\text{rate of return} = \frac{\text{annual receipts}}{\text{investment}}$$

$$= \frac{\$100}{\$1,000} = 0.10 \text{ or } 10\%$$

Instead of using the expression "rate of return," economists employ the phrase "marginal efficiency of investment." Although it has approximately the same meaning, it is a more precise term—as you will come to appreciate.

These ideas are worth repeating for emphasis.

The profit from an addition to capital is usually expressed as a percent or rate of return on the investment. Economists call the expected rate of return on an investment the *marginal efficiency of investment (MEI)*. More precisely, it is the expected rate of return over cost of an additional unit of a capital good. Thus, you might have an *MEI* or expected rate of return of 25 percent for one type of investment, 15 percent for another, and so on.

UNDERSTANDING THE MEI

You can gain a better understanding of the *MEI* by studying its graph in Chart (a) of Exhibit 8.

The chart shows that at any given time, a business firm is faced with a number of investment opportunities. These may include renovating its existing plant, purchasing new machines, acquiring additional power facilities, or installing a computer system. Each

Exhibit 8
Investment Demand in the Private Sector

(a) MARGINAL EFFICIENCY OF INVESTMENT FOR AN
INDIVIDUAL FIRM: A FIRM'S INVESTMENT
DEMAND CURVE

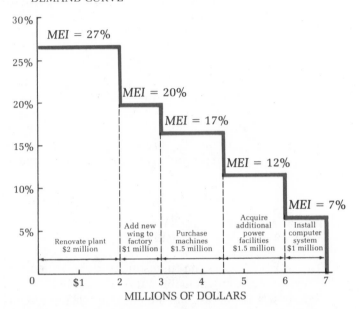

(b) MARGINAL EFFICIENCY OF INVESTMENT FOR
ALL FIRMS: THE PRIVATE SECTOR'S
INVESTMENT DEMAND CURVE

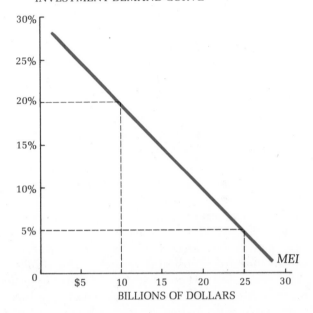

Chart (a).   *The solid stepped line is an individual firm's
MEI (or rate-of-return) curve. It shows the amount of investment the firm will undertake at various interest rates or
costs of funds at any given time. The MEI curve is thus the
firm's demand curve for investment.*

Chart (b).   *The MEI curve for all firms is a smooth continuous line obtained by summing the individual MEI curves.
It shows the total amount of private investment that will be
undertaken at various interest rates or costs. Thus, the MEI
curve in this chart is the economy's aggregate demand
curve for private investment.*

project competes for a firm's limited funds. However,
some projects are expected to be more profitable, that
is, have a higher rate of return (or *MEI*) than others. In
view of this, which projects should management select? Or, to put it differently, how much investment
expenditure should management undertake?

The first step in answering this question is to imagine that the managers of a firm *rank* alternative investment projects in decreasing order of their *MEIs*.
In the diagram, each project's cost and corresponding
MEI are shown. In Chart (*a*), the most attractive investment open to the firm is the renovation of its plant
at a cost of $2 million. For this, the firm anticipates a
rate of return or *MEI* of 27 percent. The next most
profitable investment is the addition of a new wing to
its factory at a cost of $1 million, for which the *MEI* is
20 percent. Each remaining investment project is interpreted similarly. If we assume that the risks of loss

associated with these investments are the same, the
descending order of *MEIs* suggests two things:

1. Fewer investment opportunities are available to a
firm at relatively higher, than at lower, rates of return.
For example, it is harder to find investments yielding,
say, 25 percent than 10 percent.

2. A firm will tend to choose those investment projects having the highest *MEIs*. Therefore, a project
with a higher anticipated rate of return over cost is
likely to be selected over a project with a lower one.

COST OF FUNDS: THE RATE OF INTEREST

Once the *MEI* (or rate of return) on an investment has
been estimated, the next step is to establish the cost of
funds needed to finance the investment. Only then can

you decide whether the investment is worth undertaking.

The cost of funds needed to finance an investment is expressed as a *percentage*. Thus, if a business firm borrows money for investment and agrees to pay an annual interest charge of, say, 10 percent, then that is the firm's cost of funds. Alternatively, if the firm uses its own money instead of borrowing, the interest return sacrificed by not lending the money in the financial markets (through the purchase of bonds or other securities) may be thought of as the company's cost of funds. Thus:

> The *MEI* and the cost of funds are each quoted in percentage terms. Therefore, they can be easily compared. This makes it possible to determine the amount of investment that will take place.

THE MEI AND THE INTEREST RATE

How much investment will the firm undertake? To answer this, we must understand that at any given time there is an interest rate in the market which represents the current cost of funds to the firm. It follows that a higher interest cost will mean a lower expected return and therefore a smaller volume of investment. Conversely, a lower interest cost will mean a higher expected return and hence a larger volume of investment. We may conclude that in general terms:

> Investment by a firm occurs when the *MEI* (expected rate of return) on an addition to investment exceeds the rate of interest or cost of funds that is incurred in making the investment.

For example, look again at Chart (a) of Exhibit 8. The graph shows that at an interest cost of, say, 13 percent, this particular firm would demand $4.5 million for investment. Of this amount, $2 million would be spent on renovating its plant in anticipation of a return or *MEI* of 27 percent. In addition, $1 million would be allocated to a new wing for its factory for an expected *MEI* of 20 percent. And $1.5 million would be used to buy new machines in anticipation of an *MEI* of 17 percent. If the interest cost should fall to 6 percent, the firm will demand an *additional* $2.5 million, or a *total* of $7 million. The extra amount would be invested in the next two projects—power facilities and a computer system. In general, therefore, the firm's total demand for investment funds depends on its *MEI* relative to the interest rate or cost of funds.

This analysis leads to two important principles. *At any given time:*

1. A demand curve relates the quantities of a commodity that buyers would be willing and able to purchase at various prices. For business investments, the prices are interest rates (costs of funds) to business firms. Hence, the *MEI* curve shows the amounts of investment that a firm would be willing and able to undertake at various interest rates. This is illustrated by the solid irregular line in Exhibit 8, Chart (a). It follows that *a firm's MEI curve is its demand curve for investment.*

2. Each firm's own *MEI* curve is based on its particular investment needs and expectations. If the individual *MEI* curves are summed horizontally, we get the *MEI* curve for all firms in the economy. As a result, the irregularities disappear, giving a smooth continuous line like the one in Exhibit 8, Chart (b). *The aggregate MEI curve depicts total private investment demand at different rates of interest.* For example, at an interest rate of 20 percent, the amount of private investment would be $10 billion. If the interest rate fell to 5 percent, the amount of private investment would increase to $25 billion.

DETERMINANTS OF THE MEI: SHIFTS OF THE CURVE

The *MEI* curve is an investment demand curve. Therefore, like any demand curve, it may shift to the right or left as the result of a change in one or more of the factors that determine it. At least four factors are particularly important:

1. **Expected Product Demand**   To businesses, the *expected* net return on an investment will depend largely on the demand that is anticipated for the product produced by the investment. For example, if you are a shoe manufacturer, your expected *MEI* for shoe machinery will be influenced by your anticipated demand for shoes. Similarly, for the economy as a whole, the expected return on new investment will be influenced by business executives' anticipations of total consumer spending on the products of businesses.

2. **Technology and Innovation**   Advances in technology and the introduction of new products generally require the construction of new plants or the installation of new equipment. This stimulates the demand for additional capital.

3. **Cost of New Capital Goods**   Changes in the cost of new plant or equipment affect business firms' demand for them. Thus, a rise in the cost of new capital goods shifts the *MEI* curve to the left; a fall in cost shifts the curve to the right.

4. **Corporate Income Tax Rates**   Businesses are interested in expected rates of return on investment expenditures *after* allowances for corporation income taxes. Hence, an increase in the tax rates, other things being equal, shifts the *MEI* curve to the left; a decrease in the tax rates shifts the curve to the right.

These, as well as other economic and psychological conditions, affect businesses' expected rates of return on investment. Because one or more of these factors is always changing, the *MEI* curve is continually shifting either to the right or to the left. As a result, the level of private investment in the economy fluctuates widely over the years, as shown in Exhibit 9.

Indeed:

Fluctuation in private investment is the single most important cause of fluctuations in income and employment. This, in turn, is the major reason for prosperities and recessions.

Government Demand and Net Foreign Demand

The remaining components of aggregate demand stem from government and from international sources. Government demand, which consists of public investment, depends to a large extent on public needs (such as highways, schools, and welfare) and on defense requirements. The volume of government de-

mand is independent of profit expectations and, beyond the minimum levels required by society, is determined at will by government. No scientific law or guiding set of principles exists to predict changes in the level of public investment.

Net foreign demand is the difference between our exports and our imports. In our economy, this difference is relatively minor. Indeed, net foreign demand typically constitutes a very small percentage of expenditures on GNP. Therefore, we may neglect this source of demand for purposes of income and employment analysis.

Conclusion: Reviewing the Basic Relationships

You now have the basic building blocks necessary for understanding the elementary theory of income and employment. This theory will be developed further in the following chapters. In the meantime, you can test your knowledge of the basic relationships explained thus far by making sure you understand the equations presented in Exhibit 10.

Exhibit 9
The Instability of Private Investment

The *MEI* curve is continually shifting owing to changes in the factors that determine it.

As a result, private investment spending fluctuates widely over the years.

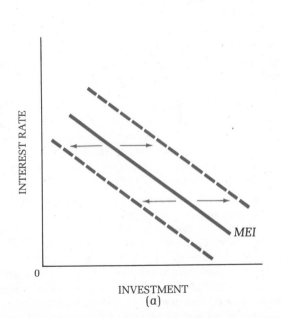

(a)

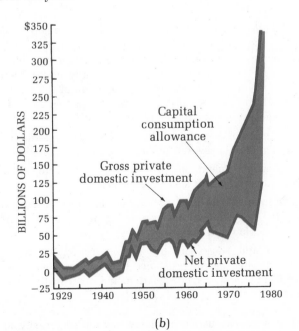

(b)

Exhibit 10
Some Key Relationships in the Theory of Income and Employment

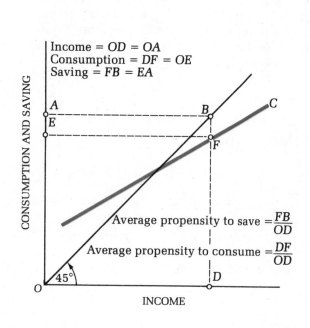

Income = OD = OA
Consumption = DF = OE
Saving = FB = EA

Average propensity to save = $\dfrac{FB}{OD}$

Average propensity to consume = $\dfrac{DF}{OD}$

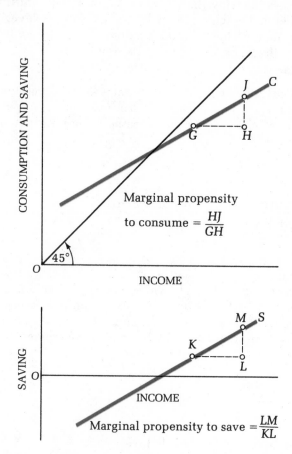

Marginal propensity to consume = $\dfrac{HJ}{GH}$

Marginal propensity to save = $\dfrac{LM}{KL}$

What You Have Learned

1. The *classical* theory of income and employment holds that in a competitive capitalistic system, supply creates its own demand: aggregate demand equals aggregate income or output. Therefore, the economy automatically tends toward full employment through the free operation of the market system. In this system, prices, wages, and interest rates are free to adjust to their full-employment levels.

2. The *modern* (Keynesian) theory of income and employment is rooted in several fundamental ideas. Among them:

○ Aggregate demand may be greater than, equal to, or less than full-employment aggregate income.

○ The interest rate need not equate intended saving and intended investment, because these are done by different people for different purposes.

○ Prices and wages are not flexible—especially on the downside—because of resistance by business monopolies, unions, minimum-wage legislation, and other institutional forces.

For these reasons, the economy may not necessarily adjust itself to full-employment equilibrium.

3. The propensity to consume, or consumption function, expresses a relationship between consumption and income. The relationship, based on observation and experience, is such that as income increases, consumption increases, but not as fast as income.

4. At any given level of income, the average propensity to consume (APC) is the proportion of income spent on consumption. Similarly, the average propensity to save is the proportion of income saved. Therefore, $APC + APS = 1$ (or 100 percent). Out of any given increase in income, the marginal propensity to consume (MPC) is the proportion of the increase spent on consumption. Similarly, the marginal propensity to save is the proportion of the increase saved. Hence, $MPC + MPS = 1$ (or 100 percent).

5. A *change in the amount consumed* means a movement along the consumption curve due to a change in income. A *change in consumption* means a shift of the entire consumption curve to a new level. This occurs because of a change in one or more of the "all other" things that are assumed to be constant when the curve is initially drawn. These factors include the volume of liquid assets owned by households, expectations of future prices and income, anticipations of product shortages, and credit conditions.

6. Investment demand, like consumption and saving, is a major variable in income and employment theory. The expected rate of return on an investment is called the marginal efficiency of investment *(MEI)*. Investment occurs when the *MEI* exceeds the rate of interest or cost of funds that is incurred in making the investment. In general, private investment spending depends on the profit expectations of businesses. These expectations are determined by such factors as expected product demand, the rate of technology and innovation, cost of new capital goods, and corporate income tax rates. For these reasons, private investment tends to be highly volatile over the years and is the major cause of fluctuations in economic activity.

For Discussion

1. *Terms and concepts to review:*

   classical economics
   New Economics
   Say's Law
   aggregate demand
   aggregate supply
   saving
   interest
   consumption
   Engel's Laws
   dissaving
   propensity to consume
   propensity to save
   average propensity
     to consume
   average propensity
     to save

   marginal propensity
     to consume
   marginal propensity
     to save
   slope
   change in amount
     consumed
   change in consumption
   absolute income
     hypothesis
   relative income
     hypothesis
   permanent income
     hypothesis
   investment
   marginal efficiency of
     investment

2. Of what significance are interest rates and prices in the classical model?

3. Does Say's Law apply to *individual* goods? Explain.

4. Why do people save? Why do businesses invest?

5. During a recession, a firm will probably increase its sales if it cuts its prices, and it will reduce its costs if it cuts its wages. It follows that the whole economy will be better off if all firms do this. True or false? Comment.

6. Express Engel's Laws in terms of the average propensity to consume *(APC)*.

7. Why does the *APC* differ from the *MPC? APS* from *MPS?*

8. What factors other than income are likely to be most important in determining consumption?

9. Complete the following table on the assumption that 50 percent of any increase in income is spent on consumption. Sketch the graphs of consumption and saving. Label all curves.

DI	C	S	APC	APS	MPC	MPS
$100	$150					
200						
300						
400						
500						
600						

10. Would you expect expenditures on consumer durable goods to fluctuate more widely than expenditures on consumer nondurable goods? Explain your answer.

11. What would be the effect on aggregate consumption if social welfare expenditures on public hospitals, parks, medical care, and so on, were financed entirely by our progressive income tax system? Does it make any difference if there are tax loopholes?

12. How would you distinguish between a "change in the amount invested" and a "change in investment"? Explain.

Portfolio
The Classical Economists: Adam Smith's "Sons" and "Daughters"

Dictionaire de l'Economie Politique, Paris: Librairie de Guillaumin, 1864.

Adam Smith

"I am a beau only to my books," remarked Adam Smith. Little did the shy, absentminded scholar suspect that though he would never marry, and probably never have any love affairs, his offspring would include numerous "children" and "grandchildren."

A Scottish professor of philosophy at the University of Glasgow, Adam Smith's masterpiece, *The Wealth of Nations* (1776), marked the beginning of *classical economics*. This body of thought dominated the Western world during the nineteenth and early twentieth centuries. Classical economists typically emphasized people's self-interest, and the operation of universal economic laws. These laws tend automatically to guide the economy toward full-employment equilibrium if the government adheres to a policy of laissez-faire or noninterventionism.

During the nineteenth century these ideas, initiated by Adam Smith, were refined and expanded by more than a dozen of his "sons" and "daughters." Among them were seven who, for different reasons, are especially worthy of mention.

Jean Baptiste Say (1767–1832)
"*Supply creates its own demand.*" This was the famous Law of Markets expounded by the French economist

Jean Baptiste Say, in his book, *Treatise on Political Economy* (1803). This work presented the first popular and systematic presentation of Adam Smith's ideas. As a result, it established Say as one of the leading economists of the early nineteenth century.

Say's Law became central to classical economic thinking. In modern terminology the Law meant simply that the level of aggregate output (GNP) always equaled the level of aggregate income (GNI). This income enabled society to buy (i.e., demand) the output produced. Therefore, general overproduction of goods (due to a deficiency in aggregate demand) was impossible. However, overproduction of specific commodities could and would occur when businesses misjudged the markets for their goods. But such errors could only be temporary and would be corrected as entrepreneurs strive to fulfill consumers' preferences by shifting resources out of the production of unprofitable goods and into the production of profitable ones.

Say's Law was occasionally challenged by some nineteenth-century dissenters. However, it took almost a century and a half for the Law of Markets to be put to rest. This was done by John Maynard Keynes in *The General Theory of Employment, Interest and Money* (1936).

Dictionaire de l'Economie Politique, Paris: Librairie de Guillaumin, 1864.

Jean Baptiste Say

Brown Brothers.

Thomas Malthus

Thomas Robert Malthus (1766–1834)
As the eighteenth century drew to a close, England found itself facing mounting social problems. Among them were widespread poverty, the growth of urban slums, and massive unemployment. These social problems resulted from economic dislocations caused by years of war with France. In addition, the factory system of production had begun, and was displacing numerous workers.

It befell a hitherto unknown English clergyman, Thomas Robert Malthus, to explain these problems. In his famous *Essay on Population* (1798, revised 1803), he expounded the belief that population would tend to outrun the food supply. The result would be a bare subsistence level of survival for the laboring class. This prophecy, of course, has become a stark reality in many of the overcrowded, poor countries of the world.

Malthus also contributed significantly to economic thought. In his *Principles of Political Economy* (1820), he developed the concept of "effective demand," which he defined as the level of aggregate demand necessary to maintain full production. If effective demand declined, he said, overproduction would result. Malthus thus not only disagreed with Say on the Law of Markets, but anticipated the Keynesian concept of full-employment aggregate demand by more than a century.

David Ricardo (1772–1823)

Generally considered to be the greatest of the classical economists, David Ricardo was the first to view the economy as an analytical model. That is, he saw the economic system as an elaborate mechanism with interrelated parts. His task was to study the system and to discover the laws that determine its behavior. In so doing, Ricardo formulated theories of value, wages, rent, and profit which, although not entirely original, were for the first time stated completely, authoritatively, and systematically. Portions of these theories became the basis of many subsequent writings by later scholars, including Marx and Keynes.

Ricardo, a businessman rather than academician, wrote a number of brilliant papers. His ideas were largely incorporated in his major work, *Principles of Political Economy and Taxation* (1817). The book was an immediate success, and attracted many disciples. As a result, Ricardo's influence became pervasive and lasting. Indeed, Ricardian economics became a synonym for classical political economy (or "classical economics," as we call it today). Fifty years were to pass before that influence waned.

Like his predecessors, Ricardo was mainly concerned with the forces that determine the production of an economy's wealth and its distribution among the various classes of society. But he was not only a "pure" theorist, as were some of the other classical economists. He also made major government policy recommendations concerning the dominant social and economic problems of his day. As a result, many of Ricardo's ideas have become pillars of economics and are as relevant today as when he first expressed them.

John Stuart Mill (1806–1873)

Known equally well as a political philosopher and as an economist, John Stuart Mill was the last of the major classical economists. His great two-volume treatise, *Principles of Political Economy* (1848), was a masterful synthesis of classical ideas. As a consequence, the book became a standard text in economics for several decades. Numerous students in Europe and America obtained their knowledge of economics from this basic work. So, too, did a number of American presidents—including Abraham Lincoln—although they did not always apply correctly the principles learned.

Mill's major objective was economic reform. Although he believed in laissez-faire, he went beyond the "natural law of political economy." He did so by advocating worker education, democratic producer cooperatives, taxation of unearned gains from land, redistribution of wealth, shorter working days, improvements in working conditions, and social control of monopoly. These measures, Mill felt, would assure to the individual worker the benefits of his or her contribution to production without violating the "immortal principles" of economics laid down by Ricardo.

It is easy to see why contemporaries of Mill often labeled him a socialist. In reality, however, he believed too strongly in individual free-

Culver Pictures, Inc.

John Stuart Mill

dom to advocate major government involvement in the economy. By today's standards Mill probably would be classified as a moderate conservative.

Jane Haldimand Marcet (1769–1858)

In addition to his four famous "sons" (and to many others who were not so famous), Adam Smith had three "daughters" who, in the nineteenth century, distinguished themselves in the classical tradition. Their fame, however, rests on their achievements in economic education—the teaching of economics—rather than on the formulation of economic principles. As Dorothy Thomson of City University of New York has remarked, "At a time when it was considered unfeminine for women to show that they have brains, it required courage for anyone to attempt to break the mold."

The first woman to break the mold was Jane Haldimand Marcet. In 1816, she published one of several economics books, *Conversations on Political Economy*. In this and subsequent works she conveyed in dialogue form the teachings of her predecessors and contemporaries—Smith, Say, Malthus, and Ricardo. Marcet thus became one of the first popular synthesizers of economic ideas. In doing so, she established an original approach to economic education and to the

Historical Pictures Service.

David Ricardo

writing of elementary-school textbooks that many teachers and writers subsequently followed.

Harriet Martineau (1802–1876)

Among the many people influenced by Jane Marcet's *Conversations,* there was one who saw in it the possibility of conveying the basic principles of economics in yet another lively dimension. That person was Harriet Martineau. To her, economics was more than a collection of principles. It was a living experience conveyed through the "natural workings of social life."

This belief led to the publication of her pioneering book, *Illustrations of Political Economy* (1834). Unlike any prior work in economics, this one was written in narrative form, almost like a collection of short stories, and was illustrated throughout with applications. The basic principles of economics were thus integrated with real-life experiences instead of being taught separately. Today the teaching of many business and some economics courses by the "case method" owes much of its success to the pathbreaking approach initially established by Harriet Martineau.

Millicent Garrett Fawcett (1847–1929)

The last great synthesis of classical economics was written by John Stuart Mill in 1848. This huge, two-volume

Culver Pictures, Inc.

Harriet Martineau

Culver Pictures, Inc.

Millicent Garrett Fawcett

work, however, was not the kind of book to be read and absorbed easily. What was needed was a more concise and simplified version—one that would present the most important principles of economics in a brief and readily understandable way.

It fell to Millicent Garrett Fawcett to write that book. A strong supporter of women's rights, she and her husband (a professor of political economy at Cambridge University) were close friends and admirers of Mill. Her *Political Economy for Beginners* (1870), based on Mill's treatise, was an enormous success. It went through 10 editions—an average of one every four years—thus ranking as one of the most enduring textbooks in publishing history.

In subsequent years Fawcett published a number of other books—two of them dealing with economic principles and issues. In these, as in the successive editions of her *Political Economy for Beginners,* she analyzed and interpreted important economic issues of her time. Her viewpoints, however, were always "classical," with an emphasis on the desirability of social reform in the spirit that John Stuart Mill would have advocated. As stated in her text, "The present system does not work so well as to be absolutely incapable of improvement . . . we ought to be ready to admit that some improvement is necessary in a community in which a considerable proportion of the population are either paupers or on the brink of pauperism."

Conclusion: Many "Grandchildren," Too

In today's terminology, it would be correct to say that the classical economists tended to be mostly concerned with macroeconomic problems. But in the 1870s, approximately 100 years after the appearance of *The Wealth of Nations,* economic thinking began undergoing a revolutionary change. A new point of view and a powerful new tool called "marginal" analysis came into existence. You have already learned about the marginal propensity to consume and the marginal propensity to save. These are only two of many marginal concepts that abound in economics.

The new view that was born in the 1870s is known as "neoclassical economics." It became the foundation of today's microeconomics. In general, neoclassical economists revised, refined, and extended many classical concepts and developed numerous new ones as well. The founders of, and contributors to, neoclassical economics, many of whose ideas are studied in modern microeconomics, may therefore be thought of as Adam Smith's "grandchildren."

Neoclassical economics dominated Western thought for seven decades—from the 1870s to the 1930s. In 1936, Keynes' great treatise, *The General Theory of Employment, Interest and Money,* gave birth to modern macroeconomics. Since then, enormous advances have been made both in macro- and in microeconomics, providing much deeper insights into how our economic system operates. However, many of the same problems that have always concerned economists are still with us. This suggests that in economics as in other social sciences, it is not usually the problems themselves that change; rather, it is our understanding of them that changes.

Chapter 8

Income and Employment Determination

Chapter Preview

How do consumption and investment combine to determine an equilibrium level of income and employment?

What influences do changes in net investment have on the level of income? Is it possible for income to change by some multiple of the change in investment?

How do changes in saving, when not offset by changes in investment, affect the level of income and output?

What pressures, either inflationary or deflationary, are created in the economy when total spending on consumption and investment fails to correspond with full-employment levels?

You have already learned that the crucial factor in determining whether we live in a state of full employment or a state of unemployment is the level of investment. The reasons for this will become increasingly evident in the following pages, where the level of investment is discussed in conjunction with the levels of consumption and saving. This will enable you to see how the three variables interact to bring about equilibrium in the economy as a whole.

After completing this chapter you will be better able to analyze the way in which economic fluctuations arise, and to evaluate government policies designed to minimize them. Those policies are of great importance. They help determine whether our economy will achieve the goals of full employment, price stability, and economic growth.

The Basic Model of Income and Employment

The time has come to construct a model that relates the concepts of consumption, saving, and investment. The model will show how these variables interact to determine the level of income and employment in an economy.

The model to be constructed is "basic" in that it focuses on the barest essentials. That is, it covers only the household and business sectors while neglecting for the time being the public and foreign sectors. In this way, as in earlier chapters, you can learn how the simplest system works before we introduce additional factors that make the model more representative of the real world. Despite its simplicity, however, the model is by no means an oversimplification of reality. Indeed, it sheds considerable light on some fundamental and rather complex economic problems.

STRUCTURE OF THE MODEL

We begin by examining the structure of the model shown in Exhibit 1. The explanation accompanying the table should be read carefully because it describes the meanings of the columns and their relationships. Once these are understood you can turn your attention to Exhibit 2—the graphs of the data in Exhibit 1.

Exhibit 1
Determination of Income and Employment Equilibrium
(hypothetical economy, billions of dollars)

(1)	(2)	(3)	(4)	(5)	(6)	(7)	(8)
Aggregate supply (output = income),* NNP = DI	Level of employment (millions)	Consumption, C	Saving, S (1) − (3)	Net investment, I	Aggregate demand, AD (3) + (5)	Inventory accumulation (+) or depletion (−) (1) − (6) or (4) − (5)	Direction of income and employment
$100	30	$140	− $ 40	$40	$180	− $80	increase
200	35	220	− 20	40	260	− 60	increase
300	40	300	0	40	340	− 40	increase
400	45	380	20	40	420	− 20	increase
500	**50**	**460**	**40**	**40**	**500**	**0**	**equilibrium**
600	55	540	60	40	580	+ 20	decrease
700	60	620	80	40	660	+ 40	decrease
800	65	700	100	40	740	+ 60	decrease
900	70	780	120	40	820	+ 80	decrease

* Includes only the private sector (households and firms), not the public sector (government) or the foreign sector. Also, households are assumed to be the sole source of saving. Therefore, NNP as a measure of aggregate supply equals NI, PI, and DI because there are no taxes, transfer payments, and so on (i.e., there is no government sector). Thus, the total income received by households (DI) equals the net value of the economy's output (NNP).

EXPLANATION OF THE TABLE:

Columns (1) and (2)   It is *assumed* that for every level of aggregate supply or output there is a corresponding level of employment. Further, these variables are directly related: As aggregate supply increases, employment increases; as aggregate supply decreases, employment decreases. (NOTE The assumption of a close relationship between output and employment is both plausible and useful for our present model. However, some exceptions will be noted in later chapters.)

Columns (3) and (4)   Consumption and saving vary directly with income [column (1)]. It is useful to think of consumption and saving as the amounts which households *plan* or *intend* to consume and save at each income level.

Column (5)   Net investment is used rather than gross investment because we are dealing with NNP in column (1) rather than GNP as a measure of the economy's output. (You should recall that net investment equals gross private domestic investment minus capital consumption allowance; actual figures are found in the front endpapers of this book.) As explained in the text, the level of net investment is *assumed* to be independent of, and therefore constant in relation to, aggregate supply [column (1)].

Column (6)   Aggregate demand is simply the sum of intended consumption and investment at each level of income, column (1). Aggregate demand thus denotes total desired spending on output, or, in other words, the total amount of consumption and investment that all sectors of the economy *plan* to undertake at each income level.

Columns (7) and (8)   The change in inventory is the difference between aggregate supply and aggregate demand, or between saving and investment. As explained in the text, the change in inventory level tends toward equilibrium— that is, zero *unplanned* or undesired accumulation or depletion. When that happens, income and employment are also in equilibrium, with no tendency to change.

Exhibit 2
Determination of Income and Employment Equilibrium
(based on data in Exhibit 1)

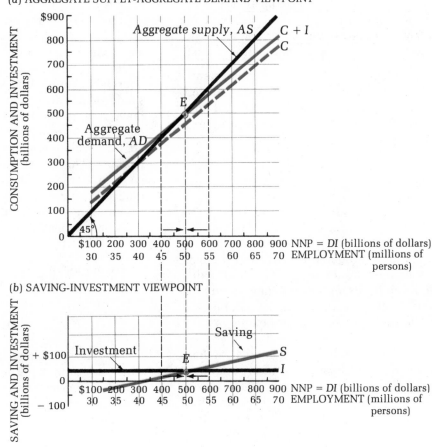

(a) AGGREGATE SUPPLY-AGGREGATE DEMAND VIEWPOINT

(b) SAVING-INVESTMENT VIEWPOINT

Upper chart		Lower chart
	At the equilibrium point E:	
Aggregate supply equals aggregate demand	*and*	saving equals investment
	To the right of E:	
Aggregate supply exceeds aggregate demand	*and*	saving exceeds investment
	To the left of E:	
Aggregate demand exceeds aggregate supply	*and*	investment exceeds saving

Several important features of these charts should be noted:

Chart (a) depicts both aggregate supply and aggregate demand. The graph of aggregate supply is the 45° line. It shows the amount of total output (consisting of consumption and investment goods), measured on the vertical axis, that will be made available for sale at each level of net national product (NNP), shown on the horizontal axis. The graph of aggregate demand shows the amount that will be spent for consumption

and investment (measured on the vertical axis) at each level of income (measured on the horizontal axis).

Charts (a) and (b) show that the graphs of consumption and saving vary directly with income. This is what you would expect from your knowledge of the propensities to consume and save.

Chart (b) also depicts the graph of net investment—a horizontal line. Why is net investment the same at all levels of aggregate supply? As emphasized in the previous chapter:

The investment plans of businesses depend on the marginal efficiency of investment *(MEI)* relative to the interest rate. The *MEI* is determined by such factors as expected product demand, the rate of technology and innovation, the cost of new capital goods, and corporate income tax rates. Therefore, the level of investment that businesses *plan* or *intend* to undertake is assumed to remain constant in relation to output. This level, however, varies widely over time, as we have already seen.

This assumption of a constant level of investment with respect to output plays a fundamental role in modern economics. Later, the assumption will be modified to permit the introduction of more complex considerations.

THE EQUILIBRIUM LEVEL OF INCOME AND EMPLOYMENT

We now have the information needed to interpret the model. The question we want to answer is: *What will be the equilibrium levels of income and employment—and why?* In other words, where will the level of output and the corresponding level of employment finally settle?

Columns (7) and (8) of Exhibit 1 point out that, at the *equilibrium* level of output, business firms are holding the precise level of inventory they desire. That is, at the equilibrium level, businesses are neither accumulating nor depleting their stock. This is because the factor determining the change in inventory, namely, the difference between aggregate supply and aggregate demand, or between planned saving and investment, is zero. The equilibrium point E in the charts of Exhibit 2 depicts these notions graphically. The vertical line shows that in our hypothetical economy equilibrium occurs at an output level of $500 billion and an employment level of 50 million persons. We have thus answered the *what* part of the question above. Now let us answer the *why*.

The best way to understand why income and employment tend toward equilibrium is to ask yourself what happens when they are not in equilibrium. For example, suppose that NNP or *DI* is greater than $500 billion—say, $600 billion. This means that businesses are paying $600 billion in the form of wages, rent, interest, and profit. At the same time, the corresponding level of total spending or aggregate demand, $C + I$, which is the amount that business firms are taking in, is $580 billion. As you can see from both the table and charts, aggregate supply exceeds aggregate demand, and the amount that households intend to save exceeds the amount that businesses intend to invest. Therefore, businesses find their sales to be less than

anticipated. This imbalance causes firms to accumulate inventories beyond desired levels, so managers cut back on production and lay off workers. As a result, output, income, and employment decrease toward their equilibrium levels as shown by the arrows in the charts.

Conversely, at any output less than the equilibrium level, say, $400 billion, the reverse occurs. In Chart (a), aggregate demand exceeds aggregate supply, and in Chart (b), businesses' intended investment exceeds households' intended saving. Households are consuming goods at a faster rate than firms are producing them. As a result, business inventories are being depleted—they are falling below desired levels. Managers then seek to expand production and to hire more workers. This causes output, income, and employment to increase toward their equilibrium levels as indicated by the arrows in the charts.

Thus, three fundamental conclusions may be drawn from this model:

1. Income and employment tend toward an equilibrium level at which aggregate supply equals aggregate demand and intended saving equals intended investment.

2. The movement toward equilibrium takes place as businesses seek to eliminate unplanned inventory changes.

3. Equilibrium can occur at *any* level of employment—not necessarily at full employment. This is because equilibrium is determined by the intersection of aggregate demand with aggregate supply (or saving with investment), as shown in the charts.

INJECTIONS AND WITHDRAWALS: THE "BATHTUB THEOREM"

A further understanding of these ideas can be gained by expressing them in terms of a physical analogy.

For example, suppose that we use the notions of "injections" and "withdrawals" to account for expansions and contractions in the economy's circular flow of income. These terms can be defined in the following way:

1. *Injections*   Expenditures that are not dependent on income. Examples are investment, government spending, and exports. The effects of these expenditures are to increase aggregate demand and thus raise the economy's level of income and employment.

2. *Withdrawals*   "Leakages" from total income. Examples are household saving, business saving, taxes, and imports. The effects of such leakages are to decrease aggregate demand and thus reduce the economy's level of income and employment.

The significance of these terms can be visualized by referring back to the diagrams in Exhibit 2. Injections may be represented by investment (I), and withdrawals or leakages may be represented by saving (S). As you have already learned, equilibrium will occur where $I = S$, the level of income and employment where injections and withdrawals are equal.

These ideas can also be illustrated in terms of a physical analogy, such as the "bathtub theorem" in Exhibit 3.

Planned and Realized Saving and Investment: Another View of Equilibrium*

The concept of equilibrium may be approached from yet another point of view. For example, it has been emphasized above that in equilibrium, *intended* saving equals *intended* investment. What does this mean? How do adjustments in inventory levels bring about stability of income and employment?

When you studied the operation of supply and demand in an earlier chapter, you saw that buyers and sellers are each influenced by different factors. Consequently, their plans or intentions as reflected by market schedules or curves do not coincide. That is, the number of units of a commodity actually purchased and sold is always equal. However, the quantities that buyers *plan* to buy and sellers *plan* to offer over the full range of their curves will always differ—except in equilibrium, where the scheduled amounts intersect.

A similar idea exists with respect to saving and investment. As you have seen, *savers and investors are different people with different motivations.* Therefore, their plans to save and invest are not identical at all levels of output. Although saving always equals actual or realized investment, saving seldom equals planned investment—except at the equilibrium level of output.

You can get a better understanding of these ideas by recalling the meaning of investment. As you learned in the study of national-income accounting in a previous chapter, investment consists of replacements or additions to the nation's stock of capital, including its plant, equipment, and inventories. In terms of what you have already learned in this chapter, investment may be divided into two parts:

1. *Planned Investment* Expenditures on plant, equipment, and inventories undertaken intentionally by businesses.

---

* NOTE TO INSTRUCTOR This section is optional. It may be omitted without affecting continuity.

Exhibit 3
Injections and Withdrawals: The "Bathtub Theorem"

Investment may be thought of as an injection into the income stream; saving may be thought of as a withdrawal. Hence, the water in the bathtub can be in equilibrium at any level as long as the inflow equals the outflow. If the inflow exceeds the outflow, the level in the tub will rise. If the outflow exceeds the inflow, the level in the tub will fall.

(NOTE In a more comprehensive sense, *injections* are expenditures that do not depend on income. Examples of injections are investment, government spending, and exports. These expenditures serve to increase aggregate demand and therefore raise the level of income and employment. *Withdrawals* are "leakages" from total income. Examples of withdrawals are household saving, business saving, taxes, and imports. These withdrawals serve to decrease aggregate demand and therefore reduce the level of income and employment.)

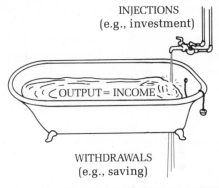

INJECTIONS (e.g., investment)

OUTPUT = INCOME

WITHDRAWALS (e.g., saving)

2. *Unplanned Investment* Changes in inventory that occur because businesses experience unexpected differences between the aggregate demand for goods and the aggregate supply of them. (NOTE Refer back to Exhibit 1, column 7, of this chapter to see how unexpected inventory changes arise.)

These concepts are summarized by the following statement:

$$\text{actual or realized investment} = \begin{cases} \text{planned investment} \\ \textit{(intentional expenditures on plant, equipment, inventories)} \\ + \\ \text{unplanned investment} \\ \textit{(unexpected inventory changes)} \end{cases}$$

This simple formula provides the basis for understanding the following ideas.

THREE POSSIBLE CASES

It has been emphasized that buyers and sellers, as well as savers and investors, are each influenced by different factors. As a result, their *plans* to buy and sell, or to save and invest, are rarely identical. That is, except in equilibrium, their market schedules or curves are not likely to be equal.

These concepts are illustrated graphically in Exhibit 4. The model is the same as the one in Exhibit 2, but the scales have been magnified so that you can see the important details more readily. Three possible cases are considered—those in which aggregate supply (AS) is either equal to, greater than, or less than, aggregate demand (AD).

Case 1: AS = AD　It is clear from Chart (a) that if businesses plan to sell an output of $500 billion, this is also the amount of C + I which the household and business sectors plan to purchase at that output. Therefore, aggregate supply equals aggregate demand and there is no inventory accumulation or depletion. Likewise, in Chart (b), the amount that households plan to save at that output equals the amount that businesses plan to invest. There are thus no unplanned or unexpected changes in inventory.

Case 2: AS > AD　Chart (a) shows that if businesses plan to sell $600 billion of NNP, households and businesses combined plan to purchase $580 billion of C + I at that output. The business sector will therefore experience unplanned investment or inventory accumulation of +$20 billion. In Chart (b), household saving exceeds planned investment of businesses by the amount of this unplanned investment. Nevertheless, saving equals actual or *realized* investment because the latter always includes both planned and unplanned (inventory) investment.

Case 3: AS < AD　Chart (a) shows that if businesses plan to produce $400 billion of NNP, households and businesses combined plan to purchase $420 billion of C + I at that output. Aggregate demand thus exceeds aggregate supply, and the difference represents unplanned *disinvestment* or negative investment. This is because the stock of inventory is being used up faster than it is being replaced. In this case it amounts to an inventory depletion of −$20 billion. In Chart (b), saving falls short of planned investment by that amount. However, saving still equals *realized* investment because unplanned (inventory) investment is negative.

CONCLUSION: FUNDAMENTAL IDENTITIES

These ideas can now be summarized briefly:

○ Saving and investment are planned by different people with different motivations. Hence, their schedules or curves are not likely to be equal—except in equilibrium.

○ Saving (like consumption) depends on the level of aggregate income or output. Saving is simply that part of society's income not consumed. Therefore, no distinction is made between planned saving and realized saving because both concepts are the same.

○ Investment is independent of aggregate income. Some investment consists of planned or intentional expenditures on plant, equipment, and inventories. Some investment may also consist of unplanned or unexpected inventory changes. However, once society incurs a given level of aggregate income, the amount of realized investment from that income includes both planned and unplanned (inventory) investment.

As a result of these conditions, the following simple equations express the key concepts you have learned thus far:

Out of any *realized* level of income, it is always true that
$$\text{income} = \text{consumption} + \text{saving}$$

and it is also true that
$$\text{income} = \text{consumption} + \text{realized investment}$$

Therefore,
$$\text{saving} = \text{realized investment}$$

These are actually fundamental identities of national-income accounting. You can verify them for any given year from the front endpapers of this book. However, you must first make the proper calculations to reflect the fact that government and the foreign sector are excluded from this basic model.

The Multiplier Principle

One of the most critical problems of macroeconomics concerns the question of how changes in net investment affect the level of income. You already know that an increase in net investment will cause an increase in income; a decrease in net investment will cause a decrease in income. But what you may not know is that *investment spending has an amplifying effect on economic activity:*

An increase in net investment will cause a magnified increase in income and output, and a decrease in net investment will cause a magnified decrease in income and output. The amount by which a change in investment is multiplied to produce an ultimate change in income and output is called the *multiplier*.

Exhibit 4
Planned and Realized Saving and Investment

Chart (a). *Unplanned investment (and disinvestment), reflected by changes in inventory, occurs at output levels where aggregate demand differs from aggregate supply.*

Chart (b). *Saving and investment, as shown by the S and*

I curves, are planned by different people with different motivations. Hence, saving and investment are not equal—except in equilibrium, where the curves intersect. But for any realized level of income, saving always equals realized investment.

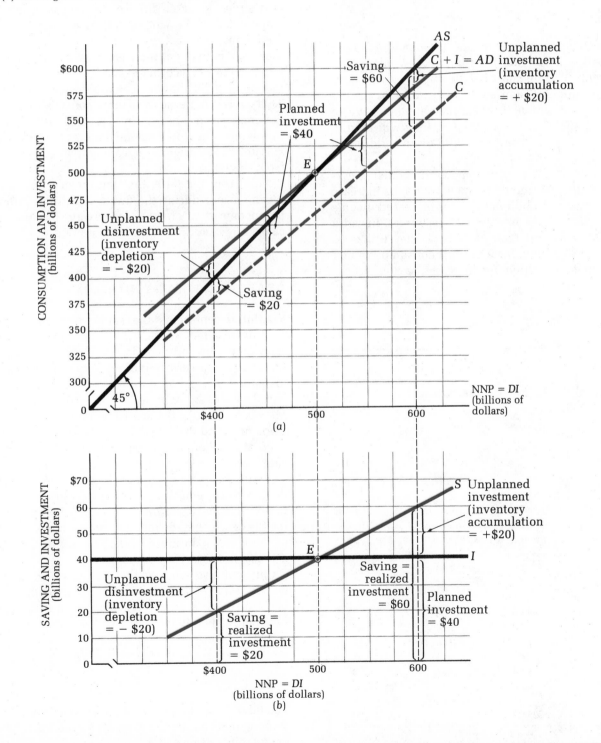

For instance, if a permanent increase in investment of $5 billion per year causes an increase in income and output of $10 billion, the multiplier is 2. If, instead, the increase in income and output is $15 billion, the multiplier is 3. How does the multiplier work? It can be illustrated in three ways: numerically by a table, graphically by a chart, and algebraically by a formula.

NUMERICAL ILLUSTRATION

Suppose that businesses decide to spend $5 billion more per year on construction of new plant and equipment. This means that unemployed workers, materials suppliers, and so on, will be hired to perform the construction. If we assume that they have an MPC of 4/5 and hence an MPS of 1/5, they will tend to spend four-fifths and save one-fifth of any additional income they receive.

The ultimate effect on income is illustrated in Exhibit 5. In the first round of expenditures the increase in investment of $5 billion becomes increased income to the owners of the newly hired resources. Because their MPC is 4/5 and their MPS is 1/5, they utilize 80 percent, or $4 billion, for increased consumption and 20 percent, or $1 billion, for increased saving.

In round 2, when the four-fifths is spent on consumption, firms find their sales increasing and their inventories decreasing. Therefore, firms hire more resources in order to increase their production, thereby creating $4 billion of income for the owners of the resources. These income recipients then utilize four-fifths, or $3.2 billion, for increased consumption and one-fifth, or $0.8 billion, for increased saving.

In round 3 and in each subsequent round, the process is repeated. Four-fifths of each increase in income is spent in the following round and is thereby added to the income stream.

Thus, a permanent increase in investment of $5 billion in round 1 has brought about an ultimate increase in income of $25 billion. The multiplier is therefore 5. This overall increase in income consists of a $20 billion increase in consumption plus a $5 billion increase in saving. The total saving increase is always the amount of the original investment, as you can verify from the table.

Note from the table that the greatest increases in income occur during the first few rounds. After that the income effects tend to fade away—like the ripples caused by a stone dropped into a pond.

GRAPHIC ILLUSTRATION

Exhibit 6 represents the same multiplier concept graphically. It shows how an increase in investment, represented by an upward shift of the $C + I$ curve in (a), or by an upward shift of the I curve in (b), causes a magnified increase in output. As before, the model is based on the assumption that the MPC is 4/5 and the MPS is 1/5. That is, the aggregate demand curve has a slope of 4/5 and the saving curve has a slope of 1/5.

Point E in both charts represents the initial equilibrium level at which aggregate demand equals aggregate supply and saving equals investment. Point E' defines a new equilibrium resulting from an increase in investment. Note from the description accompanying the charts that the increase in income is a *multiple* of the increase in investment. The multiplier, as you can see, is 5.

Can you also see that the multiplier works in reverse? What happens to income if investment falls back to its initial level? What happens if investment falls below its initial level?

FORMULA ILLUSTRATION

The tabular and graphic illustrations of the multiplier demonstrate that the increase in income is related to the marginal propensities to consume and to save. For

Exhibit 5
The Multiplier Illustrated Numerically
(all data in billions)

MPC = 4/5
MPS = 1/5
multiplier = 5

Expenditure rounds	Increase in income	Increase in consumption, MPC = 4/5	Increase in saving, MPS = 1/5
1 Increase in investment = $5 billion	$ 5.00	$ 4.00	$1.00
2	4.00	3.20	0.80
3	3.20	2.56	0.64
4	2.56	2.05	0.51
5	2.05	1.64	0.41
6	1.64	1.31	0.33
All other rounds	6.55	5.24	1.31
Total	$25.00	$20.00	$5.00

Exhibit 6
The Multiplier Illustrated Graphically

MPC = 4/5
MPS = 1/5
multiplier = 5

An increase in the level of investment by $5 billion causes an in-
crease in the level of income, or
NNP, by $25 billion. Hence, the
multiplier is 5.

What happens to income, or NNP,
if investment falls back to $40 bil-
lion? To $35 billion?

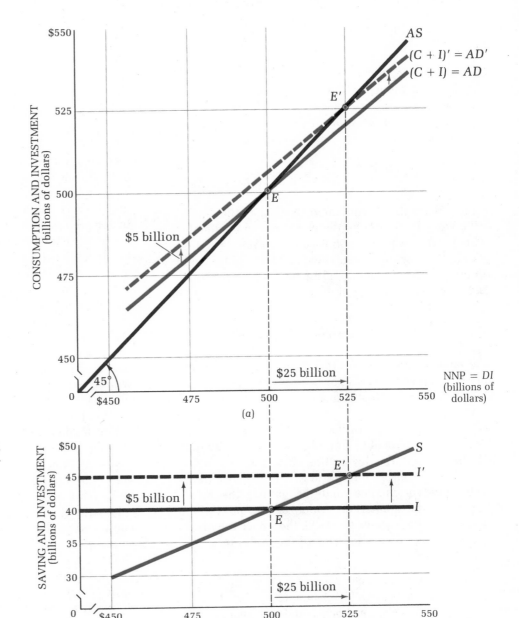

example, you have already learned from the study of the consumption function that

$$MPC + MPS = 1$$

Transposing yields

$$MPS = 1 - MPC$$

From the previous illustrations, you know that MPC is $\frac{4}{5}$ and MPS is $\frac{1}{5}$. Therefore, you can easily verify that

$$\text{multiplier} = \frac{1}{1/5} = \frac{1}{1 - 4/5} = 5$$

This is the same value of the multiplier obtained previously in the numerical and graphic illustrations.

These ideas have been stated in the form of a specific example. To be useful, they can now be expressed in terms of a general formula. Thus:

$$\text{multiplier} = \frac{1}{MPS} = \frac{1}{1 - MPC}$$

This means that if you know either the MPC or the MPS, you can determine the multiplier immediately. (This is what was done above to determine a multiplier of 5.) Then, once you know the value of the multiplier, you can predict the ultimate change in income resulting from a change in investment by the formula

$$\text{multiplier} \times \text{change in investment}$$
$$= \text{change in income}$$

The same formula applies to a decrease as well as an increase in investment. Go back and check it out in the illustrations above, just to make sure that you see how it works.

Notice that *the multiplier is the reciprocal of the MPS.* (The reciprocal of a number is 1 divided by that number.) Thus, the lower the MPS, the less withdrawal or "leakage" into extra saving that occurs at each round of income, and the greater the MPC. Therefore, the greater the value of the multiplier. Conversely, the greater the MPS, the lower the MPC. Therefore, the lower the value of the multiplier.

To summarize:

The *multiplier* principle states that changes in investment bring about magnified changes in income. This idea is expressed by the equation: multiplier × change in investment = change in income. The formula for the multiplier coefficient is thus

$$\text{multiplier} = \frac{\text{change in income}}{\text{change in investment}}$$
$$= \frac{1}{MPS} = \frac{1}{1 - MPC}$$

where MPS stands for the marginal propensity to save and MPC for the marginal propensity to consume. (NOTE This multiplier is also sometimes called the *simple multiplier* or the *investment multiplier,* to distinguish it from other types of multipliers in economics.)

The Paradox of Thrift

The multiplier principle states that any increase (or decrease) in investment sets in motion a multiple expansion (or contraction) of income. But do changes in saving or consumption also bring about a multiplied effect on income? The answer is yes—as your intuition would probably lead you to believe. But you can sharpen that intuition with some diagrams.

Take a look at Chart (a) in Exhibit 7. It illustrates the effect of an increase in saving (or equivalently, the effect of a decrease in consumption) on the nation's income or output. An increase in saving, such as from S to S', means that at any given level of income households now plan to save more than before. This might occur if they expect a recession and want to be better prepared for future contingencies.

Chart (b) in Exhibit 7 reflects the same idea as Chart (a), but now the investment curve is drawn with a moderate upward tilt. This shows more realistically that investment is not completely *autonomous*. That is, until now we have assumed for simplicity that investment is independent of income, output, and general economic activity. However, with expanding income and output, investment will grow because businesspersons become more optimistic and are willing to spend more on investment goods. We are thus relaxing the assumption of a horizontal investment curve, as was promised earlier.

This tendency of rising economic activity to stimulate higher levels of investment is called *induced investment*. Note in Chart (b) that because of a rising I curve, the multiplier effect on output resulting from an increase in saving is even greater than in Chart (a).

Looking at both charts, the new equilibrium at E' as compared to E reveals a curious phenomenon. *A small upward shift of the saving curve (or downward shift of the consumption curve) when not offset by an upward shift of the investment curve causes a multiplied decrease in income or output.* This results in an interesting paradox.

An increase in thrift may be desirable for an individual family because it can lead to greater saving and wealth. However, it may be undesirable for all of society because it leads to reductions in income, output, and employment. Also, where the investment curve is upward-sloping, an increase in thrift will actually lead to a *reduction in society's rate of saving.* This is the *paradox of thrift.*

Exhibit 7
Effect of an Increase in Saving: The Paradox of Thrift

Chart (a). *An increase in saving causes a multiplied decrease in output or income. However, at the new equilibrium point E', saving is the same as it was previously at E.*

Chart (b). *Suppose that investment depends on income so that the I curve slopes upward. Then the shift from S to S' reduces income and therefore causes investment to fall. Note that at E', saving is less than it was at E. People have tried to save more, and society has ended up saving less!*

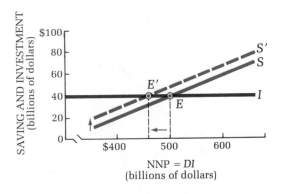

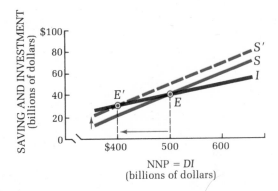

Thus, what is good for an individual is not necessarily good for everyone. (What logical fallacy is demonstrated by this paradox?)

The paradox of thrift leads to a remarkable economic implication. If the saving curve rises because households decide to save more (consume less), they should be doing exactly the opposite to improve their own and society's economic well-being. This is true unless the increase in saving can be offset by an upward shift in the investment curve. You will learn more about this implication shortly.

Inflationary and Recessionary Gaps

The modern Keynesian theory of income and employment demonstrates that the level of aggregate demand may be greater than, equal to, or less than the level of aggregate supply. These three possibilities are shown in Exhibit 8.

1. The amount by which aggregate demand *AD* (equal to *C* + *I*) exceeds aggregate supply *AS* at full employment is called the *inflationary gap*. This is shown in Chart (a). The excess volume of total spending when resources are already fully employed creates inflationary pressures that pull up prices and hence the *money* rather than the *real* value of NNP.

2. When aggregate demand equals aggregate supply at full employment, there is no gap. This is shown in Chart (b).

3. The amount by which aggregate demand falls short of full-employment aggregate supply is called the *recessionary gap*. This is shown in Chart (c). The gap occurs because the deficiency of total spending pulls down the *real* value of NNP.

In general, the economy does not move automatically toward full-employment equilibrium. An inflationary gap, for instance, could trigger further price increases as people learn to expect inflation and then include these expectations in their economic decisions. Obviously, therefore:

To close an inflationary gap, we have to find ways of reducing aggregate demand. To close a recessionary gap, we have to find ways of increasing aggregate demand.

What You Have Learned

1. The equilibrium level of NNP occurs where aggregate supply = aggregate demand. This is also where saving = investment. At this output, businesses are holding the level of inventories desired.

2. If aggregate supply exceeds aggregate demand, or planned saving exceeds planned investment, unwanted inventories accumulate. Businesses seek to reduce these surpluses by cutting back production. As a result, output, income, and employment fall. Conversely, if aggregate supply

Exhibit 8
Inflationary and Recessionary Gaps

Inflationary and recessionary gaps are always measured at the full-employment level and are shown by the vertical distances. This model assumes for simplicity that prices are constant up to the level of full employment, and thereafter turn up sharply. In reality, they would tend to turn up before the economy reached full employment and continue to rise at steeper and steeper rates.

Chart (a) Inflationary Gap. *Aggregate demand AD exceeds aggregate supply AS at full employment.*

Chart (b) No Gap. *Aggregate demand AD equals aggregate supply AS at full employment.*

Chart (c) Recessionary Gap. *Aggregate demand AD is less than aggregate supply AS at full employment.*

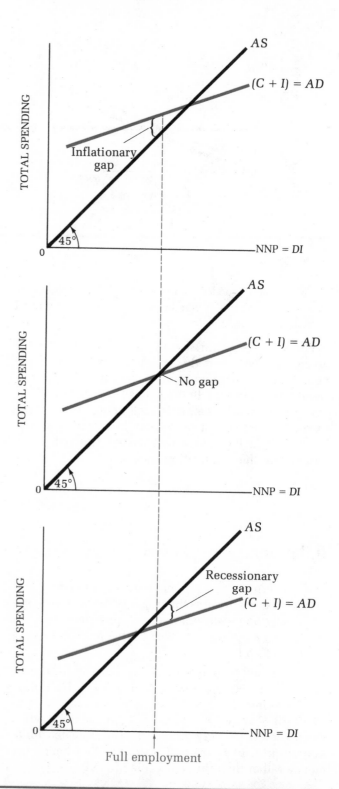

is less than aggregate demand, or planned saving is less than planned investment, inventories are depleted. Businesses try to replenish these shortages by expanding production. The result is an increase in employment as output and income rise.

3. Saving and investment are planned by different people with different motivations, and hence are not likely to be equal—except in equilibrium, where the amounts intersect. By definition, saving is that part of income not spent on consumption. Therefore, out of any realized level of income, saving always equals the amount of realized investment because the latter consists of both planned and unplanned investment.

4. Any increase (or decrease) in investment causes a multiple expansion (or contraction) of income. Any changes in consumption, or saving, similarly produce multiple effects on income. All such effects are called multiplier effects. The simple multiplier is also called the investment multiplier. It shows how changes in investment cause magnified changes in income. The multiplier is equal to the reciprocal of the marginal propensity to save.

5. The paradox of thrift tells us that although an increase in saving may be desirable for an individual, a general increase in saving by society can actually reduce income and employment. Therefore, what is good for an individual is not necessarily good for society.

6. The amount by which aggregate demand exceeds the full-employment aggregate supply is called the inflationary gap. The amount by which aggregate demand falls short of the full-employment aggregate supply is called the recessionary gap. There is no automatic tendency for aggregate demand to equal the full-employment aggregate supply. Hence, methods must be found to close inflationary and recessionary gaps if our mixed economy is to maintain full employment.

For Discussion

1. *Terms and concepts to review:*

realized investment	paradox of thrift
multiplier	inflationary gap
autonomous investment	recessionary gap
induced investment	

2. Complete the following table for a hypothetical economy. (All figures are in billions of dollars.) Assume that the propensity to consume is linear and that investment is constant at all levels of income.

NNP = DI	C	S	I	APC	APS	MPC	MPS
$100	$125		$25				
200	200						
300							
400							
500							

(a) From the data in the table, draw a graph of the consumption function and of the consumption-plus-invest-

ment function. Underneath your chart, draw a graph of the saving and investment curves and connect the two sets of break-even points with vertical dashed lines.

(b) Has there been a multiplier effect as a result of the inclusion of investment? If yes, by how much? What is the numerical value of the multiplier?

(c) What is the equilibrium level of income and output before and after the inclusion of investment?

(d) What will income be if investment increases by $10 billion?

3. How does the size of the multiplier vary with MPC? MPS? Explain why, without using any equations.

4. Distinguish between the individual and community viewpoints concerning the desirability of thrift.

5. Can you suggest at least one method of closing inflationary or recessionary gaps?

6. A student remarked to his instructor: "First you say that saving and investment are never really equal. Then you say they are always really equal. Why don't you economists make up your minds?" Can you help the student out of his muddle?

7. Suppose that a consumption function is given by the equation

$$C = 120 + 0.60DI$$

(a) What will be the amount of consumption at an income level of 100?

(b) How much income is required to support a consumption level of 420?

(c) What will be the amount of consumption if income is taxed 100 percent? How can consumption be financed under such circumstances?

(d) What is the value of the MPC? The MPS?

(e) Prepare a consumption and saving schedule, and graph the consumption and saving functions for income levels from $DI = 100$ to $DI = 500$. What is the equilibrium level of income?

8. If planned investment in Problem 7 were 50, what would be the equation for aggregate demand? Draw the aggregate demand curve and investment curve on your charts. Can you estimate the equilibrium level of income from your charts?

9. Referring to your charts in Problem 8:

(a) At a realized income of 500, how much is unplanned investment? Realized investment? Is this an equilibrium situation? Explain.

(b) At a realized income of 400, how much is unplanned investment? Realized investment? Is this an equilibrium situation? Explain.

(c) At the realized income levels in (a) and (b), does saving equal investment? Explain.

10. How does the size of the MPC and of the MPS, or the steepness of the consumption curve and of the saving curve, affect the size of the multiplier? Explain.

11. Adam Smith wrote that a spendthrift is an enemy of society, but a frugal person is its benefactor. Benjamin Franklin advised that "a penny saved is a penny earned." Evaluate these statements in light of the paradox of thrift.

Issue
Investment: Not "If," But "When" and "How Much"?

As I was going up the stair
I met a man who wasn't there.
He wasn't there again today
I wish, I wish he'd stay away.

This familiar rhyme summarizes a fundamental problem of investment. The problem is that unlike consumption expenditures, which depend heavily on the nation's income, investment expenditures to a large extent are independent of income. As a result, they fluctuate widely over the business cycle. The fluctuations cause unstable economic conditions which, like the man in the jingle, will not stay away.

Erratic investment expenditures create other difficulties as well. Among them is the possibility that business spending on plant and equipment may remain too low for long periods. When this happens, the consequences for our own and for other mixed economies are clear. The loss of jobs and incomes in the capital goods industries becomes pronounced, overall demand for goods and services declines, and the rate of economic growth is curtailed.

Situations of this type have occurred at various times. When they do, cries of "capital shortage" become commonplace. Are such cries meaningful? Will business fulfill society's investment needs, or will the nation experience prolonged periods of economic stagnation and decline?

Old Problem
At least since the time of Adam Smith, economists have known that in order for a nation to grow (i.e., experience a rising level of real GNP), society must consume less than it produces. It must also find a means whereby the difference between consumption and production is invested in capital goods that enhance productivity.

These ideas were demonstrated clearly and persuasively by the classical economists. They showed that the development of civilizations, both ancient and modern, was closely tied to capital accumulation and that the rate of accumulation was influenced by the size of the production–consumption gap—which economists call saving.

Karl Marx (1818–1883), the founder of modern socialism, contributed his own distinctive interpretation of the phenomenon. He viewed the low wages and miserable living conditions of nineteenth-century industrial workers as "forced capital accumulation"—in short, a levy or "tax" laid on them that enabled capitalists to earn higher incomes from reinvestment of profits in capital goods. Soon after the Communists took power in Russia in 1917, they instituted a program of "socialist accumulation"—which meant that the populace was required to devote a high proportion of its aggregate income to investment in capital rather than to the purchase of consumer goods.

Capital Shortage?
The problem now, according to many experts, is that our economy is likely to experience a growing deficiency of capital in the coming years. The reasons, they say, are not hard to see. Higher demands for capital are inevitable because of the need to modernize factories, improve health and safety, revitalize transportation systems, and clean up the environment. However, the supply of savings appears to be inadequate to meet these rising demands. Historically, the sum of personal and business savings (including retained profits and depreciation) has averaged around 15 or 16 percent of GNP. Some economists believe that this proportion is not likely to increase—for two reasons:

○ Corporate-profit rates, which reflect an important class of the economy's savings, have declined substantially over the long run. For example, in the mid-1960s the pretax return on invested capital of nonfinancial corporations averaged about 16 percent. Since then the figure has declined substantially.

○ Public-sector deficits will probably continue to loom large in the years ahead. Such deficits may be viewed as a claim against savings. That is, government deficits indicate that the public sector is a net consumer of resources, taking more out of the economy than is being put back. The consequence is a reduction in the production–consumption gap—a contraction of savings.

Meaningless Question
If these views are correct, a capital shortage could seriously reduce living standards. The fundamental question, therefore, is whether an actual shortage, now or in the future, is real or imagined.

As with all social and economic issues, there is more than one point of view to be considered. Many experts contend, for example, that in a free market there can be no shortage of either physical capital (plant and equipment used to produce the nation's output) or of equivalent financial capital (claims of owners and creditors against physical capital). In our economy consumer and investors state their preferences, leaving the interest rate—the price of capital—as the mechanism that clears the market. Thus, if the quantity of savings demanded for investment is greater than the quantity supplied at the existing rate, the rate will rise and thereby bring the market into equilibrium. The reverse will happen if, at the existing rate, the quantity supplied exceeds the quantity demanded. For this reason, it is meaningless to talk about a shortage of capital—or of a surplus either. As long as the market is left free to adjust to supply-and-

Charlie Chaplin, a leading comic in Hollywood's early days, depicted the declining significance of man in an age of expanding investment and technology in the movie, Modern Times (1922).

The Bettmann Archive.

demand imbalances between saving and investment, shortages and surpluses of capital—or of any other commodity—cannot occur, or at most, will be short-lived if they do occur.

Conclusion: Asking the Right Question

The trouble with all of these arguments is that they are based on an ambiguous notion of "capital shortage." From one point of view, there will *always* be a shortage as long as society's aspirations are rising. From another point of view, there will *never* be a shortage as long as interest rates are allowed to correct supply-and-demand differences in a free market. And from a third point of view, there may *sometimes* be a shortage and sometimes not, depending on general economic conditions and society's goals at any given time.

The question to be asked, therefore, is not whether a capital shortage exists or is likely to occur, for the answer to that question is both yes and no. Instead, the question is: *Given society's economic goals for a specific time in the future—such as 10 years hence—what quantities of capital will be needed to fulfill those goals?* Viewed in this way, the problem of investment and capital accumulation becomes part of a larger task of attaining a desired rate of economic growth. This, along with the objectives of attaining efficiency, equity, and stability, is one of the fundamental goals of every society.

QUESTIONS

1. "It is an economic fact of life that increased productivity is the only way to raise our standard of living. For the sake of future economic growth, the inescapable conclusion is that government policies must become more supportive of capital investment. This requires a fundamental shift in our domestic policies away from continued expansion of personal consumption and government spending and toward greater saving, investment, and capital formation."

Does this quotation, by a former political leader, mean that the *type* of investment undertaken has an effect on productivity rates and economic growth? Explain.

2. How can government, through the following measures, increase the supply of funds available to business and thereby stimulate investment and capital formation? (a) Encourage private saving; (b) reduce federal borrowing; (c) create price-indexed bonds (whose maturity values are tied directly to the general price level).

Chapter 9

Fiscal Policy for Economic Efficiency and Stability

Chapter Preview

How do changes in government spending and taxes affect aggregate demand and hence the level of income and employment?

What are the basic principles of fiscal policy? How can they be made to work to achieve the goals of continuous full employment and price stability?

Is our national, or public, debt too large? What are the real burdens of the debt? How large should the debt be?

At the end of World War II (1945), most economists and politicians feared that the United States would face widespread unemployment. Servicemen were returning to civilian life and many industries were converting from wartime to peacetime production. Accordingly, Congress passed the _Employment Act of 1946_, in which it said:

> The Congress hereby declares that it is the continuing policy and responsibility of the Federal Government to . . . create and maintain, in a manner calculated to foster and promote free competitive enterprise and the general welfare . . . maximum employment, production, and purchasing power.

This law is interpreted to mean that the government should use its fiscal powers of taxing and spending to stimulate full employment and economic growth. Since the early 1960s, increasing emphasis has been placed on achieving these objectives without causing inflationary pressures.

The noun "fisc" (from Latin _fiscus_, translated as basket, money basket, treasury) means a state or royal treasury. The adjective "fiscal" refers to all matters pertaining to the public treasury, particularly its revenues and expenditures. Thus, modern fiscal policy deals with the deliberate exercise of the government's power to tax and spend for the purpose of bringing the nation's output and employment to certain desired levels.

Introducing Government:
Enlarging the Model

In our basic model of income and employment we assumed that net national product consists of two components, consumption expenditures C, and private net investment I. We concluded that in order to close an inflationary or recessionary gap, methods must be found to alter aggregate demand. Our objective now is to show how government fiscal policy can do this.

The proper economic role of government is always controversial. Should taxes be raised or lowered? Should government spending be increased or reduced? These are among the fundamental issues of fiscal policy. They are also typical of the questions you read and hear about almost every day in the news media.

GOVERNMENT EXPENDITURES INCREASE AGGREGATE DEMAND

Government fiscal policy affects our basic model of income and employment through two major variables—taxes and spending. Let us assume for the moment that *taxes are held constant*. Then government spending (G) on goods and services becomes a net addition to total spending or aggregate demand. That is, government spending supplements household consumption expenditures (C), and business investment expenditures (I). This is illustrated in the hypothetical case of Exhibit 1, Chart (a).

The $C + I + G$ curve shows total spending at each level of net national product. The new equilibrium point at which aggregate demand AD equals aggregate supply AS occurs at E. The corresponding information in terms of saving and investment is given in Chart (b). Note that the upward-sloping line now represents saving plus taxes $(S + T)$, because taxes, like saving, denote a portion of income not spent on consumption.

REMARK   Because the basic model is now enlarged to include the public sector instead of just the household and business sectors, the existence of taxes must be recognized. Therefore, NNP in the enlarged model stands by itself—it does not equal DI as in the basic model. (Do you remember why—in terms of national-income accounting?)

Notice in Chart (a) that the AD curve includes a certain amount of government spending. However, the equilibrium NNP of $600 billion is still short of the $700 billion needed to reach the full-employment level of output. This means that in order to achieve full employment, the aggregate demand curve must be raised high enough to close the recessionary gap. This can be done by increasing any of the components of AD—namely, C or I or G. If we assume that the C and I curves remain constant, an increase in G by the amount G' will close the recessionary gap by raising the aggregate demand curve from AD to AD'.

Note that an increase in government expenditure, with taxes held constant, has a multiplier effect on NNP just as does an increase in private investment expenditure. In the diagram, an increase in aggregate demand of $20 billion, from $C + I + G$ to $C + I + G + G'$, increases NNP by $100 billion. We can infer from this that a rise in government demand has the same multiplier effect on NNP as a rise in consumer demand and in business or investment demand. This is because a rise in government demand enhances the sales and profits of firms that sell to the government. This in turn causes further increases in output throughout the economy.

Thus:

> Increased government spending may be used to raise the level of aggregate demand from an unemployment to a full-employment level. However, any additional spending which raises aggregate demand above full-employment levels will be inflationary.

Observe how the multiplier principle actually comes into play. In Exhibit 1 we know from the constant slope of the consumption curve that MPC is ⅘ at every point, and hence the multiplier is 5. Given this information, and knowing that the increase in NNP must be $100 billion to reach full employment, the increase in government spending must be $20 billion in order to achieve the desired goal. This is because 5 × $20 billion = $100 billion.

INCREASED TAXES REDUCE AGGREGATE DEMAND

What happens to the equilibrium level of NNP when government spending is constant and taxes vary? Your intuition tells you that an increase in taxes will reduce disposable income and hence consumption expenditures. This in turn will decrease output and employment. Of course, the many different kinds of taxes—direct or indirect, progressive or regressive, personal or business—may all have different effects on income and employment. For simplicity's sake, however, let us assume that an increase in personal income taxes of $20 billion is imposed on consumers in our hypothetical economy. We may represent this amount of the tax by the letter T.

Exhibit 1
Effect of Increased Government Spending on Net National Product

Assumption: MPC = 4/5; therefore, multiplier = $\dfrac{1}{1 + 4/5} = \dfrac{1}{1/5} = 5$

Chart (a). *Increased government spending by the amount G′ raises aggregate demand from AD to AD′ and produces a multiplier effect on net national product. Because the multiplier is 5, increased government spending of $20 billion increases NNP by 5 × $20 billion = $100 billion—from $600 billion to $700 billion. This closes the recessionary gap.*

Chart (b). *The multiplier effect of increased government spending G′ can also be seen in terms of a saving–investment diagram. A $20 billion increase in government spending raises the equilibrium NNP from $600 billion to $700 billion.*

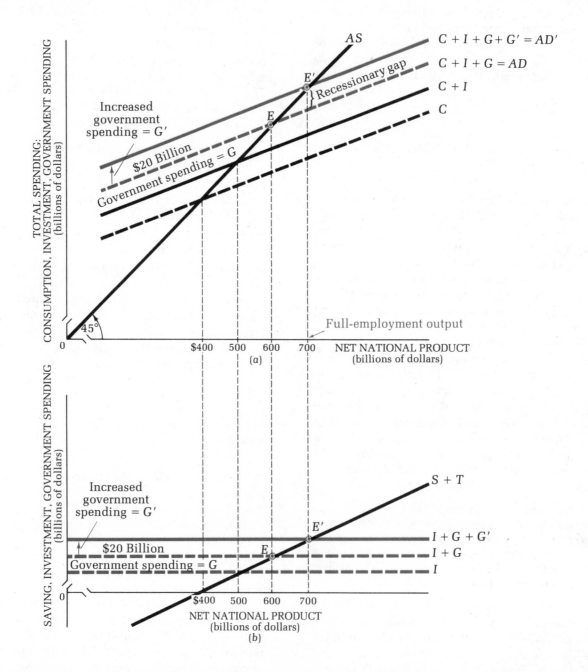

In Exhibit 2, the consumption curve C, whose MPC is ⅘, is shifted downward and parallel until it becomes C' as a result of the tax T. But has the consumption curve shifted downward by the exact amount of the tax? The answer is no:

After the tax the decrease in consumption, represented by the drop in the curve, means that at any given level of NNP people will now consume less than before. This is because their income is lower. Since the MPC is ⅘, consumption will decrease by ⅘ of $20 billion or $16 billion at every level of NNP. It follows, therefore, that saving will decline by ⅕, or $4 billion, at every level of NNP.

The tax thus causes a downward shift of the C curve according to the value of the MPC. *The amount of the downward shift equals MPC × T.* What will be the effect of T on NNP? Because the multiplier is 5, it follows that a decrease in consumption expenditures of $16 billion will reduce NNP by 5 × $16 billion = $80 billion. This is shown in Exhibit 2, where the equilibrium NNP changes from E at $400 billion to E' at $320 billion.

Exhibit 2
Effect of Increased Taxes on Consumption and on Net National Product

Assumption: MPC = 4/5; therefore, multiplier = 5.
T = tax increase of $20 billion.

The C curve will shift downward by an amount equal to MPC × T. Thus, because MPC = ⅘ and the tax increase is $20 billion, the C curve will shift downward by ⅘ × $20 billion = $16 billion. However, because the multiplier is 5, NNP will decrease by 5 × $16 billion = $80 billion. Equilibrium NNP will thus decline from E at $400 billion to E' at $320 billion.

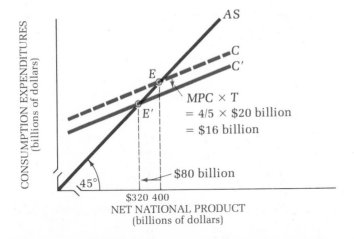

VARYING G AND T TOGETHER: THE BALANCED-BUDGET MULTIPLIER

Suppose that we now allow government spending G, and taxes T, to vary simultaneously. As you saw in Exhibit 1, the effect of a $20 billion increase in G is a $100 billion increase in NNP. This is because the added expenditure goes through the rounds of consumption and saving according to the multiplier principle. In Exhibit 2, on the other hand, the multiplier operates in reverse, to contract output as consumption and saving are reduced. Thus, the effect of a $20 billion increase in T is an $80 billion decrease in NNP.

What will be the effect if G and T are both increased simultaneously by the same amount—in our example by $20 billion? The increase in G will raise NNP by five times that amount, or $100 billion. The increase in T will lower NNP by four times that amount, or $80 billion. Therefore, the *net* effect of equal increases in G and T together will be to increase NNP by one times that amount, or $20 billion—the amount of the initial increment. This is because the increases in G and T are precisely equal or balanced, but their effects are opposite. Thus, the two multiplier processes cancel each other out—except on the very first round, when the full amount of G ($20 billion) is added to NNP. Therefore, the net multiplier effect of equal increases in G and T is 1.

We can generalize the foregoing ideas in this way:

Balanced-budget multiplier principle. If G and T are increased or decreased simultaneously by an equal or balanced amount, NNP will be increased or decreased by the same amount. For example, a balanced increase of G and T by $1 will raise NNP by $1, and a balanced decrease by $1 will lower NNP by $1.

The balanced-budget multiplier principle has two very practical implications.

1. In a full-employment economy any increase in government spending will cause an inflationary gap unless taxes are increased by *more than the increase in spending*. That is, taxes should increase by *more than enough to balance the budget.*

2. In an economy operating at less than full employment a general tax reduction will result in an increase in consumption and aggregate demand. This may be almost as effective in raising the equilibrium level of NNP as an increase in government spending. It might also have the further advantage of expanding the private (business) sector of the economy rather than the public (government) sector.

Several countries, including our own, have successfully applied this tax-cutting concept to increase their levels of output and employment. It is possible that these modern notions of fiscal policy may gain increasing use as time goes on.

Essentials of Fiscal Policy

The foregoing analyses suggest some guides for discretionary *fiscal policy*. This may be defined as deliberate actions by the government in its spending and taxing activities to achieve price stability, help dampen the swings of business cycles, and bring the nation's output and employment to desired levels.

Fiscal policies, of course, should differ according to the economy's stage of the business cycle. Government spending and taxing policies designed to cure recession should not be the same as those aimed at curbing inflation. Thus, two distinct classes of policies are necessary.

1. During recession the goal desired is to raise aggregate demand to a full-employment noninflationary level. Therefore, an *expansionary* fiscal policy is needed to close the gap. This may involve either an increase in G, a decrease in T, or some combination of both. If the federal budget is balanced to begin with, an expansionary fiscal policy will require a budget *deficit,* because the government's expenditures will exceed its revenues.

2. During inflation the goal is to lower aggregate demand to the full-employment noninflationary level. Therefore, a *contractionary* fiscal policy is needed to close the inflationary gap. This may entail either a decrease in G, an increase in T, or some combination of both. If the federal budget is already in balance, a contractionary fiscal policy would require a budget *surplus,* because the government's revenues will exceed its expenditures. Of course, a relatively small surplus may not be sufficient to do the job. The budget surplus must be large enough to induce deflationary effects if a contractionary fiscal policy is to operate effectively.

Not all fiscal activity is discretionary. Much is *nondiscretionary,* because significant changes in government spending and taxes occur automatically over the business cycle without any explicit decisions by the President or Congress. Let us now examine these changes.

AUTOMATIC OR BUILT-IN STABILIZERS

The U.S. economy has certain "built-in" stabilizers. These *automatic fiscal stabilizers* help cushion a recession by retarding a decline in disposable income and help curb an inflation by retarding an increase. They thus contribute to keeping the economic system in balance without human intervention or control, much as a thermostat balances the temperature in a house.

Four of these stabilizers are particularly important:

Tax Receipts   The federal government's chief sources of revenue are personal and corporation income taxes. The rates on these taxes—especially the former—are progressive. Thus, when national income rises, there is a more than proportional increase in government tax receipts. This tends to dampen an economic boom. On the other hand, a declining national income results in more than proportional decreases in government tax receipts. This tends to soften an economic recession.

Unemployment Taxes and Benefits   During prosperity and high employment, total tax receipts to finance the unemployment insurance program exceed total benefits paid out. This creates a surplus. During recession and unemployment, the reverse occurs. This creates a deficit.

Agricultural Price Policies   The federal government's policies toward farmers can have automatic stabilizing effects on agricultural prices and farm incomes. The Department of Agriculture may at times buy and sell farm surpluses in order to put a "floor" under falling agricultural prices. At other times these goods may be released from storage and sold in order to impose a "ceiling" on rising agricultural prices.

Corporate Dividend Policy   Corporations generally maintain fairly stable dividends in the short run. That is, their dividend payouts to stockholders do not fluctuate with each reported increase or decrease in profits. As a result, corporate retained earnings or undistributed profits, to the extent that they are saved and not invested, tend to have a stabilizing influence in both expansionary and contractionary periods.

On the whole, the automatic stabilizers tend to reduce the severity of business cycles. Some studies suggest that all the automatic stabilizers acting together may reduce the amplitudes of cyclical swings by about one-third. But automatic stabilizers merely curb the highs and lows of business cycles. To limit their spread, the Keynesian theory concludes that discretionary methods of fiscal policy as described next are needed. But first, see Box 1.

DISCRETIONARY FISCAL POLICY IN ACTION

The two basic prescriptions of discretionary fiscal policy seem to be simple and straightforward:

1. To expand the economy, cut taxes and raise government expenditures.

2. To contract the economy, raise taxes and cut government expenditures.

The principal concerns of discretionary fiscal pol-

Box 1
The Income Tax: An Unstable Stabilizer?

Our progressive income tax is supposed to serve as a powerful built-in stabilizer. During prosperity, when national income rises, government tax receipts should increase more than proportionately. During recession, when national income declines, government tax receipts should decrease more than proportionately. In this way, the extremes of business-cycle peaks and troughs are reduced, thereby curbing economic booms and recessions.

Unfortunately, the automatic stabilizing effects of the progressive income tax are actually reduced by high rates of inflation. If your income rises by 10 percent while prices remain the same, your real purchasing power increases. This is true even if your gain in income places you in a higher tax bracket. The increase in taxes is never as much as the increase in income.

What if your income increases by 10 percent when prices go up by 10 percent? In that case your nominal purchasing power increases because taxes do not rise as much as income. However, your *real* purchasing power decreases because you are in a higher tax bracket where higher tax rates apply. Further, because your tax exemptions and standard deduction remain constant, the taxable percentage of your income rises. Result: your income *after* taxes goes up less than the increase in prices, causing you to suffer a reduction in real income—a loss from inflation. Therefore, instead of helping reduce a decline in real income, the progressive income tax may actually worsen the reduction when inflation rates are high.

SOLUTION: INDEXATION

One way to overcome this problem is to index the income tax. This means to "correct" it for inflation by annually adjusting the size of exemptions and the standard deduction in proportion to the rate of inflation. The tax structure would then ensure most taxpayers that the percentage of their income paid in taxes would not increase solely because of rising prices. Government officials would also find it more difficult to finance increased expenditures. This is because high rates of inflation would no longer provide automatic increases in tax revenues.

U.S. Government Printing Office.

Indexation: Would an "inflation-proofed" income tax be more palatable?

icy thus involve ways in which the federal government (represented by the Treasury) raises and spends money, and the economic consequences of these actions. Let us examine these activities carefully.

Raising Money

First, there is a problem of how the government chooses to raise money. Basically, it has three sources of revenue: taxation, borrowing, and printing new money.

Taxation All increases in taxes tend to be contractionary because they take some purchasing power from those who are taxed. However, certain taxes, such as the sales and excise taxes, are regressive. Other taxes, such as the personal and corporation income taxes, are progressive. Some economists contend that regressive taxes tend to be more contractionary because they depress total consumer spending. Other economists argue that progressive taxes may be more contractionary because they cause a decline in both consumption and corporate investment. Similar difficulties arise in assessing the results of tax decreases. Experts are not always sure whether reductions in progressive or regressive taxes have the greater expansionary effects in terms of production and employment.

The level of taxes is not the only factor to consider. Changes in the composition and rate structure may also affect government revenues and the pace of economic activity, *depending on the MPCs of the income groups involved.* For instance, a change in tax rates which puts a greater burden on higher-income groups and a lesser burden on lower-income groups may have the net effect of stimulating total consumer demand. This would raise the general level of economic activity. (Can you explain why?) The change in tax rates may also reduce government tax revenues in the short run. This is because the great bulk of revenues comes from the lower- and middle-income groups. However, tax revenues in the long run would increase as national income rises.

Borrowing   A second way in which the government can raise money is by borrowing. This consists of selling Treasury bonds to the public, namely, households and businesses. (The government can also borrow from banks, but this involves a different set of considerations, which are explained in a later chapter.) If the public buys the bonds with income that would otherwise have been spent on consumption or investment, the public's reduction in spending will be largely offset by the government's increase. The overall economic effect will thus be approximately neutral. However, it is more likely that a significant proportion of the bonds will be purchased with income that would have been saved. Therefore, to the extent that this occurs, the sale of bonds by the government will have expansionary effects when the government receives the money and spends it.

Printing New Money   Instead of taxing or borrowing, some governments—the United States is an exception—may simply decide to print money. (Printing money is a monetary rather than a fiscal action—as you will see in a later chapter—but it is appropriate to say a few words about it here.) By printing money, a government can pay for the resources it wants without depressing private consumption and investment spending. This seems like a delightful and painless way to finance public expenditures. In fact, some Asian, African, and Latin American countries turn frequently to the printing presses to pay for armies, build highways, and meet other obligations and expenses.

But the results are not always painless—for two related reasons:

1. During high employment the effects will be infla-

tionary unless private spending is reduced by raising taxes enough to offset the increase in government spending.

2. If private spending is not reduced, the resulting inflation will act as a "tax" by raising prices throughout the economy and thereby shrinking real incomes.

These effects, however, would not necessarily occur during recession. That is, printing money to pay for public goods may not be inflationary if the increased government spending raises aggregate demand, thereby expanding real incomes as output and employment rise.

Spending Money

The second aspect of discretionary fiscal policy concerns the ways in which the government spends money. Two types of government spending are of chief concern: transfer payments and public employment expenditures. How does each affect income and employment?

Transfer Payments   As pointed out earlier, certain types of transfer expenditures act as automatic stabilizers. For example, unemployment compensation and old-age retirement benefits rise and fall in a somewhat inverse relationship with national income. Other transfer expenditures, such as veterans' benefits and interest payments on the public (i.e., government's) debt, are independent of national income and do not have this automatic stabilizing characteristic. But the *net* effect of transfer payments is expansionary to the extent that people spend them for goods and services. Otherwise, if transfer payments are not spent, their net effect tends to be neutral.

Public Employment Expenditures   Highways, parks, public buildings, rural electrification, slum clearance, and regional development are examples of *public works*. These are government-sponsored construction or development projects which would not ordinarily be undertaken by the private sector of the economy. As an instrument of fiscal policy, public works have at least three desirable features:

1. They stimulate the capital goods and construction industries, in which unemployment is usually greatest during a recession.

2. If properly planned, they can provide society with socially useful goods, such as schools, parks, dams, and highways.

3. They provide jobs which help to maintain workers' morale and self-respect.

But public employment expenditures also have certain fundamental disadvantages. They pose a difficult timing problem because they are hard to start when the need for them is greatest and hard to stop when the need for them is past. For example, it takes several years for the design, engineering, and legal work to be approved before construction of a major bridge or freeway can begin. By that time the economy may be well on its way to prosperity. Also, certain types of investment cannot be classified as either strictly public or strictly private. As a result, some public works, such as low-cost housing and perhaps power and reclamation projects, may compete with private investment. When that happens, it discourages the development and expansion of the economy's private (business) sector.

In addition to financing public works projects, government also provides public-service employment by creating jobs in government agencies. The jobs may range from leaf raking to social work, but the purpose is to provide temporary employment for people until they find jobs in the private sector.

Public-works employment and public-service employment thus comprise what is called "public employment." Its major purpose is to reduce both cyclical and structural unemployment. (See Box 2.)

DOES DISCRETIONARY FISCAL POLICY REALLY WORK? SOME DIFFICULTIES OF IMPLEMENTATION

These principles of fiscal policy, as already indicated, lead to two simple prescriptions:

1. To expand the economy, decrease taxes and increase government expenditures.
2. To contract the economy, increase taxes and decrease government expenditures.

In both cases, the multiplier tells you how large the changes must be to achieve full employment at stable prices. How well do these principles of discretionary fiscal policy actually operate? Because they require implementation by Washington, many knotty economic and political issues arise. Four broad classes of difficulties may be identified.

Forecasting and Timing

First, there is the technical problem of cyclical forecasting and fiscal timing. Although substantial advances have taken place in economic model building over the years, business-cycle forecasting is still far from being an exact science. The proper timing of appropriate fiscal measures to ward off an inflation or recession is extremely difficult. In fact, the fiscal measures are often applied after the inflation or recession has occurred rather than before.

Gaining Public Acceptance

A second problem is to gain political and public acceptance of fiscal measures. Even if business-cycle turning points are reasonably predictable, a President or Congress must decide to risk—and the public accept—unpopular fiscal measures. Among these are increased taxes and reduced government spending.

Further, there is the apparently insurmountable problem of overcoming the inherent sluggishness of the democratic process itself. It may take a year or more for Congress to hammer out a budget that incorporates the desired expenditures and taxes. By that time the fiscal needs themselves may have changed fundamentally or may no longer exist.

Coordinating Federal, State, and Local Policies

Third, there is a problem of federal versus state and local fiscal policies. Ideally, federal fiscal policies should mesh with those of state and local governments, so that all three levels of government may launch a unified countercyclical attack against inflations and recessions. In reality, however, the reverse frequently happens. During prosperity, state and local governments often run deficits in their budgets in order to build highways, schools, and public libraries. In recession, state and local governments frequently reduce expenditures so as to balance their budgets or even incur surpluses. The chief reason for these actions is that, unlike the federal government, state and local governments are much more restricted in their sources of funds. These governments cannot print money, and their opportunities for taxing and borrowing, which are considerably more limited, tend to vary directly with general economic conditions. Thus, to achieve and maintain economic stability, it becomes necessary to rely much more heavily on federal, than on state and local, fiscal policies.

Coordinating Government and Private Investment

A fourth problem is to dovetail government and private investment. As was pointed out earlier, government investment should supplement private investment and even stimulate it, but certainly not depress it. Yet government investment may clearly have depressive effects if it is competitive with private investment. To avoid this, public expenditures should be concentrated on projects that are clearly noncompetitive with private enterprise. Highway construction, slum clearance, and urban redevelopment are possibilities for such public expenditures.

Does fiscal policy really work in practice? Keynesian economists contend it does. They argue that:

Box 2
Making Jobs Through Public Employment

Like all controversial ideas, public employment has its supporters as well as critics. Proponents contend that it has two main advantages:

○ The funds to pay for it can be channeled quickly to regions where unemployment is highest. In this way, both rural and urban areas would benefit.

○ There is plenty of useful work to be done. Clerks, tree trimmers, waste collectors, police aids, hospital assistants—these and other workers are always needed at state and local levels.

Opponents, however, are quick to point out that public employment has numerous disadvantages. Among them:

High Cost   Even after deducting "savings" in unpaid unemployment compensation, reduced welfare payments, and other benefits given to unemployed persons, the net cost of a public-employment program would amount to billions of dollars annually.

Inflationary Pressures   Public-employment schemes tend to stimulate further inflation because such programs expand the less efficient public sector at the expense of the more productive private one.

Administrative Difficulties   Complex problems exist in administering public-employment programs. For example, what standards should be used to determine when a jobs program is to be initiated and when it is to be terminated? Should the standards be national or regional? Rigid or flexible?

These and other obstacles must be overcome if a public-employment program is to operate with reasonable efficiency. Otherwise, any public-employment project is likely to become an immense and wasteful make-work scheme at taxpayers' expense.

PUBLIC WORKS

The idea of creating jobs to reduce massive unemployment is not new. Large-scale public works programs were first introduced during the depression of the 1930s. Congress, urged by President Roosevelt, created the Civilian Conservation Corps (CCC) and the Works Projects Administration (WPA). The CCC employed hundreds of thousands of young men to work in national forests and in various conservation projects. The WPA was responsible for constructing many highways, dams, schools, recreational facilities, and flood-control systems, and for developing numerous cultural programs in music, theater, art, literature, and travel.

Although public-works programs are often denounced as wasteful and inflationary, many experts contend that in periods of high unemployment the creation of public jobs has social and economic advantages that far outweigh any economic shortcomings.

Culver Pictures.

Culver Pictures.

The Bettmann Archive.

○ A tax cut may stimulate business activity. Then, as national income rises, the government through our progressive tax system will collect larger revenues.

○ A cut in taxes will tend to stimulate both consumption and investment spending. This will produce a gradual rise in consumption and a magnified increase in income—just as the theories of the consumption function and the multiplier predict.

○ Too high a level of government spending, without any offsetting tax increases, will cause a demand-pull inflationary gap. This has been demonstrated for many years during periods of heavy deficit spending by government.

THE FULL-EMPLOYMENT BUDGET; FISCAL DRAG AND FISCAL DIVIDENDS

As we have just seen, the surpluses and deficits that occur from year to year in the federal budget are not entirely *discretionary*. To some extent the surpluses and deficits are *automatic* as a result of our progressive tax structure. Thus, as national income increases, the rising tax revenues of the federal government automatically push the budget toward a surplus. On the other hand, as national income decreases, the falling tax revenues automatically push the budget toward a deficit.

Therefore, with existing tax rates and spending policies, the actual budget surplus or deficit in any particular year is not necessarily the same as the one that would occur in a year of full employment. For instance, in a specific year when the economy is operating at less than full employment the government may incur a budgetary deficit of several billion dollars. With the same tax rates and the same amount of federal spending, there might be a budgetary surplus of several billion dollars if the economy were operating at full or close to full employment. Why? Because the greater level of national income during a period of high employment would have produced a larger volume of tax revenues for the government.

This prompts us to introduce a new concept called the *full-employment budget*. It may be defined as an estimate of annual government expenditures and revenues that would occur if the economy were operating at full employment. Any resulting surplus (or deficit) in this budget is called a *full-employment surplus* (or *deficit*).

Like any other surplus, the effect of a full- or even high-employment surplus is deflationary. This is because the government has taken more purchasing power out of the income stream through taxes than it has put back through spending. Under inflationary conditions this situation serves to dampen price increases. And if GNP is rising, its rate of growth will tend to be slowed. In view of this, how can we assure proper utilization of our full- or high-employment surpluses? There are two points that should be noted:

1. The automatic and more rapid increases in tax revenues relative to expenditures that an expanding economy experiences will tend to impede the economy's growth. This phenomenon is called *fiscal drag*.

2. The federal government can offset the effect of fiscal drag by declaring a "fiscal dividend" in any one or combination of several ways:

  (a) Increased federal spending on such important public goods as education, regional development, and health.

  (b) Reduced taxes on the private sector in order to increase consumption and investment.

  (c) Larger unrestricted revenue grants to the state and local governments which they can use to meet their expenditure needs.

The full-employment budget may gain increasing use by economic policy makers in Washington. The reason is that it combines the principles of discretionary fiscal policy with the concept of fiscal dividends.

Budget Policies and the Public Debt

Keynesian fiscal theory calls for budget deficits to ward off recessions and budget surpluses to combat inflations. This is the essence of countercyclical fiscal policy. What does it mean as far as balancing the budget is concerned? How does the government debt, resulting from unbalanced budgets, affect our economy?

FOUR BUDGET POLICIES

Since the early 1930s, the question has often arisen whether the federal budget should be balanced frequently, occasionally, or not at all. Four distinctly different policies have been proposed:

1. An annually balanced budget.

2. A cyclically balanced budget.

3. "Functional finance."

4. A full-employment balanced budget.

  Let us see what these policies involve.

Annually Balanced Budget

Some people argue that the budget should be balanced every 12 months. That is, annual revenues and expenditures should be equal. This policy, its advocates claim, would place the government in an economically "neutral" position by providing a constraint on runaway spending and fiscal disorder.

Is this argument correct? Obviously not. If the federal government balanced the budget each year without regard to fluctuations in the private sector, its actions would not be neutral. Such actions would, in fact, accentuate cyclical swings. In recession periods, when tax revenues are falling, tax rates would have to be increased and spending would have to be reduced in order to balance the budget. Conversely, during inflationary periods, when tax revenues are rising, tax rates would have to be reduced and spending would have to be increased in order to achieve budgetary balance.

Obviously, therefore, if the budget is to be used as a tool for countercyclical fiscal policy, adherence to annually balanced budgets is impossible.

Cyclically Balanced Budget

Another philosophy holds that the budget should be balanced over the course of the business cycle. This requires the government to incur budget deficits during depression in order to stimulate the economy. Those deficits would have to be offset with budget surpluses during prosperity in order to curb inflationary pressures and help pay off the public debt. Some economists have argued that such a policy would turn the budget into a countercyclical fiscal tool, while preserving the long-term objective of budgetary balance. In theory this is true.

In practice, unfortunately, business cycles are recurrent but not periodic, and their peaks and troughs are not ordinarily equal. Hence, it would be virtually impossible for the government to forecast its revenues and expenditures over the length of a business cycle. Further, it would be very unlikely for the surplus in any given prosperity to equal or even approximate the deficit of a previous recession.

Functional Finance

Proponents of the *functional-finance* philosophy contend that the government should pursue whatever fiscal measures are needed to achieve noninflationary full employment and economic growth—without regard to budget balancing per se. The federal budget is thus viewed in a functional sense. That is, it is seen as a flexible fiscal device to be manipulated for achieving economic objectives, not merely an accounting statement to be balanced periodically.

Functional finance is the logical consequence of the New Economics (i.e., Keynesian economic thinking).

However, functional finance is not without its critics, especially among conservatives. In their opinion, a balanced budget serves as a rough fiscal guide that should be applied with discretion. They argue that by accepting functional finance as a budget policy, the long-run goal of a balanced budget is consigned to oblivion. When this happens, both the means and criteria for preventing runaway spending and inflation are lost.

Full-Employment Balanced Budget

Can a budget policy incorporate the best features of the foregoing proposals? The Committee for Economic Development, an organization composed of some of the nation's most prominent business leaders, thinks that it can. Its plan is simple. First, determine a level of expenditures based on long-term merits without regard to stabilization considerations. Then, set tax rates to cover those expenditures at full or high employment, and, perhaps, to yield a moderate surplus besides.

This plan, in the opinion of the CED, has two major advantages:

1. It produces a balanced budget over the full course of a business cycle.

2. It rejects the use of discretionary fiscal policy, which is often difficult to apply for both political and economic reasons. Instead, it relies on the use of automatic stabilizers to keep the economy at a high level of employment.

The result of the CED plan is to produce a long-run cyclically balanced budget with automatic built-in flexibility.

According to critics, however, the plan has two major disadvantages. First, reliance on automatic stabilizers may not be enough to keep small swings from developing into big ones. Second, there are times when the private sector is either too weak or too strong, so that stabilization may require more substantial and intentional federal deficits or surpluses than the CED plan would permit.

As a general rule, therefore, a full-employment balanced budget would not necessarily assure full or high employment. Nevertheless, many economists believe that this plan would have worked quite well over the long run—probably better than actual budget policies have worked in most years. That alone is a major factor in its behalf.

THE PUBLIC DEBT: IS IT TOO LARGE?

Since the 1930s, the number of general budget deficits has far exceeded the number of surpluses. As a result, the government has accumulated a substantial debt. The size of this public debt has been the subject of a good deal of controversy and criticism. Before exploring the issues that are involved, you should examine the facts by studying the charts and statements in Exhibit 3.

Is our present public debt too large? Many people think it is. They fear that the debt will endanger the nation's credit standing and possibly lead to bankruptcy, or burden future generations unfairly. Are these dire predictions justified? Let us examine them and see.

Exhibit 3
The Public Debt and Interest Payments

Chart (a). *Much of our national debt was not incurred as a result of countercyclical fiscal policy, but to help pay for World War II (1941–1945). Further substantial increases in the debt have occurred since the 1960s.*

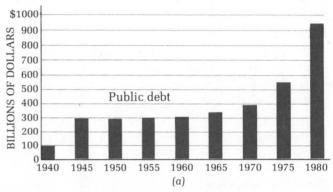

Chart (b). *The trend of a nation's debt relative to its income or GNP is the best indicator of its ability to carry that debt.*

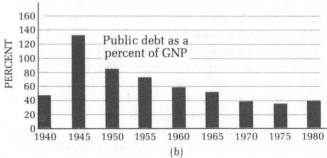

Chart (c). *The chief burdens of a public debt are the annual interest payments. The long-run trend of these payments has been upward since the 1940s.*

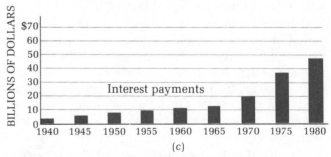

Chart (d). *The long-run trend of interest payments as a percent of GNP has been fairly stable. Note that the percentage is still relatively low.*

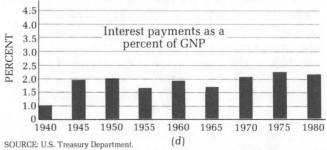

SOURCE: U.S. Treasury Department.

Endangers National Credit and May Lead to Bankruptcy

The credit standing of the U.S. government is determined, as it is for any borrower, by those who lend it money. These are the banks, insurance companies, corporations, and households that buy the bonds and other securities sold by the Treasury. Despite its large debt, the government is able to borrow (i.e., sell securities) in competitive markets at the lowest interest rates.

Bankruptcy is a term applied to a borrower who is unable to pay his or her debts. But the federal government need never go bankrupt. Even if it is unable to borrow new funds to pay off old debts, it can always raise taxes or even print money. Therefore:

> The economic consequences of government debt policies will depend on the nation's productive output, such as its real GNP, and not on the size of the debt per se. Hence, objections that a large public debt may endanger the nation's credit rating, or lead to bankruptcy, are based on psychological fears, not economic facts.

Burdens Future Generations

Many people argue that when the government incurs long-term debt it burdens future generations with the cost of today's policies. There is some merit to this argument, but several aspects of it need to be examined. First, keep in mind that the basic idea of cost involves sacrifice. The real cost of anything is not the dollars you spend for it, but the value of the alternative to it that you give up. In view of this, what are the real costs of public debt? The answer depends on the circumstances under which it is incurred:

1. If the debt is increased by deficit spending during a period of unemployment, resources are put to work that would otherwise have remained idle. Hence, the increase in debt levies no real cost on either the generation that incurs it, or on future generations. Society has benefited from the greater output, and some of it has added to the nation's capital stock inherited by later generations.

2. The situation is somewhat different if debt is increased by war. In that case the war generation bears the heaviest sacrifice because it has gone without civilian goods in order to buy military ones. In addition, spending on war usually starves the nation of capital goods, which are not replaced as fast as they are used up. That burden, more than the debt itself, may be the one borne by later generations.

What about the debt itself? To the extent that it is owed to domestic bondholders rather than to foreign ones, the payment of interest and repayment of capital are merely transfer payments. Of course, like all transfer payments, these are made by one group to another. The taxpayers who finance such payments are not identical with the bondholders who receive them. The result may be a tendency to make the rich richer (because most bondholders are in the middle- and upper-income groups) unless offset by taxation and income redistribution policies.

However, in charging past generations with burdening the future, we must remember that every economic decision helps determine the course of history. The world we live in was largely fashioned by people now dead; the decisions we make today will affect people not yet born. Society thus has an awesome responsibility and should not be too quick to incur large debts before considering both the burdens and the benefits.

WHAT ARE THE REAL BURDENS AND BENEFITS?

To conclude, here are the main burdens of a public debt.

External-Debt Burden   A debt owed to foreigners does impose a burden on future generations. This is because they must pay interest and principal without necessarily receiving corresponding benefits in return. The foreign bondholders may well spend their incomes in their own country rather than here. However, an exception can occur if the original borrowing was spent here to buy capital goods and create jobs. In that case the resulting current output may be large enough to cover most if not all of the interest and principal payments on the debt.

Capital-Consumption Burden   As we learned earlier, any increase in public debt that uses up some of the nation's capital goods without replacing them imposes a burden on future generations. This typically happens during wars, when the government shifts resources out of civilian and into military production.

Inflationary Burden   An increase in the public debt may impose inflationary burdens on the economy. This can happen if, barring any offsetting measures, the debt is incurred during full employment. An increased public debt may also be inflationary if it makes bondholders feel wealthier and thereby raises their propensity-to-consume curve above the level that would otherwise exist.

Transfer-Payments Burden   Each generation as a whole both bears the monetary costs and receives the benefits of the public debt. However, transfer payments will be a burden on present and future generations to the extent that the taxpayers are not the same people as the bondholders. As we have seen, bondholders are predominantly in the middle- and upper-income groups, whereas total tax revenues are drawn from all income groups.

Debt-Management Burden A large public debt may pose a conflict between the government's fiscal and monetary authorities. For example, the fiscal (i.e., Treasury) authorities will normally desire low interest rates in the economy in order to keep down the costs of *refunding*, or selling new bonds. On the other hand, there are times when the monetary (i.e., Federal Reserve System) authorities will desire high interest rates to help choke off inflationary tendencies. (Remember that high interest rates increase the cost of funds, thereby discouraging business investment.) The task of debt management thus raises significant problems. You will read more about them in later chapters.

In contrast, there are important benefits of a public debt. Among them:

Investment Advantages Negotiable Treasury bonds and other securities provide assured safety of principal, interest payments, and a high degree of liquidity. Because of this, these securities are a desirable investment for many families and large institutions.

Fiscal-Policy Tool Changes in the public debt, as already pointed out, can have desirable effects when used as a tool for discretionary fiscal policy. Indeed, modern countercyclical fiscal theory relies heavily on debt manipulation to achieve and maintain economic efficiency and stability.

HOW LARGE SHOULD THE DEBT BE?

In view of these arguments, should the public debt be allowed to grow without limit? There is no simple answer. However, certain principles of debt management are illustrated by the facts presented earlier in Exhibit 3. They suggest that the government's ability to pay its debt interest and refundings is determined by the taxable capacity of the nation. This in turn depends on the growth of GNP. Therefore:

There need be no adverse consequences of an indefinitely large public debt—even a debt running into the trillions of dollars. This is true, provided that:

1. The public debt does not, over the long run, grow faster than GNP. That is, the public debt as a percent of GNP should not rise for a prolonged period.

2. Taxes are used to curb inflationary pressures resulting from increases in debt.

3. Interest payments on the debt are a relatively small percentage of GNP.

In reality, many countries often suffer serious inflation due to an expanding public debt. Such inflations result from the failure of governments to adhere to these basic principles of debt management.

What You Have Learned

1. The Employment Act of 1946 requires the government to strive for the achievement of continuous full employment. Modern fiscal policy would add to this the further objective of price stability.

2. Through government spending and tax policies, aggregate demand can be altered to close inflationary or recessionary gaps. For example, an increase in government spending, with taxes held constant, will raise aggregate demand. An increase in taxes, with government spending held constant, will reduce aggregate demand. And a simultaneous and equal change in government spending and taxes will alter national income by the amount of the change. This is because of the operation of the balanced-budget multiplier principle.

3. Fiscal policy may be discretionary or nondiscretionary. Discretionary fiscal policy is "active" in that it involves conscious changes in government spending and taxation to create expansionary or contractionary effects. Nondiscretionary fiscal policy is "passive" because it relies on automatic or built-in stabilizers to keep the economy on course. Modern fiscal policy embraces some degree of both kinds of policies. However, there are differences of opinion as to the proper combination. The controversy hinges on the extent to which government should be involved in economic activity.

4. In carrying out discretionary fiscal activities, the government's sources of funds may include taxation, borrowing, or printing money. Its spending may include transfer and public-works expenditures. In brief and general terms, taxation tends to be more contractionary than does borrowing. Printing is ordinarily expansionary, and transfer payments are expansionary if they are spent. However, public-works expenditures are even more expansionary because they stimulate the capital goods and construction industries directly.

5. Those who administer fiscal policy must grapple with problems of business-cycle forecasting and timing, and the political and public acceptance of fiscal measures. Also, there are problems of the meshing of federal with state and local fiscal policies, and of government investment which may interfere with or discourage private investment.

6. The full-employment budget reflects the impact of budget surpluses and deficits on the economy's current levels of income and employment. The full-employment budget permits integration of the principles of discretionary fiscal policy with the concept of "fiscal dividends" in order to overcome the undesirable effects of "fiscal drag."

7. There is an erroneous tendency to associate some of the dangers of private debt with those of public debt. Thus, it is often argued that a large public debt can endanger the na-

tion's credit standing, lead to bankruptcy, and inevitably shift a burden of principal and interest payments to future generations. In fact, the real burdens of a debt depend on several factors. Among them: whether it (a) is externally held, (b) results in using up capital which is unreplaced, (c) induces inflationary effects, (d) imposes a transfer-payments burden due to its distribution among bondholders, and (e) creates a debt-management conflict between the fiscal and monetary authorities.

8. A large public debt may have adverse psychological consequences. However, its principal and interest must be assessed in relation to GNP and to the growth of the economy as a whole before a meaningful evaluation can be made.

For Discussion

1. *Terms and concepts to review:*

Employment Act of 1946	fiscal drag
balanced-budget multiplier	annually balanced budget
fiscal policy	cyclically balanced budget
automatic fiscal stabilizers	functional finance
public works	refunding
full-employment budget	

2. Assume that the economy is in recession, the MPC is ½, and an increase of $100 billion in output is needed to achieve full employment. Then, using diagrams if necessary, and assuming that private investment is constant:

(a) How much should government spending be increased to achieve full employment?

(b) What would happen if taxes were reduced by $10 billion? Is this enough to restore full employment? If not, how much of a tax reduction is needed?

(c) What would be the effect of a simultaneous increase in government spending and taxes of $50 billion? A si-

multaneous decrease of $50 billion? Explain why. Would the situation be different in the case of a simultaneous increase in G and T under full employment? Explain.

3. What are our chief automatic stabilizers, and how do they operate?

4. What are the government's sources of revenue and its outlets for expenditures? Which are expansionary? Contractionary?

5. In view of the difficulties of applying fiscal policies, it has been suggested that a law involving an automatic tax-rate formula be enacted. In this way tax rates could be tied to GNP and perhaps other measures and would vary automatically when these measures changed by given percentages. What are some of the chief advantages of such a proposal?

6. What fiscal-policy advantages do you see in the concept of a full-employment budget?

7. "Some increases in government expenditures, such as those for health, education, and welfare, are inflationary, whereas other government expenditures, such as those incurred for national defense and public works, are not." Do you agree? What central questions must be considered to determine whether some government expenditures are more inflationary than others?

8. Evaluate the following argument about the public debt:

No individual or family would be wise to continue accumulating indebtedness indefinitely, for eventually all debts must either be paid or repudiated. It follows that this fundamental principle applies equally well to nations, for as Adam Smith himself said, "What is prudence in the conduct of every private family can scarce be folly in that of a great kingdom."

9. Prepare a checklist of questions covering the chief factors to be considered in evaluating the consequences of a public debt.

Portfolio
The Great Depression and the Keynesian Revolution

Most people today were not alive during the economic disaster of the 1930s. Commonly known as the Great Depression, it was an era of massive unemployment and bankruptcies. One-fourth of the entire labor force was jobless. Savings of a lifetime were wiped out. Homes and farms were lost. Thousands of banks failed. All in all, the decade of the 1930s was an economic nightmare that left few families unaffected.

The accompanying photographs reveal, in human terms, the fears, anxieties, and miseries of the depression years. They also help explain why and how the federal government became the nation's largest employer and financial manager, creating programs and projects designed to absorb unemployed resources.

Enter Keynes

Because of the need to relieve unemployment, Washington experimented with a new idea. President Roosevelt decided to "prime the pump" of the nation's economy with deficit spending by the government. This, of course, is what Keynes advocated—first when he visited Roosevelt in 1934, and later in his great treatise, *The General Theory of Employment, Interest and Money* (1936).

In Keynes' view, government has an important role to play, in depression as well as prosperity. During depression, government spending should exceed tax receipts in order to generate higher levels of economic activity. During prosperity, government spending should be less than tax receipts, or at least not exceed them,

to help sustain the boom without creating inflationary pressures.

These beliefs were refreshingly illuminated by Walter Lippmann, one of the great social commentators of that era:

> In substance, the state undertakes to counteract the mass errors of the individualist crowd by doing the opposite of what the crowd is doing. It saves when the crowd is spending too much, it borrows when the crowd is saving too much; it economizes when the crowd is extravagant, and it spends when the crowd is afraid to spend. It taxes when the crowd is borrowing, and borrows when the crowd is hoarding; it becomes an employer when there is private unemployment, and it shuts down when there is work for all.

Culver Pictures.

The Great Depression started with the stock market crash of October 1929. Variety, *the news medium of show business, tried to inject some humor in the midst of national despair.*

Brown Brothers.

On Wall Street, nervous crowds gathered daily in front of the New York Stock Exchange waiting to hear whether their savings had been wiped out. At the bottom of the Depression in 1933, a share of stock in U.S. Steel could be bought for $22, General Motors for $8, RCA for $2, and Montgomery Ward for $4. The Dow Jones industrial stock average had fallen more than 80 percent from its previous high.

In short, Keynes believed that through government intervention, extreme fluctuations in the business cycle could be greatly reduced if not eliminated.

Brickbats Galore

Economists subsequently labeled these ideas the "Keynesian Revolution." Like most other revolutions, it was born during a period of adversity, and represented an extreme departure from prevailing (classical) thinking. As a result, it became a target of criticism from the right as well as the left.

To political conservatives, Keynes was a dangerous radical whose ideas favoring government intervention were a threat to the preservation of free enterprise. To political radicals, Keynes was an arch-reactionary who was striving desperately to stave off the imminent collapse of the capitalistic system. In reality, of course, Keynes was neither. In 1934, he wrote, in a letter to *The New York Times:*

> I see the problem of recovery in the following light: How soon will normal business enterprise come to the rescue? On what scale, by which expedients, and for how long is abnormal expenditure advisable in the meantime?

In 1944, as World War II was drawing to a close, Keynes played a major role in setting up an international financial system to help stabilize the world's economies. Two United Nations institutions, the International Monetary Fund and the World Bank, were created partly as a result of Keynes' efforts. These organizations were instrumental in promoting the economic development of wartorn Europe and Japan.

Like many visionaries, Keynes never lived to see the full impact of his ideas. He died in 1946, a knight and a director of the Bank of London. But his beliefs live on, and have had profound effects on the economic policies of Western nations.

Brown Brothers.

The federal government and some charitable organizations established food kitchens to provide free bread and soup for the unemployed. Free-food lines were a common sight in many towns.

United Press International.

Bank failures were the major cause of crisis during the early Depression years. In 1932, some 1,400 banks had to close their doors. Between 1930 and 1933, more than 9,000 banks failed. People waited in long lines hoping to get back a fraction of their savings.

USDA-SCS Photo.

United Press International.

Library of Congress.

Extended droughts brought massive duststorms which added to the depressed agricultural conditions. Farm foreclosures were common, and National Guardsmen were often required to preserve order among crowds of angry neighbors. Numerous dispossessed farmers packed their meager belongings and moved westward to California.

Brown Brothers.

Franklin D. Roosevelt Library.

Shantytowns—wooden and tarpaper shacks—were common sights in and around many cities. The less fortunate simply slept in open fields.

Brown Brothers.

Brown Brothers.

Some entrepreneurial spirits tried to survive by selling apples on the street. By the mid-1930s, the Works Progress Administration (WPA), a government agency created by the Roosevelt administration, had put millions of people to work. The WPA built highways and constructed buildings, bridges, airports, and parks. It planted trees, erected libraries and schools, drained swamps, and taught thousands of illiterate immigrants to read and write. The arts also benefited immensely from WPA efforts. Numerous musicians, actors, and writers were put to work, producing what turned out to be some of the best music, theater, and literature of this century.

Most experts today agree that the WPA was the right thing for its time. Nevertheless, it was not always appreciated in its own day. A few of the bridges and highways it built subsequently buckled. Some WPA funds and administrative jobs were dispensed as patronage. And a number of projects involved hardly more than leaf raking. Yet the remarkable thing is that the WPA achieved as much as it did. This is true despite its unwieldy structure, bureaucratic inefficiency, and numerous incompetent administrators. Perhaps the reason is to be found in its fundamental goal. Stated simply, the primary objective of the WPA was not to rebuild America, but to provide jobs for as many unemployed people as possible. Their productivity was a secondary concern. As a result, many authorities now concur that the WPA served several needed functions. Most important: It made people feel wanted and valued, and provided society with many useful goods and services.

Brown Brothers.

Part 3

Money, Banking, and Monetary Policy: The Fiscal–Monetary Mix

Chapter 10

Our Monetary and Banking System

Chapter Preview

What is the nature of money and of our monetary system?

Is credit the same as money? How important is credit in our economy?

What types of markets and financial institutions exist for facilitating the flow of money and credit?

What is a central bank? How is the central bank of the United States organized? What are its functions?

Most people want money. Few can define it. The average person will probably say: "It's cash, and whatever you've got in the bank." An economist may describe it in terms of the four basic functions of money—the needs it fulfills in every society:

1. *A medium of exchange*—money used as a means of payment for things.

2. *A measure of value*—money used to express the prices of things.

3. *A standard of deferred payment*—money borrowed or loaned, until it is repaid in the future.

4. *A store of value*—money saved so that it can be spent in the future.

But money and credit—which is an "extension" of money—are even more important than these functions indicate. For money and credit have a direct influence on the level of economic activity, and some economists argue that the supply of money is the chief determinant of the economy's health.

Money and Our Monetary System

A monetary system's primary task is to provide society with money that is widely acceptable. This money should also be flexible enough in supply to meet the needs of economic activity. The long history of money shows that this is no easy task. As a result, there has been a continuous evolution of monetary systems designed to achieve these two objectives.

What does it mean to say that the supply of money must be flexible? Interestingly enough, this question can only be answered in terms of the demand for money. Indeed, the demand for money, as this and the following chapters show, poses the most fundamental problem faced by our monetary and banking system.

Money and Near-Monies

What is money? The answer is by no means simple. Money has been different things at various times, and has evolved in response to our increasingly complex economy. In the United States several types of money are in use. The most familiar are coins, currency (i.e., paper money), and demand deposits (which is simply checking-account money).

Coins comprise about 1 percent of the total money supply. Coins are _token money_. This means that their value as money is significantly greater than the market value of the metals from which they are made. If this were not so, people would melt the coins down for their metallic content.

Paper money or _currency_—$1 bills, $5 bills, and so on—makes up roughly 25 percent of the money supply. Any paper money you have will almost certainly say "Federal Reserve Note" across the top. This signifies that it is issued by the Federal Reserve Banks. You will read more about them later. Federal Reserve Notes represent more than 99 percent of the total value of paper money in circulation. The rest consists of other types of paper money—some dating far back in history—which are collectors' items.

If you have a checking account at a bank, you have what is called a "demand deposit." Such deposits constitute the largest proportion of the money supply—about 75 percent. Why are demand deposits regarded as money? Because a _demand deposit_ is a promise on the part of a bank to pay immediately an amount of money specified by the customer who owns the deposit. A demand deposit is sometimes called "checkbook money," because it permits transactions to be paid for by check rather than with currency. In contrast, if you have money in a savings account, the bank can, if it wishes, require advance notice of withdrawal. Therefore, this type of account is called a _time deposit_. Such deposits are held in commercial banks and savings banks.

In addition to demand and time deposits, there are various combinations consisting of savings-type checking deposits. These permit depositors to shift their funds between demand and time deposits to take advantage of differences in interest rates. In view of this, what do we mean by "money"?

Currency, demand deposits, and certain kinds of savings deposits are readily convertible into one another. Therefore, all three constitute money.

Some other assets are almost, but not quite money. These are called _near-monies_. Their values are known in terms of money, and they can easily be converted into money if desired. The most important examples are (1) time deposits, (2) U.S. government short-term securities held by individuals and businesses, and (3) the cash value of insurance policies. The concept of near-monies is important, because people who possess near-monies may feel wealthier and hence will have a higher propensity-to-consume curve.

Several different components of money are explained in Exhibit 1.

Monetary Standards

Every nation has a _monetary standard_. This is a set of laws and practices that determines the quantity and quality of a country's money and establishes the conditions, if any, under which currency is ultimately redeemable. For instance, if a nation's money supply were based on the quantity of gold that it had, and if its currency were redeemable in gold, the country would be said to be on a gold standard.

Historically, gold and silver have been the monetary standards in most nations. However, in principle, platinum, copper, diamonds, or any commodity—even skunks or pigs—could serve as a monetary standard if the public were willing to accept it. Gold and silver have commonly been employed because they are widely accepted, limited in supply, durable, and easily divided into monetary units. Diamonds and skunks, in contrast, do not meet all these qualifications. Historically, five major monetary standards have been used in various countries at one time or another.

Gold Coin Standard

The _gold coin standard_, or simply the gold standard, is the one most people have heard about. It has several features:

1. The national unit of a currency (such as the dollar, pound, franc, mark) is defined by law in terms of a fixed weight of gold.

2. There is a free and unrestricted legal flow of the metal in any form into and out of the country.

3. Gold coins are full legal tender for all debts.

Exhibit 1

The Fed Is in the Counting House, Counting Up the Money Supply

"M-1 is up 4 percent. M-2 is up 2 percent. M-3 is down 1 percent."

This is the kind of information that is flashed weekly across the financial news wires. Every Thursday afternoon at 4 P.M., most banks in the country teletype their currency and deposit data to a federal communications station in Culpepper, Virginia. There the figures are collated and wired to Washington, where statisticians at the Federal Reserve System (the "Fed"), the nation's central bank, make the adjustments necessary to report the week's supply of money.

How is the supply of money measured? The answers differ, owing to the growing complexity of our financial system. Today there are more than a half dozen measures of the quantity of money. Six are shown for illustrative purposes, but the first three are the most important ones.

M_1 This consists of currency (and coin) in circulation plus demand or checkbook deposits. M_1 is thus the narrowest measure of the money supply.

M_{1+} This measure, an extension of M_1, consists of readily spendable money. It includes currency, demand deposits,

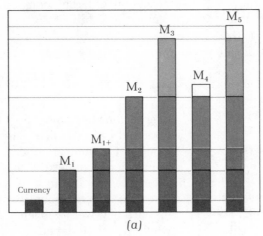

Large CDs

Thrift institution deposits

Time and savings deposits at commercial banks

Savings-type checking accounts

Demand deposits

Currency

(a)

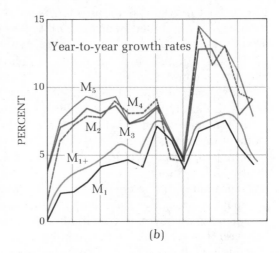

(b)

Chart (a). *The money supply is made up of several different "types." There is thus no ideal measure of money. However, M_1, M_{1+}, and M_2 are the most important measures.*

Chart (b). *Percentage increases in the money supply often vary considerably from year to year. Such wide fluctuations can be a major cause of economic instability.*

4. There is free convertibility between the national currency and gold coins at the defined rate.

5. There are no restrictions on the coinage of gold.

The gold standard reigned supreme for the United States and about fifty other countries from the late 1800s to 1914. It then prevailed on a somewhat modified basis from 1914 to the early 1930s. Since then, no country has been on the gold standard.

Gold serves as an *automatic* disciplinarian. The reason is that under a gold standard the domestic money supply is strictly determined by the amount of gold that a country has. When a nation adhered to this

standard, it found that an outflow of gold to other countries, for business or speculative reasons, would reduce the domestic money supply. This, in turn, could induce contractions in investment, income, and employment within the economy. An inflow of gold from abroad worked in the opposite way. It would increase the domestic money supply and this could have expansionary or inflationary effects at home.

The gold standard thus assured automatic contractions and expansions of the money supply. But it did not always provide such changes at the most appropriate times or in the most desirable ways. Indeed, in the early 1930s those changes were strongly adverse,

and savings-type checking accounts. Examples of the last are credit-union share drafts, negotiable orders of withdrawal accounts at thrift institutions and banks, and automatic transfer accounts which permit switching of funds between savings and checking accounts. This classification (i.e., M_{1+}) is among the most widely used measures of the money supply.

M_2 This includes not only M_{1+}, but also time and savings deposits in commercial banks. This measure is preferred by many economists who believe that changes in the nation's total money stock are the most crucial factor affecting the course of the economy.

M_3 This includes M_2 plus deposits at noncommercial-bank thrift institutions, such as accounts at savings banks and at savings and loan associations. It is thus the broadest of the four measures of money.

M_4 This is made up of M_2 plus *certificates of deposit* (CDs). These are special types of time deposits which purchasers agree to keep in banks for specified periods, usually three months or more.

M_5 This consists of M_3 plus large-denomination CDs.

The answer to the problem of measuring the money supply apparently lies in a blending of all components. Some economists are working to develop a more precise measure, one that can be used to determine the influence of money on the levels of income, employment, and prices.

The Bettmann Archive.

Richard Wood. Taurus Photos.

The nation's "counting house": headquarters of the Federal Reserve System in Washington, D.C., where the nation's money supply is tabulated and reported weekly.

prompting nations to abandon the gold coin standard during the deep depression of that era.

Gold Bullion Standard

A *gold bullion standard* defines the national unit of currency in terms of a fixed weight of gold. However, the gold is held in bars rather than in coin. Gold does not circulate within the economy, and it is available solely to meet the needs of industry (e.g., jewelers and dentists) and to settle international transactions among governments. Gold is thus largely *demonetized*. That is, its influence is removed, for the most

part, from the monetary system, except perhaps for any indirect effects that may arise through intergovernmental transactions.

The United States and most of the other advanced nations adopted a gold bullion standard when they went off the gold coin standard in the 1930s. By switching from a gold *coin* to a gold *bullion* standard, these countries felt that they would be able to "manage" their money rather than be subservient to it, while continuing to preserve confidence in their currencies both at home and abroad. However, the United States abandoned the gold bullion standard in 1971—for reasons explained in the next section.

Gold Exchange Standard

Under a _gold exchange standard_ a nation's unit of currency is defined in terms of another nation's unit of currency. The latter, in turn, is defined in terms of, and convertible into, gold. This standard was particularly popular among nations that lacked gold or were politically dependent on other nations. An example is the British Commonwealth countries' close ties to England after World War I. But with the worldwide abandonment of the gold coin standard in the early 1930s, this standard ceased to exist.

However, to encourage orderly international trade and economic growth, a modified version of the gold exchange standard was reinstituted by noncommunist nations near the end of World War II. It prevailed from 1944 to 1971, and had two distinctive features:

1. By the end of World War II, the United States owned most of the free world's gold. Therefore, the U.S. Treasury, by international agreement, made gold and dollars mutually convertible to foreign central (government-operated) banks at the rate of $35 per ounce of gold. The dollar was thus legally defined as equal to $\frac{1}{35}$ of an ounce of gold.

2. Most other noncommunist countries owned relatively little or no gold. Therefore, by international agreement, the central banks of these nations maintained a fixed par value for their currencies in terms of the dollar by buying and selling their currencies for dollars in the open market. In this way the market exchange rate between U.S. dollars and foreign currencies, such as British pounds, West German marks, and Japanese yen, was kept constant.

The gold exchange standard accomplished what it was designed to do—stimulate post–World War II international trade and development by maintaining stable prices for currencies. But in the 1960s the system began to fall apart. Excessive spending by the United States at home and abroad vastly expanded the supply of dollars, raised domestic inflationary pressures, increased American imports, and thereby flooded overseas markets with dollars.

Most of the dollars wound up in the possession of foreign central banks. These institutions increasingly chose to exchange the green paper for America's yellow metal. This put America's gold reserve under extreme financial pressure. As a result:

In 1971, after the Treasury had been drained of more than half its gold stock in less than a decade, the gold bullion standard for the United States—and therefore the gold exchange standard for other countries—came to an end. Washington announced that the Treasury would no longer convert dollars into gold to meet the claims of foreign central banks. This action completely _demonetized_ gold, preventing it from influencing our monetary system even indirectly through international transactions among governments.

Bimetallic Standard

Under a _bimetallic standard_ the national currency is defined in terms of a fixed weight of two metals, usually gold and silver. The results for the most part, have been unsatisfactory. This is largely because of the operation of an interesting phenomenon first described by Sir Thomas Gresham, a sixteenth-century financier and Master of the Mint under Queen Elizabeth I:

Gresham's Law. When two kinds of metals of differing market values circulate with equal legal-tender powers, the cheaper metal will become the chief circulating medium. At the same time the more costly metal will be hoarded, melted down, or exported, thereby disappearing from circulation. Thus, cheap money tends to drive out dear money.

Gresham's Law operates in the following way. Suppose that the government fixes the official _mint ratio_ of two metals, say silver and gold, at 15:1. This means that 15 grains of silver _(S)_ can be exchanged at the Mint (a division of the Treasury) for 1 grain of gold _(G)_, or vice versa. Thus:

$$\text{MINT EXCHANGE RATE:} \quad 15S = 1G \qquad (1)$$

On the other hand, suppose that in the free market you can exchange $15\frac{1}{2}$ grains of silver for 1 grain of gold. That is:

$$\text{MARKET EXCHANGE RATE:} \quad 15\frac{1}{2}S = 1G \qquad (2)$$

Under these circumstances, silver is costlier (overvalued) at the Mint relative to the market. In view of this, what would you do? The answer is simple:

1. Buy $15\frac{1}{2}$ grains of silver in the market for 1 grain of gold.

2. Take 15 grains of silver to the Mint and exchange them for 1 grain of gold.

3. Keep $\frac{1}{2}$ grain of silver as a profit.

It would pay, of course, for everyone to do this on as large a scale as possible. If that occurred, gold would disappear from the Mint as well as from circulation, and would be replaced by silver.

The government, of course, could counteract by reducing the price of silver (undervaluing it) at the Mint relative to the market. For example, suppose that the government changes the Mint ratio to 16:1. Thus:

$$\text{MINT EXCHANGE RATE:} \quad 16S = 1G \qquad (3)$$

In this case the reverse situation will occur. Silver will disappear and gold will become the circulating medium. Can you explain why?

"Two" Standards   You can see, therefore, that under a bimetallic standard, any change in the market value (as distinguished from the fixed official mint value) of one metal in relation to the other will cause the metal with the higher market value to disappear from circulation. This is because the metal that is relatively cheaper in the market will be taken to the mint, coined, and put into circulation. Meanwhile, coins made of the metal that is relatively dearer in the market will be taken out of circulation and hoarded, or else melted down and sold as bullion. In other words, a fixed mint ratio and a variable market ratio allow people to hold the more valuable money and pass on the less valuable.

This happened during the nineteenth century when the United States was on a *de jure* (according to law) bimetallic standard. Either gold or silver was always disappearing from circulation. Thus, during the first period of bimetallism, from 1792 to 1834, the condi-

tions described by equations (1) and (2) generally existed. That is, the Mint ratio was fixed by law at 15:1 while the market ratio tended to average 15½:1. As a result, gold usually disappeared from circulation and the country was on a *de facto* (in fact) silver standard. During the second period, from 1834 to 1873, the conditions described by equations (2) and (3) existed. Consequently, silver usually went out of circulation, and the nation was on a *de facto* gold standard.

After 1873, the situation changed again. The political power of the silver producers became strong enough to persuade Congress to overvalue silver at the Mint, thereby benefiting the western silver-mining states. As a result, gold disappeared from circulation, and the country returned to a *de facto* silver standard.

In 1900, a Republican Congress passed the Gold Standard Act, placing the country for the first time on a legal gold standard. After that, nothing particularly significant was heard of silver for several decades. Evidently, it had taken Congress more than a century to comprehend the workings of Gresham's Law and to adopt a monetary standard that overcame the inconsistencies of bimetallism. (See Box 1.)

Box 1
When Cigarettes Were Money

Would you be willing to exchange three cigarettes for a tin of cheese? How about five cigarettes for a jar of jam? Would you pay six cigarettes for a chocolate bar?

These are prices that sometimes prevailed at a prisoner-of-war camp in Italy during World War II. Allied prisoners, after receiving their weekly Red Cross food parcels, purchased goods from one another using cigarettes as money.

Cigarettes, in fact, performed all the functions of money—a medium of exchange, a measure of value, a standard of deferred payments, and a store of value. Like gold and silver coins, cigarettes were also sometimes clipped—or in this case "sweated" by rolling them between the fingers so that tobacco fell out. Additional cigarettes could then be made from the accumulated tobacco. Perhaps most interesting, however, is that cigarettes were subject to the workings of Gresham's Law. That is, a cigarette was a cigarette as far as currency was concerned. But for smoking, some brands were more popular than others. As a result, the least preferred brands served as money, while the most popular rarely circulated.

As World War II drew to a close, the prisoners' "cigarette" economy began to falter—because of the increased frequency of Allied bombings and reduced shipments of Red Cross parcels. Nevertheless, cigarettes had served as a monetary standard, thereby demonstrating the functions performed by money in an organized economy.

American Red Cross.

SUBTERRANEAN MARKETS TODAY

In more recent times, cigarettes have served as money in the "underground" economies of certain Eastern-bloc communist countries. In Rumania, for instance, 100-millimeter American cigarettes have established themselves as the medium of exchange for Scotch whiskey, leather jackets, silk scarves, and similar hard-to-get goods. However, certain preferred brands of cigarettes, particularly Kents, rarely circulate as money, thus illustrating again the operation of Gresham's Law.

Inconvertible Paper Standard

Under an _inconvertible paper standard_ the nation's unit of money cannot be freely converted into precious metals, although its value may be expressed in metallic terms. This standard has typically arisen during wars or economic emergencies when governments needed more freedom to control their money supplies than permitted by metallic standards.

During the 1930s inconvertible paper standards became universal as nations sought to manage their currencies in order to hasten economic recovery. The United States and some other advanced countries went on a gold bullion standard for international purposes and on an inconvertible paper standard for domestic purposes. Gold was used to settle international monetary claims, but removed from circulation at home. This was done by not allowing currencies to be exchanged for gold and by not making gold available for domestic monetary use (although it was always available for purchase and sale in many countries by private citizens). From a domestic standpoint, all countries have been on an inconvertible paper standard since the late 1930s.

WHAT IS THE VALUE OF MONEY?

If you cannot get gold for your money, what good is money? The answer is that the real value of money depends on its purchasing power—the quantity of goods or services that can be bought with a dollar.

You have probably heard it said that the dollar today is worth only 60 cents, or 50 cents—or perhaps even less. Such statements try to convey the idea that today's dollar buys only a fraction of what a dollar bought during some period in the past. Which period? It depends on the one you choose. The decline in the purchasing power of the dollar was much greater during some recent inflationary years than it was in the depressed 1930s.

In general:

The value of a unit of money such as the dollar is defined in terms of its purchasing power and is measured as the reciprocal or inverse of the general price level. Thus, the higher the level of prices, the lower the value or purchasing power of a unit of money, and vice versa.

These ideas are illustrated in Exhibit 2.

Exhibit 2
The Value of Money and Consumer Prices

The Consumer Price Index (CPI) is an average of prices of goods and services commonly purchased by families in urban areas. The reciprocal of the CPI thus provides a measure of the "value," or purchasing power, of the dollar.

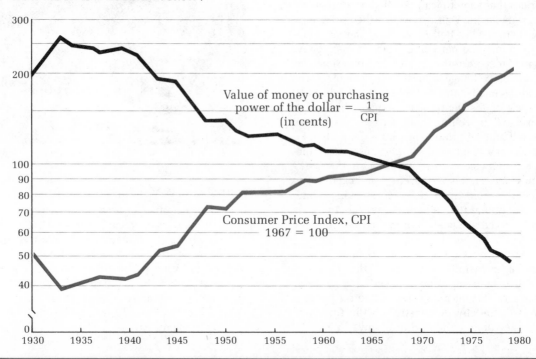

HOW MUCH IS A DOLLAR WORTH?

Value of money or purchasing power of the dollar = $\frac{1}{CPI}$ (in cents)

Consumer Price Index, CPI
1967 = 100

Debt and Credit

Who goeth a borrowing goeth a sorrowing.

Benjamin Franklin

Let us all be happy and live within our means, even if we have to borrow the money to do it.

Anonymous

Most people do not realize that debt and credit are the same thing looked at from two different sides. If a friend lends you money, his credit to you is the same as your debt to him.

The term _credit_ implies a promise by one party to pay another for money borrowed or for goods and services received. Credit may therefore be regarded as an extension of money.

The functions of debt and credit are intertwined with those of money. This is what you would expect, because credit replaces money, supplements money, and in the final analysis provides the base of the nation's money supply.

WHAT ARE THE FUNCTIONS OF CREDIT?

Credit, like money, serves at least two major functions:

1. It _facilitates trade._ The production and distribution of goods is a complex process involving exchanges of property and property rights on a credit basis. Imagine the effect on business if all credit were suddenly eliminated—if everyone in the economy had to pay cash for everything purchased.

2. It _channels savings_ into productive investment, thereby encouraging technological progress and economic growth. A credit system means that businesses can borrow savings and return them to the circular flow of society's income through investment in plant, equipment, and research.

You may be able to think of other functions of credit. For example, credit could affect the time distribution of consumption expenditures. Can you see how, if no lending were possible, a person with a large income today might have to hoard part of it for consumption later, while a person with a low income would have to do without some possible present consumption?

CREDIT INSTRUMENTS

Some credit is negotiated informally by verbal agreement between the borrower and lender, and some is handled on an open-book-account basis between business firms. For our purposes, however, the most significant part of credit is that represented by _credit instruments_. These are written or printed financial documents serving as either promises to pay or orders to pay. They provide the means by which funds are transferred from one person to another.

The principal classes of credit instruments are notes, bonds, and drafts. A _promissory note,_ or simply a _note,_ is one person's promise to pay another a specified sum of money by a given date, usually within a year. Such notes are issued by individuals, corporations, and government agencies. Firms make heavy use of notes in order to borrow working capital from banks at certain busy times of the year. The interest (or discount) on such loans is a chief source of income for commercial banks.

A _bond_ is an agreement to pay a specified sum of money (called the _principal_) either at a future date or periodically over the course of a loan. During this time a fixed rate of interest may be paid on certain dates. Bonds are issued by corporations (corporate bonds), state and local governments (municipal bonds), and the federal government (government bonds). Bonds are used for long-term financing.

A _draft_ is an unconditional written order by one party (the creditor or drawer) on a second party (the debtor or drawee) directing the latter to pay a third party (the bearer or payee) a specified sum of money. An ordinary check is an example. When you write a check, you are drawing a draft against your bank, ordering it to pay someone a certain amount of money.

The foregoing definition of a draft applies equally well to a _bill of exchange_, which is used in international trade. An exporter, for instance, draws up a bill of exchange against a customer, an importer, and discounts it—that is, sells it to the local bank at a little less than its face value. The bank then sends the bill to its correspondent bank in the city of the importer, which presents it to the importer for collection or acceptance at face value. If the bill of exchange were drawn on or accepted by a bank instead of an individual or firm, it would be called a _banker's acceptance_. This is a promise by a bank to pay specific bills for one of its customers.

THE MONEY MARKET

Markets exist for many types of credit instruments, just as for commodities. A _money market_ is a center where short-term credit instruments, such as Treasury bills and certificates, short-term promissory notes of businesses, and bankers' acceptances, are bought and sold. It is thus distinguished from the _capital market_, which deals with long-term instruments such as bonds, stocks, and mortgages. The money market is closely related to the capital market and to the foreign exchange, commodity, insurance, and bullion markets, all of which rely on the money market for credit.

In the money market the supply of short-term funds made available by lenders meets borrowers' demands for such funds. Lenders in the money market consist mainly of the Federal Reserve Banks (which are the primary source of credit for most other banks), large commercial banks, and financial institutions, such as insurance and trust companies. Borrowers are chiefly the U.S. government, brokerage houses and dealers in government securities, and investment banking houses, commodity dealers, importers, exporters, and business firms.

In general, borrowers participate in the money market by selling short-term claims against themselves to lenders. For example, the federal government each week sells 90-day Treasury bills to banks, other institutions, and the general public. Other borrowers sell promissory notes, bills of exchange, and similar credit instruments. In this way borrowers acquire the cash they need to carry on current operations.

The New York money market is the largest in the world. It attracts funds from numerous countries and performs a vital function in financing the short-term needs of the federal government and of the business sector.

THE CAPITAL MARKET

In contrast to the money market, the _capital market_ deals in long-term financial instruments maturing in more than one year or having no maturity date at all. Examples of the latter are corporate stocks and consoles (a type of bond issued in perpetuity, i.e., one with no maturity date). Together, the money and capital markets constitute the _financial market_.

Five types of instruments are bought and sold in the capital market:

1. U.S. government bonds.
2. Municipal (state and local government) bonds.
3. Corporate bonds.
4. Mortgages.
5. Corporate stock.

The yields on these securities differ from one another at any given time. The differences reflect maturity dates, coupon rates, risk of default, tax treatment, and other factors.

In general, municipal bonds tend to have the lowest yields. This is because the interest received by purchasers of such bonds is exempt from federal income taxes. Therefore, these bonds can be sold at lower yields than comparable Treasury and corporate taxable bonds. Treasury long-term bonds generally have a lower yield than comparable corporate bonds, because Treasury bonds carry no risk of default. Yields on high-quality corporate bonds are, in turn, lower than those on mortgages, which cost more to administer and are not so easily marketed.

A comparison of interest yields for these different types of securities is shown in Exhibit 3.

Financial Intermediaries

The institutions that serve the money and capital markets are known as _financial intermediaries_. They are a connecting link between lenders and borrowers, creating and issuing financial obligations or claims against themselves in order to acquire profitable financial claims against others. A chief function of financial intermediaries, therefore, is to provide _liquidity_. This refers to the ease with which an asset can be converted into cash quickly without loss of value in terms of money. In this and the next few chapters you will learn how financial intermediaries fulfill this function.

For our purposes, financial intermediaries may be divided into two broad classes: (1) commercial banks and (2) all other financial institutions. These include mutual savings banks, savings and loan associations, credit unions, insurance companies, private pension funds, finance companies, mortgage companies, and so on. As indicated above, all financial intermediaries serve as wholesalers or retailers of funds.

COMMERCIAL BANKS

All banks deal in money and credit instruments. However, a _commercial bank_ is the only type of bank primarily engaged in making short-term loans by creating demand deposits. (Remember that a demand deposit is the technical term for a checking account.) In addition, a commercial bank may engage in some of the same activities carried on by other financial institutions. These activities include taking savings accounts or time deposits, and providing life insurance. However, a commercial bank's major business is handling demand deposits.

When a commercial bank provides you with a demand deposit, it creates and issues a financial obligation or claim against itself, by agreeing to honor your checks on demand up to the amount of the deposit.

When a bank accepts your savings or time deposit, it creates a claim against itself which is legally payable after a specified time. That is, although a bank rarely does so, it can, if it wishes, require notice of

Exhibit 3
Capital Market Yields

Yields on securities tend to differ from one another at any given time, depending on risk of default, maturity dates, tax advantages, and many other factors. Note that the various yields tend to rise and fall at about the same time.

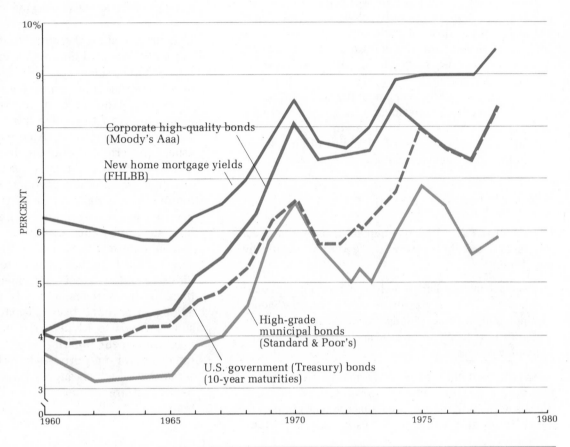

Corporate high-quality bonds (Moody's Aaa)

New home mortgage yields (FHLBB)

High-grade municipal bonds (Standard & Poor's)

U.S. government (Treasury) bonds (10-year maturities)

intended withdrawal—usually 30 days or more. Hence, a time deposit may be thought of as a claim that possesses a stipulated maturity date.

Other instruments representing time-deposit claims are savings bonds, savings certificates, and *certificates of deposit* (CDs). These are a special type of large-denomination time deposit that a purchaser agrees to keep in a bank for a specified period, usually 90 days or more. Commercial banks sell CDs (usually in $100,000 units) at rates competitive with other money-market instruments, in order to discourage corporations from withdrawing money for the purpose of investing in securities. Many CDs are negotiable and can be sold in a secondary market because they offer both liquidity (convertibility into cash) and a yield. However, they are not as liquid as demand deposits. In fact:

Demand deposits are the most liquid of all claims created and issued by financial intermediaries. Because checks written against them are instantly acceptable in ex-

change, demand deposits are included with currency as part of the money supply.

The role played by commercial banks in expanding and contracting demand deposits is of enormous importance in understanding how the economy works. Therefore, commercial banking will occupy a considerable part of our attention in this and in subsequent chapters.

OTHER FINANCIAL INTERMEDIARIES

Like commercial banks, other kinds of financial intermediaries seek to accommodate the particular needs and preferences of borrowers by creating and issuing claims against themselves.

For example, mutual savings banks and savings and loan associations issue time-deposit claims. These are very much like those provided by commercial banks—except in some cases for differences with respect to maturities and yields. The assets or claims against others that the issuing institutions acquire with the funds consist primarily of real-estate mortgages, corporate bonds, and government securities.

Likewise, credit unions issue savings-deposit claims to their members and acquire claims against others primarily in the form of consumer loans. Insurance companies issue claims in the form of policies against themselves and use most of the funds collected in premiums to purchase real-estate mortgages, corporate securities, and government bonds. In like manner, other financial intermediaries generate obligations against themselves in order to acquire funds with which to purchase profitable, but often less liquid, obligations against others.

SOME ECONOMIC IMPLICATIONS

In view of the activities of financial intermediaries, a few facts about their role in our economy should be mentioned.

> Financial intermediaries perform important economic functions. They provide the economy with the money supply and with near-liquid assets. Financial intermediaries thus facilitate investment in plant, equipment, and inventories.

As issuers of claims against themselves and as suppliers of funds to other sectors, financial intermediaries, especially banks, must observe certain practical rules for survival. Two are especially important:

Rule 1: Lend Short and Borrow Long

Banks should make short-term loans, usually for less than a year, and finance them by issuing claims against themselves for longer periods. This would give banks greater control over their short-term interest income while "locking in" their long-term interest expenses. In reality, banks sometimes do the opposite—they "borrow short and lend long." During certain periods, for instance, some banks will have 10- to 20-year loans outstanding, often to small African and Asian countries. However, the banks will be financing the loans with 90-day certificates of deposit, or with other short-term funds.

Rule 2: Spread Loans Widely

A second rule is to diversify loans among different types of borrowers. In this way, by "not placing all of their eggs in one basket," banks can reduce the risks of borrowers defaulting on their loans. In practice, banks sometimes bend this rule in order to expand their loans. As a result, when an industry that has been experiencing considerable growth suddenly takes a turn for the worse, those banks which engaged too heavily in financing the industry's expansion are likely to participate in its decline.

CONCLUSION: MAINTAINING LIQUIDITY

It seems plausible, therefore, that since the claims acquired by financial intermediaries are frequently less liquid than the claims they issue, these intermediaries may sometimes find themselves temporarily illiquid by being unable to meet unexpected demands for payment out of their own assets. This situation has occurred frequently in American history and was especially serious during the depression of the 1930s, giving rise to financial crises or panics.

To help remedy this problem, legislation to protect the public was passed providing insurance for bank deposits and setting minimum financial requirements for banks, insurance companies, and some other financial intermediaries. In addition, federally sponsored institutions have been created to provide liquidity to some financial intermediaries by lending to them or by purchasing assets from them. Notable among these have been special federal banks that supply funds to savings and loan associations and make intermediate-term loans to farmers. But most important for our purposes have been the Federal Reserve Banks, which supply funds to the commercial banks that are members of the Federal Reserve System.

The Federal Reserve System

On December 23, 1913, President Woodrow Wilson signed the Federal Reserve Act. It was, according to its preamble, "An Act to provide for the establishment of Federal Reserve Banks, to furnish an elastic currency, to afford means of rediscounting commercial paper, to establish a more effective supervision of banking in the United States, and for other purposes." Section 4 of the new statute charged the Federal Reserve Banks with making "... such discounts, advancements, and accommodations as may be safely and reasonably made with due regard for ... the maintenance of sound credit conditions, and the accommodations of commerce, industry, and agriculture."

The act marked the beginning of a new era in American banking. Periodic money panics—"runs" on banks by depositors fearing that the banks were failing—had plagued the country for many years. Based on what was learned from the great Panic of 1907, one of the most severe in American history, the act was designed to end extreme variations in the money supply and to end panics, and thus to contribute to economic stability. (See Box 2.)

Box 2
Money Panics and the Banking System

American banking history records a series of attempts to provide a currency that could expand or contract according to the demands of business.

Theoretically, the ability of commercial banks, through the lending process, to expand or contract the amount of money available should have provided for the demands occasioned by changes in business activity.

Commercial banks, however, while they could expand credit, could not add to the amount of available currency. Inasmuch as bank depositors had a legal right to withdraw their money in the form of currency and coin, banks provided for ordinary withdrawals by retaining a part of their total deposits in the form of reserves. These reserves usually consisted of currency, coin, and deposits in other banks.

What if there were a general increase in demand by depositors for their money at a time when demand deposits created by loans were already high? This could create a situation where the available amount of currency and coin might not cover the percentage of reserves which the banks had set up. An unusual demand by depositors forced banks to exchange their assets, such as securities and deposits with other banks, for currency. An attempt by one bank to supply itself with currency by withdrawing its reserve balance from another all too frequently set up a "chain reaction," which resulted in a widespread shortage of currency among many banks.

Some banks were forced to close, although their assets could have been converted into currency if sufficient time had been allowed. A widespread closing of banks resulting from unusual demands by depositors invariably brought on a period of economic depression. These unusual demands were called "money panics," and one that occurred in 1907 set into motion a thorough study of our nation's money system.

The congressional commission charged with this study found that almost all countries with a money supply that could be expanded or contracted to meet the needs of the depositors also had some form of central bank. This bank had the power to issue a currency that depositors would accept. As a result of this and other studies, Congress in 1913 passed the law that created the Federal Reserve System.

Brown Brothers.

The money crisis of October 1907 brought thousands of nervous investors to New York's Wall Street, the financial capital of the world.

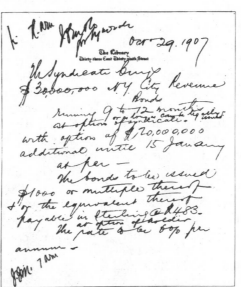

Brown Brothers.

On October 29, 1907, in the midst of the crisis, business buccaneer and financial tycoon John Pierpont Morgan wrote a personal guarantee on his library stationery to support the credit of New York.

Photoworld, Division of FPG.

OBJECTIVES, ORGANIZATION, AND FUNCTIONS OF THE FEDERAL RESERVE SYSTEM

The *Federal Reserve System* is the nation's central bank. This means that, like other central banks throughout the world, the Federal Reserve's chief responsibility is to regulate the flow of money and credit in order to promote economic stability and growth. It also performs many service functions for commercial banks, the Treasury, and the public. In specific terms, the Federal Reserve System seeks to provide monetary conditions favorable to the realization of four national objectives: high employment, stable prices, economic growth, and a sound international financial position.

The Federal Reserve System is organized essentially like a pyramid, as illustrated in Exhibit 4. It is composed of (1) member banks, (2) Federal Reserve Banks, (3) a Board of Governors, (4) a Federal Open Market Committee, and (5) other committees.

Member Banks

At the base of the Federal Reserve pyramid are the System's *member banks*. All national banks (chartered by the federal government) must be members, and state banks may join if they meet certain requirements. Of some 14,000 commercial banks, less than 6,000 are members. However, these member banks are for the most part the larger banks in the country, holding about 75 percent of all commercial-bank deposits.

Each member bank has both obligations and privileges. The obligations include holding specified reserves in its vault and/or its district Federal Reserve Bank against the demand deposits of its depositors, subscribing to the capital stock (and thus being a part owner) of its district Federal Reserve Bank, and complying with the laws and regulations of membership. The privileges include prestige of membership, ability to borrow under certain conditions from its district Federal Reserve Bank, and the opportunity to use the many facilities and services provided by the System.

Federal Reserve Banks

The country is divided into twelve Federal Reserve districts, each with a *Federal Reserve Bank*. There are also twenty-four Federal Reserve Bank branches serving areas within the districts. (See the map in Exhibit 4.)

Technically, each Federal Reserve Bank is owned by its member banks, which are the stockholders. But unlike most private institutions, the Reserve Banks are operated in the public interest rather than for profit. However, they are, in fact, highly profitable because of the interest income they earn on government securities (such as bonds) which they own. Thus, after meeting their expenses, they pay a relatively small part of their earnings to the member banks as dividends, and the major portion is returned to the U.S. Treasury. Note that the district Federal Reserve Banks (and branches) constitute the second level of the pyramid.

Board of Governors

At the peak of the pyramid is the *Board of Governors* in Washington. It consists of seven members appointed by the President and confirmed by the Senate. Members are appointed for fourteen years, one term expiring every two years, thereby minimizing political influence. The chairperson of the Board, who is also a member of the Board, is appointed by the President for a four-year term.

The Board supervises the Federal Reserve System and sees that it performs effectively. But its prime function is to influence the amount of money and credit within the economy. The Board does this by engaging in certain special activities that are explained and evaluated in subsequent chapters.

Federal Open Market Committee

The most important policy making body within the System, the *Federal Open Market Committee*, consists of twelve members—the seven Governors plus five Presidents of the major Federal Reserve Banks. Its chief function is to make policy for the System's purchase and sale of government and other securities in the open market in New York. Actual transactions are carried on by the "Trading Desk" of the Federal Reserve Bank of New York. Government securities bought outright are then prorated among the twelve Reserve Banks according to a formula based upon the reserve ratios of the various Reserve Banks.

Other Committees and Functions

Several other committees play a significant role in the System's operations. One of these is the *Federal Advisory Council*, which advises the Board on important current developments.

Like the central banks of many other countries, the Federal Reserve System also provides a number of important services to the Treasury, the public, and the commercial banks. These services include (1) performing the function of fiscal agent for the Treasury, (2) operating a nationwide "check-clearing house" for member banks, (3) providing for the wire transfer of funds from one bank to another anywhere in the country, and (4) supplying coin and currency for circulation.

Exhibit 4
Organization and Map of the Federal Reserve System

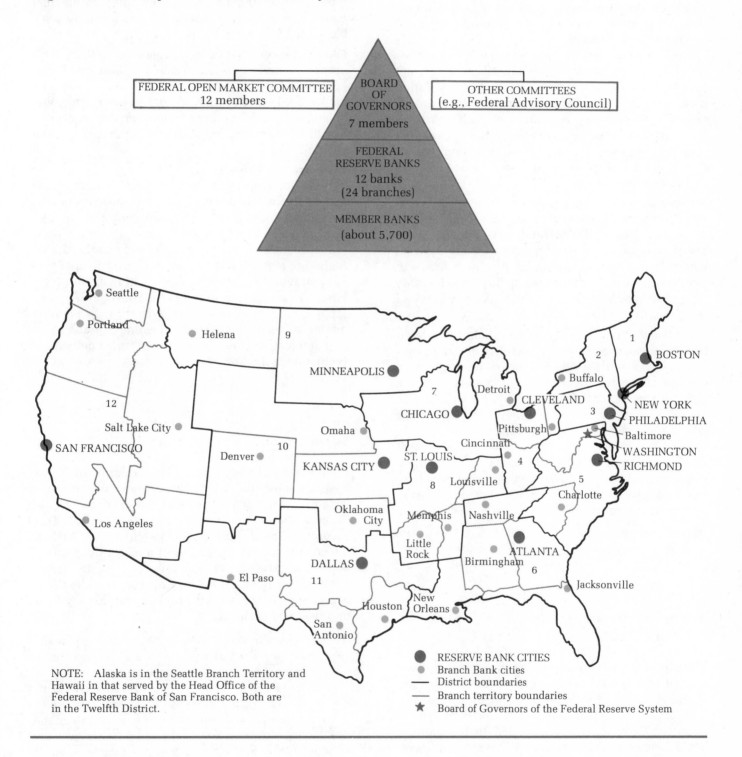

NOTE: Alaska is in the Seattle Branch Territory and
Hawaii in that served by the Head Office of the
Federal Reserve Bank of San Francisco. Both are
in the Twelfth District.

Our Dual Banking System

How is the banking system structured and supervised? This question is important because the banking industry is the largest and most important financial institution in our economy.

The United States has long had what is known as a "dual banking system." This unusual structure, not found in any other country, grew out of legislation passed during the 1860s when Congress tried unsuccessfully to shift the regulation of state-chartered banks from the state governments to the federal government. As a result, our dual banking system consists of two classes of commercial banks—national banks and state banks.

National Banks   These are commercial banks chartered by the federal government. Such banks are required to belong to the Federal Reserve System. About one-third of all commercial banks today are national banks; the rest are state banks. Although fewer in number, however, national banks hold considerably more than half the deposits of the banking system and are larger than most state banks.

State Banks   These are commercial banks chartered by state governments. State banks may become members of the Federal Reserve System by meeting certain conditions. Among them are requirements as to the types of reserves that must be held against deposits. Today, only a relatively small minority of state banks (about 10 percent) are member banks. This is mainly because it is more profitable for most banks to meet the less stringent state requirements than the more rigorous federal ones. As we shall see in later chapters, this poses difficulties for the Federal Reserve System in controlling the nation's money supply.

REMARK   You can always tell a national bank from a state bank. A national bank is required to have the word "national" in its title. If it does not, it is a state bank.

BANK SUPERVISION: A REGULATORY THICKET

The expression *dual banking system* refers to the fact that all commercial banks in the United States are chartered either as national banks or as state banks. This unusual organizational structure, rooted in America's political history, has led to the nation's banks being regulated by several government agencies.

Comptroller of the Currency   This federal agency charters all national banks. It also oversees the operations both of national banks and of those state banks that are members of the Federal Reserve System.

Federal Reserve System   The "Fed," as it is popularly known, exercises some degree of regulation over all banks, national as well as state. However, the Fed's most extensive regulatory powers apply to member banks. These consist of national banks and those state banks that belong to the System.

Federal Deposit Insurance Corporation (FDIC)   This agency supervises the operations of all insured banks (described below). These include national banks, state banks that belong to the Fed, and insured banks that do not. Relatively few banks, however, are uninsured. The FDIC, therefore, has regulatory authority over almost all banks.

State Banking Commissions   All fifty states exercise varying degrees of control over their state-chartered banks. The only banks not subject to state regulations are national banks. This is because they are federally chartered and hence subject to federal regulations.

You can see, therefore, that all banks in the United States are regulated by at least two government agencies, most are regulated by three, and many are regulated by four. As a result, there is considerable overlapping and conflicting supervisory responsibility among the regulatory agencies, leading to much waste and duplication of resources. The complex network of regulation is illustrated in Box 3.

DEPOSIT INSURANCE: PROTECTING YOUR MONEY

What happens to your money if a bank in which you have a deposit fails? Chances are you will be protected by insurance, because of the existence of the *Federal Deposit Insurance Corporation* (FDIC). This government agency came into existence in 1934 when the country was in the throes of a major depression. More than 9,000 banks had failed during the years 1930–1933, leaving depositors unprotected. The FDIC was created to correct this problem and thereby help improve bank stability.

The primary function of the FDIC is to insure deposits (demand and time) at commercial and savings banks. Each insured bank pays an annual premium of $\frac{1}{12}$ of 1 percent of its total deposits, in return for which the FDIC insures each account up to $40,000 against loss due to bank failure. In addition to its insurance function, the FDIC supervises insured banks and presides over the liquidation of banks that do fail. Two parallel agencies which perform similar functions are the Federal Savings and Loan Association, which insures deposits in savings and loan associations, and the National Credit Union Administration, which provides deposit insurance for federally chartered credit unions.

Box 3
The Bank-Regulation Thicket

Duplication of efforts leads to inefficiencies and waste of resources.

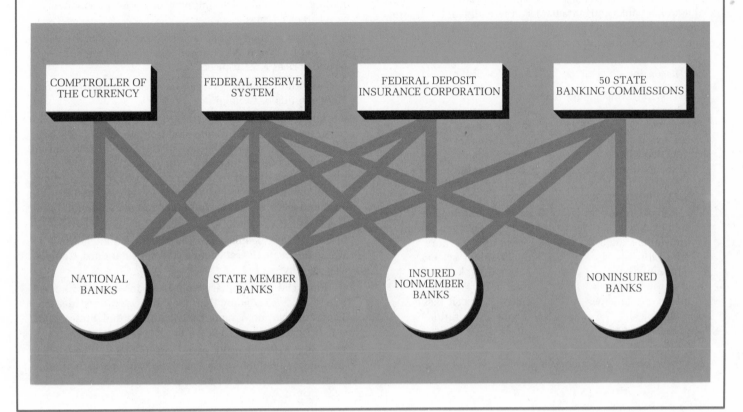

All national banks must be insured by the FDIC, and state banks may apply for coverage if they wish. Since the late 1930s, practically all banks (over 98 percent) have been covered by this insurance. Banks have thus become much more stable than was the case prior to the creation of government insurance. As a result, widespread runs on banks by panicky depositors seeking to withdraw their funds have ceased to occur.

What You Have Learned

1. Money is a medium of exchange, a measure of value, a standard of deferred payments, and a store of value. The demand for money is the most fundamental problem of our monetary and banking system.

2. The "narrowest" supply of money consists of both currency and demand deposits. A broader measure includes savings-type checking accounts. Still broader measures include near-monies, which consist of highly liquid assets such as time and savings deposits, U.S. government short-term securities, and the cash value of insurance policies.

3. Historically, the chief monetary standards of nations have been the gold coin standard, gold bullion standard, gold exchange standard, bimetallic standard, and inconvertible paper standard. Nations today are on an inconvertible paper standard.

4. In varying degrees, credit serves the same functions as money. The chief instruments of credit are notes, drafts, and bonds. Various types of short-term credit instruments are bought and sold in the money market, whereas long-term instruments are bought and sold in the capital market.

5. Financial intermediaries, such as banks, insurance companies, credit unions, and other financial institutions are connecting links between lenders and borrowers. They create and issue financial claims against themselves in order to acquire proceeds with which to purchase profitable financial claims against others. In general, they serve as wholesalers or retailers of funds.

6. The Federal Reserve System is the central bank of the United States. It consists essentially of over 5,000 member (commercial) banks scattered throughout the nation, 12

Federal Reserve Banks (plus branches) located in various cities, and a seven-member Board of Governors appointed by the President and confirmed by the Senate. The function of the System is to foster a flow of credit that provides for stable prices, orderly economic growth, and strong international financial relationships.

7. The United States has a dual banking system consisting of national banks and state banks. Practically all banks are supervised by several government agencies and almost all bank deposits (demand and time) are insured by the FDIC.

For Discussion

1. *Terms and concepts to review:*

money	bill of exchange
currency	money market
demand deposit	capital market
time deposit	financial market
near-monies	financial intermediaries
monetary standard	liquidity
gold coin standard	commercial bank
gold bullion standard	certificate of deposit (CD)
gold exchange standard	Federal Reserve System
bimetallic standard	Board of Governors
mint ratio	dual banking system
Gresham's Law	national bank
credit instruments	state bank
inconvertible paper standard	Federal Deposit Insurance Corporation (FDIC)
promissory note	
bond	

2. Which function of money is most important in today's society? Explain.

3. Which function does money perform least efficiently? Discuss.

4. How would the functions of money be affected if the value of the dollar increased from year to year?

5. The more money you have, the richer you are. Similarly, the more money a nation has, the richer it is. Therefore, nations can become rich simply by printing more money. Do you agree? Discuss.

6. If a nation is on a gold coin standard, as many nations were before World War I, what is its government supposed to do if prices rise? If prices fall?

7. Some of our money is legal tender, but most of it is not. How can this be? Explain.

8. During much of the nineteenth century, the notes (i.e., paper money) issued by state banks circulated at a discount from their face value. The rate of discount usually varied directly with the distance from the issuing bank. For example, a $1 note issued by a bank in New York might have circulated at a 15 percent discount (or at 85 cents) in Chicago and a 30 percent discount (or at 70 cents) in San Francisco. Can you explain why?

9. Today few people who understand financial history would advocate the return to a gold coin standard. Can you suggest why?

10. Financial intermediaries play a much more important role in today's economy than they did several decades ago. They are also more significant in the United States than, say, African, Asian, or Latin American countries. Why?

11. Every nation has its own central bank. Why? What minimum functions does a central bank perform that a commercial bank does not?

There is a certain proportionate Quantity of Money requisite to carry on the Trade of a Country freely and currently; More than which would be of no Advantage in Trade, and Less, if much less, exceedingly detrimental to it.
Benjamin Franklin (1729)

In addition to his many other attributes, Benjamin Franklin was a practical philosopher with a keen insight into economic problems. If he were alive today, he would readily agree that the evolution of money and banking is a history of the efforts put forth by private and public interests to attain, in his words, "a certain proportionate Quantity of Money."

Thus, prior to the American Revolution in 1775, some of the colonies experimented with the issue of paper money. However, such currency often was unredeemable for _specie_—gold and silver coins. Consequently, as business activity expanded and the colonies' needs for money grew, paper money tended to be overissued. By 1780, its value had depreciated to where $1 in specie was worth about $100 in paper currency.

Bank of the United States

After the Revolution, merchants increasingly recognized the need for banks as a source of money and credit. In the 1780s, several banks were established. Among them were the Bank of New York (started by Alexander Hamilton), and what is now the Chase Manhattan Bank (started by Hamilton's arch-rival, Aaron Burr).

But the nation needed a national bank. Such a bank, its supporters argued, would assist the Treasury in its fiscal activities. It would also provide an adequate supply of currency, which, under the new Constitution, the states were no longer permitted to issue. In 1791, largely through the efforts of Hamilton, Congress approved a twenty-year charter establishing the _Bank of the United States_.

Brown Brothers.

The Bank immediately became the nation's major financial institution. However, it placed primary emphasis on serving the commercial interests of the Northeast. As a result, numerous privately owned, state-chartered banks sprang up in frontier areas to serve the rural interests. The tendency of the frontier banks to overissue their own notes was held in check somewhat by the refusal of the Bank of the United States to accept the notes of those banks that would not redeem in specie.

The significance of this became particularly apparent after 1811. In that year, Congressional efforts to renew the Bank's twenty-year charter were narrowly defeated by agricultural groups, who feared the Bank's growing financial power. As a result, the United States was forced to fight the War of 1812–1815 without a central bank to help finance the war. Because of this, the growth of state-chartered banks and the notes they issued mushroomed to fill the void. This led to one of the worst inflations in decades.

The country's first national bank was the Bank of the United States. Granted a twenty-year charter by Congress in 1791, the Bank became more responsive to commercial than to rural interests. As a result, its charter was not renewed in 1811, even though it exercised a restraining influence on the excessive issue of notes by state banks.

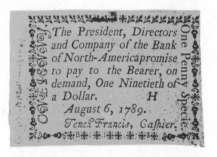

Obverse and reverse of penny note issued by first United States chartered bank, 1789. These competed with currencies issued by many local banks.

The New-York Historical Society.

Congress, convinced that a new national bank was needed, granted a twenty-year charter in 1816 to the Second Bank of the United States. The new Bank, like its predecessor, became financially powerful. But President Andrew Jackson, a strong opponent of the Bank, fought against renewal of the charter. This contemporary cartoon depicts Jackson (left) attacking the Bank and its president, Nicholas Biddle (in top hat), with a veto stick. Jackson remarked: "The lessons taught by the Bank of the United States cannot well be lost upon the American people. They will take care never again to place so tremendous a power in irresponsible hands."

Second Bank of the United States

It took a few years for Congress to become convinced that a new national bank was needed. The Second Bank of the United States was established in 1816, again with a twenty-year charter.

Like its predecessor, the Second Bank gained substantial financial power. It served as fiscal agent for the Treasury, exercised considerable control over state banks by redeeming only those notes that could be redeemed in specie at the issuing banks, issued its own notes, and financed both commercial and rural business interests. However, the Bank's generally conservative behavior caused periods of financial strain throughout the economy. But this began to change in 1828 when Andrew Jackson became President of the United States. A "hard-money" advocate, Jackson believed that neither state banks nor the Second Bank of the United States should be permitted to issue paper money. He thus under-

took measures to weaken the Bank's position. These efforts were successful. By 1836, the Second Bank of the United States had lost most of its effectiveness, and its twenty-year federal charter was not renewed.

Free Banking and the Independent Treasury

During the next twenty-five years, contrary to the wishes of Jackson and the hard-money advocates, state banking and excessive currency issue flourished. Consequently, periods of speculation, intense inflation, and severe depression became frequent occurrences. Some states reacted by prohibiting new banks entirely. Most states, however, went to the other extreme by instituting free banking—permitting anyone to form a bank without legislative approval.

The federal government, on the other hand, reacted in a different way. President Martin Van Buren, who succeeded Andrew Jackson, promoted the creation of an independent

treasury. The result was the passage of the Independent Treasury Act of 1846. This act separated the Treasury from the banking system. The law required the Treasury to receive and disburse its own funds—and thus act as its own bank—instead of dealing with state banks as it had previously done.

In addition, the independent Treasury discovered a device that permitted limited adjustments of the quantity of money in circulation. The Treasury, behaving much like a central bank, could purchase government bonds in the open market. In this way money could be fed into the economy as needed. Conversely, the Treasury could also sell government bonds in the open market. This enabled money to be siphoned out of the economy when necessary. These procedures, which more than a half-century later came to be called "open-market operations," became an integral part of the Federal Reserve System when it was established in 1913.

Greenbacks and the National Banking System

When the Civil War erupted in 1861, the Treasury soon found it necessary to relax its standards. Instead of accepting only specie in payment for government bonds, it began issuing "demand notes"—similar to paper money—to help pay for the war. This resulted in extreme inflation, which caused the market price of gold to rise far above its official price. Gold was thus hoarded, disappearing from circulation in anticipation of still higher prices. Within a few months neither

In 1836, the charter of the Second Bank of the United States was permitted to lapse. Because there was no longer a federal bank to exercise a restraining influence on state banks, the latter entered a new era of rapid growth. Currency issue became excessive as numerous banks issued their own notes. As a result, the nation experienced many periods of sharp inflation.

The $1 Bank Note (1854) typifies the imaginative designs used on bank notes from 1837 to 1863. During this period, the government of the United States had little control over paper money issues, and state and city banks throughout the country printed hundreds of notes for circulation in their locales.

The Dix or $10 note was issued by Louisiana in 1856.

the Treasury nor the banks had sufficient gold available to redeem notes.

With wartime expenditures mounting daily, Congress reluctantly authorized the Treasury to adopt a desperate measure—the printing of money. United States Notes, called green-backs, were issued. The currency, backed solely by the "faith and credit" of the government, was not redeemable in specie and was the first official legal tender money issued in the United States. The Confederate States also issued their own unredeemable currency to help pay for the War.

To facilitate further the financing of the War, Congress passed the National Banking Act of 1863. This law and related legislation provided for the following:

1. Federal chartering of banks, thus making them national banks.

2. Issuance of national bank notes—currency printed by the Treasury and backed largely by government bonds.

3. Federal taxation of state bank notes, thus forcing most of them out of existence.

4. Holding of cash reserves against both notes and deposits.

The act was thus a major step toward standardizing banking practices and reaffirming the existence of both state and national banks—our "dual banking system."

Bimetallism: Silver or Gold?

During the nineteenth century the United States was officially on a *bimetallic standard*. This meant that the dollar was defined by law in terms of both silver and gold, and could be exchanged with these metals by the U.S. Mint at the legal specified rate—called the *mint ratio*.

In practice, however, bimetallism did not really exist because there were always periods in which the free-market price of either gold or silver was higher than the official mint ratio. During such times, mine owners found it more profitable to

Brown Brothers.

It is the misfortune of war that we are compelled to act upon measures of grave importance without that mature deliberation secured in peaceful times. . . . We are about to choose between a permanent system, the National Banking System, designed to establish a uniform national currency based upon the public credit, limited in amount, and guarded by all the restraints which the experience of men has proved necessary, and a system of paper money without limit as to amount, except for the growing necessities of war.

So wrote Senator John Sherman in 1863, just prior to the creation of the National Banking System. The Confederate States had issued their own "unbacked" currency, called fiat money, to help pay their costs of the Civil War. The new National Banking System allowed national banks, acting as agents for the government, to issue currency called National Bank Notes.

sell the relatively high-priced metal on the open market than to sell it to the Mint. As a result, the cheaper metal always drove the more valuable metal out of circulation—a phenomenon known as *Gresham's Law* (described earlier in the text and defined in the Dictionary at the back of this book).

Toward the end of the nineteenth century, gold became overvalued in

During the last quarter of the nine-teenth century, the political power of the western silver-mining states was strong enough to persuade Congress to raise the price of silver at the mint. As a result, although the country was officially on the bimetallic standard, gold disappeared from circulation and the nation, for all practical purposes, was on a silver standard. Paper currency known as silver certificates were issued, and remained in circulation until the 1960s.

This $2 Silver Certificate—Series of 1896—is one of a series considered among the most artistic and interesting ever issued by the U.S. government. The design shows science presenting steam and electricity to commerce and industry.

Culver Pictures.

"You shall not crucify mankind upon a cross of gold."

the market relative to silver. Therefore, gold disappeared from circulation because it was more valuable for nonmonetary uses, while silver served with paper currency as circulating media.

In 1893, following a financial panic, President Grover Cleveland went on record advocating a strict gold standard. This caused fears of deflation. As a result, a controversy ensued which later became the chief issue of the presidential campaign of 1896. William McKinley, a gold-standard supporter, defeated easy-money advocate William Jennings Bryan, who had won the Democratic nomination on the basis of his famous "Cross of Gold" speech. Four years later, the Gold Standard Act of 1900 was passed, placing the United States on a gold standard and thereby ending more than a century of bimetallism.

A serious depression and financial panic in the early 1890s caused the presidential campaign of 1896 to focus on the nation's economic policy. It raised issues that pitted the commercial East against the agricultural West, creditor against debtor, conservative against liberal.

Republican candidate William McKinley, an Ohio legislator with impressive Civil War credentials, argued in favor of a gold standard. Democratic candidate William Jennings Bryan, a Nebraska populist with extraordinary speaking ability, advocated unrestricted coinage of silver. In a spectacular and spellbinding nomination address which ranks among the most distinguished in American political history, Bryan delivered his famous emotion-

packed "Cross of Gold" speech:

We have petitioned, and our petitions have been scorned; we have entreated, and our entreaties have been disregarded; we have begged, and they have mocked when our calamity came. We beg no longer; we entreat no more; we petition no more. We defy them! If they dare to come out in the open field and defend the gold standard as a good thing, we will fight them to the uttermost. We will answer their demand for a gold standard by saying to them: You shall not press down upon the brow of labor this crown of thorns, you shall not crucify mankind upon a cross of gold.

Federal Reserve System

By this time, the weaknesses of the national banking system were apparent. The quantity of money needed to carry on economic activity did not expand and contract smoothly enough to meet the needs of business. As a result, periods of tight money occurred, one of which produced the great Panic of 1907. This led to the creation of a presidential commission—the National Monetary Commission—to examine both American and European banking systems in order to develop a modern system for the United States. After six years of study and debate, Congress approved, and President Woodrow Wilson signed, the Federal Reserve Act of 1913.

The Act created the Federal Reserve System—the nation's first central bank. The new System had a number of interesting features. Some of them are already familiar, but many are not. For example:

○ The nation was divided into twelve districts, with a Federal Reserve Bank in each. All national banks were required to become members of the System, and qualified state banks could join if they wished.

○ Member banks were required to maintain reserves against both time and demand deposits. Reserves were held in each bank's own vaults and in its district Federal Reserve Bank—not in other commercial banks. This helped improve the stability of the System, preventing banks from pyramiding reserves at other banks, such as occurred under the National Banking System.

○ Since the nation was on a gold standard, gold served as a backing for currency. In addition, member banks were required to maintain legal reserves in gold at their district Federal Reserve Banks.

○ Member banks in need of funds could rediscount (i.e., resell) high-grade promissory notes and similar forms of commercial paper with their Federal Reserve Bank. The latter would issue paper currency—called Federal Reserve Notes—in return. These notes, which were obligations of the Treasury, were backed fully by commercial paper and 40 percent by gold.

○ During the early years of the System, the discount mechanism was the chief tool of monetary control available to the Fed. When World War I (1914-1918) broke out, the Fed helped the Treasury finance the war by allowing member banks to borrow from Reserve Banks, using government securities as collateral. The Fed thus accumulated substantial holdings of bonds, much of which were sold after the war. Through these experiences the Fed learned to conduct what is known as "open-market operations." This mechanism, as you will discover in a later chapter, soon became the System's most powerful instrument for controlling the nation's money supply.

Conclusion: Financing Growth

During the many years since the Fed's creation, our monetary and banking system has undergone numerous changes. In the 1920s, legislation was passed enabling national banks to broaden their earnings potential by permitting them to establish branch banks where permitted by state law. Banks were also permitted to make real-estate loans, and to purchase certain investment securities such as corporate bonds. The purpose of this legislation was to make national banks more competitive with state banks.

In the 1930s, several other major financial developments occurred. Because of the failure of thousands of banks, the Federal Deposit Insurance Corporation (FDIC) was created, providing protection for depositors. In addition, the United States and all other countries that were on a gold standard abandoned their commitment to the yellow metal, choosing inconvertible paper instead. In this way, governments could manage their currencies without being subject to the pressures of domestic and international market forces. This proved to be of fundamental importance during the years of World War II, 1939 to 1945.

When the war ended, American banking entered a new era. Branch banking became extensive and bank holding companies, a new form of organization, came into existence. Further changes in the structure of our financial system are still taking place, reflecting the efforts of banks to serve broader markets and acquire more access to funds.

In retrospect, it is useful to recall Benjamin Franklin's remark of 1729, quoted at the beginning of this essay. The story of money and banking, Franklin said, is largely a study of the ways in which our banking system has sought to provide "a certain proportionate Quantity of Money requisite to carry on the Trade of a Country freely and currently." You can now see how, in performing this task, banks provide much of the means for financing the nation's general economic growth.

Chapter 11

Commercial Banking: How Banks Create Money

Chapter Preview

Chapter Preview

How do commercial banks create money? How do they "destroy" it?

How does the process of credit creation by a single bank differ from that of the banking system as a whole?

What is a bank's portfolio? Of what does it consist? What goals and compromises are involved in managing a bank's portfolio?

The average person probably thinks of a bank as a place in which to deposit and withdraw money. But banks are much more than mere depositories for people's funds. They play a fundamental role in the financial and monetary structure of our economy.

In a more specific sense, banks deal in money and credit instruments. A commercial bank, as we learned earlier, is a financial institution chartered by federal or state governments. It is primarily engaged in making short-term commercial and industrial loans by creating demand or checking deposits, and retiring loans when demand deposits are repaid. In addition, a commercial bank may or may not carry on functions performed by other financial institutions. Examples include providing life insurance, holding time (i.e., savings) deposits, making long-term mortgage loans, renting safe-deposit boxes, operating a trust department, and so on.

The present chapter is concerned with surveying the basic economic functions of commercial banking.

The Fundamental Principle of Deposit Banking

You have already learned that there are different measures of money, depending on what is included in its definition. For example, you will recall that there are three main measures:

M₁ This is the narrowest measure of money. It includes currency (and coin) plus demand deposits. Coin is a negligible proportion of the money supply. Therefore, it is usually disregarded for measurement purposes.

M₁₊ This consists of readily spendable money. It includes currency, demand deposits, and savings-type checking accounts. Examples of the last are credit-union share drafts; negotiable orders of withdrawal accounts at banks and thrift institutions; and automatic transfer accounts, which permit switching of funds between savings and checking accounts.

M₂ This includes not only M₁₊, but also time and savings deposits in commercial banks.

There are still broader measures of money. However, we are interested in learning how commercial banks expand and contract the money supply. This means that the measure of money which best suits our purpose is M₁. Therefore, except where otherwise stated, the definition

$$\text{money} = \text{currency} + \text{demand deposits}$$

is the one we shall always use.

Of course, most of us are more familiar with currency than with demand deposits. In view of this, it is appropriate to ask: Who determines the amount of currency in circulation?

The answer is "the public"—you and I and everyone else. This is because currency and demand deposits are interchangeable. Therefore, you will generally cash a check when you need currency, and deposit currency in your checking account when you have more cash than you need.

Everyone behaves in much the same way. As a result, the public always holds the exact amount of cash that it wants, shifting its holdings back and forth between currency and demand deposits. On an average in a year, the economy holds about 25 percent of its money in currency and 75 percent in demand deposits. But at certain times of the year, such as Christmas and Easter, the proportion of currency in circulation increases because people desire more cash for spending. After the holidays, the proportion of currency in circulation decreases as businesses deposit their cash receipts in checking accounts.

THE GOLDSMITHS' PRINCIPLE

Because demand deposits are by far the largest part of our money supply, it is important for us to know how they come into existence and the role they play.

The credit-creation process of deposit banking is based on the following fundamental principle:

All the customers of a bank will not withdraw their funds at one time. On any given day, some customers will decrease their deposits by withdrawing funds in the form of cash and checks drawn on the bank, while others will increase their deposits by depositing funds in the form of cash and checks drawn on other banks. Under normal conditions, the volume of deposits and withdrawals will tend to be equal over a period of time.

This is a modernized version of what may be called the *goldsmiths' principle*—because it was discovered centuries ago by the English goldsmiths. They found that when people deposited gold for safekeeping, it was not usually necessary to store all the gold away. Instead, only a portion of it needed to be kept in reserve, for those individuals who might want to withdraw their gold. The rest could be "put to work" earning interest by being loaned to others with the promise of repayment.

In a bank, of course, there is always the possibility that during some periods withdrawals will exceed deposits. To meet such contingencies, reserves equal to less than 5 percent of deposits are usually more than adequate. However, for reasons of monetary control which will be explained later, the percentage of reserves that banks actually keep on hand is considerably higher than 5 percent.

THE GOLDSMITHS' PRINCIPLE AND FRACTIONAL BANK RESERVES

The ways in which demand deposits are expanded and contracted can best be illustrated in terms of changes in a bank's assets, liabilities, and net worth. These terms have special meanings.

For any economic entity such as an individual, household, or firm, _assets_ are things of value that are owned—cash, property, and the rights to property. _Liabilities_ are monetary debts or things of value which are owed to creditors. _Net worth_, or equity, is the difference between assets and liabilities. Thus, for any individual, household, or firm,

$$\text{assets} - \text{liabilities} = \text{net worth}$$

Therefore, it is also true that

$$\text{assets} = \text{liabilities} + \text{net worth}$$

As you will see shortly, the second equation is the form in which these concepts are usually presented.

When these three classes of data are grouped together for analysis and interpretation, the financial statement on which they appear is called a _balance sheet_. For example, on a bank's balance sheet, the principal assets are government securities and loans; the principal liabilities are demand deposits.

As stated above, the English goldsmiths discovered by experience that they could run a banking business by maintaining a fractional—rather than 100 percent— reserve in gold against their deposits. Although U.S. banks today do not hold gold, the law requires them to maintain fractional reserves of liquid assets against their deposit liabilities. There are three types of reserves: legal, required, and excess.

Legal Reserves   These are assets that a bank may lawfully use as reserves against its deposit liabilities. For a member bank of the Federal Reserve System, legal reserves consist of deposits held with the district Federal Reserve Bank plus currency held in the vaults of the bank—called *vault cash*. Any other highly liquid financial claims, such as government securities, are classified as *nonlegal reserves*. For a nonmember bank of the Federal Reserve System, the laws vary by state. However, almost all states permit vault cash, demand deposits with other banks, and in some cases state and federal securities to count as legal reserves.

Required Reserves   These are the minimum amount of legal reserves that a bank is required by law to keep behind its deposit liabilities. For example, if the reserve requirement is 20 percent, a bank with demand deposits of $1 million must hold at least $200,000 of required legal reserves.

Excess Reserves   These are the quantity of a bank's legal reserves over and above its required reserves.

As you can see from these definitions,

$$\text{legal reserves} = \text{required reserves} + \text{excess reserves}$$

and therefore

$$\text{excess reserves} = \text{legal reserves} - \text{required reserves}$$

It follows that anything which changes either a bank's legal reserves or its required reserves will change its excess reserves. But excess reserves, as we shall see, are the determinants of a bank's lending power. Therefore, as you study the processes by which banks expand and contract demand deposits, you should keep in mind the simple equations above.

Deposit Expansion by a Single Bank

The easiest way to understand the deposit-banking process is to examine the transactions of a single bank over successive stages.

Stage 1   Let us begin by assuming that the reserve requirement against demand deposits is 20 percent and that Bank A has the following simplified balance sheet:

BANK A: BALANCE SHEET

Stage 1: Initial Position

Assets			Liabilities and Net Worth	
Legal reserves		$ 5,000	Demand deposits	$20,000
Required	$4,000		Net worth	1,000
Excess	1,000			
Loans		16,000		
		$21,000		$21,000

Note that the balance sheet "balances." That is, the totals always conform to the equation: assets = liabilities + net worth.

Observe on the right side of the balance sheet that demand deposits are a liability because the bank is obligated to honor checks drawn by its depositors up to the amount shown. On the left side, legal reserves (which consist of vault cash plus demand deposits with the district Federal Reserve bank) are an asset. Loans are also classified as an asset because they represent financial claims, such as promissory notes, held by the bank against borrowers. Returning to the right side of the balance sheet, net worth is the difference between total assets and total liabilities. Net worth is thus a "balancing item" representing stockholders' ownership in the bank. Note that with $20,000 of demand deposits and a reserve requirement of 20 percent, required reserves (on the left side) are $4,000. Since legal reserves are $5,000, excess reserves are equal to $1,000.

Stage 2   Because the bank has $1,000 in excess reserves, it can make loans equal to this amount. Suppose you, a businessperson, borrow the funds and give the bank your promissory note in exchange. The bank then credits your account for $1,000. *Before* you write any checks, how does the bank's balance sheet look?

BANK A: BALANCE SHEET

Stage 2: After the bank grants a loan of $1,000 but before checks are written against it

Assets		Liabilities and Net Worth	
Legal reserves	$ 5,000	Demand deposits	$21,000
Loans	17,000	Net worth	1,000
	$22,000		$22,000

As shown above, demand deposits have risen to $21,000. This reflects the bank's commitment (liability) to honor your checks up to $1,000. In addition, loans have increased to $17,000, reflecting the promissory note (asset) you gave the bank for $1,000. As a result of this transaction, *the bank has created $1,000 of new money.*

Stage 3 Of course, you can take your $1,000 out in currency if you wish. However, since you are in business, you will probably find it more convenient to write checks in order to pay your bills. Suppose that you write a check for the full $1,000 and give it to a supplier from whom you purchased materials. The supplier then deposits the check in his own bank, Bank B, which in turn presents it to Bank A for payment. The effect on Bank A, as shown in the following balance sheet, is to reduce its demand deposits to $20,000 and its legal reserves to $4,000. Note that now required reserves are 20 percent of demand deposits, or $4,000—which equals the bank's legal reserves. The bank, in other words, no longer has excess reserves.

BANK A: BALANCE SHEET

Stage 3: Final Position

Assets		Liabilities and Net Worth	
Legal reserves	$ 4,000	Demand deposits	$20,000
Required	$4,000	Net worth	1,000
Excess	0		
Loans	17,000		
	$21,000		$21,000

The foregoing analysis leads to an important conclusion:

No individual bank in a banking system can lend more than its excess reserves. In other words, when a bank's excess reserves are zero, it has no unused lending power. The bank, therefore, is in "equilibrium" or *fully loaned up.*

Of course, the supplier to whom you gave your $1,000 check might have had an account in Bank A instead of Bank B. In that case the *total* demand deposits of Bank A would have been unaffected. The bank, when processing the check, would simply have reduced your account by $1,000 and increased the supplier's by the same amount. In the great majority of cases, however, this situation does not exist. Instead:

As a borrower writes checks against a deposit, his or her bank is likely to lose reserves and deposits to other banks within the banking system. Hence, a bank cannot afford to make loans in an amount greater than its excess reserves.

Deposit Expansion by the Banking System

Although a single bank cannot make loans for more than its excess reserves, the banking system can lend several times the amount. This provides another interesting example of the familiar fallacy of composition: What is true of the individual is not necessarily true of the whole. Let us see why, by continuing with the foregoing illustration. To keep matters simple, we will focus attention on relevant balance-sheet *changes* while disregarding all other items. As before, the reserve requirement is assumed to be 20 percent.

Stage 4 The $1,000 check you paid your supplier is deposited by him to his account in Bank B. The bank's demand deposits increase by $1,000 and its legal reserves (after the check clears) increase by $1,000. Assuming that prior to this transaction Bank B was fully loaned up, it sets aside 20 percent or $200 in required reserves, and hence has 80 percent or $800 in excess reserves.

BANK B

Stage 4: Bank B receives $1,000 deposit lost by Bank A

Assets		Liabilities	
Legal reserves	+$1,000	Demand deposits	+$1,000
Required	+$200		
Excess	+ 800		
	+$1,000		+$1,000

Stage 5 Bank B, of course, will try to lend $800—an amount equal to its excess reserves. Assuming it grants such a loan, its balance sheet *before* any checks are written will show that demand deposits have risen from $1,000 to $1,800 and, therefore, loans have increased by a corresponding amount. Thus:

BANK B

Stage 5: After Bank B grants a loan for $800 but before checks are written against it

Assets		Liabilities	
Legal reserves	+$1,000	Demand deposits	+$1,800
Loans	+ 800		
	+$1,800		+$1,800

Stage 6 If we assume that the borrower writes a check for the entire amount of the loan, the check will be deposited by its recipient in Bank C. This will

cause Bank B to lose $800 in deposits and (after the check clears) $800 of legal reserves to Bank C. This leaves Bank B with the following net changes:

BANK B

Stage 6: After checks for $800 are written against Bank B

Assets		Liabilities	
Legal reserves (net change = +$1,000 − 800)	+$ 200	Demand deposits (net change = +$1,800 − 800)	+$1,000
Loans	+ 800		
	+$1,000		+$1,000

Notice that the change in Bank B's legal reserves is equal to 20 percent of the change in its demand deposits. Therefore, its excess reserves are zero. Hence, Bank B is in "equilibrium" or fully loaned up.

Stage 7   Bank C receives the $800 deposit which was lost by Bank B in Stage 6, and thus (after the check clears) gains $800 in legal reserves. Assuming Bank C had been fully loaned up, it sets aside 20 percent or $160 as required reserves, and therefore has 80 percent or $640 in excess reserves.

BANK C

Stage 7: Bank C receives $800 deposit lost by Bank B

Assets		Liabilities	
Legal reserves	+$800	Demand deposits	+$800
Required +$160			
Excess + 640			
	+$800		+$800

Stage 8   Suppose that Bank C now grants a loan equal to the amount of its excess reserves. *Before* any checks are written, both its demand deposits and loans will have risen by $640.

BANK C

Stage 8: After Bank C grants a loan for $640 but before checks are written against it

Assets		Liabilities	
Legal reserves	+$ 800	Demand deposits	+$1,440
Loans	+ 640		
	+$1,440		+$1,440

Stage 9   After the borrower writes a check against the loan which is deposited in Bank D, demand deposits and (after the check clears) legal reserves in Bank C go down by $640. This leaves Bank C with the following net changes:

BANK C

Stage 9: After checks for $640 are written against Bank C

Assets		Liabilities	
Legal reserves (net change = +$800 − 640)	+$160	Demand deposits (net change = +$1,440 − 640)	+$800
Loans	+ 640		
	+$800		+$800

Because the increase in Bank C's legal reserves is equal to 20 percent of the increase in its demand deposits, its excess reserves are zero. The bank, therefore, is in equilibrium or fully loaned up.

Stage 10 and Beyond   You can see by now that a logical expansionary process is taking place. It is sufficient, therefore, to illustrate a few further steps in the sequence by noting the changes experienced by each bank on its partial balance sheet, assuming that each bank is initially fully loaned up. (All data are rounded to the nearest dollar.)

BANK D

Assets		Liabilities	
Legal reserves	+$128	Demand deposits	+$640
Loans	+ 512		
	+$640		+$640

BANK E

Assets		Liabilities	
Legal reserves	+$102	Demand deposits	+$512
Loans	+ 410		
	+$512		+$512

BANK F

Assets		Liabilities	
Legal reserves	+$ 82	Demand deposits	+$410
Loans	+ 328		
	+$410		+$410

And so on.

The deposit-creation process thus continues until all excess reserves in the system are "used up"—that is, until no bank in the system has legal reserves greater than its required reserves.

The entire process of deposit expansion is illustrated in Exhibit 1. Note that the *total* expansion of deposits created by the banking system as a whole is a multiple of the initial deposit or increase in excess reserves—in this case $5,000 for $1,000, or a ratio of 5:1.

Exhibit 1
Multiple Expansion of Bank Deposits Through the Banking System
(rounded to nearest dollar)

Cumulative expansion in deposits by the banking system as a whole, assuming a $1,000 initial deposit or increase in legal reserves and a required reserve ratio of 20 percent.

Banks	New deposits created	Required reserves at 20%	New loans (= excess reserves)	Cumulative deposits
A	$1,000	$ 200	$ 800	$1,000
B	800	160	640	1,800
C	640	128	512	2,440
D	512	102	410	2,952
E	410	82	328	3,362
F	328	66	262	3,690
G	262	52	210	3,952
H	210	42	168	4,162
I	168	34	134	4,330
J	134	27	107	4,464
All other banks	536	107	429	5,000
Totals	$5,000	$1,000	$4,000	

If all banks in the system are aligned in decreasing order of new deposits created, the multiple-expansion process can be expressed in the form of a chart.

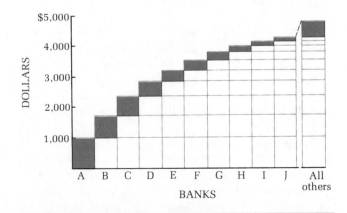

This is the same process that was illustrated above in terms of changes in the bank's balance sheets. Either approach can be used to illustrate what may be called the principle of *multiple expansion of bank deposits*. Can you express this principle in your own words? (You may want to check your definition against that in the Dictionary at the back of the book.)

THE DEPOSIT-EXPANSION MULTIPLIER

You may have noticed that the expansion in demand deposits by the banking system as a whole is determined by two factors: (1) the required reserve ratio and (2) the initial amount of excess reserves. You can verify this from Exhibit 1 by demonstrating that the reciprocal of the required reserve ratio—that is, the number 1 divided by the required reserve ratio—gives what may be called the "deposit-expansion multiplier." Thus, letting R represent the required reserve ratio,

$$\text{deposit-expansion multiplier} = \frac{1}{\text{required reserve ratio}} = \frac{1}{R}$$

Hence, if you know the required reserve ratio, you can determine the deposit-expansion multiplier immediately. For instance, the required reserve ratio was assumed to be 20 percent, or $\frac{1}{5}$. Therefore,

$$\text{deposit-expansion multiplier} = \frac{1}{\frac{1}{5}} = 5$$

This means that an increase in the banking system's *excess* reserves by $1,000 may result in as much as a $5 \times \$1,000 = \$5,000$ total expansion of new deposits for the banking system as a whole. The same formula also applies in a downward direction: A $1,000 contraction in the banking system's *legal* reserves can cause as much as a $5,000 reduction in deposits for the entire system.

These ideas can be generalized and incorporated in a simple formula. Let D represent the change in demand deposits for the banking system as a whole, E the amount of excess reserves, and R the required reserve ratio. Then,

$$D = E \times \text{deposit-expansion multiplier}$$

or

$$D = E \times \frac{1}{R}$$

To illustrate, if $R = 10$ percent or $\frac{1}{10}$, the deposit-expansion multiplier is 10. Therefore, excess reserves E

of $1,000 can result in as much as a $1,000 $\times$ 10 = $10,000 increase in the banking system's demand deposits D.

You can use the preceding formula to answer practical questions involving deposit expansion and contraction. For the latter, E would represent deficient reserves and have a negative sign.

The following definition helps summarize the basic ideas:

> *Deposit-expansion multiplier.* An increase in *excess* reserves of the banking system may cause a larger or magnified increase in total deposits. Similarly, a decrease in the banking system's *legal* reserves may cause a larger or magnified decrease in total deposits. However, the total cumulative expansion (or contraction) will at most be some multiple of the required reserve ratio.

How does this multiplier principle compare with the simple multiplier pertaining to investment and income that you studied in an earlier chapter? Do you see any analogy between the required reserve ratio and the marginal propensity to save? Now is a good time to turn back and refresh your knowledge of the simple multiplier. However, be careful not to confuse the two multiplier concepts. They involve different assumptions and applications.

A "MONOPOLY BANK" AND THE BANKING SYSTEM

It is interesting to observe how the principle of multiple expansion of bank deposits would operate if there were just one bank—a monopoly bank—instead of many independently owned banks.

A monopoly bank would behave exactly as the banking system as a whole behaves. It would receive all deposits and grant all loans. However, since it would be the only bank in the system, there would be no other banks to which it could lose reserves when checks that were drawn upon it were presented for payment. Thus, assuming a reserve requirement of 20 percent, the monopoly bank would simply continue to lend its excess reserves until it produced a 5:1 expansion of bank deposits. It would therefore be able to do what each individual bank in a system of many banks could not do.

THREE QUALIFICATIONS

The principle of multiple expansion of bank deposits assumes that the banking system will produce a magnified expansion in deposits. The expansion may be 5:1 or some other ratio, depending on the reserve re-

quirement and the assumption that banks always make loans equal to their full amount of new excess reserves. Actually, this principle is modified in practice by at least three factors.

Leakage of Cash into Circulation   A business borrowing money from a bank may take part of it in cash. Or, someone who is paid a debt by check may "cash" some or all of it, rather than deposit the entire amount. For these reasons, some money that would otherwise serve as excess reserves will tend to leak out of the banking system, thereby leaving fewer new reserves available for banks to lend.

Additional Excess Reserves   Banks do not always lend out every dollar of their excess reserves. They may desire a "safety margin" or be unable to find good investments. Thus, if the reserve requirement were 20 percent, banks might have available an average reserve of 25 percent. This, of course, would reduce the deposit-creating ability of the banking system from 5:1 to 4:1.

Willingness to Borrow and Lend   The principle of multiple expansion of bank deposits that we have shown assumes, of course, that businesses are willing to borrow and banks are willing to lend. This may not always be so. During a recession or depression, for example, when business executives are gloomy about the future, they may not borrow all that banks have available for lending. Further, banks may prefer the safety of liquidity and hence decide to maintain a higher level of excess reserves rather than risk heavy withdrawals by the public or possible default on loans.

As a result of these three factors:

> The multiple expansion of deposits actually created by the banking system is always somewhat less than the theoretical amount determined from the formula. The formula establishes the upper limit of deposit expansion—not the amount actually realized in all cases.

DEPOSIT CONTRACTION

Does the multiple expansion of bank deposits work in a downward direction? If a bank loses a deposit when all banks are fully loaned up, would this cause a cumulative contraction of demand deposits throughout the system? The answer is yes—for reasons that are essentially the reverse of those given for deposit expansion.

For example, the most obvious way for a bank to lose a deposit is for a depositor to withdraw his or her money in currency instead of by check. (A less obvious but more significant way, which will be examined subsequently, is for the Federal Reserve System to sell government securities.) Suppose, for instance, that you withdraw $1,000 in currency from Bank A. The bank's balance sheet will show a reduction in demand deposits and in legal reserves (vault cash) by that amount. Thus:

BANK A

After depositor's withdrawal of $1,000 in currency

Assets	Liabilities
Legal reserves (vault cash) −$1,000	Demand deposits −$1,000

If the reserve requirement is 20 percent, the decrease in demand deposits of $1,000 reduces Bank A's required reserves by $200. But Bank A still has a reserve deficiency of $800 against its remaining deposits. The most likely way for it to correct this deficiency is to sell some of its earning assets—primarily government securities. If the buyer of the securities pays for them with a check written against his or her deposit in Bank B, the latter institution experiences a deposit decrease of $800. Of this, 20 percent, or $160, represents a decrease in required reserves, and 80 percent, or $640, is a reserve deficiency against the bank's remaining deposits. Bank B, like Bank A, makes up this deficiency by selling some of its earning assets. The deposit contraction process thus continues in this way as indicated by the following table.

Banks	Demand deposits	Required reserves	Earning assets (e.g., government securities)
A	−$1,000	−$ 200	−$ 800
B	− 800	− 160	− 640
C	− 640	− 128	− 512
D	− 512	− 102	− 410
E	− 410	− 82	− 328
All other banks	− 1,638	− 328	− 1,310
Total	−$5,000	−$1,000	−$4,000

Note that the same end result—a reduction in deposits by $5,000 for the banking system as a whole—could have been reached by using the deposit-expansion multiplier. To illustrate, because the reserve requirement is assumed to be 20 percent, the multiplier is 5. Therefore, an initial change (decrease) in demand deposits, and hence in legal reserves, of −$1,000 results in a $5 \times -\$1,000 = -\$5,000$ change in demand deposits for the entire banking system.

To conclude:

> The multiple contraction of bank deposits is essentially the reverse of the multiple-expansion principle. It assumes initially that all banks in the system are fully loaned up. To the extent that they are not, reductions in deposits can be met out of excess reserves, thereby reducing the multiplier effect of the contraction process.

An interesting implication of our fractional reserve system is explained in Box 1.

Managing a Bank's Portfolio

As a bank expands and contracts its demand deposits, it also acquires and disposes of income-earning assets. These assets, plus the bank's cash, make up what is known as its "portfolio." Income-earning assets—or simply earning assets—consist of securities issued by federal and municipal governments and quasi-governmental institutions, and of financial obligations, such as promissory notes issued by businesses. Taken together, earning assets typically comprise between one-fourth and one-third of a commercial bank's total assets. The remaining portion of its total assets consists primarily of other loans, and to a lesser extent of demand deposits with other banks (including Federal Reserve Banks) and vault cash.

A bank's earning assets are thus an important source of its income. The manner in which banks as a whole manage their portfolios, acquiring and disposing of earning assets as the need arises, can have important impacts throughout the financial markets and on the borrowing and expenditure practices of households and businesses. It is desirable, therefore, that we look into some implications of bank portfolio management as a prelude to examining its economic effects in subsequent chapters.

OBJECTIVES: LIQUIDITY, PROFITABILITY, AND SAFETY

Imagine yourself responsible for managing a bank's portfolio. Because one of your major tasks is to acquire earning assets, the problem you continually face is to achieve a proper balance between liquidity, profitability, and safety. What do these terms mean?

Liquidity This is a complex concept, the precise meaning of which sometimes differs among economists and financial managers. For our purposes, however, it may be defined as the ease with which an asset can be converted into cash quickly without loss of value in terms of money. Liquidity is thus a matter of degree. Money is an asset which is perfectly liquid

Box 1
Why Not 100 Percent Reserves?

What would happen if banks were required to maintain 100 percent reserves against demand deposits? Improvements in banking efficiency would be dramatic, because practically all other government regulations could be dropped. Among them: a tangled web of rules and laws governing such factors as reserve levels, capital requirements, interest-rate ceilings, permissible types of asset holdings, and deposit insurance.

Would the elimination of such regulations usher in an era of financial panics similar to those that occurred before the 1930s? Clearly not. Panics occur when the public fears the inability of banks to honor their commitments. This has not happened since the creation of federal deposit insurance in 1934. Prior to that time, in the opinion of many experts, the panics that occurred were caused mainly by a government policy that promised but failed to protect bank liabilities. Under a 100 percent reserve plan, depositors would always be protected because their deposits would be fully backed. Therefore, neither deposit insurance nor many other complicated banking regulations designed to protect the public would be needed.

Despite the apparent advantages, most bankers oppose a 100 percent reserve system. One main reason is that demand-deposit inflows would no longer yield excess reserves, because currency would have to be held dollar for dollar against deposits. Demand deposits, and the interest return that banks earn, would thus be reduced. So too would the profitability of banks because they would no longer be able to create money through new deposits. Instead, banks' incomes would have to depend more heavily on fees charged for services performed.

In fact, only the Federal Reserve System would be able to expand or contract the money supply, by buying or selling government securities in the market. You will learn how this is done in the next chapter. Meanwhile, opposition to a 100 percent reserve system remains strong. Therefore, despite its benefits the system is never likely to be adopted, even though many economists have long advocated it.

2. *Collateral Value.* An asset is likely to be more liquid if it is readily acceptable to lenders as security for a loan.

3. *Contractual Terms.* An asset's liquidity is affected by the contractual conditions under which it is issued. The liquidity of a bond, for example, is greater if it has an earlier maturity date than a later one, or if it is paid off (amortized) in installments over its life instead of in a lump sum at maturity.

Profitability This is a second goal of a bank's portfolio. Profitability is measured by the difference between what you pay for an asset and what you realize when you redeem or sell it, plus any returns you receive in the interim. In the case of government (including federal and municipal) bonds, which are a major form of earning assets for banks, these variables are reflected by a single percentage figure called *yield to maturity*. A bond's yield to maturity may be 5 percent, 8 percent, or some other amount—and it will fluctuate according to market conditions. Portfolio managers, therefore, are continually changing the compositions of their earning assets, selling bonds and other securities which have lower yields in order to purchase those which have higher ones.

Safety This is a third goal in bank portfolio management. Safety refers to the probability that the contractual terms of an investment—such as the interest and principal payments on a bond—will be fulfilled by the borrower. Safety is thus a matter of degree. The safest of all financial obligations are Treasury bills, Treasury notes, and Treasury bonds. This is because these securities are backed by the good faith and taxing power of the federal government. Bonds issued by many municipal governments also rank very high on the safety scale. Interestingly enough, however, safety and liquidity do not always go together. Market prices of U.S. Treasury bonds, for example, may fluctuate substantially, thereby impairing their liquidity. However, the safety of Treasury securities—that is, payment of interest and principal—is never in doubt.

because it can be used as a medium of exchange, and it always retains the same value in terms of itself. A short-term government obligation is an asset that is almost as liquid as money, because it can be readily sold for cash with little or no loss of value. On the other hand, a bank building is a relatively illiquid asset; it cannot easily be sold and may yield a loss when it is. In general, the relative liquidity of an asset is associated with three interrelated factors:

1. *Marketability.* An asset that is bought and sold in an organized market—such as a security traded on the New York Stock Exchange—is highly salable and hence more liquid than one which is not.

THE CONFLICT BETWEEN LIQUIDITY AND PROFITABILITY

The ideal commercial-bank portfolio is liquid, profitable, and safe. But it is impossible to maximize all three objectives—for two reasons.

First, a bank's most immediate obligation is to pay cash upon demand. The moment it is unable to convert demand deposits into cash, it must close its doors. Consequently, the holding of a certain portion of its assets in the form of vault cash helps a bank to meet its liquidity needs.

Second, a bank is in business to make a profit for its owners (stockholders). The holding of earning assets is an important means of attaining this goal. Therefore:

Because a bank's vault cash yields no return, a conflict exists between liquidity and profitability. Thus: too large a proportion of a bank's assets in the form of cash provides greater liquidity but an unnecessary loss of income. Too small a proportion of a bank's assets in cash permits higher income from investment in earning assets, but at the risk of illiquidity and failure.

Evidently, a compromise between these two extremes is needed. Moreover, the compromise must be achieved with a relatively high degree of safety because banks are subject to a variety of legal and conventional constraints which limit the types of earning assets they can acquire.

The nature of the conflict between liquidity and profitability is illustrated in Exhibit 2. The axes of the chart denote the two alternatives available to a bank at any given time. For example, if you are a portfolio manager, you can keep all the bank's funds in cash, in which case the amount is represented by the vertical distance 0M. Alternatively, you can invest all the bank's funds in earning assets, in which case the

Exhibit 2
Investment-Possibilities Line

Each point along the line MN denotes a different combination of cash and earning assets. Thus, point A denotes G dollars of cash and H dollars of earning assets; point B denotes J dollars of cash and K dollars of earning assets. The portfolio manager of a bank seeks to obtain an optimum combination of cash and earning assets, subject to various legal constraints designed to assure a high degree of safety.

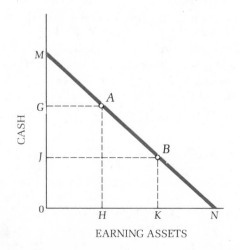

amount is shown by the horizontal distance 0N. However, neither one of these extreme choices is acceptable. Why? Because the former would leave the bank in too liquid a position to earn income, whereas the latter would leave it completely illiquid and hence unable to pay cash on demand.

If we connect the two points, the resulting line MN shows all the combinations of cash and earning assets in which you can invest the bank's funds. Therefore, it may be called an "investment-possibilities line." Of course, there is some point along the line—some combination of cash and earning assets—which is optimum for a particular bank. The challenge faced by every bank's portfolio manager, therefore, is to find that point—thereby achieving the highest possible level of earnings consistent with liquidity and safety.

PRIORITIES FOR ALLOCATING BANK FUNDS

The fundamental goals of a bank portfolio are liquidity, profitability, and safety. However, these goals are in conflict. Therefore, priorities for allocating a bank's funds must be established. Four classes of uses for such funds may be distinguished:

Primary Reserves

This category of assets receives the highest priority. It consists of a bank's legal reserves and the demand deposits it may have with other banks.

Secondary Reserves

This category of assets, which receives the second highest priority, provides "protective investment." It is made up of earning assets that are readily convertible into cash on short notice without substantial loss. Thus, it consists of such short-term financial obligations as U.S. Treasury bills, high-grade commercial paper (such as promissory notes issued by large corporations), banker's acceptances, and call loans to brokers on stock market purchases. The main purpose of this application of a bank's funds is to meet expected and more or less regular seasonal demands for liquidity such as occur during the peak business periods of Christmas and Easter.

Customer Loan Demands

The third priority in allocating a bank's funds is meeting customer credit needs. This is the fundamental purpose for which a bank is created. By fulfilling this objective, a bank enhances its profits because interest rates on loans are usually higher than on securities.

Investments for Income

The fourth priority concerns the use of a bank's funds after the three previous priorities have been satisfied. Thus, any funds which a bank has available after fulfilling the foregoing requirements are invested in long-term securities aimed at providing additional income. These investments, of course, are also subject to constraints of safety. Therefore, they consist primarily of government securities, namely, notes and bonds issued by the federal government and by state and local governments.

This order of priorities applies to all commercial banks. However, the relative distribution of funds for these four purposes differs somewhat among individual banks. In general:

The proportions of its funds that a bank allocates to cash and earning assets, and the proportions that it allocates among different types of earning assets, depend on three major factors. These are (1) legal requirements, (2) local business needs, and (3) the bank's ability to compromise the conflicting goals of liquidity and profitability at the required level of safety.

TYPES OF BANK INVESTMENTS

The types of investment a commercial bank can make are regulated by law. Consequently, three classes of securities are likely to be found in a typical bank's portfolio:

1. **U.S. Government Securities** These consist of _Treasury bills_, _Treasury notes_, and _Treasury bonds_. All are readily marketable if the bank should wish to sell them, and differ from each other by their periods of maturity. They thus contribute greatly to satisfying the liquidity requirements of commercial banks.

2. **Municipal Securities** These are marketable financial obligations issued by state and local governments. Called simply _municipals_, these securities provide holders with interest income that is exempt from all federal income taxes. This is a major reason banks purchase them.

3. **"Quasi-governmental" Securities** These consist of notes and bonds issued by various agencies of the federal government.

For the past several decades, the holdings of municipals in commercial-bank portfolios have increased substantially relative to U.S. government and quasi-governmental securities. This is largely because of the tax-exempt features of municipals.

What You Have Learned

1. Commercial banking rests on the goldsmiths' principle. This enables banks to maintain a fractional—rather than 100 percent—reserve against deposits, because customers will not withdraw their funds at the same time. Hence, the banks can earn interest by lending out their unused or excess reserves.

2. A single bank in a banking system cannot lend more than its excess reserves. When a bank's excess reserves are zero, it is in equilibrium or fully loaned up.

3. The banking system as a whole can expand deposits by a multiple of its excess reserves. This process is known as the principle of multiple expansion of bank deposits. It is of fundamental importance in banking.

4. The amount by which the banking system as a whole can expand or contract demand deposits depends on the required reserve ratio and the initial amount of excess reserves. The required reserve ratio determines the deposit-expansion multiplier, which, when multiplied by initial excess reserves, tells the maximum amount of expansion that can take place.

5. The objectives of a commercial-bank portfolio are liquidity, profitability, and safety. The portfolio manager seeks an optimum combination of cash and earning assets consistent with a high level of safety. Hence, he or she is largely limited to three major classes of investments: U.S. government securities, municipal government securities, and quasi-government securities.

For Discussion

1. *Terms and concepts to review:*

goldsmiths' principle	deposit-expansion
assets	multiplier
liabilities	liquidity
net worth	yield to maturity
balance sheet	primary reserves
legal reserves	secondary reserves
required reserves	Treasury bills
excess reserves	Treasury notes
multiple expansion	Treasury bonds
of bank deposits	municipals

2. What is meant by "fractional-reserve banking"? How did it come into existence? Is it relevant today?

3. An individual bank cannot lend more than its excess reserves. Let us see why—by observing what would happen if it tried to do so.

Suppose that the reserve requirement is 20 percent, and Bank Z is holding:

Assets		Liabilities	
Vault cash	$ 50,000	Demand deposits	
Loans and			$200,000
other assets	160,000	Net worth	10,000
	$210,000		$210,000

(a) How much are Bank Z's excess reserves?

(b) Since the reserve requirement is 20 percent or $\frac{1}{5}$, show the effect on Bank Z's balance sheet after it expands its loans in a 5:1 ratio—that is, by five times its excess reserves—but before borrowers spend their new deposits. What is the percentage of reserves to demand deposits?

(c) Suppose that borrowers write checks against their new deposits and the checks are deposited in other banks. Show the effect on Bank Z's balance sheet after all the checks are presented to it for payment. What has happened to the bank's reserves against deposits?

(d) What can Bank Z do to correct the situation? If it succeeds, how would its balance sheet look?

(e) What do you conclude from this exercise?

4. Suppose that you borrow $1,000 in currency from Midwest Bank and give the bank your promissory note in return.

(a) Show the effects on the following balance sheets:

YOUR BALANCE SHEET

Change in Assets	Change in Liabilities and Net Worth

BALANCE SHEET—MIDWEST BANK

Change in Assets	Change in Liabilities and Net Worth

(b) Complete Balance Sheet 2 below.

BALANCE SHEET 1—MIDWEST BANK

Before making $1,000 loan

Assets		Liabilities and Net Worth	
Cash	$ 3,000	Demand deposits	$20,000
Reserves	4,000	Other liabilities	25,000
Loans	15,000		
Other assets	50,000	Net worth	27,000
	$72,000		$72,000

BALANCE SHEET 2—MIDWEST BANK

After $1,000 in cash is withdrawn by borrower

Assets		Liabilities and Net Worth	
Cash	_____	Demand deposits	_____
Reserves	_____	Other liabilities	_____
Loans	_____		
Other assets	_____	Net worth	_____
	_____		_____
	=====		=====

(c) How would Balance Sheet 2 be affected if you had written $1,000 in checks against your deposit instead of withdrawing the money in cash?

5. Some people argue that "loans create deposits," while others contend that "deposits permit loans." Which statement is correct? Which is likely to be defended by economists? By bankers? Explain.

6. Assume that the reserve requirement is 10 percent. There are no currency withdrawals. Bank A's partial balance sheet is as follows:

BANK A

Assets		Liabilities	
Legal reserves	$ 16	Demand deposits	$100
Loans	84		
	$100		$100

(a) How much can Bank A expand demand deposits? Explain.

(b) If all other banks are in equilibrium, how much can Bank B lend? Bank C? What is the maximum for the whole banking system? Explain.

7. What is the deposit-expansion multiplier when (a) required reserves are 1 percent; (b) required reserves are 10 percent; (c) required reserves are 100 percent?

8. For Bank A, legal reserves are $1,000, required reserves are $800, and demand deposits are $8,000. All other banks are in equilibrium. By how much can the banking system expand its demand deposits?

9. Will the *actual* amount of deposit expansion by the banking system equal the *predicted* amount? Why or why not? Explain.

10. Fill in the gaps for the omitted banks in the following table, assuming a 15 percent reserve requirement against demand deposits. What fundamental principle does the table illustrate?

	Amount added to checking accounts	Amount lent	Amount set aside as reserves
Bank 1	—	$10,000	—
Bank 2	$10,000	8,500	$_____
...	...	...	...
Bank 11	2,315	1,968	347
...	...	...	...
...	...	...	...
...	...	...	...
...	...	...	...
Bank 20	537	457	80
All other banks	_____	_____	_____
Total—all banks	$_____	$_____	$_____

Case
Northfield Bank and Trust Co.: Portfolio Management by Linear Programming

One of the most challenging tasks faced by banks is the management of their portfolios. These consist of cash and earning assets. The latter include various types of financial claims—such as government securities, promissory notes issued by businesses, and other obligations. Banks continually change the composition of their portfolios, striving to achieve the best balance between three conflicting objectives: liquidity, profitability, and safety.

The method that many banks use to attain an optimally balanced portfolio involves a scientific technique known as linear programming. The theory underlying linear programming is mathematical, and its effective application usually requires the use of a computer. Nevertheless, you can gain some appreciation of the nature of linear programming from the following simplified example of an actual bank portfolio problem.

Investment-Possibilities Line
Northfield Bank and Trust Company has $100 million to allocate between two classes of assets—loans and securities. This task is represented in Figure 1 by the line AB, called an "investment-possibilities line." Each point along this line denotes a different possible combination of loans and securities totaling $100 million.

For example, at point A, the bank allocates $100 million to securities and nothing to loans. At point B, the bank allocates $100 million to loans and nothing to securities. At any point between A and B, the bank allocates some money to loans and some money to securities, the sum allocated to both equaling $100 million.

Of course, line AB represents the maximum attainable combinations of loans and securities totaling $100 million. If the bank decides to spend less than that amount, the combination chosen will be represented by a point to the left, or "inside," line AB.

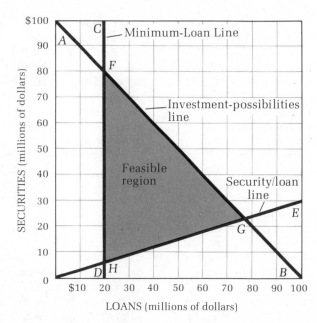

Figure 1 Constraints and Feasibility
Three intersecting straight lines establish the conditions of the bank's portfolio. The problem is to select the most profitable portfolio consist- *ing of a combination of loans and securities. This combination is represented by a point somewhere on the feasible region.*

Security/Loan Line
The bank seeks to obtain the most profitable combination of loans and securities. At the same time it does not want to incur the risk of investing too much in one of these alternatives relative to the other. From experience the bank has concluded that a minimum ratio of $30 in negotiable securities to $100 in loans provides a satisfactory balance. Therefore, line 0E represents what may be called a "security/loan line." Each point along this line denotes a different combination of loans and securities such that the volume of securities is always 30 percent of the volume of loans. For example, point H represents $20 million in loans and $6 million in securities. Point E represents $100 million in loans and $30 million in securities.

Minimum-Loan Line
Banks are in business to lend money. Although they also earn income from

other sources, lending is their most important activity. Every bank, therefore, seeks to accommodate its principal customers by fulfilling their requests for loans. In the case of Northfield Bank and Trust, it has been found that customers' aggregate demand for loans totals at least $20 million for the period under consideration. This is shown by line CD, called a "minimum-loan line." The fact that this line is vertical, intersecting the horizontal axis of the chart at $20 million, means that the bank's portfolio cannot contain less than that amount in loans, irrespective of the amount allocated to securities.

The Feasible Region
You probably realize by now that the three lines defined above represent constraints. That is, the lines impose limiting conditions on the problem. For example, the investment-possibilities line tells you that the size of

the portfolio is limited to a maximum of $100 million. The security/loan line tells you that the amount of money allocated to securities is limited to a minimum of 30 percent of the amount allocated to loans. And the minimum-loan line tells you that the amount allocated to loans must be at least $20 million.

When these ideas are put together on the chart, we obtain the shaded area *FGH*. This area may be called the "feasible region" because it designates the field within which portfolio decisions can be made. Thus, any portfolio represented by a point outside the feasible region violates one or more of the constraints. Conversely, any portfolio represented by a point within the feasible region or on any of its boundaries satisfies all the constraints. Therefore, the bank's portfolio will consist of some combination of loans and securities that can be represented by a point on the feasible region.

Income Line

In order for the bank to select the most profitable portfolio, the rate of return on loans and securities must be known. These returns will vary according to market conditions. However, suppose that for the present period the bank is earning a 10 percent return on its loans and a 5 percent return on its securities. Then, the level of income that can be earned from the portfolio depends on the amounts allocated to loans and securities.

These ideas are depicted in Figure 2. Each line, called an "income line," shows the amount of funds that must be allocated to loans and securities to earn a given income based on the above rates of return. For example, at point *J* the bank allocates $20 million to securities. Assuming a 5 percent rate of return, this produces an income of $1 million. At point K, the bank allocates $10 million to loans.

Assuming a 10 percent rate of return, this also yields an income of $1 million. Therefore, if we connect the two points, we get the income line *JK*. Each point along this line denotes a different allocation of funds to securities and to loans, the combined income from which totals $1 million.

In a similar manner, line *LM* is an income line representing $2 million. As you can see, therefore, the bank's income increases as the income line shifts outward from the origin of the chart.

The Optimum Portfolio

We now have the information needed to determine the bank's optimum portfolio. This is done by combining the essential ideas from the two previous charts, as shown in Figure 3.

The bank's goal is to select an optimum portfolio—a combination of loans and securities that yields the highest income obtainable. As you

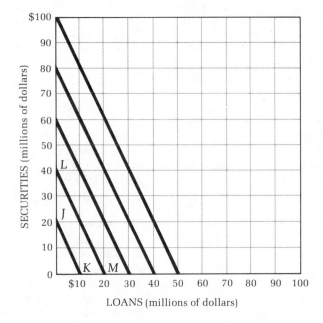

Figure 2 Income Lines
The downward-sloping lines are called "income lines." Each line shows the amount of funds that must be allocated to loans and securities to earn a given income, based on a 10 percent return on loans and a 5 percent return on securities.

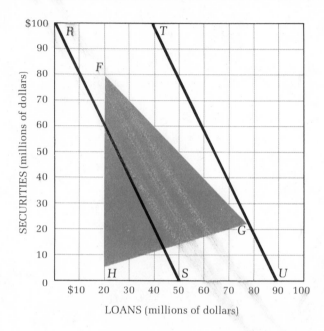

Figure 3 The Optimum Portfolio
The optimum portfolio is determined by an income line TU that lies as far as possible to the right while still touching the feasible region. This occurs at point G. The optimum portfolio thus consists of $77 million in loans and $23 million in securities.

have already learned, there are two considerations to keep in mind:

1. The optimum portfolio will be represented by a point located somewhere on the feasible region.

2. The highest income obtainable will be represented by an income line that lies as far as possible to the right while still touching the feasible region.

Does the income line *RS* determine the optimum portfolio? Evidently not. Although the line contains points that are on the feasible region, none of these points represents the most profitable portfolio.

The income line *TU*, however, does determine the optimum portfolio. This line just touches the feasible region at point G. Therefore, the most profitable portfolio is the one indicated by this point. It represents a portfolio consisting of $77 million in loans and $23 million in securities.

What will be the bank's income from this portfolio? As stated earlier, the bank earns 10 percent on loans and 5 percent on securities. Therefore, earnings will be $7.7 million on loans and $1.15 million on securities, or a total of $8.85 million on the entire portfolio.

Conclusion: A Practical Tool

Northfield Bank and Trust Co. is one of many banks that utilizes linear programming as a management tool. In practice, banks' assets are broken down into detailed categories and grouped in various ways to achieve a balance between three conflicting objectives: liquidity, profitability, and safety. Numerous constraints are then introduced which set limits on the ways in which the variables in a problem may be combined to attain the optimum result. By the use of a computer, answers are thus obtained to complex problems that would otherwise be impossible to solve.

QUESTIONS

1. On the basis of what you have read, formulate a general definition of linear programming. In the light of your definition, can you suggest how a business firm might use linear programming to improve efficiency in production?

2. (a) What constraints does Northfield Bank and Trust Co. face in its efforts to attain an optimum portfolio? (b) Is the portfolio affected by a change in any of the constraints? Explain.

Chapter 12

Central Banking: How the Fed Manages Our Money

Chapter Preview

What types of controls are available to the Federal Reserve for influencing the supply of money and the level of economic activity?

How well do these controls work? What are their favorable and unfavorable features? What sorts of difficulties arise in implementing them?

FED RAISES RESERVE REQUIREMENTS
DISCOUNT RATE INCREASED BY FED
FED TO SELL U.S. SECURITIES

The financial press often contains headlines like these. They emphasize that the *Federal Reserve System* plays not one role, but two. It is a "banker's bank," performing for member banks much the same services that member banks perform for the public. But the Fed is also an important influence on the nation's economic and monetary policy. In the preceding chapter we concentrated on the Fed's banking role. In this chapter we shall look at the part it plays in making and implementing economic decisions.

Essentially, the Fed relies on five instruments to modify or even reverse the direction of the economy. They are (1) reserve ratios, (2) discount rate, (3) open-market operations, (4) margin regulations, and (5) moral suasion. The first three are broad controls because they influence the nation's money supply and the overall availability of credit. The fourth is a selective tool aimed specifically at the stock market. The fifth is a psychological device which relies on personal talk and public opinion. It is convenient, therefore, to classify the first three as "quantitative" or "general" controls and the remaining two as "qualitative" or "selective" controls.

Before we begin, we should explain what is meant by monetary policy. The following definition indicates the central concern of this chapter:

Monetary policy is the deliberate exercise of the monetary authority's (i.e., Federal Reserve's) power to induce expansions or contractions in the money supply. The purpose of monetary policy is to help dampen the swings of business cycles and bring the nation's output and employment to desired levels.

Quantitative (General) Controls

Three types of quantitative or general controls are available to the Federal Reserve for influencing the level of economic activity. These controls consist of (1) changes in member-bank reserve ratios, (2) changes in the discount rate, and (3) open-market operations. Let us see how each helps to shape the nation's monetary policy.

RESERVE RATIOS

You already know that a member bank of the Federal Reserve System is required to maintain legal reserves against its demand-deposit liabilities. Why? Primarily to provide the monetary authorities—those who govern the central banking system—with one of several mechanisms for controlling the money supply.

As you have seen, commercial banks must maintain reserves equal to a minimum percentage of their deposits. Member banks of the Federal Reserve System may hold this minimum reserve as a deposit in a Reserve Bank and as cash in their own vaults. The minimum and maximum reserve limits are 7 and 22 percent. The exact percentages are graduated according to the size of banks' demand deposits.

You can readily see the implications of this from the following partial balance sheets. If the average required reserve ratio for member banks is 15 percent, $15 million of reserves would be needed to support $100 million of demand deposits:

MEMBER BANKS

Assets		Liabilities	
Required reserves	$15	Demand deposits	$100
Excess reserves	0		
Legal reserves	$15		

But if the average required reserve ratio for member banks is reduced to 10 percent, the amount of required reserves declines from $15 million to $10 million. This makes $5 million of excess reserves available for lending:

MEMBER BANKS

Assets		Liabilities	
Required reserves	$10	Demand deposits	$100
Excess reserves	5		
Legal reserves	$15		

The existence of excess reserves, as you already know, can lead to a multiple expansion of demand deposits for the banking system as a whole.

The reverse of this process is also true. For example, an increase in the average required reserve ratio from 10 percent to 15 percent would absorb the $5 million of excess reserves. If banks were fully loaned up and had no excess reserves, an increase in the average required reserve ratio would force them to sell some of their earning assets such as Treasury bills and commercial paper in order to raise the necessary funds to cover their reserve deficiency. This, as you have seen, causes a multiple contraction of demand deposits for the banking system as a whole.

Thus, changes in the required reserve ratio affect the economy as a whole in the following way:

> A *decrease* in the required reserve ratio tends to be expansionary because it permits member banks to enlarge the money supply. An *increase* is contractionary because it requires member banks to reduce the money supply— depending on the degree to which they have excess reserves. The Federal Reserve System can thus affect the supply of money and the availability of bank credit through its control over reserve ratios and the volume of bank reserves.

The ability to alter the required reserve ratio is the Federal Reserve System's most powerful monetary tool. But it is a somewhat blunt tool and is employed relatively seldom. The reason is that other instruments of control can be applied with greater flexibility and more refinement.

CHANGING THE DISCOUNT RATE

Federal Reserve Banks can lend money at interest to their member banks just as the member banks can lend money at interest to the public. Thus, it may be said that the Federal Reserve Banks are wholesalers of credit, while the member banks are retailers.

No Federal Reserve policy tool is as well known or as poorly understood as the *discount rate*. In reality, it is simply the interest rate charged member banks on their loans from the Reserve Banks. However, it is called a "discount rate" because the interest on the loans is discounted or deducted from the loan when it is made, rather than added on when the loan is repaid.

When a member bank borrows, it gives its own secured promissory note to the Federal Reserve Bank. The Reserve Bank then increases the member bank's reserves by the appropriate number. Why would a member bank want to borrow from the Fed? Usually, the member bank wants to replenish its reserves, which may have "run down" for one or more reasons. Some examples:

Seasonal, or Short-Term, Changes in Business Conditions   These may cause some banks to gain reserves during certain busy periods of the year and lose reserves when conditions slacken.

Trend, or Long-Term, Forces   Over a period of years, a bank that grows less rapidly than its closest competitors will often find itself with "too much" reserves. Conversely, a bank that grows faster than its competitors will frequently experience "too few" reserves.

Irregular, or Random, Forces   Unexpected short-term occurrences sometimes cause sharp changes in a bank's reserves. For example, natural disasters, such as floods or storms, or large-scale transfers of funds by corporate depositors, may subject some banks' reserves to severe pressures.

You can see, therefore, that the Federal Reserve's policy at the "discount window" (an expression widely used in banking circles) can be quite significant. It can affect not only banks' reserves but also credit conditions in the economy as a whole.

> The direct effect of changes in the discount rate is to raise or lower the price of admission to the discount window. An increase in the discount rate makes it more expensive for member banks to borrow; a reduction has the opposite effect. Indirectly, increases in the discount rate are usually associated with a rise in market interest rates and a general tightening of credit. Decreases in the discount rate tend to be associated with a reduction in market interest rates and an overall easing of credit.

The discount rate was the preeminent tool of monetary policy in the early years of the Federal Reserve System. This is no longer the case. One reason is that the Federal Reserve is very selective—its loans are deemed a privilege and not a right. As a result, banks often find it easier to replenish their reserves by selling earning assets (e.g., government securities) or by borrowing from other banks rather than by seeking loans from the Federal Reserve. Some important implications of this are explained in Exhibit 1.

OPEN-MARKET OPERATIONS: "THE FED IS IN THE MARKET"

"The Fed is in." This expression is heard frequently on Wall Street when the Federal Reserve Bank of New York buys or sells government securities. Examples of such securities are Treasury bills and Treasury bonds. The Fed deals in these, sometimes as agent for the Federal Open Market Committee, or for the U.S. Treasury, or for other banks (as part of the services rendered by the Federal Reserve System). Such transactions are commonly referred to as open-market operations. They directly affect the volume of member-bank reserves and hence the overall cost and availability of credit. These transactions are therefore the Fed's most important monetary tool for economic stabilization.

Here, essentially, is the way open-market operations work.

Buying Securities   When the Fed buys government securities in the open market, commercial banks' reserves are increased. Thus:

1. If the Fed buys securities from member banks, it pays for them by increasing member banks' reserves with the Federal Reserve Banks by the amount of the purchase.

2. If the Fed buys securities from nonbanks (such as individuals or corporations), it pays with checks drawn on itself. The sellers then deposit these checks in their own commercial banks, which in turn send the checks to the Federal Reserve Banks for collection. The Reserve Banks pay by increasing the reserves of the commercial banks.

Selling Securities   When the Fed sells government securities in the open market, commercial banks' reserves are thereby decreased:

1. If the Fed sells securities to member banks, they pay by reducing their reserves with the Federal Reserve Banks by the amount of the purchase.

2. If the Fed sells securities to nonbanks, they pay with checks drawn on commercial banks. The Federal Reserve Banks collect on these checks by reducing the reserves of the commercial banks. The commercial banks, in turn, return the canceled checks to their depositors and reduce their deposit accounts accordingly.

Illustrations with Balance Sheets

You can gain a firmer grasp of these ideas by seeing them conveyed in terms of partial balance sheets. Here are some examples. (All data are in millions of dollars.)

Case 1   Suppose that the Federal Reserve Bank purchases $1 million worth of government securities in the open market. If the seller of the securities is a member bank, the Reserve Bank pays the member bank by increasing its reserve deposit:

Exhibit 1
Application: How Changes in the Interest Rate Affect Business Investment

If you buy a debt security such as a bond, the effective rate of interest on the security is called the *yield*. The accompanying chart shows the relationship between the market price and effective yield of a $100 bond maturing one year hence with a nominal interest rate of 8 percent (paying its holder an interest of $8 per annum). The chart shows that if you could buy the bond in the market today for around $99, you would receive $100 upon maturity plus $8 in interest, which is an effective yield of about 9 percent. On the other hand, if you bought the bond today at a market price of $101, you would still get $100 back at maturity (thereby losing $1 from your purchase price) plus $8 in interest, making an effective yield of about 7 percent. Thus:

The price of a bond varies inversely with its yield.

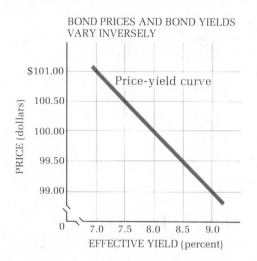

BOND PRICES AND BOND YIELDS VARY INVERSELY

PORTFOLIO EFFECTS AND BUSINESS INVESTMENT

What bearing does this inverse relationship have on longer-term interest rates? The answer can be understood in terms of the impacts on banks' portfolios of securities:

1. When the discount rate is increased, banks find it more costly to borrow. Therefore, they usually replenish their reserves by selling some of their debt securities instead. The increased sale of securities tends to lower security prices and raise their yields. These higher market yields (i.e., effective rates of interest on existing debt securities) tend to push up longer-term market interest rates on new debt se-

curities because all debt securities compete for investors' dollars. The result of higher interest rates is to discourage business investment by making it more costly.

2. On the other hand, when the discount rate is lowered, banks are likely to maintain their borrowings at a higher level than would otherwise be the case. This has effects on longer-term interest rates and business investment opposite to those given above. (Can you explain why?)

RESERVE BANK

Assets		Liabilities	
Government securities	+$1	Member-bank reserve deposits	+$1

MEMBER BANK

Assets		Liabilities
Government securities	−$1	
Reserves with Federal Reserve Bank	+$1	

Case 2 If the seller of the securities is a nonbank—such as an individual or corporation—the check received in payment from the Federal Reserve Bank will

most likely be deposited at the seller's member bank. The member bank, in turn, sends the check to the Reserve Bank for credit to its reserve account:

RESERVE BANK

Assets		Liabilities	
Government securities	+$1	Member-bank reserve deposits	+$1

MEMBER BANK

Assets		Liabilities	
Reserves with Federal Reserve Bank	+$1	Demand deposits	+$1

Note that the effect on reserves is the same in both cases. That is:

Whether the seller of securities is a bank or a nonbank, the legal reserves of the member bank are increased. The amount of the increase will be the value of the securities purchased by the Federal Reserve authorities.

Case 3   The opposite situation occurs when the Federal Reserve Bank sells $1 million of government securities in the open market. If the buyer is a member bank, it acquires $1 million in government securities and loses $1 million of reserves:

RESERVE BANK

Assets		Liabilities	
Government securities	−$1	Member-bank reserve deposits	−$1

MEMBER BANK

Assets		Liabilities
Government securities	+$1	
Reserves with Federal Reserve Bank	−$1	

Case 4   If the buyer of the security is a nonbank, the Federal Reserve Bank receives payment with a check drawn on a member bank. After the check "clears," the member bank's deposit at the Reserve Bank and the buyer's deposit at the member bank are both reduced by the value of the securities transacted:

RESERVE BANK

Assets		Liabilities	
Government securities	−$1	Member-bank reserve deposits	−$1

MEMBER BANK

Assets		Liabilities	
Reserves with Federal Reserve Bank	−$1	Demand deposits	−$1

Note in cases 3 and 4 that the ultimate effect is the same:

The legal reserves of the member bank have been reduced by the value of the securities sold by the Federal Reserve Bank.

Although these open-market operations have been illustrated for only one member bank, the same ideas apply to all member banks within the Federal Reserve System. The overall economic effects of such transactions can be summarized briefly:

Open-market purchases of government securities are expansionary. They increase bank reserves and therefore permit a multiple growth of deposits. Conversely, open-market sales of government securities are contractionary. They reduce bank reserves and hence force a multiple decline of deposits.

Qualitative (Selective) Controls

In addition to its quantitative or general controls, the Federal Reserve can make use of certain qualitative or selective tools. These, like the others, are designed to influence the supply of money and the general level of economic activity. The principal qualitative controls available to the Fed involve margin regulations and moral suasion.

MARGIN REGULATIONS

The Federal Reserve Board is empowered to set the so-called *margin requirement*. This is the percentage down payment that must be made when borrowing to finance purchases of stock. This power was granted by Congress because the excessive use of credit was a significant factor that led to the stock market crash of 1929. The higher the margin requirement, the larger the proportion of a stock purchase that must be paid for in cash. Therefore:

An increase in margin requirements discourages speculation on borrowed credit; a decrease may encourage security purchases.

The margin requirement is thus a device for dampening or stimulating activity in the securities market. This, in turn, can affect the ability of firms to sell securities in order to finance new investment.

MORAL SUASION

Of course, Reserve officials can always exert pressure on bankers by using oral and written appeals to expand or restrict credit. This process, called *moral suasion*, does not compel compliance. Nevertheless, it has been successful on a number of occasions. During recessions, it has sometimes stimulated the expansion of credit by encouraging banks to lend more. During inflations, it has sometimes discouraged lending and restricted the expansion of credit. In a more general sense, the Federal Reserve exercises moral suasion every day when it advises individual member banks on ordinary loan policy.

The Board also has the power to establish interest ceilings on member-bank time and savings deposits. In the past, it has also exercised control over installment terms for the purchase of consumer goods and mortgage terms for the purchase of houses.

To be effective, all the foregoing methods of monetary control are coordinated by the Federal Reserve. Its goal is to promote economic growth and stability through the money supply. You can gain some appreciation of the Fed's task of coordination by examining Exhibit 2.

Impact of the Treasury on Monetary Management

Interestingly enough, the Federal Reserve is not the only organization that can influence monetary management. The U.S. Treasury can, too. You can appreciate this when you realize that the Treasury raises and spends hundreds of billions of dollars annually, conducting its activities through commercial and Federal Reserve Banks. Ordinarily, such huge financial operations would wreak havoc with the banking system. To avoid this possibility, the Treasury plans

Exhibit 2
Flow of Federal Reserve Influence

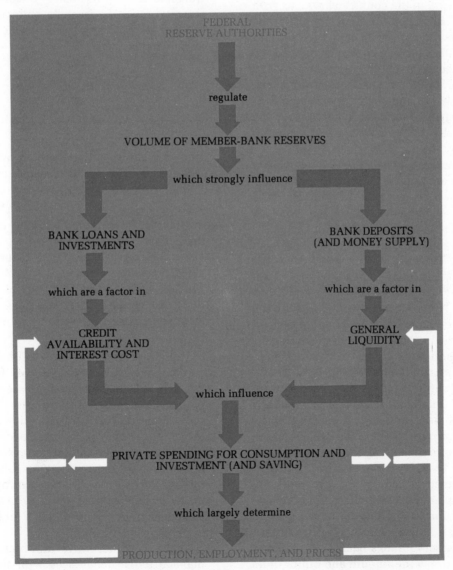

SOURCE: Board of Governors of the Federal Reserve System. Adapted.

its decisions very carefully so as to minimize the impact of its actions on Federal Reserve monetary management. Occasionally, however, the Treasury deliberately synchronizes its activities with the Federal Reserve's in order to supplement the latter's monetary policies.

To understand the Treasury's influence in monetary matters, we will examine its practices with respect to deposit banking. The ways in which its actions can be used for contractionary or expansionary purposes will then become clear.

TREASURY DEPOSITS IN THE BANKING SYSTEM

The Treasury maintains demand deposits with almost every commercial bank in the country as well as with the Federal Reserve Banks. If you send a check to the Treasury in payment of your income tax, the Treasury deposits the check in one of its approximately 14,000 commercial-bank accounts. On the other hand, if the Treasury sends you an income tax refund, its check will usually be drawn on one of its deposits at a Federal Reserve Bank. This practice is adhered to by the Treasury for virtually all its receipts and expenditures.

For example, if you have a checking account at your local bank, chances are the Treasury does too. Therefore, when you send a check to the Internal Revenue Service (a division of the Treasury) to pay your income tax, and the check is presented to your bank for payment, the bank simply transfers the funds from your account to the Treasury's. No money leaves the bank and hence the bank experiences no loss of reserves.

The Treasury, however, is constantly disbursing funds—for government payrolls, national defense, and many other purposes. In order to manage its expenditures efficiently, it periodically makes what are technically known as "calls on the banks." These are communications to banks informing them that on a certain date the Treasury intends to transfer a specified amount of funds from its commercial accounts to its Federal Reserve accounts. When the transfers are made, the reserves of commercial banks are reduced. However, when the Treasury disburses the funds with checks written against its Federal Reserve Bank accounts, the recipients deposit the checks in commercial banks, thereby increasing their reserves. On the whole, the Treasury is able to maintain fairly constant balances with the Reserve Banks because it can plan with reasonable accuracy the amount and timing of its disbursements.

To summarize:

The great bulk of the Treasury's deposits are with the nation's commercial banks. On the other hand, almost all of the Treasury's checks are drawn against the Federal Reserve Banks. This is because the money that the Treasury receives—say, from tax collections or from the sale of bonds—is deposited to its accounts in commercial banks. However, the money that the Treasury disburses—say, for tax refunds, welfare, or defense—is first transferred to its accounts at the Federal Reserve Banks and then checks are issued against those Federal Reserve deposits.

This seems like a strange way for the Treasury to conduct its transactions. However, it adheres to this policy in order to minimize the possible disruptive effects that its large-scale transactions would exert on the banks and the money market. In general, the reductions in reserves created by the Treasury's transfers are approximately offset by the increases in reserves resulting from its outlays. In this way, reasonable stability among the banks and financial markets is maintained.

CONTRACTIONARY AND EXPANSIONARY ACTIONS

You can see that the ways in which the Treasury manages its cash balances can exercise important influences on monetary policy. For example:

1. Suppose that the Treasury wishes to *contract* the availability of commercial-bank credit. In that case the Treasury can increase its average balance at the Federal Reserve Banks by transferring from its commercial accounts to its Federal Reserve accounts more funds than it intends to disburse. The effect is to reduce the volume of commercial-bank reserves and hence create a multiple contraction of demand deposits.

2. If the Treasury wishes to *expand* the availability of commercial-bank credit, it can follow the reverse procedure. That is, it can decrease its average balance by transferring deposits from the Federal Reserve to the commercial banks. This action is not as flexible as the contractionary process, because the Treasury always maintains a minimum level of Federal Reserve balances sufficient to carry on its operations. Nevertheless, the shifting of funds into commercial accounts provides the banking system with increased reserves. This may, of course, produce a multiple expansion of bank deposits.

There are other ways in which the Treasury can manage its cash balances with the intention of influencing monetary policy. In practice, however, the Treasury rarely uses any of the techniques for that purpose. Instead, it tries to perform its fiscal operations without disrupting the banks and the money market, and leaves matters of monetary management to the Federal Reserve authorities.

Is Monetary Policy Really Useful?

How effective is monetary policy in influencing economic activity? As with all policy areas of economics, this question is the subject of continuous debate. The chief pros and cons can be outlined briefly.

ADVANTAGES OF MONETARY POLICY

In evaluating the usefulness of monetary policy, it is often instructive to make comparisons with fiscal policy. This is an alternative and sometimes complementary method of fighting inflation and unemployment.

Nondiscriminatory

Monetary controls are ordinarily employed in a general way to influence the total volume of credit. The Fed is nondiscriminatory with respect to the borrowers or activities that are to be encouraged or curtailed, and leaves it to the market to be "discriminatory." The home construction industry, for example, feels the effects of tight credit more quickly than most other industries because of its dependence on the mortgage market. Fiscal policy, on the other hand, involves changes in taxation and government spending, and these changes can directly alter the composition of total production as well as its overall level.

Flexible

Because the Board of Governors controls monetary policy, changes can be made quickly and smoothly without getting snarled in administrative red tape. In contrast, fiscal policy involves budgetary considerations of taxation and spending. On such matters, Congress usually deliberates for many months before arriving at a decision.

Nonpolitical

Congress gave the Federal Reserve System political independence to assure its effective performance. It provided fourteen-year terms of office for appointed Board members, made them ineligible for reappointment, staggered their terms of office, and provided for the election of Reserve Bank presidents by their own boards of directors subject to the approval of the Federal Reserve Board. As a result, the institution can base its day-to-day decisions on economic rather than on political grounds. In contrast, fiscal policy is always partly influenced by politics.

LIMITATIONS OF MONETARY POLICY

Whereas the advantages of monetary policy are fairly general, most of its limitations arise out of specific situations and circumstances.

Incomplete Countercyclical Effectiveness

During an inflation the Federal Reserve can use its instruments of control to choke off borrowing and to establish an effective tight money policy. But during a recession, even the easiest money policy cannot ensure that businesspersons will want to borrow. If they regard the business outlook as poor, the desired increase in loans and spending will not be realized. Further, there is the possibility that commercial bankers may be unwilling to lend when they have excess reserves. For these reasons, monetary policy is far more effective as an anti-inflationary, rather than an antirecessionary, device.

Cost-Push or Profit-Push Inflation

Some observers contend that inflation often results from upward pressure on wages and prices. This pressure arises because of the monopolistic power that large unions and business firms are able to exert in the market. If this argument is true, monetary policy can do little to correct the situation. At most, actions taken by the Federal Reserve may help dampen either a cost-push or profit-push inflation, but will not eliminate either.

Conflict with Treasury Objectives

Every debtor likes low interest rates. This is especially true of the U.S. Treasury, which is the biggest debtor of all. Because the Treasury is continually refunding or selling new bonds, it wants to keep the interest cost as low as possible. Indeed, a difference of 1 percent in the interest rate on government securities can cost the Treasury several billion dollars. Reserve officials, on the other hand, regard high interest rates as an important anti-inflationary weapon. In the past these two distinctly different goals have at times resulted in a policy conflict between the Treasury and the Federal Reserve. Although compromises or "accords" were eventually worked out, they tended to reduce somewhat the full effectiveness of anti-inflationary monetary policies.

Changes in the Velocity of Money

Discretionary monetary policy, as you have seen, requires that the Federal Reserve authorities follow a two-pronged approach:

1. In prosperity, decrease the money supply to curb inflation.
2. In recession, increase the money supply to stimulate recovery.

Unfortunately, the effectiveness of these actions may sometimes be at least partially reduced by opposite changes in the velocity of money. This is simply the number of times per year that a dollar is spent. As you might expect, the velocity of money is affected by the public's confidence in the future course of the economy. For example, in prosperity, when people are optimistic, they often tend to spend more freely. Hence, velocity may increase at a time when the money supply should be reduced. In recession, when people are pessimistic, they often tend to curb their spending, Hence, velocity may decrease at a time when the money supply should be increased.

Significant changes in the velocity of money can therefore exert a direct influence on the price level. How? By causing prices to rise when velocity increases and to decline when velocity decreases. As a result, changes in velocity may offset, to some extent, the monetary authorities' efforts to stabilize the economy by contracting or expanding the money supply. We shall examine these concepts more fully in the next chapter.

Lack of Complete Control

During the past several decades, two types of situations have made it more difficult for the Reserve authorities to exercise as much control over the total volume of lending as they would like.

1. There has been a substantial growth of *financial intermediaries*—such nonbank lenders as savings and loan associations, insurance companies, personal finance companies, and credit unions. These institutions hold large volumes of savings which they are continually trying to "put to work" by investing or lending to the public. This helps to offset restrictive monetary policies of the Reserve officials.

2. Large holdings of government securities are in the hands of commercial banks and business corporations. These organizations can sell off the securities as needed to obtain additional cash.

Because both of these situations are outside the Fed's control, they tend to increase the velocity of money. This in turn can weaken the effectiveness of monetary policies.

Forecasting and Timing

Although monetary policies may be implemented more quickly than fiscal policies, monetary policies nevertheless suffer from similar kinds of forecasting and timing problems. As a result, the Federal Reserve has sometimes applied the brakes "too soon," thereby stopping economic expansions short of full employment.

The fact that there are more limitations than advantages should not lead you to believe that monetary policy is useless. It is a powerful force for stabilization and will continue to play an important role in the economy.

What You Have Learned

1. The chief responsibility of the central banking system—the Federal Reserve System—is to regulate the supply of money and credit so as to promote economic stability and growth. The ways in which this responsibility is fulfilled determine our monetary policy.

2. The chief instruments of monetary policy available to the Federal Reserve System are reserve requirements, the discount rate, open-market operations, margin regulations, and moral suasion. These tools are usually coordinated by the Reserve officials to achieve the System's overall objectives of promoting stable economic growth through the money supply.

3. The U.S. Treasury, like the Federal Reserve, can also influence monetary management. However, it usually carries on its operations in a manner that creates minimum disruption within the banking system and the money market.

4. Monetary policy has advantages and limitations as a method of economic stabilization. Its chief advantages are that it is (a) nondiscriminatory, (b) flexible, and (c) nonpolitical. Its main limitations are that it (a) may serve as an incomplete countercyclical weapon, (b) is relatively ineffective in combating inflationary forces caused by cost-push pressures, and (c) sometimes conflicts with Treasury goals. Also, it (d) may be offset by changes in the velocity of circulation of money, (e) lacks control of nonbank lending and credit operations, and (f) suffers somewhat from a lack of precision. Despite these shortcomings, monetary control will probably continue to play an integral role in our general stabilization policy.

For Discussion

1. *Terms and concepts to review:*

monetary policy	yield
discount rate	margin requirement
open-market operations	moral suasion

2. How do changes in reserve requirements, the discount rate, and margin requirements affect economic activity? Explain.

3. How do open-market operations work? When might they tend to be expansionary? Contractionary?

4. Suppose that the reserve requirement is 15 percent. If the Federal Reserve Bank purchases $1 million of government securities in the open market, a member bank increases both its legal reserves and demand deposits by that amount. (Do you remember why?) Using the axes below, construct a bar chart showing the initial net new deposit and the *potential* cumulative expansion of bank deposits that may take place at each "round" of deposit creation. (SUGGESTION You may find it helpful to construct a table showing the multiple expansion of bank deposits. The table can then be used to sketch the chart.)

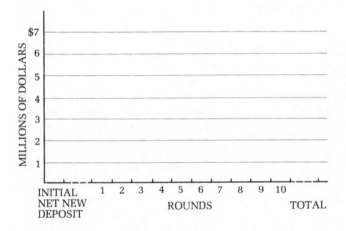

5. Suppose that the Treasury issues more paper currency than people want. (a) What will happen to bank reserves? (b) What can the Federal Reserve authorities do to offset the consequences?

6. Using two long T-accounts arranged side by side as shown, depict the positive (+) or negative (−) changes represented by each of the following transactions.

FEDERAL RESERVE BANKS		COMMERCIAL BANKS	
Assets	Liabilities	Assets	Liabilities

(a) The Federal Reserve buys $100 of government securities from a dealer. The Fed pays the dealer with a check drawn on itself, which the dealer deposits in the bank.

(b) The bank sends the $100 check to the Federal Reserve, which credits the bank's reserve deposit.

(c) The Federal Reserve buys $100 of government securities from a member bank and pays with a check on itself.

(d) The bank sends the $100 check to the Federal Reserve for credit to its account.

(e) The Federal Reserve lends $100 to a member bank by discounting the latter's note.

(f) A depositor writes a check for $100 against a demand deposit and cashes it at his or her bank.

(g) A depositor adds $100 in currency to a demand deposit.

(h) The Treasury sells $100 of securities to the nonbanking public and deposits the checks it receives in commercial banks.

(i) The Treasury transfers $100 of deposits from member banks to Federal Reserve Banks.

(j) The Treasury pays $100 for services by writing a check against its deposit at the Federal Reserve; the person to whom the check is paid deposits it to his or her account.

(k) The bank sends the $100 check to the Federal Reserve for collection.

Case
Problems of the Fed: Money + Power ≠ Happiness

Most people, if asked to identify Washington's richest and most powerful agency, would probably choose the FBI or the CIA. In reality, the Federal Reserve Board is much wealthier and usually has a far wider impact.

The Fed's income is derived primarily from the interest it receives on billions of dollars worth of Treasury securities which it holds. (Most of this interest is returned to the Treasury after the Fed deducts dividend payments to member banks plus any operating expenses deemed necessary.) The Fed's actions directly determine or influence such things as the interest rate charged on a bank loan, the minimum "down payment" needed to purchase a stock, the ability of a potential home buyer to obtain a mortgage, and many other conditions affecting people's lives.

However, despite its money and power, the Fed is almost always beset with problems. Most of them, as the following issues point out, are a reflection of the times.

Independence: Is More Regulation Needed?

When the Federal Reserve Board was created in 1913, no one perceived that it would some day exercise a powerful influence on government economic policy. In that pre-Keynesian era, the economic system was thought to be basically stable. Therefore, the Fed's primary purpose was to provide business with a proper supply of money. If that were done, it was believed, lapses from prosperity would then be temporary, and the economy would automatically restore itself to full employment.

The Great Depression of the 1930s changed these beliefs. Legislation was passed which strengthened substantially the Fed's economic powers. The Reserve Board, for example, was given complete control over open-market operations and was granted greater authority in setting reserve requirements.

This new independence has since been resented by many political leaders. One group argues that fiscal policy—government tax and expenditure actions—should take precedence over, and be accommodated by, the Fed's monetary policies. Another group believes that monetary policy should have priority over fiscal policy because the Fed's instruments of control are more powerful and faster acting. And some critics who subscribe to neither of these points of view contend that the Reserve Board's term of office should be changed to coincide with the President's. This would enable each President to choose a Board whose policies are consistent with national purpose.

These and related issues of Federal Reserve independence have been debated in Congress for years. Whatever the outcome, it is likely to have profound economic effects on everyone's life.

Discount Rate: Should Banks Be Subsidized?

When the Fed announces a change in the discount rate, the information is reported in every major newspaper.

Surprisingly, however, the discount rate is of much less functional significance than most people realize.

The discount rate determines the amount of interest member banks pay when they borrow from the Fed. This concept was conceived in 1913 when the Reserve System was created. Congress's intention was to enable the Fed to serve as a "lender of last resort" to banks in need of emergency funds. This, it was believed, would put an end to banking panics—a condition that had plagued the nation in earlier years.

The desired goal was not achieved. In 1933, the nation experienced the worst rash of bank failures in history. Washington responded by creating the Federal Deposit Insurance Corporation (FDIC), a government agency providing insurance of bank deposits. Since then, no bank panics have occurred, and there is no reason to believe they ever will.

Deposit insurance thus accomplished what the discount rate failed to do. Nevertheless, discounting was retained rather than discontinued. Over the years, it has declined in importance as a Federal Reserve tool of

monetary policy. Indeed, on a typical day, less than $\frac{1}{100}$ of the nation's banks borrow an amount equal to less than $\frac{1}{1,000}$ of the nation's deposits.

In view of this, what role does the discount rate play? More often than not, it serves as a means for subsidizing banks. Because bank borrowing at the Fed's discount window is considered a privilege and not a right, the Reserve banks are generally selective about their lending. They usually keep the discount rate several percentage points below the market rate. This enables the Fed to use the discount rate in two ways:

1. As a means of providing low-cost loans to troubled banks.

2. As a "carrot" to persuade banks to change their lending practices and policies.

Regardless of the purpose, the Fed ends up subsidizing certain banks to the tune of billions of dollars annually at taxpayers' expense.

Because of this, critics argue that discounting should be abolished, or, at least, be done at a "penalty rate." The Fed, however, feels differently. It regards the discount rate as yet another tool of monetary policy which should be available for use when needed.

Electronic Banking: Are Money and Checks on the Way Out?

The number of bad checks passed annually exceeds $1 billion, according to the FBI. But this type of dishonesty will fade into insignificance when electronic funds transfer (EFT) becomes the dominant method of paying for goods purchased.

As its name implies, EFT enables funds to be transferred instantaneously from one account to another by electronic means. A consumer, for example, selects a good and hands a plastic card to a sales clerk. The clerk inserts the card into a computerized terminal, punches a few buttons, and money is automatically transferred from the consumer's bank account to

Mimi Forsyth, Monkmeyer Press Photo Service.

Will these be replaced by EFT?

the merchant's. In a somewhat similar manner, business firms, including banks and other financial institutions, can transfer funds from one part of the country to another in a matter of seconds.

EFT, through the use of computers and telecommunications equipment, is gradually replacing cash, checks, and even credit cards as we now know them. As a result, the widespread use of EFT will accentuate certain problems of monetary policy. Two may be mentioned briefly:

1. The basic measure of the nation's money supply—defined as currency plus demand deposits—will have to be broadened. The new measure, which already exists, includes not only time deposits at commercial banks but also savings-type checking accounts. As these gain in importance, the Fed will be faced with the difficult challenge of managing a much broader category of money.

2. Certain financial regulations will have to be revised. For example, laws currently restricting interest rates on various types of deposits will create monetary-control problems for the Fed as EFT systems expand. In addition, the velocity or rate at which money is exchanged will undergo substantial change, thus affecting the prices of goods.

EFT is thus having profound effects on banks and other financial institutions. Electronic banking is revolutionizing the concept of money and is forcing the Federal Reserve System to evaluate continuously the ways in which it manages the nation's money supply.

Conclusion: Steering a Delicate Course

Although the Fed is perhaps the richest and, in many ways, the most influential agency in Washington, it is not without problems. In the Federal Reserve Act of 1913, Congress went through great effort to insulate the Fed from political and business pressures. Nevertheless, as the economy became more complex, the Reserve System's unique role as manager of the nation's money supply took on increasing importance. As a result, the Fed today often finds itself in difficult situations. It must cope with continually changing financial institutions and markets while adopting monetary policies aimed at achieving efficiency, stability, and growth.

QUESTIONS

1. Congress intentionally established the Federal Reserve System as an *independent* organization. However, many political leaders today believe that the Fed's independence is no longer appropriate. Why? Does the fact that the Fed is independent mean that it is free to undertake whatever actions it wishes?

2. The discount rate is often well below the interest rate prevailing in the money market, sometimes by as much as 2 or 3 percentage points. Can you suggest why? Would an above-market "penalty rate" be better? Explain.

3. The widespread implementation of EFT will make it increasingly difficult for the Fed to control the supply of money. Why? Of what consequence is this?

Chapter 13

Macroeconomic Equilibrium

Chapter Preview

The monetary authorities (central bank) have the power to expand and contract the money supply. How do such decisions affect the general price level? What implications does this have for monetary policy?

How is the rate of interest determined? Of what significance is the rate of interest in explaining income determination?

How do the strategic variables affecting income or GNP fit together? Can they be integrated into a coherent whole—a model of macroeconomic equilibrium?

The importance of money essentially flows from its being a link between the present and the future.

So wrote J. M. Keynes in *The General Theory of Employment, Interest and Money* in 1936. The following year he went on to say: "The possession of actual money lulls our disquietude; and the premium which we require to make us part with money is the measure of the degree of our disquietude."

The "link between the present and the future"—the "premium" to which Lord Keynes referred—is the rate of interest. This variable plays a strategic role in the explanation of income and employment determination. This fact was pointed out in an earlier chapter but must now be examined in closer detail.

It is important to understand the relationship between money and interest. The rate of interest may be directly influenced by changes in the money supply. Therefore, once the relationship between money and interest is established, the macroeconomic model of income determination will be complete. We will then see how the strategic variables in the model interrelate within the system as a whole.

Money Affects Output and Prices

You have already learned how the Federal Reserve can influence the level of economic activity by its discretionary actions. For example, to encourage economic expansion, the Fed can increase the supply of money by engaging in open-market purchases of government bonds. To initiate economic contraction, the Fed can decrease the supply of money by undertaking open-market sales of government bonds. Thus, there is a *direct* relationship between the money supply and the level of economic activity: Changes in the former can produce changes in the latter in the same direction.

The idea that changes in the money supply lead to changes in the price level was fundamental to classical economic thinking. But it was not stated with precision until the early 1900s. At that time a distinguished American economist at Yale University—Irving Fisher (1867–1947)—expressed the link between money and prices by means of an equation that soon became famous. A modernized version of that equation can be developed in the following way.

EQUATION OF EXCHANGE

You may not be able to see how fast individual dollars are spent, but you can measure the average speed of money movements as a whole rather easily. Let V stand for the *income velocity of money*. This is the average number of times per year a dollar is spent on purchasing the economy's annual flow of final goods and services—its GNP. Further, let M denote the nation's money supply as measured by the amount of money, including currency and demand deposits, in the hands of the public. Then, the income velocity of money is measured by the formula

$$V = \frac{\text{GNP}}{M}$$

For example, if in a certain year the GNP was $800 billion and the stock of money was $200 billion, $V =$ $800/$200 = 4$ per year for that year. In other words, each dollar must have been used an average of four times to purchase the economy's GNP.

The letter M in the equation above can, of course, be "transposed" to the left side so that the equation becomes

$$MV = \text{GNP}$$

Suppose, however, that we make the equation more refined by expressing GNP in terms of its component prices and quantities. Let P stand for the average price of final goods and services produced during the year and let Q represent the physical quantity of those goods and services. The *value* of final output is then price times quantity. That is, GNP = $P \times Q$, because, for example, GNP = price of apples times number of

apples, plus price of haircuts times number of haircuts, plus . . . and so on for all final goods and services produced. The equation can therefore be written

$$MV = PQ$$

This is known as the "equation of exchange." For example, imagine a highly simplified case in which the students in your class comprise an economy whose total supply of money M is $80. Further, assume that the class produces a quantity of output Q, equal to 60 units of a good, and that the average price P of this output is $4 per unit. Then the equation of exchange tells you that V must equal 3, because

$$MV = PQ$$

or

$$(\$80)(3) = (\$4)(60)$$

Each dollar is thus spent an average of three times per year on the class's output.

The equation of exchange is actually an identity because it states that the total amount of society's income *spent* on final goods and services, MV, is equal to the total amount of money *received* for society's final goods and services, PQ.

To summarize:

Equation of exchange. The quantity of money *(M)*, multiplied by the average number of times *(V)* each unit of money is spent on purchasing the economy's final output of goods and services, is MV. The average price *(P)* of final goods and services, multiplied by their quantity *(Q)*, is PQ. During a given period, society's income and expenditure are equal. Therefore, $MV = PQ$.

The equation tells us that the given flow of money can be looked at either from the buyers' or the sellers' point of view. The aggregate flow is the same in either case. As in demand and supply analysis, the quantity of a commodity purchased is equal to the quantity sold.

THE QUANTITY THEORY OF MONEY

What does the equation of exchange tell us about the role of money in influencing national income and expenditure? To answer this, we have to examine some of the components of the equation.

1. Suppose we assume that V *remains constant*. This means that by controlling M we could control GNP. For instance, if M is increased, either P or Q or both will have to increase in order to maintain equality between the right and left sides of the equation. The changes in P or Q will depend on the state of the economy. In a period of recession, Q will tend to rise relatively more than P as unemployed resources are

re-employed. In a period of high employment, P will tend to rise relatively more than Q as full utilization of resources is approached. What do you suppose would happen in a period of full employment?

2. Suppose we assume that *both V and Q remain constant*. This, in fact, is what the classical economists believed. They assumed that V was constant because it was determined by the long-run money-holding habits of households and business firms. These habits, the classicists argued, were fairly stable. Further, they assumed that Q was constant because the economy always tended toward full employment. The classical economists thus concluded that P depends directly on M. As a result, their theory has come to be known as the "quantity theory of money."

> *Quantity theory of money.* The level of prices in the economy is directly proportional to the quantity of money in circulation. That is, a given percentage change in the stock of money will cause an equal percentage change in the price level in the same direction.

The quantity theory states, for example, that a 10 percent increase in M will cause a 10 percent increase in P. Likewise, a 5 percent decrease in M will cause a 5 percent decrease in P. In general, according to the quantity theory of money, *changes in the price level are directly proportional to changes in the money supply.*

WHAT DOES THE EVIDENCE SHOW?

How well does the quantity theory of money correspond with the facts? Can changes in M be used to predict changes in P?

In evaluating the theory, it is necessary to distinguish between long- and short-term changes. The evidence suggests two major classes of findings.

1. During a number of long-run periods, changes in P have appeared to be closely tied to changes in M. For example, in the late sixteenth century, the Spanish importation of gold and silver from the New World caused major price increases in Europe. Likewise, the discovery of gold in the United States, Canada, and South Africa during the latter half of the nineteenth century brought sudden expansions in the money supply and rapidly rising prices in these countries. During more recent history, the excessive borrowing and printing of money by certain countries since the early part of this century has resulted in a continuous upward spiraling of prices. In these and various other cases prices rose directly with increases in the quantity of money. There were no corresponding increases in output, and the long-run income velocity of money remained fairly stable.

2. In the short run, V varies a good deal, even though its long-run trend has been steadily rising. This is shown in Exhibit 1. And output, of course, may also vary substantially from year to year. In addition, even if P increases as a result of an increase in M, the rise in prices might encourage an increase in V as people spend money more quickly for fear of future price increases. If this happens, P is no longer merely a passive variable dependent on M, but a *causal* variable contributing to changes in other factors.

Because of such complexities, the quantity theory of money has not yet proved suitable for predicting short-run changes in P from changes in M. However, as pointed out above, the theory provides a useful guide for judging the influence of monetary forces on long-run changes in the price level.

MODERNIZING THE QUANTITY THEORY: THE IMPORTANCE OF VELOCITY

The quantity theory of money played a critical role in classical economic thinking. Since the 1950s, it has undergone substantial revision by some economists. Notable among them has been Nobel laureate and Professor Emeritus Milton Friedman of the University of Chicago.

The revised, or "modern," quantity theory retains much of the traditional doctrine but reorients it

---

Exhibit 1
Income Velocity of Money = GNP/Money Stock

The income velocity of money (V) usually fluctuates considerably within any given year. Its long-run trend, however, has been steadily upward.

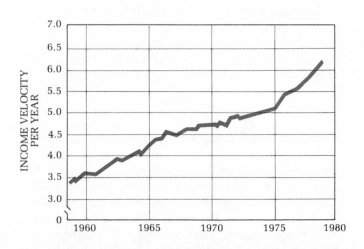

toward the importance of V. For example, V is not assumed to remain constant as in the old theory but is believed instead to be influenced by many factors. One of these is *public confidence in the economy*—or *stage of the business cycle*. If people fear unemployment or are pessimistic about the future, they will tend to refrain from spending. Therefore, they will increase their percentage of income saved. The larger the proportion of saving that occurs without a corresponding increase in investment, the more slowly money turns over. Hence, the lower its velocity.

Modern quantity theorists believe that although V fluctuates over time, its range of short-run variation is limited and, with sufficient knowledge, *predictable*. Therefore, the underlying determinant of GNP (or *PQ* in the equation of exchange) is still the quantity of money. This conclusion has important policy implications. It suggests the following "rule":

The central bank (i.e., Federal Reserve) should use its monetary instruments—such as open-market operations and control over the discount rate and reserve requirements—in a more consistent manner. That is, *it should provide a continuous expansion in the money supply at a rate sufficient to assure steady economic growth and full employment*. Failure to follow this "rule," say the modern quantity theorists, leads inevitably to economic instability.

Does this mean that diverse fiscal and monetary measures should be discarded in favor of a uniform, consistent policy that provides for steady growth in the money supply at an established rate? Many informed observers would answer yes. But many others believe that an optimum fiscal–monetary mix must be found that will assure economic stability at a high level of income and employment. However, the difficulties of attaining such a mix are considerable—for reasons that will be pointed out subsequently. (See *Leaders in Economics*, page 227.)

Determination of the Interest Rate

Any study of money must inevitably lead to a discussion of the rate of interest and to an analysis of the forces determining it. This is a matter of great importance. As you will recall from the study of investment in an earlier chapter, businesses invest in capital goods only as long as the anticipated rate of return on an additional unit of investment—called the *marginal efficiency of investment*—exceeds the cost of money capital or rate of interest. In view of this, what determines the rate of interest? The answer, as you will see, provides the final link in the Keynesian model of the macroeconomy.

The first question to be asked is: What do we mean by interest?

Interest is the price paid for the use of money or loanable funds over a period. Interest is expressed as a rate—that is, as a percentage of the amount of money borrowed. Thus, an interest rate of 5 percent means that the borrower pays 5 cents per $1 borrowed per year.

As you have already learned from the study of our nation's monetary and banking system, there is no such thing as "the" interest rate. That is, there is no single rate on all financial instruments traded in the money and capital markets. Instead, there are many different rates on specific types of notes, bonds, and so on. The rates for financial instruments depend on risks of default, maturity dates, tax advantages, and numerous other factors. Despite such differences, however, interest rates are interrelated in that they tend to increase or decrease together, although differentials between them often vary. Hence, it proves convenient to talk about "the" interest rate, thinking in terms of the whole structure of rates as rising or declining.

CLASSICAL EXPLANATION: FISHER'S THEORY

The arithmetic books tell us that interest is a payment for the use of money. This concept is adequate for most purposes. However, to the classical economists interest had a special and quite different meaning.

You recall that in the simplified circular-flow model, the total economy is divided into two parts—a household sector and a business sector. The household sector supplies the saving that the business sector borrows and invests in capital goods in order to carry on profitable production. Interest, therefore, is a price that businesses pay households to persuade the latter to consume less in the present so that they can consume more at a later date. Interest is thus a payment for "saving," for "abstinence" from consumption, or for overcoming people's preference for present as opposed to future consumption.

Why is interest necessary? The classicists believed that no household will save, and thereby forgo the pleasure of spending, unless it is offered interest in return. Likewise, no business will borrow, and thereby pay interest, without investing in profitable production. Saving, in classical theory, therefore leads automatically to spending on capital or investment goods. A flexible interest rate in the competitive money market assures this. That is, the interest rate, determined by the free play of supply and demand, adjusts to the level where every dollar saved by households is borrowed and invested by businesses. This is further explained and illustrated in Exhibit 2.

Exhibit 2
The Market Rate of Interest in Classical Theory

The interest rate is the price paid for the use of money. Like any other price, the interest rate rations the supply of a commodity, in this case money, among those who want to borrow it. Only those borrowers who are willing and able to pay the market interest rate can acquire the funds that are wanted.

The classicists theorized that the equilibrium rate of interest r is determined in the competitive money market where the supply of funds saved by households equals the demand for funds invested by businesses. They also believed that if there were a change in the investment-demand curve, say, from D to D', then the intersection with the existing saving-supply curve would determine the new rate of interest r'.

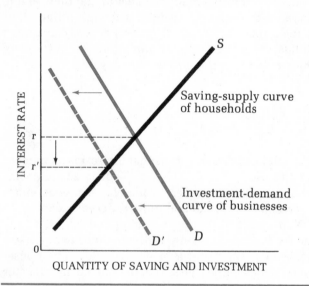

QUANTITY OF SAVING AND INVESTMENT

The Real Rate and the Market Rate

These ideas of classical economics were further developed in the early part of this century by Irving Fisher. The classical explanation of interest is also sometimes called the Fisher theory of interest. It rests fundamentally on a distinction between two kinds of interest: the real rate and the market rate.

Real Rate   The *real rate of interest* is the interest rate measured in terms of goods. That is, it is the rate that would prevail in the market if the general price level remained stable. Under such circumstances, if you lend a friend $100 today with the understanding that he will repay you $105 a year from today, you give up $100 worth of goods now for what you expect will be $105 worth of goods a year from now. The real rate of interest is therefore 5 percent. According to the classicists, this rate is established by real economic forces of demand and supply. The "real demand" for funds

by businesses is determined by the productivity (and therefore profitability) of borrowed capital. The "real supply" of funds by households is determined by the willingness of consumers to abstain from present consumption.

Market Rate   The *market rate of interest* is the actual or money rate that prevails in the market at any given time. Unlike the real rate, which is not directly observable, the market rate is the one we actually see in the markets. This is because the market rate reflects the quantity of loans measured in units of money, not goods. Hence, it is the rate people ordinarily have in mind when they talk about "the" interest rate.

A crucial point in classical theory is that the real rate and the market rate usually are not equal. Only if borrowers and lenders expect the general price level, that is, the value of a unit of money, to remain constant will both rates be the same. This does not ordinarily happen. People are always expecting prices either to rise or to fall. Therefore, the market rate of interest will depart from the real rate, depending on either of two conditions.

1. **Anticipated Inflation**   If people believe prices will rise—and hence the purchasing power of a unit of money will decline—the market rate of interest will be higher than the real rate. For example, if lenders and borrowers expect the price level to rise 5 percent per year, the market rate of interest will be the real rate plus 5 percent. This "inflation premium" is necessary to compensate lenders for their loss in purchasing power. At the same time, borrowers will be willing to pay the premium because they will be repaying their loans with money worth 5 percent less per year than the money they borrowed.

2. **Anticipated Deflation**   If people believe prices will fall—and therefore the purchasing power of a unit of money will rise—the market rate of interest will be below the real rate. The difference is a "deflation discount" (or negative inflation premium). This is necessary to compensate borrowers for their loss in purchasing power. At the same time, lenders will be willing to grant the discount because they will be repaid with money worth 5 percent more per year than the money they initially lent.

These ideas can be summarized briefly:

In classical theory, the market rate of interest may be greater than, equal to, or less than the real rate. The difference depends on whether households and businesses expect the general price level to rise, remain constant, or decline. Any differential between the market rate and the real rate represents the amount necessary to compensate lenders or borrowers for adverse changes in purchasing power resulting from anticipated inflation or deflation.

Leaders in Economics
Irving Fisher 1867–1947

Irving Fisher, a professor of economics at Yale University, was one of America's foremost economists prior to World War II. A mathematician as well as an economist, he was a profound scholar and prolific writer. In addition to twenty-eight published books, he wrote dozens of articles in professional journals. Of his books, eighteen covered diverse areas of economics and statistics. The remainder consisted of some well-known mathematics textbooks, plus several popular volumes on diet and on health—subjects that interested him because he suffered from tuberculosis as a young man.

Fisher also invented many mechanical devices. The only one to achieve commercial success was a card index system mounted on a rotary stand. Fisher received about $1 million for this, which he subsequently parlayed into $9 million in the stock market. He lost it all in the crash of 1929.

Among Fisher's major interests was the study of money and prices. In a book entitled *The Purchasing Power of Money* (1911), he stated the *equation of exchange*—which also subsequently became known as the *Fisher equation*:

$$MV + M'V' = PT$$

Here M is the quantity of currency, V its velocity of circulation, M' the quantity of demand deposits, V' their velocity of circulation, P the average price level of all goods sold, and T the volume of transactions or total quantity of all goods sold. Economists often shorten the equation to

$$MV = PT$$

by redefining M to include "money"—currency plus demand deposits.

Modern Version: $MV = PQ$
The equation, formulated long before national-income data were available, is theoretically interesting but of little practical use because it encompasses *all* transactions involving payment in money. It covers not only the sale of final goods but also the sale of raw materials, partly finished goods, securities, real estate, and used goods. Hence, it may be called the "transactions-velocity" formulation, to distinguish it from the modern and much more practical "income-velocity" formulation, $MV = PQ$. This equation encompasses only transactions for *final* goods and uses readily available GNP data. Both equations, however, have similar structural properties and permit similar interpretations.

Application
Fisher employed his equation to explain a cause-and-effect relationship between the quantity of money and the price level. He assumed that the velocity of circulation (V) and the volume of transactions (T) were constant—or at least that they always tended toward equilibrium. Therefore, he concluded, if there is "a doubling in the quantity of money . . . it follows necessarily and mathematically that the level of prices must double." Or in general, *"one of the normal effects of an increase in the quantity of money is an exactly proportional increase in the general level of prices."* From this it is evident, according to Fisher, that business cycles are not inherent in the economy but are due almost entirely to excessive expansions and contractions in the money supply—"especially in the form of bank loans." This conclusion, we shall see, is now widely accepted among many informed observers.

Many Achievements
Fisher made important contributions to the study of business cycles, capital, and interest. He also did pioneering work in the fields of mathematical economics and statistics, the integration of which is known as *econometrics.* He was honored for his many achievements by being elected president of each of the three major professional organizations concerned with the advancement of economic science—the American Economic Association, the American Statistical Association, and the Econometric Society.

Wide World Photos.

Fisher demonstrates one of his many inventions: a two-way map that could be folded into a globe or spread flat.

DERIVING THE REAL RATE: A MODERN VIEW

This classical view is held today by many informed observers. They contend that interest rates contain an inflation premium which reflects the rise in prices over the years. That is, market interest rates and prices tend to move together—just as the classicists theorized. Therefore, you can calculate the real rate of interest quite easily by subtracting the percentage change in the general price level from the market interest rate:

real interest rate = market interest rate
  − percentage change in general price level

To illustrate, here is how the formula might be employed.

First, to obtain a measure of the market interest rate, either of two figures is generally used. One is the average yield on short-term government securities—namely Treasury bills. The other is the average yield on high-grade corporate bonds—such as Moody's Aaa bond yields shown in the back endpapers of this book. (Moody's is a large private firm which sells many financial services, including ratings of, and yields on, various types of bonds.)

Second, the most comprehensive measure of the general price level is the *Implicit Price Index* (IPI), more popularly known as the GNP price deflator. This index is a weighted average of the various price indexes used to deflate the components of GNP. The IPI is also shown in the endpapers at the back of this book.

Once you have the needed information, the formula is easily applied. For example, if in a given period the market interest rate is, say, 7 percent, and the IPI has increased from the previous period by 4 percent, the real interest rate for that period is 3 percent. What if the IPI had decreased by 4 percent?

Conclusion: Prices and Interest Rates Move Together

Is the connection between prices and interest rates valid? Today's classical economists believe that it is. They point out that, historically, interest rates in the United States have risen when prices increased and have declined when they decreased. This indicates that high market interest rates reflect expected as well as actual inflation. Evidence of this can be seen in many nations. Countries that traditionally experience steep inflations generally have much higher interest rates than countries whose price levels are relatively more stable.

To conclude:

According to the classicists, increases in the quantity of money result in "too much money chasing too few goods." Consequently, prices and interest rates rise. By reducing the rate of growth in the money supply, the monetary authority (the central banking system) can retard inflation and bring about reductions in the market rate of interest.

LIQUIDITY-PREFERENCE EXPLANATION: KEYNES' THEORY

As we learned in earlier chapters, much of traditional economic thinking underwent major changes in the Great Depression of the 1930s. The person initially responsible for this restructuring of ideas was the eminent British economist John Maynard Keynes. The revised theory, which Keynes called a "general theory," resulted in the birth of the *New Economics*. You will find it helpful to refresh your understanding of this expression by looking up its meaning in the Dictionary at the back of this book.

What did Keynes have to say about the role of the interest rate and the factors determining it? We already know part of the answer:

Capital spending or investment by businesses is the strategic determinant of the level of income and employment. Such spending is undertaken as long as the marginal efficiency of investment exceeds the rate of interest. Therefore, the rate of interest is crucial in relation to investment.

As for the factors determining the rate of interest, Keynes argued that the classical theory is correct for an economy that tends automatically toward full employment. His own theory, on the other hand, is more general because it applies to an economic system that may be in equilibrium at *any* level of employment.

Keynes and the Classicists

These ideas can best be understood by comparing some of Keynes' views with those of the classicists. For example, in the classical theory, the investment-demand curve illustrated earlier in Exhibit 2 shows the amount of capital spending that businesses are willing to undertake at each rate of interest. This demand curve is the same as the marginal-efficiency-of-investment *(MEI)* curve that you studied in earlier chapters as part of the Keynesian model. You should recall, however, that in the Keynesian model, investment expenditures by the business sector are part of the economy's aggregate demand. Therefore, Keynes argued, the classicists erred by assuming that the investment-demand curve could shift *without causing simultaneous changes in the aggregate demand curve.* Such changes would, in turn, affect the level of income and hence the saving-supply curve. These ideas are illustrated in Exhibit 3.

Thus, the classical economists simply viewed interest as a "price" that equates the demand for investment with the supply of saving at the full-employment level of income. Keynes argued that because *the saving-supply curve will shift if the investment-demand curve shifts,* the rate of interest in the classical scheme cannot be determined. Nor, he said, can the equilibrium quantity of saving and investment be known, because the information provided is insufficient. In view of this, let us see how Keynes restructured the theory of interest.

Exhibit 3
Keynesian Model: Investment Affects Aggregate Demand and Income

In the Keynesian model, the equilibrium level of national income is determined by the intersection of aggregate demand *AD* with aggregate supply *AS*. But aggregate demand includes the business sector's investment demand. Therefore, a decline in investment demand will result in a decrease in aggregate demand, say, from *AD* to *AD'*, and a simultaneous drop in national income from *N* to *N'*. The corresponding saving-supply curve, therefore, will also change. Can you show this on a separate chart?

Keynes thus concluded that the classicists were wrong for believing that a change in investment demand would affect only the interest rate (as shown in Exhibit 2), not the level of income.

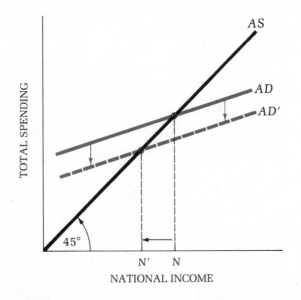

Statement of the Theory

In classical theory, interest is a reward for "waiting"— for "abstinence" from consumption. *In Keynes' theory, the rate of interest is determined entirely by the demand for and supply of money.* But two factors underlying demand and supply must be considered: liquidity preference and the quantity of money.

On the demand side, in Keynes' view, money is wanted because it is the only perfectly liquid asset. People would rather hold some of their assets in money than in any other form. Therefore, if you are to be persuaded to give up some of your perfectly liquid assets, you must be paid a reward. *Interest is the price that must be paid to overcome liquidity preference.* To put it slightly differently, *interest is the reward for not hoarding money.*

On the supply side, according to Keynes, the quantity of money is the important factor. As we have said, the quantity of money is determined by the monetary authority (central bank) through its control over open-market operations, reserve requirements, and other factors. The monetary authority can use these mechanisms to increase the money supply if the public wants to hold a larger proportion of its assets in the form of money. If the public desires to hold a smaller proportion, the monetary authority can decrease the money supply. *In Keynes' view, therefore, expansions and contractions in the money supply play a strategic role in the determination of the interest rate.*

Determinants of Demand and Supply

The demand for money is a demand for liquidity. Why should you and I and everyone else prefer to hold assets in liquid form? Keynes provided three reasons, which he called the transactions, precautionary, and speculative motives.

Transactions Motive Households and businesses must hold some of their assets in the form of money (currency and demand deposits). This is because they purchase goods and services more or less continuously from day to day, whereas they receive income only at intervals such as weekly or monthly. Therefore, a certain amount of money must be held to bridge the gap. The amount required—the transactions demand for money—does not depend on the interest rate. Instead, it is directly related to the level of economic activity. Thus, as national income rises, so does the need for money for transactions purposes.

Precautionary Motive A second reason why households and businesses want to hold part of their assets in liquid form is to meet unforeseen developments. Examples are illnesses, accidents, losses of employment, strikes, or market fluctuations. Although individuals and firms may be able to convert other assets into money at such times, the possibility of loss due to forced liquidation under unfavorable market conditions prompts them to prefer money for reserve contingencies. The precautionary demand for money is influenced primarily by national-income levels rather than by changes in the interest rate. Hence, most precautionary demand may be combined with the transactions demand for money, because both depend mainly on income. This is shown in Exhibit 4.

Speculative Motive Finally, households and businesses may prefer to hold part of their assets in the form of money to enable them to take advantage of changes in interest rates. Individuals and firms tend to hold more securities—especially long-term bonds—and less money when the interest rate is high, to take advantage of higher returns. Conversely, individuals and firms also tend to hold more money and fewer securities when the interest rate is low, because the risk of holding bonds—the possible fall in their prices—more than offsets the interest returns. As Ex-

hibit 5 demonstrates, the interest rate is inversely related to the quantity of money wanted for speculative purposes.

The transactions, precautionary, and speculative motives determine the total demand for money. What factors determine supply? As you know, the supply of money is simply the stock of money available to satisfy the demand. The supply of money is determined by the monetary authority through its control over open-market operations, reserve requirements, and discount-rate policy. Hence, at any given time the supply or stock of money is fixed. This means that it can be represented by a vertical—or in the language of economics, a "perfectly inelastic"—supply curve, as explained in Exhibit 6.

The reason for this terminology is not hard to see. Unlike most supply curves, which are upward-sloping, this one is vertical. This means that increases or decreases in the interest rate ("price" of money) do not cause changes in the stock of money. Therefore, we may say that the quantity supplied of money is unresponsive to changes in the interest rate.

Exhibit 4
Transactions and Precautionary Demands for Money

Households and businesses want to hold some of their assets in the form of money in order to carry on day-to-day transactions and to meet unforeseen contingencies. These reasons for holding money are called the *transactions motive* and the *precautionary motive,* respectively. Both demands for money depend primarily on the total level of money payments or national income. The straight line in this chart means that money demanded for transactions and precautionary purposes rises by some constant proportion of national income.

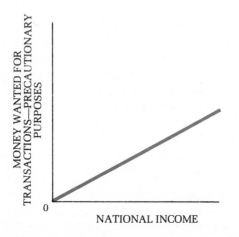

Exhibit 5
Speculative Demand for Money

Households and businesses (which comprise the private sector) desire to hold some of their assets in the form of money to take advantage of changes in interest rates. The private sector's speculative demand for money varies inversely with the interest rate. At a high interest rate, households and businesses will hold less money and more securities. At a low interest rate, more money and fewer securities will be held. Note that the line is curved rather than straight and that it tends to flatten out at its lower right end. The reasons for this are explained later.

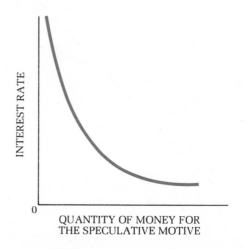

Exhibit 6
Supply of Money

At any given time, there is a quantity or stock of money available to satisfy the public's demand. This quantity is determined by the monetary authority through its open-market operations, discount-rate policy, and reserve requirements. Hence, the supply curve is a vertical line, indicating that the quantity of money supplied is unresponsive to changes in the interest rate. That is, the quantity supplied is the same at higher interest rates as at lower ones.

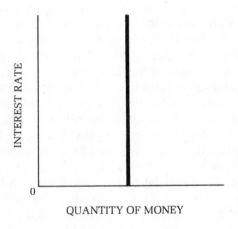

Exhibit 7
Determination of the Interest Rate by Demand for Money (L) and Supply of Money (M)

At a given level of national income, the equilibrium rate of interest r is determined by the intersection of the L curve, representing the total demand for money, with the M curve, representing total supply. Note that the L curve consists of two components. One is the transactions and precautionary demands, which depend mainly on the level of national income (but not on the interest rate). The other is the speculative demand, which depends on the interest rate and hence causes the L curve to be downward sloping. The entire L curve is the *sum* of both components.

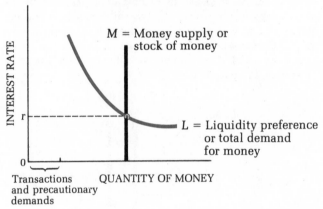

Determining the Interest Rate

Of course, as in any demand and supply problem, either variable by itself cannot determine the price. The two must be combined in order for a price to be established. This is shown in Exhibit 7. As you can see, the equilibrium rate of interest r is determined by the intersection of the liquidity-preference curve L, representing the total demand for money, with the money supply curve M, representing the stock of money. If the interest rate is higher than the equilibrium level, the quantity supplied exceeds the quantity demanded. This drives the rate down. If the interest rate is below the equilibrium level, the quantity demanded exceeds the quantity supplied. This drives the rate up. Note that the demand curve for money includes all three components of demand—as explained in the exhibit.

Like all demand and supply curves, those in Exhibit 7 are drawn on the assumption that all other things besides the interest rate that may affect demand and supply remain constant. If one of the factors changes, the relevant demand or supply curve will shift. This will bring about a new equilibrium rate of interest. For example:

1. If national income rises, the quantity of money demanded for transactions and precautionary purposes also rises. This causes an increase in liquidity preference or the demand for money at all interest rates. The L curve, in other words, shifts to the right, as in Exhibit 8. The same result might be obtained if there were a decline in business expectations. In that case, households and businesses might attempt to increase their holdings of money for precautionary purposes.

2. If the monetary authority increases the supply of money, the M curve will shift to the right. This is also explained in Exhibit 8.

To summarize:

The *liquidity-preference theory of interest* was formulated by J. M. Keynes. The theory contends that households and businesses want to hold some of their assets in the most liquid form, namely cash or checking accounts. The reason is to satisfy three motives: (1) the transactions motive, (2) the precautionary motive, and (3) the speculative motive. These motives determine the demand for money, whereas the monetary authority determines its supply. The demand for, and supply of, money together determine the equilibrium rate of interest.

Exhibit 8
Changes in the Interest Rate Resulting from Shifts in the Money-Demand and Money-Supply, or L and M, Curves

If the money-supply or M curve remains fixed, an increase in income will shift the liquidity-preference or demand-for-money curve rightward from L to L'. This causes the equilibrium rate of interest to rise from r to r'. If the money-demand or L curve remains fixed, an increase in the stock of money will shift the money-supply curve rightward from M to M'. This causes the equilibrium rate of interest to decline from r to r''.

Of course, a decrease in income or a decrease in the money supply will correspondingly shift the L and M curves leftward. Can you show what happens to the equilibrium rate of interest under such circumstances? What may happen if the L and M curves shift simultaneously in the same direction? In opposite directions?

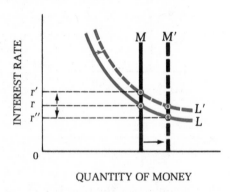

QUANTITY OF MONEY

Practical Implications of the Liquidity-Preference Theory

The liquidity-preference theory of interest is the final link in the entire Keynesian system. Without it there would be no determinate solution to our general economic model. You will gain a better appreciation of this fact as we proceed to point out the practical implications of the theory of interest within the framework of what we have already learned.

MARGINAL EFFICIENCY OF INVESTMENT AND THE INTEREST RATE

You recall from the study of income and employment that the *marginal efficiency of investment (MEI)* is the expected rate of return on an investment. More precisely, it is the *expected rate of return over the cost of an additional unit of a capital good.*

Each business firm has its own *MEI* curve. The curve shows the amount of investment a firm will undertake at various costs of money capital, expressed as interest rates. Hence, a firm's *MEI* curve is its demand curve for investment.

It follows that at any given time the sum of all firms' *MEI* curves yield an aggregate *MEI* curve. This shows the total amount of private investment that will be undertaken at various rates of interest. Therefore, the aggregate *MEI* curve is the business sector's demand curve for investment.

This idea is illustrated in Exhibit 9. In Chart (a) the equilibrium rate of interest r is determined by the intersection of the demand and supply curves of money—the L and M curves—as we have already learned. This rate is the cost of money capital to firms. Hence, in Chart (b) the amount of investment undertaken by the business sector at this rate of interest, shown by the aggregate *MEI* curve, is I.

What happens if this volume of investment is insufficient to achieve full employment? In that case the monetary authorities can lower the rate of interest by increasing the money supply—say, from Q to Q'. Assuming that the L curve remains fixed, the equilibrium rate of interest will decline from r to r', causing the amount of investment to increase from I to I'. This increase in investment, as you know, will have a magnified effect on income, owing to the operation of the multiplier. Further, since the liquidity-preference (L) curve depends on income, it will shift to the right when income rises—as you have already learned.

You can see, therefore, that the effectiveness of monetary policy for stimulating economic activity poses some challenging questions. For example:

1. To what extent will the interest rate fall as a result of an increase in the money supply?

2. To what extent will the amount of investment increase as a result of a decline in the interest rate?

3. To what extent will income rise as a result of an increase in investment?

The answer to the first question depends on the relative steepness of the L curve. The answer to the second question depends on the relative steepness of the MEI curve. And the answer to the third question depends on the size of the multiplier.

For instance, referring back to Exhibit 9, what would be the effect on the change in the interest rate and on the change in the amount of investment if both the L curve and the MEI curve were relatively flatter? Steeper? You can answer these questions by sketching some curves yourself and comparing the differences. As for the size of the multiplier, you recall that it depends on the marginal propensities to consume or to save. This is because the multiplier, as you have learned, equals $1/(1 - MPC)$, or $1/MPS$.

Exhibit 9
The Interest Rate and Investment

In Chart (a), an increase in the money-supply curve from M to M' increases the quantity of money from Q to Q'. Therefore, the rate of interest decreases from r to r'. This in-creases the amount of investment from I to I' in Chart (b), because businesses invest to the point where the MEI equals the interest rate (or cost of money capital).

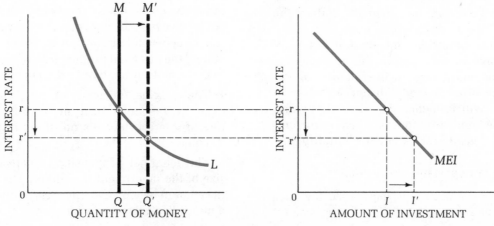

(a) DEMAND FOR, AND SUPPLY OF, MONEY

(b) BUSINESS-SECTOR INVESTMENT

THE LIQUIDITY TRAP

Should we infer from Exhibit 9 that increases in the quantity of money will always lower the rate of interest—and therefore increase the amount of investment? The answer is not a simple yes or no. As pointed out above, other factors must be considered. One of them is the shape of the L curve, which, as you saw in previous diagrams, is assumed to flatten out at its right end. As a result, the lower the rate of interest, the more resistant it becomes to further reductions, until a point is reached where the L curve becomes perfectly horizontal. From then on, it is impossible to reduce the interest rate further merely by increasing the supply of money.

This concept is illustrated in Exhibit 10. The flat portion of the curve signifies that at a low rate of interest (say, 2 percent), everyone prefers to hold money rather than risk any loss from holding long-term securities yielding poor returns. Therefore, this horizontal segment of the curve is called the *liquidity trap*. It has been used by some economists to explain why monetary policy may not be effective in inducing recovery from a deep recession if the rate of interest, although low absolutely, is still too high relative to the marginal efficiency of investment. Under such circumstances, these economists contend, there is no stimulus for business executives to increase the amount of their investment, despite low interest rates.

Exhibit 10
The Liquidity Trap

Because the L curve "flattens out" at its right end, there is some low rate of interest (say, 2 percent) beyond which an increase in the supply of money cannot reduce the rate further. Hence, the total demand for money at this low interest rate is infinite, because everyone would prefer to hold money in idle balances rather than risk the loss of holding long-term securities offering such poor yields.

In geometric terms, the *liquidity trap* exists at that rate of interest where the liquidity-preference curve becomes perfectly horizontal.

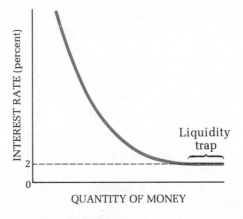

It should be emphasized, however, that this is a hypothesis; there is no concrete evidence to support it.

CONCLUSION: IMPORTANCE OF THE INTEREST RATE

The preceding analysis is based on a *given level of national income*. If national income is allowed to change, the problem becomes more complicated. This is because a change in national income will affect the rate of interest as well as the volume of saving and investment. To the extent that the amount of investment is responsive to a change in the interest rate, aggregate demand, and hence the overall level of employment, will also be affected. Further, a change in national income will influence the transactions and precautionary demands for money—which in turn influence the total demand for money for liquidity purposes.

This suggests an important conclusion:

The rate of interest is of strategic importance in income and employment analysis. It is the mechanism that establishes equilibrium between the supply of money in the economy and the amounts that people wish to hold as cash balances. Since the rate of interest is affected by the money supply, which in turn is controlled by the monetary authority, expansionary or contractionary monetary policies can influence the level of economic activity.

How does the rate of interest fit into the overall picture of income determination? As you will now see, the rate of interest is one of several strategic variables that are instrumental in establishing macroeconomic equilibrium.

Macroeconomic Equilibrium: Putting the Pieces Together

The macroeconomic theory of income determination which we set out to study at the beginning of Part 2 is now completed. (You will find it helpful to refer to the table of contents to get an overview of the ground covered thus far.) We shall now bring together the major components of the theory. This will permit certain fundamental relationships between key variables to be integrated into a meaningful whole.

OUTLINE OF THE KEYNESIAN THEORY

A summary of the Keynesian theory of income determination is outlined in Exhibit 11. The relationships may be stated briefly in the form of several propositions:

1. The level of income depends on consumption expenditure and investment expenditure.

2. Consumption expenditure depends on the propensity to consume in relation to income. Investment expenditure depends on the marginal efficiency of investment relative to the rate of interest.

3. The propensity to consume (or consumption function) expresses a relationship between consumption and income. The relationship is such that as income increases, consumption increases, but not as fast as income. Two related concepts are (a) the average propensity to consume, or ratio of consumption to income, and (b) the marginal propensity to consume, or change in consumption relative to the change in income.

4. The marginal efficiency of investment depends on expected rates of return on capital investment. The rate of interest depends on liquidity preference and the quantity of money.

5. The marginal propensity to consume affects the size of the investment multiplier. This in turn affects the amount by which an increase in investment causes a multiplied increase in income.

6. Liquidity preference—the demand for money—is determined by the transactions, precautionary, and speculative motives. In contrast, the quantity of money is controlled by the monetary authority.

These propositions contain only the main features of the theory. They do not express all the interrelations between the variables, many of which were discussed in this and earlier chapters.

SOME BASIC RELATIONSHIPS

Exhibit 12 shows an integration of important relationships. This highly simplified model conveys many of the essential ideas of macroeconomic equilibrium. In Chart (a) the equilibrium rate of interest is determined by the intersection of the demand or liquidity-preference curve for money L with the supply of money M. In Chart (b) this interest rate is brought together with the marginal efficiency of investment MEI to determine the amount of investment I. In Chart (c) this volume of investment is superimposed on the consumption function C. Hence, the intersection of the C + I or aggregate demand (AD) curve with the 45° aggregate supply (AS) curve determines the equilibrium level of income.

If this level of income is either too low or too high to correspond to full employment, the result, as we learned in the study of income and employment determination, is either a recessionary or inflationary gap. To close the gap some combination of fiscal and monetary policy is needed. But government faces problems of considerable difficulty when it tries to choose a proper blend of policies, as we shall soon see.

Exhibit 11
Outline of the Keynesian Theory of Income Determination

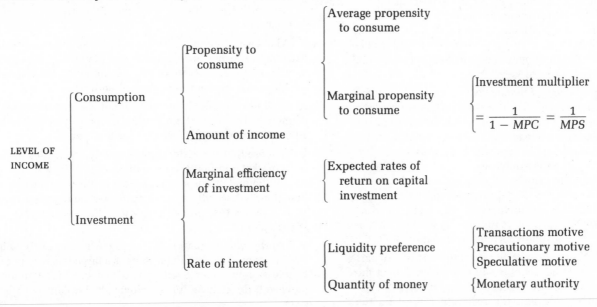

LEVEL OF INCOME
- Consumption
  - Propensity to consume
    - Average propensity to consume
    - Marginal propensity to consume
      - Investment multiplier $= \dfrac{1}{1 - MPC} = \dfrac{1}{MPS}$
  - Amount of income
- Investment
  - Marginal efficiency of investment
    - Expected rates of return on capital investment
  - Rate of interest
    - Liquidity preference
      - Transactions motive
      - Precautionary motive
      - Speculative motive
    - Quantity of money
      - Monetary authority

Exhibit 12
Simplified Keynesian Model of Income Determination

This model emphasizes the interrelationships among key variables by showing the four basic determinants of income or GNP. These are (1) liquidity preference, L; (2) money supply, M; (3) marginal efficiency of investment, MEI; (4) consumption function, C.

In Chart (a) the equilibrium rate of interest is determined by the intersection of the liquidity-preference (L) and quantity of money (M) curves. In Chart (b) the amount of investment (I) is determined by the interest rate and the marginal efficiency of investment (MEI) curve. In Chart (c) the volume of investment is superimposed on the consumption function to give the C + I or aggregate demand (AD) curve. The intersection of this curve with the 45° line or aggregate supply (AS) curve determines the equilibrium level of income.

As you can see from the charts, there can be no change in income, or NNP, without a shift of one or more of the four basic curves, L, M, MEI, and C.

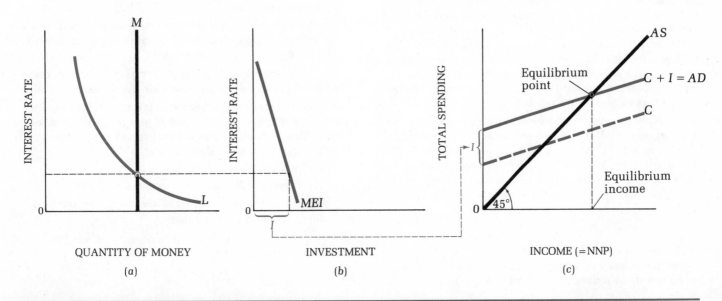

(a) QUANTITY OF MONEY   (b) INVESTMENT   (c) INCOME (= NNP)

What You Have Learned

1. The equation of exchange is $MV = PQ$. It states that the quantity of money (M), multiplied by the average number of times (V) each unit of money is spent on purchasing the economy's final output of goods and services, is equal to the quantity of final output (Q), multiplied by its average price (P). The equation is thus a truism or identity because it tells us that the same flow of money can be looked at either from buyers' or sellers' points of view.

2. The quantity theory of money, as originally formulated by Irving Fisher, assumes that the velocity of money and the volume of output are constant. Therefore, in terms of the equation of exchange, changes in the general price level are directly proportional to changes in the quantity of money. Modern quantity theorists have extended Fisher's ideas. They believe that the income velocity of money fluctuates over time, but its range of short-run variation is limited and, with sufficient knowledge, predictable. Therefore, their attention is focused on the factors influencing velocity and on the role of the money supply as a determinant of GNP.

3. In classical theory, the market rate of interest will depart from the real rate if households and businesses expect the general price level to rise or decline. Any differential between the market rate and the real rate represents the amount necessary to compensate lenders or borrowers for adverse changes in purchasing power resulting from anticipated inflation or deflation.

4. In the classical view, interest is the reward that businesses pay households for abstaining from consumption. The equilibrium rate of interest is determined in a competitive money market where the supply of funds saved by households equals the demand for funds invested by businesses.

5. In the Keynesian view, interest is the payment made to households and businesses to overcome liquidity preference. The equilibrium rate of interest is determined by the intersection of the liquidity-preference or demand curve for money with the money stock or supply curve of money.

6. Among the basic factors determining income or NNP are the state of liquidity preference, the money supply, the marginal efficiency of investment, and the consumption function. No change in NNP can occur without a change in one or more of these factors. In macroeconomic equilibrium all four variables are synchronized. Hence, a change in one of them, such as the money supply because it is controlled by the monetary authority, creates economic instability until a new equilibrium is reached.

7. An economic system may be in macroeconomic equilibrium at any level of income—not necessarily at the full-employment level. At any level of income other than the full-employment level, there will be either a recessionary or inflationary gap. Some combination of fiscal and monetary policy will therefore be needed to close the gap.

For Discussion

1. *Terms and concepts to review:*

income velocity of money	quantity theory of money
equation of exchange	interest
marginal efficiency of investment	precautionary motive
real rate of interest	speculative motive
market rate of interest	liquidity-preference theory of interest
Implicit Price Index	liquidity trap
transactions motive	

2. What basic differences are there between the equation of exchange as Fisher formulated it and the modern equation as it is used today? Is there any advantage to the modern equation as compared to Fisher's equation?

3. What has been the long-run trend of the income velocity of money (i.e., V in the equation of exchange) since the 1950s? Can you give the reasons for this trend?

4. Suppose that the Federal Reserve buys securities in the open market and that the securities are sold by a nonbank (i.e., individual or corporation). As a result of this transaction alone, what will be the directions of change, if any, of M, P, Q, V (in that order), and MV in the equation $MV = PQ$? Explain.

5. In terms of the equation $MV = PQ$, what are likely to be the effects on P, Q, and PQ if there is a large increase in the money supply under conditions of (a) substantial unemployment; (b) high or full employment. Explain your answer.

6. If the rate on short-term loans is the same as on long-term loans, what are the advantages and disadvantages to lenders of being in short-term as opposed to long-term investments? Discuss.

7. If the yield on long-term securities is greater than on short-term securities, why would anyone want to invest in the latter?

8. "The classical theory holds that the equilibrium rate of interest equates the supply of, and demand for, savings in a competitive money market. The Keynesian theory holds that the equilibrium rate of interest equates the demand for money with its supply. Therefore, there is no essential difference between the two theories." Do you agree? Explain.

9. Do the transactions and precautionary demands for holding money depend entirely on income? If not, what else do they depend on? Explain.

10. If a reduction in the interest rate does not result in an expansion of investment, what might this suggest in terms of the Keynesian theory of interest?

11. If the economy is in a liquidity trap, would an increase in the quantity of money stimulate investment? Explain.

12. Assume that the economy is in macroeconomic equilibrium. What effect would each of the following changes, considered separately and without regard to secondary results, have on income? Explain why.

(a) Increase in the money supply.

(b) Increase in liquidity preference.

(c) Increase in the marginal efficiency of investment.

(d) Decrease in consumption.

In general terms, how would secondary effects have influenced your answers?

Issue
What Price for Money?

Until near the end of the 1960s, the United States was traditionally regarded as a low-interest economy. Credit was cheap and plentiful, and three decades of a rising trend of interest rates had been tolerated because the level never got too high. But in recent history the level during some periods was well over 10 percent, causing considerable distress for consumers, home buyers, farmers, and some businesspersons.

According to traditional doctrine, interest rates are the price of funds. Therefore, like any price, interest rates perform an allocative function: They ration the supply of scarce funds—the flow of savings—to the ultimate users. Those borrowers with the most promising investment opportunities, who are willing to pay a high interest rate, bid funds away from their competitors. In this way the interest-rate structure allocates funds among households, businesses, and government, and between private and public uses.

Should Rates Be Controlled?

Of course, when interest rates rise too high, the painful effects are felt in a widening circle of individuals, industries, states and localities, and the federal government itself. Pressures are then placed on political leaders to control lending charges by legislating interest ceilings. Two major reasons for imposing controls are usually advanced:

1. Interest payments are a significant cost to business firms. Like other costs, an increase in interest rates is passed along to consumers in the form of higher prices, thereby furthering cost-push inflation.

2. Interest payments are incomes to those who grant loans. Therefore, increases in interest rates unjustly benefit lenders—especially banks—at the expense of borrowers.

Most economists do not find these arguments convincing. They believe that interest rates are a reflection of inflation rather than a cause. As a result, they oppose interest ceilings, for several reasons.

First, despite the trend of rising rates, interest charges play only a minor role in cost-push inflation. Net interest charges average less than 3 percent of total production costs of nonfinancial corporations. In contrast, labor costs average 66 percent.

Second, an increase in interest rates may be necessary to help choke off inflation. Although a rise in borrowing costs need not immediately deter spending, it sooner or later deters some consumers from buying houses, automobiles, and major appliances, and some businesspersons

from buying new plant and equipment.

But regardless of the pros and cons, the really fundamental issue rests on the basic advantage of free over controlled markets. What the United States must decide is whether it prefers a government-controlled economy or an economy in which supply and demand forces are dominant in every field—including money.

QUESTIONS

1. Market controls of any kind are likely to create distortions. But wage and price controls probably cause less damage, at least initially, than interest-rate controls. Why?

2. All of the nation's fifty states have usury statutes of one sort or another. But the laws, which set general interest-rate ceilings on various kinds of loans, are usually riddled with exemptions. As a result, in recent years, when interest rates reached their highest levels in decades, construction of owner-occupied homes in some states practically ceased, while construction of rental houses and commercial buildings continued at high levels. Can you explain why?

3. Is it possible for society to ease the burden of high interest rates on low-income families and still preserve free capital markets? Discuss.

PRIME RATE: INTEREST PAID BY TOP FIRMS ON SHORT-TERM LOANS
(prime commercial paper, 4–6 months)

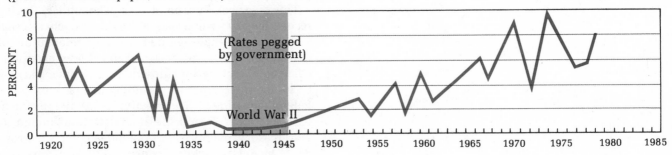

Chapter 14

Fiscalism, Monetarism, and the Fiscal–Monetary Mix

Chapter Preview

How much fiscal policy is needed to achieve full employment? How much monetary policy? Is there some ideal combination of both?

Are Keynesian ideas still appropriate for today's economy in which inflation, not just unemployment, is a fundamental problem?

It is a gloomy moment in the history of our country. Not in the lifetime of most men has there been so much grave and deep apprehension; never has the future seemed so incalculable as at this time. The domestic economic situation is in chaos. Our dollar is weak throughout the world. Prices are so high as to be utterly impossible.

The political cauldron seethes and bubbles with uncertainty. Russia hangs as usual, like a cloud, dark and silent, upon the horizon. It is a solemn moment. Of our troubles no men can see the end.

Harper's Weekly (October 1857)

Everyone agrees that times change. Yet people often see uncanny parallels between adverse economic conditions today and those of some period in the distant past. Perhaps this is because many social problems do not really change with time; rather, it is our understanding of them that changes.

This is especially true of macroeconomics. During recent history two broad policy approaches—fiscal and monetary—have guided the implementation of government measures designed to achieve economic efficiency, stability, and growth. As you have learned, fiscal actions consist of spending and taxing by the federal government. These activities are the responsibility of Congress and the administration—including the Treasury, the Bureau of the Budget, and the President. Monetary actions consist of expansions and contractions of the money supply, and of related measures affecting interest rates. Responsibility for these activities rests with the Federal Reserve System.

What are the natures of fiscal and monetary policies? How do they help alleviate two of our most important economic ills—unemployment and inflation—while promoting economic growth? These are the fundamental questions which this chapter seeks to answer. But first, a brief review of the problem is presented in Exhibit 1.

The Fiscal–Monetary Mix

You have learned that both fiscal and monetary policies are deliberate actions designed to influence economic efficiency and stability. Therefore, the question that arises is: What is the "best" fiscal–monetary mix?

Since the birth of Keynesian economics in the 1930s, economists have differed on the *relative* importance of fiscal and monetary policies as means of achieving economic efficiency and stability. The differences of opinion are complex and rest on many considerations. Nevertheless, two basic positions or schools of thought—commonly referred to as "fiscalist" and "monetarist"—may be identified.

THE FISCALIST, OR NEO-KEYNESIAN, VIEW

The *fiscalists,* also known as *neo-Keynesians* or *"new economists,"* are those persons who follow in the Keynesian tradition. Their beliefs are rooted in the fundamental equation

$$AD = C + I + G$$

The fiscalists contend that a capitalistic economy is *inherently unstable* and does not tend automatically toward full employment. This is because the level of aggregate demand does not always remain high enough to absorb the nation's full-capacity output. Therefore, the fiscalists believe, government should take up the slack by stimulating enough spending to raise aggregate demand to the full-employment level.

How can government accomplish this task? There are several ways:

1. **Reduce Taxes** This leaves the private sector with more income to spend.

2. **Increase Public Spending** This adds directly to the total demand for goods and services.

3. **Utilize Monetary Policies** These should supplement and complement the major shifts in economic activity brought about by changes in fiscal policy.

By thus adhering to an appropriate blend of fiscal and monetary policies, it is possible, in the opinion of the fiscalists, to stabilize the economy and perhaps even to "fine-tune" it.

Exhibit 1
Recessionary and Inflationary Gaps

As you recall, aggregate demand (*AD*) is the sum of consumption demand (*C*), investment demand (*I*), and government demand (*G*). The intersection of aggregate demand with aggregate supply (*AS*) determines the prevailing level of output and employment.

The line (*C* + *I* + *G*) represents the objective of a well-coordinated fiscal and monetary policy. It expresses the full-employment level of *total* spending by households, businesses, and government. A lower level of total spending such as (*C* + *I* + *G*)′ will produce a recessionary gap; a higher level will produce an inflationary gap.

What kinds of fiscal and monetary policies should be employed to close these gaps?

If a recessionary gap exists, as represented by the aggregate demand curve (*C* + *I* + *G*)′, then:

1. An appropriate fiscal policy would increase government expenditures and reduce taxes. This would increase *G*, and probably *C* and *I* as well. (Why do we say "probably" *C* and *I*? Why not "surely"?)

2. An appropriate monetary policy would increase the money supply by easing credit, thereby further encouraging business firms to increase *I*.

The result of these combined policies would be to shift the aggregate demand curve back up toward the full-employment level represented by the (*C* + *I* + *G*) curve.

On the other hand, an inflationary gap as represented by the aggregate demand curve (*C* + *I* + *G*)″ requires a different approach to fiscal and monetary policy. Can you suggest the proper guidelines?

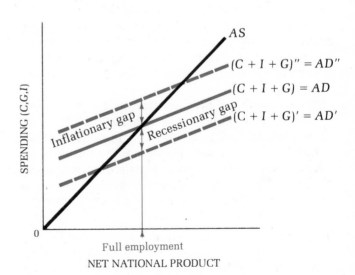

A review of the New Economics (i.e., neo-Keynesianism) ties the foregoing ideas together.

> The New Economics emerged in the 1930s from the ideas of John Maynard Keynes. In contrast with classical economic theory, it holds that a capitalistic economy does not tend automatically toward full employment. Therefore, the government should pursue active fiscal policies, supported by appropriate monetary policies, to achieve and maintain full employment, stable prices, and steady economic growth.

THE MONETARIST VIEW

In contrast to fiscalists, there is a *monetarist* group which marches to a distinctly different tune. The beliefs of the monetarists stem from the ideas expressed by Irving Fisher. These include the familiar quantity theory of money and the equation of exchange

$$MV = PQ$$

In this equation, M represents the quantity of money, V its velocity of circulation, P the average price of final goods and services, and Q the quantity of those goods and services. As you recall from the previous chapter, monetarists believe that V is relatively stable. Therefore, they say, changes in the economy's output or income *(PQ)* are due to changes in M.

NOTE   To refresh your understanding of these concepts, look up the meanings of *quantity theory of money* and *equation of exchange* in the Dictionary at the back of the book.

The monetarists contend that a capitalistic economy is *inherently stable*. Therefore, the system is not necessarily subject to business-cycle fluctuations. Major inflations and recessions, it is argued, are due primarily to one factor: *large swings in the rate of growth of the money supply.* Consequently, the monetarists conclude, fiscal policy cannot be used as a stabilizing device. Only monetary policy, in the form of consistent rather than erratic changes in the supply of money, can enable the economy to stabilize itself.

Like fiscalists, monetarists do not always agree on every point. However, monetarists are unanimous in their belief that money exercises a major influence on the economy. You can see why, by examining the main features of their argument:

1. According to monetarist theory, the amount of money people wish to hold is closely related to their level of income. Hence, if the supply of money (i.e., currency and demand deposits) increases faster than income, people will spend away the unwanted portion. This will cause inflation. On the other hand, if the supply of money increases more slowly than income, the opposite effect will occur. People will try to build up their money balances by cutting back on their expenditures, thereby causing unemployment. Therefore, monetarists conclude that *changes in the money supply cause people to alter their spending in relation to their income, thereby generating business cycles.*

2. Monetarists do not claim that business cycles result exclusively from changes in the money supply. Like the fiscalists, monetarists recognize that the economy is always in the process of adjusting to changes in such things as population, consumer habits, and competition within industries. But monetarists believe that *erratic changes in the supply of money are the dominant cause of business cycles.*

3. In view of the fundamental role of money in the economy, monetarists believe that government fiscal actions by themselves exert little, if any, influence on total spending. It is when these actions are accommodated by the Fed through monetary expansions or contractions that changes in the money supply exert a strong independent influence on total spending. Therefore, because business cycles are primarily the result of erratic fluctuations in the money supply, *control of the rate of monetary expansion or contraction is the appropriate means of stabilizing the economy.*

4. In line with the rest of their theory, monetarists believe that the market interest rate rises and falls with the general price level. The reason, they say, is that borrowers and lenders add an "inflation premium" to the real interest rate—the rate that would prevail if prices remained stable. Monetarists thus contend that *an increase in the money supply raises prices and therefore the market interest rate; a decrease in the money supply does the opposite.* (In contrast, as you recall from the previous chapter, neo-Keynesians believe that an increase in the money supply *decreases* the rate of interest. This encourages business investment and economic expansion. Conversely, a decrease in the money supply has the opposite effect.)

THE MONEY-SUPPLY RULE

The monetarists' views are strong and persuasive. To support their beliefs, monetarists cite detailed studies, some going as far back as the nineteenth century, analyzing the behavior of money and prices. Monetarists contend these studies show that changes in the money supply have larger, more predictable, and quicker effects on GNP than do fiscal-policy changes in tax rates, government expenditures, and the federal deficit. (See *Leaders in Economics,* page 241.)

Leaders in Economics
Milton Friedman 1912–

America's Best-Known Monetarist

In 1936, two contradictory events occurred that subsequently had a profound impact on economic theory and policy. In England, *The General Theory of Employment, Interest and Money* was published, in which the author, J. M. Keynes, advocated government activism to achieve full employment. In the United States, a pathbreaking article entitled "Rules Versus Authority in Monetary Policy" was published in the prestigious *Journal of Political Economy*. Written by Henry Simons, a brilliant young professor at the University of Chicago, the article made some profound observations. Among them:

A democratic, free-enterprise system requires for its effective functioning a stable framework of definite rules, laid down in legislation and subject to change only gradually and with careful regard for the vested interests of participants in the economic game. . . .

The responsibility for carrying out the monetary rules should be lodged in a federal authority, closely controlled in its exercise by a sharply defined policy. Political control in this sphere should be confined exclusively to regulation of the quantity of money and near money.

It remained for one of Simons' students to write the needed rules. That student was Milton Friedman. After receiving his Ph.D. from Columbia University in 1946, Friedman joined the economics faculty at the University of Chicago. Within a few years he was honored by the American Economic Association—the nation's major organization of professional economists—as one of its leading scholars.

Provocative Thinker

Nowadays, relatively few economists advocate the abolition of welfare, social security, graduated income taxes, and professional licensure—including the licensing of medical doctors. Milton Friedman is one who does. A Nobel laureate (1976) and professor emeritus at the University of Chicago, he is not only one of America's leading economists but also the foremost exponent of what is known as the "Chicago School" of economic thought. Like his distinguished predecessors at that renowned institution, he has an abiding faith in free enterprise and an unshakable conviction that the free market is the best device ever conceived for allocating society's resources and for ordering human affairs.

Friedman is more than a maverick economist. He has been called the most original economic thinker since John Maynard Keynes. This reputation has been earned largely because of Friedman's exhaustive criticisms of Keynesian ideas. As a result, Friedman is believed by many to equal, if not outrank, Keynes as the most influential economist of the twentieth century.

Money-Supply Rule

This belief is based primarily on Friedman's approach to money and his unique position as America's best-known monetarist. Using carefully documented research going back to the late nineteenth century, he argues that the crucial factor affecting economic trends has been the quantity of money, not government fiscal policy. Accordingly, he opposes the use of discretionary monetary policy by the Federal Reserve to achieve economic stability. Friedman advocates instead a *money-supply rule*—an expansion of the nation's money supply at a steady rate in accordance with the economy's growth and capacity to produce. Friedman gives four major reasons for this view.

1. *Past Performance of the Fed*
Throughout its history, the Fed has proclaimed that it was using its monetary powers to promote economic stability. But the record often shows the opposite. Despite the Fed's well-intentioned efforts, it has been a

Wide World Photos.

major cause of instability by permitting the quantity of money to expand and contract erratically. Therefore, the urgent need is to prevent the Fed from being a source of economic disturbance.

2. *Limitation of Our Knowledge*
Economic research has established two propositions:

(a) There are close, regular, and predictable relations among the quantity of money, national income, and prices over a number of years. Therefore, a stable price level over the long run requires that the quantity of money grow at a fairly steady rate roughly equal to the average rate of growth of the nation's output—its real GNP.

(b) The relation between the quantity of money and economic activity is much looser from month to month, quarter to quarter, or even year to year than it is over a number of years. Therefore, any attempt to use monetary policy for fine-tuning the economy is bound to create economic instability.

(Continued on next page)

3. *Promotion of Confidence*   An announced, and adhered to, policy of steady monetary growth would provide the business sector with a firm basis for confidence in monetary stability. This is more than any discretionary policy could provide even if it happened to produce roughly steady monetary growth.

4. *Neutralization of the Fed*   An independent Fed is at times too removed from political pressures and at other times unduly affected by them. Hence, a money-supply rule would insulate monetary policy both from the arbitrary power of a small group of people not subject to control by the electorate and from the short-run pressures of partisan politics.

Is the adoption of a money-supply rule technically feasible? Friedman claims that it is. Although he admits that the Fed could not achieve a precise rate of growth in the money supply from day to day or week to week, it could come very close from month to month and quarter to quarter. If and when it does, he says, it would provide a monetary climate favorable to economic stability and orderly growth. And that, Friedman concludes, is the most we can ask from monetary policy at our present state of knowledge.

In the monetarists' opinion, therefore, the government should help the economy achieve its full-employment potential by adhering to a simple and well-defined guide:

The Federal Reserve should expand the nation's money supply at the economy's growth rate or capacity to produce, which is about 3 to 5 percent per year. More than this would lead to strong inflationary pressures; less would tend to be stagnating. This guide for economic expansion advanced by monetarists is often called the *money-supply rule.*

Monetarists, in other words, believe that the Federal Reserve has the power to stabilize the economy—or at least to permit the economy to stabilize itself. How? Through the Federal Reserve's ability to control bank reserves and therefore the supply of money. In contrast, monetarists contend that the fiscalists—in their well-meant efforts to employ fiscal policy for purposes of economic stabilization—have misused monetary policy. As a result, they have magnified rather than mitigated business cycles.

Thus, the monetarists believe that the growth of the money supply, as a result of discretionary efforts by the fiscalists to "manage" the economy, has fluctuated. With the help of various charts and models, monetarists allege that *increases in the money supply have resulted in economic expansions, while decreases have caused economic contractions.*

Monetarists conclude, therefore, that even though the Federal Reserve's influence over the money supply may not be perfect, adherence to the money-supply rule would nevertheless produce better results for economic efficiency, stabilization, and growth than the flexible policy mix followed by the fiscalists.

Fiscalism Versus Monetarism: Some Unresolved Considerations

Many of the ideas advanced by the monetarists have become an integral part of modern economic thinking. Nevertheless, a number of fundamental questions remain. Some of the more important ones, which are the subject of continuing research by many economists, may be mentioned briefly.

WHAT IS MONEY?

All economists agree that it is hard to define money precisely. Monetarists have traditionally found M_1, consisting of currency plus demand deposits, too "narrow" for their purposes. They have preferred instead to use M_2, which includes M_1 plus savings accounts at commercial banks. However, this neglects the significance of M_3, which includes M_2 plus deposits in savings institutions. It also overlooks the growing importance of other forms of financial assets which substitute for money, such as Treasury bills and other highly marketable securities. Thus, because neither monetarists, fiscalists, nor anyone else can provide an ideal definition of "money," it is extremely difficult to manage.

IS MONEY A CAUSE OR AN EFFECT?

Monetarists believe that changes in the money supply *cause* changes in income and production. Is this contention correct? The answer is probably yes. But a reverse type of relation may also be true.

Thus, if spending and production increase, the expansion in business may increase the demand for money. If the Federal Reserve then enlarges the supply of money, the increase in spending will be the reason for bringing more money into circulation. In such a case the change in the money supply is an *effect* rather than a cause of total spending.

INTEREST RATES: WHICH CAUSAL CHAIN?

Neo-Keynesians subscribe to Keynes' liquidity preference theory of interest, which you studied in the previous chapter. In this theory, as shown in Exhibit 2, Chart (a), the interest rate is determined by the supply of and demand for money. Therefore, an increase in the money supply will lower the interest rate relative to the marginal efficiency of investment. This will stimulate business investment spending, as shown in

Chart (b). The result, shown in Chart (c), will be a rise in aggregate demand. This in turn will increase output, prices, or both, depending on the degree of slack in the economy. The chain of causation is thus:

NEO-KEYNESIAN VIEW:
    From Money to Interest Rates to Prices

Monetarists, on the other hand, follow in Irving Fisher's tradition. This includes the quantity theory of money and the equation of exchange. As you recall from Fisher's ideas, there is a definite distinction between the real rate of interest and the market rate. The real rate is the one that would prevail if borrowers and lenders anticipated a stable price level. The market rate, on the other hand, is the one that actually exists. It reflects borrowers' and lenders' expectations of future prices. The market rate thus includes an "inflation premium." According to the quantity theory of money, prices rise when the money supply increases.

Exhibit 2
Money Supply and the Transmission Mechanism: Keynesian View

These charts, which were presented in the previous chapter, depict the Keynesian view of macroeconomic equilibrium. The charts should be read from left to right. Thus:

Chart (a) The interest rate is determined by the intersection of the money-supply curve *(M)* and the money-demand or liquidity-preference curve *(L)*.

Chart (b) The amount of investment is determined by the marginal efficiency of investment *(MEI)* and the interest rate.

Chart (c) Equilibrium income or NNP is determined by the intersection of aggregate demand *(AD)* with aggregate supply *(AS)*.

A change in the money supply can thus initiate a series of effects. The causal chain or transmission mechanism runs from money to interest rates to prices. Thus:

money → interest rates → prices

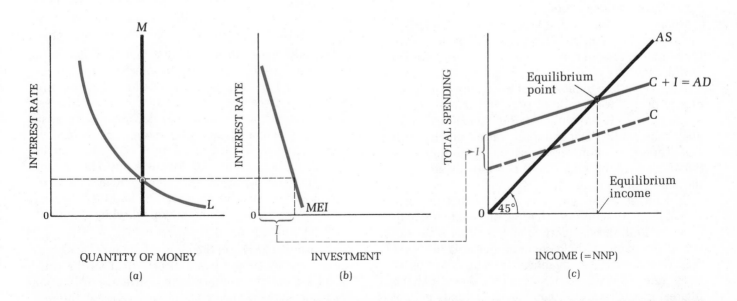

(a) QUANTITY OF MONEY   (b) INVESTMENT   (c) INCOME (=NNP)

Therefore, market interest rates also rise relative to real rates when the money supply increases. The chain of causation is:

MONETARIST VIEW:
From Money to Prices to Interest Rates

The two theories thus start from common ground. However, they lead to dramatically different conclusions. That is, both theories agree that changes in the money supply will initiate a series of effects. But the transmission mechanisms or chains of causation will differ. The neo-Keynesian theory says that an easy-money policy—an increase in the money supply—will reduce interest rates and encourage investment. The monetarist theory says that an easy-money policy will increase prices, raise interest rates and inflationary expectations, and thereby discourage investment.

REMARK   Monetarism is not based on a macroeconomic model as is neo-Keynesianism. Therefore, the monetarists' version of the transmission mechanism must be conveyed in words rather than simple charts like those in Exhibit 2.

IS VELOCITY STABLE?

You will recall from the familiar equation of exchange that

$$MV = PQ \quad \text{and therefore} \quad V = \frac{PQ}{M}$$

The second equation tells us that velocity (V) is the ratio of the economy's output (or income) to money. That is, velocity measures the speed at which money is exchanged for the economy's GNP, represented by PQ in the equations above.

Monetarists contend that V is primarily affected by the *transactions motive*. This, you recall, is the desire of the public to hold some of its assets in liquid form in order to carry on day-to-day spending.

Thus, according to monetarist belief, the amount of money people want to hold rises and falls with the economy's GNP. In terms of the second equation above, the public's demand for M varies directly with PQ. Therefore, monetarists conclude, although V fluctuates over the long run, it is relatively stable in the short run (as is GNP).

In contrast, neo-Keynesians contend that in addition to the transactions motive, people want money in order to fulfill the *speculative motive*. This is the desire of the public to hold some of its assets in liquid form in order to take advantage of changes in the interest rate. That is, neo-Keynesians believe that the interest rate determines the amount of funds people

allocate for speculative purposes. As a result, the velocity of money for transactions purposes remains relatively stable, while the velocity of money for speculative purposes fluctuates with the interest rate.

Thus in the Keynesian model, as you have already learned, a decrease in M causes a rise in the interest rate. This prompts people to spend some of their cash holdings in order to acquire more interest-earning securities such as bonds. Consequently, V increases. Conversely, an increase in M causes a decline in the interest rate. People, therefore, sell some of their securities in order to hold more cash. Hence, V decreases. Neo-Keynesians thus conclude that V is unstable and varies directly with the interest rate.

To summarize:

> According to the neo-Keynesians, an increase in M lowers the rate of interest, which in turn lowers V. A decrease in M does just the opposite. Therefore, neo-Keynesians say, in the equation of exchange $MV = PQ$, *changes in M can be more than offset by changes in V.* This contradicts the viewpoint of the monetarists, who hold that because V is relatively stable, *only changes in M will have noticeable and direct effects on PQ.*

Some further aspects of this are illustrated in Exhibit 3.

Recapitulation: The Critical Role of Money

You can now appreciate that certain differences between *fiscalism* and *monetarism* have far-reaching implications. For practical policy-making purposes, the fundamental difference concerns the effects of changes in the money supply on interest rates and prices. Two classes of effects may be distinguished.

1. *Fiscalist View*   In the fiscalist model, a change in the money supply has a direct effect on the interest rate, but not on the price level. Further, no distinction is made between market and real rates of interest. Following in the tradition of J. M. Keynes, fiscalists contend that an increase in the money supply leads to a reduction in the interest rate. This causes an increase in the amount of business investment and therefore in aggregate demand. Unemployed resources are drawn into production, and the economy thus moves toward full employment while prices adjust accordingly.

2. *Monetarist View*   In the monetarist model, a change in the money supply has a direct effect on the price level, but not on the interest rate. Further, a distinction is made between market and real rates of interest.

Exhibit 3
Money and GNP; Interest and Velocity

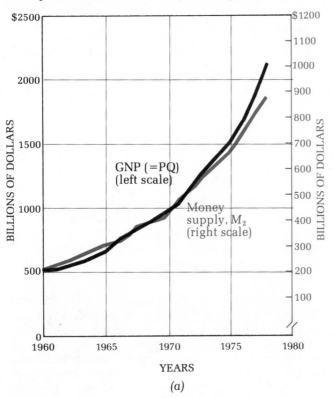

YEARS

(a)

Chart (a). *Monetarists believe that* M_2 *(consisting of* M_1 *plus savings accounts at commercial banks) comes closest to being a suitable measure of the nation's money supply. This chart shows the close relation between* M_1 *and GNP. Can you conclude from this that changes in GNP result from changes in* M_2? *Can the reverse also be true?*

Chart (b). *Neo-Keynesians prefer to measure velocity with* M_1 *because it fluctuates more widely than* M_2. *According to neo-Keynesian theory, there is a positive relationship between velocity and the interest rate: Both tend to move in the same direction. This chart suggests that some degree of relationship may exist. But can you conclude that the relationship is particularly strong?*

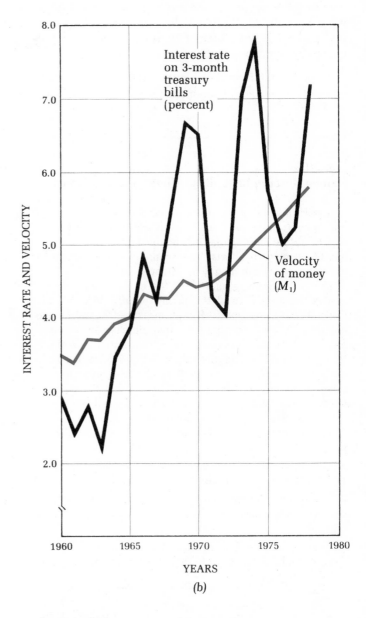

YEARS

(b)

Following in the tradition of Irving Fisher, monetarists believe that an increase in the money supply leads to an increase in prices. This causes the actual or market rate of interest to rise relative to the "real" rate—the rate that would exist if prices were stable. The difference between the market and real rate represents an "inflation premium." This is an amount that borrowers are willing to pay and lenders receive because both expect prices to continue rising.

On this basis, monetarists conclude that because the effects on aggregate demand of temporary budgetary changes are uncertain, steady monetary growth is preferable to discretionary fiscal actions.

Conclusion: Some Agreement and Disagreement

The way in which Washington manages the money supply is thus critical for public policy. Which of the two models is correct? As with all complex questions there is no simple answer. Fortunately, however, disagreements over theoretical matters need not always lead to disagreements over public policy. In economics as in medicine, there may be uniformity of opinion on treating the symptoms of an illness even though its causes are controversial. Thus:

Virtually all informed observers agree that a reasonably steady expansion of the money supply is essential for

economic stability. Much less agreement exists concerning the short- and long-run effects of changes in the money supply on interest rates and prices. Because of these differences in views, you will often encounter practical discussions in the news media concerning issues involving fiscal and monetary policy.

Exhibit 4 presents an interesting conclusion to this discussion.

Exhibit 4
Federal Reserve Instability: Money and Inflation

Monetarists contend that the Fed has focused its attention not on controlling the money supply but on controlling interest rates, something that it is unable to do. As a result, it has failed in both efforts. The economy has experienced wide swings in both money and interest rates.

The accompanying chart, say the monetarists, demonstrates the instability of the money supply, M_2, and the Consumer Price Index, CPI, both measured in percentage changes. The relationship shows that increases in the monetary-growth rate cause increases in the inflation rate about two years later. The relationship also shows that when the money-supply trend line rises over a number of years, the inflation trend line rises faster. This reflects the public's expectations that the inflation will continue, and hence that it pays to consume more and save less.

What do the monetarists prescribe as a cure? Three things. The Fed should:

1. Aim at stabilizing the monetary-growth rate and leave interest rates to be determined in the market.

2. Reduce the monetary growth rate gradually by one percentage point each year until a rate of 4 to 5 percent is reached.

3. Keep a close watch on the monetary base rather than the federal funds rate as a guide for short-term policy.*

In late 1979, the Fed announced its intention to adhere more closely to these guidelines. Many observers, however, are skeptical. They question whether the Fed will resist mounting political pressure as tighter monetary policies lead to temporary increases in interest rates and unemployment.

* The *monetary base* consists of legal reserves (i.e., currency plus commercial-bank deposits with the Fed). The monetary base supports not only member-bank deposit liabilities, but also deposits at other types of financial institutions (such as savings banks, savings and loan associations, credit unions, etc.), because these institutions maintain demand deposits with commercial banks. Therefore, the monetary base is sometimes called "high-powered" money. Its size affects the total monetary assets of the public.

The *federal funds rate* is the interest rate at which banks borrow excess reserves from other banks' accounts at the Fed, usually overnight, to keep required reserves from falling below the legal level. The Fed pays close attention to this rate as an indicator of what is happening to other interest rates.

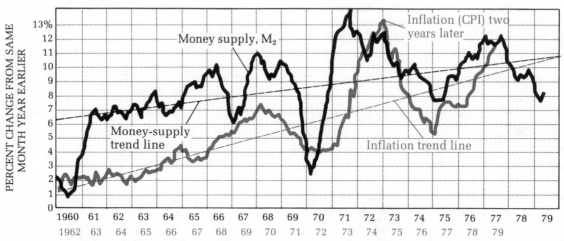

SOURCE: Adapted from *Newsweek*, August 20, 1979.

What You Have Learned

1. Which combination of fiscal and monetary policy is best? This question has concerned economists and political leaders since the birth of Keynesian economics in the 1930s. Two distinct viewpoints or schools of thought—called "fiscalist" and "monetarist"—have evolved.

2. Fiscalists are neo-Keynesians. They follow the Keynesian tradition. This means their beliefs are rooted in the fundamental equation

$$AD = C + I + G$$

and in the equation's implications. Among them:

(a) A capitalistic economy is inherently unstable and does not tend automatically toward full employment. Therefore:

(b) An active fiscal policy involving taxation and budgetary changes is needed to bring aggregate demand to full-employment levels. In addition:

(c) An appropriate monetary policy should supplement and complement the major shifts in economic activity brought about by changes in fiscal policy.

3. Monetarists are neo-Fisherians. They build upon the writings of Irving Fisher, one of the great American neo-classical economists of the early 1900s. Monetarist beliefs are rooted in the basic equation of exchange

$$MV = PQ$$

and in the quantity theory of money. These concepts have undergone substantial revision by monetarists, whose ideas emphasize the following beliefs:

(a) A capitalistic economy is inherently stable and not necessarily subject to substantial business-cycle fluctuations. Major inflations and recessions are due primarily to one factor: *erratic changes in monetary growth.* This causes people to alter their spending in relation to income, thereby generating wide swings in business activity.

(b) In the equation of exchange given above, the velocity (V) of money is relatively stable and, with sufficient knowledge, predictable. Therefore, the quantity of money (M) is of critical importance in affecting the economy's prices and output (PQ), or GNP. (In contrast, fiscalists contend that because of the speculative demand for money, V is relatively unstable and, therefore, unpredictable.)

(c) Because of the importance of monetary growth, the Federal Reserve should adhere to a "money-supply rule." That is, the money supply should be increased at the same rate as the economy's capacity to produce—about 3 to 5 percent a year. More than this would be inflationary; less would cause stagnation.

4. The fiscalist–monetarist controversy leaves many unanswered questions. Among the more important:

(a) *What is money?* There is no generally acceptable measure—one that is neither too "narrow" nor too "broad."

(b) *Do changes in the money supply affect changes in production?* There is evidence that changes in M cause changes in GNP, but there is evidence that a reverse type of relation may also exist.

(c) *Do interest rates influence prices?* Fiscalists believe that interest rates affect prices, but monetarists contend that the reverse is true.

(d) *Is velocity stable?* Fiscalists argue that V is unstable and can be more than offset by changes in M. Monetarists believe that V is inherently stable and therefore only changes in M can affect PQ.

5. There is substantial agreement among most experts that a reasonably steady expansion of the money supply is necessary to achieve stability. There is much less agreement, however, concerning the influence of money growth on other economic variables. Fiscalists believe the chain of causation runs from money to interest rates to prices. Monetarists believe the causal chain runs from money to prices to interest rates.

For Discussion

1. *Terms and concepts to review:*

recessionary gap	fiscalism
inflationary gap	monetarism
money-supply rule	

2. Monetarists are more critical of erratic changes in the money supply than of its rapid growth. The former, they contend, is a far more serious problem. Can you explain why?

3. If the money supply increased at a steady rate of about 4 percent a year, would business cycles still occur? How would a monetarist answer this question?

4. There is a close relationship between GNP and the money supply. Can you offer an explanation as to why *either one* may be the cause of the other?

5. The equation $AD = C + I + G$ says fundamentally the same thing as the equation $MV = PQ$. Do you agree? Explain.

6. Which is more important, the size of the nation's budgetary deficit or its rate of growth?

7. Is it possible for the fiscalists and monetarists to agree on public policy even though they disagree on certain fundamental matters of theory?

Case
Is Keynes Dead?

British economist John Maynard Keynes died in 1946. However, the theories he expounded ten years earlier did not. Keynesian ideas have dominated economic thought. In varying degrees, depending on the administration in Washington, the theories of Keynes became the guiding force of economic policy for decades.

But times seem to be changing. Many experts contend that the economy no longer behaves according to strict Keynesian propositions. What are those propositions? Some of the basic ones can be stated briefly:

○ GNP and employment are determined by the level of aggregate demand or total spending in the economy.

○ Government should remedy deficiencies in aggregate demand by incurring budgetary deficits.

○ Through deficit spending, government can close a recessionary gap and boost GNP by some multiple of the increase in spending.

Balanced-Budget Multiplier: Disincentives?

The third proposition can be formulated in a more general way. In the Keynesian model, an increase in government spending, even if matched by a tax increase, will raise GNP. This is because people pay their tax increases out of both savings and consumption. Therefore, if taxes are raised, the decrease in private spending is more than offset by the increase in government spending.

Conversely, if taxes are cut and government spending decreases correspondingly, aggregate demand and hence total spending decline. Therefore, so does employment.

These ideas are familar. They describe the operation of the "balanced-budget multiplier," an important principle in Keynesian theory and policy. In effect, the principle states that increases in taxes and government spending result in increases in GNP. However, the principle suffers from a basic flaw. It fails to allow for *disincentives* in production and investment that develop when tax rates rise. People undertake economic activity for income. Therefore, when marginal tax rates rise—that is, when the taxes paid on the last few dollars of wages, dividends, and interest go up—people have less incentive to work, produce, and invest. As a result, the nation's output declines, even if aggregate demand increases.

New Attitudes: "Neo" Neo-Keynesianism

Economists have been paying increasing attention to this phenomenon since the 1970s. For some years prior to that time, Keynesian ideas worked fairly well. Increased government deficits, rising tax rates, and an expanding money supply provided economic stimulation without too much inflation. But the 1970s shattered the simplistic contention that mounting inflation could somehow "compensate" for high employment. Consumers and businesspersons discovered that inflation could actually cause unemployment and recession by impairing the ability to make decisions on the basis of future expectations.

The result has caused many fiscalists or neo-Keynesians to take a new look at conservative ideas. For example:

1. There is substantial agreement with the monetarist view that steady monetary growth is an important goal.

2. There is growing acceptance of the idea that interest rates depend at least in part on inflation rates.

3. There is considerable support for the contention that inflation discourages capital spending because businesses require higher returns to offset greater risks due to instability.

4. Perhaps most dramatic of all, there is more concern than ever with the desirability of balancing the budget during prosperous times. This contrasts sharply with the doctrine of *functional finance,* which has characterized much of Washington's fiscal thinking since the 1930s.

Conclusion: Changing Ideas

Despite their changing attitudes, neo-Keynesians are not decided on how to get from here to there. On a theoretical level, new breakthroughs will be needed before any major advances can occur. But on a policy level, some substantial moves have already been made and others are likely to follow.

This does not mean that Keynesian ideas are dead. Rather, they are undergoing changes that may revolutionize economic thinking in the years to come.

QUESTIONS

1. Review your understanding of alternative budget policies studied in an earlier chapter. These include (a) annually balanced budget, (b) cyclically balanced budget, (c) functional finance, and (d) full-employment balanced budget. Which policy has government tended to follow? Which policy do you think neo-Keynesians would like to follow? What difficulties are there in doing so?

2. Which of the foregoing budget policies, if any, are compatible with monetarism?

Chapter 15

Can We Overcome Stagflation?
Alternative Policies and Proposals

Chapter Preview

Is it possible for the nation to reach a high level of employment, a low rate of inflation, and a steady increase in real GNP per capita?

What specific policies have been proposed by Washington to achieve these goals? Are the policies practical? Can they be implemented?

Since about 1970, economists and political leaders have identified certain troublesome characteristics of our economic system. Among them:

○ A tightening of fiscal and monetary policies to curb inflation may cause unemployment to rise *without* putting an end to inflation.

○ An easing of fiscal and monetary policies to boost employment may cause inflation to accelerate *without* raising the rate of employment.

These characteristics are contrary to conventional Keynesian economic thinking. Whether or not they turn out to be durable remains to be seen. Meanwhile, policies for coping with unemployment and inflation continue to be proposed. What are the natures of these policies? Can they accomplish what they are designed to do? Before answering these questions, we need a clear understanding of the problem.

Understanding Stagflation: Recession and Inflation

For many years, the chief macroeconomic problem facing our own and some other mixed economies has been *stagflation*. As the name suggests, it is a combination of two words—"stagnation" and "inflation."

The former term describes a condition resulting from slow economic growth and high unemployment. The latter term, of course, means rising prices. Other names for stagflation, therefore, are "recessionary inflation" or "inflationary recession." All of these expressions are used frequently in the news media.

PHILLIPS CURVES

Many economists believe that because inflation and unemployment can exist at the same time, there may be a relationship between them. If this is true, the relationship can be expressed by a *Phillips curve*. This idea is named after A. W. Phillips, a British economist who proposed the concept several decades ago.

The relationship is illustrated in Exhibit 1. It emphasizes the notion that if a Phillips curve actually exists, there can be only one such curve for the economy at any given time. Let us see why.

Conventional Curve

Chart (a) conveys a "conventional" Phillips curve, a type that was widely believed to exist a few decades ago. Each point on a particular curve, such as curve 1, designates a specific *combination* of unemployment and inflation. The point labeled A, for instance, represents a 4 percent unemployment rate and a 5 percent inflationary rate.

What would happen if there were a shift—for reasons to be explained shortly—from curve 1 to curve 2? In that case, a given point on the higher curve denotes at least as much of one variable plus more of the other, when compared to a point directly below or to the left of it on the lower curve. Thus, point B represents the same 4 percent unemployment rate as point A but denotes a higher inflation rate—9 percent. Point C, on the other hand, denotes the same 5 percent inflation rate as point A but a 7 percent unemployment rate. The same notion applies to any other point you may choose. Any point on curve 2 between B and C, however, represents a higher rate of both unemployment and inflation as compared to point A on curve 1. These ideas suggest that lower curves are "better" and higher curves are "poorer" for the economy as a whole.

You can now see why a Phillips curve can be defined in the following way:

A *Phillips curve* represents a trade-off between unemployment and inflation. Every point along the curve denotes a different combination of unemployment and inflation. A movement along the curve measures the reduction in one of these at the expense of a gain in the other.

The conventional Phillips curve—*if it actually existed*—would thus provide government policymakers with a menu of choices between inflation and unemployment. As one goes up, the other goes down, and conversely. The trick, therefore, would be to choose the fiscal and monetary policies needed to achieve the desired balance.

Modified L Curve: Natural Unemployment Rate

Many observers believe that the conventional Phillips curve was at one time only a temporary phenomenon. It may have existed, for example, during the 1960s. Since then, there have been periods in which inflation and unemployment have shot up simultaneously. This indicates two possibilities: Either the conventional curve has shifted so far outward as to be meaningless, or a new type of curve with a distinctly different shape has emerged. There is evidence to support both these beliefs. This suggests, as shown in Chart (b) of Exhibit 1, that the new curve may have an approximate L shape. Thus:

The modified L-shaped Phillips curve depicts a limited trade-off between unemployment and inflation. Along the lower-right segment of the curve, increased government spending through fiscal–monetary policies will raise aggregate demand and hence the inflation rate. At the same time, the increased spending will also create more jobs and thereby reduce the unemployment rate. But at some critical level of unemployment, the curve becomes vertical. Thereafter, further government spending is purely inflationary and does not reduce unemployment.

In Chart (b) of Exhibit 1 the critical level occurs at a 5 percent *natural unemployment rate*. This is the employment level at which only frictional and structural unemployment exist, not cyclical unemployment arising from a deficiency in aggregate demand. The natural unemployment rate, therefore, is not some irreducible minimum. It can be lowered by improving labor markets—through job training, combatting discrimination in hiring, and so on—but not by overexpansionary fiscal and monetary policies.

ACCELERATION CURVES: SHORT-RUN "PATHS"—A MONETARIST VIEW

Does the modified L-shaped Phillips curve really exist? Most monetarists doubt it, at least for the long run. They believe instead that the Phillips curve is a vertical line at the natural unemployment rate. Consequently, continued attempts to reduce unemployment through fiscal–monetary measures are not only futile, but lead to accelerating inflation.

Exhibit 1
A Curve Named Phillips—Then and Now
(hypothetical data)

Chart (a) Conventional Curve. *Along any given curve, a reduction in the unemployment rate can be achieved through expansionary fiscal-monetary policies. These increase aggregate demand, create more jobs, but also raise the inflation rate. This "traditional" type of Phillips curve, which at one time may have seemed plausible, has been generally discredited because both unemployment and inflation rates have frequently risen simultaneously.*

Chart (b) Modified L Curve. *Along the lower-right end of the curve (i.e., the trade-off segment) a reduction in the unemployment rate may be achieved at the expense of an increase in the inflation rate. However, at some critical level of unemployment—called the natural unemployment rate—*

the Phillips curve becomes vertical. Thereafter, further fiscal-monetary expansion merely increases the inflation rate without reducing the unemployment rate. (NOTE   The critical level in the chart—the natural unemployment rate—is 5 percent. In reality, this level cannot usually be determined so precisely. More likely, the natural unemployment rate today is somewhere between 5 and 6 percent.)

Conclusion. *There is empirical evidence to suggest that the unemployment-inflation relationship for our economy can perhaps be represented by a modified L curve. Of course, the entire curve may shift outward, thereby reflecting a higher natural unemployment rate, for reasons explained in the text.*

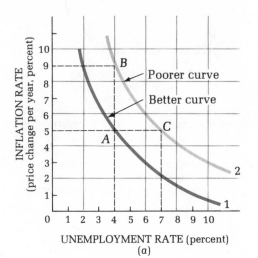

(a)

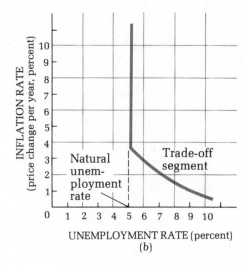

(b)

This is the meaning of the "acceleration curves" shown in Exhibit 2. In Chart *(a)*, the economy is assumed to be at point *A*, representing a natural unemployment rate *N* and a zero inflation rate. What happens if government undertakes expansionary fiscal and monetary policies to reduce the unemployment rate? The answer can be obtained by following the short-run dashed curve, representing the temporary "path" of unemployment and inflation as it passes through several stages.

Stage 1   Along the path from *A* to *B*, the increase in aggregate demand pulls up prices relative to wages. Business profits thus rise, prompting firms to increase production and hire more workers. At point *B*, the unemployment rate reaches its lowest level.

Stage 2   Workers now begin to realize that prices have been increasing faster than money wages, caus-

ing *real* wages to decline. Although unions manage to negotiate higher money wages, real wages continue to suffer. As unanticipated inflation continues, production costs rise, uncertainty mounts, and business profitability and investment incentives decline. Unemployment thus starts to increase while prices continue rising. The economy moves from point *B* to point *C*. At this point unemployment is back to its natural rate, and inflation, now fully anticipated, is at a higher level. With respect to workers, money wages have "caught up" with prices so that real wages are constant. In general, the equilibrium at *C* is *stable* (i.e., it has no tendency to change).

Stage 3   Of course, the equilibrium *can* change if government again employs stimulative fiscal-monetary measures. The economy would then follow the inflation-unemployment path shown by the dashed line *CDE*.

Exhibit 2
Acceleration Curves: Up and Down the Phillips Curve—A Monetarist View

Most monetarists believe that the Phillips curve is a vertical line at the natural unemployment rate. The line *ACE* in the charts is an example of a vertical Phillips curve. The dashed lines such as *ABC* are *acceleration curves*. They show the

temporary unemployment–inflation "path" (indicated by arrows) that the economy might follow in response to fiscal–monetary stimulation.

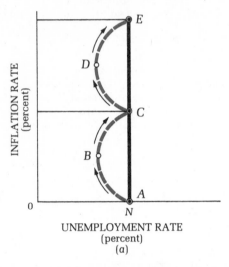

(a)

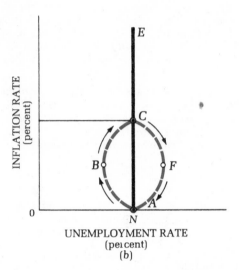

(b)

Chart (a). *Increases in government spending can temporarily reduce unemployment as the economy moves from its assumed initial equilibrium position at point A along the path to point B. However, as inflation accelerates, uncertainty mounts. Consequently, business investment declines, the unemployment rate increases, and the economy moves to a new equilibrium at C. Renewed fiscal–monetary stimulation can then push the economy into a new cycle along the path CDE. Notice that each new equilibrium position, such as C and E, represents the same natural unemployment rate accompanied by a higher inflation rate.*

Chart (b). *If the economy is at C, it can return to A along the path CFA. This would happen if government ended its fiscal–monetary stimulation, thereby causing aggregate demand to decline relative to aggregate supply. The unemployment rate would increase until the point F was reached, and then decrease as the inflation rate continued declining.*

How does the economy get back to point *A*? The answer is shown in Chart *(b)*. Let us assume that the economy is at *C*, which corresponds to *C* in Chart *(a)*. If government ends fiscal–monetary stimulation, aggregate demand declines relative to aggregate supply. As a result, the inflation rate declines and the unemployment rate increases following the path *CFA*. At point *A* the economy is again in stable equilibrium, this time at the same natural unemployment rate but at a zero inflation rate.

Against this background, we can identify some important ideas in terms of the charts.

1. The dashed lines are *acceleration curves*. These are short-run unemployment–inflation relationships showing the rapid rise in inflation that may result from attempts to increase employment through fiscal–monetary stimulation.

2. The vertical line is a Phillips curve. It connects the points A, C, and E as the economy moves from one of these stable equilibrium positions to another.

RATIONAL EXPECTATIONS: WHAT YOU FORESEE IS WHAT YOU GET

Inflation does give a stimulus . . . when it starts from a condition that is noninflationary. But if the inflation continues, people get adjusted to it. Then, when they expect rising prices, the mere occurrence of what has been expected is no longer stimulating.

Sir John R. Hicks (1967)

Hicks, a distinguished British economist and Nobel laureate, knows that economics is fundamentally concerned with predicting human behavior. Therefore, when government policymakers try to stabilize the economy, they must predict how people will respond.

But this appears to be impossible—according to a controversial theory called "rational expectations." The theory holds that people form expectations about government fiscal–monetary policies and then include these expectations in their economic decisions. Consequently, by the time the government's policies become known, the public has already acted on them, thereby offsetting the effects. As the quotation above implies, the only policy changes that can work are those that come as surprises, because they force people to revise their expectations.

Two examples will illustrate how the theory of rational expectations works.

1. If the economy is in recession, businesspersons will expect the Fed to take steps toward reducing interest rates. Investment expenditures on new plant and equipment will therefore tend to be deferred until interest rates decline, thereby worsening the recession. When the rates finally do come down they will stimulate a greater volume of investment than policy-makers intended. The result will be more rather than less cyclical instability, caused by too much rather than too little government intervention.

2. From time to time Washington proposes a reduction in corporate income taxes in order to spur business investment. According to the rational-expectations theory, such talks prompt executives to postpone many planned projects, waiting for the tax change to occur. When the change finally comes, capital spending may pick up—if a recession has not intervened.

Do these and similar examples mean that according to rational-expectations theory, the only correct public policy should be no public policy? Not quite. Proponents contend that because systematic economic policy is impotent, the only effective policy is balanced budgets and steady money growth.

The essential ideas of *rational-expectations theory* can be summarized in terms of three propositions.

> 1. Widely expected policy moves have no impact when made because they have already been incorporated into people's decisions.
>
> 2. The only policy moves that cause changes in people's behavior are the ones that are not expected.
>
> 3. Therefore, to assure economic stability, government should adhere to a policy of balanced budgets and steady growth of the money supply. Failure to do so will lead to public policies that are self-defeating and inflationary.

As stated above, rational-expectations theory is controversial. Nevertheless, it is attracting a growing number of scholars who believe there is merit in what the theory says.

CONCLUSION: SEARCHING FOR STABILITY

You have probably noticed that Phillips curves, acceleration curves, and rational-expectations theory have much in common. They try to explain, although in somewhat different ways, how inflation may result from fiscal–monetary stimulation designed to reduce unemployment.

These ideas are also related to *monetarism*. As you have learned, this doctrine holds that monetary policy is much more important than fiscal policy in affecting the economy's levels of income, employment, and prices. Because of this, sudden increases in the money supply aimed at lowering interest rates or financing government deficits may help reduce unemployment. But such measures, as acceleration curves show, are likely to work only in the short run.

In the long run, the similarity between monetarist and rational-expectation views is worth noting:

> Both the monetarist and rational-expectations theories end up with basically the same conclusion—the rejection of neo-Keynesian interventionism. But the reasons differ. Monetarist theory contends that we do not know enough about the workings of the economy to fine-tune it. Rational-expectations theory holds that the public rejects fine-tuning because everyone expects it and therefore undertakes actions which thwart its effectiveness.

These different viewpoints emphasize the enormous difficulty of achieving economic stability. Nevertheless, policymakers are not likely to abandon their attempts. It is to these efforts, therefore, that we must turn our attention.

Curing Stagflation Through the Market

Faint hearts, it is often said, do not win elections. Political leaders are acutely aware of this. In recent history, some American presidents, responding to the mounting pressures of inflation and unemployment, have resorted to desperate proposals and measures. These have included diverse policies aimed at limiting price increases, adjusting to them, and promoting more jobs.

In general, all antistagflation policies can be classified in either of two categories—market and nonmarket. Market policies, which will be considered first, seek to minimize if not avoid the bureaucracy of direct regulations that arises when nonmarket measures are employed.

FISCAL AND MONETARY POLICIES

Most authorities agree that both fiscal and monetary actions determine the level of economic activity. Although differences exist as to their relative importance, neither policy can be pursued effectively to the exclusion of the other.

The reason is not hard to see. When unemployment rises to undesirable levels, government spending is increased in order to stimulate the economy. Gradually, prices start to rise as the economy approaches high employment. To keep a lid on interest rates, the monetary authority expands the money supply. This promotes further inflation, causing additional upward pressure on interest rates. The process continues until government budgetary and monetary policies are revised in an effort to check inflation. Then the economy enters a recession and the cycle starts over again.

This scenario, more or less, is repeated almost endlessly. If it is to be avoided, measures are needed to assure greater control over government revenues and expenditures. This is part of a larger goal of limiting the size of government. An expanding federal deficit may be an indication that government is growing. If it grows faster than the national economy, command over resources is shifted from the private to the public sector.

To avoid this possibility, monetary and fiscal policies aimed at curing stagflation should seek to do three things:

○ Stabilize growth of the money supply.

○ Limit government tax revenues.

○ Curb government spending.

Conclusion: Specific Guidelines

Various economists and legislators have proposed a number of specific guidelines to achieve these objectives. Three of the guidelines have received particularly wide attention.

1. Reduce the growth of the money supply by 1 percentage point a year until it equals the long-run average growth rate of the economy—about 3 to 5 percent annually. This gradual rather than sudden reduction would cause minimum disruptions.

2. Limit government tax revenues to some specific percentage of the previous three years' average national income. As an example, a figure of about 20 percent has been suggested by many experts.

3. Link the percentage growth of federal spending to the percentage growth of GNP during periods of stable prices. If inflation exceeds a certain minimum allowable rate, the percentage increase in government spending would be reduced by deducting from the growth of GNP some specified proportion of the excess inflation. Thus:

percentage increase in federal spending

$$= \begin{pmatrix} \text{percentage} \\ \text{increase} \\ \text{in GNP} \end{pmatrix} - k \begin{pmatrix} \text{actual inflation} \\ -\text{allowable inflation} \end{pmatrix}$$

The letter k is simply a mathematical constant. To illustrate the formula, suppose Congress legislates k to equal $\frac{1}{4}$ and the allowable rate of inflation to equal 3 percent. Then, if GNP grew by 10 percent, of which 7 percent was inflation, the formula tells you that the percentage increase in federal spending should be limited to 9 percent. Thus:

percentage increase in federal spending
$$= 10\% - \tfrac{1}{4}(7\% - 3\%)$$
$$= 9\%$$

The advantages of these guidelines are apparent. They shift the focus of monetary policy from a primary emphasis on influencing interest rates to one of managing the money supply. They help assure that the public sector does not grow faster than the economy as a whole, and therefore at the expense of the private sector. And they enable the adoption of moderately flexible but specific rules of macroeconomic policy.

The guidelines thus permit compromises between fiscal and monetary policies while avoiding the extremes of either.

TAX REDUCTION: THE LAFFER CURVE

Exorbitant taxes destroy industry by producing despair. An attentive legislature will observe the point when the revenue decreases and the prejudice begins.

David Hume (1756)

I can make a profit if I sell a car for $500 and I can make a profit if I sell a car for $1,500. But I can make the most profit when I sell a car for some price in between.

Henry Ford (1930)

Hume, an eighteenth-century philosopher, and Ford, a twentieth-century industrialist, had something in common: They understood human nature as far as taxing and spending were concerned.

For instance, both men would have agreed with the idea underlying Exhibit 3. The diagram, called a *Laffer curve*, expresses a relationship between tax revenues and the tax rate. The relationship is such that as the tax rate increases from zero to 100 percent, government revenues from taxation correspondingly rise from zero to some maximum level and then decline to zero. Thus, the optimum tax rate—the one that

Exhibit 3
Professor Laffer's Famous Curve

"Except for the optimum rate, there are always two tax rates that yield the same revenues." So says Arthur Laffer of the University of Southern California.

The "Laffer curve" has received a lot of attention from many legislators and economists. Although the concept is neither new nor complicated, it may have powerful implications. Basically, it says that if tax rates are in the "normal" range, increases in the rates will yield more tax revenues. But if tax rates are in the "prohibitive" range, as Laffer and many others believe, *decreases* in the rates will actually produce more revenues by stimulating the incentive to spend and invest.

At present no one knows where the optimum point is—or even the exact shape of the curve. But there is considerable agreement that the optimum marginal tax rate is probably much less than 50 percent, perhaps around 35 or 40 percent.

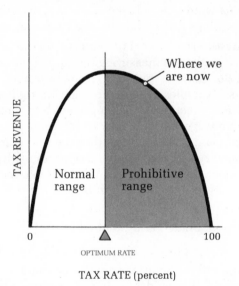

TAX RATE (percent)

produces the largest revenue—is somewhere between the two extremes.

An important feature of the curve is that it covers both a "normal" range and a "prohibitive" range. In the normal range, a higher tax rate brings higher revenues. In the prohibitive range, the tax rate is so high that it impairs incentives. Therefore, a tax cut would actually increase revenues by spurring the incentive to work and invest.

"The Wedge" and Marginal Tax Rates

Those who favor tax reduction as a cure for stagflation believe that the economy is currently operating in the prohibitive range. Their argument for a cut in taxes is based on two assumptions.

1. The difference between before-tax and after-tax incomes of resource owners has widened. This difference, called "the wedge," has reduced incentives to work and invest.

2. The decision whether or not to work or invest depends on *after-tax marginal incomes*. These are the last few dollars of wages, interest, and dividends available for spending in each tax bracket. The more that is available, the greater people's incentive to work, save, and invest.

These assumptions lead to the following obvious conclusion.

Proponents of tax reduction contend that *marginal* tax rates on economic activity should be cut. This action would make working, saving, and investing more rewarding, thereby stimulating economic activity. The result would be greater economic growth and employment, leading to higher, not lower, tax revenues.

Thus, a reduction in the marginal tax rate would promote greater efficiency and production. But there is also a danger that these benefits could be more than offset by a higher "hidden tax" of inflation. This would occur if government did not reduce its spending simultaneously with the tax cut. If that happened, the federal deficit would increase, causing even higher inflation rates. This in turn would foster still more inefficiency and waste of resources.

Conclusion: No Free Lunch

The experience of the past few decades indicates that government is not likely to restrain spending for any prolonged period. Therefore, a reduction in taxes would probably increase inflation rates rather than reduce them. In view of this, a program that includes more than tax reduction is needed.

A significant step toward stabilizing the economy would be to reduce taxes *and* government spending. A tax cut should be part of a budgetary program aimed at gradual reduction of the deficit over a number of years. Failure to do this can delude us into thinking that tax reduction by itself provides a "free lunch"—that nothing needs to be given up. This can only lead to policy failure and disappointment in the end.

REWARD AND PUNISHMENT: TIP

Do conventional fiscal and monetary measures work well enough to control today's endemic problem, stagflation? Many critics think not. A strong dose of government spending, prescribed by the Keynesian doctors to cure recession, is likely to bring the patient to an inflation high. A slow but steady increase in the money supply, ordered by the monetarist physicians, may induce a case of excessive sluggishness. And resort to radical surgery, in the form of rigid government controls over wages and prices, is regarded by many as alien to our democratic system.

It therefore comes as no surprise that economists continue to search for stagflation remedies. One of the more imaginative proposals is known as a tax-based incomes policy (TIP). Its novelty is that it uses a carrot and stick—reward and punishment—to cope with the stubborn problem of stagflation.

How TIP Works

TIP is based on the assumption that price increases are influenced strongly by wage increases. Therefore, by limiting gains in wages, upward pressure on prices will be reduced.

To implement the idea, TIP would set an annual guideline for wage increases. Through tax rewards and penalties, firms and employees would be encouraged to adhere to the guideline.

For example, each year the government would announce what it considers to be a noninflationary standard or guidepost for wage increases. The figure would be somewhere between the gain in the economy's productivity and the current rate of inflation—perhaps an average of both. A figure of about 5 percent would be a fairly likely guidepost. Firms and employees approving average wage increases in excess of the guidepost would be penalized by paying additional corporate and personal income taxes on the difference. Firms and employees approving average wage increases below the guidepost would be rewarded with corporate and personal tax cuts. Because the penalty or reward in each firm depends only on the average wage increase, individual promotions and raises are not discouraged.

Some Pros and Cons

Would the adoption of TIP help solve the economy's stagflation problem? Those who believe it would offer three basic arguments.

1. **It reduces wage inflation.**   TIP would make larger wage increases more expensive to employers and employees. Therefore, both groups would be more inclined to resist such increases.

2. **It reduces price inflation.**   TIP is based on the observation that for the economy as a whole, the margin between prices and unit labor costs is virtually constant. Consequently, because wage increases tend to be associated with price increases, reduction of wage inflation will also reduce price inflation.

3. **It permits free-market decisions.**   TIP allows business and labor to negotiate wage increases. Therefore, the market mechanism is not restricted, and hence output and employment are not adversely affected.

In contrast, critics of TIP disagree with the entire concept. Among their many reasons, three are sufficient to indicate why.

1. **It assumes "cost-push" inflation.**   TIP is based on the premise that inflation is caused by labor and business, particularly by wages pushing up prices. This assumption contradicts the monetarist view. This view holds that excessive monetary growth is responsible for inflation, which, in turn, causes workers to press for wage increases in order to maintain real incomes.

2. **It causes inefficiencies.**   TIP would require all industries, some of which are expanding and some declining, to adhere to a single guidepost. This would cause resource misallocation because firms' hiring decisions would be influenced strongly by guidepost considerations rather than by market forces alone.

3. **It causes inequities.**   TIP requires for its administration a method of measuring the equivalent average wage-rate increase resulting from improved fringe benefits. Examples of these are pension rights, medical plans, executive stock options, and numerous other nonwage enrichments which companies provide their employees. Any method devised to measure the monetary values of these benefits would obviously be enormously complex, and would create inequities that would lead to untold numbers of court tests.

Conclusion: Short-Term Solution at Best

TIP is a form of wage–price policy designed to reduce inflation without interfering with the market system. In essence, TIP provides tax benefits for those workers and firms that curb wage increases, and tax penalties for those that do not.

Would the adoption of TIP lead to a permanent cure for inflation? Probably not.

TIP is at best a short-term anti-inflationary measure. This is because it deals with the symptoms of inflation, not its cause. Among the fundamental causes of inflation are government deficit spending and excessive monetary growth. Therefore, these are the activities that must ultimately be curbed if inflation is to be controlled.

Some further aspects of this are discussed in Box 1.

INDEXATION: JUMPING ON THE ESCALATOR

If your income goes up by 10 percent when prices go up by 10 percent, your purchasing power remains the

Box 1
Washington's Knee-Jerking Policies

The late 1970s were difficult years for Jimmy Carter. To the dismay, annoyance, and alarm of many of his supporters, he launched an anti-inflation program which, experts predicted, would bring on a recession. The program consisted of sharp reductions in government spending coupled with a system of wage–price guidelines that had certain features resembling TIP.

Everyone agreed that the President's measures were dramatic. But to his monetarist critics, his actions confirmed what they had been saying all along: *Erratic government policies are the fundamental cause of economic booms and busts.*

same. However, your increased income may place you in a higher tax bracket—and thereby reduce your *real* purchasing power. The simplest way of preventing this inequity is for Congress to inflation-proof the income tax. How? By revising personal exemptions in proportion to price-level changes. This adjustment could be incorporated in the printed tax returns so that the taxpayer's task is simplified.

If you purchase some Treasury savings bonds, the money you receive for the bonds when they mature will buy less than it did when you acquired the bonds. Further, you must pay income taxes on the interest you receive while holding the bonds. Financially, therefore, you suffer a decline in real income—a loss from inflation. The simple way to correct this is for the Treasury to issue "purchasing-power bonds." These would be redeemable for a sum equal to the purchasing power of the original price. This would enable small savers to protect their savings from inflation.

Escalator Clauses

These are examples of what are known as _escalator clauses_. They are provisions in a contract whereby payments such as wages, insurance or pension benefits, or loan repayments over a stated period are tied to a comprehensive measure of living costs or price-level changes. The Consumer Price Index and the Implicit Price Index (i.e., the GNP deflator) are the most common measures used.

Many labor contracts contain "escalator clauses" providing for automatic cost-of-living adjustments in paychecks. As a result, when the price level rises, incomes covered by escalator clauses go up too—frequently in the same proportion.

Similar clauses providing protection against inflation—to creditors as well as debtors—have been proposed or incorporated in an increasing variety of long-term contracts. These include agreements involving social security benefits, pensions, and the principal and interest payments on mortgages and bonds. All told, more than 70 million Americans now receive wages or benefits that automatically rise with increases in the cost of living. Not all of these people receive pay adjustments in full proportion to increases in living costs, but they all are covered by some degree of inflation protection.

> When escalator clauses are employed systematically and on a national scale, the process is generally referred to as *indexation*. This simply means assigning escalator clauses based on measures of inflation to long-term contracts. Thus, wages, rents, and interest payments are readjusted in proportion to price changes. Even the tax system is readjusted so that corporate and individual gains due to inflation are not taxed away, thereby reducing real income.

Conclusion: No Official Adoption

A number of countries have adopted indexation as a matter of government policy. Through an elaborate set of formulas and procedures, most financial assets, contracts, and taxes undergo frequent "monetary corrections." The primary reason for indexation is to maintain equity among all participants in the economy. There is evidence, however, that in some countries indexation has also led to significant improvements in efficiency, stability, and growth.

Considering these possible benefits of indexation, will it be adopted by Washington? Probably not.

> Indexation is unlikely to be legislated as official government policy—for two reasons:
>
> 1. *It is opposed by the Treasury.* Indexed income-tax rates would reduce the government's revenues, whereas purchasing-power bonds would increase Washington's future financial obligations.
>
> 2. *It "institutionalizes" inflation.* Indexation sanctions inflation by building it into the economic system.

Indexation is thus a decision by government to live with inflation rather than to cure it by eliminating its causes. The adoption of indexation, therefore, would be an admission by political leaders that they have failed as economic policymakers.

EMPLOYMENT PROGRAMS: PUTTING PEOPLE TO WORK

Our economy faces an awesome challenge. Each year it must generate many millions of new jobs. That is what is needed to lift the country out of the quagmire of unemployment.

How can the task be accomplished? Many specific proposals have been offered. They range from the conservative position advocating a hands-off government policy to the liberal view that government should become more deeply involved. Most of the proposed measures can be grouped into one of three approaches: (1) public employment, (2) manpower policies, and (3) employment subsidies (vouchers).

Public Employment

There is a need for people to clean up parks, assist in hospitals, and fill other types of public-service jobs. Therefore, a direct way to reduce unemployment is for Washington to appropriate in advance the necessary funds for public employment. Then, when unemployment reaches a certain critical level, say, 6 percent, the money could be used to put unemployed people to work.

This statement is correct as far as it goes. However, it considers only the direct effects of a public-employment program. The indirect ones, which can be considerable, arise from the ways in which the program may be financed.

1. The funds to employ public-service workers may come from imposing higher taxes, or by borrowing from the public. In either case, households and businesses will have less money available for spending. Private-sector employment is therefore likely to decline. This decrease will have to be more than offset by the increase in public employment in order to reduce total unemployment.

2. Alternatively, government may borrow the needed funds from banks. In that case government demand will add to private demand to create new jobs. But as you have already learned, the results are likely to be inflationary even if the economy is operating at a moderate if not high level of activity.

> In reality, because of political pressures, most of the funds to pay for public employment would probably be borrowed—especially from banks. Therefore, there is a good chance that such a program would contribute significantly to inflation.

Manpower Policies

A second approach to dealing with unemployment is through *manpower policies*. These are deliberate efforts undertaken in the private and public sectors to develop and use the capacities of human beings as actual or potential members of the labor force. Manpower policies have been financed largely by government. Existing as well as future policies aim at improving job training and skills, thereby enhancing worker motivation and mobility.

Employment Subsidies (Vouchers)

Somewhat related to manpower policies as a means of reducing unemployment are employment subsidies. These are grants given to employers who hire and train unemployed persons. One way of implementing subsidies is for government to issue vouchers to the unemployed and unskilled. Those who find jobs at the minimum wage would give the voucher to their employer, who would present it to the government for redemption. The redemption value might be, say, 40 percent of the minimum wage. The employer would then be required to spend the payment on training the new workers.

Rifle or Shotgun Approach?

Critics contend that most employment programs of the above types are simply disguised "make-work" schemes. To some extent this may be true. However, well-designed employment programs can greatly reduce, if not eliminate, inefficiency and waste.

For example, by focusing on unemployment problems among particular age groups and industries, selective rather than general programs can be formulated. Several European countries, among them Sweden and The Netherlands, have followed this course, making effective use of selective labor-market techniques. These include free training programs, progressive incentive payments, and relocation grants for people willing to work in certain occupations and regions. These countries have also made some use of public-employment programs for people unable to find work in the open market. For the most part, however, a rifle approach that targets on specific problems, rather than an indiscriminate shotgun approach, has proved to be the most effective way of attacking the unemployment problem.

Conclusion: A Better Alternative

What are the economic consequences of employment programs? In general, they tend to be inflationary because they are usually financed by borrowing through the banking system. Nevertheless, well-designed programs, especially manpower policies, yield two major benefits.

1. They lower the cost to employers of hiring workers who might otherwise remain unemployed because of their low productivity.

2. They enable young people to be employed and trained for higher-paying jobs.

In view of this, what can we conclude about the desirability of manpower policies? The following practical answer is based on realistic considerations.

A comprehensive manpower strategy would be difficult and expensive to establish. But the alternative should be recognized. Government now spends many billions of dollars annually on unemployment insurance. Most of the funds produce neither new jobs nor additional output. Therefore, the money could be used instead to put people to work.

Some further aspects of this are illustrated in Box 2.

Box 2

No Trade-off Between Profits and Jobs

People sometimes find it easy to blame business for a loss of jobs. But in the long run, an expanding and thriving business sector is the only assurance of jobs. This means that in today's advancing technological society, new and expanding programs are continually needed to prepare people for the world of work. *There is no trade-off between profits and jobs.*

Paul S. Conklin/The Image Bank Germany.

Hugh Rogers, Monkmeyer Press Photo Service.

PRODUCTIVITY AND INVESTMENT: IMPROVING EFFICIENCY

Almost everyone agrees that if the nation is to make substantial progress toward reducing inflation, greater efforts will be needed to cut the costs of producing things. This means increasing the productivity of workers.

Productivity is the output of goods and services obtained from a given amount of factors of production. A rise in productivity means that the economy is getting more output, and therefore more real income, from its productive resources. A decline in productivity means the opposite. Productivity is thus a measure of an economy's technical efficiency. It follows that widespread increases in productivity make it possible for everyone to enjoy better living standards. Without such increases, efforts to provide more goods and services for the growing population must inevitably produce mounting inflationary pressures.

International Comparisons

Although every nation recognizes the importance of achieving high rates of productivity, not all are able to do so. There are numerous reasons, many of which differ between countries. In the United States, for example, management blames unions for establishing make-work rules and wasteful labor practices. Unions, on the other hand, blame management for its indifference toward, and callous disregard of, labor's needs. And both blame government for failing to pass legislation that would be conducive to stimulating greater production.

Regardless of who is at fault, there is widespread agreement that unemployment and inflation result to a large extent from a drag on output. This helps to explain why America's stagflation has, for many years, been accompanied by productivity growth rates that are among the lowest of the major industrial nations. Some interesting comparisons are shown in Exhibit 4.

CONCLUSION: INVESTING IN PHYSICAL AND HUMAN CAPITAL

What can be done to improve the nation's productive efficiency, and thereby achieve fuller utilization of resources and lower prices? Many of the answers have already been given. They include revision of the fiscal–monetary mix, broad-scale tax reductions, effective manpower policies, and special tax incentives. Adoption of these measures would go a long way toward achieving efficiency and stability.

These ideas can be stated differently. In its effort to reduce poverty, curb pollution, maintain national de-

Exhibit 4
The Productivity Race

U.S. productivity lags far behind most industrial nations'. Various experts cite a number of reasons. Three chief ones are (1) excessive government regulations, (2) slower investment growth as a result of an unfavorable economic climate, and (3) restrictive union work rules. Therefore, until major steps are taken to correct these problems, a permanent solution to the stagflation problem is unlikely.

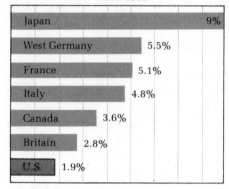

INCREASE IN OUTPUT PER WORKER-HOUR, 1965–1980

Japan	9%
West Germany	5.5%
France	5.1%
Italy	4.8%
Canada	3.6%
Britain	2.8%
U.S.	1.9%

SOURCE: U.S. Department of Labor.

fense, and attain other social goals, our society's demands on resources grow faster than the resources available. As a consequence, resource prices are bid up, resulting in inflationary instability and unemployment. Therefore:

Increased efficiency in the use of resources is necessary to expand society's output. Economic policies designed to stimulate investment in physical and human capital are the means of accomplishing this. Only with such investment can society attain the long-run growth rates necessary to absorb unemployed resources and curb inflationary pressures.

Curing Stagflation: Can Nonmarket Measures Work?

The inflation came in various forms—sometimes led by wages, sometimes by prices. Sometimes it was domestic and sometimes imported. Many programs have been launched to stop it—without durable success. Inflation seemed a hydra-headed monster, growing two new heads each time one was cut off.

President's Council of Economic Advisers

The various policies described thus far work directly through the market to overcome stagflation. As a result, these measures do not tend to limit our economic freedoms. Certain other policies, however, replace the market with extensive laws and regulations. These not only limit personal choices, but often reduce them. The chief examples of such nonmarket measures are (1) wage–price controls and (2) economic planning.

WAGE–PRICE CONTROLS: INCOMES POLICIES

One way in which government can try to cure stagflation is to impose wage and price controls. Measures of this type provide examples of what is known as *incomes policies*. These are laws aimed at curbing inflation by establishing conditions under which businesses' production costs (especially wages), prices, and profits may be allowed to increase. As you might expect, incomes policies in general, and wage–price controls in particular, are the subject of frequent debate.

Arguments Against Wage–Price Controls

Those who oppose government wage and price controls believe they have a number of undesirable effects:

Misallocate Resources   Under a system of controls, resource and product prices are determined by specific governmental rules or orders. Buyers' and sellers' responses to the free-market forces of supply and demand are thus replaced by government edicts. The wage–price structure becomes frozen. This prevents producers from responding to changes in tastes and technology as would happen if markets were unregulated. As a result, resources are misallocated and economic efficiency is impaired.

Decrease Productivity   Controls put a lid on wages and prices, keeping them from rising to their free-market levels. This diminishes productivity in three ways:

1. Millions of working hours in government and industry are wasted on administering controls.

2. To the extent that wage increases are restrained, workers' incentives are reduced and employers are prevented from paying for the high-quality workers that are wanted.

3. If ceilings are imposed on profit margins, as they were during some previous periods of control, businesses lose much of their incentive to improve efficiency. The reason is that profits above the ceiling are taxed at prohibitive rates. As a consequence, firms look for frivolous ways to increase costs. This can be done by spending lavishly on advertising and promo-

tion, buying corporate jets, providing generous expense accounts for executives, and so on—all for the purpose of cutting down profits. (See Box 2.)

Institutionalize Inflation   Wage and price controls provide at best only a temporary palliative rather than a permanent cure for inflation. They lull society into accepting inflation as a way of life instead of encouraging the public to press for eradication of the root causes. Those causes are found in the monopoly power wielded by large firms and trade unions, and in government legislation that establishes minimum wages, subsidies, tariffs, and import quotas. These monopolistic elements interfere with the effective functioning of a free market. Therefore, public policy should be directed toward eliminating them in order to achieve price stability.

The Case for Controls

On the other side of the fence, most advocates of wage and price controls are generally sympathetic with the competitive market philosophy. However, they believe that the inflationary bias has become entrenched by our failure to eliminate monopolistic elements within the economy. As a result, it is unrealistic to assume that these elements, which are now deeply embedded, will ever be significantly reduced. Therefore, the choice is not between free markets or public controls; it is between free markets and *some degree* of public controls. As many advocates of controls contend:

> Less than half the economy's private sector is responsive to reasonably competitive market forces. Within the remainder of the private sector, prices are essentially set by the great corporations in conjunction with the unions. It follows that public controls can be confined to the less competitive segment, where market power is greatest, and that they are not needed in the more competitive segment, where the market still functions.

As it happens, there is no strong evidence to support this point of view. As a result, critics have proposed other approaches—among them economic planning—as a way of reducing unemployment and inflation.

ECONOMIC PLANNING

Another method of coping with unemployment and inflation is economic planning. It may be—and often is—employed in conjunction with wage–price controls. Hence, the two approaches should not necessarily be thought of as mutually exclusive.

An *economic plan* is a detailed method, formulated beforehand, for achieving specific economic objectives.

The plan governs the activities and interrelationships of those economic organisms—firms, households, and governments—that have an influence on the desired outcome.

To repeat, the purpose of economic planning is to achieve certain objectives. Those who advocate national economic planning believe that a federal agency should be established to perform the task—both for government activities and for the private sector's actions. The government planning board would thus be directly involved in dealing with the three fundamental problems of every economic system. These problems, you recall, are WHAT to produce, HOW to produce, and FOR WHOM.

As you would expect, there is much controversy over the desirability of planning. Proponents contend that the government's central planning board would act purely in an *advisory* capacity to major industries and government agencies. The board would merely point out long-run goals or targets and suggest how they might be realized. Opponents of planning disagree strongly. They offer such arguments as the following:

1. Planning would create a new federal bureaucracy to administer economic activity. The free market—and with it consumer sovereignty—would be replaced by governmental authority and coercion.

2. The government's planning office would probably come to be dominated by the major corporations whose activities are planned. This is evidenced by the fact that many government regulatory agencies have long been influenced by the industries that are regulated. Collaboration and collusion between big business and government would thus be promoted rather than discouraged.

3. There is no evidence that government is more adept at planning than is private industry. On the other hand, there is considerable evidence based on experiences in some mixed economies that government involvement in economic planning may at best result in improvements in equity. However, this may be achieved at the cost of seriously impairing economic efficiency, price stability, and perhaps growth.

For these and other reasons, the controversy over national economic planning is likely to continue. As a result, you will often read and hear a great deal about it in the news media. (See Box 3.)

Box 3
Will Planning Work?

Can efficiency, stability, and growth be "planned" by Washington? Legislators think so—at least within limits. This is evidenced by the *Full Employment and Balanced Growth Act of 1978*. Popularly known as the Humphrey-Hawkins bill, it has three major provisions:

1. Requires the President to set long- and short-term production and employment goals, including an annual unemployment-rate target of 4 percent. It also requires the President to identify means for attaining the goals through public-employment programs, manpower policies, and so on.

2. Requires the Federal Reserve to declare semiannually its monetary policies and their relation to the President's goals.

3. Requires the government to undertake actions that will achieve the goal of full employment while striving for a zero-percent inflation rate.

These objectives, according to the bill, are to be realized by the late 1980s. Critics, however, point out that the government simply does not know how to attain full employment without creating inflation—as has been proven time and again. Congress evidently agrees. This is why the third provision of the bill, subtly worded, makes employment the primary goal and price stability an important but secondary one.

Conclusion: Economics, Politics, and Rationality

Stagflation is today's most serious economic problem. To help overcome it, numerous policy proposals have been made. Those explained in this chapter are among the most important.

Practically all of these proposals have been adopted, in varying degrees, during recent history. For example, since the early 1970s the nation has experimented with wage-price controls, wage-and-price guidelines, legislation to reduce taxes, public-employment schemes, manpower policies, and economic planning. Without evaluating specific measures, it can be said that these programs generally attack the symptoms of stagflation rather than the cause.

Stagflation is caused by improper fiscal and monetary policies. These lead to greater economic uncertainty, reduced private investment, and slower economic growth. Therefore, policies that fail to recognize the real causes of stagflation will not be successful in curing it.

Today these beliefs are held by practically all informed observers. But unfortunately, there is no consistent agreement on what constitutes the "right" fiscal-monetary mix. However, there is widespread agreement that a reasonably steady expansion of the money supply is necessary to promote greater long-run stability.

Despite this understanding, it is characteristic of our type of democracy that political considerations often outweigh economic logic. Few political leaders are willing to risk their careers on policies designed to curb inflation at the cost of increased joblessness. Consequently, legislators usually find that budget deficits accompanied by rapid monetary expansion is the easiest way of combatting unemployment. Therefore, until Congress develops some rational rules for relating government spending to revenues, stagflation resulting from large deficits and erratic fluctuations in the money supply will continue to plague the economy.

What You Have Learned

1. For many years, the chief macroeconomic problem facing our own and some other mixed economies has been stagflation. Another name for stagflation is "recessionary inflation."

2. Economists have long debated the possibility of a trade-off between unemployment and inflation. This concept is represented by a Phillips curve. A widely held view today is that the Phillips curve has a modified L shape. The vertical portion coincides with the natural unemployment rate, while the lower-right segment—the "stem"—is downward-sloping. The curve thus depicts a limited trade-off along the stem.

3. Another view—one held by monetarists—is that the Phillips curve is a vertical line at the natural unemployment rate. Along this line, therefore, fiscal–monetary stimulation to reduce unemployment leads to accelerating inflation as represented by acceleration curves.

4. The search for stability has led to some new ideas concerning public policy. One theory, the rational-expectations theory, holds that people form expectations about government fiscal–monetary policies and then include these expectations in their economic decisions. As a result, the policies become ineffective. Therefore, the best policy, according to the theory, is for government to adhere to balanced budgets and steady growth of the money supply. Failure to do so will lead to public policies that are self-defeating and inflationary.

5. A number of market measures for curing stagflation have been proposed. The chief ones, according to their advocates, are:

(a) *Fiscal and monetary policies.* These should seek to stabilize the growth of the money supply. They should also help establish closer ties among government tax revenues, government spending, and the nation's income.

(b) *Taxation and spending.* Marginal tax rates—the taxes paid on the last few dollars of wages, interest, and dividends—should be reduced. This action would make working, saving, and investing more rewarding, thereby stimulating economic activity. However, a tax cut should also be part of an overall budgetary program aimed at gradual reduction of the deficit over a number of years.

(c) *Tax-based incomes policy (TIP).* Tax benefits for those workers and firms that keep wage increases within a certain "guidepost," and tax penalties for those that do not, should be introduced. The guidepost, announced annually by the government, would be somewhere between the economy's productivity rate and the current rate of inflation, perhaps an average of both.

(d) *Indexation.* Escalator clauses based on measures of inflation should be employed nationally and systematically on a long-term basis. All payments—wages, rents, interest, taxes, and so on—would thus be adjusted automatically in proportion to price changes.

(e) *Employment programs.* A comprehensive manpower policy designed to employ and train people for higher-paying jobs should be adopted. Although such a program would be expensive, the alternative is for government to continue spending many billions of dollars annually on unemployment insurance. Most of these expenditures produce neither new jobs nor additional output.

(f) *Productivity improvement.* Measures designed to stimulate investment in physical and human capital should be undertaken. Such measures would improve productive efficiency and boost the economy's long-run growth rates, thereby helping to absorb unemployed resources and curb inflation.

6. In addition to the market measures for curing stagflation, some observers have proposed two major nonmarket policies:

(a) *Wage–price controls: incomes policies.* These are laws aimed at curbing inflation by establishing conditions under which businesses' production costs, prices, and profits may be allowed to increase.

(b) *Economic planning.* This is a program for achieving specific economic goals. A comprehensive plan would embrace the activities of households, firms, and government in a unified effort to attain desired objectives.

7. As already stated, almost all of the foregoing proposals have been adopted in varying degrees since the early 1970s. However, because stagflation is fundamentally caused by an improper mix of government fiscal and monetary policies, these are the activities that must ultimately be modified. Otherwise, any other measures can at best yield only temporary benefits, and in the long run may even be harmful.

For Discussion

1. *Terms and concepts to review:*

stagflation	tax-based incomes policy
Phillips curve	(TIP)
natural unemployment rate	indexation
	manpower policies
acceleration curves	incomes policies
rational-expectations theory	economic plan
	Full Employment and
Laffer curve	Balanced Growth Act
escalator clauses	of 1978

Issue
Growth Versus Unemployment: Okun's Unpleasant Trade-off

The Phillips-curve controversy over a trade-off between inflation and unemployment is well known. But the trade-off is only one of many in economics. Another is the trade-off between economic growth and unemployment. This relationship is based on the question: Can a rising rate of real output contribute to a decrease in the rate of unemployment? The answer is yes. Unfortunately, however, it takes a considerable amount of economic growth to produce even a small reduction in unemployment. This fact, learned through hard experience, rests on an economic principle known as Okun's Law. The principle is named after Arthur Okun, chairman of the Council of Economic Advisers under President Lyndon Johnson.

Okun's Law expresses a relationship between changes in unemployment and the rate of economic growth (measured by changes in real GNP). The law, based on long-run trends, states:

1. Unemployment decreases less than 1 percent for each percentage point that the annual growth of real GNP exceeds its long-term average.

2. Unemployment increases less than 1 percent for each percentage point that the annual growth of real GNP falls short of its long-term average.

The economy, therefore, must continue to grow considerably faster than its long-term average rate in order to achieve a substantial reduction in the unemployment rate.

What does this mean in terms of actual numbers? Over the past several decades the economy's real GNP has grown at an average rate of about 4 percent per year. In contrast, unemployment has usually fallen about one-third of 1 percent for each percentage point that the annual growth of real GNP exceeded its long-term 4 percent rate. It follows, therefore, that if these trends were to continue, the unemployment rate would be re-duced by 1 percentage point if the economy grew at 5 percent annually for three years, or at 7 percent for one year. On the other hand, the unemployment rate would be reduced by 4 percentage points—say from 9 percent to 5 percent—if the economy grew at 6 percent annually for six years. But this would be a high growth rate—one that would not likely be realized without adherence to consistent fiscal and monetary policies.

Graphic Illustration

The accompanying chart illustrates these ideas.

On the basis of Okun's Law, if the unemployment rate in the present year (Year 0) is 9 percent, as has occurred in some recent years, growth at the long-term average rate of 4 percent annually will leave unemployment unchanged. A steady growth rate of 6 percent annually would still leave more than 5.5 percent unemployed five years hence. And at the extraordinary growth rate of 8 per-

2. Explain carefully the difference between an acceleration curve and a vertical Phillips curve.

3. What legislative and fiscal actions can you recommend to *improve* the economy's Phillips curve? Before answering, explain precisely what is meant by "improve."

4. If you take a course in investments, you will learn how a modified version of the rational-expectations theory, called the "efficient-market theory," applies to the stock market. From your understanding of rational expectations, what do you suppose the efficient-market theory says about the prediction of stock market prices?

5. Many economists want to limit government spending by tying it to some percentage of tax revenues. For example, spending might be limited to, say, 103 percent of tax revenues. (a) What is the reason for allowing spending to exceed revenues? (b) Why not set the figure at 100 percent or even less? (c) Can we limit government spending by putting a ceiling on taxes?

6. Tax reduction is often seen as a device to stimulate demand. But it can also stimulate supply. Can you explain how?

7. "Indexation of the income tax and of government bonds would lower the Treasury's tax revenues. This reduction in the benefits government receives from inflation would stimulate incentives to curb inflation." Explain this statement. How does government benefit from inflation?

8. Can you give at least two arguments against indexation and two rebuttals in favor? What are your conclusions?

9. How would the position or location of our economy's Phillips curve be affected by each of the following? Explain your answer.

    (a) A reduction in tariffs.

    (b) A decrease in import quotas.

    (c) A new law making labor unions illegal.

    (d) A merger of the largest firm in each major industry

cent annually, which the United States has rarely experienced, it would take four years to bring unemployment down to the 4 percent rate that is considered to be high employment.

Bleak prospects such as these led the early-nineteenth-century classical economists to conclude that economics was a dismal science. Have today's policymakers in Washington learned enough about modern economics to alter this conclusion? The answer, to a large extent, is probably yes, but political expediencies often temper rational thinking about economic issues.

QUESTIONS

1. In science, a law is a general principle or rule—like the law of gravity in physics. Is Okun's Law such a law? How do you suppose it is derived?

2. How do such factors as (a) growth of the labor force and (b) changes in productivity affect the operation of Okun's Law?

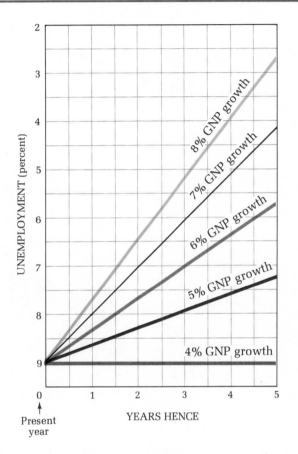

(e.g., automobiles, steel, etc.) with the second largest firm in its industry.

(e) A new law prohibiting any firm's sales from exceeding 50 percent of its industry's.

(f) Significant advances made in automation throughout most of industry.

10. Some economists and political leaders contend: "Inflation promotes growth and diminishes unemployment. We must recognize that the costs of inflation are much less than the costs of avoiding it. Therefore, we should accept inflation and learn to live with it. This can be done by recognizing that it is easier to compensate the victims of inflation than the casualties of recession." What specific compensatory measures can you propose to make inflation less painful and inequitable? Discuss.

Part 4

Economic Growth and Resource Policies

Chapter 16

Understanding Economic Growth

Economic growth has long been regarded as one of our fundamental economic goals. It has been a significant issue in political campaigns and will undoubtedly remain a major national concern for a long time to come.

Why this interest in growth? At least two reasons are already somewhat obvious:

1. Our population and labor force are expanding, making it necessary for the economy to take care of millions more people and to provide them with jobs.

2. Living standards must rise if social tensions are to be reduced without government intervention.

Our purpose in this chapter is to sketch the meaning and implications of economic growth, thus providing a theoretical basis for judging the actual growth of various economies. We shall find that there is no single "theory" of economic growth in the sense of a unified body of propositions. Instead, certain elements are common ingredients to almost all theories, and when taken together constitute the basis for most modern discussions of the subject.

What Is Economic Growth?

There is often confusion about the meaning of economic growth. This is because politicians and economists are fond of hurling statistics at each other showing growth rates of various countries or regions over different periods. Hence, an accurate definition is needed.

> *Economic growth* is the rate of increase in an economy's full-employment real output or income over time. That is, economic growth is the rise in an economy's full-employment output in constant prices. Economic growth may be expressed in either of two ways:
>
> 1. As the increase in total full-employment real GNP or NNP over time.
>
> 2. As the increase in per capita full-employment real GNP or NNP over time.

The first of these measures is usually employed to describe the expansion of a nation's economic output. The second is used to express the development of its material standard of living and to compare it with that of other nations.

In the most fundamental sense, economic growth is concerned with policy measures aimed at expanding a nation's *capacity* to produce. It thus contrasts with monetary and fiscal policies, which seek to make full and efficient use of a nation's *existing* capacity.

The concept of economic growth can be illustrated in terms of the familiar production-possibilities curves in Exhibit 1. Since each curve represents an economy's capacity to produce, an outward shift of the curve is a measure of a nation's economic growth.

MEASURING ECONOMIC GROWTH

Is the U.S. economy growing, declining, or stagnating? How does its growth compare with that of the Russian economy? The Japanese economy? The answers are determined by the way in which we measure growth. Although the definition seems clear-cut, experts do not always agree on the results, because the methods of calculation can involve some slippery procedures. Economists, therefore, simply use past measures of output or income, as suggested by the definition of economic growth, and derive long-term growth trends from these historical records. Frequently, the trends are projected into the future at various assumed compound rates of growth—like money growing at compound interest in a savings account.

The "Classical" Explanation of Growth

In the late eighteenth and early nineteenth centuries, certain classical British economists formulated theories that dealt in large part with economic devel-

Exhibit 1

Economic Growth Can Be Seen as an Outward Shift of an Economy's Production-Possibilities Curve

Economic growth is not a movement along a given curve such as from *S* to *T*, because this is merely a change in the composition of total output. Nor is economic growth a movement from a point of unemployment such as *U* to the production-possibilities curve. Economic growth is an *outward shift* of the curve.

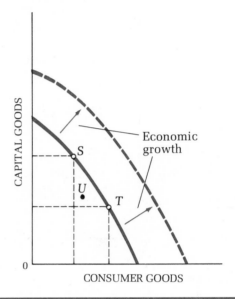

opment. These economists included Adam Smith, David Ricardo, and Thomas Malthus. The conclusions of Ricardo and Malthus were basically pessimistic. They argued that a country's economic growth must end in decline and stagnation. The ideas of these men compose what may appropriately be called the "classical" theory of economic growth. Their views are interesting and can help us to understand modern economic problems of growth.

THE SUBSISTENCE THEORY AND DIMINISHING RETURNS

The classical model of economic growth is based on a *subsistence theory*. In its simplest form the classical model can be expressed in terms of two basic propositions:

1. The population of a country tends to adjust to a subsistence level of living.

2. Increases in population, with technology and natural resources (land) held constant, result in *eventually* decreasing per capita incomes as a result of the operation of the "law of diminishing returns."

Exhibit 2
The Subsistence Theory and Diminishing Returns

In the classical model of Ricardo and Malthus, the actual level-of-living curve L depends on the size of the population (or number of workers) applied to a fixed amount of land. The population tends toward an equilibrium level at M. This corresponds to the subsistence level represented by the distance MR. Even an upward shift of the actual level-of-living curve from L to L', due to the development of new resources or new production techniques, is of short-run duration. The population simply expands to the new size at K, leaving the average output per person KT at the same subsistence level as before.

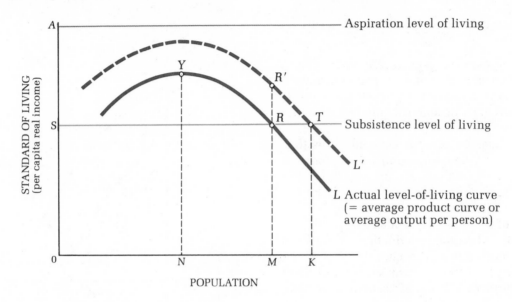

These concepts are illustrated in Exhibit 2. The population of a country is scaled on the horizontal axis, and its material standard of living as measured by per capita real income is scaled on the vertical. The curve labeled L shows the actual level of living that the society can maintain for each amount of population applied to the fixed quantity of other resources. The L curve may therefore be thought of as an *average product curve* representing the average output per person (or per worker). It results from adding more and more people to a given amount of land while production techniques are held constant.

The average product or actual level-of-living curve (L) rises to a maximum and then declines. This evidences the eventual tendency for "diminishing returns" to set in as a growing population is applied to a fixed amount of resources. The ideal or *optimum population* is therefore at N, because this yields a level of living equal to the distance NY, which is the highest level attainable on the curve. Any other combination of population and fixed resources is not optimal because it yields a lower output per person.

The classical economists contended that there was some standard of living at which the population—especially the working population—would just maintain itself, with no tendency to increase or decrease. They called this the "subsistence level." Although primarily a physical or biological level, this level is also determined by social and customary needs, which in turn influence the rearing of children.

Thus, the classicists argued that if wages per worker fell below the subsistence level, people would tend to stop having children and the population would decline, thereby increasing per capita real incomes. Conversely, if wages per worker rose above the subsistence level, people would tend to start having more children and the population would increase, thereby lowering per capita real incomes. This early-nineteenth-century classical theory is known as the subsistence theory of wages (also called the *iron*, or *brazen, law of wages*).

Although the early classical economists did not use graphs, these ideas can be expressed as shown in Exhibit 2. Suppose the standard of living at S represents the subsistence level of living. Then the equilibrium size of the population, according to the classicists, is 0M (= SR). The reason is that if the population is larger than 0M, the actual level of living will be below the subsistence level. Hence, the population will decline and per capita real incomes will therefore increase. On the other hand, if the population is less than 0M, the actual level of living will be above the subsistence level. Consequently, the population will increase and per capita real incomes will therefore decrease. Thus, it is apparent that the "subsistence level" in the classical model is a long-run equilibrium level of living for the population as a whole.

Economics—The "Dismal Science"

Because of this pessimistic theory, economics (or political economy as it used to be called) came to be known as the "dismal science." For if the subsistence level of living is a long-run equilibrium toward which society is always tending, there is no hope of ever improving the future of humanity. Even the discovery of new natural resources or the implementation of new production techniques would at best provide only temporary benefits until the population had time to adjust to these new developments. Then, a larger number of people would be left living in the same minimal circumstances as before.

For example, suppose that new natural resources are discovered, or more land becomes available, or new production techniques are developed. The effect, as shown in Exhibit 2, is to raise the average product curve from L to L', for now the same population has more or better fixed resources with which to work. However, this increase in benefits per person from MR to MR' will be of limited duration. Because average product is now above the subsistence level, the population will increase until it reaches a new equilibrium at K. At this point more people will be living at the same subsistence level, 0S (= KT), as before.

THE MALTHUSIAN SPECTER

Among the early English classical economists, there was one whose theory of population (illustrated by the above model) is especially well known. His name was Thomas R. Malthus, and his famous theory is often encountered in various social science courses.

The *Malthusian theory of population* (first published by Malthus in 1798 and revised in 1803) stated that population increases faster than the means of subsistence. That is, population tends to increase as a geometric progression (1, 2, 4, 8, 16, 32, etc.) while the means of subsistence increase at most only as an arithmetic progression (1, 2, 3,

4, 5, 6, etc.). This is because a growing population applied to a fixed amount of land results in eventually diminishing returns to workers. Human beings are therefore destined to misery and poverty unless the rate of population growth is retarded. This may be accomplished either by preventive checks, such as moral restraint, late marriages, and celibacy; or, if these fail, by positive checks, such as wars, famines, and disease.

Has the prediction of Malthus been realized? There is no doubt that it has in certain crowded underdeveloped areas of Asia, Africa, and South America. In these regions the Malthusian specter hangs like a dark cloud. Here, industrialization and economic growth are impeded because agriculture is inefficient and unable to feed both the people on farms and those who live and work in the cities. In many of these areas, wars, famines, and disease are the main curbs on population, although major efforts are now being made to encourage use of contraception.

Some Proposed Solutions

Can the underdeveloped, overpopulated countries escape from the "Malthusian trap"? Three ways out may be suggested.

One solution would be to shift millions of people from overpopulated to underpopulated regions—from the small farms in Southeast Asia, for example, to the vast jungles of South America which await development. But the many obvious political and social obstacles make this policy unrealistic.

A second possibility would be to develop new resources and production techniques. This must be done at a sufficiently rapid rate so that the upward shifts of the average product curve more than offset the growth in population. In this way the population would never catch up with the rising level of output per person, and the level of living would continually increase.

A third approach would be to seek ways of raising the "subsistence level" to the point at which it becomes an *aspiration level* or target for which to strive. In Exhibit 2, for example, the standard of living (measured along the vertical axis) might be raised from the level at S to that at A. This new level is above the maximum possible actual level of living that is attainable with any present combination of population and resources. Therefore, there might be continual pressure to reduce the existing population in order to rise higher on the average product curve. Alternatively, there might be pressure to discover and develop new resources and production techniques so as to shift the entire average product curve upward. More likely, some combination of both possibilities would probably occur.

The "Hot-Baths" Hypothesis

The second and third solutions, in varying degrees, have occurred and are continuing to occur in the economic development of some of today's advanced nations. The third approach, that of raising the subsistence level to an aspiration level, is based on a fascinating assumption. It suggests that a relationship may exist between population growth and living standards in many overpopulated, underdeveloped countries. This "connection," so to speak, can be called—facetiously—the *hot-baths hypothesis*:

> There may be a significant relationship between human fertility rates and "hot baths." That is, once a society reaches a certain minimum level of living at which it has reasonable creature comforts of life—adequate food, clothing, housing, sanitation, and so on—its desire for more and better material things as measured by its aspiration level continually rises. If this is true, the society's population will tend automatically to seek its economically optimum size, provided that its living conditions can first be brought (probably with outside help from other nations) to this minimum threshold level.

To repeat, this is only an hypothesis—a tentative proposition which has yet to be explored and tested in different nations under varying cultural and social conditions. Nevertheless, it is an interesting and important concept. Indeed, foreign aid to poor, overpopulated nations has sought, in large part, to raise living conditions in those countries to some minimum level at which their economies can break out of their stationary states and enter a new phase of more self-sustaining and self-propelling economic growth. (See *Leaders in Economics,* page 273.)

CAPITAL DEEPENING AND DIMINISHING RETURNS

The subsistence theory of wages in the classical model implies the existence of a *subsistence theory of profits* as well.

For example, the model of population growth that was developed in Exhibit 2 may be adapted to serve as a model of the growth of nonhuman capital. This includes buildings, machines, inventories, and so on. This can be done by measuring the rate of return along the vertical axis and the total stock of capital along the horizontal axis. The curve L is then the "profitability" curve of capital which results from applying different amounts of capital to a fixed quantity of other resources.

When looked at in this way, the model indicates that capital is accumulated in anticipation of future interest returns or profits. Thus, when the stock of capital in the economy is relatively low, the anticipated return on capital is high, thereby encouraging further accumulation. As capital is accumulated, however, the law of diminishing returns eventually sets in. If we suppose that $0S$ represents the "subsistence rate" of profits, capital accumulation will proceed to the level at M. Improvements in any of the fixed resources or in production techniques will, of course, shift the profit curve upward from L to L', thereby bringing about a further accumulation of capital to the amount at K.

> An increase in the stock of capital relative to other resources, especially labor, is called *capital deepening*. What are the effects of such a deepening, assuming that there are no changes in technology? Clearly, with the operation of the inexorable law of diminishing returns, the interest or profit rate on capital must *decline*. Simultaneously, the real wages of labor must *rise* as this resource becomes more and more scarce relative to the growing stock of capital.

The Wages-Fund Theory

These ideas gradually led to a reformulation of the subsistence theory of wages in the classical model. The reformulation, known as the "wages-fund" theory, existed or was implied in the writings of Smith (1776) and Ricardo (1817). However, it was best articulated several decades later in 1848 by John Stuart Mill—not only the greatest economist of his time, but also one of history's most distinguished intellectuals.

The *wages-fund theory* was a mid-nineteenth-century classical theory of wages. The theory held that the producer sets aside, from his capital, funds with which to hire the workers needed for production. The producer does this because of the indirect or "roundabout" nature of the production process: It takes time for goods to be produced, sold, and paid for. Therefore, workers must be given advanced payments—out of the producer's "wages fund"—to meet their basic needs. The amount of the wages fund, and hence the real wage of labor, depends directly on the size of the capital stock relative to the number of workers. But in the long run, as we have seen in the classical model, the accumulation of capital tends to be determined by the minimum subsistence rate of profits. Hence, the only effective way to raise real wages is to reduce the number of workers or the size of the population.

CONCLUSION: THE CLASSICAL VIEW OF GROWTH

These ideas led the English classical economists—especially Ricardo—to the conclusion that the devel-

Leaders in Economics
Thomas Robert Malthus   1766–1834

In the last third of the eighteenth century, two great problems occupied the attention of most thinking people in England. One was widespread poverty; the other was how many British subjects there were. Socialists called attention to the poverty problem with a promise of a Utopian world— a paradise—in which all would be well. The population problem had prompted Adam Smith to remark in his *The Wealth of Nations* (1776) that "No society can surely be flourishing and happy, of which the far greater part of the members are poor and miserable."

Were England's resources adequate to bring about a fulfillment of the socialists' dreams? A hitherto unknown English clergyman, Thomas Robert Malthus, thought not. In 1798, he published a treatise of fifty thousand words entitled *An Essay on the Principle of Population, As It Affects the Future Improvement of Society*. The essay was based on his observations and travels in various countries. From these he expounded his famous rule that "population, when unchecked, goes on doubling every twenty-five years or increases in a geometric ratio," but the means of subsistence can only increase in an arithmetic ratio.

Malthus became a professor of history and published a revision of his essay in 1803. In this he moderated his rigid "formula" and spoke more of a tendency of population to outrun the supply of food. Human beings, he concluded, were destined to misery

The Bettmann Archive, Inc.

and poverty unless the rate of population growth is retarded either by preventive checks such as moral restraint, late marriages, and celibacy, or if these fail by positive checks such as wars, famine, and disease.

Grim Consequences
Malthus and his population theory were severely criticized by people in nearly every walk of life—politicians, clergymen, philosophers, and journalists. All of them raised cries of heresy. Some, like the *Quarterly Review* (July 1817), admitted that it was easier simply "to disbelieve Mr. Malthus than to refute him." But some, notably Ricardo and other classical economists, made Malthus' theory the basis of their own theories of wages and rent.

The generalizations expressed by Malthus have been recognized by governments throughout the world, and by the United Nations in its efforts to assist the overpopulated, underdeveloped countries. Although there may be a tendency to dismiss the gloomy forebodings of the Malthusian theory, its warnings cannot be pushed aside. They are a stark reality for millions of people in many nations today.

Other Achievements
In addition to his population theory, Malthus made outstanding contributions to economics, notably in his *Principles of Political Economy* (1820). He was an intimate friend of David Ricardo, and it is impossible to disassociate their economic views, even though the two men were often in substantial disagreement. For one thing, Ricardo was as incapable of grasping the pragmatic and empirical approach of Malthus as Malthus was incapable of appreciating the rigor and subtle deductive reasoning of Ricardo.

Among the notable contributions that Malthus made to economic thought was the concept of "effective demand," which he defined as the level of aggregate demand necessary to maintain continuous production. More than a century was to pass before the problem of effective demand would rise again to public notice: In his *General Theory*, John Maynard Keynes paid tribute to the pioneering work of Malthus on this subject.

opment of an economy depends on the relative growth of two critical variables: *population* and *capital*. If population grows faster than capital, wages fall and profits rise. Conversely, if capital grows faster than population, profits fall and wages rise. From time to time, one of these variables may grow faster than the other, thereby causing an upward shift in the level-of-living curve of population or in the profit curve of capital. Eventually, however, both wages per worker and profits per unit of capital must tend toward a long-run level of subsistence. Land, on the other hand,

remains fixed in supply. Therefore, landlords stand to benefit over the long run as rents continue to rise with increases in population and in output per worker.

What Are the Long-Run Trends?

Have these predictions been vindicated by history? For most of the advanced or developed economies of the Western world the answer is no. Since the nineteenth century in the United States, for example, three very long-run patterns have been evident:

1. The trends of real wages and of output per worker have been sharply upward, not downward. These trends result mainly from rapid expansion in technology and growth of the capital stock at a faster rate than the population, thus resulting in a deepening of capital.

2. Interest rates or profit have fluctuated in the business cycle, with no particular upward or downward trend.

3. Land rents have moved upward only slightly, while actually declining in relation to other factor prices.

In general terms, the average product curve of the economy has shifted upward over time at a pace rapid enough to more than offset tendencies toward diminishing returns and Malthusian subsistence equilibrium. This upward shift can be attributed to changes in the conditions that are assumed to remain "fixed" when the curve is drawn. In broad terms these include improvements in the quality of labor, discoveries of new and better natural resources, and technological advances in production. We shall see shortly that these are actually the kinds of factors that determine a nation's economic growth. As a result, the classical, or "Ricardian," model is useful not only for what it includes, but also for what it excludes in explaining many of the dynamic processes of economic history. (See *Leaders in Economics,* page 275.)

What Factors Determine Economic Growth?

The classical theory of economic growth presents only a partial explanation of economic development. As yet, no unified body of principles provides what might be called a *general theory* of economic growth. However, certain factors will undoubtedly play a significant role in the development of such a theory. Our purpose at this time is to see what they are.

Let us assume that aggregate demand is sufficient to maintain full employment and that government will take the necessary monetary and fiscal measures to assure this. The growth of real GNP will then be determined by improvements in the nation's resources and the "environment" in which they are used. These major growth-determining factors include:

1. Quantity and quality of human resources.
2. Quantity and quality of "natural" resources.
3. Accumulation of capital.
4. Specialization and scale of production.
5. Rate of technological progress.
6. Environmental factors.

Because these are also the kinds of factors that influence an economy's production-possibilities curve, we shall examine the importance of each of them.

QUANTITY AND QUALITY OF HUMAN RESOURCES

On the basis of our earlier definition of economic growth, the following simple formula is a convenient guide for discussion:

$$\text{real GNP per capita} = \frac{\text{total real GNP}}{\text{population}}$$

The rate of economic growth is measured by the rate at which the left side of this equation, at full employment, increases over time. This in turn will depend, in terms of the right side of the equation, on the rate at which the numerator of the ratio, at full employment, increases relative to the denominator.

> The faster the rate of increase in total real GNP at full employment as compared to the rate of increase in population, the greater the rise in real GNP per capita at full employment and hence in the rate of economic growth.

The formula above uses population only in quantitative terms. But there are both quantitative and qualitative considerations that should be taken into account. For instance, increases in population will bring about increases in the size of the labor force—that is, in the number of people working or looking for work. The productivity of the labor force will influence the rate of economic growth. The chief factors determining labor productivity include:

○ Time spent at work, such as the average length of the workweek.

○ Education, health, and skills of workers.

○ Quantity and quality of the tools and capital equipment used by workers.

Over the past several decades, modern industrial nations have experienced a steady decline in the first of these factors along with a continuous increase in the last two.

Thus, the *quality* as well as the *quantity* of a country's human resources influence its economic growth.

QUANTITY AND QUALITY OF "NATURAL" RESOURCES (LAND)

An economy's output and economic growth also depend on the quantity and quality of its soil, minerals, water, timber, and so on. These are natural resources,

Leaders in Economics
John Stuart Mill   1806–1873

John Stuart Mill was an eminent philosopher and social scientist and the leading economist of the mid-nineteenth century. In many ways, he was one of the most unusual men who ever lived.

Any discussion of Mill must make mention of his remarkable education, based on the experiences reported in his famous *Autobiography.* He was the son of James Mill, a noted philosopher, historian, and economist. James Mill was also an intimate friend of David Ricardo and of the great utilitarian philosopher Jeremy Bentham. This intellectual background exercised a profound influence on the younger Mill, who was educated at home by his father.

At the age of three, before most children can even recite the alphabet, John Stuart was reading English fluently and beginning the study of Greek. By the time he was seven, he had read the dialogues of Plato; the great books of the ancient Greek historians Herodotus and Xenophon; the philosophical writings of Diogenes; and most of the nearly eighty works of the second-century Greek prose writer Lucian. At the age of eight, he took up the study of Latin. Before he was twelve years old, he had already digested, among other things, the major writings of Aristotle, Aristophanes, Horace, Lucretius, Sallust, and Socrates; made a comprehensive survey of algebra, calculus, and geometry; embarked on a serious study of logic through the writings of the early-seventeenth-century British philosopher Thomas Hobbes; and written, in addition to some verses, a

Brown Brothers.

"History of Rome," a "History of Holland," and the "Abridged Ancient Universal History."

At the age of thirteen, John Stuart was introduced by his father to the writings of Smith, Ricardo, and Malthus. Thus began his education in political economy—an education that eventually established him as one of the abler critics of classical economic liberalism. For although Mill as an economist is considered a member of the classical school, he actually repudiated some of its most basic premises. In contrast to Smith, for example, Mill did not believe that laissez-faire led to the best of all possible worlds. Instead, he advocated social reforms. These included the taxation and redistribution of wealth, a shorter working day, abolition of the wage system, and the establishment of democratic producers' cooperatives in which the workers would

own the factories and elect the managers to run them. It should be emphasized, however, that Mill believed too strongly in individual freedom ever to go far as a socialist. He distrusted the power of the state, and his reason for favoring producers' cooperatives was not to exalt the laboring class, but to assure workers the fruits of their labor.

Classical Synthesis

Mills' chief contribution to economics was his collection and systemization of its literature. His major two-volume work, the *Principles of Political Economy,* published in 1848, was considered to be a masterful synthesis of post-Ricardian economic writings. The book offered a calm prescription for peaceful progress and served as a standard text in economics for several decades. A noteworthy coincidence is that in the same year, an incendiary pamphlet entitled the *Communist Manifesto* was published by a then relatively unknown prophet of socialism, Karl Marx, whose ideas ultimately shook the world.

As for Mill himself, few individuals were ever held in higher esteem. Like the great and beloved Greek philosopher Plato of some 2,200 years earlier, Mill was a selfless man with a gentle, kind, and reasonable manner that endeared him to everyone. He was regarded with the deepest affection and respect—indeed, he was almost worshiped—by his contemporaries throughout the world. And, like Plato, when he died an entire nation mourned his passing.

which, in economics, are classified under the general heading of "land" as a factor of production.

Some economists contend that there is no such thing as a "natural" resource. They argue that resources provided by nature are of no value to society unless people are able to put them to use. When that happens, the resources are not natural but man-made. A nation may be rich in resources, but its material well-being or rate of economic growth will not be in-

fluenced in the slightest if these resources remain "neutral" or untapped. Consequently, demand and cost conditions must be favorable if a resource is to be converted from a neutral to a positive state. This means that there must be a high enough level of demand for the product which the resource will help to produce. There must also be an adequate supply of capital, labor, and technical skills to transform the resource to profitable use.

Of course, the quantity and quality of a nation's natural resources are not necessarily fixed. By diverting some of its *existing* labor and capital into research, a society may be able to discover or develop *new* natural resources within its own borders which will enhance its future rate of economic growth. In terms of the production-possibilities curve, this means that some consumer goods must be sacrificed in the present to enable the economy to reach a higher curve in the future.

ACCUMULATION OF CAPITAL

A society must also forgo some current consumption in order to build capital goods such as factories, machines, transportation facilities, dams, and educational institutions. The rate at which a nation can add to its stock of capital will influence its economic growth.

Why is the rate of capital accumulation greater in some countries than in others? You have already learned in the study of macroeconomic theory that many considerations may influence investment. Two, however, are fundamental: (1) profit expectations of business executives and (2) government policies toward investment. Although the influence of these conditions differs among nations, one aspect of the process of capital accumulation is relevant to all—the necessity for sacrifice.

Thus, capital accumulation is closely related to the volume of savings. This is the portion of a society's income that is not spent for consumption. In order to add to their long-run stock of capital goods, the people of a country must refrain from consuming a portion of their current output so that a part of the flow can be diverted into investment. This principle helps to explain why poor countries, like poor families, are ordinarily unable to save as much as rich ones and hence experience little or no economic growth. In general:

The *cost* of economic growth to a society is the consumption that it must sacrifice in order to save for the purpose of accumulating capital.

SPECIALIZATION AND SCALE OF PRODUCTION

The greatest improvement in the productive powers of labor and the greater part of the skill, dexterity, and judgment with which it is anywhere directed, or applied, seem to have been the effects of the division of labour.

So said Adam Smith in *The Wealth of Nations*. Smith then gave the celebrated example of a pin factory: "One man draws out the wire, another straights

it, a third cuts it, a fourth points it, a fifth grinds it. . ." and as a result there is a far greater output than if each man were to make the entire pin himself.

Smith also made the interesting point that the division of labor is limited by the "extent of the market." He observed that in a small isolated economy there will be less division of labor and a smaller scale of operations to satisfy local needs than in a large exchange economy such as Glasgow or a still larger one such as London.

These comments on specialization and scale of production provide significant insights into the process of economic growth. In the early stages of a nation's economic development, production is relatively nonspecialized and the scale of operations is small. In such circumstances "manufacturers" often produce only to supply the needs of the surrounding community, without advancing to the factory stage of production.

This situation prevailed in the United States until the end of the eighteenth century. But with the expansion of the market and advances in the technology of production, greater specialization and scale of operations became possible. Larger volumes of output at the same, if not lower, unit costs were thus realized. This has become a continuing process in the economic growth of nations and regions.

Economic growth is not just an increase in the quantity of the factors of production. Economic growth involves fundamental changes in the organization and techniques of production. These include changes in the *structure* of production as represented by the input–output relationships that characterize an economy's firms and industries.

A nation's economic growth, therefore, will be determined in part by the potential it has for increasing the specialization of its resources and the scale of its production. There are thus qualitative as well as quantitative considerations that determine economic growth.

RATE OF TECHNOLOGICAL PROGRESS

One of the most important qualitative factors influencing economic growth is the rate of technological progress. This is the speed at which new knowledge is both developed and applied to raising the standard of living.

The following remarkable series of events that took place in the United States within the short space of thirteen years, between 1790 and 1803, provides an interesting example. It demonstrates how the rate of technological progress can influence the evolution of a national economy.

In 1790, a brilliant young Englishman, Samuel Slater, employed by a merchant firm in Rhode Island, began spinning cotton thread by machine, thus marking the first effective introduction of the factory system in this country. In the same year, John Fitch constructed and operated successfully the world's first regularly scheduled steamboat. When this was later employed on western waters, it cut the costs of transportation remarkably and enabled the West to become part of the national economy.

In 1793, Eli Whitney invented the cotton gin, which made possible the extensive cultivation of cotton and subsequently transformed the economy of the South. In 1800, this same young graduate of Yale College contracted to manufacture 10,000 rifles for the government. He succeeded in producing them with precisely made interchangeable parts—the first step toward assembly-line production.

By 1803, a Philadelphia inventor named Oliver Evans achieved almost complete automation in the milling of wheat into flour by an ingenious system of machines that weighed, cleaned, ground, and packed the flour with virtually no human assistance. (See Box 1.)

These technological advances were accompanied by legal and economic innovations which had important consequences for the nation's development. Two particularly spectacular advances were critical:

1. The sudden growth of banking, including the creation of the Bank of the United States as well as more than two dozen state-chartered banks. These provided new and important sources of credit for business transactions.

2. The rapid adoption of the corporate form of business organization. This provided opportunities for accumulating large amounts of financial capital (money) with limited liability on the part of owners.

In an expanding economy where risk taking was a vital element of growth, these features made possible the financing and adoption of the technical innovations mentioned above. Clearly, therefore:

Technological progress involves more than just invention. Technological progress embraces an effort on the part of society as a whole to get the most out of existing resources and to discover new and better resources through continuous improvements in education, engineering, management, and marketing.

ENVIRONMENTAL FACTORS

All of the points considered thus far lead to an important conclusion. *The political, social, cultural, and economic environment must be favorable if significant growth is to occur.* This means, among other things, that there must be a *banking and credit system* capable of financing growth. There must be a *legal*

Box 1
Technological Progress

The steamboat and the cotton gin were two strategic inventions introduced in the early years after American independence. These and other inventions of the era played a key role in the nation's economic growth during the nineteenth century.

The Bettmann Archive.

Carding, Drawing, Roving, and Spinning in Slater's Mill, 1790.

Brown Brothers.

John Fitch's First Steamboat, Philadelphia, 1790.

Culver Pictures.

Eli Whitney's First Cotton Gin, 1793.

system that establishes the ground rules of business behavior. There must be a *tax system* that does not discourage new investment and risk taking. And there must be a *stable government* that is sympathetic to economic expansion.

It is no accident that such countries as the United States, Canada, Great Britain, Japan, and the Soviet Union have experienced periods of rapid economic growth despite their different political systems. Some Latin American and Asian countries, on the other hand, have had little or no significant economic growth for many years—and in some cases even for many decades.

CONCLUSION: THE PROBLEM OF MEASUREMENT

How important is each of the six factors discussed in determining a country's economic growth? Can we measure their separate influences? These questions are extremely difficult to answer, because some causes of growth are qualitative rather than quantitative. Consequently, there is a tendency among economists to reduce the determinants of growth to three sets of "measurable" factors:

1. Growth of the labor force.
2. Growth of capital.
3. Technical progress (i.e., "all other things").

The first two factors can be measured quite precisely, whereas the third cannot. Therefore, in measuring the causes of an economy's growth, the contributions of the first two factors to total economic growth are estimated quantitatively. Then the contribution of the third factor is viewed as a "residual" or catchall for all determinants other than labor and capital.

As a simple example, if an economy grows at the rate of 6 percent annually over a period, and 4 percent of that growth is estimated to have been due to the growth of labor and capital combined, the remaining 2 percent might be attributed to technical progress. For purposes of measurement, therefore, "technical progress" includes such things as better machinery and technology, better management, and greater labor skills.

How important is technical progress? It has been estimated that in the United States more than 80 percent of the increase in output per capita since the early part of the century has been due to the technical-progress factor. This leaves less than 20 percent to be explained by the other two factors. In terms of *total* output (as distinct from output per capita), technical progress has accounted for almost 50 percent of the growth of production in the United States and various other industrial nations. This suggests that economic growth is best envisioned as a continuous development and discovery of new and better ways of doing things, rather than just a quantitative expansion of existing inputs.

A Simple Growth Model

Modern approaches to the theory of economic growth are closely tied to analysis of business cycles. The reasons are obvious. When we studied business cycles, we learned that an economy's rate of growth will vary in different stages of the cycle. We also learned that if the consumption function is assumed to be stable, the level of income and employment is determined by net investment.

But in the study of economic growth net investment has yet another function: *It adds to the economy's capacity.* Therefore, the more the net investment undertaken in any one period, the greater will be the productive capacity of the economy in the next period. Consequently, the higher the level of investment needed to sustain aggregate demand and full employment at capacity output.

THE CAPITAL-OUTPUT RATIO

This point is illustrated by the familiar consumption-function diagram in the upper chart of Exhibit 3. For simplicity, only the private sector is represented; the influence of the public sector (government) is excluded. Let us suppose that the output at N_1 represents the economy's full-employment NNP in Year 1. Hence, the corresponding level of consumption is N_1C_1 and the corresponding level of saving is C_1S_1. We assume that this volume of saving flows into new investment, that is, that planned saving equals planned investment, so that the output at N_1 is maintained.

As a result of this new investment, the economy's capacity to produce is enlarged in Year 2 to the output at N_2. In order to produce this output, the volume of planned saving C_2S_2 must flow into new investment. If it does, the capacity of the economy will be further enlarged in Year 3 to the output at N_3.

If this process continues, the economy's ability to produce will expand by increasing amounts. Therefore, *increasing levels of investment* will be needed to sustain full employment of a *growing productive capacity.* This is further emphasized by the lower chart in Exhibit 3. Here the level of investment each year shifts upward by larger and larger amounts.

Exhibit 3
Investment and the Growth of Capacity at Full Employment

In the upper chart, let the output at N_1 be the full-employment NNP in Year 1. Then saving in that year will be C_1S_1. This amount, when invested in plant and equipment, will increase productive capacity in Year 2 by N_1N_2. Saving and investment must then rise to C_2S_2. This in turn will increase productive capacity in Year 3 by N_2N_3. Investment must thus rise by *increasing amounts*, as emphasized in the lower chart, in order to sustain full employment of a *growing productive capacity*.

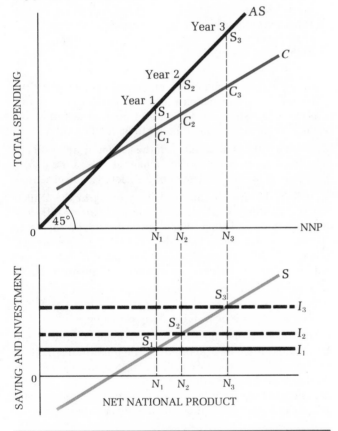

How much will the economy's productive capacity rise each year? The answer depends on the *capital-output ratio*. This is the relationship between the economy's stock of real capital and the resulting output or productive capacity. A ratio of 3:1, for instance, which has been the approximate long-run trend in the United States, means that 3 units of capital produce 1 unit of output per period.

FULL-EMPLOYMENT GROWTH RATE

We can extend the foregoing ideas to develop an important formula that is widely used as an expression of economic growth at full employment. In addition to assuming full employment, let us also assume that *saving* equals *investment* and that all investment results in an increase in *capital*.

On this basis, if we know the *average propensity to save*, that is, the proportion of the economy's income or output that is not spent on consumption, we can tell how much saving will flow into investment and hence into the creation of additional capital. Then, if we also know the capital-output ratio, we can calculate the expected full-employment growth of NNP.

The procedure is illustrated in Exhibit 4. Columns (1) and (2) show the full-employment output for each year represented by NNP. For convenience, we begin with an arbitrary NNP of $100 in Year 1. In column (3) of the table, saving equals investment or the increase in capital, and the average propensity to save *APS* is assumed to be 10 percent. This is equivalent, of course, to saying that the average propensity to consume is 90 percent. If we assume that the capital-output ratio is also 3:1, the resulting increase in output will be one-third of the increase in capital, as shown in column (4). This increase in output then becomes the next year's addition to NNP in column (2), as emphasized by the arrows. The table can thus be extended very easily by simply continuing the pattern. That is, take 10 percent of NNP, calculate one-third of that, and add the result to the current year's NNP to get next year's NNP.

Exhibit 4
The Full-Employment Rate of Economic Growth

What will be the full-employment NNP for Year 5? To find out, take 10 percent of Year 4's NNP, then calculate one-third of that, and add the result to the NNP for Year 4. The arrows illustrate the pattern to be followed.

(1)	(2)	(3)	(4)
		Saving = investment = increase in capital (APS = 0.10)	Resulting increase in output (capital/output ratio = 3/1)
Year	Full-employment output, NNP	[10% of col. (2)]	[⅓ of col. (3)]
1	$100.00	$10.00	
			3.33
2	103.33	10.33	
			3.44
3	106.77	10.68	
			3.56
4	110.33		

You may be able to estimate from the table that the full-employment output of NNP is growing at a rate of something over 3 percent per year. However, a closer estimate can be made in terms of the variables in the model by applying a simple formula. Thus:

$$\text{full-employment growth rate} = \frac{\text{average propensity to save}}{\text{capital–output ratio}}$$

This basic formula is widely used in modern theories of economic growth. It can be applied for any average propensity to consume and for any capital–output ratio. In the model above, for example, we assumed a long-run *APS* of 0.10 and a capital–output ratio of 3. Hence, the full-employment growth rate is 0.10/3 = 0.033 or 3.3 percent per year. Of course, a larger or smaller growth rate can be obtained, depending on the values of the *APS* and the capital–output ratio used in the formula.

The growth-rate formula and the simple model on which it is based are useful primarily because they illustrate important relationships. But it should be kept in mind that they assume a number of simplifying conditions. Among them: (1) a fixed capital–output ratio, (2) a fixed average propensity to save, and (3) a neglect of such real-world factors as business taxes, government monetary and fiscal policies, and changes in technology. These assumptions are the subject of much debate among economists.

What You Have Learned

1. The study of economic growth is concerned with the rate of increase in an economy's actual and potential real output or income over time. Economic growth may be viewed as an outward shift of an economy's production-possibilities curve.

2. The classical theory of economic growth, developed in the early nineteenth century, was a subsistence theory. Based on the operation of the law of diminishing returns, the classical theory held that the development of an economy depended on the relative rates of growth of population and capital. However, the returns to both in the form of wages and profit tended toward subsistence levels in the long run. Although the evidence has not borne out this theory for the advanced nations of the world, the classical model, nevertheless, is useful for explaining many of the dynamic processes of economic history.

3. Many factors determine a nation's economic growth. Among them: the quantity and quality of human and natural resources, the rate of capital accumulation, the degree of specialization and scale of production, the rate of technological progress, and the nature of the socioeconomic–political environment. For measurement purposes, however, these are usually reduced to three sets of factors: (a) growth of the labor force, (b) growth of capital, and (c) technical progress (or "all other things" not represented by the previous two measurable factors).

4. The full-employment growth of an economy's productive capacity depends on its capital–output ratio. For the United States, the ratio has had a long-run trend of about 3 : 1. A basic approach for measuring the full-employment growth rate is to divide the average propensity to save by the capital–output ratio. This formula is based, however, on a number of simplifying conditions, thus making it useful only for illustrating some important relationships.

For Discussion

1. *Terms and concepts to review:*

   economic growth

   subsistence theory
      of wages

   Malthusian theory
      of population

   capital deepening

   wages-fund theory

   capital–output ratio

2. Is our economic definition of growth "better" than the biological definition, which expresses growth as an *organic process*—a transference of material from one part of an organism (such as the human body) to another? Explain.

3. What are the shortcomings of the economic definition of growth? That is, what sort of "amenities" does the definition omit as far as the growth of a society is concerned?

4. If Ricardo and Malthus had been living in the United States rather than England during the early nineteenth century, do you think they would have developed the same theory of economic growth? Explain your answer. (HINT Think in terms of the subsistence theory and the supply of scarce resources as compared to plentiful ones.)

5. What is meant by an "optimum population"? Do you believe there really is such a thing? Is it as applicable to the United States as it is to India? Why or why not?

6. The factors that determine an economy's growth are both quantitative and qualitative. The quantitative factors are susceptible to measurement and can be incorporated in a growth model. Does this mean that such models are incomplete to the extent that qualitative factors are omitted? What can be done about correcting the situation? Explain your answer.

7. How is the full-employment growth rate of an economy influenced by the size of its *APS* relative to its capital–output ratio? Can you suggest some general policies that the government can adopt through the tax system to reduce the capital–output ratio and thus stimulate economic growth?

8. (a) It has been suggested that the income tax system, which provides equal deductions for each dependent, might be revised with the objective of regulating family size by taxation. How might this be done? Develop a specific example. (b) What do you think of a population-control plan which parallels several decades of American agricultural policy, giving subsidies for "fallow acres" and penalties for "overcropping"?

Reading
Malthus on Population

Few writings have had as much influence on social and economic thought as Malthus's classic essay on population. Although first written in 1798 and subsequently revised and elaborated at considerable length, the main theme is expressed by the following passage from Thomas R. Malthus, *An Essay on the Principle of Population* (6th ed., I, 1826, pp. 1–24).

Many extravagant statements have been made of the length of the period within which the population of a country can double. To be perfectly sure we are far within the truth, we will take a slow rate, and say that population, when unchecked, goes on doubling itself every 25 years, or increases in a geometrical ratio. The rate according to which the productions of the earth may be supposed to increase, it will not be so easy to determine. However, we may be perfectly certain that the ratio of their increase in a limited territory must be of a totally different nature from the ratio of the increase in population.

Let us suppose that, taking the whole earth, the human species would increase as the numbers 1, 2, 4, 8, 16, 32, 64, 128, 256, and subsistence as 1, 2, 3, 4, 5, 6, 7, 8, 9. In two centuries the population would be to the means of subsistence as 256 to 9; in three centuries as 4,096 to 13, and in two thousand years the difference would be almost incalculable.

In this supposition, no limits whatever are placed to the produce of the earth. It may increase forever and be greater than any assignable quantity; yet still the power of population, being in every period so much greater, the increase of the human species can only be kept down to the level of the means of subsistence by the constant operation of the strong law of necessity, acting as a check upon the greater power.

But this ultimate check to population, the want of food, is never the immediate check except in cases of famine. The latter consists in all those

Ray Ellis/Photo Researchers.

customs, and all those diseases, which seem to be generated by a scarcity of the means of subsistence; and all those causes which tend permanently to weaken the human frame. The checks may be classed under two general heads—the preventative and the positive.

The preventative check, peculiar to man, arises from his reasoning faculties, which enable him to calculate distant consequences. He sees the distress which frequently presses upon those who have large families; he cannot contemplate his present possessions or earnings, and calculate the amount of each share, when they must be divided, perhaps, among seven or eight, without feeling a doubt whether he may be able to support the offspring which probably will be brought into the world. Other considerations occur. Will he lower his rank in life, and be obliged to give up in great measure his former habits? Does any mode of employment present itself by which he may reasonably hope to maintain a family? Will he not subject himself to greater difficulties and more severe labor than in his present state? Will he be able to give his children adequate educational advantages? Can he face the possibility of exposing his children to poverty or charity, by his inability to provide for them? These considerations prevent a large number of people from pursuing the dictates of nature.

The positive checks to population are extremely various, and include every cause, whether arising from vice or misery, which in any degree contributes to shorten the natural duration of human life. Under this head may be enumerated all unwholesome occupations, severe labor, exposure to the seasons, extreme poverty, bad nursing of children, great towns, excesses of all kinds, the whole train of common diseases, wars, plagues, and famines.

The theory of population is resolvable into three propositions:

1. Population is necessarily limited by the means of subsistence.

2. Population invariably increases where the means of subsistence increase, unless prevented by some very powerful and obvious checks.

3. These checks which keep population on a level with the means of subsistence are all resolvable into moral restraint, vice, and misery.

QUESTIONS

1. Malthus and other classical economists employed the *law of diminishing returns* to explain the process of economic growth. Is this law generally valid today? In overpopulated India? In the underpopulated American Northwest?

2. "Malthus's theory implies that economic growth is impossible when there is rapid population growth." Do you agree?

Chapter 17

Problems of Economic Growth

Chapter Preview

What has been the record of American economic growth? How does it compare with that of other advanced nations? What are the sources of growth?

How fast should we grow? Are there some simple guides for understanding and measuring rates of growth?

Is economic growth "free," or does it have costs?

What obstacles must be overcome if a given rate of growth is to be sustained?

How do problems of taxation and inflation affect the rate of growth?

Until recent decades, the "goodness" of economic growth was, for most people, an article of faith. After all, economic growth brings more goods, more services, and high employment. What could possibly be wrong with such objectives?

As it turns out, quite a lot. More goods include more chemicals, petroleum products, automobiles, and other items which defile the environment and upset the ecological balance. And when unplanned, economic growth can disrupt the lives of millions of people whose skills are made obsolete by changing technology—sometimes impoverishing whole regions of the country which lose their economic base when the demand for their traditional products or raw materials declines.

These problems are not new. But society's awareness of them has been increasing. Some observers have been questioning the wisdom of growth for its own sake, and many others have been asking what *kind* of growth is beneficial—in other words, which mix of goods and services will help to make our society better.

We shall examine these issues in this chapter. But first we must compare the historical record of growth in the United States with the experience of other advanced economies, such as Great Britain and Germany. Then we shall consider the costs of growth, both financial and social.

American Economic Growth

What have been the main trends—the patterns of economic growth—in the United States?

By 1900, the United States had become the world's leading manufacturing nation, far ahead of such major producing countries as Great Britain and Germany. In terms of the rate of economic growth, the period from 1875 to 1900 was one in which America's total real GNP is estimated to have increased at an average annual compound rate of 5 to 6 percent, and per capita real GNP at 2 to 3 percent. In 1900, total GNP in current prices of that year was approximately $20 billion, and GNP per capita was about $235.

MAJOR TRENDS SINCE 1900

During the twentieth century, the *long-run trend* of *total real* GNP has been rising at an average annual rate of more than 3 percent. The *upward trend* of *per capita real* GNP has averaged a little less than 2 percent annually.

We may examine some of the implications of these trends by looking at several of the variables that play a key role in the theory of economic growth. These variables are presented in Exhibit 1. The charts reveal three important sets of features:

1. The top chart shows that NNP increased at about the same rate as the net capital stock, but the latter increased much faster than the population (as well as the labor force). Hence, there has been a substantial amount of capital deepening, that is, more capital per worker.

2. The second chart shows that the trend of real wages has been steadily upward and that their rate of growth has approximately equaled the increase in per capita output. The rise in the latter, of course, is a reflection of capital deepening and advancements in technology. Thus, labor has continued to earn approximately the same *proportion* of total output over the years.

3. The three lower charts show that along with the process of capital deepening, real wages have risen relative to the interest rate or return on capital. This is what the theory of economic growth would predict. The fact that the long-run trend of the interest rate is roughly flat, as is the trend of the capital–output ratio, can probably be accounted for by the tendency of diminishing returns to be approximately offset by advances in technology.

What conclusion can we draw from these facts? In general:

Exhibit 1
The Anatomy of U.S. Economic Development

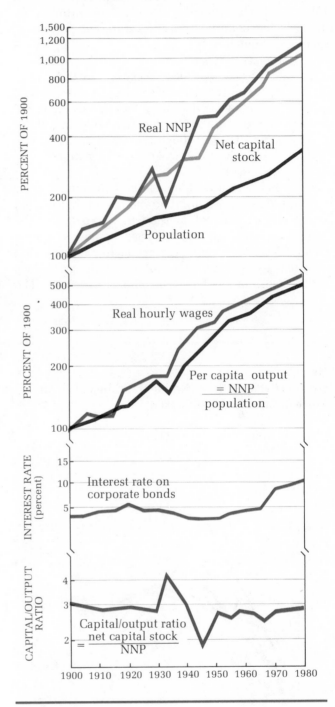

The theory of economic growth, with the inclusion of technological advance, tends to be supported by the available evidence for the United States. Similar tendencies have also been found for other advanced mixed economies.

INTERNATIONAL COMPARISONS AND THE SOURCES OF GROWTH

How does America's growth rate compare with that of other relatively advanced nations? Some information for selected countries covering different periods of time is presented in Exhibit 2.

As the facts indicate, nations may differ widely in their rates of growth. This is because growth is determined by various interacting factors, as explained earlier. For convenience, they may be summarized broadly in terms of the classification given in Exhibit 3. This table provides rough estimates of the contribution that each factor makes to the nation's total economic growth.

Note that before 1929, increases in the *quantitative* factors—the supplies of labor and capital—accounted for about two-thirds of the economy's expansion. The remaining one-third resulted from increases in such qualitative factors as improvements in education and training, technology, and "all other things." Since 1929, the situation has been almost reversed. The *qualitative* factors have played a more important role in economic growth while the quantitative factors have been less important.

Investment in Human Capital

The information suggests that improvements in education and training have become the single most important factor contributing to economic growth. In other words, the scarcest resource for our society is not land or muscle power, but brain power. The advances of modern science and technology are making this increasingly evident. Hence, our investment in human capital, reflecting a rising long-run trend in the number of high-school and college graduates and in expenditures on public elementary and secondary education, as shown in Exhibit 4, will continue to expand in the years to come. This is all the more likely in view of mounting evidence to suggest that society's returns from investment in human capital are higher than its returns from investment in capital goods.

Exhibit 2
Growth Rates of Gross National Product—Selected Countries
(percent; latest comparative data)

Chart (a). *Growth rates of real GNP.*

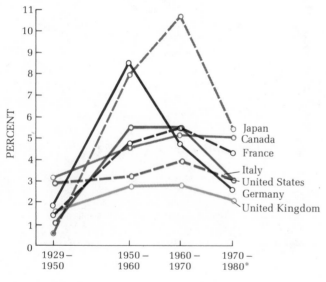

*Estimated.

SOURCE: U.S. Department of Commerce.

Chart (b). *Growth rates of real GNP per capita.*

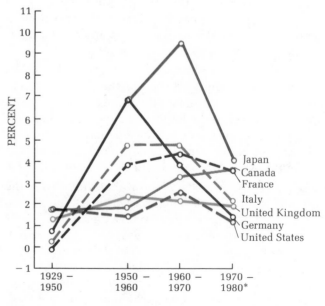

*Estimated.

Exhibit 3
Sources of U.S. Economic Growth

The factor that has been contributing most significantly to economic growth since 1929 has been a "qualitative" one, improved education and training of human resources.

Contributions to real national income	1909–1929	1930–1949	1950–1979	1980–2000*
Quantitative factors				
Increase in quantity of labor†	39%	30%	26%	24%
Increase in quantity of capital	26	21	15	12
Qualitative factors‡				
Improved education and training	13	25	30	34
Improved technology	12	18	22	25
All other things§	10	6	7	5
Total growth in real national income	100%	100%	100%	100%

* United Nations; author's estimates.
† Adjusted for decreases in the workweek.
‡ Some qualitative factors are at least partially quantitative. Improvements in education, for example, depend on the number of years of schooling as well as on the quality of schooling.
§ Consists primarily of increased economies of large-scale production resulting from the expanding size of the market.

SOURCE: Adapted with changes from Edward Denison, *The Sources of Economic Growth in the United States* (New York: Committee for Economic Development, 1962); Joint Economic Committee of the Congress, 1972; United Nations; author's estimates.

The Growth-Rate Problem: How Fast Should We Grow?

Now that we have looked at the background and history of economic growth, we may turn our attention to the future. What does it mean to talk about growth rates of 3, 4, 5 percent, or more? Should we try to set some desirable or target rate of growth?

GROWING AT COMPOUND INTEREST

First, we have to understand what is meant by the term *annual percentage rate of growth*. This expression is based on what is known as *compound interest*—interest that is computed on a principal sum and also on all the interest earned by that principal sum as of a given date. A convenient table which conveys this

Exhibit 4
Educational Attainment and Expenditures on Public Elementary and Secondary Education

A rising level of educational attainment is the same as an increase in human capital investment. The productive potential of workers is enhanced, thereby benefiting employers, employees, and society as a whole.

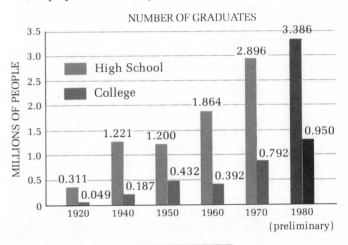

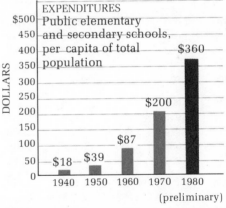

type of information is presented in Exhibit 5. This table shows the future values of $1 compounded annually at various rates of interest, and can be employed to study several types of growth problems.

EXAMPLE 1   If you deposit $1 in a savings account that pays 5 percent interest compounded annually, how much will your deposit be worth at the end of 1 year? 2 years? 10 years? 50 years?

Solution   Looking at the table in the 5 percent column, we find that a deposit of $1 will be worth: $1.050 at the end of the first year, $1.103 at the end of the second year, $1.628 at the end of the tenth year, and $11.467 at the end of the fiftieth year. (For a deposit of $100, simply move the decimal point two places to the right; for a deposit of $1,000, three places to the right, and so on.)

Exhibit 5
Growth-Rate Table

THE GROWTH OF $1 COMPOUNDED ANNUALLY AT VARIOUS RATES OF INTEREST

End of year	\multicolumn{12}{c}{Future value of $1 at:}
	1%	2%	3%	4%	5%	6%	7%	8%	9%	10%	12%	15%
1	1.010	1.020	1.030	1.040	1.050	1.060	1.070	1.080	1.090	1.100	1.120	1.150
2	1.020	1.040	1.061	1 082	1.103	1.124	1.145	1.166	1.188	1.210	1.254	1.322
3	1.030	1.061	1.093	1.125	1.158	1.191	1.225	1.260	1.295	1.331	1.405	1.521
4	1.041	1.082	1.126	1.170	1.216	1.262	1.311	1.360	1.412	1.464	1.574	1.749
5	1.051	1.104	1.159	1.217	1.276	1.338	1.403	1.469	1.539	1.611	1.762	2.011
6	1.062	1.126	1.194	1.265	1.340	1.419	1.501	1.587	1.677	1.772	1.974	2.313
7	1.072	1.149	1.230	1.316	1.407	1.504	1.606	1.714	1.828	1.949	2.211	2.660
8	1.083	1.172	1.267	1.369	1.477	1.594	1.718	1.851	1.993	2.144	2.476	3.059
9	1.094	1.195	1.305	1.423	1.551	1.689	1.838	1.999	2.172	2.358	2.773	3.518
10	1.105	1.219	1.344	1.480	1.628	1.792	1.967	2.159	2.367	2.593	3.106	4.046
11	1.116	1.243	1.384	1.539	1.710	1.898	2.105	2.332	2.580	2.853	3.479	4.652
12	1.127	1.268	1.426	1.601	1.796	2.012	2.252	2.518	2.813	3.138	3.896	5.350
13	1.138	1.294	1.469	1.665	1.886	2.133	2.410	2.720	3.066	3.452	4.363	6.153
14	1.149	1.319	1.513	1.732	1.980	2.261	2.579	2.937	3.342	3.797	4.887	7.076
15	1.161	1.346	1.558	1.801	2.079	2.397	2.759	3.172	3.642	4.177	5.474	8.137
16	1.173	1.373	1.605	1.873	2.183	2.540	2.952	3.426	3.970	4.595	6.130	9.358
17	1.184	1.400	1.653	1.948	2.292	2.693	3.159	3.700	4.328	5.054	6.866	10.761
18	1.196	1.428	1.702	2.026	2.407	2.854	3.380	3.996	4.717	5.560	7.690	12.375
19	1.208	1.457	.754	2.107	2.527	3.026	3.617	4.316	5.142	6.116	8.613	14.232
20	1.220	1.486	.806	2.191	2.652	3.206	3.870	4.661	5.604	6.728	9.646	16.367
21	1.232	1.516	1.860	2.279	2.786	3.400	4.141	5.034	6.109	7.400	10.804	18.821
22	1.245	1.546	1.916	2.370	2.925	3.604	4.430	5.437	6.659	8.140	12.100	21.645
23	1.257	1.577	1.974	2.465	3.072	3.820	4.741	5.781	7.258	8.954	13.552	24.891
24	1.270	1.608	2.033	2.563	3.225	4.049	5.072	6.341	7.911	9.850	15.179	28.625
25	1.282	1.641	2.094	2.666	3.386	4.292	5.427	6.848	8.623	10.835	17.000	32.919
26	1.295	1.673	2.157	2.772	3.556	4.549	5.807	7.396	9.399	11.918	19.040	37.857
27	1.308	1.707	2.221	2.883	3.733	4.822	6.214	7.988	10.245	13.110	21.325	43.535
28	1.321	1.741	2.288	2.999	3.920	5.112	6.649	8.627	11.167	14.421	23.884	50.066
29	1.335	1.776	2.357	3.119	4.116	5.418	7.114	9.317	12.172	15.863	26.750	57.575
30	1.348	1.811	2.427	3.243	4.322	5.743	7.612	10.063	13.268	17.449	29.960	66.212
35	1.417	2.000	2.814	3.946	5.516	7.686	10.677	14.785	20.414	28.102	52.800	133.176
40	1.489	2.208	3.262	4.801	7.040	10.286	14.974	21.725	31.409	45.259	93.051	267.863
45	1.565	2.438	3.782	5.841	8.985	13.765	21.002	31.920	48.327	72.890	163.988	538.769
50	1.645	2.692	4.384	7.107	11.467	18.420	29.457	46.902	74.358	117.391	289.002	1083.657

EXAMPLE 2   Real GNP (in 1958 prices) increased from $323.7 billion in 1948 to $487.7 billion in 1960. What was the rate of growth at compound interest?

Solution   An increase from $323.7 billion to $487.7 billion is proportional to an increase from $1 to $1.507:

$$\frac{\$487.7}{\$323.7} = \$1.507$$

Since this increase occurred over 12 years (from 1948 to 1960), we look at the 12-year horizontal line of the table and locate the closest number to $1.507; then read the interest-rate figure at the top of that column. Thus, the growth rate was between 3 and 4 percent annually—apparently about 3.5 percent. (A closer estimate can be made by interpolation if desired, but this is not usually necessary.)

EXAMPLE 3   (a) If an economy's real income as measured by its GNP per capita is $3,000, how long would it take to double that income if the economy grows at a compound annual rate of 6 percent? (b) If, in fact, the economy doubled its real income or GNP per capita in 18 years, what was its compound annual rate of growth?

Solution (a) Under the 6 percent column in the table, we note that $1 will double to $2 within 12 years (i.e., it will exactly double sometime during the twelfth year, and will be worth $2.012 at the end of the twelfth year). Hence, $3,000 will double to $6,000 in the same amount of time. (b) On the 18-year horizontal line, we find that $1 will double to $2 at an interest rate between 3 and 4 percent as shown at the top of the columns—but at a rate somewhat closer to 4 percent. We can thus conclude that the economy grew at a compound annual rate of about 4 percent—or actually a little less than that if we wish to interpolate for a closer estimate.

THE RULE OF 72

Example 3, which involves the general problem of how long it takes for a number to double when it grows at compound interest, is an extremely practical one. Businesspersons who borrow money, bankers who lend it, and people who buy bonds or other fixed income-yielding securities are often concerned with this question. For convenience, when a table is not readily available we can employ a quick way of getting good approximate answers to the problem. It may be called the "Rule of 72":

The *Rule of 72* is a simple growth formula. It states: Given the annual rate of compound interest, divide this rate into 72 to obtain the approximate number of years it takes for a quantity to double. Conversely, given the number of years it takes for a quantity to double, divide this amount into 72 to obtain the approximate annual rate of compound interest.

EXAMPLE If an economy's real GNP per capita grows at 6 percent, it will double its real income in 72/6 = 12 years. Conversely, if it takes 12 years for an economy to double its real GNP per capita, its growth rate is 72/12 = 6 percent.

The Rule of 72, as well as the principles underlying compound interest, apply to any growing quantity. This is true whether it be the growth of GNP, the growth of money in a savings account, or the growth of a tree.

IS THERE A TARGET RATE OF GROWTH?

Should we set a desired growth rate for the economy—a "target rate" for which to shoot? If so, what should the rate be? Some countries, for example, have gone through periods when their growth rates have been 10 percent or more. At this rate, an economy doubles its GNP in slightly more than seven years.

Consider what a 10 percent growth rate would mean over a period, say, of 30 years. If your income today is $10,000 per year, that amount would expand to about $175,000 per year during the next 30 years. This would be a remarkable figure, even at our long-run rate of inflation.

In real terms, our economy's long-run growth record has been more like 3 percent rather than 10 percent. At this rate it takes about 24 years for per capita income or GNP to double. If we want to grow faster than this, we have to decide how much faster, and we have to know the costs that are involved. Keep in mind that an increase in growth from 3 to 4 percent amounts to a 33⅓ percent increase in the annual rate. Looked at in this way, the difference is considerable. No wonder a country ordinarily finds it extremely difficult to raise its growth rate by an additional percentage point. Some of these difficulties are pointed out in detail below.

The Costs of Economic Growth

What are the costs of increased growth? The answer should be thought of in terms of society's *sacrifices*. These are the pleasures it must postpone today for greater future satisfactions. From this standpoint, the basic costs of economic growth are five in number:

1. The sacrifice of leisure for employment.

2. The sacrifice of consumption for investment.

3. The sacrifice of the present for the future.

4. The sacrifice of environmental quality for more goods.

5. The sacrifice of security for progress.

Let us see what each of these involves.

LEISURE VERSUS EMPLOYMENT

The rate of economic growth can be raised by using society's resources more fully. If this is done permanently rather than temporarily (e.g., by increasing the size of the labor force or the length of the workweek), the result will be a larger economic pie to be divided at any given time.

The cost of this increased growth, however, must be measured in terms of a sacrifice of leisure. What do we mean by leisure? Is it the same as idleness? Emphatically not! *Leisure is a matter of choice.* Some people may choose to use their leisure by pursuing a hobby; others will prefer "civilized loafing." But in any case the value of leisure can be expressed in various ways. One is in terms of the income that can be obtained from alternative work uses of time. Another is the contribution to the supply of goods and services that some leisure activities produce and which the person of leisure would otherwise have purchased in the market. Examples include the products of woodworking, photography, or needlework. Because these values are never actually recorded in the marketplace, they are omitted from estimates of GNP.

In contrast, idleness is not a matter of choice. Idleness tends to have no uses and to yield no income. Consequently, if we consider leisure as one of the goals of society, or part of the real income for which we work, then who is to say that a 5 percent rate of growth in real GNP is better than a 3 percent rate of growth? Indeed, the latter rate of growth may include more leisure and may in fact be preferable to the former. Therefore:

The loss of the value of leisure for the sake of more rapid growth must be recognized as one of the costs of growth. This is true even though that cost can at best be only roughly estimated rather than precisely measured.

CONSUMPTION VERSUS INVESTMENT

If an economy cannot use its resources more fully, can it still increase its output per capita or rate of growth? It probably can, provided that it is able to reduce its consumption in the present so as to achieve higher investment that will increase production in the future. The consumption that is forgone (or in fact postponed) becomes the measure of society's real cost of growth. It is somewhat easier to determine than the cost of leisure forgone, because the prices of consumer goods and services can be obtained from the market, whereas the price of leisure cannot be estimated as readily.

The amount of investment is not the only thing that matters in increasing a nation's production; the type of investment is also important. This point is significant because in most theoretical discussions it is convenient to assume a rigid relationship between investment in capital and the resulting rate of output or economic growth. This relationship is typically expressed in terms of the familiar capital–output ratio. Thus, if the ratio equals 3, an investment of $300 should increase the output rate per period by $100. In reality, however, the relationship between investment and economic growth (i.e., the productivity of investment) is not rigid. There are several reasons:

1. Investment is not restricted to the production of tangible assets such as plant and equipment. Investment also includes expenditures on the "production" of intangible assets, such as human resources and new skills, and on research and development. The returns

to society of investment in intangibles are variable and are extremely difficult to estimate with close accuracy.

2. It is not always sufficient to think in terms of capital–output ratios. Some kinds of investment, such as investment in education, yield cultural and social benefits to a nation which are not reflected by its measures of GNP.

3. Certain types of investment may contribute to GNP, but do not enhance society's material welfare if the resulting output is not wanted by consumers. For example, investment that results in the creation of large agricultural surpluses for which there are no markets at existing prices detracts from society's welfare and even wastes resources that might better be used in other ways.

Clearly, therefore:

The nature and types of investment that an economy undertakes are at least as important as the amount of its investment as far as the costs to society are concerned.

PRESENT COSTS VERSUS FUTURE BENEFITS

The greater the rate of growth, the greater the sacrifice or postponement that must be made in leisure, in consumption, or in both. This does not necessarily mean, however, that *any* gain in economic growth (defined as an increase in real output per capita) is better than none. Future income or future consumption is never worth as much as present income or present consumption. Therefore, the value or cost of the sacrifices that must be made today and tomorrow in order to achieve a given rate of growth must be compared with the value of the benefits that will be received in the future.

In comparing these costs and benefits, three basic questions must be answered.

First, what will be the increment in benefits as compared with the increment in costs? That is, how much will the economy's future income and consumption increase as a result of present and future sacrifices of consumption and leisure?

Second, how long will it take before the increased benefits are realized?

Third, is the increment in benefits and the time required to receive them worth the sacrifice? In other words, income and consumption today are worth more than the same amount of future income and consumption. Therefore, how does the *present value* of the future benefits compare with the *present value* of the future costs?

The third question provides a guide for decision making and policy formulation:

We should express the future values of costs and benefits in equivalent terms of *today's* dollars. In that way a correct comparison can be made *in the present* between the future costs and benefits involved. (In more technical language, this entails a process in financial mathematics known as "discounting.")

ENVIRONMENTAL QUALITY VERSUS MORE GOODS

Ill fares the land, to hast'ning ill a prey,
Where wealth accumulates, and men decay.
Oliver Goldsmith

Writers, poets, and artists have long warned against the headlong pursuit of riches. But their voices were seldom heeded. Now it has become uncomfortably clear that these "prophets" may have been right all along.

In America, one of the richest nations in the world, wealth continuously accumulates while the quality of life itself decays. Much of this decay must be counted as a cost of growth, even though precise measurement is difficult, if not impossible.

Does this mean that economic growth is necessarily bad? Not at all. But it does mean that the pursuit of growth for its own sake may be bad. Indeed, the thought of a nation with a per capita gross income of $175,000—as envisioned earlier—is horrifying, if much of that amount is to be made and spent as it would be today.

The result would inevitably be larger traffic jams, sprawling airports, air and water pollution at lethal levels, and lakes, rivers, and yacht marinas congested with pleasure craft. In short, we would be a nation of rich people living in extreme discomfort and almost certainly racked by associated mental ailments. Clearly:

The composition of GNP may be even more important than its rate of growth. Hence, our nation's task is to determine what that composition should be. For a free society, the solution must be found through the operation of the market system rather than by authoritarian measures. (See Box 1.)

SECURITY VERSUS PROGRESS

The costs of growth just described are applicable to all types of economic systems. But in a capitalistic system there is still another cost. It takes such forms as fluctuations in economic activity, frictional and tech-

---

Box 1
One Way to Control Pollution

How can pollution be controlled? One way is to make the free market work *against* pollution instead of for it. How? By building the cost of pollution into the price system. This involves a two-step approach:

Step 1. ***Assess the incremental or additional damage resulting from an incremental act of pollution.***   For example, what is the increased cost to society from pollution due to automobile emissions?

Step 2. ***Levy a tax on the pollution act equal to the damage.***   The tax could be levied by automobile mileage, with periodic inspections to determine the level of emissions, or the tax could be levied on gasoline.

Free Lance Photographers Guild Inc.

This free-market approach would encourage consumers (motorists) to seek ways of reducing pollution in order to avoid paying the tax. It would also encourage producers (automobile manufacturers) to respond to consumers by providing antipollution devices and systems. However, there would be some difficulties in implementing this approach. Can you point out a few? What other ways of controlling pollution can you propose?

---

nological unemployment, and obsolescence of capital and skills. This is because economic growth tends to occur in spurts rather than as a smooth and continuous process. As a result, an eminent economist, Joseph Schumpeter (1853–1950), was led to conclude that a capitalistic economy grows by replacing old methods of production, old sources of supply, and old skills and resources with new ones. To use Schumpeter's famous phrase, capitalism grows by engaging in a continual *"process of creative destruction."*

The fundamental message, therefore, is that economic growth in a capitalistic economy entails a clash between security and progress. The basic question is whether this clash is really necessary. In other words, is some economic insecurity inevitable in a dynamic economy, or must we turn to some form of command economy in order to achieve maximum security (and probable loss of some personal freedoms)? As with most issues in economics, the approach to a solution is a matter of degree. It is a problem of achieving what society regards as a desirable "trade-off" between the two extremes.

CONCLUSION: INCREASED COSTS VERSUS INCREASED BENEFITS

It is sometimes said that the best things in life are free. We can now see, however, that economic growth certainly is not one of them. Costs must be paid and sacrifices must be made to sustain any rate of growth. It is not correct to assume, therefore, that the more we grow or the faster we grow, the better off we are. Instead, alternatives must be weighed:

> It is necessary to balance the corresponding costs and benefits of alternative growth rates. In general, *the optimum rate of growth is determined where the increased costs of more growth are just offset by the increased benefits.* The optimum rate may be "high" or "low," depending on the value that society places on the advantages of growth.

Thus, if an economy is growing, say, at 3 percent, it should compare the incremental or "marginal" costs and benefits involved if it wishes to increase its growth rate to 4 or 5 percent. Clearly, the optimum rate of growth need not be the maximum rate. An economy may increase its rate by putting its population on an austerity level of living and channeling all savings thus obtained into investment. This, in varying degrees, is a policy that has been followed at one time or another by the Soviet Union, China, and some other countries.

Barriers to Economic Growth

In any society there are obstacles to economic growth. These obstacles differ according to whether the particular society is "traditional" or "advanced."

In traditional societies, the obstacles to growth are primarily cultural. They consist of social and religious attitudes toward business practices, money and interest, new productive techniques, and new institutions. In such societies, the barriers to growth are mainly the result of conflicts of values rather than conflicts of interest.

In advanced societies such as our own the obstacles to growth are chiefly economic. They take such forms as labor immobility, capital immobility, and limitations on the proportion of resources that can be committed to capital goods production. As we examine these barriers more closely, we find that they are primarily the result of conflicts of interest rather than conflicts of values.

LABOR IMMOBILITY

We have learned in a number of places in this book that labor immobility has been an important factor contributing to depressed conditions in certain industries and regions. Two typical examples are agriculture and sawmilling in several low-income areas of the South. The fundamental causes of labor immobility are ignorance of alternative employment opportunities and the costs of movement. The latter include such noneconomic factors as families' reluctance to leave their hometowns. Although these obstacles to growth will never be entirely eliminated, their reduction helps significantly to clear the path for sustained economic development.

Ignorance of employment opportunities has decreased substantially over the past several decades. This has been accomplished through the development of free government employment services, improved information facilities pertaining to job openings, and a shift of population from rural to urban areas, where the knowledge of job opportunities is more readily available.

Reductions in the cost of movement, on the other hand, are more difficult to achieve. Long-distance moving costs, in relation to income, have declined over the years. But this is only one aspect of the problem. The cost of transferring from one occupation to another, or even from one job to another, may involve a temporary decline in income while new skills are being acquired. It may also involve a permanent loss of pension rights, seniority privileges, job security, and other fringe benefits. In addition, there may be costs of entry into new jobs in the form of high license fees or union initiation fees, long periods of apprenticeship at low pay, or restrictions on the number of people admitted to an occupation.

To some extent, the costs of movement have been absorbed by federal and state governments through the provision of training programs, unemployment benefits, and the like. These have reduced the costs of labor mobility as an obstacle to growth. However, note this important point:

> Care must be taken not to shift too much of the costs of labor mobility from workers to the government. Doing so

could result in excessive labor mobility. The result might be a waste of resources, as reflected in high transfer costs resulting from frequent retraining, breaking into new jobs, and so on. These are activities that can be undertaken more productively if the workers who benefit are made to bear some of the costs.

CAPITAL IMMOBILITY

The factors that make for immobility of capital, including money and capital goods, are fundamentally the same as those that cause immobility of labor. These are ignorance and the costs of movement.

Ignorance, where capital immobility is involved, may consist of inadequate information in such areas as new markets, changes in technology, or new methods of production, distribution, and finance. In general, the significance of ignorance as a barrier to capital movement has been reduced in recent decades as a result of the growing amount of diversified information and services provided by both government and private agencies. Among these are the Departments of Agriculture and Commerce, trade associations, business publishing houses, and consulting firms.

On the other hand, it is readily apparent that specialized plants and equipment are not easily adaptable to alternative uses (which is one type of capital immobility). As a result, there are significant cost barriers to the movement of capital. But cost barriers can also arise in less obvious ways, as when government policies "protect" and thereby immobilize capital. Examples of such policies are discriminatory taxes, tariffs, quotas, subsidies, and price supports. These protective devices are given to particular industries and sectors of the economy to shelter them from the adverse effects they would experience under unrestricted competition.

The economic implications of this are apparent:

The reduced mobility of capital that results from protective government policies can be overcome—but only at a price. The problem is whether society, and its elected representatives, can be made sufficiently aware of the price to decide whether paying it is worthwhile.

RESOURCE LIMITATIONS ON CAPITAL GOODS PRODUCTION

The U.S. economy is already highly capitalized. Consequently, a substantial share of present resources must be devoted merely to replacing existing plant and equipment as it wears out. A fundamental problem, therefore, is to find ways of increasing the proportion of resources that can be applied to the production of capital goods. This proportion must be over and above that needed to keep the existing stock of capital intact.

The problem is further compounded by the fact that our "standard" or *goal* of living seems to increase about as fast as our actual level of living. As a result, the more we have, the more we want. Therefore, the proportion of income saved does not appear to be rising over the long run, and may even be declining.

REMARK Be careful to observe that this statement refers to a *long-run period* during which all factors (in addition to income) that may affect consumption and saving are allowed to vary. Hence, it does not contradict the concept of the "consumption function." This, you recall, is a principle that applies only at a *given* time when all factors other than income which may affect consumption and saving are assumed to remain constant.

Is the overall percentage of income saved likely to decline in the future? There is good reason to believe that it will. Reduced savings are encouraged by many factors. Among them:

1. The increasing availability of easy credit and the growth in real assets per capita.

2. The expanding social welfare activities of government in providing for such contingencies as unemployment and old age.

3. The possible shift in the economic attitudes of society toward a more high-consumption, "live-it-up" philosophy.

In addition, there is probably a greater chance that income and inheritance tax rates will be raised in future years rather than lowered. If this happens, it will tend to make the distribution of income less unequal, and thereby reduce still further the proportion that is saved.

For all these reasons:

The saving ratio of the economy—the average propensity to save—will probably decline gradually over the years. This means that corporate and government saving and investment will have to become increasingly important, as is already the trend, if a steady rate of economic growth is to be sustained.

Problems of Taxation, Inflation, and Economic Growth

In previous chapters dealing with fiscal and monetary policies we talked about the effects of taxation and inflation on economic growth. A few additional comments are appropriate at this time. In general, there are two questions we want to answer:

1. What role might government tax policies play in contributing to the rate of economic growth?

2. How does inflation, which we have seen is closely tied to the problems of full employment and economic growth, fit into the picture?

TAXATION AND THE INVESTMENT DECISION

We have learned that increases in investment bring about increases in productivity. This helps to sustain economic growth. We have also learned from macroeconomic theory that the *expectation of profit* is the most important factor motivating businesses to invest. This means that the volume of investment can be increased by improving the expectation of profit, or by reducing the risk of loss, or both. Taxes can be a critical factor in this respect.

For instance, when the executives of a corporation contemplate making *any* investment, they consider, among other things, three important variables:

1. The corporation income tax rate.

2. The minimum accepted rate of return on the investment after taxes.

3. The expected rate of return on the investment before taxes.

The first of these factors is written into law by Congress and is therefore known.

The second factor is predetermined in each firm as a matter of top-level corporate financial policy. It is based on the different returns and risks that are available to a firm from its alternative investment opportunities. (If you should take a course in business or corporate finance, you will find that determining the minimum acceptable rate is the single most critical economic task facing the top management of a corporation.)

The third factor, which the firm compares with other investment alternatives before deciding on the one it wants, is determined directly from the previous two by a simple formula. Thus:

$$\text{expected rate of return before taxes} = \frac{\text{minimum accepted rate of return after taxes}}{1 - \text{tax rate}}$$

For example, suppose the management of a corporation believes that a minimum rate of return of 15 percent after taxes is necessary to persuade it to invest in a project (such as a machine or a plant). If the corporation income tax rate is 48 percent, the denominator in the formula above will be $1 - 0.48 = 0.52$. Hence, the expected rate of return before taxes must be *at least* $0.15/0.52 = 28.8$ percent for the investment

to be considered. On the other hand, if the tax rate were, say, 55 percent, the expected rate of return before taxes would have to be at least $0.15/0.45 = 33.3$ percent for the investment to be eligible for consideration. Evidently, the higher the tax rate, the higher must be the expected rate of return before taxes, as is apparent from the formula.

NOTE The formula should not be taken as a rigid guide, since factors besides the tax rate influence investment and expected returns. It is merely intended to convey some basic tendencies within reasonable tax ranges.

TAX IMPLICATIONS

You learned in macroeconomic theory that there is a relationship between risk and return. At a given level of risk there are fewer investment opportunities available at higher rates of return than at lower ones. Therefore, it follows from the rate-of-return formula that the volume of investment in plant and equipment will be influenced by the steepness of the corporation income tax. Thus:

> Other things being equal, higher corporation income-tax rates tend to raise the minimum required rate of return before taxes. This closes out many investment opportunities and reduces the total volume of investment. Conversely, lower corporation income tax rates tend to reduce the minimum required rate of return before taxes. This opens up many investment opportunities and increases the total volume of investment.

Does this mean that corporation income taxes should be abolished? The answer is no, because considerations other than growth must be taken into account. What it does mean, however, is that to finance a given level of government expenditures, alternative methods of raising revenue should be considered. Other forms of taxes, such as sales taxes or personal income taxes, even if set at higher rates, may be less injurious to investment and economic growth than the corporation income tax.

How much less injurious? The answer is not yet known. But we do know that the *marginal* tax rate on personal income plays a significant role. If the marginal tax rate—that is, the tax paid on an additional dollar of income—is high, the rate of economic growth may be retarded. Why? Because, other things being equal, high marginal tax rates tend to reduce the amount of personal savings and the incentive to invest among people in the higher-income brackets. To some extent, however, this tendency may be offset by the capital-gains provisions in our income-tax laws, which permit long-term profits on investment to be taxed at special lower rates.

Income Taxes or Sales Taxes?

The possibility that steep income tax rates may stifle economic growth has prompted many economists to advocate higher sales taxes as a partial substitute for higher income taxes. Most foreign governments, in fact, obtain the bulk of their revenues from sales taxes. The United States, on the other hand, derives most of its revenues from taxes on income and wealth. Various tax studies indicate that a sales tax that exempts food and medicine is approximately proportional—taking about the same share from all income groups. It may be, therefore, that a partial reduction in income taxes and an increase in sales taxes with selected exemptions would perhaps be a desirable step to take in seeking to sustain a target of economic growth.

INFLATION AND FORCED SAVING

The relation between inflation and economic growth has been the subject of much discussion. Too rapid a rate of inflation discourages saving and thereby sets a limit on the volume of investment. This, in turn, can inhibit economic growth.

It has long been known that one way in which an economy can finance its investment to encourage economic growth is by *forced saving*. This is a situation in which consumers are prevented from spending part of their income. Forced saving may take place in different situations. Among them:

1. When prices rise faster than money wages. This causes a decrease in real consumption and hence an increase in real (forced) saving.

2. When a corporation plows back some or all of its profit for investment instead of distributing it as dividend income to stockholders. This keeps stockholders from spending part of the income on consumption.

3. When a government taxes its citizens and uses the funds for investment. This prevents the public from utilizing a portion of its income for the purchase of consumer goods.

In the United States, all three forms of forced saving, especially the second, have helped to finance economic growth. Other nations, by contrast, have leaned more toward the first or third. For example, many countries have depended heavily on the printing press to run off the money they need to pay for investment. The outcome has been prolonged and severe inflation, resulting in the first form of forced saving. At the other extreme, the Soviet Union and China have placed heavy reliance on taxation to accumulate the funds needed for capital formation, thus placing greater dependence on the third form of forced saving.

CONCLUSION: "BALANCED" GROWTH

There is general agreement that a certain amount of inflation may be inevitable in our economy. This is because of its institutions and rigidities, its tendency to generate obsolescence, and its citizens' desire to raise their general standard of living at a rate at least as fast as the system's productive capacity. The problem, of course, is to hold back inflation to a rate that is compatible with sound economic growth. Too much inflation will impede economic growth, while excessive unsound growth will tend to promote inflation. Stated differently:

> If inflation is allowed to proceed at higher rates than is compatible with a desired growth rate, the internal structure of the economy may become distorted. That is, the relationships among firms, industries, and resources within the system can become less efficient. The result is that the economy achieves a type of unbalanced or disproportional growth. This might be analogous to a biological situation in which a person's nose or ears grow too fast or too slow in relation to each other and to the rest of the head. What we seek, of course, is a healthy or "balanced" form of growth.

What You Have Learned

1. For the United States, the long-run trend of total real GNP has been upward at an average annual rate of over 3 percent. The growth trend of real GNP per capita has averaged a little less than 2 percent annually. In general, the theory of economic growth, with the inclusion of technological advance, tends to be supported by the available evidence for the United States and for other advanced Western nations.

2. International comparisons of long-term growth rates show that the United States has grown more slowly than a number of other advanced nations. Since 1929, the expansion of qualitative factors such as education and technology has been relatively more important in influencing U.S. economic growth than the increase in such quantitative factors as the amount of labor and capital. Prior to 1929, the reverse was true.

3. "Growth" is a technical notion, which for measurement purposes involves the concept of compound interest. Compound-interest tables can be used to estimate growth, and a simple growth formula such as the Rule of 72 can be employed when tables are not readily available.

4. The real costs of economic growth are expressed in terms of the sacrifices that society must bear in order to achieve growth. These include such sacrifices as leisure for employment, consumption for investment, present for the future, environmental quality for more goods, and to some extent, security for progress. The optimum rate of growth equates the increased costs of more growth with the increased benefits.

5. The chief barriers to economic growth in advanced societies are conflicts of interest rather than conflicts of values. They consist of labor immobility, capital immobility, and limitations on the proportion of resources that can be committed to capital goods production.

6. In addition to the foregoing challenges to economic growth, there are problems of taxation and inflation. Increases in corporation income taxes tend to reduce the number of investment opportunities, while decreases in taxes tend to expand them. This and other considerations suggest that a partial substitution of increased sales taxes for increased income taxes, with special exemptions for food and medicine, would be more conducive to economic growth. As for inflation, historical evidence indicates that an average annual rate not exceeding 2 percent would be compatible with full employment and with a sustained "balanced" real growth of about 3 to 4 percent annually.

For Discussion

1. *Terms and concepts to review:*

   compound interest   "process of creative
   Rule of 72   destruction"
   forced saving

2. Outline briefly the major features of U.S. economic growth from the pre-Civil War period to the present.

3. From the standpoint of economic growth, is it better for our economy to invest relatively more of its resources in machines and factories, or should it concentrate instead on education and training? What are the "costs" of choosing either one? Discuss.

4. Can you develop a rule, analogous to the Rule of 72, which tells you how long it takes for an investment to increase by 50 percent? (SUGGESTION   Use the growth-rate table in this chapter as a guide, and some trial-and-error experiments.) Using your newly derived "rule," how much better off will your children (i.e., the next generation) be if we merely grow at 2 percent? In view of your answer, do you think that an increase in growth is worth the extra costs and sacrifices that must be incurred to attain it?

5. Evaluate the statement, "The more we grow or the faster we grow, the better off we are."

6. Would industrial progress, or economic development in general, be faster or slower in a perfectly certain, as compared with an uncertain, economy? (NOTE   A perfectly certain economy is one in which the nature and time of occurrence of all future events can be predicted with certainty.) Of what significance is your answer to a welfare-oriented economy which seeks to eliminate the risks of unemployment, bankruptcy, and so on?

7. Evaluate the following suggestions that have been made by various people:

   (a) "Labor mobility, and therefore economic growth, would be increased if the government simply absorbed all costs of moving, retraining, and the like."

   (b) "The government should 'protect' important industries through tariffs, subsidies, price supports, and so on, to encourage their development to the point where they can fend for themselves. This sort of policy would also encourage general economic growth."

8. "The government should reduce income taxes, thereby leaving more savings available for investment and economic growth." If the government followed this suggestion, how would it get the revenues it needs to finance its expenditures?

Issue
The Computer That Printed "Wolf"

When Thomas R. Malthus, the early nineteenth-century economist, predicted eventual disaster because the world population would outrun the food supply, many people branded him a crackpot. More than a hundred years elapsed before the Malthusian specter was widely recognized as a grim reality in many parts of the world. And even then, it took several decades before enough people began to concern themselves with it.

Two groups that have become very much concerned with the problem are the so-called "doomsayers" and their critics. The doomsayers are best represented by the Club of Rome, an international business association which sponsored two somber best-sellers, *The Limits to Growth* (Potomac Associates, 1972) and *Mankind at the Turning Point* (Dutton, 1974). Critics of the doomsayers include many economists as well as "futurologists." Among the latter group are Herman Kahn and his associates at the Hudson Institute, a private consulting firm specializing in long-range predictions.

Doomsayers: Shades of Malthus

The doomsayers use "system dynamics" to construct a computer model that simulates the conflict between economic growth and human survival. In *The Limits to Growth* the conclusion drawn is that continued progress must take man over the edge of the abyss and result in the end of civilization sometime during the last half of the next century.

The study, which aroused worldwide interest, rested on two basic propositions:

1. Five controlling variables—population, food production, industrialization, pollution, and consumption of nonrenewable natural resources—determine the course of economic growth. These variables are all interconnected; in the language of servomechanics, the variables interact on one another by means of "feedback loops."

2. The annual increase of the five controlling variables follows a pattern that mathematicians call exponential growth. This means that the variables expand at an accelerating rate, sometimes even geometrically, thereby doubling within certain time intervals.

Alternative Scenarios

The study shows that under different sets of assumptions, interactions among the five controlling variables trace out different growth paths. However, they always lead to the same end result: the eventual collapse of civilization around the year 2075, give or take as much as 25 years.

For example, what would happen if worldwide birth-control measures were introduced? A lowered birth rate would effectively increase per capita food production and capital investment. According to the computer model, population would then expand to take advantage of the larger food supply, while increased industrialization would accelerate the pollution crisis. Even a cut in the birth rate by as much as one-third (which is highly improbable) would, according to the study, delay the impending disaster by only 20 years at best.

Similar dire results are projected when other conditions of the model are allowed to vary. For instance, if new natural resources are developed, capital investment and industrialization will be encouraged. This will stimulate population growth—and eventual collapse from pollution. Alternatively, if pollution levels are reduced, population will grow and will absorb land that would otherwise be available for agriculture. Hence, if pollution doesn't put an end to civilization, starvation will.

And so it goes, with each possible scenario leading to eventual disaster, as typified by Chart (*a*). This shows what would happen if present trends continue. Chart (*b*), on the other hand, illustrates a stabilized world model

approaching a "steady-state" or an "equilibrium" condition. This is possible, according to the study, only if (1) average family size is limited to two children, (2) capital investment is limited to replacing worn-out equipment, and (3) technological innovations such as recycling and the development of longer-lasting machinery succeed in retarding the rate of resource depletion.

Recent Findings

The *Limits* study was published in 1972. Recognizing the embryonic nature of the report, two engineering-systems scientists, M. Mesarovic and E. Pestel, turned out a revised and updated project two years later: *Mankind at the Turning Point.* Supported by a team of about sixty collaborators and consultants, the authors of the newer study again look at the world through a computer. However, instead of treating the entire globe as an undifferentiated unit, Mesarovic and Pestel construct a world model with ten regions, some developed and some underdeveloped. Using "scenario analysis"—the insertion of specific decisions in the model (such as the amount of foreign aid, investment, price of oil, etc.)—alternative policies are tested by projecting their long-term consequences. As in the earlier study, the conclusions reached in the more recent study are almost equally pessimistic: prolonged regional starvation in the underdeveloped world—particularly in South Asia—and regional, if not world, collapse, perhaps by the middle of the next century.

Can anything be done to prevent this? Perhaps, say the authors of *Mankind at the Turning Point.* The most significant step is for the overcrowded, underdeveloped countries to formulate some sort of "population-equilibrium" policy. Failure to do so, Mesarovic and Pestel believe, will drown the underdeveloped nations in a "sea of humanity."

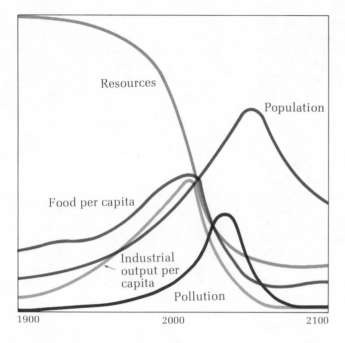

Chart (a). *If present trends continue.*

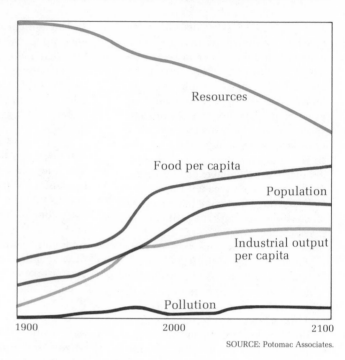

SOURCE: Potomac Associates.

Chart (b). *Approaching a "steady state" equilibrium.*

Zapping the Doomsayers

If it is possible for one book to be the opposite of another, *The Next 200 Years* (New York: Morrow, 1976), by Herman Kahn of the Hudson Institute, is the opposite of both *The Limits to Growth* and *Mankind at the Turning Point.* Kahn believes that the 200-year time frame imposes no limits to what technology can accomplish because, "In our view, the resources of the earth will be more than sufficient—with a wide margin of safety—to sustain, for an indefinite period of time and at high living standards, the level of population and economic growth we project." In a more recent book, *World Economic Development and Beyond* (Westview Press, 1979), Kahn reiterates this belief.

The main conclusions of both books can be summarized briefly:

○ World population growth will slow down as living standards in poor countries rise. Total world population will stabilize at about 15 billion—ap-

proximately four times the present level—although the earth will be able to accommodate a population of 30 billion or even more as resources become more plentiful.

○ The supply of raw materials will be more than ample to fuel the world's rising standard of living. Newfound reserves of petroleum, iron, phosphates, and other materials will expand by multiples of present levels—just as in the past. And if conventional farming is not capable of providing sufficient food, advanced technology will make up the difference. "Food will be extracted from almost any organic matter, including wood, leaves, cellulose, petroleum and even agricultural wastes."

○ Pollution will also be alleviated by technology. Indeed, "we believe that in time society will be able to cope with any technological problem," say Kahn and his associates. As a result, the world will be very rich by the end of the next century. There will be

widespread abundance of material things, and even the poorest countries will be better off, in GNP per capita, than Americans are today.

Conclusion: Quantity Versus Quality

In light of these conflicting viewpoints, is economic growth—the expansion of the nation's output or economic pie—good or bad? The issues are dramatic, and the answers are by no means simple. But there is much that is fruitful in the controversy. The "anti-growthers" force us to question the values of growth and to recognize the social costs that a heedless consumption of resources may entail. The "pro-growthers" point out that growth (rather than redistribution) will eventually eliminate poverty, and that only affluent countries can afford social services such as public assistance and free medical care for the needy. The poor countries have not achieved the rates or levels of growth that are required to provide these forms of redistribution.

But what about the *quality* of life in the next century? All things considered, the fact that the earth may be able to support a much larger population, as Kahn and his associates contend, is not necessarily the point. More fundamental is the kind of life that a larger population will experience. The idea was well expressed by the British philosopher and economist John Stuart Mill more than a century ago:

> A population may be too crowded, though all be amply supplied with food and raiment.... If the earth must lose that great portion of its pleasantness which it owes to things that the unlimited increase of wealth and population would extirpate from it, for the mere purpose of enabling it to support a larger, but not happier or a better population, I sincerely hope, for the sake of posterity, that they will be content to be stationary long before necessity compels them to it.

Hudson Institute.

Herman Kahn of the Hudson Institute: "There will be no scarcity of food in the next 200 years. If output from conventional farming isn't sufficient, let 'em eat waste."

QUESTIONS

1. The only way for us to avoid eventual self-destruction, according to the doomsayers, is to achieve world equilibrium. Is this possible without a great deal of inequality?

2. A hundred years ago, doomsayers' models like those described would quite literally have concluded that the cities of today would be asphyxiated beneath mountains of horse manure. (a) Why has this not happened? (b) What does your answer suggest about the shortcomings of such models?

3. Do you see any subtle assumptions in the doomsayers' models that are similar to the Malthusian model? Explain.

4. The doomsayers' models omit prices of resources as a strategic variable. Of what significance is this?

5. Kahn's study, *The Next 200 Years*, does not distinguish between technological feasibility and economic feasibility. Is such a distinction important?

Chapter 18

The Less Developed Countries: Special Growth Problems of Nations in Poverty

Chapter Preview

What are the chief economic characteristics of less developed countries? How do these countries compare economically with the more advanced nations?

Can a set of principles and policies be developed to provide a framework for analyzing the process of development?

What major forms of assistance have been provided to the less developed countries? Has this assistance been effective? What problems should be understood if foreign aid is to achieve the desired objectives?

While millions of inhabitants of advanced industrial nations worry about eating too much, several billion people in dozens of poverty-stricken countries worry about starving. These countries comprise most of Latin America, Africa, and Asia. It is here that most of the 3 billion citizens of the underdeveloped world live, most of them ill fed, poorly housed, and illiterate.

What is the economic destiny of nations in poverty? Because the poor nations contain three-fourths of the world's population, it is the affluent nations that are in the minority. Hence, it is important to understand both the problems faced by poor countries, and the measures that can be taken to help solve these problems.

As we shall see, nations in poverty are part of the larger study of economic growth and development. But there are international implications as well. Although there is no explicit or unified theory of economic development, some of today's most significant insights stem from Adam Smith's *The Wealth of Nations* (1776). This was written before the main thrust of the industrial revolutions, but after many important agricultural revolutions.

The Meaning of Economic Development

The poor nations are usually referred to as *less developed countries* (LDCs), underdeveloped countries, or developing countries. They are usually characterized by the following conditions:

○ Poverty levels of income (typically defined as less than $500 per capita annually), and hence little or no saving.

○ High rates of population growth.

○ Substantial majorities of the labor force employed in agriculture.

○ Low rates of adult literacy.

○ Extensive *disguised unemployment*. This is a situation in which employed resources (usually labor resources) are not being used in their most efficient ways. The concept is also known as *underemployment*.

○ Heavy reliance on one or a few items (mainly agricultural) for export.

○ Government control by a wealthy elite, which often opposes any changes that would harm its economic interests.

Among underdeveloped nations, these characteristics are tendencies rather than certainties. Exceptions can be found to all of them.

How many countries of the world are considered to be "less developed"? Which ones are they? From time to time the United Nations has designated dozens of countries as LDCs. Among them are Indonesia, Burma, India, Pakistan, Egypt, Nigeria, Syria, Morocco, Paraguay, Ecuador, Honduras, Turkey, and Colombia. (See Exhibit 1.)

WHAT IS ECONOMIC DEVELOPMENT?

The fundamental challenge facing the poor countries is to transform their economies from an underdeveloped to a developed status. Economic development is a process by which a nation attains an upward movement or transformation of its entire socioeconomic system. This means that there are improvements in the quality of resources as well as positive changes in attitudes, institutions, and values.

This is what economic development means. However, this explanation is more of a description than a definition. For economic purposes, a more precise statement is needed:

Economic development is the process whereby a nation's real per capita output or income (its GNP) increases over a long period of time. A nation's rate of economic development is thus measured by its per capita rate of economic growth.

A few words are needed to appreciate the implications of this definition.

1. By stating that economic development is a "process," we are referring to the idea that it is a continuous action or series of changes taking place in a definite manner. This suggests that certain causal forces are at work. These must be identified so that their influences on a nation's economic development can be understood.

2. By stating that economic development is measured on a "per capita" basis, we are correcting for population change. In this way, the fact is recognized that a nation which experiences an increase in total real output is not necessarily better off materially. The gain in output must more than offset any increase in population so that there are more goods for everyone.

3. By saying that economic development takes place over a "long period of time," we are distinguishing between the short and long run. A short-run spurt in economic growth may be the result of fortuitous circumstances, whereas a long-run expansion in production is generally the result of fundamental change. Thus, it is one thing for a society to experience an increase in real per capita output over a period of several years. It is quite another to sustain the increase for perhaps a decade or more.

In addition to increases in real income per capita, there are other objectives of economic development. Among these are greater equality in the distribution of income, a rising minimum level of income, and reduction of disguised unemployment. However, these are generally regarded as secondary goals—mainly because they are strongly influenced in each country by existing social structures and institutions. Therefore, in a country undergoing development, there is some likelihood that these secondary goals will be at least partially attained if the primary goal of a sustained increase in real income per capita—and more broadly an upward movement of the entire social system—is realized.

A STUDY IN CONTRASTS

It is useful to compare the gap, at different points in time, between per capita incomes in the less developed and the advanced countries. This enables us to see whether the gulf has widened, narrowed, or remained the same. Economists frequently make such comparisons, and the results are astonishing:

Over the long run, the income gap between the richest countries and the poorest ones has been widening. Indeed, in some periods the multiple has been as much as 15 or 20. As a result, an increasing proportion of all goods and services—now more than 80 percent—is produced in countries where less than 25 percent of the world's population lives.

Exhibit 1
The Less Developed Countries

Most of the less developed countries are in the Southern Temperate Zone—between the Tropics of Cancer and Capricorn. These countries comprise the underdeveloped world. Of course, there are degrees of underdevelopment, ranging from severe to relatively moderate.

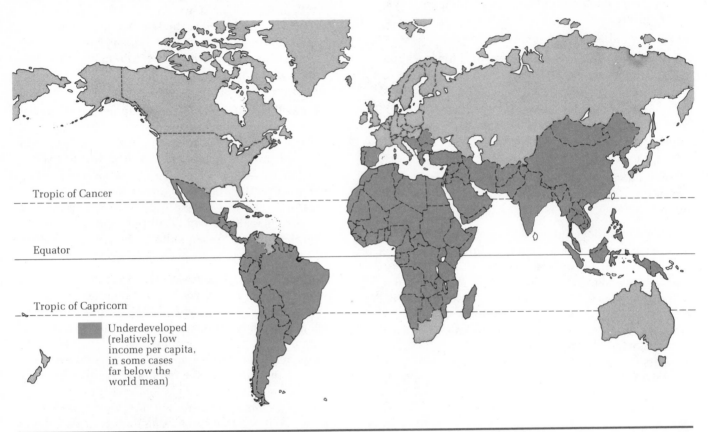

Tropic of Cancer

Equator

Tropic of Capricorn

■ Underdeveloped (relatively low income per capita, in some cases far below the world mean)

This trend portends serious consequences for the world community. However, it is not enough simply to measure differences in the economic progress of nations. We must see clearly why these differences occur. This requires us to understand the factors determining a nation's economic development. These factors include the quantity and quality of human and natural resources, the rate of capital accumulation, the degree of specialization and scale of production, and the rate of technological progress. They also include environmental factors, namely, the political, social, cultural, and economic framework within which growth and development take place. Once we comprehend the significance of these factors, it becomes easy to appreciate why the rich nations are getting richer while the poor ones are getting relatively poorer.

This point can be illustrated by comparing the United States with most underdeveloped countries. The United States has a large labor force with a relatively high proportion of skilled workers. Its business leaders are numerous and disciplined. It has a substantial and diversified quantity of natural resources, an extensive system of transportation and power, an efficient and productive technology financed by an adequate supply of savings, and a stable and comparatively uncorrupt government. And, not to be overlooked, it has a culture in which the drive for profit and material gain is generally accepted. These factors in combination have stimulated America's economic development.

In the less developed countries, on the other hand, most of these conditions are absent. Labor is largely unskilled and inefficient, and is often chronically ill and undernourished. Saving is small or even negative, resulting in low rates of investment and capital accumulation. The cultural environment favors the clergy, the military, or government administration, while frowning upon commerce, finance, and entrepreneurship. And government is often unstable or, if stable, dictatorial, corrupt, and inefficient. Paradoxically, many poor countries are rich in natural resources. However, because most of these countries lack the other ingredients, they cannot sustain economic development.

Stages of Development

The primary challenge of economic development is to get the less developed countries started on a path toward rising real income per capita. This task usually requires a major transformation of the economic and social structures of LDCs. You can gain some appreciation of what such a transformation entails by observing the stages of growth through which an LDC might pass as it progresses from underdeveloped to fully developed status.

W. W. Rostow, a distinguished economic historian who also served as special assistant to several Presidents, has constructed "models" of economic development. They consist of five phases that characterize the growth of nations. These phases are shown in Exhibit 2.

STAGE 1: THE TRADITIONAL SOCIETY

The traditional stage is the earliest form of a society's development. In this period the economy is largely primitive. It is characterized by three major conditions:

1. There is an absence of modern science and technology.

2. Resources are overallocated in agriculture and underallocated in manufacturing.

3. A rigid social structure exists which impedes economic change.

As a result of these conditions, productivity is low and real income or output per capita is barely at a subsistence level.

In terms of history, some countries and regions that belonged to the traditional stage of development included the dynasties of China, the civilizations of the Middle East and the Mediterranean, and the countries of medieval Europe.

Exhibit 2
The Stages of Development

The process of economic development, as explained by Rostow, can be divided into five stages. The model provides useful insights into the changes that occur as a nation is transformed from a traditional to a technically progressive society.

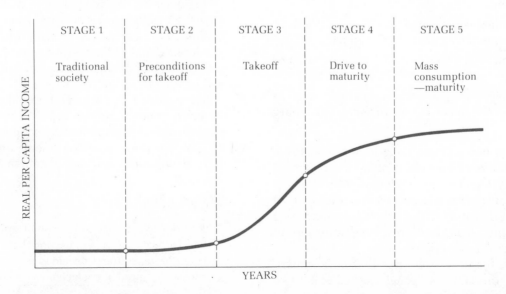

STAGE 2: THE PRECONDITIONS FOR TAKEOFF

The second stage is transitional. It is a period in which the conditions needed for upward movement are being formed. The chief characteristics of this period may be noted:

1. New scientific techniques are being applied to agriculture and manufacturing.

2. Financial institutions, such as banks, are emerging to mobilize capital and provide funds for new investment.

3. Improvements in transportation and communication are occurring, permitting a widening of commerce.

At the same time a fundamental political change—the building of a centralized national state—is taking place. Although low-productivity methods are still widespread, there may be some cases in which traditional activities exist side by side with modern ones. Obstacles to development are gradually being overcome, but real income or output per capita is rising slowly.

Historically, these conditions occurred in western Europe during the breakup of the Middle Ages. Today the majority of poor nations are in this stage of development.

STAGE 3: THE TAKEOFF

The third stage of development—the takeoff—is the great watershed of economic growth. It occurs when the old obstacles and resistances to steady expansion are finally overcome. Some important conditions that characterize this stage are these:

1. Modern technology and organizational methods in agriculture and industry are being adopted.

2. Net investment is rising, usually toward levels of roughly 10 percent of national income.

3. There is a birth of major new industries, which in turn stimulates the development of many subsidiary industries.

While this is happening, the agricultural sector is likely to be undergoing a revolutionary improvement in productivity. Labor is being released to work in the cities while farms are providing raw materials to meet the expanding demands of the industrial sector. As a result of all these conditions, real income or output per capita begins to rise significantly.

Historically, for those countries that have experienced takeoff, this stage has usually lasted about two or three decades. In Britain, for example, it covered most of the last quarter of the eighteenth century. In the United States and France, it occurred during the three decades preceding 1860. In Germany, it took place during the third quarter of the nineteenth century. In Japan, it covered the fourth quarter of the nineteenth century. And in Canada and the Soviet Union, it occurred during the quarter-century preceding the outbreak of World War I. In recent decades, several other countries, including Brazil, Egypt, Israel, Lebanon, Mexico, and Taiwan, appear to have reached the takeoff stage.

In general:

> The takeoff stage is a period in which savings are rising, there is an expanding entrepreneurial class capable of directing savings into new investment, and the economy is exploiting hitherto unused natural resources and methods of production.

STAGE 4: THE DRIVE TO MATURITY

After takeoff there follows a new stage—the drive to maturity. This is a period of sustained, if fluctuating, progress as modern technology is extended over a wide range of economic activity. Several important features of this period may be noted:

1. Investment in new plant and equipment is maintained at a relatively high rate, usually between 10 and 20 percent of national income.

2. The rapid rate of investment permits the growth of output to exceed the increase in population.

3. The economy assumes a significant role in world trade as new import requirements arise and new export commodities are developed.

On the whole, this is a period in which the economy undergoes significant structural changes as production techniques improve, the growth of new industries accelerates, and older industries level off. As a consequence, society experiences sustained increases in real income or output per capita.

Historically, it has taken advanced countries about 40 years to complete the drive to maturity. Britain, France, and the United States accomplished it during the last four decades of the nineteenth century. None of the developing countries, of course, has yet reached this stage.

In general terms:

> The drive to maturity is a period of resource diversification. The economy moves beyond the industries that initiated the takeoff and develops the capacity and technology to produce efficiently a broad range of commodities.

STAGE 5: MASS CONSUMPTION—MATURITY

The final stage of development is reached with the coming of high mass consumption. As a society achieves this level of maturity, several things happen:

1. An increasing proportion of resources is directed to the production of consumers' durables and services.

2. The percentage of skilled workers in the labor force and the percentage of urban to total population rise.

3. A progressively larger share of resources is allocated to society's welfare and security.

The stage of mass consumption is thus an age of affluence. For the United States, this period began around the end of World War I (1918). But it was in the years after World Wars I and II (1945) that the signs became most evident. A large-scale migration from rural to urban areas, from farms to factories, occurred as people became increasingly aware of and anxious to share the consumption fruits of a mature economy. Automobiles, major appliances, and social welfare services became widely diffused as real income or output per person rose to the point where society could afford to have more than just basic necessities.

In the 1950s western Europe and Japan entered this stage. The Soviet Union became technically ready for it during that period. However, political and social problems of adjustment faced by Communist leaders have often retarded the launching of this phase.

CONCLUSION: TWO SHORTCOMINGS

Does Rostow's model of the stages of development provide useful insights into the development process? There is no doubt that it does. However, the model suffers from at least two important shortcomings. These may impede its use as a guide for formulating public policy.

1. Economic development cannot be divided into precise stages. Growth is a continuous process, not a discrete one. Therefore, any attempt to separate it into distinct periods must be highly arbitrary. No two individuals viewing the past growth of a society would necessarily agree on the exact points at which one stage ended and another began. Nor would any two individuals necessarily agree on whether the society even experienced a particular stage.

2. It is not necessary for investment to rise rapidly before sustained growth can take place, as occurs in Rostow's takeoff stage. Some countries have experienced steady development resulting from gradually rising levels of investment over a long period. Nor is it necessary for an agricultural revolution—a modern-ization of farming techniques—to precede an industrial revolution in order for resources to be transferred from the rural to the industrial sector. As you shall see, experiences of LDCs since World War II indicate that agriculture and industry may expand simultaneously while sustained development is taking place.

In conclusion, therefore:

Rostow's model of the stages of development provides many useful insights into the changes that occur as a country is transformed from a traditional to a technically progressive society. Hence, the model should be viewed in this light, not as a precise explanation of a historical process.

Some Principles and Problems of Development

Although there is no single or unified theory of development, various principles and policies would undoubtedly serve as ingredients if such a theory should ever evolve. Moreover, a modern theory would have to embrace several social sciences rather than economics alone. This will become evident as we discuss the following important concepts and issues of development theory:

1. The need for agricultural development.

2. Escaping from the "population trap."

3. Investing in physical capital.

4. Investing in human capital.

5. Labor-intensive versus capital-intensive projects.

6. Small versus large projects.

7. Private versus social profitability.

THE NEED FOR AGRICULTURAL DEVELOPMENT

In underdeveloped countries the great bulk of human resources is devoted to agriculture. These resources tend to be inefficiently employed. As a result, there is a great deal of disguised unemployment or "underemployment."

Agriculture, for the most part, produces the nation's food and raw materials. Therefore, for economic development to take place out of domestic resources, agricultural efficiency must improve. This is necessary in order to produce a surplus of output over and above what the agricultural sector itself consumes. As this happens, human and material resources are spared from farms to work in manufacturing. This helps to expand the industrial sector while consuming the surplus of the agricultural sector.

This suggests a proposition of fundamental importance in economic development:

In most LDCs there is a close relationship between the agricultural and industrial sectors. The relationship is such that the growth of the industrial sector is strongly influenced by prior and/or simultaneous technical progress in the agricultural sector.

The operation of this important principle has been amply demonstrated in economic history. For example, the development of towns during the Middle Ages was accompanied by, and to a significant extent preceded by, improved methods of agricultural production. Notable was the adoption of the three-field system. And the industrial revolution of the eighteenth and nineteenth centuries in Europe and the United States was strongly influenced by an agricultural revolution. This was marked by a number of major innovations, including the introduction of root crops, horse-hoeing husbandry, four-course rotation, and scientific animal breeding. These developments were of such great importance that they actually overshadowed in certain respects the accompanying industrial revolutions. (See Box 1.)

Land Reform

Agricultural development rarely occurs without land reform. In many underdeveloped countries, agricultural land is owned by a few rich people but is farmed by large numbers of poor families. Proponents of land reform have almost always advocated the division of land ownership among the families working it. Presumably, the broadening of ownership would yield important psychological and political values as well as economic incentives.

The evidence, however, does not always bear this out. Various studies of land reform have found that the fragmenting of land ownership by itself may actually reduce farm productivity rather than raise it. This is true unless land reform is accompanied by other measures. These include:

1. The implementation of new farming techniques, such as improvements in plant strains, irrigation systems, and fertilization programs.

2. The increased availability of credit—through the creation of local banks or cooperative credit societies—for investment-minded farmers.

The need for these agricultural reforms is readily seen:

Legislation that breaks up large landholdings will also eliminate landlords, and therefore the services they provide. These are mainly tools and credit. Hence, land reform must be accompanied not only by the provision of sufficient technical and financial resources to replace what is lost, but it must also provide for the enhancement of agricultural productivity.

ESCAPING FROM THE "POPULATION TRAP"

To solve their economic problems, the less developed countries must either avoid or extricate themselves from the "population trap." That is, their real GNP must continue to increase faster than their population.

Although not all underdeveloped countries are "overpopulated," most of them are. In poor regions in Asia, parts of Latin America, and Africa, population presses heavily on physical resources. Accumulation, or saving, is therefore difficult because the level of production is low and resources are committed primarily to agriculture in order to produce the bare necessities of consumption. As long as the pressure on food supplies continues, large numbers of people must subsist at the barest survival level, making it extremely difficult if not impossible for the nation to extricate itself from the population trap.

What can be done to alleviate the problem? One approach, of course, would be for large numbers of people to emigrate from overpopulated to underpopulated regions. But numerous legal, social, and economic obstacles make this solution unfeasible.

The most practical alternative is to meet the population problem head-on. Various studies have demonstrated quite conclusively that it is cheaper to increase real incomes per capita by slowing population growth than by investing in new factories, irrigation, and so on. Studies have also shown that it is not so much the absolute *size* of the population as the population growth *rate* that lessens improvements in real income per capita. Because of this, a number of developing countries, including Indonesia, Taiwan, India, and Pakistan, have instituted family-planning programs. These have ranged from simple counseling services to large-scale voluntary sterilization schemes (usually vasectomies). A chief difficulty is that any population-control scheme may interfere with local religious traditions, thereby impeding if not preventing the development of effective programs.

An interesting *economic* approach to the problem is proposed in Exhibit 3. Although it is not likely that such a plan would ever be adopted, it provides a thought-provoking exercise for discussion.

Box 1

Agricultural Development and Economic Growth: A Novel Interpretation

It is an instructive exercise in the interpretation of economic history to consider how far the discovery of root crops (e.g., the turnip) is responsible for the development of the past three centuries.

Root crops did two main things: They eliminated the "fallow field" and they made scientific animal breeding possible. The fallow field was necessary to eliminate weeds, and the practice of planting roots in rows between which horses could hoe the ground made the fallow field unnecessary. Also, the roots enabled the farmer to feed his stock through the winter and thereby prevented the monstrous slaughter at Christmas. This made selective breeding possible, with astounding results.

1. The increased production of food probably was the principal cause of the amazing fall in mortality, especially infant mortality, in the middle years of the eighteenth century. Most of the rise in population of the Western world was due to this.

2. The extra food enabled more babies to live and thus provided the inhabitants for the industrial cities.

3. The new techniques enabled agriculture to produce a large surplus and thus made it possible to feed the hungry mouths of the new towns. Thus, even if there had been no startling changes in industrial techniques, it is probable that the agricultural revolution itself would have produced many of the phenomena we usually associate with the industrial revolution. And it is possible that the vast developments in agricultural techniques that have taken place in recent decades may foreshadow a new revolution in economic life as great as that of the last century.

SOURCE: Adapted with some changes from Kenneth E. Boulding, *Economic Analysis*, 3rd ed., New York, Harper & Row, 1955, p. 719n.

U.S.D.A. photograph.

U.S. farming methods, geared to big farms, heavy mechanization, and few farmers, often are not easily adaptable to conditions in many of the developing countries. These have many small farms that are intensively cultivated by large numbers of farmers.

Burt Glinn © Magnum Photos.

Over half the farms in most developing countries are under 12 acres in size. The type of agricultural revolution that is needed in these countries in order to make these farms as productive as those in Western nations is to provide farmers with the right incentives and the necessary agricultural inputs.

Exhibit 3
Can Population Be Controlled Through the Price System?

Can the price system be used to help plan the size of a nation's population?

Population control might be exercised through the sale of "birth rights." The government, for example, might decide that each married couple should be entitled to two "free births." Beyond that, a couple would have to pay a price if they wanted to have more children. How much would they have to pay? The answer depends on the current market price of "birth rights" or certificates, each certificate permitting a woman to have one completed pregnancy.

The government would issue a fixed amount of these certificates for a period of time. Hence, the supply curve S would be a vertical line. However, the demand curve D would be normal or downward-sloping. Through the free interaction of supply and demand, the equilibrium price would settle at P and the corresponding equilibrium quantity at Q.

Over a period of time, income (and perhaps population) would grow. Therefore, the demand curve would shift rightward to D'. The government might then decide to issue additional certificates, as shown by the new supply curve S'. This would result in a different equilibrium price at P' and equilibrium quantity at Q'. The additional certificates the government decided to issue would depend on the degree of control it wished to exercise over the market price and the size of the population.

QUESTION What are some of the social and economic difficulties in implementing such a system?

SUPPLY OF, AND DEMAND FOR, "BIRTH RIGHTS"

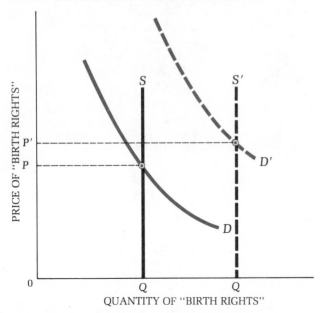

INVESTING IN PHYSICAL CAPITAL

Many economists and government officials used to believe that massive infusions of capital were alone sufficient to induce economic development. Increases in real output, it was contended, were attributable almost entirely to expansions in the stock of capital rather than to increases in labor employment or improvements in technology.

Why this unusual assumption? The answer is based on the economic concept of *marginal productivity*. This is defined as the increase in output resulting from a unit change in a variable input while all other inputs are held fixed. This concept is associated with the famous *law of diminishing returns* (the formal meaning of which you can look up in the Dictionary at the back of the book). In simplest terms, the law tells you that the more you have of a particular type of resource, the less productive or useful is one more unit of it.

Now, because most underdeveloped countries have an excess of labor, the marginal productivity of labor in such countries is low or close to zero (or perhaps even negative). And because most underdeveloped countries have an insufficient amount of capital, the marginal productivity of capital is high. Consequently, the infusion of large doses of capital appeared to be the most effective means of raising real GNP per capita.

This conclusion, although largely correct, has been greatly modified over the years. Research studies and experiences in less developed countries during the past several decades have revealed some interesting findings:

1. There are limits to the amount of new capital that LDCs can "absorb" or utilize effectively in any given period. These limits are set by such factors as the availability of related skilled labor and the level of effective demand for the output of the new capital. It does little good, obviously, to build a railroad if there is not enough skilled labor to operate and maintain it, and enough demand to support it.

2. The marginal productivity of farm labor may be low because it is employed in densely populated areas where arable land is relatively scarce. Yet in many LDCs large sections of fairly fertile lands are underpopulated for cultural, political, or locational reasons. Of course, some injections of capital may help. But increases in output would be greater if the infusions of capital were accompanied by shifts of farm labor from overpopulated to underpopulated areas.

As a general rule, therefore:

Both extra capital and extra, but related, labor are needed to obtain extra output. The notion that in the

LDCs the marginal productivity of capital is high while that of labor is low is undoubtedly correct. However, it is true only in an overall sense. When used in proper combinations, the marginal productivities of *related* classes of labor and capital are likely to be quite high.

INVESTING IN HUMAN CAPITAL

Investments in physical capital must be accompanied by investments in human capital if increased productivity is to accelerate economic development. The "quality" of a people, as measured by its skills, education, and health, is more important than its quantity in influencing a nation's cultural and economic progress. It is no accident that the populations of advanced countries have higher average levels of education and longer life spans than those of underdeveloped countries.

Four main areas call for particular attention:

1. *Emphasis on Basic Technical Training*   Underdeveloped countries usually suffer from a glut of unskilled workers and a shortage of skilled workers. These nations should place more emphasis on vocational instruction and less on academic training. For example, primary and secondary school curricula should be oriented toward technical education and on-the-job training in such fields as agriculture, commerce, industry, and construction. This would be more useful than concentrating on preparing students for passing entrance examinations at universities in Britain, France, and the United States.

2. *Development of Middle-Level Skills*   Most LDCs suffer from a relative shortage of people with middle-level as compared to high-level skills. For example, there is a relatively greater need for technicians than for scientists and engineers. To enhance productivity, universities and educational institutes should focus on the development of these middle-level skills.

3. *Utilization of Foreign Experts*   The LDCs have long suffered from a serious "brain drain." This results when their talented younger people going to universities in advanced nations remain there instead of returning to their home countries, where they are desperately needed. Underdeveloped nations may not always be able to eliminate this form of emigration. However, they can minimize it by making greater use of foreign experts in domestic education and training programs.

4. *Investment in Public Health*   Large-scale health programs are needed to reduce disease and mortality rates in LDCs. Of course, reductions in mortality rates result in greater population growth. This adds to the burden of people pressing against limited resources.

The solution, however, is not to reduce public health, but to supplement it with voluntary birth-control programs. Only when men and women gain some degree of control over their lives does investment in human capital become a force for cultural as well as economic change.

LABOR-INTENSIVE VERSUS CAPITAL-INTENSIVE PROJECTS

Should an underdeveloped country that is trying to industrialize concentrate on labor-using or capital-using investment projects? This question can be addressed in terms of what may conveniently be called a "labor-intensity" versus a "capital-intensity" criterion.

1. *Labor-Intensity Criterion*   This contends that where labor is excessive relative to capital, emphasis should be placed on projects that make maximum use of the abundant factor of production, that is, labor, and minimum use of the scarce factor, that is, capital. Such an approach will tend to reduce the degree of disguised unemployment while increasing industrial output.

2. *Capital-Intensity Criterion*   This holds that capital-using projects should be favored even if labor is excessive. The reason is that the potential gains in productivity that are achieved by maximizing the amount of capital per worker will more than offset the loss of output resulting from unemployment. This is particularly true, it is argued, when the developing country must face competition for its manufactured products from more advanced industrial economies.

To a considerable extent, the controversy over labor-intensive versus capital-intensive investments is academic and shows a lack of understanding of the real nature of modern manufacturing processes. In most industries there is little room for substitution between capital and labor. This is because production processes within plants are predetermined by technology. Combinations of labor and capital are established by engineering rather than economic requirements. A given plant is designed with a predetermined capacity to be operated by a certain number of workers. Although some variations in output may be made within a single-shift operation, multiple shifts are the only way in which large changes in output can be realized.

These facts suggest the following conclusions:

The labor-intensity versus capital-intensity criterion is usually of little practical value in implementing investment decisions within a particular industry. On the other hand, the criterion assumes greater realism when it is used to compare *interindustry* investments for the purpose of noting which projects will tend to be more labor-using (or capital-saving) and which more capital-using (or labor-saving). Such comparisons can help in deciding the types of industries that should be promoted by a developing country.

Some practical implications of this are shown in Exhibit 4.

SMALL VERSUS LARGE PROJECTS

Should LDCs try to develop large and complex production operations, or should they concentrate first on small-scale industries? Practical considerations favor the latter approach. In most underdeveloped countries it is highly probable that one or more of the necessary ingredients of industrialization is lacking. These include adequate capital, transportation facilities, suitable marketing channels, modern technical knowledge, and effective managerial skills.

Small projects demand fewer of the scarce ingredients. At the same time, they develop needed entrepreneurship, can be instituted more rapidly, and can begin to impart their beneficial economic effects to the community more quickly. Large industrial projects, on the other hand, have less chance of succeeding under these conditions, and their payoffs in terms of economic benefits to the nation are likely to lie far in the future.

The limitations of this conclusion must be recog-

Exhibit 4
Fashions in Economic Development

For many underdeveloped countries, the desire for prestige often eclipses the need for logic. The fact that the governments of many LDCs want the most modern and "fashionable" investments—regardless of how well they mesh with domestic economic needs and resources—often comes as a great shock to American economists serving as first-time consultants to these countries.

For example, there is hardly an underdeveloped country that does not have an international airline consisting of a fleet of U.S.-built jet aircraft; a modern steel mill, the ore and fuel for which must usually be imported from other countries; and an automobile assembly plant, which turns out new cars at prices two or three times higher than in the advanced countries.

These inefficient industries are protected by high tariffs and low import quotas. But the real costs, of course, are borne by the people at home.

Ethiopian Airlines.

A Boeing 707 of Ethiopian Airlines.

Jerry Frank, DPI.

Automobile assembly plant in Paraguay.

Information Service of India.

Durgapur steelworks in West Bengal.

nized, however. The distinction between "small" and "large" projects is not always clear-cut. Moreover, such projects are often complementary rather than competitive. A large manufacturing plant, for instance, will frequently stimulate the development of many small plants to provide parts and services. Hence, it cannot be stated as a firm rule that one size or scale of manufacturing is always preferable to another.

As a practical matter, the alternatives must be identified and measured in each case. For certain types of manufacturing, a large, integrated production process may be necessary in order to gain economies that will permit internationally competitive pricing. For other types of manufacturing, differences in scale may hinge on factors other than productive efficiency. Some considerations are size of market and availability of the right type of labor supply. Thus in many LDCs, modern manufacturing plants and paved roads have been provided by foreign aid, while ox-drawn wagons are used to transport the goods. Clearly, therefore, cost is not the only factor to be considered when deciding on the size of the plant to be constructed.

PRIVATE VERSUS SOCIAL PROFITABILITY

Every real investment yields two kinds of returns. One may be called the "private" rate of return; the other can be referred to as the "social" rate of return. Under certain theoretical conditions they may be identical. In reality, however, they usually differ, sometimes by a wide margin. Let us see why.

The *private rate of return* on an investment is the financial rate. This is the rate that business managers try to anticipate prior to investing their funds. It is therefore the same as the *marginal efficiency of investment* studied in macroeconomic theory. In simplest terms, the private rate of return is the expected net profit after taxes and all costs, including depreciation. The rate may be expressed as a percentage annual return upon either the total cost of the project or upon the net worth of the stockholder-owners. From the viewpoint of investors, this rate is the most important criterion, because it measures the profitability of the investment.

The *social rate of return* is the net value of the project to the economy. The social rate is estimated on the basis of the net increase in output that a project, such as a new industry, may be expected to bring, directly or indirectly, to the area being developed. The industry's contribution is measured by subtracting from the value of what it produces the cost to society of the resources used. Therefore, the concept of a social rate of return is that of a net return.

As a general rule:

A divergence usually exists between the private and social rates of return. There are two reasons:

1. The costs of various inputs to the private owner may be different from the cost to the economy.

2. The value of the sales receipts to the private owner may be different from the value to the economy of having the goods produced.

An Illustrative Example

As a practical illustration, you might think in terms of a factory in a certain area. This investment may yield a high private rate of return to its owners. If the factory employs a significant segment of the area's labor force, it may also seem to be yielding a high social rate of return. However, before we can be sure of this, we would have to analyze such offsetting factors as the pattern of resource utilization by the factory, the alternative uses of those resources, the social "disproduct" created in the area, and so on.

After these considerations are taken into account, the difference between the private and social rates may be quite substantial. Indeed, a project may have a high private rate of return and a low—possibly even negative—social rate. This might occur, for example, with a factory that pollutes its environment. Alternatively, a high social rate and a low private rate may also be encountered. This usually happens with certain types of public-works projects.

These two examples are extremes. Between them is a range of projects that are suitable for a particular community in accordance with its stock of human and material resources. This is the range that must be sought out, identified, and developed by the government agencies and organizations that are encouraging industrialization.

Some International Aspects of Development

The fundamental task of LDCs is to increase their productivity by improving their methods of production. This requires investment in physical and human capital. Examples are power facilities, factories, machines, education, public health, and the like.

Because the LDCs for the most part are poor, they do not generate enough savings to finance their own capital formation. Therefore, they must acquire the needed investment from abroad by obtaining private foreign investment, foreign aid, or a combination of the two.

ATTRACTING PRIVATE FOREIGN INVESTMENT

What economic measures might underdeveloped countries consider in order to attract investment from private foreign sources?

1. *Infrastructure Facilities*   The governments of LDCs might undertake to provide the necessary *infrastructure*. This is the economic and social overhead capital needed as a basis for modern production. Examples of infrastructure are roads, telephone lines, power facilities, schools, and public health services. Many advanced countries as well as international agencies have had a long history of providing LDCs with generous loans on relatively easy terms for the purpose of building infrastructure facilities.

2. *Insurance Protection*   Before they invest in certain politically volatile LDCs, foreign corporations are concerned with security of life and property. Insurance provisions could help reduce such risks. The governments of LDCs might consider establishing insurance companies, or contracting with foreign insurance companies, for this purpose. The plan could be financed partly by the recipient governments and partly by the governments of the lending countries. An international financing agency of the United Nations such as the World Bank (discussed later in this chapter) could provide the necessary administrative assistance. Some progress in this direction has, in fact, been made, but observers contend that much work remains to be done.

3. *Nonnationalization Guarantees*   Potential investors must be given reasonable assurance that their assets will not be nationalized (i.e., expropriated) by the governments of recipient nations. At the very least, investors should be guaranteed "fair compensation" in the event of nationalization. They should also be assured that disputed claims will be settled by the International Court of Justice at The Hague.

4. *Profit and Capital Transfers*   Businesspeople are not likely to invest in LDCs without the knowledge that a certain share of profits can be transferred out of the country each year. In addition, specific provisions are needed to permit capital mobility. For example, laws should be formulated which place minimum restrictions on the transfer of ownership between foreigners, in the event that investors wish to sell their assets.

5. *Tax Concessions*   LDCs can offer a variety of tax inducements to attract foreign capital. As examples, income taxes and property taxes on preferred types of investments can be reduced or postponed for a specific number of years. Several underdeveloped nations have had success with such policies. However, to use tax concessions effectively, care must be taken

not to drive out existing firms by giving competitive advantages to new foreign companies.

The foregoing ideas suggest this conclusion:

In order to attract foreign capital, LDCs must create a *favorable climate for investment*. This requires the adoption of economic policies designed to protect property rights, permit capital mobility, and enhance profits.

FOREIGN AID

Even under the best of circumstances, some LDCs may not be able to attract sufficient private foreign investment to meet total capital requirements for takeoff into sustained growth. In that case, help in the form of foreign aid from other nations is needed. *Foreign aid* consists of loans, grants, or assistance by one government to another for the purpose of accelerating economic development in the recipient country. Box 2 shows the results of some foreign aid.

Major Sources of Foreign Aid

Since World War II (1945), several national and international organizations have been established to assist wartorn countries with reconstruction and poor countries with development. Some of the more important agencies will be noted briefly.

Box 2
Hydroelectric Project in Ghana

This gigantic construction project, financed by foreign aid, is one of the largest ever undertaken in Africa or Asia. The huge conduits carry water from the dam to the turbine house.

Ian Berry © Magnum Photos.

World Bank   The *International Bank for Reconstruction and Development,* popularly known as the World Bank, was established by a United Nations charter in 1944. The Bank's functions are to provide loans and credit for postwar reconstruction and to promote development of poorer countries. The Bank's chief function today is to finance basic development projects, such as dams, communication and transportation facilities, and health programs. It does this by insuring or otherwise guaranteeing private loans or, when private capital is not available, by providing loans itself. The Bank has also established affiliated agencies to finance higher-risk investment projects for both private and public enterprises in underdeveloped countries.

IDCA   The most important American organization concerned with foreign assistance is the *International Development Cooperation Agency* (with the appropriate initials, IDCA). Created in 1979, it represents a major restructuring and consolidation of previous development programs operated by different U.S. agencies and various multilateral organizations. IDCA has two major functions. The first is to advise government on development policies. The second is to administer funds voted annually by Congress for the purpose of providing economic, technical, and defense assistance to nations that are identified with the free world. (IDCA includes within its organization the Agency for International Development, the government's chief foreign-aid unit which was previously part of the U.S. State Department.)

Other Nations   The United States is not the only source of assistance to underdeveloped countries. The Soviet Union, China, and other nations have come to play increasingly important roles. This is not surprising, because foreign aid may be motivated as much by political as by economic considerations.

Issues in Foreign Aid

What are some of the economic issues that arise in the provision of foreign aid? The basic questions involve the classes, amounts, conditions, and forms of aid that should be given.

1. *Projects or programs?*   Should the United States confine its aid to specific capital projects, or should it provide aid for general programs? The World Bank, the U.S. Congress, and AID have tended to follow the project approach. This is because specific projects appear more concrete and less wasteful. Economists, however (including those at AID), tend to prefer the program approach. The reason is that it permits greater flexibility, a more general use of the underdeveloped country's resources, and a recognition of the fact that capital projects which are really needed will probably be undertaken sooner or later anyhow. This latter view seems to make more sense. In the long run a nation's economic development is not dependent on single projects. Rather, it depends on a total program whose effectiveness is determined by the way in which it manages its own general resources.

2. *How much aid should the United States give?*   Various criteria for granting aid have been proposed. For example:

(a) Aid should be provided until income per capita in the recipient country has been raised by a certain percentage.

(b) Sufficient aid should be given to make up a deficit in the recipient country's balance of payments. In simplest terms, this means that when a nation's outflow of money exceeds the inflow, foreign aid should make up the difference.

(c) Aid should be provided in proportion to a recipient country's needs as measured by its income per capita.

No matter how rational these and other criteria may seem, they ignore the fact that foreign aid is more a tool of foreign policy than an application of economic logic. Demonstrations outside an American embassy, the destruction of a U.S. government facility, or the thwarting of a communist coup can influence congressional appropriations for assistance more than the rational dictates of economic experts.

3. *Should conditions be imposed on foreign aid?*   Many political leaders feel that assistance should be provided to any poor country that is trying to improve its economic position. But problems and dilemmas of a political and quasi-political nature tend to cloud this simple criterion. For instance:

Should aid be given to some communist countries, such as Poland or Yugoslavia, but not to others, such as China or Cuba?

Should we confine aid only to the noncommunist countries?

Should we see to it that the benefits of aid are spread throughout a country rather than being concentrated in a single class?

Should aid be given only to countries that accomplish reforms (such as tax, budget, and land reforms), or should it be given without restrictions?

These are typical of the problems that face the United States in its foreign-assistance programs. Some people have proposed that aid be given with no strings attached. However, this would ordinarily be a foolish course for the United States to follow. With few exceptions, it should at least approve of the goals for which the aid is to be used, and impose conditions that will assure reasonable efficiency in the attainment of these goals.

4. *Should foreign assistance take the form of loans or grants?*   The answer to this question involves not only economic, but also moral, ethical, and social considerations. In many Muslim countries, for instance, interest on loans carries an unfavorable religious connotation because it implies that the lender is taking unfair advantage of the distress of the borrower.

Nevertheless, some guide for policy decisions is needed. Perhaps the most feasible guide is an "international welfare criterion." This might be a standard that provides grants to countries whose per capita incomes are below a specified level and loans to countries above that level. In the past, our foreign-aid policies have often been inconsistent in the use of this or any other standard.

In conclusion:

Average growth rates of many underdeveloped countries have sometimes been extremely impressive for as much as a decade or more. But averages can be deceptive. Actually, there is still a wide disparity in performance among the underdeveloped nations and regions of the world. A study of the development process indicates that foreign assistance *in conjunction* with private investment is necessary if the LDCs are to make the most effective use of their human and material resources.

What You Have Learned

1. The per capita income gap between the richest nations and the poorest nations appears to be widening over the long run. This is due to differences in the factors that account for economic development. Among them: the quantity and quality of human and natural resources, the rate of capital accumulation, the degree of specialization and scale of production, the rate of technological progress, and the environmental (political, social, cultural, and economic) framework.

2. A nation may be considered to pass through various "stages" of development as it is transformed from a traditional to a technically progressive society. These stages help explain the social and economic changes that take place during growth.

3. The economic process of development can be analyzed within a framework of certain fundamental ideas. Some of the more important are these:

   (a) The need for an agricultural revolution to release underemployed resources for industrialization.

   (b) The need to reduce birth rates so as to relieve the pressure of population against resources.

   (c) The recognition that investment in physical capital alone is not the most effective way of stimulating development.

   (d) The realization that investment in human capital, as well as physical capital, is important.

   (e) The distinction between labor-intensive and capital-intensive projects.

   (f) The possible superiority of small-scale over large-scale projects.

   (g) The distinction between private and social profitability, which is a useful guide for judging the desirability of an investment project.

4. One of the ways in which LDCs can acquire capital is by attracting private foreign investment. This requires that LDCs adopt measures that will create a favorable climate for investment. Examples of such measures are provisions for the following:

   (a) Infrastructure facilities.

   (b) Insurance protection for life and property.

   (c) Nonnationalization guarantees.

   (d) Profit and capital transfers.

   (e) Tax concessions.

5. Another way in which LDCs can acquire capital as well as technical assistance is by foreign aid. The International Bank for Reconstruction and Development (World Bank), with its affiliates, helps to finance loans for investment projects in underdeveloped countries. The United States, through its technical cooperation and assistance programs, has also been a source of foreign aid. So have many other countries, including the Soviet Union and China.

6. A number of problems and dilemmas of foreign aid are of continuous concern to government officials. They involve such issues as these:

   (a) The purposes for which aid should be given.

   (b) The amount of aid to be provided.

   (c) The conditions under which aid may be extended.

   (d) The forms that aid may take.

Because political and foreign-policy considerations play a significant role in foreign aid, it is probably impossible to establish a firm set of guidelines that will be applicable in all situations.

For Discussion

1. *Terms and concepts to review:*

less developed countries	foreign aid
disguised unemployment	International Bank for
economic development	Reconstruction and
private rate of return	Development
social rate of return	International
infrastructure	Development
	Cooperation Agency

2. It is sometimes suggested that underdeveloped nations which are seeking to industrialize should simply follow the historical paths taken by the more advanced nations. After all, why not benefit from the experiences of others? Evaluate this argument.

3. In the early years of America's post–World War II aid program (1945–1955), it was argued by many critics that the provision of health and sanitation facilities to LDCs would worsen their situation rather than improve it. The reason is that health and sanitation programs would *reduce* the

LDCs' death rates. Can you explain the logic of this argument?

4. Among the first investments usually undertaken by LDCs are (a) an international airline and (b) a steel mill. Does this make sense? Explain.

5. Rapid economic development requires that a nation save and invest a substantial proportion of its income. What would you advise for the many LDCs whose savings rates are low or virtually zero because the great majority of their population is close to starvation?

6. "Rapid population growth is by far the single most serious obstacle to overcome as far as most LDCs are concerned." Can you suggest some *economic* approaches to the solution of this problem?

7. *A Gloomy Dissent on South Asia.* To Gunnar Myrdal, a leading Swedish economist and Nobel laureate, prospects for real growth in at least one part of the underdeveloped world—South Asia—are gloomy indeed. That is the clear implication of *Asian Drama*, a three-volume, 2,221-page inquiry into development in eight countries. Reporting on many years of study and observation, Myrdal concluded that growth in much of South Asia is hamstrung by hostile social, cultural, and political institutions. Thus, development plans that seek to manipulate strictly economic factors are doomed to failure. Instead, says Myrdal, countries have to massively reform their institutions before any real growth will take place. Among his proposals:

(a) Governments must be strengthened—for better policymaking and greater immunity from ethnic, social, and geographic divisions.

(b) Patterns of land ownership must be changed—to give the people who work the land an incentive to improve it.

(c) Population growth must be slowed—because, says Myrdal, it "holds the threat of economic stagnation or deterioration."

(d) Education must be modernized—to make it an instrument of development policy.

Evaluate Myrdal's proposals.

Issue
Foreign Aid: A Bottomless Pit?

America's foreign-aid programs were launched with the best of intentions after World War II. But after several decades and hundreds of billions of dollars given away, the programs started showing signs of falling apart. An increasing number of citizens—from ordinary taxpayers to political leaders and scholars—have criticized not only specific aid projects, but also the underlying philosophy of the entire aid program. The criticisms have been political as well as economic. Among them:

○ Some of the largest recipients of American aid have opposed the United States in critical international situations. India, for instance, has been helped numerous times by American food shipments, but has repeatedly denounced U.S. diplomatic and military actions. Further, critics say, why should India be given assistance if it could afford to undertake the enormous cost of developing an atomic bomb?

○ The United States has used aid as a tool for promoting foreign policy. The State Department, for example, has supported dictatorships which rule by terror and suppression.

○ Soft loans (at low interest rates) and grants to LDCs have been wasted on such inefficient monuments as steel mills, automobile assembly plants, and state airlines. If the underdeveloped countries had to rely more heavily on commercial loans, their governments would be concerned with allocating resources to agricultural and regional development programs more closely attuned to national needs.

○ The widely believed "cycle-of-poverty" thesis, which holds that poor countries are trapped in a quagmire of poverty and stagnation, is an unsupported hypothesis. All developed countries were at one time poor, with low per capita incomes and little or no accumulated capital. Yet these nations advanced, usually without significant outside capital or external grants. For example, Hong Kong, an overcrowded colony with few natural resources and a limited domestic market, has made remarkable progress since the 1960s. Other groups within nations or regions that have advanced with no significant financial or technical assistance from others include the Chinese in Southeast Asia, the Indians in East Africa, and the Lebanese in West Africa.

In light of these views, can foreign aid do for the poor countries what it did for the wartorn economies of western Europe during the 1940s and 1950s? Clearly not, according to the critics. They point out that in the western European nations the motivations and institutions favorable to development were already present. In most LDCs, on the other hand, the extension of grants and loans under the euphemism of foreign aid will amount to pouring millions of dollars into a bottomless pit.

Dissent on Development: Guilt Complex

Among the growing number of political leaders and scholars who take this position is an economist at the London School of Economics, P. T. Bauer. In various controversial books and articles, Bauer challenges the conventional wisdom that foreign aid is essential for narrowing the income gap between rich and poor countries. Income statistics, he says, often hide more than they reveal. There is no significant difference between the per capita income levels of the richest underdeveloped countries and the poorest developed ones. Further, he points out, some underdeveloped countries, such as the oil-rich Arab states, have per capita incomes that are among the highest in the world.

One of Bauer's objectives is to shatter the guilt complex of Western countries. There is an unfounded belief, he says, that advanced countries are somehow responsible for the poverty of the underdeveloped world. In a review of Bauer's writings, Edwin McDowell, a member of the *Wall Street Journal's* editorial staff, paraphrased Bauer this way:

Actually, Western prosperity was generated by its own population, not achieved at anyone's expense. Those countries were al-

FOREIGN AID: AVERAGES BY DONOR COUNTRIES
(latest comparative data)

As a percent of GNP, the average amount of foreign aid by the United States ranks near the bottom.

IN MILLIONS OF U.S. DOLLARS		PERCENT OF GNP
$401.7	SWEDEN	.72%
$428.8	NETHERLANDS	.62%
$1,638.4	FRANCE	.60%
$131.4	NORWAY	.57%
$713.4	CANADA	.50%
$721.8	BRITAIN	.38%
$1,434.6	W. GERMANY	.36%
$3,439.0	U.S.	.25%
$1,126.2	JAPAN	.25%

SOURCE: United Nations.

ready materially much more advanced than the underdeveloped countries when they established contact with the latter in the 18th and 19th centuries. Even now many developed countries, including some of the richest, have few economic contacts with the underdeveloped world.

Moreover, some of the richest Western countries were colonies in their earlier history, notably the U.S., Canada, Australia and New Zealand, and some were already prosperous while they were still colonies. This certainly does not prove that colonialism is a necessary or admirable precondition of material progress, but along with the contemporary experience of Hong Kong, it tends to refute the assumption (enunciated as a general principle by the U.N.) that colonial status and economic progress are incompatible.

Nevertheless, belief that Western economic gains were achieved at the expense of the underdeveloped world has led donors to favor economic development assistance as a form of partial restitution and has led recipients to view it as an admission of Western guilt. In part

that accounts for what the author describes as the "economics of resentment," the anomaly of donor countries beseeching poor nations not to refuse their aid, combined with recipient governments showing their thanks by pursuing policies hostile to donors.

Conclusion: Bad Economics and Bad Sociology

In a more general sense, Bauer is critical of the social implications of foreign aid. He questions the underlying premise of development—whether it is moral to try to transform human society. "The attitudes and motivations which promote material success are not necessarily or even usually those which confer happiness, dignity, sensitivity, a capacity to love, a sense of harmony, or a reflective mind." Therefore, the attempt to change fundamental attitudes and beliefs for the sake of material progress is not only bad economics, but also bad sociology.

Many people, of course, disagree with these views. Those who support foreign aid argue that the United States should not abandon its tradi-

tion of helping needy people. But as the critics point out, providing food and medicine to nations hit by disasters is one thing, while continuing massive military and economic transfusions for every country that wants them is quite another.

Whatever the outcome of the debate, two things are certain: The days of a generous U.S. aid policy are over, and it is no longer possible to discuss problems of development intelligently without coming to grips with the practical issues raised by foreign aid.

QUESTIONS

1. Much foreign aid to LDCs is in the form of military aid. Does this tend to stimulate their economies? If so, why do some critics object to such aid? If not, why is such aid given? Discuss.

2. Can you suggest some objective economic guidelines for providing aid to LDCs?

3. "It is morally wrong for rich countries not to help poor ones." Is this an economic argument? Explain.

Chapter 19

Managing Our Resources: Energy and the Environment

Chapter Preview

Chapter Preview

How have government policies affected the availability of energy? Can policies be adopted that will avoid future "shortages" or "surpluses" of energy?

The natural environment includes three major types of resources—air, land, and water. Can economic measures be devised to prevent pollution and exploitation of these resources?

Are there enough physical resources available to keep the economy growing at desired rates in the years ahead? Is our nation passing from an era of abundant natural-resource supplies into one of persistent shortages?

These questions have recently been asked with increasing frequency. Apparent deficiencies of energy and certain other raw materials, and pollution of air and water, have alerted nearly everyone to resource and environmental issues. As a result, a course in economics today would be remiss if it did not devote some time to analyzing these important problems.

This chapter focuses on economic controversies concerning two fundamental classes of resources—energy and the environment. As you will see, an understanding of the basic issues goes a long way toward formulating public policies aimed at improving efficiency and equity in the use of all types of resources.

Energy Policy: What Are the Options?

Since the early 1970s, the Arab-dominated Organization of Petroleum Exporting Countries (OPEC), through cooperation of its thirteen member nations, has managed to increase greatly the world price of oil and thereby create an energy crisis. By severely limiting output, OPEC has succeeded in boosting average oil export prices from about $2.75 to more than $20 per barrel. The consequences of this action, combined with the ability of OPEC to exercise a strong influence over world oil prices, has led political leaders everywhere to consider alternative policies for coping with future energy crises. Four distinct approaches may be explored:

1. Free markets.
2. Rationing.
3. Crude-oil allocation.
4. Demand reduction and supply expansion.

Each is intended to reduce domestic dependence on foreign sources of energy—and ideally to stabilize, if not reduce, energy prices.

Before undertaking an analysis of the policy alternatives, it is useful to keep certain facts in mind. The economics of energy resources concerns their aspects as commodities—oil, gas, and coal, as well as hydroelectric and nuclear power, both of which are produced from natural resources. As a nation's output of goods and services grows, so does its need for energy and other natural-resource commodities required to fuel that growth. Consequently, consumption of raw materials has been rising rapidly in all advanced countries, leading many observers to conclude that the world is moving from an age of relative resource abundance to an era of relative resource scarcity. But as we shall see:

The basic energy "problem" is not that the needed resources are unavailable. There are great quantities of raw materials in the ground. *The problem is economic: WHAT energy resources will society choose to extract from the ground, HOW will they be extracted, and FOR WHOM?*

FREE MARKETS

Economists may not know very much. But we do know one thing very well: how to produce shortages and surpluses. Do you want to produce a shortage of any product? Simply have government fix and enforce a legal *maximum* price on the product which is less than the price that would otherwise prevail.... Do you want to produce a surplus of any product? Simply have government fix and enforce a legal *minimum* price above the price that would otherwise prevail.

Milton Friedman and Robert V. Roosa

This quotation explains why some people argue in favor of a free market for energy, particularly for oil and natural gas. Government intervention, these critics claim, has intensified rather than alleviated our energy problem, resulting in gross inefficiencies and

inequities. Since indictments such as these affect all of us, the fundamental economic issues are worthy of examination.

Surpluses and Shortages

In Exhibit 1, the S and D curves represent the normal supply and demand curves for a commodity such as energy. The diagram shows three types of market situations that may occur. They depend on whether government legislators choose to pursue a free-market policy, a "high"-price or surplus policy, or a "low"-price or shortage policy.

1. *Free-Market Policy* Suppose that the supply and demand for energy are allowed to interact freely and that no governmental constraints are imposed on prices and quantities. It follows that the intersection of the S and D curves will determine an equilibrium price at P and an equilibrium quantity at Q. As a result, there will be no energy shortages or surpluses. The market will be cleared because sellers will be offering, and buyers will be purchasing, precisely the same quantity of energy *at the equilibrium price.*

Exhibit 1
Surpluses and Shortages of Energy

In a free market, the equilibrium price of energy will be at P and the equilibrium quantity at Q. But if government institutes measures to raise the price, say to P', the quantity supplied will exceed the quantity demanded by the distance KL. There will thus be a surplus of this amount. Conversely, governmental measures that cause a reduction in price, say to P'', will result in quantity demanded exceeding quantity supplied. There will thus be a shortage equal to the amount MN.

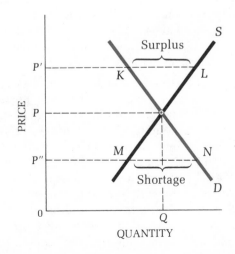

2. *"High"-Price or Surplus Policy*   What if government legislators wish to pursue a surplus policy? In that case they will adopt measures that will cause the price of energy to be higher than the free-market equilibrium price. This means that the price will rise, say from P to P'. At this higher price, the quantity supplied will exceed the quantity demanded by the distance KL. This amount, therefore, represents a surplus of energy *at the higher price.*

3. *"Low"-Price or Shortage Policy*   As a third possibility, government legislators may choose to follow a shortage policy. In that case they will adopt measures that will cause the price of energy to be lower than the free-market equilibrium price. Thus, if the price is brought down from P to P", the quantity demanded at this reduced price will exceed the quantity supplied by the distance MN. This amount, therefore, represents a shortage of energy *at the lower price.*

We are now in a position to define the correct meaning of surplus and shortage—two widely misused and misunderstood terms:

A *surplus* is an excess. It is the amount by which the quantity supplied of a commodity exceeds the quantity demanded at a given price, as when the given price is above the free-market equilibrium price. A *shortage* is a deficiency. It is the amount by which the quantity demanded of a commodity exceeds the quantity supplied at a given price, as when the given price is below the free-market equilibrium price. Therefore, because a shortage or surplus can exist only *at a given price*, the terms "shortage" and "surplus" have no meaning unless the quantities demanded and supplied of a commodity are related to a particular price.

Oil Policies

What are the implications of these ideas for America's oil policies?

For most years since the 1930s, when vast oil discoveries were made in Texas and Oklahoma, both federal and state governments have followed either surplus or shortage policies. To illustrate:

1. Prior to the early 1970s, the United States generally adhered to a surplus policy for crude oil. Legislation was enacted that permitted oil-producing states to set quotas (limits) on output and the federal government to set quotas on imports. By thus restricting our total supply, domestic crude-oil prices were kept well above world prices for several decades. As a consequence, consumers were injured because they had to pay higher prices for petroleum products. In addition, efficient producers were injured because they could not reduce costs by making fuller utilization of their

wells. For the most part, the only group to benefit from a surplus policy was the one given the most generous production quotas. This group consisted of the numerous, politically influential, but mainly inefficient small owners of property rights.

2. In the early 1970s, the United States shifted from a surplus to a shortage policy. The world price of oil rose above the domestic price as a result of the successful monopolistic export restrictions imposed by OPEC. But Washington maintained price ceilings on most oil produced domestically. Shortages prevailed because the market was prevented from clearing at the higher equilibrium price.

Efficiency and Equity   What have been the overall economic consequences of these policies? In general:

Government regulation of oil has had adverse effects on both economic efficiency and equity. Federal and state controls have resulted in *resource misallocation,* by enabling inefficient producers to survive and causing efficient ones to experience increased costs. Government controls have also created *social inequities,* by benefiting high-cost firms at the expense of both consumers and low-cost producers. On the whole, therefore, it appears that *the social costs of regulations have exceeded the social benefits.*

Natural-Gas Policies

Natural gas is a major source of energy. Like oil, large discoveries of natural gas were made in the Southwest during the 1930s. It was not until the early 1960s, however, that the Federal Power Commission (FPC), after years of litigation in the courts, was authorized to regulate the field price of natural gas. This is the price charged by producers at the wellhead.

The pricing procedure adopted by the FPC was designed to accomplish three objectives:

○ To provide just and reasonable rates to gas purchasers.

○ To yield a fair return to producers.

○ To encourage firms to explore and develop new gas.

Accordingly, the Commission established a multiple-rate structure. This consisted of a lower rate for "old" gas already flowing, and a higher rate for "new" gas not yet produced. The purpose of this pricing method was to prevent firms from reaping "unwarranted" profits that would result from a single field price high enough to encourage new exploration.

What were the consequences of these and related measures? According to the FPC's critics:

1. In seeking to establish "just and reasonable rates," the Commission neglected demand considerations by

setting prices according to a cost-plus formula. The formula based the price on the average of the industry's costs plus a "fair return to producers." Rates were consequently set below the free-market level, with the result that a natural-gas shortage was created.

2. As the shortage developed, pipeline companies found it more profitable to sell gas at free-market prices to industrial buyers (because the price to them was uncontrolled) than to contract sales at low regulated prices to the more numerous new residential and commercial customers. These nongas users, therefore, had to purchase alternative forms of energy, such as electricity and oil, for heating purposes. This raised the demand for these energy sources, causing their prices to increase. As a result, in less than a decade after price ceilings were instituted, the number of households and commercial establishments using more costly nongas fuels far exceeded the number using gas. This meant that far more people were made worse off by FPC price controls than were made better off.

3. The FPC's control over prices applied only to *interstate* (not to *intrastate*) gas sales. Consequently, consumers in large gas-producing states such as Texas, Louisiana, and Oklahoma were able to purchase all the intrastate gas they wanted at free-market prices. Consumers in most other states, on the other hand, were either restricted in their purchases or entirely excluded from the market. In relative terms, therefore, intrastate users of gas benefited from FPC controls, while interstate users, which are much more numerous, suffered.

Efficiency and Equity These criticisms, as discussed above, have been leveled by opponents of natural-gas regulation. However, there is widespread agreement—even among supporters of FPC controls—that the overall conclusions contain substantial elements of truth. To the extent that they do, it must be inferred that the net economic consequences of natural-gas regulation have not been favorable.

Federally imposed ceiling prices on interstate gas created both inefficiencies and inequities:

1. Producers were discouraged from exploration and development.

2. Industrial users along with "old" household and commercial users benefited while many more "new" household and commercial users suffered.

3. Intrastate users benefited relative to a much larger number of interstate users who suffered.

As an overall result, therefore, *the costs of regulation generally exceeded the benefits from society's point of view.*

RATIONING

A second approach to dealing with the energy problem (i.e., high prices and U.S. dependence on foreign suppliers) is for government to impose a ceiling price on fuel at some desired level below the free-market price. The limited supply could then be rationed among those who want the commodity at the ceiling price.

You can see how this would work by referring back to Exhibit 1. Because the free-market price is at P, the ceiling price would be set somewhere lower—say at P''. At this controlled price, sellers would supply the amount $P''M$. Government would then ration this quantity among those people who want the amount $P''N$.

Some Pros and Cons

Would rationing be a wise approach to solving the nation's energy problem? Those who think so offer three basic arguments:

1. *It is direct.* Rationing would reduce U.S. dependence on foreign oil while maintaining lower prices for consumers. In the case of gasoline, for example, the federal government could print coupons that would be distributed to motorists, entitling them to purchase a specified amount of gasoline each week at the regulated price.

2. *It is fair.* Rationing would assure an equitable distribution of fuel. Consumption would be based on need rather than on ability to pay.

3. *It is acceptable.* Rationing is something that the public would understand and support. People are more willing to make sacrifices when it is generally known that the burdens are being shared by everyone.

These arguments have wide appeal. However, the arguments against rationing are also impressive:

1. *It causes inequities.* No fair criteria exist for determining who would get how much. In the case of gasoline, for example, it might seem that an equal allotment to everyone based on the number of cars or on the number of licensed drivers would be equitable. But this would mean that a family with two cars or with two drivers would receive twice as much as a family with one car or with one driver. An allotment based on "need" would require that a central authority determine whose needs are "essential" and whose are "ordinary." And an allotment based on classifications of consumers would require overall criteria to be established for each classification—households, businesses, institutions, and so on—with separate criteria within each class.

2. *It causes inefficiencies.*   A massive and costly bureaucracy consisting of tens of thousands of government employees at both the national and local levels would be needed to administer a rationing system. The results would be rampant wastes and inefficiencies, with few, if any, improvements in equity.

3. *It causes black markets.*   A system of price controls and rationing is likely to encourage the creation of a <u>black market</u>. This is an illegal market in which a good is sold for more than its ceiling price. One way of avoiding this possibility is to establish a <u>white market</u>. This is a legal market in which ration coupons for a commodity are transferable, permitting people who do not want all their coupons to sell them to those who do. A white market thus reduces, but does not eliminate, the inequities and skullduggery generally associated with rationing and a black market.

Efficiency and Equity   Government rationing provides an alternative to free markets as a way of allocating scarce commodities. Despite any benefits that may result from rationing, there is evidence that the losses to society may far outweigh the gains. For example:

> Rationing creates inefficiencies and inequities in several ways:
>
> 1. Low prices discourage producers from undertaking additional investment to expand output.
>
> 2. Bureaucratic controls are required to administer allotments based on "needs."
>
> The *real* effect of rationing, therefore, is an *income transfer* from consumers of the rationed commodity to a vast new army of government bureaucrats.

There is considerable evidence to support this conclusion. The nation had three years of experience with gasoline rationing during World War II. In general, the experiment "worked." That is, private fuel consumption was severely reduced, leaving more available for military uses. However, disproportionate hardship, favoritism, and black-marketeering were rampant. These gave rise to cries of inequity and to a tide of political resentment rarely equaled in the country's history. (See Box 1.)

CRUDE-OIL ALLOCATION

A third approach to dealing with the energy problem is to allocate stocks of scarce crude oil among domestic producers (refiners) instead of consumers. This is a form of rationing without coupons. However, the rationing occurs on the supply rather than the demand side of the market.

An allocation scheme of this type, combined with a system of price controls, was implemented by Washington in the early 1970s. The program was intended to be "temporary." It contained two major features: a multilevel price structure and an oil entitlements program.

Multilevel Price Structure

The federal government decreed that there would be two levels of prices for domestically produced oil. One would be a lower price for "old" oil from wells in operation before 1972. The other would be a higher price for "new" oil from wells in operation since 1972. These prices were set substantially below the world market price of oil, thereby creating a domestic shortage. Domestic refiners, therefore, had to import oil to help make up the difference. The price that refiners paid for a barrel of oil was an average of three prices—the old oil price, the new oil price, and the world market price.

Oil Entitlements Program

Some refiners, primarily the larger ones, had access to greater amounts of domestic, lower-priced old oil than did other refiners. The government therefore designed a program to allocate old oil proportionately among all refiners, thereby tending to equalize their average total cost per barrel of oil. In essence, the program operated in the following way:

1. Refiners whose monthly holdings of old oil were below the national average were given certificates of entitlement. These could be presented to refiners whose holdings were above the national average in exchange for old oil at the ceiling price.

2. In practice, a physical exchange of oil rarely occurred. Instead, the entitlements themselves were bought and sold among refiners, with the price determined by the difference between the controlled price of old oil and the average, uncontrolled prices of new and imported oil.

3. Refiners whose monthly holdings of old crude exceeded the national average were required to purchase entitlements before processing their old oil. This assured the existence of an effective market in entitlements. As a result, refiners who would otherwise have had to rely more heavily on higher-priced new and imported oil could obtain lower-priced old oil from those who had it.

Efficiency and Equity   What were the economic consequences of this policy? On the whole:

> The crude-oil allocation system achieved its goal of reducing the average price paid by domestic refiners. But there were also adverse impacts on efficiency and equity.

Box 1
Is Rationing a Solution?

Public opinion surveys conducted from time to time reveal that if gasoline consumption is to be reduced, most people would prefer rationing to a federal-tax increase at the gas pump. Supporters of rationing contend that it is less unfair than a major price increase that penalizes lower-income motorists. What the advocates of rationing fail to recognize, however, is that a more efficient and equitable alternative is to provide lower-income people with the means (through an income-tax reduction or subsidy) to purchase gasoline, rather than to establish a cumbersome system of rationing.

In 1979, as a direct result of political uprisings in the Middle East, oil exports to the United States were reduced. Washington, therefore, again considered rationing. To save the cost of printing new coupons, the old ones were taken out of storage. But someone discovered that they were capable of activating dollar vending machines. As a result, the coupons had to be destroyed. The total cost to taxpayers for printing, storing, and burning the coupons amounted to millions of dollars.

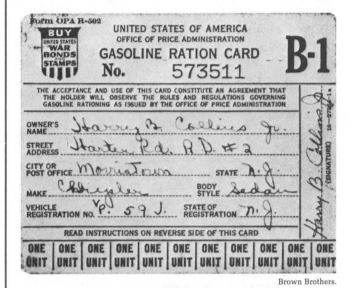

Brown Brothers.

Wide World Photos.

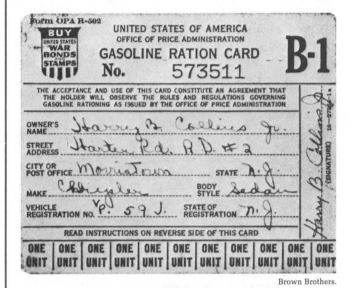

United Press International.

During World War II, gasoline was rationed through the use of coupons. As a result, people often lined up for limited supplies of rationed gas. Throughout the war, black-marketeering of gas was rampant. A white market, in which people could sell their ration coupons, would have fended off the black markets and the counterfeiting of coupons which developed.

Gasoline rationing was proposed again during the energy crisis of the early 1970s, for which the George Washington coupons were made. However, the "crisis" abated, and the coupons were never used.

Most important, domestic production of old oil was discouraged by the imposition of price controls. In other words, domestic old oil was, in effect, taxed to subsidize the purchase of imported oil.

In general, therefore, the crude-oil allocation system was an *income redistribution program* within the oil industry. The profits of large refiners, who held most of the old oil, were reduced in order to compensate smaller refiners who had to pay higher prices for new and imported oil.

DEMAND REDUCTION AND SUPPLY EXPANSION

A fourth approach to achieving greater energy independence is for the nation to seek ways of curbing energy consumption, stimulating energy production, or both. What are the economic implications of such efforts? The answer can be best understood by realizing that regardless of whether energy prices are controlled or uncontrolled, long-run trends of crude-oil and natural-gas prices are going to be upward. However, these rising price trends will have different impacts on the demand for, and supply of, energy.

Energy Demand: Present and Future Consumption

High prices for crude oil and gas will encourage conservation. Household and business consumers of energy will find it more economical to improve insulation in buildings, purchase smaller and more efficient automobiles, and pay greater attention to the energy requirement of appliances and machines. When the prices of oil and gas are high enough, consumers will also find it worthwhile to install solar-powered air-conditioning systems where geographically feasible, and seek ways of substituting other energy sources, such as coal and atomic power, for oil and gas. These effects will change the composition of energy inputs and establish a balance that reflects society's preferences for alternative energy goods.

Conservation, therefore, does not mean that energy resources must be left in the ground on the assumption that society will value these resources more highly in the future than it does in the present. Balanced use of resources today is an essential part of making our economy grow. Materials that are embodied in today's capital goods help increase tomorrow's production. Therefore:

True conservation requires that resources be managed in a manner that reflects society's preferences between present and future consumption. This means that an increase in the value of energy today, relative to its expected future value, should lead to a more rapid rate of recovery today. If government regulations and policies prevent this from happening, the nation's resources are misallocated and society suffers a net loss due to inefficiencies and inequities.

Energy Supply: Providing Incentives to Produce

Rising prices of energy will help stimulate exploration and development. But if the large capital investments needed to expand energy output are to be undertaken, producers must be given adequate incentives. Two measures would be particularly appropriate—selective price guarantees and a variable tariff.

Selective Price Guarantees   To encourage the development of new products, such as shale oil or synthetic gas from coal, the government could guarantee producers the price of these commodities for a specified number of years. If the market price of the goods rises above the guaranteed price, no government action is necessary. But if the market price falls below the guaranteed price, the government could compensate producers with direct payments to make up the difference.

The chief advantage of this proposal is that it would allow the prices of new energy to be determined in a free market by supply and demand. Government would compensate producers for the difference between the market price they receive and a higher, target price.

The chief disadvantage of the proposal is that the government would have to decide which new energy sources to support. This might discourage production of nonsupported energy sources, thereby leading to increasing government support of the total market. However, the danger of this happening can be reduced if in its legislation Congress specifies the life of the plan.

It may be noted that a plan of this type, called a *direct-payments plan,* has long existed for certain farm commodities. On the basis of this experience, there is strong reason to believe that such a plan would encourage producers to seek ways of expanding the output of energy.

Variable Tariff   To encourage domestic capital investment, producers must be protected from decisions of oil-exporting countries to disrupt the market for political or economic reasons. Government can provide this protection with a *tariff*—a tax—on the importation of oil and gas. Moreover, the tariff should be variable rather than fixed, so that upward or downward adjustments can be made quickly and easily in response to changing international conditions.

A tariff, like any other form of protection, causes resource misallocation and therefore entails economic costs. However, a tariff has less adverse consequences than the other major protective device—an *import quota*. This is a law that limits the number of units of a commodity that may be imported during a given period. Although relative prices are distorted by a tariff, it nevertheless allows the public to receive the benefits of any low-cost imports that may occur. This is because a tariff permits market forces to allocate society's resources. An import quota, on the other hand, stifles competition and creates vested interests among importers, who must apply to the government for import licenses and quota allocations. As a result, import quotas tend to become discriminatory, favoring some importers over others, at the public's expense.

CONCLUSION: EFFICIENCY AND EQUITY

The cry of "wolf" continues to be heard with each sign of an impending energy crisis. In view of this, what broad policy alternatives exist for reducing domestic dependence on foreign sources of energy?

One point of view favors a free market. By deregulating oil and natural gas, it is argued, energy prices would rise to the point where faster rates of development would be encouraged and substitution of less costly alternatives would be worthwhile. Another view holds that a free market would lead to high prices, which, in the long run, may stimulate development but at the expense of hardships borne by lower-income groups. Critics of a free market therefore advocate continuation of controls and a search for alternative fuels through various government incentives and central planning.

As with many economic controversies, there are important truths in both points of view. An appropriate resolution, therefore, would be one that recognizes the following:

Government cannot successfully program society's future energy supplies. Attempts to do so lead to prolonged surpluses or shortages—and hence to inefficiencies and inequities. Therefore, the adoption of a free market in energy, with provisions for reducing (through subsidies or tax measures) the burdens of adjustment among low-income groups, should be one of our major national goals.

Stated differently, a free market in energy would enable the economy to adjust to the new level of prices—and hence to the real cost of energy—instead of resisting the inevitable. And, in a free market, the energy sector would begin to straighten out after decades of government regulation designed to protect special interests and preserve particular groups. (See Box 2.)

Environmental Policy: What Are the Options?

The Walrus and the Carpenter
Were walking close at hand;
They wept like anything to see
Such quantities of sand:
"If this were only cleared away,"
They said, "it *would* be grand!"

"If seven maids with seven mops
Swept it for half a year,
Do you suppose," the Walrus said,
"That they could get it clear?"
"I doubt it," said the Carpenter,
And shed a bitter tear.
      Lewis Carroll, *Through the Looking Glass* (1872)

The penultimate Western man, stalled in the ultimate traffic jam and slowly succumbing to carbon monoxide, will not be cheered to hear from the last survivor that the gross national product went up by a record amount.
      John K. Galbraith

As the carpet of increased choice is being unrolled before us by the foot, it is simultaneously being rolled up behind us by the yard.
      E. J. Mishan

These quotations, particularly the last two by prominent economists, suggest that there is a direct relationship between economic growth and the level of pollution. The relationship is such that as the GNP increases, so does pollution, and both of them grow at compound (although not necessarily equal) rates.

In view of this, what policy approaches exist for curbing pollution? Before answering this question, we should examine some basic economic principles which are useful for analyzing environmental problems.

ECONOMIC ANALYSIS FOR ENVIRONMENTAL IMPROVEMENT

One major challenge of pollution stems from the widespread difference between private costs and social costs. According to classical economic theory, the operation of a free market assures that the price system will automatically allocate resources to their socially most efficient uses. But it appears that the price system is not always effective in dealing with environmental factors. For as firms seek to maximize profits, adverse side effects are generated in the form of polluted environments, which become the real costs that are borne by society. The problem, therefore, is to develop modified market as well as nonmarket mechanisms for allocating resources when the

Box 2
Energy: What Future?

The 1980s will see substantial changes in America's energy policies. Washington has come to realize that incentives are needed to spur exploration and production. Otherwise, if the gap between U.S. energy consumption and production continues to grow, it will have to be filled by energy imports. This would increase the nation's reliance on foreign sources of supply, a consequence that political leaders want to avoid.

For natural gas, the future looks particularly bright. There are enough sources underground to provide ample quantities of gas through the next century. But at what price? This remains to be seen. At high enough prices for energy, it will become profitable to convert coal into gas, and to unlock gas trapped in tight rock formations. Still more gas can come from future technologies that are known but are not yet cost-effective at present prices for energy.

SOURCE: American Gas Association.

(b) AMOUNT OF ENERGY IMPORTED TO THE U.S., PROJECTED TO 1985
(trillion British thermal units)*

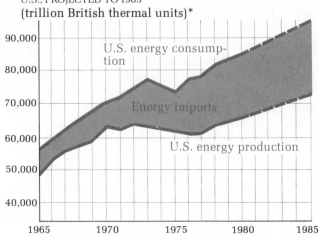

*One B.t.u.—British thermal unit—is the amount of energy needed to raise the temperature of 1 pound of water 1 degree Fahrenheit.

(a) PER CAPITA CONSUMPTION OF ENERGY IN THE U.S., PROJECTED TO 1985
(million British thermal units)*

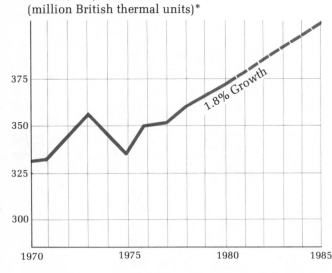

(c) SOURCES OF GAS
(trillions of cubic feet)

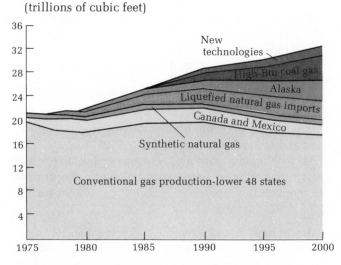

internal or private costs of firms differ substantially from their social costs. Three analytical approaches are useful for this purpose. They are called (1) marginal or incremental analysis, (2) benefit-cost analysis, and (3) cost-effectiveness analysis.

As we shall see, the ideas underlying these methods of analysis are applicable not only to pollution control, but to a wide variety of other socioeconomic problems as well.

Marginal or Incremental Analysis

One of the most fundamental rules of economics which serves as a guide for making rational decisions is the "marginal" or "incremental" principle:

The net gain of any activity is maximized at the point where the incremental (added, or "marginal") cost of that activity is equal to its incremental benefit. Thus, expenditures on pollution abatement will result in added costs as well as added benefits. But the degree of pollution will be at an optimum level from *society's* point of view when the incremental cost of reducing it further is equal to the incremental benefits derived therefrom.

For example, suppose that an upstream steel mill discharges its wastes into a river. If by spending a dollar on pollution abatement the mill can save downstream fisheries at least a dollar, it should do so—from the standpoint of society's well-being.

As was pointed out above, a problem arises because of the fundamental distinction between private costs and social costs. The upstream steel mill, for example, disposes of its wastes in a manner that affects others, but does not pay for this disposal. Instead, the mill treats the stream as a free good, and hence the mill's costs of production are lower than they would otherwise be. The downstream fisheries, on the other hand, incur higher private costs because they must absorb the pollutants of the upstream mill.

Therefore, to the extent that prices reflect all production costs, the upstream mill's prices are understated and the downstream fisheries' prices are overstated. The result is a net loss to society because of a failure of all firms concerned to equate their private and social costs. The general consequences are therefore undesirable:

1. Society gets too much steel and not enough fish.

2. Consumers of fish, by paying higher prices, subsidize consumers of steel.

3. Therefore, economic resources are not allocated in the most efficient way.

Most private decisions produce side effects of one type or another. Some may be favorable and some unfavorable. Social scientists refer to such consequences as *externalities*. In the case of pollution, the undesirable externalities can be reduced by special taxes, charges, subsidies, or laws. A fundamental challenge, of course, is to develop methods of evaluating each type of action.

Benefit-Cost Analysis

One method that has been developed for such purposes is known as *benefit-cost analysis*. As shown below, it is a technique of evaluating alternative programs by comparing, for each program, the value today—called the *present value*—of all expected benefits with all expected costs. The calculation employed to arrive at an estimate utilizes a percentage figure representing the "opportunity cost" of capital. This is a rate equal to what the funds would have earned in their best alternative use of equal risk.

EXAMPLE   Suppose that the present value of expected benefits to be derived from a particular pollution-abatement program is estimated to be $1 million, and the present value of expected costs is $0.9 million. Then the ratio of benefit to cost is 1.1 to 1. This suggests that the program may be worth undertaking, depending on how it ranks with alternative investment projects. This is because the benefit/cost ratio is greater than 1. That is, the incremental benefit exceeds the incremental cost, because each $1 of investment stands to return $1.11 in benefits. On the other hand, if the ratio turned out to be less than 1, the incremental cost would exceed the incremental benefit, and the program would not be warranted.

Benefit-cost analysis has been used since the 1930s, primarily in government investment projects for flood control and river valley development. It has also been employed to evaluate pollution-abatement projects as well as other socioeconomic programs. Among them have been manpower training, family planning, vocational rehabilitation, and disease control. Despite its extraordinary success in some of these areas, certain major limitations prevent its widespread application:

1. *Benefits are difficult to define and measure.*   In the case of a smog-abatement program, for instance, certain benefits are relatively easy to establish. Examples are the savings in painting and cleaning expenses that will result from purer air. But how do we define the effects on human life? If the program reduces the death rate from respiratory diseases, the benefit/cost ratio will rise. But if people live longer, the benefit/cost ratio will decline because older people become ill more often and require more medical care. Similarly, in a program to reduce the pollution of a lake or river, it may be possible to forecast the probable financial benefits to fisheries in terms of the higher earnings they are likely to receive. But how do we establish the nonmonetary benefits of the program to the community?

2. *Priorities may conflict with benefits.*   Even if all the monetary benefits of a program could be established, the resulting benefit/cost ratio would not always reflect the relative need for the program from society's overall standpoint. Thus, a particular pollution-abatement project may yield an expected benefit/cost ratio of 1.2 to 1. However, a program for training the hard-core unemployed may produce an expected benefit/cost ratio of 1.1 to 1. Does this mean that society's limited supply of funds should be taken from the latter and put into the former? Not necessarily. An attack on hard-core unemployment may have nonmonetary, but socially desirable, consequences that simply cannot be precisely identified for purposes of benefit-cost analysis.

Cost-Effectiveness Analysis

The difficulty of defining and measuring benefits led to the introduction of another method of efficiency planning known as *cost-effectiveness analysis*. This is a technique of selecting from alternative programs the one that will attain a given objective at the lowest cost. It is most useful where benefits cannot be measured in money. Thus, cost-effectiveness analysis is of no use in deciding whether it would be better to develop a program for abating pollution or for reducing the number of deaths from traffic accidents. However, given the decision to spend on one of these, cost-effectiveness analysis may be used to select the alternative that will cost least.

As a hypothetical example, a cost-effectiveness analysis of deaths resulting from smog might reach the following conclusions.

On the average, a reduction of one death could be achieved for each expenditure of (1) $90,000 on the development of clean-burning fuels, (2) $60,000 on the installation of furnace and engine filtering devices, (3) $45,000 on the provision of improved medical treatment, (4) $18,000 on the vigorous enforcement of existing smog-abatement laws, or (5) $150 on the production of special "gas masks" or breathing devices for all citizens. If the only factor to be considered were the cost, it follows that the last choice is the one to be adopted because it achieves the given objective at the lowest cost.

Unfortunately, there are many types of environmental problems—as well as urban and social welfare problems—where cost-effectiveness analysis has not yet demonstrated its usefulness. For example, should the limited funds available for general pollution abatement be spent for smog control, water purification, or waste disposal? This question is critical. Yet it may not be specific enough for cost-effectiveness analysis to answer. This is because a common objective must first be defined and measured, and the costs of alternative actions for achieving that objective must be identified, as in the hypothetical example above. These, of course, are the fundamental difficulties. However, as more and better information becomes available, cost-effectiveness analysis will continue to gain in importance as a powerful tool for program evaluation.

ENVIRONMENTAL POLICIES

How much does it cost to undertake antipollution programs? Who pays? These questions are at the heart of environmental policy.

Unfortunately, we do not always know the net gain—the benefits relative to the costs—of eliminating a particular waste. Hence, we may spend too much money reducing some wastes that are not very damaging and not enough reducing those wastes that are. Clearly, some specific guidelines are needed for help-ing to formulate correct judgments. Four proposals may be considered:

1. Levy emission fees on polluters.
2. Sell pollution "rights."
3. Subsidize pollution-abatement efforts.
4. Impose direct regulations.

An analysis of these alternatives will suggest some conclusions for public policy. (See also Box 3.)

Levy Emission Fees on Polluters

Many economists and legislators have increasingly emphasized the idea that the costs of pollution should be built into the price–profit system as an incentive feature. In simplest terms, this approach involves the use of metering devices to measure the amount of pollution emitted by factories. Fees would then be imposed for every unit of pollutant discharged.

A pollution-control board—a state or federal agency—could determine safe limits of emission. Then the fees it charged could be varied not only by the amount of waste emitted, but by the hour of the day, by the day of the week, and by geographic location. By setting its own multiple-fee schedules on these bases, the board could exert a strong influence on *how much, when,* and *where* pollutants were discharged. And because the emission fees would become part of a firm's costs of operation, the board would be using the price mechanism as a carrot as well as a stick.

Several arguments are offered in favor of this approach:

1. It would permit the imposition of variable charges on the generation of wastes. Historically, governmental systems for controlling waste have usually been on a yes-or-no basis. However, as indicated above, we do not yet know enough about the different kinds of waste to permit them in terms of "all or none." By levying emission fees, it would be possible to impose degrees of control as the needs arose.

2. It would enable government to distribute pollution more evenly throughout the country. By charging lower emission fees in sparsely populated areas and higher fees in the more densely populated regions, factories would be encouraged to locate away from the cities where they could pollute with less social damage.

3. It would cause firms to calculate the costs of waste, as well as the costs and benefits of abatement, and to consider these alternatives in their production and pricing decisions. Businesses would thus be stimulated to seek methods of reducing waste—perhaps by "recycling" it into production, or by developing socially harmless methods of disposal.

Box 3
Environmental Pollution

Ray Ellis, Rapho/Photo Researchers.

Chicago Sun-Times Photo.

Give me your . . . huddled masses yearning to breathe
  free,
The wretched refuse of your teeming shore.
        Emma Lazarus, *The New Colossus* (1903)

Rhoda Galyn, Photo Researchers.

Paolo Koch, Photo Researchers.

. . . And Man created the plastic bag and the tin and aluminum can and the cellophane wrapper and the paper plate.
And this was good because Man could then take his automobile and buy all his food in one place and He could save
that which was good to eat in the refrigerator and throw
away that which had no further use. And soon the earth was
covered with plastic bags and aluminum cans and paper
plates and disposable bottles and there was nowhere to sit
down or walk. And Man shook his head and cried: "Look at
this Godawful mess."

                        Art Buchwald

If you with litter will disgrace,
And spoil the beauty of this place,
May indigestion rack your chest
And ants invade your pants and vest.
            Sign at the entrance of the
            Pleasure Gardens of Ceylon

The rebuttals to these arguments can be readily anticipated. Essentially, opponents of emission fees argue as follows:

1. Only certain types of pollution can be measured with metering devices.

2. Many factors other than emission fees, such as the availability of a suitable labor supply, and access to raw materials and markets, influence the geographic location of firms.

3. Benefits and costs are impossible to measure and use precisely.

Because of these reasons, those who object to the levying of emission fees argue that such a system would at best have only limited advantages.

Sell Pollution "Rights"

A second proposal for dealing with the problem of pollution is to establish a system of marketable licenses. Each license would give its owner the "right" to pollute—up to a specified amount in a given place during a particular period of time. These licenses or rights could be bought and sold in an organized market—not unlike the stock market or the commodities market. Their prices would fluctuate according to the forces of supply and demand, reflecting the general desire of polluters to dispose of waste. The basic economic features of the proposal are explained in Exhibit 2.

At a very low price, those who wanted to pollute could do so at relatively little cost. If the price were very high, some form of supplementary rights would have to be issued to financially weaker firms in order to enable them to pollute, while limiting the opportunities for financially stronger firms through the market system. A similar type of scheme might also be developed for households.

This approach to waste control would not be adaptable to all forms of pollution. But to those for which it was suited, its fundamental advantage would be its operation through the free market and use of the price system as a mechanism for coping with pollution problems.

Subsidize Pollution-Abatement Efforts

A third approach to curbing pollution is through government subsidization schemes for firms. This system could take various direct and indirect forms. Among them: outright payments for the reduction of pollution levels, subsidies for particular control devices, and exemptions from local property taxes on pollution-abatement equipment. Also, special fast depreciation

Exhibit 2
A Market for Pollution "Rights"

One way to attack the pollution problem is through the price system. The government would determine the maximum amount of a specific type of pollution that is within safe limits—such as the number of tons of raw sewage per year dumped into a lake that would disintegrate by normal bacterial processes. It could then sell *rights to pollution* in a free market. Each "right" would permit the owner to dump a specified quantity of sewage per year into the lake.

The supply curve *S* in this case would therefore be a vertical line. The demand curve *D*, however, would be downward-sloping. This indicates that some polluters would find it cheaper to buy the pollution rights than to invest in pollution-abatement equipment, while others would not. Hence, the equilibrium price would settle at *P* and the equilibrium quantity at *Q*. Note that this quantity is less than the amount at *Q'* which would prevail if the price of pollution were zero.

Over the years, the growth in income and population would cause the demand curve to rise—say to *D'*. This would bring about a higher equilibrium price at *P'*.

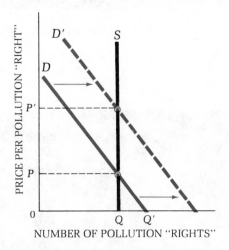

allowances and tax credits for the purchase of pollution-control equipment could be granted.

If subsidization of any type were to be employed in a pollution-control scheme, several considerations would have to be kept in mind:

1. It would be better to give firms outright payments for the reduction of pollution levels than to offer tax credits for investing in abatement equipment. Outright payments would leave businesses free to adopt the least costly means of reducing the discharge of pollutants. Tax credits, on the other hand, would discourage firms from seeking alternative methods of pollution abatement, including the possibility of burning nonpolluting fuels.

2. If firms are to be subsidized for investing in pollution controls, the subsidies should be given for equipment that is likely to enhance businesses' net profits by either adding to revenues or reducing costs. A pollution-control device that was not expected to increase profits would leave firms with very little incentive to acquire it—even if the government offered to pay part of the cost.

3. Subsidy payments should be tied to the amounts by which pollutants were reduced below the levels that would have prevailed without the payments. Such standards are extremely difficult if not impossible to estimate, especially for new firms. Yet, failure to establish guidelines of this type would make any subsidization scheme largely ineffective.

4. Subsidy payments would violate the "benefit principle" of equity if, as is most likely, the subsidies were financed out of general tax revenues. According to the benefit principle—which has strong support on moral and ethical grounds—pollution-control measures should be part of the costs of production. That is, consumers who buy products ought to pay the anti-pollution costs of production just as labor, capital, and other inputs are paid for. In other words, even though all of society benefits from subsidies to control pollution, it can be argued that consumers who buy the products that are responsible for pollution should pay the costs of reducing it.

5. Moral and ethical principles of fairness would be violated if indirect subsidies were given in the form of tax credits to firms that invest in pollution-abatement equipment. Such credits would mean that some taxpayers would have to pay higher taxes than otherwise. This would introduce further biases into the tax system, resulting in resource misallocation.

These considerations make it clear that subsidy schemes, although frequently proposed, are not necessarily the best approach for public policy.

Impose Direct Regulations

A fourth method of pollution control is to invoke the legislative powers of government at all levels. This would involve the use of licenses, permits, zoning regulations, registration, and other controls. Violators would be subject to civil and criminal proceedings. Direct regulations such as these are wholly within the province of federal and state governments, which, under the "general welfare" and "police power" clauses of the Constitution, have the authority to pass laws promoting the health and safety of citizens.

The general objection to direct regulation is the same for pollution abatement as for anything else. Regulation leads to rigidities and, in many cases, unwieldy and inefficient forms of control. A law that sets a limit on pollution levels will cause a greater misallocation of resources than, say, a system of emission fees. This is because the latter can accomplish the same overall reductions in pollution while leaving firms free to adjust to their own particular production situations as they think best.

Does this mean that direct regulations should be avoided at all costs? Not necessarily. In a capitalistic economy direct regulations may very well be needed. However, they should be adopted only after all other market-oriented mechanisms have been found unsuitable.

CONCLUSION: WHICH POLICY?

It is impossible to say which of the four approaches to pollution control—emission fees, pollution "rights," subsidization, or direct regulations—would be best. There are different kinds and sources of pollution, many of which are not well understood. Hence, a method of control that might work effectively for curbing air or water contamination might not be suitable for reducing noise levels or land exploitation. Each class of pollution problems must therefore be analyzed separately and a specific control system designed for it.

If such a procedure were followed, it might very well be found that different combinations of policies were needed for various kinds of pollution. In the meantime, most present pollution controls are in the form of direct regulation. This leaves few or no bases for judging the effectiveness of alternative control schemes.

What about technology as a solution? To many critics, technology is the culprit that has been responsible for the mess. Cans and bottles accumulate because they cannot be burned. The automobile turns cities into parking lots and greeneries into paved highways. Environmentalists now fear that people will again turn to technology—perhaps to the dream of building air-conditioned geodesic domes over the cities, or to visions of inhabiting outer space—as an answer. But these are as yet only fantasies. More realistically:

Technology will no doubt play a vital role in rescuing society from its own waste. However, our most fundamental need if we are to survive on this planet is to *create a value system that will enable us to assess the various parts of the environment.* As philosopher Lewis Mumford once stated: "Any square mile of inhabited earth has more significance for man's future than all of the planets in the solar system."

What You Have Learned

1. A surplus or shortage of a commodity can exist only at a given price. Therefore, it is meaningless to use such terms as "surplus" or "shortage" unless a specific price is understood.

2. If the United States wishes to improve the allocation of energy resources, four major options are available: (a) free markets, (b) rationing, (c) crude-oil allocation, and (d) demand reduction and supply expansion. After decades of experience with government-mandated regulations and controls, there is widespread agreement that a free market in energy would best meet the nation's goals.

3. In general, the difficulty of implementing and maintaining free markets in energy is more political than economic. Therefore, various regulations aimed at protecting special interests are likely to arise. This prevents the realizations of efficiency and equity that free markets bring.

4. The natural environment includes three major types of resources—air, land, and water. These have been polluted and exploited by businesses and households because society has failed to evaluate the real costs of using various environmental resources. That is, society has not assigned appropriate prices to cover utilization costs and has instead made the resources available "free." As a result, two methods that are gaining increasing use for correcting these shortcomings and for improving decision making about environmental issues are benefit-cost analysis and cost-effectiveness analysis.

5. Several approaches to pollution control are possible.

Among them: (a) levy emission fees on polluters, (b) sell pollution "rights," (c) subsidize pollution-abatement efforts, and (d) impose direct regulations. Because relatively little is known about the many causes and effects of pollution, it is virtually certain that no one of these policies would be suitable in all cases. Instead, various combinations would be desirable. At present, however, most policies are in the form of direct regulations.

For Discussion

1. *Terms and concepts to review:*

surplus	direct-payments plan
shortage	benefit-cost analysis
black market	cost-effectiveness
white market	analysis

2. Using supply and demand curves, illustrate the concept of direct payments. Could a direct-payments plan lead to an eventual "surplus" of oil? Explain.

3. Using supply and demand curves, describe the effects on price and output of a subsidy to sellers. How do these effects compare with those of a direct-payments plan in Question 2?

4. "If all land and inland waters were privately owned, this would be a first step in controlling pollution." Explain the justification for this statement.

5. Of the various environmental policy alternatives suggested in this chapter, which one would probably be the most practical and least costly to administer, other things being equal? Explain your answer.

Issue
Property Rights and Pollution: Who Owns What?

Curing pollution is simple. All we have to do is invoke the market system. How? By letting individuals own, buy, and sell *property rights* in what are now publicly owned resources.

If this were done, people would find it less profitable to pollute. As with any commodity, the value society places on environmental resources would reflect their best alternative uses. Only when resources are "too cheap" do they tend to be "overused" or polluted, as is the case with much of our air, land, and water.

Unfortunately, the implementation of these ideas may sometimes be difficult. The reasons, however, may be more political than economic, because private rather than public ownership may be required.

Everyone's Property Is No One's Property[1]

Pollution most frequently occurs or is conveyed through such public goods as air, rivers, lakes, oceans, and commonly owned lands, such as public parks and streets. In most cases, *rights* to use these resources (public goods)

[1] W. Lee Hopkins, "An Economic Solution to Pollution," *Business Review*, Federal Reserve Bank of Philadelphia, September 1970. Adapted.

are held by all of us in common or are simply unspecified by law. When rights to resources (goods) are vague or held in common, the rule is "first come, first served." People have less incentive to maintain the purity of a lake or stream when they do not have the right to capture the value from doing so. Water in a private lake tends to be put to its highest valued uses (including those in the future) when the owner stands to gain. If the owner can capture that value by selling the lake, he or she has an incentive to protect the quality of the water. Unfortunately, no such incentive exists for our commonly owned air, water, and land. As a result, these resources are not being put to uses most highly valued by society—they are "overconsumed" (polluted), while other goods are "overproduced." One means of coping with this problem is to specify salable property rights in our commonly owned resources (or public goods).

Privatizing Public Goods[2]

Public goods are goods which cannot be provided for some without being

[2] Abba P. Lerner, "The Economics and Politics of Consumer Sovereignty," *The American Economic Review, Papers and Proceedings,* May 1972.

provided for others. The normal market mechanism for achieving consumer sovereignty is therefore inapplicable. Those who would benefit from the provision of such goods will not pay for the benefits because they can enjoy them without paying if they are provided for anybody else. Everybody will wait for somebody else to buy them and hope to enjoy a free ride.

This is not a new problem. Indeed, in the beginning, before the invention of property rights, all goods were public. It did not pay anyone to improve on traditional procedures because any resulting increase in output would be free to everyone in the tribe. It did not pay anyone to build a house if he could instead find someone who had built one and then move in with him (or kick him out). Only with the establishment of privatization, or property, was the decentralization of decisions necessary for efficient production made possible. Our problem now is that the invention and application of the special devices needed to *privatize* the public goods have lagged behind the great increase in production of goods of all kinds. Privatizing is nothing more than establishing the institutional arrangements by which the individual or group who

Arthur Tress.

Paul Conklin, Monkmeyer Press Photo Service.

pays for the benefit gets it and the one who does not pay for it does not get it.

However, not all public goods can be privatized. There will still be services which, if provided for some, are inevitably made available for all. The market mechanism cannot work. Everybody will refrain from buying them in the hope someone else will. And nobody will be willing to pay the total cost of a benefit to all.

Need for Agreement

Where this is the case, agreement is necessary for combined action. This is what government is for. A citizen will agree to be compelled to contribute to the cost of a project, provided enough others also are compelled, so that the benefit exceeds the contribution (or tax). There is no reason for expecting such nonprivatizable services—such inherently public goods—to become more important in the future. Not all goods can be privatized, but it is our failure to privatize where privatization is possible that is responsible for most of these ills.

Ken Lambert, Free Lance Photographers Guild.

QUESTIONS

1. Is it necessary for environmental resources to be privately owned in order to reduce their pollution? How else might the market system be invoked while retaining public ownership?

2. If privatization of environmental resources is so desirable, why has it not been undertaken on a large scale?

Part 5

Using Supply and Demand. The Laws of Production and Cost

Chapter 20

Working with Supply, Demand, and Elasticity: Some Interesting Applications

Chapter Preview

To what extent do changes in the price of a good affect changes in the quantities demanded or supplied? Can these changes be measured, compared, and interpreted?

The government has influenced market prices and quantities of certain commodities by imposing price controls, price supports, commodity taxes, and subsidies. How can supply and demand models analyze the effects of these actions?

What are some of the assumptions that underlie the use of supply and demand models?

How does the price system of a market economy "filter" out buyers and sellers in the marketplace?

Is there a distinction between pure and applied science? In answer to this question, the nineteenth-century French scientist Louis Pasteur replied, "No, a thousand times no. There does not exist a category of science to which one can give the name applied science. There are only science and the applications of science, bound together as the fruit to the tree which bears it."

Supply and demand can be viewed in much the same way. You are already familiar with the "pure" side of the subject from your study of it early in this book. Now you can take a few moments to brush up on the basic concepts by reviewing the brief presentation in Exhibit 1.

In this chapter we explore the "applied" aspects of supply and demand by solving some interesting problems. When you complete this chapter you will probably agree with Pasteur that the principles and applications of supply and demand, like those of any science, are indeed "bound together as the fruit to the tree."

The Concept of Elasticity: A Measure of Responsiveness to Changes in Price

You already know from Exhibit 1 that the relationship between the price and quantity of a good is *causal*. For instance, a rise in price will cause a decrease in

Exhibit 1
Brief Review of Supply and Demand

Chart (a). *The law of demand states that the quantity demanded of a good varies inversely with its price. This means that people will buy more of a good at a lower price than at a higher price.*

Chart (b). *The law of supply states that the quantity supplied of a good usually varies directly with its price. Thus, sellers are willing to supply larger quantities at higher prices than at lower prices.*

Chart (c). *When demand and supply curves are graphed, their intersection determines the equilibrium market price and quantity. Any price above this equilibrium level results in the quantity supplied exceeding the quantity demanded, thereby driving the price down. Any price below the equilibrium level results in the quantity demanded exceeding the quantity supplied, thereby driving the price up. At the equilibrium level there are no product surpluses or shortages. Thus, the market is precisely cleared.*

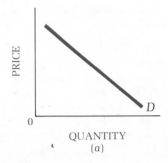
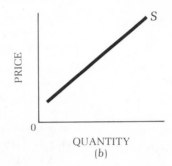
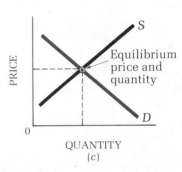

Charts (d) and (e). *A change in demand or a change in supply is represented by a shift of the given curve to a new position. Such shifts may occur as a result of changes in any of the factors assumed constant when the curves are initially drawn. In the case of demand these factors include buyer incomes, tastes, expectations, the prices of related goods, and the number of buyers in the market. In the case of supply they are resource costs, technology, sellers' expectations, the prices of other goods, and the number of* sellers in the market. Changes or shifts in demand or supply may bring about new equilibrium prices and quantities.

Charts (f) and (g). *If the demand curve remains fixed, a movement along the curve from one point to another denotes a change in the quantity demanded. Likewise, if the supply curve remains fixed, a movement along the curve denotes a change in the quantity supplied. Such changes are always associated with changes in price.*

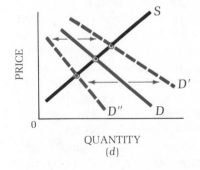
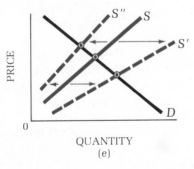
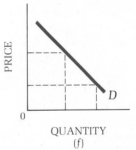
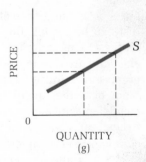

the quantity demanded and an increase in the quantity supplied. A fall in price will produce the opposite effects—an increase in the quantity demanded and a decrease in the quantity supplied.

But by *how much* will a change in price affect the quantities supplied or demanded? There is a big difference, for example, between a commodity such as salt and a commodity such as vacation trips. In the case of salt, the quantity demanded varies relatively little with changes in price. But for vacation trips, changes in price may cause relatively large changes in the quantity demanded.

How can we measure these changes? One way is to use a concept called "elasticity." This reflects the responsiveness of a change in one variable to a change in another.

The following interpretive definition of "elasticity" can be used to understand and explain its meaning:

Elasticity is the percentage change in quantity (demanded or supplied) resulting from a 1 percent change in price.

The following mathematical definition of "elasticity" can be used to calculate elasticities of supply or demand, as illustrated later:

Elasticity is the ratio of the percentage change in quantity (demanded or supplied) to the percentage change in price:

$$\text{elasticity} = \frac{\text{percentage change in quantity}}{\text{percentage change in price}}$$

You already know that the law of supply expresses a *direct* relationship between price and quantity supplied. Therefore, the coefficient you get when you calculate supply elasticity will be positive. On the other hand, the law of demand expresses an *inverse* relationship between price and quantity demanded. Therefore, the coefficient of demand elasticity will be negative. In practice, however, we often disregard the negative sign and express all elasticities as if they were either positive or zero, as you will see in the following sections.

Test Yourself

1. Suppose that you calculate the elasticity of supply for a commodity as 2.8. This means that a 1 percent increase in the price of the product will result in a 2.8 percent increase in the quantity supplied.

   (a) What would a 1 percent decrease in the price mean?

   (b) A 10 percent increase in the price?

   (c) A 10 percent decrease in the price?

2. Suppose that you estimate the elasticity of demand for a product as −0.5. This means that a 1 percent increase in the price of the commodity will result in a *decrease* in the quantity demanded of ½ of 1 percent.

   (a) What would a 1 percent decrease in the price mean?

   (b) A 10 percent increase in the price?

   (c) A 10 percent decrease in the price?

3. Instead of measuring elasticity in terms of relative amounts or percentages, why not measure it in terms of actual amounts instead? For example, suppose that you wanted to know which has the greater influence on quantity demanded—a reduction in the price of diamonds of $100 per carat, or a reduction in the price of wheat of $1 per bushel.

   (a) Would you express the price and quantity changes in terms of actual amounts or in terms of percentages?

   (b) Suppose that you chose to express the changes in terms of actual amounts. Would you be able to compare carats and bushels in order to tell which was more affected by the changes in price?

VISUALIZING ELASTICITIES FROM GRAPHS

Because elasticity measures the responsiveness of changes in quantity to changes in price, it is helpful to distinguish among the different degrees of responsiveness. This is done in Exhibit 2, where five types of elasticity are defined and illustrated. Study these diagrams and definitions carefully. Notice from the statement near the top of the exhibit that the elasticity coefficients are expressed *numerically* without regard to algebraic sign. As mentioned earlier, this practice is common in economic discussions.

There is an easy way to remember the charts in Exhibit 2. Think of them as the frames of a motion picture. In the first "frames" both curves are in a horizontal position. Then in successive frames the demand curve gradually tilts downward while the supply curve tilts upward until both curves end up in a vertical position.

Do the five different definitions of elasticity in Exhibit 2 sound intuitively reasonable? They should. After all, elasticity is nothing more than the "stretch" in quantity compared with the "stretch" in price, with both stretches being measured in percentages.

MEASURING ELASTICITY

A hypothetical demand curve is shown in Exhibit 3. Our objective is to estimate the elasticity of demand for this curve. We may choose two points near the ends of the line, such as points A and B, because they are conveniently located on at least one of the grids, and calculate the elasticity for the segment AB.

How does the change in quantity demanded compare with the change in price over this segment? Disregarding for the time being the calculations accompanying the chart, we observe from the chart alone that a movement along the curve from A to B is measured by two changes: an increase in quantity from 20 bushels to 80 bushels, and a corresponding decrease in price from about $52 to $17. A change or increase in quantity of 60 bushels is thus associated with an opposite change or decrease in price of $35. The change in quantity per unit change in price, therefore, is $60/-35 = -1.72$, or 1.72 if the sign is disregarded.

Is this the elasticity of demand? *The answer is no,* because the result is obviously affected by the units in which the quantities and prices are measured. The solution would have been different, for example, if

Exhibit 2
Five Different Kinds of Elasticity

E = numerical elasticity (i.e., algebraic signs are disregarded). The symbol < means "less than"; the symbol > means "greater than."

Case (a) Perfectly Elastic. *An infinitesimally small percentage change in price results in an infinitely large percentage change in the quantity demanded or supplied. The numerical elasticity is infinite. Thus, a change in price from P_1 to P_2 produces a change in quantity demanded or supplied from zero to a positive amount. In terms of percentages, this is an infinite change.*

Case (b) Relatively Elastic. *A given percentage change in price results in a larger percentage change in quantity. The numerical elasticity is greater than 1. Thus, a change in price from P_1 to P_2 causes a more than proportionate change in quantity from Q_1 to Q_2.*

Case (c) Unit Elastic. *A given percentage change in price results in an equal percentage change in quantity. The numerical elasticity is 1. Thus, a change in price from P_1 to P_2 causes an equal proportionate change in quantity from Q_1 to Q_2.*

Case (d) Relatively Inelastic. *A given percentage change in price results in a smaller percentage change in quantity. The numerical elasticity is less than 1 (but greater than zero). For example, a change in price from P_1 to P_2 causes a less than proportionate change in quantity from Q_1 to Q_2.*

Case (e) Perfectly Inelastic. *A given percentage change in price results in no change in quantity. The numerical elasticity is zero. Thus, a change in price from P_1 to P_2 causes no change in quantity.*

REMARK   The slope of a curve at any point is its steepness (or flatness) at that point. A straight line has the same slope at every point, but not necessarily the same elasticity. Therefore, you *cannot always infer the elasticity of a curve from its slope alone.* These charts are merely intended to help you visualize the five different kinds of elasticity.*

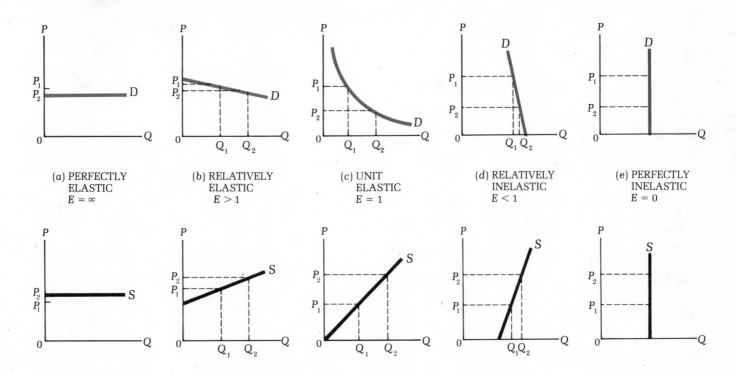

(a) PERFECTLY ELASTIC $E = \infty$ (b) RELATIVELY ELASTIC $E > 1$ (c) UNIT ELASTIC $E = 1$ (d) RELATIVELY INELASTIC $E < 1$ (e) PERFECTLY INELASTIC $E = 0$

* TECHNICAL NOTE (OPTIONAL)   If you are mathematically inclined, you may be able to see that the slope and elasticity of a curve would be the same if the *logarithms* of price and quantity were plotted in the charts. Equivalently, the slope and elasticity of a curve would be the same if it were plotted on a special type of graph paper whose vertical and horizontal axes were both scaled in *logarithms*.

The reason for this is that on a logarithmic scale, equal distances are represented by equal proportional or *relative* changes. Because elasticity is nothing more than a measure of relative change, the slope of a straight line on logarithmic scales is the same as its elasticity. It is an interesting exercise to prove these ideas algebraically.

quantities had been expressed in millions of bushels or if prices had been expressed in British pounds or in French francs. Since a chief purpose of calculating elasticity is to permit relative comparisons to be made between products, we need a measure of elasticity that is unaffected by the units in which the data are quoted—that is, we need a *coefficient of elasticity.*

The Coefficient of Elasticity

You will recall from the definition of elasticity that its measurement is simply the percentage change in quantity divided by the percentage change in price. The most common method of measuring these percentage changes is to divide the observed change in quantity by the average of the two quantities, and the observed change in price by the average of the two prices. This enables us to express the definition by the formula

$$\text{elasticity} = \frac{\begin{array}{c}\text{percentage change}\\\text{in quantity}\end{array}}{\begin{array}{c}\text{percentage change}\\\text{in price}\end{array}}$$

$$= \frac{\dfrac{\text{change in quantity}}{\text{average quantity}}}{\dfrac{\text{change in price}}{\text{average price}}}$$

You can use this formula in calculating the elasticity of demand in Exhibit 3. In doing so, however, substitute the letters P for price and Q for quantity in the formula, and attach subscripts to the letters so that you do not mix up your Ps and Qs. Thus, let

Q_1 = old quantity, or quantity before change
Q_2 = new quantity, or quantity after change
P_1 = old price, or price before change
P_2 = new price, or price after change

The formula for elasticity of demand E_D is then

$$E_D = \frac{\dfrac{Q_2 - Q_1}{(Q_2 + Q_1)/2}}{\dfrac{P_2 - P_1}{(P_2 + P_1)/2}} = \frac{\dfrac{Q_2 - Q_1}{Q_2 + Q_1}}{\dfrac{P_2 - P_1}{P_2 + P_1}}$$

Notice from the middle part of the equation that the average quantity is the sum of the two quantities divided by 2, and the average price is the sum of the two prices divided by 2. These 2s then cancel out, leaving the complex fraction at the end.

An application of this formula is illustrated by the equations in Exhibit 3. Observe that the same result is obtained whether the change is from A to B or from B

Exhibit 3
Calculating the Elasticity of Demand for the Segment *AB*

Change from A to B:
   At A: $Q_1 = 20$, $P_1 = 52$
   At B: $Q_2 = 80$, $P_2 = 17$

$$E_D = \frac{\dfrac{Q_2 - Q_1}{Q_2 + Q_1}}{\dfrac{P_2 - P_1}{P_2 + P_1}} = \frac{\dfrac{80 - 20}{80 + 20}}{\dfrac{17 - 52}{17 + 52}}$$

$$= \frac{0.60}{-0.51} = -1.2, \text{ or 1.2 } numerically$$

Change from B to A:
   At B: $Q_1 = 80$, $P_1 = 17$
   At A: $Q_2 = 20$, $P_2 = 52$

$$E_D = \frac{\dfrac{Q_2 - Q_1}{Q_2 + Q_1}}{\dfrac{P_2 - P_1}{P_2 + P_1}} = \frac{\dfrac{20 - 80}{20 + 80}}{\dfrac{52 - 17}{52 + 17}}$$

$$= \frac{-0.60}{0.51} = -1.2, \text{ or 1.2 } numerically$$

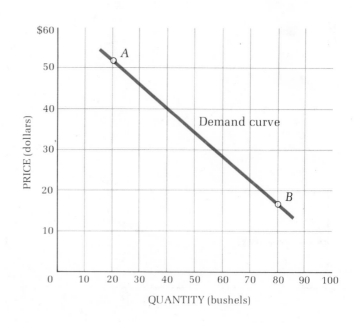

Interpretation
A 1 percent change in price results in a 1.2 percent change in quantity demanded. (Similarly, a 10 percent change in price results in a 12 percent change in quantity demanded.) Because the change in quantity demanded is more than proportional to the change in price, demand is thus relatively elastic.

to A. This is an important advantage, because many practical situations arise in which we know only two prices and two quantities, and we do not know which price and quantity came first.

EXAMPLE   The Savemore Paint Company sold an average of 300 gallons of paint per week at $10 per gallon, and 500 gallons of paint per week at $8 per gallon. What is the elasticity of demand?

The answer is −2.25, or 2.25 numerically, regardless of the values you choose for your initial price and quantity. Work it out both ways and see for yourself. How do you interpret this answer? What would you expect the percentage change in quantity to be if the price changed by 10 percent? (HINT   Refer back to Exhibit 3.)

What about elasticity of supply E_s? Do we measure it in the same way? The answer is yes. We also use the same formula. However, we let Q_1 and Q_2 stand for the quantities supplied before and after the change, and P_1 and P_2 represent the corresponding prices.

ELASTICITY OF DEMAND AND TOTAL REVENUE

In many practical situations involving the study of demand, economists find it convenient to have a simple guide for judging whether demand is elastic or inelastic. An easy method that can be used for this purpose is to compare the change in the price of the commodity with the corresponding change in the seller's gross receipts. These receipts are customarily called "total revenue." It is important to keep in mind that a seller's total revenue (abbreviated TR) is equal to price (P) per unit times the quantity (Q) of units sold. That is, $TR = P \times Q$. Thus, if a shirt manufacturer charges $10 per shirt and sells 100 shirts, the total revenue is $1,000.

Exhibit 4 provides useful visual illustrations of the relation between demand elasticity and total revenue. These charts are similar to three of the five types of demand elasticities described in Exhibit 2.

Exhibit 4
Demand Elasticity and Total Revenue

A seller's total revenue is equal to the price per unit multiplied by the number of units sold. Therefore, total revenue in all three charts can be measured by the rectangular area under the demand curve. Thus, at a price equal to the distance OP, quantity demanded is represented by the distance

OM. Therefore, total revenue is the area of the rectangle OPSM. At a price of OT, quantity demanded is ON. Therefore, total revenue is the area of the rectangle OTVN. Hence, we have the relationships shown in Charts (a)–(c).

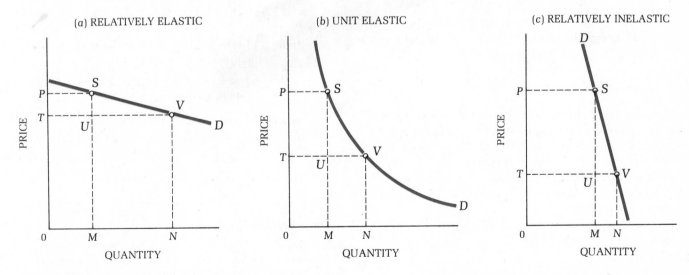

Chart (a) Relatively Elastic. *When demand is relatively elastic, a decrease in price results in an increase in total revenue, and an increase in price results in a decrease in total revenue.*

Chart (b) Unit Elastic. *When demand is unit elastic, a de-* crease or increase in price results in the same total revenue.

Chart (c) Relatively Inelastic. *When demand is relatively inelastic, a decrease in price results in a decrease in total revenue, and an increase in price results in an increase in total revenue.*

Relatively Elastic Demand

Exhibit 4, Chart (a), illustrates a relatively elastic demand curve. Suppose that the price is at P, which is represented by the distance 0P. Then the corresponding quantity demanded is at M, measured by the distance 0M. The seller's total revenue is therefore price times quantity, or 0P × 0M. This is also the area of the rectangle 0PSM, because the area of any rectangle is the product of its base and height.

Suppose that the selling firm lowers its price to 0T. The quantity demanded then increases to 0N. Hence, the seller's new total revenue is again equal to price times quantity, or the area of the rectangle 0TVN. This new rectangle is larger in area than the old one. That is, as a result of a price reduction, the seller has lost a relatively small amount of total revenue represented by the rectangle TPSU. However, the seller has also gained a larger amount of total revenue represented by the rectangle MUVN. Because the gain more than offsets the loss, the seller's final total revenue is larger after the price reduction than before.

What happens if price increases, say from 0T to 0P? The result is exactly the opposite. Total revenue declines from 0TVN to 0PSM. In other words, the large loss more than offsets the small gain.

The relationship between changes in price and changes in total revenue can be readily explained in terms of elasticity. When demand is relatively elastic:

1. A given percentage decrease in price is more than offset by a corresponding percentage increase in quantity demanded. Therefore, total revenue rises.

2. A given percentage increase in price is more than offset by a corresponding percentage decrease in quantity demanded. Therefore, total revenue falls.

Unit Elastic Demand

A second type of situation is illustrated in Exhibit 4, Chart (b). Here demand is unit elastic. At a price of 0P the quantity demanded is 0M. Hence, the seller's total revenue is the area of the rectangle 0PSM. On the other hand, at a price of 0T the quantity demanded is 0N. Therefore the seller's total revenue is the area of the rectangle 0TVN.

It is interesting to note that the rectangles are equal in area. That is, 0PSM = 0TVN. This suggests an important principle:

In any situation involving a unit elastic demand curve, the rectangular areas associated with each corresponding price and quantity are always equal. This means that a given percentage decrease (or increase) in price is exactly offset by an equal percentage increase (or decrease) in quantity demanded. Consequently, the total revenues remain the same.

This principle helps to explain why a unit elastic demand curve has such a special shape. It is the only type of mathematical curve (called a "rectangular hyperbola") that permits percentage changes in price to be exactly offset by equal percentage changes in quantity demanded. As a result, the elasticity remains equal to 1 and hence the total revenue stays constant.

Relatively Inelastic Demand

What happens in the case of a relatively inelastic demand, as in Exhibit 4, Chart (c)? The relationships are obvious. When price is reduced from 0P to 0T, total revenue decreases from 0PSM to 0TVN. Clearly, the percentage decrease in price more than offsets the percentage increase in quantity demanded. This causes total revenue to fall. The opposite occurs in the case of a price increase, say from 0T to 0P. Total revenue rises because the percentage increase in price more than offsets the percentage decrease in quantity demanded.

The foregoing ideas are helpful for analyzing and predicting the effects of price changes on sellers' total revenues. We shall encounter many practical situations in later chapters where such predictions are a useful guide to policy formulation. A brief summary of these basic concepts is appropriate.

The relationship between price and total revenue depends on whether the elasticity of demand is greater than, equal to, or less than 1. Thus:

○ If demand is relatively elastic, a change in price causes a change in total revenue in the opposite direction.

○ If demand is unit elastic, a change in price causes no change in total revenue.

○ If demand is relatively inelastic, a change in price causes a change in total revenue in the same direction.

How well do you understand these basic ideas? You can judge for yourself by answering the following questions.

Some Practical Applications

1. Public transit systems often raise their rates to offset increased costs. Some of these systems find that their gross incomes decline in the first few weeks after the rate increase, and then rise. What does this suggest about the elasticity of demand for these services?

2. A country's currency may decline in value and therefore become cheaper for foreigners to buy. When this happens, the country may experience both (a) an increase in exports and (b) an influx of tourists. How would you interpret these occurrences?

3. If your college football stadium is drawing less-than-capacity crowds, under what conditions might a price increase be desirable? A price decrease? No change in price?

WHAT DETERMINES ELASTICITY?

Once you have learned how to calculate elasticity, you have mastered only half the job. The other half is to understand the factors that determine elasticity so that you can put this important concept to use.

For example, what makes some demand or supply curves elastic and others inelastic? The answers involve three key words—"substitutes," "inexpensiveness," and "time."

1. The most important determinant of both demand and supply elasticity is the number and closeness of available substitutes.

That is, the elasticity of demand for a product depends on the ease of substitution in consumption.

For example, if a commodity has good substitutes, and if the prices of these substitutes remain the same, a rise in the price of the commodity will divert consumer expenditures away from the product and over to the substitutes. A fall in the commodity's price will swing consumer expenditures away from the substitutes and back to the product. The demand therefore tends to be elastic.

On the other hand, if a commodity has poor substitutes, consumers will not respond significantly to changes in its price. Therefore, the demand for the product will tend to be inelastic.

The foregoing principle can be applied to the elasticity of supply, which depends on the ease of substitution in production.

For example, suppose that the resources used in the production of a certain commodity can easily be increased by hiring similar resources from other occupations. Then, if the price of the commodity rises relative to its costs of production while the prices of other products remain the same, producers of the higher-priced good will find it profitable to produce more of it. As they increase the quantity supplied by hiring resources away from other occupations, the output of the more profitable commodity will increase significantly.

Conversely, a fall in the price of the product relative to its costs will cause many resources engaged in its production to shift into other occupations. This will decrease output significantly.

In both instances, supply tends to be elastic. On the other hand, if it is difficult for resources to enter or leave a particular occupation, the supply curve will tend to be inelastic.

2. The more inexpensive a good—that is, the smaller the fraction of their total expenditures that consumers allocate for a good—the more inelastic the demand for it is likely to be.

Thus, the demand for such commodities as salt, matches, toothpicks, and soft drinks tends to be relatively inelastic. This is because each is such a relatively small part of consumers' total expenditures that changes in prices result in less than proportional changes in the quantities demanded.

3. Elasticities of demand and supply for a given product tend to increase over time. That is, elasticities tend to be greater in the long run than in the short run, because buyers and sellers have more time to adjust to changes in price.

This principle is based on the observation that the longer the time that elapses after a change in price, the easier it may become for buyers and sellers to use substitutes. Demands for specific products may therefore tend to become more elastic as buyers develop new tastes and habits of consumption. Supplies of specific products may tend to become more elastic as sellers find alternative resources for production of their outputs.

Of course, you may think of exceptions to one or more of these principles. This is true of almost any principle in the social sciences. However, there is ample evidence to indicate that the principles work in most cases.

Models of Supply and Demand

Many people do not enjoy learning about a subject unless they can see how it works in the world around them. After studying supply and demand we can apply its principles to the solution of many practical problems. Some are illustrated here in the form of real-world models.

PRICE FIXING BY LAW

Government may interfere with the normal operation of supply and demand. The reason may be to establish a price that is either lower or higher than that which would rule in an unregulated market. For example, price ceilings have been placed on many consumer goods during war or other critical inflationary periods to keep prices from going "too" high. Likewise, price floors have been used to keep the hourly wages of many workers from going "too" low. What are some of the economic effects of these legally established prices?

Price Ceilings Cause Shortages

The nature of a price ceiling is illustrated by the normal supply and demand curves in Exhibit 5. The equilibrium price that would be established in the market if there were no outside interference would be at P, represented by the distance $0P$ ($= NP'$). The equilibrium quantity would be at N, represented by the distance $0N$.

What happens if the government regards the equilibrium price as too high? In that case the government might establish a ceiling price, making it illegal to sell the product at a price above $0H$. The result will be a _shortage_ equal to the amount RL, because this represents the excess of quantity demanded over quantity supplied at the ceiling price.

When this situation occurs, the limited supplies of the commodity $0R$ will be snatched up by the early buyers, leaving nothing for later customers who want the remaining RL units of the product at the ceiling price. The government, therefore, may introduce _rationing_ as an equitable method of restricting purchases. This happened during World War II, for example, when there were shortages of such price-controlled items as sugar, butter, meat, and gasoline. The government distributed ration coupons to consumers, permitting them to purchase limited quantities each week. (See Box 1.)

Exhibit 5
Price Ceilings Result in Product Shortages

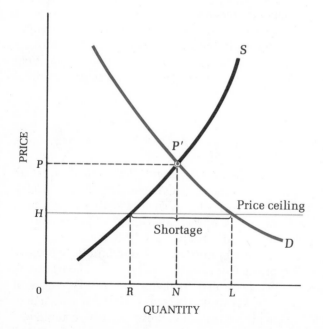

Box 1
How Rationing Works: Lessons from World War II

During World War II (1941–1945), price controls were extensive. In addition, certain commodities that were in particularly heavy demand by the armed forces were rationed for consumer use. Examples were meat, sugar, gasoline, and butter.

Consumers were issued books of ration coupons (somewhat like books of postage stamps) limiting weekly purchases of the rationed goods. Each coupon was worth a certain number of "points." This enabled consumers to purchase the rationed commodities at "point prices." For example, a homemaker buying hamburger meat might pay 25 cents per pound _plus_ 3 points worth of ration coupons.

In an attempt to minimize the imbalances between consumption and production, the government would change the point prices of goods from time to time. Thus, the ration coupons became a supplementary form of money. As a result, _the ration-coupon price combined with the dollar price performed the market function of adjusting consumption to available supplies._

Wide World Photos.

Price Floors Cause Surpluses

Price floors, which are the opposite of price ceilings, are designed to prevent a price from falling below a specified level. Although price ceilings have typically but not exclusively been a wartime phenomenon in the United States (but not in some other countries), price floors have played a continuing role in our daily lives. Two types have been particularly common: agricultural price supports and minimum-wage legislation.

In the general model of Exhibit 6, the equilibrium price and quantity that would emerge from an unregulated market are 0P and 0N, respectively. But now 0H represents a government-imposed price floor. At this price the quantity supplied will exceed the quantity demanded, resulting in a *surplus* of the amount RL.

What can be done about this surplus? In agriculture, where price floors for certain commodities have been employed during some periods, surpluses have been a recurrent phenomenon. As a result, government at various times has sought to cope with the situation in three major ways:

1. *Restrict supply.*   Acreage allotments have been imposed on farmers, thereby limiting the amount of land they can use to grow certain agricultural commodities.

2. *Stimulate demand.*   Research into new uses for agricultural products has been encouraged.

3. *Buy up surpluses.*   Certain agricultural commodities have been bought and stored by the government for future sale or disposal.

With respect to minimum wages, Exhibit 6 may be thought of as a model of the supply and demand for labor. For example, let the horizontal axis measure the quantity of labor in terms of hours of labor time, and let the vertical axis measure the price of labor in terms of wages per hour. The surplus is then the volume of unemployment RL occurring at the minimum-wage level 0H. Therefore, one way to reduce this labor surplus is to *lower* the hourly wage rate. What would this do to total payrolls if the demand for labor were relatively elastic? Relatively inelastic? Can you suggest other possible methods of reducing the unemployment surplus?

EFFECTS OF SPECIFIC TAXES AND SUBSIDIES

Supply and demand analysis can be helpful in solving problems involving certain kinds of commodity taxes and subsidies. Different degrees of elasticities affect in surprising ways the prices and quantities of some of the things we buy every day.

Specific Taxes

Suppose a *specific tax* is imposed on the sale of a commodity. That is, for each unit of a commodity sold a fixed amount of money must be paid to the government. A specific tax is thus a *per-unit tax* independent of the price of the product. Some of the taxes on cigarettes and gasoline are of this kind.

How does a specific tax on a product affect its market prices and quantities? Is the *incidence* or burden of such a tax borne by those upon whom it is initially imposed, or is it *shifted* to others? These are the practical questions that our analysis answers.

We can proceed by first examining the model in Exhibit 7, Chart (a). The curves D and S are the market demand and supply curves before the tax is imposed. The equilibrium quantity is therefore 0N; the equilibrium price is NP.

Suppose that sellers are required to pay a tax of T per unit. The results of such a tax can be analyzed in two steps:

1. The supply curve shifts leftward to the parallel position S', showing that less will be supplied at any given price. This is because the tax is an added cost to the producer at all levels of output. Hence, the *supply price*—the price necessary to call forth a given output—will be higher by the amount of the tax. For example, before the tax, consumers paid a price of NP to

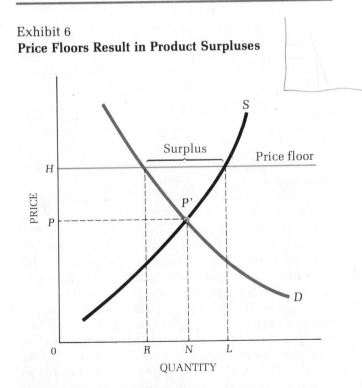

Exhibit 6
Price Floors Result in Product Surpluses

Exhibit 7
Effects of Specific Taxes and Subsidies

Taxes will affect the equilibrium prices and quantities of commodities, depending on the relative elasticities of demand and supply. Subsidies have the opposite effects of taxes, but their influence is also determined by the relative elasticities of demand and supply.

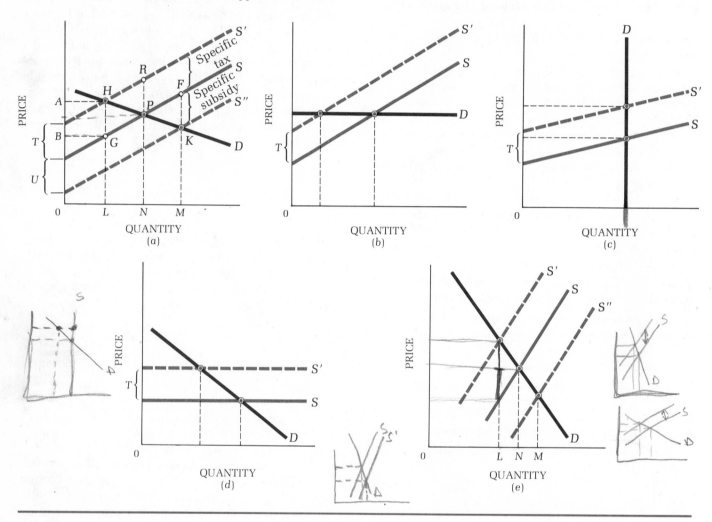

obtain the quantity ON. After the tax they must pay a price of NR to call forth the same quantity ON. When the selling firm receives NR, it will pay a tax of PR ($= T$) to the government, leaving itself with a net price of NP.

2. The tax will therefore cause the equilibrium point to shift from P to H. This movement will be associated with a decrease in quantity from ON to OL and an increase in price from NP to LH, where GH is the amount of the tax.

Importance of Elasticities

Are there any general principles that can tell us the extent to which prices and quantities will be altered as a result of the tax? Charts (b), (c), and (d) in Exhibit 7 will help answer this question.

In Chart (b), demand is perfectly elastic. As a result, any increase in price will cause sales to drop to zero. Therefore, the same price is maintained after the tax as before, but sellers compensate for the added cost of the tax by reducing their quantity. Consumers thus get fewer units of the good even though they continue to pay the same price per unit.

In Chart (c), the demand curve is perfectly inelastic. Therefore, the entire burden of the tax is shifted forward from sellers to buyers in the form of a higher price, with no reduction in the equilibrium quantity.

In Chart (d), both price and quantity are affected as a result of a perfectly elastic supply curve. The burden of the tax is shifted entirely to buyers *and* the equilibrium quantity is reduced. Note how this compares with the case in Chart *(c)*, where only price is affected, not quantity. What would have happened in Chart *(d)* if the demand curve had been perfectly inelastic?

We can now establish two important principles:

1. The more *inelastic* the demand and the supply of a commodity, the smaller will be the decline in output resulting from a given tax. [This is illustrated in Chart *(e)*, where the letters have the same meaning as before.]

2. The relative burden of a tax among buyers and sellers tends to follow the path of least resistance. That is, the tax is shifted in proportion to where the *inelasticity* is greatest.

The first principle leads to the following practical conclusion:

If we want to minimize disruptions in production, industries whose commodities are inelastic in demand and supply are better suited to commodity taxation. This is because they suffer smaller contractions in output and hence in employment.

The second principle results in another useful conclusion:

In most supply and demand situations (except the extreme ones involving perfect elasticity or inelasticity) the tax will be shared by both consumers and producers. The proportions will vary according to the relative elasticities of demand and supply.

Thus, as a result of the tax, the consumer's price will rise, but by less than the amount of the tax. Similarly, the producer's net price will fall, but by less than the amount of the tax.

REMARK   Exhibit 7 does not demonstrate the effect of a tax in the case of a perfectly inelastic supply curve. Can you illustrate such a case and explain it? Be careful; this is a tricky question. (HINT   If the supply curve is perfectly inelastic, can it shift as a result of the tax?) You will learn more about this problem in a subsequent chapter when you encounter a concept known as the "single tax." This idea has played an interesting role in American politics. In the meantime, see if you can deduce the answer yourself.

Subsidies

A *subsidy* is a payment a government makes to businesses or households to achieve a particular purpose. The subsidy enables them to produce or consume a product in larger quantities or at lower prices than they would do otherwise. Government subsidies are granted to agriculture, airlines, railroads, shipping and shipbuilding, low-income households, and to certain other groups in the economy.

A *specific subsidy* is a per-unit subsidy on a commodity. It is thus the opposite of a specific tax. In fact,

a specific subsidy can be thought of as a "negative" specific tax because the government is giving money to the seller or to the consumer rather than taking it away.

The effects of a specific subsidy on sellers are illustrated in Exhibit 7, Chart *(a)*. As a result of a subsidy equal to the amount U, the supply curve shifts downward from its normal position S to the new position S''. This is because the subsidy is like a reduction in cost to the producer at all levels of output. Therefore, the supply price will be lower by the amount of the subsidy.

For instance, the subsidy causes the equilibrium point to shift from P to K. Hence, the equilibrium price decreases from NP to MK and the equilibrium output increases from $0N$ to $0M$. At this new and larger output, buyers will pay the price MK but sellers will receive the additional amount $KF(=U)$. This, of course, is the amount of the subsidy per unit of output.

This analysis leads us to an important principle:

The more elastic the supply and demand curves, the greater will be the expansion in output and the less will be the reduction in price resulting from a subsidy.

This can be verified by comparing Charts *(a)* and *(e)* in Exhibit 7.

The economic purposes of a subsidy are to reduce price or to increase output. The latter objective is usually the primary one when the product is to be used wholly for domestic consumption. These ideas lead to an important conclusion:

If we want to increase production through the use of a subsidy, industries whose commodities are elastic in demand and supply are better suited to subsidies. This is because such industries experience larger expansions in output and hence in employment.

Subsidies are also quite common in international trade. They occur when a government subsidizes a firm or even an entire industry in order to help it penetrate foreign markets at lower prices. For example, at various times Japan has been accused by its trading partners of subsidizing the production of automobiles, electronic products, and cameras in order to encourage their export to the United States and other countries.

Other Types of Elasticities

Early in this chapter you learned that elasticity is a measure of the responsiveness of changes in quantity to changes in price. Actually, this type of elasticity, called "price elasticity," is one of many used in economics. However, it is the most common of all elasticity measures. Therefore, in any economic or business discussion, the term "elasticity" always means *price* elasticity unless otherwise indicated.

What are some other types of elasticity? Two that are especially useful are (1) the income elasticity of demand and (2) the cross elasticity of demand.

INCOME ELASTICITY OF DEMAND

When you draw a demand curve that shows a relationship between price and quantity demanded, one of the things you assume to be constant is buyers' incomes. But if incomes change, the demand curve shifts, causing a change in demand. How much of a change? The answer depends on the income elasticity of demand.

> The *income elasticity of demand* is the percentage change in the quantity purchased of a good resulting from a 1 percent change in income. This type of elasticity thus measures the responsiveness of changes in demand to changes in income.

The method of measuring income elasticity is the same as that for measuring price elasticity. As you recall, price elasticity is simply the ratio of the percentage change in quantity (demanded or supplied) to the percentage change in price. Similarly, the income elasticity of demand is the ratio of the percentage change in quantity purchased to the percentage change in income. Thus,

income elasticity of demand
$$= \frac{\text{percentage change in quantity purchased}}{\text{percentage change in income}}$$

It follows that the formula used for measuring income elasticity is the same as that for price elasticity—except for some differences in letters. Thus, let

Q_1 = old quantity, or quantity purchased before the change in income

Q_2 = new quantity, or quantity purchased after the change in income

Y_1 = old income, or income before the change

Y_2 = new income, or income after the change

The formula for the income elasticity of demand is then

$$_YE_D = \frac{\dfrac{Q_2 - Q_1}{Q_2 + Q_1}}{\dfrac{Y_2 - Y_1}{Y_2 + Y_1}}$$

NOTE   Economists usually employ the letter Y to represent income because *I* is customarily used to represent investment.

Measurement and Interpretation

How is the income elasticity of demand interpreted? What are its uses?

Before you can answer these questions, you need to understand how the income elasticity of demand is measured in a real-life situation. Exhibit 8 provides an example.

The data suggest that goods can be classified according to their income elasticity of demand. One such classification distinguishes between "superior" and "inferior" goods.

Superior Goods: $_YE_D > 0$ The income elasticity of demand for some goods may be greater than zero. That is, the coefficient may be positive. Such products are called *superior goods*. They are commodities whose consumption varies directly with money income, prices remaining constant. In the hypothetical illustration of Exhibit 8, record albums, hamburgers, and magazines are examples of superior goods. Each has an income elasticity of demand greater than zero. As you might expect, most goods are superior goods. That is, their consumption increases with income. Therefore, such goods are also called *normal goods* because they represent the "normal" situation.

Exhibit 8
Measuring the Income Elasticity of Demand

Suppose that your monthly income, and some of the things you spend it on, are shown in the table. You can calculate your income elasticity of demand for each item quite easily. The following calculation, involving record albums, provides an example.

$$_YE_D = \frac{\dfrac{Q_2 - Q_1}{Q_2 + Q_1}}{\dfrac{Y_2 - Y_1}{Y_2 + Y_1}} = \frac{\dfrac{2 - 1}{2 + 1}}{\dfrac{\$1,500 - \$1,000}{\$1,500 + \$1,000}} = \frac{\dfrac{1}{3}}{\dfrac{1}{5}} = 1.67$$

You should verify the remaining elasticities shown in the table in the same way. For each good, however, be careful to pair Q_1 with Y_1 and Q_2 with Y_2, to avoid errors.

Item	Quantity purchased per month at $1,000 income per month	Quantity purchased per month at $1,500 income per month	$_YE_D$
Albums	1	2	1.67
Hamburgers	10	15	1.00
Magazines	4	5	0.56
Movies	3	3	0
Pizzas	4	3	−0.71

Superior goods can be subclassified in terms of income elasticity. If the value of the income elasticity coefficient is greater than 1, the demand for the commodity is said to be income elastic. If the coefficient is less than 1 but greater than 0, the demand is said to be income inelastic. In Exhibit 8, record albums are income elastic while magazines are income inelastic. Hamburgers, being a borderline case, may be classified as income unit-elastic.

Inferior Goods: $_YE_D < 0$ The income elasticity of demand for some goods may be less than zero. That is, the coefficient may be negative. Such products are called *inferior goods*. Their consumption varies inversely with money income (prices remaining constant) over a certain range of income. Potatoes, used clothing, and other "cheap" commodities bought by poor families are examples. The consumption of these commodities declines in favor of more nutritious foods, new clothing, and the like as the incomes of low-income families rise. In the hypothetical example of Exhibit 8, pizza is an example of an inferior good.

In general, income elasticities of demand vary widely from commodity to commodity and from person to person. Indeed, a good that is superior for one individual may be inferior for another, and vice versa. Nevertheless, a few overall tendencies may be mentioned.

Usually, commodities that consumers regard as "necessities" tend to be income-inelastic. Examples are food, fuel, utilities, and medical services. Commodities that consumers regard as "luxuries" tend to be income-elastic. Examples are sports cars, furs, costly vacation trips, and expensive foods. Therefore, the income elasticity of demand provides an approximate guide for judging the importance of commodities to consumers.

When you draw a demand curve, you assume that buyers' incomes and the prices of other goods remain constant.

Of course, buyers' incomes may vary. If they do, the resulting change in demand is measured by the income elasticity of demand, as you have just seen. But what if prices of other goods vary? In that case the resulting change in demand is measured by a new relationship—the cross elasticity of demand.

The *cross elasticity of demand* is the percentage change in the quantity purchased of a good resulting from a 1 percent change in the price of another good. This type of elasticity thus measures the responsiveness of changes in the demand for a good to changes in the price of a different good.

Like every other type of elasticity, the cross elasticity of demand is simply a ratio of two percentage changes. Therefore, its formula is the same as all other elasticity formulas, except for the choice of letters. Thus, let

Q_{X1} = quantity purchased of product X before a change in the price of product Y

Q_{X2} = quantity purchased of product X after a change in the price of product Y

P_{Y1} = price of product Y before the change

P_{Y2} = price of product Y after the change

The cross elasticity of demand, $_+E_D$, is thus measured by the formula

$$_+E_D = \frac{\dfrac{Q_{X2} - Q_{X1}}{Q_{X2} + Q_{X1}}}{\dfrac{P_{Y2} - P_{Y1}}{P_{Y2} + P_{Y1}}}$$

Measurement and Interpretation

How is the formula used? Three practical applications are shown in Exhibit 9. The diagrams are derived from several business studies. As they show, the cross elasticities of demand for products will differ according to whether the goods are substitutes, complements, or independent.

Substitutes: $_+E_D > 0$ Substitute goods are goods that compete with one another. The more you consume of one, the less you consume of the other. Examples are butter and margarine, coffee and tea, automobile and bus transportation.

The cross elasticity of demand for substitute goods is significantly greater than zero. The coefficient is thus positive. The reason is that higher prices for one of the goods causes people to buy less of that good and more of the substitute. Hence, the quantity purchased of the substitute increases.

This idea is illustrated in Charts (a), (b), and (c) of Exhibit 9. Chart (a) shows a hypothetical demand curve for Coca-Cola. Similarly, Chart (b) shows a hypothetical demand curve for Pepsi-Cola.

What happens if there is an increase in the price of Coca-Cola? Obviously, less of it will be bought. In other words, there will be a *decrease in quantity demanded,* a movement "up" the curve. However, many people who previously bought Coca-Cola will now switch to Pepsi-Cola. As a result, there will be an *increase in demand* for Pepsi-Cola, shown as a shift of the demand curve to the right. Thus, the overall effect of an increase in the price of Coca-Cola is to reduce its sales while increasing the sales of Pepsi-Cola.

Exhibit 9
Measuring the Cross Elasticity of Demand

Substitute Goods. *In Chart (a), an increase in the price of Coca-Cola causes a decrease in quantity demanded. This, in turn, leads to an increase in demand for Pepsi-Cola, shown in Chart (b). Chart (c) estimates the cross elasticity of demand for Pepsi-Cola relative to the price of Coca-Cola.*

Complementary Goods. *In Chart (d), an increase in the price of shirts causes a decrease in quantity demanded. In Chart (e), therefore, there is a decrease in demand for ties as the curve shifts to the left. Chart (f) estimates the cross elasticity of demand for ties relative to the price of shirts.*

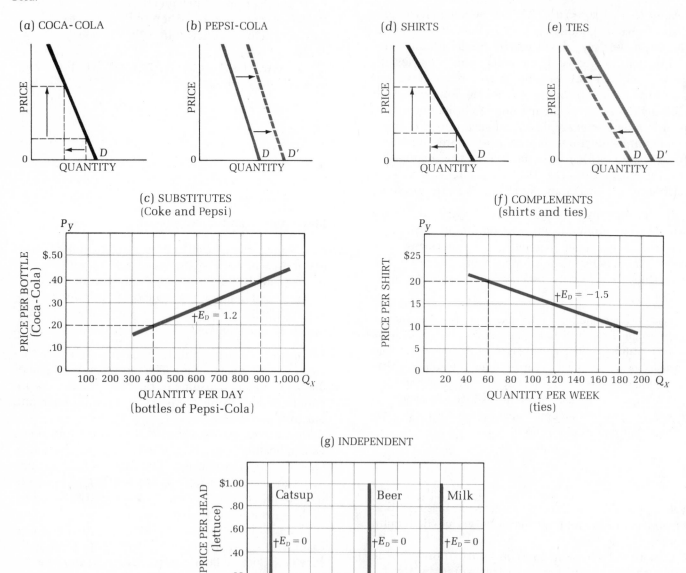

Independent Goods. *In Chart (g), changes in the price of lettuce have no effect on the demand for catsup, beer, or milk. Therefore, as shown in the graph, cross elasticities of* demand for these products relative to the price of lettuce are zero.

The opposite effects occur, of course, if there is a decrease in the price of Coca-Cola. The demand curve for Pepsi-Cola shifts to the left.

Chart (c) shows the actual consequences of changes in the price of Coca-Cola. These results are derived from a set of demand studies conducted for a chain of supermarkets. Note that higher prices of Coke result in increased purchases of Pepsi. Therefore, the cross elasticity of demand is positive. You should verify this result by applying the cross-elasticity formula to the data in the chart.

Complements: $_+E_D < 0$ Complementary goods are goods that "go together." The more you consume of one, the more you consume of the other. Examples are shoes and socks, gasoline and tires, textbooks and notebooks.

The cross elasticity of demand for complementary goods is significantly less than zero. The coefficient is thus negative. The reason is that as the price of a good increases, people buy less of it. Therefore, they also buy less of the complementary goods. The opposite effects occur, of course, if the price of a good decreases.

These ideas can be seen in Charts (d), (e), and (f) of Exhibit 9. Charts (d) and (e) show hypothetical demand curves for shirts and ties. In Chart (d), an increase in the price of shirts causes a *decrease in quantity demanded*. In Chart (e), therefore, there is a *decrease in demand* for ties as shown by a leftward shift of the curve.

Some actual relationships, based on demand studies conducted for a department store, are shown in Chart (f). The downward-sloping curve tells you that the cross elasticity of demand must be negative. You should verify the estimate by applying the cross-elasticity formula to the data in the chart.

Independent: $_+E_D = 0$ Independent goods, as the name implies, are unrelated. The consumption of one is not directly influenced by the consumption of the other. Consequently, changes in the price of one have no significant effect on quantities purchased of the other. The cross elasticity of demand is therefore zero.

An illustration of the cross elasticity of demand for independent goods is provided in Exhibit 9, Chart (g). Some examples of other pairs of independent or unrelated goods are pizza and jewelry, books and dishes, egg rolls and wristwatches.

The following rules will help you remember these ideas:

The cross elasticity of demand provides a measure of *substitutability* between products. In general:

1. Goods whose cross elasticities of demand are signifi-

cantly greater than zero may be thought of as "positive substitutes." (Examples are competing brands of goods in the same industry, such as soap, toothpaste, and television sets.)

2. Goods whose cross elasticities of demand are approximately zero may be thought of as weak or nonsubstitutes.

3. Goods whose cross elasticities of demand are significantly less than zero are complements. Such goods, therefore, may be thought of as "negative substitutes."

Some Assumptions and Conclusions

Before concluding this study of supply and demand, we must emphasize certain key assumptions that underlie the previous models. In addition, we should point out some of the implications about the overall role of supply and demand in a market economy.

TWO UNDERLYING ASSUMPTIONS

Two special assumptions are relevant to the kinds of models developed in this chapter. These serve as warnings about the limitations to the analysis.

Simple Versus Complex Considerations

Theoretical models of supply and demand assume that a particular economic action—such as the imposition of price ceilings, price floors, taxes, or subsidies—can be analyzed in terms of economic considerations alone. These models thus neglect multiple considerations involving both economic and noneconomic factors. In reality, of course, both types of conditions are usually at work.

For example, a tax on cigarettes may prompt some people to give up smoking for psychological reasons because they associate the unpleasant task of paying taxes with the act of smoking. This will cause the demand curve to shift to the left, resulting in a different equilibrium situation from the one in our model.

Likewise, in analyzing the effects of taxes, subsidies, and so on, it must be remembered that conditions vary in the real world. Supply and demand curves are always changing over time due to changes in technology, tastes, and other factors ordinarily assumed constant.

Hence, although our models have purposely been kept simple, it should be apparent that complexities such as these must be introduced if the models are to be made more realistic.

Static Versus Dynamic Models

Another important limitation of supply and demand models is that they are *static* rather than *dynamic*. In a dynamic model the influence of expectations by buyers or sellers would be recognized. This is because the process of moving toward an equilibrium position might itself cause changes in the supply and demand curves.

As an example, a fall in price might prompt consumers to postpone their purchases in anticipation of further price decreases. This would cause a fall (shift to the left) of the demand curve. Similarly, the supply curve might rise (shift to the right) as suppliers sought to offset the future effects of the expected price drop by producing and selling more now at the higher price. Situations such as these continually occur in the stock and commodities markets.

Fortunately, these limitations do not make our models too simple to be useful. They merely remind us that any model is a simplification of reality, and we should be careful not to claim more for a model than it really is.

MARKET PRICE AND NORMAL PRICE

You have learned how prices and quantities are determined under competitive market circumstances. Therefore, it is useful at this point to summarize what you know.

1. Central to supply and demand is the idea that competition among many buyers and sellers will cause market prices and quantities to move toward equilibrium.

2. Prices in a market reflect the *eagerness* of people to buy or sell. In competitive markets there will be a tendency for equilibrium prices to establish themselves automatically through the free operation of supply and demand.

3. Once equilibrium prices are established, they will have no tendency to change unless there are changes in the factors that determine supply and demand.

The third point requires some amplification. In reality, the equilibrium price is rarely, if ever, the actual price that exists at any given instant of time. The forces that are at work to determine an equilibrium price are always changing, thereby causing the equilibrium price to change. In view of this, it helps to distinguish between two kinds of price: *market price* and *normal price*.

The *market price* is the actual price that prevails in a market at any particular moment. The *normal price* is the equilibrium price toward which the market price is always tending but may never reach. (Normal price may thus be viewed as a dynamic equilibrium price.)

You can think of the market price as pursuing the normal price in much the same way as a missile pursues a moving target. The missile may never reach the target, just as the market price may never reach the dynamic equilibrium price. Yet the target is necessary to explain where the missile is heading, just as the concept of a normal price is necessary to explain where the market price is heading.

THE PRICE SYSTEM AS A RATIONING (ALLOCATIVE) MECHANISM

We now come to one of the most significant conclusions in our study of economics. It consists of an explanation of how the market system allocates scarce goods among competing buyers.

You already know that scarcity—the inability of limited resources to produce all the goods and services that people want—is an economic fact of life. In a command economy some central authority—perhaps a king, a commissar, or a committee—decides the alternative uses to which these limited resources will be put. To a large extent the central authority may also ration the fruits among the members of society, thus answering the three big questions: WHAT to produce, HOW to produce, and FOR WHOM.

In a pure market economy, on the other hand, these questions are answered by a competitive price system through the free operation of supply and demand. The concept, described in Exhibit 10, shows that the equilibrium price automatically admits certain buyers and sellers to the marketplace while simultaneously excluding others. The cost of admission to the market is the *demand prices* of buyers and the *supply prices* of sellers—two terms that are already familiar to you. The diagram and its accompanying description thus lead to the following conclusion:

A *price system* is a mechanism that allocates scarce goods and resources among competing uses. The price system accomplishes this by rationing goods among those buyers and sellers in the marketplace who are willing and able to deal at the going price.

A price system in a competitive market thus allocates goods and resources through the free play of supply and demand forces. These, in turn, result from the interaction of many sellers and buyers. But what about "noncompetitive" price systems, where buyers or sellers are relatively few? As will be shown in later chapters, this results in pricing situations quite different from the familiar supply and demand models we have studied so far.

Exhibit 10
How a Market Economy Rations (Allocates) Goods or Resources Among Buyers and Sellers

The equilibrium price serves as a highly selective filter. It admits to the market only those buyers whose demand price is greater than or equal to the equilibrium price, and those sellers whose supply price is less than or equal to the equilibrium price. All other buyers and sellers who are not able and willing to deal at the going price are excluded.

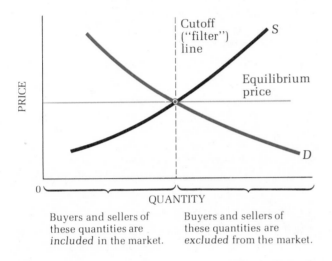

Buyers and sellers of these quantities are *included* in the market.

Buyers and sellers of these quantities are *excluded* from the market.

What You Have Learned

1. Elasticity is a basic concept in supply and demand analysis. It may be defined interpretatively as the percentage change in quantity (demanded or supplied) resulting from a 1 percent change in price. Elasticity may also be defined mathematically by the ratio: elasticity = (percentage change in quantity)/(percentage change in price).

2. The coefficient of elasticity is commonly expressed in its absolute-value or numerical form. This means that the minus signs are disregarded. There are five types of elasticity ranging from zero to infinity:

perfect elasticity	($E = \infty$)
relative elasticity	($E > 1$)
unit elasticity	($E = 1$)
relative inelasticity	($E < 1$)
perfect inelasticity	($E = 0$)

These five types apply both to supply and to demand.

3. Because elasticity is a measure of relative changes, it may vary for each segment along a curve. Our formula for elasticity gives a type of "average" elasticity over an entire segment.

4. Elasticity is *not* the same as slope. Therefore, the elasticity of a curve cannot always be judged from its slope alone. An exception occurs in the case of vertical and horizontal curves. In most other cases the exact elasticity must be calculated.

5. You can tell whether demand elasticity is greater or less than 1 by observing the effect of a price change on total revenue. If price and total revenue change in opposite directions, demand elasticity is greater than 1. If price and total revenue change in the same direction, demand elasticity is less than 1.

6. The availability of good commodity substitutes tends to make demand more elastic. Similarly, the availability of good resource substitutes tends to make supply more elastic. Goods that are relatively inexpensive tend to be more inelastic in demand. This is because they are a small part of the consumer's total expenditures.

7. Elasticities of both demand and supply tend to be greater over longer periods. The reason is that buyers and sellers can eventually adjust to the use of substitutes or to changes in price.

8. Price ceilings are imposed to keep the market price of a commodity below its normal (free-market) equilibrium price. Price floors, on the other hand, are imposed to keep the market price of a commodity above its normal (free-market) equilibrium price. Price ceilings cause product shortages and the need for rationing. Price floors cause product surpluses, which may require government action to absorb them.

9. Specific taxes tend to be shifted between buyers and sellers according to where the inelasticity is greatest. Industries whose commodities are inelastic in demand are better suited to commodity taxation because they suffer smaller contractions in output and hence in employment. On the other hand, industries whose commodities are elastic in demand are better suited to subsidies because they experience larger expansions in output and hence in employment.

10. The term "elasticity" always means price elasticity unless otherwise indicated. In addition to price elasticity, two important kinds of elasticity are (a) the income elasticity of demand and (b) the cross elasticity of demand. The first measures the responsiveness of quantity purchased of a good to changes in income. The second measures the responsiveness of quantity purchased of a good to changes in the price of another good.

11. Some important lessons are to be learned from supply and demand concepts:

(a) Simple supply and demand models do not take into account complex economic and noneconomic considerations, and are static rather than dynamic.

(b) The competitive market is always tending toward the equilibrium price, but may never reach it because the underlying forces are always changing.

(c) In a market economy, the price system allocates goods and resources by rationing them among those buyers and sellers whose demand and supply prices are sufficient to admit them to the market.

For Discussion

1. *Terms and concepts to review:*

elasticity	superior good
shortage	inferior good
rationing	income elasticity
surplus	of demand
specific tax	cross elasticity
incidence	of demand
supply price	market price
subsidy	normal price
specific subsidy	price system

2. Several studies have found that the overall demand for automobiles has an elasticity of about 1.3. (a) How do you interpret this coefficient? (b) After hearing about these studies, a Ford dealer in Chicago cut prices by 10 percent and sold 22 percent more cars. What is the elasticity of demand in this case? Does it mean that the estimate of 1.3 is incorrect? Explain.

3. Suppose that we are given the following demand schedule for a commodity:

	Price (cents)	Quantity demanded
A	20	50
B	15	100
C	10	200
D	5	400

(a) Calculate the elasticity between points A and B, B and C, C and D. (SUGGESTION   Sketch the demand curve and label it with the points A, B, C, D in order to help you "see" what you are doing.)

(b) How will your results compare if you calculate the elasticity in reverse directions (i.e., from B to A, C to B, and D to C)? Explain.

4. Fill in the blank cell in each of the following rows:

Price	Total revenue	Elasticity
increases		>1
decreases	decreases	
decreases	no change	
	increases	<1
	decreases	>1
increases		1

5. "At a given price ceiling or price floor, the size of a shortage or surplus varies directly with the elasticity of the demand and supply curves." Demonstrate this proposition graphically.

6. Many people criticize public transit systems (subways, buses, etc.) for being too crowded during rush hours. From what you know about the price system as a rationing mechanism, how would you correct the situation?

7. The R. H. Lacy Co., a department store, conducted a study of the demand for men's ties made from low-cost synthetic fibers. The store found that the average daily demand D in terms of price P is given by the equation $D = 60 - 5P$.

(a) How many ties per day can the store expect to sell at a price of $3 per tie?

(b) If the store wants to sell 20 ties per day, what price should it charge?

(c) What would be the demand if the store offered to give the ties away free?

(d) What is the highest price that anyone would be willing to pay for these ties?

(e) Plot the demand curve.

8. The demand D for sugar in the United States in terms of its price P was once estimated to be $D = 135 - 8P$. If this equation were valid today:

(a) How much would be demanded at a price of 10?

(b) What price would correspond to a demand of 95?

(c) How much would be demanded if sugar were free?

(d) What is the highest price anyone would pay?

9. The demand D for a certain product in terms of its price P is given by the equation $D = 3a - 3bP$, where a and b are positive constants.

(a) Find the price if the quantity demanded is $a/2$.

(b) Find the quantity demanded at a price of $a/3b$.

(c) How much will be demanded if the product is free?

(d) What is the highest price anyone will pay for the good?

10. PRINCIPLES OR PROVERBS? Many statements of an economic nature often parade as principles when in reality such statements are hardly more than proverbs. The differences between the two are by no means trivial. For one thing, principles are never contradictory, whereas proverbs often are. (EXAMPLE   *"Look before you leap"*; however, *"He who hesitates is lost."*) Statements such as the following are often heard. Are they principles or proverbs? Explain. Rephrase if necessary to improve the statement. Use examples.

(a) "Inexpensive products tend to have inelastic demands."

(b) "The demands of rich consumers are less elastic than the demands of poor consumers."

(c) "Products whose purchases are closely correlated with income are elastic in demand."

11. "Demand elasticity measures percentage changes in quantity demanded relative to percentage changes in price. It follows that with 10 equal demanders for a product, the elasticity will be 10 times as great as it is for one." True or false? Explain.

12. "The elasticity of demand for a product usually increases with the length of time over which a price change

persists. Thus, a 1 percent decrease in price may result at first in a less than 1 percent increase in quantity demanded, but eventually the quantity may increase by 2 percent, 5 percent, or even more." True or false? Explain why.

13. Are the following statements true or false? Explain.

(a) For most consumers, the income elasticity of demand for restaurant meals is probably lower than the income elasticity of demand for ball-point pens.

(b) For some commodities, the price elasticity of demand may be greater than 1 (i.e., relatively elastic) while the income elasticity of demand is negative.

(c) The cross elasticity of demand for commodity A relative to the price of commodity B may be quite different from the cross elasticity of demand for commodity B relative to the price of commodity A.

Case
The DuPont Cellophane Case: Using Cross Elasticity in the Courtroom

What is monopoly? It is a term that many people have heard, but few understand.

Monopoly is the absence of competition. Every business firm would like to be a monopoly in order to have greater control over its prices and profits. But monopolies, if unregulated by government, could exploit their market power at the expense of the public. For this reason, government has passed laws, called antitrust laws, that prohibit firms from obtaining or seeking a monopoly.

Defining the Relevant Market

In order to enforce the laws, the government sometimes has to specify the market for a particular product. This can be difficult. If substitution were not possible, every brand of product would have a monopoly. If substitution were extremely easy, monopoly would be virtually nonexistent. The problem is to draw the proper boundaries, that is, to *define the relevant market.*

For example, are rugs, carpets, and linoleum sold in separate markets? Or are they all sold in the floor-covering market? Should toasters and blenders be classified in separate industries? Or are they part of the electrical appliance industry?

The task of defining the relevant market has been undertaken by the courts in numerous cases. One of the most famous, which occurred in 1956, involved the use of cellophane. The E.I. DuPont Corporation, producer of cellophane, was charged by the U.S. Department of Justice with monopolizing the market.

Was the company guilty or innocent? The answer depended on the definition of the market.

1. The government (i.e., the Justice Department) argued that the relevant market was that for cellophane. Therefore, DuPont clearly had a monopoly because it controlled the entire output of the product.

2. DuPont countered with the argument that the relevant market was that for flexible packaging materials. These included cellophane, waxed papers, parchment papers, aluminum foil, pliofilm, and glassine. In that market cellophane accounted for 18 percent of the total, a figure hardly large enough to constitute a monopoly.

Conclusion: Substitutability Is Relevant

A Federal District court found in favor of DuPont. The case was appealed to the Supreme Court, and that body upheld the lower court's verdict. In both trials the courts concurred that "a relevant market exists when commodities are reasonably interchangeable by consumers for the same purposes."

Both courts also agreed that the relevant market determined the boundaries of the industry. "The cross elasticity of demand for cellophane was high and competition intense.... The relevant market, therefore, was not that for cellophane produced by the defendant . . . but for flexible packaging materials produced by various firms."

QUESTIONS

1. For several decades prior to the case, the price of cellophane was often substantially higher than the prices of other flexible packaging materials. In view of this, why would business firms, which were the main purchasers of cellophane, buy this product instead of the cheaper substitutes?

2. In the Supreme Court's minority opinion, the statement was made that "cross elasticities are not engraved in stone." Was this intended as a criticism of the majority opinion? What did it mean?

Robert Rattner.

Flexible packaging materials: substitutes for cellophane.

Chapter 21

Looking Behind the Demand Curve: Utility and Consumer Demand*

Chapter Preview

What is the basis for the law of (downward-sloping) demand?

What assumptions and principles of consumer behavior underlie the law of demand?

In economics, the term "demand," with reference to market demand, has a specific meaning. Demand is a dependent relationship revealing the quantity that will be purchased of a particular commodity at various prices—other things remaining the same. This relationship, as we have seen, can be portrayed arithmetically in the form of a demand schedule or graphically in the form of a demand curve. (It can also be represented algebraically in the form of an equation, but this is not usually necessary for understanding the basic ideas.)

What are the underlying factors that account for the law of (downward-sloping) demand? This is a question we have not yet considered. To answer it, we must turn our attention to the study of consumer behavior. This topic, which draws partially on psychology, has played an interesting and important role in the development of economic ideas.

Explaining Utility and Consumer Demand

Economists have long been interested in the factors that account for the shape of demand curves. Until now we have taken it pretty much for granted that such curves slope downward from left to right. Upon

* NOTE TO INSTRUCTOR   This chapter is optional. It may be omitted without affecting continuity.

357

closer examination we find several reasons for their negative inclination.

One explanation is based on "common sense," by which we mean observation and intuition. On the basis of our experiences it seems reasonable to expect that a reduction in the price of a product will enable a buyer to purchase more of it. Conversely, an increase in the product's price will reduce that ability.

INCOME AND SUBSTITUTION EFFECTS

A second explanation can be given in terms of what economists call "income effects" and "substitution effects."

The _income effect_ tells us that a decrease in the price of a product, while the prices of other goods and the consumer's money income and tastes remain the same, enables the consumer to buy more of the commodity and perhaps more of other commodities as well. Therefore, this results in an increase in the consumer's real income.

The _substitution effect_ says that a reduction in the price of a product, with the consumer's income, tastes, and other prices remaining constant, makes the cheaper good relatively more attractive. This enables the consumer to substitute more of that good for other products.

These concepts can be expressed in more formal terms:

1. _Income Effect_   This is the change in quantity demanded by a buyer due to the change in his or her real income resulting from a change in the price of a commodity. The income effect assumes that the buyer's money income, tastes, and the prices of all other goods remain the same.

2. _Substitution Effect_   This is the change in quantity demanded by a buyer resulting from a change in the price of a commodity while his or her real income, tastes, and the prices of other goods remain the same.

These ideas can be summarized as follows:

The total effect of a price change may be divided into two parts. One is an income effect; the other is a substitution effect. The income effect is the change in quantity demanded due exclusively to a change in real income. The substitution effect is the change in quantity demanded due exclusively to a change in the price of a good relative to the prices of other goods.

The concepts of income and substitution effects thus provide further insights into the shape of a consumer's demand curve. They tell us that the demand curve slopes downward because of the substitution effect. This means that the consumer is willing to pur-

chase more of a product when its price declines relative to other prices. The consumer's willingness, in turn, is reinforced by the income effect. This is the ability of a consumer to buy more of a product due to the gain in his or her real income resulting from the price decline. Taken together, therefore, both effects explain how a price change influences a consumer's _willingness_ and _ability_ to buy. These two terms, you recall, were emphasized when we first studied the nature of demand.

THE MEANING OF UTILITY

A third and in many ways much more fundamental explanation of the downward-sloping demand curve can be given in terms of utility. By _utility_ is meant the ability or power of a good to satisfy a want. That is, utility is the satisfaction that one receives from consuming something—whether it be pizzas, vacation trips, or textbooks.

The concept of utility was employed by the classical economists of the eighteenth and early nineteenth centuries. But the theory of utility as such did not come into full flower until the late nineteenth century, when it was formulated by certain neoclassical economists. As you study the theory in the following paragraphs, be careful not to confuse "utility" with "usefulness." At any given time, water may be much more useful than diamonds. However, the utility of either one may be quite different for various individuals.

Total Utility and Marginal Utility

Although no one knows how to measure utility, it is interesting to _assume_ that it can be measured. Suppose, for example, that a "utility meter" could be strapped to your arm to measure the units of satisfaction, called _utils,_ that you get from consuming a product. This is the same idea as a doctor strapping a meter to your arm to measure your blood pressure. What would such a utility meter reveal?

The answer is suggested by the data and curves in Exhibit 1. The table and charts show the utils, or units of satisfaction, that you might experience from consuming a hypothetical product. This model assumes that your consumption is taking place at a _given period of time during which your tastes are constant._ Otherwise, as you will soon see, it would make no sense to talk about the utility of different quantities of a product.

The exhibit illustrates that 1 unit of the commodity yields a certain amount of total utility, 2 units yield a larger amount, 3 units still more, and so on. Eventually, a level of intake is reached where total utility is at

Exhibit 1
Total and Marginal Utility

The table and charts convey the same fundamental relations. That is, as consumption of the product is increased, both total utility and marginal utility rise to a maximum and then decline. The marginal utility curve is most important, for it reveals the operation of the *law of diminishing marginal utility*. The vertical dashed line emphasizes the fact that marginal utility equals zero when total utility is at a maximum.

NOTE   *The marginal utility curve is plotted to the midpoints of the integers on the horizontal axis, because marginal utility reflects the change in utils from one unit of product to the next.*

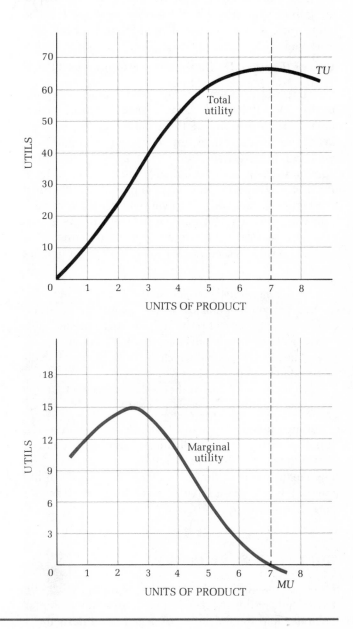

(1)	(2)	(3)
Units of product consumed	Total utility, *TU*	Marginal utility, *MU* **Change in (2)** / **Change in (1)**
0	0	
1	10	10
2	24	14
3	39	15
4	52	13
5	61	9
6	64	3
7	65	1
8	64	−1

a maximum. The consumption of any additional units results in total utility declining. This is clearly seen from the graph of total utility in the exhibit.

Much more important than total utility is *marginal utility*. This is defined as the change in total utility resulting from a unit change in the quantity of the product consumed. As you can see from column (3) of the table, marginal utility may be measured by the formula

$$\text{marginal utility} = \frac{\text{change in total utility}}{\text{change in quantity consumed}}$$

Marginal utility thus measures the *ratio of change* in the two variables. This is emphasized by the way its values are recorded in column (3) of the table—a half-space "between" those shown for columns (1) and (2). Note that its graph is plotted in the same way—to the *midpoints* of the integers on the horizontal axis—as explained in the exhibit.

Observe from the charts that the marginal utility curve reaches a maximum and then turns downward while the total utility curve is still rising. When the total utility curve reaches its maximum height, the marginal utility curve is at zero height. That is, the marginal utility curve intersects the horizontal axis, as emphasized by the vertical dashed line. The reason for this relationship is a technical one which will be explained in a later chapter—after we have learned some more about "marginal" and "total" curves.

Law of (Eventually) Diminishing Marginal Utility

It is important to emphasize that although marginal utility may at first increase, it must *eventually* decrease as more units of the product are consumed. What this means, for example, is that you might very well gain more satisfaction from the second unit of a commodity (e.g., a slice of pizza) than you gained from the first. And you might even gain more from the third than from the second. However, you must eventually reach a point where each successive unit gives you less gain in satisfaction than the previous one. This idea can be expressed more formally by an important law:

> *Law of diminishing marginal utility.* In a given period of time, the consumption of a product, while tastes remain constant, may at first result in increasing marginal utilities per unit of the product consumed. However, a point will be reached beyond which the consumption of additional units of the product will result in decreasing marginal utilities per unit of the product consumed. This is the point of diminishing marginal utility.

As suggested by the word "diminishing" in this law, it is the *decreasing* part of the marginal utility curve that is relevant. The reason will be seen shortly. The law means in effect that on the downward side of the curve, the more you have of something, the less you care about *one* unit of it.

CONSUMER EQUILIBRIUM.

How can the concepts of total and marginal utility be used to describe the economic theory of consumer behavior and the existence of negatively inclined demand curves? This is the question we set out to answer.

Imagine you are a consumer with a given amount of money to spend on two commodities, A and B. Let us designate your marginal utility for product A as MU_A, and the price of product A as P_A. Similarly, let your marginal utility for product B be represented by MU_B, and the price of product B by P_B.

Now, keep in mind that it is the *downward* side of a product's marginal utility curve that is relevant. In view of this, how should you distribute your expenditures on these two products so as to maximize your total satisfaction or utility? The answer is that you must allocate your expenditures so that the marginal

utility *per dollar* spent on the two commodities is equal. That is,

$$\frac{MU_A}{P_A} = \frac{MU_B}{P_B}$$

In other words, to achieve this result you will adjust the quantities you buy. For example, suppose that you have a combination of A and B such that the left-hand ratio is greater than the right-hand ratio. Then you can increase your total utility by giving up some of product B (thereby moving up on your MU curve of B) and buying more of product A (thereby moving down on your MU curve of A). It can be demonstrated that the gain will more than offset the loss.

For example, suppose that you have a combination of products A and B such that

$$\frac{MU_A}{P_A} = 30 \text{ utils per dollar}$$

$$\frac{MU_B}{P_B} = 10 \text{ utils per dollar}$$

If you spend a dollar less on B, you will lose 10 utils. If you spend a dollar more on A, you will gain 30 utils. The transfer of a dollar from B to A will therefore result in a net gain of 20 utils. Hence, you will make the transfer. As the transfer proceeds, the marginal utility per dollar of B rises as the amount purchased decreases. At the same time, the marginal utility per dollar of A falls as the amount purchased increases. When the two ratios are equal—say, at 20 utils per dollar—there is no further gain by transferring expenditures from B to A. At this point your total utility is at a maximum.

But what about your *money*, which is being exchanged for these products? We can think of money (symbolized m) like any other commodity. That is, the marginal utility of money to you, the consumer, is represented by MU_m and its price by P_m. The foregoing marginal-utility equation, to be complete, should now be extended to read

$$\frac{MU_A}{P_A} = \frac{MU_B}{P_B} = \frac{MU_m}{P_m}$$

But because the price of a dollar is $1, the denominator in the last ratio may be omitted and the equation becomes

$$\frac{MU_A}{P_A} = \frac{MU_B}{P_B} = MU_m$$

This equation expresses your equilibrium as a consumer. That is, the equation defines the conditions that exist when you have allocated your money and commodities in the face of market prices in such a way as to maximize your total utility. This equation is also equivalent to the following statement:

> For the consumer to be in equilibrium, the last dollar spent on A must yield the same marginal utility per dollar's worth of A as the last dollar spent on B. This, in turn, must equal the marginal utility of money (per dollar of expenditure).

This principle can be extended to any number of commodities. The point is that in order for you to be in equilibrium your marginal utility per dollar of expenditure must be equal for all commodities, which, in turn, must equal your marginal utility for money. Otherwise, you will have to increase your total utility by reshuffling your expenditures.

MARGINAL UTILITY AND DEMAND CURVES

We now wish to derive your consumer's demand curve for a specific commodity based on your utility data. The preceding equation (in color) says that for any particular commodity, say commodity A,

$$\frac{MU_A}{P_A} = MU_m$$

If we "transpose" and solve for P_A, we get

$$P_A = \frac{MU_A}{MU_m}$$

Suppose that we now simplify by assuming that in the short run your marginal utility for money is a constant positive amount. For example, let us assume that MU_m is any positive number, say 3. (The number itself makes no difference for our present purposes; any positive number can be chosen, as will be seen momentarily.) Your individual demand curve for commodity A can then be derived if your marginal utility schedule is known.

This is illustrated in Exhibit 2, where the price data in column (4) are obtained from the given information in the other columns. As you can see from the explanation accompanying the diagram, the demand curve represents the demand schedule from columns (1) and (4) of the table. This curve is negatively sloped, a fact that is uninfluenced by the constant positive value chosen for MU_m.

SOME APPLICATIONS OF UTILITY THEORY

The development of utility theory in general, and the concept of marginal utility in particular, permit us to

Exhibit 2
Deriving a Consumer's Demand Curve for a Commodity, Based on Utility Data

The demand curve is graphed from columns (1) and (4) of the table. The curve will be negatively inclined regardless of the constant positive value chosen for MU_m.

(1) Units of product, A (given)	(2) Marginal utility of money, MU_m (given)	(3) Marginal utility of product, MU_A (given)	(4) Price of product, P_A (3) ÷ (2)
1	3	15	5
2	3	12	4
3	3	9	3
4	3	6	2
5	3	3	1

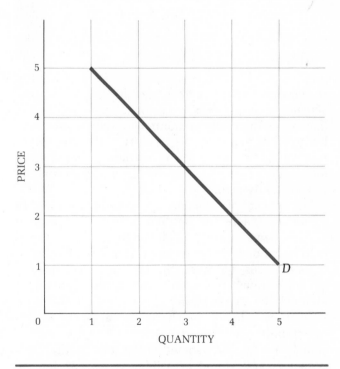

interpret more precisely problems that would otherwise be handled in relatively crude ways.

For example, a question asked earlier was: Why is the price of water low and the price of diamonds high, especially since everyone needs water but no one really needs diamonds? If we knew nothing about utility theory, the answer would be given simply in terms of "supply and demand." But we can go a step further. We can say that the marginal utility of water is ordinarily low because it is usually available in ample amounts. That is, the more we have of something, the less we care about *one* unit of it. Hence, we do not usually hesitate to use the extra water we need to sprinkle our lawns and wash our cars. The marginal utility of diamonds, on the other hand, is relatively high and their supply is scarce. Therefore, a single unit has considerable value. In a desert or on a battlefield, however, the circumstances might be exactly reversed. In those situations we might be quite willing to trade a diamond for a pint of water, or perhaps a "kingdom" for a "horse."

This suggests an interesting point:

> For some products, total utility may be high while marginal utility is low or even zero. Examples include an urban freeway during off-peak hours, a fire department when there is no fire, and a doctor's service when there is no need for it.

Can you think of other illustrations?

Consumer's Surplus

A concept directly related to utility theory is *consumer's surplus*. This is any payment made by a buyer that is less than the maximum he or she would have been willing to pay for the quantity of the commodity purchased. Consumer's surplus thus represents the difference between the buyer's *demand price* and the price actually paid.

The concept of consumer's surplus is illustrated in Exhibit 3. There the surplus is measured from a buyer's demand curve and marginal utility curve, both based on the data given previously in Exhibit 2. In both cases, however, the curves have been extended to touch the axes of the charts. Notice that although the curves seem to look alike, the scales on the vertical axes of the charts are measured in different units.

In Chart (a), the demand curve tells us that as a consumer you would be willing to pay $2 for the fourth unit of the commodity. However, you would have been willing to pay more, if necessary, for the first, second, and third units. You therefore get a consumer's surplus—a net amount of "pure" satisfaction—by paying only $2 for each of the four units. Your total expenditure is therefore $8. This is the rectangular area (equal to base × height) shown in the diagram. Your consumer's surplus, which is the right-triangular area (equal to ½ base × height), also happens to be $8 in this case. These two amounts, of course, need not always be the same, depending on the slope of the demand curve.

Exhibit 3
Measuring Consumer's Surplus from a Demand Curve and from a Marginal Utility Curve

The rectangular and triangular areas, respectively, measure total expenditure and consumer's surplus. This is true whether they are measured in dollars as in Chart (a) or in utils as in Chart (b).

(a) DEMAND CURVE

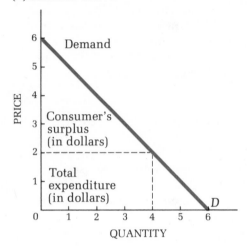

(b) MARGINAL UTILITY CURVE

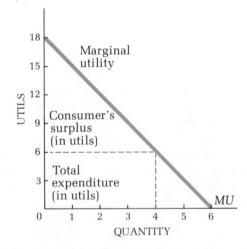

In Chart (b), we can calculate the same information in utils. Thus, your total expenditure *in utils* equals 4 × 6 = 24 utils. Likewise, your consumer's surplus *in utils* equals (4 × 12)/2 = 24 utils. Suppose that we now invoke our earlier assumption that the marginal utility of money is equal to 3 utils per dollar. Then your total expenditure in dollars comes to $8, and your consumer's surplus in dollars also comes to $8. These amounts, of course, are the same as those calculated previously from the demand curve in Chart (a).

The concept of consumer's surplus has a long and interesting history. For our present purposes, it poses two important questions:

1. Because consumer's surplus represents the "extra" value of satisfaction to a buyer, could the government tax it away without affecting either the quantity purchased or its price?

2. Suppose that a seller could measure a buyer's demand curve. Would the seller then be able to capture the consumer's surplus? For instance, could the seller charge the highest possible price for the first unit, the next highest price for the second unit, and so on—instead of charging the *same* price per unit for *all* units?

The answer to these questions is yes. However, there are limitations and conditions. Some of these are spelled out in the next section. The rest must wait until we have covered more ground in a later chapter.

Conclusion: Two Major Shortcomings of Utility Theory

As mentioned earlier, the theory of utility provides one of the more fundamental explanations of why a demand curve is downward-sloping. However, the theory suffers from serious shortcomings, at least two of which are especially important.

1. *Indivisibility of Products* The theory assumes that commodities are sufficiently divisible to be consumed in small units—such as ice-cream cones, candy bars, or cups of coffee. To the ordinary consumer who may buy one house or one piano in a lifetime, or a new and different type of car every several years, the idea of marginal utility has little or no application. This is because it is a concept that by definition refers to the consumption of increasing units of the *same commodity within a given period of time while tastes remain constant*. The theory of utility is thus weakened by the fact that many products bought by consumers are indivisible and cannot be consumed in small, successive doses.

2. *Immeasurability of Utility* A more fundamental difficulty, as mentioned at the beginning of the chapter, is that no method has yet been devised for measuring a consumer's intensity of satisfaction. That is, utility cannot be measured in the same way as we might measure the weight of an object in pounds or kilos, or the distance between two points in miles or meters. In other words, we cannot measure utility in terms of *cardinal* numbers like 10, 23, 32.7, and so on, as the theory of utility assumes.

In view of the theory's rather tenuous assumptions, must we conclude that one of its most fundamental features—the law of diminishing marginal utility—is invalid? Most economists think not.

Despite the shortcomings of utility theory, the law of diminishing marginal utility is valid for the following reason.

> Suppose that the ratio of the marginal utility of commodity A to the price of A were greater than the ratios of the marginal utilities of all other commodities to their respective prices. Then, if the marginal utilities of all other commodities remained constant as the consumption of them increased, the consumer would spend his or her entire income on commodity A and nothing on the other commodities. In reality, of course, we know that consumers do not behave in this way.

In other words, if it were not for the law of diminishing marginal utility, we would spend all of our money on the one commodity that gave us the greatest gain in satisfaction. We know, of course, that this does not actually happen. Therefore, the foregoing argument suggests the conclusion that even though there is no absolute measure of utility, the theory nevertheless permits the development of meaningful principles pertaining to consumer demand and equilibrium. (See *Leaders in Economics*, pages 365 and 366.)

What You Have Learned

1. An explanation of the law of (downward-sloping) demand can be given on the bases of observation and experience, substitution and income effects, or the theory of utility. The last assumes that utility can be measured in cardinal numbers, thus giving rise to the law of diminishing marginal utility—one of the most famous laws in economics.

2. The theory of utility shows how consumer equilibrium is obtained when the marginal utility per dollar of expenditure is equal for all commodities, including money. On the basis of this principle, a consumer's demand curve for a commodity can be derived and the concept of consumer's surplus can be demonstrated.

For Discussion

1. *Terms and concepts to review:*

income effect	consumer's surplus
substitution effect	demand price
utility	conspicuous
marginal utility	consumption
law of diminishing marginal utility	

2. Assume that Mr. R is rich and Ms. P is poor, and that both have the same marginal-utility-of-money curve (MU_m), as shown in the figure. Let Mr. R's income be $0R$ and Ms. P's income be $0P$.

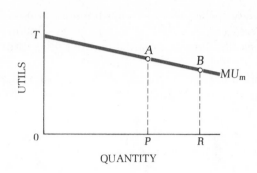

(a) What is Mr. R's marginal utility for money? Ms. P's?

(b) What is Mr. R's total utility for money? Ms. P's?

(c) If you could reallocate the total incomes of these two individuals, how would you do it so as to maximize their *combined* total utility for money? Illustrate on the diagram.

(d) Which individual would experience a loss in total utility for money as a result of this income reallocation? Which individual would experience a gain?

(e) Is the *net* effect of income reallocation a gain or a loss in the total utility for money?

(f) Does this problem suggest any implications for society as a whole? Discuss.

3. "A proportional income tax is a fair tax because, other things being the same, people with equal incomes pay equal taxes, and therefore make equal sacrifices." On the basis of this chapter, do you agree? Discuss. (NOTE Look up the meaning of *proportional tax* in the Dictionary at the back of the book.)

4. Suppose that after some minimum level of income is attained, each person's marginal utility of income changes in one of the following ways.

(a) Decreases at a rate *equal* to the percentage increase in income.

(b) Decreases at a rate *faster* than the percentage increase in income.

(c) Decreases at a rate *slower* than the percentage increase in income.

On one chart, sketch the three curves depicting the conditions outlined above. Which type of taxation—progressive, proportional, or regressive—would you suggest in order to assure equal subjective sacrifice by taxpayers? Explain your answer. (NOTE Look up the meanings of *progressive*, *proportional*, and *regressive tax* in the Dictionary at the back of the book.)

5. Fill in the empty cells in the following table:

Total utility	Marginal utility
increasing at a constant rate	
	increasing
increasing at a decreasing rate	
	zero
decreasing	

Leaders in Economics
William Stanley Jevons   1835–1882

Marginal Utility Theorist and
Mathematical Economist

Repeated reflections and inquiry have led me to the somewhat novel opinion that *value depends entirely upon utility.* Prevailing opinions make labor rather than utility the origins of value; and there are even those who distinctly assert that labor is the *cause* of value. I show, on the contrary, that we have only to trace out carefully the natural laws of the variation of utility, as depending on the quantity of commodity in our possession, in order to arrive at a satisfactory theory of exchange, of which the ordinary laws of supply and demand are a necessary consequence.

These were the words with which the great English economist Jevons introduced his major work in economics. His book, *Theory of Political Economy,* was first published in 1871, followed by three editions in later years.

Jevons is one of the towering figures in the development of economic thought. He made many significant contributions to value and distribution theory, capital theory, and to statistical research in economics. But he is perhaps best known as a leading contributor to marginal utility analysis. In one of the key passages of his book, he points out that exchange between two individuals will cease when "the ratio of exchange of any two commodities is . . . the reciprocal of the ratio of the final degrees of utility of the quantities of commodity available for consumption." This is just a clumsy way of saying that, in equilibrium, marginal utilities will be proportionate to prices.

Macmillan, Inc.

Jevons was educated in England. He majored in chemistry and the natural sciences but maintained a strong interest in philosophy, science, logic, mathematics, and political economy (i.e., economics). He served as Professor of Political Economy at Owens College, Manchester, and at University College, London. In addition to a famous study called *The Coal Question* (1865), which gained him recognition as an economist, Jevons wrote a distinguished text entitled *Elementary Lessons in Logic and Principles of Science* (1870). His main work, however, was *Theory of Political Economy,* in which he made clear his desire to develop economics as a

mathematical science. In his own words:

It is clear that Economics, if it is to be a science at all, must be a mathematical science. There exists much prejudice against attempts to introduce the methods and language of mathematics into any branch of the moral sciences. Many persons seem to think that the physical sciences form the proper sphere of mathematical method, and that the moral sciences demand some other method—I know not what. My theory of Economics, however, is purely mathematical in character. Nay, believing that the quantities with which we deal must be subject to continuous variation, I do not hesitate to use the appropriate branch of mathematical science, involving though it does the fearless consideration of infinitely small quantities. The theory consists in applying the differential calculus to the familiar notions of wealth, utility, value, demand, supply, capital, interest, labour, and all the other quantitative notions belonging to the daily operations of industry. As the complete theory of almost every other science involves the use of that calculus, so we cannot have a true theory of Economics without its aid.

Jevons also did pioneering work in statistics and business forecasting. He formulated statistical correlations and forecasts of economic data which he sold to businesses—an idea that was at least 50 years ahead of its time.

Jevons' productive efforts were brought to an untimely end. In his late thirties he began to suffer ill health, and at the age of forty-seven he drowned while visiting a health resort.

Leaders in Economics
Thorstein Bunde Veblen   1857–1929

*Great Iconoclast—Institutionalist—
"Antimarginalist"*

Theories in economics are not always accepted without reservation. Throughout their development, economic doctrines have been challenged and criticized. But no one has ever been more challenging and more critical than Thorstein Veblen—philosopher, anthropologist, sociologist, economist, "compleat" social scientist, and prophet extraordinary. Indeed, Veblen ranks as one of the most creative and original thinkers in the history of economics. He also influenced an entire generation of brilliant economic scholars who succeeded him.

Veblen was eccentric, found it difficult to get along with people, and earned a reputation for being an extremely dull and uninteresting teacher. As a result, he stumbled from one precarious teaching position to another, never reaching a rank higher than associate professor, which he held at Stanford University from 1906 to 1909. In later years he taught at the University of Missouri and at the New School for Social Research in New York City.

Veblen was part of what is known as the "institutionalist" school of economic thought. He believed that human behavior could best be understood in terms of the practices and customs of society, its methods of doing things, and its ways of thinking about things, all of which compose "settled habits of thought common to the generality of men." These habits become institutions—deeply ingrained patterns of thought and action on which all material civilization is built.

Institutions, however, are not permanent. They unfold and grow into

The Bettmann Archive.

new patterns of change. In this sense, socioeconomic behavior is more evolutionary and dynamic than it is mechanistic—more like biology than physics—because it is devoid of the "natural," "normal," "controlling principles" that are found in the writings of marginal utility theorists and other neoclassical economists.

This is the type of argument that Veblen used in hammering away at accepted economic doctrines. Thus, parodying the pseudoscientific style of some of the marginal utility theorists of his time, Veblen wrote:

What does all this signify? If we are getting restless under the taxonomy of a monocotyledonous wage doctrine and a cryptogamic theory of interest, with involute, loculicidal, tomentous and moniliform variants, what is the cytoplasm, centrosome, or karyokinetic process to which we may turn, and in which we may find surcease from the metaphysics of normality and controlling principles?

No wonder Veblen was once referred to as "the arch-disturber of the economist's academic peace of mind."

Veblen wrote more than a dozen books, all of them interesting and controversial. His first and best-known work, *The Theory of the Leisure Class* (1899; new ed., 1918), is often required reading even today for students taking courses in sociology. In this book he coined a famous phrase, *conspicuous consumption*. This meant the tendency of those above the subsistence level (i.e., the "leisure class") to be mainly concerned with impressing others through standards of living, taste, and dress—that is, through what Veblen called "pecuniary emulation"—which is the hallmark of society. This, Veblen argued, was a "commonly observed pattern of behavior" which was contrary to marginal utility theory. That is, conspicuous consumption clearly implies that people may sometimes buy more of a good at higher prices than at lower prices in order to impress others.

Thorstein Veblen, more perhaps than any other social scientist, criticized practically every phase of social life. Throughout his writings there are prophecies about the changing structure of society, many of which have materialized with astounding accuracy. History may someday record that Veblen was one of the greatest prophets of social and economic change who ever lived.

Indifference Curves

The law of diminishing marginal utility has long been used to explain the existence of downward-sloping demand curves. The chief difficulty with this explanation, as we noted earlier, lies in our *inability to measure utility*. Unlike the weight of an object or the distance between two points, utility cannot be measured in terms of cardinal numbers. It was largely because of this shortcoming that economists devised an alternative approach for explaining demand phenomena. This approach makes use of a concept known as *indifference curves*.

The Price Line or Budget Line

Imagine you are a consumer possessing, say, $2, entering the market to spend your money on goods. You are confronted with two commodities, X and Y. The price of X is $2; the price of Y is $1. In other words, the price of X is twice the price of Y. Algebraically, if P denotes price, then $P_X = 2P_Y$.

Now you could spend your entire $2 on X, in which case you could buy only 1 unit and have nothing left to spend on Y; or you could spend your whole $2 on Y and have nothing left to spend on X. The table in Exhibit 1 shows some of the combinations of X and Y that you could purchase with your $2. Thus, for $2, with P_X equal to $2 and P_Y equal to $1, you can buy

any of the combinations shown in the table as well as any other combinations that will total $2.

The diagram in Exhibit 1 illustrates the same situation graphically. In this chart, the vertical axis 0Y represents the different quantities of commodity Y that you can purchase, and the horizontal axis 0X shows the amounts of X that can be had.

Thus, if you spend your entire $2 on Y, you can purchase 2 units or an amount equal to 0M. If you spend your $2 on X, you can purchase 1 unit, or an amount equal to 0N. If we connect these two points with a line, the resulting MN is called a "price line," or "budget line."

Just what does this price line tell us? It indicates all the possible combinations of X and Y that could be purchased for a total of $2, assuming that $P_X = $2 and $P_Y = $1. Thus, point Q shows that you could purchase 1 unit of Y and ½ unit of X, for a total of $2. The same is true of any other point on MN. Notice, however, that as we move along the line from M to N, more of X can be purchased and less of Y. This is just as we should expect. Out of any given money income, the more we spend on one commodity the less we have to spend on other things. Thus:

A *price line* (or *budget line*) represents all the possible combinations of two commodities that a consumer can purchase at a particular time, given the market prices of the commodities and the consumer's money budget or income.

Exhibit 1
A Consumer's Alternative Purchase Combinations

Assumptions: consumption budget = $2; price of X = $2; price of Y = $1.

Purchase combinations	Units of X	Units of Y	Total amount spent
N	1	0	$2 + $0 = $2
Q	½	1	$1 + $1 = $2
M	0	2	$0 + $2 = $2

The price line represents all the possible combinations of commodities X and Y that you the consumer can purchase at a particular time, given the market prices of the commodities and your money budget.

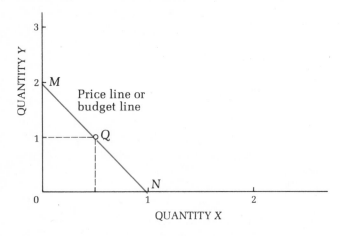

MANY POSSIBLE PRICE LINES

Suppose now that you have $4, instead of only $2. Because you have twice as much money, you can buy twice as much of each commodity, provided that their prices do not change. Thus, for $2, you were able to buy as much as 2Y or 1X, or any combination in between. Now you can buy as much as 4Y or 2X, or any combination in between. This fact is shown in Exhibit 2, where M′N′ represents the new price line at a higher income or budget of $4 and MN the old price line at a lower income or budget of $2. Obviously, for every level of income there will be a different price line corresponding to that income level. If income rises, so does the price line; if income falls, the price line falls. Thus, because an infinite number of budgets or income levels are possible, an infinite number of price lines are possible.

The Nature of Indifference Curves

Next, even though you are a consumer confronted with two commodities, X and Y, you will probably not spend your entire income on only one of these items. Instead, you will probably purchase some combination of the two. Since there are many possible combinations of X and Y that can be bought, the question is: Just which of the many possible combinations will you purchase?

Let us disregard the price relationships that were described earlier and pay attention solely to the satisfaction you would derive from possessing commodities X and Y. That is, let us forget for the moment that $P_X = \$2$ and $P_Y = \$1$ and that you have a given income.

We start by constructing what is called an *indifference schedule*. This is a list showing the various combinations of two commodities that would be equally satisfactory to you at a given time. Column (1) of the table in Exhibit 3 is an example of a possible indifference schedule for two commodities X and Y.

In this column, each combination of X and Y is

Exhibit 2
An Increase in the Price Line

An increase in your income results in the price line being shifted outward, thus enabling you to buy more of X and Y at the given market prices.

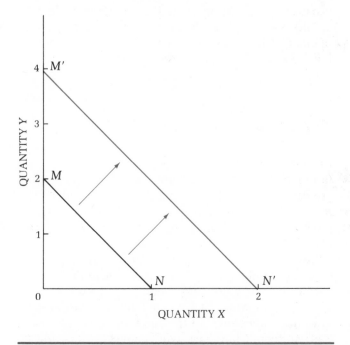

Exhibit 3
A Consumer's Indifference Schedule, Indifference Curve, and Marginal Rate of Substitution

Each combination in column (1) yields the same total utility to you, the consumer. Hence, you are indifferent as to which combination you prefer.

In column (2), the marginal rate of substitution measures the amount of commodity Y you must give up to get 1 unit of commodity X, while maintaining the same total utility. The numerical value of this ratio decreases as additional units of X are acquired.

Combina-tions	(1) Indifference schedule	(2) Marginal rate of substitution of X for Y
1	60 Y and 1X	
2	50 Y and 2X	10/1
3	41 Y and 3X	9/1
4	33 Y and 4X	8/1
5	26 Y and 5X	7/1
6	20 Y and 6X	6/1
7	15 Y and 7X	5/1
8	11 Y and 8X	4/1
9	8 Y and 9X	3/1
10	6 Y and 10X	2/1
11	5 Y and 11X	1/1

An *indifference curve* is a graph of an indifference schedule. Any point on the curve denotes a particular combination of commodities X and Y that yields the same total utility.

Note that as X increases 1 unit at a time, the amount of Y that you are willing to give up decreases. This reflects a decreasing marginal rate of substitution of X for Y.

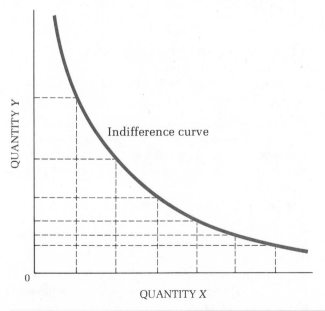

QUANTITY Y

Indifference curve

0

QUANTITY X

equally satisfactory to you. Thus, you would just as soon have combination 1, consisting of 60 Y and 1X, as you would combination 2, consisting of 50 Y and 2X, or combination 3, 41 Y and 3X, and so on. This is true because each combination yields the same total satisfaction or utility. Hence, you are completely *indifferent* as to which combination you prefer, for you prefer no one combination. All combinations are equally desirable because they *all yield the same total utility*.

Now there is this important thing to notice about an indifference schedule. Because each combination yields the same total utility, it follows that if you were to increase your X intake by one unit at a time, you would have to decrease your Y holdings by some amount in order that each successive combination continue to yield the same total utility. For example, when you possess combination 1 of 60 Y and 1X, you derive a certain amount of total utility. If you were to have 60 Y and 2X, your total utility would be greater than the total utility of 60 Y and 1X, for you would have the same amount of Y plus more of X. Therefore, in order to keep your total utility the same, you must give up a certain amount of Y for each unit increase in X. Column (1) in Exhibit 3 shows this relationship.

MARGINAL RATE OF SUBSTITUTION

Next, we should notice that as you increase your X intake, the amount of Y that you are willing to give up *decreases*. Thus, when you possess combination 1 of 60 Y and 1X, you are willing to give up 10 units of Y for 1 unit of X. This leaves you with 50 Y and 2X, or combination 2. At this point, you are willing to give up only 9 units of Y for 1 more unit of X, which would leave you at combination 3. Column (2) indicates this relationship. It shows us the amount of Y you are willing to surrender for every unit increase in your X holdings in order that the new combination yield you the same satisfaction as the previous one, that is, the same total utility.

The rate at which the consumer is willing to substitute commodity X for commodity Y is called the *marginal rate of substitution (MRS)*. It may be defined as the change in the amount of one commodity that will just offset a unit change in the holdings of another commodity, so that the consumer's total utility remains the same. Since the ratio of the change in Y to the change in X is negative (because the amount of one commodity decreases when the other increases), we may express the marginal rate of substitution by the formula

$$MRS = - \frac{\text{change in Y}}{\text{change in X}}$$

As a general rule the minus sign is understood and may be omitted in written and oral discussions.

Why does the *MRS*, as shown in column (2) of the table, decrease? You will remember that a demand curve slopes downward from left to right because the marginal utility of the commodity decreases as more of the commodity is consumed. (The more we have of something, the less we care about 1 unit of it.)

The concept of a decreasing *MRS* is similar to that of decreasing marginal utility. As X *increases* (1 unit at a time), the marginal utility of X *decreases*. As Y *decreases*, the marginal utility of Y *increases*. Thus, the more we have of X, the less we want more of it, and the less we have of Y, the less we are willing to give up more of it. That is, as we give up Y for X, the less of Y we are willing to give up for additional units of X.

For example, when you possessed 60Y and 1X, you were willing to give up a relatively large amount of Y, namely 10Y, for 1 unit of X. After that, you were willing to give up only 9 units of Y, then 8Y, and so forth, for additional units of X. This is because you care less and less for additional units of X, and hence are willing to give up less and less of Y. (Or, conversely, you care more and more for your smaller holdings of Y and you are willing to give up fewer units of it to acquire one more unit of X.)

MANY POSSIBLE INDIFFERENCE CURVES

Suppose now that we were to plot the various combinations in our indifference schedule on a chart. We would get a curve similar to the one in Exhibit 3. This curve is called an *indifference curve* because every point on it represents a particular combination of the two commodities X and Y that is equally satisfactory to you, that is, yields you the same total utility.

Just as it is possible to have an infinite number of price lines, so is it possible to have an infinite number of indifference curves. This is suggested in Exhibit 4, where point Q represents a combination of 0M of X and 0N of Y. This combination yields the same total utility as any other combination on the same curve. On the higher curve at point R, however, the consumer possesses the same amount of Y, namely 0N, plus more of X, namely 0M'. Therefore, this combination must yield a higher total utility than any of the previous combinations to be found on curve 1.

If we then compare point S on the higher curve with point Q on the lower one, we see that point S represents the same amount of X plus more of Y. Finally, if we pick any point between S and R on the higher curve, say at T, we note that there is more of *both* X

Exhibit 4
Two Indifference Curves

The higher a consumer's indifference curve, the greater the total utility. The points S and R, in comparison with the point Q, represent *at least* as much of one commodity plus more of the other. Any point between S and R, such as T, represents more of *both* commodities. Although this chart depicts only two indifference curves, an infinite number of such curves exist for every consumer.

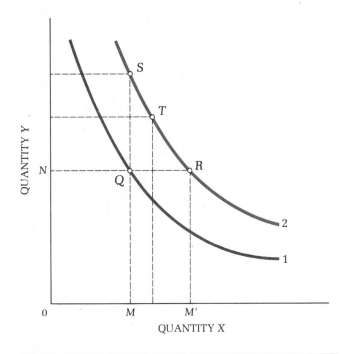

and Y *as compared with the combination denoted by point Q* on the lower curve.

These ideas suggest three important conclusions about indifference curves:

1. The higher an indifference curve—that is, the farther it lies to the right—the greater the consumer's total utility. This is because any point on a higher curve will always denote *at least* the same amount of one commodity plus more of the other.

2. A consumer will always try to be on the highest possible indifference curve. This is because it is assumed that the consumer will always try to maximize total utility.

3. Each indifference curve represents a *different* level of total utility. Therefore, indifference curves can never intersect at any point.

The Equilibrium Combination

Now let us combine the concepts of price lines and indifference curves. Superimposing one diagram upon the other, we get a result such as that depicted in Exhibit 5.

The price line MN shows us the possible combinations of X and Y that could be purchased with given prices of X and Y at a given income. Each indifference curve, 1, 2, and 3, shows various combinations of X and Y that yield the same total utility along a given curve. The higher the indifference curve, the greater the total utility. Therefore, you, the consumer, will always try to be on the highest possible indifference curve.

Given these price lines and indifference curves, precisely what combination of X and Y will be pur-

chased? The answer is based on the following fundamental notions:

1. The indifference curves represent the consumer's *subjective* valuations of X and Y. These valuations have no relationship to the *objective* facts that X and Y have certain prices and that the consumer has a certain money income to spend. These objective facts are shown by the price line.

2. Subjectively, the consumer will try to be on the highest possible indifference curve. Objectively, this goal is limited by the price line. The problem, therefore, is to reconcile this difference.

Because the price line shows all the possible combinations of X and Y that can be purchased for a given money income, it follows that there will be only one point on the price line that will also be on the highest possible indifference curve. This is point Q, where the price line is tangent to curve 2. Point Q, therefore, shows the combination of X and Y that will be purchased, namely 0L of Y and 0P of X.

Thus, as a consumer you would not want to be on curve 1, where you would purchase a combination determined by D or E, because your purchasing power as determined by the price line permits you to be on a higher indifference curve. The highest curve that you can be on and yet remain within your income as determined by the price line is curve 2. And the only place where the price line touches the highest indifference curve within your means is point Q. This point, therefore, indicates the combination of X and Y that will be purchased at the prevailing prices and income.

You are thus in a position not unlike that of the legendary Buridan's ass. The ass, it will be remembered, stood equidistant between two equal bundles of hay, and starved to death because it could not choose between them. Similarly:

All combinations on any one indifference curve are equally desirable. It is the point of tangency of an indifference curve with a price line that determines the equilibrium–purchase combination.

Exhibit 5
The Equilibrium–Purchase Combination

The tangency of the price line with an indifference curve determines the consumer's equilibrium–purchase combination. Thus, because the tangency is at point Q, you will buy 0P units of X and 0L units of Y.

A given price line may intersect any number of indifference curves, but it can be tangent to only one indifference curve.

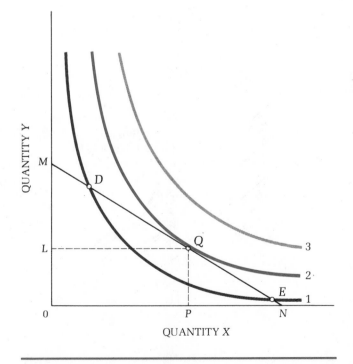

What Happens When Income Changes?

Suppose now that your income increases while the prices of X and Y remain the same. You could now purchase more of both X and Y. This condition is shown in Exhibit 6, where the price line shifts to the right from MN to M'N' to M''N'', indicating that a greater combination of both commodities can be pur-

Exhibit 6
Income–Consumption Curve

An increase in income may increase your purchases of both X and Y. The line QRS connects the tangency points of price lines and indifference curves as your income increases. It is called an income–consumption curve (ICC).

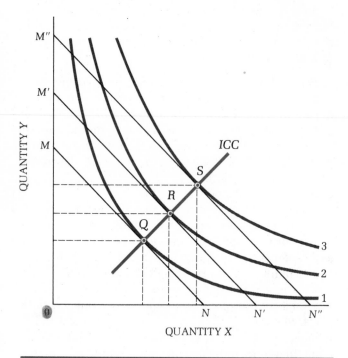

QUANTITY X

Exhibit 7
Superior and Inferior Goods

As your income increases, you may buy more of one commodity (superior good) and less of another commodity (inferior good). [NOTE The inferior good in each graph is inferior only over the range where the income consumption curve (ICC) has a negative slope, that is, bends "backward" in Chart (a) and "downward" in Chart (b).]

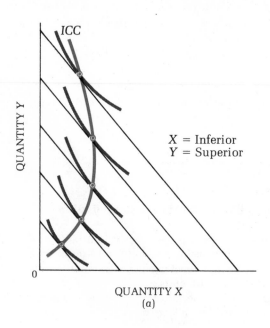

QUANTITY X
(a)

chased. At each new level of income there is a tangency with a new and higher indifference curve. Connecting these points of tangency, we get the line QRS. Then, extending vertical and horizontal lines from each of these points to the X and Y axes shows us by how much you increase your purchases of both X and Y as your income rises.

The line QRS may be called an *income–consumption curve (ICC)*. It connects the tangency points of price lines and indifference curves by showing the amounts of two commodities that you will purchase if your income changes while their prices remain constant.

It is possible, however, that as your income increases, your consumption of one commodity may increase while your consumption of the other commodity decreases. This is shown in Exhibit 7. In Chart (a), as your income rises, your consumption of Y also rises, and although X at first increases, it gradually falls off. The opposite is seen in Chart (b); as your income rises, your consumption of both X and Y increases, but Y soon decreases.

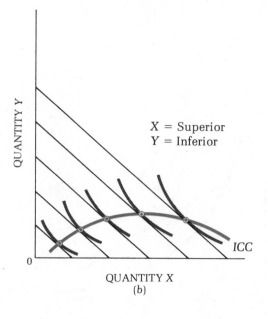

QUANTITY X
(b)

A good whose consumption varies inversely with money income (prices remaining constant) over a certain range of income is called an *inferior good*. Some classic examples are potatoes, used clothing, and other "cheap" commodities bought by low-income families. The consumption of these commodities by low-income families declines in favor of more nutritious foods, new clothing, and so on, as their incomes rise. It should be noted, however, that in a larger sense almost any good may become "inferior" at some income level. Thus, when a family "steps up" from a Chevrolet to a Cadillac because of an increase in income, the Chevrolet becomes an inferior good.

On the other hand, a good whose consumption varies directly with money income (prices remaining constant) is called a *superior good*. Most consumer goods are of this type. Superior goods are also sometimes called *normal goods* because they represent the "normal" situation. Examples include most food, clothing, appliances, and other nondurable and durable items that people typically buy.

What Happens When Price Changes?

The previous case assumed that you, the consumer, had an increased income while the prices of X and Y remained constant. Let us now allow both your income and the price of Y to remain constant, but the price of X to decrease. What happens?

The result is seen in Exhibit 8. The lower end of the price line shifts to the right from MN to MN' to MN''. This indicates that as P_X falls, more of X can be purchased. The price line thus fans outward as a result of decreases in P_X.

We can work the same idea in the other direction by permitting the lower end of the price line to shift left. For instance, let us assume that the price line to begin with is MN''. Then suppose that the price of X gradually rises while the price of Y and your income remain the same. As P_X rises, less of X can be bought, until finally the price of X is so high that it is not purchased at all. The price line then becomes the vertical line $0M$, indicating that you spend your entire income on Y.

The line QRS in the diagram is thus a *price-consumption curve (PCC)*. It connects the tangency points of price lines and indifference curves. The PCC curve thus shows the amounts of two commodities that you will purchase when your income and the price of one commodity remain constant while the price of the other commodity varies.

Exhibit 8
Price-Consumption Curve

With your income and the price of Y constant, decreases in the price of X result in your buying more of it. The line QRS connects the tangency points of price lines and indifference curves under these circumstances. It is called a *price-consumption curve (PCC)*.

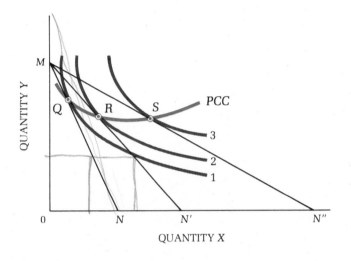

Deriving a Demand Curve

How do the principles of indifference curves and price lines relate to the law of demand? As you recall, this is the question we started out to answer.

The answer is that these two principles are together used to derive a *demand curve*. This is illustrated in Exhibit 9, where numbers are used with letters so that the computations can be followed easily.

In Chart (a), the price line MN signifies an income of $10, with $P_Y = $1 and $P_X = $2. As a consumer, you can thus purchase either 10 units of Y, or 5 units of X, or various combinations in between. The tangency of this price line with your indifference curve, however, shows that you will maximize your total utility by purchasing 4 units of Y and 3 units of X.

Suppose now that the price of X falls to $1, while your income and the price of Y remain constant. The tangency of the new price line MN' with the higher indifference curve indicates that you will be in equilibrium by purchasing 3 units of Y and 7 units of X.

We need this kind of information to derive a demand curve. For example, in Chart (b) we see the relationship between the price of X and the quantity demanded of X while all other things—namely, your

Exhibit 9
**Derivation of a Demand Curve
from Indifference Curves**

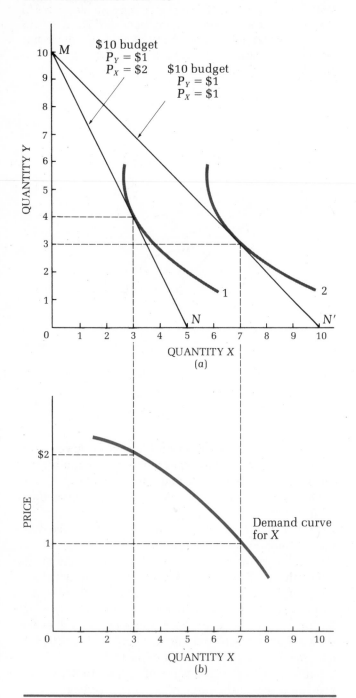

QUANTITY Y

M
$10 budget
$P_Y = \$1$
$P_X = \$2$

$10 budget
$P_Y = \$1$
$P_X = \$1$

1

2

N

N'

QUANTITY X
(a)

PRICE

$2

1

Demand curve
for X

QUANTITY X
(b)

be similarly derived), we get the demand curve for X. Clearly, then, this curve obeys the law of demand. That is, the curve is downward-sloping, indicating that the lower the price, the greater the quantity demanded.

Conclusion: Only Consumer's Preferences Are Needed

The theory of indifference curves had its origins in the late nineteenth century and reached maturity in the 1930s. It marked a major advance in the history of economics, for it freed the concept of demand from a reliance on the older and controversial concept of utility.

You can easily see the reason for this. In the indifference-curve approach, it need only be assumed that as a consumer you know your preferences. That is, you must know whether you prefer one combination of goods to another, or whether you regard them as equivalent. You do not have to know by *how much* you prefer one good to another. Hence, the older approach to demand theory, which rested on the less realistic assumption of a cardinal utility relationship (1, 2, 3, etc.), is replaced by the more realistic assumption of an ordinal preference relationship (first, second, third, etc.).

The significance is clear:

> From the standpoint of indifference-curve analysis, the inability to measure utility is no longer a problem, for such a measure is no longer needed. *A downward-sloping demand curve can be derived directly from a consumer's indifference curves and price lines without using or even assuming a "law" of utility.*

What You Have Learned

1. The theory of indifference curves relates *objective* facts determined by market prices and the consumer's income to the consumer's *subjective* valuations of commodities. The key mechanisms employed in the theory are price lines and indifference curves.

2. Through indifference-curve analysis, we can show how the consumption of goods changes when a buyer's income increases while prices are held constant. We can also illustrate how a buyer's consumption of a good changes when its price varies, while income and all other prices remain the same.

3. A consumer's demand curve can be derived directly from the tangency points of indifference curves and price lines. The law of demand can thus be established without relying on the controversial theory of utility.

income and the price of Y—remain the same. Thus, the dashed lines emphasize the fact that you will purchase 3 units of X at a price of $2 per unit, and 7 units of X at a price of $1 per unit. Connecting these two points (as well as all the in-between points that may

For Discussion

1. *Terms and concepts to review:*

   price line (budget line)   income–consumption
   indifference schedule   curve
   marginal rate of   inferior good
      substitution   superior good
   indifference curve   price–consumption curve

2. We have drawn indifference curves so that they are *convex* to the origin. What would it mean to draw an indifference curve that is *concave* to the origin? Would it make sense? Explain. (HINT   Think in terms of the *MRS*.)

3. Draw a consumer's indifference curve which represents each of the following situations:

   (a) Two commodities that are perfect complements (i.e., used in 1:1 proportions, such as left shoes and right shoes).

   (b) Two commodities that are perfect substitutes, such as nickels and dimes in the ratio 2:1.

4. Commodities such as diamonds and furs are sometimes cited as exceptions to the law of demand because some people will buy more of these at a higher price than at a lower price. Does this mean that the "demand" curve for these products is upward-sloping? Explain. (WARNING Be careful in your thinking. This is a much deeper question than is immediately apparent.)

5. In terms of indifference-curve analysis, what might be the effects of each of the following: (a) an increase in taxes; (b) an increase in the cost of living; (c) expectation of inflation.

Chapter 22

Costs of Production

Chapter Preview

What does the word "cost" mean? Is the term employed in different senses? Can we establish some definitions of costs that can be useful in analyzing and interpreting production problems?

How are costs related to production? Can this information help us understand the economic behavior of business firms?

According to a familiar saying, you have to spend money to make money. In the business world this can be translated to mean that a company must be willing to incur costs if it is to receive revenues.

What do we mean by costs? The term is by no means as simple as most people think. Engineers, accountants, and economists are all concerned with the nature and behavior of costs, but they all deal with different cost concepts in solving different problems.

For example, suppose that you were the president of a corporation and were interested in constructing a new manufacturing plant. You might employ an industrial engineer to study the cost of designing the plant, and a cost accountant to classify and analyze production costs after the plant was in operation. You might also hire an economist to advise you on the ways in which the plant's costs of production would be affected by changes in its volume of output. The economist could also provide advice as to how these costs could be used as a guide in helping you achieve the volume of production that would bring maximum profits.

Thus, the analysis of costs by engineers, accountants, and economists may be undertaken for quite different purposes. This chapter explains the basic cost concepts and relationships that are of interest to economists.

What Do We Mean by "Cost"?

As long ago as 1923, a famous economist, J. M. Clark, wrote, "A class in economics would be a success if the students gained from it an understanding of the meaning of cost in all its many aspects." Clark was prompted to make this statement because the general idea of cost can cover a wide variety of meanings. However, one meaning is common to all types of cost:

> Cost is a sacrifice that must be made in order to do or to acquire something. The nature of the sacrifice may be tangible or intangible, objective or subjective. Also, it may take one or more of many forms, such as money, goods, leisure time, income, security, prestige, power, or pleasure.

Let us amplify this definition by describing and illustrating the notion of cost.

OUTLAY COSTS VERSUS OPPORTUNITY (ALTERNATIVE) COSTS

To most of us, the concept of cost that readily comes to mind is what we may call *outlay costs*. These are the moneys expended in order to carry on a particular activity. Some examples of outlay costs to a business are wages and salaries of its employees, and expenditures on plant and equipment. Other examples are payments for raw materials, power, light, and transportation; disbursements for rents, advertising, and insurance; and taxes paid to the government. Outlay costs are also frequently called *explicit costs, historical costs,* or *accounting costs.* This is because they are the objective and tangible expenses that an accountant records in the company's books.

Economists use a more basic concept of cost: *opportunity cost.* It is defined as the value of the benefit that is forgone by choosing one alternative rather than another. This is an extremely important concept because the "real" cost of any activity is measured by its opportunity cost, not by its outlay cost. How do you identify opportunity costs? By making a comparison between the alternative that was chosen and the one that was rejected. Here are some examples:

1. To a student, the cost of attending college full time includes not only outlay costs on tuition and books. It also includes the opportunity cost of income forgone by not working full time.

2. To a business firm, the cost of advertising includes not only its outlay costs for magazine space or television time. It also includes the opportunity cost of earnings sacrificed by not putting these funds to some other use. This might consist of the purchase of new equipment or the training of more salespeople.

3. To a city, the cost of a public park includes not only the outlay costs for construction and maintenance. It also includes the opportunity cost of the tax revenues forgone by not zoning the land for residential, commercial, or industrial use.

You can probably think of other examples. It should be evident, however, why opportunity costs are often called "alternative costs."

The concept of opportunity cost arises whenever the inputs of any activity are scarce and have alternative uses. The real cost or sacrifice is then measured by the value of the forgone alternative. This principle applies at all levels of economic activity—macro as well as micro. Thus:

> For any economic entity—a society, a business, a household, or an individual—it is incorrect to confine the cost of an activity or a decision to what the entity is doing. *It is what the entity is not doing but could be doing that is the correct cost consideration.*

What About Nonmonetary Alternatives?

The principle of opportunity cost raises some important questions. For example, is it not true that the alternative cost of a given action may often involve nonmonetary considerations, such as riskiness, working conditions, prestige, and similar factors? The answer is yes. This explains, to some extent, why window washers in skyscrapers earn more than dishwashers in restaurants. Why college professors, on the average, earn less—but probably have fewer headaches—than corporation executives. Why the prices of "glamour" securities in the stock market fluctuate much more widely than the prices of public utility shares. And why some individuals may be willing to work for smaller returns in their own businesses, where they can be their own boss, rather than for higher returns in other people's.

Of course, the nonmonetary elements that help make for differences in resource allocation are often difficult to measure. But *in principle* the monetary returns plus or minus the various nonmonetary advantages and disadvantages determine the ways in which the owners of the factors of production put their human and material resources to use.

ECONOMIC COST INCLUDES NORMAL PROFIT

Once we recognize the existence of opportunity costs, it becomes apparent that there is a sharp distinction between costs in accounting and costs in economics. *Economic costs* are payments that must be made to persuade the owners of the factors of production to supply the factors for a particular activity. This definition emphasizes the fact that economic costs are supply prices or "bids" that buyers of resources must offer to attract the desired factor inputs.

Thus, a firm buys its resources, such as capital, land, and labor, in the open market. Expenditures for these resources are part of the firm's economic costs. These money outlays are the *explicit costs* that an accountant records in the company's books. But there are other types of economic costs, called *implicit costs* because they are the costs of self-owned or self-employed resources that are not entered in a company's books of account. For example, if you own a business, including the building and its real estate, and if you manage the business yourself, part of your cost includes the following implicit items.

1. The *interest* return on your investment that you are forgoing by not putting your money into an alternative investment of equal risk.

2. The *rental* receipts that you are passing up by not renting the land and building to another firm.

3. The *wages* (including the return for entrepreneurship) that you would earn if you could be hired to manage the same kind of business for someone else.

These implicit costs of ownership comprise what may be called *normal profit*. This is the least payment the owner of an enterprise would be willing to accept for performing the entrepreneurial function, including risk taking, management, and the like. Normal profit is thus part of a firm's total economic costs, because it is a payment that will keep the owner from withdrawing capital and managerial effort and putting them into some other alternative. Further, economic costs include both explicit costs and implicit costs, and implicit costs include normal profit. Therefore, any receipts that a firm may get over and above its economic costs represent *economic,* or *pure, profit.* These ideas are illustrated in Exhibit 1.

Exhibit 1
Economic Costs and Economic Profit

Suppose that you own your own business, including the building and its land. If you sell an item for $1, your economic costs and economic profit might look like this:

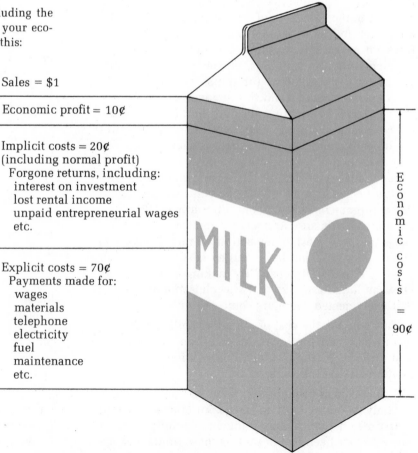

Sales = $1

Economic profit = 10¢

Implicit costs = 20¢
(including normal profit)
 Forgone returns, including:
  interest on investment
  lost rental income
  unpaid entrepreneurial wages
  etc.

Explicit costs = 70¢
 Payments made for:
  wages
  materials
  telephone
  electricity
  fuel
  maintenance
  etc.

Economic costs = 90¢

SHORT RUN AND LONG RUN

Any discussion of costs must include an explanation of two useful concepts—the short run and the long run. These do not refer to clock or calendar time, but to the time necessary for resources to adjust fully to new conditions. This is true regardless of how many weeks, months, or even years the adjustment may take.

At any given time a firm has available a certain *capacity* to produce as determined by the quantity of its equipment or the scale of its plant. If the firm experiences unexpected increases or decreases in the demand for its products, it can change its level of output by using existing plant and equipment either more or less intensively. But it cannot alter plant scale or production capacity with equal speed. Business firms do not put up new factories or discard old ones with every increase or decrease in demand, any more than colleges and universities erect new classroom buildings or abandon old ones with every rise or fall in enrollment.

This leads to an important distinction between the short run and the long run. The *short run* is a period in which a firm can vary its output through a more or less intensive use of its resources. However, it cannot vary its capacity because it has a fixed plant scale. The *long run* is a period long enough for a firm to enter or leave an industry, and to vary its output by varying *all* its factors of production, including plant scale.

These concepts of the short run and the long run suggest an appropriate passage from Henry Wadsworth Longfellow's famous poem, *The Day Is Done*:

And the night shall be filled with music,
   And the cares that infest the day,
Shall fold their tents, like the Arabs,
   And as silently steal away.

In economics as in poetry, business firms, like the Arabs to whom Longfellow referred, can also come and go by unfolding or folding their tents. But by our definition businesses can do this only in the long run, not in the short run.

The Production Function

Every businessperson is well aware that costs of production depend on two things: the quantity of resources purchased and the prices paid for them. At this point our concern is with the quantity purchased. Therefore, it will be useful to analyze a concept known as the *production function*. This is a relationship between the number of units of inputs that a firm employs and the corresponding units of output that result.

THE LAW OF (EVENTUALLY) DIMINISHING RETURNS

You have probably heard of the *law of diminishing returns*. This law is as famous in economics as the law of gravity in physics. But you are not likely to have a precise understanding of the law of diminishing returns without a prior course in elementary economics, any more than you would have a clear understanding of the law of gravity without a basic course in physics.

Exhibit 2 displays a production function based on only one variable input. The table and chart enable you to "see" the operation of the law of diminishing returns as well as to understand it in terms of the following definition.

Exhibit 2
Production Function

	(1) Units of variable factor, F	(2) Total product, TP	(3) Average product, AP (2) ÷ (1)	(4) Marginal product, MP **Change in (2)** **Change in (1)**
A	1	6	6	
				8
B	2	14	7	
				12
C	3	26	8.7	
				11
D	4	37	9.3	
				9
E	5	46	9.2	
				6
F	6	52	8.7	
				5
G	7	57	8.1	
				3
H	8	60	7.5	
				1
I	9	61	6.8	
				−3
J	10	58	5.8	

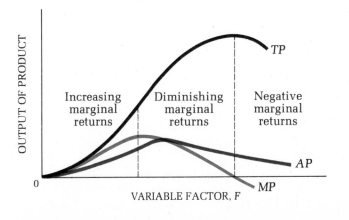

Law of (eventually) diminishing returns. Assume that the state of technology is constant. Then, the addition of a variable factor of production, keeping the other factors of production fixed, will yield increasing marginal returns per unit of the variable factor added. This will continue until an input point is reached beyond which further additions of the variable factor yield diminishing marginal returns per unit of the variable factor added. (NOTE   This law is also known by the more general name of the *law of variable proportions.*)

The law of diminishing returns was first discovered (by the great English classical economist David Ricardo) in agriculture in 1815. Considered a heroic advance in the history of economics, the law is one of the most widely held and best-developed principles in all of economics. This is because it encompasses many kinds of production functions. These range from agriculture and automobiles through retailing and textiles to zinc and zippers. The law thus has enormous significance as well as generality.

Two sets of features should be observed:

1. Note that columns (1) and (2) of Exhibit 2 are in general terms. In order to put them into specific terms, the variable input in column (1) of the table might represent pounds of fertilizer applied to an acre of land. Then the corresponding output in column (2) could be bushels of wheat. Or the variable input might be the number of workers on an assembly line in a factory and the output could be the number of units of the finished good produced. Practically any simple type of "input–output" relationship or production process could be used to illustrate the basic concepts that are involved.

2. The curves in the chart are actually "idealized" or smoothed-out versions of the data given in the table. This enables us to focus most of our attention on the graphs rather than the numbers. Thus, the horizontal axis of the chart shows the variable factor from column (1) of the table, and the vertical axis represents the corresponding output from the remaining columns.

HOW IS THE LAW INTERPRETED?

The first thing you probably noticed in the chart in Exhibit 2 is the shape of the total product or *TP* curve. As the variable input increases from zero, the *TP* curve goes through three phases. At first it rises rapidly, then it tapers off until it reaches a maximum, and finally it declines.

These three phases are reflected by the *marginal product, MP*. This is defined as the change in total product resulting from a unit change in a variable input. For measurement purposes, however, the expression "resulting from" in this definition means the same thing as "divided by." Hence, marginal product is given by the formula

$$MP = \frac{\text{change in total product}}{\text{change in variable input}}$$

You can verify these changes in *MP* from the table. *Average product, AP*, on the other hand, is simply the ratio of total product to the amount of variable input needed to produce that product:

$$AP = \frac{\text{total product}}{\text{variable input}}$$

For example, if Exhibit 2 is taken to represent the number of people working a given parcel of land in order to produce tomatoes, the results could be interpreted in the following way.

The efforts of the first person, whom we call A, applied to the fixed amount of land, have to be spread too thinly in covering all the land. Consequently, the total output is only 6 boxes of tomatoes. If a second person, B, is added who is *equally as efficient* as A, both persons can work the same amount of land and thereby increase total output to 14 boxes of tomatoes. The average output is then 7 boxes of tomatoes per person. However, the marginal product or gain in output is 8 boxes of tomatoes. Adding workers increases the total output. But as you can see, in Exhibit 2 a point is eventually reached where there are so many workers that they get in each other's way and even trample the tomatoes. When this happens, the *TP* curve passes its maximum point and turns downward. The gain in output or marginal product then becomes negative.

Marginal Returns Are the Most Important

Note, therefore, that the *MP* curve at first rises and eventually begins to fall, even though *all the workers are equally efficient.* This is an extremely important idea. The reason the *MP* curve declines is not that the last person hired is less efficient than the previous one. It declines solely for quantitative reasons. That is, the *MP* curve declines because of the changing proportions of variable to fixed factors employed, while all qualitative considerations are assumed to remain equal. This is why the term "law of variable proportions" is more often employed than "law of diminishing returns."

Mathematically, of course, the *MP* curve is derived from changes in the *TP* curve. Indeed, the *MP* curve represents the *slope* of the *TP* curve. This is because the slope of any curve is the change in its vertical distance per unit of change in its horizontal distance.

Thus, the fact that the *TP* curve first increases at an increasing rate and then at a decreasing rate is what causes the *MP* curve to rise to a maximum point and then fall. The resulting three phases—*increasing marginal returns, diminishing marginal returns,* and *negative marginal returns*—are labeled on the chart. It is to these phases—especially the first two—that the definition of the law of diminishing returns refers.

> Because all three curves rise to a maximum and then decline, it can be said that *a law of diminishing returns applies to the total product, the average product, and the marginal product curves.* Indeed, from the time the law was initially formulated in 1815 until the early part of this century, it was often stated in general terms without distinguishing between total, average, and marginal returns. But it then came to be realized that *marginal returns are of key importance for decisions involving changes in the quantities of input or output.* This idea will become increasingly apparent in subsequent chapters.

It is clear from Exhibit 2 that the point of diminishing marginal returns occurs at the input level where the *MP* curve is at its maximum. Where is the point of diminishing average returns? Diminishing total returns?

Short-Run Costs

We have seen that in the short run some resource inputs for a firm are variable while others are fixed. This is because it may be possible in a given production process, for example, to vary the number of unskilled workers or to draw down larger or smaller quantities of raw materials available in inventory. However, it may take considerable time to construct a new wing on a plant or have machines built to specification.

In view of this, what is the nature and behavior of a firm's costs in the short run? We shall answer this question by analyzing three families of cost concepts: *total cost, average cost,* and *marginal cost.*

COST SCHEDULES AND CURVES

The table in Exhibit 3 presents a company's cost schedule. It illustrates the relationship between quantities of output produced per day, as shown in column (1), and the various costs per day of producing these outputs, as shown in the remaining columns. The accompanying charts are graphs of the cost data pre-

sented in the table. Note that, as usual, output is measured on the horizontal axes of the charts and dollars on the vertical axes. Also, the graphs are idealized or "smoothed out" to show clearly their interrelationships.

Our objective is to see how the different costs in Exhibit 3 are related to output. That is, we want to know how they do or do not vary with changes in output. Because the cost curves have a number of important properties, it is important to examine them closely. Remember that we are assuming that a firm's *total costs are its economic costs and hence include normal profit.*

The Family of Total Costs

The first class of costs to be considered is the "total" group shown in columns (2), (3), and (4) of the table.

Total Fixed Costs TFC in column (2) represents those costs that do not vary with output. Examples include rental payments, interest payments on debt, property taxes, and depreciation of plant and equipment. Also included are the wages and salaries of a skeleton staff that the firm would employ as long as it stayed in business—even if it produced nothing. The *TFC* figure is $25 at all levels of output in the table and hence appears as a horizontal line on Chart *(a)*.

Total Variable Costs TVC in column (3) consists of those costs that vary directly with output. These costs rise as output increases over the full range of production. Examples are payments for materials, labor, fuel, and power. Note from Chart *(a)* that as output increases TVC increases first at a decreasing rate and then at an increasing rate. This reflects the operation of the law of diminishing (total) returns, as explained earlier.

Total Costs TC in column (4) represents the sum of total fixed cost and total variable cost. Thus, we have the basic equation

$$TC = TFC + TVC$$

This means that, for TFC,

$$TFC = TC - TVC$$

and, for TVC,

$$TVC = TC - TFC$$

You should also note from the table and Chart *(a)* that *TC* equals *TFC* at zero output. This is because there are no variable costs when there is no production. Observe too that the shape of the *TC* curve is the same as—or "parallel" to—the shape of the *TVC* curve.

Exhibit 3
Short-Run Cost Schedules and Curves for a Firm

(1)	(2)	(3)	(4)	(5)	(6)	(7)	(8)
Quantity of output per day, Q	Total fixed cost, TFC	Total variable cost, TVC	Total cost, TC (2) + (3)	Average fixed cost, AFC (2) ÷ (1)	Average variable cost, AVC (3) ÷ (1)	Average total cost, ATC (4) ÷ (1) or (5) + (6)	Marginal cost, MC Change in (4) / Change in (1)
0	$25	$ 0	$ 25	$ —	$ —	$ —	
1	25	10	35	25.00	10.00	35.00	$10
2	25	16	41	12.50	8.00	20.50	6
3	25	20	45	8.33	6.67	15.00	4
4	25	22	47	6.25	5.50	11.75	2
5	25	24	49	5.00	4.80	9.80	2
6	25	27	52	4.17	4.50	8.67	3
7	25	32	57	3.57	4.57	8.14	5
8	25	40	65	3.13	5.00	8.13	8
9	25	54	79	2.78	6.00	8.78	14
10	25	75	100	2.50	7.50	10.00	21

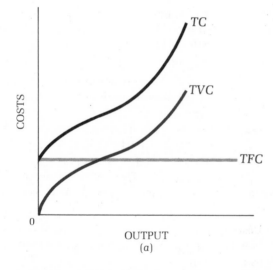

(a)

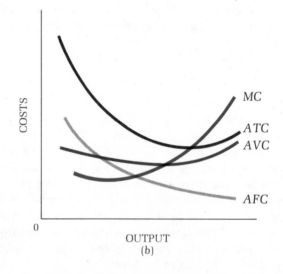

(b)

The only difference between them is the constant vertical distance represented by TFC. In other words, because total fixed cost is constant, changes in total cost are due entirely to changes in total variable cost.

The Family of Average Costs

Columns (5), (6), and (7) give us three different types of average costs. These are represented by Chart (b),. which accompanies the table.

Average Fixed Cost   AFC is the ratio of total fixed cost to quantity produced:

$$AFC = \frac{TFC}{Q}$$

Note from Chart (b) that AFC continually decreases as output increases. This is because TFC in the foregoing equation is constant. Hence, increases in Q will always reduce the value of the ratio.

Average Variable Cost   AVC is the ratio of total variable cost to quantity produced:

$$AVC = \frac{TVC}{Q}$$

Notice that as output increases, the AVC curve falls to a minimum point and then rises. The AVC curve thus reflects the operation of the law of diminishing (average) returns described earlier.

Average Total Cost   ATC is the ratio of total cost to quantity:

$$ATC = \frac{TC}{Q}$$

Hence, it is also equal to the sum of *AFC* and *AVC*:

$$ATC = AFC + AVC$$

Of course, you can also transpose either *AFC* or *AVC* in order to express the equation in terms of the other variables.

REMARK   Businesspeople often use the terms "unit cost" or "cost per unit" when they mean average *variable* cost. If you were a shirt manufacturer, for example, you might figure your cost per shirt to be $6 based on the cost of labor, materials, and other variable resources used. You would then set a "markup" price of perhaps $9 per shirt to cover "overhead" or fixed costs. Economists, on the other hand, include fixed costs with total costs right from the outset. Hence, they use unit cost, or cost per unit, to mean average *total* cost.

Notice that the vertical distance between *ATC* and *AVC* diminishes as output increases. That is, *ATC* and *AVC* come progressively closer together. This is because the difference between them, *AFC*, continually decreases as output expands.

Marginal Cost

There is an important lesson to be learned from the table and charts of Exhibit 3. The lesson is that *total cost always increases as output increases.* That is, the more a firm produces, the greater its total costs of production. This is because increased production always requires the use of more materials, labor, power, and other variable resources. Only average costs—in particular *ATC* and *AVC*—decrease as output increases until some "optimum" or best level of production is reached. Thus, when you hear a businessperson say that production needs to be increased in order to lower costs, he or she is talking about unit costs—either *ATC* or *AVC*—not *TC* or *TVC*.

The fact that total cost changes with variations in production gives rise to an important cost concept called *marginal cost*, MC. It is defined as the change in total cost resulting from a unit change in output. As you know from your previous acquaintance with marginal concepts in economics, the expression "resulting from" is used for interpretive purposes. It means the same thing as "divided by" for mathematical purposes. Therefore, marginal cost may be measured by the formula

$$MC = \frac{\text{change in } TC}{\text{change in } Q}$$

Of course, changes in *TC* are due to changes in *TVC*, because *TFC* remains constant as production varies. Hence, marginal cost can also be measured by dividing the change in *TVC* by the change in *Q*.

What does marginal cost really mean?

Mathematically, marginal cost represents the *slope* of the total cost curve (just as we saw earlier that marginal product represents the slope of the total product curve). Economically, it tells you, for any given output, the *additional* amount of cost a business firm would incur by increasing its output by one unit.

We shall see later that *for economic decisions involving changes in output, marginal cost is the single most important cost concept.*

THE AVERAGE-MARGINAL RELATIONSHIP

By this time you may have noticed an interesting geometric principle that characterizes all average and marginal curves. For convenience, Exhibit 4 groups the foregoing production curves and cost curves together, so that they may be examined simultaneously. However, we are interested for the moment only in the average and marginal curves, so these curves are shown in separate charts below their corresponding total curves.

Referring to these lower charts, we note an important set of relationships.

1. When an average curve is rising, its corresponding marginal curve is above it.

2. When an average curve is falling, its corresponding marginal curve is below it.

3. When an average curve is neither rising nor falling, that is, is either at a maximum or at a minimum, its corresponding marginal curve intersects (is equal to) it.

This set of relationships constitutes what may be called the *average-marginal relationship.*

Does the average-marginal relationship hold true for both the production-function and cost curves? The diagrams indicate that it does. But in the production diagram the marginal curve intersects the average curve at its maximum point, whereas in the cost diagram the marginal curve intersects the two average curves at their minimum points.

The sense behind the average-marginal relationship can be appreciated by a simple example. If to a class of students we add an extra, or "marginal," student whose age is above the average age of the class, the average will increase. If we add a student whose age is below the average, the average will decrease. And if we add a student whose age is equal to the average, the average will remain the same.

Exhibit 4
The Average–Marginal Relationship (*lower charts*) **and
the Total–Marginal Relationship** (*upper and lower charts*)

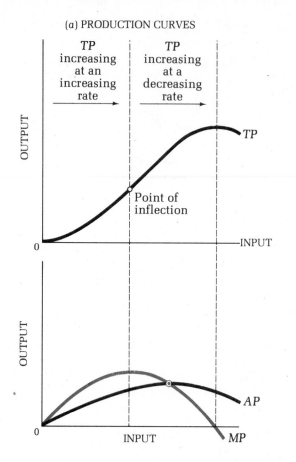

(a) PRODUCTION CURVES

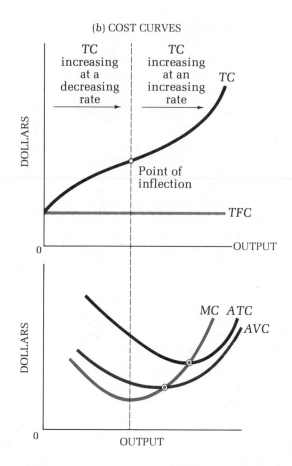

(b) COST CURVES

In later chapters we will encounter other types of average and marginal curves, but the underlying principle stated here characterizes them all.

THE TOTAL–MARGINAL RELATIONSHIP

A geometric principle is also common to all total and marginal curves. It is based on the fact that every marginal curve is a graph of the *slope* of its corresponding total curve, as we have already seen.

Referring again to Exhibit 4, this time to both the upper and lower charts, we see an interesting relationship. This is emphasized by the vertical dashed lines. Thus:

1. When a total curve is increasing at an increasing rate, its corresponding marginal curve is rising.

2. When a total curve is increasing at a decreasing rate, its corresponding marginal curve is falling.

3. When a total curve is increasing at a zero rate, as occurs when it is at its maximum, its corresponding marginal curve is zero.

This set of relationships is called the *total–marginal relationship.*

Observe from the diagrams that the point at which the rate of change of the total curve changes is called the *point of inflection.* This point corresponds to either a peak or trough of the marginal curve, as shown by the vertical dashed lines.

Note that in the foregoing statement of the total–marginal relationship, it is not necessary to include the fact that when the total curve is falling—as in the case of the TP curve at its right end—the corresponding MP curve is negative. Although negative marginal curves may exist from a theoretical standpoint, they do not ordinarily have any economic significance. An employer, for example, will not knowingly hire so many units of an input as to yield the firm a negative marginal product. (Of course, an exception might occur if the input happens to be the boss's son-in-law.)

As with the average–marginal relationship, there are several total–marginal relationships that we shall be encountering in later chapters. Nevertheless, the underlying principle presented here characterizes them all.

Long-Run Costs

It was emphasized earlier that an important difference exists between the short run and the long run. In the *short run* a firm can vary its output but not its plant capacity. Therefore, the firm will have some variable costs and some fixed costs. In the *long run* a firm can vary not only its output but also its plant capacity. Therefore, the firm has no fixed costs. That is, *in the long run all costs are variable*.

Of what practical value is this in the study of costs? We can answer this question by noting that the previous analysis of short-run costs reveals how a firm's costs will vary in response to output changes within a period short enough for the size of the plant to remain fixed. If we now extend the logic one step further, we can develop a firm's *long-run cost curve*. This shows how costs vary with output in a period long enough for all resource inputs, including plant and equipment, to be freely variable in amount. Once this is done, the resulting knowledge of the long-run cost curve can be of use to businesspeople in determining the most economical size of a plant and its general operational standards.

ALTERNATIVE PLANT SIZES

Look at the problem in this way. Suppose that you were a manufacturer whose plant had gone through a series of additions and expansions over a period of years. For each plant size with its associated complement of equipment there would be a different production function and hence a different cost structure. Each of these cost structures would be represented by a different set of short-run cost curves of the type we have already studied. To illustrate, Exhibit 5, Chart (a), presents five short-run average total cost curves, labeled ATC_1, ATC_2, and so on, for five different plant sizes. Theoretically, there could be infinitely many such curves, one for each possible plant size.

These short-run curves can be looked at from still another point of view. Suppose that you were a business manager planning to construct and equip a plant for the production of a commodity. In that case all your factors of production—and therefore all your

Exhibit 5
Short-Run Average Total Cost Curves and the Long-Run Average Cost, or Planning, Curve

Each short-run plant size or "layout" represents a different plant-cost structure. The optimum level of output is at N. Theoretically, there may be infinitely many such curves, one for each possible plant size.

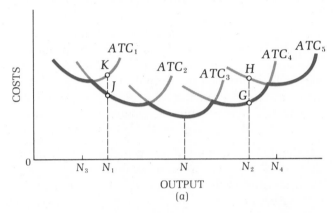

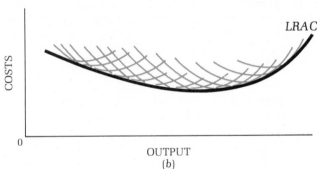

The planning curve, or long-run average cost curve, is tangent to all the short-run curves. But it can only be tangent to the minimum point of the *lowest* short-run curve. For all other short-run curves the tangency occurs on either their declining or rising sides.

costs—would be variable. Each possible plant size or "layout" would then be represented by a different cost structure, as illustrated by these short-run average total cost curves. As before, it should be borne in mind that from a theoretical standpoint there can be infinitely many such curves, one for each possible layout.

Plant Utilization

Some important lessons may be learned from Chart (a). On the basis of the information presented, it seems intuitively clear that the "optimum" output level is at N, and the lowest-cost plant for producing this output is represented by ATC_3. However, for all other levels of output two interesting principles exist—based on the assumption of infinitely many ATC curves:

1. At any output less than the optimum output at N, it pays better to "underuse" a larger plant than to "overuse" a smaller one. For example, suppose that you want to produce the output at N_1. Obviously, it is cheaper to use the larger-scale plant ATC_2 at an average production cost of N_1J per unit than to use the smaller-scale plant ATC_1 at an average cost of N_1K per unit.

2. At any output greater than the optimum output at N, it pays better to "overuse" a smaller plant than to "underuse" a larger one. For instance, suppose that you wish to produce the output at N_2. Clearly, it is cheaper to use the smaller-scale plant ATC_4 at an average cost of N_2G per unit than to use the larger-scale plant ATC_5 at an average cost of N_2H per unit.

It should be noted that these principles are true for *all* outputs—even for outputs like those at N_3 and N_4. Why? Because of the assumption that infinitely many ATC curves may be drawn. Therefore, you can sketch in the possible ATC curves for the outputs at N_3 and N_4 to demonstrate the validity of these concepts.

THE PLANNING CURVE

These principles suggest that the lower portions of the short-run average total cost curves are the only ones economically relevant to the selection of a particular plant. What would happen to these lower portions if, instead of having just five short-run curves, there were an infinitely large number of them, as we have theoretically assumed? To find out, look at Chart (b) along with the following explanation.

The heavy line, called a *planning curve*, is a *long-run average cost curve (LRAC)* that is tangent to each of the short-run average total cost curves from which it is derived. The reason for calling the *LRAC* curve a "planning curve" has already been indicated. When the plant is still in the blueprint stage and all costs are variable, the *LRAC* curve tells you the average total cost of producing a given level of output. Thus, it can be thought of as a curve that shows what costs would be like at the present time for alternative outputs if different-sized plants were built.

THE BEHAVIOR OF LONG-RUN AVERAGE COST: ECONOMIES AND DISECONOMIES OF SCALE

These ideas give rise to an important question: What causes the *LRAC* curve (or the successive ATC curves

of which it is composed) to decrease to a minimum and then rise? Or, to put the question in terms of real-world examples: Why are steel mills larger than machine shops? Why do some firms remain small while others become large?

The answers are based on what may be called *economies and diseconomies of scale*. These are decreases or increases in a firm's long-run average costs as the size of its plant is increased.

Economies of Scale

Several factors may give rise to economies of scale—that is, to decreasing long-run average costs of production.

1. *Greater Specialization of Resources*   As a firm's scale of operation increases, its opportunities for specialization are greatly enhanced. This is because a large-scale firm can often divide the tasks and work to be done more readily than can a small-scale firm.

2. *More Efficient Utilization of Equipment*   In many industries, the technology of production is such that large units of expensive equipment must be used. The production of automobiles, steel, and refined petroleum are notable examples. In such industries, companies must be able to afford whatever equipment is necessary and must be able to use it efficiently by spreading the cost per unit over a sufficiently large volume of output. A small-scale firm cannot ordinarily do these things.

3. *Reduced Unit Costs of Inputs*   A large-scale firm can often buy its inputs—such as its raw materials—at a cheaper price per unit. In other words, a large firm can obtain quantity discounts due to its larger transactions. And for certain types of equipment, the price per unit of capacity is often much less when larger sizes are purchased. Thus, the construction cost per square foot for a large factory is usually less than for a small one. The price per horsepower of electric induction motors varies inversely with the amount of horsepower.

4. *Utilization of By-products*   In certain industries, large-scale firms can make effective use of many by-products that would be wasted by a small firm. A typical example is the meat-packing industry. Here, major firms make glue from cattle hoofs, as well as pharmaceuticals, fertilizer, and other products from the remains of livestock.

5. *Growth of Auxiliary Facilities*   In some places, an expanding firm may often benefit from, or encourage other firms to develop, ancillary facilities. Examples are warehousing, marketing, and transportation systems. These facilities save the growing firm considerable costs. For example, urban colleges and universi-

ties benefit from nearby public libraries. Individual farms benefit from common irrigation and drainage ditches. And growing businesses often encourage the development of, and receive the benefit from, improved transportation facilities.

Diseconomies of Scale

At the same time that economies of scale are being realized, a point may be reached where diseconomies of scale begin to exercise a more than offsetting effect. As a result, the long-run average cost curve starts to rise, primarily for two reasons.

1. *Decision-Making Role of Management*   As a firm becomes larger, heavier burdens are placed on management. Eventually, this resource input is overworked relative to others, and "diminishing returns" to management set in. Of course, management may be able to delegate authority to others, but ultimately decisions must emanate from a final center if there is to be uniformity in performance and policy. Even the modern principles of scientific management do not eliminate these diseconomies. At most they may only be postponed, or perhaps their seriousness lessened.

2. *Competition for Resources*   Rising long-run average costs can occur as a growing firm increasingly bids labor or other resources away from other industries. This may raise the prices the firm pays for its factors and cause increases in unit production costs.

A CLASSIFICATION OF ECONOMIES AND DISECONOMIES

These causes of increasing and decreasing returns to scale are often classified according to whether they are internal or external to the firm. The distinction is important, because the internal factors may be subject to a certain amount of managerial control, whereas the external factors are not.

Internal economies and diseconomies are those conditions that bring about decreases or increases in a firm's long-run average costs or scale of operations as a result of size adjustments *within* the firm as a producing unit. They occur regardless of adjustments within the industry and are due mainly to physical economies or diseconomies. Thus, reductions in long-run average costs occur largely because the indivisibility of productive factors is overcome when size and output are increased. On the other hand, increases in long-run average costs occur because of adverse or conflicting factor interaction between management and other resources.

External economies and diseconomies are those conditions that bring about decreases or increases in a

firm's long-run average costs or scale of operations as a result of factors that are entirely *outside* the firm as a producing unit. They depend on adjustments of the industry and are related to the firm only to the extent that it is part of the industry.

On the basis of this distinction, you should be able to classify each of the various economies and diseconomies of scale listed in the two previous sections as either internal or external.

CONCLUSION: WHAT DOES THE EVIDENCE SHOW?

How have business firms adjusted to the existence of economies of scale? Do the long-run average cost curves of firms actually look like the ones shown earlier? Or do their shapes vary according to the economics of the industry in which they operate?

Relatively few studies have been done on this question. As a result, no conclusive statements can be made. Nevertheless, from the limited evidence that exists, coupled with what economists know about the theory of production and costs, it would seem that there may be three basic variations of curves. These are illustrated and described in Exhibit 6.

What You Have Learned

1. Cost is a sacrifice that must be made in order to acquire something. The sacrifice may include monetary and nonmonetary elements.

2. Opportunity costs are critical in economics because they measure the value of a forgone alternative. Opportunity costs arise because resources are limited and have alternative uses.

3. Economic costs are payments that must be made to attract resources. Such costs include not only explicit costs or money expenditures for resources, but also the implicit costs of self-owned or self-employed resources.

4. The law of diminishing returns—more accurately called the law of variable proportions—states what happens to output when a variable input is combined with fixed inputs. Although the law covers total, average, and marginal returns, the last is most important where output changes are involved. Graphically, marginal product always intersects average product at its maximum point.

5. There are three families of costs: total, average, and marginal. The family of total costs consists of total fixed costs, which do not vary with output, and total variable costs, which increase as output increases. The family of average costs consists of average fixed cost, which is the ratio of total fixed cost to quantity, and average variable cost, which is the ratio of total variable cost to quantity.

Exhibit 6
Three Typical Long-Run Average Cost Curves

The shapes of different firms' long-run average costs vary in different industries.

Chart (a). *The situation in which economies of scale out-weigh the diseconomies over a wide range of output. Examples are the aluminum, automobile, cement, and steel industries.*

Chart (b). *The situation in which diseconomies of scale set in quickly and many small firms exist side by side. Examples are the retailing, textiles, metal fabrication, and publishing industries.*

Chart (c). *The situation in which economies of scale are either quickly exhausted and diseconomies take a long time coming, or else the economies and diseconomies tend to cancel each other out. Examples are the chemical, food processing, furniture, and appliance industries.*

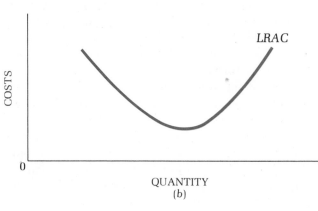

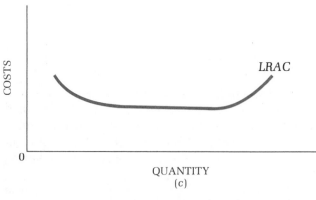

Marginal cost is a one-member family consisting of marginal cost alone. It is the change in total cost resulting from a unit change in output. Graphically, marginal cost always intersects average variable cost and average total cost at their minimum points.

6. The short run is a period long enough to vary output but not plant capacity. The long run is a period long enough to vary plant capacity. Therefore, in the short run some of a firm's costs are fixed and some are variable. But in the long run all of a firm's costs are variable because all its factors of production are variable.

7. The long-run average cost curve, or planning curve, tends to be U-shaped, reflecting first economies and then diseconomies of scale. Economies of scale result from greater specialization of resources, more efficient utilization of equipment, reduced unit costs of inputs, and fuller utilization of by-products. Diseconomies of scale arise mainly from the increasing complexities of management as a firm grows larger. Each of these economies and diseconomies can be classified as either internal or external to a firm.

8. The actual shape of a planning curve tends to vary within different industries. For example, in heavy indus-

tries, such as autos and steel, internal economies extend over a wide range of output. Hence, such industries tend to have small numbers of large firms. In light industries, such as textiles and retailing, internal economies are exhausted rather quickly over a narrow range of output. Consequently, such industries tend to have large numbers of small firms.

For Discussion

1. Terms and concepts to review:

cost
opportunity cost
normal profit
economic (pure) profit
short run
long run
production function
law of diminishing
   returns (law of variable
   proportions)
marginal product
average product
total fixed costs
total variable costs
total cost
average fixed cost
average variable cost
average total cost
marginal cost
average–marginal
   relationship
total–marginal
   relationship
long-run average cost
   curve (planning curve)
economies and
   diseconomies of scale
internal economies and
   diseconomies of scale
external economies and
   diseconomies of scale

2. Complete the accompanying table, showing the cost schedule of a firm. Graph the family of total costs on one chart and all the remaining costs on another. (NOTE   When you graph the marginal-cost curve, plot each MC figure to the midpoint between successive outputs. Thus, the first MC figure on your chart corresponds to an output of 0.5, the second to 1.5, the third to 2.5, and so on.) Discuss the various curves in terms of their shape as influenced by the law of diminishing returns. (HINT   Sketch the family of total costs on one chart and the family of average and marginal costs on a chart directly beneath it. Then see if you can draw a vertical dashed line through both charts such that the stage of increasing marginal returns is on the left side of the vertical line and the stage of decreasing marginal returns is on the right.) In your answer, account for the relative distances between ATC and AVC at different levels of output, and the reason for the intersection of MC with ATC and AVC at their minimum points.

3. Are opportunity costs entered in the accounting records of a firm? If so, what are the cost figures used for? If not, what good are they?

4. In estimating the annual cost of owning a fully paid-up $9,000 automobile, you might show the following cost entry on your books: "Interest on investment at 6 percent: $540." What would this mean? Explain.

5. Why do you suppose that some professors, who could earn considerably more by working in industry, continue to accept a lower salary by remaining in education?

6. "As a firm becomes larger and decision making more complex, the long-run average cost curve turns upward because the burden of administration becomes disproportionately greater and 'diminishing returns' to management set in." Would this statement be true of such well-managed firms as Proctor & Gamble or General Motors? Of what significance is technology, organizational structure, managerial ability, and similar factors?

7. The law of diminishing returns was originally intended to serve as an explanation of a historical process. In England, for example, as the population grew during the eighteenth and nineteenth centuries, it was predicted (by the early classical economist David Ricardo in 1817) that the marginal productivity of labor on land would decline. If this were true:

(a) What would happen to aggregrate values of agricultural land?

(b) What would happen to total land rent as a percentage share of the nation's total income?

(c) What would happen to the price of food relative to nonfood goods?

COST SCHEDULE OF A FIRM

(1) Quantity of output	(2) Total fixed cost	(3) Total variable cost	(4) Total cost	(5) Average fixed cost	(6) Average variable cost	(7) Average total cost	(8) Marginal cost
0	$100	$ 0	$_____	$_____	$_____	$_____	$_____
1	____	40	_____	_____	_____	_____	_____
2	____	64	_____	_____	_____	_____	_____
3	____	80	_____	_____	_____	_____	_____
4	____	88	_____	_____	_____	_____	_____
5	____	96	_____	_____	_____	_____	_____
6	____	108	_____	_____	_____	_____	_____
7	____	128	_____	_____	_____	_____	_____
8	____	160	_____	_____	_____	_____	_____
9	____	216	_____	_____	_____	_____	_____
10	____	300	_____	_____	_____	_____	_____

(d) How would you answer these questions with respect to the United States during most of the nineteenth century?

8. What is the effect of a technological improvement on a company's production function?

9. "If it were not for the law of diminishing returns, it would be possible to grow all the world's food in a flower-pot." Do you agree? Explain.

10. The most common type of production function is one characterized by "constant returns to scale." This means that if *all* inputs to a production process are increased in the same proportion, output is increased in that proportion. For example, if *all* inputs are expanded by 10 percent, output is expanded by 10 percent; if *all* inputs are doubled, output is doubled; and so on. In view of this, how do you account for the following situation?

(a) A suit manufacturing firm doubled the size of its factory, the number of machines in it, the number of workers, and the quantity of materials employed. As a result, output increased from 200 to 420 suits per day. Is this an example of *increasing returns to scale*, that is, economies of large-scale production?

(b) The company then doubled the quantity of managers and found that output fell to 370 suits per day. What do you suppose might have happened?

11. PHYSICAL GROWTH ANALOGIES OF RETURNS TO SCALE

(a) There is a relationship between the volume V and the surface area A of regular physical bodies. This relationship may be approximated by the "square-cube" law:

$$V = A^{3/2} = \sqrt{A^3}$$

For example, if the surface area of an object increases 4 times, its volume should increase about $\sqrt{4^3} = 8$ times. Can you use this notion to explain why there are no small warm-blooded animals in the Antarctic or in the ocean, and why the largest insect is about as large as the smallest warm-blooded animal?

(b) There is often a tendency to think that constant returns to scale should be common in economic life, yet variable returns (i.e., both increasing and decreasing) are frequently encountered. For example, we should expect that by doubling *all* inputs to a production process, the output ought to double. Yet there are examples from nature to illustrate why this is not so. Thus, if a house were scaled down so that it stood in the same proportion to a flea as it now stands to a person, the flea would be able to jump over the house. However, if a flea were scaled up to the size of a person, the flea would not be able to jump over the house. In fact, it could not jump at all because its legs would break. Can you explain why?

(c) What conclusions relevant to the size and growth of organizations can you draw from these notions? (HINT It has been said that some prehistoric monsters became extinct because they could not adjust to their changing environment. Why not?)

(d) Do you see any connection between questions (a) through (c) and the following quotation?

There is a story of a man who thought of getting the economy of large-scale production in plowing, and built a plow three times as long, three times as wide, and three times as deep as the ordinary plow and harnessed six horses to pull it, instead of two. To his surprise, the plow refused to budge, and to his greater surprise it finally took fifty horses to move the refractory machine. In this case, the resistance, which is the thing he did not want, increased faster than the surface area of the earth plowed, which was the thing he did want. Furthermore, when he increased his power to overcome this resistance, he multiplied the number of his power units instead of their size, which eliminated all chance of saving there, and since his units were horses, the fifty could not pull together as well as two.

J. M. Clark, *Studies in the Economics of Overhead Costs*, Chicago, University of Chicago Press, 1923, p. 116

Case
Sunshine Dairy Products Corporation: Constructing New Plants

Sunshine Dairy Products Corporation is a leading producer of milk, ice cream, cheese, and various other dairy products. After many years of research, the company succeeded in developing a very low calorie, low-cost, synthetic "ice cream." Extensive taste tests have indicated that this new ice cream is every bit as delicious as any of the leading regular brands. Accordingly, the management of the company has decided to produce and market the new ice cream on a test basis within one region of the country and to construct the necessary production facilities for this purpose.

The Sunshine Corporation conducted a market survey of the three largest population areas of the region. The results indicated that the company should package the product in liter-size containers, and that sales would average about 10,000, 5,000, and 2,500 liters per week in each area, respectively. An economic consultant for the company has suggested either of two alternatives with respect to the construction of ice cream plants:

1. Construct a single plant equidistant between the three population areas, with a production capacity of 20,000 liters per week at a fixed cost of $5,000 per week and a variable cost of 70 cents per liter.

2. Construct three plants (one in each market area) with weekly capacities of 12,000, 6,000, and 3,000 liters, respectively; with weekly fixed costs of $4,000, $3,000, and $2,000, respectively; and with a variable cost of only 60 cents per liter due to the reduction of shipping costs.

QUESTIONS

1. Assuming that the market survey is correct, which alternative should management select? At a price of $1.99 per liter, what would be the profit (or loss) per liter and in total?

2. If demand were to increase to production capacity, which alternative would be better?

3. Suppose that management selects the second alternative rather than the first, and that demand is at the level of production capacity in all three markets. If the company wanted to make a profit of $1 per liter in each of the three markets, what price per liter would it have to charge in each of these markets? Can management be sure of realizing its expected profit? Explain why.

4. Instead of constructing a new plant, the management of Sunshine is contemplating the purchase of an existing plant. An economic consultant has provided the following cost estimates for the plant under consideration:

(a) ATC of 5,000 liters is $12,600.

(b) AVC for 4,000 liters is $10,000.

(c) TC rises by $13,000 when production rises from 5,000 to 6,000 liters.

(d) AFC of 5,000 liters is $2,000.

(e) The increase in TC from producing nothing to producing 1,000 liters is $15,000.

(f) TC of 8,000 liters is $170,000.

(g) TVC increases by $25,000 when production rises from 6,000 to 7,000 liters.

(h) AFC plus AVC for 3,000 liters is $16,000.

(i) ATC falls by $6,000 when production increases from 1,000 to 2,000 liters.

On the basis of this information, complete the following cost schedule. [HINT First fill in all the data given in (a) through (i).]

COST SCHEDULE OF AN ICE-CREAM PLANT
(thousands of dollars per week)

Output (thousand liters per week)	TFC	TVC	TC	AFC	AVC	ATC	MC
0	$___	$___	$___	$___	$___	$___	$___
1	___	___	___	___	___	___	___
2	___	___	___	___	___	___	___
3	___	___	___	___	___	___	___
4	___	___	___	___	___	___	___
5	___	___	___	___	___	___	___
6	___	___	___	___	___	___	___
7	___	___	___	___	___	___	___
8	___	___	___	___	___	___	___

Martin M. Rotker, Taurus Photos.

Part 6

The Economics of the Firm: How Are Prices and Outputs Determined?

Chapter 23

Perfect Competition: Criteria for Evaluating Competitive Behavior

Chapter Preview

What do we mean by perfect competition?
Is it a fantasy or is it real?

How do business firms operate under
perfect competition? Do they receive
profits? Do they incur losses? How much do
they produce?

What are the economic consequences of
perfect competition? Does it have both
favorable and unfavorable features?
What would it be like to live in a world of
perfect competition?

Early in this book we learned that economics is concerned with how society allocates its limited resources, which have alternative uses, to the production of goods and services. Economists have always wanted to see this task accomplished with maximum efficiency, that is, with the least amount of waste. Hence, they have developed a theory that yields certain ideal results as far as the attainment of this goal is concerned.

This is the theory of "perfect competition," or "pure competition." (The two terms are used synonymously for most purposes, although a technical distinction that is sometimes made between them will be explained subsequently.) The theory underlies the operation of supply and demand that we studied in previous chapters. It attempts to explain how a "perfect" market economy or "pure" free-enterprise system tends to operate.

What Is Perfect Competition?

When a scientist tries to describe a complicated problem, he or she starts by constructing a simplified picture of the situation—a *model*. In this chapter we shall develop a model or theory of perfect competition.

Let us begin with a definition.

Perfect (or *pure*) *competition* is the name given to an industry or market structure characterized by a large number of buyers and sellers all engaged in the purchase and sale of a homogeneous commodity. Each buyer or seller has perfect knowledge of market prices and quantities, there is no discrimination, and there is perfect mobility of resources.

This definition contains five essential conditions which require further examination.

EXPLAINING THE DEFINITION

The expression "perfect competition" can be used in discussing either an industry or a market. The distinction is always clear from the context in which the term is used, and the definition above is applicable to both categories—industries as well as markets. Now let us analyze the rest of the definition.

Large Numbers of Buyers and Sellers

What do we mean by a "large" number of buyers and sellers? Is 1,000 large and 999 small? To answer yes would be silly; the words "large" or "small" are relative rather than absolute. Hence, our definition does not establish the size of a perfectly competitive market in terms of numbers. Instead, it uses the word "large," as we have discussed in earlier chapters, to mean *large enough so that no one buyer or seller can affect the market price by offering to buy or not to buy, to sell or not to sell.* Therefore, whether it takes 1,000 or 1 million buyers or sellers is of no relevance. The only requirement is that the market price for any buyer or seller is *given*. The individual can accept the market price or reject it, but cannot alter it by going into or out of the market.

Homogeneous Commodity

This means that all units which sellers make available must be identical in the minds of buyers. The reason for this requirement, as will be shown later, is that buyers must be indifferent as to which seller they deal with; they must be willing to purchase from the seller who offers the good at the lowest price.

Notice, therefore, that we are referring to *economic homogeneity,* not physical homogeneity. Two sellers may be selling the same physical product, but buyers may be willing to pay more to seller A than to seller B because seller A provides service with a smile, or a more attractive package, or perhaps a brand name. In that case the two products are *not* economically homogeneous.

We can illustrate this point with a concrete example. Beet sugar and cane sugar are physically the same for all practical purposes. That is, they look and taste the same. Yet in some regions of the country beet sugar sells for less than cane. Why? Because buyers do not regard them as the same. Instead, they believe that beet is somehow inferior to cane. And, because a package of sugar must be labeled either "beet" or "cane," there sometimes is a price difference between them. In this case the two products are physically homogeneous but *economically heterogeneous*. That is, they are similar but not identical. How about butter and margarine? Two nickels and a dime? Are they homogeneous? Heterogeneous?

Perfect Knowledge of Market Prices and Quantities

The third condition—"perfect knowledge"—means that all buyers and sellers are completely aware of the prices and quantities at which transactions are taking place in the market and that all have the opportunity to participate in those transactions. For example, perfect knowledge does not exist if buyers do not know that sellers across the street are charging a lower price for a certain commodity. Likewise, perfect knowledge does not exist if sellers do not know that buyers across the street are offering a higher price for a certain product. In both instances the buyers and sellers on one side of the street are not competing with the buyers and sellers on the other side, and hence are not even in the same market.

No Discrimination

This condition tells us that buyers and sellers must be willing to deal openly with one another. This means that they must be willing to buy and sell at the market price with any and all that may wish to do so. It also means that buyers and sellers must not offer or accept any special deals, discounts, or favors that are not available to everyone on equal terms. Discrimination thus has an economic meaning, not just a social one.

Perfect Mobility of Resources

The condition of perfect resource mobility requires that there be no obstacles—economic, legal, technological, or others—to prevent firms or resources from entering or leaving the particular market or industry. Further, there must be no impediments to the purchase or sale of commodities. This means that firms, resources, and commodities can be shifted about swiftly and smoothly without friction. For example, the land, labor, capital, and entrepreneurship used in wheat production can be moved quickly into corn production if it is more profitable. Potatoes stored in Idaho can be sold instantly in New York or in San Francisco if the price is right. And, in general, owners of resources and commodities are free and able to take advantage of the best market opportunities as they arise.

IS PERFECT COMPETITION REALISTIC?

Is the concept of perfect competition realistic or a fantasy? After all, no market or industry anywhere in the world exactly meets the five requirements just described. Should you infer, therefore, that the notion of perfect competition is "theoretical and impractical"?

The answer is no. As we shall see shortly, the concept of perfect competition is a *theoretical extreme*—like the concept of a perfect vacuum or the assumption of a frictionless state in physics. For example, in elementary physics it is expressly assumed in many problems of motion that there is *no friction*, although everyone knows that friction always exists in the real world. The assumption creates an idealized situation which permits simplification of a problem in order to analyze it. Similarly, the theory of perfect competition assumes a "frictionless" economic system in which the movement of goods and resources is unobstructed. Thus, like physics, economics uses idealized models in order to simplify and analyze specific problems.

But our model will not be completely unreal. Some markets do approach the conditions of perfect competition at least roughly, although none meets all the conditions precisely. The examples that come closest to the ideal are the organized commodity and stock exchanges in New York, Chicago, and many other cities, and to a lesser extent some industries producing standard raw materials. In these markets the approximation to perfect competition varies but is close enough to make the theory and conclusions of this chapter both meaningful and useful.

REMARK   As you will see, the conditions of perfect knowledge and perfect resource mobility are not absolutely essential to our theory. They are desirable, however, because they serve as "lubricating" features which tend to make a perfectly competitive system operate more quickly and smoothly than it would if these two conditions did not exist.

Costs, Revenues, and Profit Maximization in the Short Run

It follows from our explanation of perfect competition that the market price of a commodity under such circumstances would be established independently through the free operation of total supply and total demand. We have already seen how this happens. No individual buyer or seller can influence the price, yet the price emerges automatically as a reflection of the interaction of numerous buyers and sellers.

This leads us to ask a vital question: How does a seller in perfect competition, faced with a market price over which he or she has no influence, decide how much of a commodity to produce? The answer to this question is one of the most fundamental principles of economics.

TOTAL COSTS AND TOTAL REVENUES

Let us begin by turning our attention to the table in Exhibit 1, which gives the costs and revenues of a firm in perfect competition. The only costs shown are those needed for our analysis.

Columns (1) and (2) represent familiar concepts, because they contain quantities produced and their corresponding levels of total cost. As always, total cost increases as quantity increases.

Column (3) denotes *average revenue (AR)*. This is the price per unit of output or, as we shall see momentarily, the ratio of total revenue to quantity. In this case the average revenue is $10 per unit. Thus, we are assuming that the price established in the market through the free interaction of supply and demand is $10, and hence this is the price with which the firm is faced and over which it has no control. Or, to put it somewhat differently, the firm finds that it can sell all the units it wants to at the market price P of $10.

Column (4), called *total revenue (TR)*, is simply the price per unit times the number of units sold. Looking at the headings of columns (3) and (4) together, we need only the simplest arithmetic to see the connection between average revenue, total revenue, and price:

$$AR = \frac{TR}{Q} = \frac{P \times Q}{Q} = P$$

Finally, we can skip temporarily to column (8) of the table and note that *net revenue* or net profit—the difference between total revenue and total cost—is at first negative, but it rises to a peak of $15 at 8 units of output and then falls.

Graphic Illustration

The TC and TR figures are graphed in the upper chart of Exhibit 2. The TC curve has a familiar shape, but note that the TR curve is a straight line. This reflects the fact, as stated earlier, that the firm receives the same price per unit for all the units it sells.

Exhibit 1
Cost and Revenue Schedules of a Firm Under Perfect Competition

(1)	(2)	(3) Price per unit, or average revenue, P = AR (given)	(4) Total revenue, TR (3) × (1)	(5) Average total cost, ATC (2) ÷ (1)	(6) Marginal cost, MC Change in (2) / Change in (1)	(7) Marginal revenue, MR Change in (4) / Change in (1)	(8) Net revenue, NR (4) − (2)
Quantity per day, Q (given)	Total cost, TC (given)						
0	$ 25	$10	$ 0	$ —			− $25
1	35	10	10	35.00	$10	$10	− 25
2	41	10	20	20.50	6	10	− 21
3	45	10	30	15.00	4	10	− 15
4	47	10	40	11.75	2	10	− 7
5	49	10	50	9.80	2	10	1
6	52	10	60	8.67	3	10	8
7	57	10	70	8.14	5	10	13
8	65	10	80	8.13	8	10	15
9	79	10	90	8.78	14	10	11
10	100	10	100	10.00	21	10	0

The points labeled B_1 and B_2 are called *break-even points* because they designate levels of output at which a firm's revenue equals its cost. Thus, the firm is incurring neither an economic profit nor an economic loss. At any output between these two points, the firm's profit or net revenue is positive. At any output beyond the break-even points, it has a net loss (or negative net revenue) because its costs exceed its revenues.

Finally, it should be pointed out that net revenue, as represented by the vertical distance *GH,* is a maximum at 8 units of output. At this output the *slope* of the total cost curve as measured by the slope of the tangent at *H* is equal to the *slope* of the total revenue curve. This suggests an important fundamental concept:

The *slope* (steepness) of a line is the change in its vertical distance per unit of change in its horizontal distance. The slope of a straight line (such as the *TR* curve) is the same at every point, but the slope of a curved line (like the *TC* curve) differs at every point. Geometrically, you can find the slope of a curve at a point by drawing a straight-line tangent to the curve at that point. The slope of the tangent will then be the slope of the curve at the point of tangency. As you will recall from elementary mathematics, parallel lines have equal slopes. Thus, the tangent at *H* is parallel to the *TR* curve.

This important concept is amplified further in the next section and in the descriptions in Exhibit 2.

MARGINAL COST AND MARGINAL REVENUE

The use of total revenue and total cost is a valid and practical way in which to determine the most profitable level of output for a firm. However, it is not the method that economists usually employ. They prefer to use an approach which at first may seem a bit strange, but is actually much more useful for understanding and interpreting *changes* in production and costs.

Referring back to the table in Exhibit 1, note that column (5) gives average total cost, and column (6) presents marginal cost. Column (7), however, has a new term, *marginal revenue (MR)*. This is defined as the change in total revenue resulting from a unit change in output. As in previous cases, the expression "resulting from" in the definition is an interpretive term; for mathematical purposes it means the same thing as "divided by." Therefore, the formula we use for measuring marginal revenue is

$$MR = \frac{\text{change in } TR}{\text{change in } Q}$$

Marginal revenue is thus a concept exactly analogous to marginal cost. And, since the slope of a curve is the change in its vertical distance resulting from a unit change in its horizontal distance, it should now be clear that *marginal cost measures the slope of a*

Exhibit 2
Cost and Revenue Curves of a Firm Under Perfect Competition*

PROFIT MAXIMIZATION: THREE VIEWPOINTS

1. **Total Curves**   The most profitable level of output is determined where the difference between curves TR and TC, as represented by the distance GH, is a maximum. This occurs at an output of 8 units. At this output, a tangent to the TC curve, such as the tangent at H, is parallel to the straight-line TR curve. At smaller or larger outputs, such as 7 or 9 units, a tangent to the TC curve would not be parallel to the TR curve.

The break-even points are at B_1 and B_2, where TC = TR. The break-even outputs are thus 5 units and 10 units.

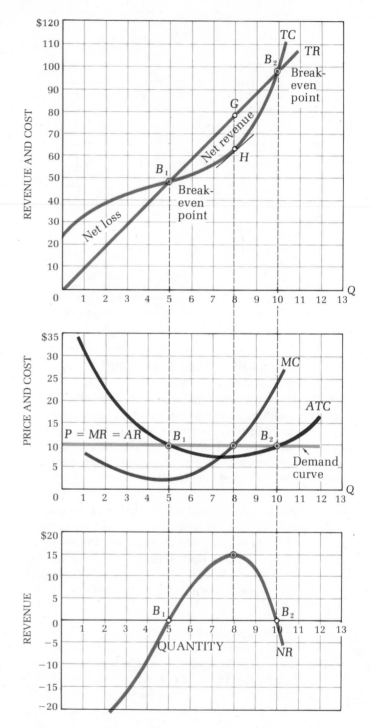

2. **Marginal Curves**   The most profitable level of output is determined where MC = MR, as explained in the text. This is also evident by following the vertical dashed line downward at 8 units of output.

The break-even points are at B_1 and B_2, where ATC = AR.

3. **Net Revenue Curve**   The most profitable level of output is determined where the net revenue curve NR (= TR − TC) is a maximum. The vertical dashed line at 8 units of output emphasizes these profit-maximizing principles in all three charts.

TECHNICAL NOTE (OPTIONAL)   If you are geometrically inclined, you may note that since parallel lines have equal slopes, the most profitable output in the top chart is the one at which the *slope* (steepness) of the TC curve equals the *slope* (steepness) of the TR curve. In the middle chart, marginal cost is the graph of the *slope* of total cost, and marginal revenue is the graph of the *slope* of total revenue. Hence, at the level of maximum profit,

$$MC = MR$$

which is the same as saying that

$$\text{slope of } TC = \text{slope of } TR$$

* The curves have been smoothed to enhance readability. As a result, the curves at some points may not correspond precisely to the data in the table.

total cost curve, and marginal revenue measures the slope of a total revenue curve.

Note that the marginal revenue figures in column (7), namely $10, are precisely the same as the average revenue or price figures in column (3). Thus, $MR = AR = P$. This is no accident. If price remains constant while quantity increases, total revenue (which equals $P \times Q$) will have to increase by the amount of the price, and this amount of change will also be the same as marginal revenue. You can verify this relationship by experimenting with a few different numbers yourself.

Finally, observe that columns (1) and (3) taken together constitute a *demand schedule*, since they disclose the price per unit that buyers will pay (and the seller will receive) for various quantities of the commodity.

Now let us see how these data look on a chart.

Graphic Illustration

When we graph the ATC, MC, and the $MR = AR$ data, we get the results shown in the middle chart of Exhibit 2. The first thing to notice is that the horizontal revenue line at the price of $10 is a demand curve based on columns (1) and (3) of the table in Exhibit 1. Indeed, it is a *perfectly elastic demand curve.* Hence, the curve is labeled $P = MR = AR$, to emphasize the fact that it represents price, marginal revenue, and average revenue—all at the same time. However, this is a special property which exists only under perfect competition. As we shall see in subsequent chapters dealing with other types of competition, a different situation arises when the demand curve slopes downward instead of being horizontal.

REMARK For graphing purposes, you should recall from previous chapters that marginal values, in this case MC and MR, are plotted to the *midpoints* of the integers on the horizontal axis, since they reflect, respectively, the change in total cost and in total revenue resulting from a unit change in quantity. Notice also from the footnote to the charts that the curves have been smoothed. Therefore, some parts of the curves may differ slightly from the data in the table.

What is the firm's most profitable level of output? We already know that the answer is 8. But we can verify it further by extending the vertical dashed line at 8 units of output from the top chart in Exhibit 2, down to the middle chart, and then to the bottom chart, which shows the graph of net revenue NR from column (8) of the table. When we do this, the middle chart, along with the other two supporting charts, reveals the operation of one of the most important principles in all of economics:

The most profitable level of output for a firm occurs where its $MC = MR$. This is a general principle which applies under all types of competition. But under the special case of perfect competition it is also true that the most profitable level of output occurs where $MC = MR = P = AR$, since the last three terms are one and the same. It is only at $MC = MR$ output that a firm's net revenue, as measured by the difference between its total revenue and total cost, is a maximum.

This $MC = MR$ rule is of such great importance that it may appropriately be called the *fundamental principle of profit maximization.* You may also verify that in the table of Exhibit 1 the demarcated section at 8 units of output shows that when NR reaches a maximum of 15, MC rises from 8 to 14, while MR remains constant at 10. The charts in Exhibit 2, of course, reveal the relationships more clearly. You should study them and their accompanying explanations carefully.

INTERPRETING THE MC = MR RULE

The $MC = MR$ rule must be elaborated more fully. In particular, we need to ask: Why does the rule "work" as a guide for profit maximization? How does a firm react to the rule within the setting of a competitive market?

Part of the answer is given in Exhibit 3. In Chart *(a)*, the market price at P and market output at N are determined by the intersection of *total* demand and *total* supply, representing the interactions of many buyers and many sellers. In Chart *(b)*, any individual seller finds that by producing to the point at which $MC = MR$, the net revenue or profit is maximized. Also, the output measured by the distance $0J$ is an infinitesimal proportion of the industry's output measured in Chart *(a)* by the distance $0N$. We may note this important principle:

Under perfect competition, each seller faces a perfectly elastic demand curve at the market price—for two reasons:

1. Because the product is homogeneous, buyers will purchase the commodity from the seller who offers it at the lowest price.

2. Because only an infinitesimal part of the total market is supplied by each seller, all of that seller's output can be sold at the going market price. The seller cannot sell any output for more than that price, and has no reason to sell any of it for less.

Thus, at any output less than $0J$, each 1-unit increase in output adds more to total revenue than it adds to total cost. That is, MR exceeds MC, so it pays to ex-

Exhibit 3
An Industry and Firm in a Perfectly Competitive Market

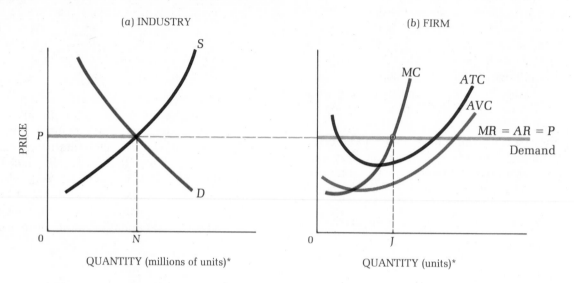

(a) INDUSTRY

(b) FIRM

*Note different horizontal scales.

Chart (a) A Perfectly Competitive Market with Many Buyers and Sellers. *The market price at P and market output at N are determined by the intersection of the total market demand and supply curves. The total market demand curve is downward-sloping, because the quantity demanded will be greater at lower prices.*

Chart (b) A Typical Firm in a Perfectly Competitive Market. *Each firm is confronted with a perfectly elastic demand curve at the market price. By producing to where its MC = MR, this firm's most profitable output at J is an infinitesimal fraction of the industry's total output at N in Chart (a).*

pand production. Conversely, at any output greater than 0J, each 1-unit decrease in output reduces total cost more than it reduces total revenue. That is, *MC* is greater than *MR*, so it pays to cut back production. Only at the point where *MC* = *MR* do we find the most profitable output 0J. Hence, we call this *MC* = *MR* point the seller's *equilibrium* position. This is because it determines the profit-maximizing output that the firm will seek to achieve and maintain under the given market conditions and the company's existing cost curves.

We can illustrate this concept with a simple example. Suppose that you were a manufacturer of bicycles. You knew that by increasing your production by a specific amount you would raise your total revenue by $10 and your total cost by $8. In that case you would try to expand output and thereby increase net profit by $2. On the other hand, if you knew that by decreasing production by a given amount, you would cut total cost by $15 and total revenue by $10, you

would try to reduce output in order to increase net profit by $5. As a general rule, the only time you would not want to alter the production rate is when profits were already at a maximum. In that case the *changes* in TC and TR would be the same—which is the same as saying that MC would equal MR.

ANALYZING SHORT-RUN EQUILIBRIUM

What is the nature of the profit-maximizing or equilibrium position which the firm is trying to attain? Some of its important properties are illustrated by the diagram in Exhibit 4.

First, note that the diagram depicts the firm in short-run equilibrium. This means that, under the existing market conditions for the inputs the firm buys and the output it sells, and the given set of cost curves with which it operates, the most profitable output is at J. Why? Because at this output *MC* = *MR* for this

Exhibit 4
Profit Maximization in the Short Run for a Perfectly Competitive Firm

At the output where a firm's MC = MR, the area of its net-revenue rectangle TULK is a maximum. This is the largest net-profit rectangle that can be drawn.

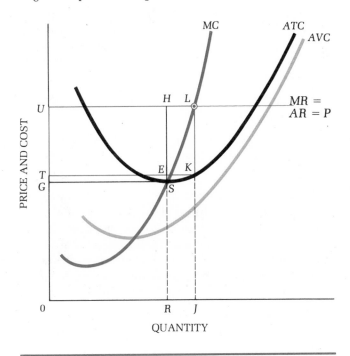

particular firm. We shall see later that in the long run certain market conditions, as well as the seller's cost curves, are likely to change. This will result in a different equilibrium position for the firm.

Next, you should verify that at the most profitable level of output 0J, the following geometric cost and revenue conditions exist. The average total cost of producing output 0J is represented by the vertical distance JK (= 0T), and the average revenue received from the sale of this output is the vertical distance JL (= 0U). The difference between these two amounts, of course, is the net revenue per unit—that is, average net revenue—as represented by the vertical distance KL (= TU). Therefore, the total net revenue can be found by multiplying the net revenue per unit by the number of units, thereby obtaining the area of the rectangle TULK.

The same result can also be arrived at in a different way. The average revenue per unit (JL) times the number of units (0J) equals total revenue, which is the

area of the large rectangle 0ULJ. Similarly, average total cost (JK) times the number of units (0J) equals total cost or the area of the rectangle 0TKJ. Therefore, when you subtract the total-cost rectangle from the total-revenue rectangle, the difference is the net-revenue rectangle TULK.

Finally, it is important to observe that profits are maximized at the output where MC = MR, even though this output may be beyond the point of minimum average total cost. Profit, in other words, is not maximized at output 0R, despite the lower average total cost of that output, namely RS. For by increasing output from 0R to 0J, the seller increases the net-revenue rectangle from GUHS to TULK. The rectangle thus gains the larger area EHLK while losing the smaller area GTES. In general, the output at which the largest net-profit rectangle can be drawn is determined by the point L, where MC = MR, and by the corresponding point K on the ATC curve. Or, to put it differently, it can be proved mathematically that any other net-profit rectangle must of necessity be smaller than the one determined by points K and L. But this is equivalent to saying that the net-revenue curve reaches a maximum at the output where MC = MR, which is a fact that you already know.

DERIVING SUPPLY CURVES FROM MARGINAL COST CURVES

When we first studied the operation of supply and demand, we learned that a supply curve expresses a relation between the price of a product and the amount that sellers would be willing and able to produce at each price. We are now in a position to show how a perfectly competitive firm's supply curve is actually derived, based on what we know about the MC = MR rule.

Suppose that we represent a firm in perfect competition by the cost curves shown in Exhibit 5. If the market price of the product is at P_1, the firm will produce an output at N_1, because this is where its MC is equal to MR_1. If the price falls to P_2, the firm will reduce its output to N_2, following its marginal cost curve. At a price of P_3 it will produce the amount N_3, but since this price is tangent to the firm's minimum average total cost curve, the firm will not be earning a positive net revenue; its net revenue will be zero. This means that the firm is only normally profitable, because average total cost includes normal profit.

We conclude from this that a perfectly competitive firm maximizes its profit by always adjusting its output so as to follow its marginal cost curve.

Exhibit 5

In Perfect Competition, a Firm's Supply Curve Is Its MC Curve Above Its AVC

The firm will always produce to where its $MC = MR$. Therefore, as the market price falls from P_1 to P_4, the firm reduces its output from N_1 to N_4, following its marginal cost curve. At P_4 the firm is just covering its average variable (out-of-pocket) costs, and hence will remain in business in the short run. At a price below P_4, the firm will go out of business—as shown by the shutdown point.

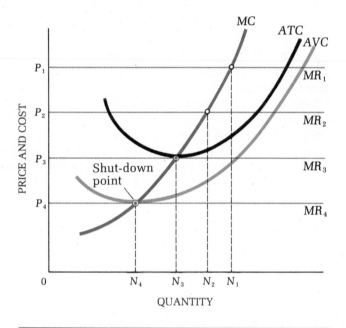

MINIMIZING SHORT-RUN LOSSES

What will the firm do if the price falls below P_3, say, to P_4? The answer is the same as before. The firm will decrease its output following its marginal cost curve, thus producing the amount at N_4. At this output the firm's net revenue will be negative, but it will be *minimizing its losses,* for the following reason.

In the short run, the firm has certain fixed costs, such as rent, property taxes, and utilities. It must continue to pay these expenses as long as it remains in business, regardless of how much it produces. Therefore, as long as the firm can get a price that is at least high enough to cover its average variable (or "out-of-pocket") costs, anything that it earns over and above this amount will go toward paying its fixed costs, which it is "stuck" with in any case.

As you can see, therefore, even at a price of P_4, the firm will lose less in the short run by operating and producing N_4 than by shutting down—as would hap-

pen if the market price should fall below the shutdown point shown in the diagram. In the long run, on the other hand, the firm must receive a price at least high enough to cover all its costs, including a normal profit, if it is to stay in business. The firm must, in other words, cover its *ATC in the long run.*

We can now summarize by stating an important principle:

> A perfectly competitive firm will determine its output by producing to where $MC = P (= MR)$. The firm will thus increase or decrease its output by following its marginal cost curve. In this way the firm will maximize its profit (or minimize its loss).

These ideas enable us to formulate two important propositions.

> 1. *A perfectly competitive firm's supply curve is the same as its marginal cost curve above the level of average variable cost.*

The reason is that the MC curve tells you how many units of the good the firm will make available at various possible prices. This, however, is the meaning of a supply curve, as you should recall from your study of supply and demand. (You should refresh your understanding by looking up the definition of *supply curve* in the Dictionary at the back of the book.)

> 2. *The industry's supply curve is the horizontal sum of the firms' marginal cost curves above their levels of average variable cost.*

In other words, you can derive a perfectly competitive industry's supply curve by summing the quantities that firms will make available at each price. This method, you should recall, was used to derive a total market supply curve when you first studied supply and demand early in this book.

Long-Run Equilibrium of a Firm and an Industry

We have seen that in the short run a firm in a perfectly competitive industry may earn profits in excess of normal profits. Can this also happen in the long run? The answer is no, because the conditions that are assumed in our definition of perfect competition prevent it from occurring. Let us see why.

THE ADJUSTMENT PROCESS

An industry is said to be in *equilibrium*—that is, in a state of "balance"—when there is no tendency for it to expand or to contract. This means that the least-profitable or borderline firm in the industry, usually called the "marginal" firm, is only normally profitable.

For instance, if any firms in the industry are earning less than their normal profit in the long run, then by definition of normal profit their owners are receiving less than the least return they are willing to accept on the basis of their opportunity costs. The owners will therefore leave the industry, causing the industry supply curve to shift to the left and the market price to rise. The remaining firms will then become more profitable. This exodus of firms will continue until the least-profitable firm is just normally profitable, at which point the industry will have no further tendency to contract.

The opposite situation occurs when the least-profitable firm is earning more than normal profits. New firms will then be tempted to enter the industry to get a share of those profits. The industry will thus expand, its total output will increase as the industry supply curve shifts to the right, and the market price will fall, thereby making existing firms less profitable. This entry of new firms will continue until the least-profitable firm is just normally profitable, at which point the industry will have no further tendency to expand.

GRAPHIC ILLUSTRATION OF LONG-RUN EQUILIBRIUM

The final adjustment to long-run equilibrium for every firm in perfect competition is illustrated in Exhibit 6. Each firm will have an average total cost curve

and a corresponding marginal cost curve for each possible scale of plant. It follows that if some firms in the industry operate with optimum-size plants when the price is higher than the long-run equilibrium level, they will earn above-normal profits. This in turn will attract new firms into the industry. Market supply will increase, market price will fall, and supernormal profits will disappear. Firms with plants that are larger or smaller than the optimum size will thus suffer losses, whereas those with optimum-size plants will earn normal profits. Therefore:

In perfectly competitive industries, firms have no choice of whether to build large-scale or small-scale plants. Firms in these industries must eventually build optimum-size plants if they are to survive in the long run.

The firm's optimum-size plant is thus ATC_3, the long-run equilibrium price is at P, and the firm's rate of output is at N. Exhibit 6 represents a model of a single firm, and a diagram similar to this could be made for each firm in the industry.

THE LONG-RUN INDUSTRY SUPPLY CURVE

We now know enough about the operation of supply and demand in competitive markets to introduce a new concept pertaining to the long-run supply price of an industry.

Each of the diagrams in Exhibit 7 represents the supply and demand situation for a different industry. We assume in each case that the industry is in equilibrium at point E. This represents the intersection of

---

Exhibit 6
Long-Run Equilibrium for a Firm in Perfect Competition

At any given time, a firm may be represented by an ATC curve and a corresponding MC curve.

In the long run, competition will force each firm in the industry to end up with an optimum-size plant such as ATC_3. At the optimum level of output for each firm, such as the output at N for this particular firm,

$$MC = P = MR = AR = ATC = LRAC$$

This equation defines the long-run conditions of equilibrium for every firm in a perfectly competitive market or industry.

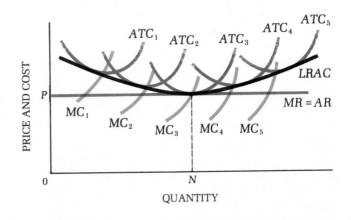

Exhibit 7
Long-Run Supply Curves for Constant-, Increasing-, and Decreasing-Cost Industries

The immediate effect of an increase in demand from D to D' is to change the industry's equilibrium from the long-run point E to the short-run point E'. At this higher price, new firms will find it profitable to enter the industry, and the supply curve will shift to the right until it reaches S'. The

industry's final equilibrium will thus settle at the long-run point E''. *The long-run industry supply curve S_L is therefore defined as the locus or "path" of the industry's long-run equilibrium points.*

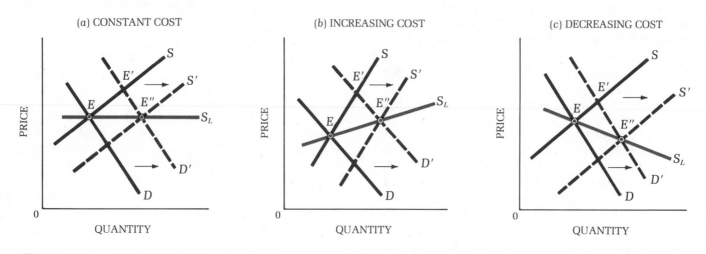

(a) CONSTANT COST   (b) INCREASING COST   (c) DECREASING COST

the industry's supply and demand curves, thus defining the industry's equilibrium price and output. Remember that the long-run supply curve of an industry is made up of the individual supply curves of all its sellers. Our purpose is to examine the nature of each industry's long-run supply curve or supply price.

Referring to the three diagrams, suppose that there is an increase (shift) in demand from D to D'. If the costs of the firms in the industry remain the same, the equilibrium point shifts from E to E'. This represents a higher market price and a larger market output than before. This expanded output occurs because firms that are already in the industry find it profitable to increase their production in response to the higher market price.

The equilibrium at E', however, is likely to be of relatively short duration. This is because the higher and more profitable price will soon attract new firms into the industry. As this happens, the supply curve of the industry will shift to the right and the market price will be driven down along the D' curve until it is no longer profitable for new firms to enter the industry. The supply curve will ultimately settle at S', and the final equilibrium will be at E'', where the new supply and demand curves intersect. The point E'' represents the *long-run equilibrium* position of the industry.

This analysis suggests an important principle.

If we connect each industry's initial and final long-run equilibrium points E and E'', we get the *long-run industry supply curve*, labeled S_L. This curve may be either horizontal, rising, or falling, depending on whether the industry is one of constant, increasing, or decreasing costs.

This principle requires an explanation of constant-cost, increasing-cost, and decreasing-cost industries.

Constant-Cost Industries

A *constant-cost industry* experiences no increases in resource prices or costs of production as new firms enter the industry. This tends to happen when an industry's demand for the resources it employs is an insignificant proportion of the total demand for those resources. In that case, new firms will be able to enter the industry and buy the labor, capital, and other inputs they need without bidding up the prices of these factors of production. The long-run industry supply curve will thus be perfectly elastic. Unspecialized resources (such as unskilled workers) which are in wide use by many industries are examples of such inputs.

Increasing-Cost Industries

An *increasing-cost industry* experiences rising resource prices and therefore increasing costs of production as new firms enter the industry. This happens because the industry's demand for resources is a significant enough proportion of the total demand that any new firms must bid up the prices of the factors of production in order to acquire them from other firms. Specialized resources (such as skilled workers) whose supplies are not readily expanded as the demand for them increases provide examples of such inputs. In general, increasing-cost industries are more common than constant-cost industries. This is especially true in our expanding scientific and technological age, when firms must make growing use of highly specialized resources. The computer, electronic, and aircraft industries are a few prominent examples of increasing-cost industries.

Decreasing-Cost Industries

A *decreasing-cost industry* experiences declining resource prices and therefore falling costs of production as new firms enter the industry and the industry expands. This, of course, is not as common as the two previous cases, but it could exist for a while as a result of substantial external economies of scale, as we have already learned. Can you give some examples?

Understanding Equilibrium

The concept of equilibrium is as fundamental in economics as in other sciences. It is important, therefore, to understand the meaning of equilibrium in the context in which it has been used here. Once you have achieved this understanding, you will be able to evaluate the social consequences of perfect competition—its effects on society as a whole.

THE EQUILIBRIUM CONDITIONS

Look back at Exhibit 6 and note carefully the properties that characterize a perfectly competitive firm in long-run equilibrium. As you can see, these properties may be described succinctly by the equations

$$MC = P = MR = AR = ATC = LRAC$$

These equations are called *equilibrium conditions*. They constitute a set of relationships that define the equilibrium position of an economic organism—in this case a firm in perfect competition. In certain advanced courses in economic theory, other sets of equilibrium conditions are studied—not only for firms, but also for households, and even for entire economies.

Our purpose is to analyze and interpret the meaning of the foregoing equations. In so doing we will see some important results of perfect competition. You may find it helpful to refer back to Exhibit 6 while reading the following explanation. Keep in mind that these characteristics apply to *every* firm in the industry.

1. **$MC = P$** This is an indicator of *economic efficiency*. It tells you that the additional cost of the resources used by the firm to produce the last unit of the product is just covered by the price which the firm receives. In other words, the value of the last unit of the good to the consumer (measured by the price he or she pays for the last unit, which is equal to the price paid for any other unit) is equal to the value of the resources used to produce that unit. Consequently:

> At the $MC = P$ level of output, the firm's resources are being allocated to the product in precise accordance with consumer preferences. At any smaller output, MC is less than P. Therefore, resources are being underallocated relative to consumer preferences. At any larger output, MC is greater than P. Therefore, resources are being overallocated relative to consumer preferences. The $MC = P$ condition is thus a standard of economic (allocative) efficiency. It measures the extent to which the firm is making full utilization of its resources to fulfill consumer preferences, given their incomes.

2. **$MC = MR$** This means that the firm is maximizing its profits and there is no incentive for it to alter its output. The firm is thus in short-run (as well as long-run) equilibrium.

3. **$MR = AR (= P)$** This tells you that the firm is selling in a perfectly competitive market. For as we shall see in the following chapters, any other type of market situation results in a firm's marginal revenue always being less than its average revenue or demand price.

4. **$ATC = AR$** This says that the firm is earning only normal profits. Therefore, there is no incentive for other firms to enter or leave the industry.

5. **$MC = ATC$** This means that the firm is operating at the minimum point on its average total cost curve. Hence, the firm is combining the variable resources available to it with its given plant so as to produce at the least cost per unit.

6. **$MC = ATC = LRAC$** This tells you that the firm is producing the optimum output with the optimum-size plant. Therefore, the firm is allocating *all* its resources in a *technically efficient* manner.

These equilibrium conditions are at the heart of microeconomics. Their implications and importance will become increasingly evident in the following pages and chapters. (Meanwhile, see *Leaders in Economics*, page 407.)

Economic Goals: Efficiency, Equity, Stability, Growth

What are the economic consequences of perfect competition? That is, to what extent does it fulfill society's four goals—efficiency, equity, stability, and growth? We can answer the question by distinguishing between favorable and unfavorable features.

FAVORABLE FEATURES OF A PERFECTLY COMPETITIVE PRICE SYSTEM

The equilibrium conditions listed above serve as a basis for describing the favorable features of an economic system composed entirely of perfectly competitive markets. Such a system would yield certain beneficial consequences in long-run equilibrium:

1. Consumer preferences, as reflected in the marketplace, would be fulfilled with the largest amount of goods consistent with the minimum (average cost) prices and known production techniques of business firms.

2. Society's resources would be allocated in the most efficient way, both within and between industries.

3. Flexible factor and product prices would assure full employment of all resources.

4. Competition among employers for inputs and among factors for jobs would cause factor owners to be paid their opportunity costs. These would be determined by the respective contributions to total output of each factor, as measured by its marginal productivity.

5. With consumer incomes and tastes given, aggregate consumer satisfaction would be maximized because goods would be distributed among consumers according to their demands.

These desirable features of a perfectly competitive price system in long-run equilibrium, and other characteristics which we have not mentioned, can be formulated as theorems which are actually proved in more advanced theoretical discussions. For our purposes it is sufficient that the favorable consequences be described as above so that they can be compared with the following shortcomings.

SOME UNFAVORABLE FEATURES

Several undesirable consequences of a perfectly competitive price system were pointed out when we first studied the laws of supply and demand early in the book. At that time we did not have a formal knowledge of the theory of perfect competition, nor did we know that it is the basis for supply and demand analysis. Now, however, we are in a better position to enrich our understanding of the various shortcomings.

Incomplete Reflection of Consumer Desires

In a perfectly competitive system, sellers react only to those preferences that consumers register through their "dollar votes" in the marketplace. Consequently, this type of system does not measure the desires of consumers for "collective" or public goods, such as national defense, highways, parks, and unpolluted air and water. Further, to the extent that incomes are unequally distributed, the competitive price system will reflect the dollar votes of the rich more than the poor. Hence, as Charles Dickens might have portrayed it, Ebenezer Scrooge could buy the milk for his cat that poor Bob Cratchit could not afford for his frail, crippled son, Tiny Tim.

Inadequate Reflection of Social Welfare

A chemical company disposes of its waste products in a nearby lake. A steel mill's smoke permeates the air of a neighboring city. A drive-in theater discharges its patrons onto a highway at the end of a movie. In each of these and many other situations, two types of costs, called "private costs" and "social costs," are involved.

Private costs are the economic costs to a firm for performing a particular act. *Social costs* are the reductions in incomes or benefits that accrue to society as a result of a particular act. In the examples above, the social costs would include the displeasures suffered by the community due to water pollution, destruction of recreational areas, and congested highways.

A similar distinction can be made in terms of benefits. If you get a good education, this act will lead to *private benefits* for you in the form of higher income. However, society will also incur *social benefits* because you will (ideally) become a more enlightened and informed citizen. Likewise, if you maintain an attractive lawn, your neighbors will be pleased. And if you bathe regularly, you are less likely to become a social outcast.

Of what significance are these distinctions between private and social benefits and costs? Because economics is a social science, a perfectly competitive price system must be evaluated in terms of its effects

Leaders in Economics
Alfred Marshall   1842–1924

Synthesizer and Pioneer in Microeconomics

In the last quarter of the nineteenth century there arose in Europe and America a system of economic thought known as the *neoclassical* school. One of the leaders of this school was Alfred Marshall, a British scholar whose landmark treatise, *Principles of Economics* (1890), will forever be regarded as a masterwork.

Marshall was born in London and educated at Cambridge University, where he majored in the classics and mathematics. "My acquaintance with economics," he once wrote, "started in 1867–1868. It commenced with reading John Stuart Mill and David Ricardo while I was still earning my living by teaching mathematics at Cambridge; and translating the doctrines into differential equations as far as they would go; and, as a rule, rejecting those which would not go."

Several decades later, John Maynard Keynes, himself a leading scholar and at one time a student of Marshall's at Cambridge, referred to his former teacher "as a scientist . . . who, within his own field, was the greatest in the world in a hundred years."

Marshall's *Principles*, which went through eight editions, was a leading text in economics for several decades. Among the major contributions of this and other works by Marshall were the distinction between the short run and the long run, the extensive use of diagrams and models to describe economic behavior, and the equilibrium of price and output resulting from the interaction of supply and demand. Marshall also systeme-

Historical Picture Services, Chicago.

tized the use of elasticity, the distinction between money cost and real cost, and many other ideas. In short, almost everything we read today pertaining to supply and demand analysis, equilibrium, and related notions was originally formulated precisely and definitively by Marshall. Few students today realize or appreciate the significant role that Marshall's ideas play in their economics education.

Although he was an adept mathematician, Marshall chose the less vigorous method of elementary geometric analysis because it served to make economic science a better "engine for discovery" in the investigation of specific problems. His approach to his predecessors was unusually conciliatory, and throughout his career he tended to phrase his own doctrines so

as to minimize the change from the classical tradition. In contrast to the earlier utility theorists, he did not take supply for granted but considered it as "the other blade of a pair of scissors." Underlying demand was marginal utility as reflected in the price offers of buyers. Underlying supply was marginal effort, reflected in the supply prices of sellers in the marketplace.

Marshall's preference for dealing with "one market at a time" rather than with "all markets simultaneously" is illustrated in typical fashion by his discussion of demand. Because the demand schedule relates solely to the relationship between price and quantity demanded, other things must be held constant, or, as Marshall has it, "impounded in *ceteris paribus*." Thus, the taste of consumers, their money incomes, the number of buyers, and the prices of other commodities are held constant in the discussion of the equilibrium determination of supply and demand. This procedure is still the accepted method of analyzing changes in demand.

By the time he retired from his professorship at Cambridge, Marshall had trained several generations of England's greatest economists. These disciples went on to assume major positions in universities and government service. Much has changed in economics since the eighth edition of *Principles of Economics* was published in 1920. However, these changes have for the most part been gradual. As a result, Marshall's neoclassical structure is still clearly identifiable today throughout the whole body of economic literature.

on society. As we know, competitive prices tend to reflect private costs and private benefits and may exclude some social costs and social benefits. Therefore, the equilibrium condition $MC = MR$ only guarantees maximum profit for a firm; it does not guarantee maximum welfare for society. To achieve the latter, the costs and benefits of production to *society* must be

incorporated in firms' activities. To the extent that they are not, the $MC = MR$ condition fails to reflect the full effect of production on social welfare.

This distinction between the private and social consequences of economic activities is important. It is discussed more fully in a number of other places in this book.

Insufficient Incentives for Progress

A third major criticism frequently leveled against a perfectly competitive system is that it dampens incentives to innovate and therefore retards economic progress. This happens because the typical firm in perfect competition is relatively small and is not likely to have access to the considerable financial resources needed to support the substantial research and development projects that often lead to major innovations. Further, even if a firm had the money to finance large-scale research, it would probably refrain from undertaking the needed capital investment because the innovation, if successful, would be adopted quickly by competing firms.

LIFE UNDER PERFECT COMPETITION— DISMAL AND DULL?

What would it be like to live in a perfectly competitive world? Most of us might find it monotonous. For example:

Goods would be standardized in each industry and the range of consumer choices severely limited.

At the grocery store, bread would be bread and ketchup would be ketchup. The modern supermarket with its endless and colorful varieties of goods would cease to exist.

The choice of an automobile, like eggs in the dairy case, might be confined to "small," "medium," and "large." In all other respects cars would be alike.

There would clearly be no need for advertising (except perhaps for industry-wide or institutional advertising such as "Eat more bread" or "Drink more milk"). Nor would there be any trademarks or brand names, and imaginative promotional campaigns, for good or evil, would be lost.

There would be no commercial television as we now know it, and newspapers and magazines (could they possibly be homogeneous?) would cost more. For in a world of perfect competition, where it would be assumed that consumers knew their alternatives, the only type of advertising needed would be that which informs rather than persuades. This means that there would be no need for anything other than, perhaps, classified advertising and the Sears, Roebuck catalog.

CONCLUSION—AND A LOOK FORWARD

Is this the kind of world you want? You must answer for yourself. For in economics the most we can do is identify the alternatives and their consequences, and leave it up to each person to make a choice. As we have already seen, although a perfectly competitive economy would have various beneficial consequences, it would also have what many people would undoubtedly regard as undesirable features.

If the imaginary world of perfect competition is so unreal, why do we study it? Does it have any practical value? The answer is simple: We do not necessarily learn about perfect competition in the vain hope of making it a reality. Instead, we study perfect competition because it provides us with a guide for evaluating and improving the real world of imperfect competition, which we shall analyze later.

REMARK   The terms "perfect competition" and "pure competition" are ordinarily used synonymously for most purposes. However, when a distinction is made, pure competition is defined simply as a large number of buyers and sellers dealing in a homogeneous commodity, without discrimination. Pure competition thus tends to operate in essentially the same way and to attain the same long-run equilibrium conditions as perfect competition. However, pure competition may not achieve these results as quickly or smoothly because the two "lubricating" features of perfect competition—perfect knowledge and perfect resource mobility, which eliminate any frictions in the system—are left out of the definition.

What You Have Learned

1. A perfectly competitive industry or market is characterized by many buyers and sellers engaged in the purchase and sale of a homogeneous commodity. Each buyer and seller has perfect knowledge of market prices and quantities, there is no discrimination, and there is perfect mobility of resources. Perfect competition is thus a theoretical extreme rather than a real-world phenomenon, although some of its features are roughly approximated in the organized commodity and stock markets.

2. In perfect competition, prices are established in the market through the interaction of many buyers and sellers. Each firm thus finds itself faced with a market price over which it has no influence. It cannot sell any of its output at a price which is the slightest bit above the market price. It can sell its entire output at the market price, and hence there is no inducement for it to sell at any lower price.

3. In terms of costs and revenues, each firm's most profitable level of output occurs where its marginal cost equals its marginal revenue. This is the output at which its total revenue minus total cost is a maximum.

4. In perfect competition, a firm's supply curve is its marginal cost curve above its average variable cost. The industry's short-run supply curve is thus derived by summing all the firms' marginal cost curves at each price above average variable cost. In the short run, a firm will operate as long as the market price is at least equal to its average variable (out-of-pocket) costs, since any price it gets over and above that will go to pay at least part of its fixed costs. In the long run, the firm will have to receive a price high enough to

cover all costs, including a normal profit, if it is to remain in business.

5. In the long run, competition will force all firms to earn only normal profits and to operate with optimum-size plants. When this occurs, the industry as well as all firms in it will be in long-run equilibrium, with no tendency to expand or contract.

6. The industry's long-run supply curve connects all of its long-run supply and demand equilibrium points. The long-run supply curve may be constant (i.e., perfectly elastic), increasing, or decreasing.

7. In long-run equilibrium, a perfectly competitive economy will have allocated its resources in the most efficient way so as to maximize consumer satisfactions. This is assured by the equations

$$MC = P = MR = AR = ATC = LRAC$$

If these are analyzed separately, they tell us that firms are maximizing their profits and making the most efficient use of their resources, given the distribution of consumers' incomes and tastes.

8. Among the favorable features of a perfectly competitive price system are the following:

(a) It fulfills consumer preferences with the largest amount of goods in the most efficient way.

(b) It allocates resources optimally and, as a result of flexible product and factor prices, tends to encourage full employment of all resources.

(c) It provides for factor payments at their opportunity costs as determined by their respective marginal productivities.

Among the unfavorable features are the following:

(a) It reflects consumer desires incompletely.

(b) It does not always measure social costs and social benefits.

(c) It provides insufficient incentives for economic progress.

For Discussion

1. *Terms and concepts to review:*

perfect competition	net revenue
average revenue	marginal revenue
total revenue	constant-cost industry
increasing-cost industry	private costs
decreasing-cost industry	social costs
equilibrium conditions	private benefits
long-run industry supply curve	social benefits

2. What is the "fundamental principle of profit maximization"? Explain. What special application of this rule applies to perfect competition? Why?

3. Is the price of a product determined by its cost of production, or is the cost of production determined by the price?

4. If new firms enter an industry, they will compete for factors of production and thereby raise the prices of those factors. How will this affect the cost curves of firms in the industry? Discuss.

5. "The farmer must receive a living price for milk." Discuss in terms of this chapter.

6. If you owned a shoestore and the shoes you carried cost you $10 per pair, would you stay in business if the highest price you could get for them was $10 per pair? Explain your answer in terms of this chapter.

7. The long-run history of the automobile industry reveals an enormous growth of output and a substantial reduction in real (inflation-adjusted) prices. How do you account for this, since we have usually assumed that larger outputs come only from higher prices?

8. Insert words in the following sentences to make them *true.* Do not delete any words. Underline your inserted words.

(a) A firm is in equilibrium when its costs and revenues are equal.

(b) A perfectly competitive firm is in equilibrium when it is producing at its minimum average cost.

(c) A perfectly competitive firm cannot earn supernormal profits.

(d) A perfectly competitive firm's supply curve is its marginal curve.

9. What are the "equilibrium conditions" for a perfectly competitive industry in long-run equilibrium? Explain their meaning.

10. "It is an indictment of our economic system that our country can spend more on such unimportant things as cosmetics or liquor than it spends on education." Evaluate this statement.

Our Farm Problem: A Case Study

American agriculture has staggered from crisis to crisis for more than a century. Although government has spent billions of dollars to alleviate farm problems, there have been few satisfactory solutions. Instead, politics has become intertwined with economics, resulting in public policies toward agriculture which have often impaired—rather than improved—the quest for efficiency, equity, stability, and growth.

The nature of the so-called "farm problem" is best understood by examining the underlying economics of agriculture as a whole.

Economics of Agriculture

The problems that farmers have traditionally faced stem largely from four conditions that characterize the agriculture sector: (1) price and income inelasticities, (2) highly competitive structure, (3) rapid technological change, and (4) resource immobility.

These conditions are not unique to American agriculture. They are prevalent in the industry in other advanced mixed economies and cause problems similar to those in the United States.

PRICE AND INCOME INELASTICITIES

The demand for most farm products, including foods and fibers, is largely unresponsive to changes in price.

As a result, people do not usually buy many more farm commodities when their prices fall, or fewer when they rise. In more technical terms, this means that the demand for most agricultural goods is relatively inelastic (unresponsive) with respect to changes in price.

The *elasticity of supply*—especially within a given year—is also less than 1 because production cannot be increased greatly in a single season. If prices are high, additional feed and fertilizer can be applied, and land farmed more intensively. But the industry's "plant"—the land itself—cannot be expanded very much.

Agricultural products tend also to be income-inelastic in demand. The *income elasticity of demand* is the percentage change in the quantity purchased of a good resulting from a 1 percent change in income. For practically all farm food products, this elasticity is less than 1.0—somewhere between 0.1 and 0.2. We may, therefore, expect a 10 percent rise in real per capita disposable income to cause only a 1 to 2 percent rise in the purchase of most agricultural food commodities.

Some Implications

Three important implications of these inelasticities should be noted.

1. Price inelasticities of demand and supply mean that small fluctuations in the output of farm products lead to large fluctuations in their prices.

2. Income inelasticity of demand means that total consumption of basic farm food products is limited largely by the rate of growth of total population. This characteristic holds in all wealthy nations. The proportion of any increase in income spent for food is always smaller in well-fed countries than in poorly fed ones.

3. As a result of both price and income inelasticities, increases in the rate of growth of farm production that exceed increases in the rate of growth of consumption will cause a downward trend in farm prices and in farmers' incomes. This has been the long-run trend in the United States. The effects are illustrated in Exhibit 1, which shows three things: an index of prices received by farmers for products sold, an index of prices paid by farmers for products bought, and a parity ratio. This is simply an index of prices farmers receive divided by an index of prices paid. The parity ratio thus provides a measure of agriculture's economic

well-being. You will learn more about this shortly in a discussion of farm policies.

HIGHLY COMPETITIVE STRUCTURE

Competition is a second major characteristic of American agriculture. By competition we mean three things:

1. There are many farms in the United States—over 2 million. As a result, virtually no single farm can influence the market price by deciding to sell or not to sell. (NOTE We say "virtually" because today there are some large farms that can exert an influence on the market price of certain commodities. This has been true only since the 1960s.)

2. Agricultural products are homogeneous—at least within broad categories. Grains, for example, are not branded products, and hence cannot be identified by

---

Exhibit 1
How Well Off Are Farmers?

The long-run trend of the parity ratio, expressed in decade averages, reached a peak in the 1940s (during World War II). This was because American farmers had to supply domestic agricultural needs as well as those of war-torn countries. Since the 1940s, the trend of the parity ratio has been downward.

However, farmers as a group are not as bad off as the figures show—for three reasons:

1. **Unreported Income** A huge proportion of farmers' incomes—about 50 percent according to government esti-

mates—comes from cash sales that are never reported for income tax purposes.

2. **Future Capital Gains** Farm property values have soared in recent decades, thereby increasing farm owners' net worth—and eventually their income when capital gains (i.e., profits) are realized from sale of the property.

3. **Tax Benefits** Farm firms receive special privileges under our tax laws that are not granted to other businesses.

For these reasons, *reported* farm income is not a true measure of farmers' economic well-being.

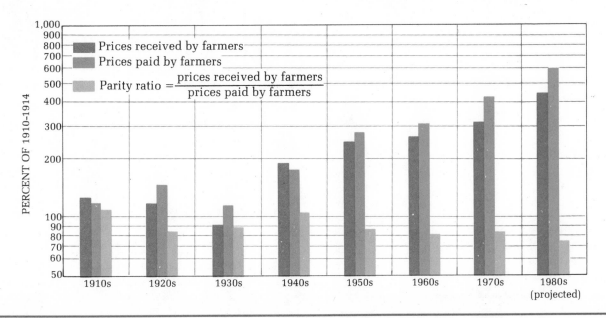

the farm they came from. Milk, meat, and produce may carry the name of a store or processor, but not usually the name of the producer. Agricultural products within each class are therefore highly substitutable, and each farmer is faced with a perfectly elastic demand curve at the market price for the goods sold.

3. As with many areas of retailing, there are few barriers to entering the agricultural industry. No licenses, union membership, or formal education are required. Anyone who wants to farm, and has a modest amount of capital, can get into the business—at least on a relatively small scale. (Large-scale farming, on the other hand, requires a considerable amount of capital.)

RAPID TECHNOLOGICAL CHANGE

American agriculture has made striking gains in productivity since 1930—greater gains, indeed, than were made in the previous two centuries.

What has been the nature of these advances? They have consisted of the introduction of new seeds, fertilizers, and pesticides; of improved breeds and feeds for livestock and poultry; and of the mechanization and electrification of farming. These advances have gone hand-in-hand with the development of improved capital and credit facilities, and with the emergence of more technically trained and educated farmers—many of them graduates of land-grant colleges. Many of these gains have been fostered by government through special taxation and subsidization programs favorable to agriculture.

These changes have wrought profound social and economic effects, as illustrated in Exhibit 2. The farm population and the number of farms have dropped over the long run, while the average size of farms, their total output, and their output per man-hour have steadily risen. However, improvements in agriculture have not been uniform. Many farmers are still poor because they lack the capital and knowledge to be-

Exhibit 2
Farms and Farm Output

The long-run trends of the farm population, number of farms, and labor input on farms have been decreasing while those of the average size of farms, their total output, and their output per man-hour have been increasing.

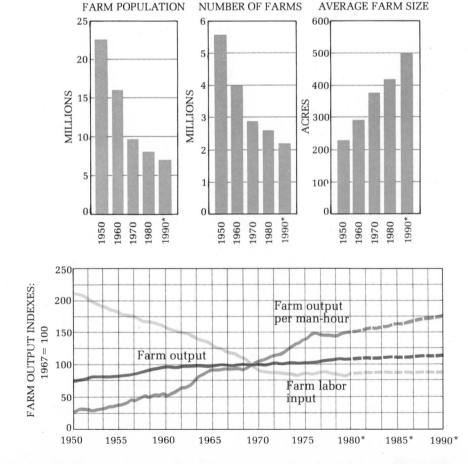

* Projected.

SOURCE: U.S. Departments of Agriculture and Commerce.

come efficient producers. This, as we shall see, has been the traditional crux of the farm problem.

RESOURCE IMMOBILITY

Although the number of farms and farmworkers has been declining, there are still too many farmers on too many farms. Why should this be? Why has agriculture, which has experienced a long-run trend of declining prices and incomes relative to the rest of the economy, failed to reduce sufficiently its stock of human and nonhuman resources? Is not this failure contrary to what the laws of supply and demand would lead us to expect?

The fundamental difficulty is that agricultural resources are relatively immobile. Farmers and farmworkers, for example, cannot use many of their skills in other activities. Hence, they tend to remain in farming because it is the only type of work they know. Further, many of them prefer to eke out an existence in rural areas rather than seek employment in the cities.

CONCLUSION: AGRICULTURE— A DECLINING INDUSTRY

The four major economic characteristics of agriculture—price and income inelasticities, a highly competitive structure, rapid technological change, and resource immobility—create a special problem in a progressive society:

> As an economy grows in wealth, it devotes less of its total resources to agriculture, and more to manufacturing and services.

The reason is simple. In technologically advanced societies, farmers can produce enough not only for themselves and their families, but also for many other people. In underdeveloped countries, on the other hand, nearly everyone is forced to farm. Productivity is so low that farmers have little left to sell after growing food and fibers to feed and clothe themselves and their families. The *relative* magnitude of the agricultural resource base is thus smaller in rich societies than in poor ones, and this base is being constantly "squeezed" as the society grows. Agriculture then becomes a declining industry in a growing economy, with the *proportion* of total resources employed in agriculture continually contracting. (See Box 1.)

Our Farm Policies

You can see from the information presented earlier in Exhibit 1 that prices paid by farmers have usually exceeded prices received. As a result, since the late 1920s government has employed policies designed to improve farmers' real incomes and to stabilize prices. Three alternative approaches which have constituted the core of our farm policy have been price supports, crop restrictions, and direct payments.

PRICE SUPPORTS

One way in which farmers might receive higher real incomes is for the government to maintain price supports for agricultural commodities. The price supports would in reality be price "floors," established at levels above those that would prevail in free markets.

The basic idea is illustrated in Exhibit 3. The diagram shows a situation at harvest time. Therefore, the demand curve D has a customary downward slope, but the supply curve S is vertical—*perfectly inelastic*—indicating that the quantity supplied is fixed or unresponsive to changes in price. The diagram indicates an important conclusion:

Exhibit 3
Price-Support Policy

At harvest time the quantity supplied is already determined. Therefore, the supply curve S is "fixed" or perfectly inelastic—unresponsive to changes in price—while the demand curve D is downward-sloping.

The diagram shows how a price-support plan establishes a price floor at some level above the free-market equilibrium price. Consumers pay and producers receive the higher parity-support price, and the resulting surplus is purchased and stored by the government.

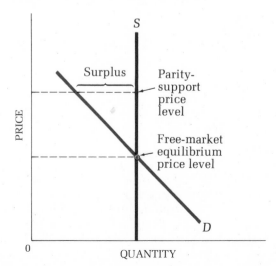

Box 1
Agriculture Responds to Adversity

The late nineteenth century saw the growth of big business and monopoly, the exaltation of commerce and the machine, and the first phase of a long-run decline of agriculture.

In the industrial sector, labor responded to its grievous loss of status by forming unions. The best known ones were the Knights of Labor and the American Federation of Labor. In the agricultural sector, farmers responded through the formation of the National Grange and the Farmers' Alliance. Both organizations worked to improve the economic position of farmers.

In several western states, the Grangers were successful in getting laws passed that set upper limits on railroad and warehouse charges, and in persuading Congress and state legislatures to create regulatory commissions. Our federal Interstate Commerce Commission (established in 1887), which regulates railroads, trucks, and other surface transportation, was partly the result of the Granger movement.

The Granger Collection.

"Gift for the Grangers" was published in Cincinnati in 1873. It exalts the virtues of farmers and emphasizes their role as the "source" of society's wealth.

The Granger Collection.

Newspaper cartoon (1873) of a farmer trying to rouse the public to the railroad menace. Railroads often engaged in economic discrimination against farmers, charging them as much as the traffic would bear instead of setting uniform rates based on distance.

Culver Pictures.

Granger meeting in Illinois in 1873. The purpose of the meeting was to protest monopolies, tariffs on imports of manufactured goods, and low farm prices.

In recent times, farmers have expressed their economic dissatisfactions and have demanded more government support by organizing tractor cavalcades to Washington.

United Press International.

Under a price-support program, consumers do not pay, nor do producers receive, the lower free-market equilibrium price at which there are no surpluses or shortages. Instead, consumers pay and producers receive the higher "parity-support price," resulting in a surplus of the commodity which government must purchase, store, and administer.

A price-support policy of this type has existed for a variety of farm products since the 1930s. The program was terminated for most, but not all, products in the early 1970s. In general, price supports have involved two major problems—selecting parity prices, and disposing of continually mounting commodity surpluses.

Parity Prices

There is a story of a farmer who, during a television interview, was asked the meaning of parity. He replied: "If a man could take a bushel of wheat to the market in 1912, sell it, and use the money to buy a shirt, then he ought to be able to do the same today. That's parity."

A dictionary will tell you that parity means the same thing as "equivalence." When applied to agriculture, therefore, a *parity price* is one that gives a commodity the same purchasing power, in terms of the goods that farmers buy, that it had in a previous base period. The period traditionally used has been 1910–1914 because it represents the "golden age of agriculture"—an era in which farmers prospered.

Over the years, the term "parity" also came to be used in a different sense to mean *parity ratio*. This, as you saw earlier in Exhibit 1, is the ratio of prices received to prices paid by farmers; it serves as an economic indicator of agricultural well-being. This ratio, whose components are updated from time to time, is calculated by the Department of Agriculture and is often quoted in the news media. A parity ratio of 80, for example, might be interpreted by some people to mean that the prices of farm products are 20 percent "too low." As a result, various farm programs are often proposed with the objective of raising farm commodity prices to 100 percent of parity, on the grounds that this would restore the fair economic status of agriculture.

Surplus Disposal

A price-support policy has, at various times, resulted in the accumulation by the government of huge surpluses—billions of bushels of wheat, millions of tons of feed grain, and so on. The costs to taxpayers—including the costs of acquisition, transportation, storage, losses on sales, and interest on investment—have amounted to billions of dollars. To alleviate the pressure, government has sought ways to reduce accumulated surpluses. The most common methods have been:

1. Foreign dumping—the sale of foods and fibers abroad at much lower prices than at home.

2. Domestic dumping—the distribution of foods to poor families and to charitable institutions.

3. Foreign aid—the donation of foods and fibers to countries in need.

4. Waste and spoilage—the willful destruction or deterioration of large quantities of commodities in order to keep them out of commercial markets.

5. Industrial uses—the expenditure of much time and effort by government and businesses to find new industrial uses for food and fibers.

Have these methods of disposing of excess farm products been socially desirable? For the most part they have not.

Informed observers generally agree that government has been inefficient in managing farm surpluses. Even foreign aid and domestic dumping, which may be desirable on humanistic grounds, frequently have been poorly administered. These practices, it is contended, should be adopted on their own merits instead of being made incidental to the disposal of surpluses resulting from inappropriate farm policies.

CROP RESTRICTION

A second way in which agricultural prices might be raised above free-market levels—and agricultural incomes thereby improved—is for government to legislate restrictions on farm production. In that way society gets less output, consumers pay higher prices, and farmers receive larger total revenues because the demand for most agricultural goods is relatively inelastic. The basic idea is explained in Exhibit 4.

At various times since the depression of the 1930s, government has attempted several methods of output restriction. The more important have been acreage curtailment, marketing quotas, and land retirement.

Acreage Curtailment

When farm surpluses accumulated in the past, government frequently sought to limit production by curtailing the amount of acreage that could be planted in particular crops. Surprisingly, however, such policies generally failed to reduce output significantly and often even increased it. The reasons are not hard to find. When farmers are required to reduce their vol-

Exhibit 4
Crop-Restriction Policy

If government requires farmers to curb output, the supply curve at harvest time is not the free-market curve S but the restricted curve S'. As a result, total output is at M rather than N, price is at J rather than H, and farmers' total revenue (equal to price times quantity) is the area of the larger rectangle 0JKM rather than the smaller one 0HLN. (NOTE Remember that the demand curve for most farm products is relatively inelastic. Therefore, higher prices result in larger total revenues. You can see that by raising the price from H to J, the gain in total revenue, HJKR, more than offsets the loss, MRLN.)

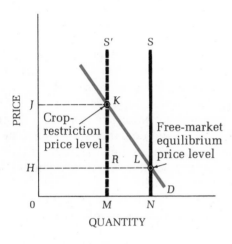

ume of acreage, they retire their poorest land and retain their best. They then cultivate the land more intensively by utilizing additional labor and capital. In this way they increase their yields per acre and often maintain, if not expand, their total output.

Marketing Quotas

Because acreage curtailment generally did not reduce output, it has been suggested that marketing quotas based on physical units would be a better method of control. Each farmer would be given certificates permitting the sale of a certain number of units of a commodity at the support price. Any production in excess of these legal quotas would be subject to high taxes.

Such marketing quotas existed for tobacco, cotton, and potatoes during the early 1930s. Similar plans have subsequently been proposed for other commodities. But Congress has rejected the idea under the pressure of middle- and upper-income farm groups who would be made worse off under such a scheme.

Land Retirement

Government has repeatedly tried, with little success, to reduce output by removing land from agricultural use. Unlike acreage curtailment, which may vary over the years, land retirement is usually fairly permanent. Many millions of acres of farm land have been retired as a result of the government purchasing and renting not only portions of farms but also entire farms. In addition, acreage-reserve programs and conservation-reserve programs have been instituted.

Land retirement is convenient, it is cheaper than price supports, and it is easier to administer than production controls. However, it has had limited, and sometimes inverse, effects on output. This is because farmers usually sell or rent their poorest lands and increase their production on the superior land they retain. When the government retires land, therefore, it must do so on a scale large enough to avoid engaging in what would otherwise be a costly and largely self-defeating activity. Failure to do so will result in the government offering higher and higher purchase prices or rental fees in order to acquire the more productive land. The people who benefit from this governmental action are landowners, who are not usually farmers.

DIRECT PAYMENTS

A third way of protecting farmers from price declines while improving farm incomes is to adopt a system of *direct payments*. This plan would eliminate parity payments to farmers and allow the prices of agricultural products to be determined in a free market by supply and demand. Government would compensate farmers for the difference between the market price they receive and some higher target price established according to a selected base period in the past. The fundamental idea is illustrated in Exhibit 5.

Direct payments are not a new idea. They were initiated in the early 1930s, introduced for a few commodities in the 1950s, and broadened to include most basic farm products in the early 1970s. In view of their importance, their economic implications are worth noting.

Are Direct Payments Good or Bad?

Under a direct-payments plan, market prices adjust freely to whatever levels are necessary to move the entire supply into consumption. As a result, the plan has the following favorable and unfavorable features.

On the positive side, the principal advantages are these:

1. It does away with the cost of storage as well as the wastes of destruction and spoilage.

Exhibit 5
Direct-Payments Policy

This plan permits consumers to pay the lower free-market equilibrium price and producers to receive the higher support or target price set by the government. The difference between the two prices is the distance *RT*. This distance times the number of units *RV* equals the area of rectangle *RTUV*—the total subsidy or direct government payments to farmers.

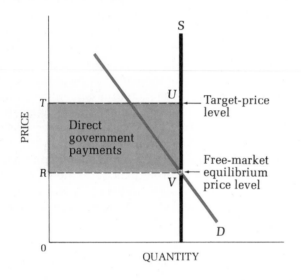

2. It brings lower prices to consumers on the domestic market.

3. It eliminates the pressure for export dumping at low prices and the resulting resentment of foreign governments.

4. It makes the farm subsidy visible, requiring it to be debated and voted upon periodically by Congress.

The principal disadvantages, on the other hand, are largely matters of costs. Direct payments are more costly to the government, and hence to the taxpayer, than price supports because direct payments cover more commodities. These costs grow as production increases. Therefore, direct payments tend to lead to stricter production controls. Land, for example, can still be taken out of crop production if the Secretary of Agriculture determines that farm output is likely to be excessive.

In general, therefore:

Under a system of direct payments, government subsidies to farmers are costly to taxpayers as long as free-market prices of farm commodities are below target prices. But if total (world) demand for farm goods increases to where free-market prices are equal to or greater than target prices, no subsidies or direct payments are required. In that case little, if any, land will be diverted from production, and the farm economy will be essentially a free-market economy.

In reality, total world demand for farm crops is rarely high enough for sufficiently long periods to eliminate *all* direct payments. As a result, subsidies to farmers, some of whom are quite rich, continue to be considerable.

Conclusion: Efficiency and Equity

The economics of agriculture is such that in an advancing economy, the proportion of resources devoted to farming tends to decline. Although this has been the long-run trend, it has been retarded by our agricultural policies. These have inhibited rather than encouraged the orderly exodus of resources from the farm sector, thus impeding agriculture's adjustment to changing supply-and-demand conditions. The results have been distortions in the utilization of farm inputs and misallocations of productive resources—at considerable costs to society.

Our agricultural policies have also created inequities among farmers by doing relatively little to correct the fundamental problem of agricultural *poverty*. Thus, despite the long-run decline in the farm population, a substantial proportion of the people living on farms may be classified as "poor." They are concentrated mostly in the South—particularly in the Appalachians and in the Mississippi Valley. For these families, who consume rather than sell most or all of what they produce, our farm policies have had relatively little effect. Instead, it is largely middle- and upper-income farmers—the ones who sell most of what they produce—who have benefited from government price- and income-support programs.

Despite these facts, our agricultural policies have been promoted as measures aimed at helping *all* farmers on the grounds that they are all poor. In reality only *some* farmers are poor; others are actually quite well off. The latter, however, are the ones who dominate agricultural organizations and political-pressure groups. This explains why Congress has done little to correct the inequities that our farm policies have created. (See Box 2.)

SOLUTION: SUBSIDIZE EXODUS

It is clear, therefore, that new policies are needed to correct imbalances existing in the agricultural sector.

Box 2
Farm Policy: Political Economy or Economic Analysis?

Many people in Congress who participate in formulating agricultural policy have personal interests in the legislation that is drafted. For example:

○ The family farm of Senator James O. Eastland, a Mississippi Democrat who served on the Senate Agriculture Committee, at times received cotton-support payments averaging about $180,000 annually.

○ Texas Representative W. R. Poage, a former head of the House Agriculture Committee and himself a farmer, who benefited financially from farm legislation, remarked:

It may be only a rationalization, but if you have—and I think you should have—people with the greatest familiarity with the situation, you get the benefit of the most knowledge. I also think that people [in Congress] who are directly involved in the truck business, the railroad business, and so forth ought to be on the committees writing transportation legislation.

For these reasons, it is easy to see that the task of formulating a sound agricultural policy may be more a problem of *political economy* than of economic analysis.

Left, *Mississippi Sen. James O. Eastland formerly received a cotton subsidy. Right, Texas Rep. W. R. Poage, when he headed the House Agriculture Committee, had farm ties.*

Wide World Photos.   Wide World Photos.

Despite predictions from time to time of world food shortages, there is no reason to believe that they will be sufficient to solve our *long-run* agricultural problem—that of *reducing the proportion of resources on farms.* We are therefore led to the following conclusion:

> The solution to our farm problem is not to provide price supports or income-maintenance programs that keep agricultural resource owners where they are. The solution is to subsidize them to get out and relocate. It would be cheaper and healthier for agriculture, and for the economy as a whole, if the government would spend money this way instead of continuing costly programs which serve to protect an artificially large agricultural sector.

What You Have Learned

1. Agriculture in the United States is characterized by (a) products that are price-inelastic and income-inelastic in demand, (b) a highly competitive structure, (c) rapid technological change, and (d) resource immobility. These characteristics mean that small fluctuations in output lead to large fluctuations in prices. Further, as the economy grows, the proportion of its total resources that it devotes to agriculture declines and the proportion that it devotes to manufacturing and services increases.

2. For many decades, prices paid by farmers have usually exceeded prices received. As a result, since the late 1920s government has employed various policies designed to improve farmers' real incomes and to stabilize prices. Three major policies that have been adopted at one time or another are price supports, crop restrictions, and direct payments.

3. Our agricultural policies have had several adverse effects. Among them: (a) the orderly exodus of resources out of agriculture has been inhibited rather than enhanced, thereby impeding the farm sector's adjustment to changing supply and demand conditions; (b) inequities have been created which have largely benefited middle- and upper-income farmers while doing relatively little or even nothing for poor ones. Society has thus borne the costs of policies that have proved to be inefficient and inequitable for agriculture as a whole.

4. Despite world food shortages that occur from time to time, America's *long-run* agricultural problem is to reduce the proportion of resources on farms. This can best be done by subsidizing farmers to leave agriculture rather than "paying" them (through price supports or income-maintenance programs) to remain in it.

For Discussion

1. *Terms and concepts to review:*

   income elasticity of demand

   parity price

   parity ratio

   direct payments

2. "The aggregate demand for agricultural products is relatively inelastic. Over the long run, aggregate demand has not increased as fast as aggregate supply. Hence, the pressure on prices has generally been downward." Illustrate this proposition graphically.

3. "Agricultural products are relatively inelastic in demand, whereas many manufactured goods are relatively elastic in demand. Therefore, a technological improvement in agriculture which results in a price reduction will bring about a decrease in the total revenue received by farmers; on the other hand, a technological improvement in manufacturing which results in a price reduction will often bring about an increase in the total revenue received by producers. This helps to explain why agriculture must decline in a technologically advancing society." Illustrate this proposition with the use of demand curves.

4. "The demand for agricultural products is such that small increases in output resulting from improved technology result in relatively large decreases in price and income (i.e., total revenue)." What type of elasticity is indicated in this statement? Illustrate with a demand curve.

5. Which is likely to have the most favorable effect on agriculture as a whole: a 10 percent decrease in farm prices, a 10 percent increase in real disposable personal income, or a 10 percent increase in population? Explain.

6. "It is only humanitarian to help the poor. Therefore, we should help farmers because they are poor." Do you agree? Explain.

7. "The government should accumulate stockpiles of agricultural goods when crops are plentiful, and sell the goods when crops are scarce. This would help stabilize farm prices and incomes without discouraging production." Discuss.

Chapter 24

Monopoly Behavior: The Other End of the Spectrum

Chapter Preview

What do we mean by monopoly? Are there different types of monopolies?

How are price and output determined under monopoly?

Are monopolies "good" or "bad"? Should something be done about them?

Can monopolies "discriminate" in price in order to earn larger profits?

How can the theory of monopoly pricing be used to help explain the pricing practices of public utilities?

Competitive systems are usually classified into several categories. Each of these categories may be regarded as occupying a position along a spectrum. Up to now we have studied only the system called perfect competition, which may be visualized at the left end of the competitive spectrum:

Perfect competition	?	Pure monopoly

In this chapter we turn our attention to the extreme opposite of perfect competition—pure monopoly. We shall find that this type of market structure is, like perfect competition, a theoretical limiting case, and that it is virtually nonexistent in its pure (unregulated) form.

Does this mean that the study of monopoly is theoretical and impractical? The answer is no. The theory of monopoly provides many useful tools and concepts for understanding the behavior of actual business firms. Against this background, the next chapter will combine the features of perfect competition and monopoly in order to help explain the competitive behavior of firms in the real world. For the time being, we represent this "real" world by a question mark in the spectrum above.

The Meaning and Types of Monopoly

What do we mean by monopoly? How do monopolies come into existence? What conditions must prevail in order for monopolies to survive? How does a monopolist determine price and output? What is wrong with monopoly and what can be done about it?

The answers to these questions comprise the basic aspects of the theory of monopoly to which we now turn our attention.

WHAT IS MONOPOLY?

A monopoly is defined as a single firm producing a product for which there are no close substitutes. This means that no other firms produce a similar product. Hence, the monopoly firm constitutes the entire industry and is thus a "pure" monopoly. A buyer who wants this particular product must either buy it from the monopolist or do without it.

REMARK   According to the dictionary, the origin of "monopoly" is the Greek *monopolion*, which means a right of exclusive sale. The dictionary, however, will also tell you that *mono* means "one" and *poly* means "many," which implies that a monopoly is one seller facing many buyers. This is the way in which we ordinarily think of monopoly. But in a later chapter relationships are studied in which one seller faces either one or several buyers. A number of interesting models will be constructed from such situations.

Pure monopolies are relatively rare, but they do exist. The electric, gas, and water companies in your locality are good examples, since each produces a product for which there are no close substitutes. But notice that a firm's degree of monopoly may vary among markets. For instance, the electric company has a monopoly in the production of electricity for lighting purposes, but for heating purposes its electricity may compete with gas, coal, and fuel oil sold by other producers. An electric company may thus be a pure monopoly in the lighting market but a "partial" monopoly in the heating market, in the sense that it faces some degree of competition from reasonably adequate substitute goods. Similarly, railroads, buses, taxis, and airlines are not pure monopolies, but they are certainly partial monopolies, depending on the extent to which buyers can substitute the products of these industries in meeting their transportation needs.

In view of this, most firms in our economy, as we shall see, may be characterized as "partial monopolies." In this chapter we shall develop a theory of pure monopoly. Many of its principles and conclusions, however, are applicable to partial monopolies as well.

SOURCES AND TYPES OF MONOPOLY

What are the origins of monopoly, and why do monopolies continue to exist? There are several possible explanations, all of which amount in one form or another to "obstacles to entry." These are economic, legal, or technical barriers that permit a firm to monopolize an industry and prevent new firms from entering. These obstacles give rise to several common types of monopolies.

Natural Monopoly

A *natural monopoly* is a firm that experiences increasing economies of scale—long-run decreasing average costs of production—over a wide range of output, enabling it to supply the entire market at a lower unit cost than two or more firms could do. Electric companies, gas companies, and railroads are classic examples of natural monopolies. The technology of these public utilities is such that once the heavy fixed-cost facilities are established (such as power generators, gas transmission lines, or railroad tracks and terminals), additional customer service reduces average total costs over a wide range of output. This permits the construction of more optimum-size plants so as to lower long-run average costs.

Legal and Government Monopolies

In some industries, unrestricted competition among firms may be deemed undesirable by society. In such cases government grants one firm in an industry an exclusive right to operate—a status of *legal monopoly*. In return for this, government may also impose standards and requirements pertaining to the quantity and quality of output, geographic areas of operation, and the prices or rates that are charged. Investor or "privately" (as distinguished from governmentally) owned public utilities are typical examples of legal monopolies.

The justification of legal monopoly is based on judicial opinions handed down for many decades by the courts. These opinions have held that a "business affected with a public interest" may qualify as a public utility (and therefore a legal monopoly) because the welfare of the entire community is directly dependent on the manner in which the business is operated.

In some states the result of this vague definition has been the establishment of numerous types of businesses as public utilities. Some examples are: common carriers of all kinds, water, gas, electricity, telephones, telegraphs, bridges, warehouses, and cemeteries. Additional examples include gristmills, sawmills, grain elevators, stockyards, hotels, docks, cotton gins, refrigeration plants, markets, and news services.

Whereas legal monopolies are privately owned but governmentally regulated, there are other monopolies, called government monopolies, that are both owned and regulated by the federal or local government. Examples are the U.S. Postal Service, the water and sewer systems of almost all local municipalities, the electric power plants of many cities, and the central banks of most countries.

Strategic-Resource Monopoly

A strategic-resource monopoly is represented by a firm that has gained control of an essential input to a production process. The possibility of this happening, however, is extremely remote. One of the only examples is the International Nickel Company of Canada, which at one time owned almost the entire world's supply of nickel reserves. Another illustration is the De Beers Company of South Africa, which today owns most of the world's diamond mines.

Patent Monopoly

A patent monopoly is a firm upon which government has conferred the exclusive right—through issuance of a patent—to make, use, or vend its own invention or discovery. A patent therefore enables a firm to profit from its invention while preventing its adoption by competitors. The National Cash Register Company and the United Shoe Machinery Company each held a series of patents on their line of products which for many years enabled them to monopolize their respective industries. Today, IBM, Xerox, Polaroid, and others have varying degrees of monopoly power through patent protection.

It is interesting to note that although a patent gives one an exclusive right to produce a specifically defined product, it does not preclude others from producing a closely related substitute good. Xerox Corporation, for example, has the exclusive right to produce copiers that function in a particular way, as described in the patents they hold, but a number of other firms produce competing copying machines. Although patents sometimes enable firms to establish pure monopolies, more often they only provide partial monopolies.

Price and Output Determination

We learned in the study of perfect competition that sellers in a perfectly competitive industry have no influence over the price at which they can sell their output. Each is faced with a perfectly elastic demand curve at the market price, and each maximizes profit by producing the output at which $MC = MR (= P)$.

A pure monopolist is in a different situation. Since the monopoly comprises the entire industry, instead of just a small part of it, the monopolist can exercise complete control over the price at which output is sold. The monopolist will thus find that more of the product can be sold at a lower price than at a higher one. This means that the market demand curve for the product will be less than perfectly elastic: It will slope downward instead of being horizontal. On the other hand, we may assume that the shapes (curvatures) of the monopoly's production function and cost curves are similar to those studied in previous chapters, because both the variable and fixed factors must be purchased in the input markets and then combined in order to produce a product. These activities are subject to the same laws of production and cost as those of any other seller.

COST AND REVENUE SCHEDULES

The cost and revenue data of a monopoly, illustrating the ideas discussed above, are shown in Exhibit 1. It should be apparent from this table that columns (1) and (2) actually compose the demand schedule facing the monopolist. Note that average revenue (= price) is inversely related to quantity. This means that in order to sell more units of a product the monopolist must charge a lower price per unit for all units sold.

Because the average revenue or price varies inversely with quantity, total revenue rises to a maximum and then begins to fall. The changes in total revenue, as always, are reflected by marginal revenue [column (7)], which now turns out to be different from average revenue because of the changes in price.

The cost schedules in the table are those used in the previous chapter for a perfectly competitive firm. This is because, as just noted, we are assuming that the shapes or curvatures of the monopolist's cost curves are similar to those of any other seller. Besides, by using the same cost data, we shall be able to see more clearly that the chief differences between the two firms originate in the output market where goods are sold, rather than in the input market where factors are bought.

A look at the table shows quite clearly that the fundamental principle of profit maximization still holds: The monopolist's most profitable level of output—the output at which net revenue [column (8)] is a maximum—is at 6 units, which is also where MC is equal to MR. Why is this so? Because as we learned in the previous chapter, at any output less than this, the added cost of an additional unit is less than the added revenue. Therefore, it pays to increase production. At

Exhibit 1
Cost and Revenue Schedules of a Monopoly

(1) Quantity per day, Q (given)	(2) Average revenue or price, AR = P (given)	(3) Total revenue, TR (1) × (2)	(4) Total cost, TC	(5) Average total cost, ATC (4) ÷ (1)	(6) Marginal cost, MC Change in (4) Change in (1)	(7) Marginal revenue, MR Change in (3) Change in (1)	(8) Net revenue, NR (3) − (4)
0	$16	$ 0	$ 25	$ —			− $25
1	15	15	35	35.00	$10	$15	− 20
2	14	28	41	20.50	6	13	− 13
3	13	39	45	15.00	4	11	− 6
4	12	48	47	11.75	2	9	1
5	11	55	49	9.80	2	7	6
6	10	60	52	8.67	3	5	8
7	9	63	57	8.14	5	3	6
8	8	64	65	8.13	8	1	− 1
9	7	63	79	8.78	14	−1	− 16
10	6	60	100	10.00	21	−3	− 40

any output greater than this, the opposite is true. Only where $MC = MR$ is the firm's output at its most profitable level.

LOOKING AT THE GRAPHS

You can visualize these ideas more easily by examining the graphs of the cost and revenue schedules rather than the data. In Exhibit 2, the monopolist's total-revenue and total-cost curves are shown in the top chart, the appropriate average and marginal curves in the middle chart, and the net revenue curve in the bottom chart. The vertical dashed line that passes through all three charts emphasizes the fact that at the most profitable level of output:

1. $TR - TC$ is a maximum.
2. $MC = MR$, since the tangents to TC and TR are parallel.
3. NR is a maximum.

Note also in the middle chart that the average-revenue or demand curve facing the monopolist slopes downward, which was not the case for a perfectly competitive seller. This means, as explained earlier, that in order to sell more units of a product the monopolist must charge a lower price per unit for *all* units sold. Since the AR curve is downward-sloping, the MR curve lies below the AR curve because of the *average–marginal relationship*, as learned in a previous chapter. You can verify this for yourself by ex-

perimenting with a few prices and quantities on your own and then sketching their graphs.

REMARK   For graphing purposes, you should recall from previous chapters that the MC and MR curves are plotted to the *midpoints* of the integers on the horizontal axis. This is because they reflect, respectively, the *change* in total cost and in total revenue resulting from a unit *change* in output. Notice also, from the footnote to the charts, that the curves have been smoothed. Therefore, some parts of the curves may differ slightly from the data in the table.

USING THE MC = MR PRINCIPLE

We must examine the profit-maximizing behavior of a monopoly more closely so that we are in a better position to evaluate the consequences of its actions. Let us therefore analyze its performance in terms of the fundamental $MC = MR$ principle, illustrated by the diagrams in Exhibit 3.

In Chart (a) the monopoly finds that the $MC = MR$ rule leads it to produce the output $0N$. At this output, the demand curve indicates that the highest price that can be charged is $NG (= 0P)$. Total profit, or net revenue, is thus the area of the rectangle shown in the chart, as explained in the accompanying information.

In Chart (b), the monopoly's costs are relatively high compared to its revenues. This is due either to an increase in the prices of the monopoly's factors of production, which causes its cost curves to shift upward, or a decrease in demand for its output, which causes

Exhibit 2
Cost and Revenue Curves of a Monopoly*

PROFIT MAXIMIZATION: THREE VIEWPOINTS

1. **Total Curves**   The most profitable level of output is determined where the difference between the curves *TR* and *TC*, as represented by the distance *GH*, is a maximum. This occurs at an output of 6 units. At this output, a tangent to the *TR* curve is parallel to a tangent to the *TC* curve, as at *G* and *H*. At smaller or larger outputs, such as 5 or 7 units, the tangents would not be parallel.

2. **Marginal Curves**   The most profitable level of output is determined where *MC = MR*, as explained in the text. You can verify this by simply following the vertical dashed line downward at 6 units of output.

3. **Net-Revenue Curve**   The most profitable level of output is determined where the net-revenue curve *NR* (= *TR* − *TC*) is a maximum. The vertical dashed line emphasizes these profit-maximizing principles in all three charts.

TECHNICAL NOTE (OPTIONAL)   If you like to think in geometric terms, remember that parallel lines have equal slopes or steepness. Hence, the most profitable output in the top chart is determined where the *slopes* of the *TC* and *TR* curves are equal, which is where the tangents are parallel. In the middle chart, since marginal cost is the graph of the *slope* of total cost, and marginal revenue is the graph of the *slope* of total revenue, it is true that at the level of maximum profit:

$$MC = MR$$

or, equivalently,

$$\text{slope of } TC = \text{slope of } TR$$

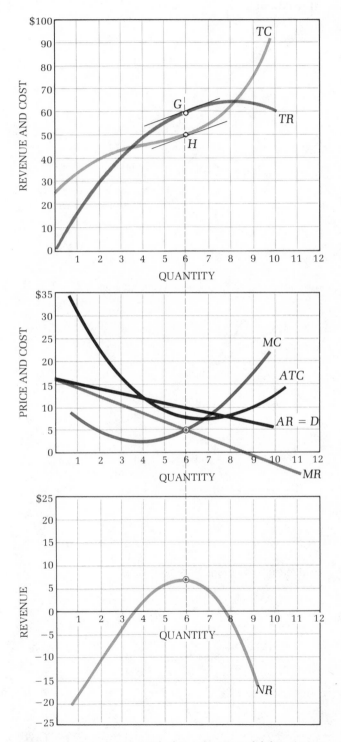

* The curves have been smoothed to enhance readability. As a result, the curves at some points may not correspond precisely to the data in the table.

Exhibit 3
Three Possible Profit Positions for a Monopolist

(a) MONOPOLIST EARNING A NET PROFIT

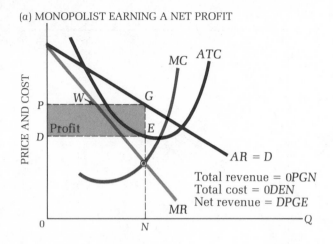

Total revenue = 0PGN
Total cost = 0DEN
Net revenue = DPGE

(b) MONOPOLIST EARNING A NORMAL PROFIT

Total revenue = 0PGN
Total cost = 0PGN
Net revenue = zero

(c) MONOPOLIST EARNING A NET LOSS

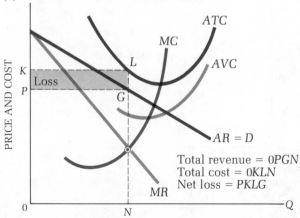

Total revenue = 0PGN
Total cost = 0KLN
Net loss = PKLG

its revenue curves to shift downward, or both. Thus, at the $MC = MR$ output, namely $0N$, the corresponding price NG is just high enough to yield a normal profit. Because the ATC curve is tangent to the AR curve at this output, the monopolist knows that any other level of production would yield losses because ATC would be greater than AR.

In Chart (c), the monopoly's ATC curve is everywhere higher than its AR curve. As before, this can be the result of an increase in costs or a decrease in demand, or both. Thus, at least for the short run, the $MC = MR$ rule still prevails because the output $0N$ and the corresponding price NG *will minimize losses*. That is, any other price and output will yield a larger loss area than the rectangle in the diagram.

You can see from these types of problems that it is essential to sketch correctly both average-revenue and marginal-revenue curves. Therefore, here is a convenient geometric rule to remember when the curves are straight lines (as they usually are):

> *An MR curve always bisects any horizontal line drawn from the vertical axis to the AR curve. Thus in Chart (a), the distance PW = WG*, and similarly for any other horizontal line that may be drawn.

This rule is based on a theorem which we shall not prove here. However, you can easily verify it for yourself by constructing your own tables and plotting the graphs. Actually, all that this rule means is that *at any given price, an MR curve is twice as steep as (or has twice the slope of) its corresponding AR curve.*

MARGINAL REVENUE IS NOT PRICE; MARGINAL COST IS NOT SUPPLY

We are now in a position to discover an important distinction between a monopoly firm and a perfectly competitive firm. When we studied the theory of perfect competition, we learned that the seller's marginal-revenue curve and average-revenue (= price) or demand curve were the same. We also learned that the marginal-cost curve was the supply curve above the level of minimum average variable cost. Do these conditions also apply to a monopolist? The answer is no, for as you can verify from the cost and revenue schedules shown earlier in Exhibit 1 and the charts in Exhibit 3:

> When a seller's demand (AR) curve is downward-sloping:
>
> 1. Marginal revenue falls faster than average revenue (= price) or demand. Thus, *marginal revenue is not price.*
>
> 2. The most profitable level of output for the seller and the most profitable price that can be charged for that

output are determined by $MC = MR$, not by $MC = AR$ ($= P$). Thus, *marginal cost is not supply.*

The reasons for these differences between price and output determination by a monopolist as compared to a perfectly competitive seller are explained further in Exhibit 4. Each diagram compares a given MC curve of a monopolist with two arbitrarily different demand or AR curves and their corresponding MR curves. A study of these diagrams and the accompanying analysis leads to the conclusion that *a less than perfectly competitive firm has no supply curve.*

In view of this, can we conclude that only under perfect competition are prices determined by supply and demand? You will have an opportunity to discuss this important question in a problem at the end of this chapter.

DO MONOPOLIES EARN "LARGE" PROFITS?

We now know enough about the behavior of a monopoly to draw three important conclusions about monopoly pricing:

1. The price charged by an unregulated monopoly is not, as Adam Smith once remarked, "the highest which can be got." This fact may surprise many people. Instead, the monopoly's price is the highest that is consistent with maximizing profits. For instance, the monopoly of Exhibit 3, Chart (a), could produce somewhat less than $0N$ and charge a price higher than NG. Then, as long as its ATC did not exceed its AR, the firm would still make a profit, but it obviously would not make the maximum profit possible.

2. A pure monopoly does not necessarily receive "high" profits just because it is a monopoly. In fact, if its profits are relatively high, the monopoly may find that the owners of some of its factors of production, such as workers or landlords, will absorb part of the surplus by demanding larger payments. This will cause the monopoly's ATC curve to rise, possibly to the point where it is earning a "small" profit or perhaps only a normal profit, as in Exhibit 3, Chart (b).

3. In the short run a monopoly may earn less than a normal profit and still remain in business, as in Exhibit 3, Chart (c). But in the long run it would have to earn at least a normal profit to continue in operation.

Thus, having a pure monopoly does not in itself assure extraordinary profit, although a monopoly is likely to be more profitable than a perfectly competitive firm. A monopolist is faced with certain market restraints that affect price and output decisions. The ability of the monopolist to cope with these restraints will affect the profitability of the firm. By adhering to the $MC = MR$ principle, the monopolist will always

Exhibit 4
No Supply Curve for a Firm with a Downward-Sloping Demand Curve

For any given marginal-cost curve, the most profitable price and output depend on the firm's particular average-revenue curve and its corresponding marginal-revenue curve. Thus, in Chart (a) the single output at N corresponds to the two prices at P and at S. In Chart (b) the two outputs at N and at L correspond to the single price at K. This suggests the following principle:

> A firm faced with a downward-sloping (or less than perfectly elastic) demand curve has no supply curve. This is because there is no single quantity that the firm will necessarily supply at a given price, and no single price at which the firm will necessarily supply a given quantity.

(a) A SINGLE OUTPUT AT MULTIPLE PRICES

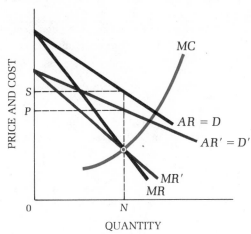

(b) MULTIPLE OUTPUTS AT A SINGLE PRICE

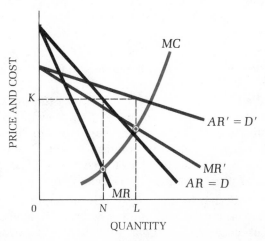

maximize profits (or minimize losses), but this principle in itself does not guarantee whether those profits will be large or small.

Evaluating Monopoly: What's Wrong with It?

You have probably heard that monopoly is "bad" but may not know exactly why. Now, however, on the basis of what you have learned from economic analysis, you can give some significant reasons.

EFFICIENCY: IT MISALLOCATES RESOURCES

The basic economic criticism of pure monopoly is this:

> By adhering to the $MC = MR$ principle of profit maximization, a monopoly misallocates society's resources by restricting output and charging a higher price than if it followed the $MC = P$ standard of competitive industry.

This basic criticism embodies certain fundamental ideas, all of which are best understood in terms of Exhibit 5.

1. In seeking to maximize profit, the monopoly produces the equilibrium output at Q and charges the equilibrium price QJ. The latter is called the _monopoly price_ because it is determined by the intersection of the MC and MR curves. Note that this price is greater than the monopoly's marginal cost at that output. This means that the value of the last unit to the marginal user (measured by the price he or she pays for the last unit, which is equal to the price paid for any other unit) is greater than the value of the resources used to produce that unit. In other words, since $MC < P$, society is not getting as much of the good that it wants in terms of what that good costs society to produce.

2. If the monopoly followed the $MC = AR (= P)$ rule of perfect competition, it would produce the larger output at N and charge the lower price NK. The latter is called the _marginal-cost price_. It is the optimum price for society because at this price, the value of the last unit to the marginal user is equivalent to the value of the resources used to produce that unit. Therefore, society is getting as much of the good that it wants in terms of what that good costs society to produce.

3. By adhering to the $MC = MR$ principle of profit maximization, the monopoly is technically inefficient because it typically "underuses" the plant by producing on the declining side of the ATC curve. Since the

Exhibit 5
Price and Output Effects of Monopoly Behavior

At the monopoly price—the price at J determined by $MC = MR$—the monopolist maximizes profit. But the price is higher, and the corresponding output is less, than if the monopolist adhered to the price at K [i.e., the marginal cost price $MC = AR (= P)$ of competitive industry]. The monopoly, therefore, is _economically inefficient_—it does not make full use of the available resources to produce the goods that society wants, given its income.

Note, too, that by adhering to the $MC = MR$ principle, the monopoly firm is _technically inefficient_—the plant is underused by operating on the declining side of the ATC curve. This condition can continue indefinitely—in contrast to perfectly competitive firms which, in the long run, operate at the minimum point of their ATC curves.

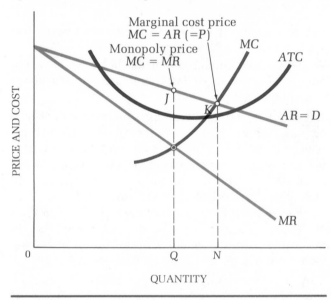

entry of other firms into the industry is blocked, the monopoly can remain in this equilibrium position indefinitely. In contrast, you will recall that firms in perfect competition are technically efficient because they operate in the long run at the minimum point of their ATC curves. Thus, society's resources are ordinarily used relatively less efficiently in monopoly markets than in perfectly competitive markets. (See also Box 1.)

REMARK   This criticism does _not_ necessarily mean that a monopoly produces less, and charges more, than a perfectly competitive industry with the same total demand curve. In fact, the opposite may often be true. In some industries, technology may widen the "spread" of the cost curves by bringing about increasing economies of scale over a broad range of output, so that one firm can supply the entire market at a lower unit cost (and perhaps at a lower price) than several. This, you will recall, is the basis of most natural monopolies, especially public utilities such as electric companies, gas companies, and railroads.

EQUITY: IT CONTRIBUTES TO INCOME INEQUALITY

A second criticism of monopoly is that it tends to create greater income inequality than would exist in a perfectly competitive economy. By restricting output and charging a higher price, the monopoly may make supernormal profits. These go to its relatively few owners, who, as corporation stockholders, are among the upper-income groups in the economy. This class thus benefits at the expense of the many consumers and resource owners who make up the rest of society.

GROWTH: IT LACKS INCENTIVES FOR INNOVATION AND PROGRESS

A third major criticism is that a monopoly, unlike a perfectly competitive firm, is not under constant pressure to develop better methods of production, and hence may retard economic progress. This is because the obstacles to entry make the monopoly relatively secure in its position; it does not face competitive pressures which would otherwise stimulate innovation. Public utilities—especially the railroads and telephone companies—are often used as illustrations of monopolies that have intentionally retarded the development of new and improved products to avoid an increase in the obsolescence rate of their existing equipment.

CONCLUSION: WHAT CAN BE DONE ABOUT MONOPOLY?

The general criticisms of monopoly are rooted in the fundamental notion of resource misallocation resulting from the restriction of output and higher prices. In view of this, what can be done about monopolies in our society? There are four major possibilities.

1. Do nothing. Sooner or later a monopoly that is not insulated by patents or other protective legislation is likely to see its position weakened. This will happen as new firms enter the industry in order to capture a share of the monopoly's market. The history of American business is replete with examples of companies that lost their dominant position due to competition from other firms, both domestic and foreign.

2. Break monopolies up into competing firms. In the United States and some other advanced countries, legislation (called "antitrust laws") exists for dealing with monopolies in this way. But the problems of implementing the laws are difficult and complex.

3. Tax away all the profits of monopolies above their normal profits. Then distribute these revenues to the public through more or improved government services. This would not drive monopolies out of business, because they would still be normally profitable. However, it would reduce the tendency for monopolies to contribute to income inequality.

4. Treat all monopolies as public utilities. That is, regulate their outputs and prices, requiring them to produce more and charge less than they would if they were completely free and unregulated. A model that illustrates this idea is explained in Exhibit 6.

No one of these approaches, nor any combination of them, would overcome completely the fundamental problem of resource misallocation. However, each

Exhibit 6
Regulating Monopolies as Public Utilities

If the government were to treat all monopolies as public utilities by regulating their prices and outputs, what pricing policy would be likely to result? According to Chart (a), there are three possibilities:

1. **Monopoly Price: MC = MR**   This price (at J) maximizes the firm's profit. But it also results in $MC < P$, and hence a misallocation of resources at society's expense. Therefore, the monopoly price is not likely to be permitted for a governmentally regulated monopoly.

2. **Marginal-Cost Price: MC = AR (= P)**   This is the pricing standard of perfect competition. The marginal-cost price (at K) is the socially optimum price—the price that maximizes society's welfare. The reason is that at this price the value of the last unit to the marginal user (measured by the price paid for the last unit, which is equal to the price paid for any other unit) is equivalent to the value of the resources used to produce that unit. But despite its desirability, the marginal-cost price is not the one that government is likely to impose on a regulated monopoly because marginal costs are usually difficult to estimate in practice.

3. **Full-Cost (or Average-Cost) Price: ATC = AR (= P)**   This price (at L) is the one at which the monopoly firm

covers all its costs, both fixed and variable, and earns a normal profit. Therefore, as explained below, this is the price that government is likely to impose.

NATURAL MONOPOLY

The situation can be different if the public utility is a natural monopoly. Under these circumstances, ATC may decline over a wide range of output, as in Chart (b). If that happens, the marginal-cost price, which is normally the socially optimum price for the welfare of society, will leave the ultility suffering a loss. This is because the marginal-cost price is below average total cost.

Conclusion: Full-Cost Price   In practice, government commissions that regulate public utilities usually try to set the full-cost price rather than the marginal-cost price. There are two reasons:

1. The full-cost price provides a fair rate of return on a utility's financial investment. This is because the full-cost price enables the firm to earn a normal profit.

2. Average costs of production can be roughly estimated from a company's accounting records, whereas marginal costs usually cannot.

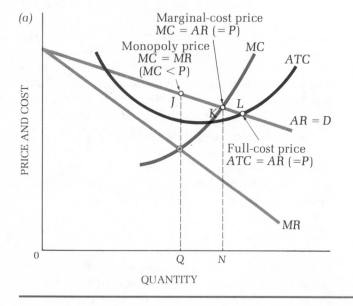

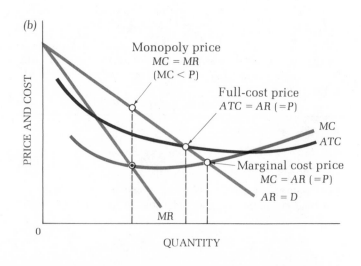

would tend to reduce somewhat the adverse effects of misallocation.

Price Discrimination

Until now we have assumed that a monopoly sells its entire output at the *same* price per unit. However, a

monopoly may sometimes find it more profitable to charge different prices instead of a single price for the units it sells. It is then engaging in what is known as price discrimination—one of the most interesting problems in the theory of monopoly.

Price discrimination may be defined as the practice of charging different prices to the same or to different buyers for the same good. Hence, it is also sometimes called *differential pricing*. In general terms, price discrimination or differential pricing is a method that some sellers may use to tailor their prices to the specific purchasing situations or circumstances of the buyer.

"TAPPING" THE DEMAND CURVE

An example of price discrimination occurs when a monopolist "taps" the demand curve of the buyer by charging lower prices for larger quantities instead of a single price per unit for all units purchased. The monopolist may also charge different prices to different classes or groups of buyers.

For example, an electric company does not usually charge the same price per unit of electricity to all buyers for all units. Instead, it *segments* the total market—that is, divides it into homogeneous submarkets consisting, say, of residential users, commercial users, and industrial users—and charges a different price to each class of user. In this way it earns more money than it would if all users paid the same price. This concept is illustrated in Exhibit 7.

Assuming that the AR curve is the demand curve of a single buyer or of a single homogeneous class of buyers, the monopoly may simply charge a price of $0P_4$ per unit and sell $0N_4$ units. In this case there is no discrimination, and the firm's total revenue is price times quantity, or the area of the rectangle $0P_4M_4N_4$.

However, the monopoly can enlarge total receipts considerably if it discriminates in price. Thus, it may charge a price of $0P_1$ for the first $0N_1$ units, giving it a total revenue of $0P_1M_1N_1$. Then it may lower the price to $0P_2$ per unit and sell an additional N_1N_2 units. After that, it can lower the price to $0P_3$ and sell an additional N_2N_3 units. Finally it can lower the price to $0P_4$, where it sells a further N_3N_4 units. Although the monopoly still ends up selling the same total number of units, namely $0N_4$, its total revenue is now the entire shaded area instead of the area $0P_4M_4N_4$ when it charged a price of $0P_4$ per unit without discrimination. Evidently, the smaller the reductions in price, the narrower the steps under the demand curve become and hence the larger the total revenue. Theoretically, the limit would be a total revenue equal to the entire area under the curve, but this would require price reductions in infinitesimal amounts. In practice, the reductions are in finite amounts for blocks of units, and the sales are made simultaneously to different classes of buyers at different price scales.

Exhibit 7
Price Discrimination Based on Quantity

A monopoly can charge a different price to the same buyer (or to the same homogeneous class of buyers) according to the quantity purchased. In that case the total revenue will be larger (shown by the shaded areas) than if the monopoly charged the same price per unit for all units purchased.

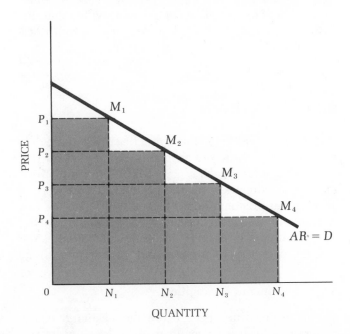

DUMPING

Another form of price discrimination occurs when a monopolist sells the same product in different markets at different prices. This practice is known in international trade as *dumping*, but its underlying principles are equally applicable to domestic trade.

The basic concept is illustrated by the diagrams in Exhibit 8. A firm that has a monopoly in the domestic market, for example, will probably find that the demand for its product at home is more inelastic than the demand abroad. This is because foreign buyers have more alternative sources from which to purchase the product. Consequently, their demand for the monopolist's product is more elastic.

Exhibit 8 shows the demand curve in the domestic market to be more inelastic than that in the foreign market. The total marginal revenue of both markets, namely $MR_1 + MR_2$, may be obtained by summing the horizontal ordinates to the MR_1 curve and the MR_2 curve in the domestic and foreign markets, or, in other words, the quantities in both markets at each marginal revenue.

The most profitable level of *total* output must be determined first. This is done in Chart *(c)*, where the MC curve in the total market is the monopoly's mar-

Exhibit 8
Illustration of Dumping

To allocate the product between the domestic and foreign markets, the most profitable level of *total* output must be determined first. This is done in Chart *(c)*. By adhering to the $MC = MR$ principle, the monopolist maximizes profit by allocating the total equilibrium output at N_3 among the two submarkets in Charts *(a)* and *(b)*. The monopolist then charges a higher price in the submarket where the demand elasticity is smaller (or the inelasticity is larger).

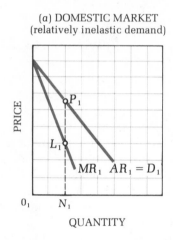

(a) DOMESTIC MARKET
(relatively inelastic demand)

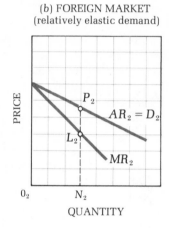

(b) FOREIGN MARKET
(relatively elastic demand)

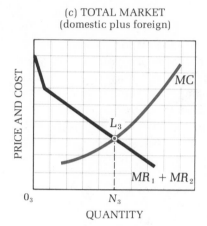

(c) TOTAL MARKET
(domestic plus foreign)

ginal-cost curve. The firm's most profitable total output is at N_3 because this is where the marginal cost of the output equals the total marginal revenue. It should be emphasized that only one marginal cost curve is assumed to exist in this case, because it makes no difference to costs whether the product is sold at home or abroad. That is, the product is still the same, and the marginal cost is determined by the total output. Hence, for the output at N_3, the monopolist's marginal cost is N_3L_3, and this is equal to N_1L_1 in the domestic market and to N_2L_2 in the foreign market.

Equilibrium in the Submarkets

How will the monopolist divide total output among the two submarkets? What price will be charged in each market? The answers to these questions follow from the $MC = MR$ principle we have already learned. In order to maximize profit, the monopolist will sell N_1 units in the domestic market at the price N_1P_1 because this is where the marginal revenue in that market is equal to the marginal cost N_1L_1. Likewise, the monopolist will sell the remaining N_2 units in the foreign market at the price N_2P_2 because this is where the marginal revenue in that market equals the marginal cost N_2L_2.

There are many illustrations of dumping at both the domestic and international level. For example, some manufacturers of appliances and various other products sell part of their output to mail-order firms and department stores (e.g., Sears and Montgomery Ward) at lower prices under different brand names. Milk cooperatives frequently sell milk at a high price to consumers and at a low price to butter and cheese manufacturers. Tire manufacturers have sold under their own brand names in the domestic market and under different brand names through other marketing channels in both domestic and foreign markets. In each case, the seller earns a higher profit by making fuller utilization of excess plant capacity—provided that the extra or marginal cost of the additional output does not exceed the extra or marginal revenue.

THE CONDITIONS FOR PRICE DISCRIMINATION

Price discrimination is thus a practice of charging different prices to different *segments* of a market for the same good, where each segment represents a distinct market or submarket for the product. If you were a seller, what practical conditions would have to exist to enable you to practice price discrimination effectively? There are three: (1) multiple demand elasticities, (2) market segmentation, and (3) market sealing.

Multiple Demand Elasticities

There must be differences in demand elasticity among buyers due to differences in income, location, available alternatives, tastes, or other factors. Otherwise, if the underlying conditions that normally determine demand elasticity are the same for all purchasers, the separate demand elasticities for each buyer or group of buyers will be approximately equal, and a single rather than multiple price structure may be warranted.

Market Segmentation

A second condition for price discrimination is that the seller must be able to partition (segment) the total market by segregating buyers into groups or submarkets according to elasticity. Profits can then be enhanced by charging a different price in each submarket. There are many ways in which a total market can be effectively segmented into submarkets. For example:

1. *Segmentation by Income*   A doctor may charge a rich patient more than a poor patient for the same operation.

2. *Segmentation by Quantity of Purchase*   A manufacturer may offer quantity discounts to large buyers.

3. *Segmentation by Geographic Location*   A state university may charge out-of-state students a higher tuition than in-state residents.

4. *Segmentation by Time (including clock time and calendar time)*   A theater, tennis club, or telephone company may charge more at certain hours than at others. Similarly, a resort hotel, restaurant, or clothing store may charge higher prices during certain seasons of the year and lower prices during others.

5. *Segmentation by Brand Name*   The same product may be sold under different brand names at different prices.

6. *Segmentation by Age*   An airline may charge less for children than for adults, despite equal time and space costs of serving them.

Segmentation by race, religion, sex, and education provide still further opportunities for partitioning a market into relatively homogeneous subgroups. Can you suggest some examples?

Market Sealing

A third condition for price discrimination is that the seller must be able to prevent—or natural circumstances must exist which will prevent—any significant resale of goods from the lower- to the higher-priced submarket. Any leakage in the form of resale by buyers between submarkets will, beyond minimum critical levels, tend to neutralize the effect of differential prices and narrow the effective price structure to where it approaches that of a single price to all buyers.

For example, a movie theater may use tickets of different color for matinees and for evenings, or for children and for adults. In this way it seals the segmented markets and prevents buyers from purchasing at the lower price and selling or using the product at the higher price. Similarly, some publishers of magazines, newspapers, and professional journals sell subscriptions to students at special rates. Of course, market sealing cannot always be accomplished with 100 percent perfection. When it is not, a certain amount of leakage will occur between submarkets, thereby reducing the effectiveness of price discrimination.

CONCLUSION: IS PRICE DISCRIMINATION LEGAL?

Price discrimination is an effective way for sellers to increase their profits. However, certain types of price discrimination are expressly illegal under our antitrust laws, while the illegality of some other forms is not clearly defined—and therefore also open to attack by the government. As a consequence, sellers must be cautious about employing certain discriminatory practices in their pricing policies.

What You Have Learned

1. A monopoly is a single firm producing a product for which there are no close substitutes. Major types are natural monopolies, legal monopolies, government monopolies, strategic-resource monopolies, and patent monopolies.

2. The most profitable output of a monopoly is determined where its $MC = MR$. Unlike a firm in perfect competition, any firm faced with a downward-sloping demand curve is a partial monopoly. It thus finds that its marginal revenue curve is not a demand curve, and its marginal cost curve is not a supply curve.

3. The basic economic criticism of monopoly is this: By adhering to the $MC = MR$ principle of profit-maximization, resources are misallocated by restricting output and charging a correspondingly higher price than if the $MC = P$ standard of competitive industry were followed. In addition, monopolies contribute to income inequality and they may lack incentives to be innovative and progressive. Four possible "solutions" are to do nothing, tax away their supernormal profits, break them up into competing firms, or regulate them as public utilities. If monopolies were regulated as public utilities, their rates would tend to accord with principles of full-cost pricing rather than monopoly pricing or marginal-cost pricing.

4. Price discrimination enlarges revenues by segmenting the market into submarkets and allowing sellers to charge different prices in each according to relative demand elasticities. Markets may be segmented by income, brand names of products, location of buyer, and various other criteria. Dumping is a typical form of price discrimination.

For Discussion

1. *Terms and concepts to review:*

monopoly
natural monopoly
legal monopoly
government monopoly
strategic-resource
  monopoly
patent monopoly
monopoly price

average–marginal
  relationship
marginal-cost price
full-cost (average-cost)
  price
price discrimination
dumping

2. Evaluate the judicial definition that a monopoly is "a business affected with a public interest."

3. Answer true or false, and explain why:

(a) A monopoly is secure since, by controlling its price and output, it can guarantee a profit.

(b) A perfect monopoly is almost as unlikely as perfect competition.

(c) A monopoly's price is higher than a perfect competitor's price in the long run.

(d) A monopoly maximizes its profit by charging the highest price it can get.

4. "A monopoly is most likely to be successful when the demand for its product is relatively inelastic." True or false? (HINT   Prove that a monopoly will never produce at an output at which the elasticity of demand is numerically less than 1. You can do this by first proving that when marginal revenue is positive, the elasticity of demand is numerically greater than 1.)

5. What is the most profitable output for a monopolist faced with a unit elastic demand curve throughout the entire length of the curve? (HINT   What is marginal revenue when demand is unit elastic?) Explain.

6. If the government wanted to extract the maximum revenue from a monopoly without driving it out of business, should the government tax profits or should it tax each unit of output? Explain.

7. "The prices of automobiles, TV sets, and cornflakes are each determined by supply and demand." Evaluate this statement in light of the fact that a less than perfectly competitive firm has no supply curve. What do "supply" and "demand" actually mean in this case?

8. Complete the accompanying table, which shows cost and revenue data of a monopolist. Sketch the following curves on three separate charts, one beneath the other, as was done in this chapter:

(a) Total revenue and total cost.

(b) Marginal cost, average total cost, average revenue, and marginal revenue.

(c) Net revenue. In the charts draw vertical dashed lines showing the most profitable level of output and the two break-even points. (NOTE   You will have to "project" the curves to obtain the second break-even point.) Label all the curves and explain their significance. Remember that marginal curves are plotted to the midpoints of the integers on the horizontal axis.

9. Suppose that you were an economic advisor to a monopoly. Can you suggest ways in which the firm could engage in price discrimination by segmenting the market on the basis of (a) quantity; (b) geographic location; (c) "time"?

10. Some critics have suggested that firms with strong monopoly power should be subsidized, or even governmentally owned, in order to have them adhere to a socially desirable pricing policy. What do you think of this argument? Be specific.

COST AND REVENUE SCHEDULES OF A MONOPOLIST

Quantity per day, Q	Average revenue or price, AR = P	Total revenue, TR	Marginal revenue, MR	Total cost, TC	Average total cost, ATC	Marginal cost, MC	Net revenue, NR
0	$21	$ 0		$22	$_____		$_____
1	20	20	$_____	37	_____	$_____	_____
2	19	38	_____	42	_____	_____	_____
3	18	54	_____	45	_____	_____	_____
4	17	68	_____	47	_____	_____	_____
5	16	80	_____	50	_____	_____	_____
6	15	90	_____	54	_____	_____	_____
7	14	98	_____	59	_____	_____	_____
8	13	104	_____	65	_____	_____	_____
9	12	108	_____	72	_____	_____	_____
10	11	110	_____	80	_____	_____	_____
11	10	110	_____	89	_____	_____	_____
12	9	108	_____	99	_____	_____	_____

Case
Cartels: "International Monopolies" and Commodity Power

In the early 1970s, the Organization of Petroleum Exporting Countries (OPEC)—a twelve-member group dominated by Arab oil nations—succeeded in escalating the world price of oil. Since then the attention of economists and political leaders has focused frequently on cartels and on the role these organizations can play in affecting global-resource allocation.

What Is a Cartel?

A cartel is often popularly referred to as an "international monopoly." More precisely, a _cartel_ is an association of producers in the same industry, established to increase the profits of its members by adopting common policies affecting production, market allocation, or price. A cartel may thus be either domestic or global in scope. However, in the United States (but not elsewhere) the term "cartel" generally applies only to producer associations operating across national boundaries.

Cartels have had a long and interesting history. The evidence indicates that cartels are generally difficult to form and even more difficult to sustain. In the past, concerted efforts by major producers to raise commodity prices substantially above free-market levels have rarely been successful for any extended period. Nevertheless, efforts at cartelization continue to be made from time to time, often for political as well as economic reasons.

How to Succeed

When a cartel is established, the goal is to raise each member's long-run profits to higher levels than would prevail under competitive conditions. To be successful, therefore, a cartel must have certain characteristics:

1. **Dominant Market Share**   A cartel must control the bulk of an industry's total output. Otherwise, the members will not have sufficient power to influence market prices.

United Press International.

2. **Cohesiveness**   The number of cartel members must be relatively small to make it feasible for members to cooperate with one another for the good of the group. Thus, a member nation will be less likely to cut its price in order to boost sales and profits at other members' expense.

3. **Income-Inelastic Demand**   The demand for the cartel's product must remain fairly stable over the long run—during recessions as well as periods of prosperity—in order to discourage members from violating the agreement when general economic circumstances change. More precisely, this means that the demand for the cartel's product must be largely unresponsive or relatively inelastic with respect to changes in buyers' income. (SUGGESTION Look up the meaning of _income elasticity of demand_ in the Dictionary at the back of the book.)

4. **Price-Inelastic Demand**   The quantity demanded of the cartel's product must also be fairly unresponsive or relatively inelastic with respect to changes in price. This means that if the price of the product is increased by some given percentage, quantity sold declines by a smaller percentage so that total revenue (price times quantity) rises.

OPEC and Other Cartels?

It is easy to see why a cartel must possess _all_ of these characteristics in order to succeed. The OPEC cartel, for example, was founded in 1960, but was not especially effective because it lacked cohesiveness—a spirit of cooperation among members. Not until the early 1970s was the needed cohesion achieved—owing partly to the Middle East war and partly to the feeling among oil-exporting countries that they had too long been exploited by the advanced nations. Whether or not OPEC continues to be effective depends on its ability to retain the necessary characteristics of a cartel.

The success achieved by OPEC has encouraged many other mineral-producing nations to consider making cartelization agreements. Several cartels—not necessarily successful—involving some of the commodities shown in Table 1 have existed for years. Ultimately, the true measure of any cartel rests on its ability to restrict output in order to sustain prices during periods of weak demand. Since cartel policy is usually based on detailed negotiation and cooperation among sovereign states with widely divergent economic and political interests, successful cartels have been relatively rare. Most, in fact, have ended up being not much more than information clearing-houses for their members.

Beating the System: Sealed Bids

But what if a cartel does succeed? Can anything be done to weaken its position and thereby bring about a reduction in prices?

One idea that merits serious consideration is the use of sealed competitive bids. A major buying nation, for example, could auction off transferable quota tickets to governments that want to bid for the right to export their commodity to the importing country. The cartel members would then have to compete in mutual ignorance, each unable to know who may be betraying the rest. At the very least, even if the cartelists agree to boycott the importing nation, a secret auction system would upset customary international market shares and exert pressure on exporting countries to reduce their prices. This, it seems, would be preferable to doing nothing at all.

Table 1. PRODUCERS OF SELECTED MINERALS

Commodity	Major producing countries
Bauxite-alumina	Jamaica, Surinam, Canada, Australia
Chromium	South Africa, Soviet Union, Turkey
Cobalt	Zaïre, Zambia, Norway, Finland
Copper	Canada, Peru, Chile
Iron ore	Canada, Venezuela
Lead	Canada, Australia, Peru, Mexico
Manganese	Brazil, Gabon, South Africa, Zaïre
Nickel	Canada, Norway
Oil	Saudi Arabia, Iran, Venezuela, Kuwait
Potash	Canada
Sulfur	Canada, Mexico
Tin	Malaysia, Thailand, Bolivia
Tungsten	Canada, Bolivia, Peru, Australia, Thailand
Zinc	Canada, Mexico, Peru

SOURCE: U.S. Bureau of Mines.

QUESTIONS

1. If a cartel maintains high prices over a long period of time, demand for the cartelized product is likely to become more elastic—and the cartel thereby weakened. Can you explain why?

2. What do you see as the single biggest economic factor capable of making or breaking a cartel?

Chapter 25

The Real World
of Imperfect Competition

Chapter Preview

Can some features of monopoly and perfect
competition be combined to develop new
and more realistic models of market
behavior?

What is the theory of monopolistic
competition? Of oligopoly? How well do
these theories serve to describe the
behavior of industries in our economy?

Do imperfectly competitive firms compete
in the same way as competitive firms? What
are the similarities? The differences?

If the world of perfect competition is largely imaginary, and the world of monopoly is relatively limited and regulated, what does the *real* world look like? In this chapter we answer that question by constructing models that come closer to approximating the kinds of markets in which most firms and industries in our economy tend to operate. We shall find that our knowledge of perfect competition and monopoly provides a basis for comparing and evaluating the consequences of these more realistic situations.

To give yourself a bird's-eye view of where you are at the present time and where you will be heading in this chapter, simply examine the following spectrum of market structures:

Perfect competition	Varying degrees of imperfect competition: monopolistic competition and oligopoly	Pure monopoly

We have already analyzed the cases of perfect competition and monopoly at the extreme ends of the spectrum. Now we turn our attention to the broad middle range in order to examine situations encompassing what is known as "imperfect competition"— market structures that are classified as "monopolistic competition" and "oligopoly." These names arise from the fact that *imperfect competition* consists of various "mixtures" of perfect competition and pure monopoly. We shall find that these mixed structures characterize most of the markets in our economy.

Theory of Monopolistic Competition

We have seen that perfect competition consists of many firms producing a homogeneous product, and monopoly consists of one firm producing a unique product for which there are no close substitutes. Both are important for economic analysis. Some industries—for example, the producers of standard raw materials, and the organized commodity and stock exchanges—operate under conditions that exhibit many characteristics of perfect competition. Other industries, such as the public utilities, have features similar to those of monopoly.

In reality, most of our economic activity occurs under conditions of imperfect competition—that is, in industries and markets that fall between the two extremes of perfect competition and pure monopoly. One in-between case which exists in a large portion of the American economy is called monopolistic competition. It may be defined as an industry characterized by a large number of firms of different sizes producing heterogeneous (similar but not identical) products, with relatively easy entry into the industry. We will study this type of competition first. The other subcategory of imperfect competition, known as "oligopoly," is examined later in this chapter.

PRODUCT DIFFERENTIATION IS A KEY FACTOR

Does the term "monopolistic competition" contradict itself? How can a market be both monopolistic and competitive at the same time?

The answer is based on the fact that in an industry characterized by monopolistic competition the products of the firms in the industry are *differentiated*. But product differentiation, like beauty, is in the eye of the beholder—and in economics the beholder is always the buyer. This means that products may be differentiated by brand name, color of package, location of the seller, customer service, credit conditions, or the smile of the salesperson—even if the products themselves are physically the same. As a result, each firm has a partial monopoly of its own differentiated product.

Monopolistic competition is found in many industries. Retailing provides a good general illustration. Some more specific examples include the manufacture of clothing, household goods, shoes, and furniture; and, in some areas, the services provided by most barbers, doctors, and dentists. In each of these industries the products sold are usually only moderately differentiated. This helps to explain why similar kinds of goods in monopolistic competition tend to have similar prices—as is usually the case in certain regions with haircuts, appendectomies, and teeth fillings. The less the degree of product differentiation in the minds of buyers, the less the disparity in prices.

PRICE AND OUTPUT DETERMINATION

When we apply these ideas to the construction of a model, we find that the theory of monopolistic competition is as much a *theory of the firm* as it is of market or industry behavior. Thus:

1. Because each seller has a partial monopoly due to product differentiation, there will be a separate AR or demand curve for each firm. These curves will be downward-sloping, indicating that a firm can raise prices to some degree without losing all of its sales.

2. We learned in the study of monopoly that a firm with a negatively inclined demand curve has no supply curve. This is because a given price may be associated with multiple outputs and a given output may be associated with multiple prices, depending on the position of the AR curve. Hence, there can be no industry supply curve; indeed, the whole concept of an industry becomes somewhat cloudy and vague in monopolistic competition because of the existence of product differentiation.

3. Because the products of competitors are close but not perfect substitutes, we may assume that their elasticity of demand is relatively high. Indeed, the degree of elasticity will vary inversely with the extent of product differentiation. And of course, the less the degree of product differentiation and the greater the number of sellers, the closer the model will be to pure competition.

The $MC = MR$ Principle Again

As always, to maximize profit, firms will seek to produce to the point where $MC = MR$. But this does not necessarily mean that they will be highly profitable. Because many firms are in the industry, and entry is relatively easy, some firms will, in the short run, earn only modest supernormal profits.

In the long run, however, there will be a *tendency* for surviving firms to be only normally profitable, but not necessarily precisely so, depending on the degree of product differentiation and the number of firms. For example, a small retail store might continue to be somewhat more than normally profitable because it happens to be in a particularly good location. On the other hand, a similar kind of store in a different location may continue to be less than normally profitable. Why? Because the seller would prefer to be his or her "own boss"—despite the economic loss that may result—rather than hire out to do the same job at a higher

Exhibit 1
Firms in Monopolistic Competition

Firm A is earning above-normal profits, firm B is receiving only normal profits, and firm C is earning below-normal profits. In the long run most firms in monopolistic competi-

tion will *tend* to be normally profitable, but there may be some exceptions due to locational factors or other special circumstances.

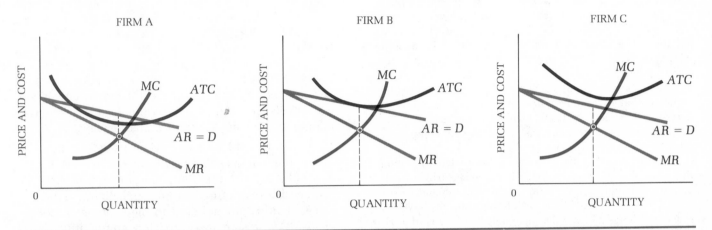

salary for someone else. Therefore, although most firms in a monopolistically competitive industry *tend* to earn normal profits in the long run, some firms do not. These possibilities are illustrated by the firms in Exhibit 1.

THE IMPORTANCE OF SELLING COSTS

Since product differentiation plays a key role in monopolistic competition, many firms spend money on advertising, merchandising, sales promotion, public relations, and the like in order to increase their profits. Marketing expenditures of this type, which are aimed at adapting the buyer to the product, are termed *selling costs*. This distinguishes them from production costs, which are designed to adapt the product to the buyer. For purposes of analysis, economists generally view all sales outlays or selling costs as synonymous with advertising.

The seller in monopolistic competition who engages in advertising seeks to attain a delicate balance between commodity homogeneity and heterogeneity. To attract customers away from competitors, the seller must convey two ideas:

1. The firm's product is not sharply differentiated from competing products, so that buyers will find it feasible to purchase the product instead of those of competitors.

2. The product is somehow superior to those of competitors, so that buyers believe there is greater heterogeneity than exists in fact.

These objectives of advertising account for the erroneous statement sometimes made about it, as explained in Exhibit 2. As you can see from the explanation accompanying the diagram, the purpose of advertising is to *shift* the demand curve to a higher position.

IS ADVERTISING "GOOD" OR "BAD"?

Advertising has been a subject of much debate among economists. The arguments have revolved around three major issues:

1. *Information Versus Persuasion* Those in favor of advertising argue that it educates and informs buyers about firms, products, and prices, and thereby tends to make markets more perfect than they otherwise would be. Those who oppose advertising reply that it seeks to persuade buyers rather than inform them, thereby creating wants that result in a distortion of "natural" preference patterns.

2. *Efficiency Versus Waste* Proponents of advertising contend that it familiarizes consumers with products and thereby broadens the market for goods. This not only encourages further capital investment and employment, but also large-scale operations that result in low-cost mass production. Critics of advertising reply that it encourages artificial product differentiation among goods that are physically similar and that advertising among competing firms tends to have a canceling effect. This duplication of effort results in a waste of resources, higher product costs, and higher

Exhibit 2
Advertising and Demand

It is often said that the seller's purpose in advertising is to make the demand curve more inelastic, thus allowing a higher price to be charged for each unit sold. If this statement were true, it would mean that the seller would prefer to be confronted with the demand curve D_1 rather than D_2. Yet if output is most profitable beyond the level at N_1, say at N_2, then D_2 is clearly preferable to D_1. Why? Because it allows for sales at a higher price, even though D_2 is more elastic than D_1. On the other hand, if output is most profitable at N_3, then D_1 would be preferred to D_2. Therefore, the argument that advertising is desirable for the seller because it results in a more inelastic demand curve may be only partially true and in many instances may be completely false.

The statement can be correctly reformulated by noting that what the seller really wants is not necessarily a more inelastic demand curve, but rather a new and higher curve *level*. This is illustrated by D_3. With this demand curve the seller can charge a higher price per unit relative to either D_1 or D_2, regardless of the most profitable output volume indicated on the chart.

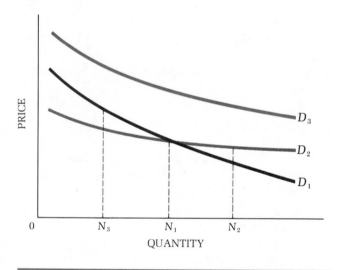

prices, so that any real economies of scale—if they exist—are lost through inefficiencies. This argument of efficiency versus waste is amplified in Exhibit 3.

3. **Competition Versus Concentration**   Defenders of advertising argue that it encourages competition by exposing consumers to competing products and enabling firms to gain market acceptance for new products more rapidly than they could without advertising. Critics of advertising contend that it facilitates the concentration of monopoly power because large firms can usually afford continuous heavy advertising, whereas new and small firms cannot.

These arguments indicate the fundamental nature of the controversy. Many students find the economics of advertising an interesting topic for a term paper. You can obtain a great deal of information on the subject in your college library, since numerous books and articles have been written about it.

CONCLUSION: MONOPOLISTIC COMPETITION AND EFFICIENCY

From what we already know about the results of perfect competition and monopoly, the more relevant social effects of monopolistic competition—those pertaining to efficiency—may be stated briefly.

1. Monopolistically competitive firms determine their production volumes and prices by the $MC = MR$ rule of profit maximization. They therefore misallocate resources by restricting outputs and charging higher prices than if they adhered to the economically efficient $MC = P$ standard of perfect competition. Note that *this is the same basic criticism that was given for monopoly*. However, in the case of monopolistic competition, the extent of resource misallocation with its associated output restriction and higher prices will depend, in each industry, on the degree of product differentiation and the number of sellers.

2. Monopolistic competition encourages <u>nonprice competition</u>—that is, methods of competition that do not involve changes in selling price. Examples include advertising, sales promotion, customer services, and product differentiation. Nonprice activities that result in greater innovation and product improvement may be desirable. However, to the extent that they result in higher production costs due to duplication of resources, excessive style changes, and so on, they tend to cause technical inefficiencies and are therefore undesirable.

3. Monopolistically competitive firms create what economists have called the <u>"wastes" of monopolistic competition</u>. This refers to the existence of "sick" industries. They are characterized by chronic excess capacity resulting from too many sellers of differentiated products dividing up markets, operating inefficiently at outputs less than their minimum average costs, and charging higher prices. Examples abound in the retail trades, such as grocery stores, clothing shops, and restaurants, as well as in the light manufacturing industries, such as textiles, shoes, and plastics.

Why do the chronically sick industries of monopolistic competition continue to exist? There are several reasons: low initial capital requirements, not much need for technical know-how, and the desire to own a

Exhibit 3
Advertising and Economies of Scale

Chart (a). In the short run, advertising raises a firm's average total cost curve by the advertising cost per unit. Thus, for the output at M, if the advertising cost per unit is DC, total advertising expenditures are equal to the area of the rectangle ABCD.

Chart (b). Advertising may also shift a firm's demand curve to the right and raise its long-run average costs, thereby influencing its economies of scale. For example, suppose that without advertising the firm would have produced the output at J for a unit cost of JE. Then, as a result of advertising, there may be several possible effects:

1. Advertising may give the firm economies of scale, enabling it to produce the larger output at K for the lower unit cost KG, even though point G is on a higher LRAC curve than point E.

2. Advertising may have a canceling effect, leaving output unchanged at J and simply increasing unit costs from JE to JF.

3. Advertising may cause diseconomies of scale, causing the firm to produce the output at L for unit costs of LH. This case is not very likely, however, since monopolistic competition results in firms of less-than-optimum size, as pointed out in the text.

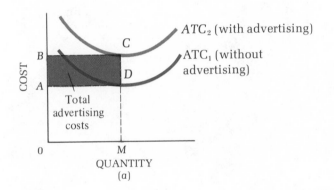

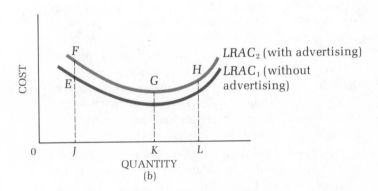

Theory of Oligopoly

When you drive a car, open a can of tuna fish, replace a light bulb, buy cigarettes, wash your hands with soap, play a phonograph record, type a term paper, or talk on a telephone, you are using products manufactured by oligopolistic industries. An *oligopoly* is an industry composed of a few firms producing either (1) a homogeneous product, in which case it is called *perfect oligopoly;* or (2) heterogeneous products, in which case it is called *imperfect oligopoly.* Oligopolistic industries are typically characterized by high obstacles to entry. These are usually in the form of substantial capital requirements, the need for technical know-how, patent rights, and the like.

Examples of perfect oligopoly are found primarily among producers of such industrial goods as aluminum, cement, copper, steel, and zinc. These goods are bought by other manufacturers who usually order

business and "be your own boss." As a result, new firms enter the industry as fast or even faster than the unprofitable ones leave it.

them by specification—that is, in a particular form, such as sheet steel, structural steel, or cold-rolled steel of a specific temper (i.e., hardness and plasticity). A specified type of steel is virtually identical whether it is made by U.S. Steel, Bethlehem Steel, Republic Steel, or any other steel company. Examples of imperfect oligopoly are found among producers of consumer goods, such as automobiles, cigarettes, gasoline, major appliances, soaps and detergents, television tubes, rubber tires, and typewriters.

In both perfect and imperfect oligopolies, the majority of sales goes to the "big three" or the "big four" companies in each industry—Alcoa, Kaiser, and Reynolds in aluminum, and General Motors, Ford, and Chrysler in automobiles. Can you think of other leading firms in some of the oligopolistic industries mentioned above?

SOME CHARACTERISTICS OF OLIGOPOLIES

In addition to fewness of sellers, high obstacles to entry, and similar if not identical products, most oligopolistic industries tend to have several other characteristics in common.

1. *Substantial Economies of Scale* Firms in oligopolies typically require large-scale production to obtain low unit costs. If total market demand is sufficient only to support a few large firms of optimum size, competition will ensure that only a few such firms survive.

2. *Growth Through Merger* Many of the oligopolies that exist today have resulted from mergers of competing firms—in some cases as long ago as the late nineteenth or early twentieth centuries. In 1901, for example, the U.S. Steel Corporation was formed from a merger of eleven independent steel producers. The purpose, as in most mergers, was to gain a substantial increase in market share, greater economies of scale, larger buying power in the purchase of inputs, and various other advantages which smaller firms did not possess to the same extent.

3. *Mutual Dependence* The fewness of sellers in an oligopolistic industry makes it necessary for each seller to consider the reactions of competitors when setting a price. In this sense the behavior of oligopolists in the marketplace may be somewhat similar to the behavior of players in such games of skill as chess, checkers, and bridge. In these games, the participants try to win by formulating strategies that recognize the possible counterreactions of their opponents.

4. *Price Rigidity and Nonprice Competition* Firms find it more comfortable to maintain constant prices and to engage in various forms of nonprice competition, such as advertising and customer service, in order to hold, if not increase, their market shares. Price reductions, when they occur, are sporadic, and usually come about only under severe pressures resulting from weakened demands or excessive inventories. These features give rise to a "live and let live" policy in most oligopolistic industries.

PRICE AND OUTPUT DETERMINATION

With these characteristics as a background, how do oligopolistic firms determine their prices and outputs?

A number of different models may be used to portray various types of oligopolistic situations. One of the most interesting possibilities is demonstrated in Exhibit 4. This model illustrates what is commonly known as the _kinked demand curve_—a "bent" demand curve and a corresponding discontinuous marginal-revenue curve, facing an oligopolistic seller.

Thus, suppose that an oligopoly's current price is at P and its output is at N. When contemplating a change in price either up or down, the firm must consider how its rivals will react. Hence, management might visualize the firm's demand curve by reasoning in the following way:

Exhibit 4
A Kinked Demand Curve Facing an Oligopolist

Given the kink at K, any price reduction below the level at P will increase sales slowly along KD because other firms will probably match any price cuts. A price increase above the level at P will reduce sales rapidly along LK because other firms will probably not match the price rise. Since marginal cost can fluctuate widely between the points G and H, the equilibrium price at P and output at N tend to be stable. However, this model leaves some price uncertainty because it does not explain why the kink happens to occur at the point K rather than at some other point.

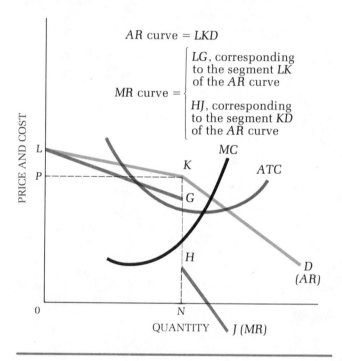

If we reduce our price below the level at P, our competitors will lose some of their customers to us and this will probably prompt them to match our price cut. Therefore, our sales will increase relatively little following the curve KD. On the other hand, if we increase our price above the level at P, our competitors probably won't match the increase and we'll lose some of our customers to them. Therefore, our sales will fall off rapidly along the curve KL.

In other words, the kinked demand curve reflects the greater tendency of competitors to follow price reductions than price increases. Price reductions take sales away from other firms and prompt them to cut prices in retaliation. Price increases do not usually invite such responses, because other firms will take sales from the firm that raises its price. It follows that the more homogeneous or standardized the product, the sharper the kink, since customers will shift more readily and sellers will therefore react more quickly to changes in prices.

As you can see, the large discontinuity in the *MR* curve between the points *G* and *H* permits the *MC* curve to fluctuate widely within this range. This helps explain why oligopolies exhibit a high degree of price stability. But there is also this seeming paradox:

> The kinked-demand-curve model leaves oligopolists with a considerable degree of price uncertainty. The model demonstrates that once the kink is *given*, the price at that point will tend to be stable. However, it does not say anything about *why* the kink happens to occur where it does instead of at some other point.

Some oligopolies have tried in various ways to reduce the state of uncertainty in which they operate. Two such methods have been collusion and price leadership.

OLIGOPOLIES IN COLLUSION

Oligopolists in some industries have occasionally colluded—"gotten together" and agreed on a single industry-wide price which they would all charge. This situation is most probable when the firms in the industry are faced with similar demands and either the same or different cost curves, as might occur in a case of perfect oligopoly. The result may then be much the same as in monopoly, except that there is more than one firm. Two interesting models can be employed to illustrate these possibilities.

Duopoly with Identical Costs

In Exhibit 5 for simplicity we assume a case of perfect oligopoly, in which the industry consists of only two firms producing a standardized product. An industry composed of two sellers is also called a *duopoly*. It may be either a perfect or an imperfect duopoly, depending on whether the product is standardized or differentiated.

In Chart (*a*) we further suppose that if the products and the prices of the two firms are identical, each firm will have a 50 percent chance of selling to any buyer, and hence the market will be divided equally between them. Therefore, the *AR* curve of the industry will be downward-sloping. At any given price such as the price at *P*, the quantity sold by each firm will be one-half the industry's total. Also, as we learned in the study of monopoly, it is mathematically true for all straight-line *MR* and *AR* curves that the *marginal revenue curve must bisect any horizontal line drawn from the vertical axis to the average revenue curve*. Hence, the *AR* curve of each firm corresponds to the *MR* curve of the industry, and so the distance *PW* =

Exhibit 5
Price and Output Determination: Two Oligopolists—A Duopoly Model

In Chart (*a*) each firm maximizes its profits by adhering to the *MC* = *MR* rule, thereby producing an amount equal to N units and charging a price of *P* per unit. Both firms may also agree to stick to this rule at all times, thereby always charging a single, industry-wide price.

(a) IDENTICAL DEMANDS AND COSTS

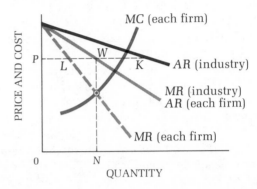

In Chart (*b*), if each firm followed the *MC* = *MR* rule, firm X represented by MC_X would prefer a price of *P*, whereas firm Y represented by MC_Y would prefer a price of *P'*. By colluding, both firms might agree on a price within this range. But through price leadership by the larger firm, firm Y may be willing to follow firm X's price of *P*.

(b) IDENTICAL DEMANDS AND DIFFERENT COSTS

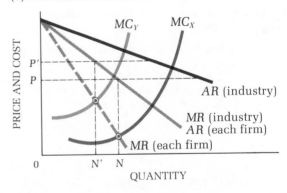

WK. Similarly, the *MR* curve of each firm is such that *PL* = *LW*.

If we assume that the two firms have identical marginal cost curves, it follows that each firm will maximize its profits by following the *MC* = *MR* rule, producing at N units of output and charging a price of *P* per unit. The two firms might also collude by agreeing not to deviate from the *MC* = *MR* rule even temporarily and to maintain a single-price policy even in the face of changing business conditions.

Duopoly with Different Costs

The identical demand conditions are also illustrated in Chart (b), but now we assume that the two duopolists X and Y have different costs. Thus, duopolist X is a larger-capacity producer than duopolist Y because the marginal cost curve of firm X as represented by MC_X is farther to the right than the marginal cost curve of firm Y as represented by MC_Y. This means that for any given marginal cost, firm X can produce more than firm Y.

In this case, by following the $MC = MR$ rule, firm X will maximize its profit by producing N units and charging a price of P per unit, whereas firm Y will maximize its profit by producing N' units and charging a price of P' per unit.

The two firms are thus in conflict. If firm X charges its preferred lower price, firm Y must charge the same price or else lose sales. If firm Y charges its preferred higher price, firm X need not do the same, in which case firm Y will again suffer the consequences.

What will the two firms do? They might collude by agreeing on a single price for both. This price may be at P, or at P', or some price in between. And it may be a price that is profitable for both firms as long as each is earning at least normal profits.

In practice, there are a number of real-world obstacles to collusion. They include:

1. The antitrust laws (to be studied in a later chapter), which make such behavior illegal.

2. The number of firms in the industry—since the larger the number, the harder it may be for sellers to "get together."

3. The degree of product differentiation—since greater differentiation makes collusion more difficult.

Despite these obstacles, cases of collusion are often uncovered by the government. (See Box 1.)

PRICE LEADERSHIP

The firms need not formally agree on a mutually satisfactory price as in Exhibit 5, Chart (b). It is possible instead that firm Y might accept a policy of *price leadership*. This is a situation in which all firms in an oligopolistic industry adhere, often tacitly and without formal agreement, to the pricing policies of one of its members. Usually, but not always, the price leader will be the largest firm in the industry, and other firms in the industry will simply go along with the leader.

Thus, in the diagram, firm X is the largest, and would probably be the price leader. It could therefore set a price at P to maximize its own profit, and firm Y would follow the leader by charging the same price. This policy avoids uncomfortable price wars, it is not

Box 1
Oligopolies in Collusion

FTC NEWS RELEASE
Federal Trade Commission   *Washington, D.C. 20580*

FTC CHARGES FOUR MAKERS OF "ANTIKNOCK" COMPOUNDS WITH UNFAIR COMPETITION

The FTC announced a complaint charging that the nation's four producers of lead-based "antiknock" additives for gasoline have engaged in practices that unlawfully reduced or eliminated competition.

The complaint alleges that the companies—Ethyl Corp., E.I. du Pont de Nemours & Co., PPG Industries, Inc., and Nalco Chemical Co.—facilitated maintenance of uniform prices by, among other things, "signaling" future price changes to competitors.

In addition to "signaling," the Commission complaint alleges that each company lessened ucertainty about price movements and facilitated maintenance of substantially uniform prices by selling only on a uniform delivered price basis. With the exception of PPG Industries, the companies are also alleged to have used "most favored" customer agreements, promising a buyer the lowest price the seller charges other buyers.

The Commission released a proposed order which, among other things, prohibits:

○ The present delivered price system and systematic freight equalization.

○ The public announcement of antiknock compound prices as well as any advance notice of price changes.

○ "Most favored" customer clauses.

regarded as illegal by the courts (unless it is proved to be the result of collusion or other monopolistic practices), and it leaves the price followers earning at least normal, although not maximum, profits. This explains why price leadership has at one time or another been a widespread practice in most oligopolistic industries. Examples include cigarettes, steel, anthracite coal, farm equipment, newsprint, tin cans, lead, sulfur, and sugar.

CONCLUSION: OLIGOPOLY AND EFFICIENCY

Oligopoly is a major form of market structure in our economy. What can be said about its social consequences? Unfortunately, the issues are extremely complex and the conclusions are by no means clearcut. Nevertheless, three aspects of oligopoly pertaining mainly to efficiency are worth noting.

1. The basic criticism of oligopoly, as a type of market structure, is the same as that of monopoly and monopolistic competition. Oligopoly misallocates resources by restricting output short of the point where $MC = P$. But this criticism does not necessarily mean that a particular oligopoly produces less, or has higher unit costs, than a perfectly competitive industry. In oligopolistic industries where technology is such that economies of scale are important (e.g., automobiles or steel), larger outputs and lower long-run unit costs may be achieved than if these industries were perfectly competitive. An automobile manufacturer, for example, could not gain significant reductions in unit costs without the technology and economies of assembly-line mass production.

2. Oligopolistic industries tend to be more progressive in research and development than perfectly competitive industries. But evidence suggests that they are considerably less progressive in research than in development, as explained further below.

3. The economic influence of oligopoly (and also monopoly) may be somewhat offset by the growth of _countervailing power_. This term means that the growth of market power by one group may stimulate the growth of a counterreaction and somewhat offsetting influence by another group on the other side of the market. For instance, powerful labor unions have grown up to face oligopolistic industries across the bargaining table; chain stores have emerged to deal with large processing and manufacturing firms; and even government has grown larger, partly in response to the growth of big business and big labor. Countervailing power therefore has some favorable competitive effects within the economy, but it does not exist with equal effectiveness in all oligopolistic industries.

To conclude:

Oligopolies are subject to the same basic criticism as monopolies and monopolistic competition. The criticism is _resource misallocation_ resulting from output restriction and higher prices. Oligopolies, however, may mitigate the problem to the extent that they realize known economies of scale, and develop and innovate with new products and techniques.

Some further aspects of this are discussed in Exhibit 6.

Do Firms Really Maximize Profits?

Now that we have completed our study of business behavior under imperfect competition, it is appropriate to ask: Do firms really strive to maximize profits as economic theory assumes? In other words, do businesspersons actually behave the way we have said they do, equating their MC and MR?

This problem often comes up in discussions of politics, labor–management relations, and other areas of current social and economic interest. Hence, we should look closely at three dimensions of the profit-maximization problem. These dimensions involve (1) definitional, (2) measurement, and (3) environmental considerations.

DEFINITIONAL PROBLEMS: WHICH CONCEPT OF PROFIT?

It is easy to define profit as total revenue minus total cost. But is this all there is to the concept of profit? The answer is not as simple as it may seem because business executives do not always know whether they are seeking to maximize short-run profit or long-run profit. Nor do executives always view the approach to profit management in the same way. As a result of these _definitional_ problems, it becomes difficult to state unequivocally that firms in the real world either do or do not strive to maximize their profits.

For example, firms often adopt policies that may reduce short-run profits but which are designed to establish a better long-run situation. Illustrations of such policies include (1) costly research and development programs for creating new products and new markets, and (2) fringe benefits to employees aimed at developing long-run loyalties. At the same time, these firms may exploit short-run market situations to the fullest advantage at the risk of adversely affecting their corporate image in the long run.

Likewise, firms often view the profit problem in discordant ways. Many studies conducted by business economists and management researchers have found that corporations tend to approach the formulation of profit policies differently. A policy that may seem wise to one firm may seem folly to another. A typical illustration of this is found in the field of employee relations. One firm may regard pension programs, health and accident plans, or even coffee breaks as means of raising labor morale and productivity. Another firm may consider them at best a necessary evil.

MEASUREMENT PROBLEMS: WHICH INDICATOR OF PROFIT?

The problems of defining a concept of profit are closely tied to the problems of measuring it. Our elementary theory of the firm has assumed that businesspersons know their marginal costs and marginal revenues and can adjust their outputs to the most profitable levels—the levels at which $MC = MR$.

Exhibit 6
Are Oligopolies Progressive in Research and Development?

Movies and television to the contrary, many of the greatest inventions of this century were not made by white-coated scientists conducting experiments in gleaming laboratories of large oligopolies. Since 1900, independent inventors working alone or in universities and small research firms have produced most of the major inventions. Among them: air conditioning, automatic transmissions, power steering, cellophane, the cotton picker, the helicopter, the gyrocompass, the jet engine, quick-freezing, insulin, the continuous casting of steel, and the catalytic cracking of petroleum.

Only a relatively small proportion of the major inventions, including nylon, tetraethyllead, the diesel electric locomotive, and transistors were developed by large private firms such as DuPont, General Motors, and Bell Telephone Laboratories.

Although basic research is conducted mainly in academic institutions and private firms, the development part of R&D is the specialty of large industrial corporations. In fact, *the great bulk of R&D outlays is for development purposes.*

On the other hand, in many oligopolistic industries, such as agricultural machinery, basic metals, and food products, relatively little has been spent on research.

In contrast, research and development in agriculture, which serves as a rough approximation of perfect competition, has been accomplished mainly by government support in federal research laboratories, experiment stations, and land-grant colleges and universities.

ENCOURAGING MORE R&D

What can be done to promote more R&D, thereby stimulating innovation, productivity, and the nation's economic growth? Several measures may be suggested.

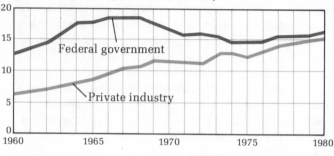

U.S. RESEARCH AND DEVELOPMENT EXPENDITURES (billions of dollars, adjusted for inflation)

SOURCE: National Science Foundation.

1. *Improve Taxation and Depreciation Benefits* Washington should broaden the tax incentives for corporate R&D spending. Also, depreciation allowances for special-purpose plant and equipment used in R&D should be liberalized.

2. *Reduce Excessive Regulations* Many government health, safety, and other regulations are viewed by business executives as too cumbersome and costly to meet. These regulations must therefore be reduced and simplified in order to stimulate corporate investment in R&D.

3. *Eliminate Antitrust Obstacles* At present, if a company gains a substantial share of a market because of an invention it has patented, it can be sued under the nation's antitrust laws for monopolizing the market. Several studies show that this factor has limited the willingness of firms to undertake heavy expenditures on R&D, especially those involving high-technology products.

But in a dynamic economic environment, where changes in technology, tastes, and other underlying forces constantly influence costs and demands, business executives cannot possibly have a precise understanding of how changes in their output will affect their costs and revenues. At best executives may be able to gain a rough idea of their costs at a few "typical" or standard volumes of output, but even this would be of relatively limited value as a guide to profit maximization in the manner described by economic theory.

As a result of these and other difficulties, business firms in imperfect competition do not, as economic theory assumes, set prices with full knowledge of their marginal costs and marginal revenues. Instead, managers establish prices on the basis of experience, trial and error, and the customs and practices of the industry of which they are a part. And prices are not usually set with the direct objective of maximizing

profits. Rather, pricing strategies often aim at attaining other objectives, including the following ones, which may (or may not) indirectly maximize profits:

1. Achieve a certain target or percentage return on investment.

2. Stabilize a firm's prices and outputs over the business cycle (i.e., over a period of years during which general economic conditions are changing).

3. Achieve a certain target or percentage share of the market.

4. Meet or match the prices of competitors.

None of these objectives is a substitute for profit maximization. All, however, influence a firm's net revenue and are usually easier for executives to use as a practical guide for profit management and control. Hence, the goals serve as *indicators* of profit rather

SOURCE: National Science Foundation.

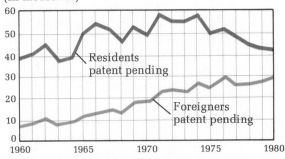

SOURCE: Bureau of Labor Statistics.

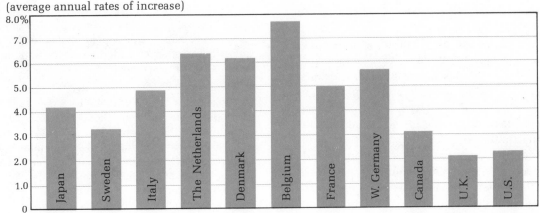

SOURCE: U.S. Department of Commerce.

than measures of profit. In studies of pricing practices of large corporations, it has been found that the first of the goals listed above is dominant, but the others also play important rules.

ENVIRONMENTAL CONDITIONS: PROFIT-LIMITING FACTORS

From a different point of view, economic conditions may encourage a firm to avoid—purposely and consciously—the maximization of (short-run) profits, although the execution of these policies may be argued to be best in the long run. Four such motives for limiting profit may be noted.

1. *Discourage Competitive Entry* If profits could be large due to higher prices rather than lower costs and superior efficiency, or if the company has a weak mo-

nopoly position in the industry, management may prefer lower profits in order to discourage potential competitors from entering the industry. In this case a long-run price policy that is in line with the rest of the industry will be more advantageous to the firm than one which exploits current market conditions for immediate profit.

2. *Discourage Antitrust Investigation* Certain monopolistic practices are illegal under our antitrust laws. Profits are one of a number of criteria used by the government as evidence of firms' monopolistic market control. This can seem somewhat paradoxical when contrasted with the previous consideration. On the one hand, management may maintain lower profits in order to exclude competitors and thereby strengthen its monopoly control. Yet the federal government's antitrusters may consider high profits, not low profits, as one of several indexes of monopoly power.

3. **Restrain Union Demands** Reducing the possibility of having to pay higher wages is another factor prompting management to restrain profits. This is particularly applicable in industries with strong labor unions. As long as the economy is prosperous and profits are rising, unions can more easily demand higher wages without inflicting damage on the firm. But if, in a recession, prices are falling faster than wages, the profit margin is squeezed at both ends. Those companies that curbed wage increases in the beginning would then have a better opportunity to cope with changing market conditions.

4. **Maintain Consumer Goodwill** Management may choose to limit profits in order to preserve good customer relations. Consumers frequently have their own ideas of a "fair" price, whether such ideas are based on "what used to be in the old days," or whether they are the results of "comparison shopping."

CONCLUSION: MAXIMIZE OR "SATISFICE"?

The profit problem is complex, making it extremely difficult to state unequivocally that firms in imperfect competition do or do not seek to maximize profits. Perhaps in reality they do not seek to maximize but to "satisfice"—that is, to attain targets of satisfactory performance such as a specific rate of return on investment, a particular share of the market, or a defined average annual growth of sales—as some scholars have suggested. In economic theory, however, we *assume* that the underlying objective is to maximize profit because, as already shown, this assumption enables us to evaluate the social performance of the firm as a resource allocator. (See *Leaders in Economics*, pages 449 and 450.)

What You Have Learned

1. Monopolistic competition exists in industries characterized by many firms producing heterogeneous products. Product differentiation, which is a matter for buyers to decide, is thus a key factor among firms in such industries. Monopolistically competitive industries are a major segment of our economy.

2. The $MC = MR$ principle serves as a guide for profit maximization in monopolistic competition. Because there is reasonable freedom of entry, firms will *tend* to earn normal profits in the long run, but there may be exceptions.

3. Advertising plays a major role in monopolistic competition because of the importance of product differentiation. The pros and cons of advertising have centered around three major issues: information versus persuasion; efficiency versus waste; competition versus concentration.

4. Monopolistic competition is subject to the same basic criticism as monopoly: Resource misallocation results from output restriction and higher prices owing to adherence to the $MC = MR$ instead of the $MC = P$ standard of production and pricing. In addition, monopolistic competition encourages nonprice competition, which may or may not be undesirable, and it results in "wastes" as well as the perpetuation of "sick" industries that are overcrowded and inefficient.

5. Oligopolistic industries consist of several firms producing either homogeneous products (perfect oligopoly) or heterogeneous products (imperfect oligopoly). These industries play a major role in our economy. Oligopolistic firms usually tend to be characterized by substantial economies of scale, a history of growth through merger, mutual dependence, price rigidity, and nonprice competition.

6. The $MC = MR$ principle applies to oligopolistic firms that seek to maximize profit. In addition, each firm tends to see itself as being faced with a kinked demand curve, indicating that competitors will follow a price decrease by any one seller, but not a price increase.

7. The kinked demand curve results in a stable price, but it leaves the seller uncertain about the determination of the price itself. This has prompted oligopolists to reduce price uncertainty either by colluding with competitors or by accepting one of the competitors as a price leader and matching that firm's price.

8. Oligopolies are subject to the same basic criticism as monopolies—resource misallocation results from output restriction and higher prices. This is due to their adherence to the $MC = MR$ rather than $MC = P$ standard of production and pricing. (However, like natural monopolies, the cost structures of oligopolistic firms may be subject to more substantial economies of scale than those of perfectly competitive firms.) In addition, oligopolies have not exhibited as much progress in basic research as might be expected. On the other hand, their market power has in some cases been mitigated by the growth of countervailing power.

9. It is difficult to state unequivocally that firms in imperfect competition either do or do not seek to maximize profits. In reality, it is quite likely that they strive to "satisfice" rather than maximize. Nevertheless, the assumption of profit maximization is fundamental in microeconomic theory because it permits an evaluation of the social function of the firm as a resource allocator.

For Discussion

1. *Terms and concepts to review:*

imperfect competition	oligopoly
monopolistic competition	kinked demand curve
selling costs	duopoly
nonprice competition	price leadership
"wastes" of monopolistic competition	countervailing power
	"satisfice"

2. Firms in monopolistic competition tend to be only normally profitable in the long run. The same is true of firms in perfect competition. Therefore, why criticize monopolistic competition?

Leaders in Economics
Edward Hastings Chamberlin   1899–1967
Joan Robinson   1903–

The theory of monopolistic competition had its origin in the early 1930s. Prior to that time there was only a theory of perfect competition and a theory of monopoly.

In the United States, the person responsible for the development of the theory was a professor at Harvard University, Edward Chamberlin. His distinguished treatise, *The Theory of Monopolistic Competition,* was published in 1933. As Chamberlin put it, the theory was needed because:

> With differentiation appears monopoly, and as it proceeds further the element of monopoly becomes greater. Where there is any degree of differentiation whatever, each seller has an absolute monopoly of his own product, but is subject to the competition of more or less imperfect substitutes. Since each is a monopolist and yet has competitors, we may speak of them as "competing monopolists," and of the forces at work as those of "monopolistic competition."
>
> It is this latter problem which is of especial interest and importance. In all of the fields where individual products have even the slightest element of uniqueness, competition bears but faint resemblance to the pure competition of a highly organized market for a homogeneous product.

In the same year, quite independently (the two were unknown to each other), an eminent economist at Cambridge University in England, Joan Robinson, published a volume entitled *The Economics of Imperfect*

Harvard University News Office.

Ramsey & Muspratt, Cambridge.

Competition. These two books by Chamberlin and Robinson formed the basis of what we know today about economic behavior in monopolistically competitive markets.

Many Similar Ideas
Both authors stressed the joint influence of competitive and monopolistic elements in the determination of equilibrium. They pointed out that the distinguishing characteristics in imperfect markets are product differentiation and consumer preferences, rather than the absence of a large number of sellers. This makes each firm a "partial" monopoly, regardless of the number of competitors in its industry.

Although there were some differences in their views, both used the critical concepts of marginal cost and marginal revenue, and both showed how the firm maximizes profits by

equating these two variables. They also discussed short- and long-run equilibrium, barriers to entry into an industry, and the role of normal profits. Chamberlin, in addition, provided a substantial analysis of the role of advertising.

One year later, in 1934, a German economist named Heinrich Von Stackelberg published a book entitled *Marktform und Gleichgewicht (Market Structure and Equilibrium),* which emphasized the interdependence of firms and the problems of oligopoly. One of Stackelberg's chief conclusions was that a democratic state cannot eliminate market structures that fail to achieve a socially desirable equilibrium, whereas authoritarian states can. He thus developed a defense of government intervention in the economy in order to bring about the results deemed best by society.

---

3. Why should firms in monopolistic competition spend so much money on advertising if much of it has canceling effects?

4. Is the kinked demand curve an objective fact of the marketplace, or is it a subjective phenomenon in the mind of each oligopolist? Explain.

5. Why is there a tendency toward some type of externally imposed price decision in oligopoly? What are some examples?

6. The need for self-protection is one reason often given for the rise of labor unions, consumer cooperatives, and agricultural cooperatives. Can you explain why in the light of this chapter?

7. One could easily argue that it is more *ethical* for people to cooperate than to compete. Therefore, why not business firms? Do you agree?

8. "Economic theory is unrealistic because it assumes that firms seek to maximize profits. Yet we know that in reality this assumption is not a valid one." Evaluate.

Leaders in Economics
Herbert Alexander Simon   1916–

Decision Doctor's R_X: "Satisfice," Not Maximize

The Nobel prize is not awarded in the fields of psychology, sociology, public administration, computer science, or applied mathematics. If the award were granted in any of these disciplines, Herbert Simon would already have received it. Instead, he is a recipient of the 1978 Nobel Prize in Economic Science.

A professor of psychology and computer science at Pittsburgh's Carnegie-Mellon University, Simon has been called by other leading scholars a "renaissance man" and "one of the few geniuses in the social sciences."

Simon is best described as a behavioral scientist. His chief interest and most of his pioneering research has dealt with the mental operations of decision making. This has led him to the study of rational behavior, human thinking processes, the creation of artificial intelligence through computer technology, and related activities.

Simon carried some of his research into economics, where he challenged one of its most basic assumptions. Economic man has to maximize for satisfaction. "That," according to Simon, "is an extravagant definition of rationality."

Wide World Photos.

According to the conventional view of economics, he wrote in his widely read book, *Administrative Behavior*:

Economic man has a complete and consistent system of preferences that allows him to choose among the alternatives open to him; he is always completely aware of what these alternatives are; there are no limits on the complexity of computations he can perform in order to determine which alternatives are best; probability calculations are neither frightening nor mysterious to him.

This assumption, according to Simon, "bears little discernible relationship to the actual or possible behavior of flesh-and-blood humans."

Simon thus criticizes the traditional microeconomic belief that firms seek to obtain maximum profits. In the modern corporation, he concludes, decision making is diffused among many departments and individuals. This often leads to conflict and dissension, not harmony. Therefore, corporate policy makers are forced to make decisions without enough accurate information to maximize profits. As a result, they aim for "satisfactory" profits rather than maximum profits. They seek to *satisfice* rather than maximize.

Most economists, however, find it difficult to accept this view. That is, they prefer to adhere to the traditional notion that firms seek to maximize profits. Otherwise, many of the conclusions and policy decisions that emerge from economists' models, both in industry and government, would be difficult to justify.

9. Are prices determined by costs of production or are costs of production determined by prices? Discuss. (SUGGESTION Think in terms of both perfect and imperfect competition.)

10. Saturn Publishing Co. publishes two monthly magazines, called *Action* and *Brisk*. The company charges the same price for both magazines, but the sales of *Brisk* are about twice those of *Action*. Both magazines are among the leaders in their field, with combined sales of 5 to 6 million copies per month. In this sales range, therefore, the marginal cost of producing the two magazines is practically constant. Further, it has been established on the basis of previous pricing experiments in various markets that the elasticity of demand is equal for the two magazines at the present price.

Recently, the president of the company posed the question of whether it is consistent with profit maximization for the two magazines to carry the same price. The sales manager replied that in order for Saturn to maximize its profits,

it ought to charge a higher price for *Brisk* than for *Action*, since demand is greater for the former.

The president has called you in as a consulting economist to settle the question. Both the president and sales manager studied a considerable amount of economics while in college and are fairly familiar with such concepts as average revenue, marginal revenue, and marginal cost. Can you provide them with an analytical (graphic) solution to the problem?

11. In the book publishing business, it is inherent in the royalty arrangement that the publisher's pricing policy results in an economic conflict between the author and the publisher. Thus, in the great majority of cases, the author's royalty is a percentage of the total revenue that the publisher receives on the sale of the book. The publisher, however, determines the price of the book (and also incurs all costs of manufacturing, promotion, and distribution). It fol-

lows that *the price which maximizes profit for the publisher is higher, and the output lower, than the price and output which maximizes royalty payments for the author.* Why? Demonstrate this proposition graphically, using marginal analysis.

12. Scrumptious Pizza Co. operates a national chain of pizza parlors on a franchise basis. The company maintains a closely controlled, uniform set of production standards and selling prices as a condition for granting franchises. One of the unique features of Scrumptious pizzas is that they are made with a special blend of imported exotic cheeses.

Recent cost increases of cheeses, dough, and other ingredients have made it necessary for the company to consider a revision of its pricing and product policies for all its franchises. Three alternatives have been proposed:

(a) Increase price by some specified percentage, but maintain quantity and quality.

(b) Reduce quantity by some specified percentage, but maintain price and quality.

(c) Reduce quality, but maintain price and quantity.

The company hired an economic consulting firm to estimate the effects on profits of each of these choices. In its report, the consulting firm submitted the following *payoff matrix*—a table showing the probable level of profit that will result from each alternative and its associated sales level.

For example, suppose that the company chooses alternative A and that its average daily national sales are 6,000 pizzas. Then its *expected profit* on those sales will be 15 percent of $2,000, or $300. On the other hand, if its sales are

Alternatives, profits, and probabilities	Average daily national pizza sales			
	6,000	7,000	8,000	9,000
Alternative A				
Profit	$2,000	$2,800	$4,000	$4,200
Probability*	0.15	0.25	0.30	0.30
Alternative B				
Profit	$1,500	$3,000	$5,000	$5,100
Probability*	0.25	0.25	0.40	0.10
Alternative C				
Profit	$1,200	$2,500	$4,500	$4,800
Probability*	0.05	0.05	0.40	0.50

* The probability of an outcome is the likelihood of its occurrence. It can be expressed as a percentage by multiplying by 100.

7,000, its expected profit will be 25 percent of $2,800, or $700. By extending this idea, you can see that the total expected profit of any alternative is simply the *sum* of the separate expected profits that comprise it. (Notice that for each alternative, the probabilities must add to 1.0, or 100 percent.)

(a) Which alternative should the company choose, assuming that it wants to maximize its profit?

(b) Which alternative should the company choose in order to maximize its sales?

(c) Is it possible to have a situation in which one alternative would maximize profit and another would maximize sales, or must the same alternative do both? Explain.

Issue
Advertising: Which Half Is Wasted?

Dozens of advertising slogans have become part of American folklore, the subject of countless jokes and of almost as many solemn academic investigations, theories, and theses. In all capitalistic industrial nations advertising is pervasive, often accounts for a surprisingly high proportion of a firm's costs, and passes its messages into the language.

Advertising provokes passionate polemics from proponents and opponents. Is it a vital source of information about available products, processes, and services? Or is it a dishonest form of promotion that either misinforms or creates a legend about a company's offerings without saying much about the reality? Those are the main lines of the debate.

Some Important Issues
Social critics generally view advertising as wasteful. They argue that it does not increase aggregate demand, but is primarily a means of one company's holding or gaining a certain share of the market. In this view, advertising of, say, freezers is a cost passed on to consumers, who are unwittingly paying for the battle for market shares waged by General Electric, Westinghouse, Frigidaire, and so on.

But is that view really correct? Certainly, each of those companies wants to increase its market share. But an important reason for advertising a *class* of product is to increase total sales. Ideally, in the minds of the industry's management, promoting the *idea* of a freezer will make many consumers regard it as a virtual "necessity."

But what happens when almost every household has a freezer? At that point, aggregate freezer sales are determined chiefly by population growth, by family incomes, and by the frequency with which households replace freezers. At this stage it is probably true to say that advertising has only a small effect on aggregate sales.

Joel Gordon.

Unfortunately, nobody knows what proportion of advertising expenditures goes to increasing aggregate sales and what to maintaining or increasing individual firms' market shares. As an eminent English businessman once said: "I know that half my advertising expenditures are wasted, but I don't know which half."

For most products, advertising helps to reduce distribution as well as production costs because products that have rapid turnover produce more revenue per unit of storage space.

Advertising, Competition, and Truth
The need to advertise greatly increases the "cost of entry" for small firms seeking to break into markets dominated by large firms. In some industries, notably cosmetics and nonprescription pharmaceuticals, advertising and packaging costs are a high proportion of total costs. In those industries only large firms can afford the heavy cost of advertising, and small firms are barred, whatever the

virtues of their products. However, advertising expenditures are only *one* cost of entry. The costs of entry are also high in certain businesses that advertise rather little, notably steel, aluminum, and other industries that require heavy capital investment and large-scale production.

A further charge against advertising is more ethical than economic in nature. Too much advertising is untruthful—despite federal and state laws requiring truth in advertising. Critics point out that the laws have discouraged specific claims that cannot be proved, and have encouraged "mood" advertising. The "Pepsi Generation" or "Coke: It's the Real Thing" are examples. They tell us nothing about the product but a great deal about the people at whom the campaign is directed. Some critics of advertising charge that such slogans are even more dishonest than the old hard-sell, because they can be neither proved nor disproved.

Although the trend is disturbing, there are those who maintain that advertising can only persuade a consumer to make the first purchase. No amount of advertising, it is argued, can sell a product a second time if the product is unsatisfactory to consumers.

QUESTIONS
1. "Advertising serves to protect existing products. It is therefore a barrier to competition and a means of monopolizing markets." Evaluate.

2. The Federal Trade Commission has charged some oligopolistic firms with (a) conspiring to share markets and (b) maintaining market shares through advertising. Are these charges logically consistent?

3. Do you agree with those critics who contend that advertising should inform rather than persuade? Do you believe that advertising bamboozles consumers into buying unwanted things? Discuss.

Chapter 26

Hiring the Factors of Production: Marginal Productivity and Income Distribution

Chapter Preview

We have already learned that the $MC = MR$ rule determines the most profitable level of *output* for a firm. Can a similar rule be developed for determining the most profitable level of *input* for a firm?

What conditions determine a firm's demand for inputs or factors of production?

Can any social implications be drawn from the principles pertaining to the hiring of factors of production?

Until now we have focused on the behavior of firms in the *output* markets by examining the principles of product pricing and production under the three classes of market conditions—perfect competition, monopoly, and imperfect competition.

But to manufacture products, firms have to buy factors of production. In this chapter we concentrate on the behavior of firms in the *input* markets in order to see how principles of resource employment can be developed. This chapter thus counterbalances some of the previous chapters by establishing microeconomic principles pertaining to the input rather than output side of the market. As you will soon see, the most interesting aspect of input principles is the way in which they parallel the ones that we learned about earlier, so that the various pieces fit together like a large jigsaw puzzle.

The Marginal Productivity Theory: How the Firm Buys Factors of Production

If you were a business executive, what principles would guide you in deciding how much of a resource you should purchase? After all, buying too little can be just as unprofitable as buying too much. A major problem facing a firm that wishes to maximize its profits is to utilize precisely the right combination of inputs. In order to do this, management must understand the nature of its demand for resources.

The demand for any resource is a _derived demand_. That is, the demand for a resource is based on what a particular factor of production contributes to the product for which it is used. For example, the demand for steel is derived in part from the demand for automobiles. The demand for land in the heart of a city is derived from the demand for the office buildings and stores that will be built upon it. The demand for college professors is derived mostly from the demand for education as measured by college enrollments. As a general rule, and as we shall see shortly, the concept of derived demand embraces the following principles:

> Other things being equal, the quantity of a factor of production that a firm demands will depend on three things: (1) the productivity of the factor; (2) the value or price of the product which the factor is used to make; and (3) the price of the factor relative to the prices of other factors.

These principles make a good deal of practical sense. For instance, they tell us that, other things remaining constant:

1. An increase in the output of a factor of production relative to its input will result in a greater demand for that factor by the firms that use it.

2. If improvements in a product or reductions in its price create a greater demand for it, the need for the factors which produce or use that commodity will also increase (e.g., electronic computers and computer programmers).

3. If the price of a factor of production becomes cheaper relative to other factors, the quantity demanded of the lower-priced factor will increase if producers begin to substitute it for the more expensive inputs (e.g., labor-saving machinery relative to high-cost labor).

PHYSICAL INPUTS, OUTPUTS, AND REVENUES

Exhibit 1 gives us a more precise understanding of a firm's demand for an input. The first three columns show how, through the law of diminishing returns, the total and marginal physical products change when a variable input such as labor is applied to fixed inputs such as land and capital. The remaining columns of the table convert these physical data into revenues on the assumption that the firm is a perfect competitor in the sale of the product to which the variable factor is contributing. The price [column (4)], therefore, is assumed to be constant at $10 per unit.

The last two columns of the table are based upon the total revenue figures [column (5)]. They introduce two new terms: _marginal-revenue product (MRP)_, defined as the change in total revenue resulting from a unit change in input; and _average-revenue product (ARP)_, which is the ratio of total revenue to the quantity of the variable input employed.

Because the firm is operating under perfect competition in the input market, the supply of labor resources is so large that the firm cannot influence the price by buying or not buying. The firm can purchase as many units as it wants at the given price. Hence, _the marginal cost of the resource will be the same as its price._

THE MOST PROFITABLE LEVEL OF INPUT

When the revenue data from the table in Exhibit 1 are graphed, we get the curves shown in the charts. In this case, since we want to relate the firm's revenues to the labor that it hires, it is easier to plot the revenue curves against input rather than output on the horizontal axis. It also helps simplify matters a bit to assume, as stated in the footnote to column (1) of the table, that there are no fixed costs. That is, the firm's fixed factors of production are available free. This means that the firm's total variable costs are the same as its total costs, and therefore the TC curve emanates from the origin of the chart instead of from a point higher up on the vertical axis.

We now ask: What is the most profitable level of input for the firm? The answer depends on the _marginal cost of the input as compared to its marginal revenue product_—that is, the amount each additional unit of the input adds to the firm's total cost as compared to the amount it adds to total revenue.

For example, Chart (a) shows that when the marginal cost or price of labor is $20 per person, the most profitable input level is 4 persons. At this input the TC_1 curve in the chart is parallel to a tangent drawn to the TR curve at D. At the same time, Chart (b) shows that at this level of input the marginal cost of the factor MCF, which is the same as the price of the factor P_F, is equal to its marginal revenue product MRP. Similarly, at $39 per person, the firm's most profitable input is 3 persons. This is again determined in Chart (b), where $MCF = P_F = MRP$. On the other hand, if the factor were available free, the most profitable input level would be 5 persons, because the TC curve in Chart (a) would lie along the horizontal axis and would be parallel to a horizontal tangent drawn at the peak of the TR curve at E. Finally, at $61 per person, the firm would just be covering its variable costs, since TC_3 is tangent to TR. Hence, the most profitable input would, theoretically, be 2.2 persons, which is

Exhibit 1
Demand for a Resource by a Firm

PERFECT COMPETITION IN THE OUTPUT MARKET; PERFECT COMPETITION IN THE INPUT MARKET

(1) Units of variable factor, F (labor)	(2) Total physical product, TPP	(3) Marginal physical product, MPP Change in (2) Change in (1)	(4) Product price, P	(5) Total revenue, TR (2) × (4)	(6) Marginal-revenue product, MRP Change in (5) Change in (1)	(7) Average-revenue product, ARP (5) ÷ (1)
0	0		$10	$ 0		$?
1	4	4	10	40	$40	40.0
2	12	8	10	120	80	60.0
3	17	5	10	170	50	56.7
4	20	3	10	200	30	50.0
5	21	1	10	210	10	42.0
6	20	−1	10	200	−10	33.3

* Labor is assumed to be the only variable input. All other inputs are fixed and are available free. Therefore, total (labor) cost equals total variable cost.

Chart (a). *The most profitable input level occurs where the distance between the TR and TC curves is a maximum. This is where a tangent to the TR curve is parallel to the TC curve. (For example, at $20 per person, the most profitable input is 4 persons, because this is the input at which the tangent at D is parallel to the straight-line TC_1 curve.)*

Chart (b). *By following the vertical dashed lines downward, it can be seen that the most profitable input also occurs where the marginal cost of the factor (MCF) or its price (P_F) equals its marginal-revenue product (MRP). Therefore, given the marginal costs or prices of the factors of production, the firm will maximize its profits by hiring each factor of production up to the point where its $MCF = P_F = MRP$. The firm's demand curve for an input is thus the MRP curve up to the maximum point on the ARP curve. As the price of the input falls, the firm hires more of it by following its MRP curve.* (NOTE   *The MRP curve, like the marginal curves in previous chapters, is plotted to the midpoints of the integers on the horizontal axis, since it reflects the change in total revenue from one unit of input to the next.*)

TECHNICAL NOTE (OPTIONAL)   Here is a simple explanation in geometric terms. Each MCF curve in the lower chart is a graph of the *slope* of its corresponding TC curve in the upper chart. Likewise, the MRP curve in the lower chart is a graph of the *slope* of the TR curve in the upper chart. The input at which the slopes are equal (or at which a tangent in the upper chart is parallel to a TC curve) is the one at which net profit is maximized. You can verify these profit-maximizing principles by following the vertical dashed lines downward at each level of input.

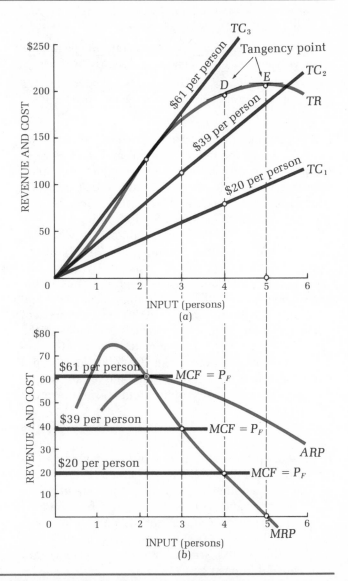

again determined in Chart (b), where $MCF = P_F = MRP$. (NOTE If you dislike the idea of measuring "fractions of persons," you can think of the horizontal axis as being scaled in terms of hours of labor time instead of numbers of persons.)

> Since the MCF or P_F line tells you the number of workers available to the firm at the particular wage, it is a *supply curve* of labor. The firm is thus faced with a horizontal supply curve of the factor in the input market just as it is faced with a horizontal demand curve for its product in the output market.

TWO IMPORTANT PRINCIPLES

Two important principles follow directly from our understanding of marginal concepts.

> When there is perfect competition in the input market, the marginal cost of an input will be the same as its price. Therefore:
>
> 1. The firm's demand curve for an input will be its *MRP* curve below the maximum point of its *ARP*.
>
> 2. The firm will maximize its profits by purchasing factors of production up to the point where $MCF = P_F = MRP$.

By this time you may have noticed a certain symmetry between the theory of input and the theory of output. For example, these two principles are analogous to the notion that in the output market a perfectly competitive firm finds that (1) its *MC* curve is its supply curve above the minimum point on its *AVC*, and (2) it maximizes its profit by producing to where its $MC = P = MR$. In fact, if you flip Chart (b) in Exhibit 1 upside down on its horizontal axis (or if you turn the book upside down and look through the back of the page while holding it up to the light), the *ARP* and *MRP* curves will resemble the *AVC* and *MC* curves of a firm in perfect competition. This is evidence of the fact that there is indeed a symmetry between the theory of perfect competition in the input and output markets, in that the curves in one market are the reciprocals of the corresponding curves in the other market.

In economic terms, why does the firm maximize its profit at the input level where $MCF = P_F = MRP$? Because at any input less than this the added cost of an additional unit is less than the added revenue, so it pays to hire another unit. At any input greater than this, the opposite is true. Hence, the fundamental principle of profit maximization—the $MC = MR$ rule which we learned in previous chapters—applies here as well. In addition, we can now state a principle of fundamental importance:

> In competitive input markets, the price paid to a factor of production will equal its marginal productivity. Therefore, each factor will be paid the value of what it contributes. This is called the *marginal productivity theory of income distribution*.

Demand for Inputs

We learned in our study of the theory of supply and demand that the market demand curve for a product is derived by summing the individual demand curves of all buyers in the market. A parallel situation exists in the market for input. Other things remaining the same, the market demand curve for a factor is derived by summing the individual demands or *MRP* curves of all firms in the market. Like any other demand curve, this aggregate *MRP* curve for a factor of production will be subject to two kinds of changes: (1) changes in demand and (2) changes in the quantity demanded.

CHANGES IN DEMAND

The market *MRP* curve for a given factor may shift from one position to another for several reasons:

1. *A Change in Demand for the Final Product* For example, a change in demand for houses will affect the price of houses and may also change the demand for lumber, bricks, carpenters, and other resources.

2. *A Change in Productivity* Improvements in the quantity and quality of the fixed factors of production will increase the productivity of the variable factor. Thus, workers who have more and better machines and land are more productive than those who do not.

3. *A Change in the Prices of Substitute or Complementary Factors* Some resources may be substitutable, some may be complementary, and some may be neither. Labor and machines provide typical examples of all three possibilities. Changes in the price of one relative to the other may encourage firms to use more or less of either or both. The choice depends on the proportions in which they must be used—such as the number of workers needed to operate a machine.

CHANGES IN THE QUANTITY DEMANDED: ELASTICITY OF DEMAND FOR FACTOR SERVICES

There are also conditions that will determine changes in the quantity demanded for a given factor. As you recall, these changes represent movements along the curve due to a change in price. Hence, these movements reflect the sensitivity or elasticity of demand for the resource. What determines this elasticity?

1. ***The Rate of Decline of Marginal Physical Product***   The rate at which the *MPP* curve declines as the variable factor is added to the fixed factors depends on the technological nature of the production process. The faster it declines, the more inelastic the resulting *MRP* curve will be and hence the less will be the change in the quantity of input demanded relative to a change in its price.

2. ***The Elasticity of Demand for the Final Product***   The greater the elasticity of demand for the final product, the more elastic the demand for the factors used in making it. For instance, if the demand for a final product is relatively elastic, a small increase in its price will result in a more than proportional decrease in the purchase of it. This will cause a relatively large drop in the quantity demanded of the resources that are used to produce it.

3. ***The Proportion of the Factor's Cost Relative to Total Production Cost***   The larger the cost of a factor of production relative to the total cost of the product, the more elastic the demand for the factor. For example, if labor costs are only 10 percent of the cost of a product, a 10 percent wage increase will raise production costs by 1 percent. Hence, the effect on the final price of the product should be small, and the quantity demanded of the factor should be relatively little affected. On the other hand, if labor costs are 90 percent of production costs, a 10 percent wage increase will have a more substantial impact on production costs as well as on final prices and sales. Therefore, the decrease in the quantity demanded of the factor is likely to be relatively large.

4. ***The Ease of Factor Substitutability***   The greater the number of different factors that can be substituted for one another in a given production process, the larger will be the elasticity of demand for any one of these factors. Thus, if copper, aluminum, and other light metals had equal conductive properties, the demand for each of them by the electrical industry would be highly elastic. But the fact is that copper is a superior conductor and hence the demand for it is relatively inelastic within its typical price ranges.

THE OPTIMUM ALLOCATION OF INPUTS

The foregoing principles apply to all factors of production that the firm may purchase. Let us assume, therefore, that the firm is buying two factors of production, labor and capital, and that these factors are substitutable for one another. There are two questions to be answered:

1. What is the least-cost combination of factors needed to produce a given output?

2. Which combination of factors yields the largest profits to the firm?

The first question is concerned with cost minimization; the second, with profit maximization.

Cost Minimization

If you were a manufacturer interested in producing a certain volume of output, in what proportion would you use the various inputs? The question is important because many different combinations will produce a given level of output, but only one combination is cheapest. Clearly, the cheapest combination depends on the relative prices of the inputs. As a manager, therefore, you would adhere to the following fundamental principle:

> *Least-cost principle*. The least-cost combination of inputs is achieved when a dollar's worth of any input adds as much to total physical output as a dollar's worth of any other input.

To illustrate, suppose that you are buying only two factors of production, A and B, in a perfectly competitive market. Letting MPP_A represent the marginal physical product of A, and P_A the price of A, and similarly for factor B, the equation of minimum cost is

$$\frac{MPP_A}{P_A} = \frac{MPP_B}{P_B} \qquad (1)$$

This indicates that if the price of an input rises, less of it should be used, thereby increasing its marginal product. Simultaneously, more of the other input should be used, thereby decreasing its marginal product. As an example, suppose that P_A and P_B are each $1, and at some given volume of output,

$$MPP_A = 10 \text{ units}$$
$$MPP_B = 8 \text{ units}$$

Assuming that you want to minimize costs at the prescribed output level, you should proceed as follows:

1. Buy $1.00 less of B, thereby reducing production by 8 units.

2. Buy $0.80 more of A, thereby increasing production by 8 units (= 4/5 of the marginal product of a dollar's worth of A).

3. Save $0.20.

This example shows how you would go about minimizing total costs for a given volume of output. Equation (1), of course, can be extended to include any number of inputs and corresponding prices. When all the ratios are equal, total costs are minimized at the established output volume. If a change should then occur in the price of one of the factors, the equality will no longer hold. This means that the cheaper factor will have to be substituted for more expensive ones until equality is restored.

Profit Maximization

The second problem concerns the question: Of all possible factor combinations, which one yields the largest profits for the firm? The answer has already been indicated and may now be expressed as a general principle:

> *Maximum-profit principle.* The most profitable combination of inputs is achieved by employing each factor of production up to the point where the marginal cost of the factor is equal to its marginal revenue product.

This principle was demonstrated in the charts in Exhibit 1. When the firm is hiring a resource in a perfectly competitive market, it will employ further units of the resource as long as the MRP of the factor is greater than its price (or marginal cost). Why? Because each additional unit adds more to the firm's total revenue than to its total cost. Conversely, the firm will release some units of the resource if the MRP of the factor is less than its price, because each reduction of one unit of the input lowers the firm's total cost by more than it lowers total revenue.

These ideas can be summarized with a formula. We know that the firm will maximize profits by hiring units of factor A up to the point where the marginal revenue product of that factor, MRP_A, is equal to its price, P_A:

$$MRP_A = P_A$$

If both sides of this equation are divided by P_A (or in other words, if P_A is "transposed" to the left side), then

$$\frac{MRP_A}{P_A} = 1 \qquad \text{(a)}$$

Similarly, the firm will buy units of factor B up to the point where the marginal-revenue product of that factor, MRP_B, is equal to its price P_B:

$$MRP_B = P_B$$

Dividing both sides by P_B (or "transposing" P_B to the left side),

$$\frac{MRP_B}{P_B} = 1 \qquad \text{(b)}$$

Since the two ratios are each equal to 1, equations (a) and (b) can be expressed as a single equation for maximum-profit equilibrium:

$$\frac{MRP_A}{P_A} = \frac{MRP_B}{P_B} = 1 \qquad \text{(2)}$$

Equation (2), like equation (1) for least cost, can be extended to include any number of inputs and their corresponding prices. In general, equation (2) defines the profit-maximizing or equilibrium conditions of a firm in a perfectly competitive input market. It shows that:

> The most profitable level of input for a firm in a perfectly competitive input market occurs where the firm earns the same increment in revenue *per dollar of outlay* from each of the factors that it hires, with each ratio equal to 1. That is, the firm hires each factor up to the point where the marginal revenue product of the factor equals its price.

It helps to translate these ideas into concrete terms. For example, suppose a firm was hiring two factors of production, labor L and capital C. If these factors were substitutable for one another, equation (2) says that the company will maximize profits in a perfectly competitive input market by hiring to the point where

$$\frac{MRP_L}{P_L} = \frac{MRP_C}{P_C} = 1$$

If this equality did not occur—that is, if the first ratio in this equation were greater than the second, and if the employment of capital were already in equilibrium at the point where $MRP_C/P_C = 1$, the firm would be earning more of an increment in revenue on its labor relative to the price of labor than it would be earning on its capital relative to the price of capital. Graphically, this means that the firm would be to the *left* of its optimum input point for labor. Hence, it would pay for the company to hire more workers, thereby reducing MRP_L until the ratios were equal. Conversely, if the first ratio were less than the second, the firm would be to the *right* of its optimum input point for labor. Therefore, it would pay for the company to reduce its number of workers, thereby raising MRP_L until the ratios were again equal.

In a more general sense, neither factor need be in equilibrium to start. You can think of the firm as juggling all its factors of production simultaneously until it achieves the desired equilibrium ratio, which is noted above.

Marginal Productivity, Income Distribution, and Equity

We have seen that when there is perfect competition in the input market, each firm will purchase factors of production up to the point where the price or marginal cost of the factor is equal to its marginal revenue productivity. Expressed in real terms, this means that each factor will be paid a value equal to what it contributes to the national output—the factor will be paid what it is "worth." This concept, as we have learned, is known as the *marginal productivity theory of income distribution.*

The theory itself was first introduced near the turn of the present century by the distinguished American economist, John Bates Clark. It was widely supported because it showed that a competitive (capitalistic) system distributed the national output in a socially "just" and "equitable" manner. However, over the years economists and social critics have pointed out three fundamental criticisms of this interpretation.

1. A large part of the market for input is imperfect rather than perfect. Thus, certain factors of production tend to be relatively immobile, and in some markets there may be only one or a few firms buying inputs instead of a large number of firms. In addition, union restrictions, patent controls, tariff barriers, and other limitations also create obstacles to a smoothly functioning market for inputs as envisioned in the competitive model.

2. Many production processes are complex. When a variety of factors are employed, it is usually impossible to divide the total output into the amounts contributed by each class of factors such as labor and capital, much less by each "subfactor," such as each type of worker.

3. Terms such as "just" and "equitable" involve normative rather than positive concepts—what *ought* to be rather than what *is.* Their meanings may also vary from time to time and from place to place according to the customs and beliefs of society. Thus, in a philosophical sense it is not necessarily "just" that a person who is twice as productive as another should be paid twice as much. It might equally well be argued, for example, that it is "just" for a family of six to receive twice as much as a family of three—regardless of their relative productivities. In other words, the *normative* question of what constitutes a just distribution of income is quite different from the *positive* question of what specific steps should be taken to alter the distribution of income. The former is a philosophical question; the latter is an economic one.

We can therefore conclude with an important generalization:

The central idea of the marginal productivity principle is that an employer will not pay more for a unit of input—whether it be a person, or an acre of land, or a dollar's worth of borrowed capital—than it is worth to the firm. The employer will continue to acquire an input as long as each unit purchased adds more to the firm's total revenue than it adds to its total cost. Because we assume in theory that the units can be infinitesimally small, the net result is that the employer's profit is maximized where the added (or marginal) cost of the input equals its added (or marginal) revenue product.

In short, the marginal productivity principle is correct in the sense that it can be deduced logically from given assumptions. However, it should be understood for what it is: *a guide for maximizing a firm's profits in the input market under prescribed market conditions.* (See *Leaders in Economics,* page 461.)

What You Have Learned

1. The marginal productivity theory explains how a firm purchases its inputs in the factor market. In general, a firm's demand for any factor of production is a derived demand based on the productivity of the factor, the price of the final product, and the price of the factor relative to the prices of other factors.

2. If a firm's production function and the market prices of the resources it purchases are given (i.e., if it is hiring factors in a perfectly competitive market for inputs), it can seek the factor combination which assures (a) least cost and (b) maximum profit. The least-cost combination requires that the marginal physical product per dollar spent on every factor be equal. The maximum-profit combination requires that the marginal revenue product per dollar spent on all factors be equal to 1. Both equilibrium conditions can be achieved simultaneously.

3. The aggregate *MRP* curve for a factor of production is determined by summing the individual *MRP* curves. Like any demand curve, the *MRP* curve is subject to changes in demand for a factor and to changes in the quantity demanded. The latter is based on a change in price and reflects the elasticity of demand for a factor.

4. The marginal productivity theory of income distribution is a guide for profit maximization in the input market. It does not purport to say what pattern of income distribution is "just" or "equitable," for this is a normative question based on philosophical rather than economic considerations.

For Discussion

1. *Terms and concepts to review:*

derived demand

marginal-revenue
    product

average-revenue product

marginal productivity
theory of income
distribution

2. What analogies do you see between a firm in the output market and a firm in the input market with respect to each of the following: (a) the profit-maximizing rule; (b) marginal cost and average variable cost, and marginal-revenue product and average-revenue product.

3. Distinguish between a change in demand for an input and a change in the quantity demanded. What are the causes of each?

4. "The way to eliminate poverty and unemployment is through minimum-wage legislation. By raising the minimum wage, workers are given more purchasing power. This creates a greater demand for goods and services, thereby putting unemployed people to work." Evaluate this argument using the graphic tools employed in this chapter. (HINT   There are *two* issues involved here. Can you identify them?)

5. "The marginal productivity theory of income distribution is a *fair* theory because it demonstrates that each worker gets what he or she deserves." Evaluate.

6. "It is meaningless to say that the equilibrium factor price will equal the marginal-revenue product, since the latter varies with the number of factor units employed." Comment. Rephrase if necessary.

Leaders in Economics
John Bates Clark   1847–1938

Marginal Productivity Theory

It is the purpose of this work to show that the distribution of the income of society is controlled by a natural law, and that this law, if it worked without friction, would give to every agent of production the amount of wealth which that agent creates.

In these words, J. B. Clark outlined the general plan for his book, *The Distribution of Wealth,* which was published in 1899. This was the first American work in pure economic theory. Prior to that time, American economists were generally interested in the socioeconomic problems of their period and with the achievement of social reforms. Clark's book still stands as one of the greatest works in economic theory published in any language.

Clark began by asking: "Is there a natural law according to which the income of society is divided. . . ? If so, what is that law? This is the problem which demands solution."

As he proceeded to answer this question, he developed a distinction between static and dynamic forces in the economy. The static forces, he said, are the result of "universal economic laws" which are always applicable to the economy, such as the law of diminishing returns, the law of diminishing utility, and so on. But the dynamic forces that exist in society—changes in population, capital, production techniques, and forms of industrial organization—are constantly causing fluctuations in production, prices, and the like. In Clark's words,

Historical Pictures Service, Chicago.

"Static forces set the standards, dynamic forces produce the variations." He went on to say:

Each unit of labor . . . is worth to its employer what the last unit produces. When the force is complete, no one body of a thousand men can withdraw without lessening the product of the whole society by the same amount that we have attributed to the one that we last set working. The effective value of any unit of labor is always what the whole society with all its capital produces, minus what it

would produce if that unit were to be taken away. This sets the universal standard of pay. A unit of labor consists, in the supposed case, of a thousand men, and the product of it is the natural pay of a thousand men. If the men are equal, a thousandth part of this amount is the natural pay of any one of them.

Actually, Clark had much in common with his great British contemporary, Alfred Marshall. Each used the static analysis, but Marshall was more realistic and analyzed many problems of dynamics and change. Clark, however, raised marginal utility analysis to its highest standard of perfection, and in so doing he founded a "marginalist school" of thought which established a pattern for teaching and research in economics that exists to this day.

The modern version of the marginal productivity theory is essentially due to Clark's treatment. His theory of wages is a demand theory which assumes a given quantity of labor in its analysis of the marginal product of labor. It was this theory, with its impeccable logic, that was widely employed by others to support the contention that a (perfectly competitive) capitalistic system distributes incomes in a "just" manner according to what each of the factors contributes.

In later decades, the development of the theory of imperfect competition and the growing power of labor unions made some of the unreal assumptions of Clark's theory more apparent.

Reading
Hicks on Wages

The essential features of the marginal productivity theory have been known to economists since the late nineteenth century. However, a systematic exposition of the theory, with an explanation in terms of relative factor shares, was first presented by a distinguished British economist and Nobel laureate, J. R. Hicks, in a book entitled The Theory of Wages *(London: Macmillan & Co. Ltd., 1932). The following selection is taken (with the kind permission of the publisher) from this classic work.*

When an entrepreneur has to choose between two different methods of producing a given output, he may be expected to choose that which costs least. For, at any rate in the first place, anything which reduces his costs will raise his profits. If employers are not using the cheapest method of production available to them, they have an incentive to change; and so there is no equilibrium.

It is this condition of minimum cost of production per unit of output which leads us directly to the law of marginal productivity. For if we suppose the prices of all the factors of production to be given, the "least cost" combination of factors will be given by the condition that the marginal products of the factors are proportional to their prices. If the

<u>marginal product of factor A</u>
price of A

is greater than

<u>marginal product of B</u>
price of B

then this means that it will be to the advantage of the entrepreneur to use a method of production which uses a little more of A and a little less of B, since in that way he will get a larger product for the same expenditure, or (what comes to the same thing) he will get an equal product at a lower cost.

Wide World Photos.

British economist and Nobel laureate, J. R. Hicks.

This condition of the proportionality of marginal products is simply another means of expressing the necessity that the method employed in a position of equilibrium should be the cheapest method of reaching the desired result. No new principle whatever is introduced; so that in practical applications we can work with the condition of minimum cost, or with the condition of the proportionality of marginal products—whichever seems more significant in the particular case.

It must, however, be observed that the above condition only states that the marginal products are proportional to the prices of the factors—it does not say that the prices *equal* the values of the marginal products. So far as the choice of methods of production is concerned, it appears that the prices of the factors might exceed,

or all fall short of, the values of the marginal products—so long as they do it in the same proportion. But if this were to be the case, it would be possible for the entrepreneur to increase his profits by expanding or contracting production without changing his methods. The condition of equality between price and cost of production would not be satisfied.

However, there can be no full equilibrium unless the wages of labor equal its marginal product; because, if this equality is not attained, someone has open to him an opportunity of gain which he is not taking. Either employers will be able to find an advantage in varying the methods of production they use, or investors and other owners of property will be able to benefit themselves by transferring the resources under their control from one branch of production to another. But we cannot go on from this to conclude that this equality of wages and marginal products will actually be found in practice; for the real labor market is scarcely ever in equilibrium in the sense considered here. In actual practice, changes in methods are continually going on; and resources are continually being transferred from one industry to another, or new resources being put at the disposal of industry, which are not uniformly distributed among the different branches of production. This ceaseless change is partly a consequence of changes in the ultimate determinants of economic activity—those things which we have to take as the final data of economic enquiry—changes in tastes, changes in knowledge, changes in the natural environment, and in the supply and efficiency of the factors of production generally. As these things change, so the marginal product of labor changes with them; and these changes in marginal productivity exert pressure, in one direction or the other, upon the level of wages.

Chapter 27

Determination of Factor Prices

Chapter Preview

Why do workers in some occupations earn
less than workers in others? Why do some
industries establish wage levels by
collective bargaining between management
and labor?

Is there any connection between the rent
paid for land and the prices received for the
products of land?

What is interest? Why does it exist?

What are the sources of profit? How are
profits determined?

Most of our nation's income consists of wages and
salaries paid to workers. The rest of the economic pie
is sliced into rent, interest, and profit. These incomes
are the payments made to resource owners who sell
their factors of production—labor, land, capital, and
entrepreneurship—in the economy's markets.

What determines the levels of wages, rent, interest,
and profit? In this chapter we seek answers to these
questions by deriving basic principles. We shall find
that many of the ideas from previous chapters dealing
with supply and demand, competition, market structures, cost and demand curves, and the like play an
integral role in determining factor prices.

What will not be so apparent, however, is that although the theory of wages, and to a somewhat lesser
extent the theory of rent, are fairly well established in
modern economics, the theories of interest and profit
involve various unsettled questions that are the subject of more advanced discussions. We shall not delve
into these issues in much detail, since our purpose at
this time is to concentrate on the main features of the
various theories rather than on the controversies that
surround them.

Theory of Wages

Wages constitute about three-fourths of the national
income. But what determines their level? Let us begin
with some definitions.

Wages are the price paid for the use of labor and are usually expressed as time rates, such as so much per hour, day, or week, or, less frequently, as piece rates of so much per unit of work performed.

Labor, as defined in economics, means all personal services, including the activities of wage-workers, professional people, and independent business-persons. "Laborers" are thus workers who may receive compensation not only in the form of hourly wages, but also in the form of annual salaries, bonuses, commissions, and the like. Our interest in this chapter is with wages as defined above, especially wages expressed as time rates.

Money wages are the amount of money received per unit of time, such as cash wages received on an hourly, weekly, or monthly basis. In contrast, *real wages* are the quantity of goods that can be bought with money wages. Real wages thus depend on money wages and on the prices of the goods that are purchased with money wages. For instance, it is quite possible for your money wages to increase while your real wages rise, remain the same, or fall, depending on what happens to prices.

THE TRENDS OF WAGES AND PRODUCTIVITY

Most of us know that wages differ between occupations and individuals. Nevertheless, it is reasonable to expect a long-run relationship between the wages of workers and their productivity. Over the years both should increase at roughly the same rate. In reality, wage gains have often outstripped increases in productivity since the late 1960s, as shown in Exhibit 1.

The gains in productivity are due partly to im-

Exhibit 1
Output and Earnings in the Private Business Sector

Wages and productivity used to increase at about the same rate over the years. But the gap began to widen in the late 1960s.

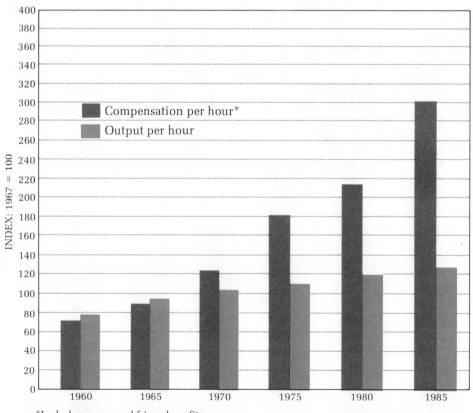

*Includes wages and fringe benefits.

SOURCE: U.S. Department of Labor.

provements in the quality of labor, which result from better education, training, and health, and partly to the remarkable growth in the quantity and quality of the other factors of production with which labor works. Since an economy's real income is the same as its real output, its income per worker is likely to keep pace with its output per worker over the long run if its markets are reasonably free and competitive. It follows, therefore, that if income and output per worker do not keep pace, we should look for reasons why.

SOME WAGE-DETERMINATION MODELS

How are wages determined in the market at any given time? The answer depends on the type of market model that is assumed to exist in a particular situation. There are several interesting possibilities.

Competitive Model: Many Buyers, Many Sellers

Suppose that there is such a large number of employers hiring a certain type of labor and such a large

number of employees selling it that no single employer or employee can influence the wage rate. We would then have a competitive model of wages as illustrated in Exhibit 2.

In Chart (a) the downward-sloping aggregate demand curve for this type of labor represents the sum of the individual MRPs of the buyers. The upward-sloping aggregate supply curve reflects the fact that if these workers are already employed, the firms buying labor will have to offer higher wages to attract workers from other occupations and localities. The equilibrium wage at W and equilibrium quantity at M are determined by the intersection of the labor supply and labor demand curves.

In Chart (b) the buying firm is faced with a perfectly elastic supply curve of labor at the market wage. The horizontal supply curve represents the marginal cost or price of the factor, as we learned earlier in the study of marginal productivity analysis. Since the firm's most profitable input is obtained by following the MCF = MRP rule, management will hire N units of labor at the corresponding market wage of W per unit.

What analogies do you see between this model and that of a perfectly competitive seller in the output market?

Exhibit 2
A Competitive Model of Wage Determination

In the competitive model, the wage at W and the corresponding quantity at M for a particular type of labor are determined in the market through the free interaction of supply and demand. Each firm can buy all the labor it wants at the market wage. Therefore, the supply curve of this

factor to any individual firm is perfectly elastic and is the same as the marginal cost of the factor. The firm's most profitable input at N and the corresponding wage at W are determined where the company's MCF = MRP.

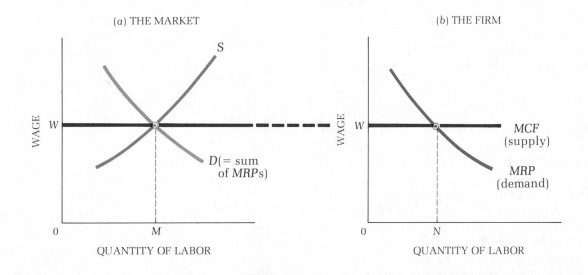

Monopsony Model: One Buyer, Many Sellers

A _monopsony_ is a market structure consisting of a single buyer and many sellers of a good or service. Hence, it may be thought of as a "buyer's monopoly." An example would be a firm that is the sole employer in a company town, as has been the case in many mining communities. Similarly, in some farm areas a single food-processing plant dominates employment for many miles around.

A monopsony wage model is shown in Exhibit 3. As you can see from the cost schedule, the monopsonist must offer a higher wage rate or price per unit for _all_ units in order to acquire more labor (just as a monopolist in the output market must charge a lower price per unit for _all_ units in order to sell more products). The result is that the marginal cost of labor will be greater than the average cost at each input, as shown in the chart.

The most profitable input level is determined, as always, where $MCF = MRP$. Thus, the monopsonist will employ L units of labor and pay the lowest possible price for that quantity of labor, namely LT per unit. As a result, input, as compared to the amount at N, will be restricted and the price per unit, as compared to the wage NW, will be lower than it would have been if the monopsonist were a perfectly competitive buyer in the input market.

What analogies do you see between this model and that of a pure monopolist in the output market?

Monopoly Model: One Seller, Many Buyers

Suppose that a labor monopoly, such as a craft union whose members include all skilled workers in a particular trade, such as printing or plumbing, faces a market composed of many buyers of that particular skill. What level of wages and what corresponding volume of labor output will result?

The model is illustrated in Exhibit 4. The curves S and D represent the normal supply and demand curves for labor in a free market. The equilibrium quantity of labor will be at N and the equilibrium wage at W. A monopoly union, however, will seek to restrict the supply of its labor in order to attain a higher wage for its members. The union will thus shift the supply curve to the left from S to S'. This will reduce the equilibrium quantity of labor to the level at N' and raise the equilibrium wage to the level at W'.

This analysis helps explain why some labor unions, especially certain craft unions, have established long apprenticeship requirements, high initiation fees, and similar obstacles to entry. Their motives, at least partly, have been to curb the supply of labor in the market and to boost wage rates. Of course, there are

---

Exhibit 3

A Monopsony Model of Wage Determination

In order to acquire more labor, the monopsonist must offer a higher price per unit for all units hired. The average cost of labor will thus rise, and the marginal cost of labor will be different from the average cost.

COST SCHEDULE OF LABOR FACTOR

Units of labor factor, F	Average cost of labor factor (= wage rate or supply price of labor), ACF or S	Total cost of labor factor, TCF	Marginal cost of labor factor, MCF
1	$5	$ 5	
2	6	12	$ 7
3	7	21	9
4	8	32	11
5	9	45	13

The MCF curve lies above the average-cost curve ACF, which is also the labor-supply curve S. By hiring to the point where $MCF = MRP$, the monopsony firm employs L units and pays the lowest price per unit consistent with that volume of input, namely LT.

The monopsony firm thus restricts its employment of resources and pays a lower price per unit of input than it would if it were a perfectly competitive buyer in the factor market.

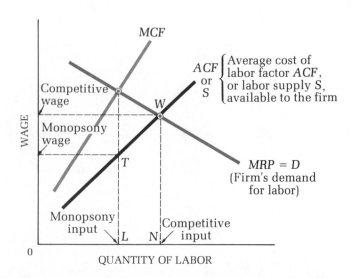

also unions that do not seek to maximize wages. They may try to maximize membership instead so that they can wield more market power. In such cases, the model in Exhibit 4 would have to be modified to reflect these objectives.

Bilateral Monopoly Model: One Buyer, One Seller

A *bilateral monopoly* is a market structure in which a monopsonist buys from a monopolist. The simplest version, which *combines the main features of the previous monopsony and monopoly models*, is shown in Exhibit 5. Both the buyer and the seller are seeking to maximize their net benefits from the transaction. Therefore, if the two parties can agree on a given quantity to be exchanged, say the amount at M, the monopsonist will wish to purchase that quantity for the lower price at U, while the monopolist will want to sell that quantity for the higher price at V. What will be the transaction price?

Economists have been trying to solve this problem for decades. Some years ago a remarkable series of controlled experiments was conducted by an economist and a psychologist at Pennsylvania State University, in which many pairs of students were involved in bargaining for real money. Out of these and other studies, there has emerged a fair amount of agreement that although the quantity figure may be determinate in a bilateral monopoly model, the price level is not. Thus, even if the two traders agree on a quantity that maximizes their *joint* net benefits, the highest price acceptable to the buyer will give the whole net benefit to the seller, and vice versa.

The solution, therefore, is logically indeterminate. That is, the price will end up somewhere between the monopsony wage rate at U and the monopoly wage rate at V, but the theory does not predict the precise level within this range.

Which Model Exists Today?

All these models are applicable to the modern economy. In the input markets, just as in the output markets, there are *degrees* of competition and monopoly. Hence, these models, or mixtures and modifications of them, can be useful in describing fundamental patterns of wage determination.

The majority of the American labor force is not organized in any labor union. Among agricultural and white-collar workers, for example, union membership is relatively slight and the situation conforms roughly to the competitive model. On the other hand, in some of the service industries, significant segments of the labor force are unorganized and relatively immobile

Exhibit 4
A Monopoly Model of Wage Determination

A monopoly union, such as a craft union composed of skilled workers like plumbers or electricians, will behave like any monopolist. It will restrict the supply of labor in order to command a higher price or wage rate as compared to the competitive case.

The curves S and D represent the free-market or unrestricted supply and demand curves. By restricting the supply of labor from S to S', the monopoly union reduces the equilibrium output from N to N', and raises the equilibrium wage from W to W'.

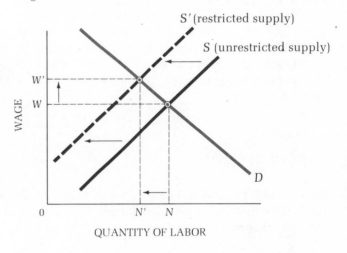

Exhibit 5
A Bilateral Monopoly Model of Wage Determination

In a bilateral monopoly, both parties may agree on some quantity such as the amount at M, but the theory does not predict the exact price. At best, we can say that the price of labor will be somewhere between the monopsony's preferred wage at U and the monopoly's preferred wage at V.

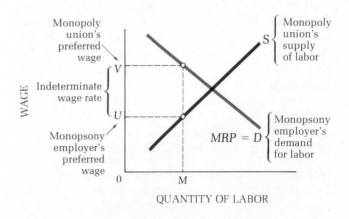

for long periods. Here, the monopsony model provides a good approximation—with an allowance for the legal minimum wage (which does not apply to many farmworkers).

Within the minority of the labor force that is organized into unions there are some segments, such as those in the garment and building trades, coal mining, and stevedoring, where the balance of power is with the unions rather than with the employers. The situation in those segments approximates that of monopoly. In most of manufacturing, transportation, and related sectors, strong unions face strong employers or employers' associations, and the bilateral monopoly model applies. In these cases, collective bargaining between unions and management is the chief means of settling issues. Thus, a wide variety of situations exists in American labor markets. These models or modifications of them can go a long way toward explaining and predicting the consequences of various outcomes.

Theory of Rent

In the early nineteenth century, a political controversy arose that was responsible for producing one of the great theoretical advances in the history of economics.

The place: England. The period: 1814–1816.

For most of the previous century, from 1711 to 1794, the price of "corn" (the generic name for all grains) had been extremely stable. But between 1795 and 1800 the price tripled, and it continued to rise over most of the following two decades. Since grain was a primary source of food, the rise in price created considerable political unrest. Many people starved, and employers reluctantly raised wages because of soaring food prices.

One group argued that the landlords were in a "conspiracy" to keep up corn prices by charging high rents to farmers. Another group, including the great English classical economist David Ricardo, argued exactly the opposite: Corn prices are high, said the "Ricardians," because of shortages resulting from the Napoleonic Wars. The high price of corn makes corn cultivation more profitable. This increases the demand for land and hence the price paid for the use of the land—namely, rent. If the price of corn fell, corn cultivation would become less profitable, and this would bring decreased rents. In Ricardo's own words:

"Corn is not high because a rent is paid, but a rent is paid because corn is high." Ricardo meant that the price of land is determined by demand and supply, and that rent is price-determined, not price-determining.

Ricardo and his followers carried on a vigorous battle for the repeal of the English Corn Laws (tariffs) of 1815 in order to bring more corn into the country, thereby increasing the supply and lowering the price.

ECONOMIC RENT IS A SURPLUS

Ricardo's argument was based on three assumptions:

1. The amount of land available is unchangeable.

2. Land used for growing corn has no alternative uses.

3. A landlord would prefer to receive any payment for the use of land rather than leave it idle and receive nothing.

In the language of modern economics, these statements amount to saying that the supply of land is perfectly inelastic, as illustrated in Exhibit 6, Chart (a).

The intersection of the supply curve S with the demand curve D establishes the equilibrium quantity at N and the corresponding equilibrium price at P. It follows that this price (or rent) per unit of land must be a surplus to the landlord. This is because the landlord would be willing to supply the same amount of land at a lower price, even down to a price of zero, depending on where the demand curve intersects the supply curve. We call this surplus "economic rent" and define it as follows:

Economic rent is any payment made to a factor of production, in an industry in equilibrium, in excess of the factor's supply price or opportunity cost—that is, in excess of the minimum amount necessary to keep that factor in its present occupation.

Note that this definition restricts the concept of economic rent to an equilibrium surplus. This is because some factors may receive surpluses while they are in a transitory stage from one equilibrium position to another and because such surpluses may exist even in long-run equilibrium. It follows that the entire rectangular area in Chart (a), OPRN, represents the total economic rent received by the landlord.

Originally, "rent" meant the payment made for the use of land. But economists eventually realized that any factor of production, not just land, may receive a surplus above its opportunity cost. Hence, they coined the expression "economic rent" to represent all such differentials. (Sometimes the term "producer's surplus" is also used.)

Exhibit 6, Chart (b), is a hypothetical model of the supply and demand for bus drivers under perfect competition. According to the chart, a quantity of bus drivers equal to 0N would each receive a wage of 0P. But only for the Nth bus driver is this wage the supply price or opportunity cost. Each of the others that make

Exhibit 6
The Determination of Rent

Chart (a). *The landlord's opportunity cost is zero. Hence, the total amount received, the area 0PRN, represents economic rent, since the landlord would be willing to supply the same amount of land at zero rent.*

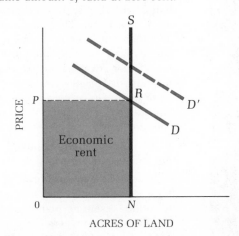

ACRES OF LAND

Chart (b). *The total amount received by the bus drivers is the area 0PRN. However, only the "Nth" driver is getting an opportunity cost. Those to the "left" are getting more than their opportunity costs, as represented by their total economic rent, the triangular area KPR.*

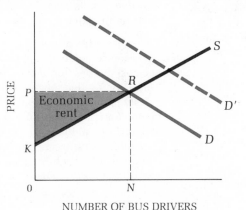

NUMBER OF BUS DRIVERS

up the amount 0N would have been willing to work for less as determined by the height of the segment KR of the supply curve. Therefore, all the other drivers are receiving a total economic rent equal to the triangle KPR. You should be able to see from the dashed lines in both diagrams in Exhibit 6 that if the supply curve remains the same, an increase in demand from D to D' will enlarge the amount of economic rent, whereas a decrease in demand will reduce it.

This leads to an important conclusion:

Economic rent arises because the owners of the various units of a particular factor of production differ in the eagerness with which they are willing to supply those units. That is, the owners differ in their supply price. If all owners had equal supply prices, the supply curve would be perfectly elastic and there would be no economic rent.

Thus, in Exhibit 6, Chart (b), the area of economic rent would diminish to zero if the supply curve were to pivot on point R so as to approach the horizontal.

Economic rent is a concept similar to that of net revenue, since both represent surpluses. The difference between them is merely a matter of reference. When the surplus is received by a factor of production, it is called economic rent; when the surplus is incurred by a firm, it is referred to as net revenue.

IS RENT A COST OR A SURPLUS? WHICH VIEWPOINT?

Contrary to Ricardo's assumptions, units of land often have alternative uses and are of different quality. This explains why the demand for an acre of real estate in the heart of a city's business district may be quite different from the demand for an acre of farm land or an acre of desert land elsewhere in the country. These differences in demand also account for the differences in rent that are paid by the users of the land.

Are these rents a cost or a surplus? The answer depends on the point of view you take. From the firm's viewpoint, rent is the price that must be paid to attract land from its alternative uses. Hence, rent is a *cost*. From the economy's viewpoint, rent is the value that society receives for making available the land provided free by nature, regardless of the alternative uses to which the land is put and the rents that are paid. Hence, rent is a *surplus*. The fallacy of composition thus plays a role in the interpretation of rent from the individual versus social viewpoint. (See *Leaders in Economics*, page 470.)

Theory of Interest

If you borrow money to buy a car or a house, or to pay your tuition, you must pay interest to the lender for the money borrowed. Therefore, interest is defined as the price paid for the use of money or loanable funds over a period of time.

Interest is always expressed as a percentage of the amount of the loan. Thus, an interest rate of 10 percent means that the borrower pays 10 cents per $1 borrowed per year, or $10 per $100 borrowed per year, and so on.

Leaders in Economics
Henry George   1839–1897

The Single Tax

Henry George was born and raised in Philadelphia by middle-class, strongly devout parents. His religious background is reflected in the missionary tendency in all his writings. After quitting school at thirteen he worked as an errand boy and clerk, went to sea while in his teens, and then lived in stark poverty in San Francisco for a number of years.

He turned his attention to politics and ran for the state legislature, but was defeated by the opposition of the Central Pacific Railroad. George vehemently opposed the land subsidy the company was receiving from the state, and the speculation occasioned by the completion of the railroad between Sacramento and Oakland. At this time the seeds of his opposition to land monopoly and exploitation were sown. In 1871 he sketched the bare outlines of his later theory in a pamphlet entitled *Our Land and Land Policy,* but did not elaborate the theme until 1879, when his famous book *Progress and Poverty* was published.

Ironically, George had difficulty in finding a publisher. But the book turned out to be a work that brought him great fame, for it was an immediate success both at home and abroad. Many millions of copies have been sold throughout the world, and it is undoubtedly the most successful popular economics book ever published.

Culver Pictures.

The central concept in George's writing is that poverty is caused by the monopolization of land by the few, who deprive the rest of the people of their birthright. Since land is endowed by nature, all rent on land is unearned surplus, and the injustice to the landless grows when, as a result of natural progress, the value of land is augmented and rent increases correspondingly. The solution, therefore, is the confiscation of rent by the government through a *single tax* on land.

No other taxes would be necessary, according to George.

Famous economists, including Alfred Marshall and J. B. Clark, debated with Henry George over the single-tax issue. Their conclusions, and those of later economists, suggested that a land tax would probably have fewer adverse effects on the allocation of society's resources than other taxes. However, a single tax on land alone would have three major shortcomings:

1. It would not produce enough revenue to meet governments' needs.

2. It would be unjust because surpluses or economic rent may accrue to other resource owners besides landlords if the owners can gain monopolistic control over the sale of their resources in the marketplace.

3. It might be impossible to administer because it does not distinguish between land and capital—that is, between the proportion of rent that represents a surplus and the proportion that results from improvements made on the land.

George entered politics again in 1886 as a candidate of the Labor and Socialist parties for mayor of New York City. By this time he was enormously popular, and it took the maximum efforts of a coalition of parties to defeat him at the polls. He became a candidate again in 1897, but the strain was too much for him, and he died during the campaign at the age of 58.

Although interest is paid for the use of money, and money, in turn, is used to buy productive resources or capital goods, you will often hear reference made to the interest on capital. What this really means, of course, is the interest on the money represented by capital invested.

In our economy there are many different interest rates on debt instruments of all types—notes, bonds, mortgages, and so on. The rates vary according to several factors:

1. **Risk**—the chance of the borrower's defaulting on the loan.

2. **Maturity**—the length of time over which the money is borrowed.

3. **Liquidity**—the ease with which the creditor can convert the debt instrument into cash quickly without loss of value in terms of money.

4. **Competition**—the extent to which lenders compete for borrowers in particular money markets.

Other things being equal, interest rates will tend to vary directly with the first two factors and inversely with the second two. If you are not sure of the reasons for this, ask yourself how these factors would affect the interest rate that you would charge if you were a banker making loans.

As a result of the wide structure of interest rates, economists find it convenient to talk about "the" rate of interest. By this they mean the theoretical *pure interest rate* on a long-term riskless loan. This rate is best approximated by the interest on long-term negotiable government bonds.

Since the interest rate is the price of money or loanable funds, we shall see shortly that it is determined by the interaction of demand and supply forces. But first, what are the sources of demand and supply?

DEMAND FOR LOANABLE FUNDS

You and I and everyone else want money. But from the economy's viewpoint we fall into three major groups: businesses, households, and government.

1. *Businesses* Businesses are the largest source of demand for loanable funds. Corporations borrow money because they want to invest the funds in new capital goods, including the building up of inventories. A firm undertakes such investments as long as it expects to receive a yield that exceeds the cost of its funds. The expected yield or rate of return on investment projects can be depicted by the marginal revenue product (*MRP*) curve of capital expressed in terms of percentages —as illustrated in Exhibit 7. You can see from the diagram that the *MRP* curve should be viewed as a cumulative investment demand curve. It tells you, for example, that the firm can earn 18 percent on the first $200,000 of investment and 16 percent on the next $100,000. Therefore, it can earn *at least* 16 percent on the first $300,000. Similarly, it can earn *at least* 14 percent on the first $400,000 invested. Interpreted in this way, we see that since the rate of interest on borrowed funds is also expressed in percentage terms, *any point on the curve shows the amount of investment the firm will undertake at various interest rates.* For example, at a 10 percent interest rate on borrowed funds, the firm will demand $600,000 for investment. If the rate is lowered to 8 percent, the firm will increase the amount of funds demanded for investment to $700,000.

The diagram thus suggests a familiar marginal principle:

Under competitive conditions, a firm will demand loanable funds up to the point where the capital purchased with those funds is such that its marginal revenue productivity is equal to the interest rate (or price) that must be paid for the loan. *The MRP curve of capital is therefore the firm's demand curve for capital.*

2. *Households* Households are the second major source of demand for loanable funds. Households borrow to buy automobiles, washing machines, vacation trips, homes, and so forth. There is some limited evidence to suggest that the household demand curve for funds is downward-sloping, indicating that households will tend to borrow larger amounts of money at lower interest rates.

3. *Government* The public sector is the third major source of demand for loanable funds. Governments at all levels—national, state, and local—borrow money to finance national defense, highways, schools, welfare, and so forth. The federal government often borrows to finance a budget deficit. Therefore, we cannot assume that the federal government's demand for loanable funds depends on the interest rate. However, there is ample evidence that this is not true for state and local governments; they tend to borrow more when interest rates are low than when they are high.

Exhibit 7
A Firm's Demand Curve for Capital

In a competitive market, the firm will demand loanable funds up to the point where the *MRP* of capital equals the interest rate or price. Thus, a decrease in the interest rate from 10 percent to 8 percent will increase the quantity of capital demanded from $600,000 to $700,000. (NOTE In macroeconomics, a firm's *MRP* curve of capital is called its marginal efficiency of investment, *MEI*.)

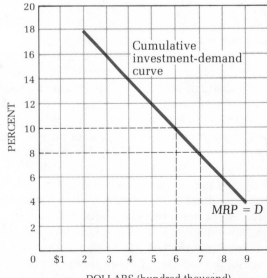

In general, as indicated by many studies:

> For all three sources—businesses, households, and government—taken together, the total market demand curve for loanable funds is downward-sloping. In addition, the demand curve is probably relatively inelastic. Therefore, changes in the interest rate are likely to result in less than proportional changes in the quantity demanded of loanable funds.

SUPPLY OF LOANABLE FUNDS

We must now turn our attention to the supply side of the picture and ask: What are the sources of loanable funds? There are two:

1. **The Central Banking System** A country's central bank (the Federal Reserve System in the United States) exercises a great deal of influence over the supply of money and hence the supply of loanable funds. This influence is intertwined with government economic measures, including taxation and spending policies, for combating recessions and inflations.

2. **Households and Businesses** These sectors of the economy supply some loanable funds to the money market out of their past or present savings. Household savings are that part of household income not spent on consumption. Business savings are mainly undistributed (plowed back) profits and depreciation reserves. Most businesses reinvest their savings in new plant and equipment, but some savings find their way into the money market. In general, very little is known about the effects of interest rates on household and business saving, but the influences are believed to be relatively slight.

DETERMINATION OF THE INTEREST RATE

The demand and supply forces generated by government, businesses, and households combine to determine the equilibrium interest rate in the market, as shown by the familiar supply and demand diagram in Exhibit 8. As mentioned above, the downward-sloping aggregate demand curve at any *given level of national income* reflects the willingness on the part of businesses to demand more funds for investment at a low interest rate than at a high interest rate. The upward-sloping supply curve, although it is based on much more complex and uncertain factors, *assumes* that household and business savers will make available somewhat larger quantities of loanable funds at a high interest rate than at a low one.

Actually, the determination of the interest rate has much deeper implications than is apparent from this simple supply and demand diagram. Further, govern-

ment monetary, taxation, and spending policies, as explained in macroeconomics, exercise a powerful influence on the forces that help determine the interest rate. As a result, the interest rate tends to be more stable and does not fluctuate as freely as do the prices of commodities that are determined by supply and demand in perfectly competitive markets.

THE RATIONING OR ALLOCATING FUNCTION OF INTEREST

Since the interest rate is a price, it performs the same rationing function as any other price by allocating the economy's scarce supply of funds among those who are willing to pay for them. Thus, in a free market, only the most profitable investment projects—those projects whose expected return or productivity is equal to or greater than the rate of interest—are undertaken. Any project whose prospective yield is below the interest rate is dropped from consideration. In this way the interest rate decides the critical question of *who* shall participate in the limited supply of capital. In so doing, the interest rate directs the growth of productive capacity in a capital-using economy.

Does the interest rate actually perform this function in our economic system? For the most part the answer is yes, but there are some qualifications:

> The interest rate in our economy is not the sole mechanism for allocating scarce funds—for two reasons:

Exhibit 8
Determination of the Interest Rate

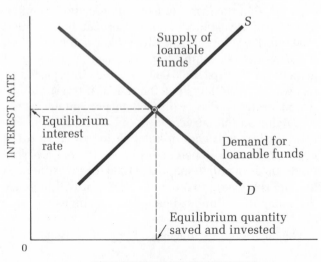

1. The government allocates some of the available capital to projects which it believes to be in the public interest, regardless of their financial profitability.

2. The unequal distribution of bargaining power among borrowers may enable many large firms to borrow on more favorable terms (at lower interest rates) than most small firms—even when the latter have relatively greater prospects for growth.

LOANABLE-FUNDS AND LIQUIDITY-PREFERENCE THEORIES

Two main theories of interest have been an integral part of economics since the 1930s. One is the loanable-funds theory; the other is the liquidity-preference theory.

The *loanable-funds theory of interest* holds that the interest rate is determined by the demand for, and supply of, loanable funds only, as distinguished from *all* money. The sources of demand for loanable funds are businesses that want to invest, households that want to finance consumer purchases, and government agencies that want to finance deficits. The sources of supply of loanable funds are the central banking system, which influences the supply of money (and hence loanable funds) in the economy; and households and businesses, which make loanable funds available out of their past or present savings.

The *liquidity-preference theory of interest* contends that people would rather hold their assets or wealth in the most liquid form, namely cash. This is necessary to satisfy three motives: the "transactions motive" to carry out everyday purchasing needs, the "precautionary motive" to meet possible unforeseen conditions, and the "speculative motive" to take advantage of a rise in interest rates. Accordingly, interest is the price or reward that must be paid to overcome liquidity preference. The equilibrium rate of interest is determined by the demand for, and supply of, money.

These two approaches should not be regarded as alternative theories of interest. Although they involve many complexities which are treated in greater detail in macroeconomic theory, they tend to supplement and complement each other rather than compete.

Theory of Profit

You have learned that *profit* or net revenue represents the difference between total revenue and total cost. Profit is thus a *residual* or *surplus* over and above normal profit, and it accrues to the entrepreneur after all costs, including explicit costs and implicit costs,

have been deducted from total revenue. What does economic theory tell us about the determinants of profit? What functions does profit perform?

The history of economics reveals a number of theories of how profits are derived. Today, three are generally recognized as being particularly relevant:

1. Friction and monopoly theory.

2. Uncertainty theory.

3. Innovation theory.

This system of classification is not all-inclusive and any one of the theories may contain elements of the others. The system merely emphasizes the main lines that have been followed in the course of thinking on the subject.

FRICTION AND MONOPOLY THEORY

By the end of the nineteenth century, the theory of a perfectly competitive economy was well on its way toward becoming a unified body of thought. Against this setting the noted American economist J. B. Clark (1847–1938) constructed a model of the economy that was intended to reconcile the static laws of theory with the dynamic world of fact.

According to Clark's "stationary" model (or the theory of perfect competition, as it is called today), the economy is characterized by a smooth and frictionless flow of resources, with the system automatically clicking into equilibrium through the free play of market forces. Changes may occur that cause a departure from equilibrium, but as long as resources are mobile and opportunities equally accessible (i.e., knowledge is perfect) to all economic entities, the adjustment to change and a new equilibrium will be accomplished quickly and smoothly. In this type of economic equilibrium all factors of production would receive their opportunity costs. The revenues of each enterprise would exactly equal its costs (including the implicit wages and interest of the owner), and no economic surplus or profit residual could result.

In the real world, however, surpluses do occur. According to the theory, they can be attributed only to the frictions (or obstacles to resource mobility) and monopoly elements that actually characterize a dynamic economy. In the long run, according to theory, the forces of competition would eliminate any surpluses, but the surpluses in reality recur because new frictions and new monopoly elements continually arise. Therefore:

Profits are the result of institutional rigidities in the social and economic system that prevent the working out of competitive forces, and are to the temporary advantage of the surplus recipient.

Many illustrations from real life substantiate the existence of friction and monopoly as a cause of economic surplus. The construction of military posts brings profit bonanzas to neighboring cities. Foreign crises often rescue domestic industries from threatening oversupplies of their products. The existence of patents and franchises enables many firms to reap profits by legally excluding competitors from the field. A favorable location for a business often results in the value of the site exceeding the rental payment for it. In general, the control of any resource whose supply is scarce relative to its demand provides a basis for pure or windfall profits. A surplus would not arise if resources were sufficiently mobile to enter the market, or if the economy were frictionless (perfect) in its competitive structure. At best, any surpluses that did arise would be short-lived and vanish entirely when the adjustments had time to exert their full effect in the market. But social processes—customs, laws, and traditions—make such rapid adjustments impossible.

UNCERTAINTY THEORY

The uncertainty theory of profit was introduced by Professor Frank Knight (1885–1972) of the University of Chicago in a remarkable doctoral thesis entitled *Risk, Uncertainty, and Profit* published in 1921. The theory is rooted in a distinction between "risk" and "uncertainty."

The Meaning of Risk

Risk is defined as the quantitative measurement of an outcome, such as a gain or a loss, in a manner such that the mathematical probability (or "odds") of the outcome can be predicted. Since the distinguishing feature of risk is predictability, the firm can "insure" itself against expected losses by incorporating them in advance into its cost structure. This is true whether the risk is of an intrafirm or interfirm nature.

Intrafirm Risk Such risk occurs when management can establish the probability of loss because the number of occurrences within the firm is large enough to be predicted with known error. For example, a factory may experience a loss of about 2 machine-hours out of every 100 machine-hours due to equipment breakdown. In this case, the cost of the production lost can be added to the cost of the production resulting from the remaining 98 machine-hours, and the profit rate altered by the revision in the cost structure. In other words, where the average expected loss for the company can be predicted for the coming period, the loss can be "self-insured" by treating it as a cost of

doing business, and hence no insurance from outside sources is necessary. Thus, small-loan companies expect a certain percentage of defaults; banks regularly charge off as bad debts a portion of their loans; and many companies institute self-insurance programs against risks for which they can prepare themselves through proper reserve accounting.

Interfirm Risk For some risks the number of observations or experiences is not large enough within any one firm for management to feel that it can predict the loss with reasonable confidence. However, when many firms are considered, the observations become numerous enough to exhibit the necessary stability for prediction. Examples of such risks are losses caused by floods, storms, fires, or deaths. Since managers are unable to predict such losses for themselves, they are able to shift the burden of the risk to insurance companies whose function is to establish the probability of such losses based on a large number of cases. Although insurance companies cannot establish that a particular individual will die or that a particular building will burn, they can predict with small error how many people will die next year or how many buildings out of a given number will burn. It follows that since a firm pays a risk premium for insurance, it can and does treat this risk premium as a cost of doing business.

The Meaning of Uncertainty

Uncertainty is defined as a state of knowledge in which the probabilities of outcomes resulting from specific actions are not known and cannot be predicted. Unlike risk, therefore, uncertainty is a subjective (rather than objective) phenomenon. No two individuals who forecast a particular outcome based on given facts will necessarily arrive at the same result because there is not enough information on which to base a strong probability estimate.

Under uncertainty conditions, decision makers must make choices based on incomplete knowledge. They may do this by forming mental images of future outcomes that cannot be verified quantitatively. It follows from this that uncertainty is not insurable and cannot be integrated within the firm's cost structure, as can risk. At best, each manager may harbor his or her own subjective probability about a future outcome, but it is nothing more than a strong hunch. According to this theory:

> The great majority of events in our society are unpredictable—they are uncertainties. Therefore, *profits are the rewards, and losses are the penalties, of bearing uncertainty.*

The uncertainty theory concludes that in a market

economy entrepreneurs undertake an activity because they *expect* but do not necessarily *receive* profits. Like a dog chasing a rabbit, the expectation of gains is the incentive that keeps entrepreneurs running.

INNOVATION THEORY

In the 1930s, one of the most distinguished economists of this century, Joseph Schumpeter, introduced a theory of business cycles based on innovations. This theory has often been extended to include the notion of innovation as a cause of profits.

An *innovation*, as economists define it, is "the setting up of a new production function"—that is, a new relation between the output and the various inputs (capital, land, labor, etc.) in a production process. Innovations may thus embrace such wide varieties of activities as the discovery of new markets, differentiation of products, or, in short, new ways of doing old things or different combinations of existing methods to accomplish new things. There is an important distinction between invention and innovation. Invention is the creation of something new; innovation is the adaptation of an invention to use. Many inventions never become innovations.

Schumpeter's original purpose in propounding the innovation theory was to show how business cycles result from these disturbances and from successive adaptations to them by the business system. His procedure was to assume a stationary (perfectly competitive) system in equilibrium—in which all economic life is repetitive and goes on smoothly, without disturbance. Into this system a shock—an innovation—is introduced by an entrepreneur who foresees the possibility of extra profit. The quietude and intricate balance of the system is then shattered as if the system had been invaded by a Hollywood-staged cattle stampede. The successful innovation causes herds of businesspeople (followers rather than leaders) to plunge into the new field by adopting the innovation, and these mass rushes create and stir up secondary waves of business activity. When the disturbance has finally ironed itself out, the system settles into equilibrium once again, only to be disturbed later by another innovation. Profits and economic activity are thus experienced as a series of fits and starts (cycles) rather than progressing smoothly and continuously. (See *Leaders in Economics*, page 477.)

FUNCTIONS OF PROFITS

As mentioned earlier, there is no single "correct" theory of profit. All three theories contribute significantly to explaining the cause of profit. They also help

us understand the two major functions of profits in our economy:

1. Profits stimulate innovation by inducing business managers to undertake new ventures and to improve production methods.

2. To the extent that markets are free and competitive, the desire for profits induces business executives to allocate their resources efficiently in accordance with consumer preferences.

As a result of these functions, you can see that profits and the profit system account for a fundamental distinction between capitalistic and socialistic systems.

What You Have Learned

1. The long-run trend of real wages in our economy has been upward, based fundamentally on the increased productivity of labor resulting from improvements in the quality and quantity of the factors of production.

2. Wages are determined in the market under different competitive conditions. Four models which explain most of the situations that exist in our economy are the competitive model, monopsony model, monopoly model, and bilateral monopoly model. The bilateral monopoly model may yield a determinate solution on quantity, but it yields an indeterminate solution on price.

3. Economic rent is a surplus which is price-determined, not price-determining. To an individual firm, rent is a cost of production just like any other cost; but to society rent is a surplus which is received for making available nature's free land.

4. Interest is the price paid for the use of money or loanable funds over a period of time. Although the interest rate is determined by the supply of, and demand for, loanable funds, it is administered by the government and is not freely fluctuating. The chief function of the interest rate is to allocate scarce funds for alternative uses, thus directing the flow of capital.

5. Profit is a residual or surplus over and above all costs, including normal profit. It may result from frictions and monopoly elements in our economy, from uncertainty, and from innovations. The chief functions of profit are (a) to stimulate economic progress by inducing business managers to invest in plant and equipment; and (b) to the extent that markets are competitive, to allocate resources in accordance with consumer preferences.

For Discussion

1. *Terms and concepts to review:*

wages	bilateral monopoly
labor	economic rent
money wages	single tax
real wages	interest
monopsony	pure interest rate

loanable-funds theory	profit
of interest	risk
liquidity-preference	uncertainty
theory of interest	innovation

2. Why has the long-run trend of real wages been upward, especially since the supply of labor today is so much larger than it was years ago?

3. Which wage-determination model best explains each of the following? Illustrate and explain each with an actual model. (a) The wages of file clerks and secretaries; (b) the wages of unskilled farmworkers; (c) the wages of typographers and longshoremen.

4. A union official once advised the members to ask for a 10 percent wage cut. Was he crazy? What economic factors might have prompted him to offer such advice?

5. "Wages are determined by the marginal productivity of labor just as prices are determined by costs of production." True or false? Explain.

6. Do you see any similarity between the concept of economic rent received by a factor of production and net revenue received by a firm? Explain.

7. Henry George ran for mayor of New York in 1886. If you had been a voter at that time, how would you have reacted to his single-tax idea?

8. Money itself is not a resource and is unproductive. Why, then, should people be willing to pay a price in the form of interest in order to acquire it? What determines the interest rate that is paid? What functions does interest perform?

9. Classify each of the following as an interfirm or intrafirm risk: (a) glassware and china breakage in a restaurant; (b) egg breakage on a chicken farm; (c) absenteeism in a factory; (d) "acts of God" (cite examples).

10. (a) From a chicken farmer's standpoint, is the price of eggs a risk or an uncertainty? (b) How about the sale of next year's Chevrolets by General Motors? Why?

11. "Economic profits should be taxed away since they result from frictions and monopolistic influences." Evaluate.

Leaders in Economics
Joseph Alois Schumpeter   1883–1950

The "Crumbling Walls" of Capitalism

One of the most famous economists of the twentieth century was Joseph Schumpeter. His reputation rests as much on his total achievements as a social scientist as on his contributions to the advancement of economics. Although many scholars have excelled in special fields, Schumpeter was one of the few who was extraordinarily well versed in many, including economics, mathematics, philosophy, sociology, and history.

Schumpeter was born in Moravia (now part of Czechoslovakia) and educated in law and economics at the University of Vienna. After a varied and successful career as a professor, cabinet minister, banker, and jurist, he accepted a teaching position at the University of Bonn in 1925. When Hitler came to power, he emigrated to the United States, and was a professor of economics at Harvard University until his death.

Schumpeter's output of books, essays, articles, and monographs was enormous, but his most important works fell broadly in the field of business-cycle theory. Perhaps his greatest theoretical contribution was the model he developed to describe how business cycles result from *innovations* by a business system under capitalism. This innovation theory was subsequently adopted by many economists as a partial explanation of how profits (surpluses) arise in a capitalistic system.

In one of his classic works Schumpeter discussed the "crumbling walls" of capitalism—that is, the eventual decay of the system due to the obso-

The Bettmann Archive.

lescence of the entrepreneurial function. In his own words:

> The economic wants of humanity might some day be so completely satisfied that little motive would be left to push productive effort still further ahead. Such a state of satiety is no doubt very far off even if we keep within the present scheme of wants; and if we take account of the fact that, as higher standards of life are attained, these wants automatically expand and new wants emerge or are created, satiety becomes a flying goal, particularly if we include leisure among consumers' goods. However, let us glance at that possibility, assuming, still more unrealistically, that methods of production have reached a state of perfection which does not admit of further improvement.

A more or less stationary state would ensue. Capitalism, being essentially an evolutionary process, would become atrophic. There would be nothing left for entrepreneurs to do. They would find themselves in much the same situation as generals would in a society perfectly sure of permanent peace. Profits and along with profits the rate of interest would converge toward zero. The bourgeois strata that live on profits and interest would tend to disappear. The management of industry and trade would become a matter of current administration, and the personnel would unavoidably acquire the characteristics of a bureaucracy. Socialism of a very sober type would almost automatically come into being. Human energy would turn away from business. Other than economic pursuits would attract the brains and provide the adventure.

Although Schumpeter was widely respected, and his many pioneering works were studied by scholars throughout the world, he never founded a "school" of economic thought or gathered a following which could eventually assume the status of a school. In other words, no "Schumpeterians" ever emerged, as occurred with some other leading scholars. Various reasons may be advanced for this. Perhaps the most significant is that his theory contained no *cause célèbre*—no fundamental challenge that could offer a rallying point. Although his innovation theory of business cycles was developed on a high theoretical plane, it offered no concrete solutions to the world's economic problems.

Reading
Ricardo on Rent

In 1817, the greatest of the English classical economists, David Ricardo, published his Principles of Political Economy and Taxation. *In this treatise he developed the theory of economic rent. This theory has remained essentially unchanged since that time. The following brief selection is taken from Ricardo's monumental book.*

Rent is that portion of the produce of the earth which is paid to the landlord for the use of the original and indestructible powers of the soil.

It is often, however, confounded with the interest and profit of capital, and, in popular language, the term is applied to whatever is annually paid by a farmer to his landlord. If, of two adjoining farms of the same extent, and of the same natural fertility, one had all the conveniences of farming buildings, and besides, were properly drained and manured, and advantageously divided into hedges, fences, and walls, while the other had none of these advantages, more remuneration would naturally be paid for the use of one, than for the use of the other; yet in both cases the remuneration would be called rent. But it is evident, that a portion only of the money annually to be paid for the improved farm, would be given for the original and indestructible powers of the soil; the other portion would be paid for the use of the capital which had been employed in ameliorating the quality of the land, and in erecting such buildings as were necessary to secure and preserve the produce.

On the first settling of a country, in which there is an abundance of fertile land, a very small proportion of which is required to be cultivated for the support of the actual population, or indeed can be cultivated with the capital which the population can command, there will be no rent; for no one would pay for the use of land, when there was an abundant quantity not yet appropriated, and, therefore, at the disposal of whosoever might choose to cultivate it.

If all land had the same properties, if it were unlimited in quantity, and uniform in quality, no charge could be made for its use, unless where it possessed peculiar advantages of situation. It is only, then, because land is not unlimited in quantity and uniform in quality, and because in the progress of population, land of an inferior quality, or less advantageously situated, is called into cultivation, that rent is ever paid for the use of it. When in the progress of society, land of the second degree of fertility is taken into cultivation, rent immediately commences on that of the first quality, and the amount of that rent will depend on the difference in the quality of those two portions of land.

When land of the third quality is taken into cultivation, rent immediately commences on the second, and it is regulated as before, by the difference in their productive powers. At the same time, the rent of the first quality will rise, for that must always be above the rent of the second, by the difference between the produce which they yield with a given quantity of capital and labor. With every step in the progress of population, which shall oblige a country to have recourse to land of a worse quality, to enable it to raise its supply of food, rent on all the more fertile land will rise.

The reason, then, why raw produce rises in comparative value, is because more labor is employed in the production of the last portion obtained, and not because a rent is paid to the landlord. The value of corn is regulated by the quantity of labor bestowed on its production on that quality of land, or with that portion of capital, which pays no rent. Corn is not high because a rent is paid, but a rent is paid because corn is high; and it has been justly observed, that no reduction would take place in the price of corn, although landlords should forgo the whole of their rent. Such a measure would only enable some farmers to live like gentlemen, but would not diminish the quantity of labor necessary to raise raw produce on the least productive land in cultivation.

Chapter 28

Stability, General Equilibrium, and Welfare Economics

Chapter Preview

What is the deeper meaning of equilibrium? Why is it important in economics (and in all other sciences)?

In what sense is our economy a "system"— a complex network in which "everything depends on everything else"?

Does the study of economics provide us with a norm for judging whether actions should or should not be undertaken to improve society's welfare?

Equilibrium is a concept of fundamental importance, and we have already made considerable use of it. But what does "equilibrium" really mean? How significant is it in economic analysis?

Equilibrium was defined in earlier chapters as a state of balance between opposing forces. An object is in equilibrium when it is at rest; it has no tendency to change its position because the forces acting upon it are canceling each other. In economics, as we have seen, the "objects" may be prices, quantities, incomes, or other variables. You cannot consider a problem solved if, at the point you terminate your analysis, the variables which are germane to the particular problem are still changing. Only when the variables settle down to steady levels, or only when their future equilibrium positions can be predicted, can you consider the solution complete.

However, the study of equilibrium is not an end in itself. We must also understand the forces that can disturb an equilibrium, and the measures that may have to be undertaken to restore it. These ideas will become more meaningful as we explore the ramifications of equilibrium in this chapter.

Stability of Equilibrium

If the forces acting upon an object at rest suddenly change, the object may not have the ability to reestablish its position. If it does, the equilibrium is stable; if it does not, the equilibrium may be either unstable or neutral. Let us examine these ideas in both a physical and an economic context.

STABLE, UNSTABLE, AND NEUTRAL EQUILIBRIUM

Exhibit 1 provides some interesting examples of the stability of equilibrium in terms of supply and demand curves.

Chart (a) illustrates a case of stable equilibrium. This represents the normal situation. In physical terms, it may be depicted by a cone resting on its base. In economic terms, it can be represented by the interaction of ordinary supply and demand curves. If the system is subjected to an external "shock" or disturbance sufficient to dislodge it from equilibrium, self-corrective forces will cause it to return to its initial position. If the price, for example, should for some reason rise above its equilibrium level at P, quantity supplied of the product will exceed quantity demanded, thereby driving the price down. If the price should fall below P, quantity demanded will exceed quantity supplied, thereby driving the price up.

Although Charts (b) through (d) do not depict typical situations, they are useful for providing deeper insights into the concept of equilibrium.

Chart (b) presents a case of unstable equilibrium. A physical example is a cone balanced on its vertex. An economic example is one in which price is determined by the intersection of supply and demand, but the supply curve is downward-sloping and cuts the demand curve from below. As you can see from the chart, the system is in a delicate state of balance; if the equilibrium is disturbed, the object will be forced away from its initial state. For example, if for some reason the price should rise above its equilibrium level, quantity demanded will exceed quantity supplied and the price will continue to rise. Conversely, if the price should fall below its equilibrium level, quantity supplied will exceed quantity demanded and the price will continue to fall. Note, however, that these conclusions would not hold if the downward-sloping supply curve cut the demand curve from above instead of from below. In that case the equilibrium would be stable. You should be able to demonstrate this by sketching the curves.

Charts (c) and (d) provide illustrations of neutral equilibrium. The physical situation can be depicted by a cone lying on its side. If the cone's equilibrium is disturbed, it simply "rolls" to some other neutral position. The analogous economic situation occurs in those ranges of price and quantity where the supply and demand curves happen to coincide. Thus, in Chart (c) any price between the points P and P' is in

neutral equilibrium—the price is "rolling" or indeterminate within this range. Similarly, in Chart (d) any quantity between the points Q and Q' is in neutral equilibrium—and therefore the precise quantity is indeterminate within this range.

STATICS AND DYNAMICS

The concepts of stable, unstable, and neutral equilibrium can also be depicted by the charts in Exhibit 2. Note from the titles of Exhibits 1 and 2 that Exhibit 1 consists of static models, whereas Exhibit 2 is composed of dynamic ones. Let us examine these concepts more closely.

A static model is one in which economic phenomena are studied without reference to time—without reference to preceding or succeeding events. In a static model, time is not permitted to enter into the analysis in any manner that will affect the results. When we construct a static model, therefore, we are taking a "snapshot" and analyzing its essential features. Each of the diagrams in Exhibit 1, and most of the other theoretical situations and charts studied in this book, are static models.

Of course, in many practical situations you want to analyze the effects of a change in one or more of the determining conditions in a static model. This method is known as comparative statics. It consists of comparing two "snapshots"—one taken before the change and one after. For example, when you analyzed supply and demand situations in previous chapters by comparing equilibrium prices and quantities before and after a shift in one or both of the curves, you were using comparative statics. Statics and comparative statics encompass most of the theory in this book—and by far the larger part of economic theory in general.

A dynamic model is one in which economic phenomena are studied by relating them to preceding or succeeding events. The influence of time is taken explicitly into account. Illustrations of the results of dynamic models are shown in Exhibit 2. Each chart depicts a possible way in which price may behave in relation to its equilibrium level over a period of time. Each of these dynamic models, therefore, is like a "motion picture" as distinguished from the "snapshot" of Exhibit 1.

Fluctuations in prices like those shown in Exhibit 2 do not continue in the same pattern indefinitely. Why? Because the underlying supply and demand curves which determine prices tend to change fairly frequently, so that different patterns are generated. At any given moment the pattern may be tending toward stable, unstable, or neutral equilibrium. However, over a period of time, prices in most markets tend toward some stable equilibrium level.

Exhibit 1
Stable, Unstable, and Neutral Equilibrium: Static Models

Chart (a) Stable Equilibrium. *The equilibrium at P is stable—like a cone resting on its base. A "shock" sufficient to disturb the equilibrium brings self-corrective forces into play which automatically restore the initial position.*

Chart (b) Unstable Equilibrium. *The equilibrium at P is unstable—like a cone balanced on its vertex. If the equilibrium is disturbed, the system is forced away from its initial state. Thus, at any price higher than the level at P, quantity demanded exceeds quantity supplied, so the price continues to rise. At any price below the level at P, the reverse is true. Note, however, that the equilibrium at P would be stable if the downward-sloping supply curve cut the demand curve from above instead of from below. Can you illustrate and explain this?*

Charts (c) and (d) Neutral Equilibrium. *In Chart (c) any price equilibrium between P and P′ is neutral. In Chart (d) any quantity equilibrium between Q and Q′ is neutral. Within their neutral ranges, price and quantity are indeterminate; they may take on any values. Hence, the situation is analogous to a cone rolling on its side.*

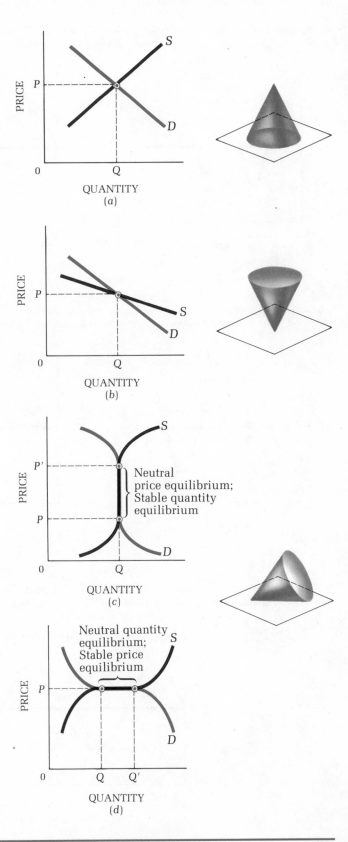

Exhibit 2
Stable, Unstable, and Neutral Equilibrium: Dynamic Models

Stable Equilibrium. *Price converges toward the equilibrium level at P. Price may oscillate or it may approach equilibrium from above or below.*

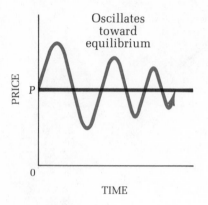

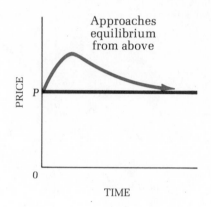

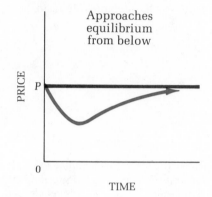

Unstable Equilibrium. *Price diverges from the equilibrium at P. Price may oscillate or it may "explode" upward or downward from the equilibrium level.*

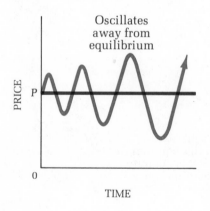

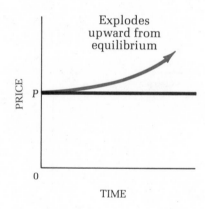

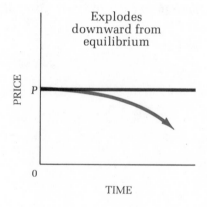

Neutral Equilibrium. *Price fluctuates around the equilibrium level at P. Price has no permanent tendency to converge toward equilibrium or diverge from it.*

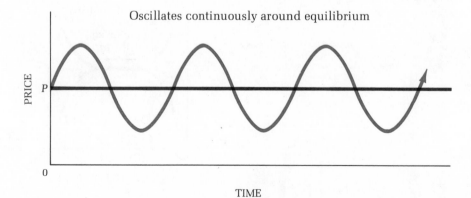

This suggests the following definition:

Stable equilibrium is a condition in which an object or system (such as a price, firm, industry, market, etc.) in equilibrium, when subjected to a shock sufficient to disturb its position, returns toward its initial equilibrium as a result of self-restoring forces. (In contrast, an equilibrium that is not stable may be either unstable or neutral.)

As you can see from this explanation, the concept of stable equilibrium is of fundamental importance. Indeed, it has occupied the interest of a number of scholars—among them Paul Samuelson, whose pioneering work on stability analysis contributed significantly to his being the first American to receive the Nobel Prize in Economic Science. (See *Leaders in Economics,* page 484.)

General Equilibrium: "Everything Depends on Everything Else"

In the early part of this century, the famous American economist Henry J. Davenport investigated relationships between the prices of corn, pork, and land. He noted part of his conclusions in a poem:

The price of pig
Is something big;
Because its corn, you'll understand
Is high-priced, too;
Because it grew
Upon the high-priced farming land.
If you'd know why
That land is high
Consider this: its price is big
Because it pays
Thereon to raise
The costly corn, the high-priced pig.

Long before Davenport observed connections between these three variables, the prominent mid-nineteenth-century French economist Frederic Bastiat expressed amazement about the Paris of his day. Hundreds of thousands of people, he remarked, live in the city, yet each day a wide variety of goods and services are provided in approximately correct quantities without coordination or planning by any single agency. "Imagination," Bastiat wrote, "is baffled when it tries to appreciate the vast multiplicity of commodities which must enter tomorrow to preserve the inhabitants from famine. Yet all sleep and their slumbers are not disturbed for a single minute by the prospects of such a frightful catastrophe."

What Davenport and Bastiat (and many other observers as well) were commenting upon is the notion that a complex economy is a vast system of interrelated components—a system in which "everything depends on everything else." We can gain a better appreciation of this idea by examining some of the features of what is known as general equilibrium theory.

PARTIAL AND GENERAL EQUILIBRIUM THEORY

Until now, almost all of our attention in microeconomics has been focused on "partial" as distinguished from "general" equilibrium theory. What do these terms mean?

Partial equilibrium theory analyzes and develops models of a particular market on the assumption that other markets are in balance. It thus ignores the interrelationships of prices and quantities that may exist between markets.

For example, ordinary supply and demand analysis is normally of a partial equilibrium nature since it focuses on a single market while neglecting others. This method of investigation can be extremely useful for gaining a better understanding of how a market works and for analyzing the effects of such things as price control, rationing, minimum wages, and commodity taxes, as was done in earlier chapters. However, by ignoring the ramifications and repercussions of price and quantity changes which may occur in other markets, we are overlooking the fact that such changes could have a significant influence on the market we are studying.

In view of this, it is necessary to think of the price system as an interrelated whole and to recognize that partial analyses can provide only approximations to a full explanation. This being the case, a "general" approach, which simultaneously takes into account all product and resource markets in the economy, is needed.

General equilibrium theory analyzes the interrelationships between prices and quantities of goods and resources in different markets, and demonstrates the possibility of simultaneous equilibrium between all markets. It thus views the economy as a system composed of interdependent parts.

General equilibrium theory is based on the assumption that if, for each particular market, all participants are given such information as consumer demand schedules, resource supply schedules, production functions, and the demand for money, equilibrium forces will cause commodity and resource prices to adjust themselves in a mutually consistent manner. The entire system can then settle down in a stable equilibrium of supply and demand.

Leaders in Economics
Paul Anthony Samuelson   1915–

America's First Nobel Laureate in Economic Science

In 1935, an extraordinary young man, born in Gary, Indiana, received his B.A. degree from the University of Chicago. He went on to pursue graduate work at Harvard University, from which he received a Ph.D. in economics in 1941. During that six-year period he published eleven major professional journal articles—most of which became classics in their own time—plus a path-breaking doctoral dissertation which later appeared as a book, *Foundations of Economic Analysis* (Harvard University Press, 1947). The impact of this treatise, which was largely conceived and written in 1937 by the then-23-year-old author, was noted in 1970 by the Swedish Royal Academy of Science when it bestowed upon Samuelson the Alfred Nobel Memorial Prize in Economic Science.

Paul Samuelson is probably the world's most widely known economist. Several generations of college students in the United States and abroad took their first course in economics from his introductory textbook. Millions of readers of American and foreign newspapers and magazines have been exposed to his articles on current economic policies. And professional economists throughout the world have studied and been stimulated toward further research by the extraordinary range of his scientific work. This includes hundreds of profound papers and several books dealing with theoretical topics in consumer behavior, business cycles, public finance, international trade,

linear programming, and other technical subjects. In all these fields, Samuelson's originality has been evidenced by his ability to develop sophisticated formulations of economic concepts through the use of advanced mathematics.

For example, among his many classic publications is a mathematical essay on the interaction of the multiplier and the accelerator—an important topic of macroeconomic theory. Samuelson wrote this celebrated article when he was a graduate student; it was initially prepared as a term paper for a seminar course in business cycles. The article reflected Samuelson's early interest in the important concept of stability.

In the *Foundations*, which immediately established his reputation as a highly creative mathematical economist, he presented a systematic analysis of static and dynamic economic theory. His approach was to describe, in mathematical form, the "state" of an economic system in equilibrium and the process or path of adjustment from one state to an-

other. He then linked statics and dynamics by what he called the *correspondence principle*—a proposition which demonstrates that in order for comparative statics (the comparison of equilibrium positions in static states) to be meaningful, it is first necessary to develop a dynamic analysis of stability.

In general, Paul Samuelson's scientific contributions—developed in precise mathematical rather than literary form—have greatly deepened our understanding of how the economic system works. He has shown the general applicability of the concept of maximization, subject to constraints, to many branches of economics. For example, the consumer tries to maximize satisfactions, subject to such constraints as income and the prices of the goods purchased. The business firm tries to maximize profit, subject to the constraints of technology, resource limitations, and costs. And government tries to maximize net social benefits, subject to various economic (not to mention political) constraints. These and many other ideas had long been part of economics, but Samuelson revealed them in new and provocative ways. As a result, he has provided a storehouse of theoretical insights which have both stimulated and facilitated important research by others.

An Institute Professor at the Massachusetts Institute of Technology, Paul Samuelson has been on the faculty of that renowned institution since 1941. He has also been active as a government consultant and as an invited speaker on many public platforms.

Any change in the determinants affecting the price and quantity of a good or resource can, however, upset the entire system and have widespread repercussions on the equilibrium prices and quantities of all other goods and resources. These ideas emphasize the fact that in the real world of imperfect competition there is often a significant degree of interdependence among various markets.

A GENERAL EQUILIBRIUM MODEL: TWO COMMODITIES

A full explanation of general equilibrium requires the use of mathematics. However, many of the basic notions can be conveyed without mathematics by a simple supply and demand analysis involving only two commodities—say, meat and fish.

In Exhibit 3, Chart (a), the intersection of the market demand curve for meat D_M and the supply curve for meat S_M determines the equilibrium price of meat P_M and equilibrium quantity of meat Q_M. Similarly, in Chart (b), the intersection of the market demand and supply curves of fish, D_F and S_F, determines the equilibrium price of fish P_F and equilibrium quantity of fish Q_F.

Before considering any change, it is important to note some of the assumptions underlying the curves. Basically, each curve in any one market is drawn on the assumption that the equilibrium price of the commodity in the other market remains constant. For example, in Chart (a) the demand curve for meat assumes that the price of fish in Chart (b) is at its equilibrium level P_F. Similarly, in Chart (b) the demand curve for fish assumes that the equilibrium price of meat in Chart (a) is at its equilibrium level P_M. Other assumptions not evident from the charts are

also made. In particular, it is assumed that (1) consumer preferences for commodities are given, (2) the stock of resources available for production is fixed, and (3) the techniques of production (the production functions for commodities) are given. These conditions are among the basic determinants of the system we are describing. Therefore, a change in any one of them will disturb the existing equilibrium pattern.

Effect of a Specific Tax

Now suppose that a *specific tax*—a tax per unit of commodity—is imposed by government on sellers of meat. In Chart (a), if the tax is equal to T per unit, it will increase the cost to suppliers by shifting the supply curve from S_M to S'_M. This will cause the equilibrium price of meat to rise to P'_M and the equilibrium quantity to fall to Q'_M. Since the price of meat compared to fish is now *relatively* higher than before the

---

Exhibit 3
General Equilibrium—A Two-Commodity Model

DEMAND AND SUPPLY CURVES FOR MEAT AND FISH

In Chart (a) the demand curve for meat (D_M) is drawn on the assumption that the equilibrium price of fish (P_F) in Chart (b) is given. Similarly, in Chart (b) the demand curve for fish (D_F) is drawn on the assumption that the equilibrium price of meat (P_M) in Chart (a) is given. The supply curves of meat S_M and of fish S_F are drawn under the same assumptions.

In Chart (a), if a specific tax of T per unit is imposed on meat sellers, the supply curve shifts from S_M to S'_M to reflect the cost increase. The equilibrium price of meat rises to P'_M

and the equilibrium quantity falls to Q'_M. Consumers, therefore, substitute fish for meat, causing the demand curve for fish in Chart (b) to shift to the right from D_F to D'_F. As a result, the equilibrium price of fish increases to P'_F and the equilibrium quantity to Q'_F.

In addition to these changes, some resources (not shown in the diagrams) are likely to move out of meat production and into fish production, causing the supply curves in both industries to shift. This process will continue until a new state of general equilibrium is reached.

(a) MEAT

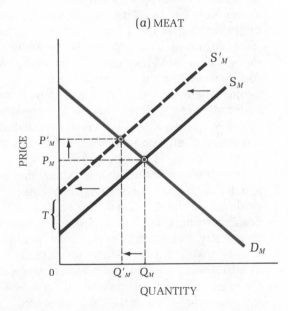

(b) FISH

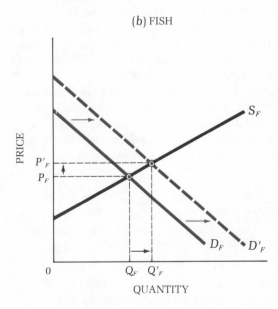

tax, consumers will substitute some fish for meat in their consumption patterns. This will cause an increase in the demand for fish—a shift of the demand curve in Chart (b) to the right from D_F to D_F'. Therefore, the equilibrium price of fish will rise from P_F to P_F' and the equilibrium quantity will increase from Q_F to Q_F'. As a result of the tax, therefore, both the price of meat and the price of fish have risen. But the quantity of meat produced and consumed has decreased while the quantity of fish produced and consumed has increased.

Under normal circumstances, various other repercussions, not shown in the diagrams, will occur. For example, after the tax, fewer resources are needed to produce the smaller quantity of meat, while more resources are needed to produce the larger quantity of fish. Therefore, the price of resources and their employment in meat production will decline, while the price of resources and their employment in fish production will rise. As a result, some resources will move out of meat production and into fish production. As this happens, the supply curves in the two industries will shift, causing market prices and quantities to change. In addition, the change in relative resource prices will cause shifts in the pattern of income distribution, and this will have further repercussions on the demand for the two commodities. This adjustment process continues until the system is once again in general equilibrium.

INTERDEPENDENCE AND THE CIRCULAR FLOW

The interdependence that exists between markets in the economy can be extended beyond what is shown in the simple model of Exhibit 3. However, the model would then be considerably more complicated. It is sufficient, therefore, to convey the overall nature of the interrelationships by means of a familiar circular-flow diagram. This is done in Exhibit 4.

The model is self-explanatory. Note that it lists the conditions that are assumed to be given or fixed in the household and business sectors, and that it emphasizes the interdependence between households, businesses, product markets, and factor markets. In general:

> The overall concept conveyed by the circular-flow model is that the quantities supplied and demanded for each product and for each factor of production must be equal. When this occurs, the economy is in a state of general equilibrium.

The earliest notion of general equilibrium was developed in the eighteenth century by a group of French economists called the physiocrats. Foremost among them was an economist named François Quesnay, who, in 1758, presented a circular-flow model to depict what he called the "natural order" of an economic system. These ideas were subsequently developed in much greater depth and with mathematical precision in the late nineteenth century by the Swiss-French economist Leon Walras (1834–1910), who ranks as one of the greatest economists of all time.

Welfare Economics

The concept of general equilibrium provides us with an overview of a perfectly competitive economy. But what are the main characteristics of such an economy? Is perfect competition "good" or "bad"? In answering these questions, we will gain some insights into what is known as welfare economics—a branch of economic theory concerned with the development of principles for maximizing society's satisfactions (i.e., its social welfare).

PARETO OPTIMALITY

To begin with, what do we mean by social welfare? The concept cannot be precisely defined, and therefore it is impossible to measure. As a result, we cannot assert objectively that any particular economic situation represents higher or lower welfare for society than another. One of the main reasons for this difficulty is that we cannot make interpersonal comparisons of utility or satisfactions; that is, the welfare of one person cannot be compared with that of another.

For example, as a rational consumer, I would feel better off if I could keep all my income, so that I could spend more for consumption. But as a good citizen I might feel better off if I gave up part of my income (through taxes and charitable contributions) and thereby consumed less, so that others who were not as fortunate as I could consume more. Similarly, some people argue that as a nation of consumers we are better off keeping all our income for ourselves. Others contend, however, that we should contribute part of our national income as foreign aid to less developed countries.

Therefore, even though we cannot make interpersonal comparisons of utility, such comparisons are made all the time. Indeed, it would be virtually impossible to have any social policy without them, for almost any social policy makes some people better off while making others worse off. Ideally, what we usually want are social policies that make some people better off without making others worse off. This involves what economists and other social scientists call "Pareto optimality."

Exhibit 4
Economic Interdependence—General Equilibrium and the Circular Flow

Households and businesses are linked through the product markets, where goods and services are exchanged, and through the resource markets, where the factors of production are exchanged. The economy is in a state of general equilibrium when the quantities supplied and demanded for goods and services and for factors of production are equal.

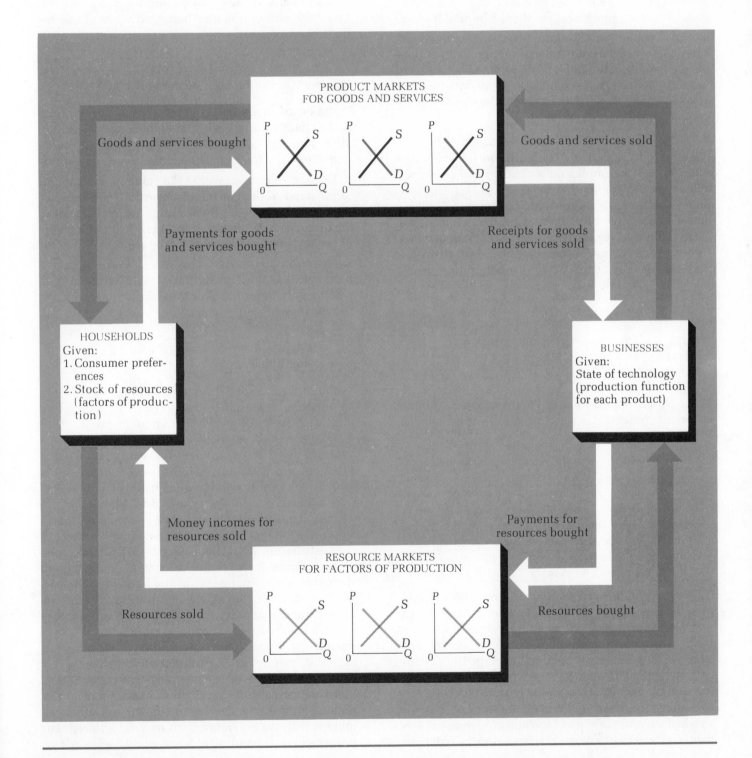

Pareto optimality is a condition which exists in a social organization when no change can be implemented that will make someone better off without making someone else worse off—each in his or her own estimation.

This concept, named after a famous Italian-Swiss sociologist and economist, Vilfredo Pareto (1848–1923), leads to two important principles:

1. Any social action that benefits at least one person without harming someone else will clearly increase social welfare, and therefore should be undertaken.

2. The effect on social welfare of any action that benefits some while harming others—the *numbers* of people are immaterial—cannot be determined because we cannot compare satisfactions and dissatisfactions among people. That is, *we cannot make interpersonal comparisons of utility.*

The first principle provides a useful guide for formulating public policies, while the second contains some interesting implications. The second principle tells us, for example, that even though a particular policy—such as the imprisonment of criminals—benefits a large majority of the people while harming a small minority, we cannot be sure that adherence to it results in an increase in social welfare. At best we can only assume that it does, but we cannot prove it in any objective, scientific way.

GENERAL EQUILIBRIUM AND PARETO OPTIMALITY—ECONOMIC EFFICIENCY AND EQUITY

What are the implications of Pareto optimality for an economic system? The answer can be stated in the form of a proposition:

> When a perfectly competitive economy achieves a general equilibrium of prices and quantities, no economic organism (individual, household, or firm) can be made better off without some other organism being made worse off. The system has therefore attained a Pareto optimum—it has achieved an *economically efficient* allocation of resources. (NOTE Certain qualifications to this statement are pointed out in the following sections.)

The proof of this proposition requires considerably more advanced economic theory than is covered in this book, but you can appreciate the sense of it on the basis of what was learned in previous chapters. For example, suppose that a perfectly competitive economy has settled down in general equilibrium. Keeping in mind the conditions that are "given"—namely, the pattern of consumer preferences, the stock of productive factors, and the state of technology—what are the main characteristics of the resulting state of balance?

Efficiency in Consumption: Household Sector

In the household sector, each consuming unit spends its income on the goods and services it wants most, given the prices it must pay. Each consuming unit therefore allocates its income so as to maximize total utility or satisfactions. In terms of Pareto optimality, this means that society has achieved efficiency in consumption because no transfer of commodities can be made between any two consuming units that will make one consuming unit better off without making the other worse off.

Efficiency in Production: Business Sector

In the business sector, as you learned in the study of perfect competition, each firm in the long run ends up producing in the output market at the level of production where the following efficiency conditions apply:

1. $MC = P$ This means that the value of the last unit of the good to the consumer (measured by the price the consumer pays for the last unit, which is equal to the price paid for any other unit) is equal to the value of society's resources used to produce that unit.

2. $MC = ATC = LRAC$ This means that the firm is producing the optimum output with the optimum-size plant, and therefore is allocating all its resources in a technically efficient manner.

Equity and Efficiency

In the input markets, firms also achieve equilibrium by adhering to marginal principles. Thus, every firm hires each factor of production up to the point where the marginal cost or price of the factor is equal to the value of what it contributes (its marginal revenue product). Each factor thus receives what it is "worth"—the value of what it contributes to total output—as determined in free markets by supply and demand. According to the *contributive standard*, therefore, society has achieved equity (economic justice) in the distribution of income. (NOTE To refresh your understanding, look up the meaning of "contributive standard" in the Dictionary at the back of the book.)

What else do the above equilibrium conditions mean? Fundamentally, they tell us that society has achieved *technical efficiency* in production by producing the largest possible volume of output with available resources. Therefore, no transfer of resources can be made between any two commodities that will increase the production of one commodity without decreasing the production of the other. In other words, the economy is on its production-possibilities curve instead of at some point inside it and hence there is full employment of all resources. Further, society has also achieved *economic efficiency* because the goods that are being produced are what people want to buy with their available incomes.

General equilibrium and economic efficiency thus go hand in hand. It is particularly interesting, however, to realize the remarkable way in which these end results come about:

> All participants in the economy—consumers, businesspersons, resource owners—acting *independently* in their own self-interest and without direction from government, make millions of market decisions daily which determine what, how, and for whom goods shall be produced. Yet the economic system, because it is perfectly competitive, is guided by Adam Smith's "invisible hand" toward general equilibrium and economic efficiency—an end result which, as Smith pointed out, is "no part of anyone's intention."

IMPLICATIONS FOR SOCIAL WELFARE

Should we conclude from this that perfect competition leads to the best of all possible worlds? As pointed out earlier, when a perfectly competitive economy is in general equilibrium, it has attained a Pareto optimum—a situation in which no person can be made better off without someone else being made worse off, each in his or her own estimation. However, there are some qualifications. The more important ones have already been discussed in several earlier chapters. Therefore, it is sufficient to summarize them briefly at this time.

1. *Social Costs and Social Benefits* Competitive prices tend to reflect private costs and private benefits while they may exclude some social costs and social benefits. Environmental pollution arising from production is a typical example of a cost to society that may not be included in a manufacturer's private costs. Likewise, flood control and conservation practices undertaken by a seller provide illustrations of benefits that accrue to many people other than those who buy the producer's product. Therefore:

> To the extent that *all* social costs and benefits are not incorporated in firms' activities, general equilibrium will not provide an optimum allocation of society's resources.

2. *Income Distribution and Equity* In a system of perfect competition, each factor of production is paid according to the "contributive standard." That is, each factor is paid what it is "worth" as measured by what it contributes to total output. This is known as the *marginal productivity theory of income distribution.* According to this principle, a person who is twice as productive as another is paid twice as much. But whether or not this is a just or equitable standard of income distribution is a normative rather than positive question which each society must answer for itself. Some might argue, for example, that it is "just" for a family of six to be paid twice as much as a family of three—regardless of their productivities. Therefore:

> To the extent that society regards the contributive standard as unjust, general equilibrium will not provide an equitable distribution of the economy's income.

CONCLUSION: NORMS OF ECONOMIC EFFICIENCY

You can now appreciate more fully the role played by modern welfare economics. In broad terms, welfare economics deals with the normative aspects of microeconomics. Welfare economics is not concerned with what the perfect world would look like, but with the changes that may be undertaken to improve the well-being of consumers and producers in *today's* world. Welfare economics does this by providing us with a norm or standard expressed in terms of economic efficiency, thus enabling us to state unambiguously whether one equilibrium position is better or worse than another.

From what we now know about microeconomics, it is clear that perfect competition, by means of Smith's "invisible hand," leads (with some qualifications) to an optimum allocation of society's resources. Other types of market structures—such as unregulated monopoly, monopolistic competition, and oligopoly—do not. This suggests that the norm provided by welfare economics can serve as a guide for government intervention in markets—either through taxes, subsidies, direct regulation, or other means—to correct for costs and gains which result when the norm is violated. In other words:

> In markets where supply and demand forces serve efficiently as mechanisms for allocating society's resources, no intervention by government is needed. But when markets fail to perform efficiently, certain types of intervention may be called for.

The nature and effects of various kinds of intervention pose many interesting problems that will occupy our attention in the following chapters. (Meanwhile, see *Leaders in Economics,* page 491.)

What You Have Learned

1. The concept of equilibrium is of fundamental importance in economics. An equilibrium position may be stable, unstable, or neutral—in a static or in a dynamic sense.

2. A static model provides a "snapshot" of the essential features of an economic phenomenon at an instant in time, whereas a dynamic model provides a "motion picture" over a period of time. Although static analysis encompasses most of economic theory, many important problems cannot be analyzed without the use of dynamics.

3. General equilibrium, as distinguished from partial equilibrium, emphasizes the interdependence that exists between markets and sectors of the economy. The notion of general equilibrium can be depicted by a circular-flow diagram.

4. The concept of general equilibrium goes hand in hand with the science of welfare economics. The latter is concerned with the development of principles for maximizing social welfare. Thus, when a perfectly competitive economy achieves a general equilibrium of prices and quantities, it has attained a Pareto optimum—an efficient allocation of resources—and therefore has maximized social welfare. Some qualifications to this conclusion may exist, however, depending on such factors as the inclusion of social costs and social benefits in firms' activities, and the extent to which society regards the contributive standard of income distribution as inequitable.

For Discussion

1. *Terms and concepts to review:*

equilibrium	specific tax
static model	welfare economics
comparative statics	Pareto optimum
dynamic model	efficiency
stable equilibrium	marginal productivity
partial equilibrium theory	theory of income distribution
general equilibrium theory	contributive standard

2. Which is more important—the stability of an equilibrium position or its "location"? Explain.

3. You have already learned the concepts of *demand price* and *supply price* in previous chapters. (To refresh your memory, look up their meanings in the Dictionary at the back of the book.) Using these notions, and thinking in terms of supply and demand curves, formulate definitions of stable and unstable *quantity* equilibrium. (HINT You may find it helpful first to formulate definitions of stable and unstable *price* equilibrium in terms of quantity supplied and quantity demanded. Then use a parallel procedure to define stable and unstable quantity equilibrium in terms of demand price and supply price.)

4. In terms of supply and demand curves, can a price equilibrium be stable for an upward movement and unstable or neutral for a downward movement, and vice versa? Is the same true for a quantity equilibrium in terms of a leftward or rightward movement? Explain.

5. If the world economy were perfectly competitive, a tariff (tax on imports) would result in a misallocation of resources and a reduction in net social welfare for the world community. Do you agree? Why?

6. Nations sometimes employ rationing as a means of distributing scarce goods. Usually, consumers are given ration coupons entitling them to purchase, say, 1 pound of meat and 1 pound of fish per week. In this way, an equal amount of each good is assigned to each consumer. Is this "fair"? Can you propose an alternative method of rationing which is more equitable?

7. It is contended by some social critics that since we do not know the actual distribution of income which will maximize satisfaction, it must be assumed that an equal distribution of income out of any given level of national income would most likely maximize satisfaction. Evaluate this argument.

Leaders in Economics
Marie Esprit Leon Walras 1834–1910
Vilfredo Pareto 1848–1923

The "Lausanne School"

Leon Walras, as he is commonly known, ranks as one of the most significant figures in the history of economic thought. His fame rests on his formulation of the theory of general equilibrium, which he developed rigorously by the use of mathematics. He thus became one of the founders of an approach to economics known as mathematical economics which has flourished to this day.

Born and educated in France, Walras studied to be a mining engineer but left engineering school before his training was completed to become a free-lance journalist. In this capacity he wrote many articles advocating economic, and especially agrarian, reform. In 1870, he was appointed to the chair of political economy at the University of Lausanne, Switzerland, where he remained until 1892.

A few years after his arrival at Lausanne, Walras published his great work, *Elements of Pure Economics.* In this book he showed how, given the mathematical equations of demand and supply at equilibrium, and the *numéraire* (the accounting unit) derived from them, the solution of the problem of general equilibrium is determinate. That is, there is a set of simultaneous equations the number of which equals the number of unknowns, with the number of prices to be ascertained. The problem, however, is determinate in a formal sense only. The necessary data cannot be obtained, and the number of simultaneous equations which would have to be solved is virtually infinite. Nevertheless, this does not destroy the

Charles Phelps Cushing.

The Granger Collection.

value of general equilibrium theory, for the virtue of the concept lies in the precise way in which it demonstrates the mutual interdependence of economic phenomena.

Walras was succeeded at Lausanne by Vilfredo Pareto, an Italian scholar who abandoned a career as an engineer to devote time to scholarly pursuits. Heavily influenced by Walras, Pareto contributed significantly to the literature of pure economics, and his expositions in mathematical economics are even today considered among the most elegant and erudite available. In his major work, *Manual of Political Economy,* he presented economic theory in an aridly pure, static, and general way in the sense that it can be applied to any economic system. Like that of Walras, Pareto's formulation of theory is one of general equilibrium under static conditions.

However, Pareto was also concerned with the problem of how to maximize total satisfactions in an economy. He developed the concept now commonly referred to as Pareto optimality—a notion that is fundamental to modern welfare economics. In passing, it should be noted that Pareto also made notable contributions to sociology. In fact, his reputation in that field is as strong as it is in economics.

Together, Walras and Pareto comprise what is known as the "Lausanne School" of economic thought. The influence of this school on subsequent writers—especially in mathematical economics, general equilibrium theory, and welfare economics—has been enormous. Indeed, modern microeconomic theory owes much of its present content to the pioneering scientific work first done at Lausanne.

Issue
Ration Gasoline?

Every student of microeconomics learns that the price system is the best device ever conceived for allocating scarce resources. Through the operation of a free market, business efficiency and reduced costs of production are encouraged, thereby benefiting consumers with lower prices.

But is this true for a commodity like gasoline? Some economists think not. They point out that the Organization of Petroleum Exporting Countries (OPEC) is a *cartel*. Hence, it is the very antithesis of a free market. As a result, these critics claim, America's oil policy has been wrong. The nation has simply accepted whatever prices the cartel has imposed. Thus, the free market, instead of nonmarket measures, has been relied upon to cope with high oil prices established by OPEC.

Rationing

What type of nonmarket measures are usually advocated? The most common is rationing. Although its disadvantages are recognized by all economists, some advocate it on the grounds that no system of rationing would be fair to everyone. There are several reasons:

1. People's dependence on automobiles varies from one region of the country to another, from one city to another, and even from one family to another. Therefore, any form of rationing must favor some groups at the expense of others.

2. Rationing involves the government in every aspect of petroleum production and distribution. The reason is that other petroleum products, such as diesel fuel and petrochemicals, are part of the industrial process that produces gasoline.

3. The administration of a gasoline rationing system requires a vast bureaucracy. This would cost taxpayers hundreds of millions of dollars annually.

Elasticity

The problem of rationing arises because consumers are not very responsive to changes in gasoline prices. The price elasticity of demand is relatively low—around 0.1 over a two-year period. This means that to reduce quantity demanded by only 1 percent, price must be increased by 10 percent. To cut quantity demanded by 10 percent, price must be increased by 100 percent (i.e., doubled). In general, to reduce quantity purchased by any given percent, price must be increased by 10 times that percent.

Because of the low price elasticity of demand, substantial reductions in gasoline consumption can be attained only by huge price increases. Government could achieve this goal by imposing excise taxes on top of existing gasoline prices. But this would raise prices at the pump to where it might cost the consumer $50 to fill the gas tank.

In recent years, government intervention in the market for gasoline has caused long lines at the pumps in many cities. A completely free market in gasoline would eliminate congestion as well as illegal practices of buyers and sellers trying to circumvent the law. Why, then, does government continue to intervene?

In states where gas was sold on "odd" and "even" days according to license-plate numbers, many people switched plates to get around the law.

Efficiency and Equity

To avoid this possibility, arguments in favor of rationing are frequently heard. Among the most cogent is one made by Seymour Zucker, an economic commentator for *Business Week* magazine.

Zucker points out that coupon rationing, combined with a ceiling price at the pump, assures each motorist a limited—but certain—supply of gasoline. If motorists are allowed to sell their ration coupons in a so-called "white market"—to prevent creation of an illegal "black market"—those motorists who want more than their allotted gasoline can purchase coupons from those who prefer cash. As a result, the coupon price plus the pump price of gasoline equals the market price that would prevail for the same limited supply of gasoline without rationing.

This type of rationing plan, therefore, turns out to be both efficient and equitable. It distributes the fixed supply to the rich and poor equally, and anyone who wants more gasoline can buy the extra coupons.

Advocates of rationing see a great deal of merit in these ideas. But the biggest advantage of rationing is that it could cut gasoline consumption by 20 percent or more, thereby turning the oil shortage into a surplus. That, according to supporters of rationing, would give the United States its best bargaining chip in dealing with OPEC.

QUESTIONS

1. A prominent political leader and critic of rationing has described it as a "no-growth approach to dealing with the energy problem." Can you explain what this means?

2. Advocates of rationing argue that high OPEC prices help cause recession. Consequently, coupon rationing, accompanied by a "white market," is needed to reduce demand. However, the price of coupons in the white market plus the pump price equals, in effect, the free-market price. The question, therefore, is: How does rationing prevent higher prices and recessionary pressures?

Part 7

Domestic Problems: Striving for Efficiency and Equity

Chapter 29

Business Behavior and the Antitrust Laws: Can Government Improve Efficiency?

Chapter Preview

Is there a "monopoly problem" in the United States?

What major laws exist to prevent monopoly and to maintain competition in our economy? How zealously are these laws enforced?

Why do firms sometimes seek to monopolize markets? What have been the major court cases dealing with monopolization and related activities?

Is our economy "monopolized" at the present time? If so, what is the extent of monopolization, and what should be done about it?

More than two hundred years ago, Adam Smith remarked in a famous passage in *The Wealth of Nations*:

> People of the same trade seldom meet together, even for merriment and diversion, but the conversation ends in a conspiracy against the public, or in some contrivance to raise prices. It is impossible indeed to prevent such meetings, by any law which either could be executed, or would be consistent with liberty and justice. But though the law cannot hinder people of the same trade from sometimes assembling together, it ought to do nothing to facilitate such assemblies; much less to render them necessary.

According to Smith, competition in business is not a "natural" practice. Given the opportunity, business executives would prefer to seek ways of avoiding competition if they could strengthen their market positions by doing so.

The history of American business suggests that this is indeed the case. As a result, the American government has, since the late nineteenth century, been engaged in constructing a body of laws and policies to assure that competition in our economy is at least maintained if not enhanced. This chapter sketches the main features of these laws, notes the interesting ways in which they have been applied in some exciting court cases, and evaluates the chief economic issues pertaining to problems of competition and monopoly in our society.

Big Business and the Monopoly Problem

In economic theory, a market is said to be monopolized when it consists of a single firm producing a product for which there are no close substitutes. This narrow definition is usually adequate for analyzing market structures. But when it comes to matters of public policy, economists, government officials, and judges in courts of law take a much broader view. They regard a market as being monopolized if it is dominated by one or a few firms—that is, if it is "oligopolized." The automobile, aluminum, chemical, and steel industries, as well as many others in the American economy, are notable examples. In each of these industries the sales of two, three, or four large firms account for a major share of the total market. This leaves a relatively minor share for smaller competitors to divide among themselves. According to this interpretation, therefore, big businesses such as General Motors, Alcoa, DuPont, and U.S. Steel, and their chief competitors, qualify as "monopolies."

BIG BUSINESSES AS "MONOPOLIES": SOME PROS AND CONS

The arguments for and against big-business monopolies have been debated for decades. Among the chief objections to monopolies are these:

1. They maximize profit by restricting output and charging higher prices than they would if they were more competitive. Monopolies thereby misallocate resources and contribute to income inequality.

2. They retard economic progress and technological advance because they are protected from the pressures of competition.

3. They exert disproportionate influences at all levels of government, giving rise to an "industrial–political complex" which favors big business at the expense of the rest of society.

Arguments in defense of big-business monopolies are these:

1. Monopolies are more effectively competitive than the numbers of firms alone indicate. This is because there is rivalry among particular products in specific markets (e.g., aluminum versus copper, steel, plastics), as well as countervailing power on the opposite side of the market exerted by monopolistic sellers of resources.

2. Monopolies permit mass-production economies at lower unit costs and prices than would be possible with large numbers of small firms.

3. Monopolies have the financial ability to support extensive research and development.

4. Monopolies have the ethical and moral sense not to exploit their monopoly power.

> To repeat: The foregoing arguments are often applied to today's big businesses, which the public erroneously equates with "monopoly." Therefore, this consideration should be kept in mind as you analyze the facts in each case before judging the relative merits of the arguments.

Reactions to Monopoly: The Antitrust Laws

The period 1879–1904 saw the first great *merger movement* in American history. During these years, an unprecedented number of firms expanded by combining or merging with others, thereby forming new single business units with huge investments, capacities, and outputs. These new business organizations were called monopolies or "trusts." In reaction to them and to subsequent economic developments Congress has passed a body of legislation known as the "antitrust laws."

The *antitrust laws* passed since 1890 commit the government to preventing monopoly and maintaining competition. There are also antitrust laws in almost every state in the country. But these are frequently ineffectual and spasmodically enforced. This is because states are powerless to control agreements or combinations in major industries whose activities extend into interstate commerce. Coupled with the states' lack of funds, this weakness has left the task of maintaining competition almost entirely to the federal government. Thus, it is the federal antitrust laws that will be of concern to us here. These laws consist mainly of the Sherman Antitrust Act, the Clayton Antitrust Act, the Federal Trade Commission Act, the Robinson–Patman Act, the Wheeler–Lea Act, and the Celler Antimerger Act.

THE SHERMAN ACT (1890)

The *Sherman Antitrust Act* was the first attempt by the federal government to regulate the growth of monopoly. The provisions of the law were concise (probably too concise) and to the point. The act declared as illegal:

1. Every contract, combination, or conspiracy in restraint of trade which occurs in interstate or foreign commerce.

2. Any monopolization or attempts to monopolize, or conspiracy with others in an attempt to monopolize, any portion of trade in interstate or foreign commerce.

Violations of the act were made punishable by fines and/or imprisonment, and persons injured by violations could sue for triple damages.

The act was surrounded by a cloud of uncertainty because it failed to state precisely which kinds of actions were prohibited. Also, no special agency existed to enforce the law until 1903, when the Antitrust Division of the U.S. Department of Justice was established under an Assistant Attorney General. (See Box 1.)

THE CLAYTON AND FEDERAL TRADE COMMISSION ACTS (1914)

In 1914, in order to put some teeth into the Sherman Act, Congress passed both the Clayton Act and the Federal Trade Commission Act. These were aimed at practices of *unfair competition,* defined as deceptive, dishonest, and injurious methods of competition. Thus, the *Clayton Antitrust Act* was concerned with four specific areas: price discrimination, exclusive and tying contracts, intercorporate stockholdings, and interlocking directorates.

1. *Price Discrimination* For sellers to discriminate in prices by charging different prices to different buyers for the same good is *illegal.* However, such discrimination is permissible where there are differences in the grade, quality, or quantity of the commodity sold; where the lower prices make due allowances for cost differences in selling or transportation; and where the lower prices are offered in good faith to meet competition. Illegality exists where, according to the law, the effect is "to substantially lessen competition or tend to create a monopoly."

2. *Exclusive and Tying Contracts* For sellers to lease, sell, or contract for the sale of commodities on condition that the lessee or purchaser not use or deal in the commodity of a competitor is *illegal* if such exclusive or tying contracts "substantially lessen competition or tend to create a monopoly."

3. *Intercorporate Stockholdings* For corporations engaged in commerce to acquire the shares of a competing corporation, or the stocks of two or more corporations competing with each other, is *illegal* if such intercorporate stockholdings "substantially lessen competition or tend to create a monopoly."

4. *Interlocking Directorates* For corporations engaged in commerce to have the same individual on two or more boards of directors is an interlocking directorate. Such directorships are *illegal* if the corporations

are competitive and if any one has capital, surplus, and undivided profits in excess of $1 million.

Thus:

Price discrimination, exclusive and tying contracts, and intercorporate stockholdings were not declared by the Clayton Act to be absolutely illegal. Rather, in the words of the law, they were unlawful only when their effects "may be to substantially lessen competition or tend to create a monopoly." On interlocking directorates, however, the law made no such qualification. The fact of the interlock itself is illegal, and the government need not find that the arrangement results in a reduction in competition.

The *Federal Trade Commission Act* served primarily as a general supplement to the Clayton Act by stating broadly and simply that "unfair methods of competition in commerce are hereby declared unlawful." In addition, it provided for the establishment of the *Federal Trade Commission* (FTC), a government antitrust agency with federal funds appropriated to it for the purpose of attacking unfair competitive practices in commerce.

The FTC is also authorized under the act to safeguard the public by preventing the dissemination of false and misleading advertising of foods, drugs, cosmetics, and therapeutic devices used in the diagnosis, prevention, or treatment of disease. It thus supplements in many ways the activities of the Food and Drug Administration, which, under the Food, Drug, and Cosmetic Act (1938), outlaws adulteration and misbranding of foods, drugs, devices, and cosmetics moving in interstate commerce.

THE ROBINSON–PATMAN ACT (1936)

Frequently referred to as the "Chain Store Act," the *Robinson–Patman Act* was passed for the purpose of providing economic protection to independent retailers and wholesalers, such as grocers and druggists, from "unfair discriminations" by large sellers attained "because of their tremendous purchasing power." The law was an outgrowth of the increasing competition faced by independents when chain stores and mass distributors developed after World War I. Supporters of the bill contended that the lower prices charged by large organizations were attributable less to lower costs than to sheer weight of bargaining power, which enabled the large organizations to obtain unfair and unjustified concessions from their suppliers. The act was thus a response to the cries of independents who demanded that the freedom of suppliers to discriminate be more strictly limited.

Box 1
Alphabet of Joyous Trusts

Although the Sherman Antitrust Act was passed in 1890, some big businesses continued to monopolize certain industries. Consequently, popular resentment toward trusts became increasingly pronounced over the next several decades. The plethora of trusts which existed around the turn of the century prompted cartoonists to depict the more objectionable monopolies in sardonic ways.

R is the Railroad Trust, always on time
To Run over the People, and get their last dime.

O is the Oil Trust, a modern Bill Sikes;
He defies the police, and does just as he likes.

B is the Beef Trust.   This heartless old sinner
Makes the People pay double or go without dinner.

U. 's the United States Rubber Trust. He Twists himself into knots, while he sobs the C. P.

S. is the Shipping Trust; when he's afloat
There's a mighty poor show for the poor People's boat.

A. is the Asphalt Trust. This is the way He shakes down the People and makes the thing pay.

The Granger Collection.

The act, which amended Section 2 of the Clayton Act relating to price discrimination, contained the following essential provisions:

1. The payment of brokerage fees where no independent broker is employed is *illegal.* This was intended to eliminate the practice of some chains of demanding the regular brokerage fee as a discount when they purchased direct from manufacturers. The argument posed was that such chains obtained the discount by their sheer bargaining power and thereby gained an unfair advantage over smaller independents that had to use and pay for brokerage services.

2. The making of concessions by sellers, such as manufacturers, to buyers, such as wholesalers and retailers, is *illegal* unless such concessions are made to all buyers on proportionally equal terms. This provision was aimed at preventing advertising and promotional allowances from being granted to large-scale buyers without allowances being made to small competing buyers on proportionally equal terms.

3. Other forms of discrimination, such as quantity discounts, are *illegal* where they substantially lessen competition or tend to create a monopoly, either among sellers or among buyers. However, price discrimination is not illegal if the differences in prices make "due allowances" for differences in cost or if offered "in good faith to meet an equally low price of a competitor." But even where discounts can be justified by lower costs, the FTC is empowered to fix quantity limits beyond which discounts may not be granted, if it believes that such discounts would be "unjustly discriminatory or promotive of monopoly in any line of commerce."

4. It is *illegal* to give or to receive a larger discount than that made available to competitors purchasing the same goods in equal quantities. Also, it is *illegal* to charge lower prices in one locality than in another for the same goods, or to sell at "unreasonably low prices," where either of these practices is aimed at "destroying competition or eliminating a competitor."

THE WHEELER-LEA ACT (1938)

An amendment to part of the Federal Trade Commission Act, the *Wheeler-Lea Act* was passed for the purpose of providing consumers, rather than just business competitors, with protection against unfair practices. The act makes *illegal* "unfair or deceptive acts or practices" in interstate commerce. Thus, a consumer who may be injured by an unfair trade practice is, before the law, of equal concern with the merchant who may be injured by an unfair competitive practice. The act also defines "false advertising" as "an advertisement other than labeling which is

misleading in a material respect." This definition applies to advertisements of foods, drugs, curative devices, and cosmetics.

THE CELLER ANTIMERGER ACT (1950)

The *Celler Antimerger Act* is an extension of Section 7 of the Clayton Act relating to intercorporate stockholdings. The Clayton Act, as stated earlier, made it illegal for corporations to acquire the stock of competing corporations. But that law, the FTC argued, left a loophole through which monopolistic mergers could be effected by a corporation acquiring the *assets* of a competing corporation, or by first acquiring the stock and, by voting or granting of proxies, acquiring the assets. Moreover, the Supreme Court in several cases held that such mergers were not illegal under the Clayton Act if a corporation used its stock purchases to acquire the assets before the FTC's complaint was issued or before the Commission had issued its final order banning the stock acquisition.

The Celler Act plugged the loophole in the Clayton Act by making it illegal for a corporation to acquire the stock *or assets* of a competing corporation where the effect may be "substantially to lessen competition, or tend to create a monopoly." The Celler Act thus bans all types of mergers. These include:

1. *Horizontal Mergers* Plants producing similar products which are under one ownership. Example: steel mills.

2. *Vertical Mergers* Plants in different stages of production which are integrated under one ownership. Example: an automobile company that owns a steel mill.

3. *Conglomerate or Circular Mergers* Dissimilar plants and unrelated product lines which are placed under one ownership. Example: a transportation company that owns a food-processing firm.

These three types of mergers are banned, provided the Commission can show that the effects may substantially lessen competition or tend toward monopoly.

It should be noted, however, that the intent of Congress in passing the Celler Act was that there be a maintenance of competition. Accordingly, the act was intended to apply to mergers between large firms or between large and small firms. The Act was not designed to apply to mergers of small firms, which may be undertaken to strengthen their market position.

ENFORCEMENT OF THE ANTITRUST LAWS

In general, the antitrust laws are applied on a *case-by-case* basis. That is, an order or decision resulting from an action is not applicable to all of industry, only to the defendants in the particular case. Cases may originate in the complaints of injured parties, suggestions made by other government agencies, or in the research of the Antitrust Division of the Department of Justice and of the Federal Trade Commission. Both of these agencies are responsible for enforcing the antitrust laws. However, most of the cases arise from complaints issued by injured parties.

The antitrust laws fix the responsibility for the behavior of a corporation on its officers and directors and makes them subject to the penalties of heavy fine or imprisonment for violating the laws. Business executives who do not want to risk violation of the law may present their proposed plans for combination or other particular practices to the Justice Department. If the plans appear to be legal, the Department may commit itself not to institute future criminal proceedings, but it will reserve the right to institute civil action if competition is later restrained. The purpose of a civil suit is not to punish, but to restore competition by providing remedies. Typically, three classes of remedies are employed:

1. *Dissolution, Divestiture, or Divorcement* Examples of these provisions include an order to dissolve a trade association or combination, to sell intercorporate stockholdings, or to dispose of ownership in other assets. The purpose of these actions is to break up a monopolistic organization into smaller but more competitors.

2. *Injunction* This is a court order requiring that the defendant refrain from certain business practices, or perhaps take a particular action that will increase rather than reduce competition.

3. *Consent Decree* This is an agreement usually worked out between the defendant and the Justice Department without a court trial. The defendant in this instance does not admit guilt, but agrees nevertheless to abide by the rules of business behavior set down in the decree. This device is the chief instrument employed in the enforcement of the Sherman and Clayton Acts.

Finally, the laws are also enforced through private suits by injured parties (individuals, corporations, or states) who may sue for treble damages including court costs. This approach to enforcement has become quite common since the 1960s.

EXEMPTIONS AND INTERPRETATIONS

A compact summary of the antitrust laws is presented in Exhibit 1. A few industries and economic groups are exempt from these laws. The most important ones

---

Exhibit 1
The Antitrust Laws in a Nutshell

1. It is flatly *illegal,* without any qualification, to:

   (a) Enter a contract, combination, or conspiracy in restraint of trade (Sherman Act, Sec. 1).

   (b) Monopolize, attempt to monopolize, or combine or conspire to monopolize trade (Sherman Act, Sec. 3).

2. When and if the effect may be substantially to lessen competition or tend to create a monopoly, it is *illegal* to:

   (a) Acquire the stock of competing corporations (Clayton Act, Sec. 7).

   (b) Acquire the assets of competing corporations (Clayton Act, Sec. 7, as amended by the Celler Antimerger Act in 1950).

   (c) Enter exclusive and tying contracts (Clayton Act, Sec. 3).

   (d) Discriminate unjustifiably among purchasers (Clayton Act, Sec. 2, as amended by the Robinson–Patman Act, Sec. 1).

3. In general, it is also *illegal* to:

   (a) Engage in particular forms of price discrimination (Robinson–Patman Act, Sec. 1 and 3).

   (b) Serve as a director of competing corporations of a certain minimum size (Clayton Act, Sec. 8).

   (c) Use unfair methods of competition (Federal Trade Commission Act, Sec. 5).

   (d) Use unfair or deceptive acts or practices (Federal Trade Commission Act, Sec. 5, as amended by the Wheeler–Lea Act, Sec. 3).

Thus, the laws taken as a whole are designed not only to prevent the growth of monopoly, but to maintain competition as well.

---

are the transport industries and labor unions. Transporters—including railroads, trucks, ships, and barges—are excluded because they are largely subject to the control of regulatory agencies such as the Interstate Commerce Commission. The exemption of labor unions was originally justified on the basis that they do not normally seek to monopolize markets or engage in methods of unfair competition. They seek instead to protect and enhance the position of labor. However, unions may be subjected to antitrust prosecution if they combine with management to violate the antitrust laws.

To summarize:

1. The Sherman Act forbade restraints of trade, monopoly, and attempts to monopolize.

2. The Clayton Act forbade practices whose effects may be to lessen substantially the degree of competition or tend to create a monopoly.

3. The Federal Trade Commission Act forbade unfair methods of competition.

But though Congress succeeded in passing these laws, it failed to define, and left up to the courts to interpret in their own way, the meaning of such terms as "monopoly," "restraint of trade," "substantial lessening of competition," and "unfair competition." As a result, judicial interpretations have been crucial in determining the economic applications and effects of the antitrust laws. In view of this, we shall attempt to sketch briefly some major issues, court decisions, and leading trends that have emerged in the past few decades—confining ourselves for the most part to the years since the end of World War II (1945).

Restrictive Agreements—Conspiracies

The state of the law as to restrictive agreements or conspiracies of virtually any type among competitors is reasonably clear, and the courts have almost always upheld the government in such cases.

In general, a _restrictive agreement_ is regarded by the government as a conspiracy of firms that results in a restraint of trade among separate companies. It is usually understood to involve a direct or indirect, overt or implied, form of price fixing, output control, market sharing, or exclusion of competitors by boycotts or other coercive practices. It makes no difference whether the agreement was accomplished through a formal organization such as a trade association, informally, or even by habitual identity of behavior frequently referred to as _conscious parallel action_—identical price behavior among competitors. The effect, more than the means, is judged.

For instance, in a major case against the American Tobacco Company in 1946, the government charged that the "big three" cigarette producers exhibited striking uniformity in the prices they paid for tobacco and in the prices they charged for cigarettes, as well as in other practices. Despite the fact that not a shred of evidence was produced to indicate that a common plan had even so much as been proposed, the Supreme Court declared that conspiracy "may be found in a course of dealings or other circumstances as well as in an exchange of words." Hence, the companies were held in violation of the law.

Thus:

No secret meetings in a smoke-filled room and no signatures in blood are needed to prove the conspiracy provisions of the Sherman Act. Any type of agreement, explicit or implicit, any practice, direct or indirect, or even any action with the knowledge that others will act likewise to their mutual self-interest, can be interpreted as illegal. This is especially true if the act results in exclusion of competitors from the market, restriction of output or of purchases, division of markets, price fixing, elimination of the opportunity or incentive to compete, or coercion.

The doctrine of conscious parallel action was partially repudiated by judges in some subsequent cases. However, it still remains as a fairly significant antitrust barometer, although the doctrine has been employed infrequently since the American Tobacco case of 1946.

THE GREAT ELECTRICAL CONSPIRACY

In February 1961, one of the most significant antitrust cases in the history of the United States was concluded. More than $2 million in fines were levied on the electrical equipment industry, and seven executives were jailed for terms of 30 days. Several dozen companies, including General Electric and Westinghouse, and a number of corporate officials were charged with unlawful price-fixing and dividing the market.

Though the fines were huge, it was the jail sentences that were more remarkable. For, although sending people to jail is not unheard of in antitrust cases, it is unusual—especially when the individuals are "pillars of the community."

NOTE   From 1890 to 1959 a total of about 200 people had received prison sentences for committing conspiracies in violation of the Sherman Act. Most of the offenders were union members and petty racketeers, and a few were wartime spies. Only seven were business executives, all of whom received suspended prison sentences. Thus, until 1959, no important business executive ever spent a day in jail for violating the Sherman Act.

In 1959, however, a Federal District Court in Columbus, Ohio, decided that four officials of garden tool companies who pleaded _nolo contendere_ (no contest or no defense) to price-fixing charges should not, as was typically the case, get off merely with fines and lectures. Accordingly, even though the government (Department of Justice) had not sought jail terms, the judge gave 90-day sentences to each of the four.

At this time, the government was also conducting its investigation of the electrical industry. The jail sentences in the garden tool case encouraged formerly reluctant witnesses to "volunteer" information to the grand jury in hopes of obtaining immunity from criminal prosecution.

As brought out in the electrical case, the conspiracy was remarkably well organized. It involved regular meetings of executives in resorts and hotel rooms, coded communications, and complicated formulas for rigging bids on government contracts. With most of the industry represented, the conspiracy directly or indirectly affected almost every dam built, every power generator installed, and every electrical distribution system set up in the United States. It even reached into the new and vital field of atomic energy. The threads wove such a fantastic pattern that Federal District Judge J. Cullen Ganey was prompted to remark:

> This is a shocking indictment of a vast section of our economy, for what is really at stake here is the survival of the kind of economy under which America has grown to greatness, the free enterprise system. The conduct of the corporate and individual defendants alike . . . flagrantly mocked the image of the economic system of free enterprise which we profess to the country and destroyed the model which we offer today as a free world alternative to state control and eventual dictatorship.

Since the electrical equipment case, there have been further indications in other cases that the courts will continue to strike down all types of restrictive agreements with increasing vigor—even to the extent of imposing jail sentences if fines alone seem to be inadequate. (See Box 2.)

Box 2

Department of Justice

News Release

TUESDAY, MARCH 6, 1979

The Department of Justice has terminated a civil antitrust case against Brink's Incorporated and Wells Fargo Armored Service Corporation.

Both companies provide armored car services. The firms had been charged with conspiring among themselves and co-conspirators to allocate customers and rig bids and price quotations for armored car services in the United States.

Both Brink's and Wells Fargo pleaded no contest to the criminal charges and were sentenced to pay fines of $625,000 and $375,000, respectively.

Combination and Monopoly

Concerning monopoly, the state of the law is less certain and the position of the courts less consistent than in cases involving restrictive agreements. There are three aspects of monopoly to be considered: monopoly per se, vertical and horizontal mergers, and conglomerate mergers.

MONOPOLY PER SE

The attitude of the courts has changed fundamentally since 1945. Before then the courts held that the mere size of a corporation, no matter how impressive, is no offense. For a firm to be in violation of the law, "unreasonable" behavior in the form of actual exertion of monopoly power, as shown by unfair practices, was required. Since the *Standard Oil* case of 1911, this had been called the *rule of reason* or, what is roughly equivalent, the "good trust versus bad trust" criterion.

But a major decision handed down near the end of World War II reversed this outlook almost completely. In the case against the Aluminum Company of America (1945) Judge Learned Hand turned the trend in judicial thinking on monopoly. It was his opinion that:

1. To gain monopolistic power even by growing with the market (i.e., by reinvesting earnings rather than by combining with others) is nevertheless illegal.

2. The mere size of a firm is indeed an offense, for the power to abuse and the abuse of power cannot be separated.

3. The company's market share was 90 percent and that "is enough to constitute a monopoly; it is doubtful whether 60 or 64 percent would be enough; and certainly 33 percent is not."

4. The good behavior of the company which, prior to 1945, would have been an acceptable defense to the court, is no longer valid, for *"Congress did not condone 'good' trusts and condemn 'bad' ones; it forbade all."*

With this decision, Judge Hand greatly tempered the rule-of-reason criterion. Subsequent court decisions have not repudiated his doctrines, although the decisions have softened his conclusions somewhat. At the present time, the judgment of monopoly is based on many factors. They include the number and strength of firms in the market, their size from the standpoint of technological development and competition with substitutes and with foreign trade, national security interests in maintaining strong productive facilities and maximum scientific research, and the public's interest in lower costs and uninterrupted production.

Box 3
The Rule of Reason

The Sherman Act outlawed every contract, combination, and conspiracy in restraint of trade. In both the Standard Oil and the American Tobacco cases of 1911—which were among the most famous in the history of antitrust—the Su-

preme Court upheld the government. But the Court went on to write the "rule of reason" into law, contending that a distinction should be made between "good" trusts and "bad" trusts.

The *Aluminum Company* case (1945) was a major milestone in the history of antitrust. It suggests that monopoly may be held illegal without requiring proof of intent and even if the power were lawfully acquired. It further implies that power may be condemned even if never abused, especially if it tends to limit or bar market access to other firms. Although the rule of reason is still an important criterion employed by the courts, it is not as strong a criterion as it was prior to 1945. (See Box 3.)

MERGERS

A merger is an amalgamation of two or more firms under one ownership. It may result from one of three types of integration:

1. *Vertical Mergers*   These unite under one ownership plants engaged in different stages of production from raw materials to finished products. Such mergers may take the form of forward integration into buyer mar-

kets or backward integration into supplier markets. They may result in greater economies by combining different production stages and regularizing supplies, thereby increasing profit margins.

2. *Horizontal Mergers* These unite under one ownership plants producing like products. The products may be close substitutes like cement from different plants, or moderate substitutes like tin cans and jars. The objective is to round out a product line which is sold through the same distribution channels, thereby offering joint economies in selling and distribution efforts.

3. *Conglomerate Mergers* These unite under one ownership unlike plants producing unrelated products. Such mergers reflect a desire by the acquiring company to spread risks, find outlets for idle capital funds, add products that can be sold with the firm's merchandising knowledge and skills, or simply gain greater economic power on a broader front.

The courts have often upheld the government by disapproving of mergers that resulted in a substantial lessening of competition or tendency toward monopoly—regardless of the type of merger involved. However, the changes in the law on corporate acquisition made in the Celler Antimerger Act of 1950 were given specific meaning in a landmark 1962 decision by the Supreme Court known as the *Brown Shoe* case.

The *Brown Shoe* Case

In the *Brown Shoe* case which involved both a horizontal and a vertical merger, the Supreme Court ruled against the defendant. The Brown Shoe Company was the nation's fourth-largest shoe manufacturer, with 4 percent of the industry's total, and it also controlled a number of retail outlets. Seven years earlier, in 1955, it had merged with the G. R. Kinney Corporation. This company operated the nation's largest retail shoe chain, accounting for 1.2 percent of national shoe sales, and also served as the nation's twelfth-largest shoe manufacturer.

Chief Justice Warren spoke for the Court in upholding a federal district court's decision ordering Brown to divest itself of Kinney. He pointed out that despite the relatively small market shares of the companies, the merger was significant. Thus:

1. The vertical aspect of the merger of Brown's manufacturing facilities with Kinney's retail outlets would probably "foreclose competition from a substantial share of the markets for men's, women's, and children's shoes, without producing any countervailing competitive, economic, or social advantages."

2. The horizontal aspect of the merger—the marriage of Brown's retailing outlets with those of Kinney—involved a retail market that could be the entire nation or a single metropolitan area. "The fact that two merging firms have competed directly on the horizontal level in but a fraction of the geographic markets in which either has operated does not, in itself, place their merger outside the scope of Section 7" of the Clayton Act. The Court must recognize "Congress' desire to promote competition through the protection of viable, small, locally owned businesses."

Conclusion: Watch Mergers Closely

On the basis of the *Brown Shoe* case and other subsequent cases, the following conclusion seems plausible:

> The government's policy is not to wage an all-out war on mergers in general. Instead, it applies its own judgment to the merits of each situation. However, both vertical and horizontal mergers are likely to be declared illegal unless the companies can clearly demonstrate that the mergers will tend to increase competition. An example is when a few small or weak firms in an oligopolistic industry merge in order to compete more effectively with the giants in the industry and thus promote the public interest.

Conglomerate or "circular" mergers, where the merging firms are neither competitors nor have a supplier–customer relationship, have proved to be the most popular form of combination, as shown in Exhibit 2. An outstanding example has been Ling-Tempco-Vought (LTV), which acquired airline, computer technology, basic steel, aerospace, electronics, car rental, meat-packing, and sporting-goods firms. Another example, one of many, has been Boise Cascade, which owns lumber, mobile homes, plastics, computer services, and land-development companies. Other well-known conglomerates are International Telephone and Telegraph, Gulf and Western, Litton Industries, and Radio Corporation of America.

Conglomerate mergers raise many difficult antitrust issues, some of which may be settled in the years to come. Until then the most that can be said is that according to the general trend of antitrust attitudes:

1. Internal growth is preferable to growth by merger.

2. Any merger in a large, concentrated, or oligopolistic industry like automobiles, chemicals, or steel will be subjected to close evaluation.

3. Any industry that has ever been charged with price fixing will automatically draw attention on a matter of mergers.

4. Mergers on the part of top companies within industries, as well as between most industries, will be scrutinized.

Exhibit 2
The Merger Movement—Recent Trends

Conglomerate mergers outweigh both vertical and horizontal mergers—in number as well as in value of assets. The most recent tidal wave of mergers occurred during the late 1960s. In that period many of today's well-known, diversified corporate giants were born.

Mergers can have adverse effects on competition by:

○ Reducing the number of firms capable of entering concentrated markets.

○ Reducing the number of firms with the capability and incentive for competitive innovation.

○ Increasing the barriers to the entry of new firms in concentrated markets.

○ Diminishing the vigor of competition by increasing actual and potential customer–supplier relationships among leading firms in concentrated markets.

ACQUISITIONS OF MANUFACTURING AND MINING FIRMS WITH ASSETS OF $10 MILLION OR MORE

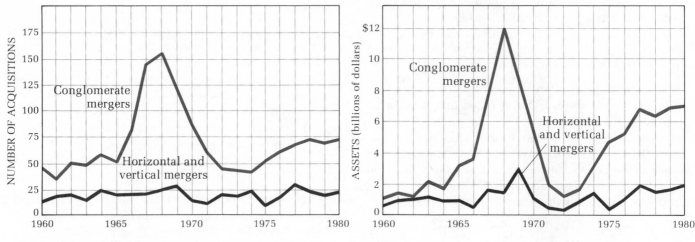

SOURCE: Federal Trade Commission. Data for 1977–1980 are preliminary.

5. The larger a company, the more carefully it will be watched, especially if it seeks merger in an industry characterized by small companies.

Patents

The Constitution of the United States (Art. 1, Sec. 8, Par. 8) empowers Congress "To promote the progress of Science and useful Arts, by securing for limited Times to Authors and Inventors the exclusive Right to their respective Writings and Discoveries. . . ." Although this power was not denied to the states, it came in time to be exercised solely by the federal government, and upon this authority the American patent and copyright system is based.

What are the economic implications of patents?

A *patent* is an exclusive right conferred on an inventor by government, for a limited time. It authorizes the inventor to make, use, transfer, or withhold an invention, which can be done even without a patent. But it also gives the inventor the right to exclude others or to admit them on specific terms, which can be done only with a patent.

Patents thus promote invention by granting temporary monopolies to inventors. But the patent system has also been employed as a means of controlling output, dividing markets, and fixing prices of entire industries. Since these perversions of the patent law have a direct effect on competition, they have been criticized by the antitrusters, and the courts have increasingly limited the scope and abuses of patent monopoly. The trends based on court decisions in each of the following areas may be sketched briefly.

STANDARD OF PATENTABILITY

Until the 1950s, the chief standard of patentability employed by the courts was the "flash-of-genius" test. Thus, in the *Cuno Engineering Corporation* case in 1941, involving the patentability of a wireless lighter, Justice William O. Douglas, speaking for the Supreme Court, said that usefulness and novelty alone do "not necessarily make the device patentable.... The device must not only be 'new and useful,' it must also be an 'invention' or 'discovery'.... The new device, however useful it may be, must reveal the *flash of creative genius,* not merely the skill of the calling. If it fails, it has not established its right to a private grant on the public domain."

The flash-of-genius test was criticized as resting on the subjective judgment of the Court, and as not taking sufficient recognition of inventions that are the product of teams rather than individuals, especially in large corporations. In response to these arguments, Congress passed the Patent Act of 1952. This law provides that in order to be patentable, a formula, method, or device must be:

1. *"New"*—unknown to the public prior to the patent application.

2. *"Useful"*—demonstrate a substantial degree of technical advance in the object invented or in the process of producing something.

3. *"Unobvious"*—not apparent to one ordinarily skilled in the art of the invention.

But the courts have not found in the Patent Act an adequate definition of "invention" and continue to rely on case law and their own judgment in determining what constitutes an invention. Consequently:

> The flash-of-genius test, tempered perhaps by the political and economic attitudes of the courts with respect to the public interest, is no longer the *chief* criterion of patentability. However, it continues to play an important role in judicial thinking. The reason is not hard to see. The above three provisions of the Patent Act are virtually equivalent to a flash-of-genius test.

RIGHT OF NONUSE

The right of a patentee to withhold an invention from use has been upheld by the courts. In numerous cases tried since the turn of the century, the courts have viewed a patent as a form of private property and hence have upheld the patentee's right to refuse putting it to use. In response, it has been argued by some that a patent is a privilege and not a right, that nonuse may retard technological progress and economic de-velopment, and hence that the courts should exercise more judgment and discretion in such cases. And even the courts in recent decades have spoken of patents as privileges contingent upon the enhancement of public welfare. But the right of nonuse appears nevertheless to be supported by the law, for as stated by the Supreme Court in the *Hartford Empire* case in 1945: "A patent owner is not ... under any obligation to see that the public acquires the free right to use the invention. He has no obligation either to use it or to grant its use to others."

What do you think? Is a patent a privilege or a right? Would society be better off if the law were changed so as to prohibit the right of nonuse? How would such a measure affect inventors' incentives and technological progress?

TYING CONTRACTS

A seller uses a *tying contract* (or tie-in sale) to require the buyer to purchase one or more additional or "tied" products as a condition for purchasing the desired or "tying" product. For the tie-in sale to be effective, the major or tying product must be difficult to substitute, not easily dispensed with, and relatively more inelastic in demand than the subsidiary or tied item. A good example occurs in block-bookings of motion pictures in which movie theaters are required to take a certain number of grade B films as a condition for obtaining grade A films. Many other examples can be cited.

An ideal opportunity for tie-in sales exists when the seller possesses an exclusive and essential patent. A classic example is the United Shoe Machinery Company, which once compelled shoemakers to purchase other materials and intermediate products as a condition for purchasing shoe machinery. In the *United Shoe* case, as well as in a number of subsequent cases involving such firms as Radio Corporation of America, International Business Machines, and International Harvester, the courts have struck down tying contracts that were found substantially to lessen competition within the meaning of the Clayton Act. On the whole:

> The trend of the courts is to disallow a tying contract of any kind, regardless of circumstances, when it is believed that the effect is to extend the scope of a patent monopoly or cause substantial injury—or even the probability of such injury—to competition.

NOTE   An extreme example was Eastman Kodak prior to 1954. The company sold amateur color film at a price that included the charge for finishing, thereby tying the sale of the film itself to the provision of finishing services. In 1954 the company signed a decree, agreeing to sell the film alone and thus admit competitors to the finishing business.

RESTRICTIVE LICENSING

Under a _restrictive license,_ a patentee sells a patented product to a licensee on restricted conditions. Typically, the restrictions include the patentee's fixing the geographic area of the licensee, the level of output, or the price at which the patented good may be sold. Usually, such licensing is motivated by considerations of reciprocal favor (e.g., the exchange of patents among competitors) or perhaps performed for the purpose of minimizing the incentive of the licensee to develop an alternative process. In any case, three major trends based on various court cases may be noted:

1. The right of a patentee to fix the licensee's prices on patented products has been and still is upheld by the courts.

2. The right of the patentee to fix the prices charged for unpatented products made by patented processes (e.g., a patented machine) is generally doubtful.

3. The use of restrictive licensing is illegal when employed for the purpose of eliminating competition among many licensees.

In general, the extent to which patent owners may license their patents is quite strictly limited. When each of several licensees accepts restrictive terms on condition or with the knowledge that others will do likewise, they are committing a conspiracy in restraint of trade in the opinion of the Court and hence are guilty of violating the law.

CROSS-LICENSING AND PATENT POOLING

"Sharing" devices such as the cross-licensing of patents or the pooling of patents for mutual benefit are not held to be illegal as such. However, they are generally declared illegal when, in the eyes of the courts, they are used as a means of eliminating competition among patent owners and licensees.

But what constitutes elimination of competition? In the _Hartford Empire_ case, decided in 1945, it was held that Hartford employed the patents in its pool to dominate completely the glass container industry, curtail output, divide markets, and fix prices through restrictive licenses. The company's use of patent pooling was therefore declared an unlawful conspiracy. In the _National Lead_ case in 1947, a cross-licensing agreement that divided markets and fixed the prices of titanium pigment was also declared illegal. And in the _Line Material_ case of 1948, the Court was most emphatic in its denunciation of a cross-licensing

arrangement that fixed the price of fuse cutouts used in electric circuits.

On the whole, it appears that patent pooling per se is not illegal. (The automobile industry is frequently cited as an outstanding example of successful and desirable patent pooling.) However, the courts will declare that abuse exists under certain circumstances:

1. When the pool is restricted to certain competitors or available only at excessive royalty payments.

2. When the pool is used as a device to cross-license competitors for the purpose of fixing prices and allocating markets.

CONCENTRATION OF PATENT OWNERSHIP

Patent concentration within a single firm has been frowned on increasingly since the late 1940s. Prior to that time, the ownership of many patents by a single firm was held to be legal. Since then, the courts have held that the concentration of patents by a dominant firm in an industry—regardless of whether the firm's patents were achieved by research, assignment, or purchase—may constitute monopolization and hence violate the antitrust laws. This is true _even if the firm did nothing illegal and did not use the patents to hinder or suppress competition._

The courts have provided strong remedies in such cases. These include compulsory licensing, sometimes on a royalty-free basis, for a company's existing patents, and on a reasonable royalty basis for future patents. They also include the provision of necessary know-how in the form of detailed written manuals and even technical consultants, available at nominal charges, to licensees and competitors.

NOTE   Thus, Eastman Kodak agreed to provide other color-film finishers with up-to-date manuals on its processing technology and to provide technical representatives to assist competitors in using the methods described. In a number of other cases involving Standard Oil of New Jersey, the Aluminum Company of America, Merck & Co., A. B. Dick, Libbey-Owens-Ford, Owens-Corning Fiberglas, American Can, and General Electric, as well as many other firms, somewhat similar measures have been adopted.

In conclusion, therefore:

Through compulsory licensing and the provision of technical knowledge, hundreds of patents involving a wide variety of manufacturing areas have been freed. Because competition was thereby significantly enhanced, it is likely that the courts will continue this policy in the future.

Trademarks

The purpose of a trademark, as originally conceived, was to identify the origin or ownership of a product. In an economic sense, however, managements have come to look upon trademarks as a strategic device for establishing product differentiation and, through advertising, consumer preference. In this way some firms have been able to establish a degree of market entrenchment that has remained substantially unrivaled for as long as several decades. Moreover, by establishing product differentiation through trademarks, firms have exploited this advantage in various ways with the aim of enhancing long-run profits. Five examples may be noted in view of their antitrust significance.

1. *Price Discrimination* This has been implemented by the use of trademarks. Until the court decided against it in 1948, Rohm & Haas sold methyl methacrylate as Lucite and Crystalite to manufacturers at 85 cents per pound, and as Veronite and Crystalex to dentists at $45 per pound. Many firms today sell branded products in one market at higher prices than they sell the same product—unbranded—in other markets.

2. *Output Control* Output control can be accomplished through the use of trademarks. United States Pipe and Foundry licensed companies to produce under its patents at graduated royalty rates on condition that they stamp their products with the trade name "de Lavaud." In 1948, the courts ruled against the company for using a trademark to control output.

3. *Exclusive Markets* These can be attained through the use of trademarks. General Electric was able to persuade procurement agencies to establish specifications requiring the use of Mazda bulbs. It licensed Westinghouse to use the name but denied its other licensees the same right. In 1949, a court ruled that General Electric had used the trademark as a device for excluding competitors from markets.

4. *Market Sharing* Market-sharing cartels have been accomplished through the use of trademarks. A *cartel* is an association of firms in the same industry, established to increase the profits of its members by adopting common policies affecting production, market allocation, or price. A cartel may be domestic or international in scope. Thus, a cartel member may be granted the exclusive right to use a trademark in its own territory. If it oversteps its market boundary, it is driven back by an infringement suit. Examples of trade names that have identified such regional monopolies include Mazda, Mimeograph, Merck, and Timken, and the trademarks of General Storage Battery, New Jersey Zinc, American Bosch, and S.K.F. Industries.

Since the 1940s, the courts have found such arrangements to be in violation of the Sherman Act. The courts have sometimes forbidden cartel members to grant their foreign partners exclusive trademark rights abroad, to sell in American markets, and to interfere with American imports.

5. *Resale Price Maintenance* This practice, popularly referred to as "fair trade," permits the manufacturer or distributor of a branded product to set the minimum retail price at which that product can be sold. It thereby eliminates price competition for the good at the retail level. Although no longer as significant as it was several decades ago, this practice has been implemented by the use of trademarks even where patents and copyrights have failed.

Concentration of Economic Power

We have examined the antitrust laws and their application. Some basic questions that remain to be answered are: (1) To what extent does monopoly power exist in the United States? (2) What should public policy be with respect to competition and monopoly?

HOW MUCH CONCENTRATION IS THERE?

The growth and importance of big business in the United States have resulted in charges, frequently made and widely believed, that (1) economic power is concentrated in the hands of a few corporate giants, (2) this concentration has grown over the years, and therefore (3) there has been a general "decline of competition." Upon close examination the evidence shows the first of these charges to be only partially true, and the second and third to be highly debatable if not unfounded. Let us see why.

A measure that is extensively used by economists and government antitrust agencies to evaluate the monopoly power of a firm is *market share*. This is the percentage of an industry's output accounted for by an individual firm. For example, if 1,000 units of a commodity were sold in a particular year, and one firm in the industry sold 500 of those units, the firm's market share for that year would be 50 percent. In practice, a company's market share is usually measured on the basis of sales, value added at each stage of production, or value of shipments.

In advanced industrial societies such as ours, where many industries tend to be dominated by a few large firms, economists and antitrust agencies have found it useful to expand the concept of market share to a measure called the _concentration ratio_. This is simply the percentage of an industry's output accounted for by its four leading firms. As in the measurement of market share, a concentration ratio is usually based on sales, value added, or value of shipments. Other measures of size, however, such as assets or employment, are also sometimes used. An illustration of concentration ratios is presented in Exhibit 3.

Do concentration ratios measure "monopoly power"? In most cases they do not, because the results can differ according to the way in which the calculations are made. Three fundamental considerations are involved: (1) the choice of an industry base, (2) the choice of a producing unit, and (3) the choice of a measure of output.

Choice of Industry Base

The degree of concentration will vary depending on the industry base chosen. Concentration ratios are tabulated by the Census Bureau, which classifies industries on the basis of physical similarities of goods produced rather than on the basis of their substitutability in the marketplace. For example, metal cans and glass jars are identified as being in two different industries, even though the products are effective substitutes and usually fall within the same market. As a result, if a concentration ratio were calculated for the food-container industry, the figure would be quite different from those that exist for either the metal-can or glass-jar industries. The same idea applies to many other industries. As a result, _concentration ratios often fail to indicate the true degree of market influence and monopoly power._

Exhibit 3
Concentration Ratios: Percentages of Industry Output Produced by Four Largest Firms in Selected Industries

Industry	Percent of industry output (value of shipments)
Primary aluminum	100
Motor vehicles	93
Cigarettes	84
Aircraft engines and parts	77
Photographic equipment	74
Tires and inner tubes	73
Aircraft	66
Soap and detergents	62
Electronic computing equipment	51
Radio and television sets	49
Construction machinery	43
Toilet preparations	38
Petroleum refining	31
Pharmaceutical preparations	26
Fluid milk	18
Bottled and canned soft drinks	14
Women's and misses' dresses	9

SOURCE: U.S. Bureau of the Census.

Since the early 1930s, many studies of concentration have been done by economists. Their purpose has been to examine the concentration of assets, employment, income, and sales in large firms. The groups studied have included financial corporations, manufacturing as a whole, particular manufacturing industries, and the output of manufactured products.

Has the long-run trend of concentration been increasing, stable, or decreasing? A synthesis of various studies reveals the following:

1. Big businesses have grown both in number and in size at a rate proportional to the economy as a whole.

2. The list of the 500 largest corporations in the economy (published annually by _Fortune_ magazine) is dynamic; many new firms are added each year and many old firms are dropped. However, in the more concentrated industries, the largest firms tend to remain.

3. The overall pattern of concentration ratios for manufacturing as a whole has exhibited two long-run trends: (a) a slight decrease for the period 1900 to 1946; (b) stability or possibly a slight increase since 1947, although the evidence is extremely murky and is currently being analyzed by many economists in and out of government.

4. Some industries, such as transportation, communication, and finance, have a moderate to high degree of concentration, while the trade and service industries are characterized by a low degree of concentration.

To conclude, therefore:

Over any long period of time, some concentration figures for individual industries, product groups, and product classes will rise while others fall. Hence, it is extremely difficult if not impossible to say whether the trend of concentration in the _economy as a whole_ has been increasing, stable, or decreasing.

Choice of Producing Unit

The degree of concentration will vary depending on the producing unit chosen, such as a plant or a firm, or a single-product or multiple-product firm. Concentration ratios apply to a heterogeneous conglomeration of industries some of which are highly competitive, some moderately so, and some virtually monopolized. Further, the ratios are obscured because they pertain to a group of the largest firms in an industry, without revealing the degree of domination by a single firm. *The ratios thus disclose little as to the extent of competition or monopoly.*

Choice of Measure of Output

The degree of concentration will vary depending on the measure of output chosen. In some cases, the concentration ratio will be seriously understated if the output figures are national and markets are regional, or if heterogeneous goods are lumped together into a single category. In other cases the ratios will be greatly overstated if the figures are limited to domestic production with competition from imports ignored. *Thus, the data on concentration may reveal little either as to the structure of markets for particular goods or as to the index of concentrated power.*

It is apparent, therefore, that measures of economic concentration are not measures of "monopoly power," as is often contended. At best, concentration ratios may reveal the results of innovation, market development, and lower costs and prices. But these ratios may also conceal the influence of potential competition, and the existence—on the other side of the market—of countervailing power. Nevertheless:

> Despite the shortcomings of concentration ratios, they are the most common measures of market power that exist. As a result, government agencies charged with enforcing the antitrust laws will continue to rely on these indicators as the best single source of information on questions pertaining to competition and monopoly in the American economy.

WHICH FUTURE POLICY FOR ANTITRUST?

What policy should society adopt to encourage competition and discourage monopoly? Three major approaches have been suggested by some economists and political leaders:

1. Public regulation or ownership of large-scale firms.

2. Vigorous enforcement of the antitrust laws.

3. Revision of the antitrust laws to make competition more workable.

Public Regulation and Ownership

Some economic and political reformers have argued that the "engine of monopoly" has overtaken the American economy. As a result, American industry is dominated by large firms with strong monopoly powers, the consequence of which is serious misallocation of society's resources.

Some who take this position—especially those with strong socialist leanings—argue in favor of greater public regulation or even public ownership of large-scale monopolies and oligopolies. The available evidence in the United States and in other Western countries, however, suggests strongly that this solution may be inferior to the two remaining alternatives.

Vigorous Enforcement of the Antitrust Laws

Many economists and political leaders argue that the growth of monopolies and oligopolies has resulted from inadequate application of the antitrust laws. These critics believe that much more competition will be encouraged if the laws are vigorously enforced. This requires, of course, that Congress appropriate larger budgets to the antitrust agencies so that they can engage in more investigations.

Supporters of this view have suggested that vigorous enforcement of the laws can be implemented in at least three ways:

1. The government should be willing to ask for, and the courts should be willing to order, dissolution (the breaking up of large firms into smaller competing firms) on a much broader scale than hitherto. This is especially true if such dissolution would not impair the efficiency or rate of technological progress of large-scale firms. For example, it has often been suggested that the Chevrolet Division, among some others, should be separated from General Motors and established as an independent corporation.

2. Congress should eliminate all exceptions to the antitrust laws so that labor unions, transport industries, and others are no longer exempt.

3. Congress should consider revising the patent laws and other protective legislation (tariffs) which aid special-interest groups and strengthen their monopolistic position.

Revision of the Laws for More Workable Competition

Finally, some economists and politicians deny that there is a significant absence of competition in big business. They argue that the antitrust laws were written too long ago to reflect the current structure of the economy. Hence, the laws may have to be revised to reflect the needs of our time.

Their position may be summarized briefly:

1. Numerous studies indicate that "effective" competition exists in large-scale enterprises. Further, the traditional assumptions of nineteenth-century atomistic competition are unrealistic and cannot be applied in our twentieth-century economy, characterized by rapid product development, market growth, and vast technological advancement. Firms compete with one another in many ways other than price—through, for example, service, convenience, quality, and style—and so competition is of a "workable" form. It is only in the manufacturing sector of our economy that the problem of unregulated monopoly exists. And even here, as we have seen, the scope is narrowed down to a select group of industries where concentration is high.

2. The tendency of economic reformers to identify the major producers in these fields as monopolies merely because of their size only serves to distort the real nature of the problem. Production in these industries is characterized by a small number of large firms, so that the antitrust problem is one of *oligopoly,* not monopoly. And economic theory does not say that oligopoly is not fiercely competitive. It only states that there may be a stronger tendency to avoid price (as compared to nonprice) competition.

3. Therefore, if the antitrust laws are to preserve or even enhance the workability of competition in our economy, a fundamental revision of these laws is necessary. Moreover, the new or revised laws should be based on the competitive structure of today's oligopolistic economy. Thus, the various forms of nonprice competition should become relevant indicators of competitive behavior, rather than price competition alone, which is too often used by the antitrust agencies and the courts because it happens to be easier to observe and measure.

You may see some elements of truth in all these viewpoints. Of course, problems of enforcement and revision of the antitrust laws are decided in Washington by the administration and Congress. But as educated citizens who are concerned about the relations between business and government, it is our responsibility to be aware of the issues. (See *Leaders in Economics,* page 514.)

What You Have Learned

1. The antitrust laws are intended to curb monopoly and to maintain competition in the American economy. The chief antitrust laws are the Sherman Act, the Clayton Act, the Federal Trade Commission Act, the Robinson-Patman Act, the Wheeler-Lea Act, and the Celler Antimerger Act. Taken together and in a broad sense, they forbid restraint of trade, monopolization, price discrimination, and unfair competition. Major groups exempt from the antitrust laws are the transport industries and labor unions.

2. The courts have consistently struck down restrictive agreements or conspiracies in restraint of trade. With respect to combination and monopoly, however, the state of the law is less certain and the position of the courts less consistent. Various court decisions suggest that:

(a) Monopoly *may* be held illegal, for the power to abuse, even if lawfully acquired and never exercised, is sufficient to rate condemnation.

(b) Vertical and horizontal mergers will be disallowed unless they increase competition, as when the smaller or weaker firms in an oligopolistic industry merge so as to compete with the giants.

(c) Conglomerate mergers may be held illegal, but the tests or standards of illegality remain to be established in future court cases.

3. Patent abuse and the power of patent monopoly have been significantly weakened in the past several decades. It appears that the courts will continue to move in the direction of preventing the abuses of the patent grant. Similarly, with respect to trademark abuse, the courts have acted increasingly to prevent the use of trademarks to promote price discrimination, market exclusion, and market sharing (i.e., cartel arrangements) among competitors.

4. Concentration ratios are typically used to evaluate the extent of "monopoly power." According to the available evidence, economic concentration in manufacturing may not be significantly greater today than it was in previous decades. In general, however, concentration ratios do not really measure monopoly power because the results can differ widely according to the way in which the calculations are made. The choice of base, unit, and index can all influence the outcome.

5. There are three broad alternatives to antitrust policy. They consist of:

(a) Public regulation or ownership of large-scale monopolies and oligopolies.

(b) More vigorous enforcement of the antitrust laws.

(c) Fundamental revisions of the antitrust laws to make competition more workable and to reflect the nature of oligopolistic competition in today's economy.

For Discussion

1. *Terms and concepts to review:*

antitrust laws	Federal Trade Commission
Sherman Antitrust Act (1890)	Robinson–Patman Act (1936)
unfair competition	Wheeler–Lea Act (1938)
Clayton Antitrust Act (1914)	Celler Antimerger Act (1950)
price discrimination	injunction
interlocking directorate	consent decree
Federal Trade Commission Act (1914)	restrictive agreement

conscious parallel action

rule of reason

merger

vertical merger

horizontal merger

conglomerate merger

patent

tying contract

restrictive license

cartel

market share

concentration ratio

2. "The rationale underlying restrictive agreements among competitors is based on the potential danger arising from the existence of the power of sellers to manipulate prices. Where this power does not exist, the laws pertaining to restrictive agreements are practically meaningless. Thus, there is no point in holding unlawful an agreement among competitors to fix prices, allocate customers, or control production, when the competitors involved are so small that they lack significant power to affect market prices." Evaluate.

3. Suppose that tomorrow morning all grocers in Chicago, without previous public notice, raised their prices for milk by 3 cents per liter. Does this action prove the existence of an agreement or constitute an offense on the part of the grocers? What would your answer be if the automobile manufacturers without notice announced a 5 percent price increase next year on all new model cars? Explain.

4. If all the companies in an oligopolistic industry quote identical prices without prior agreement by following the prices of the industry leader, is this evidence of a combination or conspiracy?

5. In an industry characterized by price leadership without prior arrangement, is there likely to be a charge of combination or conspiracy leveled against that industry if: (a) prevailing prices are announced by the industry's trade association rather than by a leading firm; (b) all firms in the industry report their prices to their industry trade association; (c) all firms in the industry quote prices on a basing point system (i.e., the delivered price is the leader's price plus rail freight from the leader's plant); (d) all firms follow the leader not only in price, but in product and sales policies as well? (These four questions should be answered as a group rather than individually.)

6. In the *Columbia Steel* case (1948), the Supreme Court said: "We do not undertake to prescribe any set of percentage figures by which to measure the reasonableness of a corporation's enlargement of its activities by the purchase of the assets of a competitor. The relative effect of percentage command of a market varies with the setting in which that factor is placed." Does this conflict with Judge Hand's statement in the *Alcoa* case? Explain.

7. "Since there are 'good' monopolies and 'bad' monopolies, a company should be judged by its total contribution to society—not by its market behavior alone." Do you agree? Explain.

8. "Many trustbusters and economists forget that *concentration is a function of consumer sovereignty,* and that the same consumers who make big businesses big can make them small or even wipe them out by simply refraining from the purchase of their products. This is a not-so-obvious principle of our free enterprise system which needs to be better understood." Do you agree? Discuss.

9. "To say that the degree of competition depends on the number of sellers in the marketplace is like saying that football is more competitive than tennis." Discuss. (HINT Can you describe different forms of competition, in addition to price competition, that exist in American industry?)

10. Suppose that General Motors, the largest firm in the automobile industry, were to reduce prices on its automobiles to levels which yield only a "fair" profit for itself, but not for its competitors. As a result, consumer purchases shift to General Motors because of its lower prices, and the other automobile manufacturers subsequently find themselves driven out of business as a result of bankruptcy. In the light of the *Alcoa* case, would General Motors be guilty of monopolizing the market and hence violating the Sherman Act?

11. It is generally stated that growth, stability, and flexibility are three primary objectives of mergers.

(a) With respect to growth, it has been said that "a firm, like a tree, must either grow or die." Evaluate this statement.

(b) Why may instability be a motive for merger? Instability of what?

(c) What is meant by flexibility as a motive for merger? (HINT Compare flexibility versus vulnerability.)

12. Section 7 of the Clayton Act of 1914 and its amendment, the Celler Antimerger Act of 1950, states:

No corporation engaged in commerce shall acquire, directly or indirectly, the whole or any part of the stock or other share capital and no corporation subject to the jurisdiction of the Federal Trade Commission shall acquire the whole or any part of the assets of another corporation engaged also in commerce, where in any line of commerce in any section of the country, the effect of such acquisition may be substantially to lessen competition, or to tend to create a monopoly.

Assume that you are a business economist for a large corporation, and you are asked to prepare a report on why this legislation should be repealed. What main points would you bring out in your argument?

Leaders in Economics
John Kenneth Galbraith   1908–

Painless Socialism

Economics, as it is conventionally taught, is in part a system of belief designed less to reveal truth than to reassure its communicants about established social arrangements.

Scientific truth in economics is not always what exists; often it is what can be handled by seemingly scientific methods.

These are typical of the criticisms John Kenneth Galbraith has leveled against traditional economic thinking. A retired Harvard professor, former ambassador to India (1961–1963), and stimulating teacher as well as scholar, the towering 6-foot 8-inch iconoclast has devoted most of his professional career to assailing the conventional wisdom of economic theories and policies. As a result, he has become a leading social critic, fulfilling in the late twentieth century a position occupied by economist-sociologist Thorstein Veblen in the early 1900s.

Galbraith has set forth his ideas in various books and articles. His arguments, concerning not only the failure of the American economic system but the failures of economics as well, can be summarized with disturbing simplicity:

The modern industrial state is not an economy of free enterprise or of consumer sovereignty. It is an economy dominated by a relatively small number of large corporations—in the United States, about 500—most if not all of them directly or indirectly dependent on government contracts. These corporations have long since experienced a separation of ownership and control so that they are governed today, not by capitalists or stockholders, but by a highly bureaucratic "technostructure" composed of the managerial and technological elite

United Press International.

who comprise the corporate sector's "organized intelligence."

The goal of the technostructure is not to maximize profits, since these would not accrue to it anyway, but to seek its own security and to produce the "minimum levels of earnings" necessary to assure corporate growth. In its quest for these goals, the technostructure *plans* the organization's future in two ways:

1. It finances corporate growth with retained earnings rather than with new security issues, thereby freeing the firm from reliance on the capital market.

2. It engages in the "management of demand" through advertising, thereby insulating the firm from the free market and from the whims of consumer sovereignty.

In seeking security and corporate growth, the technostructure is not en-

tirely on its own. It is aided by a government which establishes fiscal, monetary, and welfare policies to assure an adequate level of aggregate demand while subsidizing technological research and development.

The cooperation between the technostructure and the state depends, of course, on the consent of the people. They are taught to believe through "systematic public bamboozlement" that sustained economic growth and steadily rising incomes are *the* national goals. But this process is self-defeating, for as people become more educated they begin to realize that the costs of their material gains are the sacrifices they must make of truth, beauty, leisure, fellowship, etc.—in short, those ingredients that determine the quality of life. The result can only be mounting dissatisfaction with the prevailing system.

What is the solution for improving the quality of life? The answer is that there must be a vast expansion of the public sector—both economically and politically—in order to lessen the interest in economic growth for its own sake and permit greater emphasis on The Higher Things in Life. Otherwise, political forces must sooner or later arise that will seek to wrest the privilege of economic decision making away from the "corporate technostructure."

In short, what Galbraith advocates is closer ties between big corporations and the government. At one extreme, these ties may consist of outright government ownership of large businesses. At the other, some form of private–public partnership to assure government involvement in business decisions might be suitable. Either approach, according to Galbraith, would provide a painless transition to socialism and a more realistic response by large corporations to the public's needs and desires.

Case
Disintegrating the Big Ones

Historians may someday agree that the 1970s marked the beginning of a tough new era in antitrust enforcement. The giant American Telephone and Telegraph Company was charged with "obstructing would-be competitors"; more than a dozen of the largest U.S. oil companies were accused of being "too large for the nation's good"; and the big four cereal producers were characterized as a "shared monopoly" in the sale of ready-to-eat breakfast foods. The charges, and their numerous ramifications, will be dragged out in the courts for many years. Nevertheless, some interesting lessons can be learned from the underlying issues.

The Case Against Ma Bell

AT&T has been the target of government antitrusters for years. But in 1974, in what promises to be one of the biggest antitrust suits in history, the Justice Department accused the company of conspiring to monopolize three broad areas of activity: (1) local and long-distance phone service, (2) specialized telecommunication services, and (3) the manufacture of various kinds of telecommunication equipment. "There is no remedy for such abuses short of breaking the company up," said a Justice Department spokesman. Specifically, the antitrusters advocate the following measures:

1. AT&T should divest itself of its wholly owned manufacturing subsidiary, Western Electric. This company annually produces and sells to AT&T's subsidiary telephone companies billions of dollars worth of telephones, switchboards, and other communications equipment.

2. AT&T should surrender some or all of its Long Lines Department,

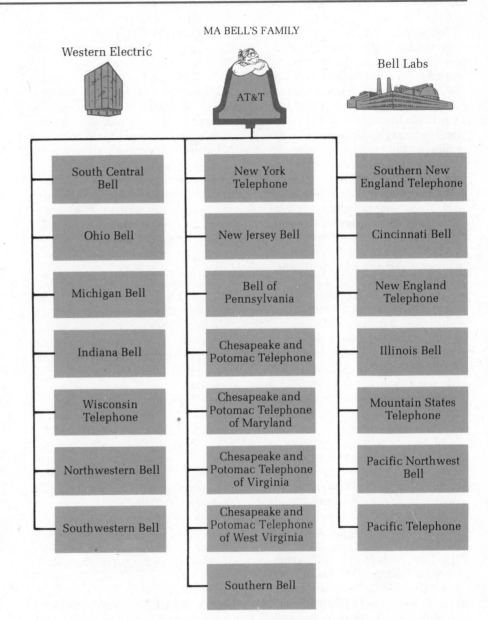

MA BELL'S FAMILY

Western Electric

Bell Labs

AT&T

Western Electric	AT&T	Bell Labs
South Central Bell	New York Telephone	Southern New England Telephone
Ohio Bell	New Jersey Bell	Cincinnati Bell
Michigan Bell	Bell of Pennsylvania	New England Telephone
Indiana Bell	Chesapeake and Potomac Telephone	Illinois Bell
Wisconsin Telephone	Chesapeake and Potomac Telephone of Maryland	Mountain States Telephone
Northwestern Bell	Chesapeake and Potomac Telephone of Virginia	Pacific Northwest Bell
Southwestern Bell	Chesapeake and Potomac Telephone of West Virginia	Pacific Telephone
	Southern Bell	

which handles about 90 percent of all long-distance calls in the United States. In addition, the company should give up a large proportion of its twenty-two regional phone companies, which own more than 80 percent of the nation's telephones.

3. AT&T should divest itself of its wholly owned research subsidiary, Bell Telephone Laboratories. This firm, which is famous for its basic research, has pioneered in the field of telecommunications and related areas.

According to the trustbusters, dismemberment of AT&T would lead to increased competition and eventual reduction of communication costs. The suit, however, does not attack local telephone service, a public-utility function that is controlled by state regulatory commissions. Instead, according to the Justice Department, it "seeks to establish the premise that control of the telephone network should not be used to dominate the field of communications equipment or to eliminate any potential competition in long-haul transmission."

AT&T's management, as well as many outside observers, see the matter differently. According to them, disintegration of the Bell System would lead to inefficiencies and higher costs to the public. Vertical integration, embracing everything from manufacture of phones to collection of bills by a central management, is the most efficient way to operate a complex telephone system. "Competition," says AT&T in its response to the Justice Department's proposals for dismemberment, "would mean loss of economies of scale as well as of improved efficiencies in network operation, both of which would increase costs to the public and degrade quality of service."

All things considered, it is unlikely that the trustbusters will get all that they want. Most informed observers, including Justice Department officials, agree with Bell's contention that the industry as presently structured has provided the world's best telephone service at fairly reasonable costs, and that Bell's profits as measured by return on invested capital have averaged only about 7 or 8 percent. But even if the Justice Department gets part of what it is asking for, the effects on the industry are bound to be enormous.

Splattering Big Oil

Throughout most of its history, the oil industry, particularly its major companies, has been subject to extensive criticisms. Among them has been the argument that the giant oil companies should be dismembered and that each firm should be permitted to operate in only one of the three segments of the industry—crude production, pipelining, or refining and marketing. Since the mid-1970s, the issue has been particularly hot as a result of the higher oil export prices brought about by the international oil cartel—the Organization of Petroleum Exporting Countries (OPEC).

Proponents of divestiture claim that disintegration would make the industry more competitive, provide stronger resistance to high-cost foreign oil, and improve efficiency in distribution from the oil well to the gasoline pump. The overall effect would be lower product prices to consumers.

The oil industry contests these arguments, claiming that the costs of divestiture would far exceed the benefits. "Rather than strengthen the industry," an oil executive says, "fragmentation would weaken our negotiations with OPEC. The results would be reduced efficiencies and costlier oil for the American public, rather than the other way around."

There may be some elements of truth and falsity in both sets of arguments. Once the rhetoric and reality are separated, however, the issues boil down to several fundamental questions. Among the more important are these:

1. Does the existence of large, integrated oil companies prevent OPEC from raising its prices still more?

Most independent oil experts, including some who are sympathetic to

United Press International.

the industry, believe that as long as OPEC's member nations retain a united front, there is little that integrated multinational oil companies can do to negotiate lower prices or weaken the cartel's power. Studies published by the Federal Trade Commission confirm this view.

2. Will dismembered firms, because of their reduced average size, be inhibited from developing alternative energy sources?

Economists who have studied the oil industry tend to agree that developmental efforts depend on profit expectations rather than on the average size of firms. If profit expectations are substantial enough, even relatively small firms can manage to acquire the capital needed, or perhaps form joint ventures, to finance new investments.

3. Would divestiture reduce the technical efficiencies inherent in vertical integration, and therefore bring about higher consumer prices?

There is no significant evidence that integration has resulted in major cost savings. On the other hand, there is substantial evidence that any economies of scale may be offset by diseconomies resulting from large-scale bureaucratic waste (as occurs in government), and that many nonintegrated firms are just as efficient as the largest integrated ones.

4. Do the major oil companies have undue market power?

On this score the oil industry comes up smelling like a rose. Indeed, by the most commonly used measures of monopoly power—market shares and concentration ratios—there is hardly a more competitive industry than oil. The facts speak for themselves. The industry's marketing concentration ratio for its largest four firms is far below the average for manufacturing as a whole (30 percent compared to 40 percent). Further, the long-run trend of profitability, a frequently used sign of monopoly power, has been only slightly above average. (The rate of return on net worth has averaged about 15 percent for the industry compared to approximately 13 percent for all manufacturing.)

On the basis of these and related facts, some of the country's leading industrial economists believe that the "big-oil monopoly" is neither big nor a monopoly. Politicians, who know when they have a hot issue, are responding to their constituents, who blame the oil companies for high prices. In the end, according to distinguished oil economist M. A. Adelman of the Massachusetts Institute of Technology, the divestiture push will prove to be a "waste of time, and therefore harmful."

Snap, Crackle, and Pop

Is conspiracy among executives possible even if there were no meetings in smoke-filled rooms? The answer is "Yes," according to the FTC, "if businesses behave as if such meetings had taken place."

Accordingly, the Commission has chosen to attack the big four cereal producers—Kellogg, General Mills, General Foods, and Quaker Oats. These companies have been accused of illegally seeking to minimize competition. How? By: (1) maintaining a "gentlemen's agreement" since 1945 to resist price cutting; (2) pressuring supermarkets to display the cereals on their shelves by company name rather than by type, thereby impeding comparison shopping; and (3) raising entry barriers to the industry through heavy advertising and excessive differentiation of essentially the same product—of which more than 150 versions have been introduced since 1950. These actions, the FTC claims, have cost consumers $128 million a year in higher prices.

The Commission is asking the court for several remedies: break up General Foods, General Mills, and Kellogg into five companies; require Kellogg, which controls nearly half the market, to license its brands to other producers on a royalty-free basis; require General Foods and General Mills to license any new brands no later than five years after they are introduced; and prohibit Quaker Oats, which is the smallest of the four, from becoming larger by acquiring a competitor.

The FTC's charges rest on a vague concept called *shared monopoly.* According to this notion, it is possible in some industries for a few large firms to dominate a market without actually conspiring to do so. Realistically, there is some doubt that the courts will uphold this view. But if

Robert Chiarello.

they do, they will be declaring one-third or more of the American economy to be illegal. The result will be open warfare against much of big business as the trustbusters apply the shared-monopoly doctrine to America's concentrated industries.

QUESTIONS

1. Does integration of large separate activities, as exists with AT&T and the big oil companies, provide lower prices through economies of scale? For example, is General Motors more efficient because it includes the Fisher Body Division as well as the Chevrolet, Pontiac, Buick, Oldsmobile, and Cadillac divisions?

2. Is there any precedence in antitrust regulation with respect to the idea and economic implications of "shared monopoly"? Discuss.

Chapter 30

Labor Practices and Collective Bargaining: Can Unions Improve Equity?

Chapter Preview

How did American labor unions evolve? What sorts of obstacles did they face? What kinds of assistance did they receive in their long and turbulent history?

What is collective bargaining? How does it work?

How do unions seek to raise wages in the labor market? Are unions "good" or "bad"?

STRIKE THREATENS TO DISRUPT PRODUCTION

UNEMPLOYMENT HIGHER IN THE GHETTOS

UNION WAGE DEMANDS ARE TOP PRIORITY

EXTRA PAY FOR HOLIDAYS A NEW TARGET

These are the kinds of headlines we frequently encounter in the news media. They describe labor problems that involve all of us, not only in our personal capacities as consumers, employees, or employers, but also as citizens concerned with significant economic issues.

We shall find in this chapter that a study of labor problems involves, in a very fundamental way, a study of unions—how they have evolved, how they bargain with management, and how they may affect the general welfare. These concepts are at best only vaguely sensed and, at worst, are generally misunderstood by most people.

We shall also learn that *the primary and continuous objective of all unions is to improve the wages and working conditions of their members by bargaining with employers.* Through a process of negotiation, unions and management work out arrangements for higher wages and salaries, new and better pension plans, holidays and vacations with pay, health and welfare plans, shorter hours, and safer working conditions. This bargaining approach to the solution of labor problems is a characteristic feature of labor economics and industrial relations in the United States and in some other advanced countries.

History of American Unionism: The Labor Movement

The development of labor unions in the United States during the nineteenth and twentieth centuries is often referred to as the *labor movement*. It is a fascinating story which plays an integral role in the nation's political and economic history.

What is a <u>union</u>? It may be defined as an organization of workers which seeks to gain a degree of monopoly power in the sale of its services so that it may be able to secure higher wages, better working conditions, and other economic improvements for its members. The development of unionism spans roughly four periods:

1. The local movement: Revolution to the Civil War.

2. The national movement: post–Civil War to the Depression.

3. The era of rapid growth: Depression to World War II.

4. The age of maturity: post–World War II to the present.

THE LOCAL MOVEMENT: REVOLUTION TO THE CIVIL WAR

Although labor organizations were started prior to the Revolutionary War, they were very short-lived and of no significant consequence. Not until the last quarter of the eighteenth century did some of the unions have sufficient durability to survive for a number of years. These were localized *craft unions* or "horizontal" unions, composed of workers in a particular trade, such as bakers, carpenters, longshoremen, printers, shoemakers, and teamsters. Throughout the history of unionism, the crafts have always been the first to organize, largely because their specialized skills or abilities put them in a relatively stronger position to gain monopolistic power in the marketplace.

In 1842, in the landmark Massachusetts case of <u>Commonwealth v. Hunt</u>, a court held a trade union to be lawful and declared that workers could legally form a union for the purpose of bargaining collectively with employers over wages, hours, and related issues.

This led to some small improvements in working conditions during the 1840s and 1850s. The most sig-

nificant developments were the gradual decline in the length of the average working day from about 13 hours to 10 or 11 hours in most factories, and the passage of 10-hour laws by many states. Laws were also passed to regulate child labor, but these were seldom enforced.

THE NATIONAL MOVEMENT: POST-CIVIL WAR TO THE GREAT DEPRESSION

After the Civil War (1865), the growth of national craft unions quickened perceptibly with the spread of industrialism across the country and the expansion of the railroads into the West. Unions became increasingly "national" as they embraced formerly local unions, which became local branches of their national organization. The movement for an 8-hour working day was begun. And the first signs of the long, bitter, and almost unbelievable hostility toward labor's struggle for union recognition and survival started to take shape.

Knights of Labor

In 1869, seven tailors met in Philadelphia and founded the Noble and Holy Order of the Knights of Labor—or simply the <u>Knights of Labor</u>. This was a national labor organization which attempted to unify all types of workers regardless of their craft, and without regard to race, sex, nationality, or creed. The organization was powerful and influential. It won several strikes against the railroads, and its membership rose rapidly to a peak of 730,000 in 1886.

> The Knights' program called for various improvements and reforms. They included: establishment of the 8-hour day; equal pay for equal work by women; abolition of child and convict labor; public ownership of utilities; the establishment of cooperatives; and, in general, the peaceful replacement of a competitive society with a socialistic system. Strikes were to be used as weapons only after all other means had failed.

The Knights were a curious group with one foot in the past, the other in the future. They championed the cause of workers in general, but rejected the traditional organizing of workers by crafts, preferring instead the mass unionization of both unskilled and skilled workers. This philosophy ultimately contributed to their decline. After 1886, membership in the Knights fell rapidly, for three major reasons:

1. Opposition by craft leaders who saw no reason why the bargaining position of labor's elite—the skilled workers—should be wasted on efforts to secure benefits for the unskilled.

2. Dissension among leading members and groups over whether a more aggressive approach through strikes and collective bargaining should replace the slower evolutionary methods of political and social change.

3. Accusations (which were never proved) that the union was connected with anarchist activities such as the violence and bombing that occurred in Chicago's Haymarket riot in 1886—a famous incident in American labor history. (See Box 1.)

As a result of these conditions, the Knights of Labor steadily lost ground in the labor movement and finally ceased to exist in 1917.

American Federation of Labor

In the early 1880s, representatives of several craft unions became dissatisfied with the philosophy and policies of the Knights and formed their own group, which became known in 1886 as the American Federation of Labor. Under the leadership of Samuel Gompers, who served as its president from 1886 until his death in 1924 (except for one year when he was succeeded by William Green), the AFL led and dominated the labor movement. Its philosophy was based on three fundamental principles:

1. *Business Unionism* This was a practical policy of seeking "bread-and-butter" improvements in wages and working conditions. These were to be achieved through evolution rather than revolution, without engaging in the class struggles of society.

2. *Federalism* This was an organizational policy of maintaining autonomous national and international craft unions, each controlling its own trade specialty.

3. *Voluntarism* This was a policy of opposition to government interference, either for or against labor. It concerned all matters pertaining to labor organization, labor negotiations with management, and related activities.

The concept of unionism adopted by the AFL was thus largely the opposite of that held by the Knights of Labor. As the Knights declined in importance, the AFL grew, with its membership exceeding 1 million shortly after the turn of the century. By World War I, after decades of extraordinary and often violent public hostility toward unions, the AFL was clearly voicing the views of a majority of organized workers. Union membership exceeded 5 million, and workers had earned substantial gains in wages and working conditions.

But then the growth of unionism started to take a turn for the worse. The government withdrew its lim-

---

Box 1

The Haymarket Riot: Haymarket Square, Chicago, May 4, 1886

By 1886 the movement for the 8-hour day had gained wide support by striking workers in many cities. In Chicago, about 80,000 workers were demonstrating when a group of anarchists took advantage of the excitement by throwing a bomb into the crowd in front of the McCormick Harvester Works at Haymarket Square. Seven policemen were killed and many people were injured. Although the anarchists bore the wrath of public indignation, organized labor in general, especially the Knights of Labor, suffered heavily.

Culver Pictures.

Box 2
Industrial Workers of the World—The "Wobblies"

THE HAND THAT WILL RULE THE WORLD—ONE BIG UNION

The early 1900s saw the formation of the Industrial Workers of the World (IWW), a labor union of immigrants who were mostly unskilled factory workers, miners, lumbermen, and dock workers. Popularly known as the "Wobblies," the organization's members had a militant style with the slogan: "Labor Produces All Wealth. All Wealth Must Go to Labor." Hence, their goals were to unite all workers into "One Big Union," tear down capitalism by force, and replace it with socialism. The IWW reached a peak membership of about 100,000 by 1912, but declined thereafter as a result of internal dissension and the imprisonment of nearly 100 of its leaders on charges of treason. The organization, however, did not become extinct.

Although still relatively small, the IWW in recent decades has concentrated mainly on organizing workers in small plants that major unions have skipped as too insignificant. According to its leaders, the Wobblies' bargaining demands today are "basically the normal types of demands for (better) working conditions and rates of pay, but flavored with a different perspective." Violence, they say, is avoided for the most practical of reasons: "The other side has more capacity."

The major publication of the IWW was a weekly magazine called *Solidarity*. The accompanying song, "Solidarity Forever," composed in 1915 by an IWW member, has long been the anthem of the entire American labor movement, and is by far the best-known union song in the United States.

SOLIDARITY FOREVER!
(Tune: "Battle Hymn of the Republic")

When the Union's inspiration through the workers' blood shall run,
There can be no power greater anywhere beneath the sun
Yet what force on earth is weaker than the feeble strength of one?
But the Union makes us strong.

Chorus:
Solidarity forever!
Solidarity forever!
Solidarity forever!
For the Union makes us strong.

Is there aught we hold in common with the greedy parasite
Who would lash us into serfdom and would crush us with his might?
Is there anything left for us but to organize and fight?
For the Union makes us strong.

It is we who plowed the prairies; built the cities where they trade;
Dug the mines and built the workshops; endless miles of railroad laid.
Now we stand, outcast and starving, mid the wonders we have made;
But the Union makes us strong.

All the world that's owned by idle drones, is ours and ours alone.
We have laid the wide foundations; built it skyward stone by stone.
It is ours, not to slave in, but to master and to own,
While the Union makes us strong.

They have taken untold millions that they never toiled to earn.
But without our brain and muscle not a single wheel can turn.
We can break their haughty power; gain our freedom when we learn
That the Union makes us strong.

In our hands is placed a power greater than their hoarded gold;
Greater than the might of armies, magnified a thousand-fold.
We can bring to birth the new world from the ashes of the old,
For the Union makes us strong.

ited protection of labor's right to organize, and employers refused to recognize labor unions. As a result, unions lost members. Lethargy and lack of aggressiveness engulfed American labor as technological changes, unfavorable court decisions, the growth of company unions, and a period of national prosperity all contributed to the dampening of union activity. By the early 1930s, union membership had declined to less than 3 million. (See also Box 2.)

THE ERA OF RAPID GROWTH: DEPRESSION TO WORLD WAR II

The fortunes of organized labor underwent a dramatic reversal during the Depression of the 1930s. The first piece of pro-labor legislation passed by Congress was the *Norris–LaGuardia Act* of 1932, which modified or eliminated the worst abuses against organized labor:

1. The hated *yellow-dog contract*, which required the employee to promise, as a condition of employment, not to join a labor union, was declared illegal.

2. The conditions under which court injunctions could be issued against unions were greatly restricted.

The stage was now set. Under President Roosevelt's administration of the 1930s, other favorable labor legislation was passed. These laws set standards for minimum wages, maximum hours, and child labor, and created the U.S. Employment Service and the social security system. But none of these was more important for the union movement than the National Labor Relations Act of 1935, which was hailed as labor's Magna Carta.

The *National Labor Relations Act* (also known as the *Wagner Act*) of 1935 is the basic labor relations law of the United States. The act has three major provisions:

1. It guarantees the right of workers to organize and to bargain collectively through representatives of their own choosing.

2. It forbids the employer from engaging in "unfair labor practices." These include:

(a) Interfering or discriminating against workers who form unions or engage in union activity.

(b) Establishing a *company union* or organization of workers that is limited to a particular firm.

(c) Refusing to bargain in good faith with a duly recognized union.

3. It established the *National Labor Relations Board* (NLRB) to enforce the act and to supervise free elections among a company's employees to determine which union, if any, is to represent the workers.

With this firm legal umbrella provided by Congress—especially the right of labor to organize and bargain collectively—the labor movement embarked on the fastest and longest upward journey in its history. Thousands of workers went back into their old unions and thousands of others joined new ones. As shown in Exhibit 1, union members totaled 10 million by 1940.

Congress of Industrial Organizations

In the mid-1930s, several union leaders in the AFL launched an attack against the craft bias of the Feder-

ation. They argued that craft unions were "horizontal" unions, which were not well adapted to the needs of workers in modern mass-production industries. Instead, *industrial unions* or "vertical" unions were needed to organize all workers in a particular industry, for example, automobile manufacturing and coal mining. Although the Federation never refused to recognize industrial unions—indeed, the insurgent leaders were all heads of industrial unions that were affiliated with the AFL—the parent organization had been relatively unsuccessful in organizing workers in mass-production industries.

A controversy thus arose within the AFL leadership that lasted for several years. Finally, in 1938, the insurgent unions were expelled from the Federation. As a result, they banded together to form an independent rival union called the *Congress of Industrial Organizations* (CIO).

The CIO was immediately successful in organizing millions of previously unorganized workers in the automobile, steel, and other mass-production industries. But the AFL also continued to make huge gains. Both the AFL and CIO emerged from World War II stronger than ever before. However, with the termination of wartime economic controls, prices rose faster than wages, and strikes broke out in many major industries during 1945 and 1946. These strikes raised a great wave of antiunion sentiment both in and out of Congress, resulting in the passage of new restrictive labor legislation. Thus came the end of an era in the history of the union movement.

THE AGE OF MATURITY: POST-WORLD WAR II TO THE PRESENT

In June 1947, after numerous major strikes, a new labor–management relations act was passed. It provided the most detailed and extensive regulation of labor unions and industrial relations in the nation's history.

The *Labor–Management Relations Act (Taft–Hartley Act)* of 1947 amended the 1935 National Labor Relations Act (Wagner Act). The Taft–Hartley Act retains for labor the rights that had been given them by the Wagner Act, but includes additional provisions:

1. Outlaws the following "unfair labor practices" of unions:

(a) Coercion of workers to join a union.

(b) Failure of a union to bargain with an employer in good faith.

(c) *Jurisdictional strikes* (or disagreements between two or more unions as to which shall perform a particular job). *Secondary boycotts* (or attempts by a union through strikes, picketing, etc., to stop one

Exhibit 1
Union Membership Since 1900

The union movement experienced its most rapid growth during the 1930s.

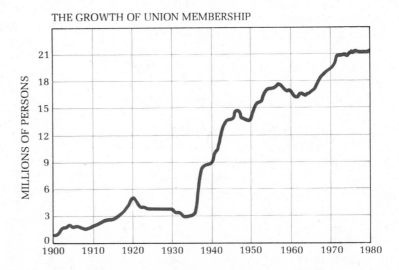

THE GROWTH OF UNION MEMBERSHIP

Since the 1950s, union membership has averaged less than 25 percent of the civilian labor force.

TOTAL UNION MEMBERSHIP AS A PERCENTAGE OF THE CIVILIAN LABOR FORCE

SOURCE: U.S. Department of Labor.

employer from doing business with another employer). _Featherbedding_ (or "make-work" rules, which are designed to increase the amount of labor or labor time on a particular job).

2. Outlaws the _closed shop_, whereby an employer makes union membership a condition of employment. But it permits the _union shop_, which allows nonunion employees to be hired on condition that they join the union after they are employed.

3. Requires unions to file financial reports with the NLRB, and union officials to sign non-Communist affidavits.

4. Prohibits strikes called before the end of a 60-day notice period prior to the expiration of a collective-bargaining agreement, in order to give conciliation agencies enough time to try to resolve disputes before a walkout occurs.

5. Enables the President to obtain an 80-day court in-

junction in order to provide a "cooling-off" period in cases involving strikes that endanger the national health or safety.

The Taft–Hartley Act also permits state legislatures to pass _right-to-work laws_. These are state laws which make it illegal to require membership in a union as a condition of employment. About 20 states, mostly in the South and Midwest, adopted such laws. Their main effect was to outlaw the union shop. In practice, however, these laws have been relatively weak in many states.

The Taft–Hartley Act was strongly denounced by unions for almost a decade after its passage. In retrospect, however, many economists and labor leaders now agree that the law does not appear to have put the unions at a disadvantage in bargaining, nor is it likely to have been a significant obstacle in the path of union growth.

The AFL–CIO

Most, but not all, labor organizations joined either the AFL or the CIO. Those unions not affiliated with any federation of labor organizations are called *independent unions*. They may be national or international and are not limited to workers in any one firm.

For a number of years during and after World War II, labor leaders in both the AFL and CIO dreamed of merging the two federations into a single and powerful union. Finally, in 1955, a single organization known as the *American Federation of Labor–Congress of Industrial Organizations* (AFL–CIO) was formed. Briefly, the purposes of the organization, as paraphrased from its constitution, are as follows: to improve wages, hours, and working conditions for workers; to realize the benefits of free collective bargaining; and to strengthen America's democratic traditions by protecting the labor movement from Communists, Fascists, and other totalitarians.

The union movement thus entered an age of maturity and power, and with it came a mounting political attack against organized labor. Some union leaders were charged with mismanagement and embezzlement of union funds, and others with extorting money from employers and employees under the threat of invoking "labor trouble." The AFL–CIO dealt with these problems by adopting Codes of Ethical Practices and by expelling several unions. In 1959, Congress passed a new law, the Labor–Management Reporting and Disclosure Act, which again indicated that the government would discipline labor as a whole in order to protect it from a few of its corrupt leaders.

The *Labor–Management Reporting and Disclosure Act (Landrum–Griffin Act)* of 1959 amended the National Labor Relations Act. Amendments include:

1. Requiring detailed financial reports of all unions and union officers.

2. Severely tightening restrictions on secondary boycotting and picketing.

3. Requiring periodic secret-ballot elections of union officers.

4. Imposing restrictions on ex-convicts and Communists in holding positions as union officers.

THE FUTURE: STABILIZATION OR EXPANSION?

What will be the future of the American labor movement? Many informed observers believe that union membership will stabilize at about 25 percent of the labor force—somewhat more than the average since the end of World War II. There are several reasons for this belief:

1. *Changing Composition of the Labor Force* The proportion of blue-collar workers, who are the chief source from which unions draw their membership, has declined steadily from almost 50 percent of the civilian labor force after World War II to about half that today. Meanwhile, the proportion of white-collar workers has increased correspondingly. Most of the unorganized blue-collar workers are employed in small manufacturing plants and in the trade and service industries, all of which are more difficult to unionize.

2. *Changing Attitudes Toward Unions* The public as well as some political leaders in Congress have become less sympathetic toward unions. This is a result of what sometimes appear to be unreasonably prolonged strikes, the discovery of fraudulent practices among union officials, and the growing belief—whether true or not—that union pressures for wage increases are a chief cause of rising prices or cost-push inflation.

3. *Changing Type of Union Leadership* Unions have become big businesses with millions of members and hundreds of millions of dollars in welfare funds. As a result, they have come increasingly to seek a new type of leadership—professional *administrators* capable of dealing effectively with Congress, management, the public, and their own rising proportion of more educated members—rather than people who are merely militant organizers.

Other labor experts contend that union membership will continue to expand since there is still a large pool of unorganized labor in agriculture, trade, and the service industries. (See Box 3.)

Collective Bargaining

The chief objective of unions has been to improve the status of workers. This goal is now achieved for the most part through the method of *collective bargaining*—a process of negotiation between representatives of a company's management and a union for the purpose of arriving at mutually acceptable wages and working conditions for employees.

If a union represents a majority of workers in a firm, it may be "certified" by the government's National Labor Relations Board and recognized by management as the collective-bargaining agent for the employees. Representatives of the union and of management then meet together at the bargaining table to work out a *collective agreement* or contract. The two sides are rarely in accord when they begin, but the bargaining process is one of give and take by both

Box 3

Bloody Battles During Labor's Formative Years

Violence and bloodshed often accompanied strikes, especially during the decades of struggle for union recognition.

Since the 1940s, labor-management differences have almost always been settled by peaceful negotiation.

Culver Pictures.

In 1940 AFL merchant sailors of the Pacific Coast fought their way through a picket line of CIO ship scalers and painters.

United Press International.

Strikers fighting National Guardsmen in the Electric Auto-Lite strike in Toledo, Ohio, May 25, 1934. Two died and many were injured.

parties until a contract is agreed upon. The union representatives then take the contract back to their members for a vote of acceptance or rejection. If the members reject it, they may send their union representatives back to continue the bargaining process or they may decide to reinforce their demands by going on strike.

When a collective agreement is ratified both by union and management, it becomes a legally binding contract as well as a guiding principle of labor-management relations for the period of time specified in the arrangement. More than 95 percent of all such agreements in existence today were successfully negotiated without any strikes or work stoppages.

Collective-bargaining contracts differ greatly in their scope and content. However, the major issues with which such agreements deal may be divided into four broad groups:

1. Wages and other benefits.
2. Industrial relations.
3. Multiunit bargaining.
4. Settling labor-management disputes.

WAGES AND OTHER BENEFITS

You may read in a newspaper that a labor-management negotiation has resulted in a 20-cent-per-hour "package," consisting of 12 cents in wages and 8 cents in other benefits. Such packages are composed of two parts:

1. *Basic Wages*—payments received by workers for work performed, based on time or output.

2. *Supplementary or Fringe Benefits*—compensation to workers other than basic wages, such as bonuses, pension benefits, holiday pay, or vacation pay.

The term "wages" is thus a complex one in many collective-bargaining discussions and may give rise to various issues and problems.

Basic Wages: Time or Incentive Payments?

If you were a worker, would you want to be paid on the basis of "time," or would you prefer some sort of incentive system which compensated you according to how much you produced?

About 70 percent of American workers in manufacturing are paid on the basis of time—by the hour, day, week, or month—with extra compensation for work done during nights, weekends, and holidays. The remaining 30 percent of manufacturing workers receive their basic compensation through some type of incentive payment that is related to output or profit. Compensation may be in the form of wages, commissions, bonuses, and so on.

> Many employers have criticized the concept of time payment by arguing that it provides no incentive for workers to produce, since it relates earnings received to time worked rather than output. Unions, on the other hand, have usually preferred time pay because it compensates workers on a uniform basis rather than penalizing the slower ones and rewarding the faster ones.

Time-payment systems tend to prevail in industries where an individual's production cannot be precisely measured and where rate of output is largely controlled by established technology. Examples include automobile, chemical, and machine-tool production. On the other hand, incentive systems have been effective in competitive industries where labor costs are a high proportion of total costs and where workers' outputs are measurable. Examples exist in some clothing and textile operations.

The great majority of unions have not strongly opposed incentive systems as such. However, they have been very much concerned with the operation of such systems and with problems they pose.

For example:

1. How should a worker be compensated if a machine breaks down or if there is a stoppage of material flow due to causes beyond his or her control?

2. Since it may be possible to measure the outputs of only certain types of workers in a plant (e.g., maintenance personnel or assembly-line operators), can an equitable incentive and time system be established for all workers in the plant?

3. Will management provide an adequate staff of accountants, time-study engineers, and personnel experts to see that the incentive system continues to operate effectively and equitably?

Profit Sharing

Many companies have introduced a different type of incentive system known as profit sharing. These firms distribute to their workers a share of the profits after certain costs, such as wages, materials, and overhead, have been covered. Profit-sharing plans of various types (including bonuses) have existed since the early nineteenth century and are by no means uncommon

in American industry. In general, profit sharing is most widespread in firms and industries with the following characteristics:

1. Consistent and relatively large profits, so that profit sharing becomes a worthwhile incentive.

2. Year-round stability of the work force (as opposed to high seasonal instability), thus permitting a permanent body of employees to build up an interest and equity in the company.

3. High turnover costs among key personnel, for whom profit sharing can have significant holding power.

4. Relatively weak or no unionization.

The first three characteristics are readily understandable, but why the fourth? The answer is that unions have usually opposed profit sharing for two major reasons:

1. It establishes an employer–employee "partnership" in profits and thereby weakens the influence of unions.

2. It makes the employee's compensation dependent on profits. These in turn are due to managerial policies (such as pricing practices, product design, and technology) over which the worker has no direct control.

As a result:

> Unions have generally opposed profit sharing, arguing that workers should be paid for what they do. They should not be penalized when a company loses money or be rewarded with a share of the profits when it makes money.

Wage Structure and Job Classification

Should all workers in a particular job classification, such as welders or assemblers, receive a single rate of pay? Or should there be a range of wages for each job based on years of experience, merit, length of service, and other factors? Such questions are obviously important for many collective-bargaining discussions.

In recent decades most manufacturing firms have adopted formal wage structures. This has been accomplished largely by the process of *job classification*. That is, the duties, responsibilities, and characteristics of jobs are described and the jobs are point-rated (perhaps by established formulas based on engineering studies of workers in such jobs). Then the jobs are grouped into graduated classifications with corresponding wage rates and wage ranges. Employers prefer job classification because it systematizes the wage structure and facilitates the handling of problems dealing with wage administration.

Some of the chief problems of job-classification plans revolve around the issue of single rates versus rate ranges for each job grouping. Unions have tended to favor the single-rate approach because it reduces friction and dissension among workers in each rank. Employers, on the other hand, have usually preferred the use of rate ranges because it permits them to grant rewards on the basis of merit within each rank.

Supplementary or Fringe Benefits

Wage supplements or fringe benefits such as pensions, insurance, and welfare plans have grown remarkably in recent decades. This trend is likely to endure as long as union negotiators continue to emphasize the need for worker "security" in their bargaining with employers. Moreover, the various plans are becoming increasingly liberal. Health plans, for example, once included only hospitalization. Now they often cover outpatient care, free eyeglasses, psychiatric and dental care, and so on. Similarly, additional benefits such as sick leaves, time off with pay, and vacation allowances have all expanded substantially.

Supplementary wages or fringe benefits raise at least two fundamental questions:

1. Whereas wages used to be paid exclusively for time worked, there is a significant trend in the payment of some wages for time *not worked*. Therefore:

> If the trend toward more and more labor costs going into fringe benefits continues, will payment for time worked decrease in importance and will our traditional mode of payment therefore become outdated?

2. To an employer, total fringe-benefit payments vary largely with the number of employees rather than with the hours worked per employee. This is because workers receive the same vacations, holidays, group insurance, and so on, whether they put in 30, 40, or 50 hours per week. This means that it may be cheaper for an employer to pay existing workers at overtime rates than to hire new employees. Therefore:

> If the growth trend of fringe benefits continues, will it add so much to employers' costs that the propensity to employ will be reduced?

INDUSTRIAL RELATIONS

A second major area of collective bargaining pertains to *industrial relations*—the rules and regulations governing the relationship between union and management. Since the subject of industrial relations is quite broad, we will focus our attention on a few of the more important topics.

Union Security

"In unity there is strength." This is the fundamental principle upon which unionism is based. It follows that a primary objective of unions is "union security." A union's ability to attain security is determined by two major factors: the type of recognition that it is accorded and its financial arrangement for collecting dues. The more common forms of union recognition are the closed shop and the union shop, and the typical method of dues collection is the "checkoff." Let us see what these concepts involve.

Closed Shop A plant or business establishment in which the employer agrees that all workers must belong to the union as a condition for employment is known as a *closed shop*. This arrangement may be advantageous to some of the parties and disadvantageous to others. Thus, it benefits the union by enabling it to control entry into the job or trade, thereby strengthening the union's bargaining position. However, it harms employers by depriving them of their right to hire whom they wish.

The Taft–Hartley Act of 1947 made the closed shop illegal for firms engaged in interstate commerce. The act only drove the closed shop underground, however. The closed shop does not exist in principle in union-management contracts, but does exist in fact in certain skilled trades and industries, such as printing, construction, and transportation.

Union Shop A plant or business establishment in which the employer is free to hire whom he or she wants, but agrees to require that the employee must join the union within a specified time after hiring (usually 30 days) as a condition for continuing in employment, is called a *union shop*.

The union shop is the most common form of union recognition found in industry today. There are two major reasons for this:

1. The Taft–Hartley Act of 1947 made the closed shop illegal.

2. There is a tendency for various industries to switch to the union shop from other less common types of union recognition arrangements.

Both the closed shop and the union shop have certain obvious disadvantages to employers—the major one being that both types of shops give the union greater bargaining strength. Hence, management has often argued in favor of the *open shop*. This is a plant or business establishment in which the employer is free to hire union or nonunion members. Unions have always opposed the open shop on the grounds that it often results in a closed nonunion shop because of the antiunion hiring preferences of many employers.

Checkoff If a union is to continue to function, it must have an efficient means of collecting dues from its members. In the old days, unions often stationed strong-arm men at plant gates on paydays in order to enforce the payment of dues. Those workers who held back their union dues risked a bloody nose or even a fractured skull. But with the growth of unionism and union recognition, the *checkoff* system was introduced. The employer, with the written permission of the workers, withholds union dues and other assessments from paychecks and then transfers the funds to the union. This simplifies the dues-collection process and assures the prompt and regular payment of dues.

Restricting Membership and Output

Many unions seek to obtain higher incomes for their members by restricting membership. This creates a scarcity of their particular kind of labor. Membership may be controlled in several ways: (1) varying apprenticeship requirements; (2) sponsoring state licensing for those in the trade (e.g., barbers, electricians, plumbers); (3) varying initiation fees; and (4) establishing seniority agreements which provide for the order in which workers may be laid off and rehired.

Many unions also seek to restrict their members' output in order to increase the demand for labor and thereby secure higher wages. Output restriction may be accomplished by shortening the working day, limiting the output per worker, and opposing the introduction of labor-saving technology.

Thus, whereas management may seek to increase profits by raising productive efficiency, unions are primarily interested in improving earnings and working conditions for their members. Because these objectives often conflict, the means that are chosen to achieve them must be ironed out around the bargaining table.

MULTIUNIT BARGAINING

Perhaps the most controversial issue in the practice of collective bargaining involves multiunit agreements.

Multiunit bargaining (sometimes inaccurately called "industry-wide bargaining") is a collective-bargaining arrangement covering more than one plant. It may occur between one or more firms in an industry and one or more unions, and it may take place on a national, regional, or local level. Although it can be national in scope and very inclusive, it is rarely completely industry-wide.

A number of examples can be used to illustrate the scope and diversity of multiunit bargaining.

○ In the automobile and steel industries, one employer such as General Motors or United States Steel owns a number of plants and bargains with a single union—the United Automobile Workers or the United Steel Workers.

○ In the construction and retailing industries, two or more employers in an industry may bargain with one or more national unions. The bargaining will usually be subdivided geographically into national, regional, and local areas.

○ In the bituminous coal industry, all employers bargain with one industrial union on a national basis. In the railroad industry, on the other hand, employers bargain with several groups and must consider the demands of all groups in arriving at a settlement.

○ In various Western cities, bargaining has developed on an area-wide basis between employer associations and unions that cut across industry lines.

○ A practice called *coalition bargaining* has also gained wide use. The AFL–CIO tries to coordinate and establish common termination dates for contracts with firms that deal with a number of unions at plants throughout the United States and Canada. In this way, the AFL–CIO can strengthen its bargaining position by threatening to close down all plants simultaneously.

Multiunit bargaining in the United States is thus a widespread and complex process that varies by industry, geography, and by the nature of the issues involved. This explains why the expression "industry-wide bargaining" is usually not completely accurate.

The chief advantages of multiunit bargaining are these:

1. It strengthens the union wage structure within markets and industries by making union–management contracts easier to negotiate and enforce.

2. It increases labor stability by making it more difficult for a rival union to enter an industry.

However, because of its large-scale and often national nature, multiunit bargaining poses several important problems:

1. It gives unions a strong degree of monopoly power which, coupled with the employer's fear of a widespread strike, often enables unions to extract highly inflationary wage settlements.

2. It tends to focus on the national settlement of basic economic issues involving wages and working conditions. It thus leaves important "noneconomic" issues like work standards and working rules for settlement at the local plant level. This often results in disproportionately higher costs to employers because they lack the funds for counteroffers after national issues have been settled.

3. It frequently allows matters of local concern to become subjects of national negotiations. This might lead to strikes, even though the issues may eventually be referred back and settled at the local level.

SETTLING LABOR-MANAGEMENT DISPUTES

The collective-bargaining process can be likened to a game of strategy between opposing players, with each side threatening to employ its own unique weapons in order to defeat the other.

The employer's major weapons include injunctions and lockouts. An *injunction* is a court order forbidding an individual or group of individuals (such as a union) from taking a specified action. Employers' use of this device has been severely restricted since the Norris–LaGuardia Act of 1932. A *lockout* is the closing down of a plant by an employer in order to keep workers out of their jobs.

The union's major weapons include boycotts and strikes. A *boycott* (sometimes called a *primary boycott*) is a campaign by workers to discourage people from dealing with an employer or buying the company's products. A *strike* is a mutual agreement among workers to stop working, without resigning from their jobs, until their demands are met.

Experience indicates that it is rarely necessary for either side to use its maximum economic strength. In general:

> Although the power to strike is labor's ultimate weapon, it is a major and costly one which unions do not use lightly. An analysis of data since 1935 indicates that on an annual basis, the amount of working time lost due to strikes has never been as high as 2 percent of total labor-days worked and has averaged less than 1 percent of that amount. This is far less than the proportion of time lost from work due to the common cold.

Arbitration and Mediation (Conciliation)

What happens if labor-management negotiations break down? In that case the unsuccessful bargainers may have to resolve their disagreements through processes known as arbitration and mediation.

Arbitration   This is a method of settling differences between two parties by the use of an impartial third party called an arbitrator who is acceptable to both sides and whose decision is binding and legally enforceable on the contesting parties. The arbitration procedure consists of the company and the union submitting their disagreement to the arbitrator. After hearing all the evidence, the arbitrator issues a deci-

sion. It is based not on what is believed to be wise and fair, but upon how the arbitrator understands the language of the contract to apply to the case at hand. Thus, an arbitrator is like a judge: An arbitrator relates the case to the contract, just as a judge relates a case to the law.

This is voluntary arbitration, which is provided for in the great majority of all collective-bargaining agreements in effect today. There is no doubt that the existence and extensive use of this type of arbitration has helped to reduce the number of strikes.

Another plan that has often been proposed as a key to industrial peace, especially in the case of prolonged strikes, is "compulsory arbitration." Obviously, however, this is not a substitute for free collective bargaining. Where it has been tried in some advanced democratic countries, it has caused more turmoil than peace and has not stopped strikes.

Mediation   This process, sometimes also called *conciliation*, is a means by which a third party, the mediator, attempts to reconcile the differences between contesting parties. The mediator may try to maintain constructive discussions, search for common areas of agreement, or suggest compromises. However, the mediator's decisions are not binding and need not be accepted by the contesting parties. The U.S. government provides most mediation services through an independent agency, the Federal Mediation and Conciliation Service, while most states and some large municipalities provide similar services.

The Economics of Unions: Efficiency and Equity

Labor unions have a measurable—though sometimes debatable—influence on the economy. Their influence on economic efficiency (resource allocation) and equity (income distribution) are particularly relevant. Let us see how.

HOW UNIONS MAY RAISE WAGES

Chief among the unions' many objectives is the raising of wages. Many interesting models of wage determination can be developed to illustrate different kinds of competitive and monopolistic market situations. Three of the more common ones are illustrated in Exhibit 2. The supply and demand curves in each diagram relate the price of labor, expressed in wages, and the quantity of labor supplied and demanded.

Exhibit 2
How Unions May Raise Wages in Competitive Markets

Chart (a) Increase the demand for labor. Through feather-bedding or other restrictive and make-work practices, unions may succeed in shifting the demand for labor to the right from D to D'. This will increase the equilibrium quantity of labor from N to N', and the equilibrium wage from W to W'.

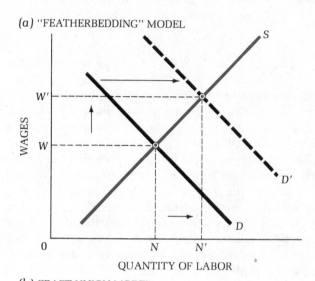

(a) "FEATHERBEDDING" MODEL

Chart (b) Decrease the supply of labor. If a craft union can restrict the supply of labor by shifting the supply curve from S to S', it will reduce the equilibrium quantity of labor from N to N' and raise the equilibrium wage from W to W'.

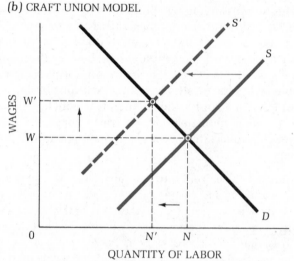

(b) CRAFT UNION MODEL

Chart (c) Organize all workers in an industry. An industrial union covering an entire industry would seek a wage level such as W', which is above the equilibrium wage at W. The supply curve of labor would thus change from its normal shape (which includes the dashed portion) to W'JS, and the equilibrium quantity would therefore decline from N to N'.

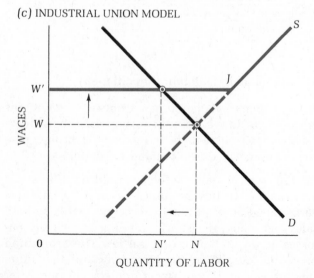

(c) INDUSTRIAL UNION MODEL

Featherbedding Model

Chart (a) of Exhibit 2 illustrates what happens when the union seeks to increase the demand for labor—that is, shift the demand curve to the right—through the use of *featherbedding* techniques. These are "make-work" rules or practices designed by unions to restrict output by artificially increasing the amount of labor or labor time employed on a particular job. For example, the Painters Union has limited the width of brushes and the sizes of rollers; the Meat Cutters Union has required prewrapped meat to be rewrapped on the job; the Trainmen's Union has demanded that railroads eliminate the use of radio telephones by crew and revert back to hand signals and lanterns; and the Railroad Brotherhood was able for years to maintain a "fireman" on diesel locomotives that have no fire.

Most featherbedding practices are imposed under the guise of promoting health or safety. But in reality they are often self-protective devices, which reflect the insecurity of workers in a declining industry. There is a fundamental need, therefore, for adequate retraining programs to permit the shifting of workers to new jobs. Otherwise, featherbedding practices, like other restrictive devices whether they are employed by unions or by business firms, must ultimately result in higher prices to consumers as well as a misallocation of society's resources.

Craft Union Model

Chart (b) represents the situation in which a craft union composed of workers in a particular trade, such as carpenters or electricians, seeks to restrict the supply of labor in order to raise wages. The union may do this by imposing high obstacles to entry for those seeking membership—such as long apprenticeship requirements, high initiation fees, or closed membership periods. In the more general sense, unions have often sought to restrict the overall supply of labor in the economy by supporting legislation to (1) curb immigration, (2) shorten the workweek, (3) reduce child labor, and (4) assure compulsory retirement. The model in Chart (b), therefore, applies to all such policies, since their effect is to shift the supply curve of labor to the left.

Industrial Union Model

The union represented in Chart (c) seeks to organize all workers in an industry and to impose a wage that is above the equilibrium wage. This changes the supply curve as explained in the exhibit. Thus, at the union-imposed wage of W', employers can hire as many as $W'J$ units of labor, and they can hire no labor at less than this wage. The new supply curve $W'JS$ is thus perfectly elastic over the segment $W'J$, signifying that the industry can buy this much labor at the union wage. If the industry wants more than $W'J$ units of labor, it will have to pay a higher wage. As shown in the diagram, the industry will demand only N' units of labor at the wage rate imposed by the union.

ARE UNIONS TOO BIG?

These models of how unions may seek to raise wages illustrate the following basic criticism often leveled against them:

Unions are monopolies. As such they engage in restrictive practices in order to achieve benefits (wages) above the free-market equilibrium levels that would exist in a competitive system. They thereby cause resource misallocation, unemployment, and inflation.

Keep in mind, however, that the same restrictive charges can equally well be leveled against any organization that has a substantial degree of monopoly power—whether it be a business firm or any other type of institution.

Exhibit 3 examines this criticism from both sides of the fence by comparing the charges often made against unions and their responses to these charges—both based on literature published by the AFL-CIO.

These and other criticisms of unions have led to suggestions that their monopolistic power should be restricted or controlled. At least four common remedies, along with an equal number of responses by unions, have been proposed:

1. *Subject unions to the antitrust laws.*

LABOR'S REPLY The antitrust laws were designed for profit-motivated corporations, not welfare-motivated unions. These laws involve complex issues which are not directly applicable to union practices and objectives, and it would be logically wrong as well as socially and economically unjust to subject unions to them.

2. *Prohibit multiunit bargaining.*

LABOR'S REPLY Multiunit bargaining enables small businesses to present a united front against union demands. Otherwise, small businesses would be overpowered by unions.

3. *Break large unions up into local bodies.*

LABOR'S REPLY Breaking up large unions into smaller ones would make them even more monopolistic in setting the price of labor. There would be several unions in each major industry, with each union monopolizing its own labor supply and seeking the highest possible wage from its employer. The union in General Motors, for example, would press for its own demands without concern for whether Ford, Chrysler, or American Motors could match those demands.

Exhibit 3
Are Unions Too Big?

THE CHARGES AGAINST UNIONS

1. Unions fix the price of labor through the exertion of their monopoly power and thereby extract excessively high wages.

2. Unions monopolize job opportunities through the use of the union shop.

3. Unions have the power to shut down whole industries as a result of multiunit bargaining.

4. Unions have become financial giants because of their tax-exempt status and the use of the dues checkoff system.

5. Unions, because of their great monopolistic power, can determine the life or death of thousands of individual businesses.

HOW THE UNIONS REPLY

1. Despite the alleged monopoly power of unions, the average worker's take-home pay is still inadequate.

2. The union shop is simply an application of the democratic principle of majority rule.

3. Multiunit bargaining is necessary in order to stabilize wage rates among competing employers.

4. The assets of unions have made possible many significant advances in social welfare, and these assets are minute compared to the assets of giant corporations.

5. Unions seek countervailing power against the firms with which they bargain. They try to benefit workers, not drive firms out of business.

---

4. *Outlaw the union shop.*

LABOR'S REPLY   Since workers elect the union that will represent them, the existence of union shops is democracy in action. Besides, eliminating the union shop would not necessarily reduce a union's ability to employ weapons such as boycotts and strikes.

The problem of union monopoly is thus a complex one. Although there is no doubt that unions possess varying degrees of monopoly power, there is no simple solution to the question of what should be done about it. Most observers would probably agree, however, that an attack against specific abuses rather than a sweeping attack against unions in general provides the most realistic and desirable approach.

What You Have Learned

1. The chief overall objective of unions is to improve the wages and working conditions of their members by bargaining with employers. Much of the history of the union movement in America can be viewed as an attempt to achieve this goal.

2. The period from the Revolution to the Civil War witnessed the beginnings of the American labor movement. Some craft unions were started despite the opposition of employers and the generally unsympathetic attitudes of the courts.

3. From the end of the Civil War to the Depression was the formative period of unionism. The Knights of Labor, followed by the American Federation of Labor, dominated the labor movement.

4. From the depression years of the 1930s until the end of World War II, the labor movement expanded rapidly. Favorable legislation was passed which guaranteed labor's right to organize and bargain collectively with employers. The Congress of Industrial Organizations emerged in this period and was extremely successful in organizing industrial unions.

5. After World War II, unions entered an age of maturity. The following have been among the chief events since then:

(a) Congress sought to curb some of the power of labor unions by passing the National Labor Relations Act (Taft–Hartley Act) of 1947. This law prohibited the closed shop, outlawed "unfair labor practices" of unions, and imposed other regulations on union practices.

(b) The AFL and CIO merged in 1955 to form one huge labor organization for the purpose of strengthening the bargaining position of workers.

(c) The Labor–Management Reporting and Disclosure Act (Landrum–Griffin Act) of 1959 constrained further the power of unions by requiring unions and union officers to submit periodic financial reports, and by imposing other restrictions on various union practices.

6. Unions try to improve the status of workers by bargaining collectively with management. Although there is no "typical" collective-bargaining agreement, the major issues usually involve matters pertaining to wages, industrial relations, multiunit bargaining, and the settlement of labor-management disputes.

7. Supply and demand models may be constructed to illustrate how unions seek to raise the wages of their members. Thus in a featherbedding model, the union tries to shift the demand curve for labor to the right. In a craft union model, the union tries to shift the supply curve of labor to the left. In an industrial union model, the union seeks to impose a wage floor above the market equilibrium level.

8. The basic criticism of unions is that they are monopolies which engage in restrictive practices in order to raise wages above free-market equilibrium levels. Hence, they cause

economic inefficiency (resource misallocation), unemployment, and inflation. Unions reply that they exert countervailing power against the firms with which they bargain and that they thereby benefit not only workers but also society as a whole.

For Discussion

1. *Terms and concepts to review:*

   union
   craft union
   National Labor Relations (Wagner) Act (1935)
   company union
   industrial union
   Labor-Management Relations (Taft-Hartley) Act (1947)
   jurisdictional strike
   secondary boycott
   featherbedding
   closed shop
   union shop
   right-to-work laws

   AFL-CIO
   Labor-Management Reporting and Disclosure Act (1959)
   collective bargaining
   industrial relations
   open shop
   multiunit bargaining
   coalition bargaining
   injunction
   lockout
   boycott
   strike
   arbitration
   mediation

2. Outline the highlights of the labor movement from the time of the Revolution to the present.

3. Some pro-labor factions have argued that the Taft-Hartley Act was a major setback to the labor movement and unfair to organized labor. If you were a *defender* of the act, how would you criticize this viewpoint? Give some examples.

4. If you were a union leader bargaining for better wages and working conditions, what criteria would you use to support your arguments? What kinds of issues might you want to negotiate?

5. What would be the probable effects of a law that required all labor-management disputes to be settled by government arbitration?

6. Which has a greater degree of monopoly power—a union's monopoly of a labor market, or a firm's monopoly of a product market? Why?

7. Do unions really raise wages? That is, do wages in unionized industries rise faster than they would if those industries were nonunionized? What are some of the basic considerations to take into account in answering these questions?

Issue
Voluntary Overtime: The Backward-Bending Supply Curve

If an employee is asked to work overtime, should he or she have the right to refuse? This has sometimes been a major issue in labor-management negotiations.

At the present time, agreements between unions and managements often stipulate that workers must put in extra hours of weekend work—at premium rates—when it is requested. Management contends that this provision in the labor contract is necessary if a business is to be operated efficiently. When demand is high, companies often have to run their plants 6 or 7 days a week. "It would be impossible," said an executive of a large agricultural implements firm, "to manage a complex system of interrelated manufacturing and assembly lines unless there is assurance of a constant work force. The decision of a few key employees not to work overtime could force the closing of our entire plant."

How do the unions reply? Their answer is simple. "Our members want the right to say 'No thanks,'" says a prominent union president. A number of other union leaders agree. Those representing a number of basic industries have declared their intention to make voluntary overtime a bargaining issue in future contract negotiations.

Varied Experiences
Many workers resist overtime because, with already large paychecks, they value their leisure more than the additional wages they would get for putting in extra hours—even at premium rates. Some observers believe, however, that this feeling is merely a by-product of prosperity. In recession, workers are faced with the difficulty of getting along on straight-time pay and are anxious to pick up any overtime they can get.

Various companies have settled the overtime question in different ways. In some firms, labor contracts require only a "reasonable amount of overtime." In others, only junior workers are required to accept it; senior employees can reject the extra hours if less-experienced workers can be found to fill the need. In still other firms, outside help is brought in to complete necessary work. But this practice is held in disfavor by most companies because it is costly and inflexible.

Regardless of what happens in various collective-bargaining negotiations, the problem of voluntary overtime is bound to surface from time to time. It is much too important an issue, both for labor and management, to lie dormant for very long.

QUESTIONS
1. Should workers be required to accept available overtime? In answering this question, keep in mind that if they refuse, they may deprive others of the right to work available overtime.

2. The refusal of an employee to work overtime means that his or her supply curve of labor is backward-bending—as shown by the S curve in Chart (a).

(a) Interpret the curve. Why does it have this peculiar shape?

(b) If the wage at J is the maximum hourly wage desired, what will be the worker's income at this wage?

3. In Chart (b), the demand and supply curves of labor for an entire industry are shown. If the equilibrium wage is at R, will this equilibrium be stable or unstable? What if the wage is at P? Explain. (HINT An equilibrium is stable when a small departure from it sets forces into motion which automatically restore the equilibrium.)

(a) INDIVIDUAL WORKER

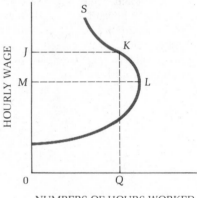

NUMBERS OF HOURS WORKED

(b) ENTIRE INDUSTRY

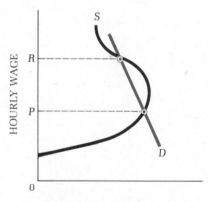

NUMBER OF HOURS WORKED

Chapter 31

Insecurity and America's Poor: Can Poverty Be Eliminated?

Chapter Preview

What chief social measures exist today to provide protection against the insecurity of old age, unemployment, disability, ill health, and death?

How can we explain the fact that in a country as rich as ours, more than 10 percent of the people are poor?

What can be done about the problems of poverty and deprivation that confront many millions of Americans? In general, what are the economic effects of proposed programs for social reform?

Security or insecurity? Welfare or illfare?

These are the alternatives that are sometimes posed in discussions of America's social problems—among them insecurity and poverty. For there are those who contend that a concern for social reform makes people dependent upon their government and is therefore contrary to the American tradition. This tradition is based on the Puritan ethic of self-reliance, industry, and thrift.

Anyone who is familiar with the history of social reform in America knows that these contentions are nothing new. From the nineteenth century to the present, we have seen the abolition of slavery, the introduction of free public education, the passage of protective legislation for labor, the provision of public charity for the needy, and the enactment of social security legislation providing some protection against the losses that may result from old age, disability, ill health, and unemployment. And always there were those who cried that such measures of protection were alien to the American tradition. In view of our history, it seems evident that our tradition may not be as simple and puritanical as these stalwart defenders make it out to be.

Thus, we shall find in this chapter that today's social reform measures are no different in their underlying philosophy from those that were introduced a century or more ago. The differences that do exist are to be found in the scope of their objectives and in the details of the specific measures.

Insecurity and Social Security

A family is insecure if it stands a chance of suffering economically from a loss of income. Such losses may occur as a result of unemployment, illness, injury, retirement, or death of the breadwinner. Because of the consequent hardships, our present program of social security was instituted during the Great Depression of the 1930s.

The *Social Security Act* of 1935 (with its many subsequent amendments) is the basic comprehensive social security law of the United States. It provides for:

1. Social insurance programs for old age, survivors, disability, and health insurance (OASDHI), and unemployment payments to insured persons.

2. A public charity program in the form of welfare services, institutional care, food, housing, and other forms of assistance.

Some of the provisions of the act are administered and financed by the federal government, some by state and local governments, and some by all three levels of government. (See Exhibit 1.)

We will now sketch some of the act's main features. You will then have a better understanding of the underlying logic and philosophy of our social security system.

SOCIAL INSURANCE PROGRAMS

The several insurance programs that are contained in the Social Security Act are diverse in their coverage, benefits, financing, and administration. They can be classified, however, into categories providing protection against (1) old age, disability, ill health, and death; and (2) unemployment.

Old Age, Survivors, Disability, and Health Insurance (OASDHI)

The OASDHI program embraces what most people commonly refer to as "social security." It is actually an annuity scheme—a special type of compulsory saving program—which provides cash benefits when earnings are cut off by old age, total disability, or death. The benefits vary according to the amount of social security taxes collected from the employer and the employee. These taxes and benefits have increased over the years, presumably to compensate for inflation. More than 90 percent of all employed persons are eligible for benefits, including retirement benefits at age 65. A similar proportion of mothers and children are eligible to receive survivors' payments if the head of the family dies. Medical and hospital in-

surance for those over 65, known as Medicare, also exists, as does Medicaid, which provides for the health needs of people with modest incomes.

Unemployment Insurance

The unemployment insurance program is administered by the individual states within a general framework established by the federal government. The program provides for *unemployment benefits*—weekly payments to covered workers who are involuntarily unemployed for a specified number of weeks. Today more than three-fourths of the civilian labor force is eligible for unemployment benefits.

CHARITABLE PROGRAMS—WELFARE

The noninsurance part of the social security system consists of charitable or welfare programs administered by federal, state, and local governments, to which the federal government contributes substantially. These programs are often referred to as special assistance programs because they are intended to help special categories of needy persons. The more important programs include aid to the disabled, medical assistance to the needy, food distribution and relief programs, housing subsidies and assistance for low-income groups, and welfare services in the form of institutional care for the needy.

In addition to these, there are general assistance programs administered and financed exclusively by various state and local governments.

EVALUATING SOCIAL SECURITY

The social security system—including both federal and state programs—provides a measure of protection against most major forms of insecurity. Nevertheless, it has been the subject of severe criticisms—particularly with respect to financing.

Social security is in no meaningful sense an insurance program—for several reasons:

○ Individual benefits are determined by many factors other than taxes ("premiums") paid.

○ Participation and "contributions" are compulsory. Thus, individuals are unable to select and pay for the particular benefits they wish to receive.

○ The tax used to finance the program is a payroll tax based on a fixed percentage of wages up to a specified minimum-wage level. Therefore, the burden of the tax is regressive, bearing most heavily on low- and middle-income groups.

Exhibit 1
Social Welfare Expenditures Under Selected Public Programs

Social welfare programs have expanded to embrace much more than "social security"—protection against loss of earnings from retirement, disability, and death as conceived in the Social Security Act of 1935.

Wide World Photos.

President Roosevelt signing original Social Security Act in 1935.

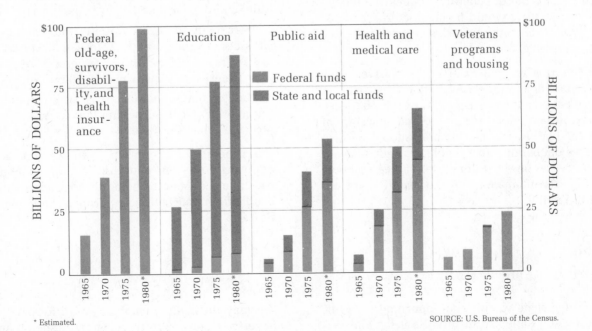

* Estimated.

SOURCE: U.S. Bureau of the Census.

In addition, the payroll tax has a destabilizing effect on the national economy. Because it is a tax on wages, increases in the tax rate legislated during recessions delay recovery by reducing income available for spending.

Financing the Program

In view of the shortcomings noted above, a different and fairer way of paying for social security is needed. Three alternative approaches to reform may be considered:

1. *Restructure the Payroll Tax* The payroll tax could be revised to permit exemptions and deductions similar to those used for the income tax. This would greatly reduce if not eliminate the tax on families in poverty. Any loss in revenue resulting from the restructuring of the tax could be made up by a small percentage increase in the income tax.

2. *Substitute the Income Tax* The payroll tax could be replaced by the income tax as a means of financing social security. This would require a substantial increase in income-tax rates in order to produce larger yields. However, since a major adjustment in the rate schedule of the income tax is not likely to be undertaken at any one time, it would probably be more feasible to restructure it in small steps. This would permit the full burden of the payroll tax to be transferred gradually in an equitable way.

3. *Finance Benefits from General Revenues* The costs of social security could be paid out of the general funds of the U.S. Treasury. Certain benefits are already financed in this way. By extending the procedure to cover all benefits out of general revenues, the financing of social security would be made more equitable because the taxes supplying the general fund are largely progressive.

These reforms are not mutually exclusive. They could be combined in various ways to produce a fairer method of paying for social security. At the very least, if the payroll tax is retained, an equitable system of exemptions for low-income families should be provided and a deliberate effort should be made to avoid worsening recessions by untimely tax increases. Some further aspects of financing social security are explained in Exhibit 2.

Affluence and Poverty: America's Underdeveloped Nation

America's aggregate wealth and opportunity are unmatched by any nation in history. Its fields and factories generate a superabundance of foods, goods, and gadgets; most of its families possess automobiles and television sets; and the great majority of families own their homes.

The signs of affluence are everywhere—except for about 25 million Americans who live in poverty and deprivation. This group is larger than the population of many countries. It is composed of men, women, and children of all races who live near or below the bare subsistence level. (See Box 1.)

WHAT IS POVERTY?

What constitutes "bare subsistence"? For many years, economists and statisticians have grappled with the problem of defining and measuring poverty. Central to the concept is the *poverty line*—a sliding income scale which varies between rural and urban locations according to family size. The level for an urban family of four—which is regarded as fairly typical—was approximately $7,000 in the late 1970s.

Of course, many of the people who fall below the line, such as a married medical school student or an elderly couple on social security who own their home and car, are poor only by definition. Nor does the poverty line distinguish between costs of living in different areas of the country. A low income goes a lot farther in Meridian, Mississippi, than in San Francisco or New York City. Nevertheless, in view of the following facts, a simple income measure of poverty understates the real dimensions of the situation:

1. A poverty-line income for a family of four allows for practically no dental or medical care. It also permits no movies, newspapers, or books, and very little clothing, meat, fruits, or vegetables.

2. More than 10 percent of the total population is classified as poor. Contrary to a widespread belief, blacks are not the majority in the group. Of 25 million poor Americans, approximately 18 million are white.

3. Most of the population lives in cities and towns. Therefore, it is not surprising that the majority of the poor are urban dwellers.

In general, there is no simple and unique definition of poverty—or even "poorness." It is an economic and psychological state of being that varies for different people from time to time and from place to place. (See Box 2.)

WHAT ARE THE CAUSES AND COSTS OF POVERTY?

We may distinguish among three different types of poverty, according to the economic, social, and personal factors that cause them.

Exhibit 2
Social Security: Will It Be There When You Need It?

Public-opinion surveys show that confidence in the social security program is ebbing. The basic reason is that the average age of the population is increasing because of reduced birth and death rates. Therefore, the social security system will be calling upon fewer workers, ages 20 to 70, to support more retired people after the turn of the century.

Does this mean that taxes to finance future social security benefits should continue to be raised? That may be one solution. A better one is to seek ways of encouraging greater investment in capital formation today, so that more and better factories and equipment will be available in the future. In that way, workers in the early part of the next century will be more productive. Hence, with their higher real incomes, they will be better able to support the aged.

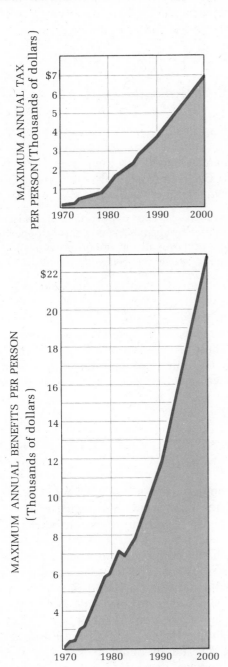

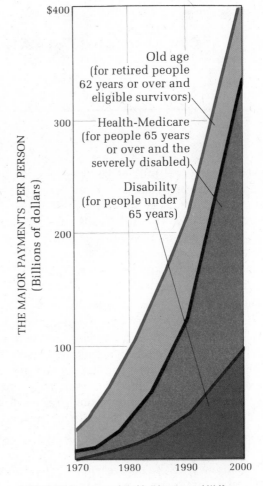

SOURCE: U.S. Department of Health, Education, and Welfare.

Maximum annual social security taxes on employee and employer, along with maximum benefits, are expected to soar in the years ahead.

Box 1

Persons Below Low-Income (Poverty) Level, by Family Status, Race, and Sex

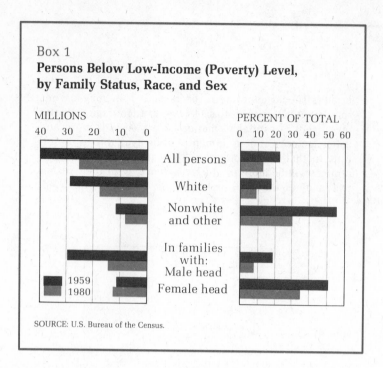

SOURCE: U.S. Bureau of the Census.

1. *Cyclical Poverty* A fall in aggregate demand for goods and services may cause a depression or a deep recession. The result is mass unemployment and widespread poverty. However, with the growth of modern macroeconomic theory and policy, political leaders have learned how to reduce such severe setbacks in the economy, and this cause of poverty is no longer as serious a problem as it once was.

2. *Community Poverty* A region may lose its economic base or its major source of income and employment, thereby leaving an entire population in a state of economic deprivation. Some geographic areas have suffered heavy unemployment because technology and machinery have replaced manual labor. This type of poverty can be remedied only through regional economic development programs or outward migration.

3. *Personal Poverty* Poverty has always existed among some individuals and families, in times of prosperity as well as in depression, in high-income regions and in low-income ones. It is due to personal and social factors, some of which are beyond the individual's control. For example, aside from that small proportion of the poor whom sociologists refer to as the "disreputable poor" (the tramps, beggars, derelicts, etc.), there are those families that are poverty-stricken because they are victims of racial prejudice, inadequate training and job opportunities, physical or mental handicaps, desertion of the breadwinner, and other causes.

Poverty levies serious social costs. Some sociological studies have concluded that poverty causes ill health and emotional disturbance and helps to spread disease. It may also cause delinquency, vice, and crime. All these impose heavy costs on the community, which must maintain more police and fire protection, more courts and jails, more public health and sanitation facilities, and more welfare programs.

Further, there is evidence that poverty breeds poverty—that the children of the poor grow up and marry others who are similarly deprived. They tend to have more children than they can provide with a proper start in life. These children are likewise raised in a poverty environment, and so the cycle perpetuates itself from one generation to the next.

Can We Eliminate Poverty?

Considering the high cost of poverty, what can be done about America's nation of the poor? In order to launch an attack on the problem, Congress passed the *Economic Opportunity Act* of 1964. This law declared that a national policy goal will be:

> to eliminate the paradox of poverty in the midst of plenty in this Nation by opening to everyone the opportunity for education and training, the opportunity to work, and the opportunity to live in decency and dignity.

The Economic Opportunity Act opened a door to waging a war on poverty. In addition, a number of specific proposals—beyond those involving improvements in the welfare system itself—have been advanced. These proposals fall loosely into three groups: (1) family allowances or guaranteed annual incomes, (2) negative income taxes, and (3) combinations of both.

FAMILY ALLOWANCES OR GUARANTEED ANNUAL INCOMES

Many sociologists and social workers have suggested the adoption of a *family-allowance system*. Under this plan, every family in the country, rich or poor, would receive from the government a certain amount of money based exclusively on the number and age of its children. Those families that are above certain designated income levels would return all or part of the money with their income taxes; those below specified income levels would keep it. More than 60 nations, including Canada and all the European countries, give such family allowances.

A modified version of the family allowance plan is the *guaranteed annual income*. This would award all families under the "poverty line" a straight allowance for each parent plus specified amounts for each child

Box 2
The Paradox of Poverty

HOUSEHOLD OWNERSHIP OF CARS AND APPLIANCES

What constitutes poverty? In some of the poorest counties of the nation, the great majority of homes lack baths and inside toilets, and a large minority have no running water. Their inhabitants, by present-day American standards, would be classified as poverty-stricken.

But let us examine the situation more closely.

In the late 1970s, among households with annual incomes under $7,500:

98 percent have refrigerators

94 percent have one or more television sets (many of them color)

72 percent have one or more cars

60 percent have washing machines

44 percent have air conditioners (including both room and central systems)

26 percent have freezers

23 percent have clothes dryers

10 percent have dishwashers

The poor in America thus have many of the accoutrements of an affluent society. This is the *paradox of poverty*. The American poor are not the same as the starving poor of India or the Far East, but they are poor nevertheless.

Bruce Davidson © Magnum Photos.

Laffont, Sygma.

In Calcutta, the "street people" live their entire lives on the city's sidewalks.

according to the size of the family. As the family's income rose, the payment would be reduced until a break-even level a little higher than the poverty line was reached.

Under both the family allowance and guaranteed annual income plans, families would not be as well or better off by not working. Nevertheless, there is substantial opposition to these proposals in Congress. This is partly because of the fear that the programs would be too costly, and partly because many legislators believe that the plans place more emphasis on governmental "big brother" paternalism than on providing jobs.

NEGATIVE INCOME TAXES

A scheme which has received widespread interest and support from liberal and conservative economists, business executives, and political leaders has been the *negative income tax*. This would guarantee the poor a certain minimum income through a type of reverse income tax. A poor family, depending on its size and private income level, would be paid by the government enough either to reduce or close the gap between what it earned and some explicit minimum level of income which might be equal to or modestly above the government's designated poverty line. The size of payments, of course, would depend on the specific formula adopted. A hypothetical illustration appears in Exhibit 3.

Several major advantages are claimed for this proposal.

1. *Administrative Efficiency* The present governmental administrative machinery—the Internal Revenue Service and the Treasury—would handle records and disburse payments, so that a new government agency would not be needed.

2. *Income Criterion* Income deficiency would be the sole criterion for establishing eligibility for subsidy, instead of the plethora of criteria that have existed in the past. Many more millions of poor families would thus be eligible. With the resulting expanded coverage, many poor families would have an income "floor" under them and could begin to break the cycle of poverty that has kept some of them on welfare for several generations.

3. *Incentive Maintenance* As the family's income increased, payments from the government would decrease by some proportion. Thus, the incentive to work in order to gain more income would not be reduced.

But despite these advantages, there are also difficulties to be recognized.

1. *High Cost* The negative income tax could not be administered, as many of its proponents claim, with only a small addition to the staff of the Internal Revenue Service. Checks would have to be sent out monthly or weekly, and effective controls established. This large task would require substantial changes in the IRS administrative structure.

2. *Opposition by Middle-Income Classes* Workers in the middle-income groups would receive no benefits from the negative income tax, as they would from a family allowance plan. In addition, they would undoubtedly resent paying taxes to subsidize families whose annual incomes were only a few hundred dollars less than their own.

COMBINING THE FAMILY-ALLOWANCE
AND THE NEGATIVE-INCOME-TAX PLANS

Both family allowances and negative income taxes have their advantages and disadvantages. In view of this, can a plan be developed which combines the best features of both? One possibility, which may be called an "income allowance plan," is illustrated for a family of four in Exhibit 4. The same model can be adapted to larger or smaller families.

Look at the table first. The essential feature of the plan is that it grants an annual monetary allowance to

Exhibit 3
How the Negative Income Tax Might Work

This is how the negative income tax plan might work for a family of four, consisting of two adults and two children:

1. As the family's income increases, the government payments decrease according to the formula:

$$\text{government payments} = \$2{,}600 - \tfrac{1}{2}\,(\text{earned income})$$

Thus, you can verify with the formula or from the chart that if earned income is zero, the family receives a government payment of $2,600 per year. If earned income rises to $1,000, the family receives a government payment of $2,100, giving it a spendable income of $3,100. Similarly, at an earned income of $2,000, the government payment is $1,600, thus making spendable income $3,600.

2. The break-even point occurs at an earned income of $5,200. At this point government payments are zero, and at higher income levels the family begins to pay income taxes.

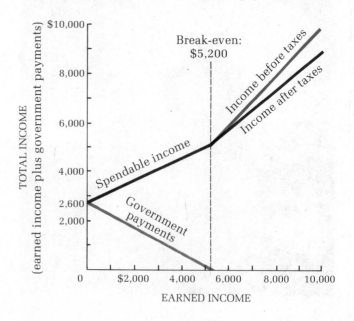

each member of a family—regardless of the family's income. (Of course, an upper limit can be set on the total amount granted to any family, and separate allowances can be provided for those covered by OASDHI insurance.) If we assume that the allowance is $500 for every man, woman, and child, and that the tax rate is 30 percent on earned income—income other than the allowance—the way in which the plan would affect a family of four is shown in the table. Note that at any level of earned income before tax, the family's earned income after the 30 percent tax plus its fixed-income allowance of $2,000 equals its disposable income.

Exhibit 4
Income-Allowance Plan for a Family of Four
(annual data—hypothetical)

Assumptions: (1) 30% tax on earned income; (2) income allowance = $2,000 (i.e., $500 per person).

Both the table and chart show that at lower-income levels, the family pays less in taxes than it receives in allowances. At higher-income levels the reverse is true. For example, when earned income before tax is $3,000, the family pays $900 in taxes and receives $2,000 in allowances, so it has a net gain of $1,100. When earned income before tax is $8,000, the family pays $2,400 in taxes and still receives $2,000 in allowances—a net loss of $400.

When the family's earned income before tax exceeds $10,000, the income allowance ceases and the present positive tax schedule goes into effect. The rate structure of the tax schedule determines the slope of the line segment AB in the chart.

Earned income before tax	Income tax at 30%	Earned income after 30% tax		Income allowance		Disposable income
$ 0	$ 0	$ 0	+	$2,000	=	$2,000
1,000	300	700	+	2,000	=	2,700
2,000	600	1,400	+	2,000	=	3,400
3,000	900	2,100	+	2,000	=	4,100
4,000	1,200	2,800	+	2,000	=	4,800
5,000	1,500	3,500	+	2,000	=	5,500
6,000	1,800	4,200	+	2,000	=	6,200
7,000	2,100	4,900	+	2,000	=	6,900
8,000	2,400	5,600	+	2,000	=	7,600
9,000	2,700	6,300	+	2,000	=	8,300
10,000	3,000	7,000	+	2,000	=	9,000

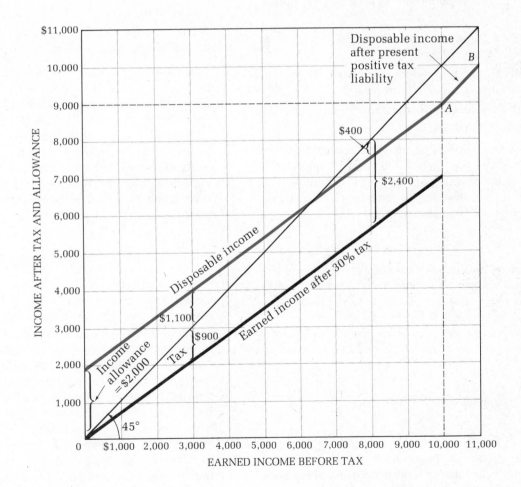

These ideas are also conveyed in the chart. The 45-degree line serves as a benchmark. Along this line, the family's earned income would equal its disposable income if there were no taxes or allowances. However, since taxes and allowances exist, their influences on income are shown by the two remaining lines.

A unique feature of this plan is that it merges the concept of a negative income tax with the existing positive-income-tax schedule. This occurs in the chart where the disposable income line reaches point A, which corresponds to an earned income before tax of $10,000 and a disposable income of $9,000. Beyond this point, income allowances are zero and the 30 percent tax no longer exists. In its place, the present positive tax schedule prevails. The rates in this schedule will determine the steepness of the line segment AB. A wide range of rates is possible, and no one need end up paying more taxes than he or she is now paying.

CONCLUSION: INCOME PLANS NOT THE WHOLE ANSWER

Virtually all income plans have at least three variables in common:

1. An income "floor"—a minimum level of income to be received by everyone.

2. A positive "tax" rate, which decreases the government allowance as income increases.

3. A break-even level of income at which the government allowance is zero.

The problem in setting up an income plan, of course, involves the correct selection of these variables while maintaining proper work incentives. The minimum-income and break-even levels should not be set so high as to subsidize those who do not need assistance.

In general:

All income plans have the same goal—to put money into the hands of the poor. At best, therefore, income plans can only relieve the symptoms of poverty—not its causes. To cure the disease itself, an income plan must be combined with proper work-incentive and job-training programs.

Attacking Poverty Through the Labor Market

One of the problems encountered in trying to eliminate poverty is that a very large proportion of the poor comprise a mixed bag of "subemployed" human resources. They include not only involuntarily unemployed, but also large numbers of discouraged jobless who have given up looking for work, part-time workers who want but are unable to find full-time employment, and full-time workers who hold jobs at inadequate pay.

In view of this, what measures besides family allowances, negative income taxes, and income allowances can be undertaken to improve the lot of America's poor—and thereby wage the war against poverty on yet another front? There are two approaches which operate directly through the labor market, rather than through income redistribution: minimum-wage adjustments, and manpower programs.

MINIMUM WAGES

Minimum-wage legislation has had a long history, both at home and abroad. The objectives of such legislation are:

1. To prevent firms from paying substandard wages when labor-market conditions enable them to do so.

2. To establish a wage floor representing some minimal level of living.

3. To increase purchasing power by raising the incomes of low-wage workers.

In the United States, the basic minimum-wage law is the *Fair Labor Standards Act* of 1938. Commonly called the Wages and Hours Law, the act has been amended from time to time for the purposes of raising the statutory wage minimum and providing coverage for broader categories of workers. Although the majority of states also have minimum-wage legislation of various forms, most of the state laws are neither well formulated nor properly enforced, as a result of which their desired effects are inadequately realized.

Pros and Cons of Minimum Wages

What are the economic consequences of minimum wages? The answers are not certain. Before examining the issues, you can gain a better appreciation of the problem by analyzing the effects of minimum wages in terms of a supply and demand model.

In Exhibit 5, the curves labeled S and D represent the supply of and demand for workers in a competitive labor market. The upward-sloping supply curve indicates that more units of labor will be supplied at a higher wage than at a lower one. The downward-sloping demand curve indicates that a larger quantity of labor will be demanded at a lower wage than at a higher one. If no minimum wage is imposed, the equilibrium price at which labor will be bought and sold—the equilibrium wage—will be at W, and the equilibrium quantity will be at N.

Exhibit 5
Effect of Minimum Wages in a Competitive Labor Market

In a competitive market the equilibrium wage at W and quantity of labor at N are determined by the intersection of the supply and demand curves for labor. If a minimum wage is imposed, a surplus of labor or unemployment results. Thus, at minimum wage 1, the surplus is JK; at minimum wage 2, the surplus is LM. In general, the higher the minimum wage, the greater the surplus.

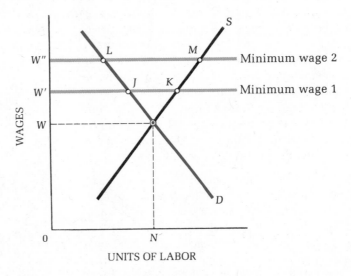

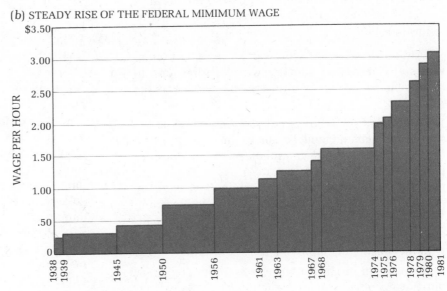

(b) STEADY RISE OF THE FEDERAL MIMIMUM WAGE

The people who are hurt by minimum-wage legislation are those who lack the skills and training to be hired at the legal wage. These are mostly young people, former homemakers entering the labor force, and some racial minority groups.

Guy Gillette, Photo Researchers.

If society feels that the equilibrium wage is too low, it will support legislation to establish a minimum wage at some higher level. Suppose that the legal minimum is set at W'. At that wage level the quantity of labor demanded will be W'J, and the quantity supplied will be W'K. There will thus be a surplus of labor equal to the amount JK. This surplus denotes a pool of labor that has become unemployed as a result of government's imposition of a minimum wage. Moreover, the higher the minimum wage, the greater the pool of unemployed. For example, if the minimum wage is raised to the level represented by W'', the new labor surplus will be the amount LM as compared to the previous smaller surplus JK.

On the basis of supply and demand analysis, opponents of minimum wages conclude that legally set wage floors cause unemployment. The workers who become unemployed are those whose productivities are not high enough to earn the legal minimum. As a result, they either remain permanently unemployed or seek work in low-wage marginal industries not covered by the minimum-wage law, thereby depressing wages in those industries still further.

How do those who favor wider use of minimum wages as a means of alleviating poverty respond to these conclusions? They offer arguments such as the following:

1. The market for labor is not as competitive as the supply and demand model assumes. Instead, there is a high degree of employer monopsony—monopolistic power—in the hiring of resources. As a result, employers are able to exploit low-skilled workers by paying them less than their productivities warrant. Therefore, by raising minimum wages and by broadening coverage, government can reduce exploitation without causing unemployment.

2. Increases in minimum wages raise both consumer purchasing power and production costs. However, low-income workers spend their increased wages quickly, creating further amplified increases in consumption and income. The resulting expansions in aggregate demand, therefore, more than offset the rise in production costs, thereby stimulating a higher rather than lower level of employment.

3. Enforced higher wages encourage employers to develop better ways of utilizing their resources. This leads to improvements in efficiency, resulting in benefits for everyone—business firms, workers, consumers, and society as a whole.

Conclusion: What Does the Evidence Show?

In view of the wide differences between opposing camps, what can be said of the link between minimum wages and poverty? This problem has been the subject of numerous research investigations, both by government and academic economists. Out of numerous studies conducted at national, regional, and industry-wide levels, covering periods of cyclical upswings and downswings, the following conclusion emerges:

Statutory wage minimums do not unqualifiedly aid the poor—as is frequently claimed. Although minimum wages help some workers, they cause unemployment among those who are the least well off in terms of marketable skills or location. These are largely the competitively disadvantaged groups of society.

Thus, although minimum-wage legislation may be an effective device for eliminating substandard wages, it is probably not an effective means of reducing poverty. This is because minimum wages attack the effect rather than the cause. Other measures, therefore, are needed if the problem of poverty is ever going to be solved.

MANPOWER POLICIES—THE DUAL LABOR-MARKET THEORY

A second approach to attacking poverty via the labor market is through manpower policies. These are deliberate efforts undertaken in the private and public sectors to develop and use the capacities of human beings as actual or potential members of the labor force. Many different groups are involved in formulating and implementing such policies. They include government agencies at the national and local levels, employers, unions, colleges, and voluntary organizations. Despite such diversity, however, there is widespread agreement that one of the nation's major manpower problems is to find adequate jobs for its poor.

Most middle-class Americans believe—because they have been taught to believe—that anyone who really wants to work can find a "good job." The facts indicate that this is not so. Evidence suggests that there exists what may appropriately be called a dual labor market. This market consists of two submarkets:

1. A primary labor market, in which jobs are characterized by relatively high wages, favorable working conditions, and employment stability.

2. A secondary labor market, in which jobs, when they are available, pay relatively low wages, provide poor working conditions, and are highly unstable.

Blue-collar workers, many of whom are union members, and white-collar workers comprise most of the participants in the primary market. In contrast, the competitively "disadvantaged poor"—the unskilled, the undereducated, and the victims of racial preju-dice—are confined to the secondary market.

In view of this:

Manpower policies for the disadvantaged, at the very least, must provide employment opportunities for individuals who want to work but are unable to find a job. More specifically, such policies must seek to accomplish two goals: (1) provide opportunities for those in the secondary market to qualify for primary employment, and (2) improve the quality of secondary employment.

What can be done to reach these goals? A number of specific measures have existed for many years. Others have been suggested, some of which are in various stages of discussion within the government. Generally speaking, all such policies follow three main avenues of attack:

1. They seek to break down discriminatory employment practices through government legislation, subsidies, and employer education.

2. They try to upgrade workers from the secondary to the primary market through training and job-experience programs.

3. They attempt to qualify people for employment in the secondary market by providing education, counseling, and related services.

Despite these efforts, manpower policies by themselves cannot solve the poverty problem. Such policies have to be coordinated with other measures—such as a negative income tax or an income allowance plan—if significant advances are to be made. But even this may not go far enough in helping to get people off the welfare roles unless our present methods of matching workers with jobs can be integrated effectively into a total manpower system.

What You Have Learned

1. The U.S. social security system is based primarily on the Social Security Act of 1935 and its many subsequent amendments. Through social insurance, the system provides a measure of protection against old age, unemployment, disability, ill health, and death. Through charity, the social security system provides welfare services for the needy. However, the payroll tax which contributes to financing the system is regressive, bearing down most heavily on low- and middle-income groups.

2. Poverty is one of today's most fundamental issues, affecting about 25 million Americans. The basic types of poverty are cyclical poverty, community poverty, and personal poverty. The great social costs of poverty have resulted in many proposals for reform.

3. Various income schemes and assistance plans have been proposed to revise and improve our welfare program. Among the most popular are family allowances, the guaranteed annual income, and the negative income tax. No matter which approach or combination of approaches is adopted, it must be combined with a work-incentive and job-training program if it is to remove people from a lifetime on the dole and make them productive, useful members of society.

4. The problem of poverty can be attacked through the labor market. Two approaches which have been considered are (a) minimum-wage adjustments, and (b) manpower programs. The preponderance of evidence indicates that the former creates adverse employment effects—particularly among competitively "disadvantaged groups." On the other hand, the latter, to be successful, must recognize the existence of a dual labor market and seek to provide opportunities for those in the secondary market to qualify for primary employment.

For Discussion

1. Terms and concepts to review:

Social Security Act (1935)	negative income tax
unemployment benefits	Fair Labor Standards
poverty line	Act (1938)
family-allowance plan	monopsony
guaranteed annual	manpower policies
income	dual labor market

2. What are the main features of our social security system? Is the system adequate? Explain.

3. Why not solve the problem of poverty by simply redistributing income equally to everyone?

4. It has been suggested that there is a remarkable inverse relationship between human fertility and "hot baths." The latter represents the reasonable creature comforts of life, such as a basic but adequate amount of food, clothing, housing, and sanitation facilities. If such a relationship exists, it might be better to break the poverty cycle by providing poor people with these goods. What do you think of this argument? (NOTE Do you think the same argument could apply to underdeveloped, overpopulated regions such as India and the Far East?)

5. In contrast to question 4, suppose that providing income allowances to poor families increased their birth rates. What might this imply about the elasticity relationship between the supply of children and family income? Explain the various implications of this.

6. Evaluate the various income plans that have been proposed for attacking the problem of poverty.

7. Two measures have often been advocated by political leaders as a means of encouraging employers to provide on-the-job training for the disadvantaged: (a) tax incentives, and (b) contract or employment subsidies. Which measure is likely to be more effective? Discuss.

Issue
Racism, Sexism, and Economics

Discrimination is a term widely used today. It generally refers to the differential treatment of persons. The most pervasive types of discrimination are racism and sexism. It is interesting to see some of the ways in which these common forms of discrimination can be analyzed in terms of supply and demand. Two practical situations which may be considered are (1) the effect of neighborhood integration on property values, and (2) discrimination in employment.

Neighborhood Integration and Property Values

You will often hear it said that when blacks move into a white neighborhood, property values decline. Although there is insufficient scientific evidence to confirm or refute this hypothesis, it is instructive to examine conditions under which it may or may not be true.

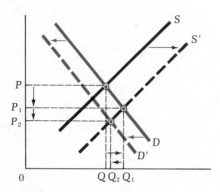

Figure 1

In Figure 1, the curves S and D represent the normal supply and demand for housing in an unintegrated (white) neighborhood. The equilibrium price of housing is at P and the equilibrium quantity at Q. Now suppose that a black family buys a house in the area. If neither the neighbors nor potential buyers harbor any racial prejudices, the supply and demand curves will be unaffected and the equilibrium price and quantity will remain at their present levels.

Suppose, however, that some of the neighbors have a prejudice against blacks. If those neighbors do not want to live in an integrated area, they might decide to sell their houses at a price below what they would have accepted earlier. The supply curve of housing will therefore shift to the right from S to S'. As a result, the equilibrium price will decline to the level at P_1, and the equilibrium quantity will increase to the level at Q_1.

Of course, sellers are not the only ones who can discriminate against blacks. Some potential buyers may, too. If buyers discriminate, they will be willing to buy less housing at any given price than they were willing to buy before. The effect of this action is to shift the demand curve to the left—from D to D' in the diagram. The intersection of the new demand curve D' with the new supply curve S' determines a still lower equilibrium price and quantity—namely, P_2 as compared to P_1, and Q_2 as compared to Q_1—than existed when sellers discriminated but buyers did not.

Three important conclusions emerge from this analysis:

1. Property values will be unaffected by neighborhood integration if neither white sellers nor white buyers discriminate against blacks.

2. Property values will be driven down by neighborhood integration if white sellers or white buyers discriminate. The amount by which property values deteriorate will depend on the intensity of discrimination—the extent to which the supply curve is shifted to the right, or the demand curve to the left—as a result of integration.

3. Property values do not decline as a result of integration per se. They decline because whites discriminate against blacks, thereby bringing about the deterioration in property values that whites fear.

Discrimination in Employment

There is a great variety of occupations which women have begun to claim as fields for individual effort from which no intelligent, refined man who views things as they really are would seek to exclude them.

Scientific American,
September 1870

More than 100 years after *Scientific American's* editorial, much evidence exists that women are still a long way from job equality with men. Despite substantial progress, recent studies show that women earn 10 to 20 percent less simply because they are women.

Much the same is also true of certain minority groups. Blacks, Orientals, homosexuals, and so forth, have long been victims of discrimination in employment. This has had several interesting economic consequences—as the following discussion points out.

Dual Market Model

An opportunity for discrimination exists when a market can be divided into homogeneous submarkets. Price and quantity can then be established in each submarket through the separate interactions of supply and demand. An illustration of this is shown in the dual-labor-market model of Figure 2. Chart (a) represents a primary labor market for males. Chart (b) depicts a secondary labor market for females. (The same model could be used to analyze discrimination between whites and blacks, skilled and unskilled, or other competing groups.)

In Chart (a), the intersection of the demand curve D for labor in the pri-

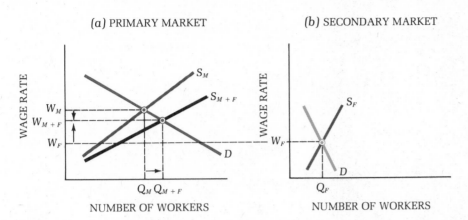

(a) PRIMARY MARKET   (b) SECONDARY MARKET

Figure 2

mary market with the supply curve of males, S_M, results in an equilibrium wage rate for males at W_M and an equilibrium quantity of male employment, Q_M. Since women are excluded from this market, they must seek employment elsewhere—namely, in the market represented by Chart (b). In this secondary market, occupations are less productive than in the primary market. As a result, Chart (b) shows that the demand for women's services is less, and the supply of females looking for jobs is smaller, than the demand for and supply of men's services in Chart (a). The economic consequence of this is that the equilibrium wage rate for females, W_F, and the equilibrium quantity of female employment, Q_F, are both less than for males.

How can the situation be cor-rected? The ideal solution would be to eliminate discrimination by per-mitting women to compete with men in the primary market. If this were done, the supply curve of females S_F in Chart (b) would be added to the S_M curve in Chart (a), yielding a new total market supply curve of males and females, S_{M+F}.

As you can see from Chart (a), the elimination of discrimination would have three major effects:

1. Total employment would be raised from the level at Q_M to the level at Q_{M+F}. This would also lead to in-creased production because women would be employed in more produc-tive jobs than before. Consequently, society would benefit by receiving a larger volume of output for the same labor input than it receives when markets are segregated.

2. The equilibrium wage of females would increase, and the equilibrium wage of males would decrease, to the level at W_{M+F}. Further, the increase in wages received by women would more than offset the decrease in wages received by men. Society, therefore, would experience a *net monetary gain*.

3. The increased wages received by women would not come at the ex-pense of reduced wages received by men. It would come from the *gain in productivity* and the additional out-put that results from the elimination of discrimination.

NOTE   These conclusions depend on the responsiveness (elasticities) of de-mand and supply, and on the relative productivities of males and females. Such considerations should be kept in mind if a more complete analysis of discrimination is undertaken.

QUESTIONS

1. If blacks rather than whites tend to buy into a newly integrated neigh-borhood, would property values de-cline? Illustrate with supply and de-mand curves.

2. "If job discrimination against fe-males were eliminated, the increase in wages received by women would more than offset the decrease in wages received by men. Therefore, society as a whole would be better off because its net satisfactions would be increased." Do you agree? (HINT What does "better off" mean?)

Chapter 32

Urban Problems: Can the Cities Be Saved?

Chapter Preview

Education, housing, and transportation are among the critical problems of our cities. What are some of the important principles and concepts that economics can offer as a guide for coping with these problems?

Many of our cities today are faced with a serious fiscal dilemma. What is the nature of this dilemma? How did it arise? What measures can be taken to resolve it in order to improve our urban environment?

The eminent philosopher Alfred North Whitehead once remarked: "The major advances in civilization are processes which all but wreck the societies in which they occur."

According to some observers, American society is already close to being wrecked. Since World War I, the everyday life of Western man has undergone greater changes than it has since the dawn of the Christian era. One of the chief reasons is that a revolution in agricultural technology has shifted a high proportion of the population from the farms to the cities.

In 1918, 50 percent of the nation's population was rural, as shown in Exhibit 1. Today, about 70 percent of the population is urban and living on only 1 percent of the land. By the year 2000, more than 80 percent of the population will be living in urban areas and much of the remaining 20 percent will be at least "semiurbanized."

This trend toward urbanization has created social and economic problems of enormous significance. Among them are problems of mass transit, suburban sprawl, medical care, education, crime control, housing, urban renewal, and ghetto unemployment, to mention only a few. As a result, the problems of American cities are among the most seriously debated issues of our time.

The social problems of urbanization are inseparable from the economic ones. To highlight and analyze

Exhibit 1
Ruralization and Urbanization

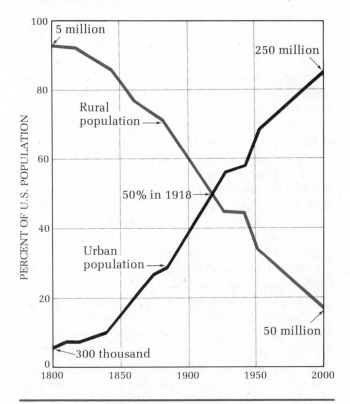

some of the more important aspects of this extremely complex subject, we shall focus most of our attention on the economic issues.

An Overview of Urban Problems

The problems of American cities result from a unique set of pressures. Some of them are deeply rooted in the nation's history; others go back only a few decades. Taken together, they have posed issues and initiated controversies that will be with us for many years to come. Because it is impossible to analyze all the problem areas, we may begin by sketching a few that are of major concern.

EDUCATION

One of the most technologically *unprogressive* segments of the economy is education. It has had to expand its resources to meet the needs of a growing population and to transmit the results of a knowledge explosion. However, it has not expanded efficiently—especially in urban areas, where the demands upon it

have been relatively greatest. Society has borne the cost in the form of higher taxes and inferior results. New ways must be sought to improve the efficiency and quality of education. Perhaps the most promising possibility is to move the public schools out of the public sector, where they have been dominated by rigid bureaucratic controls, and into the private sector, where they can compete freely for consumers' dollars. Some city governments have already taken steps in this direction, and others are giving it serious consideration.

HOUSING

American cities have long had to face the task of assuring an adequate number of decent homes for everyone. Considerable government aid has been given to the middle-income groups, but not enough to the poor. As a result, the cities are still confronted with a mounting demand for low-cost dwellings. Added to this are the problems of discrimination which blacks and other minority groups encounter in the housing market. These are among the more important difficulties that make "the housing problem" a multidimensional issue of great social as well as economic significance.

TRANSPORTATION

The ability to move goods and people is basic to the life of a city. Motor vehicles have come to play a dominant role, but cannot alone carry the burden. Hence, the cities must now create properly balanced transportation systems, including highways, buses, monorails, subways, and parking spaces. Such systems seek to optimize the use of transportation facilities with minimum congestion and maximum efficiency. At the present time many urban transportation ills are apparent: frequent overcrowding, poor service, inequitable sharing of burdens, and inadequate planning for future needs and costs. With the growth of population and industry, these problems will become progressively worse unless new transportation policies are formulated.

URBAN FINANCE

The most fundamental economic challenge facing the cities is to find ways of raising the money needed to pay for urban improvements. The problems are manifold. Increases in low-income urban populations have brought greater demands for community services such as education, public health, and public safety.

Middle- and upper-income groups, as well as businesses, have been moving out of urban areas and into the suburbs, thus depleting the tax base of the cities. Local governments have become fragmented and increasingly inefficient in their efforts to meet new and expanding area-wide needs. What steps can be taken to reduce these difficulties? There are several, but they require the will to do so at all levels of government.

A Free Market in Education

One major problem of all large cities is the public educational system. Critics have accused the public schools of being rigid bureaucracies. Conservatives, liberals, and radicals, regardless of race, have complained that the political mechanisms which are supposed to make public schools accountable to their communities have either failed to work or have worked very clumsily. As a result, only the rich now have a choice—they can either move to other school districts or they can enroll their children in expensive private schools. Middle- or low-income parents, on the other hand, have no alternative but to remain with the local public school. Parents who belong to one of several religious faiths may be able to send their children to a low-cost church school—but such schools are relatively few.

What can be done to correct the situation? One controversial suggestion is to weaken the monopoly powers of public schools by making them more competitive. The argument can be reduced to two basic propositions:

1. If public schools are to provide variety and excellence, they must be subjected to the competitive pressures of a free market in which parents and children exercise consumer sovereignty by paying their money and taking their choice.

2. If consumers are given this opportunity, they will usually choose the better schools and, in so doing, will force the quality of all schools to improve.

This argument has been advanced by numerous critics from the right and from the left. Like all panaceas, it suffers from oversimplification. Nevertheless, it has considerable merit when viewed as part of a larger, comprehensive effort at school reform. Although there are various means, political and fiscal, of encouraging a free market in education, four proposals in particular have received the greatest attention:

1. Decentralization of school systems.
2. Creation of publicly financed private schools.
3. Performance contracting.
4. The voucher system.

An analysis of each of these approaches will provide an understanding of the role that competition can play in a sorely needed program for school reform.

DECENTRALIZATION OF SCHOOL SYSTEMS

A proposal that is frequently suggested to encourage competition is for school systems to be decentralized. This would make them more responsive to the particular needs of their own communities—whether white or black, rich or poor. Most of the people who favor this approach do not base their beliefs on the benefits of competition per se. Instead, they act on the conviction that the interests of minority groups in large cities have been totally disregarded by the monopolistic system. Community leaders in these cities are therefore demanding control over the schools on the grounds that children are not only receiving an inferior education, but also one that is dominated by white middle-class values.

Would total decentralization of large school systems create the beneficial effects of competition that the advocates of this approach seek? Probably not—for several reasons:

Fragmentation of School Systems   Each relatively homogeneous community—whether white or black, rich or poor—would be given monopolistic control over its schools. This would fragment the school systems, reduce their efficiency, and return them to the situation that existed in the 1890s. At that time school administrators cried for consolidation rather than decentralization in the hope of bringing about greater economies of scale.

Resistance to Pedagogical Reform   The biases and bigotries of each community would be given a disproportionate influence over the education of its children, most of whom are not likely to remain in the same district after their schooling is completed. Further, because teachers are professionals who seek to apply professional standards, they would resent working under local pressures and find it extremely difficult to introduce pedagogical reform.

Student Immobility   Parents who are dissatisfied with the decentralized school system in one district may in principle be able to move to another. Whether they can do so *in fact* is doubtful. In New York, Chicago, and other major cities, the better schools would be unable to absorb the large numbers who would want to enroll. And in the suburbs, lower- and middle-income minority groups would continue to be effectively restricted from the better schools located in middle-income white communities.

Despite these educational drawbacks, total decentralization may yet materialize—for political rather than economic reasons. For example, the black community, too long frustrated, wants to control what its children learn and what its teachers teach. Hence, it is not likely to give much weight to the disadvantages of decentralization as a method of achieving its goal.

PUBLICLY FINANCED PRIVATE SCHOOLS

A second proposal for providing free consumer choice in education is the use of public money to create both public and private schools. The latter would be designed to meet the needs of particular minority groups. This means that a typical large city would have not only its own public schools, but also private schools run by different denominations and racial groups for their own constituents. The private schools might receive public financial support based on enrollment, community income levels, or other criteria—somewhat as certain private American universities receive partial financial aid from the federal government.

This proposal is actually another form of decentralization. The difference is that it bases decentralization on religion and race instead of geographic location. This would create competition among schools—but only in terms of ideology rather than educational quality. Even though such schools would be open to all, they would in effect be segregated by race and by religion. Admittedly, segregation has, in fact, long existed in many school districts. However, such a system would tend to perpetuate and perhaps even to encourage it—certainly not to reduce it.

PERFORMANCE CONTRACTING

A third competitive scheme proposes that each school district specify the exact educational program it wants and then invite private firms to bid for the opportunity of supplying the desired "package." The firm with the lowest price would be awarded the contract. This scheme would stimulate competition and growth in the educational systems industry, thereby encouraging the development of better teaching machines, learning materials, and other pedagogical aids. Parents, children, and taxpayers would all benefit because they would be getting the program they want at the lowest possible cost, and school districts would be making the most efficient use of the limited funds available to them.

This plan, known as *performance contracting*, has had considerable appeal. Its chief difficulty is that it requires a measurable product. Although certain parts of education are well defined and involve the acquisi-

tion of basic skills which are measurable, many other parts are ill defined and consist of learning how to relate, interpret, and appreciate. These latter parts are not ordinarily susceptible to the type of measurement that would be needed for contractual purposes. As a result, this proposal, which has been tried in some school systems, has had only limited applicability. Its greatest usefulness lies in the role that it might play as part of a more general plan.

THE VOUCHER SYSTEM

A fourth proposal for increasing competition is to give money, or more specifically "vouchers," to families with children and let them choose the school they want—public, parochial, or private. The vouchers would be equivalent in value to the community's expenditures per public-school pupil, and the city would reimburse the school by the amount of the voucher. This scheme has long been advocated by various leading educators and economists.

According to its supporters, the voucher system would promote competition in several ways.

First, schools would be pressured into stating clearly their objectives and programs—and in living up to them at the risk of being squeezed out of the market.

Second, assuming an "open-enrollment" policy, parents would be free to choose the type of school that seemed best to them—traditional or progressive, private or public.

Third, if "bonus" vouchers for poor or disadvantaged youngsters were provided, as some supporters of the plan have suggested, schools that have significant numbers of such pupils could better afford to develop programs of wide appeal to *all* students.

Fourth and finally, some of the better suburban schools, faced with mounting educational expenditures and deficits, might be encouraged into admitting many poor students from the inner city. This would help bring about a greater degree of class as well as racial integration.

The voucher system, therefore, would provide lower-income families with a range of choice in education that is roughly comparable to that enjoyed by the middle class. This by itself may make it worthy of adoption. Nevertheless, those who support the plan are well aware of its controversial nature and shortcomings. Among them:

1. It might encourage the creation of racially segregated schools—a trend that would run counter to the stated objectives of the government.

2. It would result in the public schools becoming a "last choice" for students not wanted by other schools.

3. It would lead to public support of parochial schools, thereby violating the Constitutional principle of separation of church and state.

4. It would encourage the establishment of weak schools and "diploma mills" by sharp operators seeking to exploit the public's lack of knowledge of educational programs and curricula.

Several suggestions have been made to overcome these objections. For example, racial segregation could be prevented by requiring each school to fill at least half of its openings by lottery among its applicants. Administrative controls could be introduced to minimize public subsidization of religious instruction. And, last but not least, state-supervised educational and accreditation standards could be vigorously enforced to prevent the establishment of fly-by-night schools.

The voucher system has been adopted on a limited, experimental basis by only a few, relatively small, school districts. Unfortunately, it has never been tried on a wide-enough scale to permit firm conclusions to be drawn.

CONCLUSION: COMPREHENSIVE REFORM FOR GREATER EFFICIENCY

There is substantial agreement that increased competition is needed to improve efficiency by weakening the monopolistic power of public education. The crisis that exists in public school systems today is due in large measure to their rigid, dull conformity and their failure to respond to new demands. By turning itself into an educational marketplace in which children and their parents could afford to choose the type of school they want, the school system would become more sensitive to the real needs of children and parents. However:

> Competition in education is not a complete solution. Educational quality should not be decided exclusively in the marketplace, because most parents and children are not capable of evaluating the product they are buying. Nevertheless, they should have some significant influence over it. Therefore, what is needed is a comprehensive program of reform in which some competitive elements represented by the proposals outlined above can play a part.

Housing in the Inner Cities

The desperate shortage of adequate living space for the poor is one of the major failures of American cities. Large-scale and costly efforts by government to solve the problem have met with only limited success. Nor has entrepreneurial initiative succeeded where government has failed. The provision of low-income housing in the inner cities is one activity in which exclusive reliance on private enterprise has proved to be inadequate.

What are the reasons for this? There are many, including problems of taxation, financing, technology, racial discrimination, law, and politics—to mention only a few. Because of these complexities, it is doubtful that private enterprise can ever solve the problems of low-income urban housing or the closely related problems of urban renewal, without the help of a comprehensive policy by government. Such a policy has been developing for decades, but it has been painfully slow in its evolution and frequently muddled in its administration.

GOVERNMENT HOUSING POLICIES

Although government has failed to develop an effective housing policy, it has not been unconcerned with resolving important issues. Over the years it has:

1. Regulated private housing through zoning laws, building codes, and rent controls.

2. Promoted private housing construction by making available needed supplies of credit.

3. Engaged in the ownership and operation of public housing.

4. Subsidized urban renewal programs by private builders.

Regulation of Private Housing

Government has been directly involved in the regulation of private housing in two major ways. One is by specifying the conditions under which dwellings can be built. The other is by limiting the rents that tenants must pay.

All local governments have zoning laws which control the allocation of land for commercial and industrial buildings, and for residential dwellings of the single- and multiple-family type. They also have building and housing codes which specify standards of ventilation, sanitation, and structural safety. Unfortunately, many of these laws are unduly restrictive, and their enforcement has been weakened by political influences. As a result, their economic effect has been to limit the quantity and types of housing that are most needed for large cities, and hence to contribute—along with rising population and income—to the upward pressure on rents in these areas.

To curb such pressures, particularly during war periods, government has sometimes imposed rent controls to keep rents from soaring. Rent ceilings may be necessary during emergencies, but as a permanent policy can be more harmful than beneficial—for several reasons:

1. They cause a misallocation of dwelling space, because families who can afford higher-rent apartments are encouraged to remain where they are instead of moving to make room for lower-income newcomers.

2. They limit the returns to landlords as compared with returns on invested funds in other fields, thereby encouraging neglect and even abandonment of buildings.

3. They curb the supply of rental housing and usually cause it to decline.

Over the long run, all three of these factors tend to injure tenants rather than help them. The experiences of various cities with rent controls, both in the United States and abroad, strongly confirm these conclusions. New York City, for example, long retained rent controls in one form or another for decades after World War II, largely because of political pressures, and suffered drastically from all of the effects given above. Its apartment buildings in slum areas were often without adequate heat or sanitation, and many were literally abandoned by their owners in order to obtain income-tax losses. (See Box 1.)

Promotion of Private Housing

Since the 1930s, the federal government has encouraged the construction of private housing and promoted home ownership through various agencies such as the Federal Housing Administration and the Veterans Administration. It has sought to achieve these goals by expanding the supply of housing credit—through federally chartered savings and loan associations, provisions for mortgage insurance, creation of a secondary market for mortgages, and other devices. This program has succeeded in promoting middle-income family home ownership, but it has done little to increase the supply of housing for the poor.

Public Housing

Since the 1930s government has been involved in public housing—housing that is privately designed and built but owned and operated on a rental basis by public authorities. Under the Housing Act of 1937 and its subsequent amendments, the federal government is authorized to extend financial aid to state and local governments in order to help them provide low-rent housing to low-income families. Municipal governments, through the sale of bonds, contribute 10 percent of the total capital investment for each project,

Box 1
Abandoned Buildings in New York City

Rent control in New York and some other cities has not only contributed to a housing shortage for low-income groups. It has also encouraged many landlords to abandon their buildings in favor of tax losses.

Susan Kuklin, Photo Researchers.

and the federal government pays the remaining 90 percent. The municipal public housing authorities collect the rents and operate the projects—with the objective of breaking even on operating costs. In effect, however, the federal government subsidizes virtually all these projects because interest received by municipal bondholders is exempt from federal income taxes and the projects themselves are exempt from local property taxes. Although, on the whole, public housing policies have succeeded in expanding the supply of low-rent housing, congressional appropriations have not been sufficient to meet the huge need that exists.

Urban Renewal

During the 1950s, there began a pronounced shift in emphasis from the construction of housing for the poor to the rehabilitation of the cities. Sponsored jointly by federal and municipal governments, and financed primarily by the former, the objective of urban renewal has been to rebuild old or decayed neighborhoods in order to attract industry, stimulate commercial activity, encourage the upper economic classes to return from the suburbs to the cities, and in general restore property values and tax yields.

Although urban renewal programs in the downtown centers of many cities have been impressive, they have also failed on a number of fronts. Reconstruction has been confined to limited areas without relation to an overall plan. Projects have usually been selected for their commercial value and "show appeal" instead of their usefulness to the community as a whole. Tremendous hardships have been imposed on many of the people—most of them blacks—who are evicted from renewal areas with few if any alternative areas to which they can move. And the livelihood of small-scale neighborhood businesspersons has been destroyed because they are unable to relocate at rents they can afford.

The overall effects of urban renewal in terms of its shifting the supply and demand curves are explained in Exhibit 2.

PROBLEMS OF HOUSING

The enormous need for city housing poses staggering problems of a multidimensional nature. The first and most fundamental problem is the gap between housing costs and what low-income families can pay. With the shortage of land in large cities, the kind of housing that is needed is apartment buildings, either new or rehabilitated. Even if such buildings could be made available in the quantity and density desired, government estimates show that the rental rates for a one- or two-bedroom apartment would be beyond the means of low-income families. In fact, more than two-thirds of such families could not afford to pay even *half* the estimated rents.

A second problem is that government programs to provide housing for the poor have been inadequate. Congress has created one program after another since the 1930s, but many have been insufficiently funded and very poorly conceived. In fact, they have often overlapped and even conflicted with earlier programs. As a result, they create chaos together with fantastic amounts of red tape, while exerting relatively little impact on urban problems. Nor has urban renewal been of much help. This is because most localities have been concerned with broadening their tax base

Exhibit 2

Urban Renewal Decreases the Supply of Housing

Given the demand curve *D* for housing, the destruction of blighted housing by urban renewal decreases the available supply of housing by shifting the supply curve to the left from *S* to *S'*. As a result, the equilibrium price rises from *P* to *P'* and the equilibrium quantity falls from *Q* to *Q'*. In other words, the poor pay more for less housing.

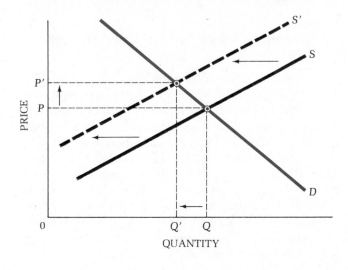

and have used urban renewal programs to construct new commercial development or upper-middle-income housing rather than to provide low-income housing.

A third problem is that while rehabilitation of slum housing is an alternative to the construction of new housing, it is not an overall solution. There are several reasons. Rehabilitation does not increase the total supply of housing units. It displaces people without successfully relocating them. It is not cheaper than new housing—especially when planning and the costs of rehabilitation are considered. And, it does not reduce the social and cultural barriers that separate the poor from the rest of society.

APPROACHES TO A SOLUTION

There is widespread agreement that ways must be found to broaden the choices available to consumers in the urban housing market. Three general approaches that would lower the price of dwellings are especially noteworthy.

Uniform National Building Code

Local building codes vary widely in the several thousand jurisdictions in the United States. Most set standards far above what is needed for safety and durability. They also specify the materials and production methods that must be used. The codes are thus designed to protect the special-interest groups, such as building-components manufacturers and trade unions, rather than to provide the largest possible supply of housing at the lowest possible prices.

To correct this situation, builders' associations, construction engineers, and governmental advisory groups have long advocated a uniform national building code. Ideally, such a code should specify performance standards rather than materials and methods. This would encourage components manufacturers as well as builders to develop new, cost-saving substitutes. Until such a uniform national code is established, there is little hope of improving production efficiency in the home-building industry—an industry that consists mainly of small firms catering to a highly fragmented housing market.

Rent Supplements

A direct approach to widening the housing market for the poor is for the government to supplement a portion of the rental payments of low-income families. This might be done by the government's making up the difference in rents for those families below a specified income level who cannot obtain decent housing at rental rates not exceeding one-fourth of their incomes. (The figure of one-fourth is typically used as a national average by budget counseling services and welfare agencies, but higher or lower figures might be more appropriate in different regions.) Thus, the tenant pays one-fourth of his or her income toward rent, and the government pays the balance up to the "fair market value." As the tenant's income rises, the government's supplement falls until the tenant is paying the full rent and the government is paying nothing.

The chief disadvantage of this plan is in its administration: Tenants and landlords must be audited periodically to see that the government is not being overcharged. But the plan has several factors in its favor:

1. It gives tenants a wider choice in seeking apartments instead of confining them to public housing projects.

2. It avoids the stigma attached to public housing.

3. It does not reduce the tenant's incentive to work.

A system of rent supplements somewhat similar to this was established by the government in 1965. Despite its advantages—including the fact that it is less costly to administer than public housing—it has been politically unpopular and has been supported on a limited scale with relatively small budgets.

Interest Subsidies

To encourage home ownership by low-income families, the government could subsidize interest payments on housing. That is, it could contribute a proportion of the monthly interest which a family must pay on its home mortgage. To help poorer families who would rather rent than buy, an equivalent arrangement could be made. With this system, the government would pay the landlord a proportion of the contractual interest and the landlord in turn would reduce the tenant's rent. In both instances, the government's interest subsidy varies inversely with the family's income. As the latter rises toward some specified level, the former declines toward zero.

This type of plan was adopted in the Housing and Urban Development Act of 1968. However, it was geared toward helping families whose incomes are just above the poverty line instead of below it. On the whole, the act made a substantial start toward expanding the supply of new dwellings for low- and moderate-income families. But it was only a start. Extensions are needed if decent housing is to be provided for the poorest segments of the population.

An analysis of rent supplements and interest subsidies in terms of supply and demand is presented in Exhibit 3.

CONCLUSION: A UNIFIED PLAN FOR GREATER EQUITY

Any solution to city housing problems requires some sort of government subsidy. There is a gap between what low-income families can pay for housing and what private enterprise can supply at a reasonable profit. Subsidies are a realistic means of closing this gap.

The most common types of subsidy, in the form of below-market interest rates, rent supplements, and long-term mortgages, can continue, but more extensive plans are also needed:

An effective and far-reaching program would be one in which the federal government acquires the land it needs, provides for the construction of dwelling units by private enterprise, and pays no property taxes as long as the buildings are occupied by low-income families. However, since the cities cannot afford to lose the taxes on these properties, the federal government could relieve them of all health, education, and welfare costs, since these services are a national concern.

Exhibit 3
Rent Supplements and Interest Subsidies Increase the Demand for Housing

(a) SHORT RUN

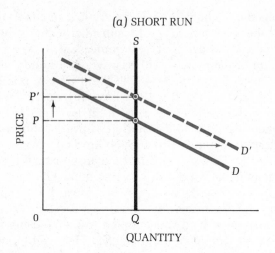

Chart (a). *In the short run the stock of housing in existence is fixed. Therefore, the supply curve S is a vertical line—perfectly inelastic or unresponsive to changes in price. Consequently, factors that tend to increase the demand for housing, such as rent supplements and interest subsidies, cause the demand curve to shift to the right—from D to D'. This brings about a rise in the equilibrium price from P to P' while the equilibrium quantity Q remains the same. As a result, the entire increase in housing expenditure is absorbed by landlords as increased rents.*

(b) LONG RUN

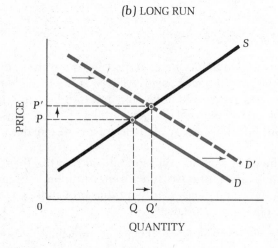

Chart (b). *In the long run the supply of housing has been found to be relatively elastic. That is, it has been highly responsive to changes in price. Consequently, an increase in demand from D to D' leads to a higher equilibrium price P' and a larger equilibrium quantity Q'.*

The adoption of such a plan would improve social equity by permitting business and government to work together in meeting the housing needs of all low-income groups.

Transportation Systems

Any discussion of urban problems must include transportation. The central task is to correct the imbalance that exists between automobiles and other forms of transportation, such as subways and monorails. Why this imbalance? A significant cause is the Federal Highway Act itself. This law allows 90 percent federal funding for freeways, thereby providing cities with virtually costless highways, which have been too tempting to resist. The result has been mounting traffic congestion, a tearing apart of the cities as well as the countryside, and the creation of distorted transportation systems which tend to increase the private and social costs of movement.

A city's transportation system consists of all the vehicles and "fixed plant" necessary to move people and goods from one place to another. It may thus include not only automobiles, taxis, buses, and subway trains, but also streets, freeways, stations, parking spaces, and similar facilities. There is no doubt that continued investment in all of these will occur in many large cities during the coming years. However, it is desirable that the growth of urban transportation systems be economically sensible. Therefore, two classes of policy proposals should be considered:

1. Transportation pricing.

2. Technological improvements and innovations in transportation systems.

TRANSPORTATION PRICING

We know from the study of supply and demand that a price system rations the use of existing goods among buyers who are willing to pay the market price, and guides the distribution of resources to their most rewarding alternatives. Can a price system be used to help correct urban transportation problems?

There is excessive traffic congestion in our cities because of an imbalance between automobiles and other forms of transportation. Most cities have created this imbalance themselves by subsidizing the use of automobiles and discouraging the use of mass transit. They have done this by constructing and maintaining streets and freeways without charging users sufficiently high fees to allow a proper allocation of this resource. Therefore, if the situation is to be corrected, a fundamental principle must be recognized:

> At any given time the supply of streets, bridges, and other traffic facilities is fixed. If during some period there is congestion on the roads or shortages of parking spaces, this means that the quantity demanded of the facility at that moment exceeds the quantity supplied. Therefore, a higher price is needed to bring the two quantities into balance—to "clear" the market.

At the present time, the use of most roads is allocated to users on the basis of time delays that motorists are willing to tolerate. Thus, everyone who uses a road at any given moment enjoys the same service. But during rush hours, a person whose time is more valuable pays a higher price in terms of delays than the person whose time is less valuable. This means that the former individual, in effect, "subsidizes" the latter.

Variable Tolls

A *variable toll system* would greatly reduce if not eliminate the overall problems of "congestion" and "shortage." For example, if higher tolls were charged during morning and evening rush hours on major freeways connecting the suburbs with the cities, users whose time was relatively more valuable to society would still travel regularly at those hours. However, others would shift their travel to alternative roads or to off-peak times, or else seek different forms of transportation, such as rapid transit.

Of course, there may be some technical problems in implementing such a proposal, but the solution is well within the grasp of modern technology. In some cases it would be feasible to introduce existing toll systems of the types currently found on various turnpikes and highways. But these could be gradually replaced with modern roadway devices such as magnetic car identifiers and automated computer systems. Such systems would permit motorists to be billed monthly for the benefits they derive from the use of roads. A considerable amount of research on this has already been conducted in the United States and other countries. In fact, some of the world's largest cities have been experimenting with differential pricing systems in which fares or tolls are based on time, distance, and direction of travel.

Economic analysis thus suggests that with the development of diverse transportation facilities in the cities, the adoption of a variable toll system would correct much of the imbalance that exists between private automobile and public transportation. With this system, motorists would continue to have a free choice as to the alternative streets and the amount of street space they wish to utilize. Thus, scarce public streets would be allocated according to the <u>benefit principle</u>. This principle holds that people should be "taxed" for a service in proportion to the benefit they receive from it.

Public Transit Systems

Variable tolls, as opposed to flat fares, are equally desirable for public transit systems, including subways and buses. Such systems are used at full capacity during the morning and evening peak periods, and are usually underutilized the rest of the time. Low or even free off-peak fares would relieve much of the rush-hour congestion. Further, this pricing scheme could be adopted at little or no additional cost to the transit system (other than the expense of installing new turnstiles or fare boxes). This is because the cost of operating the vehicles is substantially the same whether they are full or empty.

It is sometimes contended that differential transit fares would burden the poor, since they rely heavily on public transportation. There are three major weaknesses in this argument.

First, the poor tend to live closer to the inner cities and to travel shorter distances. Hence, a fare based on mileage would actually benefit them.

Second, many of the poor who travel to get to work, such as those who perform domestic service in the suburbs or work as cleaning personnel in office buildings, travel against the major flow of traffic or at off-peak times. Therefore, they too would benefit from a differential fare system.

Third, some studies have shown that the poor tend to rely as much or more on public transportation for nonwork trips, so a lower fare during off-peak hours would be to their advantage.

In general, therefore, although some lower-income families would undoubtedly be hurt by a differential fare structure, it appears that many more would benefit.

TECHNOLOGICAL IMPROVEMENTS AND INNOVATIONS

In addition to establishing an appropriate pricing system for rationing the use of transportation facilities, various technological improvements and supplemental policies are possible. Three independent classes of proposals, none of which would require a massive investment in new facilities, may be considered.

1. *Electronic Control Systems*   These would regulate access to urban freeways through strategically placed sensors and traffic signals. Such controls have been

employed successfully in a number of cities in the United States and Europe. They are likely to gain large-scale adoption in the coming years.

2. *Subsidies* These can be used to reorient bus services in the inner cities. Various studies indicate that present bus systems often do not provide adequate connection and transfer points to meet the needs of the working poor—especially those who must commute by bus to work in the suburbs.

3. *Taxicab and Jitney Services* These can be expanded. Merely by relaxing somewhat the restrictions which almost all cities exercise on the supply of taxis, their number could be increased and the rates reduced. And by permitting the use of jitneys—that is, cars or station wagons which carry passengers at nominal rates over a regular route (a very common form of public transportation in many foreign and in some American cities)—much of the problem of automobile congestion in the cities would be eliminated.

CONCLUSION: AN EFFICIENT "TRANSPORT MIX"

The cities can do a great deal at relatively little cost to relieve the transportation pressures they now face. Experimentation with new and flexible approaches is needed to find an efficient "transport mix"—one suited to the special requirements of each city. The money that can be saved from optimum use of a well-designed transportation system might better be spent on education, housing, pollution abatement, and other measures that will make the city a more desirable place to live. (See Box 2.)

Financing Local Government: Our Urban Fiscal Dilemma

Any discussion of urban policies must eventually deal with the difficult problem of financing public services. Why does a problem exist? Mr. Micawber in the novel *David Copperfield* described a situation that epitomizes the financial squeeze which many of our cities are experiencing today:

> Annual income twenty pounds, annual expenditure nineteen six: result, happiness.

> Annual income twenty pounds, annual expenditure twenty pounds ought and six: result, misery.

This is indeed the essence of America's urban fiscal dilemma. The reasons for it can be summarized briefly:

1. As our population expands and our economy grows

richer, we not only purchase more goods and services from the private sector, but we also increase our demands on the public sector.

2. To meet these demands, urban governments have to increase their expenditures on virtually all types of public services. These include sanitation, police and fire protection, education, health, welfare, transportation, recreation, and cultural facilities.

3. While cities have been left to grapple with soaring municipal costs, the groups that pay the heaviest share of taxes—business firms and middle-income families—have for decades been moving to the suburbs. These groups have been replaced by an ever-expanding population of the poor, who need but cannot afford the more expensive education, welfare, health services, and other public benefits.

These conditions have forced most cities to face a growing fiscal problem. To raise the revenue needed to pay for public services, taxes must be increased. However, taxes in the cities are already burdensome, and further increases may only hasten the exodus of people and businesses to nearby suburbs, where taxes and other amenities are more favorable.

Most cities have frequently had deficits amounting to many millions of dollars—deficits which they covered by dipping into reserves, by borrowing against future budgets, and by selling long-term notes. Not since the depression of the 1930s, however, has the plight of many city treasuries been as bleak as in recent years.

How should the various levels of government direct their limited resources to combat poverty, crime, pollution, eyesores, and ghetto unemployment, while improving education, housing, mass transit, and the other amenities of a better urban America? The solution rests on finding more effective ways of raising revenues while improving the efficiency of local government. Several proposals for achieving these objectives may be considered:

1. Minimize fiscal disparities.

2. Utilize revenue sharing.

3. Impose user charges.

4. Restructure the property tax.

5. Establish metropolitan government.

A broad approach to financing urban government should draw on all these proposals.

MINIMIZE FISCAL DISPARITIES

Cities provide many goods and services whose benefits and costs are not appropriately apportioned. People benefit in varying degrees from the expendi-

Box 2
**Urban Transportation: Economic
Solutions to Imbalances**

The major transportation problem facing large cities is to get hundreds of thousands—and in some cases millions—of people to and from work in the central business districts with minimum congestion and reasonable comfort. The economic difficulties of accomplishing this include problems of costs, revenues, pricing, and financing.

Costs are a problem because mass-transit systems such as commuter trains and subways suffer from a limited ability to adjust variable costs to fluctuations in passenger volume. They also require large amounts of capital investment to provide for modernization and expansion.

Revenues are inadequate because political pressures have forced regulatory agencies to keep tolls and fares low—too low to meet operating costs, let alone replace obsolete equipment. Pricing policies create other difficulties; distorted fare structures have caused some facilities to be overused while others are relatively idle. Financing is hard to obtain because efforts to support mass-transit operations out of general funds have met with considerable resistance. Many people feel that mass transit benefits only commuters, rather than the public as a whole; and most cities and states are financially hard-pressed.

Fast, efficient mass transit is vital to the economic health of our big cities. Two guidelines for policy may be suggested:

○ Public funds should subsidize both capital investment and operating costs of mass transit. Attempts to cover constantly rising operating expenses by increasing fares have diverted commuters to highways.

○ Tolls for the use of highways, bridges, and tunnels should more closely reflect the private and social costs of commuting by private car. The excess revenues should be allocated to mass transit. Such action would help to offset current highway-biased subsidy arrangements.

Charles Harbutt © Magnum Photos.

John Bryson, Rapho/Photo Researchers.

Can variable toll systems which charge higher prices during peak periods and lower prices during off-peak periods help reduce imbalances in the utilization of facilities?

Ray Ellis, Rapho/Photo Researchers.

tures of local governments, and they pay in varying degrees for the values they receive. But the disparities between costs and benefits may be wide because the people who work in the city and the people who visit the city are not always the same people as the taxpayers who own property or live in the city. As a result of these misalignments, there tend to be wide differences not only in the taxable bases and expenditure requirements of the more than 80,000 local governmental units in the United States, but also in the quantity and quality of services provided by these units.

"Spillover" Effects

The divergencies of costs and benefits have created extensive "spillover" effects among a wide array of urban government expenditures. These range from health, education, and welfare services to environmental control. Two examples of the many "spillover" effects may be given.

1. The mounting education and welfare budgets of most major cities have been due in large part to our national agricultural policy. In recent decades, Washington has promoted the subsidization and mechanization of the South's cotton and tobacco fields, driving out millions of workers, who have then streamed into the cities looking for jobs. Most of these people are poor, unskilled, and usually illiterate. Hence, they have either become public charges or at best have been able to find menial employment at the minimum wage. Meanwhile, many of the "expatriates"—the former residents of the cities—continue to work in the cities and hold the higher-paying jobs while turning over the bulk of their tax bills to the suburban municipalities in which they reside.

2. In the area of environmental control, it was once thought that air and water pollution were strictly local problems peculiar to a few cities. But now it is recognized that geographic boundaries in such matters are largely irrelevant and that the issues are of national or even international concern. Canadian residents, for example, have filed suits in U.S. federal courts against American firms for contaminating the air over Canada.

In these and many other situations, the disparities between costs and benefits should be minimized. The most effective way to accomplish this is for the federal government to absorb a much larger share of the financial burden. At the present time, state and local governments pay almost all the costs of public safety, transportation (except highways), elementary and secondary education, water supply and treatment, parks and recreation, and garbage collection. In addition, they pay a substantial part of the costs of health,

welfare, and social security programs. If a larger portion of the costs of these local activities could be transferred to Washington, many of the spillover effects would be greatly reduced or eliminated and the city governments would be relieved of enormous tax responsibilities.

UTILIZE REVENUE SHARING

An approach for relieving the mounting fiscal pressures facing states and cities is for the federal government to engage in *revenue sharing*. Such a plan requires that the federal government *automatically* turn over a portion of its tax revenues to state and local governments each year. The justification for this is based on certain fundamental facts and relationships involving both revenues and expenditures.

First, the federal government collects most of the taxes levied; state and local governments collect a relatively minor proportion. The federal government's chief source of revenue is the income tax. Because of its progressive rate structure, the tax yields approximately a 1.5 percent increase in revenues for every 1 percent increase in the nation's total output of final goods and services—its gross national product (GNP). The state and local governments, on the other hand, receive the great bulk of their revenues from property, sales, and other taxes. These tend to increase by about 1 percent for every 1 percent increase in GNP.

Second, state and local spending has been increasing at rates of about 7 percent to 10 percent per year—roughly twice as fast as the growth in GNP. At the same time, state and local governments have met growing public resistance to increases in taxes, the imposition of new taxes, and the sale of bonds—these being the only methods available to finance rising municipal expenditures. Federal government spending, on the other hand (except for extraordinary military needs), *may* tend to rise less than federal revenues when the economy is expanding, thereby leaving a *fiscal dividend*.

According to the revenue-sharing advocates, *the salvation of states and cities lies in sharing the fiscal dividend*. Of course, the federal government has long poured out money to states and localities, but this has been largely in the form of grants-in-aid for specific programs to which Washington attaches many bureaucratic strings and controls. What the governors and mayors want is a kind of philosophical Jeffersonianism. This is an arrangement whereby the federal government gives out blocks of grants for broad general purposes while allowing all or most of the spending decisions to be made at state and local levels. In this way, by sharing a percentage of its revenues on a fixed basis with hard-pressed states and cities, the federal government can encourage much greater local initiative.

Revenue sharing was approved by Washington in 1972. Although state and local government leaders often complain that the program is inadequate and has not been consistently implemented, there is widespread agreement that revenue sharing in general has been successful.

IMPOSE USER CHARGES

Local governments obtain their revenues from various sources. These include taxation, license fees, interest earnings, special assessments, sale of property, charges for municipal services, and so on. The last item, often called "user charges," offers promising opportunities for additional revenues.

At present, many people receive the benefits of city hospitals, public housing, treated water, mass transit, refuse collection, and public schools. Many people also help support part of the costs of these locally provided services through special payments, rents, and fees, as well as through taxation. The issue is whether the cities should revise their systems of user charges for these services, and whether they should charge for services which are presently financed out of tax revenues.

The answer to both questions is yes—for several reasons:

First, a revision of user charges is based on the recognition that if certain types of services are available too cheaply or at flat rates, their limited supply will be rationed by congestion whenever the quantity demanded exceeds the quantity supplied at the existing price. As we mentioned earlier, mass-transit facilities during rush hours serve as striking illustrations. In such cases a *differential* pricing structure rather than a single price would not only provide a better rationing mechanism, but would provide a larger total revenue as well.

Second, by imposing charges on certain services which are currently financed entirely from tax revenues, and by varying the charges according to their use, a more efficient utilization of resources and a greater volume of total revenue can be realized. Public libraries and marinas provide typical examples. The services of these facilities are usually offered free or at little cost to residents of the suburbs as well as the cities. Because the poor make relatively less use of these amenities, the overall effect is for middle-income households to be subsidized in large measure from taxes paid by low-income groups.

User charges have a number of advantages. Among the more important are these:

1. They enable the municipal government to know the value of its services to its users.

2. They reduce benefit spillovers resulting from geographic differences.

3. They permit greater efficiency of production, less oversupply of services, and larger total revenues than would occur with tax financing.

But user charges also have at least two closely related limitations. First, they are inappropriate for financing "public goods"—goods whose benefits are available to everyone—such as clean streets, traffic lights, and public safety. Second, they are difficult to apply where specific benefits to users are hard to identify and measure.

RESTRUCTURE THE PROPERTY TAX

A fourth approach to improving the finances of local governments is to revise the existing structure of the property tax. This tax, with its diverse rates and bases, is imposed only at the state and local levels, not at the federal level. Although local governments have other sources of revenue, such as sales and excise taxes, income taxes, utility revenue, and liquor store revenue, the property tax is nevertheless their largest single source of funds. This tax helps pay the local share of school costs as well as a large part of the expenses incurred for public safety, sanitation, street lighting, and the bulk of other community services.

Despite its widespread use, the property tax suffers from a number of shortcomings. Three are particularly important.

1. It requires tax assessors to "guess" the market value of taxable property. This is because the true market value cannot be known unless the property is sold. As a result, wide differentials and inequities of assessment exist both within and between districts.

2. The tax is extremely regressive. It bears down much harder on poorer families than richer ones because housing is such a large part of consumer spending for lower-income groups.

3. It causes "fiscal zoning"—that is, the control of land use in order to maximize the tax base. For example, it encourages laws requiring large minimum lot sizes, thereby raising land costs and discouraging the construction of smaller homes for moderate-income families.

These and other factors make the property tax one of the most controversial in the entire tax structure.

Nevertheless, it continues to exist, partly because it raises so much revenue and partly because it is the major tax which local governments are permitted by their states to levy.

The Land Value Tax

The many bad economic effects of the property tax have resulted in various proposals for its revision. The most desirable and feasible way to correct its deficiencies would be to restructure it in favor of a land value tax. This is a tax on bare sites exclusive of buildings that stand on them. This idea was first proposed by the American economist Henry George in his book, *Progress and Poverty* (1879). But unlike George, who advocated a tax on land as a "single tax" to replace all others, it is suggested here as a partial but substantial substitute for the property tax.

The fundamental idea is to tax the annual unearned gains from land. This is the economic rent or surplus that accrues to the owners of land not because of improvements they have made upon it but because of community development and population growth which have caused the market value of land to rise. Three chief arguments are advanced in favor of such a tax.

1. It discourages land from being held out of productive use.

2. It encourages the building of structures on the land.

3. It returns to society the increases in the value of land resulting from economic growth.

The major criticism of the tax is that it is difficult to administer. This is because it cannot distinguish between increases in the value of land resulting from economic growth and increases due to improvements made on the land.

Even though this criticism is valid, its adverse effects can certainly be mitigated through appropriate tax laws. Experience in other countries which make use of land value taxation, including mixed economies such as Canada, Australia, and New Zealand, indicates that such laws are feasible and workable.

At present, the property tax in the United States is relatively light on land and heavy on buildings. Hence, the tax favors landowners, who tend to be in the higher-income groups, and speculators, who find it more profitable to hold land for future resale than to build upon it. By restructuring the property tax so that it bears down relatively heavier on land than on buildings, these undesirable effects would be greatly reduced without causing revenue losses to local governments. In fact, various studies have concluded that a land value tax which averages about 5 percent nationally would yield the same total revenue that is now produced by property taxes on land and buildings.

ESTABLISH METROPOLITAN GOVERNMENT

A fifth means of coping with the challenges facing local governments is one which realizes the need for regional attacks on pressing urban problems. This approach is as much political as economic. It is based on the recognition that local government authority in most metropolitan areas is too fragmented to provide for overall balanced systems of land use, transportation, public health, and the like. For example, many large urban areas, such as Chicago, New York, Philadelphia, and Pittsburgh, have considerably more than 500 local governmental units each. The effects of such proliferation are fiscal duplication, administrative inefficiency, and suburban separatism, which hurts minority groups.

To help correct these deficiencies, some form of consolidation is needed. One of the more feasible possibilities is to set up a "two-tier" system of metropolitan government in urban regions. Such a system could consist of an area government and local governments, with functions assigned to each. At the area level, the functions assigned could be those which have broad overlapping interests or which offer advantages of economies of scale. Examples are planning, zoning, water supply, sewage disposal, transportation, and public health. At the local levels, community governments could administer their own police departments, fire services, and education. Some functions, of course, could also be shared at both levels, where it is advantageous to do so.

There are three major advantages to such a plan.

1. Efficiency would be increased by consolidating some of the functions of smaller governmental units.

2. Governmental units at all levels would become more responsive to human needs and preferences as a result of decentralizing some of the functions of the larger cities.

3. The relationship of local governmental units to the states and federal government would be strengthened by a more rational allocation of functions among the various levels.

Metropolitan government has been adopted in varying degrees by some cities in the United States and Canada. But most local officials oppose the idea because they fear the loss of power. Consequently, the majority of states have been reluctant to pass the necessary enabling legislation. Ideally, if Washington would expand the program of grants which it already provides for some regional activities, it could offer additional incentives to the states and local governments by rewarding them financially if they initiate plans for the establishment of some form of metropolitan government.

What You Have Learned

1. Critics have accused the public schools—especially those in large cities—of being rigidly controlled educational monopolies. This makes them insensitive to community desires and unresponsive to the need for change. By subjecting them to competition in a free market, it is argued, the quality of all schools will improve. Four proposals have been advanced for increasing competition: decentralization of school systems; creation of publicly financed private schools; performance contracting; and the voucher system.

2. The inner cities have long been faced with the problem of providing adequate housing for the poor. Government has tried to help but sometimes has done more harm than good. The ultimate solution rests on developing a proper system of federal subsidies to help support low-income housing. The federal government should also absorb the health, education, and welfare costs of the cities so that the latter can afford to exempt all low-income housing from property taxes.

3. The transportation crisis of the cities is due primarily to an imbalance between private automobile and public transportation. This results in congestion, time delays, and a general misallocation of transportation facilities. Two broad steps can be taken toward developing a balanced transportation system.

   (a) Introduce an appropriate pricing system, in the form of variable tolls, to ration the use of scarce transportation facilities.

   (b) Introduce technological improvements and innovations such as electronic control systems, mass-transit subsidy schemes, and relaxed restrictions on the use of taxicab and jitney services.

4. The most fundamental problem of the cities is to finance needed urban improvements. This requires that they resolve their present fiscal dilemma. Recommended measures are: minimize fiscal disparities; utilize revenue sharing; impose user charges; restructure the property tax; and establish metropolitan government.

For Discussion

1. *Terms and concepts to review:*
   benefit principle   fiscal dividend
   revenue sharing

2. Can you propose some guidelines for improving public education in the United States by suggesting the kinds of decisions that should be centralized and decentralized at different levels of state and local government?

3. "If the government would stop interfering in the housing market, the price of housing would adjust to the free interaction of supply and demand and there would be no problem." Do you agree? Explain.

4. Various public transit systems have considered raising their fares during morning and evening rush hours and lowering them at other times. Despite the advantages of such schemes, they have rarely been adopted. Why?

5. If the cities need more money to finance urban improvements, why do they not simply raise taxes or borrow?

6. It may be argued that when a city makes available "free" museums, "free" golf courses, "free" tennis courts, "free" marinas, and so on, it is redistributing income *from the poor to the rich!* How might this happen? What can be done about it?

Case
Protecting the Public: When Are the Benefits Worth the Costs?

How much is your college education worth? One way to find out is to conduct a _benefit-cost analysis_. This rather complex procedure generally consists of three basic steps:

1. Estimate the value today—the so-called _discounted_ or _present value_—of future lifetime earnings you expect from your education. To do this, you must guess not only your future annual earnings, but also the value of the nonmonetary advantages your education will provide. The result you obtain will be a dollar figure representing the _benefit_ of your college education.

2. Next, estimate the discounted or present value of your annual educational expenses. These include the prices of books and tuition and the opportunity (alternative) cost of lost income which results from going to school instead of working. The resulting dollar figure represents the _cost_ of your investment in a college education.

3. Finally, assuming that _all_ the benefits and costs—monetary and non-monetary—have been correctly identified and estimated, compare the benefit of your college education with the cost. Obviously, the benefit must equal the cost in order for the investment to be repaid by its net receipts. If the benefit turns out to be less than the cost, the investment has not been worthwhile.

Benefit-cost analysis helps to provide a guide for achieving increased efficiency in the allocation of scarce resources. Economists are making increasing use of benefit-cost techniques for evaluating government investment projects—among them job-training programs, pollution-abatement schemes, and weapons systems. One of the more novel approaches, however, involves the use of benefit-cost analysis for judging the effectiveness of legislative measures designed to protect the public.

Applications: Government Safety Programs

Should a pharmaceutical company be required to submit proof of a drug's effectiveness before it is marketed—even if the delay results in a substantial cost to the public in terms of pain or perhaps loss of life?

Should auto seatbelts be required even if the security they afford encourages more reckless driving and the possibility of more accidents?

These and similar questions about the benefits and costs of government safety regulations are being increasingly raised by economists. On the basis of extensive research, some startling conclusions have emerged.

Among them:

1. A federal law requiring pharmaceutical manufacturers to prove the efficacy of new drugs before marketing them has perhaps done more harm than good. Since the legislation was enacted, the rate of introduction of new drugs has declined more than 50 percent, while the average testing period has more than doubled. Further, there is no evidence that the average effectiveness of new drugs has improved as a result of the law. On the other hand, costs to society of the government's regulatory efforts have been astronomical. According to one study, drug-research expenses have soared, approval of new drugs has been impeded, and competition among pharmaceutical manufacturers has been greatly impaired because new firms have been effectively barred from entering the market to compete with producers of established drugs.

2. A federal regulation requiring the installation of auto seatbelts has resulted in substantial reductions in driver injuries and fatalities. But the same legislation may also give motorists a false sense of security, encouraging them to take greater risks—and thereby cause more accidents. This is an argument advanced by a University of Chicago professor of law, Sam Peltzman. An ardent free-market advocate, Peltzman claims that his research shows strong evidence of many more, rather than fewer, automobile mishaps resulting from legislation requiring safety belts. It should be noted that some critics disagree, claiming that Peltzman's data are not conclusive and do not support his strong assertions.

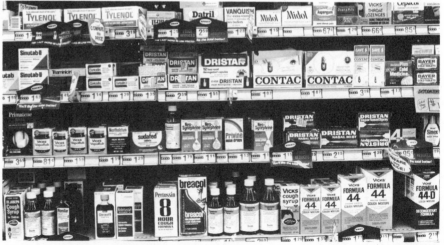

Robert Chiarello.

Robert Chiarello.

Value of a Life

Regardless of the findings, the purpose of Peltzman's studies is to arrive at benefit-cost estimates of government regulations and programs. In most cases the studies require a value to be placed on human life. Economists contend that this is done implicitly when a community decides on the size of a police force, fire department, or public hospital to be built. Benefit-cost analysis, however, forces explicit recognition of the issue. Where a human life is concerned, the economic value is usually based on a prediction of the individual's expected lifetime earnings, discounted at an appropriate interest rate. The resulting present value is then compared with the current investment outlay to determine whether the anticipated benefits are worth the costs.

The results can sometimes be disturbing, if not shocking. The poor, the retired elderly, and the young, for example, tend to have low present values because of their low productivities, and thus their earnings are either zero or very low. As a result, government programs undertaken on behalf of these groups may not always be

economically justifiable. For example, Burton Weisbrod of the University of Wisconsin has shown that the development of polio vaccine had relatively low economic benefits to society because polio is primarily a childhood disease. The social return might have been greater if the same investment had been made in preventing a more common disease—say, cancer—instead of polio.

Minimizing Risk

Despite the technical precision permitted by benefit-cost analysis, some economists contend that the method is incorrect when it is used to estimate the value of a lifesaving government program. Their reasons are based on three fundamental arguments:

1. The object of a government safety program is to reduce the risk of death. The value of reducing the risk should be determined and paid by those who benefit from it—the individual, his family, or even society as a whole.

2. The lower the risk of death, the greater the value to the beneficiaries. Therefore, the relationship between risk and value measures the worth of a human life.

3. In general, the economic value of a life is the amount of money that beneficiaries would be willing to pay to minimize the risk of death. This amount is ordinarily much greater than the present-value figure established by conventional benefit-cost procedures based on expected lifetime earnings, because the gains from risk reduction to *all* beneficiaries (including family and society) must be taken into account.

Conclusion: Increasing Use

On the basis of these arguments, some studies have placed the value of an "average" human life in excess of $500,000. This compares to estimates of one-half that amount derived from conventional benefit-cost studies using expected lifetime earnings as the relevant measure.

Of course, the risk-reduction approach to benefit-cost analysis is broader and more difficult to apply than the narrower earnings approach. Nevertheless, the risk-reduction approach is gaining increasing attention among government leaders concerned with utilizing sophisticated benefit-cost concepts in designing new safety programs to be supported by taxpayers' dollars.

QUESTIONS

1. The evaluation of government programs raises difficult problems—more so with the measurement of benefits than of costs. Can you explain why?

2. The economic worth of any asset—a machine, a factory, and so forth—is determined by the present value of expected earnings during its assumed life. Can this method of valuing an asset be applied to measuring the value of a human life? (Keep in mind that a human being can be viewed as an asset, generating income over a given time period.) Discuss.

Part 8

International Economics and the World's Economies

Chapter 33

International Trade: The Commerce of Nations

Chapter Preview

What are the chief highlights of world trade? Are there significant regional patterns of trade for the United States?

Why do nations trade? What benefits do they receive? What costs do they incur?

Why do countries impose obstacles to trade? Are their reasons valid?

How does international trade affect income and employment? Is there a relationship between a country's imports, exports, and national income?

The study of international economics is timely because the countries of the world are increasingly interdependent economically. Many of the issues that can either tie nations closer together or drive them apart have roots in economics.

In general, international economics is concerned with the same fundamental questions as domestic economics. Thus, the problems of WHAT to produce, HOW MUCH, and FOR WHOM are still foremost. The difference is that these questions are studied for several economies or nations rather than for one.

On the microeconomic side, for example, international economics may show how the price systems of different countries interact to affect resource allocation and income distribution. On the macroeconomic side there may be concern with the ways in which imports, exports, and investment expenditures among nations affect income, employment, and economic growth. Both microeconomic and macroeconomic principles are often employed simultaneously in the study of international economics.

To begin with, we will concentrate on one broad segment of international economics—trade among nations. The remaining aspects of international economics, dealing with principles of international finance and with results of various commercial and financial policies, will be considered later in this chapter.

Major Features of World Trade

It is appropriate to begin the study of international trade by asking two questions: (1) Of what relative significance is world trade to nations? (2) What are the distributional patterns of trade between the United States and the major regions of the world?

THE IMPORTANCE OF WORLD TRADE

American students are not as familiar with the importance of international trade as are students in most other countries. This is because in many nations the volume of exports or imports may be as much as 40 percent of GNP. But less than 10 percent of the GNP of the United States is sold abroad, and approximately the same percentage is purchased abroad.

However, neither the dollar volume of U.S. trade nor the U.S. products involved are trivial—as you can see from Exhibit 1. In total dollar volume, the amounts are far larger than the trade carried on by other countries. In terms of relative importance, agricultural goods represent less than 20 percent of what we import and export, whereas nonagricultural goods represent more than 80 percent of these totals.

PATTERNS OF U.S. TRADE

Where do our imports come from? Where do our exports go? Exhibit 1 shows clearly that the least industrialized areas of the world are neither America's biggest suppliers nor its biggest customers. Europe, which includes most of the leading industrial countries of the world, along with Canada and Asia, notably Japan, are America's largest markets for purchases and sales of goods.

Of course, changes in the world's economies since the early part of this century have brought changes in our patterns of trade. For example, trade with Asia has grown in relative importance, while trade with Europe, although still large in absolute terms, has declined substantially.

Why Do Countries Trade?

Imagine what would happen if you tried to be completely self-sufficient. You would have to grow your own food, make your own clothing, build your own means of transportation, construct your own shelter, make your own furniture, treat your own illnesses, and provide for all your needs and desires. Obviously, you would not be able to do many things because you lack the necessary material resources, time, and skills. Hence, your level of living would be much lower than it is now.

How could you correct the situation? You could *specialize*—that is, concentrate on the things you do best. In that way, you could produce more than enough for yourself and sell or trade your surpluses for the other things you want. That is essentially what we all do. A carpenter, a salesperson, a doctor, a teacher, a bricklayer—each "specializes" in the activity that he or she does best and thereby earns enough to buy the goods and services produced by others.

Specialization also exists among nations:

> Resources are distributed unevenly throughout the world. Some countries have more or better land, or labor, or capital than others, so it may pay for them to *specialize*. In this way, a larger quantity and greater variety of goods are produced, which nations can exchange with one another. As with individuals, the quantity and variety of goods would be less if each nation tried to be self-sufficient.

These ideas can be better understood by examining the principles and consequences that underlie the exchange of goods between nations and regions.

LAW OF ABSOLUTE ADVANTAGE

The simplest and most obvious reason for trade is provided by what is known as the *law of absolute advantage*. This principle states that a basis for trade between regions exists when each, because of natural or acquired endowments, can provide the other with a good or service for less than it would pay to produce the product at home.

Thus, the United States buys coffee from Brazil, and Brazil buys machinery from the United States. Libya buys lumber from Sweden, and Sweden buys oil from Libya. Flordia buys cars made in Michigan, and Michigan buys oranges grown in Florida.

In general, this kind of trading helps both parties. Imagine how costly it would be, for example, if some Florida business managers tried to acquire the factories and skilled workers needed to make automobiles, or if some Michigan business executives tried to build the huge hothouses that would be needed for growing orange trees.

NOTE For convenience, we ordinarily speak of "countries" or "regions" as buyers and sellers of products. But the governments of those areas are not doing all the buying and selling. Most international trade is carried on by private firms. Only in command economies do governments engage significantly in trade.

Exhibit 1
Foreign Trade of the United States

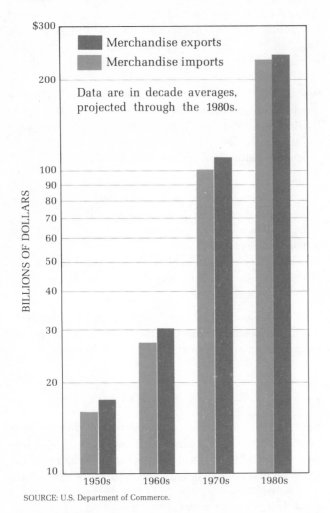

Merchandise exports
Merchandise imports

Data are in decade averages, projected through the 1980s.

BILLIONS OF DOLLARS

1950s   1960s   1970s   1980s

SOURCE: U.S. Department of Commerce.

U.S. MERCHANDISE EXPORTS AND IMPORTS, 1978

	Merchandise exports	Merchandise imports
	(billions of dollars)	
Item		
Agricultural products	$ 29	$ 15
Nonagricultural products*	112	157
	$141	$172
Region		
Africa	$ 5.9	$16.9
Asia	40.0	58.3
Australia and Oceania	3.5	2.4
Europe	43.6	38.0
Canada	28.4	33.6
Mexico and Central America	11.0	12.6
South America	10.9	10.3

* Minerals, fuels, chemicals, manufactured goods, and machinery.

SOURCE: U.S. Department of Commerce.

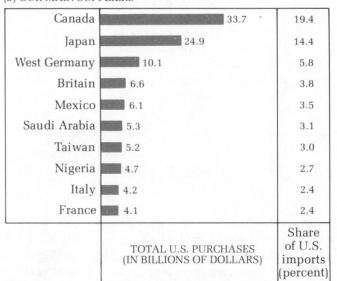

(a) OUR BEST CUSTOMERS

	TOTAL U.S. SALES (IN BILLIONS OF DOLLARS)	Share of U.S. exports (percent)
Canada	28.4	19.8
Japan	12.9	9.0
Britain	7.1	4.9
West Germany	7.0	4.9
Mexico	6.7	4.7
Netherlands	5.7	4.0
Saudi Arabia	4.4	3.1
France	4.2	2.9
Venezuela	3.7	2.6
Iran	3.7	2.6

(b) OUR MAIN SUPPLIERS

	TOTAL U.S. PURCHASES (IN BILLIONS OF DOLLARS)	Share of U.S. imports (percent)
Canada	33.7	19.4
Japan	24.9	14.4
West Germany	10.1	5.8
Britain	6.6	3.8
Mexico	6.1	3.5
Saudi Arabia	5.3	3.1
Taiwan	5.2	3.0
Nigeria	4.7	2.7
Italy	4.2	2.4
France	4.1	2.4

THE CONCEPT OF COMPARATIVE ADVANTAGE

The reasons for trade are not always obvious as in the examples given above. Trade between individuals or nations can be profitable even if one of the parties can produce *both* products more efficiently than the other. This involves a concept known as "comparative advantage."

For example, some doctors may be good typists. Yet a doctor generally hires a typist, even though the typist may not type as well as the doctor does. This is because the time spent at medical practice is more profitable than the time spent at the typewriter. Thus, suppose a doctor can do a necessary day's typing in 1 hour, whereas the typist who is hired takes 3 hours to do the same amount of typing. If the doctor earns $60 per hour by practicing medicine, and pays the typist $6 per hour, the doctor gains $42 per day by performing only medically related tasks. To put the example in a different but equivalent way, the doctor can earn enough money in 18 minutes by practicing medicine to pay for 3 hours of the typist's time.

An Application to Nations

Applying the same principle to nations, let us take the case of England and Portugal, both producing two products—cloth and wine. (This was the kind of example used in 1817 by the great English classical economist David Ricardo, when he first explained the mutual advantages of trade between nations in terms of what is now known as the law of comparative advantage.)

An illustration based on hypothetical data appears in Exhibit 2. It is clear from the table that Portugal is equally as efficient as England in the production of cloth, but three times as efficient as England in the production of wine. Therefore, Portugal has a comparative (or relative) advantage in wine production.

In the charts of Exhibit 2, the data are presented in the form of production-possibilities curves. The "curves" in earlier chapters appeared as curved lines that were bowed outward. However, here the curves are shown as straight lines. This is because we are assuming for simplicity that production takes place under conditions of constant rather than increasing costs.

Thus, in England, the intersection of the production-possibilities curve DE with the two axes of the chart tells us that 1 day's labor can produce either 30 yards of cloth or 10 gallons of wine, or any particular combination in between as determined by any given point along the line. Hence, the steepness (slope) of DE measures the relative cost of the two products in England and is constant at the ratio 3:1. Similarly, in Por-

Exhibit 2
The Law of Comparative Advantage

The curves *DE* and *D'E'* are production-possibilities curves for each country. Without trade between the two nations, England may choose to be self-sufficient in both cloth and wine by producing a combination represented by point K. Similarly, Portugal may choose to be self-sufficient by producing a combination represented by point K'.

PRODUCTION FROM 1 DAY'S LABOR AT FULL EMPLOYMENT

	Cloth output (yards per day)	Wine output (gallons per day)	Cost ratio (cloth/wine)
England	30	10	3/1
Portugal	30	30	1/1

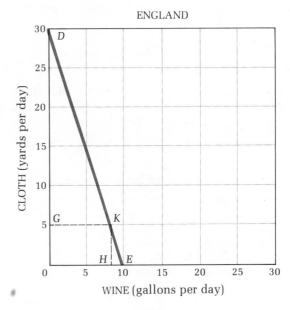

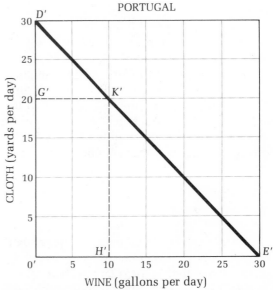

tugal, the intersection of $D'E'$ with the two axes signifies that 1 day's labor can produce either 30 yards of cloth or 30 gallons of wine, or any specific combination in between as determined by any given point along the line. Therefore, the steepness of $D'E'$ measures the relative cost of the two products in Portugal and is constant at the ratio 1:1.

How much will each country produce? It is impossible to answer this question without knowing the demands for each product in the two countries. However, if we assume that there is no trade between them, it may be inferred that each will try to be self-sufficient by producing some cloth and some wine, as denoted by any given point on each nation's production-possibilities curve. Thus, England might choose the point K representing $0G$ yards of cloth and $0H$ gallons of wine. On the other hand, Portugal might choose the point K' representing $0'G'$ yards of cloth and $0'H'$ gallons of wine.

Introducing Trade

What will happen if the two countries decide to engage in free and unrestricted trade? Let us assume for simplicity the following conditions:

1. There are no transportation costs between the two countries.

2. Competitive conditions prevail in both nations.

3. Labor is the only scarce factor of production and hence prices of the products are equal to their relative labor costs.

This means that the costs, and therefore the prices, in both countries are as follows:

price in England: 3 yards cloth = 1 gallon wine
price in Portugal: 1 yard cloth = 1 gallon wine

Obviously, *cloth is cheaper in England and wine is cheaper in Portugal.* Therefore, England will import wine from Portugal and Portugal will import cloth from England. As exports of Portuguese wine enter England, the supply of wine in England will increase and its price will fall. Similarly, as exports of English cloth enter Portugal, the supply of cloth in Portugal will increase and its price will fall.

THE GAINS FROM TRADE

The price ratios in England and Portugal will thus become equal to one another. Why? Because we have assumed above that there is competition in both nations and there are no trade restrictions or transportation costs between them. Therefore:

The two countries will comprise in effect a *single market* with a *single price ratio.* At this new price ratio, it will pay for England to specialize in the production of cloth and for Portugal to specialize in the production of wine. Then both nations can trade a portion of these outputs with one another. In that way the two countries can end up with more wine and more cloth than if each country tried to produce both products by itself.

The point is illustrated graphically in Exhibit 3. Chart (a) is constructed by combining the two previous charts from Exhibit 2. Thus, the chart for England is in the same relative position as before, but the chart for Portugal is "flipped over" so that its origin is in the upper right-hand corner at $0'$. The construction procedure is shown in Chart (b).

Chart (a) has several interesting features:

1. The dashed line DL defines the trading possibilities for both countries. Since it is a straight line, it has a constant price ratio (or slope) which is somewhere between the price ratios represented by the old production-possibilities curves, DE and $D'E'$.

2. An "exchange point" will tend to be established in the vicinity of P because at a point such as this both England and Portugal can have more cloth and more wine by specializing and trading than by trying to be self-sufficient. For example, suppose that England specializes entirely in cloth and produces $0D$ yards of it. If it consumes $0M$ yards of cloth, it can export the remaining MD yards and acquire $0N$ ($=MP$) gallons of wine in return. It thus ends up at the point P where it has *more* cloth than when it was self-sufficient at the point K.

3. Similarly, if Portugal specializes completely in wine, it can produce $0'E'$ gallons. If it consumes $0'N'$ of this, it has left over $N'E'$, which it can export to England in return for $0'M'$ yards of cloth. In this way Portugal also ends up at the point P, where it consumes *more* of both cloth and wine than when it was self-sufficient at the point K'.

4. Both countries thus benefit from international specialization and exchange. The amount by which a country benefits from trade is called the *gains from trade.* This concept plays an important role in the trading policies of nations.

It is interesting to note from the chart that only in the vicinity of point P along the line DL will both countries gain by having more of both wine and cloth. At exchange points which are much higher or lower, one country may gain while the other loses, as compared to when each was self-sufficient without trade. At point S, for example, England will gain by having more cloth and more wine than it had at point K, but Portugal will lose by having more wine and less cloth than it had at point K'. At point T, on the other hand,

Exhibit 3
The Terms of Trade and the Gains from Trade

Chart (a) combines the two separate charts of Exhibit 2, as shown here in Chart (b).

The lines DE and D'E' are the production-possibilities curves from the previous exhibit. Before trade begins, England is producing at point K and Portugal at point K'. As a result of trade, both countries may extend their production frontiers to the point P, where each country receives more of both goods than before. These increased benefits of trade are called the *gains from trade*.

The dashed line DL is the new price line representing the trading possibilities of both nations. Its steepness (slope) measures the *terms of trade*. This is the amount of goods that each nation must give up (or export) for one unit of goods that it receives (or imports). The line must fall somewhere between the two old price lines DE and D'E' in order for trade to occur. If it falls to the left of DE (or to the right of D'E'), it will be cheaper for England (or for Portugal) to produce both products and not trade.

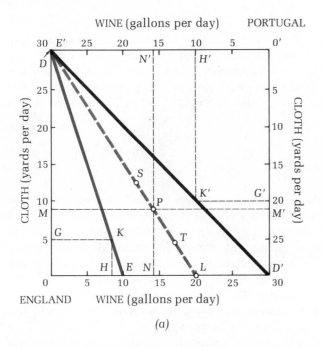

(a)

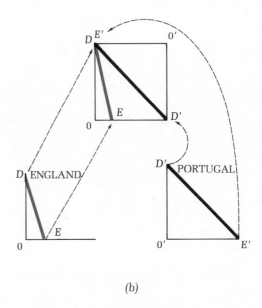

(b)

England will have comparatively less cloth and more wine, while Portugal has more of both. Therefore:

> Only in the vicinity of point P can *both* countries experience the mutual benefits of having more of *both* products. Hence, under conditions of competition and unrestricted trade, the exchange point will tend to settle at or near P.

THE TERMS OF TRADE

Each country thus gains by specializing in what it can produce with the greatest comparative or relative advantage. The gains will then be divided between the two countries according to the new price ratio, which, as we have seen, is simply the slope of the trading-possibilities line DL in the chart.

Thus, the closer that the line DL is to DE, the higher will be the price of wine relative to cloth, and hence the greater the gain to Portugal as compared to England. If DL should coincide with DE, which is unlikely, Portugal will receive all the gains from trade and England will receive none. The converse of these principles, of course, is equally applicable if the line DL shifts in the opposite direction toward D'E'.

In general, the new price line DL must always be somewhere between the old price lines DE and D'E' in order for trade to occur. For if DL is, say, to the left of (or steeper than) DE, the trading price of wine will be *greater* than the old price ratio in England. England will then find it cheaper to produce its own wine than to import it from Portugal. Similarly, if the line DL is to the right of D'E', it will pay for Portugal to produce its own cloth instead of trading with England.

These ideas involve what is known as the *terms of trade*. It is simply the number of units of goods that must be given up for one unit of goods received by each party to a transaction. (Graphically, the terms of trade are measured by the slope of the line *DL* in the chart.) In any transaction, the terms of trade are determined by the relative demands of the trading parties. In general:

> The terms of trade are said to move in *favor* of the party which gives up less units of goods for one unit of goods received, and *against* the party which gives up more units of goods for one unit of goods received.

As we shall see, the terms of trade play a vital and intensely practical role in evaluating exchange relationships between nations.

CONCLUSION: AN IMPORTANT LAW

The foregoing ideas permit us to formulate a principle of fundamental significance in economics, especially in international economics. It is based on the concept of comparative advantage which was developed earlier, but the concept may now be expressed more formally as a law.

The *law of comparative advantage* states that if one nation can produce each of two products more efficiently than another nation, and if the former can produce one of these commodities with comparatively greater efficiency than it can the other commodity, it should specialize in production of the product in which it is most efficient and leave production of the other product to the other country. The two nations will then have more of both goods by engaging in trade. This principle is also applicable to individuals and regions as well as to nations.

The law of comparative advantage thus leads to an important conclusion:

> Free and unrestricted trade among nations encourages international specialization according to comparative advantage. It thereby *tends* to bring about three favorable results:
>
> 1. The most efficient allocation of world resources as well as a maximization of world production.
>
> 2. A redistribution of relative product demands, resulting in greater equality of product prices among trading nations.
>
> 3. A redistribution of relative resource demands to correspond with relative product demands, resulting in greater equality of resource prices among trading nations.

It is important to emphasize that these outcomes are *tendencies* rather than certainties, because they are based on such idealistic assumptions as the existence of competition and the absence of trade restrictions (including transportation costs). Since these assumptions are not entirely realized in practice, the consequences of free trade will deviate from the above-mentioned tendencies.

Instruments of Protection

Despite the fundamental advantages of free trade—namely, encouragement of the most efficient allocation of world resources and the maximization of world production—nations have not been quick to adopt it. They have often chosen instead to institute various methods of protecting their home industries by imposing barriers to free trade. The reasons usually advanced for such actions will be explained later. But first, the chief forms of protection may be noted briefly.

TARIFFS

Tariffs have played a very significant role in various political and sectional disputes in the United States. A *tariff* is a customs duty or tax imposed by a government on the importation (or exportation) of a good. Tariffs may be specific, based on a tax per unit of the commodity, or ad valorem, based on the value of the commodity. There are a number of reasons, some of them rather complex, why a government might impose a tariff. For present purposes, however, it will be simplest for us to think of a tariff as a tax on imports exclusively, and to assume that it is imposed for the primary purpose of protecting domestic industry from foreign competition, or for providing the government with more revenue.

Exhibit 4 presents a history of tariff levels in the United States. Because a tariff is a law which must be approved by Congress, it is often named after the legislator who sponsored it. As the chart shows, the trend since 1930 has been sharply downward, with average rates less than 10 percent since 1970.

QUOTAS AND OTHER NONTARIFF BARRIERS

Tariffs are not the only means that nations employ to protect their home industries. Another common instrument of protection is the *import quota*. This places a precise legal limit on the number of units of a commodity that may be imported during a given period. Countries may also impose other nontariff barriers to

Exhibit 4
Average Tariff Rates in the United States
(duties collected as a percent of dutiable imports)

Tariffs have often been a political football in American history. Although rates have fluctuated widely, the trend has been sharply downward since the early 1930s. Since the post–World War II years, America has been a leading low-tariff nation.

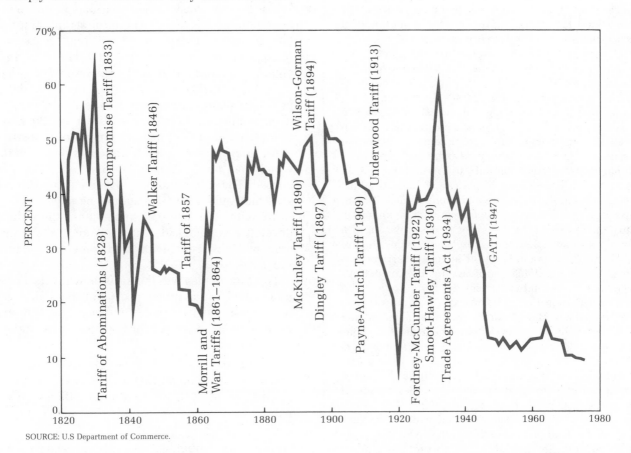

SOURCE: U.S Department of Commerce.

trade. Examples are customs procedures and laws involving import financing; foreign exchange requirements; and regulations involving labeling, health, safety, and shipping, some of which are expressly designed as protectionist devices. Quotas and other nontariff barriers have become relatively more significant than tariffs as protective instruments in many countries, including the United States. (See Box 1.)

What are the economic consequences of protection? In general:

All forms of protection tend to impede the full advantages of international specialization that are to be gained from free or unrestricted trade. When a nation adopts protective devices such as tariffs or quotas, it causes a shift of resources from more efficient to less efficient uses, and restricts consumers' freedom of choice.

Arguments for Protection

Despite the fact that the law of comparative advantage and the economic benefits of free trade have never been successfully refuted—although there have been many heroic attempts to do so—efforts by special-interest groups to obtain protection are common. American history, for example, is replete with long and eloquent pleas by business managers, union representatives, and political leaders contending that theirs is a "different" situation requiring special consideration. Most of these arguments for protection can be grouped into one of the following categories:

1. Infant-industry argument.

2. National-security argument.

3. Diversified-economy argument.

Box 1

Nontariff Barriers: When Is a Salami a Bologna?

In France, it is illegal to advertise whiskey and gin—allegedly because they are bad for the health. Without the pressures of advertising, the French tend to drink domestic wines and brandies instead of importing scotch and gin.

Similar restrictions on trade exist in other countries. The United States, for example, prohibits the importation of French candies—presumably because their colorants are unsafe. Japan prohibits the exportation of calculators containing integrated circuits made in other countries. And The Netherlands prohibits exports of pharmaceuticals not manufactured by members of a Dutch trade association.

But perhaps most interesting is the question: When is a sausage not a sausage? The not-so-simple answer is: When it is exported and bumps into another country's definition of a sausage. The definition may be expressed in terms of size, shape, casing, color, the mix of ingredients, and, in some instances, the number of pieces per link. Anything that does not conform to a particular country's definition of a sausage is ruled a nonsausage and may not be imported.

Thus, the classic nontariff barrier is the provision of a German tariff law of 1902, now obsolete, affecting the import of cows. This granddaddy of nontariff barriers was designed to exclude Dutch and Russian cattle competitive with German types, but to allow entry of Swiss cattle. It did so with a definition that gave an extra low duty rate to "large dappled mountain cattle or brown cattle reared at a spot 300 meters above sea level and which have at least one month's grazing at a spot at least 800 meters above sea level."

The old German law, while not mentioning any country, achieved its aim with what amounted to a description of Swiss cattle-raising practices. Modern nontariff barriers, however, are not so diplomatic. The catalog of such barriers seems infinite, and as research develops, almost every country, including the United States, is seen to be a prime offender.

4. Wage-protection argument.

5. Employment-protection argument.

We shall see below that there are fallacies in all these arguments. But before we do, the following fundamental point should be understood:

We can sell abroad only if we buy abroad. When the United States imports from foreign countries, those countries earn most of the dollars they need to purchase American exports. In general, *exports are the cost of trade, imports the return from trade,* not the other way around. Over the long run, a nation must export (sacrifice goods) in order to import (acquire goods).

As you will see in the following paragraphs, this basic principle is essential for understanding the fallacies that underlie almost all arguments for protection—*including those for both tariffs and quotas.*

INFANT-INDUSTRY ARGUMENT

When George Washington was inaugurated in 1789, he appointed Alexander Hamilton as the first Secretary of the Treasury. In 1791, Hamilton issued his famous *Report on Industry and Commerce.* In this volume he articulated with remarkable depth and clarity the economic problems of the time and proposed the nation's first protective tariff system. A fundamental justification for this system was the new nation's need to protect its growing infant industries.

An *infant industry* is an underdeveloped industry which may not be able to survive competition from abroad. The infant-industry argument for protection says that such industries should be shielded temporarily with high tariffs or quotas until the industries develop technological efficiency and economies of scale which will enable them to compete with foreign industries.

This type of plea was the basis on which tariffs were established for a number of industries during the nineteenth and twentieth centuries. But economists have come to recognize three major shortcomings of this argument:

1. Tariffs or other protective devices become the vested interests of particular business and political groups and as such are extremely difficult to eliminate.

2. Some protected industries never grow out of the "infant" stage—that is, they never become able to compete effectively with more mature industries in other countries.

3. An increase in tariffs or quotas results in higher prices to domestic consumers. Therefore, if an industry must be shielded from foreign competition, a subsidy would be more desirable because it tends to increase output as well as to reduce costs and prices. Above all, a subsidy is visible and must be voted periodically by Congress.

NATIONAL-SECURITY ARGUMENT

From time to time, representatives of various industries have made major efforts, through government and the news media, to gain protection from the onslaught of foreign competition. For example, some years ago the chairman of the board of the U.S. Steel Corporation asked a congressional committee: "Can we be assured of the strong industrial base in steel we need for modern defense if one-quarter or more of the steel we require were imported from countries lying uncomfortably close to the Soviet Union or China?"

This quotation provides a superb illustration of the "national-security argument." The argument contends that a nation should be as self-sufficient as possible in the production of goods needed for war and defense. On the face of it, this plea for protection seems persuasive, but on closer examination the following criticisms become apparent:

1. It is a political and military argument rather than an economic one. Therefore, it should be decided by the proper authorities in a calm and rational manner without the distortions of people who have a direct business interest in the outcome. The economist can help by pointing out the costs of protection in terms of resource misallocation and a reduced standard of living.

2. Many industries are important for defense or national security and could qualify equally well for increased protection.

3. As in the infant-industry argument, if some form of shielding is necessary, a subsidy is preferable to a tariff or quota.

DIVERSIFIED-ECONOMY ARGUMENT

"Don't put all your eggs in one basket." This maxim is as true for nations as it is for individuals—according to the "diversified-economy" theorists. They contend that increased protection is desirable because it enables a nation to build up a variety of industries for greater economic stability. In that way, they say, a highly specialized economy—such as Bolivia's tin economy or Chile's copper economy—will be less susceptible to adverse swings in the world's demand for its exports.

This argument contains some elements of truth. A single-crop or single-product economy is highly vulnerable to swings in demand—which may be permanent. For example, the introduction of man-made fibers has impoverished or severely damaged economies that concentrated on production of natural fibers.

But the diversified-economy argument also contains some shortcomings:

1. It is of little significance to economies that are already diversified and advanced, such as the United States.

2. It assumes that the government is more clairvoyant than private investors, and thus more able to envision the future economic benefits flowing from new and diversified industries.

3. It overlooks the inefficiencies that may result from forced, "unnatural" diversification, and the consequent increase in cost, which may more than offset any economic gains.

WAGE-PROTECTION ARGUMENT

Because wages in the United States are higher than in most other industrialized nations, some people argue that tariffs or quotas are needed to protect American workers from the products of cheap labor abroad.

In essence, advocates of this argument are contending that a high-wage nation cannot compete with a low-wage nation. In reality, however, the contention is false. The products of high-wage U.S. labor compete daily in world markets with the products of low-wage labor. The fact is that for many products, high wages do not of themselves prevent or even hinder trade among nations.

Three criticisms and qualifications of the wage-protection argument are particularly important:

1. It assumes that labor is the only resource entering into production. In fact, labor is a resource that is combined in each nation with varying quantities of capital and land. As a result, the products of countries may often by characterized as *labor-intensive, capital-intensive,* or *land-intensive,* depending on the relative proportions of resources that are employed in production.

2. Low-wage countries will have an advantage over high-wage countries *only* with products that are labor-intensive. These are goods for which wages are a large proportion of total costs. High-wage countries may be better off not competing with low-wage countries in these products.

3. Even where labor-intensive products are concerned, however, high-wage countries may be able to compete effectively with low-wage countries if labor productivity in the former is high enough to compensate for lower wage levels in the latter. (See Box 2.)

EMPLOYMENT-PROTECTION ARGUMENT

Supporters of trade protection often argue that tariffs or quotas are desirable because they reduce imports relative to exports and thus encourage a favorable balance of trade—that is, a surplus of exports over imports. This, in turn, stimulates the export industries and helps to bring about a higher level of domestic income, employment, and production.

Is this a valid plea for protection? Like the previous arguments it may seem persuasive, but the following considerations should be kept in mind:

Box 2
Labor Fights for Quota Protection

The American labor movement has been actively supporting protectionism since the late 1960s. Liberal trade policy, its leaders contend, is an anachronism. Quotas are needed to protect high-paid American workers from the products of cheap labor abroad.

Wide World Photos.

1. Any benefits in the form of higher income and employment, if they occur, are not likely to last long. The history of tariffs and quotas shows that in the long run, nations tend to retaliate with their own protective measures, leaving all nations worse off than before.

2. Tariffs and quotas tend to result in higher prices, thus penalizing domestic consumers while benefiting inefficient domestic producers. In the long run this encourages a movement of resources out of more efficient industries into less efficient (protected) ones, thereby raising costs and reducing comparative advantage.

3. In international trade, goods pay for goods, and hence in the long run a nation which exports must also import. Protective measures tend to impede the operation of this principle and therefore in the long run limit rather than encourage higher real income and employment.

CONCLUSION: TARIFFS PREFERRED TO QUOTAS

It is clear from these arguments that any kind of protective measure benefits some groups at the expense of the rest of society. Nevertheless, it is likely that

nations will always employ certain forms of protection—for political as well as for economic reasons. If this is so, which type of protection is economically preferable—tariffs or quotas? The answer is best understood in terms of a society's four major goals—efficiency, equity, stability, and growth.

Efficiency

A tariff causes less resource misallocation and permits greater efficiency in domestic markets than an import quota. This is because under a tariff, although imports are taxed, the foreign supply of the commodity available in the domestic market is nevertheless flexible. As a result, an increase in the domestic demand for the good can be met by a corresponding change in the volume of imports, with little or no change in the domestic price or in production. Even if the domestic price should rise, it can never exceed the world price by more than the import duty.

Under an import quota, on the other hand, the foreign supply of the commodity available domestically is inflexible. Consequently, an increase in domestic demand simply raises the domestic price relative to the world price without any limit as to the differential between them.

In general therefore:

A tariff causes less resource misallocation than an import quota. This is because market adjustments take place mostly in terms of changes in import quantities under a tariff, and changes in domestic prices under an import quota.

Equity

A tariff provides less inequity than an import quota. With a tariff, dependency of domestic buyers on particular suppliers is reduced, and there is greater assurance that the benefits of such low-cost imports as may occur are fully realized by the public rather than by the recipients of quota allocations. With an import quota, on the other hand, importers must apply for government licenses. The allocation of licenses is usually determined by noneconomic factors—without relation to consumer choice and producer cost. Thus:

Import quotas, unlike tariffs, tend to be discriminatory. The reason is that such quotas favor some importers over others, enabling the former to reap larger profits at the latter's and at the public's expense.

Stability and Growth

Tariffs and quotas cause higher domestic prices, but a tariff permits greater price stability than does a quota. This is because the foreign supply of a commodity available in the domestic market is flexible under a tariff but inflexible under a quota. Consequently, changing supply and demand conditions results in smaller fluctuations in price, but greater fluctuations in import quantities, under a tariff than under a quota.

Finally, with respect to growth, it is true that both tariffs and quotas encourage expansion of protected industries. However, in the long run, the final result of either is a net loss in the economy's overall growth as resources shift out of industries in which the nation has a comparative advantage into protected industries which entail relatively high costs of production.

To conclude:

Both a tariff and an import quota entail economic costs. Although relative prices are distorted by a tariff, it nevertheless permits market forces to allocate society's resources. Alternatively, an import quota stifles competition, creates vested interests in quota allocation, and is discriminatory in its effects. Therefore, if some degree of trade protection in a commodity is desired for whatever reason, the country would be better off with a tariff than with an import quota.

A fitting conclusion to this discussion of trade protection is presented in Box 3.

The Foreign-Trade Multiplier

How does foreign trade affect a nation's income and employment? To answer this question, we must think of imports and exports in a special way. Imports should be regarded as *withdrawals* from a nation's circular flow of income because they represent money earned at home but not put back into the income

---

Box 3
Who Will Be the Sacrificial Lamb?

Despite all the economic arguments that can be presented in favor of free trade, many prominent people, including some business executives, labor leaders, and politicians, continue to plead for protection.

There is no question that my industry's needs for price relief from the below-cost-of-production price levels now prevailing in the so-called "world" market will cost consumers more and will contribute to further inflation.

However, if such relief is not provided, much, if not all, of the domestic sugar producing industry will disappear. The inflationary effect of what my industry seeks will pale into nothing compared to that induced by total or even greater reliance on foreign suppliers for this vital commodity.

A. E. Benning
Chairman and Chief Executive Officer
The Amalgamated Sugar Co.
Ogden, Utah

South African ferrochrome producers, using predatory prices, are destroying producers in a drive to control U.S. supply of this critical material. Without import relief, there would then be nothing to prevent a South African ferrochrome cartel from extracting monopoly prices or withholding supply from U.S. steel producers and thus substantially disrupting this essential industry.

A. D. Gate
Committee of Producers of High
Carbon Ferrochrome
Washington, D.C.

A very large proportion of the imported footwear is produced in factories owned or controlled by American manufacturers. It is sold in the American market at the same price it would command if it had been made here. Thus the cost differential between the low-wage foreign operation and the modest wages of American shoe workers becomes a profit differential for manufacturers, wholesalers and retailers. The consumer gets no share in it.

Are we now to tell the typical shoe worker, aged 50, that he must cheerfully surrender his job to a 12-year-old girl in Taiwan or a peasant working behind his cottage in Spain? Can we make him whole by offering him a course in bricklaying or bus driving? He will not buy it. And neither, we think, will the nation.

George O. Fecteau, President
United Shoe Workers of America

Thousands of our members have become sacrificial lambs on the altar of foreign trade.

The flood of foreign-made tires is being felt by our members in that segment of the rubber industry. If nothing is done to check this trend, thousands of tire plant jobs will be eliminated. We cannot and will not stand still for this.

Our people don't want to hear ideological phrases of the learned economists' theories on free trade. What all our members really want is a steady job.

Peter Bommarito, President
United Rubber Workers

Comparative advantage [says] let each country produce what they make best and we have unlimited free trade and the end result is prices are cheaper and everybody's life is better.

There is one catch. If the comparative advantage is that some countries work children, have no minimum wage, no 40-hour workweek, no other protections, no free unions, then obviously they have an advantage of exploitation and it should not be subsidized by the workers of this country. In fact, it ought to be opposed.

Edmund G. Brown, Jr.
Governor, State of California

stream through consumption expenditures. Thus, if students in the United States decide to buy more Hondas and fewer American-made motorcycles, the American motorcycle industry will sell less. As a result, it will reduce its investment expenditures and lay off workers. These unemployed workers will then buy fewer television sets, vacation trips, automobiles, and other goods. Their reduced demands for these products and services will in turn result in a further decline in investment and employment. The initial increase in imports, therefore, will eventually bring about a *multiplied* decrease in national income and output.

Exports should be regarded as *injections* into a nation's circular flow of income because they represent money received from foreigners who have bought American goods. For example, if Germans decide to buy less of their own goods and more American commodities, some American firms will find the demand for their products increasing. These firms will then expand their investment in plant and equipment and hire more workers, who in turn will buy more of other products and thereby encourage the expansion of other industries. The initial increase in exports, therefore, eventually brings about a *multiplied* increase in national income and output.

These ideas suggest the existence of a "foreign-trade multiplier"—one of many multiplier concepts in economics. It may be described in the following way:

> The *foreign-trade multiplier* is a principle which states that fluctuations in exports or imports may generate magnified variations in national income. This principle is based on the idea that a change in exports relative to imports has the same multiplier effect on national income as a change in autonomous expenditures does. Similarly, a change in imports relative to exports has the same multiplier effect on national income as does a change in withdrawals from the income stream.

In general, an increase in exports tends to raise domestic income, but the increased income also induces some imports. These imports act as "leakages": They tend to reduce the full multiplier effect that would exist if imports remained constant. The foreign-trade multiplier is thus analogous in certain ways to the investment multiplier studied in macroeconomic theory.

What You Have Learned

1. Trade is important in the world economy. In quantitative terms, merchandise imports or exports range anywhere from about 4 to 40 percent of GNP for many major countries. In qualitative terms, many goods that countries import are virtually impossible to produce domestically.

2. Nations can raise their material standards of living by specializing and trading instead of trying to be self-sufficient. Two basic principles of specialization are the law of absolute advantage and the law of comparative advantage. The latter is more general because it demonstrates that nations can mutually benefit from specialization and trade even if each has only a relative rather than a complete advantage over the other in the production of commodities. The *gains* from trade are the benefits that nations receive, whereas the *terms* of trade are the real sacrifices they must make in terms of the goods they give up in return for the goods they receive.

3. Despite the mutual benefits of free and unrestricted trade, nations have instituted various forms of protection. These common instruments of protection consist of tariffs, import quotas, and other protective devices, such as unusual types of customs procedures and laws pertaining to import financing, foreign exchange requirements, and regulations involving labeling, health, safety, and shipping.

4. Many pleas may be advanced in favor of protection. Each needs qualification and most involve logical fallacies. In general, if some form of protection is to be imposed, a tariff is less objectionable on economic grounds than an import quota.

5. The foreign-trade multiplier is one of many multiplier concepts in economics. It is a principle which states that fluctuations in a nation's exports or imports may cause magnified changes in its national income.

For Discussion

1. *Terms and concepts to review:*

    law of absolute advantage
    gains from trade
    terms of trade
    law of comparative advantage

    tariff
    import quota
    infant industry
    foreign-trade multiplier

2. Examine the following production-possibilities table based on hypothetical data:

Country	Labor input (days)	Output of: Shoes (pairs)	Beef (pounds)
Italy	3	100	75
Argentina	3	50	60

(a) Which country, if any, has an absolute advantage in production? A comparative advantage? Explain.

(b) What is the *range* of possible barter terms—that is, the range within which the two countries may exchange goods? (HINT   What are the *domestic terms of trade* in each country?)

(c) What will determine the actual terms of exchange? Explain carefully.

3. The Constitution of the United States (Article 1, Sec. 10) states: "No State shall, without the consent of the Congress, lay any imposts or duties on imports or exports, except what may be absolutely necessary for executing its inspec-

tion laws." Do you think the Founding Fathers were wise to pass this law? What would happen to the American standard of living if each state were allowed to impose protective barriers to trade?

4. "If you believe in the free movement of goods between nations, you should logically believe in the free movement of people, too. This means that cheap foreign labor should be admitted to the United States, even if it results in the displacement of American labor." Do you agree? Explain your answer.

5. An editorial in the *Washington Inquirer* stated that:

The United States should develop a large shipbuilding industry. Such an industry would provide more jobs and higher incomes for workers. Moreover, the ships could be used for passenger and cargo service in peacetime, and could be quickly converted for military purposes in case of war. In view of these advantages, it would be wise for the U.S. government to protect the domestic shipbuilding industry from foreign competition until it can grow to a stronger competitive position.

Do you agree with this editorial? Explain.

6. Abraham Lincoln is reputed to have remarked: "I don't know much about the tariff. But I do know that when I buy a coat from England, I have the coat and England has the money. But when I buy a coat in America, I have the coat and America has the money." Can you show that Lincoln was correct only in the first sentence of his remark?

7. The foreign-trade multiplier is ordinarily smaller than the domestic-investment multiplier. Why?

Issue
Should the United States Trade with the U.S.S.R.?

Not so long ago, most informed observers believed that prospects for sizable trade with communist countries were dim. Whenever occasional steps were taken to expand U.S.–Soviet trade, the efforts were generally met with strong opposition in the United States. Consumer groups organized boycotts of Russian-made goods, municipalities passed ordinances forbidding the sale of communist products, and dockworkers at major ports refused to handle shipments arriving from, or being sent to, the Soviet Union. As far as U.S. critics were concerned, trading with the Russians was far more advantageous for them than for us. "They get American machinery, technology, and the benefits of our know-how, whereas all we get are some furs and vodka," remarked a former U.S. congressman.

Interestingly enough, many Russian leaders were equally opposed to trading with the United States. In Moscow, the arguments often heard were that the country was exporting important resources needed for Soviet development, that such resources helped strengthen Western economies, and that the added production resulting from increased exports was not needed to bolster Russia's economic growth.

It is easy to see how such attitudes and beliefs served to limit the development of U.S.–Soviet economic relations. Until the early 1970s, for example, less than 1 percent of America's imports and exports consisted of trade with Russia.

United Press International.

Changed Outlook

These views underwent a complete reversal by the mid-1970s. The turnabout was a result of many conditions. In the United States three major factors lent credence to the belief that trade should be expanded:

1. The Soviets can import virtually anything they want from Western Europe and Japan. Therefore, by refusing to sell to the Russians, the United States is missing out on profitable sales that other countries are making to Russia.

2. The Soviet Union provides a huge potential market for American goods.

By establishing strong trade relations with Russia, the United States strengthens its export industries, promotes fuller utilization of its resources, and raises the level of national income and employment.

3. The Soviet Union possesses a vast storehouse of raw materials—roughly one-half the world's known reserves of oil, coal, and natural gas, plus huge stocks of antimony, iron ore, chrome, lead, and numerous other metals. Many of these products constitute an ever-expanding list of raw materials which the United States must import to meet the growing demands of American industry.

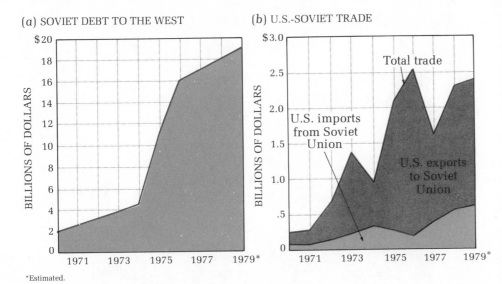

(a) SOVIET DEBT TO THE WEST

*Estimated.

(b) U.S.-SOVIET TRADE

raised to help finance large projects. However, it is also true that Japan and the advanced Western European countries can meet virtually all of Russia's capital and technological needs. Therefore, the Soviets do not stand to lose very much even if trade relations with the United States fail to improve significantly.

Conclusion

Both the United States and the U.S.S.R. have commodities and raw materials that could be useful to the other country. Each nation also possesses the means to pay for the goods it wants. Given these conditions, the basis for mutually beneficial trade exists. The question is whether these conditions should be exploited, or whether a policy of "no trading with the enemy" should be made an integral part of our overall foreign policy.

At the same time that the United States began expressing a growing interest in trade with Russia, the Soviets adopted similar attitudes. For example, Moscow declared that the "planned extension of trade relations with countries outside the communist sphere, on terms mutually convenient to the parties involved, was a desired policy." The reasons, according to the official Soviet newspaper *Pravda,* are not difficult to understand:

○ The U.S.S.R. possesses the largest reserves of most of the world's raw materials. By trading some of these natural resources for needed capital equipment and technology produced by advanced noncommunist coun-

tries, the Soviets can help to assure their nation's steady rate of growth while assuming a dominant role in the world economy.

○ The Soviet Union's planned growth rate is about 7 percent a year. The nation's output from any imported capital investment would be planned to exceed this rate. This would enable the initial outlay to be recovered in about 10 years. Thereafter, further output from the investment would accrue as a net gain to Soviet society.

○ The Soviets would prefer to trade with major American corporations because they have access to Wall Street—the world's best-developed capital market, where funds could be

QUESTIONS

1. Some critics have contended: "We should not sell agricultural commodities (such as wheat) to Russia because domestic supplies are thereby reduced, causing prices of the goods to rise. Americans thus end up paying more for food, while Russians benefit." Evaluate this argument.

2. Should the U.S. government permit unlimited private trade with Russia—even to the extent of allowing American firms to sell military weapons to the Soviets? Discuss.

Chapter 34

International Finance: The Payments of Nations

Chapter Preview

What is the foreign exchange market? What important economic functions does it perform?

How are money flows into and out of a country recorded? Can we analyze the nature and sources of such flows?

What are the economic implications of an imbalance or disequilibrium in a nation's money inflows and outflows?

What are the methods and effects of correcting a disequilibrium in a nation's international money flows?

At one time the study of international economics dealt primarily with the problems of trade between nations. But this has long since ceased to be true. The economic relationships among countries depend as much on financial considerations as on trade. Hence, an understanding of international finance is essential in dealing with world economic problems.

What do we mean by international finance? In the most general sense it deals with the monetary side of international trade. International finance is therefore concerned with the nature of international transactions—their forms of payment, the ways in which they are recorded for purposes of analysis and interpretation, their economic effects on the nations that are involved, and the methods by which their undesirable consequences can be minimized. Once you have some familiarity with these complex issues, you will better understand many of the most critical problems faced by nations today.

International Payments and Foreign Exchange

Each nation has its own unit of currency. This means that when transactions are conducted across national borders, one currency must be converted into another.

For example, if a French importer buys machinery from the United States, the American exporter eventually receives payment in dollars, not French francs. Similarly, if an American tourist visits England, he pays for his hotel room, restaurant meals, and other goods and services in British pounds, not dollars. The instruments used to make international payments are called *foreign exchange*. They consist not only of currency, but also to a much larger extent of checks, drafts, or bills of exchange, which are simply orders to pay currency.

FUNCTION OF THE FOREIGN EXCHANGE MARKETS

International transactions go on all the time. As a result, some people have dollars which they want to exchange for pounds, and others have pounds which they want to exchange for dollars. How do these people acquire the foreign exchange they desire?

The answer is that foreign exchange is bought and sold in organized markets through dealers, just as stocks, bonds, wheat, and many other commodities are bought and sold. In the United States, the foreign exchange dealers are the large commercial banks located in New York, San Francisco, and other major cities. Overseas, the major foreign exchange centers include London, Zurich, Paris, Brussels, Tokyo, and Hong Kong. Therefore, if you want to acquire or dispose of foreign exchange, you can easily do so by communicating directly with a dealer or by going through any local commercial bank, which will arrange the transaction through one of the large banks dealing in foreign exchange.

The most fundamental function performed by the foreign exchange markets is that they provide a means for transferring purchasing power from one country to another and from one currency to another. Without foreign exchange markets, international trade would be virtually limited to barter.

EFFECTS OF INTERNATIONAL TRANSACTIONS

Suppose that an American exporter sells a machine to a British importer. The importer might pay for it by purchasing a draft from the bank—that is, an order to pay a specified number of pounds sterling to the American exporter. The exporter then converts the draft into dollars by selling the draft to a foreign exchange dealer. The number of dollars the dealer pays for the draft depends on the rate of exchange between dollars and pounds. (The dealer, like any broker, will also impose a commission charge.)

The American exporter now has the dollars, and the dealer has a draft payable in British pounds. What will each of them do? Since they are in business, they are likely to deposit the funds in their own commercial-bank accounts so that they can continue to write the checks they need to carry on their activities. Thus, the American exporter will deposit the dollars in an American bank, and the American foreign exchange dealer will send the draft to England for deposit in a British bank. The dealer, by having such an account, can write a draft or check against it and sell it to an American importer who needs pounds to pay for goods purchased from a British exporter.

What are the results of these activities? In general, international transactions have two economic effects:

1. An export transaction increases the supply of money in the exporting country and reduces it in the importing country. The converse of this, resulting from an import transaction, is also true. (Can you explain why?)

2. By exporting, a nation obtains the foreign monies it needs to acquire imports. In other words, a nation that sells abroad can also buy abroad. (Japan, for example, sells motorcycles, television sets, and other goods to the United States and is thereby able to obtain the dollars it needs to buy American machines, agricultural goods, and other products.)

The Balance of Payments

So far, we have assumed that economic relationships among nations are based solely on international trade. In reality, this is not the whole story. Foreign exchange is demanded and supplied as a result of various other important types of transactions besides importing or exporting. It is necessary, therefore, that we examine the nature of these transactions.

Corporations prepare periodic reports, such as balance sheets and income (or profit and loss) statements, summarizing in money terms the results of their business activities. These reports are used by bankers, business executives, stockholders, creditors, or any other interested parties—even by the government—to evaluate a company's financial position.

Each nation also prepares a somewhat similar periodic report called a "balance of payments." The report summarizes in money terms the results of a nation's international economic activities by showing how some transactions cause an outflow of funds and others an inflow. It should be apparent, therefore, that a nation's balance of payments is of concern not only to economists, but also to business managers, bankers, government leaders, and anyone interested in world affairs.

AN ILLUSTRATIVE MODEL OF THE BALANCE OF PAYMENTS

What does a balance-of-payments statement actually look like? How is it interpreted? We can best answer these questions by first analyzing the structure of an idealized balance-of-payments form such as the one shown in Exhibit 1. This illustration is a generalized model; that is, it clearly emphasizes the major categories and subcategories that should be understood. You will find yourself referring back to this model quite often because, as will be seen later, most countries do not publish their balance-of-payments statements in such a convenient form.

As was pointed out above, a nation's balance of payments is a financial summary of its international transactions. The first thing to notice is that these money flows are represented in the last two columns of the statement by "debits" and "credits"—two terms that are widely used in discussions involving the balance of payments:

> A *debit* is any transaction that results in a money outflow or payment to a foreign country; it may be represented on a balance-of-payments statement by a negative sign. A *credit* is any transaction that results in a money inflow or receipt from a foreign country; it may be represented in a balance-of-payments statement by a positive sign. (NOTE   These definitions are applicable only in international economics. If you take a course in accounting, you will find that the terms "debit" and "credit" are defined in different ways.)

The balance-of-payments model shown in Exhibit 1 is self-explanatory. All you have to do is go down the list to see that each item would logically result in either an outflow or inflow of money, and hence would be recorded as either a debit or credit.

The balance of payments is divided into four major categories. These are ranked in what is for most countries the following (decreasing) order of importance: (1) current account, (2) capital account, (3) unilateral transfer account, and (4) official reserve transactions account. In the first category, the subclassification at the top denoting merchandise trade usually involves the largest debits and credits in balance-of-payments statements. Thus, a merchandise import is a debit item because it results in a money outflow or payment to the exporting country. Conversely, a merchandise export is a credit item because it results in a money inflow or receipt to the importing country.

The remaining items can be interpreted in a similar way. In the last category, confusion will be avoided by thinking of international reserve assets like any other commodity as far as debits and credits are concerned. Thus, imports of such assets are debits; exports are credits.

Exhibit 1
General Model of the Balance of Payments

	Debit (money outflows or payments) (−)	Credit (money inflows or receipts) (+)
I. Current account		
A. Merchandise trade		
1. Merchandise imports	×	
2. Merchandise exports		×
B. Service transactions		
1. Transportation		
a. Rendered by foreign carriers	×	
b. Rendered by domestic carriers		×
2. Travel expenditures		
a. In foreign countries	×	
b. By foreigners here		×
3. Interest and dividends		
a. Paid to foreigners	×	
b. Received from abroad		×
4. Banking and insurance services		
a. Rendered by foreign institutions	×	
b. Rendered to foreigners by domestic institutions		×
5. Government expenditures		
a. By home government abroad	×	
b. By foreign governments here		×
II. Capital account		
A. Long-term		
1. Purchased securities from foreigners	×	
2. Sold securities to foreigners		×
B. Short-term*		
1. Increase of bank balances abroad	×	
2. Decrease of foreign-held bank balances here	×	
3. Increase of foreign-held bank balances here		×
4. Decrease of bank balances abroad		×
III. Unilateral transfer account		
A. Private		
1. Remittances sent abroad	×	
2. Remittances received from abroad		×
B. Governmental		
1. Grants to other countries	×	
2. Grants from other countries		×
IV. Official reserve transactions account		
A. Increase in government-held international reserve assets	×	
B. Decrease in government-held international reserve assets		×
Errors and omissions		

* Also includes private currency holdings and claims not listed.

SOURCE: Adapted with substantial changes from Delbert Snider, *Introduction to International Economics*, 5th ed., Homewood, Ill., Irwin, 1971.

THE BALANCE OF PAYMENTS ALWAYS BALANCES (IN ACCOUNTING)

If you take a basic course in accounting, you will learn to apply a principle known as *double-entry bookkeeping*. This principle holds that every transaction is of a twofold nature and must be expressed for accounting purposes in the form of *both* debits and credits. In more general terms, for any given debit there must be one or more credits whose total will precisely equal the debit. Conversely, for any given credit there must be one or more debits whose total will precisely equal the credit.

This idea can be illustrated with reference to the balance-of-payments model in Exhibit 1. Suppose, for example, that an American firm exports equipment worth $1 million to a foreign country. This part of the transaction is a merchandise export and appears as a credit item on the U.S. balance of payments. The importing country may pay for the goods in any one or a combination of several ways, all of which are recorded as debit items on the U.S. balance of payments. For instance, the importing country may pay in dollars by decreasing its foreign-held bank balances in the United States. Or it may pay in its own currency, which has the effect of increasing U.S. bank balances held abroad. Or it may receive the equipment as a gift under the U.S. foreign-aid program, in which case it is a unilateral transfer similar to a grant.

Double-entry bookkeeping assures in principle that *total debits equal total credits*—or, in other words, that the *balance of payments always balances* in an accounting sense. In practice, however, since a country's balance of payments summarizes millions of individual international transactions, it is rarely accurate down to the last dollar. Hence, total debits will either be less than or greater than total credits. To correct this situation, a balance-of-payments statement will often show an item called "errors and omissions." This equals the difference between actual total debits and actual total credits, and is added to the smaller of these two totals to bring the total payments into balance.

In a more fundamental sense, however, there is an obvious realistic reason why a balance-of-payments statement always balances:

A country, like a household, cannot spend more than its current income unless it draws on its cash reserves, sells some of its assets, borrows, or receives gifts. All of these are credit items on its balance-of-payments statement. Conversely, a country cannot spend less than its current income unless it accumulates cash reserves, acquires some assets, lends, or gives gifts. All of these are debit items. Therefore, total debits must always equal total credits.

THE FOUR MAJOR ACCOUNTS

The balance-of-payments model, as we have seen, contains four major accounts. Let us survey briefly the contents of each.

1. *Current Account*   This includes all imports and exports of goods and services, and is the most basic account in the balance of payments. It is the "stuff" of which international economic relations are composed. The other three accounts fulfill what are largely auxiliary functions by facilitating the flow of goods and services.

2. *Capital Account*   This is composed entirely of paper claims and obligations. The long-term component consists of loans and investments maturing in more than one year. The short-term component consists of claims maturing in less than one year and of foreign exchange and bank balances. These short-term capital movements may flow into or out of a country to make up for differences in payments and receipts resulting from a gap between imports and exports or from other transactions.

3. *Unilateral Transfer Account*   This account is somewhat like the capital account, except that it involves capital movements and gifts for which there are no return commitments or claims. Thus, a personal remittance to a resident of a foreign country involves no commitment for repayment and is classified as a unilateral transfer.

4. *Official Reserve Transactions Account*   This consists of changes in international reserve assets—those used for settling accounts between government central banks. As you will see, such intergovernmental settlements usually arise because of deficits or surpluses in the other three major classes of accounts—current, capital, or unilateral transfer. Therefore, international reserve assets serve to finance those deficits and surpluses. Examples of international reserve assets are convertible currencies (i.e., those in wide demand and therefore readily exchangeable, such as U.S. dollars and German marks) and gold.

Against this background, let us summarize what is meant by "balance of payments":

The *balance of payments* is a statement of the money value of all transactions that take place between a nation and the rest of the world during a given period. These transactions may consist of imports and exports of goods and services, and movements of short-term and long-term investments, gifts, currency, and gold. The transactions may be classified for convenience into several categories: current account, capital account, unilateral transfer account, and official reserve transactions account.

THE UNITED STATES BALANCE OF PAYMENTS

The U.S. balance of payments is shown in Exhibit 2. Note that the balance of trade is not the same thing as the balance of payments, although many people confuse the two. The *balance of trade* is that part of a nation's balance of payments which deals with merchandise imports and exports. A "favorable" balance of trade exists when the value of a nation's exports exceeds the value of its imports. An "unfavorable" balance of trade exists when the value of a nation's imports exceeds the value of its exports.

What about the "balance" in the balance of payments? Here the concept is somewhat more complicated. In simplest terms a nation's overall balance of payments always balances by virtue of the principle of double-entry bookkeeping. However, certain types of specific balances shown in Exhibit 2 may be important for some purposes. As a result, the remainder of this chapter is devoted to a discussion of essential ideas involving balance-of-payments adjustments. (See also *Leaders in Economics,* page 592.)

Economic Balance and Imbalance

Although a nation's balance of payments always balances in the accounting sense—in the sense that total debits always equal total credits—it need not balance in an economic sense. Among the reasons for economic imbalance are the lack of appropriate relationships among exchange rates, prices, income, and capital movements. In order to comprehend the underlying economic forces that are at work, we must understand two important sets of concepts associated with balance-of-payments analysis. These are (1) autonomous and compensatory transactions and (2) equilibrium and disequilibrium.

AUTONOMOUS AND COMPENSATORY TRANSACTIONS

It is useful to think of a nation's balance of payments as a record which reports two very different types of transactions—autonomous and compensatory.

Autonomous Transactions   These are undertaken for reasons that are independent of the balance of payments. Referring back to the general model in Exhibit 1, we see that the main classes of autonomous transactions are merchandise trade and services, long-term capital movements, and unilateral transfers. The reasons for calling these autonomous are not hard to see. Merchandise trade and services are a response to rel-

ative differences in prices at home and abroad. Long-term capital movements are a response to relative differences in expected rates of return on financial investments at home and abroad. And unilateral transfers are a response to private and governmental decisions based on personal, military, or political considerations. These autonomous transactions are thus unrelated to the balance of payments as such, and may result in total money receipts being greater or less than total money payments.

Compensatory Transactions   In contrast, these are undertaken as a direct response to balance-of-payments considerations. Compensatory transactions may be thought of as balancing items which arise in order to accommodate differences in money inflows and outflows resulting from autonomous transactions. Looking back at the general model in Exhibit 1, we see there are two main classes of compensatory transactions. These are short-term capital movements and shifts in the official reserve transactions account (consisting of international reserve assets such as major currencies and gold holdings). Since these involve primarily changes in bank balances and in international reserve assets at home and abroad, it seems clear that they serve largely as adjustment items to correct for imbalances in autonomous transactions. Thus, in a sense, a person who borrows to pay a debt is financing a deficit in his or her personal "balance of payments" by means of a compensatory transaction—the money borrowed.

EQUILIBRIUM AND DISEQUILIBRIUM

How do autonomous and compensatory transactions affect the economic position of a nation in relation to other nations? The answer to this question involves the notion of equilibrium and disequilibrium. As you already know, an economic "object" (such as a market price or quantity) is in equilibrium when it is in a state of balance among opposing forces. Conversely, it is in disequilibrium when there is an absence of such a state of balance. The same ideas of equilibrium or disequilibrium can be applied to a nation's international economic position as reflected in its balance of payments:

Balance-of-payments disequilibrium exists when, over a given period (usually several years), the sum of autonomous credits does not equal the sum of autonomous debits. A *deficit disequilibrium* occurs when total autonomous debits exceed total autonomous credits. Conversely, a *surplus disequilibrium* occurs when total autonomous credits exceed total autonomous debits.

The existence of compensatory transactions is evidence of a nation's balance-of-payments disequilib-

Exhibit 2
United States Balance of Payments, 1978

The balance on goods and services shows the value of our net trade of merchandise and services. The balance on current account reflects current patterns of trade and the net flow of gifts and grants to foreign countries.

Line		Credits (+), debits (−) (millions of dollars)
1	Merchandise exports	141,844
2	Merchandise imports	175,988
3	Merchandise trade balance	−34,144
4	Military transactions, net	531
5	Investment income, net	19,915
6	Other service transactions, net	2,814
7	**Balance on goods and services**	**−10,885**
8	Remittances, pensions, and other transfers	−2,048
9	U.S. government grants (excluding military)	−3,028
10	**Balance on current account**	**−15,961**
11	*Not seasonally adjusted*	
12	Change in U.S. government assets, other than official reserve assets, net (increase, −)	−4,657
13	*Change in U.S. official reserve assets (increase, −)*	872
14	Gold	−65
15	Special Drawing Rights (SDRs)	1,249
16	Reserve position in International Monetary Fund (IMF)	4,231
17	Foreign currencies	−4,543
18	**Change in U.S. private assets abroad (increase, −)**	**−54,963**
19	Bank-reported claims	−33,957
20	*Nonbank-reported claims*	−2,256
21	Long-term	33
22	Short-term	−2,289
23	U.S. purchase of foreign securities, net	−3,389
24	U.S. direct investments abroad, net	−15,361
25	*Change in foreign official assets in the United States (increase, +)*	33,967

Line		Credits (+), debits (−) (millions of dollars)
26	U.S. Treasury securities	24,063
27	Other U.S. government obligations	656
28	Other U.S. government liabilities	2,810
29	Other U.S. liabilities reported by U.S. banks	5,043
30	Other foreign official assets	1,395
31	**Change in foreign private assets in the United States (increase, +)**	**29,293**
32	U.S. bank-reported liabilities	16,860
33	*U.S. nonbank-reported liabilities*	1,676
34	Long-term	−49
35	Short-term	1,725
36	Foreign private purchases of U.S. Treasury securities, net	2,248
37	Foreign purchases of other U.S. securities, net	2,899
38	Foreign direct investments in the United States, net	5,611
39	Allocation of SDRs	
40	*Discrepancy*	11,449
41	Owing to seasonal adjustments	
42	Statistical discrepancy in recorded data before seasonal adjustment	11,449
	Memoranda: Changes in official assets:	
43	U.S. official reserve assets (increase, −)	872
44	Foreign official assets in the United States (increase, +)	31,157
45	Changes in Organization of Petroleum Exporting Countries (OPEC) official assets in the United States (part of line 25 above)	−570
46	Transfers under military grant programs (excluding lines 1, 4, 9)	274

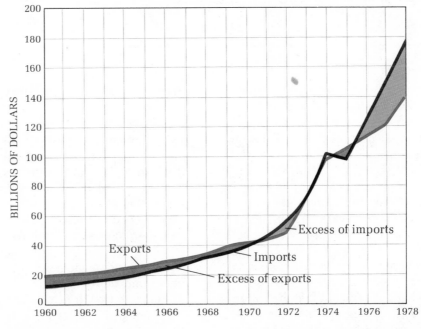

EXPORTS AND IMPORTS OF MERCHANDISE

SOURCE: U.S. Department of Commerce.

Leaders in Economics
Thomas Mun   1571–1641

Mercantilist

At the end of the fifteenth century, a new philosophy of *statism* emerged in Western Europe. Absolute monarchy had replaced the decentralized structure of feudalism; the oceans had been conquered and were no longer considered barriers to trade; and the expansion of world commerce had occurred simultaneously with the development of banking and credit institutions. These factors encouraged dramatic struggles for power by kings and princes, resulting in ultranationalistic policies that tended to make all states enemies, as each sought to achieve world military and economic leadership.

These developments gave rise to what is known as <u>mercantilism</u>—a set of doctrines and practices aimed at promoting national prosperity and the power of the state. This was to be achieved in three ways:

1. Accumulating precious metals (mainly gold and silver) through the maintenance of favorable trade balances, or excesses of exports over imports.

2. Achieving economic self-sufficiency through imperialism.

The Bettmann Archive.

3. Exploiting colonies for the benefit of the mother country by monopolizing the raw materials and precious metals of the colonies while reserving them as exclusive markets for exports.

Mercantilism reached its peak in the seventeenth century, serving as a political and economic ideology in England, France, Spain, and Germany.

The majority of those who wrote on mercantilist theory were businesspeople. The most notable was Thomas Mun, a leading English merchant and for many years a director of the famous British East India Company. His book, *England's Treasure by Forraign Trade,* was published posthumously by his son in 1664. This treatise is regarded as the outstanding exposition of mercantilist doctrine. It stressed the importance to England of maintaining a favorable balance of trade—a doctrine of fundamental significance in mercantilism since it was a key means of accumulating bullion. The book was also the first work to show that it was not the specific balance of trade with any particular nation that was the important consideration, but the total balance with all nations. The former could be unfavorable, according to Mun, as long as the latter was favorable.

In Germany, the chief goal of mercantilism was to increase the revenue of the state. Hence, it became known as <u>cameralism</u> (after *Kammer,* the name of the royal treasury), and its principles were extensively implemented as government policy during the eighteenth century.

---

rium. In practice, of course, we do not always expect the sum of autonomous receipts and payments to match each other exactly—any more than we expect total supply and demand in a competitive market to be precisely equal at all times. This is because of the numerous decision-making entities (mostly households and firms) that are involved. But we do expect periodic deficits and surpluses to balance out approximately over a period of a few years. When such a tendency is not apparent there is reason to suspect trouble.

The most common situation is one in which a country suffers from a persistent deficit disequilibrium for a number of years. This means that the nation is spending more than it is earning, and hence must be either drawing on its cash reserves, selling its assets, borrowing, or receiving gifts from other countries.

Adjusting to Equilibrium

How can a nation correct a disequilibrium in its balance of payments? The answer is straightforward. Since disequilibrium is the result of a gap between a country's total autonomous payments and receipts, the factors that determine these autonomous transactions must undergo a change so that the nation's total money outflows and inflows can be brought into equality. We can best approach the problem by analyzing the adjustment process that would take place under four sets of circumstances: (1) freely fluctuating exchange rates, (2) price and income changes, (3) the gold standard, and (4) government controls. Let us see how adjustments in the balance of payments are brought about under each of these conditions.

ADJUSTMENT THROUGH FREELY FLUCTUATING EXCHANGE RATES

The _foreign exchange rate_ is the price of one currency in terms of another. If in the wheat market the price of wheat were $1 per bushel, this would mean that anyone could take $1 to the market and exchange it for a bushel of wheat and anyone could take a bushel of wheat to the market and exchange it for $1. Similarly, if in the foreign exchange market the price of British pounds in terms of dollars were $2 = £1, it would mean that anyone could take $1 to the market and exchange it for the equivalent of £½, or anyone could take £1 to the market and exchange it for $2.

The foreign exchange market is a competitive market which behaves according to the laws of supply and demand. This means that fluctuations in the price of foreign exchange are the result of changes in the demand and supply curves of buyers and sellers. The basic idea is illustrated in Exhibit 3. In this simple model, the "commodity" being bought and sold is British pounds and the price is expressed in terms of dollars. (A similar situation could be depicted in which the commodity is dollars and the price is expressed in terms of British pounds.) For simplicity, we are assuming that there are only two countries, the United States and Britain. The interaction of the demand curve for pounds with the supply curve of pounds thus determines the equilibrium price at P and the equilibrium quantity at N.

In the foreign exchange market Americans (such as importers, tourists, etc.) are always looking to buy pounds; and Britons are always looking to buy dollars. Hence, at any given time there are "dollars looking for pounds" and there are "pounds looking for dollars." This makes an active market in foreign exchange.

The Adjustment Process

In order to understand how international adjustments take place under freely fluctuating exchange rates, let us begin by assuming a state of equilibrium in which the exchange rate in Exhibit 3 is at P and there is neither a deficit nor a surplus in the American balance of payments. If American imports of British goods should now rise, and if this increase is not offset by long-term capital movements or unilateral transfers from Britain to the United States, the American demand for pounds will also increase. That is, the demand curve will shift to the right from D to D'. As the price rises toward the new equilibrium level at P', British pounds will become more expensive for Americans to buy, thereby causing the United States to reduce its purchases of British goods. Conversely,

Exhibit 3
Supply of, and Demand for, British Pounds

An increase in demand for British pounds will raise the equilibrium price from P to P' and the equilibrium quantity from N to N'.

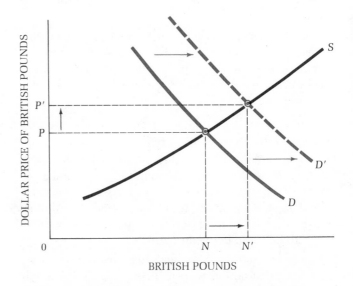

American dollars will become cheaper for Britons, thereby causing Britain to expand its purchases of American goods. This slowing down of American imports from Britain and expansion of American exports to Britain will continue until a new equilibrium in the U.S. balance of payments is reached which accords with the equilibrium price in the foreign exchange market. Thus:

Freely fluctuating exchange rates perform at least three important functions:

1. They automatically correct a disequilibrium in the balance of payments through the free play of international market forces.

2. They may make imports cheaper and exports dearer. or vice versa, by altering the price of foreign exchange without *necessarily* affecting domestic or foreign price levels.

3. To the extent that they operate independently of domestic price and income levels, they bear the burden of balance-of-payments adjustments without imposing constraints on the domestic economy (as will be explained shortly).

Despite these desirable features, freely fluctuating exchange rates involve some disadvantages:

1. They make it difficult and risky for traders to commit themselves for weeks or months in advance to international transactions, since the exchange rate may change between the time that goods are ordered and the time that they are received. This uncertainty may reduce trade between nations.

2. Freely fluctuating exchange rates turn the terms of trade against a nation whose currency is depreciated in the foreign exchange market. For example, an increase in the demand for British pounds results in a price increase or appreciation in the dollar price of pounds and a price decrease or depreciation in the pound price of dollars. This means that the United States must export more goods to Britain to earn the same total revenue as it earned before.

3. Freely fluctuating exchange rates *may* stimulate or depress a nation's export industries by making its currency either cheaper or dearer in international markets. This could tend to encourage fluctuations in income and employment.

ADJUSTMENT THROUGH PRICE AND INCOME CHANGES

A moment's reflection will make it evident that if exchange-rate adjustments can conceivably bring about an equilibrium in the balance of payments while domestic price and income levels remain stable, the converse principle is also true. That is, changes in domestic price and income levels can restore equilibrium in a nation's balance of payments while exchange rates remain stable. Let us see why.

Price Changes

In terms of our previous example, if there is a deficit in the U.S. balance of payments due to an excess of imports over exports, a deflation of American prices can have the same effect as a depreciation of the dollar in the foreign exchange market. For if prices in the United States are reduced, it becomes cheaper for Britons to buy American goods. American exports to Britain will therefore increase, and this will tend to eliminate the U.S. balance-of-payments deficit. (Equivalently, an inflation in Britain can have the same effect as an appreciation of the pound in the foreign exchange market. Can you explain why?)

How might a deflation be brought about? There are three possibilities:

1. Some deflationary pressures will be induced automatically through market forces because the excess of American imports over exports will cause a reduction in the United States money supply.

2. Contractionary monetary and fiscal policies may have to be invoked in order to exert a downward push on prices.

3. U.S. manufacturers may try to reduce or stabilize prices so as to compete with foreigners.

It is possible that a trade-off exists between price changes and the level of employment. To the extent that this is true, reductions in prices will tend to increase unemployment and thereby bring about a recession. The question, therefore, is whether such a high cost should be incurred in order to achieve balance-of-payments equilibrium. Many political leaders believe that it should not and that some other solution should be sought.

Income Changes

A country's balance of payments is also related to its national income. Thus, if the domestic level of income increases while exchange rates and domestic prices remain stable, people will tend to import more goods from abroad and to take more trips abroad. (For balance-of-payments purposes, an American tourist visiting a foreign country is equivalent to the United States importing "scenery" from that country.) A deficit in the U.S. balance of payments, therefore, can be corrected through a decrease in the domestic level of income. (Equivalently, it can also be corrected through an increase in other nations' levels of income, since American exports will increase if foreign income rises.)

The disadvantages of adjustment through domestic income reduction, however, are essentially the same as those of price deflation. Contractionary monetary and fiscal policies would have to be invoked in order to cause a downward pressure on national income. This in turn would probably induce a recession and unemployment—a trade-off which most people would not willingly accept for the sake of achieving balance-of-payments equilibrium.

Before proceeding with this important problem, it will be helpful to conclude our discussion thus far with an important principle:

The influence of adjustments in exchange rates, price levels, and income levels on a balance-of-payments disequilibrium will depend on the relevant responses or elasticities involved.

For example, the effect of a general 10 percent reduction in domestic prices, with foreign prices remaining the same, depends on demand elasticity or responsiveness to changes in price. The reduction in prices would have the same effect as a 10 percent depreciation in the exchange rate as far as corrections in a deficit are concerned, although the reduction would have quite different effects in other respects.

Likewise, the influence of income changes on a country's trade depends, among other things, on its income elasticity of demand for imports. That is, it depends on a country's demand responsiveness to changes in its income.

For example, what happens if the country's income elasticity of demand is less than 2 (i.e., less than proportional to the change in income)? Greater than 1? Factors such as these are of considerable practical significance. Indeed, they have played extremely important roles in the international financial policies of nations, as we shall see later. (NOTE   You will find it helpful to look up the meaning of *income elasticity of demand* in the Dictionary at the back of the book.)

ADJUSTMENT UNDER THE GOLD STANDARD: THE CLASSICAL MODEL

A very interesting process of adjustment takes place when the trading nations' monetary systems are on a gold standard. This situation existed for several dozen countries during the half century before World War I and for a short time thereafter until the onset of the depression in the early 1930s. From a theoretical standpoint, international adjustments under a gold standard can be considered part of the classical (i.e., pre-1930s) model of income and employment. As you will see, however, the model has important implications for today's world economy.

The Gold Standard

If a nation were on a gold standard, it would be obliged to buy and sell gold to the public in exchange for paper money at a *fixed legal rate,* and permit gold to be imported and exported without restrictions. Under these circumstances, the exchange rate would tend to be stable and would never fluctuate beyond very narrow limits.

In 1930, for example, when the United States and England were both on a gold standard, the U.S. Treasury was required by law to buy and sell gold to the public at a price of $20.67 per fine ounce. Similarly, the Bank of England was required by law to buy and sell gold at a price of £4.25 per fine ounce. It follows that since an ounce (which is equal to 480 grains) of gold could be exchanged for $20.67 in the United States or for £4.25 in England,

$$\$20.67 = £4.25 \quad (= 1 \text{ ounce gold or } 480 \text{ grains})$$

Therefore, the par rate of exchange between the two countries was determined by the ratio $20.67 ÷ £4.25, or

$$\$4.86 = £1 \quad (= 0.24 \text{ ounce gold or } 113 \text{ grains})$$

In 1930, the cost (including insurance and freight) of shipping 0.24 ounce or 113 grains of gold between New York and London was about $0.02. As a result, the exchange rate or dollar price of pounds remained within the range of $4.84 to $4.88, for the following reasons:

1. If the price of pounds in the foreign exchange market rose, say, to $4.89, it would be cheaper for an American importer to acquire 113 grains of gold for his $4.86 and then ship the gold to London at a cost of 2 cents in order to pay the British exporter. The importer would *in effect* be paying $4.88 for a pound instead of $4.89.

2. If the price in the foreign exchange market fell, say, to $4.83, a British importer would be better off to acquire gold for his £1 (= $4.86) and then ship the gold to New York at a cost of 2 cents in order to pay the American exporter. The importer would *in effect* be getting $4.84 for a pound instead of $4.83.

The upper and lower limits of foreign exchange were thus $4.88 and $4.84, respectively. These were known as the *gold points*—a technical expression which represents the range within which the foreign exchange rates of gold standard currencies will fluctuate. Thus, the gold points are equal to the par rate of exchange plus and minus the cost (including insurance) of shipping gold. The upper and lower gold points for a nation are called its *gold export point* and *gold import point,* respectively, because gold will be exported when the foreign exchange rate rises above the upper level and imported when the rate falls below the lower level. One nation's gold export point is thus another nation's gold import point, and vice versa.

We may, therefore, conclude:

Since a gold standard provides free convertibility between paper money and gold, as well as the unrestricted shipment of gold into and out of the country, the exchange rate under such circumstances tends to remain stable within the limits set by the gold points.

The Adjustment Process

How does the existence of a gold standard affect the restoration of equilibrium due to a trade deficit in a nation's balance of payments? This in effect was a key question which the classical economists asked. Their answer was that the adjustment is brought about automatically through changes in the price level. Why? Because they assumed that the price level is directly related to the quantity of money in circulation, which in turn is tied to the volume of gold holdings.

Thus, if a country experiences a disequilibrium in its balance of payments as a result of a trade deficit, its demand for foreign exchange will rise at least to the gold export point. As gold leaves the country, the quantity of money will decrease, which in turn will reduce prices. With lower prices, the country's exports will rise and its imports fall, thereby correcting the disequilibrium.

What happens if a country experiences a disequilibrium in its balance of payments due to a trade surplus? The process is exactly the opposite. The country's demand for foreign exchange will fall, gold will be imported, prices will increase, and exports will fall while imports rise until equilibrium is again restored.

This explanation of the adjustment process, it should be emphasized, was the classical solution. Logically, it was an integral part of the classical theory of income and employment because it assumed two conditions:

1. *Full employment.*   Therefore, an increase in the quantity of money would assure an increase in the general price level.

2. *Flexible prices and wages.*   Therefore, prices and wages respond readily to changes in total spending.

Are these assumptions valid? With the development and extensions of economic ideas since the 1930s, the first assumption of full employment has been recognized by many economists as a special rather than a general case. Further, the second assumption of flexible prices and wages—especially on the downward side—is obviously incorrect in our modern economy, where both big businesses and big unions exert monopolistic influences in the marketplace.

We can, therefore, come to a further conclusion:

The gold standard has both desirable and undesirable features. On the one hand, it provides for stable exchange rates, which tend to reduce risks and encourage international trade while automatically correcting international disequilibrium. On the other hand, it requires that each nation submit to painful processes of deflation (or inflation) by subordinating its domestic economy to the dictates of external economic relations in order to achieve international equilibrium.

ADJUSTMENT THROUGH GOVERNMENT CONTROLS

The methods of adjustment described thus far rely on market forces to correct a disequilibrium in the balance of payments. Now we turn our attention to a final and radically different method of adjustment—one which suppresses market forces by imposing direct government controls on international transactions. The list of specific controls is almost endless, but for analysis they can be grouped into two categories: exchange controls and trade controls.

Exchange Controls

One way in which a nation might seek to correct a deficit in its balance of payments is to limit the freedom of its residents to import goods and services and to export funds. To accomplish this objective, the government would impose direct controls over those types of international transactions that are to be curbed, while leaving others relatively uncontrolled or even "free."

Under such a system, all foreign exchange earnings must be sold to the government and all foreign exchange needed to pay for international transactions must be bought from the government. The rates at which the government buys and sells foreign exchange are officially established and need not be equal. The typical method of doing this is by the adoption of a "multiple exchange system." Thus, the government may set a relatively high price or rate of exchange on the foreign exchange needed to import unessential luxury goods, and a relatively low rate on the importation of vitally needed raw materials and capital goods. It may also designate some types of transactions as unrestricted and sell portions of its foreign exchange to the highest bidders.

In general:

Exchange controls require that the government, rather than the free market, decide the order of priority for the importation of goods and services. This decision may then be implemented by allocating the limited supply of foreign exchange among competing uses.

Nations have instituted exchange controls for various reasons. The more important ones have been to provide better centralized control over the economy, to reduce wide economic fluctuations, to eliminate persistent deficits in the balance of payments, and to assure essential imports for hastening economic growth and development. The chief advantage of controls is that *some* method of adjustment must be employed to correct a significant balance-of-payments deficit disequilibrium. Exchange controls are usually the least undesirable and least painful of the various choices that have been discussed.

On the other hand, exchange controls also have several disadvantages:

1. By preventing or even limiting the importation of certain goods, controls may shift the demand for these goods to domestic producers. The effect may be to stimulate inflation at home as well as an exodus of resources out of export industries. This will encourage a drop in exports and aggravate rather than cure the deficit disequilibrium.

2. Since exchange controls prevent the free expression of market forces, they encourage the creation of an illegal black market in foreign exchange.

3. By curbing imports, controls help bring on deflation in those countries whose export industries are adversely affected. This may encourage retaliatory measures by the injured nations, thereby reducing trade.

Trade Controls

A government may use another general class of measures, called *trade controls,* to adjust a balance-of-payments deficit disequilibrium. These may take such forms as tariffs and quotas to curb imports, special taxes on outflows of capital and on tourists going abroad, and subsidies to encourage the export industries. Measures such as these, as we have already learned, prevent the operation of the law of comparative advantage, misallocate world resources, and discourage the flow of trade. As with exchange controls, trade controls may also invite retaliation by other nations.

What You Have Learned

1. Since nations carry on their business in different currencies, foreign exchange markets exist where currencies and related instruments can be bought and sold, or "converted." The existence of such markets enables nations to engage in international transactions.

2. The international transactions of nations are summarized periodically in a financial statement known as the balance of payments. This records money inflows and outflows, classified in categories of accounts.

3. In accounting terms, a nation's balance of payments always balances. This is because the sum of money inflows must equal the sum of money outflows—by virtue of the principle of double-entry bookkeeping. But in an economic sense, the balance of payments may not balance because certain transactions may not be sustainable.

4. Balance-of-payments disequilibrium may be corrected by (a) movements in exchange rates; (b) adjustments in price and income levels; (c) gold flows, with consequent price and income adjustments if nations are on a gold standard; and (d) government controls over foreign exchange and foreign trade. The first three rely on market forces to bring about the needed adjustment; the fourth suppresses market forces by substituting the hand of government.

For Discussion

1. *Terms and concepts to review:*

foreign exchange
debit
credit
balance of payments
balance of trade
mercantilism
cameralism
autonomous transactions
compensatory transactions
balance-of-payments disequilibrium
foreign exchange rate
gold points

2. In a free market, if the dollar rate of exchange on French francs rises, what happens to the French rate of exchange on dollars? Explain.

3. How does each of the following transactions affect the supply of money in the United States?

(a) The United States sells Chevrolets to England.

(b) France sells perfume to the United States.

(c) An American tourist visits Japan.

(d) A Japanese tourist visits the United States.

4. Which of the following transactions results in a debit, and which in a credit, in the U.S. balance of payments?

(a) An American student buys a new Honda motorcycle.

(b) An American tourist flies Air France to Paris.

(c) General Motors pays a dividend to a British stockholder.

(d) The U.S. Army builds a new military base overseas.

(e) An American resident buys shares of stock in a British corporation.

(f) An American resident sends money to his relatives in another country.

5. Can there be a net positive or net negative balance in the balance of payments?

6. Why are autonomous debits and credits not likely to be equal?

7. Compare the processes of adjustment to disequilibrium under (a) freely fluctuating exchange rates; (b) price and income changes; (c) the gold standard; (d) government controls. (SUGGESTION   Think in terms of what these systems have in common, and develop your answer accordingly.)

Case
Trading in Foreign Exchange: The Fastest Game in Town

Do fluctuating currency values affect businesses engaged in international trade? Would a company dealing abroad be incurring undue risks if it failed to protect itself against changes in the value of the dollar? The answer to both questions is yes. However, management can achieve the financial protection required by trading in the most universal of all commodities—money. Two sets of institutions exist for meeting this need:

1. *The Interbank System*—a network of currency-trading desks at the world's major banks. These mainly serve large corporations dealing in lots of $1 million or more at a time.

2. *The International Monetary Market*—an organized exchange in which currencies are traded through brokers in a public market. Participants are primarily smaller corporations and individuals.

Dennis Brack, Black Star.

Both institutions comprise what is called the "foreign exchange market." It is a money center in which the world's leading currencies—dollars, marks, pounds, yen, francs, and so forth—are bought and sold. Some are traded by investors seeking protection against future currency fluctuations, the rest by speculators hoping to make a profit. As a result of these divergent goals, international trade is able to flourish in a world of fluctuating exchange rates.

Fast Action

Who are the currency traders? As with the stock and commodity markets, the foreign exchange market has its own mixed bag of participants. Among them: banks, corporations, oil-rich sheiks from the Middle East, millionaires from almost every country, businesspersons, and ordinary citizens. The leading professionals in the field, however, are

mainly major banks and individual specialists. But these experts, popularly referred to as the "gnomes of Zurich," have had their share of setbacks, as recent history attests:

○ New York's Franklin National Bank, the twentieth-largest bank in America, and West Germany's Herstatt Bank, one of Europe's biggest, suffered financial failure (bankruptcy) as a result of foreign exchange losses.

○ Union Bank of Switzerland and the Swiss branch of Lloyd's Bank—both highly reputable institutions—lost $150 million and $75 million, respectively, from dealings in foreign exchange.

○ The Vatican, acting on the advice of an eminently successful Italian financier, lost $60 million on foreign exchange transactions.

If these experts are unable to beat the fast-moving foreign exchange market,

how can a company dealing abroad hope to do so? The answer is, it cannot; therefore, it should not try. Instead, it should write forward contracts, thereby shifting the consequences of exchange-rate fluctuations to speculators who are willing to bear the risks.

How Forward Contracts Work

The essential idea behind a forward contract is simple. The seller of the contract agrees to deliver a stipulated amount of foreign exchange for a specified price at a certain future date. The buyer promises to accept. Basically, the entire process consists of five steps:

Step 1 A U.S. manufacturer agrees to export goods to an English buyer six months from now in exchange for £1,000. The manufacturer, however, does not know what £1,000 will be worth in U.S. dollars in six months.

Foreign-exchange trading, whether in the international monetary market or in the trading rooms of the world's major banks, is a hectic experience for both buyers and sellers.

Régis Bossu, Sygma.

Therefore, he wants to protect himself from risk exposure.

Step 2 The manufacturer writes (sells) a contract to a U.S. bank, agreeing to deliver £1,000 in six months in exchange for $1,900 at that time. The bank is thus guessing that the exchange rate in six months will be $1.90 = £1.

Step 3 The U.S. bank telephones its correspondent bank in London and borrows £1,000 *today*. Assuming that the exchange rate today is $2.00 = £1, the U.S. bank sells the pounds for $2,000 and lends out the money to its U.S. customers for six months.

Step 4 Six months later, the U.S. manufacturer delivers goods to the English buyer and is paid £1,000. The manufacturer then takes pounds to the U.S. bank and receives $1,900 as agreed (step 2). The U.S. bank also gets back its $2,000 in repaid loans (step 3).

Step 5 The U.S. bank pays back the £1,000 it borrowed six months earlier from the London bank. The remaining dollars cover the U.S. bank's service charges, interest expenses on pounds borrowed, and profits.

This is one of the more common ways in which forward contracts operate. As a result of selling a contract, the manufacturer has "hedged" his risk by protecting himself against a fall in the price of pounds.

Conclusion: Promotes Trade

Two groups, each with different goals, participate in the foreign exchange market. One group, the *hedgers*, is concerned with *reducing risks* of currency fluctuations. Another group, the *speculators*, seeks to *earn profits* by assuming risks that hedgers wish to avoid. Speculators, therefore, engage both in buying and selling forward contracts in the hope

of profiting from fluctuations in currency prices. Of course, speculators who guess future currency prices incorrectly can incur huge losses—as often happens. Nevertheless, speculators are a necessary part of the foreign exchange market—a market that facilitates international trade by enabling business firms to hedge their risks of currency losses.

QUESTIONS

1. In the example of forward-contracts given above, who is the hedger? The speculator? Explain. What would have been the effect on the respective parties if the price of pounds six months later (step 4) had fallen to $1.80? Risen to $2.20?

2. "Speculators are no different from gamblers. Like gamblers, speculators create no product and hence perform no useful social function." Evaluate.

Chapter 35

International Economic Problems and Policies

Chapter Preview

What economic changes took place during World Wars I and II that led to a weakening and disintegration of the world economy?

How did nations respond to these changes after World War II?

What problems of international economic adjustment have nations come to face? What can be done to solve these problems?

The late Lord Rothschild, a world-famous financier, was once asked by a friend to explain the international financial system. He replied, "My dear chap, there are only two men in the world who understand the international financial system—a young economist in the Treasury and a rather junior man in the Bank of England. Unfortunately, they disagree."

There is no doubt that most people are unfamiliar with the international monetary system. This is true despite the fact that the dollar is often under attack by foreigners; our gold policy (or lack of it) is regarded by some groups as a national scandal; and American tourists visiting abroad are sometimes astounded to discover that the value of their dollars, in terms of foreign currencies, can decline considerably between breakfast and dinner.

These are only a few of the events that occur in the complex world of international finance. But important happenings also take place in the area of international trade. In this chapter we shall review the background and consequences of these developments and discuss recommendations for improving the community of sovereign nations held together by economic interdependence.

The Interwar Period: Weakening and Disintegration of the World Economy

In the decades before World War I, most major countries were closely integrated through a well-developed network of trade and finance. The essential features of this complex system may be characterized briefly:

1. Nations and regions tended to specialize on the basis of their factor endowments, thus making multilateral trade necessary.

2. Tariffs for the most part affected only moderately the international flow of goods according to the principle of comparative advantage.

3. London was the center of finance and trade, with its supporting facilities of banks, brokerage houses, insurance companies, shipping firms, and communication lines extending throughout the world.

4. Almost all major nations and many minor ones—several dozen in all—were on the gold standard, thus permitting the easy convertibility of currencies that is needed for carrying on international transactions smoothly and efficiently.

This was also an era of rapid advances in technology and large migrations of labor and capital. These fundamental changes were assimilated, though not, to be sure, without some major political and economic upheavals. The balances of payments of most trading nations tended to adjust fairly smoothly to gold movements, while exchange rates remained stable.

This, briefly, was the nature of the relatively harmonious international economic setting that prevailed until the eve of World War I. In the next three decades, however, the world economy experienced a series of deep disturbances. These included: (1) structural weakening during the 1920s, (2) disintegration during the 1930s, and (3) disruption during World War II.

STRUCTURAL WEAKENING DURING THE 1920s

World War I destroyed the economic relations between nations that had developed through almost five decades of peace in Europe. International commercial and financial links were broken, markets were disorganized, and the marketing system was shattered. All belligerent nations except the United States abandoned the gold standard; the American government officially discouraged gold withdrawals from banks; and gold exports were subjected to strict legal controls. These steps were necessary to prevent the hoarding of gold and its flight to safer havens in neutral nations—common occurrences in periods of crisis.

After the war there were violent inflations in continental Europe, and the restoration of the gold standard became a major objective of international policy. Between 1925 and 1929, more than 40 countries returned to gold; only a few continued to operate on the basis of inconvertible paper. But the new gold standard established during this period was based on economic conditions and philosophies different from those that existed before 1914. Some of the more important changes that took place may be noted briefly.

Changes in National Objectives

Governments began to place less emphasis on the automatic operation of an international monetary system provided by the gold standard and more emphasis on *domestic* economic stability. The war and postwar years brought severe monetary disturbances, inflation, and then depression. With the establishment of the Federal Reserve System in the United States just before World War I and the creation of similar institutions in many other countries during the 1920s, government officials became increasingly involved in efforts to stabilize prices and economic activity through central-bank monetary policy.

Increased Government Intervention

In many countries, the decade after the war was marked by the beginnings of a retreat from laissez-faire as farmers, labor unions, consumers, and other special-interest groups pressed for greater government protection and reforms. This gave rise to growing nationalism. As a result, the United States and other nations, including Australia, Great Britain, India, and Japan, enacted new protective trade legislation during the 1920s.

Conclusion: Increased Importance of the U.S. Economy

The changing national objectives and government policies weakened the international monetary mechanism by making it more rigid. At the same time, the United States gained increasing dominance in the international economy. By 1929, it had become the world's largest exporter, the second largest importer (after Great Britain), and chief creditor. This meant that with other nations heavily dependent on it, the United States would have to maintain a stable, high level of income and employment, and a steady flow of lending to other nations if the well-being of the world economy was to be preserved. Any sudden changes in American economic stability, tariff rates, or credit flows could affect access to markets and produce severe international repercussions. This, as we shall see, is precisely what happened.

DISINTEGRATION DURING THE 1930s

In the United States, prosperity began its rise in 1922 and reached a peak in the first half of 1929. During this period American investment, income, and employment climbed to unprecedented heights. But then the overall decline in economic activity set in—first with a drop in industrial production in July 1929, then with a collapse of the stock market three months later, and finally with a precipitous decline in American spending and investment abroad.

How did the major trading nations respond to these depressing effects on world commerce? There were several types of reaction, which we shall now examine. As will be seen later, these reactions significantly affected the international economic policies of nations after World War II.

Higher Tariffs

In the United States and other major countries there was a marked tendency to subordinate internctional trade to national interests. The United States made access to its domestic market difficult by passing the Smoot–Hawley Tariff of 1930. This new law broadened the range of protected commodities to over 25,000, and provided for increases in some 800 rates covering a wide variety of both agricultural and industrial goods. Great Britain, which had been the citadel of free trade for 80 years, abandoned its policy and adopted a protective tariff in 1932. Similarly, other countries attempted to controy their foreign trade by establishing tariffs, quotas, special exchange allocations, bilateral trade agreements for the trading of specific products, and monopolistic state-controlled trading systems. In general, the actions undertaken during this period more than offset years of effort by the League of Nations to establish freer international trade.

Financial Crisis and the Abandonment of Gold

A second major development of international significance occurred in the spring of 1931. Two major European banks failed due to technical insolvency—their liabilities exceeded their assets. The fear of further bank failures spread, causing financial panics accompanied by heavy "runs" on nations' gold and foreign-exchange reserves. In Britain, which was especially hard hit because British banks were overextended on loans to foreigners, the gold drain reached crisis proportions. Consequently, on September 21, 1931, Parliament announced that the Bank of England would no longer be required by law to sell gold. This meant, of course, that Britain had officially gone off the gold standard.

In the months that followed, the international depression deepened and financial panics were repeated in various nations. As a result, by the end of 1932, twenty-four countries had followed England in abandoning the gold standard.

Devaluation of the Dollar

The United States was not, of course, immune to the effects of the Depression. The period 1929–1932 was one of severe deflation. Moreover, some 5,000 banks—about one-third of the nation's total—became insolvent. As a result, early in 1933, a wave of currency and gold hoarding ensued. This forced President Roosevelt to declare a bank "holiday," to place an embargo on the export of gold, and to prevent banks and the Treasury from paying out the precious metal. These steps placed the United States on a *gold bullion standard* in which gold was nationalized by the Treasury, taken out of domestic circulation as money, and made available in the form of gold bullion only for industrial uses and international transactions in return for other money.

In addition, the government made a further attempt at currency stabilization when it devalued the dollar in 1934.

> *Devaluation* is an official act which makes a domestic currency cheaper in terms of gold or foreign currencies. Historically, it was typically undertaken to increase a nation's exports and to reduce its imports.

Thus on January 31, 1934, the United States devalued the dollar relative to gold by approximately 41 percent, by raising the Treasury's buying and selling price of gold from $20.67 per ounce to $35 per ounce. This act made it cheaper for foreigners to buy dollars, and more expensive for Americans to buy foreign currencies.

Consequences of Devaluation

Other countries responded to the devaluation by imposing higher tariffs and other trade restrictions. But the devalued dollar, which was now stabilized in relation to other depreciated currencies, exerted mounting balance-of-payments pressures on the remaining gold standard countries with their overvalued currencies. During the mid-1930s this, in combination with the growing fear of war in Europe, resulted in a heavy net inflow of capital and gold to the United States for safekeeping. Between 1934 and 1938, the remaining gold standard nations—Belgium, Switzerland, France, and The Netherlands—unable to sustain any further drain, abandoned gold and devalued their currencies. Thus came the end of an era. (See Box 1.)

Conclusion: International Agreements

By the eve of World War II, the leading trading countries of the Western world had learned at least two important lessons:

By releasing their currencies from gold, nations could be free to manage their economies by fiscal and monetary means without the fear of losing reserves and without the need to be regulated by international gold movements. Devaluation, however, is not ordinarily a one-way street; it usually causes opposing reactions by other nations in the form of trade restrictions or retaliatory devaluation.

The remaining highlights of the immediate pre-World War II years may be summarized briefly.

1. The United States and most Western European countries entered an agreement which, for international purposes, represented a compromise between the rigidities of the gold standard and domestic currency management. Thus:

(a) Each country established its own government stabilization fund to buy and sell foreign exchange in the open market in quantities necessary to maintain reasonable stability of its own currency in relation to foreign currencies.

(b) Competitive devaluation for the purpose of expanding exports was renounced.

(c) The central banks of the participating countries were authorized to buy gold without limit, but gold served largely as an equilibrating device for balance-of-payments purposes.

On the whole, exchange-rate equilibrium was restored among the democratic trading nations, while

---

Box 1
Dollar Devaluation and the Gold Standard

In the winter of 1934, a famous crime occupied the attention of most Americans. Dollar devaluation was only a secondary concern. Hence, when the United States devalued the dollar on January 31, 1934, few people anticipated the worldwide implications of this act. Within the next four years the gold standard faded into extinction, never again to be restored by any nation.

totalitarian countries like Germany and Russia maintained tightly controlled systems for allocating foreign exchange.

2. In the area of international trade, the United States established a *Reciprocal Trade Agreements program*. This was a plan for expanding American exports through legislation which authorized the President to negotiate U.S. tariff reductions with other nations in return for parallel concessions. The program consists of the Trade Agreements Act of 1934, with subsequent amendments, and related legislation. An interesting feature of the Reciprocal Trade Agreements program has been the widespread use of what is known as a *most-favored-nation clause*. Its inclusion in a trade treaty means that each of the signatories agrees to extend to the other the same preferential tariff and trade concessions that each may in the future extend to nonsignatories, that is, the same treatment that each gives to its "most-favored nation." The great majority of trading countries have adhered to this principle since 1948.

DISRUPTION DURING WORLD WAR II: LEND LEASE

World War II (1939–1945) disrupted world trade. The belligerents as well as the leading neutral nations were largely prevented from engaging in exchange transactions with the United States and the Allies. In order to help the allied nations to buy the goods they needed but could not pay for, the United States instituted a system of Lend Lease in 1941. It provided advances in goods and supplies in return for "reverse" Lend Lease by the recipient countries in the form of care and housing for American troops. In money terms, the value of the grants given by the United States far exceeded the value of the services that it received in return. But as Prime Minister Winston Churchill remarked to Parliament, Lend Lease was not intended to provide for an equal exchange; indeed, it was "the most unsordid act in the history of any nation."

Post–World War II International Commerce

In the summer of 1944, few people were concerned about the problems of international trade and finance. Allied troops were engaged in the great battle of the Normandy beachhead; a group of German army officers had tried unsuccessfully to assassinate Adolf Hitler; and a politically obscure man named Harry S Truman was emerging as the potential running mate of President Roosevelt in his bid for a fourth term.

At the same time, an event of less colorful but highly durable significance was taking place in the lovely rural setting of Bretton Woods, New Hampshire. There, in the Mount Washington Hotel, at the foot of New England's highest mountain, the United Nations Monetary and Financial Conference was holding an international meeting destined to affect the world's economic structure for decades to come. Present at the meeting were representatives from 16 governments, including Lord Keynes in his capacity as advisor to the British treasury.

The primary result of this historic gathering was the formation of a plan for a new and remarkable international financial system. The original agreement was developed largely by the British and American delegations. It was signed by 35 nations, but the membership subsequently increased to more than three times that number. We shall find it useful to examine the nature of this system and related aspects of world trade.

EUROPEAN ECONOMIC RECOVERY

When the war ended, the European economy was devastated. For five years after the war, Europe's balance of payments on current account suffered from a substantial trade deficit. Among the factors that were responsible for this deficit were the pressure of inflation, the reduction of productive capacity caused by the war, and the loss of overseas export markets.

The immediate task, of course, was to rebuild the European economy while financing its deficit. Most of the responsibility fell to the United States, which extended approximately $17 billion in foreign aid between 1945 and 1948, about half of which was in the form of outright gifts and half in the form of loans. But it was recognized that these were merely stopgap measures and that more consistent and far-reaching policies were necessary. The result was the formulation of two important types of American aid programs that have had a substantial influence on the economic development of other nations.

European Recovery Program (Marshall Plan)

On June 5, 1947, Secretary of State George C. Marshall delivered a commencement address at Harvard University in which he proposed what came to be known as the *European Recovery Program* (ERP) or *Marshall Plan*. Financed by the United States, the plan was a comprehensive blueprint for the economic recovery of European countries. The plan's purposes were to (1) increase the productive capacity of these countries, (2) stabilize their financial systems, (3) promote their mutual economic cooperation, and (4) reduce their dependence on U.S. assistance. Out of this came the Organization for European Economic Cooperation, an association consisting initially of 17 European countries which sought to cooperate in assuring their own economic recovery.

The Marshall Plan ended in 1951, after providing over $10 billion in aid. About 90 percent of this was in outright grants and the rest in loans. There is widespread agreement that the program was a success. It contributed substantially to raising the average level of industrial production among participating nations by more than half their 1947 level and to suppressing a decade of rapid inflation.

Mutual Security Administration

By late 1951, American emphasis had shifted from direct economic aid to containment of communism. The immediate cause of this change in attitude was the outbreak of the Korean War in June 1950. The ERP was absorbed by the Mutual Security Administration, which provided both military and economic assistance to various nations throughout the world. Since the early 1950s, a substantial part of American economic aid has been directed at the underdeveloped countries in Africa, Asia, and Latin America. A great deal of aid has gone to countries which are regarded as bulwarks against communism. The results have not always been favorable. America has been criticized for propping up repressive regimes and is often regarded by the peoples of such countries as a supporter of dictatorship and even of political terrorism.

TRADE LIBERALIZATION AND REGIONAL INTEGRATION

Even during World War II, it was evident to many political leaders that a new multilateral trading system would be needed after the war—one which provided for liberalization and economic integration of world trade. A significant step in this direction, as we have seen, was the Reciprocal Trade Agreements program adopted by the United States. This program empowered the President to agree on mutual tariff reductions with other countries and to incorporate most-favored-nation clauses in such agreements. After the war, various trading nations endorsed and adopted additional measures designed to strengthen world commerce. The more important ones are examined briefly.

General Agreement on Tariffs and Trade (GATT)

The first major postwar step toward liberalization of world trade was the *General Agreement on Tariffs and Trade* (GATT). An international agreement signed in 1947 by 23 countries, including the United States, it is dedicated to four basic principles: (1) nondiscrimination in trade through adherence to unconditional most-favored-nation treatment, (2) reduction of tariffs by negotiation, (3) elimination of import quotas (with some exceptions permitted), and (4) resolution of differences through consultation. The number of nations participating in GATT has since increased by several dozen, and it has been an important and successful force for the liberalization of world trade.

Regional Integration

Despite the fact that nations have erected trade barriers to shield themselves from one another, the underlying desire for free trade has nevertheless been persistent. Although worldwide free trade may never become a reality, regional free-trade agreements among two or more nations are commonplace. Such agreements have typically taken three forms: free-trade areas, customs unions, and common markets.

1. *Free-Trade Area* This is an association of trading nations whose participants agree to impose no restrictive devices, such as tariffs or quotas, on one another. However, each country is free to impose whatever restrictions it wishes on nonparticipants. The best-known example is the European Free Trade Association (EFTA), established in 1960. Its members have included Austria, Great Britain, Sweden, Norway, Denmark, Switzerland, and Portugal. Similar organizations have been established or proposed among Latin American, Asian, and African countries.

2. *Customs Union* This is an agreement among two or more trading nations to abolish trade barriers such as tariffs and quotas among themselves, and to adopt a common external policy of trade (such as a common external tariff) with all nonmember nations. The most familiar example is Benelux (i.e., Belgium, The Netherlands, and Luxembourg). Similar plans have been adopted or proposed in other geographic areas.

3. *Common Market* This is an association of trading nations which agrees to (a) impose no trade restrictions, such as tariffs or quotas, among participants; (b) establish common external barriers (such as a common external tariff) to nonparticipants; and (c) impose no national restrictions on the movement of labor and capital among participants. The most significant example has been the European Economic Community (EEC) or European Common Market, established in

1958. Among its members have been Belgium, Denmark, France, Great Britain, West Germany, Ireland, Italy, Luxembourg, and The Netherlands.

A free-trade area, a customs union, and a common market (in that order) represent increasing degrees of economic integration. Of these, the common market is the most significant. What can be said about its economic effects?

On the favorable side:

A common market yields two major benefits:

1. It encourages a more efficient allocation of member nations' resources in accordance with the laws of comparative advantage.

2. It expands the size of the market for member nations, thereby enabling their industries to gain the economies (lower unit costs) of large-scale production.

On the unfavorable side:

A common market places a trade barrier—typically a tariff wall—between the member countries as a whole and all nonmember nations. The result may be a diversion of trade between the two groups, thereby causing an economic loss for all parties concerned.

Reduction of Trade Barriers

The United States has long sought to foster greater economic unification with other nations. Toward this end it has passed various "trade acts" as part of its Reciprocal Trade Agreements program. These laws, designed to encourage U.S. trade expansion, have widened the powers of the President by enabling him to reduce trade barriers. Specifically, the President can:

1. Negotiate reductions in tariff and certain nontariff barriers for broad categories of goods instead of on specific commodities.

2. Lower tariffs by substantial percentages on the basis of reciprocal trade agreements, provided that such agreements include most-favored-nation clauses so that the benefits of reduced tariffs are extended to other countries.

3. Grant vocational, technical, and financial assistance to American employees and business leaders whose industries are adversely affected by tariff reduction.

As a result of these trade-expansion acts, numerous nations have become involved in duty reductions. However, some countries whose industries were injured by tariff reductions have found themselves faced with increased pressures for protection and have either adopted or are considering adopting various forms of nontariff barriers to trade. Among these are quotas, license requirements, and border taxes.

Post–World War II International Finance

The postwar developments in international trade were paralleled by equally momentous changes in international finance. When the representatives of the allied nations met in Bretton Woods in 1944 to construct an orderly system of international monetary cooperation that would be conducive to global trade, the experiences of the 1930s were still fresh in everyone's mind. It was clear that neither a system of freely fluctuating exchange rates nor one of fixed rates which permitted easy devaluations was the way to strengthen the financial relationships of nations in the postwar world.

INTERNATIONAL MONETARY FUND

One of the most important products of the Bretton Woods conference was the formation of the *International Monetary Fund* (IMF). This is an organization established by the United Nations in 1944 for the purposes of eliminating exchange restrictions, encouraging exchange-rate stability, and providing for worldwide convertibility of currencies to promote multilateral trade based on international specialization. Today well over 100 nations are members of the Fund.

The IMF has helped many countries to overcome temporary balance-of-payments deficits. It has also served as a powerful force in helping to maintain relatively stable exchange rates. These and related matters are taken up in further detail later in the chapter.

FROM DOLLAR SHORTAGE TO DOLLAR SURPLUS

The United States emerged from the war as a large creditor to the allied countries. After the war, American lending continued to mount into the billions of dollars as the United States shifted its emphasis from the provision of military goods to the provision of civilian goods to the war-torn nations. The latter, of course, had little if anything to export in return. Nor did they have the gold or dollar reserves with which to pay for the American goods that they received. Hence, a "dollar shortage" became one of the most talked-about problems of the postwar decade as the United States continued to show a rather persistent deficit in its balance of payments after 1950.

Further, since gold and dollars were the major source of international monetary reserves, the dollar (and to a lesser extent the pound sterling) became known as a *key currency*—in effect, a substitute for gold in meeting international obligations. This meant that during the 1950s, while the United States was accumulating a huge deficit in its balance of payments, other countries—mainly the European nations—were adding to their reserves, primarily in the form of dollar deposits in U.S. banks or of short-term government securities.

By the mid-1950s, the European and Japanese economies were not only rehabilitated, but thriving. The United States, however, was still maintaining heavy troop commitments overseas, providing economic aid to underdeveloped countries, and experiencing a mounting outflow of American tourists going abroad. All this added up to continued deficits, and by the late 1950s it was recognized throughout the world that the dollar shortage had been *transformed* into a serious and dangerous dollar surplus.

"DEFENDING THE DOLLAR"

How might the deficit be corrected? There were three plausible choices: (1) domestic deflation, (2) devaluation of the dollar, and (3) reductions in foreign outlays. The first two choices would increase international earnings by expanding U.S. exports relative to imports; the third would simply decrease U.S. expenses.

The first choice was ruled out because deflation would lead to an increase in the unemployment rate in the United States, which was already averaging close to 5 percent. The second choice was also ruled out because devaluation by a major trading country such as the United States would undoubtedly have brought on a chain of competitive devaluations by most other countries. This left the third choice—reduction of foreign outlays—as a means of "defending the dollar."

The measures adopted in the early 1960s took several major forms. Families of servicemen stationed overseas were sent back to the United States. The limits on duty-free goods which could be brought back by returning American tourists were cut. European countries were exhorted to carry a larger share of the mutual defense burden and of foreign aid. An "interest equalization tax" and "voluntary restraints" were imposed on the outflow of American capital. Nations in debt to the United States were asked to speed up their payments. Trading nations were urged to end their remaining restrictions against American imports. And so on.

What were the consequences? At worst, they did not succeed in eliminating the deficit. At best, they may have merely helped to keep the deficit from becoming still larger. But in any case they were more than straws in the wind, for they portended a series of international monetary crises that shook the financial world.

INTERNATIONAL MONETARY CRISES

In terms of what it set out to do, the 1944 conference at Bretton Woods was a smashing success. It stabilized exchange rates and created an international monetary system that was highly productive of world trade and investment. This was accomplished by establishing a modified type of gold exchange standard with two distinctive features:

1. The dollar was tied to gold, and the U.S. Treasury agreed to make gold and dollars mutually convertible to foreign central banks at the rate of $35 per ounce of gold.

2. Each nation fixed an exchange rate or par value for its currency in relation to the dollar and agreed to maintain that rate within a 1 percent range by buying and selling its currency against the dollar.

This meant that business managers anywhere in the world could trade with Britain, for example, and be certain that the value of the pound would not vary by more than a few cents above or below its established rate. As before, however, nations still needed monetary reserves to settle their international monetary deficits. Under the pure gold standard, such reserves consisted of gold; however, under the postwar modified gold exchange standard, reserves consisted primarily of gold and dollars, and to a lesser extent of British pounds. The dollars, as we have seen, were derived largely from U.S. deficits and held mainly in the form of bank deposits and short-term government securities. Because of this, the United States became known as the "world's banker," with the dollar serving as the key or reserve currency.

As American and British deficits continued to mount, and as inflationary forces pushed up prices not only in the United States but also in England and various other important trading nations, the accumulation of pressures erupted in large speculative flows of major currencies, thereby endangering the international payments system. Recurring doubts arose as to whether the United States would be willing and able to maintain convertibility of the dollar into gold at the fixed price of $35 for an ounce of gold. As a result, increasing proportions of dollars were converted into gold during the 1960s by foreign speculators and others who thought it would be safer or more profitable to hold the yellow metal instead of the green paper.

Finally, in the late 1960s, three sets of events capped a decade of international monetary crisis.

Special Drawing Rights ("Paper Gold")

After 1958, the European countries began to press the United States to reduce its balance-of-payments deficit. The United States, in return, urged throughout the 1960s that a plan be developed for increasing international liquidity in the absence of dollar outflows. After almost five years of discussion and four years of negotiation, *Special Drawing Rights* (SDRs)—popularly known as "paper gold"—were approved by the International Monetary Fund in 1969.

> SDRs are supplementary reserves in the form of account entries or "claims" on the books of the IMF. The claims are allocated among participating countries in accordance with their relative economic strength as determined by their national income, population, and volume of world trade. SDRs can be drawn upon by governments to help finance balance-of-payments deficits. It is hoped that the "paper gold" will provide an orderly growth of reserves to meet the expanding needs of world trade.

Further aspects of SDRs are described in Exhibit 1.

Devaluation

On November 19, 1967, the twenty-sixth Sunday after Trinity, churchgoers in England heard a somber and particularly apt text from Anglican pulpits. The lesson was from *St. James*, Chapter 5, Verses 1 to 3:

> Go to now, ye rich men, weep and howl for your miseries that shall come upon you.
> Your riches are corrupted, and your garments are motheaten.
> Your gold and silver is cankered; and the rust of them shall be a witness against you, and shall eat your flesh as it were fire. Ye have heaped treasure together for the last days.

Why this curious reading from scripture? The answer is that while the creation of SDRs was being discussed among governments, Britain was indulging herself with an easy-money policy that was contrib-

Exhibit 1
The Implications of Special Drawing Rights

What do SDRs mean for the United States?

Until 1971, the United States used its gold stock or its "credit line" with the IMF to absorb unwanted dollars that accrued to foreign central banks as the result of the U.S. deficit. With the introduction of SDRs, the United States has (within internationally agreed-upon limits) had the additional option of exchanging the unwanted dollars for SDRs. This has aided conservation of the U.S. gold stock and thus

contributed to the viability of the existing international payments mechanism.

The introduction of SDRs may eventually modify the role of the dollar as a reserve currency. The view that the dollar cannot and should not be expected to meet the world's future needs for growth of reserves was the underlying rationale for the introduction of the SDRs. Meanwhile, however, the SDR's role in international transactions has been less significant than initially expected.

THE CHANGING MIX IN WORLD RESERVES

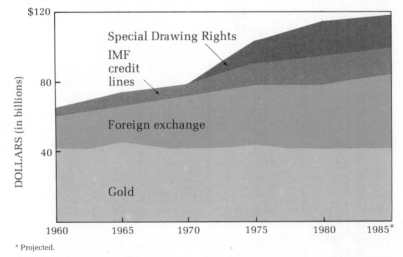

* Projected.

SOURCE: International Monetary Fund.

uting to inflation, trade deficits, and financial strains. On November 18, 1967, she succumbed to international economic pressures and devalued the pound from $2.80 to $2.40, a decrease of 14.3 percent. This was the third devaluation for Britain in 36 years. It was intended to give the country a sharper competitive edge in world markets as well as the breathing time needed to repair its foundering economy and deficit-ridden balance of payments.

Whether or not a devaluation succeeds in eliminating a deficit depends on many factors—among them the various policy measures taken at home to curb inflation. Such measures, which Britain adopted, included heavy new taxes, broad wage controls, and a tight national budget. In the long run, if an austerity policy is sufficiently harsh and if it is combined with an appropriate restrictive monetary policy, it can succeed in curbing inflation and thereby make a devaluation yield lasting economic benefits.

A Two-Tier System for Gold

Following the devaluation of the pound in 1967, confidence in the dollar was further weakened by inflation in the United States and the expectation that the dollar would have to be devalued. Consequently, a rush to buy gold developed late in the year. Most of the buyers were speculators who expected to make a quick profit by reselling the gold at the higher price.

In the meantime, seven countries known as the Gold Pool nations—the United States, Great Britain, West Germany, Belgium, Italy, The Netherlands, and Switzerland—had, since 1961, been holding the free-market price of gold in European markets and in other locations at the American price of $35 per ounce by pooling their gold and standing ready to buy or sell as the need arose. With the onset of the new "gold rush," there was a danger that the gold holdings of these nations would be depleted, thus endangering the entire international monetary system. The speculative fever reached a dramatic climax in March 1968 with the announcement of a two-tier (or two-price) system for gold by the Gold Pool nations. Henceforth, they said, their central banks would exchange existing gold stocks among themselves at the historic official price of $35 per ounce, and would no longer buy or sell gold in private markets. This would leave the price of gold to rise or fall like that of any other commodity.

This action further demonetized gold—that is, reduced its influence in the monetary system and thereby removed its threat to the dollar. Thus, by the end of the 1960s, the dollar seemed victorious over gold for several reasons. The West German mark had been revalued upward, and the French franc had been

devalued, both to more realistic levels. Britain's trade balance had improved. And South Africa, the world's largest producer of gold, was mining the metal faster than the free market could absorb it, thus creating a huge "overhang" of potential supply. These factors contributed to bringing the free price of gold down to the near-$35 level that had prevailed for most of the three previous decades.

END OF AN ERA

For a brief time it seemed as if the period of recurring international monetary crises was over. But these hopes were short-lived. To the dismay and disapproval of foreign governments, the United States continued to spend more overseas than it earned and refused to take measures that would enable it to pay its own way in the world.

By 1970 the chronic deficit had ballooned to the point of crisis. U.S. imports were rising far faster than exports; banks and corporations were putting billions of dollars annually into investments abroad; and defense spending, swollen by the Vietnam war, was a hemorrhage through which other billions of dollars leaked out.

Moreover, foreigners were holding billions of dollars they did not want. In the summer of 1971 certain countries, headed by France and Switzerland, rushed to convert their dollar holdings into gold. By July only $10 billion was left in Fort Knox. The crunch came on August 15, 1971. On that day President Nixon announced to the world that the U.S. "gold window" was closed; henceforth, the government would no longer exchange dollars for gold with foreign central banks. Thus, the system of fixed exchange rates based on the Bretton Woods agreement with which the free world had lived for 27 years came to an end.

RECENT DEVELOPMENTS: "DIRTY" FLOATING

Events since the termination of Bretton Woods have been accompanied by further changes in international economic relations. The more important developments may be summarized briefly:

○ In December 1971, and again in February 1973, the United States devalued the dollar—first against gold and then against SDRs. In addition, the German mark and Japanese yen were revalued upward, resulting in a substantial net, or effective, dollar devaluation.

○ In November 1973, the two-tier system for gold was abandoned by the Gold Pool nations. This left them free to pursue whatever actions they wished with respect to gold.

○ In 1972 and 1973, after several further monetary crises, the Japanese yen, the British pound, and some other important currencies were set "afloat"—their values determined by the free play of supply and demand. Subsequently, various other nations' currencies were officially swept afloat by the tidal waves of selling that continued to strike the U.S. dollar. Experience has shown, however, that floating rates tend to be "dirty" rather than clean: Central banks frequently intervene in the market to keep their weak currencies from falling too sharply. Despite these efforts, some currencies decline while others rise, reflecting international confidence—or lack of it—in a country's economy.

As a result of these developments, representatives of the United States and other major trading nations have met on a number of occasions since 1973 to work out an improved world monetary system. The key question that must be answered is whether new rules of the game can be devised which will permit greater exchange-rate stability in international economic relations. (See Box 2.)

Problems of International Adjustment Under Fixed Exchange Rates

Looking back over these historical developments, it is appropriate for us to ask why international monetary crises have occurred. The reasons can be easily summarized. Under a system of fixed exchange rates such as prevailed in the Bretton Woods agreements:

1. The international supply of a nation's currency tended to exceed the demand for it when that country ran a *deficit* in its balance of payments. This occurred when the nation payed out more money than it took in, by spending, investing, or giving it away. To buy its currency back, the monetary authority had to spend

---

Box 2
Can Exchange Rates Be Stabilized?

Whenever exchange rates seem to be settling down, something happens to create a new round of instability. In most cases a nation's currency loses value in relation to other currencies because of a higher rate of inflation.

These developments emphasize the difficulty—or impossibility—of maintaining stable exchange-rate agreements once the market decides that a particular currency is overvalued.

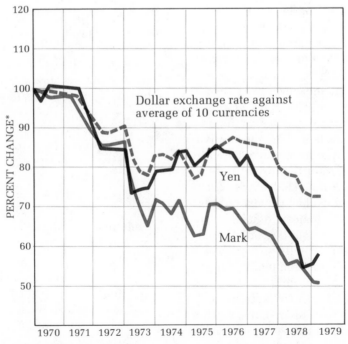

* Index: fourth quarter 1969 = 100

its reserves of convertible currencies or gold (by selling the gold to foreign central banks) or borrow from the International Monetary Fund.

2. Conversely, the international demand for a nation's currency tended to exceed the supply of it when the country ran a *surplus* in its balance of payments. In that case the nation was taking in more money than it was paying out, and to meet foreign demand the central bank had to sell its currency in return for foreign exchange. This resulted in an accumulation of reserves, mostly dollars, which the central bank in the surplus country did not always wish to hold.

3. The international monetary system was threatened whenever major nations continued to run large deficits or surpluses for prolonged periods of time. The problem, therefore, was for each of the leading trading countries to maintain a tendency toward balance between its money inflows and outflows.

What difficulties did nations encounter in achieving international monetary balance? It is to this problem that we now turn our attention.

THE RELUCTANCE TO ADJUST

The heart of any international monetary system is its adjustment mechanism—the process by which nations achieve payments balance.

Under the old gold standard, the adjustment was automatic; a nation with a deficit in its balance of payments tended to lose gold, and the loss of gold brought about a domestic deflation which resulted in increased exports and decreased imports. This meant, however, that the domestic economic goal of full employment through appropriate fiscal and monetary policies had to take second place to international economic adjustment—a situation that all nations found untenable.

Under the Bretton Woods system, exchange rates remained fixed, and so the process of adjustment was left to nations themselves. This meant that countries had to be willing to adopt either deflationary policies to correct persistent balance-of-payments deficits, or "reflationary" policies to reduce balance-of-payments surpluses. Of course, the pressure on deficit nations to change their domestic policies depended on how long their reserves held out or how long they could continue to borrow. Surplus nations, on the other hand, tended to gain reserves, and hence were able to avoid adjustment almost indefinitely.

In general, nations that are committed to the maintenance of full employment do not find it easy to adopt a policy of domestic deflation. Under fixed exchange rates, the United States and Britain were prime examples. Both went through long periods of deficits,

but both were able to delay adjustments because the dollar and the pound served as reserve currencies. Eventually, when the United States was forced to adjust in the 1960s because it was losing gold, it took the easier and less effective route of employing indirect forms of exchange controls—such as interest equalization taxes and the imposition of limits on capital exports, corporate overseas investing, and bank lending abroad.

In terms of historical experience, it appears that under a system of fixed exchange rates such as existed in the Bretton Woods era, the most positive approach a government could take to correct an imbalance was to change the par value of its currency. But this was considered to be the most drastic of measures. Thus, if a country had been suffering from deficits, a depreciation of its currency in order to restore balance involved a sacrifice of international prestige, for its political leaders were thereby admitting to the world that they had been unable to manage domestic economic affairs properly. On the other hand, if a country had been experiencing surpluses in its balance of payments, an appreciation or upward revaluation of its currency may have caused some domestic unemployment, especially in its export industries, and hence was a step which elected political leaders were not easily persuaded to take.

THE INEVITABILITY OF ADJUSTMENT

Ultimately, of course, nations had to adjust, because the forces that create international imbalances—inflation or deflation—also caused domestic economic difficulties which required correction. But the adjustment was often a long time in coming, and in the meantime nations bumped along from one crisis to another.

Was this the world that those at Bretton Woods envisaged in 1944? The answer is no. They never thought that the dollar would remain the world's key currency for several decades after the war, nor that it would be a currency whose supply might someday exceed the quantity that central banks wished to hold. Likewise, they never foresaw the possibility that there would someday be a huge market for *Eurodollars*. These are dollar deposits in banks outside the United States, mostly in Europe. Eurodollars are held by American or foreign banks, corporations, and individuals, and represent dollar obligations which are constantly crossing national frontiers in search of the highest return. Hence under fixed exchange rates, Eurodollars could affect balances of payments and even turn pressure on a currency into an international monetary crisis. Some interesting aspects of this are described in Box 3.

Box 3

Eurocurrency: Questions and Answers That Worry Some Experts

When interest rates soar at home, domestic companies often seek cheaper loans in the "Euromarket." Although it originated in Europe, the Euromarket has become a world market in which leading banks, large corporations, governments, and wealthy individuals negotiate short- and long-term financing in major currencies.

WHAT IS EUROCURRENCY?

It is money on deposit in financial institutions outside the country of its origin. Examples are U.S. dollars on deposit at banks outside the United States, Swiss francs outside Switzerland, German marks outside West Germany, and so on. The quantities involved, which determine the size of the Eurocurrency market, are equivalent to *trillions* of dollars.

ARE EURODOLLARS THE SAME AS EUROCURRENCY?

No. Eurodollars are the portion of Eurocurrency denominated in dollars. Until the late 1960s, Eurodollars constituted almost the entire Eurocurrency market. Since then, marks, francs, pounds, and yen have gained in importance. However, the supply of Eurodollars amounts to hundreds of billions of dollars—considerably more than America's basic money supply consisting of currency and checking-account deposits.

WHAT IS SO SPECIAL ABOUT THE EUROMARKET?

It is largely unregulated, and there are no reserve requirements. Therefore, banks can make cheaper loans and pay higher interest to depositors because there are no laws requiring a certain percentage of deposits to be kept idle as reserves.

WHY ARE GOVERNMENT OFFICIALS WORRIED ABOUT IT?

For two reasons:

1. If the Eurocurrency market continues to expand relative to domestic markets, central banks will find it increasingly difficult to control the volume of money and credit.

2. Some central bankers believe that the Euromarket increases the severity of foreign exchange fluctuations.

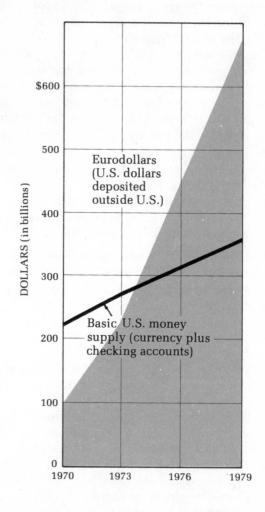

For both reasons, therefore, it is felt that the Euromarket is becoming an important contributor to world economic instability. Some experts, however, disagree. They contend that the Euromarket has caused increased competition among large banks, resulting in more foreign loans than in the past.

Floating, Adjustable, or Crawling Rates?

In view of this historical background, what can be done to improve the world's monetary system? Central bankers and economists are interested in three types of proposals: floating exchange rates, adjustable pegs, and crawling pegs.

FLOATING EXCHANGE RATES

Floating exchange rates leave currencies uncontrolled and free to fluctuate according to supply and demand. Thus, a decrease in the price of a nation's currency in the foreign exchange market encourages that country's exports and discourages its imports. Conversely, an increase in the price of a nation's currency has the opposite effect. The chief advantages of freely floating exchange rates, therefore, are that (1) they provide for automatic adjustment in the balance of payments without the intervention of a central authority; and (2) they eliminate the need for stabilization funds and international reserves. The chief disadvantages are that (1) they may restrict the expansion of world trade by leaving importers, exporters, creditors, and others in a greater state of uncertainty about future exchange rates; and (2) they may encourage speculation in foreign exchange which could accentuate price swings and cause a destabilization of world trade. These undesirable consequences might eventually lead to more rather than fewer trade controls. As a consequence, central banks may intervene to prevent exchange rates from fluctuating *too* freely. (See also Exhibit 2.)

ADJUSTABLE PEGS

An *adjustable peg* system permits controlled changes in the par rate of exchange after a long-run disequilibrium in the balance of payments. It also allows for short-run variations in the exchange rate within a few

---

Exhibit 2
Currency Protection in the Forward Exchange Market
(90-day forward spread—hypothetical data)

Forward exchange is foreign exchange that is bought (or sold) at a given time and at a stipulated current or "spot" price, but is payable at a future date. By buying or selling forward exchange, importers and exporters can protect themselves against the risks of fluctuations in the current exchange market.

The spread between spot and future prices can vary considerably, as the chart shows. Currencies that are in strong demand tend to sell at a premium, while those that are in a weaker position sell at a discount. In the more recent months shown, for example, French importers from Germany paid heavily by buying forward marks at a premium, thus restricting their purchases of Volkswagens. But German importers found forward francs so cheap they could afford to buy a lot more French wine.

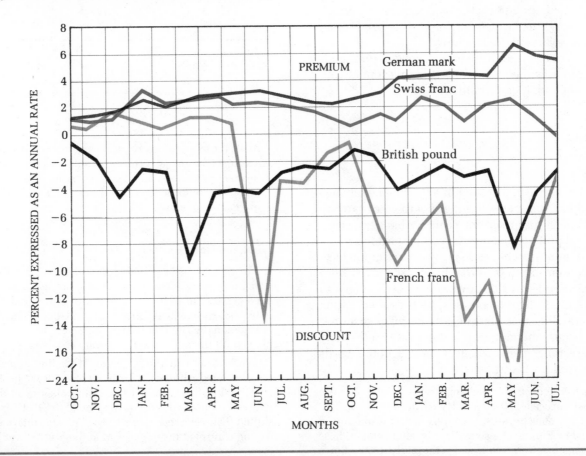

percentage points around the par value. (This was essentially the Bretton Woods system.) The most desirable feature of such a system is that it operates efficiently only if the par rate is consistent with the nation's long-run equilibrium in its balance of payments, so that the adjustment problem is then entirely of a short-term nature. The most undesirable feature is that the threat of speculation and disruption of foreign exchange markets exists when a change in the basic par rate becomes necessary.

CRAWLING PEGS

Under a _crawling peg_ system the par value of a nation's exchange rate changes automatically by small increments, downward or upward, if in actual daily trading on the foreign exchange markets the price of its currency persists on the "floor" or "ceiling" of the governmentally established range for a specified period of time. The changes in the par value are small and gradual (probably about 3 percent annually) so as to discourage speculation, yet sufficient to correct for fundamental imbalances in the balance of payments.

The crawling peg system thus represents a compromise between floating exchange rates and the adjustable peg. Although the crawling peg does not eliminate the need for international reserves, it permits fewer reserves to be needed than with fixed rates. And, since everyone knows how far and in what direction exchange rates are moving, speculation tends to be minimal while world trade and investment continue to expand. (See Exhibit 3.)

CONCLUSION: PERMANENT AGREEMENT DOUBTFUL

The choice between a system of adjustable exchange rates and one that permits either floating or crawling rates has been discussed for years by bankers, economists, and political leaders. Governments tend to believe that an adjustable exchange-rate system is best. Many economists, on the other hand, especially those in the academic world, have come increasingly to favor the more flexible systems, such as the floating rate or crawling peg. Despite international meetings held to discuss the matter, it is doubtful whether any enduring arrangements will ever emerge. In the words of one European central banker:

> The system of fixed exchange rates [under Bretton Woods] _succeeded because it was needed._ It accomplished its objectives—to encourage world trade and to stimulate Europe's economic development. Those achievements were realized by the early 1960s. Since

Exhibit 3
How the Crawling Peg Would Work

Under the crawling peg system a deficit nation finds that its exchange rate stays at the lower level of the allowable band of fluctuation. So its exchange rate moves downward in predictable fashion until the impact of a lower exchange rate brings its balance of payments back into equilibrium. On the other side, the exchange rate of a surplus nation increases in a manner that gradually reduces its surplus. The merit of the crawling peg is that its movements are predictable and it facilitates the adjustment process on the part of both deficit and surplus nations.

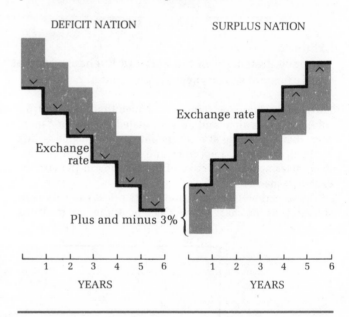

then, the lesson of history has been that it is unrealistic to assume that any government would go along with a permanent policy of exchange rates based on some agreed-upon mechanism that could easily be discarded in a period of adversity.

What You Have Learned

1. For several decades before World War I, most national economies were closely integrated through a well-developed network of trade and finance. Despite rapid advances in technology and heavy migrations of labor and capital, the international economic setting remained relatively harmonious until the outbreak of the war.

2. World War I disrupted national trading and financial relationships. Although efforts were made at postwar reconstruction, there was a structural weakening of the international economy during the decade of the 1920s as nations shifted their economic goals toward greater internal stability and control at the expense of automatic external adjustment.

3. The world economy, particularly the interdependence of nations, underwent major deterioration during the Depression of the 1930s. Governments sought to protect themselves from economic crises by imposing higher tariffs, by going off the gold standard, and by devaluing their currencies. Although some significant steps toward international economic reform were made during the late 1930s, the outbreak of World War II prevented further progress.

4. After World War II, most of the war-torn nations of the world became beneficiaries of American economic aid. Major steps were taken toward trade liberalization through GATT and toward economic integration through the development of common markets. In the area of international finance, the Bretton Woods conference of 1944 established the IMF and a world monetary arrangement that was enormously successful in encouraging international trade.

5. By the 1960s, however, it was apparent that economic conditions had changed so much that the world's monetary system was out of date. The volume of world trade increased faster than reserves, causing international monetary crises that resulted in exchange controls and devaluations. Among the measures taken to alleviate the pressures were the introduction of SDRs and a two-tier (or two-price) system for gold. Finally, in the face of continued adversity, the Bretton Woods system of fixed exchange rates was abandoned in late 1971. Since then, countries have allowed their currencies to float in foreign exchange markets.

6. Three proposals have been suggested to improve the world's monetary system: (1) floating exchange rates, (2) an adjustable peg system, and (3) a crawling peg system. Political considerations being what they are, however, it is unlikely that any system of exchange-rate stability will be adhered to by all nations under all circumstances.

For Discussion

1. *Terms and concepts to review:*

gold bullion standard
devaluation
Reciprocal Trade
  Agreements program
most-favored-nation
  clause
European Recovery
  Program (ERP)
General Agreement on
  Tariffs and Trade
  (GATT)
free-trade area
customs union
common market
International Monetary
  Fund (IMF)
Special Drawing Rights
  (SDRs or "paper gold")
Eurodollars
floating exchange rates
adjustable peg
crawling peg
forward exchange

2. What major features would you stress if you were to write a research paper on the history of international commercial and financial policies?

3. If a country's balance of payments is in equilibrium and the nation experiences a decline in exports, does its balance of payments go into disequilibrium? What happens if floating exchange rates prevail?

4. Devaluation (or exchange depreciation) stimulates a nation's exports while curbing its imports; upward revaluation (or exchange appreciation) has the opposite effect. In view of this, would you recommend the use of devaluation and revaluation as useful countercyclical policies to combat recessions and inflations, similar to the way we currently use fiscal–monetary policies for such purposes? Explain.

5. From the experiences of the 1960s, would you say that the dollar was overvalued or undervalued in world markets? What could have been done to correct the situation?

6. Why do you suppose that many "anti-Keynesians" often propose that the United States go on a gold standard?

7. The various economic regions of the United States (e.g., Northeast, Southwest) are somewhat like countries, each with its own particular type of economy. However, unlike countries, they all use the same currency, dollars, which puts them in effect on a fixed exchange rate with respect to one another. What happens when some of these regions experience deficits and others surpluses? How do they adjust? How does the regional adjustment process compare with that of nations?

8. Deficits in the U.S. balance of payments were welcomed in the early 1950s but viewed with great concern a decade later. Why?

9. It is often said that the Bretton Woods arrangement resulted in a compromise between fixed and floating exchange rates. Is this true? Explain. What would have been a better compromise?

Case
Multinational Corporations: The "New" Foreign Investment

The great English classical economist David Ricardo demonstrated in the early nineteenth century that unrestricted operation of the law of comparative advantage makes everybody better off. Each nation, he said, should be free to specialize in the products in which it is most efficient and leave the production of other things to the countries that can do so most efficiently. The world economy will then have more goods by engaging in trade.

Today the neon signs of American, European, and Japanese multinational corporations light the skylines of most of the major cities throughout the world. These companies have spawned subsidiaries and branches in order to exploit their own comparative advantages. They have discovered that economies of scale can be enhanced by locating in foreign markets, and that the advantages of such economies outweigh the regulations and financial risks that global operations may entail.

The international economic implications of multinationals are discussed frequently in the news media. The more important issues, therefore, are worth examining.

What Are Multinationals?
Boeing, Lockheed, McDonnell-Douglas, and other U.S. aircraft manufacturers do business around the globe, but are they multinationals? Not really, because virtually all of their manufacturing is done in the United States. Accordingly, they are *international* rather than *multinational.*

Are all multinationals American? Most lay observers think they are. But, in fact, the first companies with manufacturing, mining, or oil-producing facilities in several countries were British and Dutch. Some companies survive, among them the mighty Royal Dutch/Shell group of companies, one of the world's largest oil concerns, and the Anglo-Dutch Unilever group. In recent years other

Robert Rattner.

large European and Japanese companies have entered the multinational ranks. But even if it is hard to define a multinational precisely, recognition is somewhat simpler:

A multinational is a large company that produces in at least four countries, does business still farther afield, and employs people of many nationalities.

Under Attack
Multinationals have been severely criticized for being too big, too powerful, and too rich. Some critics, for example, point to General Motors' annual sales being larger than the gross national products of some of the countries in which it does business and suggest that GM is more powerful than those nations. But a top executive at IBM rebuts that charge as nonsense. "Wherever a multinational operates," he says, "it must observe local laws. And if a country wishes to, it can expropriate the local subsidiary. Can a multinational expropriate a country?" Not now, perhaps; but it was not so long ago that the United Fruit Company controlled some 4 million acres of land in Latin America and that Liberia was known as the "Firestone Republic."

Today, the financial resources of the major multinationals are so huge that they can challenge or even wreck some nations' economic and monetary policies. Rightly or wrongly, the

multinationals as a group have often been blamed for causing, or at least intensifying, the international monetary problems that have damaged the world economy in recent decades.

The reason, quite simply, is that if the multinationals' corporate treasurers decide a nation's currency is overvalued, they will shift into a safer one, thereby raising demand for it, and reducing demand for the one they have quit. Similarly, the multinationals may withhold investment in those countries which they think are politically unstable or subject to chronic inflation and put their money in those nations offering better prospects. Good business, yes; but the corporations' individual and collective decisions can have a profound influence on the wealth of nations.

In contrast, the purely national corporation, because it is usually smaller than the typical multinational and is committed to one country, enjoys less freedom to shift money and resources around the world as the prospect of profit dictates. Nor can the national company as easily shift manufacturing operations from a high-cost country to one characterized by low wages. Multinationals can, and frequently do; understandably, labor unions accuse them of exporting jobs. However, the multinational frequently has little choice,

MAJOR AMERICAN MULTINATIONALS
(sales of each exceeds $10 billion annually)

Company
Exxon
General Motors
Ford Motor
Texaco
Mobil Oil
Gulf Oil
General Electric
International Business Machines
International Tel. & Tel.
Chrysler

MAJOR FOREIGN MULTINATIONALS AND THEIR INVESTMENTS IN THE UNITED STATES

Foreign investor	Country	U.S. company	% owned	Industry
1. Royal Dutch/	Netherlands	Shell Oil	69	Oil
Shell Group	UK	Asiatic Petroleum	100	Oil
2. Anglo American	South			
Corp of South Africa Ltd	Africa	Engelhard Min. & Chem.	29	Industrial materials
		Inspiration Consol Copper	73	Copper
		Terra Chemicals Int'l	51	Chemicals
3. Tengelmann Group	Germany	Great A&P Tea	42	Supermarkets
4. British Petrol Co Ltd	UK	Standard Oil Ohio	52	Oil
		BP Pipelines	100	Alaskan pipeline
5. Friedrich Flick Group	Germany	W.R. Grace	28	Chemicals, consumer activities
		U.S. Filter	35	Pollution control, chemicals
6. B.A.T. Industries Ltd	UK	Brown & Williamson Ind.	100	Tobacco, retailing
		BATUS	100	Paper, cosmetics
7. Solvay & Cie SA	Belgium	Allied Chemical	5	Chemicals, oil and gas
		Soltex Polymer	100	Chemicals
		Hedwin	100	Plastics processing
8. Cavenham Ltd	UK	Grand Union	100	Supermarkets
9. Richard Gruner	Liechtenstein	American Airlines	5	Airlines
10. Robert Bosch GmbH	Germany	Borg-Warner	10	Chemicals, automotive parts, air conditioning
		American Microsystems	10	Computers
		Robert Bosch Corp.	100	Electronics
11. Philips NV (stockholders)	The Netherlands	North American Philips	62	Electronics
12. Unilever NV	The Netherlands	Lever Brothers	100	Consumer goods
		Thomas J. Lipton	100	Food
		Nat'l Starch & Chemical	100	Chemicals, starch, adhesives
13. Seagram Co Ltd	Canada	Joseph E. Seagram & Sons	100	Liquor, oil and gas
14. Nestlé SA	Switzerland	Nestlé Co	100	Food
		Libby, McNeill & Libby	100	Food
		Stouffer	100	Food, restaurants
		Alcon Laboratories	100	Drugs
15. Bayer AG	Germany	Mobay Chemical	100	Chemicals
		Miles Laboratories	100	Drugs
		Cutter Laboratories	100	Drugs
16. Thyssen AG	Germany	Budd	100	Automotive products
17. George Weston Ltd	Canada	Peter J. Schmitt	87	Supermarkets
		National Tea	74	Supermarkets
		Interbake	100	Bakeries
		Eastern Fine Paper	100	Paper
		Ruperts Certi-Fresh Foods	82	Fish processing
18. Imperial Chemical Industries Ltd	UK	ICI Americas	100	Chemicals
		Fiber Industries	38	Man-made fibers
19. Henkel KGaA	Germany	Clorox	19	Consumer products
		Henkel Corp	100	Specialty chemicals
20. "C.I.P." SA	Luxembourg	A.E. Staley Mfg	9	Food ingredients, animal feeds

SOURCE: Forbes.

because to compete effectively against products already being produced in low-cost countries it must move to them.

Furthermore, many manufacturing operations in developing nations produce components that are exported for assembly in the multinationals' major markets—which are the rich industrial countries. In that sense, the strategy may even create jobs at home.

A favorite governmental charge against the multinationals is that they avoid taxes by "transfer-pricing" techniques. That is, multinationals allegedly manipulate the prices that subsidiaries pay to each other so as to take profits where taxes are lowest, thereby depriving higher-tax governments of their revenues. There is plenty of evidence that some multinationals do indeed use this technique, but they point out that tax avoidance is no crime and ask rhetorically whether their strategy should be to take their profits where taxes are highest.

Conclusion: International Regulation?

Quite clearly, the multinationals will continue to be under attack for a long time, not only for the practices outlined above, but also for their sheer size and nature. To many observers, including some leading business executives, the spectacle of a giant corporation run by a few people making decisions that affect the lives of millions of people and perhaps dozens of countries is extremely distasteful. The attack on multinationals is thus as much political as economic.

The probability is that out of all the scrutiny and discussion will emerge an international consensus on the regulation of these giant corporations, with the majority of countries adopting identical or very similar laws. The process is likely to be slow, however. Although most nations agree that the multinationals need regulation, agreement for the movement virtually ends there, with each country having its own distinct ideas about the rules to be observed.

QUESTIONS

1. A multinational company may have operations in—among other countries—the United States and South Africa. In the United States the company supports the ideal of equal opportunity regardless of race and religion. In South Africa it goes along with discrimination against blacks. Is the company merely being prudent, or is it morally flawed? How should it behave?

2. A U.S. company has the choice of serving export markets by building a plant in North Carolina or Taiwan. In North Carolina it can expect a net profit after taxes equaling 5 percent of sales. In Taiwan it can expect 15 percent. Where should it locate?

3. In some Middle Eastern countries bribes to government officials are not only customary—they are also the price of doing business. Should a multinational pay the bribes and take the business, or follow strict ethical principles and let the business go?

Chapter 36

Radical Viewpoints, Old and New

Chapter Preview

What major types of radical philosophy
have grown up as reactions to capitalism?

Who was Karl Marx? What radical theories
did he propose that virtually shook the
world?

What are the strengths and weaknesses of
Marx's theories? What can we gain from
understanding them?

How do concepts of socialism and
radicalism today differ from those
developed by Marx in the third quarter of
the nineteenth century?

The history of radicalism is a history of social protest.
Protest against what? All the economic, social, political, and cultural ailments of capitalism.

Social protest is by no means new, of course. It can
be found in writings dating back at least as far as the
Old Testament. But two characteristics distinguish
radicalism from most earlier rebellions against established orders.

First, it is avowedly economic in nature. Second, it
is international in scope and appeal. Radicalism, as we
know it today, has roots less than two centuries old.
But in that time—brief, as history goes—the movement
has split into two factions. The first, socialism, seeks to
right wrongs primarily through democratic procedures. The second, communism, regards parliamentary democracy as a tool of capitalism.

Each of these broad factions has, in turn, split into
further groups. But despite the many different types of
radical theory that flourish in various parts of the
world, all groups have this much in common: *They
seek to change the structure of capitalistic institutions
and to establish new institutions for the purpose of
building a better world.*

Reactions to Capitalism:
Four Radical Philosophies

Modern socialism, like capitalism, grew out of the industrial revolution. You have already learned that early British classical economists such as Adam Smith, Thomas Malthus, and David Ricardo sought to explain and justify the economic transformation that took place in England during the late eighteenth and early nineteenth centuries. Therefore, they advocated policies of economic liberalism, namely laissez-faire and free or unrestricted international trade. At the same time, however, other scholars, both in Britain and on the Continent, were challenging the classicists with ideas of their own.

In England, for example, the factory system had already taken hold. Critics of the new order saw frightful working conditions (including cases of cruelty toward young children in the factories and mines), crowded and filthy cities, and mobs of angry workers displaced by the introduction of new machines. In France, years of wars and waste had brought crushing taxes for the support of a corrupt government, resulting in the Revolution of 1789, one of the greatest social upheavals in world history. And in Germany, manufacturers were seeking to build up industrial establishments that could compete with those in Britain.

Against this setting arose several major reactions to capitalism. They took the form of four great radical philosophies:

1. Utopian socialism.

2. Marxian socialism and communism.

3. Syndicalism.

4. Christian socialism.

We sketch briefly the historical backgrounds of these movements before proceeding to a closer examination of the second and most important one, Marxian socialism and communism.

UTOPIAN SOCIALISM

There have always been people who have dreamed of a better world. In that sense, it is correct to refer to such individuals as "socialists"—that is, as social reformers.

The first and perhaps the best book on social reform was written by Sir Thomas More (1478–1535), the famous English statesman under Henry VIII, as well as saint and martyr in the Roman Catholic Church. More's great satirical classic, Utopia (which is often required reading in English literature courses), was an attack on the evils of poverty, waste, idleness, and the institution of private property. The last, of course, is fundamental to capitalism. More was critical of conditions in England and certain other European states during the early sixteenth century. As a solution, he proposed creation of a "utopia"—an ideal city-state (somewhat similar to Plato's Republic). In this society everyone would be happily employed, there would be ample opportunity for cultural enrichment, and democracy would prevail, with all citizens working for the good of society. (The name Utopia, incidentally, which was invented by More, is Greek for no place.)

More's book stimulated a flood of publications advocating social reform—a flood that has lasted until the present day. First among the reformist writers were the utopian socialists. These were English and French theorists of the early nineteenth century who proposed the creation of model communities, largely self-contained, where the instruments of production were collectively owned, and government was primarily on a voluntary and wholly democratic basis. The chief propagators of such plans were, in England, Robert Owen (1771–1858) and, in France, Charles Fourier (1772–1837).

Robert Owen was by far the best known of the utopian socialists. In the gloomy squalor of factory life in Britain, this young Horatio Alger rose from apprentice to co-proprietor and manager, in his twenties, of a huge cotton mill at New Lanark in Scotland.

Here, in the first quarter of the nineteenth century, he built a model community of neat houses and free schools for his workers and their families. The community attracted many thousands of visitors, including political dignitaries, social reformers, writers, and businesspeople from around the world. He shortened the workday, improved working conditions, and rewarded each employee in proportion to his actual hours of labor. Later he constructed similar model communities—one of them in the United States, in New Harmony, Indiana. All of them, however, turned out to be administrative and financial failures.

Owen's place as a social reformer is significant. He played a key role during the early nineteenth century in giving England its first effective factory laws for the protection of workers. In retrospect, of course, it is now evident that Owen was a prophet of improvements he never lived to see, for his ideas profoundly influenced the betterment of industrial life in Britain and the United States.

In 1884, a movement known as Fabian socialism was founded in England. An outgrowth of utopian socialism. it advocated gradual or evolutionary reform within a democratic framework. The movement attracted many prominent people over the years. Some of its most active supporters were economists Beatrice and Sydney Webb, who helped to build the British Labour Party; the distinguished Anglo-Irish dramatist George Bernard Shaw; and the noted economist and historian G. D. H. Cole.

MARXIAN SOCIALISM AND COMMUNISM

Toward the middle of the nineteenth century, there occurred in Europe a series of events that strongly influenced the future course of the world.

In December 1847, on one of London's typically damp and cold winter days, a small but clamorous group of labor leaders met at a convention of the newly formed Communist League. There were strong currents of anxiety and trepidation in the air, for although England was relatively calm at the time, the Continent was on the verge of an upheaval. Through an almost continuous belt stretching from France to Russia there was seething discontent over the long-prevailing miseries of poverty, injustice, and political and social intolerance. No one doubted that a series of revolutions would sweep Europe in the coming months.

Among those who attended this historic meeting were two relatively young and unknown intellectual radicals. One was Karl Marx, aged twenty-nine; the other was his close friend and associate, Friedrich Engels, aged twenty-seven. They had been commissioned by the League to prepare a statement of principles and a program for action that would help incite the masses and foment revolt against the existing order of society. Their tract opened with the following inflammatory, dramatic, and ominous words:

A spectre is haunting Europe—the spectre of Communism. All the powers of old Europe have entered into a Holy Alliance to exorcise this spectre; Pope and Czar, Metternich and Guizot, French radicals and German police-spies.

After pages of historical analyses and predictions, their treatise ended with the following exhortation:

The Communists disdain to conceal their views and aims. They openly declare that their ends can be attained only by the forcible overthrow of all existing social conditions. Let the ruling classes tremble at a Communist revolution. The proletarians have nothing to lose but their chains. They have a world to win.
Working men of all countries, unite!

In the following month, January 1848, this statement of principles and objectives was published as a pamphlet under the title, *Communist Manifesto*. It is significant not for its economic content, for it had practically none. Its importance lies in the manner in which it presented Marx as a brilliant and forceful revolutionary.

But there is another side to Marx—that of a ponderous scholar and deep philosophical economist—which is of much greater significance. In most of the three decades that followed publication of the *Manifesto*, Marx devoted almost all his working time to developing an extensive and extraordinary "scientific" theory, which was eventually published as a mammoth treatise entitled *Das Kapital* (vol. I, 1867). This was the "Doomsday Book of Capitalism"—a powerfully written work in which Marx predicted the revolutionary overthrow of the capitalistic system and its ultimate replacement by a *classless* society composed only of workers, or proletarians, who would own and operate the means of production for the benefit of all.

Marx called this ultimate state "communism" in order to distinguish it from various "unscientific" forms of socialism, such as utopian socialism, which existed during his time. Much of the spirit of his ideas was incorporated in the Russian, Chinese, and Cuban revolutionary systems of communism that were established in the twentieth century. In contrast, in some Western nations various evolutionary or moderate Marxian systems were also founded, represented largely by social-democratic types of political parties. These groups have preferred to retain the title of socialism in order to help bridge the gap between certain features of Marxian theory and the rest of the socialist movement. In general, Marxism is by far the most significant of the radical philosophies to have emerged as a reaction to capitalism.

SYNDICALISM

The third great radical philosophy spawned by the industrial revolution was syndicalism. This movement, which was both a strategy of revolution and a plan for social reorganization, was influenced by the wave of anarchism that spread through parts of Europe during the late nineteenth and early twentieth centuries.

The advocates of *syndicalism* demanded the abolition of both capitalism and the state, which they viewed as instruments of oppression, and the reorganization of society into industry-wide associations or syndicates of workers. Thus, there would be a syndicate of all the steel mills, which would be owned and operated by the workers in the steel industry; a syndicate of all the coal mines made up of workers in the coal industry; and so on. In this way, the syndicates, which were fundamentally trade unions, would replace the state, each syndicate governing its own members in their activities as producers, but leaving them free from interference in all other matters. The chief exponent of syndicalism was the French social philosopher Georges Sorel (1847–1922). Ironically, his views later influenced the growth of fascism.

In the United States, the syndicalists organized a revolutionary industrial union in 1905 called the Industrial Workers of the World (IWW). The union was founded in Chicago by Eugene V. Debs, William D. Haywood, and Daniel De Leon—all of them well-known names in the history of radicalism. The group's avowed aim was to overthrow capitalism and to establish socialism by calling a general strike throughout industry, locking out employers, and seizing the nation's factories. Despite the organization's success in gathering a peak membership of 100,000 before World War I and in leading over 150 strikes, it suffered from growing internal dissension and almost fell apart after the war. However, it continued to survive. Today, with its distinctly moderate philosophy, it is a small but vigorous union.

CHRISTIAN SOCIALISM

The late nineteenth century also saw the rise of the Christian socialists, whose ideas were the most moderate of the four great radical philosophies. The movement was started in France by a Catholic priest. It then spread to England, where it caught on among a number of Protestant intellectuals and clerics, and subsequently reached the United States. Variations of it still exist in these and other countries.

In general, _Christian socialism_ is a movement of various church groups to preach the "social gospel"—a type of social legislation and reform that is grounded in theology. It seeks to improve the well-being of industrial workers by advocating the formation of labor unions, the passage of legislation, and above all by appealing to employers to respect the dignity of workers as people and as Christians, rather than as so much muscle or physical power. It also repudiates the Marxian doctrine of the class war or revolution. Among the leading forces of this movement have been Pope Leo XIII, the "working-man's Pope," whose famous encyclical _Rerum Novarum_ (1891) enunciated these principles; Pope Pius XI, whose encyclical _Quadragesimo Anno_ (1931) reaffirmed them; and the Protestant theologians Reinhold Niebuhr and Paul Tillich.

The Economic Theories of Karl Marx

None among the various radical philosophies that emerged as reactions to capitalism during the nineteenth century has had deeper or more widespread effects than that of Karl Marx. Indeed, his views, in one form or another, are the basic beliefs of more than one-third of the inhabited globe.

Marx, a "philosophical economist," was deeply influenced by the writings of the eminent early-nineteenth-century German philosopher Georg Hegel, and in particular by the Hegelian _dialectic_. This technical term denotes a method of logic or reasoning in Hegelian philosophy. It holds that any concept, which may be called a _thesis_, can have meaning only when it is related to its opposite or contradictory concept, called an _antithesis_. The interaction of the two then forms a new concept of understanding called a _synthesis_. Thus, the concept of "high" (thesis) evokes the opposite concept of "low" (antithesis), and the two then interact to form the new concept of "height" (synthesis). Similarly, contradictory concepts like "light" and "dark," "truth" and "falsity," "being" and "not being," interact to form new concepts, each of which brings us a step closer to understanding the ever-changing nature of the real world.

In Hegelian philosophy, the dialectic process, through its reconciliation of opposites, becomes a method of interpreting history. Thus, in the evolution of cultures we observe a process in which the higher form of culture triumphs over the lower form. In the development of art, one "period" is succeeded by another. In the history of religion, primitive and simplistic types of worship give way to more sophisticated forms and concepts. In general, history is a record of progress from lower to higher manifestations of the dialectic principle.

How did these Hegelian ideas influence Marx's thinking? We can seek to answer this question by sketching briefly the fundamental doctrines that appear in his enormous work _Das Kapital_ (translated _Capital_), Volume I of which was published in 1867:

1. Economic interpretation of history.

2. Theory of value and wages.

3. Theory of surplus value and capital accumulation.

4. The class struggle.

5. Theory of socialistic and communistic evolution.

These doctrines constitute the framework of Marxian theory. Although they are attributed to Marx, they were formulated during his many years of association with his close friend and intellectual collaborator, Friedrich Engels. Each man had a profound influence on the other.

ECONOMIC INTERPRETATION OF HISTORY

Marx sought to discover the basic principles of history. His method was to construct what he regarded as a completely logical system in which he presented in scientific fashion the laws of historical development, the sources of economic and social power, and a prediction of the inevitable future.

In order to predict the future course of events, Marx had to understand the causal forces that were at work. This, he believed, could only be done by studying the past. Hence, he looked for the fundamental causes of historical events, and he found them in the economic environments in which societies develop.

> According to Marx, all great political, social, intellectual, and ethical movements of history are determined by the ways in which societies organize their social institutions to carry on the basic economic activities of production, exchange, distribution, and consumption of goods. Although economic motives may not always be the sole cause of human behavior, every fundamental historical development is basically the result of changes in the way in which one or more of these economic activities is carried out. This, in essence, is the *economic interpretation of history*.

Thus in the Marxian system economic forces are the prime cause of change—the alpha and omega of history—which operate with the inevitability of natural laws to determine the development of a society. Even the Protestant Reformation of the sixteenth century, which for all intents and purposes was a major religious movement in world history, was cloaked in ideological veils according to Marx, thereby concealing its true causes, which were basically economic.

Dialectical Materialism

This philosophy became known as *dialectical materialism*. It was a method of historical analysis used by Marx which employed the philosopher Hegel's idea that historical change is the result of conflicting forces and that these forces are basically economic or materialistic. In the Marxian view of history, every economic system, based on a set of established production, exchange, distribution, and consumption relationships, grows to a state of maximum efficiency and then develops internal contradictions or weaknesses which cause it to decay. By this time the roots of an opposing system have already begun to take hold. Eventually this new system displaces the old while absorbing its most useful features. This dynamic process continues, with society being propelled from one historical stage to another as each new system triumphs over the old.

THEORY OF VALUE AND WAGES

The second major doctrine in Marxian economics is the theory of value and wages. This, of course, was also a fundamental area of concern to the classical economists who preceded Marx—including Smith, Ricardo, and others. But Marx, unlike the classical economists, used these concepts to a different end in explaining the historical development and future course of capitalism.

To Marx, the term "value" had the same meaning as it had to other orthodox economists both before and after. *Value* is the power of a commodity to command other commodities in exchange for itself. This power is measured by the proportional quantities in which a commodity exchanges with all other commodities. Likewise, to Marx and other economists, the *price* of a commodity is its power to command money in exchange for itself. Price is simply the "money name" of the value of a commodity.

But what determines the value of a commodity? The answer, according to Marx, is labor. In his words:

> That which determines the magnitude of the value of any article is the amount of . . . labor-time socially necessary for its production. . . . Commodities, therefore, in which equal quantities of labor are embodied, or which can be produced in the same time, have the same value. The value of one commodity is to the value of another, as the labor-time necessary for the production of one is to that necessary for the production of the other. As values, all commodities are only definite masses of congealed labor-time.

In general terms, therefore, if it takes twice as much labor-time to produce coats as hats, the price of coats will be twice the price of hats. Note from the last sentence of the quotation that Marx did not restrict his concept of labor-time to direct labor spent on the production of commodities. He included indirect labor as well, such as the labor-time necessary to construct the factories and machines which are then used to produce other goods. Therefore:

> *Since capital and other commodities are congealed labor,* they are all reducible to the common denominator of labor-time and will exchange for one another at prices that are proportional to the amount of labor-time they contain.

From this theory of value, it was a short step for Marx to develop his theory of wages. In his view, a mature capitalistic society consists of only two classes—a capitalist class, which owns and controls the means of production, and a working class, which owns and controls nothing and is subservient to the capitalist class. (The land-owning class, at this relatively advanced stage of capitalism's development, had declined to a position of minor importance.) This leads to the following theory of wages:

> The capitalist class finds, in its competitive struggle to earn profits, that it must pay the lowest possible level of wages to the working class. The wages it will pay, therefore, will be at a subsistence level—a wage level that is just high enough for the working population to maintain itself, based primarily on its physical or biological needs and to a lesser extent on its social and customary needs.

This theory of wages, it may be noted, did not originate with Marx. It was the familiar *subsistence theory of wages* which Marx adopted from the classical economists who preceded him.

THEORY OF SURPLUS VALUE AND CAPITAL ACCUMULATION

When Marx combined his theories of value and wages, the logical outcome was the third feature of his theoretical system: the doctrine of surplus value. From this, there emerged the natural process of capital accumulation.

Surplus Value

In Marx's model, surplus value arises in the following way. When workers are employed in the production of a commodity, it is the capitalist who sets the length of the working day. Thus, on the one hand, the value of what the workers produce is determined by the labor-time embodied in the commodity. On the other hand, the wage that the workers receive is determined by the "subsistence level" of living. The workers do not stop production when the value of what they create is equal to their subsistence wage. Instead they continue to produce, and the value that they create over and above their subsistence wage represents "surplus value," which goes to the capitalist. In numerical terms, the capitalist may set the working day at 12 hours, but the workers may each produce a value equal to their subsistence wage in 7 hours. The remaining 5 hours of their labor-time is, therefore, surplus value which is literally appropriated or stolen by the capitalist.

To Marx, surplus value is the driving force of the capitalistic system—the key incentive that prompts capitalists to carry on production. Efforts on the part of capitalists to increase surplus value may take the form of increasing the length of the working day, intensifying or speeding up the workers' production (by offering "piece rates" or other incentives), and introducing labor-saving machinery, thereby permitting some workers to be released while those who remain are made to work longer hours or more intensively.

Capital Accumulation

What do capitalists do with the surplus value which, according to Marx, has been literally stolen from the labor of workers? Marx's answer is that capitalists use part of the surplus for their personal consumption and part to acquire more labor and machines. They acquire these, of course, because they expect to get back more money than they lay out. The inflow of surpluses, over and above the capitalists' money outlays, continues in an unending series from one production operation to the next, thereby generating a sequence of capital accumulations. Thus, whereas other economists contended that capitalists were engaging in "abstinence" or "saving" when they acquired funds to hire more labor for production, Marx argued that the funds which capitalists "saved" were stolen from workers in the form of surplus value.

These ideas, which lie at the heart of the Marxian model of capitalism, may be summarized briefly:

> *Surplus value* is the difference between the value that workers create as determined by the labor-time embodied in a commodity that they produce, and the value that they receive as determined by the subsistence level of wages. Surplus value is not created by capitalists, but is appropriated by them through their exploitation of the worker. Hence, capitalists are robbers who steal the fruits of the laborers' toil. The accumulation of capital comes from surplus value and is the key to, as well as the incentive for, the development of a capitalistic system.

It is interesting to note that Marx harbored no particular animosity toward capitalists as such, even though they were characterized by Marx as greedy robber barons. In Marx's view it was the competitive capitalistic system itself that was evil. Capitalists were merely participants in the great race. They had to exploit and accumulate or else they would be exploited and accumulated.

THE CLASS STRUGGLE

What are the consequences of capitalistic production? In order to answer this question, Marx turned to an examination of the past, and again used the method of dialectical analysis—thesis and antithesis—to interpret the historical process.

All history, he said, is composed of struggles between classes. In ancient Rome it was a struggle between patricians and plebeians and between masters and slaves. In the Middle Ages it was a conflict between guildmasters and journeymen and between lords and serfs. And in the modern society that has sprouted from the ruins of feudal society, class antagonisms have narrowed down to a struggle between two opposing groups—the oppressing capitalist or bourgeois class and the oppressed proletariat or working class. The former derive their income from *owning* the means of production and from exploiting the labor of workers. The latter own nothing but their labor power and, since they are dependent for a living upon the receipt of a wage, must sell their labor power in order to exist.

What is the role of the state in this two-class society? Marx's answer was precise: "The state," he said, "is nothing but the organized collective power of the possessing classes." It is an agency controlled by the bourgeoisie to advance its own interests, and its power "grows stronger in proportion as the class antagonisms with the state grow sharper." The state, in short, is an agency of oppression.

The Consequences of Capitalist Production

The class struggle might go on indefinitely, according to Marx, were it not for certain "contradictions" that automatically and inevitably develop within the capitalistic system. Among the more important ones are these:

1. *Increasing Unemployment*   The capitalists' drive to increase their surplus value and to accumulate capital results in the displacement of labor (i.e., in modern terminology, technological unemployment), and in ever-increasing misery as a "reserve army of the unemployed" builds up.

2. *Declining Rate of Profits*   As capital accumulates, a growing proportion of it goes into physical capital such as labor-saving machinery, which yields no surplus value, while a declining proportion of it goes into human capital or labor, which is the sole producer of surplus value. Hence, the capitalists' rate of profit—or the surplus value that they appropriate from labor—tends to be a declining percentage of the total capital that is accumulated.

3. *Business Cycles*   With increasing unemployment, a declining rate of profit, and the tendency for wages to remain at the subsistence level, uncertainty and instability are inevitable. Depressions recur "each time more threateningly" as capitalists find themselves under continual competitive pressure to acquire more physical capital and to displace workers.

4. *Concentration and Monopolization of Capital*   Competition among capitalists thus becomes increasingly intense. A dog-eat-dog situation develops as small capitalists are either fatally weakened or absorbed by a few larger ones. In this way capital becomes concentrated in large-scale industrial units or monopolies. As Marx put it, "hand in hand with this centralization" of capital goes the "expropriation of many capitalists by the few."

5. *Finance Capitalism and Imperialism*   Marx implied that a fifth "contradiction" would emerge from the monopoly stage of capitalistic development. The nature of this contradiction was amplified in the early twentieth century by V. I. Lenin, the founder of Soviet Russia. Lenin argued that the growing tendency toward concentration and monopolization of capital would produce an economy dominated by "finance capital." In this situation, huge business trusts or monopolies, in conjunction with a handful of large banks, control and manipulate the masses. Those who manage finance capital will then reach out beyond their own national boundaries, forming cartels and international combines to dominate and control the markets and resources of other nations. When this happens, the economy has reached the stage of "capitalistic imperialism"—the highest stage of capitalism.

Summary

Marx concluded that these conditions, especially the first, imposed miseries and hardships on workers which they would not tolerate indefinitely. The working class, he said, would eventually revolt against the capitalist class and bring about a system in which economic justice prevails. Before we examine the nature of this change, let us summarize the foregoing Marxian ideas briefly.

> The *class struggle* represents an irreconcilable clash of interests between the bourgeoisie or capitalist class and the proletariat or working class. The source of this clash is the surplus value which capitalists steal from workers. This results over the long run in increasing unemployment, a declining rate of profit, business cycles, concentration of capital, and finance capitalism and imperialism.

According to Marx, the class struggle will eventually be resolved when the proletariat overthrows the bourgeoisie and establishes a new and equitable economic order.

THEORY OF SOCIALIST AND COMMUNIST EVOLUTION

Marx held that capitalism must someday receive its death blow at the hands of the workers. When this happens, capitalism will be succeeded by socialism, which Marx regarded as a *transitory stage* on the road to communism. This stage will have two major characteristics:

1. *"Dictatorship of the proletariat."* This is a state of affairs in Marxian socialism in which the bourgeoisie have been toppled from power and are subject to the control of the working class. In other words, the "ex-

propriators have been expropriated," and capitalists' properties are under the management of the proletariat, who are also in control of the state.

2. *Payment in accordance with work performed.* This means that laborers will earn wages, each worker receiving "for an equal quantity of labor an equal quantity of products," and "he who does not work, shall not eat."

Socialism, in Marxian ideology, may thus be defined as a transitory stage between capitalism and full communism. That is, Marxian socialism is a stage in which the means of production are owned by the state, the state in turn is controlled by workers ("dictatorship of the proletariat"), and the economy's social output is distributed by the formula: from each according to his ability, to each according to his labor.

> *Communism*, in Marxian ideology, is the final, perfect goal of historical development. It means:
>
> 1. A classless society in which all people live by earning and no person lives by owning.
>
> 2. The state is nonexistent, having been relegated to the museum of antiquities "along with the bronze ax and the spinning wheel."
>
> 3. The wage system is abolished and all citizens live and work according to the motto: *"from each according to his ability, to each according to his needs."*

This last quotation, it may be noted, represents the essence of pure communism and is one of the most famous phrases in all of literature. (See *Leaders in Economics*, page 627.)

Evaluation of Marxian Theory

Now that we have sketched the main features of Marxian theory, it is appropriate for us to discuss its achievements and failures. It is evident that Marx sought to reach three major objectives:

1. To develop a *theory of history* that would explain the fundamental causes of capitalistic development.

2. To formulate *theories of value, wages, and surplus value* that would describe the basic processes at work in the capitalistic economy.

3. To establish a foundation for *revolutionary socialism and communism.*

We may evaluate Marx's theories in terms of these objectives.

THEORY OF HISTORY

As you recall, Marx's interpretation of history was based on *economic* thesis and antithesis. Although he recognized that political, social, and other factors influenced historical development, he regarded them as distinctly subordinate. To him, the basic or causal forces were fundamentally economic, centering around the activities and institutions relating to production, exchange, distribution, and consumption of goods.

Critics have pointed out that this is a one-sided, oversimplified interpretation because it leaves out or fails to give sufficient weight to the many noneconomic forces and institutions in history. Despite this criticism, many distinguished historians have long believed that Marx's interpretation of history provided the first deep awareness of the importance of economic forces in the historical process.

In the past several decades modern historians have increasingly incorporated economic causation in their historical studies. Although it cannot be said that Marx was solely responsible for this trend, there is general agreement that his approach to the study of history played a significant role.

THEORIES OF VALUE, WAGES, AND SURPLUS VALUE

Marx's theory of value, we have seen, was a *labor theory of value.* In essence, his argument can be stated in the form of a syllogism. This is a type of reasoning in formal logic consisting of two premises or assumptions, and a logical conclusion which follows directly from the premises. Thus, according to Marx:

Labor creates all value.

Labor does not receive all the value it has created.

Therefore, labor is being cheated.

It should be remembered, of course, that according to Marx the first premise is true because capital and all other commodities are nothing more than congealed labor. The second premise is true because labor receives a subsistence wage which is less than the value it creates. And the conclusion is true because capitalists literally appropriate or steal the surplus value of labor for themselves.

Was Marx correct? We can answer this question by offering the following criticisms of his ideas, based on economic principles and concepts learned in previous chapters.

Neglect of Entrepreneurial Functions

By attributing all value to labor alone, Marx neglected the functions performed by the entrepreneur as a risk taker and organizer of the factors of production. Without the entrepreneur, labor would be an amorphous mass. It is the entrepreneur who gives "shape

Leaders in Economics
Karl Heinrich Marx   1818–1883

If it is true that people are ultimately judged by the influence of their ideas, then Karl Marx surely ranks as one of the most important individuals who ever lived. For his thoughts have shaped the policies of nations and have affected the lives of millions of people.

Who was Karl Marx? He was born in Treves, Germany, the son of a successful lawyer with liberal philosophical leanings. The young Marx was educated at the Universities of Bonn and Berlin, and received his doctorate in philosophy from the University of Jena in 1841 at the age of twenty-three.

In Marx's undergraduate years his radical ideas began to flourish when he fell in with an extremist student group called the Young Hegelians—disciples of the German philosopher Georg Hegel. During the 1840s, while Marx was still in his twenties, he spent short periods in Germany, France, and Britain, always one step ahead of the police, who continually sought to expel him because of his incendiary articles extolling communism and revolution in newspapers and other periodicals, and his attacks against religion and utopian socialism. "Religion," he once wrote in a quotation that has since become famous, ". . . is the sigh of the oppressed creature . . . the opium of the people." As for utopian socialism, it was "unscientific" because it lacked an understanding of the role of history and of the certainty of the class struggle.

It was also during the 1840s that Marx became involved with the two most important people of his life. One of them was Jenny von Westphalen, daughter of an aristocrat who was a district attorney of Treves. The other was a gallant named Friedrich Engels, son of a wealthy industrialist.

Marx married Jenny, whom he had known since childhood; she was literally "the girl next door." The match itself was a study of opposites. She was slender, beautiful, and genteel; he was short, stocky, and caustic. But they loved each other deeply, and she gave up her refined and prestigious life in Treves in return for his unstinting devotion to her and to their children. Their life together was one of great hardship and extreme poverty as they moved from one slum to another while Marx struggled to earn a living—a task which, as a writer, he never mastered.

Marx met Engels during a brief stay in Paris in 1843. The two men struck up an immediate intellectual rapport. This fact was especially surprising because Engels' father was a rich businessman who owned factories in Germany and England, and the young Engels never exhibited any aversion to the social and monetary advantages which this background afforded him. Engels became Marx's lifelong friend, collaborator, and alter ego, as well as his benefactor. Indeed, there is no evidence that Marx ever had any other close friends.

In 1849, after being hounded by police and expelled from three countries, Marx moved to London, where he lived, except for brief intervals, until the time of his death. Here he existed in the depths of poverty, depending for bare survival on small and irregular remunerations of $5 to $10 that he received for articles submitted to the *New York Tribune,* and on the benevolence of Engels, who, for some unexplained reason, led a double life. He was fully in accord with Marx's anticapitalistic views, yet he also managed his father's factory in Manchester and even held a seat on the Manchester Stock Exchange.

Marx sacrificed everything for his research, an activity which engaged his full time and effort from morning until night in the great library of the British Museum. The result, after many years of painstaking work, was the publication of his enormous treatise, *Das Kapital* (vol. I, 1867). But his health was never too good. In 1881, after the death of two of his five chil-

Historical Picture Service, Chicago.
Friedrich Engels (left) *with Karl Marx and his family.*

dren, his devoted and tired wife Jenny also passed away, and Marx followed her two years later. His eulogy was delivered by Engels and the funeral was attended by eight persons.

Engels labored on Marx's notes for the next several years, thereby making possible the publication of volumes II and III of *Das Kapital* (1885, 1894). Four additional volumes entitled *Theorien über den Mehrwert (Theories of Surplus Value)* were published from still other notes in the period 1905–1910. On the basis of these and other writings, Marx has come to be regarded as an economist of major significance. But note this important point: It was Lenin, not Marx, who fashioned the content of communism. Marx predicted its eventual occurrence, while it remained for Lenin to design the final structure. This he did in his writings and speeches during the first two decades of the present century, and in his founding of Soviet Russia after the Revolution of 1917.

and form" to labor by bringing workers together, providing them with capital, and giving them a purpose for working. In a socialistic or communistic society, these functions might be performed by the government or by a committee of workers, but they are functions that must be performed by somebody.

Failure to Recognize Demand

Marx's theory of value, based as it was on the labor-time embodied in a commodity, failed to recognize that the normal value of a good is as much a result of demand as of supply. As we know already, in a competitive capitalistic system the concept of long-run normal value is that of an equilibrium value which reflects diverse consumer demands bidding for the services and products of scarce factors of production. This means that consumers must be willing and able to buy and to express their preferences through the price system if prices are to serve the function of inducing both human and nonhuman resources into production. Marx did not fully understand this role of the price system, and hence his theory of value provided an inaccurate and unrealistic measure of the real values at which commodities are exchanged.

Inadequate Theoretical Support of Surplus Value

Surplus value, according to Marx, arises because workers are paid a subsistence wage which is less than the value of the commodities that they create. The question we must now ask is whether this theory of surplus value is plausible. The answer appears to be no, for the following reasons:

1. *Definition of subsistence is vague.* Marx did not use the concept of subsistence in a consistent manner, nor did he define it as a determinate quantity. At certain times he employed the term in a biological sense to refer to the goods needed for physical well-being, and at other times he used it to mean the "conventional" goods to which people become "socially accustomed."

2. *Competition will eliminate the surplus.* Marx placed strong emphasis on the competitive forces that exist in a capitalistic society—and in particular the highly competitive relationships among capitalists themselves. This means that if wages are sufficiently flexible to adjust to the "socially accustomed" level of living, there is every reason to believe that the surplus itself will be eliminated as capitalist employers bid higher and higher wages for the services of employees. For if a worker yields a surplus to *his* or *her* capitalist employer, it will pay for *some other* capitalist employer to hire the worker away at a higher wage. Competition among capitalists will thus bid wages up to a level at which the surplus no longer exists.

These are among the chief reasons to conclude that Marx's theory of surplus value lacks theoretical support. Further, there is no concrete evidence to indicate that there exists in the capitalistic system a fund of value of the type that Marx conceived in his concept of surplus value. This does not necessarily mean, however, that a surplus does not exist. Modern radical economists believe that it does, as you will see later in this chapter.

REVOLUTIONARY SOCIALISM AND COMMUNISM

Marx predicted that the increasing misery of workers would prompt the proletariat class to overthrow capitalism and to replace it first by socialism and then by communism. This, he said, would be the inevitable result of the "internal contradictions" that were inherent in capitalism and that would eventually destroy it.

Was Marx's prediction correct? For the most part, no—at least not in the sense that he meant. But despite the mistakes that exist in the Marxian model, the views of its author have long been accepted by hundreds of millions of people in many nations. In some totalitarian countries his theory was adopted intact; in many nontotalitarian nations a brand of "modified" or "revised" Marxism developed. We may refer to the latter as *post-Marxism*. This type of socialism is not necessarily antagonistic to capitalism. However, it seeks to achieve socialistic goals through a much greater degree of government regulation and control than exists in market-oriented capitalistic systems. More will be said about this later.

CONCLUSIONS: THREE QUESTIONS

We may conclude this evaluation of Marxian theory by answering briefly three fundamental questions that are often asked.

Have Marx's Deductions Been Borne Out?

Some of Marx's deductions of the "economic consequences of capitalist production" have evidently not been realized. There are several reasons.

First, the proletariat, far from experiencing increasing misery, has in fact experienced a long-run growth of real wages and a rising standard of living.

Second, the rate of profits has not declined, nor have business cycles been entirely an overproduction phenomenon as Marx claimed.

Third, the proletariat and the capitalist, at least in the United States, have not congealed into two distinct and opposing classes. Indeed, they often overlap to the extent that the great majority of corporation stockholders are also workers. And in the United States, most corporate stock is owned by households, not only directly, but also indirectly through pension funds.

There is thus no question that some of Marx's most important theoretical deductions have turned out to be fallacious.

Are There Elements of Truth in Marx's Predictions?

Despite his incorrect predictions of economic events, we cannot conclude that Marx was totally wrong. Some of his prophecies contained important truths. For example:

1. It would be foolish to deny that technological, cyclical, and structural unemployment have continued to plague the capitalistic system.

2. There has certainly been a growth in the concentration of capital and monopoly power since the time of Marx's writing during the third quarter of the nineteenth century. (However, there is considerable disagreement among economists as to the direction of monopoly trends during most of the present century.)

3. Although capitalism has not ended in final collapse, it was certainly dealt a serious blow in 1930 with the emergence of a prolonged and desperate depression that eventually ushered in many new measures of social reform.

On this score, therefore, some of Marx's prophecies were disturbingly meaningful.

What Is the Value of Marxian Theory?

We are thus led to conclude that Marx put his finger on some of the most important economic problems of our society. Among them: unemployment, business cycles, and industrial concentration and monopoly, to mention a few. Most of our efforts in previous chapters were devoted to the development of methods for curing these ills within a framework of capitalism. It is appropriate, therefore, that we now turn our attention to examining the ways in which modern socialism—a system rooted in Marxian ideology—seeks to solve these and other basic economic problems.

Development and Meaning of Socialism

When the nineteenth century drew to a close, Marxism had already become an international movement of considerable significance. But it was a movement whose members had divergent viewpoints. As a result, the followers of Marx began to divide into two factions. One of these consisted of a large and heterogeneous majority called "revisionists"; the other was composed of a smaller but more homogeneous minority known as "strict Marxists."

The basic philosophies of these two groups are implied by their names:

> The revisionists believe that the theories of Marx must be *revised* in order to accord with conditions of the times, and that socialism should be achieved by peaceful and gradual means through a process of evolution rather than revolution. The strict Marxists, on the other hand, adhere to a literal interpretation of their master's teachings, contending that the workers of the world form one great brotherhood which must revolt in order to overthrow the capitalistic system and establish a dictatorship of the proletariat.

Since the early part of this century, the revisionists have been in control of most of the socialist parties of Western nations. Further, since the first third of this century, socialistic governments have been in power at one time or another in a number of democratic countries. These include England, France, Sweden, Norway, Denmark, Australia, and New Zealand. In most of these and various other nations, socialist leaders were placed in office—and subsequently voted out of office—through free elections. This suggests that when we talk about socialism we are referring to *democratic* socialism of the liberal reformist type, as distinguished from authoritarian socialism such as exists in the Soviet Union, Eastern Europe, Cuba, and China.

SOCIALISM BETWEEN WORLD WARS I AND II

In order to appreciate the meaning of modern democratic socialism, it is desirable that we sketch briefly the historical development of socialist thought and practice in the period between the two world wars.

During the 1920s and 1930s, socialists of peaceful Marxian persuasion both in Europe and America launched a renewed and vigorous attack against the shortcomings of capitalism. Expressions like "economic inequality," "chronic unemployment," "private wealth and public poverty," and "degeneration of social and cultural values" became familiar shibboleths. In Europe, social democratic parties were strongly committed to revisionist Marxism, the solidarity of the working class, and the ultimate establishment of socialism by democratic means as a way of correcting the deficiencies of the capitalistic system. This was an era of great ferment in socialist activity.

The Theoretical Model

At the same time, some economists at European and American universities began to grapple with a question that eventually evolved into one of the most interesting controversies in the history of economics. The essence of the problem may be summarized by recalling that in the theoretical or pure model of capitalism there are at least three important features:

1. The means of production are privately owned.

2. Product and resource prices are freely determined in competitive markets.

3. Resources are allocated efficiently in accordance with consumer and occupational choice.

Now, if we adopt the classical definition of socialism as an economy in which the means of production are owned by society, the question we ask is this:

> Can a socialistic economic system, seeking to be democratic rather than authoritarian, and lacking the prices that are freely established in competitive markets, achieve the same degree of efficiency in resource allocation as the pure model of capitalism, without destroying the basic economic freedoms of consumer and occupational choice?

This question, it may be noted, is the fundamental theoretical problem of democratic socialism.

Notice that the issue is complicated by the fact that the system must remain democratic. It might be easier to achieve greater efficiencies in resource use by *telling* consumers what they can have and by *ordering* workers to their jobs, but such actions would be completely contrary to the basic philosophy of democratic socialism.

This problem became the subject of widespread discussion in the 1930s and was finally resolved in 1938 with the publication of a remarkable theoretical model of a socialist economy. The chief architect of the model was a well-known Polish economist, Oskar Lange.

According to this theoretical model, a democratic socialist economy could be administered by a Central Planning Board which would set prices *as if* the competitive market had set them. The Board would, for example, manipulate prices in the product and resource markets with the objective of equating supplies and demands, thereby assuring that equilibrium was maintained without surpluses or shortages. In this way the Board, through *trial and error,* would guide the factors of production into their most efficient uses in accordance with the wishes expressed by households—*all through the operation of a price system which permits freedom of consumer and occupational choice.*

This type of economy, the socialist theorists contended, would yield a double benefit.

First, it would achieve efficient resource utilization as in the theoretical competitive model of capitalism.

Second, and simultaneously, it would overcome the major disadvantages of real-world capitalism. How? By bringing about (1) a more equitable distribution of income resulting from the elimination of private ownership, (2) an adjustment of production according to consumer demands, and (3) a continuous high level of employment assured by stable investment policies by government.

POSTWAR DEVELOPMENTS: THE MEANING OF MODERN SOCIALISM

The outbreak of World War II prevented these ideas from being pursued further. Nor were they taken up again after the war—for three major reasons:

1. Mixed capitalistic countries of Western Europe experienced high rates of economic growth during the postwar years, thereby discrediting the widely held socialistic belief that capitalism was an outmoded economic system.

2. Several conservative governments in Western Europe adopted many far-reaching social-welfare measures which socialist leaders supported with pride.

3. Various nationalization policies (i.e., government takeovers of major industries) in some West European nations turned out unsuccessfully, creating problems of excessive bureaucratization and inefficiency which were even greater than the problems that nationalization was designed to solve.

These developments led to a substantial change in orthodox socialist thinking. Many social democratic parties abandoned their traditional opposition to private property and their goal of *total* social ownership, and turned their attention instead to "improving the mix" in already mixed economies. As a result, the following definition of socialism reflects the views of contemporary socialist thinkers:

> *Socialism* is a movement that seeks to improve economic efficiency and equity by establishing (1) public ownership of all important means of production and distribution, and (2) some degree of centralized planning to determine what goods to produce, how they should be produced, and to whom they should be distributed.

As you can see, therefore, the core of socialism is *economic.* Socialism's goal is to transform capitalism by altering its most fundamental feature—the institution of private property.

Radical Socialism—The New Left

Since the decade of the sixties, a new wave of radical socialism has swept across the major Western democracies. Frequently referred to as the New Left, the members of this movement are mostly political and social activists who take an aggressive stand on many fundamental issues. For example, they press for greater social and economic equality, more "worker control" over economic enterprises, nationalization of large firms, and an end to war and imperialism by advanced nations. Unlike many other socialists, the newer radicals regard centralized authority with disdain. Hence, they are not admirers of the Soviet Union or of any system that suppresses freedom of expression.

The radical socialists have not developed a complete philosophy or body of thought. However, they have many interesting things to say about economic matters. We can gain an appreciation of some of their main ideas by focusing attention on two fundamental areas: the problem of resource allocation and the nature of surplus value.

RESOURCE ALLOCATION: FREE MARKETS VERSUS COOPERATIVE PLANNING

As you have seen in a number of earlier chapters, the free market plays a central role in capitalistic societies. Through the unhampered interaction of supply and demand, the market mechanism accomplishes several major objectives:

1. It provides producers with information about consumer preferences.

2. It allocates society's resources in accordance with these preferences.

3. It encourages the most economical choice of production techniques.

4. It synthesizes the individual buying and selling decisions of millions of households and firms.

For these reasons, it is understandable why the free market has often been extolled by distinguished political as well as economic leaders. (See Box 1.)

Despite these apparent virtues, adherents of the New Left are not persuaded that the free market is the most desirable device for allocating resources. On the contrary, they believe strongly that the market mechanism is both socially and economically objectionable—even evil—for the following reasons:

1. The free market creates economic instability in the form of unemployment and inflation. Government policies may at times succeed in reducing instability, but history shows clearly that government policies are often ill conceived and improperly administered because they are designed to preserve the market mechanism rather than replace it.

2. The market system perpetuates economic and social inequalities—unjustified disparities in the distribution of income, wealth, and power. Two fundamental institutions of capitalism, private property and inheritance, are among the root causes of economic inequality, while a third institution—the market system—permits inequalities to continue.

3. The free market causes an inefficient distribution of resources between private and social goods—a lack of *social balance*. This happens because the market system, through advertising and promotion, favors the production of private goods (such as automobiles, television sets, and stereos) for which consumers can voluntarily express their preferences by prices offered. At the same time, the free market suppresses the production of social goods (such as schools, libraries, and public hospitals) which come into existence only through compulsory taxes. In other words, as a result of the market system, too much private expenditure goes to satisfy superficial wants artificially created, while many fundamental public needs are neglected because they cannot compete successfully for the same resources.

Supporters of the New Left thus conclude:

> The market system is inefficient, inequitable, and immoral. It perpetuates a class structure that associates wealth with privilege, and poverty with oppression. These problems cannot be solved within the framework of existing capitalistic institutions. Therefore, the institutions themselves must be changed before any significant improvements in human welfare can be realized.

In other words, radical socialists believe that the market system should be replaced by some alternative decision-making process which promotes society's well-being—economic as well as moral and cultural.

Cooperative Planning

If free markets are strongly opposed by New Leftists, what mechanism do they advocate for providing information and allocating resources? The most obvious answer would appear to be central planning—a method used in varying degrees by socialistic countries for decades. Under central planning, the government decides what goods will be produced, how they will be produced, and to whom the output will be distributed. At the very least, therefore, central planning requires government to exercise substantial control over most, if not all, important phases of economic activity.

Box 1
The Free Market

The free market is not only a more efficient decision-maker than even the wisest central planning body, but even more important, the free market keeps economic power widely dispersed. It is thus a vital underpinning of our democratic system.

John F. Kennedy

United Press International.

I am convinced that if it were the result of deliberate human design, and if the people guided by the price changes understood that their decisions have significance far beyond their immediate aim, this mechanism would have been acclaimed as one of the greatest triumphs of the human mind. Its misfortune is the double one that it is not the product of human design and that the people guided by it usually do not know why they are made to do what they do.

Friedrich A. Hayek

United Press International.

Today's New Leftists do not subscribe to these views of President Kennedy or Nobel prize winner Hayek. To the radical socialists, the market mechanism fosters inequality and oppression rather than equity and freedom.

This solution poses a basic problem for New Leftists. Most of them are as strongly opposed to traditional forms of central planning as to free markets—for two reasons:

1. *Bureaucratic Inefficiency* Experiences in socialistic countries show that central planning leads to bureaucracy—excessive multiplication and concentration of power in administrative bureaus—with resulting inefficiency and waste. The benefits of central planning are thus lost to society through resource misallocation and reduction of output.

2. *Authoritarian Management* The growth of bureaucracy, as the evidence also shows, results in autocratic or "top-down" decision making. Sacrifices are imposed upon workers without their prior advice or consent.

New Leftists are thus led to the conclusion that a third method of resource allocation—one that avoids what they regard as the undesirable consequences of both the free market and central planning—is needed. The method they advocate may be called "participative decision making" or "cooperative planning."

According to New Leftists, cooperative planning is the ideal method of resource allocation. Cooperative planning entails (1) educating people to their "true needs," (2) eliminating "economic waste" caused by unproductive labor, and (3) preserving democratic traditions through worker participation in decision making at both the company and national levels. Adoption of cooperative planning would lead to "production for use" rather than for profit, within a social framework oriented toward collaboration (rather than competition) for mutual benefit.

These ideas—particularly the expressions in quotation marks—require some further comment. As we shall see, they are directly related to the notion of *surplus value*, a concept of fundamental importance both in Marxian and New Left thinking.

THE NATURE OF SURPLUS VALUE

As you recall, Marx defined a society's "surplus" as the difference between the value of goods created by workers and the subsistence wage they actually receive. In other words, Marx viewed a capitalistic economy's surplus as consisting of profits, rent, and interest—the sum of which rightfully belongs to workers but is expropriated (literally stolen) by capitalists.

New Leftists believe that Marx's definition of surplus was adequate for his time, but that the concept must be broadened to reflect the greater complexity of today's advanced capitalistic economies. Accordingly, adherents of the New Left define economic surplus in a capitalistic society as the *difference between the* market value of all final goods and services produced during a period and the socially necessary costs of producing them. Thus, if the total market value of all final goods and services produced in the economy during a given year—called gross national product or GNP—is $1 billion, and the socially necessary costs of producing that output are $400 million, then the society's economic surplus for that year is $600 million.

The question that must be asked, of course, is what is the meaning of "socially necessary costs"? New Leftists define this concept for measurement purposes as the sum of three types of expenditures:

1. *Replacement Investment*   This is the value of plant and equipment used up or depreciated each year in producing the nation's final output—its GNP.

This amount of investment expenditure is thus necessary to replace that part of GNP which is worn out.

2. *Payments for Productive Labor*   This class of expenditures consists of wages paid to workers producing "socially useful output"—an expression widely employed but not clearly defined by New Leftists. They hold that in a capitalistic economy, a substantial share of the surplus is used to support largely "unproductive" activities—among them excessive advertising and administration (both in business and government). In a socialistic economy, most of these expenditures would be socially unnecessary, leaving a larger proportion of society's resources to be employed in more constructive activities.

3. *Minimal Costs of Government*   This class of expenditures includes only those costs of government needed to carry on essential services—education, public health, judicial administration, police and fire protection, planning, and so on. All other expenditures on government in capitalistic societies—such as expenditures for war and imperialism—are wasteful, and serve only to absorb a large part of the surplus that could better be used for producing needed social goods.

In summary, therefore:

Modern radical socialists (New Leftists) define economic surplus as consisting not only of profits, rent, and interest as Marx contended, but also of socially unnecessary costs in both the private and public sectors. This concept of economic surplus is, therefore, much broader than the view held by Marx.

These ideas can be expressed by two simple equations.

According to Marx:

economic surplus = profits + rent + interest

According to the New Leftists:

economic surplus = profits + rents + interest
+ socially unnecessary costs

What Happens to the Surplus?

Radical socialists believe that over the long run, the economy's surplus tends to rise—both in absolute terms and as a percentage of GNP. According to some estimates, the surplus today in the United States is more than 60 percent of GNP, having risen from somewhat less than 50 percent since the 1930s.

This growing surplus, the radicals say, exists because of insufficient consumption and investment opportunities available in a mature capitalistic economy. As a result, resources are increasingly utilized in "unproductive" outlets and activities. These include:

1. *Nonprice Competition*   This consists of methods of competition that do not involve changes in selling price, such as advertising, product differentiation, superficial model changeovers, and so on.

2. *Bureaucracy*   This is the overabundance of administrative bureaus and agencies, especially in government.

3. *War and Imperialism*   These are military activities and the exploitation of weaker nations by both government and large corporations in a vast "military–industrial complex."

New Leftists thus conclude that these inherent contradictions within capitalism must eventually lead to its collapse—either through revolution or war, or through a fundamental transformation of its basic institutions. In fact, according to many radical socialists, the end of capitalism may already be in sight, as evidenced by the social and economic disruption, warlike policies, and growing importance of government that characterize today's advanced capitalistic countries.

CONCLUSION: IDENTIFYING FUNDAMENTAL ISSUES

You can see from the foregoing analysis that radical economists have had much to criticize about capitalism's institutions and processes. What solutions to society's ills do New Leftists offer? The answer is not clear. Although the radicals advocate public ownership of capital, administration by "workers' councils," and cooperative planning, these are only means toward an end. There is much that the radicals do not explain. For example:

How can resources be allocated without markets?

How can planning be achieved without bureaucracy?

How can greater social and economic equality be realized without competition?

How can collective ownership exist without destroying individual initiatives?

And, in general, how can national governments of large, complex societies make important social and economic decisions without seriously impairing efficiency and democratic processes?

In view of this, what conclusion can we draw about the merits of radical socialism?

Perhaps the chief contribution of the New Left has been its identification of important issues. By pointing out the shortcomings of our economic system, radical socialists have made us more aware of capitalism's failure to achieve desired goals of efficiency and equity. And, by focusing attention on such problems as ownership, the distribution of wealth and power, externalities and market failures, and social values in general, the New Left has put its finger on some of the most fundamental issues of our time.

What You Have Learned

1. The major reactions to capitalism have been utopian socialism, Marxian socialism and communism, syndicalism, and Christian socialism. Of these, the Marxian reaction has had the most significant impact on the political and economic relationships of nations.

2. Karl Marx was strongly influenced by the early-nineteenth-century German philosopher Georg Hegel, and particularly by the latter's use of the dialectic—the reconciliation of opposites—as a method of interpreting history. This approach provided much of the basis for Marx's (and Engels') theories. There are five major features of the Marxian system which are the pillars of Marx's model: (a) economic interpretation of history, (b) theory of value and wages, (c) theory of surplus value and capital accumulation, (d) the class struggle, and (e) theory of socialist and communist evolution.

3. Critics of Marx have pointed out that (a) his economic interpretation of history is oversimplified and one-sided, although there has indeed been a growing emphasis on economic causation in modern historical studies; and (b) his theories of value, wages, and surplus value neglected the entrepreneurial functions, failed to recognize the role of demand in the determination of value, and rested on inadequate theoretical foundations. Despite these criticisms, there are elements of truth in Marx's predictions, and much is to be gained from a knowledge of Marxian theory in understanding some of the pronouncements and policies of communist nations today.

4. Socialism in most of the Western world is conceived as a democratic process—in the sense that socialist leaders may be voted into or out of office in free elections. The goal of the majority of today's democratic socialists is the establishment of the "welfare state" through evolutionary rather than revolutionary methods.

5. An important force in modern socialism is the "New Left." Its adherents, who are radical socialists (as distinguished from conventional democratic socialists), oppose free markets, bureaucratic central planning, and in general the social and economic inequities inherent both in market and in command economies. Although many fundamental problems have been identified by New Leftists, it is not clear that their proposed methods of solution (through public ownership, cooperative planning, etc.) are superior to those available in present-day mixed economies.

For Discussion

1. *Terms and concepts to review:*

utopian socialism	price
Fabian socialism	subsistence theory
syndicalism	of wages
Christian socialism	surplus value
economic interpretation	socialism
of history	"dictatorship of the
dialectical materialism	proletariat"
value	

2. Why should a student of today be familiar with the nature and origins of radical ideas, some of which are well over a century old?

3. What is meant by an "interpretation of history"? Can you suggest several different types of interpretations? In your previous history courses in high school or college, which interpretations were stressed?

4. Marx was aware of the fact that direct labor is only one of several inputs used in production, and that raw materials, machines, and other resources were also necessary. How, then, could he argue that labor alone was the basis of value?

5. According to Marx, would there be such a thing as surplus value if capitalists paid workers "what they were worth"? Explain.

6. Do you believe that there is such a thing as a "class struggle" in the Marxian sense? Why or why not? (HINT Can we divide a complex social structure into dichotomous or opposed subclasses? By what criteria?)

7. If we prove that Marx's theory of surplus value is logically incorrect, does this mean that workers *in fact* are not exploited in our capitalistic system? Explain by defining what you mean by "exploitation." (HINT If you were a profit-maximizing employer, would you hire someone to work for you if the added value he or she created were less than the wages you paid?)

8. What major shortcoming do you find in the Marxian model of capitalism?

9. Marxism, it has been said, is like religion: "For those who believe, no explanation is necessary; for those who do not believe, no explanation is possible. Logical arguments, therefore, are not the grounds for acceptance or rejection. It is emotion, not logic, that is the influencing factor. This is why Marxism remains as the basic ideology of several nations and many millions of people throughout the world." Do you agree? Can you add anything to the proposition?

10. Radical socialists have referred to democratic socialists as "coddlers of capitalism." Can you suggest why?

11. Is it possible to have political and social freedom in a command economy? Is it possible to have a market economy without political and social freedom? Explain.

Issue
Is Capitalism Dying?

The United States has experienced several recessions during the latter half of this century. In recent years, unemployment and inflation rates of 9 percent and 12 percent, respectively, have not been uncommon. These strains on the economic system have stirred debates among scholars as to whether American capitalism has entered its final era—a crisis stage leading to decline and fall, perhaps before the end of this century.

Notable among the supporters of this belief are many of today's New Leftists—radical socialists whose ideas of impending disaster stem largely from the writings of Karl Marx. According to the New Left, what the United States has experienced since the mid-1970s has not just been severe business cycles, as most conventional economists contend, but rather wrenching changes in the system's fundamental structure. To support this view, radicals offer the following analysis.

Marxian Dynamics

In Marxian theory, as well as in modern New Left thinking, an advanced capitalistic economy develops certain "contradictions" which lead eventually to the system's collapse. Many of today's radicals believe that these contradictions are already apparent—as evidenced by certain developments in recent history:

○ *Business cycles.* The depression of 1974–1975 was the worst one experienced by capitalistic countries in four decades. In accordance with Marxian logic, the sharp downturn was the result of the growing influence of two long-term trends:

1. The drive for capital accumulation, particularly labor-saving equipment, resulting in the displacement of labor and in an ever-increasing level of unemployment.

2. A declining rate of profit, arising from the inability of physical capital (as distinguished from human capital, i.e., labor) to produce surplus value.

○ *Market concentration.* With the worsening of economic conditions—manifested especially by a declining rate of profit—capitalists have sought ways to protect their self-interest by absorbing weaker firms. This has led to the concentration of capital in large-scale industrial units or monopolies.

○ *Imperialistic multinationalism.* The effects of monopolization are ultimately realized on an international scale with the emergence of a new form of business enterprise—the multinational corporation. Operating across national boundaries, the huge multinational organizations dominate markets and control the resources of other countries. This is what Lenin called the stage of "capitalistic imperialism"—the highest and final stage of mature capitalism.

The radicals conclude that the United States entered this last stage in the 1960s, followed shortly thereafter by Japan and West Germany. Therefore, it is only a matter of time, probably not more than a few decades, before these bastions of capitalism

Table 1.   SALES, PROFITS, AND STOCKHOLDERS' EQUITY, IN ALL MANUFACTURING CORPORATIONS (billions of dollars)

Year	Sales	Profit after federal income taxes	Stockholders' equity
1950	$ 181.9	$12.9	$ 83.3
1955	278.4	15.1	120.1
1960	345.7	15.2	165.4
1965	492.6	27.5	211.7
1970	708.8	28.6	306.8
1975	1,065.2	49.1	423.4
1976	1,203.2	64.5	462.7
1977	1,328.1	70.4	496.7
1978*	1,095.2	71.2	495.3
1979*	1,237.5	73.2	501.1
1980*	1,301.6	74.1	503.3

* Estimated from preliminary data.

SOURCE: Federal Trade Commission.

either collapse or else are drastically transformed by the internal dynamics of their own system.

What Future?

Today's Marxists recognize that policymakers in government and in business seek ways to escape from crisis and to sustain steady growth. Among the tools and techniques used for these purposes are fiscal and monetary policies, the laying off of workers, the cutting of services, and intermittent experiments in wage–price controls and economic planning. But these are only temporary palliatives,

for there is no escape from the growing dilemma of inflation versus unemployment. As the squeeze on workers continues, they will respond increasingly with strikes and demonstrations, thereby sowing the seeds for what will be a revolution at worst or an extreme leftward shift in political ideology at best. In any case, a sure sign of these impending developments, the radicals contend, is the growing oppression which the working class is experiencing as a result of government's failure to resolve the contradictions inherent in today's advanced capitalistic societies.

QUESTIONS

1. Radicals base much of their belief in the eventual collapse of capitalism on a declining rate of profit. Do the data in Table 1 support the radicals' contention? (SUGGESTION What are the long-term trends of percentage rate of return on stockholders' equity and on sales?)

2. What do you think is the strongest argument the radicals have to support their view? Do you believe the argument will be resolved? If not, is capitalism doomed, as many radicals contend? Explain.

Chapter 37

Economic Planning: The Visible Hand in Mixed and in Command Economies

Chapter Preview

Why do some nations engage in economic planning? Are there particular tools and techniques of planning that countries use?

What can we learn from the experiences of nations that plan?

Is a gradual convergence taking place between communism and capitalism—an eventual meeting between East and West?

As you know, the market system is the basis of capitalism and is a fundamental mechanism for allocating resources in mixed economies. Through the unhampered interaction of supply and demand, producers are provided with information about consumer preferences, society's resources are allocated in accordance with these preferences, the most economical choice of production techniques is encouraged, and the individual buying and selling decisions of millions of households and firms are synthesized. This method of resource allocation, including its achievements and failures, has occupied our attention in most of the earlier chapters.

An alternative way in which a society can allocate its scarce resources is by economic planning. An *economic plan* is a detailed scheme, formulated beforehand, for achieving specific objectives by governing the activities and interrelationships of those organisms—firms, households, and governments—that have an influence on the desired outcome. This method of resource allocation plays a key role in command economies. However, certain types of economic plans are also employed in many mixed economies.

Why should we study economic planning? There are two reasons. First, *planned economies*—economic systems in which the government directs resources for the purpose of deciding WHAT to produce, HOW, and possibly FOR WHOM—are playing an increasingly important role in today's world. Second, the problems that economic planning tries to solve are fundamental to every type of economic system. Therefore, an understanding of planning principles and experiences can provide us with guides for evaluating and improving public policies.

Why Plan? Four Fundamental Goals

Why do some countries undertake economic planning? The reason is obvious. Countries plan in order to achieve specific economic goals which, it is believed, would not be realized, or would be attained too slowly, if markets were allowed to operate freely. What are these economic goals? As you recall, four that are fundamental to all economies—mixed as well as command—are efficiency, equity, stability, and growth. A review of these concepts will help refresh your understanding of certain fundamental ideas.

EFFICIENCY

In general, *efficiency* is the ability to make the best use of what is available to attain a desired result. Two important types of efficiency are "technical" and "economic."

REMARK   These terms were discussed many times in earlier chapters. If you do not recall their specific meanings and implications, you should look them up *now* (under "efficiency") in the Dictionary at the back of the book.

Technical efficiency, which exists when a society is on its production-possibilities curve, is a primary goal of *all* economies because every society wants to make maximum use of available resources. Economic efficiency, which includes technical efficiency while also reflecting consumer preferences, is a primary goal of market-oriented economies but not necessarily of command economies, because their planners are not always interested in fully satisfying the wants of consumers. As a result of these differences in goals, you can appreciate why we are not always able to compare performances of command economies with market-oriented ones.

EQUITY

Every economic system seeks answers to three fundamental questions: WHAT goods should society produce? HOW should goods be produced? FOR WHOM should goods be produced? The first two questions deal with resource-utilization problems. Therefore, they are concerned with matters of efficiency. The third question deals with income distri-

bution—the division of society's output among people. Hence, it is concerned with matters of equity or justice.

As you learned in previous chapters, equity is a philosophical *concept* and it is also an economic *goal*. There is no scientific basis for concluding that a particular standard of income distribution is either just or unjust. As a result, although many standards of distribution are possible, three have received the widest attention:

1. **Contributive Standard** "To each according to the market value of his or her contribution to society's output."

2. **Needs Standard** "To each according to his or her needs."

3. **Equality Standard** "To each, equally."

Do you recall from earlier chapters the economic implications of these distributive standards? You can review them now by looking up the terms in the Dictionary at the back of the book.

STABILITY AND GROWTH

Stability and growth are the two remaining fundamental goals of every economic system. These terms have close economic interrelations. By maintaining stability, an economy avoids substantial inflationary and deflationary price movements and is better able to promote continuous full employment of all resources. This in turn leads to a robust volume of economic activity and to the encouragement of steady *economic growth*—a rising level of real output per capita. As a result, all income groups in society benefit even if each receives a constant proportion of an expanding economic pie.

CONCLUSION: HOW MUCH PLANNING?

Every society seeks four fundamental economic goals: efficiency, equity, stability, and growth. Some societies, however, try to attain these goals by constructing plans—schemes of action or procedure designed to accomplish certain objectives. When an economic organism such as a household, firm, or government undertakes planning, it seeks to do a systematic job of setting goals, determining resources needed to meet the goals, and matching the two according to a time schedule. Although centralized planning is a key feature of command economies, most democratic countries also engage in some degree of planning. A chief problem these countries face, of course, is to achieve what they regard as a proper compromise or middle ground between free markets and centralized control. (See Box 1.)

Box 1
The Many Shades of Capitalism

Capitalism is a system characterized by private ownership of the means of production. This implies that there is a relatively free market in which entrepreneurs can enter businesses of their choice, and that production is motivated by the drive for profit.

Capitalism is also usually associated with personal freedom. In reality, however, the two may be independent. For example, Nazi Germany (1933–1945) was capitalist because most of its industries were privately owned. But the government was a dictatorship which deprived people of political and social freedoms. Yugoslavia, on the other hand, is also a dictatorship. However, most industries are state-owned, and are managed by workers within a relatively free-market framework.

Further "models" can be identified among the world's leading capitalist countries:

UNITED STATES AND WEST GERMANY

These countries come closest to the traditional concept of capitalism. Most businesses are privately owned and operated for profit. Government provides certain basic services (education, national defense, post office) and exercises varying degrees of regulation over certain others. Government also tries to direct the economy toward higher levels of efficiency and stability by employing tax, spending, and money-supply policies.

BRITAIN, FRANCE, AND ITALY

Most industries in these countries are privately owned, except for those deemed "basic." Among them are coal, railroads, and steel in Britain, some oil refineries and an auto company in France, and public transportation systems as well as some financial institutions in Italy. France has also

adopted so-called "indicative planning." That is, government and industry representatives jointly establish broad production targets for key industries. These industries then receive government tax and credit incentives to achieve desired goals.

SCANDINAVIA: DENMARK, NORWAY, SWEDEN

Scandinavian capitalism, which is often mistaken for socialism, is more accurately called "welfare statism." The Swedish version is the most thoroughly developed. Although about 90 percent of Sweden's enterprises are privately rather than governmentally owned, profits and income taxes are as high as 80 percent. These revenues are used to promote investment and to finance an extensive system of social benefits providing cradle-to-grave care for everyone. As a result, the Swedish standard of living is one of the highest in the world. But these benefits have been accompanied by considerable inflationary pressures—due largely to budget deficits incurred to finance social programs.

JAPAN

Most Japanese enterprises are privately owned. But industry and government work closely together. The largest firms, especially those engaged heavily in exporting, receive substantial government preferences. These include tax privileges, easy credit from state-connected banks, and similar benefits. Japan's economic system is thus a type of industry–government cartel. Both sectors cooperate to achieve maximum production and employment. This is accomplished in part by limiting imports and by dumping in overseas markets, thereby "exporting" unemployment to Japan's major trading partners.

Tools of Economic Planning

If economic planning is to be effective, government efforts must be directed toward influencing behavior at both macro- and microeconomic levels. What analytical procedures are available for such purposes? There are several, but those that have gained increasing use as tools of economic planning are econometric models and input–output analysis.

ECONOMETRIC MODELS

If you were in a high government position responsible for overall economic planning, one of your chief functions would be to establish relationships between important variables that have an influence on the

economy's performance. Some examples of such variables are consumption expenditures, investment expenditures, interest rates, prices, production, money supply, employment, and productivity. How would you go about combining these and other factors into a set of meaningful relationships that can be used as a guide for forecasting and planning?

One way of attacking the problem is by the use of *econometrics*. This approach integrates economic theory, mathematics, and statistics. That is, it expresses economic relationships in the form of mathematical equations and verifies the resulting models by statistical methods. By constructing theoretical models that can be quantified and tested with actual data, econometrics seeks to explain economic behavior.

Econometric models were first introduced on a

substantial scale during the 1930s. Among the pioneers in the field were Professors Ragnar Frisch of Norway and Jan Tinbergen of The Netherlands. In recognition of their monumental contributions, both men were honored in 1969 by becoming the first recipients of the Alfred Nobel Memorial Prize in Economic Science. Today, as a result of the trailblazing efforts of Frisch and Tinbergen, large-scale econometric models have gained wide use. They consist of hundreds of equations and are employed as forecasting and planning devices by some corporations as well as by a number of national governments.

Planning in The Netherlands

The nation that has made the greatest use of econometrics for government planning is The Netherlands. Denmark, Norway, and Sweden have also placed heavy reliance on this planning technique. The approach used by the Dutch, however, may be regarded as typical of the way in which econometric planning procedures can be employed by a government that wishes to use them.

In The Netherlands, a Central Planning Bureau founded by Jan Tinbergen serves as the planning agency for the Dutch economy. The Bureau constructs econometric models which are designed to do two things—*forecast* and *simulate*. Both activities provide the basis for planning.

When used for forecasting, the models are employed to predict the short- and long-term course of such economic variables as consumption expenditures, investment expenditures, prices, interest rates, and gross national product. These predictions serve the government as a guide for judging future trends in the economy.

When used for simulation, the models are employed to reproduce operations within the economy and the outcomes of different policies. The government may want to know, for example, what the effects will be on total output, income, interest rates, and employment if personal income taxes are increased by 10 percent, or decreased by 5 percent. The alternative tax rates are fed into the model, and the resulting outcomes are computed. Similarly, alternative raw materials quantities, factory utilization rates, and so on, are "plugged" into the model to determine how much production will be available to fulfill anticipated demands at specified prices.

In these ways, the Central Planning Bureau arrives at numerical estimates of the various inputs needed to reach alternative targets. The Bureau then provides the information to representatives of labor, management, and government, all of whom work together to construct a final plan.

An illustration of an econometric model is presented in Exhibit 1. You can see from the explanation why such models are gaining increasing use in many countries as tools for forecasting and planning.

INPUT–OUTPUT ANALYSIS

If the demand for automobiles were to increase by 20 percent, how much of an increase could be expected in the sales of rubber, steel, automobiles, and glass to the automobile industry? One way of answering this question is by the use of input–output analysis.

Input–output analysis is a method of studying the interrelations between industries (or sectors) of an economy. A model in the form of a table is constructed in which each of the economy's industries is listed twice: once down the left side as a seller of outputs and once across the top as a buyer of inputs. Within the body of the table are squares called "cells," depicting in numerical terms the sales–purchase relationships between the industries comprising the model.

A highly simplified illustration of an input–output model for an economy composed of four industries is shown in Exhibit 2. A more realistic model would contain dozens or even hundreds of industries. The model is interpreted in the following way:

1. Each row (reading across from left to right) shows the value of output each industry at the left sold to the industries listed across the top of the table. For example, in the period covered, the rubber industry sold $300 million worth of goods to itself for further production, $100 million to the steel industry, $500 million to the automobile industry, and nothing of significance to the glass industry. The interindustry sales total was therefore $900 million. In addition, direct consumption of rubber by other sources amounted to $200 million. The rubber industry's total output was therefore $1,100 million.

The remaining rows for each industry are interpreted similarly. Thus, the dollar figure in each cell tells you how an industry's total output shown at the right end of the table was distributed among the various buyers listed across the top.

2. Each column (reading down from top to bottom) shows the value of input each industry at the top purchased from the industries listed along the left side of the table. For example, in the period covered, the steel industry bought $100 million worth of goods from the rubber industry, $400 million worth of steel for its own use, $200 million worth of goods from the automobile industry, and nothing of significance from the glass industry. In addition, it purchased $900 million worth of "other resources." Therefore, the value of total input purchased by the steel industry was $1,600 million.

Exhibit 1
Mathematizing the Economy—An Econometric Model

Although an econometric model is usually an elaborate system of mathematical equations, some of the flavor of econometrics can be experienced from a simple model. This is illustrated by the following five-equation system that describes a national economy:

$$\text{consumption expenditures} = a + b \left(\text{national income} \right) \tag{1}$$

$$\text{investment expenditures} = c + d \left(\text{profits in previous period} \right) \tag{2}$$

$$\text{taxes} = e \left(\text{gross national product} \right) \tag{3}$$

$$\text{gross national product} = \left(\text{consumption expenditures} \right) + \left(\text{investment expenditures} \right)$$
$$+ \left(\text{government expenditures} \right) \tag{4}$$

$$\text{national income} = \left(\text{gross national product} \right) - (\text{taxes}) \tag{5}$$

In the equations above, each of the letters a, b, c, d, and e are mathematical constants, called parameters. Each represents some particular number derived by statistical procedures. Once the parameters are determined, the model can be "solved" by making various substitutions and calculating the results.

The first three equations in the model are "behavioral." They tell how the dependent variable on the left side behaves in relation to the independent variable on the right. Thus, the first equation states that consumption expenditures depend on—are a function of—national income. The second says that investment expenditures are a function of the previous period's profits. The third states that taxes are a function of—or some proportion of—gross national product.

The last two equations are "definitional." They express identities or truisms about the economy. Equation (4), for example, shows that gross national product is the sum of three classes of expenditures—consumption, investment, and government. Equation (5) says that national income is the difference between gross national product and taxes.

Of course, since the model is intended to be a simplification of reality, the equations necessarily omit certain variables that might be included in a more detailed model. Nevertheless, even this basic model could be used reasonably well for forecasting the dependent variables—those on the left sides of the equal signs. First, however, good estimates must be obtained of the five parameters a through e and of the two variables, "profits in the previous period," shown in equation (2), and "government expenditures," shown in equation (4). Once the forecasts are made, planning can be facilitated by organizing resources to meet desired goals.

Guy Gillette, Photo Researchers.

Exhibit 2
Input–Output Table for an Economy with Four Industries
(millions of dollars; hypothetical data for a given period)

An input–output table shows certain interdependencies between industries in an economy. Reading from left to right, the dollar figure in each cell tells you the sales (outputs) that each industry listed at the left made to the industries shown across the top. Conversely, reading down from top to bottom, the dollar figure in each cell tells you the *purchases* (inputs) that each industry shown across the top acquired from the industries listed at the left. The numbers in parentheses are called *input coefficients*. They indicate the proportions of total inputs (shown at the bottom) which the industries at the top of each column received from the industries at the left. Of course, for each industry at the top of the table, the sum of its input coefficients must equal 1 (or 100 percent).

Output (sellers) \ Input (buyers)	Rubber industry	Steel industry	Automobile industry	Glass industry	Interindustry sales total	Direct consumption*	Total output
Rubber industry	$300 (0.27)	$100 (0.06)	$500 (0.25)		$900	$200	$1,100
Steel industry	$200 (0.18)	$400 (0.25)	$600 (0.30)	$100 (0.17)	$1,300	$300	$1,600
Automobile industry	$100 (0.09)	$200 (0.13)	$400 (0.20)	$200 (0.33)	$900	$1,100	$2,000
Glass industry			$400 (0.20)	$100 (0.17)	$500	$100	$600
Other resources	$500 (0.45)	$900 (0.56)	$100 (0.05)	$200 (0.33)	$1,700		$1,700
Total input	$1,100	$1,600	$2,000	$600	$5,300	$1,700	$7,000

* Consists of all other sales, including direct sales to households, government, foreign sources, and sales for capital formation (i.e., investment goods).

The remaining columns for each industry are interpreted in the same way. The dollar figure in each cell shows how an industry's total input shown at the bottom of the table was distributed among the various sellers listed at the left.

3. With this information given, the table enables us to calculate the value of each input needed to produce an additional dollar's worth of output. The resulting numbers, called *input coefficients*, are shown in parentheses in each cell. Each input coefficient is obtained from the formula

$$\text{input coefficient} = \frac{\text{industry's specific input}}{\text{industry's total input}}$$

For example, reading down from the top of the table, the steel industry's specific input from the rubber industry was $100 million, while the steel industry's total input was $1,600 million. Therefore, the steel industry's input coefficient, IC, for rubber is

$$_{\text{STEEL}}\text{IC}_{rubber} = \frac{\$100}{\$1,600} = 0.06$$

Similarly, reading down again from the top of the table, the glass industry's specific input from the automobile industry was $200 million, while the glass industry's total input was $600 million. Hence, the glass industry's input coefficient for autos is

$$_{\text{GLASS}}\text{IC}_{autos} = \frac{\$200}{\$600} = 0.33$$

The remaining input coefficients for each industry are calculated similarly. Notice that the sum of the input coefficients in each column must equal 1.

Application to Forecasting and Planning

The input–output table can now be used to answer the question posed at the beginning of this section:

If the demand for automobiles were to increase by 20 percent, how much of an increase could be expected in the sales of rubber, steel, automobiles, and glass to the automobile industry?

A 20 percent increase in the demand for automobiles would increase their direct consumption from $1,100 million to $1,320 million. This additional output of $220 million worth of automobiles would be matched by the following input increases in the automobile industry:

$$
\begin{array}{rl}
rubber: & 0.25 \times \$220 \text{ million} = \$\,55 \text{ million} \\
steel: & 0.30 \times \$220 \text{ million} = 66 \text{ million} \\
automobiles: & 0.20 \times \$220 \text{ million} = 44 \text{ million} \\
glass: & 0.20 \times \$220 \text{ million} = 44 \text{ million} \\
other\ resources: & 0.05 \times \$220 \text{ million} = \underline{11 \text{ million}} \\
\text{Total value of additional inputs:} & \$220 \text{ million}
\end{array}
$$

The total value of additional inputs to the automobile industry thus equals the value of its additional output, $220 million.

NOTE There are also numerous secondary, tertiary, etc., effects on the automobile and other industries because of the interactions they have on each other's production decisions. For example, more automobiles require more steel, rubber, etc., which also require more automobiles, and so on.

You can now appreciate the usefulness of input–output analysis:

An input–output model serves two important planning functions:

1. It indicates the impacts of changes in demand on industry supplies.

2. It suggests where potential bottlenecks may arise in the flow of goods between industries.

In these ways, input–output analysis permits changes to be anticipated before they occur. This enables plans to be formulated in order to minimize disruptions in resource use.

Uses and Difficulties

The pioneering work on input–output analysis was done by Wassily Leontief at Harvard University. Leontief devoted most of his professional career—some forty years, from the 1930s to the 1970s—to deriving the data needed for compiling massive input–output tables encompassing hundreds of industries. In 1973, in recognition of his scholarship, the Swedish government awarded Leontief the Nobel Prize in Economic Science. As a result of his efforts, many corporations and some governments (including the Russian government) today make substantial use of input–output analysis for forecasting and planning their economic activities.

Despite the advances made in input–output analysis, it still suffers from certain problems. Among them:

○ The data in input–output tables are based on past relationships in the economy. To be more useful for forecasting and planning, the dollar flows and coefficients should ideally reflect current, if not future, relationships. This will be impossible, however, until more and better information, and improved methods of analyzing it, become available.

○ The division of an economy into specific industries raises many problems of definition and classification. Should television production be treated as a separate industry, or should it be grouped with television equipment, electronic equipment, or communications equipment? One classification may be too narrow or refined; another, too broad or aggregated.

These and other difficulties have only retarded, rather than prevented, the implementation of input–output techniques. Much progress has already been made in overcoming these obstacles.

CONCLUSION: MORE SCIENTIFIC PLANNING

During the past several decades, a growing number of corporations and governments have placed increasing reliance on scientific planning techniques—including econometrics and input–output analysis. The reasons can be attributed to two major factors:

1. Continuing integration of economic theory and mathematics. This makes possible the formulation of complex economic concepts in precise mathematical terms.

2. Rapid advances in computer science. This enables huge quantities of data to be processed and analyzed.

As a result, models of economic systems can now be constructed on much larger scales than were previously possible. This suggests the following conclusion:

In the final analysis, the usefulness of any model depends on the accuracy and completeness of its information. As research and data-collection methods improve, econometrics and input–output analysis will gain wider adoption as scientific planning tools in industry and government.

It is significant to note that econometrics, input–output analysis, and related techniques are more than just analytical tools. As a result of their development

.and implementation, much of the nature of economics has undergone dramatic changes in recent decades. (See *Leaders in Economics,* page 645.)

Planning in the Soviet Union

Any study of economic planning would be remiss without a discussion of the Soviet Union. This nation has been actively engaged in planning longer than any other country.

Modern Russia came into existence as a direct reaction to capitalism. In November 1917, the revolutionary Bolshevik (later known as Communist) party of Russia, under the leadership of V. I. Lenin, overthrew the government and, five years later, established the Union of Soviet Socialist Republics. The ultimate objective of the party, which identified itself with the "dictatorship of the proletariat," was to establish Marxian socialism and eventually full communism in Russia and throughout the world. This, it was said, would end the "want, misery, and injustice of capitalist society."

Has this goal been achieved? We can best answer the question by examining the present structure of the Soviet economy within a framework of four distinguishing features:

1. Soviet economic institutions and organizations.
2. Soviet economic planning.
3. The challenge of economic growth.
4. Reorganization and changes in the Soviet economy.

SOVIET ECONOMIC INSTITUTIONS AND ORGANIZATION

Every society is characterized by certain institutions—established ways of doing things based on customs, practices, or laws. Acting in combination, they affect the society's organizational structure. We examine here the more important institutions in the Soviet economy.

Social Ownership of Industry

The Soviet Union defines its economic system as socialist, not communist. Socialism, according to Marxian doctrine, is a preparatory stage in the attainment of full communism. Unlike the United States, therefore, all means of industrial production in the U.S.S.R. which require the use of hired labor are owned by "society," represented by the government. Although individuals such as professionals and artisans can work for themselves, they must do so without the help of hired labor. Except for a few special cases (e.g., domestic servants), no individual may employ another for a wage or for private gain.

In general, the publicly owned enterprises in the U.S.S.R. are not significantly different in form from similar types of American publicly owned firms such as the Tennessee Valley Authority, the U.S. Postal Service, and municipally owned public utilities. However:

> Public ownership in Russia does not apply to consumer goods. Virtually all consumer goods are privately owned. And, as in the United States, people may own automobiles, houses, furniture, clothing, government bonds, savings deposits, and so on.

Social Ownership of Agriculture

Agriculture in the U.S.S.R. is organized along somewhat more complex lines. Two types of farms are in operation, both socially owned:

1. *State Farms* These are agricultural lands owned and operated as state enterprises under government-appointed managing directors. Workers and administrators are hired to run the farms and are usually paid set wages as well as bonuses if their work exceeds basic norms of output.

2. *Collective Farms* These are agricultural cooperatives. They consist of communities of farmers who pool their resources, lease land from the government on a long-term basis, and divide the profits among the members according to the amount and kind of work done by each. Collective farms, which are subject to detailed government regulation, are the dominant form of agriculture in the Soviet Union.

Collective farms were introduced in the late 1920s as a compromise between socialistic principles and political expediency. They were meant to reduce the hostile resistance of the agrarian class (at that time about 80 percent of the Russian population) to total centralization and control of agriculture. Under the collectivization laws, the farms must sell the bulk of their output to the government at low preset prices, and can dispose of the rest as they wish—usually through farmers' markets or bazaars. These are free markets where prices and quality are invariably higher than in government stores.

Economic Incentives

A fundamental feature of the Soviet economy is its widespread use of monetary rewards. They are used to induce people to exert the efforts needed for accomplishing specific tasks. Two major forms of economic incentive exist:

Leaders in Economics
Ragnar Frisch 1895–1973
Jan Tinbergen 1903–
Wassily Leontief 1906–

Econometrics and Input–Output Analysis

Adam Smith and Karl Marx founded systems of economic thought. Yet it is doubtful whether these intellectual giants, if they were students today, could pass a graduate course in economic theory. The reason is based on the two men's lack of mathematical sophistication in explaining economic ideas. Smith's *The Wealth of Nations* (1776) confines its examples to the use of arithmetic, while Marx's *Das Kapital* (vol. I, 1867) never goes beyond simple algebra. Today the highest status—not only in economics but in all the social and management sciences—is accorded those whose competence in their particular field is buttressed by the ability to use higher mathematics in formulating essential ideas.

The evidence of this on an international scale became apparent in 1969 when the Swedish Royal Academy of Science bestowed jointly on Norway's Ragnar Frisch and Holland's Jan Tinbergen the first Alfred Nobel Memorial Prize in Economic Science. Both men, the Academy noted, had distinguished themselves since the 1930s by developing pioneering applications of higher mathematics to economic theory and measurement—the integration of which is known as "econometrics."

In 1973 an American economist— Wassily Leontief—who had immigrated from Russia several decades earlier and had spent most of his professional career at Harvard University, became another recipient of the Nobel Prize in Economic Science. Leontief was honored for his outstanding work in developing input-

output analysis—a highly sophisticated approach to studying complex relationships among industries, regions, and sectors of an economy.

Today econometrics and input–output analysis are standard tools for forecasting and planning in various countries. As societies become more complex, these tools and other procedures employing advanced mathematical techniques will gain increasing use by governments and corporations. Hence, there is no doubt that if Adam Smith and Karl Marx were students today, and aspiring social scientists, they would be devoting a good deal of their efforts to mastering differential and difference equations, matrix algebra, statistics, and other subjects in higher mathematics.

UPI Cablephoto.

Ragnar Frisch

UPI Cablephoto.

Jan Tinbergen

United Press International.

Wassily Leontief

1. *Differential Rewards* These are paid to persons in occupations requiring different skills. For example, within the high-income groups are academic research scientists, ballet and opera stars, and university professors of science. In the middle-income groups are engineers, physicians, teachers, and skilled workers. In the lower-income groups are technicians, semiskilled workers, and unskilled workers.

2. *Productivity Incentives* These are provided for workers and managers. Thus, basic pay rates for workers in industry and on state farms are usually calculated not in relation to hours of work, but in terms of units produced. In addition, special graduated rates are paid to those who exceed the norm. (It is interesting to note that in the United States and other noncommunistic countries, piecework payments of this type have long been bitterly criticized by labor unions as exploitative.) Managerial incentives, on the other hand, consist of bonuses and various types of fringe benefits, including housing and free meals at the plant.

Are economic incentives of this type contrary to Marxian thinking? The Soviets think not:

> In a *socialistic* society, the Russians say, people have not yet been prepared for full communism. Therefore, incentives may be needed to persuade individuals to produce at their full potential.

Freedom of Consumer and Occupational Choice

In the competitive model of capitalism, there is both consumer sovereignty and freedom of consumer choice. That is, consumers register their demands for goods through the price system, and producers compete with one another to fulfill those demands. In such a system the consumer is theoretically king. This means that the consumer not only decides *what* is produced, but also is free to choose *how much* is wanted from the supplies that are available.

In the Soviet economy the state decides which and how many consumer goods will be produced (except for the free-market portion of goods produced by collective farms). It then places these goods in government stores—normally without rationing—at equilibrium prices that it believes will clear the market in a given period. Consumers are free to purchase the products or not, as they see fit, at the established prices. Hence, it is correct to say that, generally speaking, there is freedom of consumer choice in the Soviet Union, but there is not consumer sovereignty.

Under normal conditions there is also freedom of occupational choice. As was suggested above, the state sets differential wage and salary structures according to types of occupation, skill, geographic location, and other conditions. Workers are largely free to choose the kinds of jobs for which they can qualify.

Broadly speaking, therefore:

> Soviet households have much the same freedoms of consumer and occupational choice as do households in the United States and most other countries. Although there are exceptions, the Soviet leaders have found through hard experience that the preservation of such freedoms provides for more orderly markets and much greater administrative efficiency.

Money and Taxes

The monetary unit in the Soviet Union is the ruble. But in effect two kinds of money circulate:

1. *Currency* This is used for transactions within the household sector and between households and the state.

2. *Bank Money* This is used in the government sector among state enterprises.

These currencies are convertible into one another for business purposes (e.g., to pay wages), but such conversion is under strict government control. The dual monetary system is designed to prevent the excessive issue of currency in the household sector and to facilitate budgetary control over state enterprises.

Taxes in the Soviet Union, as a percentage of national income, are much higher than in the United States, and probably higher than in most other countries. The reason is the Soviet government's greater proportion of total expenditures. These include: military outlays; welfare spending on socialized medicine, free education, and numerous other benefits; complete operation of state enterprises; and financing of most new investment in industry, trade, communication, and transport. What are the chief sources of the revenue that pays for these expenditures? In the United States it would be primarily a graduated personal income tax and to a lesser extent a corporation income tax. The latter averages roughly 50 percent of corporate profits. In contrast:

> The bulk of the Soviet government's revenue comes from a profits tax on state enterprises and a sales tax—called a "turnover" tax—on goods sold to the public. Although the rates vary, the profits tax has tended to bring in about 40 percent of the state's annual revenue and the sales tax about 30 percent.

SOVIET ECONOMIC PLANNING

The Soviet Union has been a planned economy since the 1920s, but its economic plans have varied from time to time. Economic plans have taken the form of enormous comprehensive blueprints for coordinating the parts of most or all of the economy. Beginning in 1928, the state embarked on a series of Five-Year Plans (with occasional shorter or longer ones at different times), each with the purpose of achieving certain objectives. There is no need for us to explore the details of each of these plans. However, it will be useful to examine their general features.

The Problems of Balance and Flexibility: Input–Output Analysis

Some of the difficulties that arise very early in the planning process involve the problems of achieving appropriate balance and flexibility among the interrelated parts of the economy.

In formulating a five-year plan, for example, production targets are established not only for enterprises and industries but also for geographic regions of the economy. If the plan is to be ideal, it must utilize fully all resources in the most efficient way. This is the task of input–output analysis—a basic tool of planning in the Soviet Union. Thus, the quantities of inputs to be produced, such as iron, steel, and glass, must be balanced by the quantities of outputs, such as houses, automobiles, and agricultural machinery, which utilize these inputs. Otherwise, there will be excess production of some of these commodities relative to others, with the result that certain resources will be used inefficiently.

These difficulties are further complicated by the fact that the planned balances must be dynamic rather than static. That is, they must allow for growth in the quantities of outputs and inputs to be produced over a period of time. This requires that the plan be sufficiently flexible to permit readjustment of any of its parts at any point during the life of the plan in the event that the desired targets are not being met as originally intended.

The Formulation of Objectives

The various five-year plans that have guided the Soviet Union since 1928 have emphasized different objectives based on economic, social, political, and military considerations. For the most part, the biggest problem has been deciding on the proportion of the nation's limited resources to be devoted to the production of consumer goods, capital goods, and military goods. In general, the plans have had four major objectives:

1. To attain the highest standard of living in the world by overtaking the advanced capitalistic countries in output per capita as rapidly as possible.

2. To build a major military complex with the most modern nuclear capabilities.

3. To provide for universal health and education so as to further the nation's growth and scientific progress.

4. To achieve a substantial degree of economic independence from the outside world.

On the whole, the effort to attain these goals has made it necessary for the Soviet planners to follow a threefold strategy.

First, place a major reliance on agriculture to supply the food and raw materials needed for rapid industrialization.

Second, give high priority to the use of the country's limited resources for the development of heavy industry, such as steel, machine building, fuel, and power.

Third, give low priority to the production of consumer goods.

The consequences of these policies on the Soviet Union have been painful. Standards of living have remained low compared to the United States, and agriculture has experienced repeated failures and setbacks, which have been the cause of serious concern to government leaders.

The Details of Planning

A comprehensive economic plan of the type prepared in the Soviet Union is extraordinarily detailed. It includes a number of "subplans," such as an output plan, a capital budget or expenditures plan, a financial plan, a labor utilization plan, and various regional plans. A few words may be said about the problems of preparing the first two of these plans: the output plan and the capital budget.

Output Plan   In the preparation of the output plan, the government leaders must be concerned both with consumer preferences and sacrifices in production.

The Soviets recognize that, on the one hand, it would be irrational to produce goods that consumers desire if the production of such goods interfered with the overall objectives of the plan. On the other hand, it would be equally irrational to produce goods that consumers do not desire—that is, would not purchase in sufficient quantities at specified prices. This helps explain why advertising exists in the Soviet Union, although on a much smaller scale than in the United States. Advertising not only seeks to influence the marketing of new products, but also helps to clear the market of unsold goods.

Soviet planners must take alternative production costs into account when they set output targets. Labor costs are relatively easy to measure because they are reflected by wage rates, which serve as an indication of the "real costs" of labor—the sacrifices in production that must be made in order to attract labor out of alternative employments. But the means by which the Soviet leaders measure nonlabor costs of production are not always so clear. For example, some experts in the field believe that the Soviet authorities do not attempt to include in their estimates of money costs all the real sacrifices in production resulting from the use of natural resources, capital funds, and land. Nor do they include the costs of distributing goods (e.g., warehousing, transportation, etc.) in their calculation of national income, because they regard distribution activities as unproductive. Thus:

> Soviet attitudes toward alternative costs and distribution are due partly to the difficulties of measurement, partly to the influence of Marxian ideology, and partly to the belief that certain types of price and cost calculations are "capitalistic economics." As a result, there is no doubt that the Soviet planners often sacrifice economic efficiency in order to attain desired objectives.

Capital Budget   How do the Soviet authorities determine the output of specific types of producers' goods. For example, how do they decide between a bulldozer and a power shovel, or between a truck and a railroad flat car?

Such decisions are governed by the capital budget. This is a list of specific investment projects arranged in decreasing order of priority according to each project's *coefficient of relative effectiveness* (CRE). This technical term, used in the Soviet Union, means the expected payoff or percent rate of return on a capital investment. It is akin to the concept of "marginal efficiency of investment" used in Western economics. A particular investment project is thus either accepted or rejected by the planning authorities according to whether its CRE is above or below the prescribed minimum. In general:

> The CRE is a device for rationing the scarce supply of capital among alternative uses. The method of calculating the CRE is quite similar to procedures used by business economists and financial managers in the United States. The factors that enter into the calculation include economic costs, interest rates, and the returns and expenses expected on the project over its estimated life.

Adoption and Supervision of the Plan

When the Soviet planners complete their plan, it is reviewed by the government, by the representatives of labor and management, and by the Communist party. The advice and suggestions of these groups may then be incorporated by the planners before they submit it to the Politburo—the highest organ of the Communist party—for the resolution of disputes and final approval. Supervision of the plan is then entrusted to various agencies whose responsibility is to see it through to fulfillment. In the process of supervision, however, the plan is revised periodically to correct for unforeseen developments and errors. In effect, therefore, the "plan" is actually a series of plans rather than a rigid once-and-for-all arrangement.

Reorganization and Changes

Of course, an effective plan should be responsive to changing needs. In recognition of this, Soviet planners have at times instituted various reforms. For example:

○ Decision making at the enterprise level has been partially decentralized. Company managers are given greater freedom in hiring workers, setting wages, varying product mixes, contracting with suppliers, and making small investments in new equipment.

○ Incentive systems to encourage greater output have been introduced. Workers and managers can strive for bonuses and other benefits based on the efficiency of their enterprise. Efficiency is measured by the ratio of a firm's profit to total assets (i.e., by a firm's return on assets). This relates the productivity of assets to goods *sold* rather than merely to goods produced.

○ Marketing programs to stimulate consumer demand have been instituted. Advertising is employed to help move goods from dealers' shelves, and prices are reduced when sales become sluggish.

What have been the results of these reorganizations and changes? In general:

> Soviet reforms have been introduced to encourage greater overall efficiency. However, the reforms in large part have met with limited success—for political as well as economic reasons. Thus:
>
> 1. Central planners have not been willing to surrender the real power needed to make decentralization work.
>
> 2. The economy has not undergone the organizational and administrative changes required to permit the introduction of new production and distribution methods.
>
> 3. Soviet workers have not been sufficiently interested in monetary incentives because of the limited consumer goods available on which increased incomes can be spent.

As a consequence, greater pressures are frequently put on the Kremlin to provide a larger quantity and better quality of consumer goods.

ACCOMPLISHMENTS AND FAILURES

The major economic goal of the Soviet Union has been the attainment of rapid growth. Other objectives—stability, equity, and efficiency—have not been neglected. However, they have been of secondary importance. How successful have the Soviets been in realizing their desired ends?

Growth

Unfortunately, various problems of definition and measurement are encountered in dealing with Soviet data. These difficulties make comparisons with mixed economies that much harder. Nevertheless, the available figures suggest the following growth patterns:

1. Since 1950, the growth of real gross national product (GNP) in the Soviet Union has averaged approximately 6 percent per year. This compares with about 4 percent for the United States and somewhat higher rates for West Germany and Japan.

2. Real GNP in the Soviet Union has increased relative to the United States, but the rate of increase has slowed down. In 1950, for example, Russia's real GNP was one-third that of the United States; in 1960 it was 44 percent, and since 1970 it has averaged close to one-half. (See Exhibit 3.)

How can we explain this substantial growth record? Is Soviet success based on some magic formula? The answer is no. The growth record is due simply to a consistent economic policy which has stressed several underlying factors:

1. The maintenance of a high proportion (between one-fourth and one-third) of gross investment to GNP.

2. The granting of major priority to the development of heavy industries such as steel, machine building, and power, all of which have magnified or multiplier effects on income and output.

3. The construction and importation of vast quantities of modern equipment.

4. The training of hundreds of thousands of technicians to operate and maintain the physical plant.

These factors have been combined with a rapid increase in the nonagricultural labor force, thereby helping to provide the supply of labor needed in the industrial sector.

Stability, Equity, and Efficiency

The remaining results of Soviet planning, expressed in terms of stability, equity, and efficiency, may be summarized briefly.

With respect to stability, fluctuations in investment expenditures are the chief cause of business cycles. In a command system, where government makes the strategic decisions, it is easier to manage such expenditures than in a capitalistic system, where decisions

Exhibit 3
Economic Growth—U.S.S.R. and U.S.A.

Since 1950, Russia has grown somewhat faster than the United States—but still lags far behind in total output. At present, the Russian economy is roughly half as big as that of the United States.

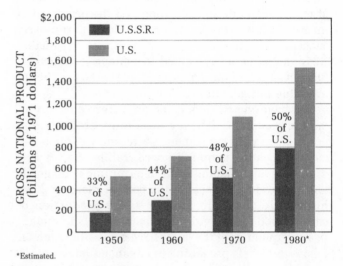

*Estimated.

SOURCE: U.S. Department of State.

are left up to each firm. As a result, the Soviet economy has maintained high employment and stable prices for much longer periods than have mixed economies.

Concerning equity, the distribution of income in the U.S.S.R. is quite uneven. Enterprise managers, for example, not only earn much higher salaries than ordinary workers but also receive substantial fringe benefits in the form of superior housing, longer vacations, and in some cases a free car. Similarly, physicists, opera singers, and others in certain preferred occupations (determined by government) are paid considerably more than semiskilled and unskilled workers. Therefore, contrary to Marxian doctrine, *incomes are not generally distributed according to "needs."* However, there are not the extremes of high and low incomes in Russia that exist in many mixed economies, and all Soviet citizens receive state-subsidized education, health care, housing, and other benefits at relatively little or no direct costs. On the whole, therefore, the distribution of income—both money and real—is substantially more equal in the Soviet Union than in most advanced mixed economies.

Finally, the Soviet Union has been considerably less successful with respect to efficiency than with its other goals. The factors responsible have been both technical and economic. The agricultural sector has lagged far behind the industrial sector in productivity. The reasons are due mainly to short growing seasons, inadequate incentives to stimulate productivity, and heavy investment of resources in industry and defense at the expense of agriculture. Productivity has also suffered in the industrial sector. This is evidenced, as mentioned earlier, by the fact that various reforms designed to increase output—including efforts at management decentralization and the provision of incentives for workers—have not been particularly successful. On the whole, therefore, it may be said that Russian planners have failed to achieve technical efficiency—the maximum ratio of physical outputs to available physical inputs.

Nor have the Soviets come anywhere close to attaining economic efficiency—maximum production in accordance with consumers' preferences. This is because a central planning board, rather than a free market, is the mechanism for determining what goods will be produced. Because the central planners have historically given top priority to the production of capital goods relative to consumer goods, the quantities and qualities of the latter have generally fallen far below the levels prevailing in advanced mixed economies.

CONCLUSION: BETTER PLANNING

As a consequence of these experiences, the Russians have given up on broad reform. They have undertaken instead to improve central planning and management systems in order to reduce inefficiencies and improve productivity. In general:

> Since about 1970, Soviet emphasis has shifted from more planning to better planning—through the application of modern economic and scientific management principles. Imports from the West, ranging from agricultural goods to advanced equipment and systems, are rising as a result of these efforts. The ultimate goal is to meet the needs of restive consumers—whose living standards are far below those in other industrial nations.

Planning in China

In 1949, the Communist People's Liberation Army swept victoriously into Peking, the ancient capital of China. Under the leadership of Mao Tse-tung, it took control of a largely underdeveloped, war-devastated economy containing one-fourth of the world's population in an area one-third larger than the continental United States.

During the next thirty years, China pursued policies aimed at achieving three broad socioeconomic goals:

1. A *classless* society, in which all people are equal.

2. A *collective* society, in which all resources are publicly owned and employed for the nation's benefit.

3. A *cooperative* society, in which everyone lives, works, and sacrifices for the common good.

The ideological goals of China under Chairman Mao can thus be summed up in three words: *classless, collective,* and *cooperative.* Although the country did not achieve all three objectives, Chinese society came closer than any other communist nation in realizing its goals.

In the late 1970s, after the death of Mao, China underwent a change in political leadership. As a result, the nation's ideology has been somewhat modified. However, the economy continues to be characterized by certain special features, as explained below.

ORGANIZATION: INDUSTRY AND AGRICULTURE

One of the distinguishing characteristics of the Chinese economy concerns the way in which its industrial and agricultural sectors are organized. Both were gradually transformed from private to public ownership during the first decade of communist rule. Consequently, since 1960 almost all economic activities of any significance have been state-controlled.

The organization of the industrial sector was patterned after the Soviet system. Ministries of production were created to serve as administrative agencies within individual industries or groups of industries. There is a Ministry of Electric Power, a Ministry of Steel, a Ministry of Textiles, and so on. In most cases the various ministries are part of a complex network designed to direct government investment, production, and marketing plans—both nationally and locally. Although some degree of decentralization exists, its advantages are outweighed by bureaucratic structures that have been built up between the various ministries and enterprises. As a result, inefficiency and waste are common in the administration of many industries, and the resulting losses in productivity are reflected at all levels.

The agricultural sector, which provides China with most of its food and raw materials, is the foundation of the economy. Agricultural activity is organized into communes. These are groups of villages which own their own land and assign production teams to farm it. The communes consume a portion of the output produced and sell the rest. State farms also exist, but these are government-owned enterprises operated as agricultural experiment stations for the purpose of developing new and improved farming methods.

To conclude:

China's industrial and agricultural sectors are organized in such a way as to facilitate centralized economic planning. Although a certain amount of decentralization exists, enterprise managers are given limited discretion in determining prices, resource utilization, and output volumes, provided their decisions do not conflict with political ideology and national goals.

PLANNING STRATEGIES AND EXPERIENCES

Economic planning has occupied the attention of Chinese political leaders for decades. What have been the results of their efforts? This question can best be answered by sketching some of the highlights of China's recent planning experiences.

Efficiency

As you know, an economy is said to be economically or allocatively efficient when it has achieved maximum output with its available resources and is producing goods that consumers are willing and able to purchase. Does China's command economy meet this test of efficiency? The answer is no—for two major reasons:

1. In China the production of most goods is determined by the state—not by consumers through their spending decisions. Consequently, there is freedom of consumer choice in that consumers can select from the goods available. But there is relatively little consumer sovereignty because markets do not play a dominant role in relating consumer preferences to production decisions.

2. China suffers from considerable disguised unemployment, best termed _underemployment_. There are many reasons. For example, most of the labor force is unskilled and uneducated, making it difficult for workers to adapt to modern technology, even when it is available. Transportation facilities are largely primitive, slowing down the movement of goods and people. And restrictions are imposed on specialization and resource mobility, limiting the migration of workers between industries and between farms and cities.

Equity

In a capitalistic economy, the four classes of income payments are wages, rent, interest, and profit. In China, rent and interest are confined to special state-determined uses for the purpose of influencing resource allocation. Profits, on the other hand, are encouraged. But they are either remitted to the state or used by enterprises for reinvestment and expansion, and for incentive bonuses to workers and managers. Wages, therefore, remain the major form of income payment.

The government's policy has been to narrow inequalities in income over the years. This has been accomplished in various ways:

1. Properties of the rich were either confiscated or taxed away during the 1950s. Consequently, there is no wealthy class. Nor is there any destitute or poverty class, because no one is permitted to fall below a minimum standard of living.

2. Various social benefits have been instituted. Among them are free education, health care, old-age homes, and retirement facilities. In addition, there are vocational, cultural, recreational, and child-care programs.

3. Price and wage policies designed to reduce class differences have been implemented. As a result, a discriminatory pricing system exists which provides lower prices for "essential" goods and higher prices for nonessentials. In addition, the long-run goal of the wage policy is to reduce the gap between the lowest and highest wage rates by gradually increasing the lowest relative to the highest.

Although these accomplishments are noteworthy, they do present an exaggerated view of China's gains in equity. Many wide differences in income per capita still exist. Certain professionals and factory managers, for example, earn many times more than the average worker. And in the urban sector, the average level of income is approximately four times higher than in the rural. Despite these disparities, however, China has made considerable progress toward eliminating the extremes of low and high incomes. Box 2 provides examples of this progress.

Stability

The achievement of relatively stable wages and prices has been one of the notable accomplishments of China's central planners. Stability has been attained through the coordination of several major policies:

1. _Incentive Systems_ By the use of incentives, employees are continually encouraged to put forth their greatest productive effort. In addition, many enterprises have cooperative committees which permit workers to participate with managers in decision-making activities. Taken together, all these measures are designed to stimulate productivity within the framework of China's ideological goals.

Box 2
China: Striving for Efficiency and Equity—with Tears

China's struggle for greater efficiency has been impeded by many factors, cultural as well as economic. As a result, the nation must make do with a good deal of primitive capital and obsolete technology in the long struggle toward industrialization. Thus, bicycles, carts, horses, and manpower are the chief means of moving people and goods in the country's industrial areas. In addition, China lacks modern capital equipment to undertake most large-scale construction activity. Consequently, large numbers of workers are employed continuously to build dikes, canals, roads, and bridges.

In its struggle for equity, the nation's policies have had a profound influence on Chinese society and culture. Never before in the country's long history have so many people been changed in such a short time. In the past few decades, legal equality was established between the sexes. Medical and sanitation facilities were greatly expanded in the cities and villages. Education was revised and extended by establishing full-time day schools, part-time evening and correspondence schools, and combined work-study programs. And language reform was undertaken to promote unification and simplification—with the eventual goal of replacing the characters with more easily learned phonetic symbols. While China is still poor in comparison to Western nations, there is no doubt that most of its people have acquired more material necessities in the latter half of this century than they ever had in previous centuries.

However, these achievements have not been painless. China is still a monolithic, oppressive totalitarian state. Terror and brutalities exist (although they are often hidden) and life is controlled. Consequently, China, with its hundreds of millions of people, is a difficult country for advanced democracies to understand. But it is a country which, in today's world, is even more difficult to ignore.

United Press International.

United Press International.

Eric Kroll, Taurus Photos.

United Press International.

Eastfoto.

Eastfoto.

2. *Wage-Price Policy*   Of course, gains in productivity result in declining unit labor costs and therefore rising profit margins. How do China's planners distribute the benefits of higher profits? In two ways. One is by decreasing prices while keeping wages constant, thereby increasing workers' real incomes. The other is by investing a percentage of profits in new capital, thereby enlarging the base for achieving future gains in productivity and real income. China's wage-price policy thus consists of converting a portion of productivity improvements into higher real income. This is done partly by reducing prices and partly by raising wages.

3. *Fiscal-Monetary Controls*   China's fiscal and monetary policies have helped considerably to maintain price stability. Fiscal control is exercised through the national budget, and most government expenditures are financed by taxes. Monetary control is exercised by the nation's central bank—the People's Bank of China—which holds accounts of all enterprises and determines the allocation of financial resources. Because the government limits deficit financing, minimizes borrowing from abroad, and maintains a stable money supply, much of the upward pressure on prices that prevails in mixed economies has been considerably less pronounced in China.

As pointed out above, none of these policies is pursued independently. All three are coordinated by China's planners to assure a high degree of wage-price stability.

Growth

The Chinese regard capital investment as an important requirement for growth. Accordingly, China's planners have adhered to a low-wage policy—for two major reasons. One is to provide more funds for capital formation. The other is to minimize inflationary pressures by keeping the aggregate demand for consumer goods in line with the limited supply of such goods. The result of this policy has been a continuous high rate of capital investment. It is estimated to average between 30 and 40 percent of gross national product—and in some periods as high as 40 to 50 percent—compared with a range of only 10 to 20 percent for most mixed economies.

The consequence of China's investment planning has been a steady expansion of economic growth at an average rate of about 4 percent per year. This is approximately in line with long-run growth rates experienced by the United States and some other mixed economies. However, by Western standards China is still a very poor country with a low average level of living. Therefore, whether Chinese leaders can turn their country into an economic superpower by the year 2000 depends on the nation's ability to adhere to an optimum policy capable of sustaining a high rate of growth.

FOUR MODERNIZATIONS: "THE NEW LONG MARCH"

In 1978, China's new leaders announced a monumentally ambitious plan designed to launch the nation into the twenty-first century. Called the Four Modernizations, the plan is a twenty-year blueprint for improving agriculture, industry, science, and the military. The details of the plan, including projected growth rates of production and real income, undergo frequent revisions. Nevertheless, the Four Modernizations, which China's news media have called The New Long March, consists of three phases:

Phase 1   Nationwide mechanization of agriculture accompanied by a reorganization of industry.

Phase 2   Large and sustained annual increases in factory and in agricultural production.

Phase 3   Diversification of production, with greater emphasis on sophisticated consumer goods and high-technology items such as electronic products and computers. As for the military, it appears that this will be given the lowest priority in the overall plan for mechanization.

The first two phases are to be completed during the 1980s. The third phase can then be initiated and completed by the end of this century.

CONCLUSION: LIMITED MARKET SOCIALISM

China, in 1978, thus made a complete turnaround from the previous thirty years of communist rule and isolation. In an effort to modernize itself and become an economic superpower by the year 2000, it has opened its doors to the advanced nations. Whether the turnaround will continue remains to be seen, for China is still a totalitarian nation with a somewhat divided leadership. Nevertheless, it is a nation whose economic system is now substantially different from the preceding one.

China's current economic system may be described as limited market socialism. That is, the means of production are still owned by government. However:

○ Cooperation and trade with foreign nations are recognized as important conditions for growth.

○ Wages more closely match each worker's output, and profit-sharing bonuses are used as incentives for workers and managers.

○ Managers make greater use of anticipated profits as a guide for determining what goods to produce and how to produce them.

○ Government makes greater use of realized profits as a guide for allocating credit to particular industries.

The Chinese, it is said, are always looking for a quick solution to their problems. At present, they are focusing on rapid modernization. But the difficulties of achieving their desired goals are likely to be much greater than China's leaders imagine.

For example, the nation's GNP must grow considerably faster than the average annual rate of 4 percent experienced thus far. In addition, the country must maintain political stability, curb population growth, and greatly improve productive efficiency in agriculture and manufacturing. Otherwise, China will be unable to expand exports in those commodities in which it has comparative advantages. Hence, it will not be able to earn the funds necessary to import modern plant and equipment from other countries.

These facts, as well as those presented in Exhibit 4, are a few of the hard realities that China must face as it tries to race toward modernization.

The Convergence Hypothesis: A Meeting of East and West?

The only choice is either bourgeois or socialist ideology. There is no middle course.

V. I. Lenin

Is this view of Lenin's really true? Some scholars in both the East and West think not. They believe in a *convergence hypothesis*. This is a theory which proposes that capitalism and communism, driven by the process of industrialization, will eventually merge to form a new kind of society. In it, the personal freedoms and profit motive of Western capitalistic democracies blend with the government controls that exist in a communistic (especially in the Soviet) economy.

Perhaps the most dramatic statement of this rapprochement between East and West was made some years ago by the distinguished Soviet physicist Andrei Sakharov. In a 10,000-word essay that was smuggled to the West, he wrote:

The continuing economic progress being achieved under capitalism should be a fact of great theoretical significance for any dogmatic Marxist. It is precisely this fact that lies at the basis of peaceful coexistence and it suggests, in principle, that if capitalism ever runs into an economic blind alley it will not necessarily have to leap into a desperate military adventure. Both capitalism and socialism are capable of long-term development, borrowing positive elements from each other and actually coming closer to each other in a number of essential aspects.

The only hope for world peace, Sakharov concluded, was a coalescence of socialistic and capitalistic systems. Otherwise, we stand on the brink of disaster.

THREE BASIC ASSUMPTIONS

The convergence hypothesis, of course, is an adaptation of the familiar Marxian doctrine that economic forces determine a nation's political and social devel-

---

Exhibit 4
Can China Catch Up?

China's leaders announced their new plans for economic growth in 1978. But their chances of catching up to the U.S.S.R., not to mention the United States, by the year 2000 are practically zero.

For example, China's 1978 GNP must grow at an average annual rate of 5 percent in order to match the Soviet Union's 1978 GNP by the end of the century. The comparable growth rate needed to equal America's 1978 GNP is 8 percent.

LATEST COMPARABLE DATA, 1978

	United States	U.S.S.R.	China
Gross national product, GNP	$2.1 trillion	$1.2 trillion	$445 billion
Steel production	135 million tons	166 million tons	34 million tons
Grain production	294 million tons	259 million tons	325 million tons
Average annual wage	$13,400	$3,000	$360
Population	220 million	262 million	1 billion
Proportion of labor force engaged in agriculture	3.3%	25%	85%

SOURCE: Central Intelligence Agency; U.S. Department of Commerce; Joint Economic Committee of Congress.

opment. But it departs from orthodox Marxism by challenging the conviction that communism is the only route to attaining the highest form of social evolution. Thus, in the simplest sense, the key factor is the ongoing process of industrialization. As former Harvard economist John Kenneth Galbraith put it years ago, advancing technology has different implications for the United States and for the Soviet Union. In the United States it must lead to increased intellectual curiosity and freedom; in the Soviet Union, to much greater government planning and control.

The convergence hypothesis rests on three basic assumptions:

1. Industrialization leads to urbanization and to many common challenges of effective resource organization and management. The skills, training, and desires of a steel worker in Pittsburgh are not significantly different from one in Magnitogorsk. Hence they tend to evolve toward a similar way of life.

2. Industrialization inevitably produces a more complex society with problems of specialization and exchange that are common to all advanced economies.

3. Industrialization raises living standards and improves economic well-being. This, in turn, leads to intellectual independence and probably to ideological nonconformity.

CONCLUSION: MANY GAPS REMAIN

On the basis of these assumptions, there appear to be more surface similarities today between the United States and the Soviet Union than there were several decades ago. Thus, in order to make its economy work better, the United States has accepted a degree of "socialism" and welfare statism which in the more distant past would have been unthinkable. The Soviet Union, on the other hand, has followed a policy of greater freedom and decentralization since the mid-1960s.

Are we to conclude from this that the convergence hypothesis is becoming a reality? The answer is no:

Even if communism is capable of achieving its economic goals, the evidence does not show that the political and social objectives of the United States are anywhere present in communist countries. Indeed, there is at least as much evidence to suggest that social and political inequalities are widening, thereby bringing into question some of the underlying implications of the foregoing assumptions. We are thus led to the conclusion that even if the Soviet Union and the United States actually do come closer in the economic sphere, there are still major if not unbridgeable gaps between the traditions, value systems, and goals of the two societies.

What You Have Learned

1. Countries engage in economic planning to achieve specific economic goals. The chief ones are efficiency, equity, stability, and growth.

2. Among the basic tools of scientific economic planning are econometrics and input–output analysis. These techniques are gaining increasing use by corporations as well as by governments.

3. Since the late 1920s, the Soviet system has been a command economy. Its primary objective has been to raise itself to the status of a major industrial and military power. Through state ownership of industry and extensive planning, it has succeeded in achieving these goals. But its citizens have paid a heavy cost in terms of deprivation of consumer goods and lack of political and economic freedoms.

4. Chinese leaders, in their formal planning efforts, are emphasizing a high rate of investment in heavy industry, accompanied by a reorganization of agriculture to achieve greater efficiency in food and raw materials production. Despite some serious setbacks, the long-run growth of China's GNP under communist leadership has been reasonably satisfactory—averaging about 4 percent annually. Its ability to sustain this rate of expansion will depend on whether it can maintain political stability, curb population growth, improve agricultural productivity, and expand exports in those commodities in which it has comparative advantages—such as agricultural and handicraft products.

5. Some observers contend that the process of industrialization must lead eventually to a convergence of communism and capitalism—a meeting of East and West. Even if this hypothesis were valid on economic grounds, which is doubtful, it overlooks the traditions and goals which make the Soviet Union and the United States vastly different in their institutions and value systems.

For Discussion

1. *Terms and concepts to review:*

economic plan	state farms
planned economy	collective farms
efficiency	coefficient of relative
economic growth	effectiveness (CRE)
econometrics	underemployment
input–output analysis	convergence hypothesis

2. In terms of goals, political leaders often place a higher priority on equity than on efficiency, stability, or growth. Can you suggest why?

3. Fill in the required data, including the input coefficients, for the accompanying input–output table.

(a) Suppose that there is a 10 percent increase in foreign demand for manufactured goods. Would any of the numbers in the table be affected? Explain.

(b) Would other sectors of the economy be affected by an increase in foreign demand for manufactured goods? Does it make any difference if the manufacturing sector is operating at full capacity or at less than full capacity? Discuss.

INPUT–OUTPUT TABLE FOR AN ECONOMY

(millions of dollars; hypothetical data)

Output (sellers) \ Input (buyers)	Agricultural sector	Manufacturing sector	Service sector	Intersector sales total	All other sales	Total output
Agricultural sector	$100 ( )	$200 ( )	$50 ( )		$150	
Manufacturing sector	$300 ( )	$400 ( )	$200 ( )		$100	
Service sector	$50 ( )	$150 ( )	$100 ( )		$100	
Other resources	$50 ( )	$250 ( )	$50 ( )			
Total input					$350	

(c) In terms of your answer to part (b), can you explain why an input–output table may serve as a model to depict an economy in general equilibrium?

4. Since the Soviet Union is a centrally directed and collectivist economy, there is no competition as in American capitalism. True or false? Explain.

5. Why would a socialist economy such as that of the Soviet Union want to employ the capitalistic device of providing economic incentives? What types of incentives do they use?

6. Is there freedom of consumer choice in the Soviet Union? Is there consumer sovereignty? Explain.

7. Which would you suggest as a better guide for judging the efficiency of firms in the United States and in the Soviet Union: profits or sales? What are some of the assumptions underlying your answer?

8. What criteria would you use in judging whether one nation's economy is better than another's? Are there non-economic criteria, too?

9. Why do the Soviet authorities want to engage in the complex and difficult task of planning? Why do they not simply let a free-market system allocate the resources and distribute the income for them?

10. What are some of the "capitalistic" practices that the Soviet Union has adopted over the years? Do the Soviets view these as a step toward capitalism? Explain.

11. What is the economic function of profits, and of the anticipation of profits, in a market economy? In the Chinese economy?

12. There is considerable evidence that in advanced Western societies and even in the Soviet Union, the use of material incentives serves to spur worker productivity and thereby encourage greater output. In view of this, why did Chinese leaders under communism (i.e., pre-1978) usually oppose the use of material incentives?

Portfolio
China: "The New Long March"

Joan Lebold Cohen, Photo Researchers.

Chinese newspaper headline translates: "The New Long March."

Billboards and posters are major communications media in China.

Many of them glorify the New Long March toward modernization.

The Chinese people's march toward the great goal of the Four Modernizations echos from the foothills of the Yenshan Mountains to the shores of the Yellow Sea to all corners of the world. It has aroused worldwide attention. We are setting out to conquer on our New Long March the mountains, seas, plains, oilfields and mines of our motherland. We want to scale the heights of science and technology. We want to develop normal trade relations with other countries of the world.

The Peking *People's Daily*

To achieve their goals, China's leaders have embarked on a dramatic and ambitious journey. The new doctrine does not represent an abandonment of, but rather a retreat from, the repressive communist ideology that prevailed from 1949 to 1978.

Paolo Koch, Photo Researchers.

"Take advantage of every moment to race to the year 2000."

Andanson/Sygma.

I. Alex Langley, DPI.

Agricultural development has one of the highest priorities in China's plans. Most farms are organized into communes. These are groups of villages that own their own land and *assign production teams to farm it. The communes consume a proportion of the output and sell the rest. Because the organization of most communes is relatively primitive,* *the greatest difficulties will be encountered in trying to mechanize them. The Chinese, however, expect to achieve this goal by the late 1980s.*

Thus, the once sacred goals of national self-reliance and independence from outside resources are now gone. In their place, China's leaders have instituted new forms of "market socialism." For example:

○ Greater initiative and autonomy are encouraged at the individual enterprise level.

○ Realistic pricing practices designed to allocate goods and resources are being implemented in certain industries.

○ Steady wage increases, bonuses, paid vacations, and other material incentives are being employed to spur greater production and productivity.

○ Thousands of students and plant managers are being sent to Japan and the advanced Western democracies to study "capitalistic" technology and management methods. In addition, huge contracts are being signed with

major firms in these countries to set up new plants in China.

○ Tourists are encouraged to visit China and to exchange cultural experiences. The Middle Kingdom now hosts hundreds of thousands of tourists annually, compared to a relative handful prior to 1978.

What do China's leaders promise the people in return for their efforts? A higher material standard of living—a greater quantity and variety of consumer goods—than the nation has ever had. Ideally, this will also be accompanied by more political and social freedoms than the Chinese have hitherto experienced.

An Optimum Economic Policy

What steps should China take to assure a steady and self-sustaining expansion of GNP?

China's long-run policy should seek to accomplish three major goals:

1. ***Reduce Population Growth*** This requires organized educational birth-control programs on a national scale.

2. ***Improve Agricultural Efficiency*** This requires the adoption of new technology and practices, such as the use of improved seeds, fertilizers, pesticides, and farm equipment.

3. ***Expand Foreign Trade*** This requires specializing in the production of labor-intensive commodities embracing a wide array of agricultural and handicraft products, along the lines dictated by the law of comparative advantage.

China's economic planners, in varying degrees, have been pursuing these objectives for many years. Whether the country's leadership, however, is capable of sustaining a large-scale organized effort in this direction for the next several decades remains to be seen.

Georg Gerster, Rapho/Photo Researchers.

Andanson/Sygma.

Audrey Toppino, Rapho/Photo Researchers.

Eric Kroll, Taurus Photos.

The ultimate goal of China's modernization plans is to achieve a higher material standard of living. Larger quantities and varieties of consumer goods are thus being introduced to a much greater extent than ever before.

China has invited an economic invasion by Western democracies. Pierre Cardin has been hired to design high-fashion clothing. Coca-Cola is being sold throughout much of the country. U.S. Steel is helping to build giant iron ore refining facilities. Pan American Airways is developing a luxury hotel chain. The Japanese and Germans are building steel mills and chemical plants. The British are supplying industrial equipment. The Dutch are providing port facilities. The Swedes are constructing railroads. And the French are developing telecommunications satellites and nuclear power plants. Meanwhile, the Chinese are learning English and other foreign languages in an effort to establish closer contact with the formerly "barbaric" foreigners.

Index

Dictionary of Economic Terms and Concepts

This dictionary catalogs the definitions of every technical word, phrase, and concept given in the text, plus definitions of many other terms as well. It also presents cross references and brief examples that explain the significance of important terms. Hence the Dictionary will be a convenient and permanent source of reference—not only for this course, but for future courses you may take in economics, business administration, and other social sciences.

A

ability-to-pay principle: Theory of taxation which holds that the fairest tax is based on the financial means of the taxpayer—regardless of any benefit he may receive from the tax. Financial means may be determined by either wealth or income. The U.S. personal income tax is founded on this idea.

absolute advantage, law of: Principle which states that a basis for trade exists between nations or regions when each of them, as a result of natural or acquired superiorities, can provide a good or service that the other wants at a lower cost than if each were to provide it for itself. This law accounts for much of the world's trade.

absolute income hypothesis: Proposition which states that a family's propensity to consume (i.e., the amount it spends on consumption) depends on its *level* of income—the absolute amount available for spending. This concept of the propensity to consume was the one used by Keynes. (*Contrast with* **relative income hypothesis; permanent income hypothesis.**)

acceleration curves: Short-run inflation–unemployment relationships showing how the inflation rate speeds up with expansionary fiscal–monetary policies and slows down with contractionary ones. (*See* **Phillips curve.**)

accelerator principle: Proposition that net investment in capital goods depends upon *changes* in the level of output (i.e., GNP). This is because capital goods are durable. Therefore, if existing production capacity is adequate, it is possible to produce a constant level of output with existing equipment, replacing it as it wears out. No net investment needs to be undertaken. But if aggregate demand increases, the economy, operating at full capacity, will have to undertake additional investment in order to produce an increase in output. Therefore, net investment is a function of *changes* in the level of output. Thus:

$$\text{net investment} = \text{accelerator} \times \text{change in GNP}$$

and hence

$$\text{accelerator} = \frac{\text{net investment}}{\text{change in GNP}}$$

The accelerator itself is a mathematical constant—a number such as 1.0, 1.5, 2.0, etc.—which is estimated by statistical procedures.

accounts payable: A company's debts to suppliers of goods or services.

accounts receivable: Amounts due to a firm from customers.

accrued expenses payable: Obligations such as wages and salaries, interest on borrowed funds, and pensions.

adjustable peg: System which permits governmentally controlled changes in the par rate of foreign exchange after a nation has had long-run disequilibrium in its balance of payments. It allows also for short-run variations within a narrow range of a few percent around the par value.

ad valorem subsidy: Fixed percentage subsidy based on the price or value of a commodity.

ad valorem tax: Fixed percentage tax on the price or value of a commodity. *Examples:* sales taxes, property taxes, and most import duties.

aggregate demand: Total value of output that all sectors of the economy are willing to purchase at any given time or level of income.

aggregate supply: Total value of output produced or available for purchase by the economy at any given time or level of income.

Agricultural Adjustment Act (1938): Basic farm law (with subsequent amendments) of the United States. It has, at various times, provided for (1) price supports of selected farm products at specified levels; (2) production control through acreage allotments of certain crops; (3) marketing agreements and quotas between the Department of Agriculture and producers in order to control the distribution of selected commodities; (4) payments to farmers and others who follow approved soil conservation practices; and (5) parity payments to farmers for selected agricultural staples.

allocative efficiency: *See* **efficiency.**

Aluminum Company of America case (1945): Major antitrust case against Alcoa. The company was the dominant firm in aluminum production, accounting for 90 percent of the nation's output. Even though Alcoa did not aggressively seek to attain a monopoly, but rather had it "thrust upon" itself, the company was a "passive beneficiary" of monopoly. Therefore, Judge Learned Hand found the company in violation of the Sherman Act. This stringent interpretation was thus contrary to the traditional *rule of reason* that had prevailed since the Standard Oil case of 1911. As it happens, Judge Hand's rigid interpretation was greatly tempered in subsequent antitrust cases, and has not been strictly applied since 1945.

American Federation of Labor–Congress of Industrial Organizations (AFL–CIO): League of labor unions formed in 1955 by a merger of the AFL and CIO. Its purposes are to improve the wages, hours, and conditions of workers, and to realize the benefits of free collective bargaining. It exercises no authority or control over member unions other than requiring them to abide by its constitution and code of ethical practices.

American Tobacco case (1911): Major antitrust case in which the Supreme Court found the "tobacco trust" to be in violation of the Sherman Act. The trust consisted of five major tobacco manufacturers controlling 95 percent of domestic cigarette production. However, the Court did not condemn this. It was the trust's "unreasonable" market behavior, driving competitors out of business, that caused the Court's condemnation.

annually balanced budget: Philosophy which holds that total revenues and expenditures in the government's budget should be balanced or brought into equality every year.

antitrust laws: Acts passed by Congress since 1890 to prevent monopoly and to maintain competition. The chief ones are (1) the Sherman Antitrust Act (1890); (2) the Clayton Antitrust Act (1914); (3) the Federal Trade Commission Act (1914); (4) the Robinson–Patman Act (1936); (5) the Wheeler–Lea Act (1938); and (6) the Celler Antimerger Act (1950).

Aquinas, St. Thomas (1225–1274): Medieval philosopher who wrote on economic problems during the early stages of modern capitalism. He attempted to harmonize reason with faith by applying principles of Aristotelian philosophy to biblical teaching and canonical dogma. Thus he held that the individual's right to private property accords with natural law; commerce is to be condoned to the extent that it maintains the household and benefits the country; fairness and truthfulness in commercial dealings are essential virtues; and so on. In general, these and other ideas of Aquinas make him one of the important leaders in early economic thought.

arbitrage: Act of buying a commodity in one market and simultaneously selling it in a dearer market at a higher price. Arbitrage tends to equalize prices of a commodity in different markets, except for differences in the costs of transportation, risk, and so on.

arbitration: Settlement of differences between parties (such as a union and management) by the use of an impartial third party called an arbitrator who is acceptable to both sides and whose decision is binding and legally enforceable on the contesting parties. The arbitrator issues a decision based not on what he thinks is wise and fair, but on how he thinks the language of the contract applies to the case.

assets: Resources or things of value owned by an economic entity, such as an individual, household, or firm. *Examples:* cash, property, and the rights to property.

automatic fiscal stabilizers: Nondiscretionary or "built-in" features that automatically cushion recession by helping to create a budget deficit and curb inflation by helping to create a budget surplus. *Examples:* (1) income tax receipts; (2) unemployment taxes and benefits; (3) agricultural price supports; and (4) corporate dividend policies.

autonomous consumption: Consumption independent of income. It is that part of total consumption which is unrelated to income. (*Compare* **induced consumption.**)

autonomous investment: Investment independent of income, output, and general economic activity. (*Compare* **induced investment.**)

autonomous transactions: Settlements among nations that arise from factors unrelated to the balance of payments as such. The main classes are merchandise trade and services, long-term capital movements, and unilateral transfers.

average cost price: *See* **full cost price.**

average fixed cost: Ratio of a firm's total fixed cost to the quantity it produces. Also, the difference between average total cost and average variable cost. Thus

$$\text{average fixed cost} = \frac{\text{total fixed cost}}{\text{quantity of output}}$$

Also,

average fixed cost

$$= \text{average total cost} - \text{average variable cost}$$

average–marginal relationship: Relationship between all corresponding average and marginal curves such that: when an average curve is rising, its corresponding marginal curve is above it; when an average curve is falling, its corresponding marginal curve is below it; and when an average curve is neither rising nor falling (i.e., it is either at a maximum or at a minimum), its corresponding marginal curve intersects (is equal to) it.

average product: Ratio of total output or product to the amount of variable input needed to produce that volume of output. Thus

$$\text{average product} = \frac{\text{total product}}{\text{variable input}}$$

average propensity to consume: Ratio of consumption to income:

$$\text{average propensity to consume} = \frac{\text{consumption}}{\text{income}}$$

It thus reveals the proportion of income that is spent on consumption.

average propensity to save: Ratio of saving to income:

$$\text{average propensity to save} = \frac{\text{saving}}{\text{income}}$$

It thus reveals the proportion of income that is saved (i.e., not spent on consumption).

average revenue: Ratio of a firm's total revenue to its quantity of output sold—or equivalently, its price per unit of quantity sold. Thus

average revenue

$$= \frac{\text{total revenue}}{\text{quantity}} = \frac{(\text{price})(\text{quantity})}{\text{quantity}} = \text{price}$$

average revenue product: Ratio of total revenue to the quantity of an input employed. Thus

$$\text{average revenue product} = \frac{\text{total revenue}}{\text{quantity of input employed}}$$

average tax rate: Ratio or percentage of a total tax to the base on which it is imposed. *Example:*

average personal income tax rate

$$= \frac{\text{total personal income tax}}{\text{total taxable income}}$$

average total cost: Ratio of a firm's total cost to the quantity it produces. Also, the sum of average fixed cost and average variable cost. Thus

$$\text{average total cost} = \frac{\text{total cost}}{\text{quantity of output}}$$

Also,

average total cost

$$= \text{average fixed cost} + \text{average variable cost}$$

average variable cost: Ratio of a firm's total variable cost to the quantity it produces. Also, the difference between a firm's average total cost and average fixed cost. Thus

$$\text{average variable cost} = \frac{\text{total variable cost}}{\text{quantity of output}}$$

Also,

average variable cost

$$= \text{average total cost} - \text{average fixed cost}$$

B

Bain index: Measure of a firm's monopoly power, based on the divergence between price, P, and average total cost, ATC. A modified version of the index in which the divergence is expressed as a proportion of price is

$$\text{Bain index} = \frac{P - ATC}{P}$$

The index will be zero (no monopoly power) when the firm is earning only normal profit (i.e., $P = ATC$). On the other hand, the index will be greater than zero when the firm is earning an economic or excess profit (i.e., $P > ATC$). Basic shortcomings of the index are that (1) large profits do not necessarily indicate the existence of strong monopoly power, since large profits may be the result of greater efficiency or of different accounting methods used for depreciation and asset valuation; (2) it is a static rather than dynamic measure and therefore cannot be applied to firms that experience rapid changes in technology, demand, and so on.

balanced budget: Budget with total revenues and total expenditures that are equal.

balanced-budget multiplier: Principle which asserts that if government spending and taxes are increased or decreased simultaneously by a balanced or equal amount, NNP will be increased or decreased by the same amount. *Example:* A balanced increase in government spending and taxes of $1 will raise NNP by $1, and a balanced decrease of $1 will lower NNP by $1. The reason for this is that the effects of balanced increases in government spending and taxes are equal but opposite, and hence the two multiplier processes cancel each other out—except on the first round, when the full amount of government spending is added to NNP.

balance of payments: Statement of the money value of all transactions between a nation and the rest of the world during a given period. These transactions may consist of imports and exports of goods and services, and movements of short-term and long-term investments, gifts, currency, and gold; they may be classified as current account, capital account, unilateral transfer account, and official reserve transactions account.

balance-of-payments disequilibrium: Circumstance that exists when, over an unspecified period lasting several years, a nation's autonomous credits do not equal its autonomous debits. A deficit disequilibrium exists when total autonomous debits exceed total autonomous credits; a surplus disequilibrium occurs when total autonomous credits exceed total autonomous debits.

balance of trade: That part of a nation's balance of payments dealing with merchandise imports and exports. A "favorable" balance of trade exists when the value of exports exceeds the value of imports; an "unfavorable" balance exists when the value of imports exceeds the value of exports.

balance sheet: Statement of a firm's financial position on a given date. It shows what the firm owns (its assets), what it owes (its liabilities), and the residual or equity of the owners (the net worth).

Bank of the United States: Chartered for the period 1791 to 1811, the Bank's function was to assist the Treasury in its fiscal activities and to provide an adequate supply of currency to meet the needs of business. The Bank's performance was generally satisfactory, but its charter was not renewed. Primary opposition came from farmers, who felt that the Bank favored urban commercial interests over rural agricultural ones, and that the Bank's financial power was too great.

banker's acceptance: Bill of exchange drawn on or accepted by a bank instead of an individual or firm. It is a promise by a bank to pay specific bills for one of its customers when the bills become due. (*See also* **bill of exchange; draft.**)

barter: Simple exchange of one good for another without the use of money.

basic wages: Payments received by workers for work performed, based on time or output.

benefit-cost analysis: Method of evaluating alternative investment projects by comparing for each the (discounted) present value of all expected benefits or net receipts with the (discounted) present value of all expected costs or sacrifices. Once such comparisons are made, a rational basis exists for choosing one investment project over the other.

benefit-cost (B/C) ratio: Ratio of the present value of benefits (net receipts) of an investment to the present value of costs:

$$B/C = \frac{\text{present value of benefits}}{\text{present value of costs}}$$

The B/C ratio thus gives the present value of net receipts per dollar of investment cost. The ratio must equal at least 1 in order for the investment to be recovered (i.e., repaid by its net receipts).

benefit principle: Theory of taxation which holds that a fair tax is one which is levied on people according to the services or benefits they receive from government. The chief difficulties are that: (1) for many goods, benefits cannot be readily determined (e.g., national defense, public education, police and fire protection); and (2) those who receive the benefits are not always able to pay for them (e.g., recipients of welfare or unemployment compensation).

bilateral monopoly: Market structure in which a monopsonist buyer faces a monopolist seller. The equilibrium quantity may be determinate. However, the price level for that quantity is logically indeterminate. That is, the price will end up somewhere between the minimum price preferred by the monopsonist and the maximum price preferred by the monopolist.

bill of exchange: Draft (or type of "check") used between countries. (*See also* **draft.**)

bimetallic standard: Monetary standard under which the national unit of currency (such as the dollar) is defined in terms of a fixed weight of two metals, usually gold and silver. The United States was on this standard during the nineteenth century, but it usually worked unsatisfactorily due to the operation of Gresham's Law. (*See also* **Gresham's Law; mint ratio.**)

black market: Illegal market in which a good is sold for more than its legal ceiling price. The good may or may not be rationed. If it is, experience indicates that the criteria used for rationing are virtually certain to create skullduggery and inequities. (*Compare* **white market.**)

Board of Governors: Group of seven people that supervises the Federal Reserve System. Members are appointed by the President and confirmed by the Senate for terms of 14 years each, one term expiring every 2 years.

bond: Agreement to pay a specified sum (called the "principal") either at a future date or periodically over the course of a loan, during which time a fixed rate of interest may be paid on certain dates. Bonds are issued by corporations, and by the federal, state, and local governments. They are typically used for long-term financing.

boycott: Campaign to discourage people from dealing with a particular firm. (Sometimes called a "primary boycott.")

break-even point: Level of output at which a firm's total revenue equals its total cost (or its average revenue equals its average total cost) so that its net revenue is zero. At a break-even point as defined in economics, a firm is normally profitable, since total cost in economics includes normal profit.

Brown Shoe case (1962): Major antitrust case in which the Supreme Court struck down a merger between Brown Shoe and Kinney Shoe as a violation of the Clayton Act. Although both companies were shoe manufacturers and retailers with relatively small market shares, the merger, it was held, would nevertheless "foreclose competition from a substantial share of the market for shoes without producing countervailing economic or social advantages." The Court also held that the merger might increase market concentration in a few cities where both companies had retail stores.

budget: Itemized estimate of expected revenues and expenditures for a given period in the future.

budget deficit: Budget in which total expenditures exceed total revenues.

budget surplus: Budget in which total revenues exceed total expenditures.

Burns, Arthur Frank (1904–): American economist and expert on business cycles, fiscal policy, and monetary policy. He served as President of the National Bureau of Economic Research, as a professor of economics at Columbia University, and in various high-level government positions as head of the President's Council of Economic Advisors and as Chairman of the Board of Governors of the Federal Reserve System.

business cycles: Recurrent but nonperiodic fluctuations in general business and economic activity that take place over a period of years. They occur in aggregate variables such as income, output, employment, and prices, most of which may move at approximately the same time in the same direction, but at *different rates.* Business cycles are thus accelerations and retardations in the rates of growth of important economic variables.

C

cameralism: Form of mercantilism extensively implemented by German governments during the eighteenth century. Its chief objective was to increase the revenue of the state. (The word comes from *Kammer,* the name of the royal treasury.)

capital: 1. As a factor of production, capital is a produced means of further production (such as capital goods or investment goods in the form of raw materials, machines, or equipment) for the ultimate purpose of manufacturing consumer goods. Hence human resources are also part of an economy's capital. **2.** As money, capital represents the funds which businesspersons use to purchase capital goods.

3. In accounting, capital may sometimes represent net worth or the stockholders' equity in a business.

capital consumption allowance: Expression used in national-income accounting to represent the difference between "gross" and "net" private domestic investment. It consists almost entirely of depreciation and is often used synonymously with it.

capital deepening: Increases in an economy's stock of capital at a faster rate than the growth of its labor force, thus expanding the volume of capital per worker and raising average output per worker.

capitalism: Economic organization characterized by private ownership of the means of production and distribution (such as land, factories, railroads) and their operation for profit under predominantly competitive conditions.

capital market: Center where long-term credit and equity instruments such as bonds, stocks, and mortgages are bought and sold.

capital/output ratio: Concept sometimes used in a "total" sense, and sometimes in a "marginal" sense. Thus: **1.** The "total" capital/output ratio is the ratio of an economy's total stock of real capital to the level of its income or output. **2.** The "marginal" capital/output ratio is the change in an economy's income or output resulting from a unit change in its stock of real capital. Thus a ratio of 3/1 means that three units of additional capital produce one unit of additional output.

capital stock: Unit of ownership in a corporation. It represents the stockholder's proprietary interest. Two major classes are common stock and preferred stock.

capital widening: Increases in an economy's stock of capital at the same rate as the growth of its labor force, thus maintaining the same volume of capital per worker and hence the same average output per worker.

cartel: Association of producers in the same industry, established to increase the profits of its members by adopting common policies affecting production, market allocation, or price. A cartel may be domestic or international in scope. In the United States, organizations of independent business enterprises established for mutually beneficial purposes are called *trade associations*, not cartels. The latter term has been reserved exclusively for foreign or international associations. However, when a trade association or similar group fixes prices, restricts output, or allocates markets for its members, it behaves *in effect* like a cartel.

Celler Antimerger Act (1950): Major antitrust law. An extension of Section 7 of the Clayton Antitrust Act, it prohibits a corporation from acquiring the stock *or assets* of another corporation if the effect would be a substantial lessening of competition or tendency toward monopoly. *Note:* Prior to this law, only the acquisition of *stock* by competing corporations was illegal under the Clayton Act.

certificate of deposit (CD): Special type of time deposit which a purchaser agrees to keep in a bank for a specified period, usually three months or more. Many CDs are negotiable, and hence can be sold in a secondary market because they offer both liquidity and a yield. Banks began to offer CDs in the early 1960s at rates competitive with other money market instruments, in order to discourage corporations from withdrawing money for the purpose of investing in securities.

Chamberlin, Edward Hastings (1899–1967): American economist who was one of the pioneers in developing the theory of monopolistic competition. His doctoral dissertation, *The Theory of Monopolistic Competition* (Harvard, 1933), became a standard work in the field. In this and in subsequent editions and articles, Chamberlin emphasized the role of product differentiation, advertising, and differences in consumer preferences as factors contributing to the existence of "partial" or "competing monopolists." Chamberlin thus identified a new form of market structure, monopolistic competition, the theory of which has become an essential part of microeconomics.

change in amount consumed: Increase or decrease in the amount of consumption expenditure due to a change in income. It may be represented by a movement along a consumption-function curve.

change in consumption: Increase or decrease in consumption, represented by a shift of the consumption-function curve to a new position. The shift results from a change in any of the factors that were assumed to remain constant when the curve was drawn. These may include (1) the volume of liquid assets owned by households, (2) expectations of future prices and incomes, (3) anticipations of product shortages, and (4) credit conditions.

change in demand: Increase or decrease in demand, represented by a shift of the demand curve to a new position. The shift results from a change in any of the factors that were assumed to remain constant when the curve was drawn. These may include (1) buyers' money incomes, (2) the prices of related goods, (3) buyers' tastes or preferences, (4) the number of buyers in the market, and (5) buyers' expectations about future prices and incomes.

change in quantity demanded: Increase or decrease in the quantity demanded of a good due to a change in its price. It may be represented by a movement along a demand curve.

change in quantity supplied: Increase or decrease in the quantity supplied of a good due to a change in its price. It may be represented by a movement along a supply curve.

change in supply: Increase or decrease in supply represented by a shift of the supply curve to a new position. The shift results from a change in any of the factors that were assumed to remain constant when the curve was drawn. These may include (1) the state of technology, (2) resource prices or the costs of the factors of production, (3) the prices of other goods, (4) the number of sellers in the market, and (5) sellers' expectations regarding future prices.

checkoff: Procedure by which an employer, with the written permission of the worker, withholds union dues and other assessments from paychecks and then transfers the funds to the union. This provides an efficient means by which the union can collect dues from its members.

Christian socialism: Movement, since the late nineteenth century, by various church groups to preach the "social gospel"—a type of social legislation and reform that seeks to improve the well-being of the working classes by appealing to Christian ethical and humanitarian principles.

circular flow of economic activity: Model demonstrating the movement of goods, resources, payments, and expenditures among sectors of the economy. A simple model may include the household and business sectors, and the product and resource markets—but other models may be constructed which are more complex.

Clark, John Bates (1847–1938): Leading American economist whose major treatise, *The Distribution of Wealth* (1899), was the first American work in pure economic theory. The book developed what is essentially the modern version of the marginal productivity theory. This theory demonstrates that a (perfectly competitive) capitalistic system distributes incomes to resource owners in proportion to the market values of their contribution to production. The theory was thus used by others to justify capitalism as a fair (equitable) system. Clark, it should be noted, had much in common with his British contemporary, Alfred Marshall. Both used similar methodologies in analyzing economic problems. Clark, however, tended to be more theoretical and abstract.

classical economics: Body of economic thought dominant in the Western world from the late eighteenth century until the 1930s. Among its chief proponents were Adam Smith (1723–1790), Jean Baptiste Say (1767–1832), Jeremy Bentham (1748–1832), Thomas Robert Malthus (1766–1834), David Ricardo (1772–1823), Nassau William Senior (1790–1864), and John Stuart Mill (1806–1873). It emphasized man's self-interest, and the operation of universal economic laws which tend automatically to guide the economy toward full-employment equilibrium if the government adheres to a policy of laissez-faire or noninterventionism.

class struggle: In the theories of Karl Marx, an irreconcilable clash between the bourgeoisie or capitalist class and the proletariat or working class, arising out of the surplus value which capitalists appropriate from workers. The class struggle will eventually be resolved when the proletariat overthrows the bourgeoisie and establishes a new and equitable economic order.

Clayton Antitrust Act (1914): A major antitrust law aimed at preventing unfair, deceptive, dishonest, or injurious methods of competition. It declares as illegal, where the effect is a substantial lessening of competition or tendency toward monopoly: (1) price discrimination, except where there are differences in grade, quality, or quantity sold, or where the lower prices make due allowances for cost differences in selling or transportation, or where the lower prices are offered in good faith to meet competition; (2) tying contracts between sellers and purchasers; and (3) intercorporate stockholdings among competing corporations. It also makes illegal, regardless of the effect on competition: (4) interlocking directorates if the corporations involved are competitive and if any one of them has capital, surplus, and undivided profits in excess of $1 million.

closed shop: A firm which agrees that an employee must be a union member before he is employed, and must remain a union member after he is employed. Outlawed by the Labor–Management Relations (Taft–Hartley) Act of 1947.

coalition bargaining: Method of bargaining by which a federation of unions (such as the AFL–CIO) tries to coordinate and establish common termination dates for contracts with firms that deal with a number of unions at their plants throughout the economy. Its purpose is to enable the federation to strengthen union bargaining positions by threatening to close down all plants simultaneously.

cobweb theorem: Generic name for a theory of cyclical fluctuations in the prices and quantities of various agricultural commodities—fluctuations which arise because for certain agricultural products: (1) the quantity demanded of the commodity at any given time depends on its price at that time, whereas (2) the quantity supplied at any given time depends on its price at a previous time when production plans were initially formulated. Hogs and beef cattle have been notable examples.

coefficient of relative effectiveness (CRE): Term used in the Soviet Union to mean the expected payoff or percent rate of return on a capital investment; akin to the concept of marginal efficiency of investment in Western economics.

coincident indicators: Time series that tend to move approximately "in phase" with the aggregate economy, and hence are measures of current economic activity.

collective agreement: A collective-bargaining contract worked out between union and management, describing wages, working conditions, and related matters.

collective bargaining: Negotiation between a company's management and a union for the purpose of agreeing on mutually acceptable wages and working conditions for employees.

collective farms: Agricultural cooperatives in the Soviet Union, consisting of communities of farmers who pool their resources, lease land from the government, and divide the profits among the members according to the amount and kind of work done by each. This type of farming, which is subject to detailed government regulation, dominates agriculture in the Soviet Union.

collective good: *See* **public good.**

command economy: Economic system in which an authoritarian government exercises primary control over decisions concerning what and how much to produce; it may also, but does not necessarily, decide for whom to produce. (*Compare* **planned economy.**)

commercial bank: Financial institution, chartered by federal or state governments, primarily engaged in making short-term industrial and commercial loans by creating demand or checking deposits, and retiring loans by canceling demand deposits. It may also perform other financial functions, such as holding time or savings deposits and making long-term mortgage loans.

common market: Association of trading nations which agrees to: (1) impose no trade restrictions such as tariffs or quotas among participants; (2) establish common external barriers (such as a common external tariff) to nonparticipants; and (3) impose no national restrictions on the movement of labor and capital among participants. *Example:* European Economic Community (EEC).

common stock: Shares that have no fixed rate of dividends, and hence may receive higher dividends than the fixed rate on preferred stock if the corporation's earnings are sufficiently high.

Commonwealth (Mass.) v. Hunt (1842): The first case in which a (Massachusetts) court held a trade union to be a lawful organization. It declared that workers could form a union to bargain collectively with employers.

communism: 1. In the theories of Karl Marx, the final and perfect goal of historical development, characterized by: (*a*) a classless society in which all men live by earning and no man lives by owning; (*b*) a nonexistent state; and (*c*) a wage system which is completely abolished and all citizens live and work according to the motto: "from each according to his ability, to each according to his needs." **2.** In most communist countries today, an economic system based on (*a*) social ownership of property, including most of the means of production and distribution; (*b*) government planning and control of the economy; and (*c*) a scheme of rewards and penalties to achieve maximum productive effort. *Note:* Communist leaders claim that the system which exists in communist countries today is socialism of the type which Marxian ideology holds as being preparatory to the attainment of full communism.

company union: A labor union limited to a particular firm. It is usually unaffiliated with any other union.

comparative advantage, law of: Principle which states that if one nation can produce each of two products more efficiently than another nation and can produce one of these commodities more efficiently than the other, it should specialize in the product in which it is most efficient and leave production of the alternative product to the other country. The two nations will then have more of both goods by engaging in trade. This principle is applicable to individuals and regions as well as to nations.

comparative statics: Method of analysis in which the effects of a change in one or more of the determining conditions in a static model are evaluated by comparing the results after the change with those before the change. *Example:* Comparing the effects on equilibrium prices and quantities (in a supply and demand model) resulting from a shift in supply or demand curves. It is like comparing two "snapshots" of a phenomenon—one taken before the change and one after.

compensatory (accommodating) transactions: Settlements among nations that are a direct response to balance-of-payments considerations. They may be thought of as balancing items which arise to accommodate differences in money inflows and outflows resulting from so-called autonomous transactions. The two main classes are short-term capital movements and shifts in gold holdings.

competition: Rivalry among buyers and sellers of goods or resources. Competition tends to be directly related to the degree of diffusion (as opposed to the concentration) of market power and the freedom with which buyers and sellers can enter or leave particular markets. It is sometimes used to mean perfect (pure) competition, depending on whether it is employed in that context.

complementary goods: Commodities which are related such that at a given level of buyers' incomes, an increase in the price of one good leads to a decrease in the demand for the other, and a decrease in the price of one good leads to an increase in the demand for the other. *Examples:* ham and eggs; hamburgers and buns. (*Compare* **substitute goods.**)

compounding: Process by which a given amount, expressed in dollars, is adjusted at interest to yield a future value. That is, interest when due is added to a principal amount and thereafter earns interest. *Example:* At 6 percent, a principal of $1, plus interest, amounts to a sum of $1.06 after one year, and to an additional 6 percent or a sum of $1.124 after two years, and so on. Compounding is thus the opposite of **discounting.**

compound interest: Interest computed on a principal sum and also on all the interest earned by that principal sum as of a given date.

Comptroller of the Currency: Federal agency which charters all national banks. It also oversees the operations of national banks and of those state banks that are members of the Federal Reserve System.

concentration ratio: Percentage of an industry's output accounted for by its four largest firms. The percentage (or ratio) is usually based either on sales, value added, or value of shipments. Sometimes, however, other measures of size, such as assets or employment, are used.

conglomerate merger: Amalgamation under one ownership of unlike plants producing unrelated products. It reflects a desire by the acquiring company to spread risks, find outlets for idle capital funds, add products which can be sold with the firm's merchandising knowledge and skills, or simply gain economic power on a broader front.

conscious parallel action: Identical price behavior among competing firms. It may or may not be the result of collusion or prior agreement but has, nevertheless, been held illegal by the courts in various antitrust cases.

consent decree: A means of settling cases in equity among the parties involved (such as a defendant firm and the Department of Justice). The defendant does not declare himself guilty, but agrees nevertheless to cease and desist from certain practices and abide by the rules of behavior set down in the decree. This is the chief instrument employed by the Justice Department and by the Federal Trade Commission in the enforcement of the Sherman and Clayton Acts. The majority of antitrust violations are settled in this manner.

conspicuous consumption: Expression originated by Thorstein Veblen (1857–1929) to mean that those above the subsistence level (i.e., the so-called "leisure class") are mainly concerned with impressing others through their standard of living, taste, and dress—that is, through what he called "pecuniary emulation." ("Keeping up with the Joneses" is a popular expression of this concept.)

constant-cost industry: Industry which experiences no increases in resource prices or in costs of production as it expands, despite new firms entering it. This will happen only when the industry's demand for the resources it employs is an insignificant proportion of the total demand for those resources.

constant dollars: Expression reflecting the actual prices of a previous year or the average of actual prices of a previous period of years. Hence economic data are often quoted in constant dollars. (*Compare* **current dollars.**)

Consumer Price Index (CPI): Average of prices of goods and services commonly purchased by families in urban areas. Generally referred to as a "cost-of-living index," the CPI is published by the Bureau of Labor Statistics of the U.S. Department of Labor.

consumer sovereignty: Concept of the consumer as "king"—in the sense that the consumer registers his preferences for goods by his "dollar votes" in the marketplace. In a highly competitive economy competition among producers will cause them to adjust their production to the changing patterns of consumer demands. In less competitive circumstances, where monopolistic forces and other imperfections exist, resources will not be allocated in accordance with consumer wishes.

consumer's surplus: Payment made by a buyer that is less than the maximum amount he would have been willing to pay for the quantity of the commodity that he purchases.

consumption: Expenditures on consumer goods and services.

consumption function: Relationship between consumption expenditures and income such that as income increases, consumption increases, but not as fast as income. The expression **propensity to consume** is often used synonymously. (*Note:* Since the word "function" is employed here in its mathematical sense to mean a variable whose value depends on the value of another variable, the expression "consumption function" can also be used to designate any type of relationship between consumption and income—not necessarily the type defined above. However, the above type is the most common one.)

contributive standard: Criterion of income distribution popularly expressed by the phrase, "To each according to his or her contribution." It means that if the market value of one person's production is twice that of another's, then the first person should be paid twice as much as the second. This is the predominant criterion of income distribution in market-oriented economies. You will consider the contributive standard a just or equitable one only if you believe that each person is entitled to the fruits of his or her labor. (*Compare* **equality standard; needs standard.**)

convergence hypothesis: Conjecture that capitalism and communism, driven by the process of industrialization, will eventually merge to form a new kind of society in which the personal freedoms and profit motive of Western capitalistic democracies blend with the government controls that exist in a communistic (especially Soviet) economy.

corporation: Association of stockholders created under law, but regarded by the courts as an artificial person existing only in the contemplation of the law. The chief characteristics of a corporation are (1) limited liability of its stockholders; (2) stability and permanence; and (3) ability to accumulate large sums of capital for expansion through the sale of stocks and bonds.

correspondence principle: Proposition which demonstrates that in order for comparative statics (the comparison of equilibrium positions in static states) to be meaningful, it is first necessary to develop a dynamic analysis of stability.

cost: Sacrifice that must be made to do or to acquire something. What is sacrificed may be money, goods, leisure time, security, prestige, power, or pleasure.

cost-effectiveness analysis: Technique of selecting from alternative programs the one that attains a given objective at the lowest cost. It is a type of analysis most useful when benefits cannot be measured in money.

cost-push inflation: Condition of generally rising prices caused by factor payments to one or more groups of resource owners increasing faster than productivity or efficiency. It is usually attributed to monopolistic market power possessed by some resource owners, unions, or business firms. "Wage-push" and "profit-push" are the most common forms of cost-push inflation.

countervailing power: Proposition that in the United States the growth of market power by one group may tend to stimulate the growth of a counterreaction and somewhat offsetting influence by another group. *Examples:* Big labor unions face big corporations at the bargaining table; chain stores deal with large processing and manufacturing firms; and big government faces big business and big unions.

craft union: Labor union composed of workers in a particular trade, such as bakers, carpenters, and teamsters. It is thus a "horizontally" organized union.

crawling peg: System of foreign exchange rates which permits the par value of a nation's currency to change automatically by small increments, downward or upward, if in actual daily trading on the foreign exchange markets the price in terms of other currencies persists on the "floor" or "ceiling" of the governmentally established range for a specified period.

credit: In international economics, any transaction which results in a money inflow or receipt from a foreign country. It may be represented on a balance-of-payments statement by a plus sign.

credit instrument: Written or printed financial document serving as either a promise or order to transfer funds from one person to another.

creeping inflation: Slow but persistent upward movement in the general level of prices over a long period of years, typically at an average annual rate of up to 3 percent.

cross elasticity of demand: Percentage change in the quantity purchased of a good resulting from a 1 percent change in the price of another good. Thus:

cross elasticity of demand

$$= \frac{\text{percentage change in the quantity purchased of X}}{\text{percentage change in the price of Y}}$$

$$= \frac{(Q_{X2} - Q_{X1})/(Q_{X2} + Q_{X1})}{(P_{Y2} - P_{Y1})/(P_{Y2} + P_{Y1})}$$

where Q_{X1} and Q_{X2} represent quantities purchased of X before and after the change in the price of Y, and P_{Y1} and P_{Y2} represent the corresponding prices of Y before and after the change. The cross elasticity of demand thus measures the responsiveness of changes in the quantities purchased of a good to changes in the price of another good. In general, the higher the coefficient of elasticity, the greater the degree of substitutability. (For example, competing brands of goods in the same industry, such as soap, toothpaste, and television sets, have high positive cross elasticities.) A coefficient of zero indicates goods that are nonsubstitutes or unrelated. (Examples are lettuce and beer, hats and books.) A negative coefficient indicates goods that are complementary. (Examples are watches and watchbands, cameras and film, shirts and ties.)

"crowding out": Hypothesis that deficit spending (i.e., expansionary fiscal policy) creates upward pressure on interest rates, which in turn discourages private investment. There are two underlying reasons. (1) An expansionary fiscal policy, by raising GNP, also increases the public's demand for money to carry on larger volumes of transactions. (2) An increased supply of government bonds on the market depresses their prices and raises interest rates, because bond prices and interest rates vary inversely. Therefore, if the money supply is not increased, interest rates rise and some private investment is reduced (i.e., "crowded out" by government deficit spending).

currency: Paper money. (Coins are not part of currency.)

current assets: Cash and other assets that can be turned quickly into cash.

current dollars: An expression reflecting actual prices of each year. Hence economic data are often quoted in current dollars. (*Compare* **constant dollars.**)

current liabilities: Debts that fall due within a year.

customs union: Agreement among two or more trading nations to abolish trade barriers such as tariffs and quotas among themselves, and to adopt a common external policy of trade (such as a common external tariff with all nonmember nations). *Example:* Benelux (i.e., Belgium, Luxembourg, and The Netherlands).

cyclically balanced budget: Philosophy which holds that total revenues and expenditures in the government's budget should be balanced or brought into equality over the course of a business cycle.

cyclical unemployment: Unemployment which results from business recessions or depressions because aggregate demand falls too far below the full-employment level of aggregate output and income.

D

death taxes: Taxes imposed on the transfer of property after death. They consist of estate and inheritance taxes, and are imposed by federal and state governments at progressive rates.

debit: In international economics, any transaction which results in a money outflow or payment to a foreign country.

It may be represented on a balance-of-payments statement by a minus sign.

decreasing-cost industry: Industry which experiences decreases in resource prices or in its costs of production as it expands because of new firms entering it. This situation might arise for a while as a result of substantial external economies of scale.

deduction: In logical thinking, a process of reasoning from premises to conclusions. The premises are more general than the conclusions, so deduction is often defined as reasoning from the general to the particular. (Opposite of **induction.**)

deflation: **1.** Statistical adjustment of data by which an economic time series expressed in current dollars is converted into a series expressed in constant dollars of a previous period. The purpose of the adjustment is to compensate for the distorting effects of inflation (i.e., the long-run upward trend of prices) through a reverse process of "deflation." **2.** Decline in the general price level of all goods and services—or equivalently, a rise in the purchasing power of a unit of money. (*Compare* **inflation.**)

demand: Relation expressing the various amounts of a commodity that buyers would be willing and able to purchase at possible alternative prices during a given period of time, all other things remaining the same. This relation may be expressed as a table (called a **demand schedule**), as a graph (called a **demand curve**), or as a mathematical equation.

demand curve: Graph of a demand schedule, showing the number of units of a commodity that buyers would be able and willing to purchase at various possible prices during a given period of time, all other things remaining the same.

demand deposit: Promise by a bank to pay immediately an amount of money specified by the customer who owns the deposit. It is thus "checkbook money" because it permits transactions to be paid for by check rather than with currency.

demand, law of: Principle which states that the quantity demanded of a commodity varies inversely with its price, assuming that all other things which may affect demand remain the same. These "all other" things include (1) buyers' money incomes; (2) the prices of related goods in consumption; and (3) tastes and other nonmonetary determinants such as consumer preferences, number of buyers in the market, or composition of buyers.

demand price: Highest price a buyer is willing to pay for a given quantity of a commodity.

demand-pull inflation: Condition of generally rising prices caused by increases in aggregate demand at a time when available supplies of goods are becoming more limited. Goods may go into short supply because resources are fully utilized or because production cannot be increased rapidly enough to meet growing demand.

demand schedule: Table showing the number of units of a commodity that buyers would be able and willing to purchase at various possible prices during a given period of time, all other things remaining the same.

deposit-expansion multiplier: Proposition which states that an increase in *excess* reserves of the banking system can cause a magnified increase in total deposits; similarly, a decrease in the banking system's *legal* reserves may cause a magnified decrease in total deposits. The total cumulative expansion (or contraction) will at most be some multiple of the required reserve ratio. The deposit-expansion multiplier can be expressed by the formula

deposit-expansion multiplier

$$= \frac{1}{\text{required reserve ratio}} = \frac{1}{R}$$

Therefore, if we let D represent the change in demand deposits for the banking system as a whole, and E the amount of excess reserves, then

$$D = E \times \text{deposit-expansion multiplier}$$

or

$$D = E \times \frac{1}{R}$$

Example: If $E = \$1,000$ and $R = 10$ percent, then $D = \$1,000 \times 1/0.10 = \$10,000$. Thus excess reserves of $1,000 can result in as much as a $10,000 increase in demand deposits.

There are "leakages," however, which prevent this multiplier from exerting its full impact. They include (1) the leakage of cash into circulation, since some deposits will be withdrawn in cash and some checks will be "cashed" instead of deposited; (2) a margin of excess reserves which banks for one reason or another may not lend out; and (3) the failure of businesspersons to borrow all that the banks want to lend.

depreciation: Decline in the value of a fixed asset, such as plant or equipment, as a result of wear and tear, destruction, or obsolescence resulting from the development of new and better techniques.

depression: Lower phase of a business cycle in which the economy is operating with substantial unemployment of its resources, and a sluggish rate of capital investment and consumption resulting from little business and consumer optimism.

derived demand: Demand for a product or resource based on its contribution to the product for which it is used. *Examples:* The separate demands for bricks, lumber, and so on, are derived partly from the demand for construction; the demand for steel is derived partly from the demand for automobiles.

devaluation: Official act which makes a domestic currency cheaper in terms of gold or foreign currencies. It is typically designed to increase a nation's exports while reducing its imports.

dialectical materialism: Logical method of historical analysis. In particular, it was used by Karl Marx, who employed the philosopher Hegel's idea that historical change is the result of inherently conflicting or opposing forces in society, and that the forces are basically economic or materialistic.

"dictatorship of the proletariat": Expression used by Karl Marx to describe a stage of Marxian socialism in which the bourgeoisie or capitalist class has been toppled from power and, along with its properties, is under the management of the proletariat or working class, which is also in control of the state.

diminishing marginal utility, law of: In a given period of time, the consumption of a product while tastes remain constant may at first result in increasing marginal (i.e., incremental) satisfactions or utilities per unit of the product consumed, but a point will be reached beyond which further units of consumption of the product will result in decreasing marginal utilities per unit of the product consumed. This is the point of diminishing marginal utility. *Note:* Even though marginal utility may rise at first, it *must* *eventually fall.* It is the diminishing phase of marginal utility that is relevant and serves as the basis for the law.

diminishing returns (variable proportions), law of: In a given state of technology, the addition of a changing or variable factor of production to other fixed factors of production may at first yield increasing marginal (i.e., incremental) returns per unit of the variable factor added, but a point will be reached beyond which further additions of the variable factor will yield diminishing marginal returns per unit of the variable factor added. This is the point of diminishing marginal returns. *Note:* Even though marginal returns may rise at first, *they must eventually fall.* It is the diminishing phase of marginal returns that is relevant and serves as the basis for the law.

direct payments: Method of subsidizing sellers while permitting the price of a commodity to be determined in a free market by supply and demand. If the price turns out to be "too low," sellers are compensated by a subsidy from the government for the difference between the market price received and some higher, predetermined target price. If the market price turns out to be equal to or greater than the target price, no subsidized compensation is provided. Under this system, therefore, consumers pay and sellers receive the market price of the commodity, but sellers *may in addition* receive a subsidy. (*Note:* A plan of this type has long existed for certain farm commodities.)

direct tax: Tax that is not shifted—that is, its burden is borne by the persons or firms originally taxed. *Examples:* personal income taxes, social security taxes paid by employees, and death taxes.

discounting: Process by which a given amount, expressed in dollars, is adjusted at interest to yield a present value. *Example:* At 6 percent, $1.06 one year hence has a present value of $1; $1.124 two years hence has a present value one year hence of $1.06, and a present value today of $1. Discounting is thus the opposite of **compounding**.

discount rate: Interest rate charged to member banks on their loans from the Federal Reserve Banks. It is called a "discount rate" because the interest on a loan is discounted when the loan is made, rather than collected when the loan is repaid.

disequilibrium: State of imbalance or nonequilibrium. *Example:* a situation in which the quantities supplied and demanded of a commodity at a given price are unequal, so there is a tendency for market prices and/or quantities to change. Any economic organism or system, such as a household, a firm, a market, or an economy, which is not in equilibrium is said to be in disequilibrium.

disguised unemployment (underemployment): Situation in which employed resources are not being used in their most efficient ways.

disinvestment: Reduction in the total stock of capital goods caused by failure to replace it as it wears out. *Example:* the consumption or using up of factories, machines, etc., at a faster rate than they are being replaced so that the productive base is diminishing.

disposable personal income: Income remaining after payment of personal taxes.

dissaving: Expenditure on consumption in excess of income. This may be accomplished by drawing on past savings, borrowing, or receiving help from others.

dividend: Earnings which a corporation pays to its stockholders. Payments are usually in cash, but may also be in property, securities, or other forms.

division of labor: Specialization in productive activities among workers, resulting in increased production because it (1) permits development and refinement of skills; (2) avoids the time that is wasted in going from one job to another; and (3) simplifies human tasks, thus permitting the introduction of labor-saving machines.

double coincidence of wants: Situation which is necessary in a barter exchange, because each party must have what the other wants and must be willing to trade at the exact quantities and terms suitable to both.

double taxation: Taxation of the same base in two different forms. A typical example is the corporate income tax: the corporation pays an income tax on its profits, and the stockholder pays an income tax on the dividends he receives from those profits.

draft: Unconditional written order by one party (the creditor or drawer) on a second party (the debtor or drawee) directing him to pay a third party (the bearer or payee) a specified sum of money. An ordinary check, therefore, is an example of a draft.

dual banking system: Expression referring to the fact that all commercial banks in the United States are chartered either as national banks or as state banks. This organizational structure, not found in any other country, is a unique outgrowth of American political history.

dual labor market: Labor market consisting of two submarkets: (1) a primary labor market in which jobs are characterized by relatively high wages, favorable working conditions, and employment stability; and (2) a secondary labor market in which jobs, when they are available, pay relatively low wages, provide poor working conditions, and are highly unstable. Blue-collar workers, many of whom are union members, comprise most of the participants in the primary market, whereas the competitively "disadvantaged poor"—the unskilled, the undereducated, and the victims of racial prejudice—are confined to the secondary market.

dumping: Sale of the same product in different markets at different prices. *Example:* A monopolist might restrict his output in the domestic market and charge a higher price because demand is relatively inelastic, and "dump" the rest of his output in a foreign market at a lower price because demand there is relatively elastic. He thereby gains the benefit of lower average total costs on his entire output (domestic plus foreign) and earns a larger net profit than if he sold the entire output in the domestic market—which he could do only by charging a lower price per unit on all units sold.

duopoly: Oligopoly consisting of two sellers. Hence it may be either a perfect duopoly or an imperfect one, depending on whether the product is standardized or differentiated.

dynamic model: One in which economic phenomena are studied by relating them to preceding or succeeding events. The influence of time is therefore taken explicitly into account. A dynamic model is thus like a "motion picture" as distinguished from a "snapshot." (*Compare* **static model.**)

E

econometrics: Integration of economic theory, mathematics, and statistics. It consists of expressing economic relationships in the form of mathematical equations and verifying the resulting models by statistical methods.

economic costs: Payments made to the owners of the factors of production to persuade them to supply their resources in a particular activity.

economic development: Process whereby a nation's real per capita output or income (its GNP) increases over a long period of time. A nation's rate of economic development is thus measured by its per capita rate of economic growth.

economic efficiency: See **efficiency.**

economic good: Scarce commodity—that is, any commodity for which the market price is greater than zero at a particular time and place. (Opposite of **free good.**)

economic growth: Rate of increase in an economy's full-employment real output or income over time—that is, the rise in its full-employment output in constant prices. Economic growth may be expressed in either of two ways: (1) as the increase in total full-employment real GNP or NNP over time, or (2) as the increase in per capita full-employment real GNP or NNP over time. The "total" measure is employed to describe the expansion of a nation's economic output or potential, whereas the "per capita" measure is used to express its material standard of living and to compare it with other countries.

economic indicators: Time series of economic data, classified as either leading, lagging, or coincident indicators. They are used in business-cycle analysis and forecasting.

economic interpretation of history: Proposition advanced by Karl Marx (and others) that the great political, social, intellectual, and ethical movements of history are determined by the ways in which societies organize their social institutions to carry on the basic economic activities of production, exchange, distribution, and consumption of goods. Thus economic forces are the prime cause of fundamental historical change.

economic man: The notion that each individual in a capitalistic society, whether he or she be a worker, businessperson, consumer, or investor, is motivated by economic forces and hence will always act to obtain the greatest satisfaction for the least sacrifice or cost. Satisfaction may take the form of profits to a businessperson, wages or leisure hours to a worker, pleasure to a consumer from the goods that he or she purchases, and so on.

economic plan: Detailed method, formulated beforehand, for achieving specific economic objectives by governing the activities and interrelationships of those economic organisms, namely firms, households, and governments, that have an influence on the desired outcome.

economic (pure) profit: Payment to a firm in excess of its economic costs, including normal profit. It is the same as **net revenue.**

economic rent: Payment to an owner of a factor of production, in an industry in equilibrium, in excess of the factor's supply price or opportunity cost—that is, in excess of the minimum amount necessary to keep that factor in its present occupation. It is thus a surplus to the recipient.

economics: Social science concerned chiefly with the way society chooses to employ its limited resources, which have alternative uses, to produce goods and services for present and future consumption.

economic system: Relationships between the organisms or components of an economy (such as its households, firms, and government) and the institutional framework of laws and customs within which these organisms operate.

economies (diseconomies) of scale: The decreases (increases) in a firm's long-run average costs as the size of its plant is increased. Those factors that give rise to economies of scale or decreasing long-run average costs of production as the plant size increases are (1) greater specialization of resources; (2) more efficient utilization of equipment; (3) reduced unit costs of inputs; (4) opportunities for economical utilization of by-products; and (5) growth of auxiliary facilities. Diseconomies of scale may eventually set in, however, due to (1) limitations of (or "diminishing returns" to) management in its decision-making function; and (2) competition among firms in bidding up the prices of limited resources.

efficiency: Ability to make the best use of what is available to attain a desired result. Two specific types of efficiency are "technical" and "economic." **1. Technical efficiency.** Condition which exists when a production system—a firm, an industry, an economy—is achieving maximum output by making the fullest utilization of available inputs. The system is then on its production-possibilities curve. This means that no change in the combination of resources can be made which will increase the output of one product without decreasing the output of another. **2. Economic (allocative) efficiency.** Condition which exists when a production system has achieved technical efficiency *and* is fulfilling consumer preferences by producing the combination of goods that people want—are willing and able to purchase—given their incomes. This means that no change in the combination of resources or of output can be implemented which will make someone better off without making someone else worse off—each in his or her own estimation. (*Note*: Economic efficiency is synonymous with **Pareto optimality.**)

elasticity: Percentage change in quantity demanded or supplied resulting from a 1 percent change in price. Mathematically, it is the ratio of the percentage change in quantity (demanded or supplied) to the percentage change in price:

$$\text{elasticity, } E = \frac{\text{percentage change in quantity}}{\text{percentage change in price}}$$

$$= \frac{(Q_2 - Q_1)/(Q_2 + Q_1)}{(P_2 - P_1)/(P_2 + P_1)}$$

where Q_1 and Q_2, and P_1 and P_2, denote the corresponding quantities and prices before and after the change. This coefficient of elasticity is usually stated numerically without regard to algebraic sign, and may range from zero to infinity. It may take any of five forms:

perfectly elastic	$(E = \infty)$
relatively elastic	$(E > 1)$
unit elastic	$(E = 1)$
relatively inelastic	$(E < 1)$
perfectly inelastic	$(E = 0)$

The above definition refers to what is known as *price elasticity* of demand or supply. It is one of several types of elasticities that exist in economics and is the one that is commonly understood unless otherwise specified. In general, elasticity may be thought of as the responsiveness of changes in one variable to changes in another, where responsiveness is measured in terms of percentage changes.

Employment Act of 1946: Act of Congress which requires the government to maintain high levels of employment, production, and purchasing power. To assist the President in this task, the act authorizes him to appoint a panel of experts known as the Council of Economic Advisors.

Engel's Laws: Set of relationships between consumer expenditures and income, derived by a nineteenth-century German statistician, Ernst Engel, based on research into workingmen's purchases in Western Europe during the

1850s. The relationships state that as a family's income increases: (1) the percentage it spends on food decreases; (2) the percentage it spends on housing and household operations remains about constant (except for fuel, light, and refrigeration, which decreases); and (3) the percentage it spends on all other categories and the amount it saves increase (except for medical care and personal care items, which remain fairly constant). In general, the *total* amount spent increases as a family's income increases. *Note:* Strictly speaking, only the first relationship above is attributed to Engel; the other two are modernized versions of his early findings, based on more recent research.

entrepreneurship: Factor of production which designates the function performed by those who assemble the other factors of production, raise the necessary money, organize the management, make the basic business policy decisions, and reap the gains of success or the losses of failure. The entrepreneur is the innovator and the catalyst in a capitalistic system. He need not be exclusively an owner or a manager; the entrepreneurial function may be performed by both, depending on the size and complexity of the firm.

equal advantage, law of: In a market economy, owners of resources will always transfer them from less desirable to more desirable uses. As this happens, the occupations *out* of which resources are transferred often tend to become more desirable while the occupations *into* which resources are transferred tend to become less desirable. This transfer process continues until all occupations are equally desirable. At this point there is no gain to be made by further transfer of resources. Hence the economy is in equilibrium. *Note:* The term "desirable" includes both monetary and nonmonetary considerations. The latter helps explain why permanent differences in monetary rewards may exist between various occupations.

equality standard: Criterion of income distribution popularly expressed by the phrase, "To each, equally." You will regard the equality standard as a just or equitable one only if you assume that all people are alike in the *added* satisfaction or utility they get from an extra dollar of income. If this assumption is false—if an additional dollar of income actually provides a greater gain in utility to some people than to others—then justice is more properly served by distributing most of any increase in society's income to those who will enjoy it more. In reality, there is no conclusive evidence to suggest that people are either alike or unlike in their capacities to enjoy additional income. Therefore, no scientific basis exists for assuming that an equal distribution of income is more equitable than an unequal one. (*Compare* **contributive standard; needs standard.**)

equation of exchange: Expression of the relation between the quantity of money (M), its velocity of circulation (V), the average price (P) of final goods and services, and the physical quantity (Q) of those goods and services:

$$MV = PQ$$

The equation is actually an identity which states that the total amount of money spent on goods and services (MV) is equal to the total amount of money received for goods and services (PQ). (*See also* **quantity theory of money.**)

equilibrium: State of balance between opposing forces. An object in equilibrium is in a state of rest and has no tendency to change.

equilibrium conditions: Set of relationships that defines the equilibrium properties of an economic organism such as a household, a firm, or an entire economy.

equilibrium price: 1. Price of a commodity determined in the market by the intersection of a supply and demand curve. (Also called **normal price.**) **2.** Price (and corresponding equilibrium quantity) that maximizes a firm's profit.

equilibrium quantity: 1. Quantity of a commodity determined in the market by the intersection of a supply and demand curve. **2.** Quantity (and corresponding equilibrium price) that maximizes a firm's profit.

equity: Justice or fairness. In economics, equity refers to justice with respect to the distribution of income or of wealth within a society. Equity is thus a philosophical concept but an economic goal. However, there is no scientific way of concluding that one standard or mechanism for distributing income is just and therefore "good" while another is unjust and therefore "bad." Each society or type of economic system establishes its own standards of distribution. Nevertheless, economics can help to evaluate the material consequences of a standard which a society adopts. (*See also* **contributive standard; equality standard; needs standard.**)

escalator clause: Provision in a contract whereby payments such as wages, insurance or pension benefits, or loan repayments over a stated period are tied to a comprehensive measure of living costs or price-level changes. The consumer price index and the implicit price index (GNP deflator) are the most common measures used.

estate tax: Progressive (graduated) tax imposed by the federal government and by most state governments on the transfer of all property owned by a decedent at the time of death. Exemptions, deductions, and rates vary widely among the states.

Eurodollars: Dollar deposits in banks outside the United States, mostly in Europe. They are held by American and foreign banks, corporations, and individuals, and represent dollar obligations which are constantly being shifted from one country to another in search of the highest return.

European Recovery Program (ERP): Commonly known as the "Marshall Plan" (after Secretary of State George C. Marshall, who proposed it in 1947), this was a comprehensive recovery blueprint for European countries, financed by the United States, for the purposes of (1) increasing their productive capacity; (2) stabilizing their financial systems; (3) promoting their mutual economic cooperation; and (4) reducing their dependence on U.S. assistance. The ERP was terminated in 1951 after considerable success, and its functions were absorbed by other government agencies and programs.

excess reserves: Quantity of a bank's legal reserves over and above its required reserves. Thus:

excess reserves = legal reserves − required reserves

Excess reserves are the key to a bank's lending power.

excise tax: Tax imposed on the manufacture, sale, or consumption of various commodities, such as liquor, tobacco, and gasoline.

exclusion principle: Basis for distinguishing between nonpublic and public goods. A good is nonpublic if anyone who does not pay can be excluded from its use; otherwise, it is a public good.

explicit costs: Money outlays of a firm recorded in its books of account. (*Compare* **implicit costs.**)

external economies and diseconomies of scale: Conditions that bring about decreases or increases in a firm's long-run average costs as a result of factors that are entirely outside of the firm as a producing unit. They depend on adjustments of the industry and are related to the firm only to the extent that the firm is a part of the industry. *Example:* External economies may result from improvements in public transportation and marketing facilities as an industry develops in a particular geographic area; however, diseconomies may eventually set in as firms bid up the prices of limited resources in the area.

externalities: External benefits or costs of activities for which no compensation is made. (Externalities are also called **spillovers.**)

F

Fabian socialism: Form of socialism founded in England in 1884. It emerged as an outgrowth of utopian socialism by advocating gradual and evolutionary reform within a democratic framework.

factors of production: Human and nonhuman productive resources of an economy, usually classified into four groups: land, labor, capital, and entrepreneurship.

Fair Labor Standards Act (Wages and Hours Law) of 1938: An act, with subsequent amendments, which specifies minimum hourly wages, overtime rates, and prohibitions against child labor for workers producing goods in interstate commerce.

family-allowance plan: Plan that provides every family, rich or poor, with a certain amount of money based exclusively on the number and age of its children. Families above certain designated income levels return all or a portion of the money with their income taxes, but those below specified income levels keep it. More than 60 countries have family allowance plans.

Fawcett, Millicent Garrett (1847-1919): English economic educator whose book, *Political Economy for Beginners* (1870), was largely a simplification and abridgment of classical economics as expressed by Mill in 1848. (*See* **Mill, John Stuart.**) Her book was highly successful, went through ten editions over a period of forty years, and established her as an outstanding popularizer of classical economic ideas.

featherbedding: Labor union "make-work" rules designed to increase the labor or labor time on a particular job. Outlawed by the Labor-Management Relations (Taft-Hartley) Act of 1947.

Federal Advisory Council: Committee within the Federal Reserve System that advises the Board of Governors on important current developments.

Federal Deposit Insurance Corporation (FDIC): Government agency which insures deposits (demand and time) at commercial and savings banks. Each insured bank pays an annual premium of 1/12 of 1 percent of its total deposits, in return for which the FDIC insures each account up to $40,000 against loss due to bank failure. In addition to its insurance function, the FDIC supervises insured banks and presides over the liquidation of banks that do fail. Two parallel agencies which perform similar functions are the Federal Savings and Loan Association, which insures deposits in savings and loan associations, and the National Credit Union Administration, which provides deposit insurance for federally chartered credit unions. National banks (chartered by the federal government) are required to be insured by the FDIC and state-chartered banks may apply if they wish. Since the late 1930s, practically all banks have been covered by insurance, thereby eliminating bank runs and permitting greater bank stability.

federal funds rate: Interest rate at which banks borrow excess reserves from other banks' accounts at the Fed, usually overnight, to keep required reserves from falling below the legal level. In general, the lower the volume of excess reserves, the higher will be the federal funds rate. Therefore, the federal funds rate is an important indicator which the Fed watches to decide whether it should add to banks' reserves or take them away. For short periods of time the Fed can largely control the federal funds rate. For example, the rate can be raised by selling Treasury bills to the banking system, thereby pulling out reserves. Conversely, the rate can be lowered by buying bills from the system, thereby putting in reserves. As part of its policy-making function, the Fed tries to maintain a federal funds rate that is consistent with other monetary goals.

Federal Open Market Committee: The most important policy-making body of the Federal Reserve System. Its chief function is to establish policy for the System's purchase and sale of government and other securities in the open market.

Federal Reserve Bank: One of the 12 banks (and branches) which make up the Federal Reserve System. Each serves as a "banker's bank" for the member banks in its district by acting as a source of credit and a depository of resources, and by performing other useful functions.

Federal Reserve System: Central banking system created by Congress in 1913. It consists of (1) 12 Federal Reserve Banks—one located in each of 12 districts in the country; (2) a Board of Governors; (3) a Federal Open Market Committee and various other committees; and (4) several thousand member banks, which hold the great majority of all commercial bank deposits in the nation.

Federal Trade Commission: Government agency created in 1914. It is charged with preventing unfair business practices by enforcing the Federal Trade Commission Act, and exercising concurrently with the Justice Department the enforcement of prohibitive provisions of the Clayton Antitrust Act as amended by the Robinson–Patman Act.

Federal Trade Commission Act (1914): A major antitrust law of the U.S. Its chief purpose is to prevent unfair (i.e., deceptive, dishonest, or injurious) methods of competition and, as amended by the Wheeler–Lea Act (1938), to safeguard the public by preventing the dissemination of false and misleading advertising of food, drugs, cosmetics, and therapeutic devices.

financial intermediaries: Business firms that serve as middlemen between lenders and borrowers by creating and issuing financial obligations or claims against themselves in order to acquire profitable financial claims against others. Examples of such firms are commercial banks, mutual savings banks, savings and loan associations, credit unions, insurance companies, and all other financial institutions. In general, they are wholesalers and retailers of funds.

financial markets: The money and capital markets of the economy. In the former, short-term credit instruments are bought and sold; in the latter, long-term credit and equity instruments are dealt in.

firm: Business organization that brings together and coordinates factors of production—capital, land, labor, and entrepreneurship—for the purpose of producing a good or service.

First Bank of the United States: *See* **Bank of the United States.**

fiscal drag: Tendency of a high-employment economy to be held back from its full growth potential because it is incurring budgetary surpluses. Such surpluses may arise because, other things being equal, a progressive tax system tends to generate increases in revenues relative to expenditures during periods of high employment.

fiscalism: Macroeconomic theory and policies which follow in the tradition of John Maynard Keynes. Fiscalists contend that an increase in the money supply leads to a reduction in the interest rate. This causes an increase in the amount of business investment and therefore in aggregate demand. Unemployed resources are drawn into production, and the economy moves toward full employment while prices adjust accordingly. The fiscalist model is thus characterized by (1) a predominantly monetary theory of the interest rate, (2) a predominantly nonmonetary theory of the price level, and (3) no distinction between market and real rates of interest. (*Contrast with* **monetarism.**)

fiscal policy: Deliberate exercise of the government's power to tax and spend in order to achieve price stability, help dampen the swings of business cycles, and bring the nation's output and employment to desired levels.

Fisher equation: *See* **equation of exchange.**

Fisher, Irving (1867–1940): One of America's foremost economists during the first half of the twentieth century. A professor at Yale University, he authored many books and articles on diverse topics, including statistics and monetary theory. Among his many contributions was the "Fisher equation," which he used to explain the cause-and-effect relationship between the money supply and the price level. (*See* **equation of exchange** and **quantity theory of money.**)

fixed assets: Durable assets of an enterprise used to carry on its business, such as land, buildings, machinery, equipment, office furniture, automobiles, and trucks.

fixed costs: Costs that do not vary with a firm's output. *Examples:* rental payments, interest on debt, property taxes.

floating exchange rates: Foreign exchange rates determined in a free market by supply and demand.

"forced" saving: Situation in which consumers are prevented from spending part of their income on consumption. Some examples include: (1) prices rising faster than money wages, causing a decrease in real consumption and hence an increase in real (forced) saving; (2) a corporation which plows back some of its profit instead of distributing it as dividend income to stockholders; and (3) a government which taxes its citizens and uses the funds for investment, thereby preventing the public from utilizing a portion of its income for the purchase of consumer goods.

foreign aid: Loans, grants, or assistance from one government to another for the purpose of accelerating economic development in the recipient country.

foreign exchange: Instruments used for international payments. Such instruments consist not only of currency, but also of checks, drafts, and bills of exchange (which are orders to pay currency).

foreign exchange rate: Price of one currency in terms of another.

foreign-trade multiplier: Principle which states that fluctuations in exports or imports may generate magnified variations in national income. It is based on the idea that a change in exports relative to imports has the same multiplier effect on national income as a change in autonomous expenditures; similarly, a change in imports relative to exports has the same multiplier effect on national income as a change in withdrawals from the income stream. In general, an increase in exports tends to raise domestic income, but the increased income also induces some imports which act as "leakages," tending to reduce the full multiplier effect that would exist if imports remained constant.

forward exchange: Foreign exchange bought (or sold) at a given time and at a stipulated current or "spot" price, but payable at a future date. By buying or selling forward exchange, importers and exporters can protect themselves against the risks of fluctuations in the current exchange market.

forward prices: Proposed plan for reducing price uncertainty and encouraging greater stability in agriculture through the use of the price system as an adjustment mechanism. Under the plan, a government-appointed board would predict in advance of breeding or seeding time the equilibrium prices of commodities, based on expected supply and demand. The government would then guarantee those predicted or forward prices in two ways: by storage programs and direct payments to farmers if actual prices should fall below forward prices, and by a direct tax on farmers if actual prices should rise above forward prices.

free good: Good for which the market price is zero at a particular time and place.

free-rider problem: Tendency of people to avoid paying for a good's benefits when they can be obtained free. Public goods (e.g., national defense, air-traffic control, etc.) provide examples because the benefits of such goods are indivisible and therefore cannot be denied to individuals, whether they pay or not. Those who do not pay are thus "free riders." If many people become free riders, there might be no way of knowing how much of a public good should be provided. In that case, some form of collective action, usually through government, is taken.

free-trade area: Association of trading nations whose participants agree to impose no restrictive devices such as tariffs or quotas on one another, but are free to impose whatever restrictive devices they wish on nonparticipants. *Example:* The European Free Trade Association (EFTA).

frictional unemployment: Unemployment due to maladjustments in the economic system resulting from imperfect labor mobility, imperfect knowledge of job opportunities, and a general inability of the economy to match people with jobs instantly and smoothly. A common form of frictional unemployment consists of people who are temporarily out of work because they are between jobs.

Friedman, Milton (1912–   ): A leading American economist and Nobel laureate (1976) who did pioneering work in the study of consumption theory, monetary economics, and other fields. Most of his career was spent as a professor at the University of Chicago, where he was the foremost exponent of the "Chicago School" of economic thought. This approach to economics extols free markets, a minimal role for government, and other libertarian views. Friedman thus follows in the tradition of Adam Smith and most other classical economists.

full cost (average cost) price: Price for a given volume of output which is at least high enough to cover all of a firm's costs of production—that is, its average total cost for that volume of output. If demand is great enough to enable the firm to sell its entire output at that price, the firm will earn a normal profit. If it can sell its output at a still higher price, it will earn an economic or pure profit.

full employment: Condition in which all the economy's resources available for employment are being utilized with maximum efficiency. In terms of society's human resources (which serve as an imperfect but practical representation of "all" resources), full employment means that the entire civilian labor force is working, except for those who are temporarily out of work or who are changing jobs.

Full Employment and Balanced Growth Act (1978): Federal law with three major provisions. (1) Requires the President to set long- and short-term production and employment goals, including an annual unemployment-rate target of 4 percent, and to identify means for attaining the goals through public-employment programs, manpower policies, etc. (2) Requires the Federal Reserve to declare semiannually its monetary policies and their relation to the President's goals. (3) Requires the government to undertake actions that will achieve the goal of full employment while striving for a zero-percent inflation rate.

full-employment budget: Estimate of annual government expenditures and revenues that would occur if the economy were operating at full employment. Any resulting surplus (or deficit) is called a full-employment surplus (or deficit).

"functional finance": Philosophy which holds that the government should pursue whatever fiscal measures are needed to achieve noninflationary full employment and economic growth—without regard to budget balancing per se. The federal budget is thus viewed functionally as a flexible fiscal tool for achieving economic objectives, rather than as an accounting statement to be balanced periodically.

functional income distribution: Payments in the form of wages, rents, interest, and profits made to the owners of the factors of production in return for supplying their labor, land, capital, and entrepreneurial ability.

G

gains from trade: Net benefits or increases in goods which a country receives as a result of trade.

Galbraith, John Kenneth (1908–): American economist whose writing, in the tradition of the "institutionalist school," is perhaps closest to that of Thorstein Veblen. Like Veblen, Galbraith criticized America's capitalistic institutions and processes. Among his chief propositions are these: (1) The market system, dominated by big business, does not perform the way the "conventional wisdom" of traditional economics says that it does. (2) Modern industry is run by a "technostructure" of elite specialists who bamboozle consumers through advertising, thereby insulating big business from the free market. (3) A larger public sector is needed, both economically and politically, to reduce the power of large corporations and to "educate" the people to appreciate "the higher things in life."

General Agreements on Tariffs and Trade (GATT): International commercial agreement signed in 1947 by the United States and many other countries for the purpose of achieving four basic long-run objectives: (1) nondiscrimination in trade through adherence to unconditional most-favored-nation treatment; (2) reduction of tariffs by negotiation; (3) elimination of import quotas (with some exceptions); and (4) resolution of differences through consultation.

general equilibrium theory: Explanation or model of the interrelations between prices and outputs of goods and resources in different markets, and the possibility of simultaneous equilibrium among all of them. It is primarily of theoretical interest, but focuses attention on the fact that in the real world markets are often interdependent.

general price level: Expression representing the "average" level of prices in the economy. It is often represented by the **Implicit Price Index,** although no index can accurately reflect all prices.

George, Henry (1839–1897): Prominent American economist whose book, *Progress and Poverty* (1879), ranks as one of the most widely read economic treatises of all time. In the book he advocated a *single tax* on land as the source of all government revenue. The reason, he contended, is that unlike other factors of production, land is provided by nature. Therefore, rent to landlords is an unearned surplus which increases as population grows, depriving the landless of their birthright to a share of the surplus. The solution is government taxation of all land rent. If this were done, no other taxes would be needed. (*See* **single tax.**)

gift tax: Progressive (graduated) tax imposed by the federal and by some state governments. It is paid by the donor or person who makes the gift, not the donee or recipient of it. Exemptions, deductions, and rates vary widely among the states.

Gini coefficient of inequality: A measure of the degree of inequality in a distribution. On a Lorenz diagram, it equals the numerical value of the area between the Lorenz curve and the diagonal line, divided by the entire area beneath the diagonal line. The ratio may vary between 0 (no inequality) and 1 (complete inequality).

GNP deflator: *See* **Implicit Price Index.**

gold bullion standard: Monetary standard under which (1) the national unit of currency (such as the dollar, pound, mark, etc.) is defined in terms of a fixed weight of gold; (2) gold is held by the government in the form of bars rather than coin; (3) there is no circulation of gold in any form within the economy; and (4) gold is available solely to meet the needs of industry (e.g., jewelry, dentistry) and settle international transactions among central banks or treasuries. This is the standard that the United States and most advanced nations adopted when they went off the gold coin standard in the early 1930s.

gold (coin) standard: Monetary standard under which (1) the national unit of currency (such as the dollar, pound, franc) is defined by law in terms of a fixed weight of gold; (2) there is a free and unrestricted flow of the metal in any form into and out of the country; (3) gold coins are full legal tender for all debts; (4) there is free convertibility between the national currency and gold coins at the defined rate; and (5) there are no restrictions on the coinage of gold. Nearly 50 countries of the world were on this standard in the late nineteenth and early twentieth centuries.

gold exchange standard: Monetary standard under which a nation's unit of currency is defined in terms of another nation's unit of currency, which in turn is defined in terms of, and convertible into, gold. This standard prevailed in the noncommunist world from 1944 to 1971 and is primarily of international economic significance. Thus in this period, the U.S. dollar was defined as equal to $\frac{1}{35}$ of an ounce of gold and was convertible to foreign central banks at this rate. Each foreign central bank, in turn, defined the par value of its own currency in terms of the U.S. dollar and maintained it at that level. The entire system operated by international agreement (under the **International Monetary Fund**).

gold points: Range within which the foreign exchange rates of gold standard countries will fluctuate. Thus the gold points are equal to the par rate of exchange plus and minus the cost (including insurance) of shipping gold. The upper and lower gold points for a nation are called its "gold export point" and "gold import point," respectively, because gold will be exported when the foreign exchange rate rises above the upper level and will be imported when the rate falls below the lower level. One nation's gold export point is thus another nation's gold import point, and vice versa.

goldsmiths' principle: Banks can maintain a fractional—rather than 100 percent—reserve against deposits, because customers will not ordinarily withdraw their funds at the same time. Hence the banks can earn interest by lending out unused or excess reserves. This principle was discovered centuries ago by the English goldsmiths, who held gold in safekeeping for customers.

goodwill: One of the "intangible" assets of a firm (like patents and trademarks), the value of which is arbitrarily established on a company's balance sheet.

government monopoly: Monopoly both owned and operated by either a federal or local government. *Examples:* The U.S. Postal Service, many water and sewer systems, and the central banks of most countries.

grants-in-aid: Financial aid at the intergovernmental level. The aid which consists of (1) revenues received by local governments from their states and from the federal government; and (2) revenues received by state governments from the federal government. These revenues are used mainly to help pay for public welfare assistance, highways, and education.

Great Leap Forward: Ambitious economic plan undertaken by China during 1958–1960 to enormously accelerate its rate of economic growth. The plan was unrealistic and forced the country into a major economic crisis.

greenbacks: Paper money (officially called United States Notes) issued by the Treasury to help finance the Civil War, 1861–1865. The currency was not redeemable in specie (gold or silver coins) and was the first official legal tender money issued by the federal government. (*Note:* The U.S. dollar today is sometimes called a "greenback," but this is a colloquial rather than a literal term.)

Gresham's Law: Principle which asserts that cheap money tends to drive dear money out of circulation. Thus, if two kinds of metals, such as gold and silver, circulate with equal legal tender powers (as happened in the United States under the bimetallic standard during the nineteenth century), the cheaper metal will become the chief circulating medium while the dearer metal will be hoarded, melted down, or exported, thereby disappearing from circulation. The law is named after Sir Thomas Gresham, Master of the Mint under Queen Elizabeth I during the sixteenth century. (*See also* **mint ratio; bimetallic standard.**)

gross national disproduct: Sum of all social costs or reductions in benefits to society that result from producing the gross national product. *Example:* Pollution of the environment is part of gross national disproduct, to the extent that it is caused by production of the gross national product.

gross national expenditure: Total amount spent by the four sector accounts of the economy (i.e., household, government, business, and foreign) on the nation's output of final goods and services. It is equal, by definition, to gross national product.

gross national income: The equivalent of gross national product from the "income" viewpoint. It consists of national income at factor cost (i.e., the sum of wages, rent, interest, and profit) plus two nonincome or business expense items: indirect business taxes and capital consumption allowance.

gross national product: Total market value of all final goods and services produced by an economy during a year.

growth: *See* **economic growth.**

guaranteed annual income: Plan that awards all families under a certain "poverty line" level a straight allowance for each parent plus specified amounts for each child according to the size of the family. No family receives less than a designated amount, and as a family's income rises the payment from the government is reduced until a break-even level, which is a little higher than the poverty line, is reached.

H

hard-core unemployed: People who are unemployed because they lack the education and skills for today's complex economy. (Discrimination may also be a contributing factor.) They consist mainly of certain minority groups, such as Negroes, Mexicans, the "too-old," the "too-young," the high-school dropouts, and the permanently displaced, who are victims of technological change.

Hicks, John R. (1904–   ): Leading British economist and Nobel laureate. He contributed significantly to the reconstruction of demand theory through the development of indifference-curve analysis. His work thus follows in the tradition of general equilibrium theory as formulated by Leon Walras and Vilfredo Pareto in the late nineteenth century. Among Hicks' other leading contributions have been a refinement of the marginal productivity theory of wages and an integrated analysis of Keynesian with classical theory.

"high-powered money": *See* **monetary base.**

hog–corn price ratio: Number of bushels of corn required to buy 100 pounds of live pork:

$$\text{hog–corn price ratio} = \frac{\text{price of live hogs per 100 pounds}}{\text{price of corn per bushel}}$$

When the ratio is relatively low, hog production decreases because farmers find it more profitable to sell their corn in the market than to use it for feeding hogs. Conversely, when the ratio is relatively high, hog production increases because farmers use the corn to feed more hogs, and to market them at heavier weights.

horizontal equity: Doctrine which states that "equals should be treated equally." *Example:* Persons with the same income, wealth, or other taxpaying ability should, in order to bear equal tax burdens, pay the same amount of tax. (*Compare* **vertical equity.**)

horizontal merger: Amalgamation under one ownership of plants engaged in producing similar products. The products might be close substitutes, such as cement, or moderate substitutes, such as tin cans and jars. The objective is to round out a product line which is sold through the same distribution channels, thereby offering joint economies in selling and distribution efforts.

household: All persons living in the same home. A household may thus consist of one or more families.

human resources: Productive physical and mental talents of the people who comprise an economy.

Humphrey–Hawkins bill: *See* **Full Employment and Balanced Growth Act (1978).**

hyperinflation: Situation in which prices are rising with little or no increase in output; hence it is also sometimes called "runaway" or "galloping" inflation.

hypothesis: A working guess about the behavior of things, or an expression about the relationship between variables in the real world. In economics, the "things" may include consumers, workers, business firms, investors, and so on, and the variables may include prices, wages, consumption, production, or other economic quantities.

I

imperfect competition: A classification of market structures that falls between the two extremes of perfect competition and monopoly. It consists of monopolistic competition and oligopoly.

implicit costs: Costs of self-owned or self-employed resources that are not recorded in a company's book of account. *Example:* the alternative interest return, rental receipts, and wages that a self-employed proprietor forgoes by owning and operating his own business.

Implicit Price Index (GNP deflator): Weighted average of the price indexes used to deflate the components of GNP. Thus for any given year:

$$\text{GNP in constant prices} = \frac{\text{GNP in current prices}}{\text{Implicit Price Index } (= \text{IPI})}$$

Therefore,

$$\text{IPI} = \frac{\text{GNP in current prices}}{\text{GNP in constant prices}}$$

Because of its comprehensiveness, the IPI is the best single measure of broad price movements in the economy.

import quota: Law that limits the number of units of a commodity that may be imported during a given period.

incidence: Range of occurrence or influence of an economic act. It is a term used primarily in the study of taxation and refers to the economic organism such as a household or a firm that bears the ultimate burden of a tax.

income: Gain derived from the use of human or material resources. A flow of dollars per unit of time. (*Compare* **wealth.**)

income-consumption curve: In indifference-curve analysis, a line showing the amounts of two commodities that a consumer will purchase when his income changes while the prices of the commodities remain the same. Geometrically, it is a line connecting the tangency points of price lines and indifference curves as income changes while prices remain constant.

income distribution: Division of society's output (i.e., the income society earns) among people. Income distribution thus concerns the matter of who gets how much, or what proportion, of the economy's total production. (*See* **functional income distribution; personal income distribution.**)

income effect: Change in quantity of a good demanded by a buyer due to a change in his real income resulting from a change in the price of a commodity. It assumes that the buyer's money income, tastes, and the prices of all other goods remain the same. (*Compare* **substitution effect.**)

income elasticity of demand: Percentage change in the quantity purchased of a good resulting from a one percent change in income. Thus,

income elasticity of demand

$$= \frac{\text{percentage change in quantity purchased}}{\text{percentage change in income}}$$

$$= \frac{(Q_2 - Q_1)/(Q_2 + Q_1)}{(Y_2 - Y_1)/(Y_2 + Y_1)}$$

where Q_1 and Q_2 represent the quantities purchased before and after the change in income, and Y_1 and Y_2 represent the corresponding levels of income before and after the change. Thus the income elasticity of demand denotes the responsiveness of changes in quantity purchased to changes in income, where responsiveness is measured in terms of percentage changes.

income statement: Financial statement of a firm showing its revenues, costs, and profit during a period. Also known as a profit-and-loss statement.

income tax: Tax on the net income or residual that remains after certain items are subtracted from gross income. The two types of income taxes are the personal income tax and the corporation income tax.

income velocity of money: Average number of times per year that a dollar is spent on purchasing the economy's annual flow of final goods and services—its GNP. It equals the ratio of GNP to the quantity of money. (*See also* **equation of exchange.**)

incomes policy: Laws aimed at curbing inflation by establishing conditions under which businesses' production costs (especially wages), prices, and profits may be allowed to increase. *Examples:* Wage and price controls.

inconvertible paper standard: Monetary standard under which the nation's unit of currency may or may not be defined in terms of any metal or other precious substance; however, there is no free convertibility into these other forms. Historically, this standard has existed on a domestic basis in all countries since the worldwide abandonment of gold in the 1930s.

increasing-cost industry: Industry which experiences increases in resource prices or in its costs of production as it expands because of new firms entering it. This will happen when the industry's demand for the resources it employs is a significant proportion of the total demand for those resources.

increasing costs, law of: Principle which states that on an economy's production-possibilities curve relating two kinds of goods, the real cost of acquiring either good is not the money that must be spent for it, but the increasing amount of the alternative good that the society must sacrifice or "give up" because it cannot have all it wants of both goods.

Independent Treasury Act (1846): Law that created the Independent Treasury System (1846–1863). During its life, the law enabled the Treasury to act as its own bank, receiving and disbursing its own funds, thus making it independent of the banking system. The Independent Treasury System also engaged in the purchase and sale of government bonds, thus affecting the quantity of money. This procedure, which decades later was called *open-market operations,* became an integral part of the Federal Reserve System after its establishment in 1913.

independent union: Labor union not affiliated with any federation of labor organizations. It may be national or international, and is not limited to workers in any one firm.

indexation: Assignment of inflation-adjusting escalator clauses to long-term contracts. Thus wages, rents, interest payments, and even the tax system can be readjusted in proportion to price changes so that people's gains due to inflation are not taxed away, thereby reducing real income. *Example:* If your income goes up by 10 percent when prices go up by 10 percent, you have no more purchasing power than before. Yet your income tax will rise because you will be pushed into a higher tax bracket. This situation can be avoided by indexing the income tax, thereby "correcting" it for inflation. (See **escalator clause.**)

index numbers: Figures that disclose the relative changes in a series of numbers, such as prices or production, from a base period. The base period is usually defined as being equal to an index number of 100, and all other numbers in the series both before or after that period are expressed as percentages of that period. Index numbers are widely used in reporting business and economic data.

indifference curve: Graph of an indifference schedule. Every point along the curve represents a different combination of two commodities, and each combination is equally satisfactory to a recipient because each one yields the same total utility.

indifference schedule: Table showing the various combinations of two commodities that would be equally satisfactory or yield the same total utility to a recipient at a given time.

indirect tax: Tax that can be shifted either partially or entirely to someone other than the individual or firm originally taxed. *Examples:* sales taxes, excise taxes, taxes on business and rental properties.

induced consumption: That part of total consumption which is related to income.

induced investment: Tendency of rising income, output, and economic activity to stimulate higher levels of investment. That part of total investment which is related to aggregate income or output. It may also be directly related to induced consumption, which in turn is related to income. (*Compare* **autonomous investment.**)

induction: Process of reasoning from particular observations or cases to general laws or principles. Most human knowledge is inductive or empirical since it is based on the experiences of our senses. (Opposite of **deduction.**)

industrial relations: Rules and regulations governing the relationship between union and management. It often deals with such matters as union security (e.g., the type of recognition that the union is accorded, or its financial arrangement for collecting dues) and methods of controlling the quantity and kind of union membership through apprenticeship requirements, licensing provisions, initiation fees, and seniority rules.

industrial union: Labor union consisting of all members from a particular industry, such as a union of coal miners or a union of steel workers. It is thus a "vertically" organized union.

industry: Group of firms producing similar or identical products.

infant industry: Underdeveloped industry which, in the face of competition from abroad, may not be able to survive the early years of struggle before reaching maturity.

inferior good: A good whose consumption varies inversely with money income (prices remaining constant) over a certain range of income. *Examples:* potatoes, used clothing, and other "cheap" commodities bought by poor families. The consumption of these commodities declines in favor of more nutritious foods, new clothing, and the like as the incomes of low-income families rise.

inflation: Rise in the general price level (or average level of prices) of all goods and services—or equivalently, a decline in the purchasing power of a unit of money (such as the dollar). The general price level thus varies inversely with the purchasing power of a unit of money. For example, if prices double, purchasing power decreases by one-half; if prices halve, purchasing power doubles.

inflationary gap: Amount by which aggregate demand exceeds aggregate supply at full employment, thereby causing inflationary pressures.

infrastructure: A nation's economic and social overhead capital needed as a basis for modern production. *Examples:* roads, telephone lines, power facilities, schools, and public health.

inheritance tax: Tax imposed by most state governments on property received from persons who have died. It is primarily progressive (graduated) in rate structure, but exemptions, deductions, and rates vary widely among the states.

injunction: Court order requiring that a defendant refrain from certain practices, or that he take a particular action.

innovation: Adoption of a new or different product, or of a new or different method of production, marketing, financing, and so on. It thus establishes a new relation between the output and the various kinds of inputs (capital, land, labor, etc.) in a production process. In a more formal sense, it is the setting up of a new production function.

innovation theory: Explanation originated by Joseph Schumpeter (1883–1950) which attributes business cycles and economic development to innovations that forward-looking businesspersons adopt in order to reduce costs and increase profits. Once an innovation proves successful, other businesspersons follow with the same or with similar techniques, and these innovations cause fluctuations in investment which result in business cycles. The innovation theory has also been used as a partial explanation of how profits arise in a competitive capitalistic system.

institutions: Those traditions, beliefs, and practices which are well established and widely held as a fundamental part of a culture. *Example:* Institutions of capitalism include private property, economic individualism, laissez-faire, and free markets. (*Note:* In sociology, social systems are often characterized by their institutions. Examples of sociological institutions are marriage, the family, etc. Institutions are thus the pillars or foundations on which a social system rests.)

interest: 1. Return to those who supply the factor of production known as "capital" (i.e., the payment for supplying the funds with which businesspersons buy capital goods). 2. Price paid for the use of money or loanable funds over a period. It is stated as a rate—that is, as a percentage of the amount of money borrowed. Thus an interest rate of 5% means that the borrower pays 5 cents per $1 borrowed per year, or $5 per $100 borrowed per year, and so on.

interlocking directorate: Situation in which an individual serves on two or more boards of directors of competing corporations.

internal economies and diseconomies of scale: Conditions that bring about decreases or increases in a firm's long-run average costs or scale of operations as a result of size adjustments within the firm as a producing unit; they occur irrespective of adjustments within the industry and are due mainly to physical economies or diseconomies. *Example:* Internal economies may result from greater specialization and more efficient utilization of the firm's resources as its scale of operations increases, but internal diseconomies may eventually set in because of the limited decision-making abilities of the top management group.

International Bank for Reconstruction and Development (World Bank): Established by the United Nations in 1945 to provide loans for postwar reconstruction and to promote development of less developed countries. The Bank's chief function is to aid the financing of basic development projects such as dams, communication and transportation facilities, and health programs by insuring or otherwise guaranteeing private loans or, when private capital is not available, by providing loans from its own resources and credit. Affiliated agencies also exist to help finance higher-risk investment projects in underdeveloped countries.

International Development Cooperation Agency (IDCA): The most important American organization concerned with foreign aid. Created in 1979, it represents a major restructuring and consolidation of previous development programs operated by different U.S. agencies and various multilateral organizations. IDCA has two major functions. The first is to advise government on development policies. The second is to administer funds voted annually by Congress for the purpose of providing economic, technical, and defense assistance to nations that are identified with the free world. (IDCA includes within its organization the Agency for International Development, the government's chief foreign-aid unit which was previously part of the U.S. State Department.)

International Monetary Fund (IMF): Established by the United Nations in 1944 for the purposes of eliminating exchange restrictions, encouraging exchange-rate stability, and providing for worldwide convertibility of currencies so as to promote multilateral trade based on international specialization. Over 100 nations are members of the Fund.

inventory: Stocks of goods which business firms have on hand, including raw materials, supplies, and finished goods.

investment: Spending by business firms on new job-creating and income-producing goods. It consists of replacements of or additions to the nation's stock of capital, including its plant, equipment, and inventories (i.e., its nonhuman productive assets).

"invisible hand": Expression coined by Adam Smith in *The Wealth of Nations* to convey the idea that each individual, if left to pursue his self-interest without interference by government, would be led as if by an invisible hand to achieve the best good for society.

involuntary unemployment: Situation in which people who want work are unable to find jobs at going wage rates for the related skills and experiences they have to offer.

isoquant: Curve along which each point represents a different combination of two inputs or factors of production (such as capital and labor), and each combination yields the same level of total output.

J

Jevons, William Stanley (1835-1882): English neoclassical and mathematical economist who made major contributions to value and distribution theory, capital theory, and to statistical research in economics. He is best known as a leading contributor to marginal utility analysis. "Value," he pointed out, "depends entirely upon utility." In equilibrium, marginal utilities are proportionate to prices. "From this, the ordinary laws of supply and demand are a neces-

sary consequence." Jevon's major work in economics was his book, *Theory of Political Economy* (1871).

job classification: Process of describing the duties, responsibilities, and characteristics of jobs, point-rating them (perhaps by established formulas based on engineering time studies of workers in such jobs), and then grouping the jobs into graduated classifications with corresponding wage rates and wage ranges.

jurisdictional strike: Strike caused by a dispute between two or more craft unions over which shall perform a particular job. Outlawed by the Taft–Hartley Act, 1947.

K

Keynes, John Maynard (1883-1946): British economist and founder of the New Economics. His most widely known work was his book, *The General Theory of Employment, Interest and Money* (1936), in which he reorganized thinking about macroeconomic problems. The following chief features characterize the so-called Keynesian "system."

(1) The dependency of consumption on income, called the **consumption function.**

(2) The **multiplier** relationship between investment expenditures and income.

(3) The **marginal efficiency of investment** as a measure of businesses' demand for investment.

(4) The use of **fiscal policy** and **monetary policy** to maintain full employment.

In contrast to the classical theory, Keynes showed that our economic system could remain in equilibrium at any level of employment, not necessarily full employment. Therefore, he concluded, active fiscal and monetary policies by government are needed to maintain high levels of resource utilization and economic stability.

kinked demand curve: A "bent" demand curve, and a corresponding discontinuous marginal revenue curve, facing an oligopolistic seller. It signifies that if the seller raises his price above the kink, his sales will fall off rapidly because other sellers are not likely to follow his price upward; if he drops his price below the kink, he will expand his sales relatively little because other sellers are likely to follow his price downward. The market price, therefore, tends to stabilize at the kink.

Knights of Labor: National labor organization founded in 1869. It rejected the traditional organizing of workers by crafts, preferring instead the mass unionization of both unskilled and skilled workers. The Knights championed the cause of workers and achieved many liberal improvements and reforms, but began to decline in the late 1880s due to several factors: (1) opposition by craft leaders who preferred organization along craft lines; (2) internal dissension among leading members and groups; and (3) suspicion—unproved—of its involvement in Chicago's Haymarket riot and bombing of 1886. By 1917 it ceased to exist.

Kuznets, Simon Smith (1901–): Russian-born American economist who made major contributions to the study of national income accounting, economic growth, productivity, and related areas. He is the "father" of national income accounting because much of his efforts toward improving the theory and measurement of national income during the 1930s became a foundation for subsequent methods by the U.S. Department of Commerce. In 1971, at the age of 70, Kuznets was awarded the Nobel Prize in Economic Science.

L

labor: 1. Factor of production which represents those hired workers whose human efforts or activities are directed toward production. **2.** All personal services, including the activities of wageworkers, professional people, and independent businesspersons. "Laborers" may thus receive compensation not only in the form of wages, but also as salaries, bonuses, commissions, and the like.

labor force: The employable population, defined for measurement purposes as all people 16 years of age or older who are employed, plus all those who are unemployed but actively seeking work.

Labor–Management Relations (Taft–Hartley) Act (1947): An amendment to the National Labor Relations (Wagner) Act of 1935. It retains the rights given to labor by the 1935 Act, but also (1) outlaws "unfair labor practices" of unions, such as coercion of workers to join unions, failure to bargain in good faith, jurisdictional strikes, secondary boycotts, and featherbedding; (2) outlaws the closed shop but permits the union shop; (3) requires unions to file financial reports with the NLRB and union officials to sign non-Communist affidavits; (4) prohibits strikes called before the end of a 60-day notice period prior to the expiration of a collective-bargaining agreement; and (5) enables the President to obtain an 80-day court injunction against strikes that endanger national health or safety.

Labor–Management Reporting and Disclosure (Landrum–Griffin) Act (1959): Act which amended the National Labor Relations Act of 1935 by (1) requiring detailed financial reports of all unions and union officers; (2) severely tightening restrictions on secondary boycotting and picketing; (3) requiring periodic secret-ballot elections of union officers; and (4) imposing restrictions on ex-convicts and Communists in holding positions as union officers.

Laffer curve: Relationship between tax revenues and the tax rate. The relationship is such that as the tax rate increases from zero to 100 percent, tax revenues rise correspondingly from zero to some maximum level and then decline to zero. The optimum rate is thus the one that produces the maximum revenue. Rates that are lower than optimum are deemed "normal" because tax revenues can be increased by raising the rate. Rates that are higher than optimum are regarded as prohibitive because they impair personal and business incentives and are thus counterproductive. Therefore, when the tax rate is in the prohibitive range, tax reductions should bring increased economic activity and higher, not lower, tax revenues.

lagging indicators: Time series that tend to follow or trail aggregate economic activity.

laissez-faire: "Leave us alone"—an expression coined in France during the late seventeenth century, but which today is interpreted to mean freedom from government intervention in all economic affairs.

land: Factor of production which includes land itself in the form of real estate as well as mineral deposits, timber, water, and other nonhuman or "natural" resources.

law: Expression of a relationship between variables, based on a high degree of unvarying uniformity under the same conditions. (Often used synonymously with **principle.**)

leading indicators: Time series that tend to move ahead of aggregate economic activity, thus reaching peaks and troughs before the economy as a whole.

legal monopoly: Privately owned firm which is granted an exclusive right by government to operate in a particular market, in return for which government may impose standards and requirements pertaining to the quantity and quality of output, geographic areas of operation, and the prices or rates that are charged. The justification of legal monopoly is that unrestricted competition in the industry is socially undesirable. Public utilities are typical examples of legal monopolies.

legal reserves: Assets that a bank may lawfully use as reserves against its deposit liabilities. For a member bank of the Federal Reserve System, legal reserves consist of deposits held with the district Federal Reserve Bank plus cash in the vaults of the member bank—called "vault cash." For a nonmember bank, legal reserves vary by state law, but they commonly include vault cash, demand deposits with other banks, and in some cases state and federal securities.

Lerner index: Measure of a firm's monopoly power, based on the divergence between price, P, and marginal cost, MC, expressed as a proportion of price. Thus

$$\text{Lerner index} = \frac{P - MC}{P}$$

When a firm is in equilibrium, the index will range between 0 and 1. It will be zero (no monopoly power) for a firm in perfect competition, since $P = MC$. At the other extreme, the index will be 1 (complete monopoly power) in the rare case of a firm whose marginal costs are zero. Basic shortcomings of the formula are that (1) marginal-cost data for a firm are not generally known and cannot be readily derived; and (2) it is a static rather than dynamic measure.

less developed (underdeveloped) country: A nation which, in comparison with the more advanced countries, tends to exhibit such characteristics as (1) poverty level of income and hence little or no saving; (2) high rate of population growth; (3) substantial majority of its labor force employed in agriculture; (4) low proportion of adult literacy; (5) extensive disguised unemployment; and (6) heavy reliance on a few items for export.

liabilities: Monetary debts or things of value owed by an economic entity (such as an individual, household, or business firm) to creditors.

limited liability: Restriction of the liability of an investor, such as a stockholder in a corporation, to the amount of his investment.

liquidity: Ease with which an asset can be converted into cash quickly without loss of value in terms of money. Liquidity is thus a matter of degree. Money is perfectly liquid, whereas any other asset possesses a lower degree of liquidity—depending on the condition above.

liquidity preference (theory of interest): Theory formulated by J. M. Keynes (1883–1946) contending that households and businesses would rather hold their assets in the most liquid form—cash or checking accounts, to satisfy three motives: (1) the "transactions motive," to carry out everyday purchasing needs; (2) the "precautionary motive," to meet possible unforeseen conditions; and (3) the "speculative motive," to take advantage of a change in interest rates. These motives determine the demand for money, whereas the monetary authority determines its supply. The demand for, and supply of, money together determine the equilibrium rate of interest.

liquidity trap: Condition in which an increase in the supply of money will not reduce further the rate of interest, because the total demand for money at that relatively low interest rate (expressed in terms of a liquidity-preference curve) is infinite. This means that at the low rate of interest, everyone would rather hold money in idle balances than risk the loss of holding long-term securities offering poor yields. (In geometric terms, the liquidity trap exists at that rate of interest where the liquidity-preference curve becomes perfectly horizontal.)

loanable funds theory of interest: Theory which holds that the interest rate is determined by the demand for, and supply of, loanable funds only, as distinguished from *all* money. The sources of demand for loanable funds are businesses that want to invest, households that want to finance consumer purchases, and government agencies that want to finance deficits. The sources of supply of loanable funds are the central banking system, which influences the supply of money (and hence loanable funds) in the economy, and households and businesses that make loanable funds available out of their past or present savings.

lockout: Closing down of a plant by an employer in order to keep workers out of their jobs.

logarithmic scale: Special type of scale used in graphing. The scale is spaced in logarithms. As a result, equal *percentage* changes between numbers are represented by equal distances along the scale. For example, a 100 percent change is always the same distance on the scale whether the change is from 1 to 2, 2 to 4, 3 to 6, 5 to 10, 10 to 20, 50 to 100. In contrast, a conventional scale is spaced arithmetically. Therefore, equal *amounts* of change between numbers are represented by equal distances along the scale. Thus the changes from 1 to 2, 2 to 3, 6 to 7, 15 to 16, and so on, are all the same distances on an arithmetic scale. A logarithmic scale is useful for comparing *ratios* of change between data. In contrast, an arithmetic scale is used to compare *amounts* of change between data.

long run: Period that is long enough for a firm to enter or leave an industry, and to vary its output by varying all its factors of production, including its plant scale.

long-run average cost curve (planning curve): Curve that is tangent to, or envelops, the various short-run average total cost curves of a firm over a range of output representing different scales or sizes of plant. Thus it shows what the level of average costs would be for alternative outputs of different-sized plants.

long-run industry supply curve: Locus or "path" of a competitive industry's long-run equilibrium points. That is, the long-run industry supply curve connects the stable equilibrium points of the industry's supply and demand curves over a period of time, both before and after these curves have adjusted completely to changed market conditions. The long-run industry supply curve may be either upward sloping, horizontal, or downward sloping, depending on whether the industry is an increasing-, constant-, or decreasing-cost industry.

Lorenz diagram: Graphic device for comparing cumulative percentage relationships between two variables. It is often used to compare a society's actual distribution of income with an equal distribution. For example, each axis of the chart is scaled from 0 to 100 percent, and the cumulative percentage relationships between two variables such as "percent of income" and "percent of families" are plotted against each other. The resulting (Lorenz) curve of actual income distribution is then compared to a 45° diagonal line representing equal income distribution. The degree of departure between the two curves indicates the extent of income inequality. Similar curves may be constructed to show other types of distributions (e.g., distribution of wealth, distribution of wages in a factory).

M

macroeconomics: That part of economics which studies and theorizes about the economy as a whole, or about large subdivisions of it. It analyzes the economic "forest" as distinct from its "trees."

Malthusian theory of population: First published by Thomas Malthus in 1798 and then revised in 1803, this theory states that population tends to increase as a geometric progression (1, 2, 4, 8, 16, 32, etc.) while the means of subsistence increase at most only as an arithmetic progression (1, 2, 3, 4, 5, 6, etc.). This is because a growing population applied to a fixed amount of land results in eventually diminishing returns to workers. Human beings are therefore destined to misery and poverty unless the rate of population growth is retarded. This may be accomplished either by (1) preventive checks such as moral restraint, late marriages, and celibacy, or if these fail then by (2) positive checks such as wars, famines, and disease.

Malthus, Thomas Robert (1776–1834): English classical economist. Best known for his theory which held that population would tend to outrun the food supply. The result would be a bare subsistence level of survival for the laboring class. (See **Malthusian theory of population.**) Malthus, in his book, *Principles of Political Economy* (1820), also developed the concept of "effective demand," which he defined as the level of aggregate demand necessary to maintain full employment. If effective demand declined, he said, overproduction would result. He thus anticipated a fundamental concept in modern macroeconomics.

manpower policies: Deliberate efforts undertaken in the private and public sectors to develop and use the capacities of human beings as actual or potential members of the labor force.

Marcet, Jane Haldimand (1769–1858): English economic educator whose book, *Conversations on Political Economy* (1816), conveyed in dialogue form the teachings of her classical-economic predecessors and contemporaries—Smith, Say, Malthus, and Ricardo. She thus contributed significantly to the teaching of economics.

marginal cost: Change in total cost resulting from a unit change in quantity. It is measured by the ratio

$$\text{marginal cost} = \frac{\text{change in total cost}}{\text{change in quantity}}$$

Marginal cost is also the change in total variable cost resulting from a unit change in quantity, since total cost changes because total variable cost changes, whereas total fixed cost remains constant. In general, marginal cost measures the gain in total cost from an additional unit of quantity produced.

marginal cost price: Price (or production) of output as determined by the point at which a firm's marginal cost equals its average revenue (demand). This is an optimum price for society, because the value of the last unit to the marginal user (measured by the price he pays for the last unit, which is equal to the price he pays for any other unit) is equivalent to the value of the resources used to produce that unit. However, this marginal cost price will leave the firm suffering a loss if it results in a price below the firm's average total cost.

marginal efficiency of investment: Expected rate of return on an addition to investment. More precisely, it is the expected rate of return over the cost of an additional unit of a capital good. It is determined by such factors as (1) the demand for the product which the investment will produce;

(2) the level of production costs in the economy; (3) technology and innovation; and (4) the stock of capital available to meet existing and future market demands.

marginal product: Change in total product resulting from a unit change in the quantity of a variable input employed. It is measured by the ratio

$$\text{marginal product} = \frac{\text{change in total product}}{\text{change in a variable input}}$$

Marginal product thus measures the gain (or loss) in total product from adding an additional unit of a variable factor of production.

marginal productivity theory of income distribution: Principle which states that when there is perfect competition for inputs, a firm will purchase factors of production up to the point where the price or marginal cost of the factor is equal to its marginal revenue productivity. Therefore, in real terms, each factor of production will be paid a value equal to what it contributes to total output—that is, it will be paid what it is "worth."

marginal propensity to consume: Change in consumption resulting from a unit change in income. It is measured by the ratio

$$\text{marginal propensity to consume} = \frac{\text{change in consumption}}{\text{change in income}}$$

It thus reveals the fraction of each extra dollar of income that is spent on consumption.

marginal propensity to invest: Change in investment resulting from a unit change in aggregate output. It is measured by the ratio

$$\text{marginal propensity to invest} = \frac{\text{change in investment}}{\text{change in aggregate output}}$$

marginal propensity to save: Change in saving resulting from a unit change in income. It is measured by the ratio

$$\text{marginal propensity to save} = \frac{\text{change in saving}}{\text{change in income}}$$

It thus reveals the fraction of each extra dollar of income that is saved.

marginal propensity to spend: Change in total spending on consumption and investment resulting from a unit change in aggregate output or income. The marginal propensity to spend, *MPE*, consists of the marginal propensity to consume, *MPC*, and the marginal propensity to invest, *MPI*. Thus out of any change in aggregate output or income,

$$MPE = MPC + MPI$$

marginal rate of substitution: In demand theory, the rate at which a consumer is willing to substitute one commodity for another along an indifference curve. It is the amount of change in the holdings of one commodity that will just offset a unit change in the holdings of another commodity, so that the consumer's total utility remains the same. Thus, along an indifference curve,

$$\text{marginal rate of substitution} = \frac{\text{change in commodity Y}}{\text{change in commodity X}}$$

The marginal rate of substitution is always negative because one commodity must be decreased when the other is increased in order to keep total utility the same (i.e., to remain on a given indifference curve).

In production theory, the marginal rate of substitution is

the change in one type of productive input that will just offset a unit change in another type of productive input, so that the total level of production (along an **isoquant**) remains the same. Some examples of productive inputs are capital and labor, fertilizer and land.

marginal revenue: Change in total revenue resulting from a unit change in quantity. It is measured by the ratio

$$\text{marginal revenue} = \frac{\text{change in total revenue}}{\text{change in quantity}}$$

Marginal revenue thus measures the gain (or loss) in total revenue that results from producing and selling an additional unit.

marginal revenue product: Change in total revenue resulting from a unit change in the quantity of a variable input employed. It is measured by the ratio

$$\text{marginal revenue product} = \frac{\text{change in total revenue}}{\text{change in a variable input}}$$

Marginal revenue product thus measures the gain (or loss) in total revenue from adding an additional unit of a variable factor of production.

marginal tax rate: Ratio, expressed as a percentage, of the change in a total tax resulting from a unit change in the base on which it is imposed. *Example:*

marginal personal income tax rate

$$= \frac{\text{change in total personal income tax}}{\text{change in total taxable income}}$$

marginal utility: Change in total utility resulting from a unit change in the quantity of a commodity consumed. It is given by the ratio

$$\text{marginal utility} = \frac{\text{change in total utility}}{\text{change in quantity consumed}}$$

Marginal utility thus measures the gain (or loss) in satisfaction from an additional unit of a good.

margin requirements: Percentage down payment required of a borrower to finance purchase of stock. This rate is set by the Federal Reserve System's Board of Governors. An increase in margin requirements is designed to dampen security purchases; a decrease, to encourage it.

market economy: Economic system in which the questions of what to produce, how much to produce, and for whom to produce are decided in an open market through the free operation of supply and demand. There are no "pure" market economies, but several specialized markets (such as the organized commodity exchanges) closely approximate some of the properties of a pure market system. (*Compare* **command economy.**)

market price: Actual price that prevails in a market at any particular moment.

market rate of interest: Actual or money rate of interest which prevails in the market at any given time. (Contrast with **real rate of interest.**)

market share: Percentage of an industry's output accounted for by an individual firm. Measures of output usually employed are sales, value added, or value of shipments.

Marshall, Alfred (1842–1924): English economist who synthesized neoclassical thinking around the turn of the century and made many pioneering contributions as well. Among them: the distinction between the short run and the long run, and the equilibrium of price and output resulting from the interaction of supply and demand. Also: the concept of elasticity, the distinction between money cost and real cost, and many other concepts. Much of modern microeconomics stems from Marshall's work. His best-known book, *Principles of Economics,* went through eight editions and was a standard reference and text in economics from 1890 until the 1930s.

Martineau, Harriet (1802–1876): English economic educator whose book, *Illustrations of Political Economy* (1834), emphasized the teaching of economics through applications and real-life experiences. She was thus a pioneer in the use of the "case method" of teaching—along the lines used today in many business and in some economics courses.

median: Special type of average that divides a distribution of numbers into two equal parts—one-half of all cases being equal to or greater than the median value, and one-half being equal to or less.

mediation: Method of settling differences between two parties (such as a union and management) by the use of an impartial third party, called a mediator, who is acceptable to both sides but makes no binding decisions. The mediator tries to maintain constructive discussions, search for common areas of agreement, and suggest compromises. Federal, state, and most large local governments provide mediation services for labor–management disputes. Mediation is also sometimes called "conciliation."

member bank: Bank which belongs to the Federal Reserve System. All national banks (chartered by the federal government) must be members. State banks may join if they meet certain requirements.

mercantilism: Set of doctrines and practices aimed at promoting national prosperity and the power of the state by (1) accumulating precious metals (mainly gold and silver) through the maintenance of favorable trade balances; (2) achieving economic self-sufficiency through imperialism; and (3) exploiting colonies by monopolizing their raw materials and precious metals while reserving them as exclusive markets for exports. Mercantilism reached its peak in the seventeenth century, serving as a political and economic ideology in England, France, Spain, and Germany.

merger: Amalgamation of two or more firms under one ownership. The three common forms are: (1) *horizontal,* uniting similar plants and products; (2) *vertical,* uniting dissimilar plants in various stages of production; and (3) *conglomerate,* uniting dissimilar plants and products.

microeconomics: That part of economics which studies and theorizes about the specific economic units or parts of an economic system, such as its firms, industries, and households, and the relationships between these parts. It analyzes the "trees" of the economy as distinct from the "forest."

Mill, John Stuart (1806–1873): Last of the major English classical economists. His two-volume treatise, *Principles of Political Economy* (1848), was a masterful synthesis of classical ideas. Mill advocated laissez-faire, but he was also a strong supporter of social reforms. Among them: worker education, democratic producer cooperatives, redistribution of wealth, shorter working days, taxation of unearned gains from land, and social control of monopoly. Mill supported these measures because he mistrusted government and wanted to assure to individual workers the benefits of their contributions to production. Therefore, although Mill was often called a socialist, he was in fact a "moderate conservative" by today's standards. He believed too strongly in individual freedom to advocate major government involvement in the economy.

mint ratio: Under a bimetallic standard, the ratio of the weight of one metal to the other, and their equivalent in terms of the national unit of currency (such as the dollar) as defined by the government. For example, during the nineteenth century when the United States was on a bimetallic standard, the government defined the mint ratio for many years as

$$15 \text{ grains of silver} = 1 \text{ grain of gold} = \$1$$

The mint ratio was therefore 15:1. Since it remained fixed by law, it resulted in either gold or silver being driven out of circulation, depending on the relative market values of the two metals. (*See also* **bimetallic standard; Gresham's Law.**)

Mitchell, Wesley Clair (1874–1948): Leading American economist during the first half of the twentieth century. Mitchell was a professor of economics at Columbia University and a founder of the National Bureau of Economic Research, one of the world's major centers for quantitative research in aggregative economic activity. Mitchell's lifework was devoted to the study of business cycles, their history, nature, and causes. Much of what is known today about economic fluctuations has roots in the pioneering research done by Mitchell.

mixed economy: Economic system in which the questions of what to produce, how much to produce, and for whom to produce are decided for some goods by the free market and for other goods by a central government authority. There are varying forms and degrees of mixed economies.

model: Representation of the essential features of a theory or of a real-world situation, expressed in the form of words, diagrams, graphs, mathematical equations, or combinations of these.

monetarism: Macroeconomic theory and policies which follow in the tradition of Irving Fisher. Monetarists contend that an increase in the money supply leads to an increase in prices. This causes the actual or market rate of interest to rise relative to the "real" rate—the rate that would exist if prices were stable. The difference between the market and real rate represents an "inflation premium." This is an amount which lenders require and borrowers are willing to pay because both expect prices to continue rising. Monetarists conclude from their analysis that the effects on aggregate demand of temporary budgetary changes are uncertain. Therefore, steady monetary growth is preferable to discretionary fiscal actions. Thus, stated in concise terms, the monetarist model is characterized by (1) a predominantly monetary theory of the price level, (2) a predominantly nonmonetary theory of the interest rate, and (3) a distinction between market and real rates of interest. (*Contrast with* **fiscalism.**)

monetary asset: Claim against a fixed quantity of money, the amount of which is unaffected by inflation or deflation. *Examples:* bonds, accounts receivable, savings deposits, promissory notes, and cash. For every monetary asset, there is an equal monetary liability. (*See also* **monetary liability.**)

monetary base: *Net* monetary liabilities of government—the Fed and the Treasury—held by the public. It equals the sum of currency held by the public, currency in the vaults of commercial banks, and member-bank deposits at the Federal Reserve. The monetary base thus consists of currency plus member-bank reserves. The monetary base is also referred to as "high-powered money" because it can be used as reserves by commercial banks to expand demand deposits by more than the amount of reserves.

monetary liability: Promise to pay a claim against a fixed quantity of money, the amount of which is unaffected by inflation or deflation. For every monetary liability, there is an equal monetary asset. (*See also* **monetary asset.**)

monetary policy: Deliberate exercise of the monetary authority's (i.e., Federal Reserve's) power to induce expansions or contractions in the money supply in order to help dampen the swings of business cycles and bring the nation's output and employment to desired levels.

monetary standard: Laws and practices which determine the quantity and quality of a nation's money, and establish the conditions, if any, under which its currency is ultimately redeemable.

monetary theory (of business cycles): Explanation of economic fluctuations in terms of financial factors, such as changes in the quantity of money and credit, and changes in interest rates. Upswings occur when credit and borrowing conditions become favorable enough for businesspersons to borrow; downswings occur when the banking system begins to restrict its expansion of money and credit.

money: Anything which has at least these four functions: (1) a medium of exchange for conducting transactions; (2) a measure of value for expressing the prices of current and future transactions; (3) a standard of deferred payments which permits borrowing or lending for future repayment with interest; and (4) a store of value which permits saving for future as well as current spending.

money illusion: Situation in which a rise in all prices and incomes by the same proportion leads to an increase in consumption, even though real incomes remain unchanged.

money income: Amount of money received for work done. (*Compare* **real income.**)

money market: Center where short-term credit instruments such as U.S. Treasury bills and certificates, short-term promissory notes, and bankers' acceptances are bought and sold.

money-supply rule: Guide for economic expansion advanced by some economists, especially by Milton Friedman. The "rule" states that the Federal Reserve should expand the nation's money supply at a steady rate in accordance with the economy's long-term growth trend and capacity to produce, such as 3 to 5 percent per year for the United States. More than this would lead to strong inflationary pressures; less would tend to be stagnating if not deflationary.

money wages: Wages received in cash. (*Compare* **real wages.**)

monopolistic competition: Industry or market structure characterized by a large number of firms of different sizes producing heterogeneous (similar but not identical) products, with relatively easy entry into the industry.

monopoly: Industry or market structure characterized by a single firm producing a product for which there are no close substitutes. The firm thus constitutes the entire industry and is a "pure" monopoly.

monopoly price: Price (and production) of output as determined by the equality of marginal cost and marginal revenue ($MC = MR$)—but with marginal cost less than average revenue or price ($MC < P$). It is the profit-maximizing price for an imperfect competitor. At this price, the value of the last unit to the marginal user (measured by the price he or she pays for the last unit, which is equal to the price paid for any other unit) is greater than the value of the resources used to produce that unit.

monopsony: Market structure consisting of a single buyer of a good or service. It may be thought of as a "buyer's monopoly."

moral suasion: Oral or written appeals by the Federal Reserve board to member banks, urging them to expand or restrict credit but without requiring them to comply.

most-favored-nation clause: Provision in a trade treaty by which each signatory country agrees to extend to the other the same preferential tariff and trade concessions that it may in the future extend to nonsignatories (i.e., the same treatment that each gives to its "most favored nation"). Most trading countries have adhered to this principle since 1948.

multiple expansion of bank deposits: Process by which a loan made by one bank is used to finance business transactions, and ends up as a deposit in another bank. Part of this may be used by the second bank as a required reserve, and the rest lent out for business use so that it is eventually deposited in a third bank; and so on. The total amount of credit granted by the banking system as a whole will thus be a multiple of the initial deposit. (*See also* **deposit-expansion multiplier.**)

multiplier: Principle which states that changes in investment bring about magnified changes in income, as expressed by the equation: multiplier $\times$ change in investment = change in income. The multiplier coefficient is given by the formula

$$\text{multiplier} = \frac{\text{change in income}}{\text{change in investment}}$$
$$= \frac{1}{MPS} = \frac{1}{1 - MPC}$$

where *MPS* stands for the marginal propensity to save and *MPC* the marginal propensity to consume. (*Note:* This multiplier is sometimes called the "simple multiplier" or the "investment multiplier" to distinguish it from other types of multipliers in economics.)

multiunit bargaining: Collective-bargaining arrangement covering more than one plant. It may occur between one or more firms in an industry and one or more unions, and it may take place on a national, regional, or local level. It is sometimes inaccurately called "industry-wide bargaining," although it is rarely completely industrywide.

municipals: Marketable financial obligations—mostly bonds—issued by state and local governmental authorities (the latter including cities, towns, school districts, etc.). Interest income paid to their owners is exempt from federal income taxes, and usually from state income taxes of the state in which they are issued.

N

national bank: Commercial bank chartered by the federal government. Such banks are required to belong to the Federal Reserve System. A minority of banks today are national banks, but they hold considerably more than half the deposits of the banking system and are larger than most state-chartered banks.

National Banking Act (1863): Legislation aimed at standardizing banking practices and reaffirming the existence of our dual banking system. The law contained the following main provisions. (1) Opportunities for banks to be federally chartered, thus making them national banks. (2) Issuance of Treasury currency backed largely by government bonds.

(3) Federal taxation of state bank notes, thus forcing them out of existence. (4) Holding of cash reserves against notes and deposits.

national income (at factor cost): 1. Total of all net incomes earned by or ascribed to the factors of production—that is, the sum of wages, rent, interest, and profit which accrues to the suppliers of labor, land, capital, and entrepreneurship. [*Note:* It should not be confused with the total income received by people from all sources (i.e., personal income). The difference between the two is based on various accounting considerations.] **2.** In general terms and in theoretical discussions, the expression "national income" is often used in a simple generic sense to represent the income or output of an economy.

National Labor Relations (Wagner) Act (1935): Basic labor relations law of the United States. It (1) guarantees the right of workers to organize and bargain collectively through representatives of their own choosing; (2) forbids employers to engage in "unfair labor practices" such as discrimination or interference; and (3) authorizes the National Labor Relations Board to enforce the act and supervise free elections among a company's employees.

National Labor Relations Board: Government agency established under the National Labor Relations Act of 1935 to enforce that act; investigate violations of it; and supervise free elections among a company's employees so as to determine which union, if any, is to represent them in collective bargaining.

Natural Gas Act (1938): Legislation granting the Federal Power Commission (FPC) authority over the interstate transportation of natural gas and empowering the Commission to regulate rates and services.

natural monopoly: Firm which experiences increasing economies of scale (i.e., long-run decreasing average costs of production) over a sufficiently wide range of output, enabling it to supply an entire market at a lower unit cost than two or more firms. Electric companies, gas companies, and railroads are classic examples.

natural unemployment rate: Employment level at which only frictional and structural unemployment exist, not cyclical unemployent arising from a deficiency in aggregate demand. The natural unemployment rate can be lowered by improving labor markets—through job training, combating discrimination in hiring, and so on—but not by overexpansionary fiscal and monetary policies.

near-monies: Assets which are almost, but not quite, money. They can easily be converted into money because their monetary values are known. *Examples:* time or savings deposits, U.S. government bonds, and cash values of insurance policies.

needs standard: Criterion of income distribution popularly expressed by the phrase, "To each according to his or her needs." This is the distributive principle of pure communism and an approximate criterion for apportioning income in most families. If you regard the needs standard as a just or equitable one, you are assuming that a central authority is capable of determining what constitutes yours and everyone else's needs. (*Compare* **equality standard; contributive standard.**)

negative income tax: Plan for guaranteeing the poor a minimum income through a type of reverse income tax. A poor family, depending on its size and other income, would be paid by the government enough either to reduce or close the gap between what it earns and an explicit minimum level of income. That level might be equal to or above the government's designated "poverty line." As the family's income increases, the government's payment declines to zero.

neoclassical economics: Approach to economics which flourished in Europe and the United States between 1870 and World War I. Among its leaders were William Stanley Jevons in England, Carl Menger in Austria, Leon Walras in Switzerland, Vilfredo Pareto in Switzerland, Alfred Marshall in England, and John Bates Clark and Irving Fisher in the United States. The neoclassicists were primarily concerned with refining the principles of price and allocation theory, "marginalism," the theory of capital, and related aspects of economics. They made early and extensive use of mathematics, especially differential and integral calculus, in the development of their analyses and models. Much of the structure of modern economic science is built on their pioneering work.

net national product: Total sales value of goods and services available for society's consumption and for adding to its stock of capital equipment. It represents society's net output for the year and may be obtained by deducting a capital consumption allowance from gross national product.

net-profit ratio: Ratio of a firm's net profit after taxes to its net sales. It is one of several general measures of a company's performance.

net revenue: A firm's "pure" or net profit—equal to its total revenue minus its total cost.

net worth: Difference between the total assets or things of value owned by a firm or individual, and the liabilities or debts that are owed.

New Economics: Body of economic thought which originated with the British economist John Maynard Keynes (1883–1946) in the 1930s. It has since been extended and modified to the point where its basic analytical tools and methods are now used by practically all economists. In contrast to classical economics, which emphasized the automatic tendency of the economy to achieve full-employment equilibrium under a government policy of laissez-faire, the New Economics demonstrates that an economy may be in equilibrium at any level of employment. It therefore concludes that appropriate government fiscal and monetary policies are needed to maintain full employment and steady economic growth with a minimum rate of inflation.

nonprice competition: Methods of competition that do not involve changes in selling price. *Examples:* advertising, product differentiation, and customer service.

normal good: A good whose consumption varies directly with money income, prices remaining constant. Most consumer goods are normal goods. (Same as **superior good.**)

normal price: The dynamic equilibrium price toward which the market price is always tending but may never reach.

normal profit: Least payment that the owner of an enterprise will accept as compensation for his entrepreneurial function, including risk taking and management. Normal profit is part of a firm's total economic costs, since it is a payment which the owner must receive in order to keep him from withdrawing his capital and managerial effort and putting them into an alternative enterprise.

normative economics: Approach to economics which deals with what "ought to be" as compared to what "is." It involves statements which are value judgments, and hence much of it cannot be empirically verified. (*Compare* **positive economics.**)

Norris–La Guardia Act (1932): Act of Congress which outlawed the yellow-dog contract and greatly restricted the conditions under which court injunctions against labor unions could be issued.

notes payable: Promises to pay the holder, such as a bank, a sum of money within the year at a stated rate of interest.

O

Okun's Law: Relationship between changes in unemployment and the rate of economic growth (measured by changes in real GNP). The law, based on long-run trends, states that unemployment (1) decreases less than 1 percent for each percentage point that the annual growth of real GNP exceeds its long-term average, and (2) increases less than 1 percent for each percentage point that the annual growth of real GNP falls short of its long-term average. The economy, therefore, must continue to grow considerably faster than its long-term average rate in order to achieve a substantial reduction in the unemployment rate. (The law is attributed to Arthur Okun, chairman of the Council of Economic Advisors under President Lyndon Johnson.)

oligopoly: Industry or market structure composed of a few firms selling either: (1) a homogeneous or undifferentiated product—the industry is then called a "perfect" or "pure" oligopoly; or (2) heterogeneous or differentiated products—the industry is then called an "imperfect" oligopoly. Some examples of perfect oligopoly are the copper, steel, and cement industries; some examples of imperfect oligopoly are the automobile, soap, detergent, and household appliance industries.

oligopsony: Industry or market structure composed of a few buyers of a commodity. *Example:* Natural-gas pipeline companies are oligopsonists in that there are only a few of them that purchase gas for transportation from any given field.

open-market operations: Purchases and sales of government securities by the Federal Reserve System. Purchases of securities are expansionary because they add to commercial banks' reserves; sales of securities are contractionary because they reduce commercial banks' reserves.

open shop: Business firm in which the employer is free to hire either union or nonunion members.

operating profit ratio: Ratio of a firm's operating profit to its net sales.

opportunity cost: Value of the benefit that is forgone by choosing one alternative rather than another. Also called "alternative cost," since it represents the implicit cost of the forgone alternative to the individual, household, firm, or other decision-making organism. Opportunity costs are not entered in a firm's public accounting records. (*Compare* **outlay costs.**)

outlay costs: Money expended to carry on a particular activity. They are the explicit costs which are entered in a firm's public accounting records, such as its income statement, to arrive at a measure of profit. *Examples:* wages and salaries, rent, and other money expenditures of a firm.

overinvestment theory (of business cycles): Explanation which holds that economic fluctuations are caused by too much investment in the economy as businesspersons try to anticipate rising demands during an upswing, and from sharp cutbacks in investment during a downswing when businesspersons realize they expanded too much in the previous prosperity.

P

paradox of thrift: Proposition which demonstrates that if people as a group try to increase their saving, they will end up by saving less. The conclusion of the paradox is that an increase in saving may be desirable for an individual or family, but for an entire economy will lead to a reduction in income, employment, and output if it is not offset by an increase in investment. The concept was first introduced by Bernard Mandeville in *The Fable of the Bees* (1714) and was later recognized in the writings of several classical economists.

Pareto optimality: Condition which exists in a social organization when no change can be implemented which will make someone better off without making someone else worse off—each in his own estimation. Since an economic system is a type of social organization, Pareto optimality is synonymous with *economic efficiency.* (*See also* **efficiency.**)

Pareto, Vilfredo (1848–1923): Italian economist and sociologist who developed many elegant mathematical formulations of economic concepts, especially those pertaining to general equilibrium theory. His work provided a foundation for indifference-curve analysis. He showed that a theory of demand could be developed without dependence on utility, by observing consumer purchases of combinations of goods that are equally acceptable. Pareto was heavily influenced by Leon Walras, and succeeded him as Professor of Political Economy at the University of Lausanne, Switzerland. (*See* **Pareto optimality.**)

parity price: Price which yields an equivalence to some defined standard. *Examples:* (1) In agriculture, a price of an agricultural commodity which gives the commodity a purchasing power, in terms of the goods that farmers buy, equivalent to that which it had in a previous base period. (2) In international economics, the price or exchange rate between the currencies of two countries that makes the purchasing power of one currency substantially equivalent to the purchasing power of the other.

parity ratio: In agriculture, an index of the prices farmers receive divided by an index of the prices they pay. It is used to measure the economic well-being of agriculture as a whole.

partial equilibrium theory: Explanation or model of a particular market, assuming that other markets are in balance. It thus ignores the interrelationships of prices and quantities that may exist between markets. *Example:* Ordinary supply and demand analysis is normally of a partial equilibrium nature, since it usually focuses on a single market while neglecting others.

participation rate (labor force): Number of people in the civilian labor force as a percentage of the civilian population. Only persons 16 years of age or older are included in the calculation.

partnership: Association of two or more individuals to carry on, as co-owners, a business for profit. The partners are solely responsible for the activities and liabilities of the business.

patent: Exclusive right conferred by government on an inventor, for a limited time. It authorizes the inventor to make, use, transfer, or withhold his invention, which he might do even without a patent, but it also gives him the right to exclude others or to admit them on his own terms, which he can only do with a patent. Patents are thus a method of promoting invention by granting temporary monopolies to inventors.

patent monopoly: Firm which exercises a monopoly because the government has conferred upon it the exclusive right—through issuance of a patent—to make, use, or vend its own invention or discovery.

perfect competition: Name given to an industry or market structure characterized by a large number of buyers and sellers all engaged in the purchase and sale of a homogeneous commodity, with perfect knowledge of market prices and quantities, no discrimination in buying or selling, and perfect mobility of resources. (*Note:* The term is usually employed synonymously with *pure competition,* although there is a technical distinction: pure competition does not require perfect knowledge or perfect resource mobility, and hence does not produce as smooth or rapid an adjustment to equilibrium as does perfect competition. However, both types of competition lead to essentially the same results in economic theory.)

permanent income hypothesis: Proposition which states that a family's propensity to consume (i.e., the amount it spends on consumption) depends on its anticipated long-run or permanent income—the average income expected to be received over a number of years. In addition, the theory holds that a family's consumption is approximately proportional to its permanent income. This hypothesis is thus an alternative theory of the consumption function. (*Contrast with* **absolute income hypothesis; relative income hypothesis.**)

personal income: In national-income accounting, the total income received by persons from all sources.

personal income distribution: Shares of total income received by people. The shares are often expressed in terms of percentages of aggregate income received by each fifth of all families, or in terms of the percentage of families falling within specific income classes.

Phillips curve: Curve which represents a trade-off between unemployment and inflation. Every point along the curve denotes a different combination of unemployment and inflation, and a movement along the curve measures the reduction in one of these at the expense of a gain in the other.

Phillips Petroleum case (1954): Major regulation case in which the Supreme Court authorized the Federal Power Commission to regulate natural-gas prices that producers charge interstate pipeline companies. This was the first time in the nation's history that the Supreme Court ordered a regulatory commission to expand the scope of its authority.

planned economy: Economic system in which the government, according to a preconceived plan, plays a primary role in directing economic resources for the purpose of deciding what to produce, how much, and possibly for whom. A planned economy may or may not be a command economy, depending on whether the government operates within a substantially authoritarian or democratic framework. (*See also* **command economy.**)

plant: Establishment that produces or distributes goods and services. In economics, a "plant" is usually thought of as a firm, but it may also be one of several plants owned by a firm.

Point Four Program: Part of the Foreign Economic Assistance Act of 1950. The Program seeks to raise living standards in the underdeveloped countries by making available to them U.S. technical and financial assistance, largely in the areas of agriculture, public health, and education. Much of this work is now carried out by agencies of the United Nations and by the U.S. Agency for International Development.

positive economics: An approach to economics which deals with what "is" as compared with what "ought to be." Much of positive economics involves the use of statements that can be verified by empirical research (i.e., by an appeal to the facts). (*Compare* **normative economics.**)

poverty line: Measure of poverty among families, defined in terms of a sliding income scale which varies between rural and urban locations according to family size.

precautionary motive: Desire on the part of households and businesses to hold part of their assets in liquid form so that they can be prepared for unexpected contingencies. This motive is influenced primarily by income levels rather than by changes in the interest rate and is one of the chief sources of demand for loanable funds in the modern theory of interest.

preferred stock: Shares of stock that receive priority (i.e., preference) over common stock at a fixed rate in the distribution of dividends, or in the distribution of assets if the company is liquidated.

prepayments: Business expenditures made in advance for items that will yield portions of their benefits in the present and in future years. *Examples:* advance premiums on a fire insurance policy; expenses incurred in marketing a new product.

present value: Discounted value of future sums of money. The discount is taken at a specified interest rate for a specified period of time. Present value is thus a sum of money adjusted for interest over time.

price: The exchange value of a commodity, i.e., the power of a commodity to command some other commodity, usually money, in exchange for itself.

price–consumption curve: In indifference-curve analysis, a line which connects the tangency points of price lines and indifference curves by showing the amounts of two commodities that a consumer will purchase when his income and the price of one commodity remain constant while the price of the other commodity varies.

price discrimination: Practice by a seller of charging different prices to the same or to different buyers for the same good.

price leadership: Adherence by firms in an oligopolistic industry, often tacitly and without formal agreement, to the pricing policies of one of its members. Frequently but not always, the price leader will be the largest firm in the industry, and other firms will simply go along with the leader, charging the same price as he charges.

price line (budget line): In indifference curve analysis, a line representing all the possible combinations of two commodities that a consumer can purchase at a particular time, given the market prices of the commodities and the consumer's money budget or income.

price system: Mechanism that allocates scarce goods or resources by rationing them among those buyers and sellers in the marketplace who are willing and able to deal at the going prices. The term is often used to express the way prices are established through the free play of supply and demand in competitive markets composed of many buyers and sellers. In reality, of course, there may be "noncompetitive" price systems in markets where buyers or sellers are relatively few in number.

primary reserves: A bank's legal reserves (consisting of vault cash and demand deposits with the Federal Reserve Bank) and demand deposits with other banks.

prime rate: Interest rate charged by banks on loans to their most credit-worthy customers.

principle: Fundamental law or general truth. It is often stated as an expression of a relationship between two or more variables. (*See also* **law**.)

private benefit: Utility that accrues to an individual, household, or firm as a result of a particular act. (*Compare* **social benefit**.)

private cost: Disutility (including economic cost) that accrues to an individual, household, or firm as a result of a particular act. (*Compare* **social cost**.)

private property: Basic institution of capitalism which gives each individual the right to acquire economic goods and resources by legitimate means, and use or dispose of them as he wishes. This right may be modified by society to the extent that it affects public health, safety, or welfare.

private rate of return: The business or financial rate of return on an investment—that is, the rate which business-persons try to anticipate before investing their funds. In financial terms, it is the expected net profit after taxes and all costs, including depreciation, and may typically be expressed as a percentage annual return upon either the total cost of a project, or upon the net worth of the stockholder owners.

private sector: That segment of the total economy consisting of households and businesses, but excluding government.

"process of creative destruction": An expression coined by the economist Joseph Schumpeter (1883–1950) to describe the growth of a capitalistic economy as a process of replacing the old with the new—that is, old methods of production, old sources of supply, and old skills and resources with new ones.

Producer Price Index (PPI): Average of selected items priced in wholesale markets, including raw materials, semi-finished products, and finished goods. The PPI is published by the Bureau of Labor Statistics of the U.S. Department of Labor.

production function: Relationship between the number of units of inputs that a firm employs and the corresponding units of output that result.

production-possibilities curve: Curve which depicts all possible combinations of total output for an economy, assuming that there is (1) a choice between producing either one or both of two kinds of goods; (2) full and efficient employment of all resources (i.e., no underemployment); and (3) a fixed supply of resources and a given state of technological knowledge.

product markets: Markets in which businesses sell the outputs that they produce (in contrast with resource markets in which they buy the inputs they need in order to produce).

profit: 1. Return to those who perform the entrepreneurial function. The residual (if any) after the payment of wages, rent, and interest to the owners of labor, land, and capital. **2.** Difference between total revenue and total cost. It is the same as net revenue, a residual or surplus over and above normal profit that accrues to the entrepreneur-owner after all economic costs, including explicit (outlay) costs and implicit (opportunity) costs, have been deducted from total revenue.

program-planning-budgeting system (PPBS): Method of revenue and expenditure management based on (1) determination of goals, (2) assessment of their relative importance to society, and (3) allocation of resources needed to attain the goals at least cost. In more general terms, PPBS is a budgeting method which relates expenditures to specific goals or programs so that the costs of achieving a particular program can be identified, measured, planned, and controlled.

progressive tax: Tax whose percentage rate increases as the tax base increases. The U.S. personal income tax is an example. The tax is graduated so that, other things being equal and assuming no loopholes, a person with a higher income pays a greater percentage of his income and a larger amount of tax than a person with a lower income.

promissory note: Commitment by one person to pay another a specified sum of money by a given date, usually within a year.

propensity to consume: Relationship between consumption expenditures and income such that as income increases, consumption increases, but not as fast as income. The expression **consumption function** is often used synonymously.

propensity to save: Relationship between saving and income such that as income increases, saving increases, but faster than income.

property resources: Nonhuman productive resources of an economy, including its natural resources, raw materials, machinery and equipment, and transportation and communication facilities.

property tax: Tax on any kind of property, such as real property in the form of land and buildings, or personal property, such as stocks, bonds, and home furnishings.

proportional tax: Tax whose percentage rate remains constant as the tax base increases; hence the amount of the tax paid is proportional to the tax base. The property tax is an example. Thus, if the tax rate remains constant at 10 percent, a taxpayer who owns $10,000 worth of property pays $1,000 in taxes; a taxpayer who owns $100,000 worth of property pays $10,000 in taxes.

proprietorship: Simplest form of business organization in which the owner or proprietor is solely responsible for the activities and liabilities of the business.

prosperity: Upper phase of a business cycle in which the economy is operating at or near full employment, and a high degree of business and consumer optimism is reflected by a vigorous rate of capital investment and consumption.

psychological theory (of business cycles): Explanation of economic fluctuations in terms of people's responses to political, social, and economic events. These responses, it is contended, set off cumulative waves of optimism and pessimism, causing cycles in economic activity.

public choice: Study of nonmarket collective decision making. It is thus the application of economics to political science.

public good: Commodity not subject to the exclusion principle. That is, the good's benefits are indivisible and hence no one can be excluded from its consumption for not paying. Therefore, most public goods, but not all, are produced by the public sector because the private sector is usually unable or unwilling to provide them. Other characteristics of a public good are (*a*) very low or even zero incremental or marginal costs, and (*b*) spillover costs to some groups and spillover benefits to others. *Examples:* national defense, fire protection, air traffic control, radio broadcasting, most television transmission, and fireworks displays.

public sector: That segment of the total economy consisting of all levels of government. It is thus exclusive of the household and business segments which comprise the private sector.

public works: Government-sponsored construction, defense, or development projects which usually (but not always) entail public investment expenditures that would not ordinarily be undertaken by the private sector of the economy.

pure competition: *See* **perfect competition** for similarities and differences.

pure interest rate: Theoretical interest rate on a long-term, riskless loan, where the interest payments are made solely for the use of someone else's money. In practice, this rate is often approximated by the interest rate on long-term negotiable government bonds.

pure market economy: Competitive economic system composed of many buyers and sellers, so that prices are determined by the free interaction of supply and demand.

Q

quantity theory of money: Classical theory of the relationship between the price level and the money supply. It holds that the level of prices in the economy is directly proportional to the quantity of money in circulation, such that a given percentage change in the stock of money will cause an equal percentage change in the price level in the same direction. The theory assumes that the income velocity of circulation of money remains fairly stable, and that the quantity of goods and services is constant because the economy always tends toward full employment. (*See also* **equation of exchange.**)

R

rate of return: The interest rate which equates the present value of cash returns on an investment with the present value of the cash expenditures relating to the investment. That is, the rate of return on an investment is the interest rate at which the investment is repaid by its net receipts (i.e., difference between total receipts and total costs).

ratio (logarithmic) scale: Scale on a chart such that equal distances are represented by equal percentage changes. (It is equivalent to plotting the *logarithms* of the same data on an ordinary arithmetic scale.)

rational-expectations theory: Belief that people form anticipations about government fiscal–monetary policies and then include these anticipations in their economic decisions. Consequently, by the time the government's policies become known, the public has already acted on them, thereby offsetting the effects. This means that to assure economic stability, government should adhere to a policy of balanced budgets and steady growth of the money supply. Failure to do so will lead to public policies that are self-defeating and inflationary. In other words, the theory holds that the only policy moves that cause changes in people's behavior are the ones that are not expected. Once the public learns to expect a policy, it no longer alters behavior.

rationing: Any method of restricting the purchases or usage of a good when the quantity demanded of the good exceeds the quantity supplied at a given price.

real asset: Claim against a fixed amount of a commodity or the right to a commodity, the money value of which is affected by inflation or deflation. *Examples:* house, car, and most other goods and services. (*See also* **real liability.**)

real income: Purchasing power of money income or the quantity of goods and services that can be bought with money income. (*Compare* **money income.**)

realized investment: Actual investment out of any realized level of income. Equal to the sum of planned and unplanned (inventory) investment.

real liability: Promise to pay a fixed amount of a commodity, or right to a commodity, the money value of which is affected by inflation or deflation. (*See also* **real asset.**)

real output: Value of physical output unaffected by price changes.

real rate of interest: In classical theory, the interest rate measured in terms of goods. It is the rate which would prevail in the market if the general price level remained stable. Factors determining it are "real demand" for funds by businesses and "real supply" of funds by households. The former, in turn, is determined by the productivity of borrowed capital, and the latter by the willingness of consumers to abstain from present consumption.

real wages: Quantity of goods that can be bought with money wages. Real wages thus depend on the prices of the goods bought with money wages.

recession: Downward phase of a business cycle in which the economy's income, output, and employment are decreasing, and a falling off of business and consumer optimism is reflected by a declining rate of capital investment and consumption.

recessionary gap: Amount by which aggregate demand falls short of full-employment aggregate supply, thereby pulling down the real value of the nation's output.

Reciprocal Trade Agreements program: Plan for expanding American exports through legislation which authorizes the President to negotiate U.S. tariff reductions with other nations in return for parallel concessions. The program consists of the Trade Agreements Act of 1934, with subsequent amendments, and related legislation.

recovery: Upward phase of a business cycle in which the economy's income, output, and employment are rising, and a growing degree of business and consumer optimism is reflected by an expanding rate of capital investment and consumption.

refunding: Replacement or repayment of outstanding bonds by the issue of new bonds. It is thus a method of prolonging a debt by paying off old obligations with new obligations.

regressive tax: Tax whose percentage rate decreases as the tax base increases. In this strict sense there is no regressive tax in the United States. However, if we compare the rate structure of the tax with the taxpayer's net income rather than with its actual base, the term "regressive" applies to any tax which takes a larger share of income from low-income taxpayers than from high-income taxpayers. Most proportional taxes are thus seen to have regressive effects. A sales tax, for instance, is the same for rich people as for poor people, but the latter spend a larger percentage of their incomes on consumer goods and hence the sales taxes they pay—assuming that there are few if any exemptions—are a greater proportion of their incomes.

Regulation Q: Law which (1) empowers the Federal Reserve System to set ceiling interest rates paid by banks on time and savings deposits, and (2) prohibits commercial banks from paying any interest on demand deposits. The law was passed during the depression of the early 1930s when the rate of bank failures was high. The purpose was to reduce competition among banks by discouraging them from making risky loans at high interest rates.

rent: Return to those who supply the factor of production known as "land."

relative income hypothesis: Proposition which states that a family's propensity to consume (i.e., the amount it spends on consumption) depends on its previous peak level of income and/or the relative position that the family occupies along the income scale. A family's spending behavior is thus influenced by the highest past income levels to which it has become accustomed and by the incomes of other families in the same socioeconomic environment. This hypothesis, therefore, is an alternative theory of the propensity to consume. (*Contrast with* **absolute income hypothesis; permanent income hypothesis.**)

required reserves: Minimum amount of legal reserves that a bank is required by law to keep behind its deposit liabilities. Thus, if the reserve requirement is 10 percent, a bank with demand deposits of $1 million must hold at least $100,000 of required legal reserves.

resale price maintenance: Practice whereby a manufacturer or distributor of a branded product sets the minimum retail price at which that product can be sold, thereby eliminating price competition at the retail level.

resource markets: Markets in which businesses buy the inputs or factors of production they need to carry on their operations.

restrictive agreement: Conspiracy of firms that restrains trade among separate companies. It may involve a direct or indirect form of price fixing, output control, market sharing, coercion, exclusion of competitors, and so on, and is illegal under the antitrust laws.

restrictive license: Agreement whereby a patentee permits a licensee to sell a patented product under restricted conditions. The restrictions may include the patentee's fixing the geographic area of the licensee, his level of output, or the price he may charge in selling the patented good.

return on net worth: Ratio of a firm's net profit after taxes to its net worth. It provides a measure of the rate of return on stockholders' investment.

return on total assets: Ratio of a firm's net profit after taxes to its total assets. It measures the rate of return on, or productivity of, total assets.

revenue sharing: Plan by which the federal government turns over a portion of its tax revenues to state and local governments each year.

Ricardo, David (1772–1823): English classical economist, generally regarded as the "greatest of the classical economists." Ricardo was responsible for refining and systematizing much of classical economic thinking. He formulated theories of value, rent, wages, and international trade, some of which have since been modified but many of which have endured to the present. In general, Ricardo held a scientific view of the economy; therefore, the task of economists, he believed, was to discover the laws that determine economic behavior. Among Ricardo's chief contributions that are of major relevance today are the **law of diminishing returns**—one of the most fundamental laws of economics; the theory of economic rent (studied in microeconomics); and the **law of comparative advantage** (studied in international economics).

right-to-work laws: State laws which make it illegal to require membership in a union as a condition of employment. These laws exist mostly in southern and midwestern states; their main effect is to outlaw the union shop, but in practice they have been relatively ineffective.

risk: Quantitative measurement of an outcome, such as a gain or a loss, in a manner such that the mathematical probability (or "odds") of the outcome can be predicted. Because risk is predictable, losses that arise from risk can be estimated in advance and can be "insured" against—either by the firm itself or by an insurance company. *Examples:* The losses resulting from rejects on an assembly line can be "self-insured" by being built into the firm's cost structure; the possibility of fire damage can be externally insured by an insurance company.

Robinson, Joan (1903–): English economist who is best known for her distinguished treatise, *The Economics of Imperfect Competition,* published in 1933. In this book she identified and developed the new concept of monopolistic competition (which she called "imperfect competition"). This type of market structure, she emphasized, was characterized by "partial monopolies" producing similar products in order to fulfill diversified consumer preferences. Imperfect competition, she said, was thus a realistic market structure, the theory of which must be understood in order to evaluate the market behavior of a major segment of the private sector.

Robinson–Patman Act (1936): A major antitrust law of the United States, and an amendment to Section 2 of the Clayton Antitrust Act dealing with price discrimination. Commonly referred to as the "Chain Store Act," it was passed to protect independent retailers and wholesalers from "unfair discriminations" by large sellers who enjoy "tremendous purchasing power." The act declared the following illegal: (1) payment of brokerage fees where no independent broker is employed; (2) granting of discounts and other concessions by sellers such as manufacturers to buyers such as wholesalers and retailers, unless such concessions are made to all buyers on proportionately equal terms; (3) price discrimination, except where the price differences make "due allowances" for differences in cost or are offered "in good faith to meet an equally low price of a competitor"; and (4) charging lower prices in one locality than in another, or selling at "unreasonably low prices," where either of these practices is aimed at "destroying competition or eliminating a competitor."

rule of reason: Interpretation of the courts (first announced in the Standard Oil case of 1911) that the mere size of a corporation, no matter how impressive, is no offense, and that it requires "unreasonable" behavior in the form of actual exertion of monopoly power, as shown by unfair practices, for a firm to be held in violation of the antitrust laws. This interpretation, also known as the "good-trust-versus-bad-trust" criterion, was largely reversed in the Aluminum Company of America case in 1945, as well as in subsequent cases.

rule of 72: Approximate formula for expressing the relationship between the number of years, Y, required for a quantity to double if it grows at an annual rate of compound interest, R. Thus

$$YR = 72$$

Therefore,

$$Y = \frac{72}{R} \quad \text{and} \quad R = \frac{72}{Y}$$

Example: At 6 percent interest compounded annually, a quantity will double in $Y = \frac{72}{6} = 12$ years. Conversely, if a quantity doubles in 12 years, the compounded annual rate of growth is $R = \frac{72}{12} = 6$ percent.

S

sales tax: A flat percentage levy imposed on retail prices of items.

Samuelson, Paul Anthony (1915–): Leading American economist and the first American to receive the Nobel Prize in Economic Science. Samuelson's publications are extensive. His first treatise, *Foundations of Economic Analysis* (1947), based on his doctoral dissertation, explored the notion of equilibrium in many new and provocative ways. It also developed a concept of economic dynamics which was highly original and sophisticated. His hundreds of articles range through numerous areas of economics. Many of these articles, dealing with both macroeconomic and microeconomic topics, have become classics. In addition, Samuelson authored an introductory text which served as the standard work in the field for several decades.

"satisfice": A concept to convey the idea that in reality firms do not seek to maximize profit but to achieve certain levels of satiation. *Example:* Firms try to attain a particular target level or rate of profit, and they try to achieve a specific share of the market or a certain level of sales.

saving: That part of income not spent on the consumption of goods and services.

Say, Jean Baptiste (1767–1832): French classical economist. He is best known for his popularization of Adam Smith's *Wealth of Nations* (1776) and for formulating the "Law of Markets"—the classical doctrine that supply creates its own demand. Say's Law thus asserted the impossibility of general overproduction. This idea was central to classical economic thought, because it led to the conclusion that markets were "self-correcting" if left free of government intervention.

Say's Law: An assertion that "supply creates its own demand." That is, the total supply of goods produced must always equal the total demand for them, since goods fundamentally exchange for goods while money serves only as a convenient medium of exchange. Therefore, any general overproduction is impossible. This assertion, named after the French economist Jean Baptiste Say (1767–1832), was fundamental in classical economic thought, for it led to the conclusion that the economy would automatically tend toward full-employment equilibrium if the government followed a policy of laissez-faire.

scarcity, law of: Principle which states that at any given time and place economic goods, including resources and finished goods, are scarce in the sense that there are not enough to provide all that people want; these scarce goods can be increased, if at all, only through sacrifice.

Schumpeter, Joseph Alois (1883–1950): Leading Austrian–American economist. His theories can be expressed in the form of several fundamental propositions. (1) The entrepreneur (i.e., businessperson) is the central actor—the prime mover of capitalism. (2) In striving for profit, the entrepreneur innovates by introducing new production techniques and new organizational methods. (3) Innovations cause economic growth, but they are also responsible for business cycles, which ultimately lead to the erosion of capitalism. (4) This erosion is already occurring because capitalistic institutions which encouraged and nurtured entrepreneurship in the nineteenth and early twentieth centuries have either disappeared or undergone substantial change.

scientific method: A disciplined mode of inquiry represented by the processes of induction, deduction, and verification. The essential steps of the scientific method consist of (1) recognition and definition of a problem; (2) observation and collection of relevant data; (3) organization and classification of data; (4) formulation of hypotheses; (5) deductions from the hypotheses; and (6) testing and verification of the hypotheses. All scientific laws may be modified or challenged by alternative theoretical formulations, and hence the entire cycle consisting of these six steps is a self-corrective process.

seasonal fluctuations: Short-term swings in business and economic activity within the year which are due to weather and custom. *Examples:* upswings in retail sales during holiday periods such as Christmas and Easter; changes between winter and summer buying patterns.

secondary boycott: Attempts by a union through strikes, picketing, or other methods to stop one employer from doing business with another employer. Outlawed by the Labor–Management Relations (Taft–Hartley) Act of 1947.

secondary reserves: A bank's earning assets that are near-liquid (i.e., readily convertible into cash on short notice without substantial loss). *Examples:* short-term financial obligations such as U.S. Treasury bills, high-grade commercial paper, bankers' acceptances, and call loans.

Second Bank of the United States: Chartered for the period 1816 to 1836, the Bank's functions were to serve as fiscal agent for the Treasury, issue its own notes, and finance both rural and commercial business interests. However, the Bank's generally conservative policies caused periods of financial strain throughout the economy. When Andrew Jackson, a "hard-money" advocate who opposed the issue of paper money by banks, became the nation's President in 1828, he undertook measures to weaken the Bank's effectiveness. As a result, when the Bank's federal charter expired in 1836, it was not renewed.

selling costs: Marketing expenditures aimed at adapting the buyer to the product. *Examples:* advertising, sales promotion, and merchandising.

separation of ownership and control: The notion that in a modern large corporation there is a distinction between those who own the business (the stockholders) and those who control it (the hired managers). If stock ownership is widely dispersed, the managers may be able to keep themselves in power for their own benefit rather than for the primary benefit of the corporation and its stockholders.

shadow prices: Estimates of a commodity's prices that would prevail in a highly competitive market composed of many buyers and sellers. Shadow prices are established for accounting purposes as a means of valuing goods and resources which are not valued in the desired way by the price mechanism.

Sherman Antitrust Act (1890): A major antitrust law of the United States. It prohibits contracts, combinations, and conspiracies in restraint of trade, as well as monopolization or attempts to monopolize in interstate trade or foreign commerce. Violations are punishable by fines and/or imprisonment.

shortage: Any type of deficiency. *Example:* the amount by which the quantity demanded of a commodity exceeds the quantity supplied at a given price, as when the given price is below the free-market equilibrium price. (*Compare* **surplus.**)

short run: Period in which a firm can vary its output through a more or less intensive use of its resources, but cannot vary production capacity because it has a fixed plant scale.

simple multiplier: *See* **multiplier.**

single tax: Proposal advanced by the American economist Henry George (1839–1897) that the only tax a society should impose is a tax on land, because all rent on land is unearned surplus which increases as a result of natural progress and economic growth. Three major shortcomings leveled against this thesis are that the single tax would (1) not yield enough revenues to meet government's spending needs; (2) be unjust, because surpluses may accrue to other resource owners besides landlords if the owners can gain some monopolistic control over the sale of their resources in the marketplace; and (3) be difficult to administer because it does not distinguish between land and capital—that is, between the proportion of rent that represents a surplus and the proportion that results from improvements made on the land.

slope: Rate of change or steepness of a line as measured by the change (increase or decrease) in its vertical distance per unit of change in its horizontal distance. It may be measured by the ratio

$$\text{slope} = \frac{\text{change in vertical distance}}{\text{change in horizontal distance}}$$

Hence a horizontal line has a zero slope; a vertical line has an "infinite" slope. All straight lines which are upward or positively inclined have a slope greater than zero. (Analogously, all straight lines which are downward or negatively inclined have a slope less than zero.) Parallel lines have equal slopes. The slope of a straight line is the same at every point, but the slope of a curved line differs at every point. Geometrically, the slope of a curve at a particular point can be found by drawing a straight line tangent to the curve at that point. The slope of the tangent will then be equal to the slope of the curve at the point of tangency. In economics, all "marginals" are slopes or rates of change of their corresponding "totals." *Examples:* The marginal propensity to consume represents the rate of change or slope of its corresponding total propensity to consume; a marginal cost curve is the slope of its corresponding total cost curve; a marginal revenue curve is the slope of its corresponding total revenue curve; and so on. The concept of slope or rate of change (i.e., "marginal") is unquestionably the most powerful and important analytical tool of economics.

Smith, Adam (1723–1790): Scottish philosopher and author of *The Wealth of Nations* (1776). This was the first comprehensive, systematic study of economics. The treatise earned Smith the title Founder of Economics. In the book, he analyzed such concepts as specialization, division of labor, value and price determination, the distribution of income, the accumulation of capital, and taxation. He argued that if individuals were left alone to pursue their self-interests, their behavior would, as if guided by an "invisible hand," lead to maximum benefits for society. He thus concluded that laissez-faire (i.e., nonintervention of government) was essential to a society's economic efficiency. (*Note:* Smith's ideas became the foundation upon which was constructed the whole subsequent tradition of classical economics.)

social balance: Existence of an optimum distribution of society's resources between the private and public sectors—the former represented by the production of private goods, such as cars, clothing, and television sets, and the latter by the production of certain types of social goods, such as libraries, public health, and education.

social benefit: Utility that accrues to society as a result of a particular act, such as production or consumption of a commodity. (*Compare* **private benefit.**)

social cost: Disutility that accrues to society as a result of a particular act, such as production or consumption of a commodity. It includes real costs, the costs of sacrificed alternatives, and reductions in incomes or benefits caused by the act. It thus includes noneconomic as well as economic costs. (*Compare* **private cost.**)

socialism: 1. In the theories of Karl Marx, a transitory stage between capitalism and full communism, in which the means of production are owned by the state, the state in turn is controlled by the workers (i.e., "dictatorship of the proletariat"), and the economy's social output is distributed by the formula: From each according to his ability, to each according to his labor. **2.** In its contemporary form, a movement which seeks primarily to improve economic efficiency and equity by establishing (a) public ownership of all important means of production and distribution and (b) some degree of centralized planning to determine what goods to produce, how they should be produced, and to whom they should be distributed.

social rate of return: Net value of a project to an economy (i.e., a town, city, state, or country). It is estimated on the basis of the net increase in output which a project such as a new industry may be expected to bring, directly or indirectly, to the area being developed. The industry's contribution is determined by subtracting from the value of what it produces the cost to society of the resources used. Hence the measure is intended to reflect all economic and social benefits as well as costs. (*Compare* **private rate of return.**)

Social Security Act (1935): A basic comprehensive social security law of the United States. It provides for two types of social security: (1) social insurance programs for old age, survivors, disability, and health insurance (OASDHI), and for unemployment, both of which yield payments to insured persons or their survivors; and (2) a public charity program in the form of welfare services, institutional care, food, housing, and other forms of assistance. Some of the provisions of the act (with its many subsequent amendments) are administered and financed by the federal government, some by state and local governments, and some by all three levels of government.

social security tax: Payroll tax which finances the U.S. compulsory social insurance program covering old-age and unemployment benefits. The taxes are paid by both employees and employers, based on the incomes of the former.

Special Drawing Rights (SDRs or "paper gold"): Supplementary reserves (established in 1969) in the form of account entries on the books of the International Monetary Fund. SDRs are allocated among participating countries in accordance with their quotas, and can be drawn upon by governments to help finance balance-of-payments deficits. They are meant to promote an orderly growth of reserves that will help the long-run expanding needs of world trade.

specialization: Division of productive activities among individuals and regions so that no one person or area is self-sufficient. Total production is increased by specialization, thus permitting all participants to share in a greater volume of output through the process of exchange or trade.

specie: Money in the form of gold or silver coins. The nominal or stated value of the coin should equal the market value of the metal contained in the coin, but this does not usually happen. The reason is that the market value of the gold or silver in the coin fluctuates according to supply and demand. Therefore, the metallic value of the coin may be greater or less than the nominal value stated on the coin. (*See* **mint ratio.**).

specific subsidy: Per unit subsidy on a commodity. (*See also* **subsidy.**)

specific tax: Per unit tax on a commodity. (*See also* **tax.**)

speculation: Act of buying or selling goods or securities in the hope of making a profit on price movements.

speculative motive: Desire on the part of households and businesses to hold part of their assets in liquid form so that they can take advantage of changes in the interest rate. This motive is thus tied specifically to the interest rate and is one of the chief sources of demand for loanable funds in the modern theory of interest.

spillovers: External benefits or costs of activities for which no compensation is made. (Spillovers are also called **externalities.**)

stable equilibrium: Condition in which an object or system (such as a price, firm, industry, or market) in equilibrium, when subjected to a shock sufficient to disturb its position, returns toward its initial equilibrium as a result of self-restoring forces. (In contrast, an equilibrium that is not stable may be either unstable or neutral.)

stagflation: Combination of "stagnation" and "inflation." It is a condition characterized by slow economic growth, high unemployment, and rising prices. Stagflation thus combines some of the features of recession and inflation.

Standard Oil case (1911): Major antitrust case in which Standard Oil of New Jersey was ordered broken up by the Supreme Court. The Court held Standard Oil to be in violation of the Sherman Act because the company had engaged in "unreasonable market practices, including the attempt to drive others from the field and to exclude them from their right to trade." In this case, the Court introduced an important new criterion for judging monopoly behavior. (*See* **rule of reason.**)

state bank: Commercial bank chartered by a state government. Such banks may become members of the Federal Reserve System by meeting certain conditions—among them requirements as to the types of reserves that must be held against deposits. Today only a relatively small minority of state banks are member banks—primarily because it is more profitable for most banks to meet the less stringent state requirements than the more rigorous federal ones.

state farms: Lands in the Soviet Union that are owned and operated as state enterprises under elected or governmentally appointed managing directors. Workers and technicians are hired to run the farms, and are usually paid set wages as well as bonuses if their work exceeds basic norms of output.

static model: One in which economic phenomena are studied without reference to time—i.e., without relating them to preceding or succeeding events. Time, in other words, is not permitted to enter the analysis in any matter that will affect the results. A static model is thus like a "snapshot" as distinguished from a "motion picture." (*Compare* **dynamic model.**)

static multiplier: The multiplier without regard to the time required to realize its full effect. (*Compare* **truncated multiplier.**)

stock: Units of ownership interest in a corporation. The kinds of stock include common stock, preferred stock, and capital stock.

strategic-resource monopoly: Firm which has a monopoly because it controls an essential input to a production process. *Example:* DeBeers of South Africa owns most of the world's diamond mines.

strike: Agreement among workers to stop working, without resigning from their jobs, until their demands are met.

structural inflation: Condition of generally rising prices caused by uneven upward demand or cost pressures in some key industries such as automobiles, construction, or steel, even if aggregate demand is in balance with aggregate supply for the economy as a whole.

structural unemployment: Type of unemployment, usually prolonged, resulting from fundamental alterations or "structural" variations in the economy, such as changes in technology, markets, or national priorities. Most types of workers—unskilled, skilled, or professional—are subject to structural unemployment as a result of any of these factors.

subsidy: Payment (usually by government) to businesses or households that enables them to produce or consume a product in larger quantities or at lower prices than they would otherwise.

subsistence theory of wages: Theory developed by some classical economists of the late eighteenth and early nineteenth centuries. It held that wages per worker tend to equal what the worker needs to "subsist"—that is, to maintain himself and to rear children. If wages per worker rose above the subsistence level, people would tend to have more children and the population would increase, thereby lowering per capita real incomes; conversely, if wages per worker fell below the subsistence level, people would tend to have fewer children and the population would decline, thereby increasing per capita real incomes. Wages per worker would thus tend to remain at the subsistence level over the long run. This theory is also known as the "brazen" or "iron law of wages."

substitute goods: Commodities which are related such that at a given level of buyers' incomes, an increase in the price of one good leads to an increase in the demand for the other, and a decrease in the price of one good leads to a decrease in the demand for the other. *Examples:* gin and vodka; beef and pork. (*Compare* **complementary goods.**)

substitution effect: Change in quantity of a good demanded by a buyer resulting from a change in the good's price while the buyer's real income, tastes, and the prices of other goods remain the same. (*Compare* **income effect.**)

sunspot theory: Theory of business cycles proposed in England during the late nineteenth century. It held that sunspot cycles (disturbances on the surface of the sun) exhibited an extremely high correlation with agricultural cycles for a number of years; therefore, sunspots must affect the weather, the weather influences agricultural crops, and the crops affect business conditions. This theory received worldwide popularity when it was first introduced, but then fell into disrepute because the high correlation between sunspots and agricultural cycles did not endure; it was the result of accidental rather than causal factors.

superior good: A good whose consumption varies directly with money income, prices remaining constant. Most consumer goods are superior goods. (A superior good is also called a **normal good** because it represents the "normal" situation.)

supermultiplier: An enlargement of the simple multiplier, reflecting the inclusion of the marginal propensity to invest, *MPI*. It may be expressed by the formula

$$\text{supermultiplier} = \frac{1}{1 - (MPC + MPI)} = \frac{1}{1 - MPE}$$

where *MPE* denotes the marginal propensity to spend.

supplementary (fringe) benefits: Forms of compensation to workers other than basic wages, such as bonuses, pension benefits, and holiday and vacation pay.

supply: A relation expressing the various amounts of a commodity that sellers would be willing and able to make available for sale at possible alternative prices during a given period of time, all other things remaining the same. This relation may be expressed as a table (called a supply schedule), as a graph (called a supply curve), or as a mathematical equation.

supply curve: Graph of a supply schedule, showing the number of units of a commodity that sellers would be able and willing to sell at various possible prices during a given period of time, all other things remaining the same.

supply, law of: Principle which states that the quantity supplied of a commodity usually varies directly with its price, assuming that all other things which may affect supply remain the same. These "all other" things include (1) resource prices; (2) prices of related goods in production; and (3) the state of technology and other nonmonetary determinants, such as the number of sellers in the market.

supply price: Least price necessary to bring forth a given output. Hence it is the lowest price a seller is willing to accept to persuade him to supply a given quantity of a commodity.

supply schedule: Table showing the number of units of a commodity that sellers would be able and willing to sell at various possible prices during a given period of time, all other things remaining the same.

surplus: Any type of excess. *Example:* the amount by which the quantity supplied of a commodity exceeds the quantity demanded at a given price, as when the given price is above the free-market equilibrium price. (*Compare* **shortage.**)

surplus value: In the theories of Karl Marx, the difference between the value that a worker creates as determined by the labor-time embodied in the commodity that he produces and the value that he receives as determined by the subsistence level of wages. This surplus, according to Marx, is appropriated by the capitalist and is the incentive for the development of a capitalistic system.

surtax: Tax imposed on a tax base in addition to a so-called normal tax. *Example:* a surtax on income in addition to the normal income tax. Note that a surtax is imposed on an existing tax base; it is not a "tax on a tax" as is popularly believed.

syndicalism: Economic system which demands the abolition of both capitalism and the state as instruments of oppression, and in their place the reorganization of society into industry-wide associations or syndicates of workers. The syndicates, fundamentally trade unions, would replace the state. Each syndicate would then govern its own members in their activities as producers but leave them free from interference in all other matters. The chief exponent of syndicalism was the French social philosopher Georges Sorel (1847–1922), some of whose views later influenced the growth of fascism.

T

tariff: Customs duty or tax imposed by a government on the importation (or exportation) of a good. Tariffs may be (1) specific, based on a tax per unit of the commodity; or (2) ad valorem, based on the value of the commodity.

tax: A compulsory payment to government. Its purposes may be to influence (1) efficiency through resource allocation (so as to produce more of some commodities and less of others); (2) equity through income and wealth distribution; (3) economic stabilization; and (4) economic growth.

tax avoidance: Legal methods or "loopholes" used by taxpayers to reduce their taxes. (*Compare* **tax evasion.**)

tax base: An object that is being taxed, such as income in the case of an income tax, or the value of property in the case of a property tax, or the value of goods sold in the case of a sales tax.

tax-based incomes policy (TIP): A proposal for curbing inflation. The program provides tax benefits for those workers and firms that keep wage and price increases within an established guidepost, and tax penalties for those that do not. The guidepost, based on the economy's productivity and the current rate of inflation—perhaps an average of both—would be announced annually by government. In general, TIP is at best a short-run anti-inflation measure because it deals with the symptoms of inflation, not the cause. The fundamental cause of inflation is rooted in fiscal and monetary policies.

tax evasion: Illegal methods of escaping taxes, such as lying or cheating about income or expenses. (*Compare* **tax avoidance.**)

tax incidence: Burden of a tax—that is, the economic organisms, such as households, consumers, or sellers, that ultimately bear the tax.

tax rate: Amount of tax applied per unit of tax base—expressed as a percentage. *Example:* A tax of $10 on a base of $100 represents a tax rate of 10 percent.

tax shifting: Changing of the burden or incidence of a tax from the economic organism upon which it is initially imposed to some other economic organism. *Example:* Sales and excise taxes are imposed on the products of sellers, but these taxes are shifted in whole or in part through higher prices to buyers of the goods.

technical efficiency: *See* **efficiency.**

terms of trade: Number of units of goods that must be given up for one unit of goods received, by each party (e.g., nation) to a transaction. In general, the terms of trade are said to move in favor of the party that gives up fewer units of goods for one unit of goods received, and against the party that gives up more units of goods for one unit of goods received. In international economics, the concept of "terms of trade" plays an important role in evaluating exchange relationships between nations.

theory: Set of definitions, assumptions, and hypotheses put together in a manner that expresses apparent relationships or underlying principles of certain observed phenomena in a meaningful way.

time deposit: Money held in a bank account of an individual or firm for which the bank can require advance notice of withdrawal.

time preference: Human desire for a good in the present as opposed to the future. The desire is reflected by the price people are willing to pay for immediate possession of the good as opposed to the price they are willing to pay for future possession.

time series: A set of data ordered chronologically. Most of the published data of business and economics are expressed in the form of time series.

time value of money: The notion that dollars at different points in time cannot be made directly comparable unless they are first adjusted by a common factor—the interest rate. For example, if your money can earn 6 percent annually, then $1 today is worth $1.06 to you one year from today. Similarly, $1.06 next year is worth, two years from today, an additional 6 percent, or $1.124. Conversely, $1.06 one year from today is worth $1 to you today; $1.124 two years from today is worth $1.06 a year from today, and is worth $1 today. (*See also* **compounding; discounting.**)

TIP: *See* **tax-based incomes policy.**

token money: Any object (usually coins) whose value as money is greater than the market value of the materials of which it is composed. *Example:* pennies, nickels, and so on.

total cost: Sum of a firm's total fixed costs and total variable costs.

total fixed costs: Costs that do not vary with a firm's output. *Examples:* rental payments, interest on debt, property taxes.

total-marginal relationship: Relationship between all corresponding total and marginal curves such that when a total curve is increasing at an increasing rate, its corresponding marginal curve is rising; when a total curve is increasing at a decreasing rate, its corresponding marginal curve is falling; and when a total curve is increasing at a zero rate, as occurs when it is at a maximum, its corresponding marginal curve is zero. (*Note:* The case of decreasing total curves gives rise to negative marginal curves, but these situations need not be included in the definition because they are not ordinarily relevant or realistic in an economic sense.)

total revenue: A firm's total receipts; equal to price per unit times the number of units sold.

total variable costs: Costs that vary directly with a firm's output, rising as output increases over the full range of production. *Examples:* costs of raw materials, fuel, labor, and so on.

trade association: Organization of independent business enterprises (usually but not always in the same industry) established for mutually beneficial purposes. (*Note:* A trade association which behaves illegally by fixing prices, restricting output, or allocating markets for its members is similar to a cartel.) (*See also* **cartel.**)

Trade Expansion Act (1962): Part of the U.S. Reciprocal Trade Agreements program, this act broadened the powers of the President to (1) negotiate further tariff reductions on broad categories of goods; (2) lower or eliminate tariffs on those goods for which the European Common Market and the United States together account for at least 80 percent of total world exports; (3) lower tariffs by as much as 50 percent on the basis of reciprocal trade agreements, provided that such agreements include most-favored-nation clauses so that the benefits of reduced tariffs are extended to other countries; and (4) grant vocational, technical, and financial assistance to American employees and businesspersons whose industries are adversely affected by tariff reduction.

transactions motive: Desire on the part of households and businesses to hold some of their assets in liquid form so that they can engage in day-to-day spending activities. This motive is influenced primarily by the level of income rather than by changes in the interest rate and is one of the chief sources of demand for loanable funds in the modern theory of interest.

transfer payments: Expenditures within or between sectors of the economy for which there are no corresponding contributions to current production. *Examples:* social security payments, unemployment compensation, relief payments, veterans' bonuses, net interest paid on government bonds and on consumer loans, and business transfers (such as charitable contributions, and losses resulting from theft and debt defaults).

Treasury bills: Marketable financial obligations of the U.S. Treasury, maturing in up to 1 year from date of issue.

Treasury bonds: Marketable financial obligations of the U.S. Treasury, maturing in more than 7 years from date of issue. (These are *not* U.S. Savings Bonds, with which most people are familiar.)

Treasury notes: Marketable financial obligations of the U.S. Treasury, maturing in 1 to 7 years from date of issue.

trend: Long-run growth or decline of an economic time series over a period of years.

truncated multiplier: The multiplier applicable to a finite number of time periods. Its size approaches that of the static multiplier as the number of periods increases. However, it always realizes more than half the effect of the static multiplier within the first few periods. Thus the truncated multiplier for, say, four periods is measured by the formula

truncated multiplier for four periods
$$= 1 + MPC + (MPC)^2 + (MPC)^3$$

tying contract (tie-in sale): Practice whereby a seller requires the buyer to purchase one or more additional or "tied" products as a condition for purchasing the desired or "tying" product. *Examples:* block bookings of motion pictures in which movie theaters are required to take grade B films as a condition for obtaining grade A films; the United Shoe Machinery Co., which once required shoemakers to purchase other materials as a condition for purchasing shoe machinery.

U

uncertainty: State of knowledge in which the probabilities of outcomes resulting from specific actions are not known and cannot be predicted because they are subjective rather than objective phenomena. Uncertainties, therefore, are not insurable, and cannot be integrated into the firm's cost structure.

underconsumption theory (of business cycles): Explanation of economic fluctuations which holds that recessions result from consumer expenditures lagging behind output because too large a proportion of society's income is not spent on consumption. According to the theory, society distributes income too inequitably to enable people to purchase all the goods produced.

underemployment (disguised unemployment): State of affairs in which employed resources are not being used in their most efficient ways.

unemployment: Situation which exists whenever resources are out of work or are not being used efficiently. There are various types of unemployment, such as technological, frictional, structural, disguised, involuntary, and cyclical.

unemployment benefits: Weekly payments to "covered" workers who are involuntarily unemployed.

unfair competition: Deceptive, dishonest, or injurious methods of competitive behavior. Such practices are illegal under the antitrust laws.

union: Organization of workers which seeks to gain a degree of monopoly power in the sale of its services so that it may be able to secure higher wages, better working conditions, and other economic improvements for its members.

union shop: Business firm whose owner allows a nonunion member to be hired on condition that he join the union after he is employed.

U.S. Steel case (1920): Major antitrust case against U.S. Steel Corporation. The company, formed from a consolidation of many independent firms in 1901, accounted for nearly half the national output of iron and steel. Nevertheless, the Court found no evidence of wrongdoing, and refused to order the breakup of the company. "The law does not make mere size an offense, or the existence of unexerted power an offense," said the Court. This was thus an application of the *rule of reason* by the Court, one of many such applications that have been used.

utility: Ability or power of a good to satisfy a want as determined by the satisfaction that one receives from consuming something.

utopian socialism: Philosophy advanced by a group of English and French writers in the early nineteenth century which advocated the creation of model communities, largely self-contained, where the instruments of production were collectively owned and government was primarily on a voluntary and wholly democratic basis. The leading propagators were Robert Owen (1771–1858) in England and Charles Fourier (1772–1837) in France.

V

value: Power of a commodity to command other commodities in exchange for itself, as measured by the proportional quantities in which a commodity exchanges with all other commodities.

value added: Increment in value at each stage in the production of a good. The sum of the increments for all stages of production gives the total income—the aggregate of wages, rent, interest, and profit—derived from the production of the good.

value-added tax: Type of national sales tax paid by manufacturers and merchants on the value contributed to a product at each stage of its production and distribution.

variable costs: Costs that vary directly with a firm's output, rising as output increases over the full range of production. *Examples:* costs of raw materials, fuel, labor, and so on.

variable proportions, law of: *See* **diminishing returns, law of.**

Veblen, Thorstein Bunde (1857–1929): American institutional economist and critic of neoclassical economics. He emphasized the role of social institutions (i.e., customs and practices) as major determinants of economic behavior. Among his many books, his first and best-known one was *The Theory of the Leisure Class* (1899). In this book he coined the famous phrase "conspicuous consumption" as a characteristic of the "leisure class." (*See* **conspicuous consumption.**)

verification: Testing of alternative hypotheses or conclusions by means of actual observation or experimentation—that is, by reference to the facts.

vertical equity: Doctrine which states that "unequals should be treated unequally." *Example:* Persons of different income, wealth, or other taxpaying ability should, in order to bear equal tax burdens, pay different amounts of tax. (*Compare* **horizontal equity.**)

vertical merger: Amalgamation under one ownership of plants engaged in different stages of production from raw materials to finished products. It may take the form of forward integration into buyer markets or backward integration into supplier markets. The chief objective is to achieve greater economies by combining different production stages and by regularizing supplies, thereby increasing profit margins.

W

wages: 1. Payment to those owners of resources who supply the factor of production known as "labor." This payment includes wages, salaries, commissions, and the like. **2.** The price paid for the use of labor. It is usually expressed as time rates, such as so much per hour, day, or week, or less frequently as rates of so much per unit of work performed.

wages-fund theory: Classical theory of wages best articulated by John Stuart Mill in 1848. It held that producers set aside a portion of their capital funds for the purpose of hiring workers needed for production. The amount of the fund depends on the stock of capital relative to the number of workers. In the long run, however, the accumulation of capital is itself limited or determined by the tendency toward a minimum "subsistence rate" of profits; hence the only effective way to raise real wages is to reduce the number of workers or size of the population. (*Note:* This theory was a reformulation of the **subsistence theory of wages.**)

Walras, Leon (1834–1910): French economist whose major work, *Elements of Pure Economics* (1874), was done at the University of Lausanne, Switzerland. He is regarded as one of the greatest economic theorists of all time. This is due to his mathematical formulations of the theory of general equilibrium "under a system of perfectly free competition." The model links the various markets of the economy through systems of equations, and shows the conditions needed to determine equilibrium prices and quantities. The Walrasian system thus represents the perfection of classical and neoclassical economics.

"wastes" of monopolistic competition: Expression used to denote overcrowded "sick" industries of monopolistic competition; the wastes are characterized by chronic excess capacity and inefficient operations. *Examples:* retail trades; textile manufacturing.

wealth: Anything which has value because it is capable of producing income. A "stock" of value as compared to a "flow" of income. (*Compare* **income.**)

welfare economics: Branch of economic theory concerned with the development of principles for maximizing social welfare.

Wheeler–Lea Act (1938): Amendment to the Federal Trade Commission Act. It was passed primarily to protect consumers, rather than just business competitors, from unfair (deceptive, dishonest, or injurious) methods of competition. Thus injured consumers are given equal protection before the law with injured merchants. The act also prohibits false or misleading advertisements for food, drugs, cosmetics, and therapeutic devices.

white market: Legal market in which ration coupons for a commodity are transferable, permitting people who do not want all their coupons to sell them to those who do. A white market thus reduces, but does not eliminate, the inequities and skullduggery generally associated with rationing and a black market. (*Compare* **black market.**)

Y

yellow-dog contract: Contract that requires an employee to promise as a condition of employment that he will not belong to a labor union. Declared illegal in the Norris–La Guardia Act of 1932.

yield: Effective or going market rate of interest on a secu-rity. In a broader sense, it is the effective rate of return on any type of investment.

yield curve: Graph which shows, at a given time, the relationship between yields and maturities for debt instruments of equal risk (e.g., treasury bonds). The yield curve thus expresses the *term structure of interest rates* for a particular class of debt instruments, which are alike in all respects except their maturity dates.

yield to maturity: Percentage figure reflecting the effective yield on a bond, based on the difference between its purchase and redemption price, and any returns received by the bondholder in the interim.

General Business and Economic Indicators

POPULATION, EMPLOYMENT, WAGES, AND PRODUCTIVITY

Year	(28) Population	(29) Civilian labor force	(30) Unemployment	(31) Unemployment as percent of civilian labor force	(32) Average weekly hours of work — Total non-agricultural private sector	(33) Average gross hourly earnings — Total non-agricultural private sector	(34) Output per hour of all persons — Private business sector	(35) Compensation per hour — Private business sector
	Millions of persons			Percent	Hours	Dollars	1967 = 100	
1929	121.9	49.2	1.6	3.2	—	—	—	—
1930	123.2	49.8	4.3	8.7	—	—	—	—
1931	124.1	50.4	8.0	15.9	—	—	—	—
1932	124.9	51.0	12.1	23.6	—	—	—	—
1933	125.7	51.6	12.8	24.9	—	—	—	—
1934	126.5	52.2	11.3	21.7	—	—	—	—
1935	127.4	52.9	10.6	20.1	—	—	—	—
1936	128.2	53.4	9.0	16.9	—	—	—	—
1937	129.0	54.0	7.7	14.3	—	—	—	—
1938	130.0	54.6	10.4	19.0	—	—	—	—
1939	131.0	55.2	9.5	17.2	—	—	—	—
1940	132.1	55.6	8.1	14.6	—	—	—	—
1941	133.4	55.9	5.6	9.9	—	—	—	—
1942	134.9	56.4	2.7	4.7	—	—	—	—
1943	136.7	55.5	1.1	1.9	—	—	—	—
1944	138.4	54.6	0.7	1.2	—	—	—	—
1945	140.0	53.9	1.0	1.9	—	—	—	—
1946	141.4	57.5	2.3	3.9	—	—	—	—
1947	144.1	59.4	2.3	3.9	40.3	1.131	53.6	36.0
1948	146.6	60.6	2.3	3.8	40.0	1.225	55.6	39.0
1949	149.2	61.3	3.6	5.9	39.4	1.275	56.5	39.7
1950	151.7	62.2	3.3	5.3	39.8	1.335	61.0	42.4
1951	154.3	62.0	2.1	3.3	39.9	1.45	62.7	46.6
1952	157.0	62.1	1.9	3.0	39.9	1.52	64.5	49.6
1953	159.6	63.0	1.8	2.9	39.6	1.61	66.5	52.8
1954	162.4	63.6	3.5	5.5	39.1	1.65	67.6	54.5
1955	165.3	65.0	2.9	4.4	39.6	1.71	70.3	55.8
1956	168.2	66.6	2.8	4.1	39.3	1.80	71.2	59.5
1957	171.3	66.9	2.9	4.3	38.8	1.89	73.2	63.4
1958	174.1	67.6	4.6	6.8	38.5	1.95	75.1	66.2
1959	177.1	68.4	3.7	5.5	39.0	2.02	77.5	69.0
1960	180.7	69.6	3.9	5.5	38.6	2.09	78.7	71.9
1961	183.8	70.5	4.7	6.7	38.6	2.14	81.1	74.6
1962	186.7	70.6	3.9	5.5	38.7	2.22	84.8	78.1
1963	189.4	71.8	4.1	5.7	38.8	2.28	88.1	81.0
1964	192.1	73.1	3.8	5.2	38.7	2.36	91.6	85.3
1965	194.6	74.5	3.4	4.5	38.8	2.45	95.0	88.7
1966	197.0	75.8	2.9	3.8	38.6	2.56	98.0	94.9
1967	199.1	77.3	3.0	3.8	38.0	2.68	100.0	100.0
1968	201.2	78.7	2.8	3.6	37.8	2.85	103.3	107.6
1969	202.7	80.7	2.8	3.5	37.7	3.04	103.5	114.9
1970	204.9	82.7	4.1	4.9	37.1	3.23	104.2	123.1
1971	207.1	84.1	5.0	5.9	36.9	3.45	107.7	131.4
1972	208.9	86.5	4.8	5.6	37.0	3.70	111.4	139.7
1973	210.4	88.7	4.3	4.9	36.9	3.94	113.6	151.2
1974	211.9	91.0	5.1	5.6	36.5	4.24	110.1	164.9
1975	213.6	92.6	7.8	8.5	36.1	4.53	112.4	181.3
1976	215.1	94.8	7.3	7.7	36.1	4.86	116.4	197.2
1977	216.9	97.4	6.9	7.0	36.0	5.25	118.6	213.0
1978	218.7	100.4	6.1	6.0	35.8	5.69	119.2	231.2
1979	220.6	102.9	5.6	5.8	35.7	6.16	118.1	252.8

PRODUCTION AND BUSINESS ACTIVITY

Year	(36) Index of industrial production — 1967 = 100	(37) Total new construction — Value put in place — Billions of dollars	(38) Business expenditures for new plant and equipment — Billions of dollars	(39) Manufacturers' new orders — Millions of dollars
1929	21.6	10.8	—	—
1930	18.0	8.7	—	—
1931	14.9	6.4	—	—
1932	11.6	3.5	—	—
1933	13.7	2.9	—	—
1934	15.0	3.7	—	—
1935	17.3	4.2	—	—
1936	20.4	6.5	—	—
1937	22.3	7.0	—	—
1938	17.6	6.9	—	—
1939	21.7	8.2	—	—
1940	25.4	8.7	—	—
1941	31.6	12.0	—	—
1942	36.3	14.1	—	—
1943	44.0	8.3	—	—
1944	47.4	5.3	—	—
1945	40.6	5.8	—	—
1946	35.0	4.3	—	—
1947	39.4	20.0	19.33	15,256
1948	41.0	26.1	21.30	17,693
1949	38.8	26.7	18.98	15,614
1950	44.9	33.6	20.21	20,110
1951	48.7	35.4	25.46	23,907
1952	50.6	36.8	26.43	23,204
1953	54.8	39.1	28.20	23,586
1954	51.9	41.4	27.19	22,335
1955	58.5	46.5	29.53	27,465
1956	61.1	47.6	35.73	28,368
1957	61.9	49.1	37.94	27,559
1958	57.9	50.0	31.89	27,002
1959	64.8	55.4	33.55	30,724
1960	66.2	54.7	36.75	30,235
1961	66.7	56.4	35.91	31,104
1962	72.2	60.2	38.39	33,436
1963	76.5	64.8	40.77	35,524
1964	81.7	67.7	46.97	38,357
1965	89.8	73.7	54.42	42,100
1966	97.8	76.4	63.51	46,402
1967	100.0	78.1	65.47	47,062
1968	106.3	87.1	67.76	50,684
1969	111.1	93.9	75.56	53,967
1970	107.8	94.9	79.71	52,068
1971	109.6	110.0	81.21	55,990
1972	119.7	124.1	88.44	64,162
1973	129.8	137.9	99.74	76,183
1974	129.3	138.5	112.40	87,151
1975	117.8	134.5	112.78	85,082
1976	130.5	151.1	120.49	99,184
1977	138.2	174.0	135.80	112,451
1978	146.1	206.2	153.82	128,488
1979	152.2	230.0	176.37	143,918